Nineteenth-Century Literature Criticism

Guide to Gale Literary Criticism Series

For criticism on	Consult these Gale series
Authors now living or who died after December 31, 1999	*CONTEMPORARY LITERARY CRITICISM (CLC)*
Authors who died between 1900 and 1999	*TWENTIETH-CENTURY LITERARY CRITICISM (TCLC)*
Authors who died between 1800 and 1899	*NINETEENTH-CENTURY LITERATURE CRITICISM (NCLC)*
Authors who died between 1400 and 1799	*LITERATURE CRITICISM FROM 1400 TO 1800 (LC)* *SHAKESPEAREAN CRITICISM (SC)*
Authors who died before 1400	*CLASSICAL AND MEDIEVAL LITERATURE CRITICISM (CMLC)*
Authors of books for children and young adults	*CHILDREN'S LITERATURE REVIEW (CLR)*
Dramatists	*DRAMA CRITICISM (DC)*
Poets	*POETRY CRITICISM (PC)*
Short story writers	*SHORT STORY CRITICISM (SSC)*
Black writers of the past two hundred years	*BLACK LITERATURE CRITICISM (BLC)* *BLACK LITERATURE CRITICISM SUPPLEMENT (BLCS)*
Hispanic writers of the late nineteenth and twentieth centuries	*HISPANIC LITERATURE CRITICISM (HLC)* *HISPANIC LITERATURE CRITICISM SUPPLEMENT (HLCS)*
Native North American writers and orators of the eighteenth, nineteenth, and twentieth centuries	*NATIVE NORTH AMERICAN LITERATURE (NNAL)*
Major authors from the Renaissance to the present	*WORLD LITERATURE CRITICISM, 1500 TO THE PRESENT (WLC)* *WORLD LITERATURE CRITICISM SUPPLEMENT (WLCS)*

ISSN 0732-1864

Volume 122

Nineteenth-Century Literature Criticism

Criticism of the
Works of Novelists, Philosophers, and Other
Creative Writers Who Died between 1800
and 1899, from the First Published Critical
Appraisals to Current Evaluations

Lynn M. Zott
Project Editor

GALE®

Detroit • New York • San Diego • San Francisco • Cleveland • New Haven, Conn. • Waterville, Maine • London • Munich

THOMSON

GALE

Nineteenth-Century Literature Criticism, Vol. 122

Project Editor
Lynn M. Zott

Editorial
Jessica Bomarito, Jenny Cromie, Kathy D.
Darrow, Elisabeth Gellert, Edna M. Hedblad,
Jelena O. Krstović, Michelle Lee, Thomas J.
Schoenberg, Lawrence J. Trudeau, Maikue
Vang, Russel Whitaker

Research
Nicodemus Ford, Sarah Genik, Tamara C. Nott,
Tracie A. Richardson

Permissions
Debra Freitas

Imaging and Multimedia
Robert Duncan, Lezlie Light, Kelly A. Quin

Composition and Electronic Capture
Gary Leach

Manufacturing
Stacy L. Melson

LIBRARY OF CONGRESS CATALOG CARD NUMBER 84-643008

ISBN 0-7876-6353-0
ISSN 0732-1864

Printed in the United States of America
10 9 8 7 6 5 4 3 2 1

Contents

Preface vii

Acknowledgments xi

Literary Criticism Series Advisory Board xiii

Preface

Since its inception in 1981, *Nineteeth-Century Literature Criticism* (*NCLC*) has been a valuable resource for students and librarians seeking critical commentary on writers of this transitional period in world history. Designated an "Outstanding Reference Source" by the American Library Association with the publication of is first volume, *NCLC* has since been purchased by over 6,000 school, public, and university libraries. The series has covered more than 300 authors representing 29 nationalities and over 17,000 titles. No other reference source has surveyed the critical reaction to nineteenth-century authors and literature as thoroughly as *NCLC*.

Scope of the Series

NCLC is designed to introduce students and advanced readers to the authors of the nineteenth century and to the most significant interpretations of these authors' works. The great poets, novelists, short story writers, playwrights, and philosophers of this period are frequently studied in high school and college literature courses. By organizing and reprinting commentary written on these authors, *NCLC* helps students develop valuable insight into literary history, promotes a better understanding of the texts, and sparks ideas for papers and assignments. Each entry in *NCLC* presents a comprehensive survey of an author's career or an individual work of literature and provides the user with a multiplicity of interpretations and assessments. Such variety allows students to pursue their own interests; furthermore, it fosters an awareness that literature is dynamic and responsive to many different opinions.

Every fourth volume of *NCLC* is devoted to literary topics that cannot be covered under the author approach used in the rest of the series. Such topics include literary movements, prominent themes in nineteenth-century literature, literary reaction to political and historical events, significant eras in literary history, prominent literary anniversaries, and the literatures of cultures that are often overlooked by English-speaking readers.

NCLC continues the survey of criticism of world literature begun by Gale's *Contemporary Literary Criticism* (*CLC*) and *Twentieth-Century Literary Criticism* (*TCLC*).

Organization of the Book

An *NCLC* entry consists of the following elements:

- The **Author Heading** cites the name under which the author most commonly wrote, followed by birth and death dates. Also located here are any name variations under which an author wrote, including transliterated forms for authors whose native languages use nonroman alphabets. If the author wrote consistently under a pseudonym, the pseudonym will be listed in the author heading and the author's actual name given in parenthesis on the first line of the biographical and critical information. Uncertain birth or death dates are indicated by question marks. Single-work entries are preceded by a heading that consists of the most common form of the title in English translation (if applicable) and the original date of composition.

- The **Introduction** contains background information that introduces the reader to the author, work, or topic that is the subject of the entry.

- A **Portrait of the Author** is included when available.

- The list of **Principal Works** is ordered chronologically by date of first publication and lists the most important works by the author. The genre and publication date of each work is given. In the case of foreign authors whose works have been translated into English, the list will focus primarily on twentieth-century translations, selecting those works most commonly considered the best by critics. Unless otherwise indicated, dramas are dated by first performance, not first publication. Lists of **Representative Works** by different authors appear with topic entries.

- Reprinted **Criticism** is arranged chronologically in each entry to provide a useful perspective on changes in critical evaluation over time. The critic's name and the date of composition or publication of the critical work are given at the beginning of each piece of criticism. Unsigned criticism is preceded by the title of the source in which it appeared. All titles by the author featured in the text are printed in boldface type. Footnotes are reprinted at the end of each essay or excerpt. In the case of excerpted criticism, only those footnotes that pertain to the excerpted texts are included. Criticism in topic entries is arranged chronologically under a variety of subheadings to facilitate the study of different aspects of the topic.

- A complete **Bibliographical Citation** of the original essay or book precedes each piece of criticism.

- Critical essays are prefaced by brief **Annotations** explicating each piece.

- An annotated bibliography of **Further Reading** appears at the end of each entry and suggests resources for additional study. In some cases, significant essays for which the editors could not obtain reprint rights are included here. Boxed material following the further reading list provides references to other biographical and critical sources on the author in series published by Gale.

Indexes

Each volume of *NCLC* contains a **Cumulative Author Index** listing all authors who have appeared in a wide variety of reference sources published by the Gale Group, including *NCLC*. A complete list of these sources is found facing the first page of the Author Index. The index also includes birth and death dates and cross references between pseudonyms and actual names.

A **Cumulative Nationality Index** lists all authors featured in *NCLC* by nationality, followed by the number of the *NCLC* volume in which their entry appears.

A **Cumulative Topic Index** lists the literary themes and topics treated in the series as well as in *Classical and Medieval Literature Criticism, Literature Criticism from 1400 to 1800, Twentieth-Century Literary Criticism,* and the *Contemporary Literary Criticism* Yearbook, which was discontinued in 1998.

An alphabetical **Title Index** accompanies each volume of *NCLC*, with the exception of the Topics volumes. Listings of titles by authors covered in the given volume are followed by the author's name and the corresponding page numbers where the titles are discussed. English translations of foreign titles and variations of titles are cross-referenced to the title under which a work was originally published. Titles of novels, dramas, nonfiction books, and poetry, short story, or essay collections are printed in italics, while individual poems, short stories, and essays are printed in roman type within quotation marks.

In response to numerous suggestions from librarians, Gale also produces an annual paperbound edition of the *NCLC* cumulative title index. This annual cumulation, which alphabetically lists all titles reviewed in the series, is available to all customers. Additional copies of this index are available upon request. Librarians and patrons will welcome this separate index; it saves shelf space, is easy to use, and is recyclable upon receipt of the next edition.

Citing *Nineteenth-Century Literature Criticism*

When writing papers, students who quote directly from any volume in the Literary Criticism Series may use the following general format to footnote reprinted criticism. The first example pertains to material drawn from periodicals, the second to material reprinted from books.

Kim McQuaid, "William Apes, Pequot: An Indian Reformer in the Jackson Era," *The New England Quarterly,* 50 (December 1977): 605-25; excerpted and reprinted in *Nineteenth-Century Literature Criticism,* vol. 73, ed. Janet Witalec (Farmington Hills, Mich.: The Gale Group, 1999), 3-4.

Richard Harter Fogle, *The Imagery of Keats and Shelley: A Comparative Study* (Archon Books, 1949), 211-51; excerpted and reprinted in *Nineteenth-Century Literature Criticism,* vol. 73, ed. Janet Witalec (Farmington Hills, Mich.: The Gale Group, 1999), 157-69.

Suggestions are Welcome

Readers who wish to suggest new features, topics, or authors to appear in future volumes, or who have other suggestions or comments are cordially invited to call, write, or fax the Project Editor:

Project Editor, Literary Criticism Series
The Gale Group
27500 Drake Road
Farmington Hills, MI 48331-3535
1-800-347-4253 (GALE)
Fax: 248-699-8054

Acknowledgments

The editors wish to thank the copyright holders of the excerpted criticism included in this volume and the permissions managers of many book and magazine publishing companies for assisting us in securing reproduction rights. We are also grateful to the staffs of the Detroit Public Library, the Library of Congress, the University of Detroit Mercy Library, Wayne State University Purdy/Kresge Library Complex, and the University of Michigan Libraries for making their resources available to us. Following is a list of the copyright holders who have granted us permission to reproduce material in this volume of *NCLC*. Every effort has been made to trace copyright, but if omissions have been made, please let us know.

COPYRIGHTED MATERIAL IN *NCLC*, VOLUME 122, WAS REPRODUCED FROM THE FOLLOWING PERIODICALS:

American Literature, v. 35, November, 1963; v. 72, March, 2000. © 1963, 2000 Duke University Press. Both reproduced by permission.—*American Studies,* v. 27, Spring, 1986. Reproduced by permission.—*Anales Cervantinos,* v. XXII, 1984 for "The Spanish, English, and American Quixotes" by Sally C. Hoople. Reproduced by permission of the author.—*Australian Slavonic & East European Studies,* v. 10, 1996. Reproduced by permission.—*Canadian Slavonic Papers,* v. XXVI, March, 1984. Reproduced by permission.—*Early American Literature,* v. XVI, Spring, 1981; v. XVI, Fall, 1981; v. XVIII, Fall, 1983; v. 25, 1990; v. 26, 1991. Copyright © 1981, 1983, 1990, 1991 by the Department of English at the University of North Carolina, Chapel Hill. All reproduced by permission of the University of North Carolina Press.—*ESQ: A Journal of American Renaissance,* v. 20, Winter, 1974 for "The Americanization of Faust: A Study of Charles Brockden Brown's *Wieland*" by Joseph A. Soldati. Reproduced by permission of the publisher and the author.—*Germano-Slavica,* v. 9, 1995-96. Reproduced by permission.—*Irish Slavonic Studies,* n. 10, 1993 for "One Man and His Dogs: An Anniversary Tribute to Ivan Turgenev" by A. D. P. Briggs; n. 10, 1993 for "Superfluous Women and the Perils of Reading 'Faust'" by Peter I. Barta. Copyright © 1993 *Irish Slavonic Studies* and contributors. Reproduced by permission.—*Journal of European Studies,* v. 14, September, 1984. © 1984 by Science History Publications Ltd. Reproduced by permission.—*Novel: A Forum on Fiction,* v. 8, Winter, 1975. Copyright © NOVEL Corp, 1975. Reproduced by permission.—*Philological Quarterly,* v. 64, Spring, 1985. Reproduced by permission.—*Scando-Slavica,* v. 34, 1988 for "Determinism in the Novels of Turgenev" by James B. Woodward. Copyright © 1988 by the Association of Scandinavian Slavists and Baltologists. Reproduced by permission of the author.—*South Atlantic Review,* v. 49, November, 1984. Reproduced by permission.—*Studies in American Fiction,* v. 12, Spring, 1984; v. 18, Spring, 1990. Copyright © 1984, 1990 Northeastern University. Both reproduced by permission.—*Studies in American Humor,* n.s. v. 3, 1995. Reproduced by permission.—*Studies in the Novel,* v. 9, Summer, 1977; v. 14, Spring, 1982. Copyright 1977, 1982 by North Texas State University. Both reproduced by permission.

COPYRIGHTED MATERIAL IN *NCLC*, VOLUME 122, WAS REPRODUCED FROM THE FOLLOWING BOOKS:

Allen, Elizabeth Cheresh. From "Turgenev's Last Will and Testament: Poems in Prose," in *Freedom and Responsibility in Russian Literature: Essays in Honor of Robert Louis Jackson.* Edited by Elizabeth Cheresh Allen and Gary Saul Morson. Northwestern University Press, 1995. Copyright © 1995 by Northwestern University Press. Reproduced by permission.—Axelrod, Alan. From *Charles Brockden Brown: An American Tale.* University of Texas Press, 1983. Copyright © 1983 by the University of Texas Press. Reproduced by permission.—Brouwer, Sander. From *Character in the Short Prose of Ivan Sergeevic Turgenev.* Rodopi, 1996. Reproduced by permission.—Traill, Nancy H. From *Possible Worlds of the Fantastic: The Rise of the Paranormal in Fiction.* University of Toronto Press, 1996. © University of Toronto Press 1996. Reproduced by permission.—Costlaw, Jane T. From "'Oh-La-La and No-No-No': Odintsova as Woman Lone in 'Fathers and Children,'" in *A Plot of Her Own: The Female Protagonist in Russian Literature.* Edited by Sona Stephan Hoisington. Northwestern University Press, 1995. Copyright © 1995 by Northwestern University Press. Reproduced by permission.—Costlow, Jane. From "Abusing the Erotic: Women in Turgenev's 'First Love,'" in *Engendering Slavic Literatures.* Edited by Pamela Chester and Sibelan Forrester. Indiana University Press, 1996. © 1996 by Indiana University Press. Reproduced by permission.—Davidson, Cathy N. From *Revolution and the Word: The Rise of the Novel in America.* Copyright © 1988 by Oxford University Press, Inc. Used by permission of Oxford University Press, Inc.—Eekman, Thomas. From "Turgenev and the Shorter Prose Forms," in *Text and Context: Essays to Honor Hils Ake Nilsson.* Edited by Peter Alberg Jensen & others. Almqvist & Wiksell International, 1987. © Stockholm Studies in Russian Literature. Reproduced by per-

Literary Criticism Series Advisory Board

The members of the Gale Group Literary Criticism Series Advisory Board—reference librarians and subject specialists from public, academic, and school library systems—represent a cross-section of our customer base and offer a variety of informed perspectives on both the presentation and content of our literature criticism products. Advisory board members assess and define such quality issues as the relevance, currency, and usefulness of the author coverage, critical content, and literary topics included in our series; evaluate the layout, presentation, and general quality of our printed volumes; provide feedback on the criteria used for selecting authors and topics covered in our series; provide suggestions for potential enhancements to our series; identify any gaps in our coverage of authors or literary topics, recommending authors or topics for inclusion; analyze the appropriateness of our content and presentation for various user audiences, such as high school students, undergraduates, graduate students, librarians, and educators; and offer feedback on any proposed changes/ enhancements to our series. We wish to thank the following advisors for their advice throughout the year.

Wieland

Charles Brockden Brown

The following entry presents criticism of Brown's novel *Wieland; or, The Transformation* (1798). For information on Brown's complete career, see *NCLC*, Volumes 22 and 74.

INTRODUCTION

Charles Brockden Brown's most highly-regarded novel, *Wieland,* is widely considered the first gothic novel produced by an American. Written in epistolary form, the work draws on the traditions of both Gothic and sentimental novels, and includes such narrative elements as murder, suicide, seduction, and insanity. Although *Wieland* has often been interpreted as an indictment of Puritanism, some scholars maintain that the novel is an historical parable or even a self-referential allegory of the writing process itself.

PLOT AND MAJOR CHARACTERS

The title character of the novel is Theodore Wieland, whose sister Clara narrates the family's story, beginning with the arrival of their father from England. Believing it his duty to spread Christianity among the Indians, Theodore and Clara's father is at first distracted by worldly pursuits, and later, when he has achieved sufficient wealth to pursue his calling, his efforts are thwarted by the Indians themselves. Believing he has failed, he retreats to his temple at midnight for private worship and dies following a flash of light and an explosion. The event is described as a case of spontaneous combustion. The children's mother dies soon after, but Theodore and Clara are raised in material comfort with enlightened attitudes on religion and human nature.

When the children reach adulthood, Theodore marries Catherine Pleyel, a family friend, and the couple settles into a life of privilege on the family estate, where Clara lives in her own house on the grounds. Catherine's brother Henry visits from Europe, and the two men affably debate about philosophy and religion, with Pleyel's rationalism in opposition to Wieland's belief in religion and the supernatural. Their contentment is soon disturbed, however, by a mysterious disembodied voice

and by the appearance of a stranger named Carwin, who joins their intellectual circle although he is not their social equal. The voice claims that Pleyel's betrothed has died in Europe, and when this is later confirmed, Wieland becomes convinced the voice is divine in nature.

In time, Clara falls in love with Pleyel, but he has overheard a conversation between Clara and Carwin that suggests her virtue has been compromised and he rejects her. Wieland, meanwhile, determines that the voice is God's, and that god is commanding him to murder his wife and children. He obeys but then believes he must also murder his sister and Pleyel as further proof of his devotion and obedience. Clara is saved by the intervention of neighbors and her brother is taken to prison. Carwin confesses that he is a ventriloquist and is responsible for the mysterious voices the family has heard. Because of his own attraction to Clara, he was determined to turn Pleyel against her—he orchestrated the conversation Pleyel overheard that implicated Clara. Carwin denies, however, any involvement with the voice Wieland heard commanding him to murder his family. When Wieland escapes from prison and returns to kill his sister, Carwin saves her by speaking to Wieland as God—this time telling Theodore that he has been deceived. Wieland realizes the enormity of his crimes and commits suicide.

The novel concludes three years later, when Clara has fled to Europe and has married Pleyel. At this time Clara feels that she has recovered from the effects of the events and is able to begin writing her account of the family's tragedy. Carwin has retreated to the country-side and has become a farmer.

MAJOR THEMES

Most critics and scholars interpret *Wieland* as a caution-ary tale on the dangers of religious fervor or as an in-dictment of patriarchal institutions. The actions of the two Wieland men, father and son, represent for some critics a study in madness; others read the pair as em-bodiments of the Faustian theme, or more specifically, as American versions of Faust. Issues of interpretation and the dangers of reaching conclusions based on insuf-ficient knowledge are also prominent themes. Since the novel leaves questions unanswered and problems unre-solved, some have argued that Brown may have been pointing out the inability of humans to know the truth with any degree of certainty.

CRITICAL RECEPTION

Many early critics assessed *Wieland* as a flawed novel filled with inconsistencies and ambiguities caused by Brown's lack of skill as a writer. The work was consid-ered unsophisticated and too dependent on the conven-tions of the Gothic novel and the sentimental novel of seduction. More recently, however, *Wieland* has been reevaluated and its ambiguities are now often regarded as deliberate strategies by the author. James R. Russo refutes the common notion that Brown was an inferior writer and suggests that readers must separate the au-thor from his narrator: "*Wieland* is told by a confessed madwoman, Clara Wieland, and her narrative seems in-coherent at times because she is confused, not because Brown is."

Joseph A. Soldati maintains that the work is highly complex: "Innovatively employing the myths of Icarus and Narcissus in its exploration of the Faustian hero's dark psyche, *Wieland* is the precursor of the psycho-logical tales of Poe, Hawthorne, Melville, Faulkner, and others." But Soldati points out that there is a difference between the American Faust and his European prede-cessors; the level of violence and destruction associated

with Theodore Wieland is much more extreme and "re-flects the New World's violent temper." Other critics have also considered *Wieland*'s tragic events as an in-dictment of American ideology. Roberta F. Weldon claims that the family's isolation and self-involvement led to a "dangerous myopia," and she suggests that Brown was predicting a similar fate for the emerging nation as a whole if its ideals were allowed to promote the rights of the individual to the detriment of the com-mon good. According to Weldon: "By focusing on the error of the Wieland family, the novel examines the flawed design underlying the American ideal. The Wielands believe with Emerson that 'the individual is the world' but experience the danger of self-absorption and are destroyed by it." Edwin Sill Fussell suggests that *Wieland* is concerned with its author's struggle to break with the literary conventions of the past and to create a new, uniquely American, literature. According to Fussell, "in *Wieland* Charles Brockden Brown was writing about writing . . . about that American litera-ture not yet in existence but coming into existence as he confronted and incorporated the stiffest resistance imaginable, his own impossibility."

Much scholarly interest has centered around possible source material for *Wieland*. Critics have suggested the Old Testament story of Abraham as an obvious inspira-tion for the slaying of Wieland's family by God's com-mand. Other critics's suggestions for possible sources include Milton's *Paradise Lost*, several of Shake-speare's plays—among them *Hamlet, Macbeth, Othello,* and *Much Ado about Nothing*—and most commonly, two contemporary accounts of New England men who murdered their families claiming they had been ordered by God to do so.

PRINCIPAL WORKS

Alcuin: A Dialogue (fictional dialogue) 1798

Wieland; or, The Transformation. An American Tale (novel) 1798

Edgar Huntly; or, Memoirs of a Sleep-Walker (novel) 1799

Ormond; or, The Secret Witness (novel) 1799

Arthur Mervyn; or, Memoirs of the Year 1793. 2 vols. (novel) 1800

Clara Howard (novel) 1801; revised as *Philip Stanley; or, The Enthusiasm of Love* (novel) 1807

Jane Talbot, a Novel (novel) 1801

A View of the Soil and Climate of the United States [translator] (nonfiction) 1804

*Carwin, the Biloquist, and Other American Tales and Pieces. 3 vols. (unfinished novel and short stories) 1822

The Novels of Charles Brockden Brown. 7 vols. (novels) 1827

The Rhapsodist, and Other Uncollected Writings (essays and novel fragment) 1943

The Novels and Related Works of Charles Brockden Brown. 6 vols. (novels and unfinished novels) 1977-87

Memoirs of Stephen Calvert (unfinished novel) 1978

Carwin, the Biloquist and *Memoirs of Stephen Calvert* were published earlier in William Dunlap's *The Life of Charles Brockden Brown: Together with Selections from the Rarest of His Printed Works, from His Original Letters, and from His Manuscripts Before Unpublished,* 1815.

CRITICISM

William M. Manly (essay date 1963)

SOURCE: Manly, William M. "The Importance of Point of View in Brockden Brown's *Wieland.*" *American Literature* 35, no. 3 (November 1963): 311-21.

[*In the following essay, Manly suggests that* Wieland *has more in common with the darker works of Poe and Hawthorne than the sentimental tradition with which it is often associated.*]

Students of Charles Brockden Brown's **Wieland** have often noted its relationship to the Richardsonian sentimental novel. Fred Lewis Pattee was the first to suggest similarities when he wrote in his early Introduction: "The book is to be classed with the seduction novels so popular at the close of the 18th Century—a book of the *Clarissa Harlowe* type."[1] Leslie Fiedler later elaborated the sentimental seduction theme into the major experience of the novel,[2] and a more recent reading has found **Wieland** to be a sentimental novel with a reactionary middle.[3]

Surely there are sentimental-seduction materials in **Wieland**: Clara, the narrator, swoons at several critical moments; she is occasionally dithyrambic with emotion over her would-be lover Pleyel; Carwin, the villain of the piece, at one point confesses to a desire to ravish Clara; and in the denouement he confesses that he has seduced Clara's maid. Yet I would suggest that for all these incidental trappings, the emotional power of **Wieland** does not rely in any essential way on the traditional appeals of the sentimental novel. The felt literary experience which Brown's early novel provides is far closer to the dark ambiguities of reason and emotion in Poe, Hawthorne, and Henry James than to the palpitating excesses of Richardson. Sentiment is only one aspect of the narrator's sensibility, and not the dominant aspect; seduction is only one of a cluster of threats that assail her, and not the dominant threat. The astonishing intensity which Brown generates in such an unevenly written novel reflects his ability to convey through a first-person narrator the shifting instability of a mind swayed between objective logic and subjective terror, creating thereby a tension which is not resolved until the final pages. The controlling drama of this novel is suggested by another of Pattee's early insights: "The Wieland family is abnormal, but the reader holds the key to this abnormality. The novelist has skillfully furnished all the materials for a clinic. The book is a study in dementia: all four of the main characters are touched with it."[4]

I

The sensibility of Clara Wieland filters two preoccupations which occur throughout Brown's writing: his avowed interest in rationalism, truth, and purpose; and his equal fascination with the disruption of these qualities in the bizarre, the Gothic, and the sentimental. Though critics have claimed **Wieland** for one or the other of these preoccupations,[5] it seems clear that Brown constructed his tale not around one, but around both—the one leading dramatic force to the other—and that the dramatic tension so generated is the key to **Wieland**'s central fascination despite its surface flaws. To be fully logical and guided by common sense is, in the mental world of this narrator, to be fully sane; to give reign to one's susceptibilities to supernatural and mystical speculation on mysterious events is to move toward madness. This unresolved dramatic tension begun in the early pages and continued until the final ones not only gives a heretofore slightly regarded unity to this early tale but is clearly its guiding genius.

Clara displays from the beginning a far more rational and controlled intelligence than that of the typical sentimental heroine. Even random samplings of her conversation have a philosophic rigor unknown to Clarissa: "We recalled and reviewed every particular that had fallen under our observation," "he merely deduced from his own reasonings," "I labored to discover the true inferences deducible from his deportment and words." Her analysis of her brother's possible delusion seems to be taken from Locke or Hume entire: "The will is the tool of the understanding, which must fashion its conclusions on the notices of sense. If the senses be depraved it is impossible to calculate the evils that may flow from the consequent deductions of the understanding" (p. 39). The highly rational Pleyel says of her: "I have contemplated your principles, and been astonished at the solidity of their foundation, and the perfection of their structure" (p. 138). This common sense side of Clara reveals the impact of Brown's reading in Locke and Hume, his early interest in Voltaire and the French Deists, and his association with Deistic thinkers in America like Benjamin Franklin. But beyond this, we see in Clara's rationalism Brown's own innate philosophic habit of mind which caused comment among friends and critics alike.

Yet Clara has a more dangerous aspect to her sensibility, a tendency to veer from objective common sense into a melodramatic world of haunting speculation. Working against her tendency to set forth her narrative logically and clearly are sudden shifts as her imagination becomes overwhelmed with horror. Before describing Carwin she writes "My blood is congealed: and my fingers are palsied when I call up this image. Shame on my cowardly and infirm heart!" (p. 56). Three times she pauses to recover herself from soaring sensations which threaten to overwhelm her senses, and toward the end of the tale she morbidly looks toward her own death: "Let my last energies support me in the finishing of this task. Then will I lay down my head in the lap of death. Hushed will be all my murmurs in the sleep of the grave" (p. 248). The indulgence of Clara's imagination sets up an emotional rhythm in the novel which is constantly tugging at the factual foundations on which the tale seems to be based, and injects a hint of instability into the whole.

This tension which Brown is at pains to create through Clara's conflicting predisposition is initiated in her early description of her father's strange death. On the one hand the event is informed with scientific objectivity. The description of her father's day and of the symptoms with which the fatal evening begins are almost clinical; significantly, a man of science, a doctor (Clara's uncle), related the facts to her because she was too young to have understood them at the time. This same rational and scientific uncle will enter the tale in the final scenes to start Clara back on the road to mental health. Clara says of him: "My uncle's testimony is peculiarly worthy of credit, because no man's temper is more skeptical, and his belief is unalterably attached to natural causes" (p. 21). Even the description of her father's body after the mysterious accident is unemotionally realistic: "My father, when he left the house, besides a loose upper vest and slippers, wore a shirt and drawers. Now he was naked, his skin throughout the greater part of his body was scorched and bruised. His right arm exhibited marks as of having been struck by some heavy body. His clothes had been removed, and it was not immediately perceived that they were reduced to ashes. His slippers and his hair were untouched" (pp. 19-20). It is not surprising that the precisely observed details of this description came from an actual journal report of a similar accident: Clara's tone of factual authenticity is unmistakable.

Yet though she is disposed to view her father's death with a certain objective reserve, another more "Gothic" appeal manifests itself. Throughout the episode Clara dwells intermittently on her father's feeling that he might be doomed by some supernatural agency, and on

her mother's thoughts that fatal night. The episode when seen from the eyes of her mother is bathed in emotionalism: "What was it she feared? Some disaster impended over her husband or herself. He had predicted evils but professed himself ignorant of what nature they were. When were they to come? Was this night, or this hour to witness the accomplishment?" (pp. 17-18). This impressionistic speculation on her mother's thoughts long after the event is evidence at the outset of a tendency to color events subjectively, a tendency with which the reader sympathizes—the death is, after all, a mystery—but on which he can only reserve judgment. The peculiar irresolution of the elder Wieland's death is in part the irresolution of Clara's attitude toward it, an irresolution which the tale will demonstrate to have dangerous consequences.

Brown's dramatization of opposed tendencies in Clara's consciousness is structurally reinforced by the externally opposed personalities of the ultra-rational Pleyel and the ultra-religious Wieland. Their conflicting, and ultimately irreconcilable, attitudes toward experience are defined early: "Pleyel was not behind his friend in knowledge of the history and metaphysics of religion. Their creeds, however, were in many respects opposite. Where one discovered only confirmations of his faith, the other could find nothing but reasons for doubt. Moral necessity, and calvinistic inspiration, were the props on which my brother thought proper to repose. Pleyel was the champion of intellectual liberty, and rejected all guidance but that of his reason" (p. 28). Pleyel, being an outsider, is untouched by the morbid inheritance of a mysterious death which appears to haunt the Wielands; his perspective is like that of Clara's uncle whose nature was "unalterably attached to natural causes." Pleyel is inclined to regard the mysterious voice which Wieland first hears with sociable good humor and skeptical reservation. Wieland, on the other hand, consistently exhibits a mind prone to supernatural brooding and tends to color events with his own interpretation of them. The mysterious voices cause Wieland to fall into a prolonged, introspective meditation which partially isolates him from his friends. Clara remarks of her brother that he always regarded his father's death as "flowing from a direct and supernatural decree," and that he was in some respects an "enthusiast" in religious matters.

Clara is clearly the inheritor of her brother's introspective disposition, which she gradually comes to realize is leading to dangerous alienation from reality, but which she is powerless to control by the application of objective logic. Her emotional commitment to supernatural interference is deepened by her second encounter with the mysterious voice, this time heard not only by Wieland but by Pleyel. She cannot contain an upwelling of enthusiasm: "The tales of apparitions and enchantments did not possess that power over my belief which could even render them interesting. I saw nothing in them but ignorance and folly, and was a stranger even to that terror which is pleasing. But this incident was different from any that I had ever before known. Here were proofs of a sensible and intelligent existence, which could not be denied. Here was information obtained and imparted by means unquestionably superhuman" (p. 51). Her use of "proofs" and "unquestionably" at this juncture, while Pleyel is bemused but uncommitted, is an ominous shifting of Clara's mental balance in the direction of Wieland's "enthusiasm"; her assured invocation of the supernatural to explain appearances runs against an underlying tenor of skeptical "scientism" and rationality which has vied for the reader's attention from the beginning.[6] Through Clara's brooding and extravagance Brown begins subtly to establish that the mind which filters the experience of the tale is itself a biased glass which warps the proportions of the events seen; in this respect, the complex tension of the tale becomes focused not on typical sentimental or Gothic situations, but on the problem of separating appearances from realities, truths from fictions, in a manner which suggests Henry James's later technique in "The Turn of the Screw." Clara's vacillation at this point is merely an early tremor in her mental stability but it is a tremor which subtly prepares the reader for those later oscillations between madness and sanity which dominate the tale's central scenes.

Clara grows more and more frenzied as frustration and isolation continue to exacerbate an already divided sensibility. Her tone takes on a desperate quality: "You will believe that calamity has subverted my reason, and that I am amusing you with the chimeras of my brain, instead of facts that really happened. I shall not be surprized or offended, if these be your suspicions" (p. 74). As her instability mounts, her naturally rationalistic, philosophic temper becomes steadily weakened: "I now speak as if no remnant of doubt existed in my mind as to the supernal origin of these sounds; but this is owing to the imperfection of my language, for I only mean that the belief was more permanent, and visited more frequently my sober meditations than its opposite. The immediate effects served only to undermine the foundations of my judgment and precipitate my resolutions" (p. 168).

II

The subtle dislocation of Clara's narrative is further emphasized by her inexplicable first-sight reaction to Carwin, the ventriloquist villain, a reaction which the reader can neither share nor understand. Having had only a glimpse of Carwin's face (he appears as a rustic stranger), and hearing only a snatch of his conversation to her maid, she is not only moved to tears, but his image continues to preoccupy her for days. The instability which she displays at this juncture is confusing even to

herself: "The manner in which I was affected on this occasion, was, to my own apprehension, a subject of astonishment. The tones were indeed such as I never heard before; but that they should, in an instant, as it were, dissolve me in tears, will not easily be believed by others, and can be scarcely comprehended by myself" (p. 59). Clara's involuntary fantasies soon veer to a morbid preoccupation with her father's mysterious death and her own legacy of possible madness; Carwin the stranger is thus only the occasion for a fresh release of melancholy as his image provokes foreshadowings of doom.

This curious reaction, taken together with her response to the voices in the closet plotting her murder, and the warning in the recess—all the startling and inexplicable situations that make up the fabric of this tale—gradually isolate Clara from the free and healthy social intercourse of the novel's beginning, to press her toward the private hell of doubt and uncertainty which characterizes its climax. The progression appears as preordained as a Greek tragedy. We follow those early premonitions and warnings which have intruded into her consciousness and watch them become inexorably realized in the real and threatened mental disintegration of Wieland and Clara herself. One of Brown's major foreshadowing devices, which has heretofore received insufficient, if not irrelevant, treatment, is the dramatic impact and subsequent effect of Clara's dream of Wieland, a dream which not only subtly prepares the reader for Wieland's disastrous transformation in the climactic scenes of violence but gives Clara a dim insight into her own possible mental disintegration if she follows her brother's course. After falling asleep in an isolated summer bower, she dreams she is walking in the evening twilight to her brother's habitation: "A pit, methought, had been dug in the path I had taken, of which I was not aware. As I carelessly pursued my walk, I thought I saw my brother, standing at some distance before me, beckoning and calling me to make haste. He stood on the opposite edge of the gulph. I mended my pace, and one step more would have plunged me into this abyss, had not some one from behind caught suddenly my arm, and exclaimed, in a voice of eagerness and terror, 'Hold! hold!'" (p. 71)

In a curious way, Clara both sees and does not see the pit toward which she is headed in her carelessness; it is a course which her conscious mind neglects but which her subconscious intuits as destructive. The dream is appropriately mysterious; it is an "abyss" toward which her brother beckons her, but with what intention? Recent criticism of **Wieland** has been inclined to interpret the abyss and Clara's fears of her brother as a latent horror of incest,[7] despite the complete lack of objective evidence for such a view within the novel. Clara at no point fears seduction or rape by Wieland but at several points fears the homicidal possibilities of a latent, and perhaps inherited, insanity in her brother. The image of an "abyss" is present at two other crucial points in the narrative, where it is clearly used to mean the gulf of insanity.[8] Furthermore, Clara herself interprets her own dream toward the end of the tale as a prophetic intuition of her brother's incipient transformation into a maniac,[9] an intuition which is repeated in the following waking episode that takes place shortly after her dream.

Alone and in a disturbed state, Clara enters her bedroom prepared to peruse a manuscript, but at her closet door she hesitates, inexplicably overcome with terror: "A sort of belief darted into my mind, that some being was concealed within, whose purposes were evil" (p. 96). She is suddenly haunted by the vision of "An hand invisible and of preternatural strength, lifted by human passions, and selecting my life for its aim," and in the instant the dream of Wieland's temptation to destruction is recalled. She is led to the irresistible conclusion that Wieland is within the closet—"What monstrous conclusion is this? my brother!" (p. 99) Once again the dream warns her subconscious of danger, but it is quite obviously not sexual assault which she fears but homicidal violence. The very ambiguity of her thoughts and actions in this scene indicates that it is not only Wieland's madness which is dimly presaged, but the scene itself dramatizes a threat to her own sanity that the reader cannot fail to remark. Her irrational compulsiveness here is a subtle prelude to that terrifying compulsive and fanatic behavior of the later Wieland. The disturbed mind faltering in darkness which so fascinates Brockden Brown in this and other novels could well stand as a metaphor for the entire action of this strange tale.[10]

It is not Wieland who emerges from the closet, but Carwin, and this brief direct encounter of Carwin and Clara has been a key scene for those critics who desire to view the tale as Richardsonian. Here, if nowhere else in the novel, sexual assault is presented as a momentary threat. But in the same breath that Carwin alludes to his opportunity to ravish Clara, he professes his inability to do so because she is protected by a "higher power." The scene is short and fraught with mysterious, apologetic behavior on the part of Carwin, who does not appear either here, or anywhere else, as a lusty Lovelace. Even this scene of avowed momentary passion for Clara is later confessed to be a sham expedient, designed to make him seem more flamboyant. Carwin, in fact, is for the most part a shadowy background figure whose final confessions reveal him to be more of a pathetic bumbler than a figure of soaring sexual passion.[11] Though he is the mechanism behind mysterious events, the dramatic heart of the novel is not in the events themselves but in the reaction of Clara and Wieland to them. When the mysteries are brought to light they appear trivial and uninteresting; they have their meaning in the agonies they have produced. Which is only to say again

that the central drama of the novel lies not in sex or sensationalism per se, but in Clara's consciousness as she copes with a growing isolation from the sane and normal preoccupations of daily life.

III

The mysterious alienation of Pleyel (later found to be the work of Carwin) is one more instance of this isolation. The sentimental attraction of Pleyel for Clara is precisely why her isolation from him is so dismaying, for once again the strange has intruded itself into the intimate and familiar to disturb the very foundations of Clara's sanity. To be sure, part of this alienation results from a too scrupulous conventionality which Clara regrets, but this is hardly the most important reason for the alienation, nor is it the point of the whole episode. The incident is organically integrated into Brown's carefully constructed chain of isolation and frustration which with fateful relentlessness is pressing Clara closer and closer to possible disaster, as her emotions and imagination gain control over her reason.[12]

At the climax of the tale those intimations and omens which have plagued Clara from the beginning come to fruition. Wieland's murdered wife and children are discovered, and Wieland himself takes over the narrative for a time (by means of a trial transcript) to portray the consequences of a morbidly hypersensitive sensibility when it is cut loose from any balancing skepticism. Wieland's transcript, which begins so rationally and ends in such horror, is a logical extension of the path on which Clara has been walking, and from which she is only fortuitously saved. In the culminating scenes of the tale, Clara is brought to the brink of complete disorientation: she falls into frenzies, she becomes delirious, and just before Carwin enters for the last time, she is on the point of suicide.

But with Carwin's confession comes catharsis: rationalism begins to be restored and the healthy perspective of fact begins to replace the instability of fancy. This resolution in explanation is actually begun slightly before the confession with the appearance of her uncle, whose rationality and scientific interests take the place of the missing Pleyel. Facts of family history are given, and a medical explanation of Wieland's condition is provided. Yet, as her uncle shows Wieland's madness to be inherited, Clara's dread of her own mental transformation is increased. Shortly after the climactic events she takes to her bed delirious; once again the ominous image of an abyss, the symbolic inheritance which has haunted her from the beginning, is recalled in a phantasmagoric dream: "Sometimes gleams of light were shot into a dark abyss, on the verge of which I was standing, and enabled me to discover for a moment, its enormous depth and hideous precipices" (p. 264). The ultimate purgation breaking the concatenation of terrors that has dominated her fancy is achieved through a fire from which she is physically and symbolically rescued, a fire which sweeps away the scenes of her past and jars her into a fresh start for the future. As it was fire which destroyed her father to begin the inexorable tragic chain of frustrations and fears that make up **Wieland,** so it is fire that at last breaks that chain to allow Clara to return to a normal life.

This fresh start is the true ending of the novel; from this point on Clara's few pages of "tying up loose ends" act simply to draw out the purgation that Carwin's confession inaugurated and bring the reader back into a world of cause-and-effect sanity. That Brown was careless with some of his details is undeniable, but such carelessness leaves the central experience of the novel untouched. This reading has tried to show that Brown's over-all achievement in **Wieland** is far more of a piece than most critics will acknowledge who approach this early work more as a mine of literary-cultural materials than as a powerful psychological experience. If one must find a tradition for **Wieland,** it must surely lie with those peculiarly American explorations of the tormented psyche which seem ambiguously and resonantly to hover between appearance and reality, fact and imagination, daylight and dream. Brockden Brown is clearly the first of those many in American letters who have grasped the dramatic importance of "point of view" in fiction.

Notes

1. Fred Lewis Pattee, Introduction to Charles Brockden Brown's *Wieland or the Transformation,* "Hafner Library of Classics" (New York, 1958), p. xxxvi. All page references (hereafter in text) are to this edition.

2. Leslie Fiedler, *Love and Death in the American Novel* (New York, 1960), Chap. ii.

3. Larzer Ziff, "A Reading of *Wieland,*" *PMLA,* LXXVII, 51-57 (March, 1962).

4. Pattee, Introduction, p. xl.

5. Critics in recent years have swung to the rationalistic view of Brown's fiction. David Lee Clark began the trend in an early dissertation, *Charles Brockden Brown, a Critical Biography,* Columbia University, 1923. Brown's sentimental and Gothic side have been emphasized by Harry Warfel, *Charles Brockden Brown, American Gothic Novelist* (Gainesville, Fla., 1949).

6. In addition to Clara's rationalistic tone, and the emphasis on reason in the tale, Brown's preface serves further to bias the reader toward a realistic solution by promising that "appearances" will be solved in accordance with "known principles of human nature" (*Wieland,* p. 3). See also in this connection Brown's footnotes (pp. 21 and 202) where the naturalistic tendency of the tale is upheld by documentation outside it (unavailable, of course, to Clara).

7. Fiedler, *op. cit.,* began the incest trend, along with a number of other distortions, such as, for example, his statement that "Brown does not dare openly imagine even murder between characters of one blood—only the approach to it" (p. 36), about a tale in which a man murders his wife and four children, and attempts to murder his sister. The incest idea has been revived more recently by Ziff, *op. cit.,* who writes: "The horrors of incest and inherited depravity which Clara forces back from the threshold of her consciousness by turning to thinking about thinking are not to be explained away by the *tabula rasa*" (p. 54).

8. When the impact of Wieland's madness has dawned on her, Clara writes, "Now was I stupified with tenfold wonder in contemplating myself. Was I not likewise transformed from rational and human into a creature of nameless and fearful attributes? Was I not transported to the brink of the same abyss?" (pp. 202-203). Again when in a delirious dream, the image of an abyss again haunts her imagination as the threat of insanity: "Sometimes I was swallowed up by whirlpools, or caught up in the air by half-seen and gigantic forms, and thrown upon pointed rocks, or cast among the billows. Sometimes gleams of light were shot into a dark abyss, on the verge of which I was standing, and enabled me to discover, for a moment, its enormous depth and hideous precipices" (p. 264).

9. "I recollected the omens of this destiny [she is in danger of "perishing under the grasp of a brother"]; I remembered the gulf to which my brother's invitation had conducted me; I remember that, when on the brink of danger, the author of my peril was depicted by my fears in his form: Thus realized, were the creatures of prophetic sleep, and of wakeful terror!" (p. 214). When we add to this Clara's early reservations about Wieland's excessive morbidity, which she claimed "argued a diseased condition of his frame which might show itself hereafter in more dangerous symptoms" (p. 39), Ziff's contention that Wieland's insanity is a "leap rather than a development" (*op. cit.,* p. 56) is rather too simple and condescending—Brown is not interested in "developing" Wieland's madness but in developing Clara's—and to the extent that Clara intuits her brother's condition it is sufficiently prepared for.

10. Clara's crisis of consciousness before a door suggests later treatments of the idea in both Poe's "Fall of the House of Usher," and Henry James's

"Jolly Corner." In these tales, as in *Wieland,* the protagonist has been driven to the edge of sanity before confronting the door, and in each case the door represents the barrier beyond which some terrifying conception lurks which threatens mental equilibrium.

11. Carwin is perhaps the most overrated villain in American fiction, and has been the subject of many distortions. Richard Chase, convinced of Carwin's central role, writes that he "has little difficulty" in convincing Clara at the end of his ventriloquistic endeavors that "if he is a criminal he is a high-minded one whose actual crimes are venial, being merely the result of a certain necessary unscrupulousness in the choice of means to ends" (*The American Novel and its Tradition* [New York, 1957], p. 33). This is clearly wrong. Leslie Fiedler, who misreads the Clara-Carwin relationship in a different way, wishes to make Carwin into a sex-crazed ravisher.

12. Ziff, *op. cit.,* in attempting to prove that the focus of *Wieland* is a rather confused attack on sentimentalism which is not carried through, misses the larger and deeper unity of Brown's work. Leaving aside the assumption that Brown and his intellectual milieu were in a state of optimistic innocence as he started to write, a view which I find untenable, his view of Clara-Pleyel misunderstanding as simply anti-sentimental is superficial.

Joseph A. Soldati (essay date 1974)

SOURCE: Soldati, Joseph A. "The Americanization of Faust: A Study of Charles Brockden Brown's *Wieland.*" *ESQ: A Journal of the American Renaissance* 74, no. 1 (1974): 1-14.

[*In the following essay, Soldati discusses the blending of the Icarus and Narcissus myths achieved by Brown in the characterization of Theodore Wieland and his sister Clara.*]

In Western literature, especially during the Romantic Period, man has often been represented by two heroic figures—Prometheus and Faust. Peter L. Thorslev has correctly claimed that since Prometheus "is the Romantic hero apotheosized, he is pure allegory; there is nothing in him of the Gothic, nothing of the dark mystery or taint of sin of the other Romantic heroes."[1] Prometheus, therefore, represents the most benign aspects of man—his altruistic endeavors in the service of his fellowman.[2] Faust, however, is completely shrouded in "the dark mystery or taint of sin" of the Romantic hero, and his appeal for our culture has been as great as, if not greater than, the appeal of Prometheus. In-

deed, Schopenhauer, in *The World as Will and Representation* (1819), observed that Faust's anguished striving embodies not only the essence of man but also the essence of the cosmos. Even more emphatically, Oswald Spengler states in *The Decline of the West* that the "prime symbol" of the Faustian soul is "pure and limitless space," calls Western civilization the Faustian culture, and designates Faust as the primary representative of Western Man.[3] Faust, totally unlike the altruistic Prometheus who strives for the ultimate well-being of others, strives only for the ultimate satisfaction of himself. Faust, then, represents the more malign aspect of man—his selfishness and egocentrism—at the same time that he represents the ethereal glory of trying to soar with the gods.

Surrounded as Faust is in an aura of mystery—his dark liaisons with devils, spirits, and gods—it is not surprising that the dominant villain-heroes of the Gothic novel are Faustian men. It is not enough to claim, as Mario Praz does, that the Gothic hero-villain is a perverted, metamorphosed descendant of Satan in a black cape of Romantic erotic sensibility; for the Gothic hero-villain is also a Faustian man in the tradition of Marlowe's Faustus and Goethe's Faust.[4] What has not been observed is that the Faustian man incorporates the myths of Icarus and Narcissus, and that the configurations of these myths reveal the psychological, metaphysical, and structural components of the Gothic novel. For the Faustian protagonist of the Gothic novel, the Narcissistic (internal) plunge into the Self and the Icarian (external) leap above human frailty are in constant, relentless tension. Utilizing this tension extant between its heroes' internal and external impulses, the Gothic novel—as a genre of the Faustian literary tradition—is thus a paradigm of man's dangerous egocentrism (Narcissism) and his soaring search for forbidden knowledge and subsequent fall (Icarianism). The Gothic novel is, then, a retelling of the myth of man's fall, the fall brought about by his attempts to gain the secrets of the universe—his attempts to be the equal of the gods.

To be the equal of the gods, however, man must disassociate himself from mortal existence. And principle of all the Faustian characteristics is the individual's drive to leave the earth of men. Such a drive has in fact been called by psychologists the Icarus complex,[5] deriving from the myth of Icarus, the youth who, after escaping the earth, flew too close to the sun which melted the wax of his wings and caused him to plunge to his death in the sea. One can associate the Icarus complex with numerous American and European fictional characters, but nowhere is the complex more apparent than in the Gothic novel. Indeed, it is not unreasonable to observe that, in the Gothic novel, the Faustian prototype is characteristically possessed by an Icarus complex. It is as though he, like Icarus, leaves the earth to experience the ethereal and that this dizzying experience of dwelling in the stratosphere of the gods blurs his perception of his own mortal existence. Joseph L. Henderson has written that "Faust had failed to live out to the full an important part of his early life. He was, accordingly, an unreal or incomplete person who lost himself in a fruit-less quest for metaphysical goals that failed to material-ize. He was . . . unwilling to accept life's challenges to live both the good and the bad."[6] This refusal to face the earthly realities of life and the tendency to substi-tute instead a metaphysical quest may well be dominant characteristics of the Icarus complex.

The psychological concept of the Icarus complex, ac-cording to Ogilvie (p. 31), is a "compound of *ascen-sionism* (the wish to overcome gravity), *narcissism* (a craving for attention and admiration), and the *anticipa-tion of falling* (unwanted or accidental descents)." In the Gothic novel ascensionism (the major feature of the Icarus myth because Icarus actually attempted to fly from the earth to the heavens) is, of course, not usually manifest in the protagonist's actual flight; rather he en-deavors to raise himself above ordinary human exist-ence and seeks godlike status. Ascensionism is revealed in the Faustian man through his "fantasies of rising, fly-ing, and floating; in a fondness for height (tall people, trees, towers, mountains) and for flying objects . . . in bursts of enthusiasm, extravagant flights of fancy and rapid elevations of confidence; in wishes for a spectacu-lar rise in social status or prestige; and so on" (Ogilvie, p. 31). Constantly believing in his own supremacy, the Faustian man refuses to surrender himself to the world of his fellowman, and, at least in his own mind, he pulls away from that world.

Christopher Marlowe's Doctor Faustus obviously as-pires to higher-than-human goals, and the first chorus of the drama links the doctor with Icarus:

> So much he profits in divinity,
> The fruitful plot of scholarism grac'd,
> That shortly he was grac'd with Doctor's name,
> Excelling all and sweetly can dispute
> In the heavenly matters of Theology;
> Till swoln with cunning, of a self-conceit,
> His waxen wings did mount above his reach,
> And, melting, heavens conspir'd his over-throw.[7]

Faustus' self-conceit is, of course, only his ego in tri-umph—in ascension—over all other concerns. Glutted with learning, he mixes idealism with over-confidence, over-estimates his abilities, and refuses to recognize his limitations as a man. This, then, is the meaning of the Icarus myth: "The human ego can be exalted to experi-ence godlike attributes, but only at the cost of over-reaching itself and falling to disaster" (Henderson, pp. 112-113).

It is, therefore, the dual nature—the soaring and the falling—of the Faustian hero that is most intriguing. Like Marlowe's Faustus, Goethe's Faust is also imbued with self-conceit:

> Of course, I am smarter than all the shysters,
> The doctors, and teachers, and Scribes, and Christers.[8]

And he early describes his own existence as apart from other men:

> I, image of the godhead, that began
> To dream eternal truth was within reach,
> Exulting on the heavens' brilliant beach
> As if I had stripped off the mortal man.

> *(Faust* I, 614-617; p. 111)

This is the beginning of the Icarian leap, for Faust's stripping off the human veneer of mortality is tanta-mount to man's disastrous exaltation of his ego. In such a deluded state, Faust does not know that in his soaring is also his fall. Mephistopheles, however, does know this, and commands the spirits to "dazzle him with dream shapes, sweet and vast. / *Plunge him into an ocean of untruth*" (*Faust* I.1510-1511; p. 171, my italics). In his desire to soar, the Faustian-Icarian cannot check his inevitable fall.

It is Narcissism, however, that is the primary source of the Faustian hero's Icarianism. Implicit in the Gothic novel is, as Harold Bloom observes of many Romantic works, a complex exploration into "the Romantic my-thology of self."[9] Thus the Faustian man is the embodi-ment of the Romantic writers' preoccupation with self-indulgence. This internal, Narcissistic allure of the Self seemingly conflicts with the hero's external, Icarian im-pulse to soar above mortals. Yet it is the psychological nature of the hero's Narcissism that generates his out-ward metaphysical quest. If one can imagine the hero's Narcissism as a metal spring being wound tighter and tighter and then suddenly releasing, one can understand the inward, psychological impulse of the hero's Narcis-sism and the outward, metaphysical release of his Icari-anism. Both impulses are generated by the same spring, so to speak. Thus, the Faustian villain-hero of the Gothic novel is a Narcissist because his Icarian quests for forbidden knowledge and godlike status are really exercises in the idolatry of Self and are therefore dan-gerous. His ultimate spiritual, and in some cases physi-cal, reflections invert the ancient, classical myth of Nar-cissus and are horrible instead of beautiful. Herbert Marcuse, in "The Images of Orpheus and Narcissus," discusses the relationship of both Orpheus and Narcis-sus to Western culture with pertinence to the nature of the Faustian hero's Narcissism.[10] These images, Mar-cuse writes, explode the reality of the world and "are committed to the underworld and to death. At best they are poetic, something for the soul and the heart. But they do not teach any 'message'—except the negative one that one cannot defeat death or forget and reject the call of life in the admiration of beauty" (p. 165). Ulti-mately, like the mythological Narcissus, the Faustian hero is victim of his own self-enamoration.

Narcissism, the primary force in the Faustian hero's belief that he can overcome the horror of mortal existence, ensnares him with its dark allure. Enraptured with the reflection of his Self in the metaphysical pool of possibility, the hero recognizes perfection in his own ego. Then, unable to sustain this euphoric vision of his perfect being, he compensates for over-estimating his ego by what Erich Neumann characterizes as "a depressive self-destruction which, in the form of *Weltschmerz* and self-hatred, often culminates in suicide. . . ."[11] But it is the dark side of the Self that the Narcissistic reflection really projects. "The dark side of the Self is the most dangerous thing of all," writes M.-L. von Franz, "precisely because the Self is the greatest power in the psyche. It can cause people to 'spin' megalomanic or other delusory fantasies that catch them up and 'possess' them. A person in this state thinks with mounting excitement that he has grasped and solved the great cosmic riddles; he therefore loses all touch with human reality. A reliable symptom of this condition is the loss of one's sense of humor and of human contact."[12] At the height of the Faustian hero's megalomania, the dark side of his Self becomes the dominant, destructive side, and his reality is totally subjective. Any action he takes will usually be at the expense of others, often those closest to him. Hence Narcissism—the plunge into the Self—destroys not only the Faustian hero but also those around him.

There is, however, a distinction between the Faustian hero's Narcissistic plunge into the Self and his Icarian plunge, or fall, away from his ethereal goals—even though the two plunges are complementary. The Narcissistic plunge is the direct and psychological result of the Faustian hero's inward brooding and mesmerization with his Self. The Icarian plunge is the indirect and metaphysical result of the hero's attempt to soar above human frailty. For the Faustian hero it is the Icarian plunge that is his greatest fear—his anticipation of falling—the fear that he will lose favor with the gods he has sought to imitate and will be hurled back to the earth of mere men. When he is hurled back, he often falls into what is, metaphorically speaking, the underworld—that real or imaginary dark labyrinth of the human condition. But the Faustian hero of the Gothic novel, regardless of the motives or the stimuli that influence him to emulate Icarus, is not engaged in mere folly. Indeed, he seems to typify the man who desires to dwell apart in both degree and kind from his fellowman. But he is only the challenger, and seldom, if ever, the victor. The Faustian hero, then, is one who takes the fatal Narcissistic plunge into the Self and, simultaneously, the Icarian leap away from human frailty to challenge the gods.

Charles Brockden Brown's *Wieland; Or, The Transformation* (1798) is the American Romantic successor of the Faustian tradition. Innovatively employing the myths of Icarus and Narcissus in its exploration of the Faustian hero's dark psyche, *Wieland* is the precursor of the psychological tales of Poe, Hawthorne, Melville, Faulkner, and others.[13] The two myths not only are subjacent to the Icarus complexes inherent in the elder Wieland and his son Theodore, but are also thematic and, to a lesser extent, structural entities as well. Brown's *Wieland* achieves an effective synthesis of the two myths so that they become psychological configurations which dominate and reflect both Wielands' Faustian endeavors. *Wieland* is more than a novel about the madness of two men; it is an artistic, literary structuring of that madness.[14] To examine *Wieland* is to explore the Icarian-Narcissistic elements which pervade the novel and which expose the dark and terrible labyrinth of Faustian existence.

I

The first chapter of the novel reveals the beginning of the elder Wieland's Icarian nature. A brooding and remorseful man, he "spent all his time pent up in a gloomy apartment, or traversing narrow and crowded streets" until he discovered the book of the Comisards and the Bible.[15] The knowledge he finds in these works lifts him to the apex of ecstasy as often as it drops him into the abyss of fear. Thus he experiences the ascensionism and the anticipation of falling which are symptomatic of the Icarus complex. As Brown writes: "He was alternately agitated by fear and ecstasy. He imagined himself beset by the snares of a spiritual foe, and that his security lay in ceaseless watchfulness and prayer" (p. 15). But the elder Wieland becomes possessed by this "spiritual foe," which he calls his Deity, and after emigrating to America and settling on the Schuylkill River (near Philadelphia), he builds a temple for it. Set on a cliff above the river, the temple "was no more than a circular area, twelve feet in diameter, whose flooring was the rock, cleared of moss and shrubs, and exactly levelled, edged by twelve Tuscan columns, and covered by an undulating dome" (p. 18). By constructing the temple on the bluff above the river, the elder Wieland manifests not only his growing religious fanaticism but also an Icarian fondness for high places. The temple, then, becomes a monument to his religious ecstasy, to his Icarian soaring.

In spite of old Wieland's fantastical imagination and its accompanying religious fanaticism, he never insists that his wife, his two children—Clara and Theodore—or anyone else worship as he does. In fact:

> His deportment to others was full of charity and mildness. A sadness perpetually overspread his features, but was unmingled with sternness or discontent. The tones of his voice, his gestures, his steps, were all in tranquil uniform. His conduct was characterized by a certain forebearance and humility, which secured the esteem of those to whom his tenets were most obnoxious. They

might call him a fanatic and a dreamer, but they could not deny their veneration to his invincible candour and invariable integrity. His own belief of rectitude was the foundation of his happiness.

(p. 19)

The old man's appearance as a fair and charitable man is misleading, however. For as he substitutes his fanaticism for earthly reality, he becomes more and more alienated from his family: the world of his Deity is his primary concern, the world of men secondary. Yet one must not forget that he had *knowledge* of his Deity, and that, in spite of his overt fanaticism, he knew what other men did not know; he had gained access to an electrifying spiritual world. It is not important that he never reveals the mysteries of this other world. What is important is that knowledge of the Deity's world came only after he turned away from the human world.

But, as with all Icarians, his ecstasy, his happiness does not last. The anticipation of falling is always present:

Suddenly the sadness that constantly attended him was deepened. Sighs, and even tears, sometimes escaped him. To the expostulations of his wife he seldom answered anything. When he designed to be communicative, he hinted that his peace of mind was flown, in consequence of deviation from his duty. A command had been laid upon him, which he had delayed to perform. He felt as if a certain period of hesitation and reluctance had been allowed him, but that this period was passed. He was no longer permitted to obey. The duty assigned to him was transferred, in consequence to his disobedience, to another, and all that remained was to endure the penalty.

(p. 20)

The ultimate penalty is, of course, death; but for the elder Wieland, Icarian that he is, it is really the fall from his former ethereal fantasy that is most painful. Unable to sustain the ecstatic soaring quality between himself and his Deity, he believes he has lost the Deity's favor and has been cast down:

He did not describe the penalty. It appeared to be nothing more for some time than a sense of wrong. This was sufficiently acute, and was aggravated by the belief that his offence was incapable of expiation. No one could contemplate the agonies which he seemed to suffer without the deepest compassion. Time, instead of lightening the burden, appeared to add to it. At length he hinted to his wife that his end was near. His imagination did not prefigure the mode or the time of his decease, but was fraught with an incurable persuasion that his death was at hand. He was likewise haunted by the belief that the kind of death that awaited him was strange and terrible. His anticipations were thus far vague and indefinite: but they sufficed to poison every moment of his being and devote him to ceaseless anguish.

(p. 20)

But the old man's haunting premonitions of his "strange and terrible" death are only partly illustrative of his final suffering. The death itself is also symbolic of the terrible consequences of his dark knowledge. On a night when his inquietude is the greatest, he is mortally injured by a severe blow and vicious burns. Of the mysterious circumstances which occurred that night, only this is revealed:

It appeared, that while engaged in silent orisons, with thoughts full of confusion and anxiety, a faint gleam suddenly shot athwart the apartment. His fancy immediately pictured to itself a person bearing a lamp. It seemed to come from behind. He was in the act of turning to examine the visitant, when his right arm received a blow from a heavy club. At the same instant, a very bright spark was seen to light upon his clothes. In a moment, the whole was reduced to ashes.

(p. 26)

His is a lingering, stinking, horrible death of fever, delirium, and "insupportable exhalations and crawling putrefaction" (p. 26). As Icarus was destroyed by the heat of the sun, old Wieland dies from spontaneous combustion—explosion and fire—as if fulfilling his tormented apocalyptic vision.[16]

In the interval between old Wieland's death and young Theodore Wieland's own fanatical transformation, the elder Wieland's wife dies. Clara and Theodore are raised by a maiden aunt and remain at the family home where they are educated away from "the corruption and tyranny of colleges and boarding schools" (p. 28). The isolation of their youth continues into their adulthood despite the coming of Catharine [sic] Pleyel, who becomes Theodore's wife, and later of Henry, Catharine's brother. In the "six years of uninterrupted happiness" (p. 34) following their marriage, Theodore and Catharine have four children and become the guardians of fourteen-year-old Louisa Conway. Suddenly the isolated tranquility of their lives is broken by the mysterious Carwin who, unknown to the others, practices ventriloquism—a practice which helps precipitate Theodore Wieland's transformation from eccentric scholar to homicidal maniac and suicide.

Carwin, however, is only the catalyst: Theodore Wieland is his own executioner. To understand completely how and why Wieland operates, one must closely examine the major components of his Icarus complex—his Narcissism and Icarian ascensionism. For these, the inner workings of his psyche outwardly expressed, not only make him the extraordinary fictional character he is, but also set the Icarian rise-fall pattern that carries throughout the novel.

Wieland, like Narcissus, becomes the victim of his egocentrism and, like Icarus, attempts to soar above human frailty. Wieland's turn inward, as well as his desire to raise himself above all mortals, originates from two acceptable civilized endeavors—scholarship and religion. Although the younger Wieland's drive for knowledge exceeds his father's in its relentlessness, it parallels the traditional forms of which the reader is familiar in both Marlowe's and Goethe's Fausts: "My brother was an indefatigable student," writes Clara, and adds that "the chief object of his veneration was Cicero" (p. 32). This mention of Wieland's scholarly character takes on a new importance when one remembers that Cicero was also an egoist who sought perfection in his arguments. And Wieland is not content just to understand the works of his Latin hero: "He was anxious to discover the gestures and cadences with which they ought to be delivered. He was very scrupulous in selecting a true scheme of pronunciation for the Latin tongue, and in adapting it to the words of his darling writer" (p. 32). One soon discovers to what depths Wieland immerses himself in his studies, and in what inane results he glorifies: "His favorite occupation consisted in embellishing his rhetoric with all the properties of gesticulation and utterance. Not contented with this, he was diligent in settling and restoring the purity of the text. For this end, he collected all the editions and commentaries that could be procured, and employed months of severe study in exploring and comparing them. He never betrayed more satisfaction than when he made a discovery of this kind" (p. 33). Totally committing himself to the rational mechanics of scholarship, Wieland is actually engaged in producing trivia. His study is merely for his own self-glorification.

But academic excellence is not enough to satisfy Wieland's ultimate metaphysical goals. He is like Goethe's Faust who realizes that

> Two souls, alas, are dwelling in my breast,
> And one is stiving to forsake its brother.
> Unto the world in grossly loving zest,
> With clinging tendrils, one adheres;
> *The other rises forcibly in quest*
> *Of rarefied ancestral spheres.*

(I, 1112-1117; p. 145; my italics)

In evidence here are the two souls, or Selves, of Faustian man. One Self recognizes the earthly concerns of human love and responsibility; the other, trapped in the dark web of the ego, advances toward the forbidden realms of the gods. Like Faust, Wieland wants absolute truth; unlike Faust, however, Wieland turns toward religion for ultimate knowledge and truth and becomes an adamant Calvinist.

Characteristic of Wieland's basic Calvinism is a marked distrust of society-at-large and a constant distrust of his own intelligence. He permits himself only the company of his family and a few select friends, and he is mistrustful of anything foreign—his inherited European es-

tates, for example. His brooding over religious matters, however, destroys his intellectual awareness to the extent that he is in a constant quandary whether or not to trust even his senses when he hears the voice. While all of this is occurring, he remains, curiously enough, exhilarated—his enlarged Calvinism transforming into a soaring, destructive fanaticism as he slowly succumbs to the belief that he is in personal contact with God.

Wieland's religious fanaticism, then, is really his ruling passion. Infused as he is with the belief that his father's death was the result of a "direct and supernatural decree" (p. 45), Wieland can only believe that the voice he hears for the first time in the temple is God's. (It is really Carwin using ventriloquism to keep from being discovered.) This first voice incident catalyzes Wieland's religious fanaticism with his Narcissistic tendency and instigates his Icarian leap. In other words, Wieland's inward Narcissism is the nucleus of his outward Icarian release. Thus, the extent of Wieland's fanaticism must be understood in terms of his perception of the significance of the voice for him. Clara observes that "the will is the tool of the understanding, which must fashion its conclusion on the notices of sense. If the senses be depraved, it is impossible to calculate the evils that may flow from the consequent deductions of the understanding."[17] The reader along with Wieland discovers the presence of the young man's dark Self—one which writhes in Narcissistic-Icarian tension. And there is evidence that Wieland feels the influence of his dark Self, for shortly after the first voice incident, on a dark night, he wishes aloud that "not only the physical but moral night be dispelled" (p. 46).

Wieland's metamorphosis has now begun; the voice has inextricably enmeshed him in the entanglements of his fanatical religious uncertainty.[18] When Clara asks him what he thinks of the incident, he exclaims: "There is no determinate way in which the subject can be viewed. Here is an effect; but the cause is utterly inscrutable. To suppose a deception will not do. Such is possible, but there are twenty other suppositions more probable. They must all be set aside before we reach that point" (p. 46). What is important about this first encounter with the voice is that it marks the beginning of Wieland's transformation from eccentric scholar to fanatical madman. It marks the cessation of his scholarly pursuits and the increase of his religious pursuits. It is the point from which he begins his long journey into his dark Self, the point at which he is so powerfully captivated by his ego that he cannot escape himself nor concern himself with others, the point from which he must begin his escape from the earth of men to fit the self-imposed majesty that will find favor in the eyes of his inscrutable God; it is the point from which his Narcissism and his Icarianism become more and more intense.

Because Wieland is unwilling to suspect he is being deceived by a human voice, his fantasy now governs his actions, and the voice of his imagination demands that he kill his wife. The murder obviously illustrates the extreme violence of Wieland's Faustianism. But such an act, he believes, will dramatize his religious faith and propel him into the ethereal realm of God. After strangling Catharine, Wieland is raised to heights of religious rapture, as if he truly had left the earth of frail men:

> This was a moment of triumph. Thus had I successfully subdued the stubbornness of human passions; the victim which had been demanded was given; the deed was done past recall.
>
> I lifted the corpse in my arms and laid it on the bed. I gazed upon it with delight. Such was the elation of my thoughts, that I even broke into laughter. I clapped my hands and exclaimed, "It is done! My sacred duty is fulfilled! To that I have sacrificed, O my God! thy last and best gift, my wife!"
>
> *For a while I thus soared above frailty.*
>
> (pp. 196-197; my italics)

But Wieland's rapture quickly subsides to sorrow—the expected human emotional reaction: "*I imagined I had set myself forever beyond the reach of selfishness*: but my imaginations were false. This rapture quickly subsided" (p. 197; my italics). This resulting premature descent from ecstasy is unexpected and almost unbearable: "I will not dwell upon my lapse into desperate and outrageous sorrow. The breath of heaven that sustained me was withdrawn, and I sunk into *mere man*" (p. 197). The ideal has not been reached; the sacrifice is not complete if he is to have perfect spiritual understanding, or so he believes; and he is given another chance at the total rapture he experienced earlier:

> I thank my God that this degeneracy was transient,— that he deigned once more to raise me aloft. I thought upon what I had done as a sacrifice to duty, and *was calm*. My wife was dead; but I reflected that though this source of human consolation was closed, yet others were still open. If the transports of a husband were no more, the feelings of a father had still scope for exercise. When remembrance of their mother should excite too keen a pang, I would look upon them and *be comforted*.
>
> While I revolved these ideas, new warmth flowed in upon my heart—I was wrong. These feelings were the growth of selfishness. Of this I was not aware, and, to dispel the mist that obscured my perceptions, a new effulgence and a new mandate were necessary.
>
> From these thoughts I was recalled by a ray that was shot into the room. A voice spoke like that which I had before heard:—"Thou has done well. But all is not done—the sacrifice is incomplete—thy children must be offered—they must perish with their mother!—."
>
> (pp. 197-198)

Although Doctor Faustus and Faust endeavored to reach their material-spiritual nirvanas at the expense of themselves and loved ones, Wieland is the first to brutally murder so many to escape his mortal boundaries. Marlowe's Faustus is damned; Goethe's Faust, although later reprieved, destroys Gretchen; but Wieland annihilates his whole family, his wife and all his blood heirs—Benjamin, William, Constantine, little Clara—and even his ward, Louisa Conway.

It is the savagery of Wieland's Faustianism—its utter violence and total destructiveness—that sets him apart from his European predecessors and reflects the New World's violent temper.[19] Wieland's terrible crimes—the result of apocalyptic brooding coupled with fanatical pursuit of an ideal—point the way for protagonists of numerous later American novels. Some even surpass Wieland as does Ahab, who sacrifices his ship's company for Moby-Dick. But the Americanization of Faust is Brown's creation, and Wieland is the first Faust in our literature to use such totally destructive means to achieve his ends.

Like all Faustian men, however, and like his father before him, Wieland anticipates his fall. After murdering his wife, he admits that his aspirations to set himself "beyond the reach of selfishness" (p. 197) were false. His "breath of heaven" withdrawn, he falls only to rise again by murdering his children. His final anticipation of falling occurs during his last confrontation with Clara. In perhaps his most rational moments after the murders, he asks: "Sister, . . . I have acted poorly my part in this world. What thinkest thou? Shall I do better in the next?" (p. 253). Later he exclaims: "My wife and babes have gone before. Happy wretches! I have sent you to repose, and ought not to linger behind" (p. 253). He has become destructive to the point of self-destruction, and, perhaps consciously, he anticipates his own suicide.

Because he falls from his God's favor, Wieland, like all Faustian men, is finally "restored to the perception of truth"—the human truth of his delusion and depravity. It is not the fall but the abrupt realization of his own human truth that destroys him. For Wieland's fall and ultimate sorrow obliterate all his links with the human and spiritual world. When Wieland believes Carwin's admonishing words ("Man of errors . . .") to be God's, both the human and the ethereal worlds are negated. Is he lunatic? Has he cherished merely a delusion? These questions seem to race through his astonished and perplexed mind. He mutters incomprehensibly an appeal to heaven which "implied doubt as to the nature of the impulse that hitherto had guided him, and questioned whether he had acted in consequence of insane perceptions" (p. 260).

But Wieland is unable to bear even these flickerings of doubt. Before Carwin had spoken Wieland had been ready to murder his sister. Now he stumbles randomly around the room; his face twitches, and his lips move

but utter no sound. He is beyond help as a human being, beyond fitting himself into the human spectrum,
and beyond bearing the excruciating abstractions of his
mind:

> For a time his movements seemed destitute of purpose.
> If he walked; if he turned; if his fingers were entwined
> with each other; if his hands were pressed against op-
> posite sides of his head with a force sufficient to crush
> it into pieces; it was to tear his mind from self-
> contemplation; to waste his thoughts on external ob-
> jects.

(p. 261)

Even Clara can see no purpose for him to go on living:

> Oh that thy frenzy had never been cured! that thy mad-
> ness, with its blissful visions, would return! or, if that
> must not be, that thy scene would hasten to a close!—
> that death would cover thee with its oblivion!
>
> What can I wish for thee? Thou who hast vied with the
> great Preacher of thy faith in sanctity of motives, and
> in elevation above sensual and selfish! Thou whom the
> fate has changed into parricide and savage! Can I wish
> for the continuance of thy being? No.

(p. 261)

It is as if the word "No" now symbolizes for Wieland
the complete loss of his Icarian gamble. Only his ego
remains, and he presses his hands against his head as if
to smother it within the fierce recesses of his mind.
Then, his Faustian role complete, in a frenzied yet enlightened gesture, he grasps his knife and plunges it
into his neck.

II

If *Wieland* is an exploration of the Faustian hero's dark
psyche, it is Clara's point of view that reveals that
darkness, for she not only narrates nearly all the novel,
she is also her brother's Narcissistic image. It is by
Clara that the reader comes to understand Wieland. And
although there is hardly an implication of incest between Wieland and Clara, Brown's *Wieland* is the first
American novel to disclose the Narcissism between
brother and sister. Clara virtually mirrors herself in her
brother's early happiness and final despair; the more his
mind becomes distorted by his fanatical delusions, the
more she reflects his grotesque agony: "My state was
little different from that of my brother. I entered, as it
were, into his thoughts. My heart was visited and rent
by his pangs" (pp. 260-261). Even after Wieland kills
himself, Clara seems mesmerized by his dead body—
the Narcissistic reflection in utter refraction: "I was incapable of sparing a look or thought from the ruin that
was spread at my feet" (p. 262).

This sibling Narcissism in American fiction is based on
subtle psychological factors, rather than on physical attraction between brother and sister. Although William

Hill Brown—no relation—introduced the incest motif
in the American novel in *The Power of Sympathy*
(1789), it is Brockden Brown's treatment of sibling
Narcissism that is used later by Poe with Roderick and
Madeline Usher ("The Fall of the House of Usher")
and, even more strangely and more dynamically, by
Faulkner with Henry and Judith Sutpen (*Absalom,
Absalom!*), Horace and Narcissa Benbow (*Sanctuary
and Sartoris*), and Quentin and Caddy Compson (*The
Sound and the Fury*). Each of these brothers finds an
alter-ego in his sister; conversely, each sister sees in her
brother a reflection of herself.

Wieland's own Narcissism is reflected not only by his
sister, Clara, but by his wife, Catharine. Together they
form a mutual admiration society, acting out their innate Narcissism. Clara herself attests to this fact: "Every day added strength to the triple bonds that united
us. We gradually withdrew ourselves from the society
of others, and found every moment irksome that was
not devoted to each other" (pp. 28-29). Outwardly they
seem representative of the highest ideals of civilized
man. Yet the closed triangle of their exclusive man-
sister-wife relationship actually represents a retreat from
the reality of the outside world. At the same time, of
course, it represents an advance toward the prison of
the individual ego.

When Henry Pleyel joins their select group, he merely
becomes another reflection in the mutual mirror. Clara
tells of his place in the group: "This new friend, though
before his arrival we were sensible to no vacuity, could
not now be spared. His departure would occasion a
void which nothing could fill, and which would produce insupportable regret" (p. 34). The little society
now exhibits major characteristics of Narcissism—withdrawal from the outside world, submersion into the ego,
and a complete selfishness. Like the mythic Narcissus,
the group becomes infatuated with images and not with
actualities. All four believe the illusion that they are
somehow immune to the harsh realities of the outside
world and that, because they put complete trust in their
own rationality, they are somehow infallible as well.
Furthermore, the group Narcissism is indicative of the
tensions extant in Wieland between his Narcissistic
plunge (inner egotism) and his Icarian rise-fall (outer
egotism).

The group's central figure is always, of course, Wieland.
Not only is he the primary figure which projects the
Narcissistic image to and from Clara, Catharine, and
Pleyel, but he is also the energizing force of those images. From him and through him the destructive elements of Narcissism emanate. Indeed, Wieland's Narcissism is so strong that he not only represents the
tyranny of the harsh outside world the group had attempted to shut out, but he also, ironically, symbolizes
the tyranny within the group and within the human

mind. In other words, "Wieland . . . becomes a symbol for civilized man's savage potential" (Kimball, p. 215).

To understand the composition of Wieland's savagery, one must understand that, coming as it does from his ego, it is directed primarily against Catharine and Clara—his Narcissistic reflections—the two people who are most like himself, and whom he most loves. Narcissus loved his reflection and perished because he did. Wieland's own Narcissism parallels the myth, then exceeds it; and the results are even more disastrous. The reflection he sees of himself in his sister and wife is not enough to maintain the majesty of his ego. Because his Narcissism is compounded by religious fanaticism, he must seek his alter-ego not in human-kind but in his God. He therefore must destroy his earthly reflections. One view purports that Wieland's religious fanaticism is "a practical companion piece to Abraham's trial of which S. Kierkegaard brings so many versions in *Fear and Trembling,* seeing in it the highest expression of faith."[20] But this view seems insupportable because, by sacrificing his family, Wieland seeks not so much to express his rigid faith as to rise above his human state. His actions are more to satisfy his self-love than his love of God. Although Abraham's love of his son and Wieland's love of his family are diametrically opposed to the love of God, Wieland's self-enamoration is even more opposed to God's love. Abraham is not a Narcissist, whereas Wieland's actions reveal that he has all the components of the Narcissist—"excessive egocentricity, self-complacency, and self-absorption."[21] Most obvious is that Wieland, like Narcissus "rejects love and then becomes fatally infatuated with his own reflection" (Neumann, p. 89). He finally turns away both from Catharine and Clara and from the importunate demands that must be met when one loves others rather than himself. Thus Wieland fully rejects the love of his wife and sister and sets out to destroy them.

While he succeeds in killing his wife, he does not succeed in murdering Clara who is the primary reflection of his Narcissism. Wieland's attempt to kill Clara can be read as an attempt to destroy this major image of himself; therefore, it is an attempt to strike out against his earthly self in order to attain demi-god status. His alter-ego (Clara) must be destroyed if his own ego is to triumph. Erich Neumann has written of the Narcissist's "preservation of a relation to himself in opposition to love of the environment and of an outside object."[22] Wieland, by killing his sister, will preserve his egocentric relation to himself, thereby cancelling out the love of his sister. Searching for the rationale to kill her, he exhorts: *"Thou angel whom I was wont to worship!* fearest thou, my sister, for thy life?" (p. 263; my italics). That he will sacrifice Clara, whom he worshipped as the other half of his Narcissistic reflection, illustrates how total his Narcissism has become: he no longer needs the outward, physical reflection of himself. And,

interestingly enough, when Wieland cannot kill his sister—he is stopped by Carwin's voice—he kills himself. It cannot be otherwise. Under the tenets of his religious philosophy, Wieland's self-preservation depends on his murdering Clara. Without her sacrifice Wieland will be confronted with the reality of his actions, and that reality, for him, would be unendurable. If his ego in attempting to soar cannot have its sacrifice, it must, paradoxically, sacrifice itself. His suicide, then, is the ultimate plunge into Narcissism.

III

Along with the Narcissism theme, the Icarian rise-fall pattern functions throughout **Wieland.** Icarian soaring (ascensionism), manifested by Wieland's fanaticism and evident throughout as he experiences spasmodic bursts of enthusiasm and flights of fancy, is countered by Icarian falling (unwanted descents), manifested by the depressive "lows" Wieland experiences after each inordinate event. These unwanted descents are, of course, important to the novel's overall effect; but Brown continually keeps Wieland's ascensionism before the reader. This ascensionism is most obvious on the night he kills the members of his family, as he voices in confessing the murders before the court:

> *For a time my contemplations soared above earth and its inhabitants.* I stretched forth my hands; I lifted my eyes, and exclaimed, "Oh, that I might be admitted to thy presence! that mine were the supreme delight of knowing thy will, and of performing it!—the blissful privilege of direct communication with thee, and of listening to the audible enunciation of thy pleasure!"
>
> (p. 190; my italics)

Completely bewildered by his flight on the night of the murders, he confesses "that the relations of time and space were almost obliterated from my understanding" (p. 190). As time and space dissolve in the ether of his ego, Wieland believes he sees a spectre, which he describes as "a lustre," an "irradiation," "the element of heaven," "a fiery stream": "The lineaments of that being whose veil was now lifted and whose visage beamed upon my sight, no hues of pencil or of language can portray" (p. 191). It is this spectre—evidence of the hallucinatory effects Wieland's ascensionism has had upon him—that commands Wieland to slay his wife. If not totally separated from reality, Wieland experiences at least a terrible distortion of it.

After Wieland is captured and imprisoned, he relentlessly attempts to regain the ecstatic heights he achieved on the night of the murders. Indeed, Wieland's two escapes from prison are actually physical movements *upward* and are indicative of his obsessive ascensionism. It is as though to soar again he must first ascend from the dungeon. Furthermore, the escapes themselves are characteristically ascensionistic because of the fantastic aura about them—as if denizens of the supernatural world had helped Wieland to execute the escapes. His first escape is almost superhuman, occurring as if "by some miracle," since "his chains, and the watchfulness of his guards, were redoubled" (p. 215). Then he is captured at his sister's house. But his second escape, no less difficult, is more successful, and he finds Clara (with Carwin) in her room. His two escapes have had but one objective—to slay his sister and experience again the ecstasy of acting out what he believes is his God's will: "Father! I thank thee. This is thy guidance. Hither thou hast led me, that I might perform thy will. Yet let me not err; let me hear again thy messenger! . . . Poor girl! a dismal fate has set its mark upon thee. Thy life is demanded as a sacrifice. Prepare thee to die" (p. 246). He has risen from the dungeon to attempt again to soar above human frailty.

Yet even when Carwin admits to Wieland that he, Carwin, was the source of the voices (though he was not the source of the voice which compelled Wieland to slay his family), Wieland's ascensionism remains. He is still caught in the majesty of his ego: "Thinkest thou [Clara] that thy death was sought to gratify malevolence? No. I am pure from all stain. I believed that my God was my mover!" (p. 253). Wieland is still driven to kill Clara, and he attempts to rationalize Carwin's participation in his own actions, thus exhibiting the inescapability of his Icarian torment: "Clara . . . thy death must come. This minister [Carwin] is evil, but he from whom his commission was received is God. Submit then with all thy wonted resignation to a decree that cannot be reversed or resisted. Mark the clock. Three minutes are allowed to thee, in which to call up thy fortitude and prepare thee for thy doom" (p. 255). But Wieland is deterred from murdering his sister by Carwin, who, during the three-minutes, had left the room. Ironically, Carwin uses his ventriloquism, which earlier had helped perpetrate Wieland's fantasy, to stop the murder: "A voice, louder than human organs could produce, shriller than language can depict, burst from the ceiling and commanded him—*to hold!*" (p. 259). All that is left is Carwin's final admonishment: 'Shake off thy frenzy, and *ascend* into rational and human. Be lunatic no longer" (p. 259; my italics).

The ascension into rationality and humanness is, for Wieland, a descent. And here, in the last climactic pages of the novel, the Icarian pattern of rise and fall fully asserts itself: "*Fallen* from his lofty and heroic station; now finally restored to the perception of truth; *weighed to earth* by the recollection of his own deeds; consoled no longer by a consciousness of rectitude for the loss of offspring and wife,—a loss for which he was indebted to his own misguided hand,—Wieland was transformed at once into the *man of sorrows!*" (p. 260; my italics).[23] Further ascension is no longer possible. Stripped of his delusions, Wieland is transfigured back to earthly man,

one "weighed to earth by the recollection of his own deeds." The voice only Wieland could hear had demanded he sacrifice his family; now, with the symbolic gesture of thrusting his knife into his throat, he silences the voice forever.[24] Wieland's ultimate Narcissistic plunge is therefore no less the inevitable Icarian fall—the fall from the soaring heights of ecstasy and the frenzied rejoicing in the total ego to the self-destruction of the complete "*man of sorrows.*"

Notes

1. *The Byronic Hero: Types and Prototypes* (Minneapolis: Univ. of Minnesota Press, 1962), p. 112.

2. I refer here solely to the Aeschylean Prometheus—the rebellious, suffering champion of man—rather than to the cunning, trickster Prometheus of Hesiod's *Theogeny* or to the Roman Prometheus *plasticator* who, as M. K. Joseph observes, in the "Introduction," Mary W. Shelley, *Frankenstein; Or, The Modern Prometheus* (London: Oxford Univ. Press, 1969), p. viii, "was said to have created or re-created mankind by animating a figure made of clay."

3. *The Decline of the West,* trans. Charles Francis Atkinson (New York: Knopf, 1932), I, 183.

4. All students of the Gothic novel owe much to Mario Praz's invaluable study, *The Romantic Agony,* trans. Angus Davidson, 2nd ed. (New York: World, 1967). My study here of the Faustian nature of the Gothic villain is but a departure from, not a refutation of, Praz's general thesis.

5. See Daniel M. Ogilvie, "The Icarus Complex," *Psychology Today,* 2 (1968), 31-34, 67; and Henry A. Murray, "American Icarus," *Clinical Studies of Personality,* ed. A. Burton and R. F. Harris (New York: Harper, 1955), pp. 614-641. It seems extremely fortuitous that as the Romanticists seized upon the ancient myths, so too have twentieth-century psychologists seized upon them and applied them to the twentieth-century experience.

6. "Ancient Myths and Modern Man," *Man and His Symbols,* ed. Carl G. Jung (New York: Dell, 1969), p. 112.

7. *The Tragical History of Doctor Faustus,* ed. Frederick S. Boas (London: Methuen, 1949), I,i,15-22; pp. 56-57.

8. *Faust,* trans. Walter Kaufmann (Garden City, N.Y.: Doubleday, 1963), I, 366-367; p. 93. Hereafter, references to this edition will appear in the text.

9. Harold Bloom, in the "Afterword" to his edition of Mary Shelley's *Frankenstein, Or, The Modern Prometheus* (New York: New American Library, 1965), p. 215. In determining that Narcissism is an active force working upon the Gothic protago-

nist, I am referring mainly to the most popular story of Narcissus—the story of the beautiful youth who, falling in love with his own reflection in a pool, becomes so enamored with himself that he rejects the love of everyone else. Pausanias' story of Narcissus—the story of the love between Narcissus and his twin sister—does, however, influence my discussion of sibling Narcissism later in the essay.

10. "The Images of Orpheus and Narcissus," *Eros and Civilization: A Philosophical Inquiry into Freud* (Boston: Beacon Press, 1966), 159-171. I am using this essay only as it pertains to Narcissism; I am not here concerned with the connections of the Faustian hero of the Gothic novel with the Orpheus myth.

11. *The Origins and History of Consciousness,* trans. R. F. C. Hull (New York: Pantheon, 1954), p. 123.

12. "The Process of Individuation," *Man and His Symbols,* ed. Carl G. Jung (New York: Dell, 1969), p. 234.

13. I am, of course, aware that *Wieland* has its English successors—among them Mary Shelley's *Frankenstein* (1818) and Emily Brönte's *Wuthering Heights* (1847).

14. Much has been written about the madness in *Wieland.* Harry R. Warfel, *Charles Brockden Brown: America's Gothic Novelist* (Gainesville, Fla.: Univ. of Florida Press, 1949), p. 195, writes that *Wieland* is a terror story organized, "unlike most Gothic tales, around the theme of mental balance and the ease with which that balance is destroyed." Fred Lewis Pattee, in his "Introduction" to *Wieland; Or, The Transformation* (New York: Harcourt, Brace, 1926), p. xl, calls the novel "a study in dementia," in which the reader holds the key to the Wieland family's abnormality. William M. Manley, "The Importance of Point of View in Brockden Brown's *Wieland,*" *American Literature,* 35 (1964), 319, suggests that "the disturbed mind faltering in darkness . . . could well stand as a metaphor for the entire action of this strange tale." And Kenneth Bernard, "Charles Brockden Brown," *Minor American Novelists,* ed. Charles Alva Hoyt (Carbondale and Edwardsville: Southern Illinois Univ. Press, 1970), p. 5, has labeled Theodore Wieland as a creature springing "from the nonrational corners of the mind," whose sustenance comes from "darkness and mystery."

15. Charles Brockden Brown, *Wieland; Or, The Transformation* (Garden City, N.Y.: Doubleday, 1962), p. 14. Hereafter, references to this edition will appear in the text.

16. Much of what Ann Y. Wilkinson, "*Bleak House*: From Faraday to Judgment Day," *ELH,* 34 (1967),

225-247, says about Krook's spontaneous combustion and the apocalyptic vision of *Bleak House* can be applied to the elder Wieland. See also Elizabeth Wiley, "Four Strange Cases," *Dickensian,* 58 (1962), 120-125, who discusses spontaneous combustion in *Wieland, Bleak House,* Marryat's *Jacob Faithful,* and Melville's *Redburn.*

17. P. 45. Larzer Ziff, "A Reading of *Wieland,*" *PMLA,* 77 (1962), 50-51, has correctly pointed out that Clara's observation here sums up the whole psychology of *Wieland.*

18. See Paul Levine, "The American Novel Begins," *American Scholar,* 36 (1966), 134-148, who suggests that *Wieland,* in a sense, resembles Kafka's *Metamorphosis.*

19. Arthur Kimball, "Savages and Savagism: Brockden Brown's Dramatic Irony," *Studies in Romanticism,* 6 (1967), 214, has pointed out Brown's skepticism of man's innate virtue and of the overly optimistic hopes for the new world: "that from the hidden corners of man's mind there is likely to issue as much darkness as light. That darkness, in the form of savage violence, is a central theme in *Wieland.* . . ." Ziff, p. 57, writes that in *Wieland* Brown "penetrates beneath the principles of the optimistic psychology of his day, and recognizes the claims which Calvinism makes on the American character."

20. John G. Frank, "The Wieland Family in Charles Brockden Brown's *Wieland,*" *Monatshefte,* 42 (1950), 350-351.

21. Neumann, *The Origins and History of Consciousness,* [Princeton: Princeton University Press, 1954,] p. 122.

22. *Art and the Creative Unconscious: Four Essays,* trans. Ralph Manheim (New York: Pantheon, 1959), pp. 185-186.

23. Although Wieland's transformation into a "man of sorrows" seems to be a reference to Christ—the traditional "man of sorrows"—there is no other evidence in the novel that Brown is suggesting an analogue between Wieland and Christ.

24. Kimball, p. 216, suggests that Wieland's stabbing himself in the neck is an "attempt to kill the voice."

Wayne Franklin (essay date 1975)

SOURCE: Franklin, Wayne. "Tragedy and Comedy in Brown's *Wieland.*" *Novel: A Forum on Fiction* 8, no. 2 (winter 1975): 147-63.

[*In the following essay, Franklin suggests that the primary sources for* Wieland *were Shakespeare's* Hamlet *and* Much Ado About Nothing.]

Many critics and scholars have written extensively about the various sources of Charles Brockden Brown's novel, *Wieland; or The Transformation* (1798), yet what may be the most pervasive general influence—that of Shakespeare—has been overlooked entirely so far. The sources enumerated certainly are important for an understanding of Brown's immediate use of other writers, as well as for a grasp of his translation of historical events into fiction. Thus, one critic has stressed the role of the Godwinian "novel of ideas" in the make-up of *Wieland,* while others have focused on such diverse things as the presence of the Gothic formula, the influence of various German works, the historical background of the spontaneous combustion motif, or the story of one American farmer whose execution of his family, reported in contemporary newspapers, bears an obvious relation to the "sacrifice" effected by Theodore Wieland. What I would argue, however, is that these immediate sources are all partial, while a reference to Shakespeare—to *Hamlet* and *Much Ado About Nothing,* in particular—can provide us with a fairly thorough guide, not only to the origins of Brown's novel, but also to its multiple meanings. My intent is not finally to point out specific Shakespearean sources for *Wieland,* though Brown's deep and continuing fascination with Shakespeare makes such an approach both attractive and sensible. What I want to suggest, rather, is a more general parallelism between Shakespeare's typical generic distinctions and that mixing of genres which, it seems to me, is one of the most interesting of Brown's achievements in this book.

I

The most outright reference to Shakespeare in the novel is the use by Carwin the "Biloquist" of a snatch of verse from *Macbeth*—"Hold! Hold!"—as a warning to various characters in various situations. But this reference, though it is the only one openly acknowledged in the book, is far less important dramatically than those from which, as I hope to show, *Wieland* derives a good deal of its strength. The Carwin line certainly has thematic importance, for it implies that his intrusion into the world of the Wielands is benevolent (or at least partly so): it is, after all, "heaven" which may "peep through the blanket of the dark / To cry 'Hold, Hold!'" in Lady Macbeth's soliloquy.[1] For the time being, I want to leave aside the question of Carwin's nature and his role in the book, and to turn to other issues.

First of all, to the plot, which is essentially dual. There is the tale of Wieland's loss of reason, his murder of his family, his attempted murder of his sister. But then there is the often independent story of that sister herself, which is in many ways more complex. It involves not simply the courtship of Clara and Pleyel (which, blunted and frustrated as it is, finally succeeds in marriage), but also the threatened seduction of Clara by

Carwin, and the attempted murder of her by Theodore, as well as her own illness and recovery. Yet even here Clara's story does not end, for there is beyond all these separate elements of her tale the very act of telling that tale, the plot of attempting to plot the past, to explain and order it. As William Manly has argued, the point of view in Brown's book is of crucial importance, is in itself highly engaging: ". . . the central drama of the novel," Manly writes, "lies not in sex or sensationalism per se, but in Clara's consciousness as she copes with a growing isolation from the sane and normal preoccupations of daily life."[2]

Clara's view of her suffering continually impinges on our own as we read the book, so much so, in fact, that we may accept her interpretations of her past at face value. But surely a good portion of Brown's subject here is the limitation of Clara's view. She is partial from the outset—not from evil intent, to be sure, but partial nonetheless. And if we fail to see that the way in which she understands and tells her story is limited, then we will fail to appreciate the essential complexity of life in the book. There is so much put-on and deceit, so much mistake and error in *Wieland,* that it is simply impossible for any one character to provide us with the last word on what is real or important. We may *want* that final word, but Clara cannot give it to us.

Clara's mistakes are numerous. Some are caused merely by the limitation of her senses or by the paucity of her information. And at times the intersection of her own simple errors of perception with those of other characters creates more elaborate mistakes—as when she and Pleyel both are in error on that "fatal" night (he thinks she is by the river with Carwin; she thinks he *is* Carwin, come back to assault her, as he stands outside her door; and so forth). From this mutual mistake evolves the breakdown of their courtship, as well as Pleyel's voyage to Europe and Clara's first bout with delirium. That closed door before which Pleyel pauses, behind which Clara stands trembling: isn't it used by Brown to represent all those bars to perception, all those closed doors of vision and hearing and even of thought, which literally abound in *Wieland*?

The episode of the door may suggest, at first, a Shakespearean analogue which is more misleading than illuminating. I refer not to the famous knocking at the gate in *Macbeth,* but to the comic passage at tongues in *The Comedy of Errors* (III.i). Dromio of Syracuse, safe inside the house of Antipholus of Ephesus, keeps its owner and his servant from entering. "Who talks within there?" Antipholus asks (III.i.38)—it is a question that well might ring through *Wieland*—and the scene easily becomes a microcosm of the confusion and error which control the world of Shakespeare's play. Indeed, the thematic ambience of the play, though not its tone, is very close to that of Brown's novel, and the scene at the gate clearly acts as a symbolic embodiment of the theme, just as the scene at the door in *Wieland* does. *The Comedy of Errors* is fraught with misperceptions and unwitting deceit, and the characters who are forced to deal with those "errors" begin to doubt not only their own sanity but also the justness of the universe. "And here we wander in illusions," Antipholus of Syracuse remarks (IV.iii.38), while in the next scene the conjurer Pinch concludes of the two Ephesians that

> . . . *both man and master is possessed*;
> *I know it by their pale and deadly looks.*
> *They must be bound and laid in some dark room.*
>
> (IV.iv.89-91)

—and the remarks of both characters would fit in not simply with the atmosphere of *Wieland,* which is charged with illusions, but also with its action, for it is precisely to a "dark room" that the madly violent Theodore is condemned (he ends up "at the bottom of a dungeon loaded with chains" after killing his family).[3] And even more fitting, given Brown's subtitle, is Dromio of Syracuse's question: "I am transformèd, master, am I not?" (II.ii.194)

Confusion, of course, is at the heart of much comedy, so what these lines from *The Comedy of Errors* can do for our appreciation of *Wieland* is more generic than specific. The point is that the stuff out of which Brown created his book is not by necessity tragic, and this point is, as we shall see soon, of immense importance in our reading of *Wieland.* Error, mistake, misperception, confusion: all these things, so central to the plots of the novel, are not absolute in nature. Their human meaning derives not from what they are in themselves but from what they do to people, and from how people react to them. We should remember, nevertheless, that regardless of the farcical nature of Shakespeare's play, the confusion at one point verges on violence: swords are drawn, oaths sworn, and death is foreseen. What saves the play from violence, in the end, is the presence in the theater of someone who knows what is what—for it is the knowledge of the audience, as much as anything else, that keeps the play comic. Are we willing to imagine a production which uses identical twins (two sets of them), and which gives us no clues to which is which? Such a production would fail, fail miserably, not just because it would confuse the audience, but also because it would upset the basic balance of the universe of the play. In the end, it is confusion that is apparent, not the realities and identities which it momentarily obscures, and the sanity of the audience rests on this crucial fact.

Yet *Wieland* is, in many ways, a book of "errors" in the Shakespearean sense. The difference between the novel and the play lies, as I have said, in tone rather than theme. What is lacking in Brown is just the kind of audience which Shakespeare absolutely requires. As readers, we never know exactly what has happened; we never can say, as we can in viewing or reading *The Comedy of Errors,* that everything has happened because of a simple, circumstantial doubling of identities. To be sure, we can attribute some of the mistakes to the doubling, the biloquism, of Carwin. But in *Wieland* there never occurs that complete resolution of doubt on which Shakespeare's comedy rests. The twins in the play suspect at various times that they are being tricked by other people, that witches or devils are playing with them, or that they themselves are mad. So, too, various characters in *Wieland* see Theodore's transformation as the work of devils or angels (Wieland himself accepts the latter view almost to the very end), while others attribute it to Carwin (who is a devil in Clara's view, anyway), or to a derangement of Wieland's mind. Bewitchment, trickery, and madness thus are the three explanations in both the play and the novel; but only in Shakespeare do we know for sure which has caused the problem (and actually it is none of the three, but just "circumstance"). In Brown, we remain puzzled and upset. We are an audience which has been taken into the action, and we are only sure that each of the three agencies has had some role in the events, if only from the subjective viewpoint of the various characters.

It is at this juncture that Clara once more emerges as an important figure in the novel, for in her act of telling Brown's story she assumes an omniscience which she does not really possess. And as Clara sees the story, it is in essence tragic, not because of her brother's murderous violence, but because of her own imminent death. Again and again as she writes out her account of the confusing world in which she lives, she tells us that she has but one wish: she hopes that she will live long enough to explain everything to us, and, that done, she will sink down to the grave. In her mind, ending and end are synonymous, life-story and life are indistinguishable. Hence, when the curtain falls, the actress must fall too, and she never will rise again. Clara, in other words, orders her life by reference to artistic canons, not just in the act of turning that life into art, but in the very living of it as well. Her expectation of death is aesthetic, not terrific.

But even in this imagination of disaster, of grand finale, Clara is mistaken. She has misread not simply the particular events of her experience, but even its overall form. Thus the seemingly fatuous conclusion to Brown's novel, the postscript written three years later at Montpellier, is simply the last in a series of confusions and reversals. Like the humorous endings of so many Beethoven pieces, in which the "last" note is sounded and then sounded again and again, the postscript catches us off-balance. Prepared for tragedy, we are jolted by the happiness which meets us. We are not so much relieved as puzzled.

It is in this aspect of the novel that Shakespeare becomes most relevant, for Clara's confusion of comedy and tragedy is the kind of thing which plagues Shakespeare's heroes and heroines over and over again. Even *The Comedy of Errors* is a case in point, for the characters in that play are astounded by the turnabout at its end. Thus the Abbess-Mother proclaims "After so long grief such Nativity!" (V.i.408), and though she is referring particularly to the long period of separation undergone by her family, her words ring true for the shorter "grief" of the play itself. Yet if we use the same words regarding Clara's remarkable rebirth, we use them questioningly, not in simple wonder. Her marriage to Pleyel after the fiery death of her old life seems incredible—not because it is generally implausible, but because Clara has prepared us for the fire of cremation rather than that of the Phoenix.

Yet even here is a Shakespearean analogue, one that is particularly appropriate for *Wieland.* We recall the scene of confusion with which we started: Clara has been home alone, has been accosted by Carwin (who has been lurking in her closet), and has then been delivered from what looks like Carwin's intended rape. Pleyel in the meantime is coming home to his guest room in her house, and as he passes by the river bank on his way, he hears what he takes to be Clara and Carwin making love. He is appalled, of course, and rushes into the house. Hesitating before Clara's chamber door, he decides not to enter the room, but instead goes into his own across the hall. Clara, meanwhile, thinks that Pleyel is Carwin. Then, believing wrongly that he has left the house again, she sneaks downstairs to lock the doors behind him. But her problems are not over. In returning to her room, she is heard by Pleyel, who thinks that she is coming back from her supposed "midnight assignation" with Carwin (p. 118). He waits until morning to accost her, insult her, and then leave her house for good. Later, she learns from Theodore what it is that Pleyel thought he witnessed; and later still, she hears Carwin's account of the night. Carwin tells her, in effect, that Pleyel has been the dupe of a fiction, that he himself imitated her voice—not out of malice, but for the sheer delight of tricking this "man of cold reserves and exquisite sagacity" (p. 236).

The Shakespearean parallel in this case is marvellously to the point. For in *Much Ado About Nothing,* a play shot through with all kinds of fictions, pretenses, and deceptions, there is a scene which surely seems like Brown's particular model. The play concerns the love of Claudio and Hero, the enmity of Don John for his forgiving brother Don Pedro, and the loving enmity of Beatrice and Benedick. It is with the first two pairs that the parallel deals. Don Pedro has wooed and won Hero for Claudio (and even this romantic masquerade causes problems), and Don John, looking for some way to get even with his brother, decides to disrupt Claudio and

Hero's impending marriage. His plan of disruption is simple. Don John and his operatives fake a midnight interview between Borachio and Hero's servant, Margaret, who pretends to be Hero herself. Claudio and Pedro are brought to watch the interview, and to conclude from it that Hero is nothing more than "a common stale" (IV.i.63). Claudio waits until the next day for revenge, which he achieves by insulting Hero in public during the wedding ceremony. As she leaves she falls into a swoon, accused of profligacy not only by her lover but also by her father. Inept villain as he is, Don John has succeeded, for the moment at least, in toppling the polite world of his brother to the dust.

The parallels between this scene and the elements of Brown's plot discussed above are numerous. But even more telling are other details from *Wieland.* Clara thinks, after talking to her brother but before speaking with Carwin, that the latter probably tricked Pleyel by having "some vile and abandoned female . . . mimic [her] voice" (p. 126). Now this is exactly what happened in Shakespeare's play, and it might just as well have happened in the novel, for in *Wieland* as in *Much Ado About Nothing* there is an unfaithful servant girl: Judith, Clara's maid, is Carwin's secret consort, much as Margaret is Borachio's.

Other parallels are deeper. As Claudio rushes off from Hero, we recall, she has swooned, and it is feared that she is dead: Claudio's words, in effect, have laid her low. Pleyel, like Claudio, waits until the next day to upbraid his love, and his upbraiding, though not immediately, has the same effect. Thus when he leaves Clara confused about his charges against her, she cannot rest content, but follows after, seeking an interview with him at his house below the city. And that interview ends as does Claudio and Hero's during the wedding. Rough and violent in his language, Pleyel causes Clara to cry out as he leaves the room: "Pleyel! Art thou gone? Gone forever?"—after which, Clara later recalls, "A painful dizziness seized me, and I fainted away" (p. 135). Thus, one of Pleyel's first impulses on hearing the midnight interview by the river almost has been fulfilled: "I was governed by an half-formed and tempestuous resolution," he later tells Clara, "to break in upon your interview, and strike you dead with my upbraiding" (p. 152).

We suspect, of course, that Pleyel's words would not be able, as Claudio's are not, really to kill his love. Yet the motif of death is an important one. In the play, after all, the counterplot of Leonato and Hero and their friends involves the feigning of Hero's death. And, I would argue, Clara herself indulges in a similar ruse. Her imagined disaster, that death waiting for her after her "finis," is in effect merely another one of those unending pretenses in the book. In the end, her life is embraced by the same comic form which embraces Hero's; but before that end, and the reconciliation which makes it possible, neither Hero nor Clara can view events comically. For both, life is potentially tragic until it proves otherwise. The pall of death hangs over both until the startling "nativity" which concludes the novel and the play alike.

Yet there are differences between the lingering deaths of these two wronged women. Most importantly, Hero is aware of her fiction, aware that the tragedy which exists at the center of her comedy is feigned—even though she doesn't know for sure that things will turn out right in the end. Clara, on the other hand, takes her fiction for fact; she is dead not in pretense but in anticipation. After she first faints in Pleyel's house, her experience to the close of her woeful tale is one long swoon. She remains in a sense unconscious until the postscript reveals her awakening, remains submerged in a world of seeming death which for her is terribly real. The tragedy of her life is certain; the comedy of it is dead.

It is this difference between Clara's experience and Hero's which underlines most strongly Brown's theme of human limitation. It has seemed to some readers that the comic ending of *Wieland* is an outrageously false move on Brown's part, that it violates the whole force and direction of his story to that point. In bringing Clara back from the grave, such readers complain, the author has sold out his art for the sake of a transparently happy ending.[4] I disagree, for that ending seems to me an immensely shrewd ploy. How better to inculcate the announced moral of human misperception and its consequences than to present us with a narrator who doesn't understand her tale—to show us, in other words, not merely the local mistakes and confusions and deceptions of the plots as they develop, but also the general confusion of the very person who spends so much time harping on these and other errors? Clara's act of structuring her tale by reference to tragic canons is simply the grandest mistake of *Wieland.* "The will is the tool of the understanding, which must fashion its conclusions on the notices of sense. If the senses be depraved it is impossible to calculate the evils that may flow from the consequent deductions of the understanding" (p. 39)—so Clara announces just after Wieland hears the first strange warning voice, and the idea, clearly enough, is Brown's. But it does not remain mere idea in *Wieland.* Every incident, every misperception and false conclusion, every wrong action—all derive from the theory as Clara expresses it. But so, too, does the tale Clara herself tells. She is so overwhelmed by her experience that her largest "deduction of the understanding"—her story—is itself the most convincing proof of Brown's idea. "What but ambiguities, abruptnesses, and dark transitions," Clara asks, "can be expected from the historian who is, at the same time, the sufferer of these disasters?" (p. 166)—and her question goes to the heart of her own failures as narrator.

It is on this level that the parallels between *Much Ado About Nothing* and *Wieland* become most meaningful. The point is that all the time Clara thinks she is dying, she is living in a world that turns out (in terms of her love life, at least) to be surprisingly like that lived in by Claudio and Hero. Clara's feigned extremity, in other words, is simply much ado about nothing, or too much ado about something. She herself admits this point in her postscript. The last words of her tale proper—"And now my repose is coming—my work is done!" (p. 262)—allow no extension of either life or art. Yet extension is precisely what we get, and we get it, what is more, coated with a moral sugar that helps us swallow it. Clara admits that she had been "enamoured of death," yet now, three years later, she is "not destitute of happiness." How can such a radical change come about? Her answer sounds almost flippant: "Such is man," she writes. "Time will obliterate the deepest impressions. Grief the most vehement and hopeless, will gradually decay and wear itself out" (p. 262).

What has been decayed in her is not merely grief; all the tumultuous feelings wrought in her mind by the events of her earlier life have disappeared, and she now looks back "upon the sensations and reasonings of that period with wonder and humiliation" (p. 263). Everything had seemed to be rushing, as in her dreams, toward the inevitable precipice of madness and death; but the tragic catastrophe has been averted, not by a *deus* or *dea ex machina,* but by "time," by the simple course of daily events. Clara had talked earlier about her "destiny" (p. 262), yet tragic agents of that sort are absent from her private world. The push and press of dreadful event that are so important in tragedy, the inevitability of doom and disaster—these are replaced in Clara's world by the slow but certain healing process of temporality. And nothing could be farther from the tragic spirit, both as Clara imagines it to be present in her experience and as great writers have used it in their works, than this curative sense of time. "To-morrow, and to-morrow, and to-morrow," says Macbeth,

> *Creeps in this petty pace from day to day*
> *To the last syllable of recorded time,*
> *And all our yesterdays have lighted fools*
> *The way to dusty death.*

> (V.v.19-23)

And though Clara might say, as he does, "Out, out, brief candle!"—though she might say this while telling her tale, she presents a far different view in her postscript. "To-morrow" is for her restorative rather than deathly; "as day follows day," she remarks, "the turbulence of our emotions shall subside, and our fluctuations be finally succeeded by a calm"—and it is a calm of peace and prosperity, not of death (p. 262).

Clara's story may seem, at times, to be that "tale told by an idiot" referred to in Macbeth's speech; but there is a method in Clara's madness, as there is in Hamlet's. Her insanity is temporary (in the root meaning of that term), and when the "depravity" of her senses (and hence of her understanding and her will) has been cured through the introduction of new sensations, of "a new train of images, disconnected with the fate of [her] family" (p. 268), she returns quickly to normality. Reason regains control of her, and no longer can she say of her life, as she had on the second page of her story: "The experience of no human being can furnish a parallel: That I, beyond the rest of mankind, should be reserved for a destiny without alleviation, and without example!" (p. 6). For in fact nothing is more common in life, as opposed to art, than the balm of forgetfulness and the cooling breeze of a new morning. "Futurity has no power over my thoughts," Clara had said at the outset (p. 5); but she was wrong, absolutely wrong. It is, in the end, futurity itself that saves her, that relieves her suffering, that makes her story comic rather than tragic. It is futurity that effects her final, hopeful transformation. Carwin himself, regardless of his own errors of perception, saw at least this much of the truth of Clara's character: that though a "momentary sadness" might affect her, she is "impregnable to any permanent and heartfelt grief" (p. 233).

II

Clara's final, ironic transformation underscores the power of that theme in general in **Wieland.** As Scott Garrow has shown, for example, every major character and various minor ones suffer from radical internal changes in the course of the narrative, and not all these changes are as reassuring as Clara's.[5] For Theodore, the thematic ambience of *Much Ado About Nothing* is ridiculously inappropriate: his life, unlike his sister's, *is* fully tragic. There is at the core of it a truth of suffering and disaster which is definitely unfeigned, a reality which the future is powerless to change. But the larger irony of the novel is that, during all the time that Clara views herself as a tragic victim, Theodore sees his murderous actions comically—sees them, that is, as the fulfillment of divine law, sees himself as aligned with God rather than against Him. Hence his ending, like Clara's, is a disabusal; he commits suicide when he realizes the tragedy of his mistake. His fiction of divine command, like hers of divine abandonment, shatters against the truth.

Clara, of course, is involved centrally in Wieland's tragedy, so her view of it is important for any reading of Brown's book. And that view presents yet a further irony, for Clara refuses throughout her tale to admit that her brother has any primary responsibility for his acts. Carwin, in her way of seeing things, is the "author" of the tragedy which enveloped Theodore (p. 255): "Thou art the author of these horrors!" she exclaims to him— "O! Carwin! Carwin! What hast thou to answer for?"

she asks (p. 252). "There is thy betrayer," she tells Theodore (p. 245). And even though, in light of Theodore's recognition of his fault and Carwin's admission of his own role in prompting Wieland's insanity, Clara is given the information necessary for a right conclusion, she persists to the end—even into her postscript—in blaming Carwin far more than he deserves. It is true that her hysterical accusations of Carwin now seem tempered; but so does every other memory of the tumultuous past which she longs to put behind her. And her last words in the novel reveal, I believe, that she persists in her delusion of Carwin's essential guilt, not only for her temporary falling-out with Pleyel, but also for her brother's irredeemable tragedy.

The only fault in Theodore which Clara will admit is a general human frailty, one shared by other characters in the novel. Thus she claims that, although it is a "mournful consideration" that "virtue should become the victim of treachery," nonetheless "the evils of which Carwin and Maxwell were the authors, owed their existence to the errors of the sufferers." Yet what kind of "error" is it in Wieland that contributed to his downfall? Clara's answer is far too simple, and it is so with very good reason. She joins her own troubles vis-à-vis Pleyel with Theodore's: "If Wieland," she explains in her final sentence, "had framed juster notions of moral duty, and of the divine attributes; or if I had been gifted with ordinary equanimity or foresight, the double-tongued deceiver would have been baffled and repelled" (p. 273).

In the words of Donald A. Ringe, "Such a conclusion . . . will not do."[6] Part of Clara's return to normalcy—a return seemingly exemplified in these closing words— ought to lie in her acceptance of what has happened to Theodore and his family. Yet does Clara, in saying what she does in her postscript, really accept the truth? Isn't she, in effect, substituting yet another fiction for reality? What I mean is this: Wieland's tragic flaw, Brown clearly wants us to believe, is a certain mental trait which, under the early influence of Carwin's put-ons, develops an insidious energy of its own. Carwin's "double tongue," in other words, serves merely to call forth a deep doubleness in Theodore's own character, and it is the latter doubleness which is primarily to blame for the tragedy. The first voices Theodore hears are simple ventriloquisms, but the later ones—the ones he himself mistakes for divine commands—are in fact the delusions of a very unbalanced mind. Now Clara never does accept the implications of this fact. Even her final sentence in the novel continues the illusion which she entertains all along—namely, that the voices, each and every one of them, were the work of Carwin. In her view, the "errors" of Wieland were intellectual; they were traceable to a perverted sense of God and justice. She does not say, after all, that Theodore imagined he heard voices which he took to be God's; she says that he took the voices which he *did* hear to be divine rather than human, and that if he had possessed better ideas of "the divine attributes," he never would have made such a mistake. She does admit that he was "mad," to be sure. Yet what that admission signifies is that, given the "depraved" state of his senses (as caused by Carwin's external "depraving" of them—not, as Larzer Ziff maintains, by some internal "depravity" of his nature),[7] Wieland could not help suffering from a false understanding, and that his will accordingly led him to wrong actions. In her view, all humanity was aptly categorized by Apemantus in *Timon of Athens*: "Who lives that's not depravèd or depraves" (I.ii.133), that philosopher asks, and Clara's answer might be almost laughably simple—for Theodore is pure victim in her version of his tragedy, while Carwin is pure victimizer. Her brother's only fault is to be found in the unfortunate fact that his received notions of God and morality did not counteract (or perhaps even re-enforced) the evil machinations of his undoer.

What this explanation leaves out is the very heart of Brown's portrait of Theodore. And Clara leaves it out because its truth bears too closely on her own continued sanity. Wieland is mad, mad in a grand and tragic way, and because he is her brother, the danger clearly exists that she, too, may be infected. Indeed, her dreams of him—often taken to be concerned strictly with incest—are also to be read as fantasies of the mental contamination which Wieland's fate threatens for her.[8] Her whole concept of herself as tragic victim, as a Job-like sufferer, is a projection born of her fears: if she can remain a mere innocent victim, a passive thing in the control of great malignant forces, then she need not face the fact she fears most, which is her incipient madness. But she does not rest merely at her own victimization. She must create in her tale the additional illusion that Theodore, too, is a victim. His only fault is an excess of piety, an Abraham-like submission to the will of God as he is given to see that will. It is Carwin, this stranger, this outsider, this double-tongued villain, who is to blame. Notice that even in the passage in which she admits that the "errors" of Wieland contributed to his sufferings, she still calls Carwin, almost unconsciously, the *author* of the evils which overwhelmed her brother. Indeed, she is so undiscriminating as to speak of Carwin and the truly evil Maxwell in one breath, as though the obviously great differences between these two characters were totally missed by her. Maxwell clearly *is* a villain, while both Clara's uncle and Pleyel testify to the basic truthfulness of Carwin's confessions. They both accept, and hope Clara will too, that Carwin's only fault was his incessant and uncontrollable "curiosity." Yet on Clara this idea is completely lost; even in her postscript she cannot judge truly of Carwin's role in the events she has narrated. To be sure, she writes at the end of the tale proper that her correspondent has excused Carwin from blame in her brother's tragedy. But her language at this point is very tricky: "Talk not to me, O my revered friend!" she writes, "of Carwin. He has told thee his tale, and thou exculpatest him from all direct concern in the fate of Wieland. This scene of havock was produced by an illusion of the senses. Be it so: I care not from what source these disasters have flowed; it suffices that they have swallowed up our hopes and our existence" (p. 261).

Now on the surface this passage seems to indicate that Clara (even before the purifying fire and her trip to Europe) has accepted the notion of her brother's insanity. Yet even here Clara is distracted; she is repeating her correspondent's ideas with an air of resigned indifference, is mouthing the authorized version of her own tale. And, what is more, she is distorting that authorized version even in listlessly repeating it. Her uncle's explanation, based on the "*mania mutabilis*" of Erasmus Darwin, was that Wieland's "illusions were maniacal" (p. 202)—that they were the result of madness rather than a simple tricking of the senses. Yet when Clara herself uses that phrase "an illusion of the senses" she is being ambiguous at best—for the early voices heard by others besides Wieland were also sensory illusions, though they came from external causes. Darwin's own theory had made it plain that this particular mania, like others related to it, involved "increased actions of the organs of sense"—that is, illusions internally produced.[9] But no such clarity exists in Clara's analysis. Indeed, her postscript suggests that she herself does not really believe the scientific explanations put forward by her uncle. She writes there that Carwin "sought my uncle, and confided to him the tale which he had just related to me. He found a more impartial and indulgent auditor in Mr. Cambridge, who imputed to maniacal illusion the conduct of Wieland, though he conceived the previous and unseen agency of Carwin, to have indirectly but powerfully predisposed to this deplorable perversion of mind" (pp. 267-68). Cambridge's explanation, in other words, is an imputation, an opinion, and Clara implies a certain unconscious doubt on her own part merely in presenting it as such. Cambridge is not simply more "impartial" than she—he is also more "indulgent," and that word opens a long vista into Clara's mind, a vista which reveals a good many persistent doubts and fears lingering in her even after her supposed rebirth. It is always dangerous in Brown to hang too much on single words, but when, as in the case of Clara's treatment of Carwin, ambiguities and distortions surface again and again, there is a meaning in the resultant pattern. Clara, I would argue, is still struggling, three years later, with the implications of her tale and the life it only darkly mirrors.

Clara's vision of her brother's "tragedy," then, is influenced by her own needs and desires. She refuses to admit his primary responsibility for what has occurred because in doing so she would be forced to front her own, related disorder. Hence the tale she tells is far less tragic than Theodore's life seems to be on its own. Underplaying the complicity of her brother in his downfall, she gives us the impression that he is the victim of malignant forces akin to those which she believes have been persecuting her. Absent from her Hebraic sense of tragedy is the Greek (and Shakespearean) idea that some inherent and central flaw in the tragic figure finally causes the tragedy which engulfs him. Clara suggests almost unknowingly that Carwin is a vastly enhanced (and successful) Don John, and that the evil in her family's world is all traceable to the machinations of this one "bad" man. Such a view is of the essence of comedy, which always (and especially in its melodramatic guise) simplifies evil, which banishes it entirely from the field of vision, or which embodies it in such a gross and palpable form that the audience sees it all in one person—sees it operate and then fail, as it does in Don John's case. But tragedy either makes that gross form of evil less gross and more sympathetic (and hence more problematic) or disperses evil throughout the human world. I do not mean to imply that, in the case of *Much Ado About Nothing,* for example, Claudio and Don Pedro or even Leonato are free from flaws. Yet the flaws they possess (hastiness, short-sightedness, credulity) hardly come off as evils. They are follies rather than deep faults. And the best proof of this view is in the ending of the play: Don John has fled (but will be caught), the operatives Conrade and Borachio have been arrested, and everything works out in the end as it might have originally. *Much Ado About Nothing* flirts with tragedy, with death, violence, and evil; but at its close the beautiful motions of the dance overcome all disharmonies.

In **Wieland,** even as Clara sees things, the flirtation is fatal. Yet Clara would confine the evil within Carwin's character; she refuses steadfastly to admit the general contagion of her universe. And she even manages, in her postscript, to perform what is, in terms of narrative form, something like a dance. She is again, "not destitute of happiness."

But it is not *Much Ado About Nothing,* nor comedy in general, which ultimately explains **Wieland.** Carwin in reality is nothing more than the trigger which sets Theodore hurtling off into madness—just as, in Shakespeare, the witches spur but do not cause Macbeth's ambition, or Iago aggravates but does not originate Othello's jealousy. Wieland is not duped, as Claudio wholly is, but is merely set in motion; and once he is going he proceeds under his own power, relentlessly and mercilessly. It is wholly appropriate that, once informed of his errors, he kills himself—for his end *is* comparable to that of Othello. Indeed, the placing of the dead Catherine on Clara's bed, suggestive as it is in terms of the incest motif, surely cues the reader to the parallel between the statures, flaws, and misdeeds of

Othello and Wieland. Of course, jealousy is not an issue in **Wieland** (unless we follow the incest spoor, again); but mistaken murder is—mistaken murder that leads to a recognition of guilt and then to suicide by stabbing.

Yet if Theodore's death suggests a strong parallel to *Othello,* the conception of his character and the role of the voices he hears derive rather from *Hamlet* than from this other play. *Hamlet* is *par excellence* the Shakespearean study of madness, real and feigned, and (regardless of his use of such things as Cajetan Tschink's *The Victim of Magical Delusion* or Schiller's *Der Geisterseher*)[10] Brown would seem to have used that play consciously in writing his novel. Even the opening tale of the elder Wieland reveals the influence of *Hamlet*—for, like Shakespeare's young prince, the old fanatic loses his "peace of mind" because of his "deviation from his duty" (p. 14). And Theodore's father is even more like the elder Hamlet than the younger. There are important differences between the two, of course—the ghost of Theodore's father does not actually appear to his son, for example—yet the reader of both works certainly feels the crucial bearing of the fathers' lives on those of their sons.

We never know with the elder Wieland, as we do with Shakespeare's prince, exactly the "duty" that has been imposed. We may suspect the Abraham-Isaac motif (one rendered more possible by the fact that C. M. Wieland, the family's German namesake, wrote *Der Geprüfte Abraham*)[11]—but to the end the duty remains a mystery. All we know is that it "was transferred, in consequence of his disobedience, to another"—to Theodore? we are forced to wonder—and "all that remained was to endure the penalty" (p. 14). It is clear, at any rate, that the duty spoken of is not, as Ziff argues, the one which first urged him to emigrate to America (the conversion of the Indians to Christianity), and that the "penalty" does not end with the father's death: for why else would he warn his wife, before his combustion in the temple, to be ready for the "calamities" which await her? (p. 16).[12]

Clara herself doubts whether the eerie end of her father was the "penalty of disobedience" to God, or whether it resulted simply from the "irregular expansion of the fluid that imparts warmth to our heart and our blood" (pp. 21-22): she is torn, that is, between supernatural and scientific explanations. But the important point about his death is not its cause—rather, its effect, especially on his son. The early association of the "voices" with the father's old temple surely suggests that this building has been resanctified, that the Deistic weapons of art, music, and philosophy with which Theodore has usurped the structure have been countered by the militant resurgence of the faith of his father. Supremely, rigidly rationalistic, that Deistic world is obviously ready for an outburst of repressed enthusiasm, a kind of Second Great Awakening of fervid fundamentalism.

Hence the presence of those voices in the temple and then elsewhere is indeed like a ghostly visitation from the grave, a return of the father's word into the world of the son. Like the deep intonings of the ghost-father in *Hamlet,* these voices seem like righteous sounds come from the past to cleanse the present. And, given the peculiar mentality and heritage of Theodore, sacrifice, that ritual of rituals, might seem the perfect vehicle of such a cleansing. Hence the tale of the elder Wieland (as of Clara's maternal grandfather, who heard voices and jumped off a cliff in obedience to them) forms a vitally important backdrop to the experience of Wieland. We are led to believe, by virtue of those earlier experiences of the family, that the voices Wieland seems to hear—even if not divine—could appear to be so to him. And all this leads us slowly but surely into the tragedy which follows. Like the moody midnight scene which opens Shakespeare's play, the beginning account of the elder Wieland creates the right atmosphere for the action we are to witness. We see no ghosts in the novel; but the father's spirit broods over **Wieland** as ominously as it does over *Hamlet.*

Further parallels between the two works can be traced in the characters of their two protagonists. Wieland is no carbon-copy of Hamlet, but he does share some of the most famous traits of the prince. His sister, for example, sees "a sort of thrilling melancholy" (p. 25) as his main mental trait—and, like Hamlet, he is somewhat aloof and given to thoughtfulness, abstracted and rather strict in his view of morality. Both Wieland and Hamlet, what is more, tend to be mystical—as when Clara calls her brother an "enthusiast" in religious matters (p. 40), or when Hamlet himself discounts the ability of "philosophy" to explain everything which happens in earthly experience. Both are willing to believe that mere empiricism and rationality are insufficient guides to life—and both are provided by their creators with alter-egos (Horatio and Pleyel) who are mouthpieces for the opposite view.

The main difference between Wieland and Hamlet—aside from the former's total lack of that playfulness which is one of Hamlet's most engaging characteristics—is simply the fact that Brown's protagonist actually is mad, while Hamlet probably is not. Yet even here there is a perverse similarity, for if Hamlet's stratagem throughout is to pretend madness, then Wieland's pretense is that he is sane, that he is acting as any other normal person would act under a divine command. The split between appearance and reality, which in the play occurs mainly between Hamlet and his uncle's court, is moved by Brown into the very mind of his hero. But because we see so little of that mind (except for the very effective courtroom statement, which functions as a soliloquy in the novel)—because we see so little of Wieland's mind, this theme of psychological ambiguity is treated by Brown mainly in its social aspects, as it is

seen by others rather than as it is felt by Wieland. His choice of Clara as narrator allows him to give his readers the kind of outside view of his hero which, in Shakespeare, is developed in the court scenes. And Clara's lamentations over her brother's fate sound very much like many of those comments, naive or cynical, which Hamlet's feigned madness elicits in the play.

It is, first of all, Claudius who says to Rosencrantz and Guildenstern:

> *Something have you heard*
> *Of Hamlet's transformation—so call it,*
> *Sith nor th' exterior nor the inward man*
> *Resembles that it was.*
>
> (II.ii.4-7)

—and his description might fit Wieland just as well. Indeed, there are echoes of this very theme in Brown's book, not simply in the subtitle and the plot, but in a good number of particular scenes. Clara keeps lamenting that someone as exalted as her brother should have fallen so low, and her language recalls that of Ophelia in particular. Hence Clara asks Carwin if he knows that he has destroyed Wieland: "Hast thou not made him the butcher of his family; changed him who was the glory of his species into worse than brute; robbed him of reason, and consigned the rest of his days to fetters and stripes?" (p. 222)—a view of the tragedy which echoes Ophelia's description of the crazed Hamlet just after he has urged her to go to a "nunnery":

> *O, what a noble mind is here o'erthrown!*
> *The courtier's, soldier's, scholar's, eye,*
>   *tongue, sword,*
> *Th' expectancy and rose of the fair state,*
> *The glass of fashion and the mould of form,*
> *Th' observed of all observers, quite, quite*
>   *down!*
>
> (III.i.150-54)

And there is an echoing in **Wieland** of events as well as ideas, for the scene in which Ophelia reports how Hamlet came to her "with his doublet all unbraced / . . . As if he had been loosèd out of hell / To speak of horrors" (II.i.78; 83-84) is substantially and emotionally parallel to that in which Theodore comes into Clara's room, speaks to his voices, and then hurries out. Or, indeed, that Ophelia-Hamlet scene (as reported by her), taken together with the interview of Hamlet and his mother in her chamber, goes a long way toward illuminating both of those scenes in **Wieland** in which Theodore confronts Clara in her room. In the interview of Hamlet and Gertrude, we recall, Hamlet's mother feels he is threatening her with violence (as Clara feels Wieland is in their second scene)—while Hamlet, like Wieland in both his interviews with Clara, speaks to his "ghost," though neither woman hears an answer.

There is something of both Ophelia and Gertrude in Clara's make-up. One can argue, in fact, that her whole sense of herself as tragic victim is modelled on an idea similar to that used by Shakespeare in drawing the character of Hamlet's lover. Ophelia's exclamation—"O, woe is me / T' have seen what I have seen, see what I see!" (III.i.160-61)—is fairly close to Clara's tone throughout her narration (with the added irony that Clara's suffering, unlike Ophelia's, is not really empathetic, but selfish), and I am tempted to say that Clara's dread of the contagion of Wieland's madness suggests the similar contagion in the relationship of Hamlet and Ophelia. It is, after all, the dread of drowning that seems foremost in Clara's mind when she dreams of death during her feverish recovery.

Yet all these echoes or parallels are fairly tenuous when compared to the greatest single connection between the play and the novel, which is to be found in the theme of delusion. Horatio first raises the idea in *Hamlet* when he warns Hamlet of the dangers posed to him by the ghost:

> *What if it tempt you toward the flood, my lord,*
> *Or to the dreadful summit of the cliff*
> *That beetles o'er his base into the sea,*
> *And there assume some other horrible form,*
> *Which might deprive your sovereignty of reason*
> *And draw you into madness?*
>
> (I.iv.69-74)

The danger, never literally realized in *Hamlet,* is one which goes to the heart of Brown's book. The experience of Clara and Theodore's maternal grandfather is perhaps the first thing called to mind—but of even greater interest is the consonance of Horatio's warning with the obsessive imagery of Clara's dreams and fantasies. For her, madness is associated with some cliff above an abyss throughout the book—as, indeed, it is in the novel generally (in, for instance, the placement of the temple, that locus of enthusiasm, at the verge of a hill above a stream). And more instructive than this imagistic connection of the Horatio passage to *Wieland* is its bearing on the fate of Theodore himself. The fate suggested by Horatio is essentially that which overcomes Brown's protagonist—so much so that the novel seems like a rewriting of *Hamlet* with a single basic change. For *Wieland* is what *Hamlet* would have been had the prince's doubts about the ghost been correct— and had Hamlet neither raised them himself nor listened to them when they were expressed by Horatio. And in this way, *Wieland* is both simpler in plot and more complex in its psychological insights than Shakespeare's play.

The death of Hamlet, though surrounded by a general slaughter of innocent and guilty alike, is in some sense an affirmation. The duty imposed on him has been fulfilled, and at last the air of Denmark is clear of the foulness and duplicity which have emanated from Clau-

dius. Such is not the case in Brown's novel. The tragedy there is caused not by the relentless flow of events but by a simple error. It is all a mistake; the spilled blood neither redeems nor purifies the world. In a profound way, Shakespeare's play is a study of the tension between truth and fiction, between the deep commands of the ghost and the sugared and smooth words of Claudius, between the pretense of normalcy in Denmark and the reality of corruption beneath the surface of the state. Hence the play-within-the-play, nominally a fiction, ironically speaks the truth; Hamlet's contrived reality (unlike those of Don John or Iago or Carwin) is not a deception but a revelation. Not so with the contrivances of Wieland's fantasy. *They* are the fiction; and the end of Brown's drama, as a result, is vastly different from the end of Shakespeare's.

Horatio's comment about Hamlet early in the play— "He waxes desperate with imagination" (I.iv.87)—fits Wieland's life far better than it does Hamlet's. For Brown's book is, on almost all its levels, concerned with the desperate imagination—with the delusive voices of Wieland, but also with the delusive "voice" of Clara as she narrates her tale. Yet if Brown derived this theme or others from Shakespeare, he worked his own "transformation" in them while writing his novel, just as he translated Shakespeare's typical distinctions between tragedy and comedy into a domestic idiom more suitable for his "American tale." Shakespeare was not a burden to him, but a liberating influence, and **Wieland** is all the better for the debts incurred in its writing. It is a rich book, not a juvenile one; a pioneering effort in psychological fiction, not a mere melodrama. And it is more, for in mixing comedy and tragedy, renewal and disaster, as thoroughly as he did in this novel, Brown laid the foundation of a peculiarly American style of fiction, a way of seeing and writing which was to be almost "natural" for later novelists. That style of fiction, the ironic novel, is the peculiar generic possession of such authors as Melville and Hawthorne, Twain and James, Fitzgerald and Faulkner; but it was Brown who first broke the ground in this field, and he did so by using Shakespeare without becoming overwhelmed by his example—without becoming, in effect, a mere "biloquist."

Notes

1. *William Shakespeare: The Complete Works,* ed. Alfred Harbage (Baltimore: Penguin, 1969), p. 1114 (I.v.51-52).

2. "The Importance of Point of View in Brockden Brown's *Wieland,*" *American Literature,* 35 (1963), 320.

3. *Wieland; or The Transformation,* ed. Fred Lewis Pattee (New York: Hafner, 1958), p. 182.

4. See Donald A. Ringe, *Charles Brockden Brown* (New York: Twayne, 1966), p. 34; and Larzer Ziff, "A Reading of *Wieland*," *PMLA*, 77 (1962), 53.

5. "Character Transformation in *Wieland*," *Southern Quarterly,* 4 (1965-66), 308-18.

6. *Charles Brockden Brown,* p. 42.

7. "A Reading of *Wieland*," p. 54; see Samuel Johnson's *Dictionary, s.v.* "deprave."

8. See Manly, p. 318.

9. Erasmus Darwin, *Zoonomia; or, The Laws of Organic Life. Part Second* (Philadelphia: T. Dobson, 1797), I, 450.

10. Harry R. Warfel, "Charles Brockden Brown's German Sources," *MLQ* [*Modern Language Quarterly*], 1 (1940), 357-65.

11. John G. Frank, "The Wieland Family in Charles Brockden Brown's *Wieland*," *Monatshefte,* 42 (1950), 351.

12. Ziff, p. 55; contrast with Pattee's "Introduction" to *Wieland,* p. xl.

J. V. Ridgely (essay date 1975)

SOURCE: Ridgely, J. V. "The Empty World of *Wieland*." In *Individual and Community: Variations on a Theme in American Fiction,* edited by Kenneth H. Baldwin and David K. Kirby, pp. 3-16. Durham: Duke University Press, 1975.

[*In the following essay, Ridgely studies the various transformations of Brown's characters in* Wieland.]

Wieland is a nocturnal tale, a nervous melodrama played out in the uncertain illumination of candle, lamp, fire, moon, stars. To a degree, of course, Brown's darkened stage set is a literary convention; in folk tale as well as in the contemporary Gothic novel of terror, night is the time when creatures of mystery and danger are expected to walk abroad. But Charles Brockden Brown was a self-proclaimed novelist of purpose, and the titillating shudder, though he employed it as a time-tested lure for readership, he condemned as an end in itself. In his preface he announced that he aimed at no less than the "illustration of some important branches of the moral constitution of man,"[1] and he attached a didactic tag to the end of the novel to assure that no one could underestimate his fundamental seriousness. Unfortunately, this conclusion can too lazily be taken as a sufficient summation of the tale's entire import. Certainly, as recent criticism has made us aware, *Wieland* is far more complex in structure and in meaning than its narrator, Clara Wieland, intimates by moralizing in her final sentences only on the "errors" of the Stuarts, of Wieland, and of herself. For, as Brown himself proclaims, Man is the protagonist; and the theme is conceived as universal: when the light of reason becomes dimmed or is extinguished by superstition, by trickery, or by unusual experience which is misconstrued as preternatural, horror is loosed in the world. This horror is that of man's darkened mind; and its state may be externalized, as here, by false appearance, by the urge to destroy reason in others, by murder, by self-destruction. *Wieland* is a warning to beware of the quality of sense perceptions, an appeal to cultivate and protect the light of reason; for, once benighted, some men may not find their way back out of the blackness.

This is Brown's manifest message; but, as several recent commentators[2] have argued, Brown's apparent dedication to Lockean sensationalist psychology is compromised by other ramifications of the tale. Thus Larzer Ziff sees Brown as the first American novelist "to face the confusion of sentiment and an optimistic psychology, both of which flowed through the chink in the Puritan dike, and to represent American progress away from a doctrine of depravity as a very mixed blessing indeed."[3] William M. Manley, disputing Ziff's focus on sentimental-seduction materials in the novel, still finds that the "astonishing intensity which Brown generates . . . reflects his ability to convey through a first-person narrator the shifting instability of a mind swayed between objective logic and subjective terror, creating thereby a tension which is not resolved until the final pages."[4] And Donald A. Ringe summarizes: "To show that Brown made use of sensationalist psychology in his book does not necessarily mean that he accepted it uncritically, for the developing action of the novel calls its validity into serious question."[5] Despite their different emphases, all three critics reach what is certainly a valid conclusion: the manifest and the latent content of *Wieland* appear to be at odds. Yet all, in arriving at this point, overlook an aspect that is an even more fundamental peculiarity of the tale. For the world of *Wieland* is not only nocturnal; it is also a remarkably empty one. Confined to a few characters and some set locales, it is curiously without a wider social reference: state, city, church—even other families—remain mere shadows lurking in the general gloom. It is this world devoid of those authoritative institutions by which sense impressions could be weighed and judged which I wish later to emphasize. But I would like, first, to demonstrate just how Brown brings each of his principal characters—Clara, Pleyel, and Wieland—to the ultimate state of dangerous illusion, to that "transformation" to which the subtitle refers.

I

As several critics have correctly emphasized, an early comment of Clara's furnishes the key to Brown's method of putting his leading players to the test. "The will," writes Clara, "is the tool of the understanding, which must fashion its conclusions on the notices of sense." And, she continues sententiously, "If the senses be depraved it is impossible to calculate the evils which may flow from the consequent deductions of the understanding" (39). These maxim-like statements provide the philosophical basis for Brown's employment of light and dark patterns. For if "depravity" of the senses is crucial it is but a step to positing that the light of full day may be linked with the light of unclouded reason; or, to formulate the principle in the reverse manner, that if the senses are required to function in natural gloom, in artificial (hence "false") light, or in darkness, mental perception is correspondingly obscured. The degree and the quality of illumination, then, are all-important. It is this point which Wieland, Pleyel, and finally Clara spectacularly fail to comprehend.

Brown's narrative ultimately depends for force upon the cumulative effect of misapprehended experience; but, for purposes of discussion, it may be divided into four main parts: (1) *a prolog,* dealing with the elder Wieland's background in Europe and with his death in Pennsylvania; (2) *a central action,* constructed around the eight voices produced by the ventriloquist Carwin and reaching a climax in Clara's discovery of the body of Wieland's wife; (3) *a denouement,* in which Clara learns that Wieland has murdered his family and that Carwin is the agent of the voices; and in which Carwin's confession, Wieland's threat of death to her and his suicide bring on her mental collapse; (4) *an epilog,* written in France three years after these last events, in which Clara tells of her restoration to rationality and of her union with Pleyel. What now follows is a synoptic analysis of **Wieland** in accordance with this structure, with particular reference to Brown's schematic employment of light-dark contrasts.

1. The Prolog (chs. I-II). The elder Wieland, convinced that his religion has been "expressly prescribed to him" (14), builds a classical temple to his deity and retires there for worship each noon and midnight (the midpoints of light and darkness). His religion has the appearance of the light of reason (the classical temple and midday), but it is also associated with the darkness of unreason (revelation and midnight). On the final evening of his life he goes alone to his shrine. There his "fancy" pictures a "person bearing a lamp" and at the same moment a "spark" lights upon and consumes his clothes. Watching from a window, his wife and her brother (Clara's uncle) see "gleams" and "rays." Running to the temple, the uncle discovers that the elder Wieland's body is scorched; before his death he describes the fiery doom that had overtaken him. This harrowing event, occurring during Clara's childhood, becomes obsessively the subject of her thoughts. Two explanations are presented to her: either the "Divine Ruler interferes in human affairs" or "the [dangerous] condition of [her fa-

ther's] thoughts" caused a natural physical reaction— i.e., spontaneous combustion, a "scientific" theory supported by her uncle (a surgeon) and by Brown himself in a footnote. The circumstances of the death (fire, night) set up the light-dark structure for the whole book and underscore Brown's use of the temple as a locale for misapprehended experience.

2. The Central Action (chs. III-XVII). Left orphans, Clara and Wieland grow up on isolated properties outside Philadelphia. Since her education was modeled on "no religious standard" but rather left to the guidance of her own "understanding," Clara leans to the deistic. Her brother, though, scholarly, speculative, and moody like his father, pursues "the history of religious opinions" (26). These views are scoffed at by his friend Pleyel, "the champion of intellectual liberty, and [one who] rejected all guidance but that of his reason" (28). Upon Wieland's marriage to Pleyel's sister Catharine, Clara moves to a house nearby, but all meet regularly in the temple for intellectual amusements.

First voice: Wieland goes at night to the temple to retrieve a letter. The moon is for a moment hidden by a cloud (his senses are darkened) and he sees a "glimmering" (false light) that reminds him of the fate of his father (36). It is then that he hears a voice, which he takes to be that of his wife, warning him of danger ahead and urging him to return to the house. The voice, as we learn later, is projected by Carwin; but as the bright moon comes out again Wieland sees no one. Back in the house, he is told that his wife has not stirred, and Pleyel attributes hearing of the voice to a "deception of the senses" (38).

Second voice: Some time later, Clara and Catharine are sitting at home awaiting the return of Wieland and Pleyel. As the clock strikes midnight, the men enter and relate that while talking in the temple they have heard Catharine's voice informing them that Pleyel's intended bride is dead. The experience shakes Pleyel's rationalism; it only confirms Wieland's belief in revelation.

Third voice: Carwin now makes his first open appearance. Dressed as a rustic but speaking with a musical and educated voice he is initially seen by Clara in afternoon sunlight. But next day arises in "darkness and storm" (61), a signal that though Carwin is outwardly a man of reason (his arrival in daylight) he is dark and perverted within. As night returns, the storm ceases; Clara spends "the darksome hours" (62) musing on death. Retiring to bed, she listens to the clock (which her father had owned) striking twelve; then she hears voices at her bed's head whispering threats of murder. In panic she flees to Wieland's house, where she faints.

Fourth voice: A voice of "piercing shrillness" (68) calls the occupants to Clara's aid. As she recovers, Clara reflects on the occurrences of the voice; she can no longer doubt its reality. But she fails to realize that it has always been heard in semidarkness and that the understanding may thus have been duped.

Fifth voice: Clara goes at sundown to her summerhouse near the river and falls asleep. She dreams that as she is walking to her brother's house in twilight she comes upon a deep pit; beyond it her brother beckons her forward. As she is about to step into the abyss, someone catches her from behind and a voice cries "Hold! hold!" She awakens in "deepest darkness," with her "faculties still too confused" for her to find her way up the bank. Then comes a voice, which she recognizes as one of those which whispered near her bed. It promises her safety if she will avoid the summerhouse and not reveal what has happened. Without "the faintest gleam" to guide her steps, she remains motionless till she sees a "ray" (71-72). The "first visitings of this light [call] up a train of horrors," as she thinks of her father's end and of the warning voice (flickering light is associated with superstition). But now a "new and stronger illumination" (73) bursts upon her; it is Pleyel bearing a lantern. Confused, she tells him nothing of her experience.

Next evening Clara meets Carwin at Wieland's and learns that Pleyel had known him in Europe. The "voices" become a main topic for their discourse and three conflicting theories emerge: (1) Carwin holds for a "ready and plausible solution" (natural causes), but conceals his own role (reason deceiving by partial truth); (2) Wieland again maintains "the probability of celestial interference"; (3) Pleyel still accepts no testimony but that of his senses (83-85).

Sixth voice: In her bedroom, Clara goes to a closet; inexplicably a voice again cries "Hold! hold!" Terrified, she searches for its source, but in the faint moonlight from the windows she can discover no one. "Dark is less fertile of images than the feeble lustre of the moon," she muses (96-97). Suddenly recalling her dream, she now first consciously associates danger with her brother; and in a "phrenzy" she calls for him to come forth. But it is of course Carwin who emerges from the closet; and, dissembling for his own purposes, he says that he had come to ravish her but that the voice of warning had saved her. Actually, he has been prowling through her effects and has no intention of sexual attack. Carwin leaves in moonlight, and Clara is left to her "bewildering ideas" (105).

Seventh voice: Pleyel tells Wieland that he has heard voices which have convinced him that Clara has given herself to Carwin; later, in his own home, he relates to Clara his experience while denouncing her supposed fall from virtue. He had been on his way to tell her that Carwin was a fugitive from justice; as he passed her summerhouse in moonlight he became aware of voices he took to be Clara's and Carwin's. "My sight was of

no use to me. Beneath so thick an umbrage, the darkness was intense," he recalls—not comprehending that he should have mistrusted his *other* senses. Sadly he tells her, "I yielded not but to evidence which took away the power to withhold my faith" (154). Clara protests vainly; as Pleyel stalks out of the room, she notices that "the light was declining" (155). The light of reason has now been dimmed in Pleyel too.

Eighth voice: Carwin writes asking for an 11 P.M. interview at Clara's house to explain his threat of rape. Though Clara thinks, with justice, that "the writer had surely been bereft of his reason" (156), she decides to return home. Arriving, she arms herself with a penknife and starts up the stairs. But again there is a cry of "*hold! hold!*" and she is confronted by a mysterious face, which then vanishes. Remarkably continuing up the stairs anyway, she enters her room. She discovers not Carwin but a note from him warning of a horrible sight to come. Carrying a light "in order to dispel any illusive mists that might have hovered" before her eyes (170), she comes upon the body of Catharine. Her death Clara immediately attributes to Carwin; and when Wieland enters in a distracted state she mourns the "extinction of a mind the most luminous and penetrating that ever dignified the human form" (174)—supposing that grief has driven him mad. With these two erroneous conclusions of Clara's the pattern of mystification in the novel ends.

3. The Denouement (chs. XVIII-XXVI). Clara, discovering next that Wieland's entire family has been murdered, sinks into delirium. As she recovers, she puts the blame upon Carwin, but her uncle gives her some documents to read, informing her that the "execution was another's" (182). The death-dealing hand was Wieland's own, she learns. In his confession, light and dark are again given their schematic roles. Before the court Wieland recalls his moment of "illumination." Having gone to Clara's house in search of her, he had entered her darkened room. Satisfied of her absence, he turned to leave; but on the stairs he was "dazzled" by a "lustre" which burst upon his vision: "I opened my eyes and found all about me luminous and glowing. It was the element of heaven that flowed around. Nothing but a fiery stream was at first visible; but, anon, a shrill voice from behind me called upon me to attend" (188). A visage, he continues, now beamed upon his sight and he was enjoined to kill his wife and (later) his children as sacrifices. The intensity and quality of this false light are important; they signify the force of his delusion.

Reading through this account, Clara cannot at first realize that the voice which Wieland heard was *not* that which had addressed herself and the others on previous occasions. Told by her uncle that Wieland was a victim of religious mania, she counters that "this madness, if madness it were, had affected Pleyel and myself as well as Wieland" (202).

Clara is not long left in doubt. Returning to her bedroom in order to destroy her journal, she sits in the twilight of her closed house, the darkness "suiting the colour of [her] thoughts" (218). As she contemplates suicide, Carwin enters and confesses to being the source of the eight voices through his power of "biloquism" (225-241). His hidden motivation (which Brown reveals more fully in *Memoirs of Carwin, the Biloquist*) derives from his association with a secret anarchistic order like the Illuminati; what he tells Clara is: "I cannot justify my conduct, yet my only crime was curiosity" (231). Emphatically he denies any responsibility for the "voice of God" heard by Wieland or for the murders. While Clara is pondering these explanations, Wieland, having escaped from prison, rushes in and tells her she is the predestined final victim demanded by his "angel." But Clara points at Carwin and charges him with being the source of the "angel" voice. Wieland challenges him, but Carwin will admit only to some deception. Wieland orders him out and is able for a moment to see part of the truth: "If I erred, it was not my judgment that deceived me, but my senses" (251-252). He thanks God for this last "illumination"—i.e., knowledge of Carwin's power to defraud. However, suddenly irrational again, he argues that though the messenger was evil the commissions must have come from God, and he will carry out the final order. Carwin reenters, unseen by Wieland, and for the ninth and last time in the novel he employs his feigned voice. Crying "*hold!*" he stays Wieland's hand; then he orders him to "ascend into rational and human": "not heaven or hell, but thy senses have misled thee to commit these acts." Wieland is shaken: "A beam appeared to be darted into his mind." This beam is the emblem of right reason, for he is "restored to perception of truth" (257-259). But his recovered rationality brings immediate awareness that he cannot live in the world of daylight, and he commits suicide.

4. The Epilog (ch. XXVII): written in France by Clara three years later. After Wieland's suicide, Clara's will to live was destroyed and she sank into a heedless state. But one night she was shocked into awareness by a light-filled dream: "Sometimes I was swallowed up by whirlpools, or caught up in the air. . . . Sometimes gleams of light were shot into a dark abyss, on the verge of which I was standing, and enabled me to discover, for a moment, its enormous depth and hideous precipices. Anon, I was transported to some ridge of Aetna, and made a terrified spectator of its fiery torments and its pillars of smoke" (264). Coming out of this phantasmagoria, Clara realized the house was ablaze; and, in a scene in which Brown draws obvious parallels with the death of her father, she was rescued. But whereas the inner fire of his delusion destroyed him, actual flame was for Clara a purifying agent. She

now agreed to her uncle's plea to leave the nightmare-producing scene behind; together they have come to live in France, the home of the Enlightenment.

Brown now clumsily drags in the Stuart-Conway-Maxwell subplot which he had introduced early and neglected—but not before he restores Pleyel too. Pleyel had married his foreign bride, but she has conveniently died in childbirth. Now, having heard from Carwin the truth about Clara, he comes back to her; and Brown is able to marry restored reason to reason in fact as well as symbol.

II

As I have said, Brown is content in his conclusion simply to let Clara bemoan the "errors" of passion and foresight which had brought catastrophe to the Stuart and Wieland families. But these errors, as we have seen in detail, are really the result of the immediate granting of ultimate authority to the last recorded sensory data. Quite unaccountably, Brown does not allow Clara to ponder the process by which she and Pleyel have been able to restore themselves: it is by a return to society, by the recognition that one must verify sense impressions in the context of a world which is broader than the limiting locales of the central action.

Brown does, indeed, sketch in for the reader all the necessary background. As the extended prolog makes evident, a fatal pattern has been initiated in previous generations, on both the paternal and maternal sides of Clara's family; and the human danger in this fallacy is pointed up by the early and isolated deaths of the fathers. The paternal grandfather married beneath his social level, cut himself from familial ties, devoted himself to literature and music, and "died in the bloom of his life" (7). His son, Clara and Wieland's father, was taken under the protection of a London merchant, given duties that were "laborious and mechanical," and "spent all his time pent up in a gloomy apartment," where he devoted himself to dismal religious speculation. His only attempt at broader social contact—a move to America in an effort to become a missionary of his faith to the Indians—was a failure. He then married a "woman of a meek and quiet disposition" and eventually retired to his sequestered farm with his small family. Clara herself underscores the ultimate isolation from the wider world which his religious fanaticism produces: "He allied himself with no sect, because he perfectly agreed with none. Social worship is that by which they are all distinguished; but this article found no place in his creed. He rigidly interpreted that precept which enjoins us, when we worship, to retire into solitude, and shut out every species of society" (12). The deadly consequences of his act are thus foreordained: testing his sense of a divine proscription given to himself alone against no established religious body, he goes to the solitary and fiery death which is brought on, as Clara surmises, by the "condition of his thoughts." In a later scene, Clara's uncle reveals to her the similarly spectacular demise of her maternal grandfather: believing that his own end "would be inevitably consequent on that of his brother, [he] waited from day to day in expectation of the stroke which he predicted was speedily to fall upon him." Finally, the "summons" comes and he throws himself from a cliff (201-202). His illusions Clara's uncle simply classifies as "maniacal."

Brown would have us understand, then, that a tendency toward a private belief which leads to insane conclusions is inherent in the Wieland family: it is a trait which is to be revived in the younger Wieland, Clara's brother. In the preferred isolation of his country home, Wieland devotes himself to "long and abstruse deductions from the system of divine government and the laws of our intellectual constitution" (39-40), and his only diversion is meeting with the limited family circle which gathers in the temple where his father had died. It is Clara who first sees the family propensity reemerging: "There was an obvious resemblance between him and my father, in their conceptions of the importance of certain topics, and in the light in which the vicissitudes of human life were accustomed to be viewed" (26). Both in his own and his father's cases an inner conviction that God speaks directly to a single individual leads to a corrupted vision of one's duty toward mankind at large. As Wieland boasts in his confession, "my contemplations soared above earth and its inhabitants" (187).

This familial predisposition toward damaging introspection accounts not only for Clara's solitary intellectual pursuits but also for her obsessive dwelling on her father's fate and for the intuitive dread of Wieland which is released in her dreams. Indeed, the death of the father is clearly represented as the key incident which drives the family into a mistaken sense of its own uniqueness: "We gradually withdrew ourselves from the society of others, and found every moment irksome that was not devoted to each other" (23). Like her father and brother, Clara is eventually led by her untested perceptions into mental disorientation. Yet she alone has the means for survival. Both the love which she has felt for Pleyel and the disturbing fact of the intrusion of an outsider, Carwin, prove to be her salvation. As she tells us, the shock of Wieland's murderous actions and his own suicide drove her to seek the seclusion of her house and to communicate with no one. Only gradually, she remarks in her postscript, did she become aware that continued obsessive brooding on her family's fate and refusal to reenter society would have proved fatal to her as well:

> I now see the infatuation and injustice of my conduct in its true colours. I reflect upon the sensations and reasonings of that period with wonder and humiliation.

> That I should be insensible to the claims and tears of my friends; that I should overlook the suggestions of duty, and fly from that post in which only I could be instrumental to the benefit of others; that the exercise of the social and beneficent affections, the contemplation of nature and the acquisition of wisdom should not be seen to be means of happiness still within my reach, is, at this time, scarcely credible.
>
> (263-264)

For the fire which demolished her home had also destroyed her past:

> This incident, disastrous as it may at first seem, had, in reality, a beneficial effect upon my feelings. I was, in some degree, roused from the stupor which had seized my faculties. The monotonous and gloomy series of my thoughts was broken. My habitation was levelled with the ground and I was obliged to seek a new one. A new train of images, disconnected with the fate of my family forced itself on my attention, and a belief insensibly sprung up, that tranquillity, if not happiness, was still within my reach. Notwithstanding the shocks which my frame had endured, the anguish of my thoughts no sooner abated that I recovered my health.
>
> (265-266)

Clara's "transformation" back to normality is, of course, completed by her union with Pleyel, that alleged man of reason who also too easily trusted to his unverified sense perceptions. Through her uncle's efforts, Pleyel is at last brought to hear Carwin's confession of his unseen role, and Clara is immediately restored to Pleyel's "good opinion." But why did Pleyel on his own never think of confronting Carwin? Why, when all his memories of Clara cried out against belief in her sexual fall, did he refuse to accept her own denials? The answer is that, though he had wider social contacts and interests than did the Wieland family, he had been infected by an unfounded pride in his intellect as sole judge of the truth; like the others, he admitted of no institutions by which he might have challenged his erroneous perceptions. Now, in the settled society of Europe, amid contacts which emphasize man's role as social animal, his mind functions as it should.

We may ask, finally, whether Brown intends some deeply significant contrast between young open America and old crowded Europe in the final scenes set in France. The question is difficult to answer with assurance, because the intrusion of the Maxwell-Stuart subplot obfuscates what might have been clear-cut definition. But it may well be that, writing in a decade which followed upon the sundering of America from the parent country, Brown himself was experiencing the deprivation of a fostering social order, of those traditional institutions by which the individual self attempts to gauge its proper role. True, some intellectual comfort could be found in optimistic sensationalist psychology, in the *tabula rasa* with which each individual started anew:

America's slate too had scarcely been scratched. Yet the terrible emptiness of the world of **Wieland** and the demonstrable falsity of dependence upon unmediated sensory perception suggest that Brown perceived America's need for greater awareness of otherness, for some replacement for severed parental ties. Perhaps even more strongly than the Wieland family did their literary creator feel the loss of the father.

Notes

1. *Wieland or The Transformation,* ed. Fred Lewis Pattee, Hafner Library of Classics (New York, 1958), p. 3. All subsequent references are to this edition, which follows closely the first printing of 1798, and are included in the text.

2. See Larzer Ziff, "A Reading of *Wieland,*" *PMLA,* 77 (March, 1962), 51-57; William M. Manly, "The Importance of Point of View in Brockden Brown's Wieland," *American Literature,* 35 (Nov., 1963), 311-321; Donald A. Ringe, *Charles Brockden Brown* (New York, 1966), pp. 25-48.

3. Op. cit., p. 54.

4. Op. cit., pp. 311-312.

5. Op. cit., p. 27.

Michael T. Gilmore (essay date 1977)

SOURCE: Gilmore, Michael T. "Calvinism and Gothicism: The Example of Brown's *Wieland.*" *Studies in the Novel* 9, no. 2 (summer 1977): 107-18.

[*In the following essay, Gilmore claims that Milton's* Paradise Lost *provided the inspiration for Brown's* Wieland.]

Charles Brockden Brown's "Gothic" novel **Wieland; or The Transformation** (1798) was long read as an expression of Enlightenment rationality. The author's purpose, according to this view, was to caution readers "against credulity and religious fanaticism."[1] But the rationalist interpretation has come under spirited attack in recent years, partly as a result of a reassessment of *le genre noir* in general, and the Calvinist underpinning of Brown's tale has begun to gain the recognition it deserves.[2] Nevertheless, the misreadings persist in one form or another, and even Larzer Ziff, who properly insists that "Brown ends his journey through the mind by approaching the outskirts of Edwards' camp," misconstrues the novel's denouement as a conventional happy ending. Further, Ziff's analysis of the sentimental seduction theme is a source of confusion, the effect of which is to trivialize Brown's principal concern.[3] For the Carwin-Clara-Pleyel triangle has little to do with

sentimental love: rather it is Brown's version of the temptation in the garden, and **Wieland** itself is his retelling of the biblical fable of the Fall of Man.

It is well known that William Godwin's *Caleb Williams* had a major impact on Brown and that its publication in 1794 prompted the American to turn to the writing of fiction. Much stressed by critics, the Godwinian influence is usually cited as proof of Brown's radicalism and hostility to religion. As Joel Porte has recently shown, however, *Caleb Williams* possesses an "exacerbated Calvinist framework" and breathes the spirit of *Paradise Lost.* With Falkland in the role of the harsh Divinity and Caleb as the sinful Adam, it charts a course of guilt, suffering, and relentless persecution, ending with a reversal in which the eponymous hero, having succeeded in vindicating himself in a court of law, is overcome by remorse and acknowledges that "he is precisely the 'monster of depravity' whom he had been represented as being all along." In the ruined Gothic world of *Caleb Williams,* argues Porte, there is no hope, no prospect of grace or redemption.[4]

And yet the conclusion of Godwin's novel would seem to suggest that the author did in fact have a scheme of salvation, a scheme which is unmistakably Calvinist and may even have derived from his reading of Jonathan Edwards.[5] *Caleb Williams,* which Godwin wrote, as he claimed in the preface, in order to expose "Things as They Are," is profoundly antilaw in outlook and expounds the view that the English legal system is a tool of class oppression. On a different or deeper level, however, the book is addressed to the issue of salvation by works or faith. Mr. Raymond, captain of a band of thieves patterned after Robin Hood's mythical crew, declares to Caleb that "either . . . we all of us deserve the vengeance of the law, or law is not the proper instrument of correcting the misdeeds of mankind." As Old Testament God, Falkland uses the "remorseless fangs of the law" to hound Caleb with the threat of extinction; but once the wretched victim is imprisoned and arraigned for judgment, the pursuer declines to appear to press charges. Jehovah becomes Christ in an unexpected *volte-face*; and Caleb, who has doggedly protested his innocence, thereby denying his need for grace, is transformed into Cain or the Wandering Jew. In the novel's postscript, he goes to a magistrate and turns the law against Falkland himself, who is convicted and dies after three days. He will not rise again for Caleb Williams. For the latter, having figuratively slain Christ—"A nobler spirit lived not among the sons of men," he now says of Falkland—awakens too late to his corrupt nature and participation in the primal crime. He might have secured himself from damnation, he realizes, if "I had opened my heart to Mr. Falkland, if I had told to him privately the tale I have now been telling . . ."— if, in short, he had thrown himself upon the mercy of the Redeemer and made a confession of sin.[6] What Godwin's residual Calvinism reduces down to is the conviction that only through Christ and the covenant of grace can mankind be saved; given human depravity, there is no salvation through law or good works.

Crane Brinton, in his work on the French Revolution, has commented on the resemblance between Protestant and Robespierrean theology, arguing that "the men who made the Terror were compeers of the first Crusaders, of Savonarola, of Calvin."[7] Brinton's thesis is perfectly illustrated by Godwin, whose radicalism bears the indelible stamp of his orthodox upbringing. In the case of Brown, who was raised as a Quaker, the Calvinist mood informing both *Wieland* and the fragment *Memoirs of Carwin the Biloquist* probably stems as much from the eighteenth-century American background as from his immersion in Enlightenment literature. The *Memoirs of Carwin,* which was composed at roughly the same time as *Wieland* but not published until 1803, strongly evinces the traces of both Godwin and native religious thought. Brown's closest friend, Elihu Hubbard Smith, was a graduate of Yale who introduced the novelist to Timothy Dwight, the grandson of Jonathan Edwards; and it is not impossible that Brown was familiar with the great theologian's writings. But Brown himself hinted at another source of influence, a source conned by Edwards and Godwin alike: John Milton. While Carwin perfects his ventriloquism, for example, he peruses Milton's *Comus* (p. 281);[8] and although *Paradise Lost* is not actually mentioned by name in the fragment, its theme is crucial and pervasive. Carwin is consumed by a perverse lust for knowledge which his father denounces as "incorrigible depravity" (pp. 275-76). After an almost supernatural fire that burns down his father's barn—a reminder, perhaps, of the fiery sword that the Angel Michael waved behind Adam and Eve as he drove them from Paradise—Carwin leaves the pastoral setting where he was born, wanders to the city, and catches the eye of the mysterious Ludloe, who proposes to finance him on a voyage to Europe. A Utopian schemer and apparent Illuminatus, Ludloe plays Falkland to Carwin's Caleb Williams. He seems to possess preternatural powers of which his protégé stands in awe. Like Milton's God, he projects a new Eden, and like Edwards's Christ, he demands a full and sincere confession from those seeking membership in the exalted order to which he belongs. "Perdition or felicity will hang upon that moment" (p. 344), says Ludloe in reference to the confession, adding that "concealment is impossible" and that every secret must be divulged (p. 350). Carwin, however, resolves to withhold the knowledge of his biloquism from his confessor; and shortly thereafter Brown abandoned the manuscript, leaving unanswered the question of his protagonist's fate.

It is in *Wieland,* of course, that he furnishes the answer, an answer that has been foreshadowed by Carwin's insatiable curiosity, his unwillingness to confess all, and

his transformation into a Spanish Catholic: This last detail is especially significant in light of the conventional Gothic technique of displacing the action to a Catholic setting, with its ubiquitous decaying abbeys, monasteries, and catacombs. To embrace Catholicism, as Protestant authors indoctrinated with the theology of John Calvin knew in their bones, was to ensure perdition, since Catholics clung to the misguided belief that salvation could be won by spurning the world or performing good works within it. This was to deny the need for divine election and to gloss over the universal depravity of mankind, which rendered truly virtuous actions impossible without an infusion of the Holy Spirit. On the issue of salvation by works Catholics and Protestant Armenians locked arms, and what has passed as the anticlericalism of the Gothic school might more properly be viewed as a veiled protest against the waning of Calvinist dogma around the turn of the eighteenth century. That the Gothicists themselves frequently shared in the general disquietude of the age is true, but at the same time they were too thoroughly steeped in Puritanism to find the Catholic or Armenian alternative a meaningful one. William Godwin, after all, went from Calvinism to atheism but was never tempted by the Church of England, and his hunger for inner-worldly sainthood surely accounts at least in part for his attraction to the French Revolution. Carwin's adoption of Catholicism, to which Brown alluded again in *Wieland,* is not, therefore, simply a convenient device for endowing the villain with an aura of exoticism. Instead it is an outgrowth of the explicitly Calvinistic bias of the Gothic school and stamps Carwin as one of the damned, an unrepentant sinner who counts upon the false security of the legal covenant to preserve him from the vengeance of a righteous God. It is altogether consistent with his repudiation of Christ-Ludloe and his subsequent protests of innocence throughout the novel. Despite having set in motion the train of events that culminates in the younger Wieland's suicide, he will defend himself against Clara's accusations of depravity, allowing that his morals are "far from rigid" but insisting that he is not the "desperate or sordid criminal" that she charges him with being (p. 230).

And yet the almost oppressive theological temper of Brown's tale is barely sensed at the outset, the participants themselves confidently consigning it to the past. Although Clara concedes that the history of her father's strange death, which she recounts in the introductory chapters, has left an impression on her that "can never be effaced" (p. 21), the idyllic middle-class landscape inhabited by herself, her brother, Catherine, and Pleyel retains few traces of the morbid spirituality to which the elder Wieland fell prey. Brown's subtitle "An American Tale" suggests that he saw in his central foursome a microcosm of the bourgeois American society that by 1798 stood in defiant opposition to the Puritan past. Surely it is no coincidence that at one point in the narrative Pleyel refers to a Ciceronian oration that makes "the picture of a single family a model from which to sketch the condition of a nation" (p. 34). Unruffled rationality, moderation, and middle-class ease are the distinguishing marks of the Mettingen setting; the temple that the senior Wieland kept bare—"without seat, table, or ornament of any kind" (p. 12)—and consecrated to the worship of the Deity has been cluttered with a harpsichord, pedestal, and bust of Cicero, Enlightenment trappings that symbolize a rejection of the austere Protestantism of an earlier day. The God-charged universe of Cotton Mather and Jonathan Edwards has narrowed to a common sense world that would have gladdened the heart of Benjamin Franklin. Even the childhood environment of the younger Wielands has been scrupulously based on enlightened principles, with special emphasis on the golden mean: "our education," comments Clara, "had been modeled by no religious standard" (p. 24), the aunt who raised her and her brother seldom deviating "into either extreme of rigor or lenity" (p. 22). Once a guide for personal conduct, religion has become merely a subject for casual debate, and assembled at their "fane" on the Schuylkill, the circle of intimates whiles away the hours in aimless cultural pursuits.

If the Wielands have renounced the past, however, Theodore has not succeeded in exorcising the ghost of his father, which continues to haunt him in the form of an inchoate longing for what the Puritans would have called a conversion experience. "Moral necessity, and calvinistic inspiration," according to Clara, "were the props on which my brother thought proper to repose" (p. 28). She further describes him as grave, thoughtful, and given to melancholy. But Brown has taken pains to distinguish Wieland from authentic Calvinists and to spell out the dangers inherent in his background and sensibility. While apprenticed to a merchant in England, the senior Wieland had come into contact with the doctrines of the Camissards, a Huguenot sect notorious for its antinomian excesses. Having emigrated to America with the intention of preaching to the Indians, he had connected himself to no established church and abjured all forms of social worship. A separatist and enthusiast, he had lived in daily expectation of a direct message from the Almighty. Even the mother of Clara and Theodore, although not a fanatic like their father, did not belong to any congregation and was a devout disciple of the mystical Count von Zinzendorf, whose separatist impulses were a thorn in the side of Gilbert Tennent. The aunt who reared the younger Wielands was a separatist of a different order, but a separatist nonetheless. She preserved her charges, in Clara's words, "from the corruption and tyranny of colleges and boarding-schools" (p. 22); and Theodore and his sister have carried on the family tradition in their own enlightened fashion. Fortunate enough to find their temperaments duplicated in Catherine and Pleyel, they have gradually withdrawn from "the society of others, and found every moment irksome that was not devoted to each other" (p. 23).

Thus Brown has carefully sketched in the flaws of upbringing and character that will eventually issue in Wieland's antinomian mania and Clara's fits of madness. Whereupon he introduces into the narrative the figure of Carwin, and his implicit criticism of American life begins to move in the direction of epic, as it becomes increasingly clear that the fable underlying his novel is Milton's *Paradise Lost*. Clara is utterly captivated by the appearance of Carwin, who begs at her door for water dressed in virtual rags. That a stranger who reminds her of a rustic clown should exert so powerful a hold on her imagination would seem absurd were it not for the fact that her portrait of him so strikingly resembles the fallen Angel Lucifer or the Wandering Jew Ahasuerus:

> yet his forehead, so far as shaggy locks would allow it to be seen, his eyes lustrously black, and possessing, in the midst of haggardness, a radiance inexpressibly serene and potent, and something in the rest of his features, which it would be vain to describe, but which betoken a mind of the highest order, were essential ingredients in the portrait.
>
> (p. 61)

The faded grandeur that Clara detects in Carwin's countenance plunges her into a maze of mournful associations which call into question the Edenic bliss of her present life, and for the first time since the tragedy of her father she is troubled by intimations of mortality: "Death must happen to all" (pp. 62-63). Although she argues that her infatuation with the mysterious wanderer should not be mistaken for love, there is good reason to believe that Clara is sexually drawn to him, and that the storm which rages outside her window while she studies his picture is both an omen of future disaster and an emblem of the tumultuous passions aroused by his presence. Indeed, it is a Miltonic storm such as accompanied the transgression in Eden, a circumstance which is entirely appropriate in view of the fact that Carwin will bring death and sin into the garden of *Wieland*. For he is Brown's Gothic tempter, and Clara has become the novelist's American Eve.

It is worth noting, for example, that the biloquist has but a single name. The absence of a surname or Christian name—for the reader never knows which one it is that Carwin lacks—implies an estrangement from society that brands him as an outcast and misfit. In spite of the apparent ease with which he insinuates himself into the Mettingen setting, Carwin's ultimate failure to shed his solitude places him in the company of archetypes such as Lucifer, Cain, and Ahasuerus. Bumbler that he proves to be, the biloquist is nevertheless modeled on

Milton's conception of Satan. So extensive, in fact, are the parallels between *Wieland* and *Paradise Lost* that it is hard to imagine how they have been overlooked. Carwin's eloquence is an obvious case in point. Overhearing him converse with her servant, Clara is forcibly struck by the sweetness of his voice; and his uncanny powers of speech occasion the numerous misunderstandings that shatter the novel's surface tranquillity. Repeatedly Clara is under the misapprehension that he is speaking directly into her ear; in Milton's classic, Satan is discovered squatting like a toad, "close at the ear of Eve" (4.800). Envious of Eve's love for Adam, the Arch-Fiend is filled with wonder when he first beholds the primal parents, and the sight of their beauty, refulgent with the image of God, almost swerves him from his sinister purpose. Similarly, Carwin is jealous of Clara's passion for Pleyel, although he also expresses admiration for the latter's "exquisite sagacity" (p. 236), and he hesitates to employ his verbal skills against them. Clara in particular captures his fancy, Judith having told him that her mistress's "perfections were little less than divine" (p. 227). In *Paradise Lost,* Satan addresses Eve as scarcely inferior to the angels, and entering the sleeping form of the serpent, he literally licks the ground on which she treads (9.526).

There are, moreover, striking affinities between the dream in which Lucifer appears to Eve and entices her to the tree of knowledge, and that in which Wieland beckons Clara to the edge of an abyss. Clara's dream has generated a host of conflicting interpretations. To critics who favor the sentimental seduction reading, for example, the chasm evokes a latent fear of incest; to William H. Manly, it stands for the insanity that runs in the Wieland family.[9] Another interpretation, one based on Brown's indebtedness to Milton, seems more probable, however. In both the novel and the epic, the dreams eventually come true; beguiled by Satan, Eve eats of the forbidden fruit, and Clara is physically menaced by Theodore, who believes himself under a divine injunction to slay her. But the physical threat is less important, ultimately, than the fact that her brother compels Clara to confront the evil within herself. We will return later to this decisive turning point in her narrative; for the present, it is enough to suggest that the pit toward which she hastens is hell—the hell that awaits those who taste of the fruit of the tree of knowledge of good and evil. There are several hints to this effect. Clara is stopped short in her progress by a voice crying "Hold," by which Brown may have wished to recall the heavenly prohibition imposed on Adam and Eve. Further, the mysterious voice summons Clara to "Remember your father, and be faithful"; and she shudders with fright, as if she beheld "suspended over me, the exterminating sword" (pp. 72-73).

But the portent of the dream is temporarily lost sight of, even by Clara herself, after the scene in which she ap-

proaches the closet door and is again arrested by the command to "Hold!" Imagining because of her dream that Theodore is her enemy, she leaps to the conclusion that he is the person hiding within the closet and calls to him to come out, exclaiming "I know you well." But the person who steals forth is Carwin, not Theodore, and the focus of danger is thus shifted to the biloquist (pp. 96-102). The brother becomes the other in a dramatic turnabout which has the effect of seeming to isolate evil in an external agent. The importance of this scene for Clara's development cannot be overstressed, since she will continue almost to the end of her narrative to regard the intruder as the sole cause of the sufferings that destroy her family's happiness. As Milton's God was careful to explain to the angels, however, He created man able to withstand temptation, thereby rendering him inexcusable for having sinned. Clara will only grasp this truth at the last.

This is not to say, of course, that Carwin is guiltless. Although her brother will eventually undermine Clara's conviction of her own innocence, it is the "double-tongued" wanderer who brings about her fall in the eyes of Pleyel. This is what the controversial seduction episode is really about: deceived by Carwin's ventriloquism, and convinced that Clara has succumbed to the villain's wiles, Pleyel charges her—in accents unmistakably Miltonic—with having committed the primal sin: "O wretch!—thus exquisitely fashioned—on whom nature seemed to have exhausted all her graces; with charms so awful and pure! how art thou fallen! From what height fallen! A ruin so complete—so unheard of!" (p. 117). Pleyel goes on to accuse Clara of consummate depravity, despairing that "In thy ruin, how will the felicity and honor of multitudes be involved" (pp. 117-18). He describes Carwin as the blackest of criminals, a Satanic schemer whose devices "no human intelligence is able to unravel" and who has leagued with infernal spirits in order to wage "a perpetual war against the happiness of mankind" (pp. 148-49). Clara herself now says of the biloquist that "this a foe from whose grasp no power of divinity can save me" (p. 126). As her words indicate, Carwin has completely replaced her brother as the source of her fears. And indeed Pleyel pictures Clara, in what appears to be a deliberate allusion to her dream, as "rushing to the verge of a dizzy precipice," led on by the cunning seducer (p. 147). The denunciations that he hurls at her, and her indignant protests of purity, recall the bickering between Adam and Eve after the Fall:

> Thus they in mutual accusation spent
> The fruitless hours, but neither self-condemning,
> And of their vain contest appeared no end.
>
> [9. 1187-89]

"Neither self-condemning"—Milton's words go to the core of the novel's concern, and underline the mutual failure of Clara and Pleyel to assume responsibility for their transgressions. What is more, as the confrontation at Pleyel's house demonstrates, both are unwilling to go beyond reliance on the legal covenant. Pleyel takes upon himself the office of unforgiving judge—Clara calls him "inexorable" (p. 129)—and he denies her the Christian charity that might have repaired the misunderstandings engendered by Carwin's duplicity. He holds her to the relentless letter of the law:

> An inscrutable providence has fashioned thee for some end. Thou wilt live, no doubt, to fulfil the purposes of thy maker, if he repent not of his workmanship, and send not his vengeance to exterminate thee, ere the measure of thy days be full. Surely nothing in the shape of man can vie with thee!.
>
> (p. 135).

Clara likewise spurns the message of Christ and demands justice instead of mercy. "I come hither not to confess," she informs her accuser, "but to vindicate" (p. 133). Here the Godwinian aspect of Brown's tale comes to the fore, and here too the true meaning of the secrecy theme is cast into bold relief. The issue for Brown is manifestly the reluctance of sinful man to lay bare his heart—an ordeal that Poe, for one, considered impossible, and that Edwards regarded as essential for salvation. Although Clara hears out Pleyel in silence and persists in believing herself blameless, she has been guilty of concealing her true feelings from him, and her concealment has contributed to their estrangement as much as Carwin's officiousness. She has also kept secret the interview with the would-be murderer whose summons interrupted her dream at the summerhouse—an interview, as Pleyel rightly surmises, that took place with the Satanic biloquist, albeit that Clara was then ignorant of his identity. The reader knows, however, from Clara's own words, words written after the fact but inserted into her narrative prior to the climactic scene with Pleyel, that her "scruples were preposterous and criminal. . . . My errors have taught me thus much wisdom; that those sentiments which we ought not to disclose, it is criminal to harbour" (p. 90).

Clara's fall, like that of the primal couple, ushers sin and death into the Edenic world of **Wieland.** Having left Pleyel's house—significantly, he has announced his intention of setting out on a long journey—she returns to a Mettingen despoiled by her brother's murderous rampage. Overcome by what she sees, she casts the entire burden of guilt on Carwin. She assumes that he is the murderer of her brother's family; and even Theodore's confession does not shake her belief that the author of woe is the biloquist, to whom she attributes supernatural powers. This is to deny man's complicity in the Fall and to reject—in Edwards's words—"The Great Christian Doctrine of Original Sin." To Clara's disordered mind, evil is extrinsic, not integral to human nature:

> O brother! spare me, spare thyself: There is thy betrayer. He counterfeited the voice and face of an angel, for the purpose of destroying thee and me. He has this moment confessed it. He is able to speak where he is not. He is leagued with hell, but will not avow it; yet he confesses that the agency was his.
>
> (p. 245)

In this speech, Clara is implicitly proclaiming her own innocence as well as Theodore's and taking refuge in the legal covenant—the covenant predicated on the mistaken notion that fallen man is essentially unfallen, and that Lucifer alone is responsible for sin. Moments later, however, she is brought up sharply by the discovery that she is prepared to defend herself against Wieland's attack by plunging her penknife into his heart, a weapon that she has all along insisted that she will use only against herself. This realization sets off a reversal of sentiment that recalls Caleb Williams's despair after the trial of Falkland:

> I estimate my own deserving; a hatred, immortal and inexorable, is my due, I listen to my own pleas, and find them empty and false: yes, I acknowledge that my guilt surpasses that of all mankind: I confess that the curses of a world, and the frowns of a deity, are inadequate to my demerits. Is there a thing in the world worthy of infinite abhorrence? It is I
>
> (pp. 249-50)

Admittedly, the act that Clara contemplates is one of self-defense—but that is precisely Brown's point. For although any court of law would deliver a verdict of justifiable homicide (just as Caleb Williams is vindicated in a court of law), Clara—finding herself capable of slaying her own brother—has ceased to think in terms of the law. She has finally accepted the fact of human corruption: the "adders" of sin are now lodged in her own breast (p. 256).

Clara is prostrated with grief and self-loathing after the death of her brother. Much like Milton's Eve, she craves "quick deliverance from life and all the ills that attend it" (p. 261), and she revolts against the inevitable decree that she must quit the scene of her former bliss:

> O unexpected stroke, worse than of Death!
> Must I thus leave thee, Paradise: thus leave
> Thee, native soil, these happy walks and shades,
> Fit haunt of gods?
>
> [9.268-71]

Clara has accepted her culpability, but she still shrinks from its consequences. It is not until her home is consumed by flames—as in the **Memoirs of Carwin,** the conflagration recalls Michael's fiery sword—that she resigns herself to banishment from the garden and agrees to accompany her uncle on a voyage to Europe. The last chapter of the novel is therefore dated at Montpellier in France, and is written, significantly enough, three years after the narrative proper. It finds Clara chastened but "not destitute of happiness" (p. 262), for her sanity has been restored and she has been reunited with her American Adam. She now admits that "no human virtue is secure from degeneracy" (p. 270), and she has made a full confession of her former sentiments to Pleyel. Inevitably one is reminded of Eve's moving speech to Adam in *Paradise Lost*: "Living or dying, from thee I will not hide / What thoughts in my unquiet breast are risen . . ." (9.974-75). In Calvinist terms, Clara has been reborn through the agency of Christ: she has bared her soul and given her assent to the doctrine of original sin. "It will not escape your notice," she writes, "that the evils of which Carwin and Maxwell were the authors, owed their existence to the errors of the sufferers" (p. 273). Man is partner with Satan in the Fall.

In the last book of *Paradise Lost,* Adam almost rejoices over his sin because of Michael's prophecy of the coming of Christ; by the concluding pages of Brown's novel, Clara has grown to a measure of self-awareness that was beyond her when she dwelt in the Mettingen Eden. The transformation of Brown's title refers, then, both to the Fall and the promise of redemption; and it is altogether fitting that Hawthorne's *Marble Faun* (1860) was published in England under the title *Transformation,* its subject being the Fortunate Fall. As for Carwin, the ventriloquist acknowledges his misconduct, but, as he correctly insists, he has committed no crime punishable by human law. "I cannot justify my conduct," he tells Clara, "yet my only crime was curiosity" (p. 231). Caleb Williams's crime was no different: curiosity, after all, is the primal sin. Escaping the clutches of Ludloe, Carwin makes his way into a remote district of Pennsylvania, where he engages "in the harmless pursuits of agriculture" (p. 268). Blind to his own depravity, ignorant of his need for grace, the villain returns to the garden from which Clara and Pleyel have been expelled and becomes an "innocent" American yeoman. This is Brown's devastating judgment on Franklin's America: it no longer has any place for those who penetrate to the truth of the human heart. Clara is doomed to permanent exile from a land which has lost the sense of sin.

The apologetic tone of Brown's "advertisement," and his apprehensions concerning his tale's reception, are reminiscent of the somewhat defensive posture adopted by Edwards in the preface to *The Great Christian Doctrine of Original Sin Defended* (1757). Barely forty years separate the publication of the two works, both of which deal, as Brown announced in his "advertisement," with "the moral constitution of man" (p. 3). Edwards, writing in the aftermath of the Great Awakening, still retained some hope of restoring his countrymen to "the principles and scheme of religion maintained by our pious and excellent forefathers."[10] No such hope animates Brown's "veiled sermon," as Fred Lewis Pattee once

called it.[11] And so it is fitting that **Wieland** is built on the fable of *Paradise Lost.* For in going back to Milton for his inspiration, Brown was doing more than paying tribute to the greatest of Puritan authors. He was also addressing a theme that was to engage a host of later American novelists: the promise of America, he strongly suggests, is the "paradise lost" in **Wieland.**

Notes

1. David Lee Clark, *Charles Brockden Brown: Pioneer Voice of America* (Durham: Duke Univ. Press, 1952), pp. 168-69. See also Harry R. Warfel, *Charles Brockden Brown: American Gothic Novelist* (Gainesville, Fla.: Univ. of Florida Press, 1949), pp. 104-5.

2. For important reassessments of the Gothic novel, see Lowry Nelson, Jr., "Night Thoughts on the Gothic Novel," *The Yale Review,* 52 (Winter 1963), 236-57; Robert D. Hume, "Gothic Versus Romantic: A Revaluation of the Gothic Novel," *PMLA,* 84 (1969), 282-90; and the essays in G. R. Thompson, ed., *The Gothic Imagination: Essays in Dark Romanticism* (Pullman, Wash.: Washington State Univ. Press, 1974), particularly Joel Porte's "In the Hands of an Angry God: Religious Terror in Gothic Fiction," pp. 42-64. The religious theme in Brown has been noted by Larzer Ziff, "A Reading of *Wieland,*" *PMLA,* 67 (1962), 51-57; and Donald A. Ringe, *Charles Brockden Brown* (New York: Twayne Publishers, 1966), pp. 25-48.

3. See Ziff, pp. 51-57.

4. Porte, pp. 52-55.

5. On Edwards's influence on Godwin, see Alfred Owen Aldridge, "Jonathan Edwards and William Godwin on Virtue," *American Literature,* 18 (1947), 308-18.

6. William Godwin, *Caleb Williams,* ed. David McCracken (New York: Oxford Univ. Press, 1970), pp. 233, 273, 278-79, 296, 323, 325-26.

7. Crane Brinton, *A Decade of Revolution: 1789-1799* (New York: Harper Torchbooks, 1963), pp. 158-61. The similarity between the Puritan and French Revolutions has been examined in detail by Michael Walzer, *The Revolution of the Saints: A Study in the Origins of Radical Politics* (Cambridge, Mass.: Harvard Univ. Press, 1965).

8. I will be referring to Fred Lewis Pattee's edition of *Wieland; or The Transformation,* which includes the fragment *Memoirs of Carwin the Biloquist* (New York: Harcourt, Brace & World, 1926). Page references will appear in the text.

9. Ziff, p. 54; also see Leslie A. Fiedler, *Love and Death in the American Novel,* rev. ed. (New York:

Dell, 1966), pp. 74-104, 126-61; and William M. Manly, "The Importance of Point of View in Brockden Brown's *Wieland,*" *American Literature,* 35 (1963), 317-18.

10. Jonathan Edwards, *The Great Christian Doctrine of Original Sin Defended,* ed. Clyde C. Holbrook (New Haven: Yale Univ. Press, 1970), p. 102.

11. Introduction to *Wieland,* p. xxviii.

James R. Russo (essay date 1981)

SOURCE: Russo, James R. "'The Chimeras of the Brain': Clara's Narrative in *Wieland.*" *Early American Literature* 16, no. 1 (spring 1981): 60-88.

[*In the following essay, Russo disputes common theories that attribute the perceived incoherence of* Wieland's *plot to Brown's incompetence as a writer, claiming that it is not Brown, but his narrator, who is responsible for the incoherence.*]

Modern criticism has found one major fault with *Wieland*: its loose and unbalanced structure.[1] The alleged incoherence of its plot is attributed to Charles Brockden Brown's carelessness as a writer, a notion so firmly entrenched in Brown criticism that it persists all but unchallenged despite much evidence to the contrary.[2] A better explanation for the seeming incoherence of *Wieland* is possible only if we set aside the a priori reasoning that Brown was an inferior artist. Clara Wieland herself provides us with the key when she makes the following damaging admission: "What but ambiguities, abruptness, and dark transitions can be expected from the historian who is, at the same time, the sufferer of these disasters?"[3] Indeed, *Wieland* is told by a confessed madwoman, Clara Wieland, and her narrative seems incoherent at times because she is confused, not because Brown is. "My narrative may be invaded by inaccuracy and confusion" (p. 147) Clara admits, but her very admission may, ironically, prevent the reader from taking her warning seriously. When she confesses that her version of various actions and motivations depends upon "a coincidence of events scarcely credible" (p. 139), the literal truth of her assertion may escape the most alert reader. Even Pleyel only partially perceives the truth about Clara when he accuses her of having "a sensibility somewhat too vivid" (p. 123).

William Manly has correctly argued that *Wieland* is Clara's story, not her brother's, and that Brown conveys "through a first person narrator the shifting instability of a mind swayed between objective logic and subjective terror."[4] I wish to take Manly's argument one step further by demonstrating that Clara actually flits back and forth between imagination and reality throughout the novel, and that many of the inconsistencies which have bothered the critics actually provide the evidence for such a reading. Clara does not intentionally lie to the reader; she simply does not know the truth.[5]

The novel itself provides the reader with numerous reasons for questioning Clara's mental stability. First, she has inherited insanity from *both* sides of her family. We are informed through Clara's uncle, Mr. Cambridge, that her maternal grandfather committed suicide in a sudden fit of madness by jumping off a cliff (p. 179). Clara herself contemplates suicide more than once. On the paternal side, the family instability is traced in detail in the opening chapters of the novel that culminate in the bizarre death of Clara's father, when she is still a child. Both brother and sister, it seems, have inherited a legacy of violence and mental instability, yet it is interesting to note how each child chooses to deal with that legacy. Of the two, Theodore's approach is the more reasonable. It is true that he believes, as did his father, that God at times may choose to communicate directly with individual men, and this belief will eventually undo him. However, it must be stressed that such a tenet is not a radical one. It is only Pleyel, whose rationalistic views are radical themselves in the novel's historical context, who would object to it. Throughout the novel, Clara herself vacillates on this same philosophical point of whether one can communicate directly with God. Therefore, it makes little sense to see Theodore's commonly held world view as a "potential for mania,"[6] for such a reading ignores the more significant attempts that Theodore makes to break free from his legacy of violence and insanity. For instance, he converts his father's temple, the scene of the elder Wieland's fanatical devotions and violent death, into a summerhouse, and symbolically refutes his father's religious mania by placing in its center a bust of Cicero. Indeed, the son shows himself to have a more stable and inquiring mind than the father had, and while he lacks the complete religious skepticism of his friend Pleyel, he shows no sign whatever of being unbalanced until the voices begin.[7] Therefore, Franklin's claim that Wieland is not so much duped by the voices as merely started on a course that he would have inevitably followed, as Othello is through Iago's aggravations or Macbeth through the instigation of the witches, is not precisely true.

Theodore's sane approach to life is even more evident when we compare him to his sister, for numerous details suggest that Clara has been less successful than her brother in breaking away from the Wieland legacy, despite her claim to be the more rational of the two. Where Theodore attempts to tear away from the past, Clara preserves and nourishes it. Where Theodore rejects his father's fanaticism by converting the elder Wieland's shrine into a summerhouse, Clara hoards her lunatic father's possessions and cherishes his memory as "sacred." In her closet she keeps his memoirs and reads them late at night before going to sleep. In her bedroom she keeps the antique clock which chimed her father to his death. It is Clara, not Theodore, who constantly broods over their father's strange death whenever she sees a flash of light, and it is Clara who causes us to feel, as Franklin puts it, that "the father's spirit broods over *Wieland* as ominously as it does over *Hamlet*."[8] We should not ignore the way violence continually creeps into Clara's waking and sleeping thoughts. Not only does she conjure up the vivid image of Pleyel's drowned corpse and other like phantasms, but she also admits that these ugly visions have a soothing effect upon her, learning to enjoy as she does through the course of the novel "that terror which is pleasing" (p. 45).

Clara's insanity, her inability to perceive reality, may best be illustrated by examining the major dramatic incidents of the novel: the events that cluster around her first encounter with the voices in her closet, her dream by the river and the warning voice that speaks through the lattice, her discovery of Carwin in her closet, the murder of Catherine, Carwin's confession, and her final confrontation with her brother. In each of these episodes it can be clearly demonstrated that Clara loses touch with reality, and that the events simply could not have happened as she reports them.

Before Clara Wieland hears the voices in her closet plotting her murder, others have heard strange voices. Theodore has heard his wife's voice warn him not to ascend to the summerhouse. Another voice, again sounding like Catherine's, has informed Wieland and Pleyel of the death of the latter's fiancee (though this information turns out to be false). Clara informs us that in the case of these first two voices the agent must have been supernatural: "that there are conscious beings besides ourselves in existence, whose modes of activity and information surpass our own, can scarcely be denied" (p. 45). She also feels that the agent must be benevolent, and that her brother's obedience to the first voice "perhaps saved him from a destiny similar to that of my father" (p. 46). While there may be nothing outwardly sinister in these opinions, it should be noted that the pleasure Clara feels when the voice informs Pleyel of his fiancee's death is unsettling, even though we realize that Clara herself is in love with Pleyel: "Propitious was the spirit which imparted these tidings. Propitious he would perhaps have been, if he had been instrumental in producing as well as in communicating the tidings of her death" (p. 46). At best, the above passage shows Clara to be selfish enough to view as "propitious" the death of another human being. At worst, it shows that she, even if only subconsciously, condones violence for personal ends, for she tells us that the voice would merit her approval even if it had *caused* the death of Pleyel's Teresa, and not merely reported it.

It is shortly after the appearance of Carwin that Clara hears the voices in her closet. One sunny afternoon Clara spies Carwin on the Wieland property; a while later he appears at her door requesting a drink of water. The impression he makes on Clara is extreme, and she weeps piteously when she hears him speak. Later in the afternoon she draws his portrait and spends most of the night awake staring at it. She herself admits that this reaction to Carwin is most unusual: "The manner in which I was affected on this occasion was, to my own apprehension, a subject of astonishment" (p. 52). Yet if Clara is astonished, the reader needn't be, for the reaction of the young girl is natural enough in that it is completely physical. Where she is romantically attached to Pleyel, her reaction to Carwin is quite different, as is made clear by her long physical description of him. (Pleyel, we should remember, is never described in physical detail by Clara.) Clara's description of Carwin is highly ambivalent, portraying accurately her simultaneous attraction and repulsion. Carwin is a large man who radiates strength, and despite his pallid cheeks, his large irregular teeth, and his discolored skin, Clara finds that there was "something in the rest of his features which it would be vain to describe, but which served to betoken a mind of the highest order" (p. 53). And, it is Carwin's *physical* presence which causes Clara to blush when the man comes upon her "accidentally" when returning the borrowed cup. The meeting causes Clara a "confused sense of impropriety" (p. 53), and the phrase itself suggests that her response is a physical one. In short, Clara is, at least subconsciously, confronted with her own sexuality, and as she stares at Carwin's portrait that night, her state of mind is mirrored in the violent storm outside her bedroom window. She spends the entire next day looking alternately at the storm and the portrait, though she does not understand why she does so. She does admit, however, that "you will perhaps deem this conduct somewhat singular" (p. 54).

While the awakening of the young woman's sexuality is perhaps not as "singular" as Clara thinks, what follows as night falls *is* morbidly "singular." As she stares past the portrait of Carwin out her bedroom window into the darkness, Clara finds that her thoughts turn melancholy. She begins by questioning the meaning of the storm which has just ceased: "Why was my mind absorbed in thoughts ominous and dreary? Why did my bosom heave with sighs and my eyes overflow with tears? Was the tempest that had just passed a signal of the ruin which impended over me?" (p. 54). Of course, the "tempest" which Clara refers to has a double meaning. She asks in the literal sense whether the violent outer storm might be an evil omen, but the reader must realize, even if Clara does not, that the same question applies to her inner storm occasioned by the physical presence of Carwin. The question of whether Clara's inner struggle, her battle with her own sexuality, predicts dire consequences takes on added force when in her musing state she foreshadows the tragedy which is to happen months later:

> My soul fondly dwelt upon the images of my brother and his children; yet they only increased the mournfulness of my contemplations. The smiles of the charming babes were as bland as formerly. The same dignity sat on the brow of their father, and yet I thought of them with anguish. Something whispered that the happiness we at present enjoyed was set upon mutable foundations. Death must happen to all.
>
> (P. 54)

There might not be anything so sinister in Clara's thoughts if it were not that they turn to violent death, not merely abstract death. When her thoughts become "insupportable," she tries to dispel them with the songs and poetry of her paternal grandfather (who is briefly mentioned in the first chapter of the novel). The ballad she chooses contains "scenes of violence and carnage which were here wildly but forcibly portrayed" (p. 55). It is in this state of mind ("thronged by vivid but confused images") that Clara finally falls asleep. She tells us that she is awakened at midnight by the sound of the clock—the same one, she reminds us, that called her father to the temple that tragic night—and she begins to ponder her father's bizarre death. These reflections are interrupted by voices in her private closet, which Clara informs us is always locked. After listening to a rather lengthy dialogue in which the two voices plan her murder, Clara finally jumps from bed and rushes outside (though "scantily robed") to her brother's house. She admits that she can "hardly recollect the process of turning the keys and withdrawing the bolts" (p. 58). She tells us that she faints upon her brother's door-step and is found there by Theodore and Pleyel, who have been awakened by a shrieking voice. Despite her furious departure she has managed not to awaken Judith, the maid, whom they find fast asleep upon their return.

Given Clara's state of mind when she went to sleep, the opinion of Pleyel and Theodore that the whole episode was a dream is plausible. The inability of the dreamer to run away despite danger, the lunatic discussion of the two voices attempting to resolve the method of her execution, and the fact that the whole thing begins at midnight (the time of her father's death) by the stroke of the fateful clock, all suggest that Clara is dreaming. So does the fact that she flees through a series of locked doors without remembering unlocking them. Carwin's confession later in the novel may lend some validity to the bizarre episode, but when the reader remembers that his confession comes to us via Clara and that his confession is itself contradictory, incoherent, and improbable, that reader has legitimate cause to doubt the truth of the reported events. Furthermore, the reader may well notice a pattern emerging. The only tangible result of this episode is that Pleyel agrees to come and live with Clara; he resides in the vacant chamber across

from her own. Earlier, another voice has prevented Pleyel from leaving for Europe by informing him (falsely) of the death of his fiancée. From Clara's point of view the voices are indeed "propitious."

It is some weeks later when Clara again hears a voice, and this time there is even more justification for doubting her version of the event, for in this instance, her own language reveals that she has temporarily lost touch with reality. Clara reports that she has taken a walk during the late afternoon and found herself at one of her favorite retreats, the small summerhouse in the recess of the river bank. She falls asleep on a bench while listening to the "lulling sounds of the waterfall" in a state of mental and physical "utmost supineness" (p. 62). Perhaps it is Clara's "hereditary dread of water" (p. 83) that causes her sleep to be "molested . . . with dreams of no cheerful hue" (p. 62). The vivid one that Clara recounts has been much discussed by critics;[9] however, it is less important to interpret the dream in which Clara's brother beckons her toward an abyss, than it is to establish its boundaries—that is, to determine whether what follows is really part of the same dream. Clara tells us that she is awakened from it by a voice which exclaims, "Hold!" She informs us that both the voice and the arm that pulls her back from the brink of the abyss are part of the dream itself. However, once she is "awake," she hears a voice identical to the one that has just finished speaking *in her dream*; this voice warns her to "avoid this spot" because "the snares of death encompass it" (p. 63).

Although Clara informs us that she was dreaming when her brother beckoned her toward the pit, but was awake when the voice spoke to her through the lattice, warning her away from the summerhouse, her testimony should be doubted. Even Carwin's confession later in the novel does not make her statement plausible, for he himself must admit that "the coincidence of your dream in the summerhouse with my exclamation was truly wonderful" (p. 206). Furthermore, Clara's own words suggest that the voice which warns her to stay away from the summerhouse in the river recess is part of the same dream in which her brother beckons her toward the abyss, for after the voice "awakens" her, she confesses that "images so terrific and forcible disabled me for a time from distinguishing between sleep and wakefulness, and withheld from me the knowledge of my actual condition" (p. 62). Though she wishes to return to her house, her "faculties were still too confused" (p. 63) to find the path. Yet despite this confusion of the senses, she insists that the voice in the lattice warning her away from the river, which is identical to the one in her dream, is real. Her certainty upon this crucial point is undercut, however, when she is rescued by Pleyel and reluctantly admits: "I was almost dubious whether the pit into which my brother had endeavored to entice me, and the voice that talked through the lattice, were not part of the same dream" (p. 64). She also realizes that her readers will be "dubious": "You will believe that calamity has subverted my reason, and that I am amusing you with the chimeras of my brain instead of the facts that have really happened. I shall not be surprised or offended if these be your suspicions" (p. 65). However,, by acknowledging that her account is preposterous she does not make it less so.

There are several additional reasons to believe that the voice coming from behind the lattice is part of the dream of the abyss. First, the episode contains many of the same characteristics of the earlier episode in which Clara heard voices in the closet; again there is the inability to flee from danger, the dark confusion of the senses, the less than coherent dialogue of the warning voice. After telling Clara to avoid the spot, the voice admonishes her to "Remember your father, and be faithful" (p. 63). Despite Carwin's later confession, we cannot believe it possible for him to have said this to Clara, because at this time he had no knowledge of her father's history. He has been by his own admission (that is, Clara's report of his admission) eavesdropping upon the Wieland family's conversations in the temple-summerhouse, but since there is no reason to suggest that the Wielands have been casually discussing the matter of the elder Wieland's death, and since even according to Carwin's confession he had not yet begun perusing Clara's diary or examining the contents of her closet, then we must conclude that the voice behind the lattice cannot have been his.

If all of this were not enough, the evidence presented by Pleyel also discourages our trust in Clara's narrative. When Pleyel comes searching for her by the river bank, he repeatedly calls out her name, yet for some time she does not respond, claiming that "such was the tumult of my thoughts that I had not power to answer him till he had frequently repeated his summons" (p. 64). A few evenings later, according to Pleyel, he has the occasion to view a letter that Clara is writing (presumably to Carwin) requesting *another* interview at midnight. This, in connection with other evidence he is soon to receive, causes Pleyel to conclude that Clara is having an illicit affair with Carwin. Indeed, Clara never does explain the letter that Pleyel glimpses, except to say that it was an entry in her diary and the words he saw were taken out of context. However, she never establishes the context whereby we are to understand her desire for *another* interview, nor does she until later inform us of her reported "trepidation and blushes" when Pleyel accidentally witnesses part of what she has written. It appears that she would have passed over the incident entirely had it not been for Pleyel's accusations. He reports that she questions him eagerly to find out how much of the letter he has read. Later, when he mentions his rescue of Clara to Carwin, the latter also becomes visibly uneasy for no apparent reason.

If we consider the possibility that both the abyss into which Clara is beckoned and the subsequent voice behind the lattice are parts of the same dream, then that dream makes a good deal more sense than critics have previously been able to find. For if the dream is a dual one in which two dangers are subconsciously presented to the dreamer, then those two dangers are not difficult to identify. Despite the attempts of some critics to see the dream in which Theodore beckons Clara toward the pit as representing a threat of incest, the rest of the novel does little to encourage such a reading. After all, Theodore has done nothing at this point to suggest that he might be a threat to Clara (although she might irrationally consider him to be a threat). As one critic has pointed out, however, the pit into which Clara nearly falls in her dream is more suggestive of violence than sex.[10] Her brother represents for her the potential for violence she has inherited from their parents, and for that reason she later suspects that it is he concealed in her closet and intending to do her harm. Yet the danger represented by the voice in the lattice is even clearer, for that one warns her away from the summerhouse in the recess of the river bank, the scene of her alleged rendezvous with Carwin. Here the threat is expressly sexual, and Clara's conscious dread of becoming a "polluted" woman is responsible for the subconscious warning in the form of the disembodied voice. To Clara's conscious mind death is preferable to such "pollution," and the two are so closely linked that when she first sees the light from Pleyel's lamp, she recalls the flash of light that was a prelude to her father's death.

Seen in these terms, *Wieland* is a struggle between Clara's conscious and subconscious desires. The two are so disparate and so violently opposed that she becomes in effect a schizophrenic, flitting in and out of reality. She reports as fact "dreams" or rather delusions that cover up the truth her conscious mind cannot accept. Her dreams, like the one of the warning voice in the river recess, are true in the mind of the pure Clara who narrates her tale, and only gradually, as evidence relentlessly accumulates to incriminate her, does the reader realize that another Clara exists—though she is well hidden. Just as there are two summerhouses, one open, close to heaven on an austere cliff, the other secret, dark, in the hidden recess of the river bank, so are there two Claras, each as different as the summerhouses they alternately inhabit. The Clara of the sunny, open summerhouse narrates her tale as truthfully as she can, but, unaware as she is of what is transpiring beneath the cliff in the hidden recess, she can only lead herself and the reader astray.

On the night that Clara reports finding Carwin in her closet we discover that she has once again worked herself into a mental state bordering on frenzy, just as she had done on the night when she first heard the voices in her closet. And again there is evidence that she loses touch with reality. Pleyel and the Wielands have agreed to meet during the afternoon for a dramatic recitation of a new German romance characterized by its "adventurous and lawless fancy." Like her grandfather's romance, which Clara had been reading on the evening when she first heard the voices, this romance contains both passion and violence "portrayed in wild numbers and with terrific energy" (p. 78). When Pleyel does not arrive at the time designated for the rehearsal, the Wielands become anxious for his safety, and when his absence is protracted, Clara bursts into tears, informing the reader that her heart was "ready to burst with indignation and grief" (p. 81). She vacillates between anger and disappointment and informs us that she had intended that evening to reveal her love to him. Thus, when Pleyel does not arrive, she illogically feels jilted, exclaiming: "Blind and infatuated man! . . . Thou sportest with happiness. The good that is offered thee thou hast the insolence and folly to refuse" (p. 81). That night, as Clara continues to muse about Pleyel's failure to keep his appointment, she conjures up vivid images of his anticipated violent death by drowning, picturing his "livid corpse which the tide may cast, many days hence, upon the shore" (p. 83).

Although Clara perceives that she is allowing herself to be thus "tormented by phantasms of my own creation" (p. 83), she nevertheless continues to indulge her imagination, which has begun to torment her since allowing the "inroad of a fatal passion." Because Clara does not specify what passion she refers to, the reader is left to ponder whether she means her conventional, romantic infatuation with Pleyel or her sexual passion for Carwin. Whichever she refers to, one thing is clear; she makes no attempt to control her vivid imagination, for as she puts it, her new passion may "dig for me an untimely grave" (p. 83). After imagining Pleyel's death, her thoughts then progress "by no violent transition" to the bizarre death of her father whom she "cherished with the utmost veneration" (p. 83). She informs us that she has saved "every relic concerned with this fate" and that these are locked in her closet. It is ostensibly to read her father's memoirs that Clara decides to enter her closet, and the reader should note that she becomes frightened of what she may find within *before* she has any reason to suspect that someone may be concealed there. Given her state of mind, we should not be surprised that inside the closet she finds the horror she anticipates.

What happens when Clara tries to open her closet door is clearly imaginary. Once again, all the marks of a dream are present. Though terribly frightened, Clara cannot run away, and she tells us that her refusal to do so was "dictated by frenzy." In fact, instead of running away when she finds that someone is within the closet preventing entry, she irrationally begins to bang on the door and cry out; she explains, "Surely I was bereft of

understanding" (p. 88). That she is indeed "bereft of understanding" becomes clearer when Carwin finally emerges from the closet and begins an insane monologue in which he informs Clara that her guardian spirit is too strong to allow him to fulfill his intended schemes of violence upon her. Even Carwin's alleged confession later in the novel makes no sense in this regard, for we are asked to believe that while Carwin has the necessary physical strength to prevent Clara's entry into the closet, he instead decides to reveal himself and confess to contemplated rape and murder in order to avoid having to admit to trespassing! Furthermore, Clara would have us believe that he shares her compulsion to read her lunatic father's memoirs late at night. Such an explanation of his motives only serves to make Clara's account more ludicrous.

This vivid and complete delusion, which Clara reports as fact, can only be correctly interpreted when we understand the symbolic significance to Clara of her closet. As the receptacle of Clara's diary, which she admits contains the secrets of her heart, and as the receptacle of her past, because it holds her father's memoirs and her grandfather's poetry, the secret, locked closet represents Clara's very identity—her inner self. The preternatural voice which warns her not to open the door and examine what is within is really warning her against probing too deeply into that secret inner being. The suggestion is that there is something within Clara that might, if she were to be made consciously aware of it, be too much for her to face. This highly significant symbol stands for the human mechanism by which a part of the mind screens from the self those things that it cannot manage to live with.

Yet Clara's closet suggests further symbolic meanings as well. That it is also a sexual symbol is difficult to deny, and while Freudian critics will be interested in Clara's irrational fear that her brother is in this symbolic closet, the far more interesting feature of the episode, at least as I see it, is that Clara's entire delusion is a subconscious and symbolic *confession* of truth that her conscious mind, because of its inhibitions, cannot grapple with. When she tells us that *Carwin was in her closet,* she is, in a sense, telling us the truth, for she is at the moment not in her bedroom as she reports, but rather with Carwin in the summerhouse recess where the two are overheard by Pleyel. The voice in her dream which tells her to "Hold!" and tries to prevent her from looking inside her closet (that is, from understanding herself) attempts to spare her the self-perception that would doubtless destroy her. Yet the fable related to us by the conscious mind of the pure Clara is on this level a thinly veiled allegory that reveals the truth about the other Clara with whom the pure one is unacquainted. Brown provides us with a subtle clue that makes such a reading unavoidable when he tells us that just before opening her closet door, Clara hears through her open window in the dead stillness of the night "the murmur of the waterfall" that cascades beside the river recess where the preternatural voice has warned her that destruction awaits. Thus Clara's fear of water, which she associates with death, and her fear of opening her closet door, which represents at once her own secret identity and her cherished virginity, merge into a complex, artistic expression of the truth, although the teller of the tale is, by authorial design, unaware of it.

What happens after Carwin allegedly leaves Clara's bedroom also supports the reading I have argued. Rather than immediately seeking safety and counsel in her brother's house, as indeed we might expect her to do if her reported encounter with Carwin were real, Clara instead remains in her own house ruminating over what has occurred and not even bothering to lock the front door. She tells us that her thoughts return to Pleyel and again she imagines him dead: "I dwelt, with an obstinacy for which I cannot account, on the idea of his death. I painted to myself his struggles with the billows and his last appearance. I imagined myself a midnight wanderer on the shore, and to have stumbled on his corpse, which the tide had cast up" (p. 101). Of course, this vision of Pleyel's death presents some ironic truth. Subconsciously aware of her "pollution" through her connection with Carwin, Clara realizes that Pleyel is, in a sense, dead to her. Ironically, he, not she, is the actual midnight wanderer of the vision, and it is he who finds Clara in the summerhouse with Carwin and overhears their dialogue.

Pleyel's accusations of Clara's conduct confirm the arguments I have been presenting above. Critics have often regarded those accusations as the natural result of Pleyel's dependence upon his senses.[11] He makes the mistake, they argue, of assuming that since the voice he hears sounds like Clara's, the speaker must then actually be Clara. Such a reading, however, does not do Pleyel justice, for it is not merely the sound of the voice that he hears that convinces him that Clara is corrupt, but rather the things that the voice says, things that only Clara could know. The female voice that Pleyel overhears in the river recess discusses Clara's "former deeds of dishonor" and "the circumstances of the first interview that took place," as well as the unfortunate interruption by Pleyel and the speaker's inability to invent on the spur of the moment a suitable excuse for being in the summerhouse at night, thereby making Pleyel call out her name repeatedly. If this evidence were not damaging enough, the voice "dwelt upon incidents of which only you [Clara] could be conscious, incidents that occurred on occasions on which none besides your family were witnesses" (p. 135). Furthermore, according to Pleyel, the very idiosyncratic expressions of the speaker's language were Clara's own. Far from jumping to conclusions based solely upon sense perceptions, as critics have alleged, Pleyel, as he himself puts

it, "yielded not but to evidence which took away the power to withhold my faith" (p. 135). Clara does the best she can to explain away the strong proofs urged against her by Pleyel, but even the explanation we get in Carwin's alleged confession (which is, we remember, relayed through Clara) does not truly answer Pleyel's accusations. We are given to believe that Carwin has been able to counterfeit accurately such a detailed conversation because he has been eavesdropping for months upon the Wieland family. On occasions when Clara might be expected to return home any moment, Carwin has nonetheless stolen into her bedroom, opened her locked closet door and read her diary. (Though he is supposed to be having an illicit relationship with Clara's maid, Clara would have us believe that Carwin's real desire is to read her diary, and that having finally been caught in this act, he tried to convince her that his intention was rape, not curiosity.) Clara herself sums up the situation when she admits that "the events of that night are marvellous. Few to whom they should be related would scruple to discredit them" (p. 111).

Pleyel presents further evidence that also suggests the falsity of Clara's narrative. According to Pleyel, after hearing her in the river summerhouse, he returns to Clara's house (where he is then residing) and, finding the front door open, goes upstairs to his room. Shortly afterward he hears Clara enter, lock the front door, and climb the stairs to her own room. Clara's account of these same events is preposterous, but no more so than is necessary to explain the testimony of Pleyel, who has no reason to lie. According to Clara, she is already in her locked room, Carwin having left, when she hears footsteps upon the stairs. She never even considers the possibility (though it occurs to the reader), that these might belong to Pleyel, who is, after all, living there, nor does that possibility occur to her even when she reports the footsteps entering his room. Instead, she assumes that the footsteps must belong to Carwin, who, for some strange reason, has changed his mind and returned to menace her once more. But the most ludicrous part of the story is her reported resolution to venture downstairs to lock the front door. According to Clara, she has heard the footsteps enter Pleyel's room; after a short time she decides that whoever it was that entered Pleyel's room must have mysteriously left again (though she has not heard him do so). Despite having convinced herself that the intruder has left the premises, she nevertheless would have us believe that she *tip-toed* downstairs to lock the front door. That done, she informs us that she returns upstairs without taking any precautions about noise. In this fashion Clara explains, albeit lamely, how it is that Pleyel, in the very next room has heard only the ascending steps and not the descending ones. But her tale makes no sense. If she believes the intruder left the house, why sneak quietly downstairs? If she believes he still might linger on the premises, then why not use stealth upon her return?

Compared to Pleyel's tale, which is plausible, logical, and consistent in every detail, Clara's version of this event is totally unconvincing, yet when Clara approaches her brother with this feeble tale, she invites him to examine the circumstances, which she admits are of an "ambiguous nature," and to compare her story with Pleyel's. The criteria she wishes her brother to employ in judging the truth of the two tales is simple enough: "If there be anything in his story inconsistent with mine, his story is false" (p. 109).

Clara's attempts to reconcile her story with Pleyel's testimony on the ascending footsteps may suggest the possibility, at least, that Clara is not self-deluded, as I have argued, but rather a conscious liar. (Would a genuinely deluded Clara feel the need to reconcile her tale with Pleyel's?) Such a reading is tempting in a number of instances. For example, when Clara discovers that Pleyel has read the portion of her journal entry in which she allegedly requests *another* meeting with Carwin, she quickly questions Pleyel to discover how much he has read. Admittedly, such behavior is more suggestive of conscious than subconscious guilt. Nevertheless, this kind of reading poses enormous difficulties. First of all, such a reading entirely negates Brown's emphasis on epistemology and severely undercuts Clara's repeated ironic comments about how little self-awareness men are capable of. But more important, if Clara were a conscious liar, would she tell the kinds of lies she tells? One would think that a conscious liar would be able to do much better. And plausibility is not the only issue here. For instance, if Clara were in fact alone with Carwin in the summerhouse where they are overheard by Pleyel, why would a rational Clara not only claim to be in her own bedroom but also accuse Carwin of concealing himself in her closet there, thus pointing the finger at the very man she would naturally wish to protect? And, of course, if Clara is a deliberate liar attempting to conceal her own degradation, why would she later blame Carwin, her lover, for inciting Theodore to murder his family when, by remaining silent, she could let her brother take the blame? To a conscious liar we must assign conscious motives. In fact, the utter absurdity of Clara's untruths is the best evidence we have for believing that an unstable, deluded woman is telling them.

Despite the fact that Clara boldly asserts the truth of her own report, her language does little to strengthen her case. Upon hearing the loud voice warning her not to open the closet door, Clara says that she notices a resemblance between it and the voice she heard exclaiming "Hold!" in her dream in the summerhouse. At this point she is so certain that the previous voice was part of the dream that she claims "there are means by which we are able to distinguish a substance from a shadow, a reality from the phantom of a dream" (p. 86). However, later in the novel Clara tells us that the voice in her "dream" was real, that Carwin actually shouted "Hold!"

and that this exclamation, by a strange coincidence, happened to coincide with her dream, though why Carwin would shout "Hold!" at a sleeping woman we are left to ponder.

Ultimately then, we are forced to conclude that Clara is not as capable of distinguishing substance from shadow as she claims to be, and as the novel progresses, other instances arise to illustrate her inability to do so. For instance, on the day when Clara goes to Philadelphia to attempt a reconciliation with Pleyel, she becomes utterly confused by what she reports as his ambivalent treatment of her. When they first meet, Pleyel repeats his harsh accusations, informing her that "God may repent of his workmanship" and "send his vengeance" to destroy her; we are told that he then leaves the room, whereupon Clara shrieks and faints. Awakening shortly thereafter, Clara finds a changed Pleyel: "All the fury and scorn which the countenance of Pleyel . . . lately expressed had now disappeared, and was succeeded by the most tender anxiety. . . . 'My senses must have been the victim of some inexplicable and momentary frenzy. Forgive me, I beseech you; forgive my reproaches. I would purchase conviction of your purity at a price of my existence here and hereafter'" (p. 119). Clara cannot understand Pleyel's rapid change of heart (nor can the reader), but she is even more baffled when a few moments later he returns transformed yet again: "The tenderness which he had lately betrayed had now disappeared, and he once more relapsed into chilling solemnity" (p. 120). The only suitable explanation for Pleyel's reported vacillation is to see that his momentary softening is totally in the imagination of the narrator and in fact is another of her dreams. Though she has Pleyel tell us that *he* has been a temporary victim of a frenzy disrupting his senses, the reader must see that *Clara* is the one who suffers such a lapse. She desperately wants and needs to hear Pleyel say that he believes her to be pure, and so, in her imagination, he does.[12]

Clara's state of mind later that day when she returns to Mettingen distorts both her perception and her account of what she finds when she gets there. Although it is getting late when she leaves Pleyel's home, Clara stops at Mrs. Baynton's house in the city where she finds a letter from Carwin waiting for her. This circumstance alone is incriminating enough, for it suggests that she has informed Carwin of her intention of going to Philadelphia and stopping at Mrs. Baynton's; neither circumstance could Carwin reasonably be expected to anticipate. His letter requests another interview, this time at eleven o'clock. Given the story Clara has told us, she has great difficulty explaining just why she intends to comply with his request without even informing her brother. The best she can do is to say that she trusts her heavenly protector (the voice) to defend her, and that she hopes Carwin may be found willing to help in "unraveling the maze in which Pleyel is bewildered" (p. 141).[13]

After she arrives home at Mettingen, the nature of the reported events of the evening indicate that Clara is once again flitting in and out of reality. According to her story, Clara arrives at her brother's house shortly before eleven o'clock and is surprised then to find Wieland and Catherine absent. Though the light is dim, she goes from room to room looking for them, but she can find no sign of either the parents or the children. Clara tells us that she feels "some vague solicitude as to the condition of the family" (p. 143) and seeks out Louisa Conway, who is asleep in her chamber. Louisa informs Clara that Wieland and Catherine have been waiting for her return. Clara then goes to her own house where she finds the body of Catherine, who has been murdered in her bed. Clara tells us that she sits by the bed "for more than an hour" with Catherine's corpse without reporting the murder. Her brother then arrives and is making threatening overtures toward Clara when Mr. Hallet and the others appear on the scene and effect her rescue.

This sparse outline of events is unlikely enough, even pruned as it is of most of its startlingly contradictory details. Somehow it appears that the paths of Clara and her now maniac brother have crossed without either's knowledge. He has murdered his wife in Clara's bedroom, presumably while Clara is conversing with Louisa Conway. When Clara goes to her own house to meet Carwin, she would have us believe that her brother returns to his house and kills the rest of his family while she sits idly with the corpse of his wife, this despite the fact that *both* Wieland and Clara testify that each stood alone on the staircase at exactly eleven; each witnesses a strange face and hears a loud voice. After murdering his children, Wieland is then supposed to have murdered Louisa Conway so savagely that "not a linement of her face remained" (p. 157). This detail, perhaps more than any other, should suggest to the reader that there is more to the truth than Clara is telling, for when we read Wieland's own statement of the case, we find no indication that he has been commissioned to kill Louisa; nor does he make any mention of having done so in the portion of his deposition that we are allowed by Clara to read. This is surely a strange circumstance in view of the fact that Louisa's execution is by far the most brutal; her face is so battered that every feature is eradicated. Such brutality seems foreign to Theodore's inmost nature and violates the laws of human nature that Brown alludes to in the advertisement. Our perplexity is augmented when we examine Wieland's murder of Catherine, which we read about in his deposition. Though he strangles her, Wieland relents more than once, loosening his grasp. He informs us that he regrets

making her suffer, for his duty is to take her life, not torture her. After the murder, Wieland places her body gently on the bed and suffers great remorse.

If the details of Louisa's unusually brutal murder seem unaccountable, the dreamlike quality of Clara's narration and her admitted "confusion of faculties" must reinforce our doubts that we have been told the whole truth. First of all, on the way up the stairs to her own room before discovering Catherine's corpse, Clara has another "vision" and hears another voice. Carwin's later confession, which attempts to explain this voice and face, is hardly satisfactory. When Clara turns around on the staircase, she sees at the bottom of the stairs a face that seems to be in the act of screaming. The sound, however, comes to her from another direction.[14] All of this is later explained by Carwin's admitted ventriloquism, but other details of the encounter can have no explanation except in terms of Clara's imagination. For one thing, the face she sees is clearly not human: "The eyes emitted sparks, which, no doubt, if I had been unattended by a light, would have illuminated like the corruscations of a meteor" (p. 148). This "meteoric refulgence" is never explained in Carwin's confession for the simple reason that it cannot be; it is pure fantasy, pure dream. Clara admits at this point that "my narrative may be invaded by inaccuracy and confusion" (p. 147), and that "this visage was, perhaps, portrayed by my fancy" (p. 148), but she does not understand the lunacy of suggesting, as she does, that whatever caused the "refulgence" of the face at the bottom of the stairs might be of the same "nature of that which accompanied my father's death" (p. 149).[15] That Clara takes seriously such an intuitive connection suggests that she has indeed lost touch with reality. Her plight is emphasized when, an hour later, her real rescuers arrive, but appear to her imaginary: "For a time I questioned whether these were not shapes and faces like that I had seen at the bottom of the stairs—creatures of my fancy or airy existence" (p. 154). At this point in the narrative then, Clara has become so confused that not only do the creatures of her imagination seem real, but the beings of the real world seem to her unsubstantial.

Concerning this episode, then, it may be argued that both the events themselves and the way they are reported contribute to the suspicions of the careful reader that there is more to the truth than the narrator clearly understands and tells. For instance, why does Wieland, who has not heard a voice since the voice he and Pleyel heard in the summerhouse, suddenly hear one on the night of the murder? Why does the voice he hears suggest Clara's bedroom as the place for Catherine's execution? Why, when, and by whom is Louisa Conway murdered? And finally, why does Clara go completely mad after these events?

The question of why Theodore Wieland begins hearing voices on that night has been a thorny problem for critics. It is frequently asserted that Carwin's previous vocal imitations have acted as a catalyst, setting the potentially insane Wieland in motion,[16] but the obvious problem with such a theory is that Wieland, according to Clara, has heard no voices for months, and even more significantly has shown no signs of instability during that interregnum or on the very day of the murder. According to Wieland's deposition, the voice begins suddenly and without warning. Under these circumstances there can be only one rational explanation for why Theodore Wieland suddenly hears a voice after so long a time, and that is that the voice urging him to murder his family *is real*—that it is deliberately produced by someone who wants the violence to occur, someone who has a stronger motive than the intellectual curiosity ascribed to Carwin, someone acting through cold malevolence, someone who will find in that violence a catharsis. Only one person has such a motive, though it must be seen as operating subconsciously. Clara Wieland's is the voice that urges her brother to murder.

When we look back upon the novel, we find a cumulation of suggestions that Clara has been at least indirectly responsible for two of the earlier voices. Admittedly, we know that the first voice, which warns Theodore away from the summerhouse on the cliff, is Carwin's. Brown's outline for the novel, discovered among Elijah Brown's papers, makes clear this fact. However, each subsequent voice appears to act on Clara's behalf. Even though Carwin is no doubt responsible for the voice that informs Theodore and Pleyel that Teresa de Stolberg is dead, we must suspect that this communication can only have been instigated by Clara. Granted, Carwin derives great pleasure from his biloquial powers, and it would be entirely in character for him to indulge those powers by speaking to the two men, if only to mystify them. But Carwin has nothing to gain by telling them that Teresa is dead, for it is of no consequence to him whether Pleyel leaves the country or not, and his confession on this point is hardly convincing. Clara informs us that the voice was "propitious," and indeed it is strikingly so, for it is Clara, not Carwin, who is mortified by the prospect of Pleyel's departure. It is extremely doubtful, as I have argued above, that the third voice, which shrieks outside the Wieland house on the night Clara is discovered in a faint on its doorstep, involves Carwin at all. At any rate, the fact that the episode takes place on an evening when Pleyel "chanced" to be staying the night with the Wielands, suggests that the voice, if not Clara's own, was operating on her behalf, and the end result, of course, is that Pleyel is induced to move into Clara's spare bedroom. Clara is at a loss to explain why the voice seems always to operate with her best interests in mind, but the reader should note that as the novel progresses Carwin's agency, with each subsequent voice, is less significant and certain.

Therefore, when a voice again influences Theodore and convinces him to murder his family, we must see that as part of a pattern connected with Clara, not her brother. The murdered people symbolize the goodness and chastity Clara has lost. Only by seeing this sense of loss as the real motive for the murders can we understand why Louisa Conway too is murdered, for she is not one of Wieland's family, and it makes little sense for Theodore to murder her as if she were. She must die simply because she is a chaste, innocent young woman; her death is dictated by her relationship to *Clara,* not Theodore. Furthermore, the utter savagery of her murder, and the fact that the deed is never mentioned in the portion of Theodore's deposition that we are allowed to read, suggests that Clara is guilty of the act. We remember it is she who enters Louisa's room before going to her own house to meet Carwin. Again, Louisa's is not a murder committed by a man who believes himself acting under divine injunction, for such a man would not enjoy violence for its own sake. Clara, however, does have a motive for brutally eradicating Louisa's "lineaments," for Louisa represents Clara's lost purity. Therefore, she is not simply killed, but her identity erased, the innocence and beauty of her face completely annihilated. Moreover, such a reading makes clear why Catherine, who represents a different kind of chastity—that which derives from matrimonial fidelity—must be murdered in Clara's bed rather than her own: the voice that compels Wieland directs him to commit the crime in his sister's house because Clara, as stage manager, is symbolically destroying and punishing herself by having Catherine, the actual victim, murdered in Clara's bed.[17] It is for this reason that Clara so unreasonably blames Carwin for everything that happens in the novel, because to her mind her seduction is the ultimate cause of the later murders. Even when her rescuers appear on the scene, Clara invites them to look heavenward and see Carwin's sparkling visage and mocking contempt. She actually believes his face is there, following her. Clara goes mad at this point, not because she has witnessed a brutal crime, but rather because she has occasioned it.

The sanity to which Clara is restored by her rationalistic uncle is less than complete. After her bout with raving deliriums, she is subject to fits of imagination, and she still believes these fantasies to be real. She remains suicidal but does not understand the irony of her own words when she says, "My life is marked for a prey to inhuman violence" (p. 189). She continues to regard Carwin (though now we understand why) as the cause of the entire tragedy, and she admits that she finds relief in having an "object . . . on which we may pour out our indignation and our vengeance" (p. 190). She tells us that she believes Carwin to be a kind of preternatural demon and that "evil spirits existed, and that their energy was frequently exerted in the system of the world" (p. 180). Despite Clara's continued instability, however, she does at this point come as close to conscious self-perception as she does anywhere in the novel. In contemplating her brother's tragedy she says: "Now I was stupified with tenfold wonder in contemplating myself. Was I not likewise transformed from rational and human into a creature of nameless and fearful attributes? Was I not transported to the brink of the same abyss? Ere a new day should come, my hands might be imbrued with blood, and my remaining life be consigned to a dungeon and chains" (p. 179). Indeed Clara has been transformed into a "creature of nameless and fearful attributes," and, as I maintain, hers is the transformation Brown refers to in the novel's subtitle.

Clara's final return to her own house, the scene of her last confrontation with her brother, is as dreamlike a scene as the others already discussed. Her stated reason for her return is to destroy the diary that she says Pleyel unfortunately caught a glimpse of and misinterpreted. Without informing her uncle of her design, Clara travels to the site of the recent tragedy unattended. As we have seen her do on previous occasions, she works herself into a highly emotional state, this time by stopping at the family graveyard "to ponder on the emblems and inscriptions . . . on the tombs of Catherine and her children" (p. 192). She also walks past the recess in the river bank where, I allege, she has met with her lover, Carwin. By the time she actually arrives at her house, she has reached such an emotional pitch that "slight movements and casual sounds were transformed into beckoning shadows and calling shapes" (p. 193). Though she quickly secures her diary, Clara inexplicably remains in the house until she collapses "incoherent and half-articulate," calling out Carwin's name.

Given these circumstances, we should hardly be surprised when Carwin does appear to Clara, though we must understand that he only appears in the young girl's imagination. Clara begs heaven to produce him before her, and, in the dim light produced by *a ray of light streaming through the keyhole of her closet door,* Carwin noiselessly appears. As I have suggested previously, Clara's closet symbolizes her own identity, and it is appropriate that out of the misty half-light of that identity Carwin should appear to her and confess to all that she herself is guilty of. Although Carwin is little more than Clara's scapegoat in *Wieland,* the picture that we get of him has been enshrouded in the "chimeras" of the narrator's brain. He is guilty of none of the things he allegedly confesses to in this scene; however, he is guilty of the one thing that his "confession" denies: he has seduced Clara.[18]

There is other evidence that Carwin does not actually return to Clara's house to confess. First, it is extremely unlikely that he *would* do so, when we recall that he is an escaped convict and that there is now a warrant for his arrest. Why would he return to the scene of the crime at all, and how do we account for the fact that after all these months he appears on the scene at the very hour that Clara herself arrives? Even more convincing evidence is presented when Theodore Wieland appears on the scene and does not even seem to notice Carwin. According to Clara, she and Carwin hear footsteps on the stair, but the latter makes no move to escape, though for all he could know, the person approaching is in pursuit of him: "His [Carwin's] confusion increased when the steps of one barefoot were heard upon the stairs. He threw anxious glances sometimes at the closet, sometimes at the window, and sometimes at the chamber door; yet he was detained by some unexplicable fascination. He stood as if rooted to the spot" (p. 217).

Carwin's unreasonable behavior (his failure to flee from danger) is explicable only when we see that he is part of Clara's dream and cannot run away any more than she, in an earlier dream, could run away from the imaginary person concealed in her closet. The dream will not admit of escape. Therefore, although Carwin is a large, powerful man, in Clara's dream he becomes a whimpering little coward upon the arrival of the smaller, emaciated, unarmed Wieland. Furthermore, it seems that Carwin is visible only to Clara: "His [Carwin's] station was conspicuous, and he could not have escaped the roving glances of Wieland; yet the latter seemed totally unconscious of his presence" (p. 217). Although Clara repeatedly attempts to draw her brother's attention to "Carwin," and while she tells us that Wieland finally *does* see him, we have reason to doubt Clara's testimony on this point, for the questions purportedly addressed to Carwin by Wieland appear rhetorical in nature. "Man . . . what art thou? The charge has been made. Answer it" (p. 219). Furthermore, the questions that follow could just as readily have been addressed to Clara herself, and not the phantom Carwin. For instance, Wieland asks, "The visage—the voice at the bottom of the stairs—to whom did they belong? To thee?" (p. 219). When we remember that Clara, according to her own narrative, was supposedly herself ascending the stair at eleven o'clock on the night of the murder, and that she has testified that Wieland was not present there at eleven, we see that their version of events can in no way be reconciled. If he was on the stair at eleven (as he testifies), then she cannot have herself been present, unless, as I maintain, it is Clara who is concealed at the bottom of the staircase and taunts her brother to murder his wife. The question "to whom did they [the face and voice at the bottom of the stairs] belong?" is addressed to her. Furthermore, the reply to the question, which Clara ascribes to Carwin, is likewise her own: "'I meant nothing—I intended no ill, if I understand—if I do not mistake you—it is too true—I did appear—in the entry—did speak. The contrivance was mine, but—'" (p. 220).[19] When we realize that this confession, ascribed to Carwin by Clara, is in reality her own, then her brother's response is understandable; rather than becoming justifiably enraged, as we might expect if Wieland were really confronting Carwin, Wieland becomes subdued and allows the guilty party to withdraw with the admonition, "Go and learn better. I will meet thee, but it must be at the bar of thy Maker" (p. 220). Wieland, at last undeceived, is a broken man, but he has no desire to murder his own sister, regardless of the enormity of her crimes. That Clara subconsciously wants to be punished is clear, for she says that when "Carwin" was allowed to retreat with this admonition, she is unwilling to let him go: "I thirsted for his blood, and was tormented with an insatiable appetite for his destruction" (p. 221). She further hints at the chimerical quality of her projected scapegoat and at her own debased nature when she says, "Surely thou [Carwin] wast more than man, while I am sunk below the beasts" (p. 221).

The dreamlike quality of what follows can only be explained when we realize that Clara cannot perceive reality accurately. The guilty part of Clara's schizoid personality has confessed the truth to her brother, but that confession is related to us as Carwin's. The still pure part of Clara, however, does not accept responsibility, except subconsciously, and therefore calls down curses upon her scapegoat, Carwin. Her brother, who now finally perceives the truth, attempts to convince Clara that she should not blame Carwin. Although the latter has supposedly left the room at this point, Wieland's words suggest that he has never been present: "'Clara! . . . be thyself. Equity used to be a theme for thy eloquence. Reduce its lessons to practice, and be just to that unfortunate man'" (p. 225). Wieland does not understand that by calling down curses upon Carwin, part of Clara is begging for self-punishment, but there can be little doubt that this is true when we remember that the voice that earlier taunted Wieland to kill his family instructed him to kill Clara as well. As Wieland himself recalls, "Once it was the scope of my labours to destroy thee, but I was prompted to the deed by heaven" (p. 224). He had been about to carry out that portion of Clara's mad design when she was rescued by Mr. Hallet and the others, for it had been her plan to destroy herself along with the rest of the family. Now, facing her brother for the last time, she gives him yet another opportunity to kill her; however, having learned the truth, that he is not under divine injunction, Wieland proves refractory. He simply hands the knife to Clara and says that she has nothing to fear from him.

Her final perverse attempt at self-destruction foiled in this manner, Clara finds that she cannot accept her brothers's passivity; in order to reach the desired conclusion she must resurrect Carwin and his magic voice once more. According to Clara's narrative, shortly after Wieland tells her that she need not fear him, he nevertheless begins to undergo a swift and radical change similar to those Pleyel was reported to have gone through earlier. To Clara, it seems that "a new soul appeared to actuate his frame, and his eyes to beam with preternatural luster" (p. 225). This new Wieland is once again unaccountably bent upon his sister's destruction, despite his recent avowal of nonviolence, and he informs her that "thy death must come" (p. 226). But as Wieland approaches to kill Clara, she notices the phantomlike Carwin reappearing noiselessly in the room. Again he is unnoticed by Wieland, and although Wieland's barefoot approach was heard distinctly, Carwin enters without a sound, emphasizing yet again the insubstantial, imaginary quality of his presence in Clara's mind. When Clara beseeches him to save her, Carwin pays no attention, but rather turns around and "glides" through the doorway. Wieland himself "seemed to notice not the entrance or exit of Carwin" (p. 228), nor does he seem to grasp the fact that Clara is holding the knife in her hand. The dream marks are all too clear; we are once more at the mercy of Clara's imagination.

The final voice that Clara hears is also, even more clearly than the others she has heard, the result of that imagination. She informs us that Wieland is approaching, intent upon killing her; *however, we remember, that she, not he, is holding the knife.* As she wields the knife against her brother, "a voice, louder than human organs could produce, shriller than any language can depict, burst from the ceiling and commanded him—to hold!" (p. 229). Although Clara informs us that the command was issued to *him,* we must see that in reality the voice of her imagination is commanding *her,* for she is the one with the weapon, and she is the one about to strike her brother with it. The rest of that voice's inhibiting warning also applies to Clara, not her brother: "'Man of errors! cease to cherish thy delusion; not heaven or hell, but thy senses, have mislead thee to commit these acts. Shake off thy frenzy, and ascend into rational and human. Be lunatic no longer'" (p. 230). These words do not apply to Wieland, who had become calm, rational, and resigned much earlier in the scene when the cause of the voices was explained to him. He has been true to his word in that, once undeceived, he never menaces Clara, whom he simply pities. The warning voice functions, as indeed it so often does throughout the novel, as Clara's conscience. Just as it earlier warned her to stay away from the recess in the river bank, now it warns her against the murder of her brother. This time the warning is louder—louder than *human organs* could produce—because the crime is more serious. As in the previous case, however, Clara does not heed the warning. She informs us that she unconsciously lets the knife drop from her hand, whereupon her brother picks it up and plunges it to the hilt into his own neck. But Brown provides us with a physical detail which belies the truth of that assertion, having Clara tell us, "My hands were sprinkled with his blood as he fell" (p. 232). Thus Clara's earlier prediction, that someday she would awaken with her own hands imbrued with blood, comes to pass, and the young girl is seen to exhibit fully the Wieland legacy of insanity and violence.

Theodore Wieland, then, is murdered by his sister, and Carwin's presence from the beginning of the scene is purely imaginary. After the murder of Theodore, Clara's own language with regard to Carwin reinforces this truth yet again: "Carwin . . . had left the room; but he still lingered in the house. My voice summoned him to my aid; but I scarcely noticed his re-entrance, and now faintly remember his terrified looks . . . (p. 232)." Later, when Clara tells us that Carwin does finally leave her alone in the house, she says: "When he left me, I was scarcely conscious of any variation in the scene" (p. 232).

That Clara reaches some degree of self-awareness at this point seems probable in view of her words and actions. Too few readers have taken her seriously when she truthfully informs us: "I listen to my own pleas, and find them empty and false; yes, I acknowledge that my guilt surpasses that of all Mankind; I confess that the curses of the world and the frowns of a deity are inadequate to my demerits. Is there a thing in the world of infinite abhorrence? It is I" (p. 223).

Having reached this conclusion, Clara attempts one last time to fulfill her insane design. Despite the pleadings of her uncle, she refuses with "ferociousness and frenzy" to leave her house, the scene of all the tragedies. On the last page of her primary narrative, Clara hints at her intended suicide: "And now my repose is coming—my work is done" (p. 233). Shortly thereafter she has to be rescued from her burning house. As it burns, Clara, inside, dreams again of the symbolic dark abyss at whose brink she stands. Below are whirlpools and jagged rocks. She is witnessing the eruption of a volcano, which corresponds to both her physical and mental state as she sleeps in the burning house, when she is again rescued, having failed to do for herself what her brother earlier refused to do. From the cleansing fire of that interior volcano and the corresponding exterior one, Clara emerges purified, but totally self-deceived: "I was, in some degree, roused from the stupor which had seized my faculties. The monotonous and gloomy series of my thoughts was broken" (p. 237). Clara thus regains her sanity in so far as she puts the tragedy behind her, but she does not perceive the truth of her experience. Clearly, the truth would be too much for her to bear.

Admittedly, there are features of the novel that are not attributable to Clara Wieland. First, there is the "Advertisement" at the beginning of the novel, and second, the matter of the learned footnotes throughout the text; these come to us directly from Charles Brockden Brown, not Clara. If Brown were writing the kind of narrative that I have argued above, would he not have provided the reader with some hint of his intentions? For it is one thing to argue that the narrator of *Wieland* has deceived us, but another matter entirely to argue that its author has. In fact, the "Advertisement" to *Wieland* presents strong evidence in favor of the reading presented above. In it Brown admits that "the incidents related are extraordinary and rare." He mentions specifically the ventriloquism of Carwin and the religious delusion of Wieland, but his footnotes make clear that he also includes in this category the spontaneous combustion of the elder Wieland and the curious suicide of Clara's maternal grandfather. However, while Brown states that there are records of such "miraculous" events, he hopes that "intelligent readers will not disapprove of the manner in which appearances are solved. . . ." Furthermore, he says that "the solution will be found to correspond with *the known principles of human nature*" (my italics). He suggests then that the novel hinges not so much on scientifically verified data (though he concedes that one historical instance is "a sufficient vindication of the Writer") as it does upon human nature. He seems to have agreed with Coleridge that the one thing never permissible, if the reader is to suspend disbelief, is insufficient character motivation. The "Advertisement" suggests that Brown is less interested in documenting the events themselves than he is investigating what he terms "the latent springs and occasional perversions of the human mind." Far from being "temporary" (topical) in its treatment of odd scientific occurrences, he hopes *Wieland* will illustrate "some important branches of the moral constitution of man." Clearly then, there is nothing in Brown's preface which is incompatible with the reading given above.

That Brown wishes us to look for a human solution to the mysteries of *Wieland* is also apparent when we examine his learned footnotes, especially the one on "spontaneous combustion." Indeed, the episode of the elder Wieland's bizarre death and its accompanying footnote plainly discredit the scientific explanation—spontaneous combustion—in favor of a more human one. A close examination of the incident and Brown's source—an account of the death of an Italian priest—reveals that Brown intended for his "intelligent readers" to conclude that Clara's father was murdered.[20] The facts are these. Old Wieland, who seems to know that his death is approaching, climbs the hill to his temple on the cliff to pray. It is midnight. He is gone some time when his wife hears a loud report and sees a gleam of light. When Clara's uncle arrives at the scene, the light vanishes, and he finds only the charred body of Wieland, who, before he dies, gives an account of what happened. He says that his first impression was that someone was approaching him with a lamp, but before he could turn around, he received a blow to the right arm. Then he saw a spark drop into his clothes, igniting both them and him. These details—the loud report, the blow to the arm, the spark that ignites the clothes—do little to suggest that Wieland was a victim of spontaneous combustion. Neither does the fact that his hair—the most flammable part of the human body—and his slippers are not burned. It would appear that the fire originated in his clothes, not his body; it is extinguished before it reaches the extremities of the body.

A careful examination of Brown's source surely supports my reading and discourages the theory of spontaneous combustion. The account in the *American Museum* is composed of two parts. The first contains the testimony of the physician who attended the dying priest, Bertholi. Many of the details are identical to those given in **Wieland,** and there can be no doubt that the account was Brown's principal source. There is a loud report, a flash of light, a blow to Bertholi's right arm, and a "spark" which drops into the man's clothes. When Bertholi is found, his body is badly burned, but his hair is untouched. The physician concludes that Bertholi was a victim of spontaneous combustion—that he was "killed by an electrical commotion, the cause of which resided in his own body." However, the second part of the account contains an analysis of the physician's conclusions, and the writer of this portion pointedly disagrees with the doctor's reasoning. He too mentions that it is illogical for Bertholi's hair to remain unburned. He too mentions that the combustion theory in no way explains the loud report, the blow to the arm, and is at best neutral on the matter of the fatal spark. Even more persuasively, the writer points out that the lamp in Bertholi's room had been full of oil before the incident but was found to be dry afterwards, though the wick was visibly charred. Clearly, the evidence pointed more toward human malice than spontaneous combustion.

One thing is undeniable. Since Brown used the *American Museum* account as a source for **Wieland,** he could not have been unaware of the ambiguity of the details. He could not have been unaware that the writer of that account argued convincingly *against* the spontaneous combustion theory. Yet Brown himself did not delete the compromising details. Instead he added to them. First, where Bertholi was obese and an alcoholic as well—the two details that led the physician to suspect combustion—Wieland is neither, a fact which renders the combustion theory in the latter case even weaker. Next, Brown adds two significant details not in the original. He allows Wieland to inform the reader that his first impression was that someone was approaching him with a lamp. But the most suggestive detail—also absent from the source—is that, according to Clara's uncle, "there was somewhat in his [Wieland's] manner that indicated an imperfect tale. My uncle was inclined to believe that half the truth had been suppressed" (p. 18).[21]

After telling us the details of this bizarre event, Clara presents us with a philosophical dilemma that she has been a lifetime trying to resolve. She cannot make up her mind whether her father's death was the result of divine edict (as a punishment for not obeying a divine command), or whether it was a pure accident, the result of spontaneous combustion. Brown's point is that the dilemma she presents herself and the reader is a false one, for it ignores a third possibility—indeed the most plausible explanation—that her father was murdered. Even at the end of the novel Clara is still debating the question she begins her narrative with. Though she comes to accept the possibility that evil demons exist, she cannot see that they may be human. Indeed, human malice is never a reality for Clara, and her refusal to consider its existence is reflected in her inability to interpret correctly her own motives and desires as the novel progresses.

The final paragraph of the novel, in which the reader is left to moralize upon the tale, also suggests that the postscript is not merely an appendage. When Clara says, ostensibly of Louisa Conway's mother, that "If the lady had crushed her disastrous passion in the bud, and driven her seducer from her presence when the tendency of his artifices was seen" (p. 244), the tragedy need not have taken place, the reader should understand this, in view of the argument presented above, as applying to Clara's relationship with the seducer Carwin, which sets in motion the entire tragedy of **Wieland.** Clara ends the novel by wishing that she herself "had been gifted with ordinary equanimity or foresight" (p. 244), but she does not understand that the "double-tongued deceiver" is not Carwin, but herself.

Although most critics stress the psychological aspects of the novel (as, in fact, I have done), we must also see that **Wieland** is a philosophical novel of some stature. Ultimately, it deals with the complex issue of epistemology. It thoroughly refutes "Franklinesque" optimism and the philosophy upon which that optimism was founded, for the novel's major tenet seems to be that Man is incapable of obtaining true knowledge since he is incapable of perceiving things correctly. Clara, contemplating her own deceived senses, asks: "What is man, that knowledge is so sparingly conferred upon him?" (p. 102). The world of **Wieland,** like the world of Brown's other novels, is one of imposture, falsehood, and deception, all of which coexist with honesty and sincerity. The self, which colors all perceptions, is the greatest uncertainty of all. Even those characters in the novel who are not self-deceived are nevertheless incapable of making rational judgments based on sense perceptions. Theodore Wieland is deceived by clever mimicry into committing outrageous acts that are abhorrent to his gentle nature. Pleyel, who comes closer to the truth than anyone else in the novel when he correctly suspects the true relationship that exists between Clara and Carwin, nevertheless finally allows himself to be deceived by her lover's lies and even ends up marrying her. To know and to accept what one knows are different matters. And Pleyel would have done well to heed his own warning, which is also Brown's admonition to the reader: "It is better to know nothing than to be deceived by an artful tale" (p. 127).

Notes

1. One notable exception is Michael D. Butler in "Charles Brockden Brown's *Wieland*: Method and Meaning," *Studies in American Fiction,* 4 (1976), 127-42.

2. Larzer Ziff in "A Reading of *Wieland,*" *PMLA,* 77 (1962), 53, explains the novel's faults this way: "To be sure, Brown was a hasty, careless writer, and rather than go back and revise his novel . . . he . . . wrote a number of *deus ex machina* explanations."

3. Charles Brockden Brown, *Wieland: or, the Transformation; Memoirs of Carwin, the Biloquist,* ed. Sidney J. Krause (Kent, Ohio, 1977). All subsequent references to this edition are included in the text.

4. William Manly, "The Importance of Point of View in Brockden Brown's *Wieland,*" *American Literature,* 35 (1963), 311-21.

5. It is curious that Clara's insanity should have been overlooked by critics, for her madness is more demonstrable than that of her brother or—as James Soldati in "The Americanization of Faust: A Study of Charles Brockden Brown's *Wieland,*" *Emerson Society Quarterly,* 20 (1974), 4, would have it—Carwin. The novel's subtitle, "The Transformation," is more applicable to Clara than her brother, because, as Ziff points out, Theodore's transformation "is not followed in detail by Brown. . . . His insanity is a leap rather than a development" (Ziff, p. 56). Clara's mental breakdown, on the other hand, is portrayed in a careful, subtle, gradual manner and, as Wayne Franklin puts it in "Tragedy and Comedy in *Wieland,*" *Novel,* 8 (1975), 153: "How better to inculcate the announced moral of human misperception than to present us with a narrator who does not understand her tale?"

6. Ziff, p. 56.

7. Butler disagrees. For his analysis of the situation see pp. 132-33.

8. Franklin, p. 160.

9. See Leslie Fiedler, *Love and Death in the American Novel* (New York, 1960), p. 54; David Lyttle, "The Case Against Carwin," *Nineteenth Century Fiction,* 26 (1971), 259; Manly, pp. 317-19; Donald Ringe, *Charles Brockden Brown* (New York, 1966), p. 36, and Ziff, p. 54.

10. Manly, p. 319.

11. See especially Butler, p. 135 and Ringe, pp. 32-33.

12. This scene presents strong evidence that Clara is not a conscious liar. If she were, she would either inform us that she convinced Pleyel of her innocence or tell us that he refused to believe her. But surely she would not portray him as vacillating, for to do so would be needlessly complicated, pointless, and improbable. Pleyel's reported schizophrenic behavior is a feature of *Clara's* mind and is symbolic of her inability to deal with external reality.

13. In fact, it seems that later on, Carwin does tell Pleyel that Clara is innocent and thereby reconciles them. However, the reader must judge for himself whether what Carwin tells Pleyel is the truth. If Carwin is Clara's lover, as I maintain, would he not lie for her (and himself) about this matter?

14. Brown does not seem to have understood that ventriloquism is an illusion. In both *Wieland* and *Carwin, the Biloquist* he suggests that it is possible literally "to throw the voice."

15. Here too, it is difficult to argue that Clara is a conscious liar, because, presumably, a rational person would do much better. Surely she would not go out of her way to strain credulity.

16. In "The Voices of Carwin and Other Mysteries in Charles Brockden Brown's *Wieland,*" *Early American Literature,* 10 (1975), 307-09, Robert Hobson argues that Carwin actually produces the voice that urges Wieland to murder his family.

17. Brown's source for the murders was an account of a multiple murder perpetrated by one James Yates. This account was published in both *The New York Weekly Magazine* (July 1796) and *The Philadelphia Minerva* (August 1796). Though there can be no doubt that this account served as Brown's source, it is interesting to note that Brown changed his source significantly. He adds the brutal murder of Louisa Conway, who is not a member of the Wieland family; in Brown's source Yates murders only those members of his own family. Furthermore, where James Yates chases his wife through the fields and finally murders her there, Brown has Theodore murder Catherine in Clara's bedroom. Each of these changes supports the reading I give above.

18. In this regard it is interesting to examine Brown's fragment, *Carwin, the Biloquist,* which was in-

tended as a sequel to *Wieland.* It follows the career of Carwin as a young man before the events at Mettingen. Few readers of this fragment have noted the importance of Carwin's role as a seducer. Though he has unusual biloquial powers, we see that Carwin employs them repeatedly for the purpose of seduction. For instance, when Carwin goes to Spain, he informs us that he frequently uses his ventriloquism "to annihilate the scruples of a tender female," and he further admits that "if voluptuousness, never gratified at the expense of health, may incur censure, I am censurable" (p. 275). Even more significant is the episode which is left incomplete at the end of the fragment. Here Carwin has been befriended by a man named Ludloe who belongs to a secret society which practices deceit while requiring total honesty among its members. Ludloe warns Carwin that in order to join the group the latter must confide every aspect of his past life, and that if the young man attempts to withhold anything, his death will be the result. Carwin, however, decides not to inform Ludloe of his biloquial powers, but he leads the reader to believe that he has told Ludloe everything else about his past. As it turns out, however, Carwin has concealed, not only from Ludloe, but from the reader as well, one important episode from that past, and when the fragment breaks off, Carwin has just been presented by Ludloe with evidence of the young man's seduction of a young lady in Toledo. In addition to this, Carwin informs us that it is Ludloe's plan to marry him to a rich widow named Mrs. Bennington presumably to gain control of her fortune. In the entire fragment then, Carwin's biloquial powers are secondary in importance to his role as a seducer. Brown portrays him as a young man on the make, not unlike the author's later Arthur Mervyn.

19. This confession is confusing at best if we take it at face value as coming from Carwin. It contradicts what he has allegedly just finished telling Clara. He claims in his earlier confession to her that he had nothing to do with the voice that urged Wieland to murder his family, and he further comments that he did not even know about the tragedy. Yet when Wieland asks him (according to Clara's account) whether it was his face at the bottom of the stairs, and whether it was his voice that urged him to commit murder, Carwin reportedly stammers that this is true. The resulting contradiction has led Hobson to conclude that Carwin must have actually incited Wieland to commit murder. The problem is that Carwin can have no motive for such an act, since cold-blooded murder is a different matter from intellectual curiosity— the motive usually ascribed to Carwin in the case of the earlier voices.

20. "Letter respecting an Italian priest, killed by an electric commotion, the cause of which resided in his own body," *American Museum,* 11 (April 1792), 146-49.

21. I have already argued how the changes Brown made in his source concerning the Yates murders support my reading of the novel. See note 18. Brown's other two learned footnotes also do nothing to discourage my thesis. On ventriloquism, Brown tells us that "The power, is, perhaps, given by nature, but it is doubtless improvable, if not acquirable, by art." And in the novel itself Carwin informs us that "it is an art which may be taught to all." Finally, concerning the strange madness of Clara's maternal grandfather, Brown refers us to Erasmus Darwin's *Zoonomia.* The "mania mutabilis" to which Brown alludes turns out to be a type of schizophrenia whereby "Patients are liable to mistake . . . imagination for realities," just as I have argued that Clara does throughout her narrative. The example Darwin gives, interestingly enough, is that of a woman who "imagined that she heard a voice say to her one day as she was at her toilet, 'Repent, or you will be damned'" (*Zoonomia; or, The Laws of Organic Life* [London, 1756], II, 356-58).

Cynthia S. Jordan (essay date 1981)

SOURCE: Jordan, Cynthia S. "On Rereading *Wieland*: 'The Folly of Precipitate Conclusions.'" *Early American Literature* 16, no. 2 (fall 1981): 154-74.

[*In the following essay, Jordan suggests that* Wieland's *ending, often considered flawed, represents a deliberate strategy of the author to caution readers about hastily-drawn conclusions.*]

Starting with William Dunlap, author of the first critical biography of Charles Brockden Brown, critics of Brown's novels have persistently resorted to external data—especially Brown's "headlong rapidity of composition"—to account for apparent inconsistencies in the texts, the most prominent of these being the characteristically "muddled" ending.[1] Critical readings of *Wieland,* for example, have offered various extratextual explanations—apologies—for its conclusion: on the one hand, Brown is portrayed as a "careless writer" whose inattention to revision forced him to concoct an improbable "*deus ex machina* denouement"; on the other, his opportunities for revision are shown to have been severely limited by the page groupings of the proofs and thus "the very professionalism of the printer" is blamed for the various abruptnesses of the final chapter.[2] Only recently have critics begun to shift some of the blame for the bothersome ending onto the narrator, Clara, and yet what is seen as her final "artistic confusion"[3] is still shown to be the inevitable result of "Brown's own indecision," his "contradictory and unresolved"[4] notions about the role of fiction.

I offer the following rereading of *Wieland* in defense of this author who continues to be touted with such faint praise. Brown, America's first professional novelist, has too long been a victim of the attitude that pre-nineteenth-century American writers wrote with an "innocence" (read "lack") "of technique" because they had no "valid concept of fiction."[5] By traditionally relying on extratextual data the resulting readings, however helpful they have been in revealing to us the man or the intellectual climate of the period, have frequently failed to do justice to the works themselves. In what follows I will show that by reading *Wieland* as a self-explanatory text, we may better understand how Brown's "muddled" endings serve his fictional design.[6]

Before doing so, however, I shall try briefly to generate an overall sense of the thematic issues engendered by Brown's irregular narrative endings. For example, *Wieland*'s conclusion *is* bothersome, not only because of Clara's rapid attempt to tie up all loose ends, but also because of its cavalier optimism after some two-hundred pages of deepening moral chaos, and, especially, because of its heavy dependence on what Leslie Fiedler has rightly called "broad coincidences hard to credit."[7] But to attribute such blatant aesthetic deviance to Brown's lack of fore-thought, discipline, or aesthetic principles is to overlook certain salient features in the catalogue of his fiction. That is, it seems notable that five of his six novels are written in an epistolary format, an authorial decision that signals that the narrator's point of view should constitute a thematic concern and that also effectively frees an author from the obligation to create, as Fielding pointed out, "regular beginnings and conclusions."[8] Furthermore, Brown left large fragments of two unfinished novels, *Stephen Calvert* and *Memoirs of Carwin the Biloquist,* and a third, *Arthur Mervyn,* was published in two parts, its ending delayed for over a year. On the basis of this evidence, we should at the very least allow that Brown was aware of, if not actively concerned with, the problems entailed in making satisfactory endings.

Evidence of the latter possibility, however, may be found once we turn to the actual texts, where, if intentionality be at issue, it would seem appropriate to say that Brown went out of his way to impress those problems on his readers: all of his novels have endings that call attention to themselves—that call into question not only their own credibility, but also the belief in the possibility of "endings" per se. *Edgar Huntly,* for example, ends with a letter describing the assumed death of the archvillain, Clithero Edny, after which the writer, Sarse-field, concludes: "With the life of this wretch, let our regrets and our forebodings terminate. . . . May this be the last arrow in the quiver of adversity! Farewell!"[9] I say "assumed death" because what actually happens is that Clithero jumps from a boat into the water and is "seen no more" (p. 280). Only fifty pages earlier Sarsefield had seen Edgar plunge "into a rapid stream, from a height from which it was impossible to fall and to live." "You sunk to rise no more," he told the miraculously surviving Edgar, and yet, "'My eyes, my ears bear testimony to your existence now, as they formerly convinced me of your death. What am I to think? What proofs am I to credit?'" (p. 232). Such questions recur throughout the book—"What should I think?" (p. 10), asks Edgar, "How was I to consider this act . . . ? . . . What are the conclusions to be drawn by dispassionate observers?" (p. 88)—and cut to the heart of a novel replete with "consequences . . . that cannot be foreseen" (p. 87); outcomes that are "contradictory to precedent events" (p. 185); "exception[s] to all the rules that govern us in our judgments of human nature" (p. 43); and in particular, stories, such as the one Clithero tells Edgar, which are "completely the reverse of all . . . expectations" (p. 86). Given this emphasis on the extreme difficulty of drawing conclusions and this backlog of thwarted expectations, readers who credit—or discredit—Brown with his villain's convenient "suicide" in the final chapter surely do so with as much credulity as Sarsefield, who foresees an end to adversity. In other words, it is this narrator's sanguine sense of an ending, not Brown's, that warrants our skepticism: there is no absolute proof of Clithero's death, and in light of Edgar's survival in a strikingly similar situation, we are obliged to suspect that both Clithero and the contingent threat of further adversity are still at large in a naive America. If we are left with any certainty at all, it is that Edgar is correct in exclaiming, near the end of his portion of the narrative, "How little cognizance have men over the actions and motives of each other! How total is our blindness with regard to our own performances!" (p. 267).

The pervasiveness of this dual theme—for it appears in various forms in all the novels—necessarily fuels our skepticism regarding the credibility of Brown's other narrative endings, of his other self-satisfied narrators. In *Ormond,* for example, Sophia Westwyn bases her conclusions and her optimism for the future solely on her estimation of Constantia's character, although in fact neither she nor the reader has actually seen what transpired between her friend and the villain Ormond behind closed doors. We are left with the suspicion that Sophia's case parallels Constantia's—i.e., that perhaps "a bias . . . swayed her thoughts in numberless ways, though she knew not that they were swayed"[10]—and thus, that her admitted dedication to the "ultimate restoration of tranquility" (p. 241)—to happy endings—has made her an unreliable narrator. Both *Jane Talbot* and

Clara Howard end with seemingly resolved misunderstandings, declarations of undying love and pledges to marry, and yet throughout these novels, which are structured as series of impassioned and hastily dispatched letters, we have witnessed decisions and revisions that mere minutes have reversed, including reversals of sentiment within any given letter: "Skip the last couple of sentences," writes Jane, "or think of them as not mine: I disown them"; her lover writes back, concluding, "In this long letter I have not put down one thing that I intended."[11] Indeed, what proofs are readers to credit when characters know their own hearts and minds so imperfectly, and when we have been specifically warned in *Jane Talbot* that "Passion may dictate large and vehement offers upon paper, which deliberating prudence would never allow to be literally adhered to" (p. 99)? The very tidiness of such endings calls attention to itself and to the possibility that the narrators have been and will continue to be blind to their own performances, for Sophia, Clara, and Jane have all repeatedly witnessed the ubiquity of the "unexpected" and the "unforeseen"—two frequent epithets in Brown—and seem yet to be unwary of "the folly of precipitate conclusions."[12]

The last phrase is used by Arthur Mervyn near the beginning of his tale, and although he seems, in the early stages, to be circumspect enough to realize that "it may by no means be uncommon for men to *fashion* their conclusions in opposition to evidence and *probability* . . ." (p. 77; italics Brown's), he quickly goes the way of all Brown's characters, developing a myopic pride in his own "power of arranging . . . ideas and forming conclusions" (p. 117). Throughout the novel Arthur is repeatedly shown to misinterpret the actions and motives of others—of Welbeck, Wallace, and Mrs. Fielding, his (perhaps) future wife, to name but a few—and to be blind to his own performances: his professed good intentions more often than not cause others anger or anguish, and at times, physical harm. Again, in light of this character's overwhelming lack of insight, we must come to doubt his self-professed powers of deduction.

And it is not surprising that, in the last paragraphs, after musing with ambivalence over his planned marriage—to one of the first Dark Ladies in American literature—he comes to an impasse:

> this is but the humble outline of the scene; some thing is still to be added to complete our felicity.
>
> > What more can be added?
> > What more? . . .
> > But why am I indulging this pen-prattle?

His final act as narrator is to abjure his pen "till all is settled" regarding his future, "till Mervyn has been made the happiest of men" (p. 230). In other words, there is no "regular" or satisfactory conclusion. Like

the villainous Clithero, Arthur's ambivalence is merely seen no more—the moral conflict is repressed rather than resolved—and though the written narrative stops, the action quite obviously does not. It seems unlikely that a con—and conned—man like Arthur will ever be the happiest of men, but the larger issue here is determined by the final metaphorical act. We are forced to consider whether a narrative ending is ever significant of anything more than an "Arthur" / author's[13] laying down of the pen for lack of knowing "what more can be added"—i.e., whether endings are possible when, as Arthur's situation has shown, "Life is dependent on a thousand contingencies, not to be computed or foreseen" (p. 136).

What I have been trying to suggest is that the unsatisfactoriness of Brown's endings is consistent with the vision of reality that emerges as these various texts progress: his novels blatantly and repeatedly challenge the reader's sense of an ending. Specifically, Brown's fictional worlds are governed by coincidence, "contingencies"; as a result, unforeseen complications are ever imminent, and thus narrative closure, the tying together of all the loose strands of a story, is impossible. On the other hand, since human actions and motivations are always shown to be ambiguous, then hindsight is ultimately as unreliable as foresight, and thus, denouement, the *un*tangling of the various strands of a story, is equally impossible.[14] In such worlds the human condition is that suggested by Ormond when he berates Constantia, "Thou seest not an inch before thee or behind" (pp. 211-12): narrators are necessarily unreliable because no one can ever know the whole story.

And yet nearly all Brown's characters eventually take on the role of narrator, or more specifically, of "author"—in *Edgar Huntly* alone, Edgar (p. 171), Clithero (pp. 49, 71, 78), Mrs. Lorimer (pp. 40, 265), her brother Arthur (p. 44), and, by virtue of their letter writing, Sarsefield and Waldegrave are all "authors"—to the extent that we must assume that authorship, too, i.e., storytelling, is an aspect of the human condition. Contrived narratives, whether oral stories, letters, journals, manuscripts, or books, abound in these novels as representations of their authors' attempts to impose order on an anarchic reality; for example, I have already discussed Arthur Mervyn's pride in his talent for "arranging . . . ideas and forming conclusions," and at the beginning of her tale, Clara Howard informs her correspondent that she has put "the enclosed letters . . . into a regular series."[15] Brown's emphasis is always on the contrivance of regularity, the artificiality, of such narratives, which emphasis gives rise to his frequent metaphors of verbal trickery: forgery in *Ormond* and *Jane Talbot,* counterfeiting in *Arthur Mervyn* and *Ormond,* and ventriloquism in *Wieland.* But he is also careful to show that the success of such trickery is dependent not only on the talent of the storyteller, but also, as Clara Wieland will partially understand, on the "errors"—the credulity—"of the sufferers."[16] Thus, to be human is to create and to believe in stories which must inevitably be false, which must be partial and biased renderings of events that are ultimately inscrutable. "Disastrous and humiliating is the state of man!" exclaims Edgar Huntly, "By his own hands is constructed the mass of misery and error in which his steps are forever involved" (p. 267).

In effect, Brown's novels bespeak a theory of fiction similar to that described by Frank Kermode, whose apt phrase, "the sense of an ending," I have been using throughout: "Men in the middest make considerable imaginative investments in coherent patterns which, by the provision of an end, make possible a satisfying consonance with the origins and with the middle."[17] "Men exist more for the future than the present," we are told in **Clara Howard,** "We are busy marking the agreement between objects as they rise before us, and our previous imaginations" (pp. 338-39). Very simply, Brown's characters hope to foresee, or to "fashion," endings to their various stories in order to give stability to their lives and meaning to the fearfully random events in the middest; they need fictional structures; they need to believe in authority. What makes Brown's work unique, however—and singularly appropriate for an American author writing only twenty-odd years into the "middest" of the American experiment—is his insistence on the extreme danger attendant on any rigid belief in the finality of human stories, and thus, of human authority over the temporal flow of events: his characters suffer—and occasionally die—as a result of a too-ready reliance on their own sense of an ending.

In the following discussion of **Wieland** I delineate more fully the complexities of this theory of fiction that focuses so fearfully on misperceived endings. In particular, I discuss Clara Wieland's role as unreliable narrator, her spurious "conclusions" and what they tell us about stories and storytellers; and in closing, I try to derive, from the evidence of this text, what Brown considered to be the proper uses of fiction, for when contrived endings are used so consistently and self-consciously to represent palpable threats to human well-being, two of the more obvious questions to arise are, Why write fiction? and, perhaps more important, Why read it? Indeed, these questions are raised to thematic concern in Brown's works: "Why do I write?" asks Clara Howard's would-be lover, "for whose use do I pass my time thus?" (p. 289); Clara Wieland questions her own responsibilities as storyteller—"Why should I rescue this event from oblivion?" (p. 228)—and elsewhere, after reading from the text of her brother's confession, will ask, as a reader to readers, "Will you not . . . be astonished that I read thus far? What power supported me through such a task I know not" (p. 174). Terence Martin and more recently Michael Davitt Bell have argued

that, having been strongly influenced by the Scottish Common Sense school of thought, "the conventional wisdom of his age," Brown "feared that fiction would unsettle the mental balance of novel readers" and therefore wrote novels to dramatize "the dangers of novel-reading."[18] I do not believe this to be the case, however, for in worlds such as the ones Brown creates, in which *all* reasoning processes are shown to be fictive, mere storytelling, the gravest danger lies in immediate action. As a result, written stories serve both their authors and their readers as precautionary mediations, never finally foolproof, but useful nevertheless if for no other reason than for their very duration. In what follows I argue that **Wieland** presents a hierarchy of fictional forms and thus, a hierarchy of dangers, and that characters encounter greater perils when they stop writing, when they stop reading—when they engage actively in "the folly of precipitate conclusions."

Clara Wieland begins her narrative with statements of bleak despair, revealing that since "every remnant of good" has been wrested from her life "and exterminated," she has resigned herself to "a destiny without alleviation" (p. 6). In recalling the dire events of her recent past, first the loss of a lover as a result of a con man's tricks, and next, the death of her immediate family at the hands of a brother who believed he was obeying divine commands, she becomes more and more confirmed in her hopelessness and foresees no alternative but death: "Why not terminate at once this series of horrors? . . . I will die, but . . . only when my tale is at an end" (p. 228). Eventually, after she has described her brother's similarly inspired attempt on her life, his awakening to remorse, and his suicide, we read, "And now my repose is coming—my work is done!" (p. 233). But if we have taken her at her word and expect her to die after this final, breathless exclamation point, we are mistaken, for on the next page we find a continuation of her work "Written three years after the foregoing, and dated at Montpellier," and of her life, which has regained its "ancient tranquillity" (pp. 234-37).

Setting aside for a short while the specifics of the questionable conclusions drawn in this sequel, what we have in effect is a narrator who has projected two distinct endings, neither of which come to pass, and who has produced a third, the sequel itself, which, as Clara herself admits—and as critics have wholeheartedly concurred—bespeaks "events the least probable" (p. 234). What has not been generally recognized, however, is that Clara's inability to satisfy her audience's expectations with a consummate ending has been prefigured throughout as a family trait. Clara's uncle, for example, tells the story of her maternal grandfather, who literally jumped to a hasty and mortal conclusion.[19] While on a picnic the grandfather had suddenly told his companions that he had just received a "summons" from his dead brother, and "before their surprise would allow them to understand the scene," he had rushed to the edge of a cliff and thrown himself over, leaving his immediate audience and future audiences, such as Clara, "unacquainted with particulars" of what he actually heard. Moreover, the uncle's personal conclusion to this story, that his father had "unquestionably" suffered "maniacal" illusions, is unsatisfactory to Clara: "I was far from accounting for [such] appearances in my uncle's manner" (pp. 178-79). Thus we are presented with an inconclusive story within an inconclusive story, a dubious heritage for any author. Finally, the Wieland side of the family is no more fortunate, its endings no less precipitate. Clara's questionable success as narrator is specifically foreshadowed in the authorial, or storytelling, experience of her brother and her father.

Early in the novel we learn that the younger Wieland had begun work on a book about "that mysterious personage, the Daemon of Socrates." His "skill in Greek and Roman learning was exceeded by that of few, and no doubt the world would have accepted a treatise upon this subject from his hand with avidity; but alas! this and every other scheme of felicity and honor, were doomed to sudden blast and hopeless extermination" (p. 48). On a purely phenomenal level, we are presented with a written text that does not end according to plan—that never ends—and with the image of a reading audience left with no conclusive knowledge. Thematically, Theodore's unfinished treatise provides a more specific analogy to his sister's ultimately unsatisfactory narrative, for the "Daemon" in question was perceived to be a personal demon by his accusers and a Satanic visitor by the later Church Fathers.[20] This unresolved historical debate virtually resurfaces in *Wieland*: once the disembodied voices begin, Theodore maintains "the probability of celestial interference" (p. 75), and Clara entertains both possibilities, that of "evil geniuses" (p. 132) and of a "mysterious monitor" (p. 85) whom she goes so far as to call "*my* heavenly friend" (p. 94). Furthermore, Theodore's accusers impute his acts to "the influence of daemons" (p. 176), and Carwin the biloquist will declare that "some daemon of mischief seized me" (p. 201). Essentially, any final interpretation of the plot of *Wieland* depends on the reader's evaluation of the nature of the "daemonic" voices, and Clara's seemingly complete book is hardly more helpful than her brother's unfinished one in enabling us to draw our own conclusions. That is, even though Brown himself ostensibly weights the evidence in favor of Carwin's guilty agency—with a scientific, authorial footnote explaining "*Biloquium,* or ventrilocution" (p. 198)—readers are never given any direct proof of what young Wieland hears on the night of his crime: the source of the voice that orders him to kill his family remains shrouded in mystery.

Readers are not permitted to witness the incidents immediately leading to the crime. We get all our informa-

tion from stories told after the fact: Wieland's confession, for example, is first delivered orally in a courtroom, then copied down by an unknown person (p. 163), and finally copied down again by Clara, who incorporates only a part of the text into her own story—she stops "in the midst of the narrative" (p. 175) and picks up again "near the conclusion" (p. 176). Her action alone suggests the type of material "transformation" (consider the full title of the book) that stories undergo in the telling, and we are led to suspect what one of Brown's later heroines will declare, that "second-hand" narratives have "all the deductions and embellishments which must cleave to every story as it passes through the imaginations" (*Clara Howard,* p. 355)—and the pens—of its various tellers.

The unreliability of the story-evidence we receive is confirmed once Wieland and Carwin begin to change their own stories, to revise their former conclusions. Originally, Wieland says, and unquestionably believes, that he had heard a "direct communication" (p. 167) from God, ordering him to kill his wife and children, while Carwin says that he was not even in the house at the time the voice was heard. Later confronted by both Clara and a fierce Wieland, a shaken Carwin admits, "I did appear—in the entry—did speak. The contrivance was mine, but—" (p. 220); and Wieland here concludes that he had been "guilty of . . . error" in believing he had heard God's voice, that he "had been made the victim of human malice." Within seconds, however, he changes his story a second time; he apparently receives a new "illumination" regarding Carwin's agency, which he communicates to Clara: "'The form thou hast seen was the incarnation of a daemon. The visage and voice which urged me to the sacrifice of my family, were his. Now he personates a human form: then he was invironed with the lustre of heaven . . . he from whom his commission was received is God'" (pp. 225-26). Wieland is once again confirmed in his belief, but readers are further than ever from being able to draw a conclusion. And at this point we are presented with a final source of contention, "new sounds . . . uttered from above." Carwin having withdrawn from the room after his truncated confession, a voice tells Wieland that "not heaven or hell, but thy senses have misled thee to commit these acts. . . . Be lunatic no longer." Although Clara admits that her brother "reflected not" that this voice might be as spurious as the original murderous commands, she tells us that Wieland has been "restored to the perception of truth" (p. 230), and she describes his overwhelming remorse and the resulting suicide, which he effects "with the quickness of thought" (p. 231)—the phrase suggests yet another hastily drawn conclusion.

Given this multiplicity of evidence, what proofs are we to credit in determining what Theodore Wieland actually heard on the night of his crime? Bell's reading recapitulates Clara's own conclusions and seems representative of the critical consensus, that "Carwin is only indirectly responsible for Wieland's madness," that his previous vocal tricks have "only unsettle[d] Theodore's ability to distinguish between fact and fiction, leading him [on the night of the crime] to accept the reality of voices produced by his own imagination."[21] But to say that Wieland was insane and imagined hearing voices is to overlook certain unanswered questions. For example, how do we account for Carwin's admission that he was in the house and "did speak" to Wieland on that night? "The contrivance was mine, but—": his confession remains significantly inconclusive. Since we never know the extent of his "contrivance," and since he had previously admitted his betrayal of Clara's lover, Pleyel, "a man of . . . exquisite sagacity," by a vocal "imposture" that "amounted to proof which the most jealous scrutiny would find to be unexceptional" (pp. 209-10), it seems *probable* that the voice that ordered Wieland to sacrifice his family was real, was Carwin's. Probability is all Brown allows us, however, and even to say the voice was Carwin's does not resolve the final problem: What is the source of Carwin's vocal powers? I have said that Brown himself provides a seemingly authoritative footnote to acknowledge the existence of "ventrilocution," but buried among the scientific information is the admission that "unsatisfactory speculations are given on the means by which the effects are produced. . . . This power is difficult to explain" (p. 198). In the midst of the confrontation scene, Clara had declared that "whether [Carwin] were infernal, or miraculous, or human, there was no power . . . to decide" (p. 227), and I believe readers are left in a similar position, powerless to determine the actual source of Carwin's "voice." He himself "know[s] not by what name to call it" (p. 198); he can only explain ambiguously, "the mode in which heaven is said by the poet to interfere . . . [is] somewhat analogous to my province" (p. 203), and elsewhere admits to being controlled by a "daemon" (p. 201). I later discuss the implications of Carwin as an artist figure. Here I conclude that because we do not have absolute knowledge of what Wieland heard, we cannot reject the *possibility* that he heard the audible enunciation of God's will[22] (cf. the "story" of Abraham), and more important, that Clara's "treatise" on daemons is as inconclusive as her brother's because, as one of Carwin's former acquaintances affirmed, the biloquist's powers are "such as no human intelligence can unravel" (p. 130).

If Theodore's unfinished book foreshadows the ultimate functional inadequacy of Clara's narrative, its inability to communicate the reality behind events, her father's "imperfect tale," which is the first story we encounter in *Wieland,* suggests another, more integral cause of narrative imperfection: not only does external reality remain inscrutable, but storytellers themselves are shown to be unreliable. The elder Wieland's fate was similar in many particulars to that of his son and remains, for future generations, as inexplicable. He had been an extremely religious man, whose final night was spent in expectation of a direct communication (in his case, a retribution) from his God. He was found alone in his place of worship, his body "scorched and bruised," his clothes "reduced to ashes," and when asked for an explanation on his deathbed, "the sum of the information which he chose to give" added up to an "imperfect account." "There was somewhat in his manner that indicated an imperfect tale," and Clara's uncle "was inclined to believe that half the truth had been suppressed" (p. 18). "What are the conclusions that we must form?" (p. 19), asks Clara, an ironically appropriate question for a woman who has inherited the same dubious authority as a storyteller.

It seems incredible that critics have so long taken Clara at her word, have faulted Brown rather than her for *Wieland*'s doubtful ending, when she admits that her "opinions were the sport of eternal change" (p. 180) and that her "narrative may be invaded by inaccuracy and confusion" (p. 147); and when she is repeatedly presented as a suppressor of information, a distorter of truth. Early in the novel she herself describes her duplicitous treatment of Pleyel, her willful withholding of "the true state of [her] affections" (p. 79), in order to make him jealous enough to make his own declaration. Even though, writing in retrospect, she recognizes the errors of such self-serving contrivances, there is further evidence which suggests that her conscious suppression of the truth in this instance may be merely the external manifestation of her repressed nature throughout. In the sequel, for example, we learn that during the period of her separation from Pleyel, during his marriage, though she tried to view him as a "friend," her "passion . . . was merely smothered for a time": "my passion was disguised to myself" (pp. 237-38). A number of critics have commented on Clara's thinly disguised incestuous desires for her brother, and this tendency to obfuscate "passions" and motives even to herself is figuratively reinforced for us by the many instances in which Clara describes her narrow escapes from dangers that she perceives to emanate from a dark "recess," a word she often associates with her closet (e.g., pp. 87, 207). Kimball has written very persuasively that "Clara's symbolic private closet" serves as "a striking metaphor for Locke's 'dark room of the mind.' . . . Like Edgar Huntly's wilderness cave, it harbors the shadowy nightside of the id. . . . The closet contains at different times the 'memoirs' of her father, the incarnate irrationality which is Carwin, a 'lancet and other small instruments' with which Clara contemplates suicide, a manuscript of her innermost secrets, . . . and a host of other vague terrors of physical violence, death, seduction and incest, which . . . remain in obscurity."[23] I would add two things. First, that she keeps her father's manuscript locked in her closet metaphorically strengthens the idea that she has inherited the psychological limitations implicit in his imperfect authority, and second, that her own journal of secret transactions, linked as it is with this dark recess, provides more specific insights into her authorial psychology. That is, Pleyel says that Clara always "wrote much more than [she] permitted [her] friends to peruse," and that when interrupted, she "hurried the [journal] out of sight" (p. 125). More figuratively, Clara's journal is written in shorthand. On a phenomenal level, we perceive that the original information, "disguised" as *it* may be, is virtually transformed into a symbolic representation that offers only partial data to readers; thematically, we are given metaphorical evidence that our narrator habitually uses language in order to conceal the truth. Thus Clara Wieland shows herself to be, by nature and by design, an eminently unreliable narrator.

The next question must be, then, What has Clara suppressed or repressed in the telling of *Wieland*? I maintain the distinction because I believe two of her "conclusions" remain suspect by virtue of these closely aligned tendencies. The first is her final testimony regarding Wieland's death. As he and Clara were alone in the room at the time, we only have her word that he killed himself. Furthermore, in describing her preparations for the confrontation scene, she has revealed herself capable not only of premeditated "self-defense" against Carwin—"in a fold of my dress an open penknife was concealed" (p. 223)—but also of murderous passion. Convinced that Carwin had willfully tricked Wieland into murdering his family, she admits that she "thirsted for [the biloquist's] blood, and was tormented by an insatiable appetite for his destruction" (p. 221). In addition she admits to having been capable of killing her brother to save her own life, and this memory precipitates an outburst of the inveterate desire for self-censure: "O, insupportable remembrance! hide thee from my view for a time; hide it from me that my heart was black enough to meditate the stabbing of a brother!" (pp. 222-23). Like Wieland and Carwin during this final sequence, Clara changes her story frequently, and although she contends that she had been finally "incapable" of "self-defense," the rapid changes in her state of mind undermine our certainty. For example, what motivates Clara to account for the fact that when she is found she has Wieland's blood on her hands (p. 232)? The inclusion of this detail is reminiscent of Carwin's artful "narratives": "Those that were . . . most minute, and, of consequence, least entitled to credit, were yet rendered probable by the exquisite art of this rhetorician" (p. 74). I suggest that just as Wieland's actual death is caused by Clara's penknife, "plunged . . . to the hilt in his neck" (p. 231), so might his "suicide" have been effected solely by Clara's pen; that Clara might have killed her brother and suppressed half the truth in the later telling.[24]

I want to make clear, however, that I am arguing only for the possibility that Clara murdered her brother, and I argue thus because I believe that it is the unreliability of conclusions per se that demands our attention in *Wieland,* and not any one of Clara's conclusions; and that the issue of whether Clara is a murderer is itself subsumed in her conclusion regarding Carwin. Her final word on this man who has been variously described as "an imp of mischief" (p. 123), an "enemy of God and man" (p. 216), is that he is "probably engaged in the harmless pursuits of agriculture" in "a remote district of Pennsylvania" (p. 239). This is the story Carwin told Clara, which she has believed. But in our first meetings with him, we learned that "he had formerly declared that it was his purpose to spend his life" (p. 68) in Spain. The point is stressed: Pleyel "was *taught* to believe that Carwin should never leave that country" (p. 72; italics mine), and yet Carwin has shown up to perpetrate his deceptions on the American scene. The biloquist himself admits that he is "destined perpetually to violate [his] resolutions" (p. 206), that "the temptation to interfere" is, for him, "irresistible" (p. 200), and he is described as a villain who "sets his engines of destruction . . . against every object that presents itself" (p. 130). The Satanic overtones are not gratuitous, for as Gilmore has shown in delineating the parallels between *Wieland* and *Paradise Lost,* Carwin has brought "death and sin into the garden of *Wieland.*" In Brown's "American Tale," Carwin may be seen as evil incarnate, and if he is, and if, as Clara contends, he has turned his energies to "harmless" gardening, then surely evil has died out in America—a highly unlikely conclusion.[25] Like Milton's Satan, that first "author of evil" (*Paradise Lost,* VI, 262), Carwin is presented as an "author" of "evils" (p. 50), of "unheard-of disasters" (p. 160). The specific nature of his evil, however, is that he is an artful storyteller, one who fashions tidy fictions with endings that seem absolute; and Clara Wieland has a constitutional need to believe in such stories, which, by providing an end, make a satisfying consonance with her interpretation of what has gone before.[26]

But if to accept a happy ending is to satisfy a need for order, it is also to repress knowledge of a truly anarchic reality, to indulge in the delusive comforts of "better thoughts." In the midst of her difficulties, Clara had admitted the extent of Carwin's demonic hold over her with images that showed him quite literally lurking in her mind: "Carwin was the phantom that pursued my dreams" (p. 157); "the image of Carwin was blended in a thousand ways with the stream of my thoughts" (p. 148). But "better thoughts grew up in my mind imperceptibly," she tells us at the beginning of her sequel, and she emphasizes that the change was not the result of conscious effort: "perhaps it merely argues a fickleness of temper, . . . a defect of sensibility" (p. 235), i.e., an unconscious desire to forget the darker implications arising from her past experience. Clara's willingness to believe in Carwin's seductive story shows that she has substantially repressed her former horror regarding his power to effect evil—a power that might at any moment resurface; and, by extension, that she has repressed the horrifying extent of her own capacity for evil, perhaps her ability to kill even a brother. Her removal to Europe at the end heightens our sense that she has cut herself off from any direct knowledge of the evil potential that still lurks in America and in her own Americanness. To sum up, Clara's various conclusions—that Wieland was merely mad, that she was a powerless bystander, that Carwin has repented of his storytelling—are indeed the comforting products of her better thoughts, but the ending of **Wieland** leaves her, and any credulous readers, on the brink of a dangerous future, unprepared.

And this brings us to two of the central issues raised by this text: what, then, for Clara has been the benefit in writing her story, and for us, in reading it? It is not enough to say that Clara writes to achieve peace of mind, for surely the more important aspect is that we are allowed to see on what shaky ground that peace is founded. But it is also not enough to say that readers achieve a healthy distrust of reading fiction, for it is not reading but acting that generates the gravest danger in this book. **Wieland** presents a hierarchy of fictional forms and a variety of writers and readers, and to understand more fully the proper uses of fiction as suggested by this novel, we must turn our attention back to the "middest."

First of all, it should not escape our notice that Clara's writing has kept her alive and relatively sane. We are told that friends tried to withhold from her "the implements of writing; but they quickly perceived that to withstand would be more injurious than to comply with [her] wishes" (p. 235). Clara firmly believed that she would "die . . . only when [her] tale [was] at an end" (p. 228), and one of her authorial outbursts reveals what she saw as the terrifying alternative to writing: "Why not terminate at once this series of horrors?" she asks, "—hurry to the verge of the precipice, and cast myself for ever beyond remembrance and beyond hope?" (p. 228). For Clara, the image of the precipice is equated with both death and insanity, and insanity is portrayed as having to encounter, without mediation, the dark side of the human psyche, e.g., the "heart . . . black enough" to entertain "insupportable" desires. Thus her fervent drive to suppress and to repress throughout, and her insistence on maintaining her own "author"-ity, which is threatened from without but even more fearfully from within.

In other words, **Wieland** presents a subtle and highly sophisticated defense of literary art as a means of keeping an anarchic human nature in check. In an early dream Clara's fears of encountering what Kimball has

called "the shadowy night-side of the id" (in this instance incestuous desires) and her salvation from such an encounter are revealed: "A pit, methought, had been dug in the path I had taken, of which I was not aware. . . . I saw my brother, standing at some distance before me, beckoning and calling me to make haste. He stood on the opposite edge of the gulph. I mended my pace, and one step more would have plunged me into the abyss, had not some one from behind . . . exclaimed, in a voice of eagerness and terror, 'Hold! hold!'" The voice, which we later learn to be Carwin's quoting from *Macbeth,* awakens her to "images so terrific" that they "disabled [her], for a time, from distinguishing between sleep and wakefulness, and withheld from [her] the knowledge of [her] actual condition" (p. 62). The final phrase holds the key to what might seem at first mere Gothic melodrama, for the scene acts as a metaphor for the psychological complexities of the creative process and, in particular, its dependence on sublimation. Clara has been literally saved from experiencing the primal depths of her incestuous desires, her "actual condition," by a poet's words projected out of the dark "recess" (p. 61) where her dream originates.

I have already said that Clara uses the word "recess" elsewhere to describe the closet where her writings are kept and from which they eventually emerge; Brown also used the word himself, in an earlier poem in which he had depicted his own—less urgent—experience in "Fancy's . . . enchanting maze":

> In this recess I sat
> And saw, or dream'd I saw, an airy shape,
> And heard aerial notes, a voice . . .

that he would also call "my genius, my divine / Instructress, better angel, heavenly friend . . . my Muse."[27] Later in the novel, Clara will call the voice that warns her away from the dangers brewing in her psychic closet "*my* heavenly friend" (p. 94) and after one vocal warning will wonder whether the phenomenon exists "in [her] fancy or without" (p. 147). It would seem that, among his numerous functions in this book, Carwin also serves as a creative impetus, as Clara's muse: just as he "taught" Pleyel to believe in stories, his fictions instruct and inspire Clara in the art of storytelling as an art of self-defense. The dream scene shows how Clara's poetic imagination, under Carwin's (and Shakespeare's) tutelage, enables her to transform potentially harmful energies into compelling "images," into something less harmful to herself and to others.[28] Similarly throughout, though her narrative of sublimation keeps her from acknowledging her true capacity to do evil, it also keeps her, for the duration of her tale, from such doing. We must remember that it was when Clara was trapped in an actual encounter with the murderous Wieland that she began to see no alternative but to become a murderer herself; the immediacy of the danger had forced her to a hasty conclusion. And Clara's is not an isolated case: once Theodore leaves off writing his book on Socrates' Daemon, he must encounter the dangers of daemons face to face; without benefit of mediation, his violent passions surface all too tragically, with the "quickness of thought."

The quickness of thought is the true culprit in *Wieland,* for although Clara's authorial experience does provide intriguing insights into Brown's theory of creativity, the larger significance of the writing metaphor lies in the time factor. The thematic complement to the defense of literary-art-as-mediation is the warning against *un*mediated response, against action based on precipitate conclusions, and this helps to illuminate the psychological seductiveness of Carwin's treacherous "author"-ity. What makes this multifarious character dangerous as an artist figure in his own right is the immediacy of his art: he is literally a *teller* of tales. In the world of *Wieland* unsatisfactory narrative endings represent the insufficiency of conclusions derived by unreliable mental processes; consequently, in such a world the only safety lies in postponing those conclusions, metaphorically, in lengthy narratives committed to paper. Carwin's vocal fictions, however, induce the most immediate misperceptions in (as in one of Clara's experiences) "interval[s] . . . too brief to be artifically measured" (p. 85). A similar and more enlightening phrasing occurs in Brown's *The Man At Home,* published in the same year: "Our curiosity is proportioned, among other circumstances, to the shortness of the interval, and thus slightness of the bar between us and knowledge."[29] "Seeming slightness" is surely more accurate (for the Man is, of course, another of Brown's victims of credulity). Throughout *Wieland,* the human mind is shown to be infinitely fallible, and yet characters are driven to *know,* to jump the bar—or to strike through the mask, as a later American writer would have it. Carwin's vocal fictions are effective precisely because they allow his conclusion-seeking victims insufficient time for doubtful reflection; they seem to provide direct knowledge.

Finally, we must follow the logic of Brown's metaphorical fictions one more step: if written narratives are privileged over oral ones, then a reading audience must be privileged over a listening one, by virtue of the longer mental "interval." And as usual, *Wieland* delineates this order by inversion. Theodore, for example, not only abandons his writing, but also becomes "less disposed than formerly to . . . reading" (p. 35), once Carwin's vocal tricks begin: thus an end to reading helps pave the way into the chaotic abyss of direct experience. Pleyel is the most noteworthy reader in this novel, however, and as such, his behavior serves as a warning to *Wieland*'s readers in three respects, each showing by contrast the value of circumspect reading.

First, Pleyel's situation is somewhat analogous to our own, in that he becomes a motivated reader in order to discover the real nature of Carwin's character, and in that the information he reads has literally undergone several transformations. The Philadelphia newspaper article, which was a notice of an escaped convict named Carwin, had been "copied from a British paper" (p. 133). When Pleyel tracks down the printer, he finds that the article had been forwarded by a Mr. Hallet, who had received the clipping in a letter from one Ludloe, which letter—a damning accusation against Carwin—Pleyel also reads. At this point he believes he has the whole story regarding Carwin, but readers of *Wieland* must suspect the veracity of such emphatically second-hand narratives. The second way in which Pleyel serves as a warning is that, like Wieland, he too is seduced from reading to acting. Armed with what he believes to be absolute proof of Carwin's villainy, he departs for Clara's house and on his way, hears the false scenario that convinces him of her degeneracy. He later admits that though "hearing was the only avenue to information," his "uncertainty vanished": "I yielded not but to evidence which took away the power to withhold my faith" (pp. 134-35). Blinded by jealously, Pleyel thus fails the test of experience in one of Brown's fateful intervals. Finally, the jealousy just mentioned provides the most important clue to Pleyel's credulity in accepting the printed evidence against Carwin, and to his main significance to us as readers. What had originally precipitated his research into Carwin's background had been his *mis*reading of Clara's journal. Glancing over her shoulder at a text written in shorthand, of which he caught "only parts of sentences" and random words— "*summer-house, midnight . . . another* interview" (p. 125)—he immediately harbored suspicions of her involvement with the biloquist; but, like the elder Wieland's reading of the Camisard manuscript (which inspired the religious fanaticism that in some way led to *his* downfall), "his constructions of the text were hasty and formed on a narrow scale" (p. 9). Although Pleyel saw the "necessity of resorting to other means of information" (p. 126), his vision was already distorted by unconscious motives, and he never questioned his further reading. Thus at the outset Pleyel is shown to be a poor reader, one who reads superficially and jumps to hasty conclusions. And the end result is that we become forewarned, having learned from indirect experience.

I began with the question, What are the proper uses of fiction as suggested by *Wieland*? It should be obvious by now that this novel presents a world in which *all* mental processes are shown to be fiction-making, first, because external realities, e.g., the motives and actions of other people, are ever inscrutable, and thus any interpretations of such realities must remain inconclusive "stories"; and second, because the human mind itself, in trying to interpret experience, is ever subject to unconscious impulses—passions—that can transform even the most well-intentioned testimony into sheer fiction. Thus Brown originates epistemological themes that have come to be recognized as quintessentially American, themes long acknowledged in the works of our major writers, Hawthorne, Melville, and James.[30] What makes Brown's work unique, however, is the skillful and consistent use of his own "figure in the carpet": the precipitate conclusion. This figure, in fact, is precisely what allows us to see that there *are* proper, and discriminating, uses of fiction. In **Wieland** Brown uses writing and reading fictitious narratives as metaphors for time well spent, as necessary mediations between human beings and their dangerously unpredictable futures. If anything, **Wieland** serves as a defense of reading fiction, for what it can tell us about the complexities of human nature. In particular, **Wieland**'s readers learn to distrust happy endings and to turn their attention back to the "middest," to a careful scrutiny of the psychological complexities, especially the disguised self-interest, leading to action. Its subtitle, "An American Tale," was surely not a gratuitous flourish. But Brown's message to a young nation, nurtured from its infancy on stories promising its own happy ending, as the New Jerusalem, has only too recently begun to be heard.

Notes

1. Fred Lewis Pattee, Introduction, to Charles Brockden Brown, *Wieland, or The Transformation, Together with Memoirs of Carwin the Biloquist* (New York, 1926), p. xliii; Paul Witherington, "Charles Brockden Brown: A Bibliographical Essay," *Early American Literature,* 9 (1974), 180. For a recent and very persuasive reassessment of the extent and the effects of Brown's haste in composition, see Sydney J. Krause, "*Ormond*: How Rapidly and How Well 'Composed, Arranged and Delivered,'" *Early American Literature,* 13 (1978/79), 238-49.

2. Larzer Ziff, "A Reading of *Wieland,*" *PMLA,* 77 (1962), 53; Witherington, p. 181, citing Joseph Katz, "Analytic Bibliography and Literary History: The Writing and Printing of *Wieland,*" *Proof,* 1 (1971), 8-34.

3. Michael Davitt Bell, "The Double-Tongued Deceiver: Sincerity and Duplicity in the Novels of Charles Brockden Brown," *Early American Literature,* 9 (1974), 148.

4. Mark Seltzer, "Saying Makes It So: Language and Event in Brown's *Wieland,*" *Early American Literature,* 13 (1978), 85.

5. Terence Martin, *The Instructed Vision: Scottish Common Sense Philosophy and the Origins of American Fiction* (Bloomington, Ind., 1961), p. 135.

6. My purpose in this essay is not so much to argue a consummate consciousness on Brown's part, as

to try to correct the usual portrait of him as a demented hack. For example, while I agree with James Russo's recent claim that Brown "was a careful craftsman who was far ahead of his time in narrative technique" ("The Tangled Web of Deception and Imposture in Charles Brockden Brown's *Ormond,*" *Early American Literature,* 14 [1979], 225), I believe that Michael Davitt Bell's assessment—that Brown ultimately "lacked the skill" of such later writers as Poe, Hawthorne, and Melville (p. 160)—provides a necessary qualification and helps explain Brown's long-delayed recognition as a serious artist. (Russo's study of *Wieland* [in *Early American Literature,* 16 (1981)] appeared too late to be accommodated here.)

For important reassessments of Brown's artistry, focusing on the intricacies of his symbolism and metaphor, see Arthur G. Kimball, "Savages and Savagism: Brockden Brown's Dramatic Irony," *Studies in Romanticism,* 6 (1967), 214-25; Wayne Franklin, "Tragedy and Comedy in Brown's *Wieland,*" *Novel,* 8 (1975), 147-63, citing extensive Shakespearean parallels; Michael T. Gilmore, "Calvinism and Gothicism: The Example of Brown's *Wieland,*" *Studies in the Novel,* 9 (1977), 107-18, showing parallels between *Wieland* and *Paradise Lost*; and Seltzer, using a Todorovian approach in "Saying Makes It So."

7. Leslie Fiedler, *Love and Death in the American Novel* (New York, 1975), p. 155.

8. Fielding's Preface to *Familiar Letters Between the Principle Characters in David Simple* (1747), cited by Frank Kermode, *The Sense of an Ending: Studies in the Theory of Fiction* (New York, 1966), p. 174.

9. Charles Brockden Brown, *Edgar Huntly, or Memoirs of a Sleepwalker* (Port Washington, N.Y., 1963), p. 280. All further references to this edition will appear in parentheses within the text.

10. Charles Brockden Brown, *Ormond, or The Secret Witness* (New York, 1937), p. 30. All further references to this edition will appear in parentheses within the text.

11. Charles Brockden Brown, *Jane Talbot* (Port Washington, N.Y., 1963), pp. 75, 102. All further references to his edition will appear in parentheses within the text.

12. Charles Brockden Brown, *Arthur Mervyn, or Memoirs of the Year 1793* (Port Washington, N.Y., 1963), p. 58. All further references to this edition will appear in parentheses within the text.

13. Bell has pointed out the pun (p. 156).

14. See J. Hillis Miller, "The Problematic of Ending in Narrative," *Nineteenth-Century Fiction,* 33

(June 1978), 3-7. Miller argues the possibility of interpreting any given narrative ending as either a closure or a denouement; Brown's novels seem to argue the *im*possibility of a narrative's achieving either.

15. Charles Brockden Brown, *Clara Howard* (Port Washington, N.Y., 1963), p. 287. All further references to this edition will appear in parentheses.

16. Charles Brockden Brown, *Wieland, or The Transformation: An American Tale* (Kent, Ohio, 1978), p. 244. All further references to this edition will appear in parentheses within the text.

17. Kermode, p. 17.

18. Bell, pp. 146-47.

19. I agree with Kimball (p. 221) that "Brown has been underrated as an ironist."

20. See *OED* entry for "Demon."

21. Bell, p. 146.

22. Brown states, in his "Advertisement," that some of the incidents related in *Wieland* "approach as nearly to the nature of miracles as can be done by that which is not truly miraculous" (p. 3); but I believe this to be an authorial disclaimer of the type found throughout the novel—inconclusive. For example, I find it highly suggestive that in this book full of authors of fictions, God is twice identified as an "author," pp. 74, 166.

23. Kimball, p. 216.

24. That Brown's self-professedly virtuous characters are capable of murder is demonstrated later in *Ormond*: "the violence of Ormond had been repulsed by equal violence" on the part of Constantia Dudley, who ironically chooses to kill rather than to lose her "virtue" (p. 240). James R. Russo, in "The Tangled Web," provides detailed evidence of the moral inconstancy of Constantia. See also Kenneth Bernard, "*Edgar Huntly*: Charles Brockden Brown's Unsolved Murder," *Library Chronicle*, 33 (1967), 30-53, in which Bernard argues that Huntly, the narrator, "is in fact guilty of Waldegrave's murder, and his internal drama of guilt is played out with Clithero as alterego . . ." (cited in Witherington, p. 182).

25. Gilmore, p. 112. I maintain my qualification—*if* Carwin is to be seen as evil incarnate—because I believe Brown has ironically designed a situation in which readers must argue by "fictional" analogy, in which we must confront the fictional bases of our own conclusions. That is, we are forced to judge not on proofs, but on the basis of Clara's and Carwin's Miltonic metaphors. Are they not both "double-tongued" deceivers, using another's "voice" to tell stories of their own devising? Unquestionably, Carwin fulfills Satanic functions, but as I will argue, he also serves as Clara's muse, and at such times represents the lesser of two evils. His multiple role, like his truncated confession in the confrontation scene, makes it impossible to draw any hard-and-fast conclusion.

26. Clara's need to believe in stories that ostensibly tie up loose ends helps to account for her inclusion of the Conway-Maxwell story in her sequel. Larzer Ziff, "A Reading of Wieland," sees this story as evidence of Brown's poor planning, his need, since he had lost control of Carwin's characterization, to invent a new seducer to enact the crimes for which the Biloquist had originally been slotted; and Joseph Katz, "Analytic Bibliography," sees it as proof that Brown had insufficient time to revise. The new story does fulfill important thematic functions, however. By recounting another con man's seduction and destruction of a family, Clara is more able to justify her own unlikely story and to reinforce her belief in authoritative conclusions: "the evils of which Carwin and Maxwell were the authors owed their existence to"— and she gives four plausible explanations. Moreover, the story serves as an ironic parallel to Clara's own in ways she does not perceive, and perhaps as a final paradigm for all stories, for though Clara attributes the central villainy—the murder—to Maxwell, she admits that "the author of this reason could not certainly be discovered," and the story ends with the unsettling comment that Maxwell "disappeared from this scene" (p. 244). Such details reinforce our suspicions that all stories originate to explain away—for a time—the inexplicable.

27. The poem, first printed in the *American Register* in 1794, is called "Devotion. An Epistle," and is partially reprinted in Pattee's introduction to *Wieland*, p. xv.

28. A strikingly literal example of just this type of literary transformation occurs in *Jane Talbot*, in a letter from Jane to her lover, Henry Colden: "I should certainly bestow upon thee a hearty—*kiss* or two. My blundering pen! I recall the word. I meant *cuff*, but my saucy pen, pretending to know more of my mind than I did myself, turned . . . her *cuff* into a *kiss*," p. 110.

29. Reprinted in Charles Brockden Brown, *The Rhapsodist and Other Uncollected Writings*, ed., Harry R. Warfel (New York, 1943), p. 43.

30. A number of critics have commented on the epistemological anxiety that informs so much nineteenth-century American fiction. See, for ex-

ample, Richard Chase, *The American Novel and Its Tradition* (Garden City, N.Y., 1957); Richard Poirier, *A World Elsewhere: The Place of Style in American Literature* (New York, 1966); Joel Porte, *The Romance in America: Studies in Cooper, Poe, Hawthorne, Melville, and James* (Middletown, Conn., 1969); and Richard Brodhead, *Hawthorne, Melville, and the Novel* (Chicago, 1976). Porte's discussion of *The Scarlet Letter* is especially suggestive of the thematic heritage that links Brown's Gothicism with Hawthorne's romances; e.g., see Porte's comment that "Without 'guilt' there can be no 'craft,' but the avenue to insight about the human condition ultimately opened up by the artist's work finally justifies both that work and the normally forbidden or avoided experiences that provoked it" (p. 98).

Michael Kreyling (essay date 1982)

SOURCE: Kreyling, Michael. "Construing Brown's *Wieland*: Ambiguity and Derridean 'Freeplay.'" *Studies in the Novel* 14, no. 1 (spring 1982): 43-54.

[*In the following essay, Kreyling explores* Wieland's *decentered universe by means of the Derridean theory of endless freeplay.*]

> Every man discriminates between the voluntary acts of his mind and his involuntary perceptions, and knows that to his involuntary perceptions a perfect faith is due. He may err in the expression of them, but he knows that these things are so, like day and night, not to be disputed.

Emerson wrote in the hortative mode. This passage from "Self-Reliance" must be read as a wish in the blank face of fact: would that the voluntary acts of the mind and one's involuntary perceptions were as surely distinguishable as night and day; would that a perfect faith in either one, or in the distinction between the two, were possible. Thus would ambiguity be banished. Good and evil, truth and fiction, reality and appearance would appear without disguises. Language in this Emersonian wish-world would also be perfect, for our voluntary mental acts (words) would never fail to find the link with our involuntary perceptions.

The wish erects a wall around language and is expressive of the great fear that language reveal itself as the master of man and not his tool. Language, as an act subject to the human will, is quarantined in the conscious Emersonian mind, restricted from any residence whatever in the unconscious. In his wish to keep language in the realm of the conscious, Emerson places himself at odds with the romantic mode. As Northrop Frye has observed, the romantic mode liberates lan-

guage to play in the realms of the pre- and unconscious.[1] That Emerson, as spokesman for an American tradition of optimistic idealism, is an authoritarian realist where language is concerned, seems to be an assertion that cuts against the grain. But Emerson is a brilliant spot in a long American tradition supporting the authority and objective reality of the Ideal, for underlying that tradition is the religious belief in the Word as God. Take away Emerson's distinction (that is, consider the word as unrestricted in its movement through consciousness, fix no residence for the word on a level of the human psyche) and the Word is demoted to a word. The center of the universe vanishes.

The darker works of Poe, Melville, and Hawthorne risk such a decentered universe. But the process of its creation—or decreation—can first be seen years earlier in Charles Brockden Brown's *Wieland, or The Transformation.*[2] For the significance of the subtitle let me suggest the transformation (or decreation) of a centered universe to a decentered one. And let me use some recent and still largely controversial critical methodology to make my point.

II

Wieland, published in 1798, has fascinated critics of American fiction. It is, as Donald Ringe has written, a "remarkable achievement" in spite of frequent lapses in craft and "ludicrous" convolutions in diction.[3] *Wieland* challenges the critic to make coherent sense of a narrative that often dramatizes the failure of sense-making by "rational" characters who are confused and ultimately mentally "blasted" by their failure.

The consensus of criticism of *Wieland* calls this theme in the novel ambiguity, and indicates by the choice of that term that there is a legitimate meaning or truth available to the characters if they can only discern it. The critical approach is usually to discern couplings of concepts, forces, or values which become one concept, force, or value through the unmasking of the other as untrue or evil. In this approach most critics have shown their staunch support of the Emersonian distinction. They set limits to the term "ambiguity" by analyzing it as the issue of a defect in "involuntary perception." Once that defect is repaired, the interpretations hold, the real good, or the desirable alternative, is instantly perceived and chosen. The center is thereby restored, and the world spins on smoothly once again.

Ringe, one of the first critics to follow the literary historians who had placed *Wieland* in the tradition of the English sentimental novel, finds that the characters of *Wieland* confuse appearance and reality (p. 27). Larzer Ziff sees Calvinist depravity struggling with the eighteenth-century's optimistic rationalistic psychology.[4] William Manly sees "objective logic and subjective terror" locked in a battle which the former happily wins.[5] Michael Davitt Bell sees a division between sincerity and duplicity, respectively buttressed by "Lockean rationalism and the power of the irrational."[6] Michael Butler reads *Wieland* as an investigation of the competing claims of social and private man, with a resolution favorable to "some ultimately optimistic ideas about social man's limitation and capabilities."[7] John Cleman and Mark Seltzer adopt a more skeptical view of the novel; they doubt that *Wieland* is a text susceptible of conclusive interpretation.[8]

This digest of critical interpretations of *Wieland* is impressive in at least two ways. It testifies to ongoing critical concern in Brown's novel, and it illustrates how devoted is the act of interpretation to the stability of meaning. This essay, coming after much discussion, aims at a redefinition of our critical bases in ambiguity of theme and structure. My viewpoint, or beginning, is all-important, for I will try to avoid the presumption of knowable meaning in describing the nature of ambiguity in *Wieland.* The work of one critic who has had much to say about the nature of ambiguity in language and literature—Jacques Derrida—is central to the reading and interpretation I wish to offer. The implications of Derrida's critiques of philosophical and literary discourse are now being felt. In altering our thinking on the theme of ambiguity in literary texts, he can be of much help.

In "Structure, Sign, and Play in the Discourse of the Human Sciences" Derrida attempts to define "freeplay."[9] His definition proceeds from another concept, that of the centered structure. The center of any structure is that part of the structure which is not subject to the substitutions of elements or terms—the structurality of structure. A centered structure, then, is one in which substitution of elements (change) is limited by the presence of the center. The notion of presence—which holds with Emersonian assurance that mind can and does act *voluntarily* in the control of language and knowledge—is the notion that Derrida subjects to "deconstruction." "Freeplay" is the free substitution that, by a convention of philosophy, occurs everywhere except in the center of the structure. Derrida elaborates:

> The concept of centered structure is in fact the concept of a freeplay based on a fundamental immobility and a reassuring certitude, which is itself beyond the reach of the freeplay. With this certitude anxiety can be mastered, for anxiety is invariably the result of a certain mode of being implicated in the game, of being caught by the game, of being as it were from the very beginning at stake in the game.

> (p. 248)

This very anxiety, I think, is what Emerson-as-realist wishes so ardently to deny. With the perverseness of romance, however, Brown's text sets forth the very thing that the conscious mind fears: the erasure of presence-at-the-center which it has claimed for itself.

Ambiguity, it seems to me, is too often thought of as a "centered structure," for we preserve the "reassuring certitude" that some significance will emerge. Derridean freeplay, in the present context, seems to be more radical than ambiguity. Elsewhere in his essay Derrida says:

> Freeplay is the disruption of presence. The presence of an element is always a signifying and substitutive reference inscribed in a system of differences and the movement of a chain. Freeplay is always an interplay of absence and presence, but if it is to be radically conceived, freeplay must be conceived of before the alternative of presence or absence; being must be conceived of as presence or absence beginning with the possibility of freeplay and not the other way around.

> (pp. 263-64)

The shifting of the mind from residence in a centered structure to a decentered structure, in which freeplay describes the continuous movement or disappearance of meaning, involves a seismic upheaval. *Wieland,* with its variety of such shocks, is well-suited as a test of the applicability of the Derridean theory to literature.

III

The significance of the family history of the Wielands has been explored by nearly every critic who addresses the novel. It is no less crucial to the following presentation. Clara's father, desiring refuge from an amorphous gloom and a life that seems mired in meaningless routine, fatefully embraces a text attributed to the Camissards. The Camissards, Huguenot zealots who rebelled against the Catholic King of France, Louis XIV, were motivated by the visions of a few leaders to believe in personal revelation and the imminence of apocalypse. They had succumbed, in the terms of Frank Kermode's *Sense of an Ending,* to the consolations of apocalyptic time: the elimination of the uncertain by a divine conflation of *chronos* and *kairos.*[10] There was no nonmeaning for the Camissard, no ambiguity. All occurrences testified to the imminent parousia; all signs dwelled in the glow of the transcendental signified.

The elder Wieland absorbed this apocalyptic fervor along with the certitude it imparted. He emigrated to America where he intended to convert the savages. That, he was convinced, was to be his unambiguous mission from God. But, as Larzer Ziff points out, America foiled him by making him rich instead of holy, and he lived in a prosperous gloom the rest of his life waiting for the unambiguous penalty that a thwarted God was sure to visit upon him.[11] He had gone into the wilderness only to be dragged back into the world's time, ordinary *chronos.* Vengeance came in the certain form of spontaneous combustion in his Tuscan temple overlooking the sublime Schuylkill.

The Wielands' uncle, the same admirable and rational man who picks up the pieces and fits them into a jerry-built explanation for Clara at the close of the novel, suspects that the fatally injured Wieland is withholding a key clue, for the story of the luminous cloud that incinerates him is, to the uncle, "an imperfect tale" (p. 20). Like Emerson, the uncle believes that whatever mysteries arise in the order of things, the order of things will solve. For Wieland père, however, the end of his life is no mystery: his sin of failure brought the Deity's inevitable retribution. Uncle Thomas Cambridge, whose surname suggests English commonsense and whose first name echoes the most famous case of doubt of parousia in the Christian Bible, is ensconced in history, the centered universe. To the Wieland children he becomes an alternative father centered in rationality.

Thus is the Wieland family determined from the outset of the novel. Signifiers and signified do not coincide, are not coeval; there are some facts for which there are no signs, and some signs which might attach to several facts. The uncle's centered universe flows over past events assuaging the anxiety of the Wieland orphans. They grow to maturity clinging to rationality and to language as a centered discourse. A center of their universe ensures order.

Theodore marries Catharine Pleyel, a girl virtually the image of his sister Clara (p. 23). Clara professes love for her sister-in-law and gradually reveals her attraction for her brother-in-law, Henry. Two pairs of brothers and sisters living in close proximity imply a premium on familiarity and order. Indeed the elder Wieland's temple, stark and empty in his day, is refurnished with a bust of Cicero and a harpsichord. Critics have placed various constructions on these two items, but that they reinforce the thrust for order and away from a previous generation's unhealthy fancy (p. 97) is not disputed.

There is, however, a decentering disaster percolating beneath the confident surface of Mettingen, and Pleyel's decomposition from "gay young rationalist"[12] to confused inquisitor is the least complicated of the several instances of its impact. A mysterious voice, first heard by Wieland alone, brings tidings to Pleyel that his beloved has died in Germany. Pleyel, who had scoffed at Wieland's faith in the voice, now fails to reject its news for him, and he withdraws into a Wielandesque moody solitude where fancy can begin the erosion of his vaunted logic. Clara, narrating these events, also jumps instantaneously to the conclusion that the voice issues from a "superhuman" source: "That there are conscious beings, besides ourselves, in existence, whose modes of activity and information surpass our own, can scarcely be denied" (p. 51). This assumption could be denied rather easily. Pleyel had done so once; he is powerless to do so again, however, when the information imparted has meaning for himself.

From this point forward Pleyel becomes a wooden-headed and woodenhearted cad. Ziff's estimation of him as Brown's sample of the sentimental hero in all of his limitations is valid.[13] The disintegration of Pleyel also dramatizes the swiftness with which decentering can demolish "logic."

Pleyel hears what he takes to be "evidence" that his ideal woman, Clara, has been conducting a secret and lascivious commerce with the interloper, Carwin. Placing an Emersonian "perfect faith" in these "involuntary perceptions," he accuses Clara of lust. Clara can and does dismantle the certitude in Pleyel's interpretation by pointing out how he has permitted the involuntary and voluntary to mix. Her defense is to resort to her "character," her good name. By all of her past life, Clara pleads (p. 138), she has composed a character which shall be signified by her name. Her argument implies a kind of social language in which all agree to collaborate the better to know one another and thereby to preserve the community in and through which each has his or her existence. By accepting contrary evidence—Clara later calls the evidence "signals"—Pleyel commits an elementary act of treason. He abets deconstruction in the "language" of character by allowing freeplay to infiltrate the "fundamental ground" which had hitherto been sacrosanct. With the substitution of each new piece of "evidence" Pleyel surrenders more of the center.

Pleyel's defection, however, is the least of Clara's worries. Wieland's utter destruction, likened by one critic to the noble fall of Icarus,[14] presents Clara with a more immediate shock. She had venerated her brother's intellect, had worshipped him as the first among men. To see him driven mad by doubt and brutalized by solitary confinement in prison breaks Clara's tough and admirable mind.

Theodore Wieland has obviously been deeply affected by the mysterious voice that disrupts the Mettingen idyll. His symptoms have been present from the early pages. He had inherited his sire's gloom and, with his name, the father's preference for a theo-centered universe. Hearing the disembodied voice before any of the others gives Wieland *fils* a head start toward decentering. He maintains, in the face of Pleyel's mild derision, that he did hear the voice of his wife, although he knows she did not and could not have uttered the sounds that he heard. Wieland subsequently tells his sister that "'the understanding has other avenues'" besides the five senses. He will, he pledges, find the cause of the voice—for he still believes in causes and effects—by eliminating all false explanations (p. 41). But the pressure of living with a multiplicity of changing truths—freeplay—destroys him.

In the transcript of his address to the court that sentences him for the murder of his wife and children,

Wieland displays the agents of his decentering. It has been more violent than Pleyel's. First he marvels to the court at the freeplay in his own name. All present have known "Wieland," he claims, as a certain bundle of characteristics (p. 184). All that is honorable is included; all baseness is excluded. Now that sign ("Wieland") must also admit murder and madness in the freeplay of substitutions.

He had clung to his name as an unambiguous sign, but it proved false. The center of his universe, his own consciousness, has dropped out of sight. Praying to the Word for coherence, Wieland exclaims: "'Would that a momentary emanation from thy glory would visit me! that some unambiguous token of thy presence would salute my senses!'" (p. 187). But God, Wieland's namesake, does not speak the Word. Wieland has instead taken the antics of Carwin as a sign from the unambiguous, and the result is tragic error. When Carwin confesses that he was in fact not the speaker of the words that sent Wieland to murder his family, the decentered Theodore turns his knife upon himself as the only way to end endless freeplay.

Carwin, himself uncentered, is the presumptive center of the ordered but stricken universe of which Mettingen with its close-knit inhabitants is the emblem. His intrusion seems to cause the decomposition of this Eden; in fact, the flaws that bring it down have always been present in the fictions of its perfection.

Carwin is the antithesis of Mettingen and of all that the retreat stands for—the familiar, reliable correspondence between characteristic and character, signifier and signified. Pleyel relates Carwin's chameleonlike transformation into a Spaniard and seems astonished that Carwin could so successfully change his appearance and his identity as to fool Pleyel himself. In the light of Pleyel's own shortcomings, his acumen in assessing character must not be overvalued.

Carwin's most crucial relationship—more crucial than the murky, one-sided relationship he strikes with Wieland—is the one with Clara. The importance of their initial meeting is central to the issues of ambiguity and language. Clara is the third to hear the mysterious voice. Her brother's report of his encounter with a mysterious voice thrills her. And Pleyel's testimony leads her to believe that the voice not only possesses infallible information, but is perhaps using this information to direct fate by removing her rival for Pleyel's attention. Thus is she prepared for a more crushing fall when Carwin enters, for she has begun to permit "voluntary" and "involuntary" to fraternize.

Clara, returning to her house, sees an ill-dressed vagabond in the neighborhood but thinks little more about him. Outsiders are rare in Mettingen, but not totally unknown. She sits out of sight of her front door when a man knocks and requests of her maid, Judith, a drink of water. The voice is so hypnotically attractive that Clara's awareness is completely drawn to it. She does not hear flirtatious badinage; she hears the voice of a romantic Heathcliffean figure. She constructs a character to be consistent with the voice: "My fancy had conjured up a very different image. A form, and attitude, and garb, were instantly created worthy to accompany such elocution; but this person was, in all visible respects, the reverse of this phantom. Strange as it may seem, I could not speedily reconcile myself to this disappointment" (p. 60). The sight of the actual speaker, the neighborhood vagabond, plunges Clara into a sudden anxiety, "a fit of musing" (p. 60).

Clara had construed a character from the evidence of one sense on the premise that characteristics—tone of voice, vocabulary, rank, class—are consistent with other characteristics under the rubric of the unity of character. Wieland and Pleyel operate under the premise of the stability of the character, the word, as well. Clara implies that this is a natural or "involuntary" law for the discovery of significance, for she uses the passive verb: "were instantly created." When the actual, Carwin, fails to coincide with the character Clara had construed, the ground beneath her construction vanishes, and she is left so "disappointed" that she is physically weakened. She finds herself caught in the game, as Derrida would say, not the toy of suppressed fantasies or "depraved" senses, but of the very language by which she is to know the difference between corrupted senses and truth. Clara experiences in this moment the "freeplay" in language and its precedence over meaning.

The imperative to interpret still holds, however. After Clara hears the mysterious voice, she presents us with a sample of her reasoning. At first she reasons that the evidence of her ear—a voice so close that it seems to originate from beside her on her pillow—is a mere figment, "some casual noise transformed into the voice of a human nature" (p. 65). This is recognizable as Pleyel's logical tack. With the second occurrence, however, Clara is not so steadfast. Threats of death and worse unseat her composure and she flees to her brother's house, fainting at his door. A voice rouses the men, Wieland and Pleyel, who find nothing in Clara's dwelling to explain the situation. Pleyel then consents to lodge there, but he is little comfort, for he ridicules Clara's fears.

Carwin's presence in the midst of the inward-facing Mettingen community illustrates its unnaturalness. The community tries to interpret him, to give him a character, unsuccessfully. Clara confesses that the more the community knows of Carwin, the less its members can say exactly who he is: "He afforded us no ground on which to build even a plausible conjecture" (p. 81). He is and remains a bundle of characteristics without a center.

Carwin explains that the voices heard by Wieland and Pleyel are probably imitations of Catharine's voice perpetrated by an unknown person (p. 85). The cry of help that brought Wieland and Pleyel to Clara's aid was uttered, Carwin says, by someone on the spot (p. 86). To each phenomenon Carwin gives an explanation which is not only plausible but, since he himself performs the actions, also "true." But his "mode of explaining" does not satisfy the Mettingen group, for whom (Clara explains) "it is such, perhaps as would commend itself as most plausible to the most sagacious minds, but it was insufficient to impart conviction to us" (p. 86).

Brown, by the simple series of incidents—the hearing and interpretation of a mysterious voice—maneuvers his innocents into the position of rejecting the plausible as "insufficient." They, unlike the putative villain, Carwin, have entered a state in which characteristics, sensory evidence, and "reality" itself are no longer significant, i.e., generative of meaning. They are now truly lost in a game of freeplay in which any sign may be substituted for any other, where the rigors of objective existence no longer exert any centering control. No resolution, no return to a steady state in which the true can be winnowed from the false, reality from appearance can be attained. Centeredness (certitude) is permanently subordinated to freeplay. Order is a fiction.

The climatic murders of the novel are presaged by an abortive attempt by the innocents to reimpose the lost order on their crumbling lives by rehearsing a play. The play would have furnished them with knowable characters, dialogue, a plot; there would have been few if any options to transform the play into something other than the text of it. Where there is text, there is order. But the rehearsal never occurs. Instead, events accelerate toward the decentering of Clara's consciousness when her brother appears and tries to attack her.

When Pleyel does not appear for the rehearsal, Clara breaks the cardinal rule of logical interpretation, (the maintenance of checks on freeplay) by speculating in advance of the facts. Impatient with the slow arrival of explanation, she rushes ahead with her own fancy. Pleyel, she imagines, has drowned. Although she is aware of the fanciful nature of her reverie, Clara nevertheless indulges in it. The "economist of pleasure" goes on something of an imaginative binge, casting rationality to the winds. She soon recognizes that her mind is operating beyond her willed control. But she surrenders all desire to regain control and follows the "train of reflections," or associations, which carries her out of the safe world in which freeplay is limited.

First she thinks of her father, whose memory she venerates, whose possessions are protected by her as "reliques" (p. 94). One of these mementoes is a narrative which Clara now desires to read for its ordered arrangement of a life. Once again a text is sought when order is failing. The manuscript is kept in her closet, but when she approaches this room the voice frightens her away. In a chaotic state Clara recalls the fitful dream in which she had perceived her brother on the opposite side of an abyss beckoning her to cross to his side. Why would she consider her brother, whom she worships as she does her father, as a threat to her safety? Fear of the anarchy of incest or the psychomoral transgression of narcissism have been offered as explanations.[15] But the arbitrary barrier erected by Emerson seems to offer a less controversial explanation. Father and brother have become conflated in Clara's mind; both have crossed the barrier into the realm of "involuntary perceptions." Clara still prefers the barrier, although she is swayed by the argument that involuntary acts of the mind might be as reliable as voluntary, and that seemingly involuntary perceptions (her dream) might in fact be voluntary on a level unknown to her. She hazards the generalization: "Ideas exist in our minds that can be accounted for by no established laws. Why did I dream that my brother was my foe?" (p. 99).

Morning brings some relief from the tangled and troubling "logic" of Clara's night. She hopes that a calmer explanation will be forthcoming from Pleyel. He, however, shocks her with accusations, based on his "evidence" of the previous night, of her assignation with Carwin. Clara's analysis of Pleyel's logic brings her close to "biloquism": she speculates that Carwin has trained another woman to imitate her voice (p. 126). She hazards a visit with Pleyel in order to reinstate logic, but the effort, as we have seen, miscarries because of his obtuseness.

Pleyel indicts Carwin as an "imp of mischief" (p. 140), a demonic and cunning improvisor whose "character," that sign by which he is to be known, is not a stable entity but a shifting bundle of appearances that he can and does alter at will. That Carwin alone, in carrying this improvisational "reality" to Mettingen, infects the unnatural paradise with the ordinary world, is the strong implication of Pleyel's news. It would be simple and even desirable to restore Mettingen by loading the blame for chaos on Carwin and thus brand the world as unnatural.

Clara, however, cannot completely resolve the story in this way. She begins to ponder a possible answer that is far more troubling since it admits of no resolution at all. Thinking of Pleyel's story, Clara, her sense of being wronged now becalmed, sees the situation from his point of view. "In what other way was it possible for him to construe these signals?" (p. 158) she asks herself, thus allowing the principle of multiple, but not complementary, explanations or interpretations of the same signals. The "perfect faith" that Emerson desired is thus thrown out of balance.

In the climactic scene of the novel Wieland threatens Clara. That Carwin rescues her underlines "freeplay" as a dominant issue and Carwin as its agent. Wieland tries to pile the guilt upon the intruder's shoulders, just as Pleyel had, calling Carwin a devil dispatched from hell to wreck the Arcadia of Mettingen. But the load topples with a fine ironic twist. Just after Wieland dismisses Carwin as an "incarnation of a demon" (p. 253), the demon returns in answer to Clara's prayer for rescue from her homicidal brother (p. 254). This "form," Carwin, exercising its power of improvisation, of freeplay, is both demon and angel, destroyer and rescuer.

IV

Three years later, purged by fire and harrowed by illness, Clara writes from Montpellier, France. She is regaining her health. Pleyel's intended, who was not dead, has since married him and then, incontrovertibly, died. The widower surfaces as Clara's suitor. Carwin, like Dick Diver, is out there in the expanse of the American hinterland, an inextinguishable spark of romance. Narrative loose ends are perfunctorily tied up.

There is, however, no resolution except on this level of the makeshift. Carwin's confession is not sufficient when it belatedly comes from him. He weakly says: "'I have acted, but my actions have possibly affected more than I designed'" (p. 220). There is no catharsis in this.[16] The presence of Clara's uncle, Thomas Cambridge, who supplies the Maxwell story, is also a makeshift device that only calls attention to its lameness. By the end of the novel we are persuaded that rational explanation is a necessary fiction, not a necessary reality, to which the straying Clara happily retreats for psychic survival.

The spreading freeplay and decentering of **Wieland** present "reality" as a fiction, the play of points of view, contending constructions, the inertia of the mind to stay in one groove of assumptions regardless of the "facts" (p. 61). Wieland's mind is tortured and eventually blasted by the great void where reality ought to have been in a centered universe and by his fatal impatience with freeplay. Clara is brought to the precipice, then retreats to tell her tale. The tale concerns the play of signals, the problematic nature of perception, the unstable character conventionally ignored by the use of proper names, the absence of the Word or cause as center of a knowable and structured universe. Without causes, adequate or not, the human consciousness is decentered and alienated, thrown into a game in which it is at stake.

The game of which Derrida speaks, so different from what we have been used to call ambiguity, never ends. Ends themselves, Kermode has suggested, are fictions,

respites, in the game.[17] Thus "ending" is one of our most desired yet impossible achievements. In such a playful condition is Clara Wieland when her narrative (she thinks) ends. She is back in Montpellier, France, in the Cevennes, the territory of the Camissards, whose text her father had "construed" in the beginning.

Notes

1. Northrop Frye, *Anatomy of Criticism* (1957; rpt. New York: Atheneum, 1968), pp. 304-5.

2. Charles Brockden Brown, *Wieland, or The Transformation,* ed. Fred Lewis Pattee (New York: Harcourt Brace Jovanovich, 1926). All references to *Wieland* are taken from this edition and will appear in parentheses in the text.

3. Donald Ringe, *Charles Brockden Brown* (New York: Twayne, 1966), pp. 48, 44.

4. Larzer Ziff, "A Reading of *Wieland,*" *PMLA,* 77 (March 1962), 51-57.

5. William Manly, "The Importance of Point of View in Brockden Brown's *Wieland,*" *American Literature,* 35 (Nov. 1963), 312.

6. Michael Davitt Bell, "'The Double-Tongued Deceiver': Sincerity and Duplicity in the Novels of Charles Brockden Brown," *Early American Literature,* 9 (Fall 1974), 144.

7. Michael Butler, "Charles Brockden Brown's *Wieland*: Method and Meaning," *Studies in American Fiction,* 4 (Autumn 1976), 127.

8. John Cleman, "Ambiguous Evil: A Study of Villains and Heroes in Charles Brockden Brown's Major Novels," *Early American Literature,* 10 (Fall 1975), 190-219; Mark Seltzer, "Saying Makes It So: Language and Event in Brown's *Wieland,*" *Early American Literature,* 13 (Spring 1978), 81-91.

9. Jacques Derrida, "Structure, Sign, and Play in the Discourse of the Human Sciences," in Macksey and Donato, eds., *The Structuralist Controversy* (Baltimore: The Johns Hopkins Univ. Press, 1972), pp. 247-73.

10. Frank Kermode, *The Sense of an Ending* (New York: Oxford Univ. Press, 1967), pp. 47, 50.

11. Ziff, p. 54.

12. Ringe, p. 28.

13. Ziff, p. 52.

14. Joseph A. Soldati, "The Americanization of Faust: A Study of Charles Brockden Brown's *Wieland,*" *ESQ,* 20 (First Quarter 1974), 13.

15. Ziff, p. 54, suggests incest. Joseph A. Soldati, throughout his essay, argues for combined Narcissistic and Icarian complexes.

16. William Manly, p. 321, asserts that catharsis does accompany Carwin's confession.

17. Kermode, p. 144.

Edwin Sill Fussell (essay date 1983)

SOURCE: Fussell, Edwin Sill. "*Wieland*: A Literary and Historical Reading." *Early American Literature* 18, no. 2 (fall 1983): 171-86.

[*In the following essay, Fussell suggests that Clara Wieland's struggle to produce the narrative of her family story parallels Brown's struggle to produce a new American literature.*]

> I entreated him to tell me . . . what progress had been made in detecting or punishing the author of this unheard-of devastation.
>
> "The author!" said he; "Do you know the author?"
>
> "Alas!" I answered, "I am too well acquainted with him. The story of the grounds of my suspicions would be painful and too long."[1]

Dark Transitions

Born January 17, 1771, in the proprietary colony of Pennsylvania, a presumably loyal subject of the crown; five years old when the American Revolution broke out; twelve years old when the Treaty of Paris was signed; eighteen years old when the Constitution was ratified: if not in 1776 or 1783 then certainly in 1789, Charles Brockden Brown underwent a change of political allegiance and was henceforth a citizen of the United States of America. Although his opinion or preference was never consulted in these matters, it is likely he thought about them, thought about them to most purpose when he was writing and publishing *Wieland; or The Transformation. An American Tale* in 1798. At some point during those twenty-seven nationally turbulent yet spectacularly developmental years he strangely had become a different person, as his patria ceased to be one comparatively clear thing and became quite another thing, not clear at all. Indubitably, there had been a transformation. He took the word for his first subtitle and his theme.

His second subtitle was also his theme, for of course he was engaged in the creation of an American literature—his need to define and embody the typifying communal experience of that new polity, to write the nation into an existence more deeply and genuinely constitutional than the merely assertive and legalistic, to give it a character, a personality, and a soul. What if on reflection it appeared as if an earlier generation of writers, the polemical patriots, as one might call them, had in very fact or inflamed fancy written a predecessor patria out of existence and what if it were the very patria Brown had been born to? Then the creation of the new literature must somehow depend on the destruction of the old patria, it must admit and assess the extent and the cost of that disallegiance, only then to incorporate that destructive knowledge and, with it, to move on. The new American writer must by birth and profession inhabit the old world and the new. To be an American he must have been transformed. Born into the Society of Friends, it must also have been second nature for Brown to ask how it was that the most glorious nation God ever shone his face at happened to commence in widespread hatred, mass murder, willful blindness, possible psychosis.

His ambivalences were many and in themselves doubtful, including a bit of the hysterical and paranoid bewilderment of those polemical patriots, with their mixed motives of *ad fontes* and stand-pat; his own mixed attitudes toward that precedent generation, which had altered his nationality for him and landed him in his present plight (whether they were to be thanked or cursed, they could hardly be ignored); was it by their doing that he now found himself in the odd position of asking for, and answering the call for, an American literature, when indeed there was no such thing, nor easy prospect of it, the best available models (the English) being anathema? It was a most quixotic undertaking.[2] The revolution was itself so literary in a sort—not his sort—that literature encapsulated the other dilemmas and might justly have been seen as the direct or indirect cause of them. The national agony in letters, and thus in national identity, was owing to writers, and Brown's particular agony was both the fault of the tribe and a unique problem of his own. Writing was the imaginable source of woe, yet still more writing was the only exit from woe. And so he wrote a diatribe against writing but within that context he split the indictment in order to show an irresponsible writer wreaking havoc and wretchedness on a hapless populace while quite another kind of writer—his kind—was quietly restoring a semblance of reason and peace to such of those people as chanced to survive. *Wieland* is a furious contest between villainous confused Carwin and our doughty daughter of the American Revolution, Clara Wieland, Brown's narrator. Clara wins, but the price of her victory is exile. Having finished her novel, she removes to Europe, never more to confront the monstrosity of these States.

An author so circumstanced as Brown could hardly avoid thinking of himself as tantamount to the historical process yet by no means in control of it. Especially in her guise as Columbian Fair, sufferer and inditer of the new American literature, Clara Wieland in her fictive torments is Charles Brockden Brown in his, and the language she lavishes on her situation can easily be applied to the author of her being:

My ideas are vivid, but my language is faint; now know I what it is to entertain incommunicable sentiments. . . . Yet I will persist to the end. My narrative may be invaded by inaccuracy and confusion; but if I live no longer, I will, at least, live to complete it. What but ambiguities, abruptnesses, and dark transitions, can be expected from the historian who is, at the same time, the sufferer of these disasters?

(P. 147)

Clara Wieland tells us that when her father died she was "a child of six years of age. The impressions that were then made upon me, can never be effaced" (p. 19). Clara's course runs nicely parallel with her creator's and they both run parallel with their broader constituency. Clara's lover, Pleyel, "urged, that to rely on the exaggerations of an advocate, or to make the picture of a single family a model from which to sketch the condition of a nation, was absurd" (p. 30), but it is just this exaggeration and absurdity upon which *Wieland* is constructed and from which it derives its wild yet public power. As Clara says, "How will your wonder, and that of your companions, be excited by my story! Every sentiment will yield to your amazement. If my testimony were without corroborations, you would reject it as incredible. The experience of no human being can furnish a parallel" (p. 6). The experience of Charles Brockden Brown can, and the experience of the youthful United States can. They are all three the same.

DEVILS AND DUPES

"Ventriloquism" is an old world but Brown had "biloquist" a decade before the *OED*.[3] "One who can speak with two different voices" naturally suggests moral obliquity, all the more as it is only one person who speaks, and it may also suggest a literary situation in which a newly nationalized writer must talk both English and American, using the same lexicon and syntax for roughly opposite, and even inimical, ends. The latter duality dates as far back as the revolutionary slang-whangers (Irving's and Paulding's term, in *Salmagundi*), especially those poetical satirists who concocted anti-British invectives in the metrical modes of Dryden and Pope. "'Yes, said I, this, it is plain, is no fiction of the fancy'" (p. 44). Indeed, it is not. It is literary history. "I have not formed this design upon slight grounds, and . . . I will not be finally diverted from it" (p. 49). Pleyel says the first and Clara the second. *Wieland* is full of helpful hints. After all, ventriloquism comes in two stages, the imitation of the voice and the physical (geographical) displacement of it, both stages making apt analogies with literary creation in the art of the novel. They are two stages of mimesis.[4] In addition to "ventriloquism" and "biloquism," these also are loaded words in *Wieland*: "narrative," "narrator," "tale," "plot," "writing," "audience," "war," and "author." (In the present essay, hardly a quotation but contains one or more of them.) Whether viva voce or by the pen, each

of the following is an "author": the grandfather Wieland, the Wieland father, the Wieland of the title, Pleyel, Carwin, and, encompassing all these as well as herself, Clara Wieland. Except for the first named, in Brown's novel each of them is reversibly an audience. Finally, in *Wieland* the vox humana and the scribal habit are perpetually being confounded. "'You saw me in the very act of utterance'" (p. 214), Carwin says to Clara, with more pertinence to theme than to any ordinary view of things.

Talkers and listeners, writers and readers, not only reverse but concatenate. "Such was my brother's narrative. It was heard by us with different emotions. Pleyel did not scruple to regard the whole as a deception of the senses" (p. 34).[5] On this occasion Carwin was first the narrator and Wieland was his audience but then Wieland becomes the narrator and Clara and Pleyel are his audience. Pleyel is also a narrator in his own right, in addition to being a secret audience (reader) of Clara's secret journal (about him). Perhaps for better reasons than we have supposed, the writer of the day is by the nature of his calling reclusive, or as the wife remarks in Crèvecoeur's *Letters From An American Farmer* (1782), "Let it be as great a secret as if it was some heinous crime. . . . I would not have thee, James, pass for what the world calleth a writer; no, not for a peck of gold, as the saying is."

Crèvecoeur's *Letters* and Brown's *Wieland* resemble each other in thematic progression from idyl through regrettable action to paradise lost—one view of the American Revolution, not necessarily Loyalist. "The storm that tore up our happiness, and changed into dreariness and desert the blooming scene of our existence, is lulled into grim repose," as Crèvecoeur has it. "How had my ancient security vanished!" (p. 60) is perhaps the briefest of Brown's many perorations on the modalities of pathos, and a good question. According to Huckleberry Finn, "That's the peculiarity of a revolution—there ain't anybody intending to do anything when they start in."[6] (Who is "anybody" and who are "they"?) It is plain enough what kind of view *Wieland* takes of incontinent authors and their instigations—a dim one. Clara expostulates to and about Carwin: "And thou, O most fatal and potent of mankind, in what terms shall I describe thee? What words are adequate to the just delineation of thy character? How shall I detail the means which rendered the secrecy of thy purposes unfathomable? . . . Let me tear myself from contemplation of the evils of which it is but too certain that thou was the author" (pp. 49-50). This is not the view of the author commonly found in English literature nor is it yet that fearful conservative distaste for the imagination (Scotch Common Sense philosophy) supposedly universal in American colleges and universities—Brown attended none of them—which is considered responsible for the dearth of imagination in our early national literature. Brown's view of literature in this novel is far worse than that, more inclusive, more realistic, purely American, distinctly a product of pos-trevolutionary backlash, composed in about equal parts of horror and contempt. By unholy cross with such attributes of omniscience as "the author of creation" and "the author of our being," the concept of author is raised to almost infinite powers but with no commensurate responsibility or benevolence. He is, in a word, the devil.

WRITERS AS THE BANE OF OUR EXISTENCE

According to *Wieland,* writers do not merely reflect and record the disasters of social disruption; they are positively the prime cause of it. No matter that he peddles his wickedness by voice rather than by pen, Carwin clearly stands in for the American writer in times not so very long ago when he was busy producing his diabolical revolution. Brown's attitude toward him is as threatened and disdainful as that of the farmer's wife in Crèvecoeur toward the whole lot of them. As Clara frames the charge with her customary vehemence: "His tale is a lie, and his nature devilish. As he deceived me, he likewise deceived my brother, and now do I behold the author of all our calamities!" (p. 216). The tone is biblical, prophetic, and angry; the word "author" recurs like clockwork.

Nor are disclaimers by way of intention of any use. The personages of Brown's fiction are strictly accountable for the results of their behavior, let their intentions be what they might, and this simplistic moral asperity is applied with special rigor to anyone engaged in the act of writing, or indeed of communicating by whatsoever means with other persons, the latter being held defenseless in a degree.[7] Carwin's extenuations are feeble bleats and are as quickly dismissed. "Had I not rashly set in motion a machine, over whose progress I had no controul, and which experience had shewn me was infinite in power? . . . This is the extent of my offenses'" (pp. 215-16). It is too much to be borne, the extent is so boundless. Men are supposed to be responsible for what they set in motion, all the more so as the machine—speech, writing, publication in any form—is indirect in operation. "'Carwin may have plotted,'" Clara's uncle tries to interpose, insouciant and reasonable, "'but the execution was another's'" (p. 161). Clara, herself a writer, will never be brought to agree. What she knows is that the writer will be held responsible for whatever the audience takes it into its sweet head to do. She will herself so hold, in continuous outrage. It avails Carwin no whit to mumble, "'I meditated nothing'" (p. 201). He is simply damned by virtue of damage irretrievably done. Few will fully share Brown's judgments of these matters but none will deny their necessitarian clarity and sweep.

It is all Clara can do to write about it. "Yet have I not projected a task beyond my power to execute? If thus, on the very threshold of the scene, my knees faulter and I sink, how shall I support myself, when I rush into the midst of horrors such as no heart has hitherto conceived, nor tongue related? I sicken and recoil at the prospect" (p. 49). Nearly all such remarks in *Wieland* may be understood, really must be understood, in various applications extending from the most limited to the most inclusive. The horrors from which Clara sickens and recoils are the family murders, or they are Carwin, the cause of them, or they are the American writer in his capacity as inflammatory revolutionist, or they are the problems of American literature *tout ensemble.* (Such readers as wish may still have Carwin as a ventriloquistical clown.)

Yet we must be equally mindful that Clara never ascribes to her own writing any such baleful effect on a potential audience as she so stridently ascribes to Carwin. And in his "Advertisement," or preface, Brown strikes a perfectly normal tone of self-confidence and self-esteem, touched with becoming modesty. "The following Work is delivered to the world as the first of a series of performances, which the favorable reception of this will induce the Writer to publish. His purpose is neither selfish nor temporary. . . . The incidents related are extraordinary and rare." Notably Brown capitalized "Work" and "Writer," asserted the purity and permanence of his achievement, and for good measure sent a copy crosstown to Thomas Jefferson, the vice president, with a long letter, which Jefferson answered briefly but politely.[8] As for the ambiguity of reference, there is something curiously reciprocal, maybe perverse, in the American writer answering his own demand for an American literature with an American Work or Works, and it may be the perversity of the situation that partly accounts for the unceasing animosity against Carwin. It is, as almost always, Clara crying out: "'O wretch! once more hast thou come? Let it be to abjure thy malice; to counterwork this hellish stratagem. . . . Testify thy innocence or thy remorse: exert the powers which pertain to thee, whatever they be, to turn aside this ruin. Thou art the author of these horrors! . . . I adjure thee, by that God whose voice thou hast dared to counterfeit'" (p. 227). It is not in the long run Carwin, however, but Clara who turns aside this ruin, she who exorcises the horrors of him by writing about them—by writing about his writing, as one might say. It is plain enough that Clara exists for us, as does Brown, only as she writes. "A few words more and I lay aside the pen for ever. . . . I have justly calculated upon my remnant of strength. When I lay down the pen the taper of life will expire: my existence will terminate with my tale" (p. 221). In that termination American literature is born. These are the birth pangs.

EXCHANGES OF WRITERS AND READERS, WITH SOME CULPABILITY OF THE AUDIENCE

Two generations earlier the grandfather, an unmoved mover, began it all. He was a composer, and he was a writer—gifted with a famous writer's name—and even yet Clara can hardly confront one of his ballads without its suggesting "a new topic in the horrors of war" (p. 55). "War" is one of those black-magic words of **Wieland** but it is not the French and Indian War that is in question but a worse one, closer to home.[9] The father emigrates to the American plantations and devotes his religious fanaticism to converting the Indians through Scripture, i.e., the written word: "[T]o disseminate the truths of the gospel among the unbelieving nations" (p. 10), which sounds innocuous until we remember how gullible some people are and wonder how it will be when Thomas Paine is scattering his atheistical fire-brands among our amber fields of grain. As father Wieland is also a writer, he constitutes one more splendid reason for disbelief in the whole train of unreliable narrators, especially as the American writer might be conceived—it must have been tempting in 1798—as having imported dangerous doctrine from Europe only in his mad success to export it back again. **Wieland** is a tissue of dubieties concerning causation: "There was somewhat in his manner that indicated an imperfect tale. My uncle was inclined to believe that half the truth had been suppressed" (p. 18). This is the father Wieland. He has written an autobiography that sounds like an early American masterpiece, idealized; in Clara's language, "the narrative was by no means recommended by its eloquence; but neither did all its value flow from my relationship to the author. Its stile had an unaffected and picturesque simplicity. The great variety and circumstantial display of the incidents, together with their intrinsic importance, as descriptive of human manners and passions, made it the most useful book in my collection" (p. 83).

That author's son, titular hero of **Wieland,** brother to Clara, is a chip off the old block, the new or proto-American through and through, madness multiplied. "His brain seemed to swell beyond its continent. . . . His words and motions were without meaning. . . . I beheld the extinction of a mind the most luminous and penetrating that ever dignified the human form. . . . I had not time to reflect in what way my own safety would be affected by this revolution, or what I had to dread from the wild conceptions of a mad-man. . . . Confused clamours . . ." (pp. 153-54). The diction is suggestive: "continent" and "without meaning" and "extinction" and "revolution." Out of these clamors the younger Wieland writes literally a criminal confession. Upon reading it, Clara (now audience, now speaker) tells us: "The images impressed upon my mind by this fatal paper were somewhat effaced by my malady. They were obscure and disjointed like the parts of a dream. I was desirous of freeing my imagination from this chaos" (p. 175). This document, which she does and does not wish to read, she calls a "tale" and a "narrative" (pp. 175, 176). Even its author admits that it will hardly be believed. This is the same he who at the beginning of **Wieland** was so "diligent in settling and restoring the purity of the text" (p. 24), the text being Cicero. Of him, Clara's uncle says to her, she for a while supposing him to mean Carwin, "'Thou art anxious to know the destroyer of thy family, his actions, and his motives. Shall I call him to thy presence, and permit him to confess before thee? Shall I make him the narrator of his own tale?'" (p. 162). Hearing Carwin's voice, and acting on it, Wieland was audience; now he is author to the shattered Clara, who doubles as audience and writer both.

The parade of narrators and auditors continues unabated. Pleyel, the lover she will lose and regain, literally takes notes on Clara his inamorata, even she so novelistically inclined, she so nationally representative: "'I was desirous that others should profit by an example so rare. I therefore noted down, in writing, every particular of your conduct. . . . Here there was no other task incumbent on me but to copy; there was no need to exaggerate or overlook, in order to produce a more unexceptionable pattern. . . . I found no end and no bounds to my task. No display of a scene like this could be chargeable with redundancy or superfluity'" (p. 122). Perhaps one reason he notes her down *in writing* is that she so often appears to partake not only of the American literary enterprise but of the republic itself. In that last passage she is referred to as a "scene." "'Here, said I, is a being, after whom sages may model their transcendent intelligence, and painters, their ideal beauty. Here is exemplified, that union between intellect and form, which has hitherto existed only in the conceptions of the poet'" (p. 121). Comparable remarks were frequently made about the Constitution, with its new institutions; like them, Clara was worth writing down; Pleyel sounds like an infatuated version of *The Federalist Papers*. "'I have marked the transitions of your discourse, the felicities of your expression, your refined argumentation, and glowing imagery; and been forced to acknowledge, that all delights were meagre and contemptible, compared with the audience and sight of you.'" Listening and looking are again conflated. "'I have contemplated your principles, and been astonished at the solidity of their foundation, and the perfection of their structure'" (pp. 121-22), and now she is just like a poem of some length. All this was written in the administration of John Adams.

Clara points out that Pleyel's narrative is in turn dependent on an antecedent telling, which in turn depends on the rather mindless susceptibilities of a previous audience. "Here Pleyel paused in his narrative, and fixed his eyes upon me. Situated as I was, my horror and astonishment at this tale gave way to compassion for the anguish which the countenance of my friend betrayed. I reflected on his force of understanding. . . . Carwin had constructed his plot in a manner suited to the characters of those whom he had selected for his victims"

(p. 133). Pleyel persists in being an arrant gull: "'I can find no apology for this tale. Yet I am irresistibly impelled to relate it. . . . Why then should I persist! yet persist I must'" (p. 134). He must, they all must, because of Charles Brockden Brown's unrelenting purposes. His is that kind of a world.

Clara not only composes the entire novel in a series of letters (chapters) lacking salutation or signature, but in it she tells of composing still another document, the secret tale of her abortive passion for Pleyel. "I was tempted to relinquish my design"—of returning to her house—"when it occurred to me that I had left among my papers a journal of transactions in short-hand. I was employed in this manuscript on that night when Pleyel's incautious curiosity tempted him to look over my shoulder. . . . I had regulated the disposition of all my property. This manuscript, however, which contained the most secret transactions of my life, I was desirous of destroying" (pp. 190-91). Not only does Pleyel look over her shoulder, but Carwin takes the key to her chamber, lets himself in, and reads the whole thing. Like Pleyel, he is a great admirer of the native American character, or muse, so bountifully burgeoning in young Clara: "'Your character exhibited a specimen of human powers that was wholly new to me. . . . I perused this volume with eagerness. The intellect which it unveiled, was brighter than my limited and feeble organs could bear. . . . You know what you have written. You know that in this volume the key to your inmost soul was contained. If I had been a profound and malignant imposter, what plenteous materials were thus furnished me of stratagems and plots!'" (pp. 205-06) Who but Charles Brockden Brown could conceive an imposter who was "profound"? Like nearly every other character in the novel, Carwin is an audience as well as an author, but he is a very immoral audience, specifically a peeping Tom and an eavesdropper. He is also a plagiarist, once removed: "'I exerted all my powers to imitate your voice, your general sentiments, and your language. Being master, by means of your journal, of your personal history and most secret thoughts, my efforts were the more successful'" (p. 210). If in the early years of the republic, writing was a most dangerous business, and reprehensible as well, reading was about as bad. They went together and were together suspect. The story of suspicions was painful and long.

Carwin as American Revolutionary And Post Revolutionary Writer

As given to us in Clara's narration, Carwin is first and foremost a voice, a sweet talker, and mighty irresistible. She reports his verbal advent in language suggesting the advent of the new American literature as well: "The words uttered by the person without, affected me as somewhat singular, but what chiefly rendered them remarkable, was the tone that accompanied them. It was

wholly new." It will never be easy to say in an old language (English) what the new tone is, but Clara patriotically plows ahead: "I cannot pretend to communicate the impression that was made upon me by these accents, or to depict the degree in which force and sweetness were blended in them. They were articulated with a distinctness that was unexampled in my experience." If Clara's description owes something—not much—to the traditions of sensibility, we will value its transcendence the more, here put to new uses, public, literary, historical. Clara goes on. "The voice was not only mellifluent and clear, but the emphasis was so just, and the modulation so impassioned, that it seemed as if an heart of stone could not fail of being moved by it. It imparted to me an emotion altogether involuntary and incontroulable. When he uttered the words 'for charity's sweet sake,' I dropped the cloth that I held in my hand, my heart overflowed with sympathy, and my eyes with unbidden tears" (pp. 51-52). Clara's reaction is vastly in excess of its cause, and once more it would seem that the Work or Works of literature are likely to be dangerous, lies and deception, wonderfully sweet, reducing the audience to abject debaucheries of pleasing emotion, with loss of reason, loss of will.

At first, Carwin seems the nearly ideal audience for "the tale" of "the inexplicable events that had lately happened" (p. 73), i.e., the death of the elder Wieland, but soon we find roles reversed, and the others are captive audience to his "disquisition," to his "narratives" ("all the effects of a dramatic exhibition"), and in general to "the exquisite art of this rhetorician." Yet even Clara in her admiration observes that "his narratives, however complex or marvellous, contained no instance sufficiently parallel to those that had befallen ourselves, and in which the solution was applicable to our own case" (pp. 74-75), as was so regularly complained of English fiction of the times by American literary patriots, especially such as were out of patience with republican women who swooned over dukes. Brown's fable manages to glance at nearly all the literary hopes and fears of that brusque but unconfident epoch. If *Wieland* were an allegory, it would be nonsense for Carwin to represent the American writer, in his worst badness, while at the same time bringing to mind the preposterous irrelevance of English literature. But in Brown's loose fable he can suggest all manner of thing, perhaps most how transitional the literary situation was, with the muse forever migrating to these shores, or about to, momentarily delayed, weary of wing, inevitable, and even so late as Whitman's "Song of the Exposition" (1871). Let Carwin be vague, multiple, forward looking. As Pleyel says to Clara: "'It would be vain to call upon Carwin for an avowal of his deeds. It was better to know nothing, than to be deceived by an artful tale'" (p. 127). Pleyel is promptly deceived by an artful tale. As a general rule, Carwin's victims are remarkably complicit in their own duping, and even Providence—

novelistic Providence—is made to conspire: "Carwin's plot owed its success to a coincidence of events scarcely credible. The balance was swayed from its equipoise by a hair" (p. 139).

Through the melodramatic rhetoric, Carwin enacts what seems to be Brown's conception of the revolutionary and even the post-revolutionary American writer, he who wrought great evil—but maybe in the fullness of time he will wreak some good—without quite willing it, by possessing powers whose extent neither he nor his audience might have understood in advance. Perhaps it was part of Brown's purpose to persuade a later audience, with these analogues of military and political events only a little while back, of the awesomeness of literary power in a society where the written word was so boundlessly on the march; perhaps he meant also to suggest a heightened moral responsibility on the part of himself and his fellows, whence benefit might yet evolve from sin, as in *Paradise Lost.* Culpable Carwin is a veritable model of literary laceration, a classic case against the dire effects of literature out of control, an exemplary enactment of late eighteenth-century American political and literary hysteria, culminating in the American Revolution, now slowly receding in the popular mind. "'I will fly. I am become a fiend, the sight of whom destroys. Yet tell me my offense! You have linked curses with my name; you ascribe to me a malice monstrous and infernal. I look around; all is loneliness and desert! . . . My fear whispers that some deed of horror has been perpetrated; that I am the undesigning cause. . . . My actions have possibly effected more than I designed. . . . I come to repair the evil of which my rashness was the cause, and to prevent more evil. I come to confess my errors'" (pp. 195-96). To whom Clara cries: "Wretch!" Continuing on, ever loquacious, righteously wronged, at the top of her bent: "Who was it that blasted the intellects of Wieland? Who was it that urged him to fury, and guided him to murder? Who, but thou and the devil, with whom thou art confederated?" (p. 196). She continues to vilify "the author of these dismal outrages" and he poorly replies: "'Wretch as I am, am I unworthy to repair the evils that I have committed? . . . I have deceived you: I have sported with your terrors: I have plotted to destroy your reputation. I come now to remove your errors; to set you beyond the reach of similar fears; to rebuild your fame as far as I am able.'" His best line is: "'All I ask is a patient audience'" (p. 197).

Whether or not Clara is in some of her permutations the young nation herself, it is surely that young nation, more or less represented by the Wieland family and what happens to them, that is most damaged by Carwin's acts of imitation. As in Crèvecoeur, it is not so much an individual who is outraged and devastated as it is an entire family, with suggestions of the countryside around. Carwin's is the true voice of the American bard

imposing his own exile for monstrous unspeakable crimes against the people, and it sounds as if he is talking about the American Revolution: "'I had acted with a frenzy that surpassed belief. I had warred against my peace and my fame: I had banished myself from the fellowship of vigorous and pure minds: I was self-expelled from a scene which the munificence of nature had adorned with unrivalled beauties, and from haunts in which all the muses and humanities had taken refuge'" (p. 211). He even seems to blend with the audience of the bard and is not only he who incites to violence but those incited. It is impossible to imagine Brown in 1798 or any other time an unreconstructed Loyalist, but it is easy to imagine him a good enough Quaker to wonder if that transformation from colonial to national condition might have been accomplished with less violence.

WRITING AND ACTION AND WRITING

For history, the inclusive point is that writing is both the cause and the effect of action; in this instance, the American Revolution was at least partly caused by writers, then that revolution, now won, necessitates an American literature to justify it and to ensure its fruits to posterity. There is plainly in **Wieland** just such a cause-effect-cause triad where Charles Brockden Brown in the process of helping create a national literature records in analogue how the opportunity and obligation of doing so arose from a war of rebellion induced by his literary precursors. It is rather a matter for definition, as there can hardly be an American literature, in the full sense of the term, until there is a United States of America. Historians of ideas notwithstanding, colonial American history is colonial American history.

With respect to the polemics of political uprisings, **Wieland** surely takes cognizance of the well-known fact that literary produce as a cause of war increases with the increase in the reading public—at least the violence is sooner likely to come to a boil. But as the audience is also more widely spread, so the more various and complex is likely to be the interplay between expression and physical action and the more various and complex the timing of these interactions, so that our awareness of the relations of history and literature (neither of them a simple cause of the other, nor a simple effect of some third cause, seldom specified, but locked in their reciprocities) must also be correspondingly more various and complex. In the new, comparatively democratic society, more and more persons were not only readers but writers, and literature was no longer the preserve or responsibility of a ruling class; then if guilt should come into question, as it certainly does in **Wieland** the guilt can be generously shared, which is maybe a comfort. With public rhetoric abounding, it must have been evident that the line between speaking and writing was increasingly blurred, the line between the political speech delivered orally to a small crowd and that same speech set in print and delivered up at large. Would that wider readership be more or less inflamed? Who could know ahead of time? Historians might be able to tell us later. Who would then be responsible? Everybody, if they wanted to live.

Fortunate as we are to have so revealing a document as **Wieland,** it seems the rankest folly to read it mainly as a Gothic novel or other divertissement in the annals of literary types. Spontaneous combustion, religious mania in a homicidal degree, ventriloquism—the topics are not especially American, they are not even topics of adult interest. It seems a terrible confession of weakness in historical reasoning to define the field of American literature in political terms, precisely in terms of the break with the parent country, followed by the desire to create an independent culture, primarily in literature, the most accessible of the arts for a new nation, and then go looking for the evidence in the junkyards of universal infantilism, psychologically or existentially construed. **Wieland** is more important to us than that. It is conceivably the major literary landmark between the Declaration of Independence and the appearance of *The Pioneers* by James Fenimore Cooper in 1823, and the reasons for its importance must be of the same order as the claim. What is hardest to grasp, yet at the heart of the rest, is that in **Wieland** Charles Brockden Brown was writing about writing, including his own, i.e., about that American literature not yet in existence but coming into existence as he confronted and incorporated the stiffest resistance imaginable, his own impossibility. It sounds more Alexandrine than it is, human achievements, both individual and collective, so conspicuously effectuating themselves in present actions that look to the future at the same time as they ride the waves of the past, and all in one unitary mode.

Notes

1. Charles Brockden Brown, *Wieland and Memoirs of Carwin the Biloquist,* ed. S. W. Reid, Sydney J. Krause, and Alexander Cowie, Bicentennial Edition (Kent, Ohio, 1977), p. 160; quotations will hereafter be cited parenthetically in the text.

2. It may be further quixotism to attribute the shortcomings of early American literature to subservience to such imports as sentimentality, Gothicism, or Scotch Common Sense philosophy. Early American literature is its own sufficient cause.

3. Ventriloquism further appears in the fragmentary "Memoirs of Carwin the Biloquist" (1803-05) (*Wieland,* pp. 252-53, 259). Also of special interest are Brown's variations in formula, as "my biloquial faculty" (p. 259), "my bivocal projects" (p. 276), "my bivocal faculty" (p. 284), and "some bivocal agency" (p. 308). Ventriloquism, but with-

out the American literary theme, is in *Arthur Mervyn; or Memoirs of the Year 1793,* ed. Sydney J. Krause, S. W. Reid, Norman S. Grabo, and Marvin L. Williams, Jr., Bicentennial Edition (Kent, Ohio, 1980), p. 194, and in *Ormond; or the Secret Witness,* ed. Ernest Marchand (New York, 1937), pp. 95-96. These two novels were published in 1799 and 1799-1800, respectively.

4. Ventriloquism as a mode of imitation is strenuously discussed in a chapter called "Animal Magnetism" by James Fenimore Cooper in *Gleanings in Europe; France,* ed. Robert E. Spiller (New York, 1928).

5. "This scene of havock was produced by an illusion of the senses. Be it so: I care not from what source these disasters have flowed; it suffices that they have swallowed up our hopes and our existence" (p. 233). But no more than Scotch Common Sense philosophy is Lockean psychology the subject of *Wieland.* It is a condition of the subject.

6. "Tom Sawyer's Conspiracy," in *Hannibal, Huck & Tom,* ed. Walter Blair (Berkeley, Calif., 1969), p. 168.

7. It is not only in sentimental novels of seduction that the nubile young are led astray; our highly rationalistic Clara also succumbs. "The impulses of love are so subtile," she reasons, "and the influence of false reasoning, when enforced by eloquence and passion, so unbounded, that no human virtue is secure from degeneracy" (p. 241). Neither is all degeneracy sexual, any more than all eloquence and passion are spent in the pursuit of erotic happiness. Thus Carwin is "the grand deceiver" but he is also "the author of my peril . . . the author of this black conspiracy; the intelligence that governed in this storm. Some relief is afforded in the midst of suffering, when its author is discovered or imagined; and an object found on which we may pour out our indignation and our vengeance" (pp. 189-90). Author, author, author—it is all his fault, and always.

8. Both letters are in David Lee Clark, *Charles Brockden Brown: Pioneer Voice of America* (Durham, N.C., 1952), pp. 163-64.

9. "These events took place between the conclusion of the French and the beginning of the revolutionary war" ("Advertisement"). The statement is plausible only if taken to mean that one war leads to another, with private disasters in between. In the text proper, there are echoes of a war actually going on, and the only question is, which one? "The Indians were repulsed on the one side, and Canada was conquered on the other" (p. 26) is diversionary or maladroit, for it is hard to know how "furnishing causes of patriotic exultation" to the Brit-

ish Empire fits "An American Tale." In the same passage, Brown refers to "revolutions and battles." There were no revolutions in the French war but in 1798 the American Revolution was still active—violently so—in Brown's imagination.

Alan Axelrod (essay date 1983)

SOURCE: Axelrod, Alan. "New World Genesis, or the Old Transformed." In *Charles Brockden Brown: An American Tale,* pp. 53-96. Austin: University of Texas Press, 1983.

[*In the following essay, Axelrod examines possible old world and new world sources for several of the characters and narrative elements in* Wieland.]

James Yates, known to the community of Tomhannock, New York, as a naturally gentle man, industrious, sober, and kind, threw his Bible into the fireplace, deliberately demolished his own sleigh, killed his wife, his four children, and his horse shortly after nine on a December evening in 1781. That afternoon, a Sunday, there being no church nearby, several neighbors had gathered at Yates's house to read Scripture and sing psalms. So cordial were his spirits that he persuaded his sister and her husband to remain until nine, long after the others had left. They engaged in serious, interesting, and affectionate conversation, Yates addressing his wife in more than commonly endearing terms. He spoke of his happy home and of how, tomorrow, he would treat his wife to a sleigh ride as far as New Hampshire. Before his sister and her husband left, they all sang one more hymn.

Upon his capture and interrogation Yates told how he took his wife upon his lap and opened the Bible to read to her. Their two sons, a five-and a seven-year-old, were in bed. Eleven-year-old Rebecca sat by the fire, while the baby, a daughter aged six months, slumbered at her mother's bosom.

"Instantly a new light shone into the room," and two Spirits appeared before Yates, one at his right and the other at his left. The latter bade him "destroy all his *idols,* beginning with the Bible." Although the Spirit at his right hand attempted to dissuade him, Yates obeyed the first, calling it his "good angel," and cast the book into the flames. Bolting from her husband's lap, Mrs. Yates snatched the Bible from the fire, but before she had time to utter a word, Yates threw it in again, holding his wife fast until the book was completely consumed.

Seizing an axe, Yates ran out the door and broke up his sleigh. He ran to the stable and killed one horse, striking another, which, however, escaped. When he returned to the house to tell his wife what he had done, the "good

angel" reappeared: "You have more idols, (said he) look at your wife and children." Without a moment's hesitation, Yates ran to the bed of his two sons, caught the older one up in his arms and threw him against the wall with such force that he "expired without a groan." He next seized the younger boy by the feet and dashed his "skull in pieces against the fireplace" before the child could even awaken.

Seeing that his daughter and wife had fled with the baby, Yates again took up his axe "in pursuit of the living." His wife was running with the baby to her father's house half a mile away. Yates called to her, but she only screamed, redoubling her pace. Within thirty yards of her, Yates hurled his axe, gashing the woman's hip and causing her to drop the baby girl. Gathering the infant in his own arms, Yates threw her against a log fence. He had now lost sight of his wife, though the track her bleeding hip left in the snow was easy enough to follow.

Within eyeshot of her father's house—inexplicably— she turned and ran across an open field back to Yates's own door, whereupon all her husband's *natural feelings*" welled up within him: "Come then, my love (said I) we have one child left, let us be thankful for that— what is done is right—we must not repine, come let me embrace you—let me know that you do indeed love me." With that, she embraced Yates in her "trembling" arms, pressing her "quivering" lips to his cheek.

"This is also an idol!" a voice spoke behind him, and breaking instantly from her, Yates wrenched a stake from the garden fence. He leveled her with a single stroke. Realizing that the blow might only have stunned her, he struck again and again until he himself could not recognize one feature of her face.

Then he heard moans and sobbing coming from the barn. It was Rebecca, who begged her father's mercy so affectingly that once again *natural pity*" took possession of Yates. He thought now "that to destroy *all* my idols, was a hard task." So, taking her by the hand, he asked her to sing and dance for him. And while she danced and sang, Yates pondered: this pity and these feelings were not "in the line of my duty." Convinced of his momentary error, he caught up a "hatchet that stuck in a log." Presently, Rebecca's forehead was "cleft in twain."

Theodore Wieland's ritual murder of his family had its genesis in the James Yates tragedy. Brown suggested in his prefatory "Advertisement" to **Wieland** that "most readers will probably recollect an authentic case, remarkably similar to that of Wieland." As early as 1801 a reviewer recognized this as an allusion to the murders in Tomhannock, a case (Carl Van Doren concluded in a 1914 article for *The Nation*) indeed familiar to Brown's contemporary readers. Perpetrated in 1781, the Yates atrocity was not news by July of 1796 when it first reached print as a complete account in *The New York Weekly Magazine.* However, it did excite sufficient interest among the public to merit reprinting a month later in the *Philadelphia Minerva.*[1]

In his *Nation* article, Carl Van Doren cataloged enough parallels between the Tomhannock and *Wieland* tragedies to confirm the 1801 reviewer's speculation that the actual case had inspired the fictional one. In addition to the generally parallel situations of "divinely inspired" murder, *Wieland* shares with the Yates atrocity such details as the murderer's extended confession, a wife killed with her four children (two boys and two girls—the baby, in each case, a girl), and the mangling of a corpse beyond recognition (Yates's wife and Wieland's foster-daughter Louisa Conway). Both Yates and Wieland protest their innocence not of the deed, but of crime, insisting that they obeyed the will of a superior Being. Both are cast into dungeons and loaded with chains: Yates escapes twice and is recaptured, while Wieland also twice escapes and is twice retaken, only to escape a third fatal time. Wieland attempts after his third escape to kill Clara, as Yates had attempted to kill his sister immediately after the slaughter of his wife and children.[2]

An outline Brown apparently drew up shortly before the composition of *Wieland* reveals the influence of the Yates murders in even greater detail than the finished novel.[3] We first note that, in the outline, Theodore is called Charles, and, like James Yates, he has a wife and four children. Like the Theodore of the finished novel, he also has an adopted daughter. His conversation with his family on the night he kills them is "affectionate, solemn, foreboding misfortune," as Yates's conversation had been "grave . . . but interesting and affectionate." At midnight Charles hears "vocal sounds" and sees a "light" and a "figure," much as "a new light [had] shone into the room" when Yates looked up to behold "two Spirits." The "figure" Charles sees "forewarns against Idolatry"—echoing the idol motif that is very much a part of the Tomhannock murders, although absent at least in explicit form from *Wieland.* Then Charles (433):

. . . Destroys 1 some favourte [*sic*] ⁱⁿ⁻animate object. an organ.

	2. greyhound.	
		200.
	3. children 2.	
omen	4. ~~Wife~~ Ward.	
Command	5. ~~Ward~~ Wife.	
Repugnan[c]e	6. Sister.	

Resolute
~~Interval of~~
Repenting

Yates had conducted himself similarly, destroying (1) his sleigh, (2) a horse, (3) two children, (4) his infant daughter and his wife, and (5) his older daughter. He ended (6) by attempting to murder his sister. Twice Yates faced his "Command" with "Repugnan[c]e" and had intervals of at least near repentance. But he is finally and fatally "Resolute."

More significant than the details Brown drew from the account of the Yates atrocity is the central thematic concern *Wieland* shares with the Tomhannock murders; these murders, like Brown's novel, dramatically manifest the complex effects of New World extremity. *Wieland* bears two subtitles. The first, "The Transformation," reflects the horrible change Theodore (like Yates) suffers, turning from a civilized, gentle family man to, from all appearances, a monster. What we shall be exploring now is how this transformation reflects the national environment and culture: the "American Tale" that is the second subtitle.

James Yates, the Charles Wieland of Brown's outline, and Theodore Wieland in the finished novel each delivers, upon capture, confessional narratives aimed at justifying the transformation they have undergone. James Yates exhibits nothing but contempt for his accusers. After coolly relating his deeds, he refuses "to confess his error or *join* in prayer," praying instead to a deity he addresses as "Father": "My father, thou knowest that it was in obedience to thy commands, and for thy glory that I have done this deed." This seems to have impressed Brown, who, in sketching Charles's confession, elaborated upon Yate's contempt, particularly emphasizing its intellectual ramification:

> Thou, omnipotent & holy! Thou wast the prompter of my deed. My hands were but the instruments of thy will. I know not what is crime. Of what action caused [?] evil is the ultimate result. Thy knowledge as thy power is reverenced[?]. I lean[?] upon thy promise I cheearfully [*sic*] sustain the load of pain of [infaming] hatred wh[ich] erring [?] men lay upon me. In thy arms of thy protection I entrust my safety. In the fullness of thy justice I confide for my reward.

Charles now addresses judge and jury:

> You say that I am criminal, Presumptuous man! Thou deservest that the arm of righteous [?] vengeance should crush thee. Thus impiously to usurp the prerogative of thy creator! To count thus rashly on the comprehension of thy views: on the fall [frail?] pervading property of thy foresight!
>
>   (437)

Having acted at what he believes the behest of God, Charles sees himself placed far above the faulty "comprehension" and "foresight" of presumptuous mankind. While much of Charles's outline confession finds its way into *Wieland* substantially unchanged (see pp. 176-

7), the intellectual significance of revelation is further developed in the finished novel. Theodore Wieland's religious mania is depicted as the result of an intellectual errand, a quest for absolute truth. Theodore testifies:

> My days have been spent in searching for the revelation of [God's] will; but my days have been mournful, because my search failed. I solicited direction: I turned on every side where glimmerings of light could be discovered. I have not always been wholly uninformed; but my knowledge has always stopped short of certainty.
>
> (165)

Having isolated the intellectual dimension of the Yates-Wieland murders, we may decide that they are not so much "American" as biblical. It is as if both Brown *and* Yates had drawn upon Genesis, the twenty-second chapter, in which Abraham, hearing the voice of God command the sacrifice of his son Isaac, obeys, like Yates and Wieland, without hesitation. Abraham puts aside the dictates of what James Yates called "natural feelings" (for Isaac is his only son, whom he loves) in obedience to what he perceives as an absolute truth transcending them. It is this leap of faith, of course, that inspired the epistemological fable Søren Kierkegaard, in *Fear and Trembling,* embroidered upon Genesis, chapter 22. The self, a vessel of "natural feelings," is itself the means through which the absolute truth of God's command contrary to those feelings must be apprehended. Like Abraham, Yates and Wieland believe implicitly in their ability to apprehend divine truth. The transformation from loving husband and father to murderer they see as a transformation from the state of fallible mortality motivated by the relative truths of nature to an infallible state of divinity as agent of God's truth. Pondering the mortal consequences of his divine deed, Yates for a moment considers dragging all the dead into his house, setting it afire, and attributing the carnage to Indian massacre. "I was preparing to drag my wife in, when the idea struck me that I was going to tell a *horrible lie*; and how will that accord with my profession [that the killings were an act of divine truth]? . . . No, let me speak the truth, and declare the good motive of my actions, be the consequences what they may" (28). Absolute truth must not be pleaded with lies before the relative justice of men.

The manner in which the Abraham and Isaac story became an American tale is complex, likely involving more than the direct use of "native" materials. This we shall examine presently; but first, and more simply, we should observe that Brown's version of the biblical episode is a grotesque criticism of the intellectual blindness behind the Abrahamic leap of faith. This critical view is abetted by—may even have been inspired by—the extremity of wilderness life. Although Brown may have been familiar with Michel Guillaume Jean de Crèvecoeur's observation that vast wilderness space fosters among Americans a (healthy) "religious indifference" because zeal cannot be transmitted over any great distance,[4] the novelist would have seen that, in the case of James Yates, precisely such wilderness conditions nurtured fanatic notions. Yates's Tomhannock, remote from city and established church (Yates was accustomed to conducting impromptu services himself) concentrated in itself the newness of the New World. Yates's act, like Theodore Wieland's, was born of that world, a wilderness isolated from the emotionally and intellectually tempering influence of city civilization and organized religion. Their immediate environment helped make antinomians of Yates and Wieland, each of whom is convinced that he enjoys an original relation to the absolute.

If the wilderness offers nothing to check a misguided leap of faith, it does, ironically, provide a model after which the tragic consequences of the leap may be fashioned. The blackest irony of James Yates's action is that in performing what he sees as God's will he commits an atrocity worthy of the stereotyped "godless" American Indian. His project of slaughter bears more than a casual resemblance to a particular account of Indian atrocity written by a young gentlewoman named Ann Eliza Bleecker. Her *History of Maria Kittle* ("A Pathetic Story Founded on Fact")[5] was popular enough to go through two printings before 1800. Set in Tomhannock, the hometown both of Mrs. Bleecker and of James Yates, the story relates with pornographic zeal the lurid details of cruelties practiced by Indians upon Maria and her household. The Indians attack primarily with their "tomahacks," cleaving in twain as handily as Yates the foreheads of their victims. Not content with a single deadly stroke, they beat their victims' corpses beyond recognition. Maria's pregnant sister-in-law falls victim to a "tomahack" blow between her eyes:

> Her fine azure eyes just opened, and then suddenly closing for ever, she tumbled lifeless at [her attacker's] feet. His sanguinary soul was not yet satisfied with blood; he deformed her lovely body with deep gashes; and, tearing her unborn babe away, dashed it to pieces against the stone wall.
>
> (35-6)

The Indian's "tomahack" can be readily recognized in the axe Yates uses to destroy his sleigh, kill his horse, and wound his wife, before battering her lifeless face beyond recognition with a fence stake. The hatchet he drives between his daughter's eyes is even more closely identifiable with the Indian weapon. (The word is of French origin, but the *OED* indicates that *hatchet* was almost automatically associated with the Indian by the end of the eighteenth century.) When he does not resort to hatchet, axe, or fence stake, Yates dashes members of his unfortunate family against the nearest wall or fireplace. Recall, too, that after he surveyed the slaughter,

Yates contemplated blaming it on Indians, as if to certify the completion of his "savage" transformation.

As a group of phenomena, the Yates case, *Maria Kittle,* and *Wieland* do not so much represent a chain of influence as they do a web of culture. Mrs. Bleecker might have drawn the violence of *Maria Kittle* directly from examples of Indian hostility in upstate New York; or she may even have modeled her book's violence on the crime of her white Tomhannock neighbor, who proved himself so precocious a student of Indian-style mayhem. Beyond doubt, Mrs. Bleecker knew Yates and knew of the murders. Bound with *Maria Kittle* in Bleecker's *Posthumous Works* (1793) is a letter dated December 1781 to Miss Susan Ten Eyck, the person to whom the epistolary *Maria Kittle* also is addressed. "JAMES YATES," Mrs. Bleecker writes, "a few nights ago murdered his wife, four children" and (as she reports it) more than one horse as well as a cow. Mrs. Bleecker further remarks that "by all appearances [Yates] is a religious lunatic" (151). Though she forbears to relate to Miss Ten Eyck the particulars "of cruelty too horrid to mention" (unwonted reticence from the author of *Maria Kittle!*), she had apparently seen Yates at close quarters after the murders. The *New York Weekly Magazine* account of the murders mentions that after his capture Yates was held some time at the house of a "Mrs. B-----r," and a year after the murder a "Mr. Bl-----r" (note that there are enough blanks for the "eecke") sent some fruit to Yates in his Albany "dungeon."

We may speculate on how conscious Brown was of the profound implications of the Yates story when he appropriated it for *Wieland.* Did he realize, consciously and articulately, that Yates had partaken of that "eucharist" Richard Slotkin described, the act betokening New World transformation through "communion" with the wilderness? Brown does make Clara Wieland say, after she has read the first part of her brother's confession, that Theodore's deed "was worthy of savages trained to murder, and exulting in agonies" (174). Advised to leave the country because Theodore will not rest until he has killed her along with the others, Clara protests: "I live not in a community of savages; yet, whether I sit or walk, go into crouds, or hide myself in solitude, my life is marked for a prey to inhuman violence" (189). The white residents of James Yates's Tomhannock were entitled to similar protests, no doubt. But the town's very name sounds like "tomahack."

While the evidence is very convincing that Brown was familiar with the Tomhannock murders and used them in *Wieland,* Edwin Fussell suggests that the book also owes a debt directly to *Maria Kittle.*[6] And it is true not only that the *Posthumous Works* of Mrs. Bleecker were published by T. and J. Swords, the firm that was to print much of what Brown wrote, but also that Ann Eliza's nephew, Anthony Bleecker, was a member with

Brown of the intimate New York Friendly Club.[7] In this manner Brown must have found himself caught up in a complex web of influences that made up the conditions of existence in his nation and that caught him up in the writing of an American tale. Brown's outline for *Wieland* suggests that he was not moved to compose his tale directly. The invention of an American Abraham proceeded along a circuitous route, apparently, via Yates and *Kittle,* the Bible, of course, but also through Europe in the form of a minor poem by the novel's namesake, Cristoph Martin Wieland. By recalling what Brown told John Bernard about his habits of composition, how literary ideas worked in his mind unbidden and practically divorced from consciousness, and by examining the outline for *Wieland,* we can speculate on how the novelist wove the variegated strands of multiple influence into the fabric of his book.

Preceding Brown's outline proper are columns of more than one hundred names, among which we recognize Conway, Bedloe, Lorimer, Dudley, Pleyel, Edny, Wyatte, Inglefield, Carwin, and Welbeck as characters in Brown's fiction. Not "Wieland," but "Weyland" appears twice in the list. "Weiland" occurs in a shorter list near the end of the outline, and "Wieland" appears twice in a list of book titles. The columns are a quarry sufficient to supply a dozen novels with character names. We know from Elihu Hubbard Smith's diary that Brown was fond of drawing up plans and programs for literary projects, and perhaps the name lists were part of such a plan. Indeed, following the names in the outline is a list of titles, quite possibly drawn up as a prospectus for a literary career:

Sky-walk, or the man unknown to himself

Wieland, or, the Transformation

~~Carwin~~. or [subtitle obliterated]

Bedloe. or the self devoted

Gower, or The dead recalled

More remarkable is this catalog of themes found at the end of the outline:

Tales. passions poutrayed.
Hallucination
    ulation

Somnamb.	Mimicry
person. Simil	~~personal Similitude~~
Melanaema*	
Hallucinat.	Ventriloquizm
Love of Country	Dissimulation

*Melanaema: "A condition of suffocation in which the blood throughout the body assumes a dark or black color" (*OED*).

Although a penchant for drawing up lists and literary programs tends to contradict the impression of spontaneous composition Brown conveyed to Bernard, the lists themselves exhibit a kind of "automatic" writing. They are neither systematic nor wholly random. Such alliterative clusters as "Barwell / Bertrand / Carew / Caster" occur frequently and even suggestions of imperfect rhyme, as in "Heene / Mayne." "Welbeck" follows "Beckworth," and the sound of "Car" seems particularly to have appealed to Brown:

Carrington		Caring
Carling, —		Carey.
Charlton,		Carton.
Carlingford.		Carford.
Carlington.		—Carfield
Carbourg.		
		Carobury
Carsey		
		Carlosteen
Carlette.	Carney	
Carwin.	Carhill	
Carrell.	Carlhurst	
Cardale.		
Carville.		
Carhuyson.		
Carry.		
Carborough.		

One of the names Brown recorded struck in him a conscious intellectual chord. The "Weyland" of the name list is transformed into the title list's "Wieland," a name familiar to Brown (and to most of literary America and Europe) as that of an enormously popular and influential German pre-Romantic poet.[8] Early in his novel (7), Brown has Clara Wieland acknowledge her family's literal kinship with Christoph Martin Wieland (1733-1813). Best known to Brown and his contemporaries as the author of the epic poetic fantasy *Oberon* and several novels, Wieland appealed to Brown (and to many another nascent Romantic) for both aesthetic and political reasons. Attuned to the ideas of Rousseau and Godwin, C. M. Wieland was also an intellectual idealist whose Platonism was filtered through Shaftesbury. One student of the poet's work sees his career as a "continual struggle for certitude, for the right answers," suggesting further that "epistemology is the key to a deeper understanding of Wieland's personality and accomplishments."[9] Given what we have already determined about Brown's place in the intellectual tradition of the American novel, it is little wonder that the novelist's freely flowing thoughts should have paused at Wieland's name. For Brown, like Christoph Martin Wieland—and Theodore Wieland, like his German namesake—was engaged in continual struggle for certitude.

At least two other German sources—Friedrich Schiller's *Der Geisterseher* and an imitation of it by Cajetan

Tschink, bearing the same title—also probably figured in the composition of *Wieland*;[10] but an early effort of Christoph Martin Wieland seems to have exerted the greatest influence. *Der Gepryfte Abraham,* a minor verse epic retelling the Abraham and Isaac story, appeared in 1754 and was translated into an English prose version, *The Trial of Abraham,* issued by the Norwich, Connecticut, press of John Trumbull in 1778. Like *Wieland, The Trial of Abraham* is to a large extent an intellectual elaboration upon Genesis, chapter 22, probing the psychological and moral consequences of absolute obedience born of absolute faith. Like Theodore Wieland and James Yates, C. M. Wieland's Abraham consciously subdues "natural affection" to the command of divine will. Natural affection is real, but revealed truth transcends it. While C. M. Wieland's Abraham pondered God's awful command, "his musing soul in a scale of speculation ascended from truth to truth, till it brightened up, that every painful sentiment dissolved in the radience [*sic*] of inspired wisdom."[11] Still, like Yates and Theodore, Abraham consciously has to suppress the immediate promptings of nature. In order to achieve certitude a man must attain the realm of pure thought, which (in C. M. Wieland's Platonic cosmogony) is the realm of God. "Silence, Nature," bids the loving father of Isaac. "My will is dedicated to God" (35).

There is a striking psychological and intellectual similarity not only among *The Trial of Abraham,* *Wieland,* and the Yates atrocity but also among the physical phenomena associated with the moment of "divine" revelation in each case. James Yates reported the presence of "a new light" as the two "Spirits" appeared before him. The display to which C. M. Wieland treats his Abraham is more spectacular:

> And now a sudden effulgence diffuses itself over the hill, and with increasing radiancy, like a cloud of light, moved through the azure sky: Abraham lifted up his eyes, felt the presence of the Deity; an angel, by God's intuitive [?] command, descended invisible, to strengthen the patriarch's eyes: At one look, for only of one is the human soul capable, he saw the divine glory through inconceivable ranks of adoring angels, between them Jehovah inthroned on cherubs; celestial scene, which verbal description would obscure!
>
> (3)

None of this is present in the austere description of the scene in Genesis, chapter 22; however, most of the elements C. M. Wieland includes are also to be found in Theodore Wieland's confession. He tells the court how he entered his sister's house, its total darkness requiring caution in descending the stairs. As Theodore reached for the balustrade—

> How shall I describe the lustre, which, at that moment, burst upon my vision!
>
> I was dazzled. My organs were bereaved of their activity. My eye-lids were half-closed, and my hands withdrawn from the balustrade. A nameless fear chilled my

veins, and I stood motionless. This irradiation did not retire or lessen. It seemed as if some powerful effulgence covered me like a mantle.

As with Abraham's vision, the revelation is too intense to be borne by mortal senses.

> I opened my eyes and found all about me luminous and glowing. It was the element of heaven that flowed around. Nothing but a fiery stream was at first visible but, anon, a shrill voice from behind called upon me to attend.
>
> I turned: It is forbidden to describe what I saw: Words, indeed, would be wanting to the task. The lineaments of that being, whose veil was now lifted, and whose visage beamed upon my sight, no hues of pencil or of language can pourtray.
>
> (167-8)

For Theodore Wieland, as for the German poet's Abraham, the experience of the absolute is beyond words.

Whatever the order in which Brown read *The Trial of Abraham* and read about Yates, it is the American situation—and Brown's own deepest ambivalent response to it—that drew Abraham and Isaac, Christoph Martin Wieland, Theodore Wieland, and James Yates together. Indeed, despite its remote origins in the German poet's fatherland and in the biblical land of Moriah, *The Trial of Abraham* employs the very epistemological metaphor most immediately available to the American writer. On the eve of the day appointed for his sacrifice, Isaac relates to Abraham and Sarah an adventure that befell him and his friend Abiasaph in the wilderness of Haran. The youths, wandering along the frontier, spy a beautiful bird, its song the sweetest music, its wings a rainbow. Isaac would capture it as a present for Ribkah (Rebecca, his future wife), and with Abiasaph he follows the bird into the forest. Oblivious to all but the gorgeous bird, they are soon lost. Worse, they wander into the domain of Tidal and Gog, grandsons of Nimrod, who plan to sacrifice the youths to their god Adramelech. There is little hope, until Elhanan, Isaac's guardian angel, intervenes, rescuing both young men.

Isaac and Abiasaph's adventure in the wilderness, far more a product of C. M. Wieland's imagination than of the Old Testament, is crucial to the poet's intellectual reinterpretation of the Abraham and Isaac story. The bird that the boys blindly follow is a metaphor of sublunary sensual reality. Lured by "too much love to God's creatures" (in both his attraction to the bird and to Ribkah, for whom the bird is intended), Isaac forgets himself and is lost in the creature's realm, a chaos of sensuality ruled by a deity who, appropriately, demands actual, physical sacrifice, rather than the ideal, symbolic sacrifice finally enjoined by Abraham's God. The moral of the parable is found in Abraham's words to Sarah as he and Isaac embark for Moriah: "Yet, oh guard thine heart, lest too much love to God's creatures insensibly stifle the thoughts of God" (30). Intellectually considered, the wilderness of *The Trial of Abraham* is a version of Plato's cave. By no means is Brown's American wilderness so one-dimensional as the German poet's, but something like it does figure in the precarious balance of Brockden Brown's ambivalence toward civilization and the wild.

The Yates murders served as the American nexus upon which other "sources" converged. Yates became an Abraham, flourishing tragically in the isolation and violence of a New World frontier town. And Abraham, through Christoph Martin Wieland, became an actor in a drama of epistemology. In Brown's work, the Old World is repeatedly tested by the New World as, compulsively, certitude falls before skepticism, doubt, error, and the frailty of human perception. Recall that Brown, in his outline for **Wieland,** identified himself with two seekers of certitude: he named his first Wieland "Charles," having drawn "Wieland" from his list of names likely because it resonated so tellingly with the surname of a German poet engrossed in themes of knowledge and knowing. The American nexus of the Yates tragedy, then, became for Brown the correlative of an intensely felt intellectual conflict.

What **Wieland** wonderfully illustrates is how Brown's American subjects serve to focus and concentrate his "wildering" thoughts into an artifact of culture burst through the mere peculiarities of an environment. The essence of Brown's "Americanism," of his relation to his time and place, consists precisely in his uneasy command of both Old and New World sources. **Wieland** suggests that, for Brown, to be an American, especially an American author, meant a life lived in emotional conflict born of restless skepticism about the truth of thought and perception. The novelist found that what had been a comfortable confidence in one's "eastern" mind could become an agonizing doubt as one forced consciousness to a "western" frontier. Brown carried a great deal of the Old World into his New World fictions, using the Bible and *Der Gepryfte Abraham* to translate the Yates murders into the tale of Theodore Wieland.

The creation of Theodore's father required even more of the Old World.

The man who would become the father of Clara and Theodore Wieland, smothered by seven years of spiritual aridity as apprentice to a London trader and charged with a zeal born of radical religious reading, was overwhelmed one day by an awakening of the religious affections, which prompted him to leave England for the banks of the Schuylkill outside Philadelphia. His intention (for so he believed God had commanded) was to preach to and convert the Indians; but fear of the Indians, which had tormented him even before he left Europe, was "revived [upon reaching America], and a nearer survey of savage manners once more shook his resolution" (10). Cheap land and black slaves "gave him who was poor in Europe all the advantages of wealth," so that for fourteen years, setting aside the zeal of youth, he prospered as a farmer. Having earned a degree of leisure, he took up Scripture and theology once again until "his ancient belief relative to the conversion of the savage tribes, was revived with uncommon energy" (10). Missionary labors, undertaken at last, "were attended with no permanent success." A minor spiritual victory here and there was poor compensation for the derision and insults to which Wieland was subject. The extremities of wilderness life, fatigue, hunger, sickness, and solitude also took their toll. "The license of savage passion, and the artifices of his depraved countrymen, all opposed themselves to his progress" (11).

Discouraged, essentially broken by his wilderness missionary sojourn, Wieland came back to his family. Eschewing conventional and social religion, he worshiped in complete solitude daily at noon and midnight, building for this purpose "what to a common eye would have seemed a summer house" (11). Slight and airy, it "was no more than a circular area, twelve feet in diameter, whose flooring was the rock, cleared of moss and shrubs, and exactly levelled, edged by twelve Tuscan columns, and covered by an undulating dome" (11). We shall see in a later chapter that this "temple" is of a piece with Palladian designs Brown sketched in fragmentary manuscripts that are probably parts of a youthful and abortive utopian project. This does not explain, however, the incongruity of having the senior Wieland conduct his "gothic" religious exercises in a monument to the neoclassical sensibility.

The picture Clara Wieland paints of her father's religious beliefs is grimly fanatical. It was the chance reading of "a book written by one of the teachers of the Albigenses, or French Protestants" that sent the senior Wieland on his ill-fated mission to America. A consideration of this religious background figured in the earliest stages of the composition of the novel. Wieland "contracted a gloomy & religious sprirt [sic]," Brown noted in his outline, "from the perusal of the works of the first reformers. He built up a system of his own. The Savoyard protestant faith was his. See Chambers Cyclopaedia" (427).

Ephraim Chambers's *Cyclopaedia* does not have an article on "Savoyard protestants," nor are they mentioned under the main "Protestant" entry. Perhaps Brown intended a reference to the entry under "Waldenses" in Chambers, since these Protestants were "Savoyards," residents of the Savoy Piedmont. The religious persecution they perpetually suffered culminated in the "massacre" of April 24, 1655, that is the subject of John Milton's Sonnet 18. But this resolutely independent yet simple and mild sect hardly seems a likely source for a "gloomy," let alone fanatical, religious spirit. The Waldenses were, however, often confused with their neighbors to the east, the Albigenses, with whom, theologically, they had very little in common. Chambers's *Cyclopaedia,* in its article on the Albigenses, stresses the sect's Manicheanism. Their belief was in "two Gods, the one infinitely good, the other infinitely evil . . . the good God made the invisible world, and the evil one that which we live in." Some later commentators have observed that the Albigenses were actually a direct outgrowth of the Persian Manichees. Chambers enumerates additional Albigensian heresies, including a belief in two Christs (one good, the other evil), no resurrection of the body, the uselessness of baptism and other holy rites and sacraments, the absence of confession and penance, and the belief that marriage is both unholy and unlawful. Later writers mention the Albigenses' fanatical asceticism, which may culminate in suicide among the sect's "perfected" as a means of evading mortal sin. For once an Albigensian has been initiated through a laying on of hands known as the "*consolumentum,*" a single sin of the flesh forfeits eternal salvation. Suicide was generally by starvation.[12]

Melancholy, foreboding, fanaticism, self-loathing, deprecation of the physical and elevation of the spiritual: Brown could have found enough of these in the Albigensian doctrine to supply two generations of Wielands. Why, then, attenuate the gothic effect of such a religion by having its American disciple worship in the bright product of the age of reason? The incongruity is made the more striking by the sedate temple's location "on the top of a rock whose sides were steep, rugged, and encumbered with dwarf cedars and stony asperities" (11), a "sublime" landscape that anticipates *Edgar Huntly.* If the admixture of classical restraint with fanaticism and the sublime is a product of Brown's incongruous nature, it was an incongruity he shared with his culture. As conspicuously out of place in the American landscape as the "dungeon" Edgar Huntly projects into it, Wieland's temple has its source in a similar reaction to the extremity of wilderness experience. Wieland, all but destroyed by his missionary endeavors, erects a symbol of classical order at the edge of the wilderness that had debilitated him. Upon the Albigensian passion that sent him into the wilderness in the first place, he imposes a symbol of passionless order; and where once he had worshiped in limitless American wilds, he now confines religious meditation daily behind twelve Tuscan columns at noon and at midnight exactly. The rage for order Edgar Huntly and the senior Wieland manifest is part of the impulse that led the "gothic novelist" himself to sketch drawings of Palladian buildings. And these designs, like the "dungeon" and "temple" Huntly and Wieland respectively project into the wilderness, may be located along the same cultural continuum that moved a Thomas Jefferson to build Monticello.

If the senior Wieland's architectural reaction to the wilderness can be accounted typically American, his religion, despite its familiar missionary element, seems quite alien. It is initially puzzling that Brown failed, say, to tap the rich vein of Puritanism Hawthorne would later discover. After all, as Larzer Ziff has suggested, in *Wieland,* "Brown . . . penetrates beneath the principles of the optimistic psychology of his day, and recognizes the claims which Calvinism makes on the American character. . . . Beginning consciously in the camp of the benevolent Philadelphians of the American Philosophical Society . . . Brown ends his journey through the mind by approaching [Jonathan] Edwards' camp." Brown "was the first [American novelist] to face the confusion of sentiment and optimistic psychology, both of which flowed through the chink in the Puritan dike, and to represent American progress away from a doctrine of depravity as a very mixed blessing indeed."[13]

While Ziff is correct in remarking the similarity of intellectual tone between *Wieland* and Puritan theology, it is an oversimplification to declare that Brown sided with the Puritans in order to attack facile optimism. It is true that the novel explores the horrors of an irrationality against which reason proves powerless; and it is also true that in the blind fate of Wieland, father and son, and in the motiveless malignity of the "biloquist" Carwin, we do see a species of "depravity." However, if Brown can be said to attack anything, it is fanaticism; and the novelist must have seen that neither of the Wieland men could be literally Puritans. Required were solitary figures whose religion, like that of James Yates, had developed in isolation. Puritanism, for all its potential extremity (especially as it might have been popularly perceived), was simply too social an institution, providing too many of the checks and balances of rational civilization to serve the novelist's purpose.

While Albigensianism, a long-dead schism originating in medieval Toulouse, may at first seem a gratuitously exotic choice for the Wieland religious background, the sect can be seen as a caricature of the more sulfurous aspects of Calvinist doctrine. The Albigensian's Manichean cosmogony of absolute good and evil and its rigorous doctrine of natural depravity resonate powerfully with the kind of religion that would appeal to the literary sensibilities of Hawthorne and Melville. Much as *Edgar Huntly* translates European gothicism into terms of the American wilderness, *Wieland* uses an exotic Old World religion to help define in the New World wilderness the intellectual themes that, we have already suggested, mark Brown as an American author. The shadowy Albigensian background of the senior

Wieland—which manifests itself in the next generation as the "calvinistic inspiration" (25) of Theodore—is meant to expose and explain the tragic errors to which a blind leap of faith may lead. Resonant with, perhaps even inspired by, the particular situation of the American Puritans, *Wieland* was written neither to approve of nor to condemn them.

Whatever their "calvinistic inspiration," the two Wielands are what the eighteenth century called "enthusiasts," a kind of fanatic the Reverend Charles Chauncy described and cautioned against in a sermon written during that violent spasm of revivalist emotion in America known as "The Great Awakening": "He mistakes the working of his own passions for divine communications, and fancies himself immediately inspired by the SPIRIT of GOD, when all the while, he is under no other influence than that of an over-heated imagination."[14] Men like Chauncy feared that error lay behind the upheaval of religious affections, egocentric error that could lead to such disasters as the Yates murders, which, like the Awakening, were in part fostered by the conditions of wilderness life. What might begin as belief in a divine commission to "deliver [God's] message to the world" (6), Chauncy observes, may evolve into unmitigated horror:

> Sometimes [enthusiasm] appears in their imaginary peculiar intimacy with heaven. They are, in their own opinion, the special favourites of God . . . and receive immediate, extraordinary communications from him. The tho'ts, which suddenly rise up in their minds, they take for suggestions of the SPIRIT; their very fancies are divine illuminations; nor are they strongly inclin'd to any thing, but 'tis an impulse from GOD, a plain revelation of his will.

> And what extravagances, in this temper of mind, are they not capable of, and under specious pretext too of paying obediences to the authority of GOD? Many have fancied themselves acting by immediate warrant from heaven, while they have been committing the most undoubted wickedness.

(4)

In just this manner did the seeds of the senior Wieland's enthusiasm bear deadly fruit in the son.

As thoroughly as Chauncy's description anticipates the Wielands, it is of course impossible simply to infer that Brown had read the sermon, which, after all, had appeared more than a half-century before *Wieland,* and in Boston, a city Brown may never even have visited. More important is what "Enthusiasm Described and Cautioned Against" suggests about the nature of faith in America. It shows us how the religious theme in *Wieland* reaches beyond Calvinism as such and toward broader questions about the assumptions on which men habitually construct "truth." While this is not so peculiarly American a theme as Puritan Calvinism, such phenomena as the Yates atrocity show that it is no less a function of culture and physical environment.

Chauncy's sermon is related thematically to a document we do know that Brown used in the composition of **Wieland.** Chauncy recommends Scripture and reason as antidotes to the egocentricism of enthusiasm, yet he observes that "in nothing does the *enthusiasm* of these persons discover itself more, than in the disregard they express to the Dictates of *reason.*" Both James Yates and Theodore Wieland are contemptuous of the reasonings of their captors. In Chauncy's terms, "They are above the force of argument" (5). Enthusiasm is actually beyond the power of reason, for "'tis properly a disease, a sort of madness," the result of "bad temperament of the blood and spirits" (3). Here the minister anticipates a treatise to which Brown refers in a footnote to **Wieland** (179). Erasmus Darwin, Brown points out, described Theodore Wieland's disorder in his *Zoönomia; or The Laws of Organic Life,* which was published in a complete American edition the year before Brown wrote his novel. Darwin defines "Mania mutabilis" as a state of delusion wrought by some "physical defect"— thought to be hereditary—in the nervous system or sensory organs. Instances of the mania Darwin recounts include a woman who hallucinates the presence of an angel, another who hears a voice commanding "Repent, or you will be damned," and others of like nature.[15] Somewhat ironically, perhaps, Darwin illustrates his "scientific" description of Mania mutabilis with a number of religious examples, whereas the clergyman Charles Chauncy defines this malady of the religious affections scientifically. Larzer Ziff was right to note elements of something like the Calvinist notion of innate depravity in **Wieland,** but Chauncy's "medical" definition of enthusiasm comes even closer to precisely what we find in the novel. The roots of enthusiasm are not to be explained theologically, but physiologically, as a "disease, a sort of madness: And there are few; perhaps none at all, but are subject to it" (Chauncy, 3).

In a similar vein, at the conclusion of the misadventures of **Edgar Huntly,** Brown has Huntly's friend Sarsefield declare: "Consciousness itself is the malady, the pest, of which he only is cured who ceases to think." In this strictly intellectual sense, depravity is a fact of human existence. In the world of Brown's novels, to think is to invite error, and to act upon thought is to invite calamity. As Edgar Huntly himself concludes: "Disastrous and humiliating is the state of man! By his own hands is constructed the mass of misery and error in which his steps are forever involved. . . . How little cognizance have men over the actions and motives of each other! How total is our blindness with regard to our own performances!" (267). And Clara Wieland cries out from the pages that recount her brother's life of holy error: "What is man, that knowledge is so sparingly conferred upon him!" (102).

While Brown's absorption in intellectual themes suggests that he was no simple product of a Calvinist heritage, the fact remains that his themes do at least smack of such a background. Ziff suggests, in effect, that Brown's use of depravity, predestination, even the hellfire spontaneous combustion attending the senior Wieland's demise, is reason enough to enroll the novelist with such Calvinist-influenced writers as Hawthorne and Melville in an important tradition of the national literature. But William L. Hedges, in a 1974 article, raises a well-founded objection to this view. He concedes that "concepts such as innocence, puritanism and the Protestant ethic might be adequate to discussions of Brown if liberally enough construed," but when "the construction is too strict . . . we risk forgetting that Charles Brockden Brown the Quaker and Young Goodman Brown the New England puritan are not identical." When we stop to consider that Brown grew up not in Puritan Boston but Quaker Philadelphia, that his parents were indeed Quakers, and that his only formal education was the six years he spent at the Friends' Latin School, we are inclined to second Hedges's objection that Larzer Ziff "approaches . . . an . . . untenable extreme in arguing that in [**Wieland**] Brown reverts to something like a Calvinist doctrine of 'inherited depravity' and a 'confused acceptance of supernatural causation.'"[16] But, turning back to the novel itself, we *do* see in Theodore Wieland something very like inherited depravity. And rather than a display of William Penn's gentle doctrine of the Inner Light we are treated to the Day-of-Doom spontaneous combustion of Theodore's zealot father.

How do we reconcile the biographical fact of Brown's Quaker background with the aesthetic fact of his most famous novel, the darkness of whose themes suggests the Calvinist heritage of a Hawthorne or Melville? To begin with, we can no more call Brown simply a Quaker than we can call him simply a Calvinist. True, his parents were Quakers; but of their six children, four, including Charles, married non-Quakers (Warfel, 19-20). Moreover, an exchange between Brown's closest friends, Smith and Dunlap, reveals that the novelist's marriage to Elizabeth Linn, the daughter of a Presbyterian minister, was not his first romance "outside the Meeting." On March 29, 1798, Elihu Hubbard Smith showed William Dunlap a letter in which Brown described himself "as assiduously writing Novels & in love" (Dunlap, *Diary,* 236). By April 24 Smith was calling a Miss Susan A. Potts Brown's "Mistress" (Smith, 439-40), while Dunlap, a few days later, was content to identify her as "CBB's wished for" (Dunlap, *Diary,* 252). But at the end of September Dunlap tersely recorded that Brown had related to him "the manner in which his mother breaks off his connection with Miss Potts" (Dunlap, *Diary,* 343). It is most likely that Mrs. Brown's objection was made on religious grounds: Susan Potts was not a Quaker (Clark, 195).

No hard evidence exists that Brown harbored ill will toward either his mother or Quakerism; however, interestingly enough, in *Arthur Mervyn* (Part 1, published the year after *l'affaire Potts*) Brown puts the young title character through a romantic experience analogous to his own. Arthur, who is not a Quaker, falls in love with a Quaker farmer's daughter but dejectedly puts off proposing to her because he knows her father will object to the marriage on religious grounds. Brown, conveniently, kills off the father and has Arthur acknowledge that the old man's death has removed the only obstacle to marriage. Even if we take the episode from *Arthur Mervyn* as evidence of Brown's covert rebellion against the religion that may have cost him his Miss Potts, we must still conclude that his attitude toward Quakerism was ambivalent rather than wholly antagonistic. For he is careful to paint the old Quaker of the novel as a kindly, mild, and generous man. Perhaps the extent and longevity of such ambivalence toward the religion of his parents is most fully suggested by a document he wrote the year before his death. In *An Address to the Congress of the United States, on the Utility and Justice of Restrictions upon Foreign Commerce,* an 1809 pamphlet directed against Jefferson's embargo, Brown counseled that the President's action was not only ineffectual, but immoral, an act of war, greed, and vengeance. "There are [some] who will pass me by as a visionary," Brown wrote:

> And some, observing the city where I thus make my appearance [Philadelphia], may think my pacific doctrine, my system of rational forbearance and forgiveness carried to a pitch of *Quaker* extravagance. The truth is, I am no better than an outcast of that unwarlike sect, but cannot rid myself of reverence for most of its practical and political maxims.[17]

Cast out from the Meeting—perhaps, indeed, because of his marriage—Brown yet retains a reverence for the Friends, or, at least for their "practical and political maxims."

The novelist's religious ambivalence suggests that, while Charles Brockden Brown indeed was not Young Goodman Brown the Puritan, neither was he, say, John Woolman or William Penn the Quaker. We should, in any case, avoid stereotyping Quakerism as the mild religion of Woolman and Penn; it could, of course, take other forms as well. Though Brown found his bride outside the Meeting, he would not have had to venture that far in order to find a germ he might nurture into the full-blown fanaticism of both the senior and junior Wieland. Available to the novelist in the collection of the Library Company of Philadelphia was William Smith's *History of New-York* (London: 1757; reissued in Philadelphia: 1792), in which Brown would have come across the story of Lewis Morris. Appointed Chief Justice of the New York Supreme Court in 1692 and governor of New Jersey in 1702, Morris nevertheless

had been "a little whimsical" in his youth. Bridling under the zealous Quaker tutelage of a certain Hugh Coppathwait, young Morris played a practical joke on him one day: "The pupil taking advantage of [Coppathwait's] enthusiasm, hid himself in a tree, and calling to him, ordered him to preach the gospel among the Mohawks. The credulous quaker took it for a miraculous call, and was upon the point of setting out when the cheat was discovered."[18]

We can do little more, really, than wonder if Brown actually had this comical episode in mind when he wrote of the senior Wieland's call to preach to the Indians or when he had son Theodore heed the "divine" command—which may well have issued from the ventriloquist Carwin—to sacrifice his family. But, considered with the evidence of Brown's ambivalence toward the religion of his parents, the case of Hugh Coppathwait does tell us at least one thing definitely: it is a mistake to label Brockden Brown's religious influences with the stereotyped tags that commentaries have furnished to date.

We turn now to a particular influence upon Brown, about which there has so far been no hard speculation: Robert Proud, author of the first history of Pennsylvania and the schoolmaster of the future novelist. Proud, as master of the Friends' Latin School, was certainly a professed Quaker. Harry R. Warfel describes him as "tall as a tower and commanding in presence, with a prominent Roman nose and bushy brows arching over a large face"—a symbol of "the old patriarchal order." Warfel drew this description from Charles West Thomson's "Notices of the Life and Character of Robert Proud, Author of 'The History of Pennsylvania'" (1826) either directly or through the redaction of it in *The Dictionary of American Biography* (*DAB*). But Warfel added on his own a judgment for which neither Thomson nor the *DAB* gives unambiguous warrant. "Wise, calm, mild, energetic, resourceful, affectionate," Warfel declares, Proud "was the living embodiment of the Quaker philosophy" (Warfel, 22-3).

Charles West Thomson did meet a former student of Proud's who described the schoolmaster as "mild, commanding, and affectionate"; but when Thomson himself, as a boy, caught a glimpse of Proud it was his stern bearing that made the greatest impression.[19] "I well remember the imposing effect, which the curled, gray wig, the half-cocked, patriarchal-looking hat and the long, ivory-headed cane, had on my boyish imagination." Likely that effect was terrifying, especially on a "boyish imagination," which would undoubtedly as well as painfully connect the ivory-headed cane with the profession of schoolmaster. In fact, Proud, "obscure and retiring," emerges from the traces that remain of his life—including the 1797 *History of Pennsylvania*—as a malcontent and misanthrope, desperately forlorn among a nation and people he did not cherish. Thomson wished to record Proud's life precisely because, by 1826, memory of the man had all but vanished.

Born in Yorkshire, England, in 1728, Robert Proud showed such early genius that his parents precipitously steered him into a medical career. But, much as the youthful Brown would himself become disgusted with the profession of law for which he had been trained, so Proud bolted from medicine. This or financial troubles (which were something of a plague upon Proud) may have caused his abrupt departure from England for America in 1759. There were rumors circulating that Proud had actually fled England because of an unhappy love affair—financial embarrassment barred marriage—but Thomson gives these stories no credit; though, it is true, Proud did remain a bachelor lifelong. Whatever his reasons for emigrating, two years after his arrival in Philadelphia he was engaged as a master of the Friends' Latin School, where he presented a figure so stern that he quickly became known as "Dominie Proud." There is no evidence that he discouraged this appellation, though it better suits a Scots Calvinist than an English Quaker.

If the epithet suggests Presbyterian sternness, this bearing actually masked a melancholy as morbid as any found in the diaries of Cotton Mather or Michael Wigglesworth, or, for that matter, in the youthful letters of Brockden Brown himself. Among some verses Proud left in manuscript at his death is "A Plaintive Essay, attempted by R. P. in 6 mo., 1781, after several years of great distress, dejection, and trouble of mind," which Thomson included in an appendix to his biographical sketch of Proud. The schoolmaster addresses God, who, unaccountably, has of late seen fit to forsake his faithful servant:

> But oh! why now this grievous fall,
>   Why am I left forlorn?
> Why am I thus deprived of all,
>   Why was I ever born?

In 1770 Proud had resigned as master at the Latin School to embark upon a financially ruinous decade of foreign trade. The "Plaintive Essay" was written the year after he returned to the school, quite broke, and just a year before Brockden Brown enrolled.

> Oh! why in my declining years,
>   Hast Thou forsaken me!

A commercial failure, Robert Proud never felt at home in America. Furthermore, politically and philosophically conservative, he was a Loyalist Tory during the Revolution, and felt himself doomed to perish:

> Far distant, in a foreign land . . .
> Where death and darkness, understood,

> Possess the human mind,
> Rebellion, wrath, revenge, and blood,
>   The actions of mankind!

The "Plaintive Essay" concludes with a quatrain "Motto":

> Our early days are best but quickly gone,
> Disease with pain and sorrow soon come on,
> Labor and care soon introduce decay,
> And death resistless hastens all away.

Such effusions are hardly the work of a "living embodiment of the Quaker philosophy."

At the very least, Proud may well have nurtured in Brown the melancholy that would become a characteristic of the vision embodied in his fiction. Moreover, and more importantly, the schoolmaster may have shaded his somber-hued lessons with tones specifically religious and thereby may have influenced not only the emotional tenor of his pupil's future work but also its themes. The single sentence devoted to Robert Proud in *The Literary History of the United States* mentions the "almost medieval spirit" in which the pedagogue argued "that men were born to obey."[20] Better to have called this spirit Calvinist; for Proud's Toryism was as much the result of religious as of political conviction. These lines from "Vox Naturae, An Elegy," another of the poems printed by Thomson, depict Proud as an exile among a people doomed by their rebellion to everlasting damnation:

> Hence eternal reason's voice
> I will follow in my choice;
> For, as happiness alone
> By obedience first was known,
>   But was lost
> By rebellion, so no more
> Shall be known, upon this shore,
> That true glory, peace, and joy,
> Which did former days employ,
>   On this coast.[21]

In a letter to his brother William dated "12 mo. 1st '77," Proud cranks his rhetoric to a pitch just flat of "Sinners in the Hands of an Angry God." Prophesying that America shall surely suffer for its "unnatural Rebellion," he summons up an image of the "over-ruling Hand of Divine Providence, which disposes the Events of Things, and inflicts the Scourge of his wrath on Mankind, for their Depravity and Revolt from the true Means of their real Interest and Felicity." Revolution is itself the punishment for unnatural rebellion, "the grand Punishment assigned by the Almighty for the wickedness of the human Race, while in the State of Existence."[22]

In the June 1799 issue of his *Monthly Magazine* Brown published a review of Proud's single claim upon posterity, his *History of Pennsylvania* (1797). Judging the author no artist, and the work an exhaustive collection of material rather than a genuine history, Brown nevertheless praised the "humble, honest, and industrious compiler. If his merit were measured by the labour which so large a compilation cost him, it would not be accounted inconsiderable."[23] Nor is it an inconsiderable labor to read the *History,* whose choked syntax recalls the densest passages of Cotton Mather's *Magnalia Christi Americana.*

More significant are the Matherian sentiments Proud entertains in his "Preface Dedicatory," where he conceives history as an interaction of Providence and the perpetual legacy of original sin. Divine Providence ordains government, Proud maintains, but "a constant decay [operates] in human affairs" to undermine it.[24] Through "folly or depravity" men rebel against the felicity of providentially ordained governments. "For the history of all nations abounds with instances of the same nature, operating in all descendants of *Adam* and *Eve,* which we are told, prevailed in these first parents, as representatives, of mankind" (6). Despite the lessons of history, "the interdicted tree, with its *forbidden fruit,* is still as tempting as ever it was" (7). "Ambition is rooted in human nature"—a human nature forever depraved when Adam and Eve first foolishly sought change—and ambition

> demands restraint; it assumes all manner of appearances whatsoever, and is now working wonders, in the world, under the name of *equality* and *the rights of man*;—Hence to mistake innovation for renovation, and a love of change for melioration, connected with such an idea of *self-dependency,* as is inconsistent with the enlargement of civilization, or of the social happiness of mankind, in any great or extensive degree, . . .
>
> (14)

So Proud's "sentence" itself decays, syntactically, in the course of another quarter-page.

As we cannot declare with certainty that Proud's evident melancholy fostered Brown's own, so we cannot say for sure that the novelist's "Quakerism" was that of his schoolmaster. We do know some things for certain: Brown's formal education was the work of Robert Proud; Brown respected the schoolmaster's *History*; and the novelist apparently maintained contact with Proud, at least through September 1, 1800, when he addressed a melancholy letter to "R. P." reporting his convalescence from some unspecified emotional wound, possibly the broken engagement with Miss Potts (Dunlap, *Life,* 2: 101). And we know, too, that the ostensibly Quaker novelist produced in *Wieland* a drama of depravity and fatality in which "Inner Light" seems but the product of hallucination and spontaneous combustion.

Without doubt, the best-known episode of *Wieland* or any other Brown novel is that in which the father of Clara and Theodore unaccountably bursts into flame while making his midnight obeisances in his "temple." This instance of "spontaneous combustion" is also the novel's most sensationally "Calvinist" incident—as far as a narrowly popular view of Calvinism is concerned—redolent of the sensibility behind revival sermons, Wigglesworth's *Day of Doom,* and even calling to the mind of the modern reader a famous scene in Melville's *Redburn.*[25]

In addition to considering a scientific explanation for her father's death, Clara Wieland does speculate that his horrible end might have been "the penalty of disobedience"—punishment, apparently, for his vacillation and failure in missionary life—"the stroke of a vindictive and invisible hand." If so, it is the hand of an Angry God, and the senior Wieland's death is "fresh proof that the Divine Ruler interferes in human affairs, meditates an end, selects and commissions his agents, and enforces by unequivocal sanctions, submission to his will" (19). Once again, though, we must avoid narrow interpretations; while popular Calvinist lore may have influenced the origin of the spontaneous combustion scene, it is as a metaphor informing the book's intellectual themes that the episode is more important. As usual, Brown abstracts the literal particulars of his material and raises them to the level of contemplation.

A light emanates from the temple, followed by an explosion. Clara Wieland's uncle runs to his brother's aid and sees "a blazing light . . . between the columns of the temple."

> Within the columns he beheld what he could no better describe, than by saying it resembled a cloud impregnated with light. It had the brightness of flame, but was without upward motion. It did not occupy the whole area, and rose but a few feet above the floor. No part of the building was on fire.

As soon as the uncle enters the temple, the light vanishes, plunging all into darkness (17). The scene is an early climax in the crescendo of the *Wieland* gloom. Yet, in this visually gloomy novel, the scene is also one of only two instances of bright light. The combustion of father Wieland, and son Theodore's description of the "divine" illumination that inspires him to "sacrifice," luridly punctuate the otherwise visually austere novel's pattern of images.

Brown admits light but grudgingly into most of *Wieland.* When seen, it is fleeting, vanishing upon approach, as the temple's illumination dies the instant Clara's uncle passes between the columns. Most often, images of flitting light are associated with the character in whom Brown distills the essence of deception, the enigmatic Francis Carwin, who insinuates himself into the world of the Wielands with little purpose beyond confounding them with his "biloquistic" talents. Years after his father's death, Theodore, on his way to the temple to fetch a letter he has left there, sees "a glimmering between the columns." Naturally, this recalls to him his father's combustion years earlier, but he continues toward the temple until arrested by what is later revealed as Carwin imitating the voice of Theodore's wife Catharine.

Another instance: one night, while Clara sleeps and dreams—like Edgar Huntly—in the wilderness environs of her home, she hears the biloquist's voice. What she dreams is Theodore beckoning her toward a pit into which she surely would have fallen had not "some one" caught her arm, exclaiming "in a voice of eagerness and terror, 'Hold! Hold!'" At this she wakes—like Huntly, into the very wilderness of her dream—and hears the warning again. This time she recognizes the voice as one she had heard earlier, in the closet of her own bedroom, a voice that had threatened to murder her. It warns her of danger now, tells her to flee. Convinced that her life is in peril, Clara is also aware of the hazards of flight through a woods that is as dangerous and dark as any dream-image of it, a place where one "could not take a step without hazard of falling to the bottom of the precipice." The darkness is unrelieved until, pondering whether to stay or leave,

> I perceived a ray flit across the gloom and disappear. Another succeeded, which was stronger, and remained for a passing moment. It glittered on the shrubs that were scattered at the entrance, and gleam continued to succeed gleam for a few seconds, till they, finally, gave place to unintermitted darkness.

As it had for her brother, such a flitting gleam recalls the horror of her father's death. The girl is paralyzed by fear until she beholds the "new and stronger illumination" of a "lanthorn" carried by Henry Pleyel, the most rational (and pedestrian) figure in Brown's novel (62-4).

And, a final example. Chapter 15 closes with Clara entering the deathly silent parlor of her brother's house, "in which a light was just expiring in the socket" (142). Leaving the apparently deserted house, she walks toward her own, and, at the beginning of Chapter 16, is startled to see a light in her chamber window. "As I eyed it, it suddenly became mutable, and after flitting to and fro, for a short time, it vanished" (145). The next sound she hears is, again, Carwin's piercing "hold! hold!" She gets a glimpse of his face—its eyes emitting sparks—finds a fragment of his writing, and, lastly, discovers the corpse of Catharine Wieland (142-51).

The association of Carwin with these images is not casual. His function in the novel is to counterfeit knowledge; the "illuminations" Carwin furnishes are as evanescent as lights that appear one moment, only to vanish the next. Since images of illumination are common in everyday speech as metaphors for discovery, revelation,

and knowledge ("I see the light," for example), it is easy to overlook their apparently casual occurrence throughout *Wieland.* We might not think much about Clara's observation that, although Carwin quickly became an intimate of her tight little family and social circle, he "left us wholly in the dark, concerning that about which we were most inquisitive" (71-2). Nor would we be particularly apt to remark Clara's desire to reflect "some light . . . on the actual situation of" Carwin (127). Common as such figures of speech are, Brown takes pains to make his reader conscious of the link between the physical darkness of his story and the figuratively dark state of human knowledge. One evening, shortly after Carwin's biloquism first manifests itself as Catharine Wieland's warning voice, Clara remarks to her brother: "'How almost palpable is this dark; yet a ray from above would dispel it.' 'Ay,' said Wieland, with fervor, 'not only the physical, but moral night would be dispelled'" (36).

Would that all humankind enjoyed the privilege of Abraham: a ray from above, a revelation of absolute truth. "'But why,'" Clara asks Theodore, "'must the Divine Will address its precepts to the eye?' He smiled significantly. 'True,' said he, 'the understanding has other avenues'" (36). Perhaps, then, we should say that the evanescence of light in *Wieland* figures as something even more than metaphor. For, as this conversation suggests, light is literally the means of "seeing," of acquiring knowledge: the chief means by which "the Divine Will addresses its precepts" to humankind. Locke, as Brown well knew, held that knowledge was the product of the senses. Yet, like Carwin's counterfeited voices of revelation, which address the understanding through another of its sensory "avenues," the light of *Wieland* is deceptive, vanishing as quickly as it appears: "What is man, that knowledge is so sparingly conferred upon him!"

Ironically, the second explosion of light in the otherwise flickering visual scheme of *Wieland,* the "illumination" that bursts only upon the deranged mind of Theodore, is, of all the lights that flicker through the book, by far the steadiest and most certain. All of his life, Wieland tells judge and jury, has been spent "searching for the revelation of [God's] will." Hitherto the search has failed: "I turned on every side where glimmerings of light could be discovered." Although never "wholly uninformed," his "knowledge has always stopped short of certainty." But that night of the murders, entering the dark house of Clara, revelation was total and blindingly brilliant. "I had no light. . . . The darkness required some caution in descending the stair. I stretched my hand to seize the balustrade by which I might regulate my steps. How shall I describe the lustre, which, at that moment, burst upon my vision!" Dazzled, blinded, chilled by a nameless fear, Theodore closes his eyes; but still this "irradiation did not retire or lessen. It seemed as if some powerful effulgence covered me like a mantle."

Opening his eyes, he finds all about him "luminous and glowing. It was the element of heaven that flowed around. Nothing but a fiery stream was at first visible; but, anon, a shrill voice from behind called upon me to attend," and the sacrifice was demanded (165-8). This most intense "illumination," a product of Mania mutabilis, lacks the physical substance of the father's spectacular combustion—or, for that matter, lacks the substance of any of *Wieland's* other and dimmer lights. Its unflickering brilliance fueled exclusively by Theodore's imagination, the truth of its revelation is but the certainty of solipsism.

As the senior Wieland's spontaneous combustion is significant on the level of image and beyond its more specific resemblance to Calvinist pyrotechnics, so the drama of light and dark, of which the combustion is a spectacular part, extends beyond the immediate story of *Wieland.* By linking the two literally brightest moments of his novel to the darkness of error rather than to the illumination of truth, Brown inverts the very metaphor that informed an "Age of Enlightenment."[26]

It was an age for which Joel Barlow spoke in 1787, when he brought before the public his *Vision of Columbus.* Barlow depicted America as the political, moral, and religious utopia for which Christ himself had died. In images of light and flame Barlow welds reason to religious revelation on the free soil of the United States:

> In no blest land has fair Religion shone,
> And fix'd so firm her everlasting throne.
> Where, o'er the realms those spacious temples shine,
> Frequent and full the throng'd assemblies join;
> There fired with virtue's animating flame,
> The sacred task unnumber'd sages claim;
> The task, for angels great; in early youth,
> To lead whole nations in the walks of truth,
> Shed the bright beams of knowledge on the mind,
> For social compact harmonize mankind,
> To life, to happiness, to joys above,
> The soften'd soul with ardent zeal move;
> For this the voice of Heaven in early years,
> Tuned the glad songs of the life-inspiring seers,
> For this consenting seraphs leave the skies,
> The God compassionates, the Saviour dies.[27]

In *Wieland,* Barlow's shining religion and shining temples, worshippers fired with virtue's flame, become the fuel for spontaneous combustion; and the voice of heaven becomes that of Francis Carwin, biloquist. Not that Brown necessarily had Barlow in mind when he wrote his dark book, but he knew the poem, praised it in a review, and had been, in his youth, almost certainly influenced by it. But the popular *Vision of Columbus,* like its later reworking as the *Columbiad* (1807), and like Philip Freneau and Hugh Henry Brackenridge's

Poem, on the Rising Glory of America (1772), did draw upon conventional images emblematic of a national optimism.[28] We shall, in the next chapter, examine in some detail Brown's relation to Barlow's *Vision* and the vision it embodied. For the present, though, we might observe that the novelist's praise for the poem suggests an impulse to share in its optimism; but, speaking in the voice most his own—the voice of fiction—Brown intoned Barlow's pious images reversed, as it were, in a kind of Black Mass.

Barlow's vision is of a rational America, and his images of illumination reflect the dominance of reason. In *Wieland,* light suggests revelation rather than reason, and, at that, false revelation. Nevertheless, the temple, in which the first spectacular "illumination" takes place, is an architectural *hommage* to an age of reason. As such, it might be seen as a simple moral icon, caging behind its neoclassical columns the flames of enthusiasm. Furthermore, as if to suggest that reason endures while passion burns itself to ash, the temple survives the conflagration to be appropriated by Wieland's children and their friend Henry Pleyel for classical study and harpsichord music, rational amusements that seem better suited than religious worship to the structure's twelve Tuscan columns and undulating dome.

Converted by Theodore and the others of his circle ostensibly to serve the cause of Enlightenment reason, the structure actually continues—even under Pleyel and the Wieland progeny—as a *temple.* It is sacred to Marcus Tullius Cicero, whose bust, commissioned by Theodore from an "Italian adventurer," presides on a pedestal opposite the harpsichord (23-4). For the "chief object of [Theodore's] veneration was Cicero."

> He was never tired of conning and rehearsing his productions. To understand them was not sufficient. He was anxious to discover the gestures and cadences with which they ought to be delivered. He was very scrupulous in selecting a true scheme of pronunciation for the Latin tongue, and in adapting it to the words of his darling writer. His favorite occupation consisted in embellishing his rhetoric with all the properties of gesticulation and utterance.

Theodore worships Cicero almost as his father had worshipped his dark Albigensian God. Theodore collected all the editions and commentaries he could find, employing "months of severe study in exploring and comparing them" in order to settle and restore "the purity of the text" (24).

The rationality suggested by the architecture of the temple notwithstanding, Theodore's veneration is not for Cicero the archapostle of Roman reason, but for Cicero the orator, persuader of men and instigator of their actions. If Theodore's enthusiasm betrays an excess of zeal, it is not without some basis in the conventional critical opinion of Brown's day. The Scots rhetorician Hugh Blair, whose *Lectures on Rhetoric and Belles Lettres* was almost a household book in America, expressed great admiration for Cicero, pointing out, however, that his chief and almost too artful appeal is to the emotions, and that in purely intellectual argument he is inferior to the Greek Demosthenes.[29]

Theodore's weakness for the Roman orator both foreshadows and reveals his susceptibility to the voices of Carwin. Clara herself attests to Carwin's powers as an orator. When she first saw Carwin he appeared to her rustic, ungainly, malproportioned, unprepossessing, and unremarkable. Then he spoke—asked for a simple cup of water. Clara instantly became obsessed with his image and voice. Theodore's voice and Pleyel's "were musical and energetic," but Carwin's surpassed even theirs. "It was wholly new."

> I cannot pretend to communicate the impression that was made upon me by [Carwin's] accents, or to depict the degree in which force and sweetness were blended in them. They were articulated with a distinctness that was unexampled in my experience. But this was not all. The voice was not only mellifluent and clear, but the emphasis was so just, and the modulation so impassioned, that it seemed as if an heart of stone could not fail of being moved by it. It imparted to me an emotion altogether involuntary and incontroulable [*sic*].
>
> (52)

In moving "especially the softer passions," Hugh Blair observed, Cicero "is very successful. No man knew the power and force of words better than Cicero." As Carwin's verbal emphasis was always just, so the structure of Cicero's sentences "is curious and exact to the highest degree." Full, flowing, never abrupt, "Ciceronian eloquence"—whether that of Cicero or Carwin—is almost too "dazzling by its beauties," its rhetoric at times "showy rather than solid" (2: 204-6).

One day, while "bandying quotations and syllogisms," Theodore and Pleyel fall to friendly argument over the merits of Cicero's oration for Cluentius. Pleyel, genial contestor of Cicero's divinity, holds that the orator had embraced a bad or doubtful cause, and criticizes the logic of his argument. Although there is nothing in the *Defense of Aulus Cluentius Habitus* that bears directly upon *Wieland,* Brown's citation of this oration is not without significance. Among the more dramatic of Cicero's speeches, its narrative and "plot" are surely the most complex, involving charges and countercharges, and the guilty accusers' baroque obfuscations of the truth. The novelist who would soon prove himself capable of the gnarled second part of *Arthur Mervyn,* and who was already manifesting a fondness for sub-subplot in the relatively direct *Wieland* (follow, for example, the alive-dead-alive-dead fate of Pleyel's shadowy European fiancée, Theresa de Stolberg), was understandably attracted by Cicero's command of a complex narrative. Hugh Blair himself had singled out the *Pro Cluentio* for careful analysis and praised Cicero (though he cited another speech) for his "very remarkable" talent of narration (2: 281-98, 394-6). Clara Wieland's appraisal of Carwin's early discourses on mysterious voices from invisible sources might well have expressed her brother's (or even Blair's) admiration for the Cicero of the *Pro Cluentio*:

> [Carwin's] narratives were constructed with so much skill, and rehearsed with so much energy, that all the effects of a dramatic exhibition were frequently produced by them. Those that were most coherent and most minute, and, of consequence, least entitled to credit [!?], were yet rendered probable by the exquisite art of this rhetorician. For every difficulty that was suggested, a ready and plausible solution was furnished.
>
> (74)

Thus Carwin is curiously identified with Cicero—and (we may reasonably infer) like the Cicero of *Pro Cluentio,* he is also identified with the novelist, whose business it is to furnish plausible solutions for every difficulty suggested.

Brown, who at an early stage of composition bestowed upon Wieland his own first name, also shared something of Theodore's regard for Cicero. While the orator was Theodore's "darling author," Brown's own favorites were Shakespeare and Milton, as well as Cicero, whose Latin Robert Proud had taught the boy, sometime between his tenth and sixteenth years, "to cherish" (Warfel, 9 and 225). Much later the novelist would make Cicero the hero of a forty-eight-page tale incongruously bound in the third slim volume, second edition, of ***Edgar Huntly.*** "The Death of Cicero, a Fragment" tells the story of the orator's last days as he is pursued by agents of the Triumvirate, which, declaring him an enemy of Rome, have ordered his execution. At first glance the "fragment" appears to be a straightforward celebration of Cicero's stoic valor. The orator, weary of the ignominy of flight, resigns himself to death despite the expostulations of his companion Tiro, who argues that to die at the hands of the Triumvirate is more ignominious. Over Tiro's objections, confronted at last by his enemies, Cicero orders his retainers to put up their swords. One Papilius Laenas, whom Cicero had once defended in court, executes the sentence of the Triumvirate.

Though it picks up the story of Cicero's flight *in medias res,* "The Death of Cicero" is essentially a complete tale; so we might question why Brown chose to call it "A Fragment." Perhaps it was intended as part of a projected fictional treatment of Cicero's life. More likely, Brown was acknowledging the emotionally unsettling and dramatically unsatisfying ambivalence of the piece's denouement, which leaves the tale at loose ends. Tiro, telling the story of Cicero's death in a letter addressed to Atticus, concludes his narration entirely of two minds about the orator's "heroic" resignation. He should have seen escape as his duty, Tiro asserts, only to end by suggesting that perhaps Cicero had been right to choose a dignified death after all. The pattern of ambivalence in "The Death of Cicero" is a familiar one in Brown's writing. Brown would announce to his brother the aim of creating in Arthur Mervyn a model of moral rectitude; the result was a figure as ambiguous as Melville's Pierre. Brown set out to celebrate the heroic moral conviction of his favorite Roman author, only in the end to question the basis of Cicero's heroism. We are left with the unspoken possibility that Cicero's stoicism is akin to the Wieland fanaticism.

It is therefore no surprise that Brown implies an identification of Carwin with Cicero. To be sure, Brown nowhere equates the two, but the identification, pivoting on Theodore Wieland's weakness for rhetoric, suggests that Cicero's powers make him a potential Carwin—and, for that matter, Carwin's powers (had he developed commensurate moral principles) make him a potential Cicero. Further to compound an already complex system of identification, Brown, as a creator of narrative, implicitly associates himself with Carwin/Cicero, and, as a seeker of certitude, with Theodore ("Charles") Wieland. Nothing in Brockden Brown's writings illustrates more strikingly the "double mental existence" the novelist explained to John Bernard. Brown projects himself into *Wieland* as both the deceiver and the deceived. What is more, the "deceiver" in him is the novelist, a Carwin/Cicero, yes, but also the Christoph Martin Wieland/Theodore Wieland seeker of certitude. The novel, for Brown a means of discovering truth, is also a rhetorical exercise in which the novelist, like the Cicero of *Pro Cluentio*—and like Carwin—is obliged merely to furnish a "ready and plausible solution" for every difficulty suggested. Perhaps it was a growing awareness of an irreconcilable tension between "seeker" and "deceiver" that led Brown to abandon fiction, to relinquish "romance" in favor of "history." For history (he explained in his 1800 *Monthly Magazine* article, "The Difference between History and Romance") catalogs surfaces only, while romance is always speculative.[30] And in speculation Brown always found space for the disturbing doubleness of his mental existence.

In *Wieland* he was unwilling to relinquish either half of the doubleness, though both must have distressed him. He passes no absolute judgment against Carwin, except obliquely in the epigraph to the novel:

> From Virtue's blissful paths away
> The double-tongued are sure to stray;
> Good is a forth-right journey still,
> And mazy paths but lead to ill.

But even this apparently "forth-right" condemnation of doubleness and duplicity has its twists. Those "mazy paths" recall the "pleasant paths" in the "metaphysic wilderness" of **"Devotion: An Epistle."** While the young poet of 1794 had recognized a duty to "beat with indefatigable heels, / Th' highway" of reason, the mazy paths of darker speculation simultaneously attracted and disturbed him.

There are some more obvious means by which Brockden Brown seeks to extenuate the guilt of Carwin. The biloquist is himself pictured as a victim. The fragmentary *Memoirs of Carwin the Biloquist,* begun immediately after the completion of *Wieland,*[31] detail the protagonist's naïve association with the sinister and powerful Ludloe. Carwin is pictured also as the victim of an ignorant and brutal father. Finally, Brown leaves the extent of Carwin's involvement in the Wieland murders so much in doubt that the subject has become a matter of critical controversy.[32]

The potential Carwin in Cicero, the classical orator whose greatest appeal is ultimately to the passions, recalls the flames at the heart of the temple. It is not enough merely to oppose enthusiasm with reason: the always speculative, ever ambivalent Brown shows himself wary of an enthusiasm to be found at the heart of reason itself. It is likely, as Larzer Ziff argues, that Brown is critical of the early Republic's facile rationality, but not only because it was impotent to deal with an irrational element at the core of human nature. The young Republic of the United States was, to use Howard Mumford Jones's phrase, founded on "Roman virtue," which permeates architecture no less than government.[33] Cicero, the embodiment of Roman virtue, emerges ambiguously, as Brown depicts him, both through his identification with Carwin and through his actions in "The Death of Cicero" fragment. Like Hawthorne after him, Brown was critical of those who serve a principle of "reason" reared irrationally as a homemade god. Both male Wielands, like Roger Chillingworth, or Rappaccini, or Aylmer, or Ethan Brand, serve gods they themselves have created and to whom they sacrifice their love and heart's desire, relinquishing at last nature itself.

Brown's uneasy examination of the classical background behind his nation's culture does not stop with his ambivalent criticism of Cicero. "My brother's skill," Clara observes, "in Greek and Roman learning was exceeded by that of few." Where he had earlier concerned himself with the textual problems of Cicero's works, after the first two manifestations of Carwin's voice Theodore begins "collecting and investigating the facts which relate to that mysterious personage, the Daemon of Socrates" (48).

Socrates, as Plato represents him to us, refers to his Daemon a number of times, describing it most succinctly in the "Apology":

> You have often heard me speak of an oracle or sign which comes to me, and is the divinity which Meletus ridicules in his indictment. This sign I have had ever since I was a child. The sign is a voice which comes to me and always forbids me to do something which I am going to do, but never commands me to do anything.[34]

Little wonder that Theodore had taken sudden interest in the subject. When Carwin's mysterious voice made its debut it was to warn Wieland, who was walking to the temple, to stop: "There is danger in your path" (33). The second manifestation of the voice, heard by Wieland and Pleyel, interrupted their debate about the merits of Pleyel's plan to visit his betrothed in Europe. Pleyel, endeavoring to convince Wieland to accompany him abroad, was just suggesting that Catharine, as a good wife, would abide by Theodore's decision, when "a negative was clearly and distinctly uttered from another quarter" before Wieland could answer. This voice goes on to "warn" against making a useless journey: for Pleyel's fiancée (it says) is dead (44).

The resemblance to the Daemon of Socrates, which warns rather than commands, is unmistakable. As Edgar Huntly reacts to the horrifying newness of the pit by making of it a horrible but more familiar dungeon, or as Theodore's father recoiled from the wilderness by building the Palladian temple, so Wieland launches upon a study of a classical parallel for the mysterious voice, as if to bring it within the range of what is not only familiar, but venerable. The Daemon of Socrates, one modern writer reports, has been the subject of numerous commentaries and has given rise to any number of interpretations, both ancient and modern.

> Apuleis treated it as a private god. The Fathers of the Church were completely divided about it. Some, like Tertullian, St. Cyprian and Lactantius held it came from Satan; others, like Justin Martyr, Clement of Alexandria, Eusebius and St. Augustine thought of it as some kind of angel. Today certain people think it may have been a type of hallucination that occurs in epilepsy. Still others have seen nothing more in it than Socrates recognizing the voice of conscience.[35]

Brown's linking Carwin with the Daemon, a figure subject to ambiguous interpretation, reflects the complexity of the novelist's own identification with the biloquist. Indeed, in at least one way, Carwin seems to be associated with the clearly benevolent voice of warning. Seven of the nine confirmed instances of biloquism in the novel are warnings: to Theodore, not to approach the temple (32ff.); to Theodore and Pleyel, not to go to Europe (41ff.); again to Theodore and Pleyel, to aid Clara, who had fainted after hearing "murderers" in her closet (59); to Clara, preventing her dream-fall into a

dream-pit, and warning her to avoid a certain secluded wilderness nook (63ff.); and again to Clara, forestalling her discovery of Carwin behind her closet door (85). Lastly, Carwin saves Clara from death by uttering his favorite monosyllabic injunction—"Hold! Hold!"—as her brother is about to execute upon her, as he had upon wife, children, and ward, the sentence of God (299).

But neither does Brown let us see Carwin as a genius of pure benevolence. The first two instances of biloquism proceed not so much from malice, as from Carwin's perverse and diabolically unconscious curiosity. The third is the product of this same curiosity, Carwin having created the closet dialogue between two "murderers" (he says) simply to test Clara's courage. When Clara panics, running out of her house, collapsing in a dead faint at her brother's threshold, Carwin, alarmed himself at the effect of little more than a deadpan practical joke, cries: "Awake! arise! hasten to succour one that is dying at your door!" (59). A more deliberate motive is behind Carwin's wilderness warning to Clara: he wishes to secure the privacy of an amorous retreat—he is intimately occupied with Judith, Clara's chambermaid. Also self-serving is his warning Clara not to open her closet door; he is inside, reading a personal memoir left Clara by her father.

The motive for his final biloquistic performance would seem the least suspect. That he exhibits enough presence of mind to exercise his powers to prevent Clara's murder redeems Carwin from, at least, absolute villainy. Yet this instance of Carwin's benevolence is supremely ironic, since it was necessitated by his previous mischief. Even if Carwin is not directly guilty of the Wieland atrocities, his biloquistic stunts in large measure set the stage for Theodore's madness. Carwin's last injunction—his final "Hold! Hold!"—merely denies madness its consummation. To compound the irony, in a gesture typical of Brown's "do-gooders," Carwin is not content to stop with the utterance of his "favorite monosyllable," but continues, addressing Theodore: "Man of errors! cease to cherish thy delusion: not heaven or hell, but thy senses have misled thee to commit these acts. Shake off thy phrenzy, and ascend into rational and human. Be lunatic no longer" (230). Where the "delusion," called the "delicious idea" by Erasmus Darwin in *Zoönomia,* "produces pleasurable sensations, as in personal vanity or religious enthusiasm[,] it is almost a pity to snatch [the maniac] from [his] fool's paradise, and reduce [him] again to the common lot of humanity."[36] So reduced, "transformed at once in the *man of sorrows*" by Carwin's final "benevolence," Theodore plunges Clara's penknife into his own neck (230-1).

Isaiah prophesied that, despised and rejected, the Messiah would be "a man of sorrows" (53:3). This is the ironic measure of divinity Brown at last allows Wieland:

identification with Christ as the man of sorrows, but incarnated in the "Man of errors." And though we would despise and reject that man, he, surely, bears "our griefs and carrie[s] our sorrows" (Isaiah, 53:3-4); for, as Christ was sent among us as our sorrowful advocate, so Wieland, the man of errors, is even more our representative. Charles Chauncy defined enthusiasm as a "disease" endemic perhaps to all men. "Consciousness itself," Sarsefield declares in **Edgar Huntly,** "is the malady." And so Clara's lament—"What is man, that knowledge is so sparingly conferred upon him!"—sadly inverts the Paul of Hebrews 2:6-7. "What is man," the Apostle rejoices, "that thou art mindful of him?" Man—"a little lower than the angels" and crowned with glory and honor!

Carwin is not evil, but the moral basis for his motives is in no way commensurate with his powers. His talents enable him to approach Cicero in forensic skill and the Daemon of Socrates in authority, but Carwin lacks the moral principles by which he might regulate his powers. The association of Carwin with Cicero and the Daemon ameliorates his character at the same time as it underscores its weaknesses, answering to the needs of Brown's ambivalent identification with the biloquist. The association seems also a response to the broader ambivalence of Brown's relation to some of his nation's adopted cultural values. Not only does the identification of Carwin with Cicero and the Daemon fail to vindicate Carwin unequivocally, it also fails to elevate the classical figures by contrast. Their association with the biloquist diminishes their status as cultural models.

In modern English the distinction between *daemon* and *demon* is not always clear. Defining *demon,* the *Oxford English Dictionary* shows how *daemon,* for Socrates a *"divinum quiddam . . .* a certain divine principle or agency, an inward monitor or oracle," evolved pejoratively through the interpretations of Socrates' accusers and the Christian Fathers into what we understand by the modern English word *demon.* The blurred distinction between *daemon* and *demon* suggests the ambivalence with which the idea of any inspirational voice or spirit has traditionally been regarded. In the case of **Wieland,** Brown frequently associates Carwin with demons in the sense of the word given by Samuel Johnson in his *Dictionary,* as a "spirit; generally an evil spirit; a devil."

But, curiously, whereas Johnson spells the word *demon,* Brown persists in *daemon,* as if to preserve through orthography the idea of a *divinum quiddam* even as he calls Carwin a devil. Pleyel, Clara, Theodore, and even the elusive Ludloe identify the biloquist as—to use Brown's spelling—a *daemon.* Ludloe (who has tenaciously as any "demon" fastened himself upon Carwin) says that the biloquist is "in league with some infernal spirit" (130). The reasonable Pleyel sees the "daemons"

with whom Carwin is leagued as nothing more substantial than metaphors of man's darker side. "As to an alliance with evil geniuses," he explains to Clara, "the power and the malice of daemons have been a thousand times exemplified in human beings. There are no devils but those which are begotten upon selfishness, and reared by cunning" (132). But Clara, despite her rational education, entertains more literal notions of Carwin's daemons: "Where is the proof, said I, that daemons may not be subjected to the controul of men?" (180). Brought before the bar of justice, Theodore denies that he acted under the "influence of daemons" (176), meaning, presumably, evil spirits or devils.

Yet it is Theodore who finally and positively defines Carwin as a "daemon," not a "demon," but something of a *divinum quiddam.* Theodore had made good a third escape from his dungeon for the purpose of "sacrificing" Clara. But Carwin's stammering and ambiguous confession forestalls him. Enraged beyond revenge after Carwin's "incoherent confessions," Wieland contemptuously orders the biloquist from the room. Apparently disabused of his errors now, Theodore is about to spare Clara—but, suddenly: "A new soul appeared to actuate his frame, and his eyes to beam with preternatural lustre."

> Clara! [he exclaims] I must not leave thee in doubt. I know not what brought about thy interview with the being whom thou callest Carwin. For a time, I was guilty of thy error, and deduced from his incoherent confessions that I had been made the victim of human malice. He left us at my bidding [actually, Wieland had threatened him], and I put up a prayer that my doubts should be removed. Thy eyes were shut, and thy ears sealed to the vision that answered my prayer.
>
> I was indeed deceived. The form thou hast seen was the incarnation of a daemon. The visage and voice which urged me to the sacrifice of my family, were his. Now he personates a human form: then he was invironed with the lustre of heaven.

"Clara," Wieland concludes, "thy death must come" (225).

Theodore claims to have seen and heard a "daemon" when he murdered his family, not a devil or an evil spirit, but a being "invironed with the lustre of heaven." Now the hapless Wieland recognizes Carwin as the "incarnation" of that "daemon," personating "a human form"; for Carwin's "visage and voice" (Wieland says) urged the sacrifice of his family. In this, his penultimate moment upon earth, Theodore comes to regard Carwin much as Socrates had regarded his own Daemon. Of course, Brown does not mean to call Socrates and the classical tradition of rational inquiry evil; but the novelist's spirit could not rest in a Socratic symposium anymore than it could in a Ciceronian temple. Some imp of the perverse seems always to knock down whatever figure Brown's imagination suggests, no matter how exemplary. Abraham, Cicero, Socrates—in *Wieland* all wobble on their pedestals.

The philosopher whose rational method triumphed over the mysticism of Anaximides, Parmenides, Heraclitus, and Empedocles, also allowed for the influence of the irrational. One modern student of Socrates finds the source of the philosopher's originality in the remarkable union of "a critical mind, a gift for analysis, a taste for free investigation and doubt, and a wonderful practical sense, with a sincere religious faith, deep burning enthusiasm and a tendency to ecstasy, or at least toward the possibility of it."[37] For Brown such a happy synthesis was not possible. Carwin, as Brown's version of the Socratic Daemon, does indeed have an affinity for the rational mind—but as a cat for the mouse. Carwin's stunts can operate successfully only upon the rational individual who has quite reasonably come to depend upon the truth of what his senses tell him.

Conceived in the American halcyon of John Locke's epistemology, Brown's Carwin must have appeared as an extraordinarily dangerous figure. Though the biloquist deals in illusion, the voices are real enough in their appeal to the senses; and in an epistemology where ideas are ultimately the products of sensation, Carwin is able to create and interpose his private universe of mysterious voices between mind and nature itself. Pleyel, the reasonable Lockean, is merely duped by Carwin's counterfeit of Clara's seduction. Although the result is upsetting, even emotionally painful, for both Clara and Pleyel, it is hardly tragic. But when Carwin works his tricks upon an individual in whom both the rationalist and the enthusiast contend, then the biloquist finds he has "rashly set in motion a machine, over whose progress I had no controul, and which experience [shows as] infinite in power" (215-6). The tragedy, however, does not proceed from any grand malice. Why, for example, did Carwin counterfeit a terrifying dialogue between "two" murderers in Clara's closet? Because "some daemon of mischief seized me" (201).

As a youth, doubtless prompted by the same "daemon," Carwin delighted in making people think his spaniel talked. The dog "asserted the dignity of his species and capacity of intellectual improvement. The company [that had gathered in amazement to hear the animal] separated lost in wonder, but perfectly convinced by the evidence that had been produced" (***Memoirs of Carwin the Biloquist***, 260). This harmlessly impish parlor trick is actually of a piece both with the "murderous dialogue" counterfeited for Clara and with a divine command to murder that Carwin may have counterfeited for Wieland. Ludloe, the youthful biloquist's mysterious mentor, explains how men

> believed in the existence and energy of invisible powers, and in the duty of discovering and conforming to their will. This will was supposed to be sometimes made known to them through the medium of their senses. A voice coming from a quarter where no attendant form could be seen would, in most cases, be ascribed to supernal agency, and a command imposed on them, in this manner, would be obeyed with religious scrupulousness. Thus men might be imperiously directed in the disposal of their industry, their property, and even of their lives. Men, actuated by a mistaken sense of duty, might, under his influence, be led to the commission of the most flagitious, as well as the most heroic acts.
>
> (***Carwin***, 263-4)

The spaniel's name was "Daemon."

Ludloe, a hyperambitious member of the Illuminati, insinuates a motive for the exercise of talents such as Carwin's: "If it were [a man's] desire to accumulate wealth, or institute a new sect, he should need no other instrument" (264). Such motives are not always admirable, but they are reasonable, and are therefore by no means Carwin's. Spurred only by a "daemon of mischief," Carwin's *primum mobile* is, in fact, a *mobile* without motive, to use Edgar Allan Poe's definition of his own version of the daemon of mischief, "a motive not *motivirt*":

> Through its promptings we act without comprehensible object; or, if this shall be understood as a contradiction in terms, we may so far modify the proposition to say, that through its promptings we act, for the reason that we should *not*. In theory, no reason can be more unreasonable; but, in fact, there is none more strong. With certain minds, under certain conditions, it becomes absolutely irresistible.

Poe called this the "Imp of the Perverse." "Beyond or behind this, there is no intelligible principle" (Poe, 6:150).

"It is a radical, a primitive impulse," Poe's narrator says of the Perverse, "—elementary" (6:147). Certainly, Carwin obsessed Brown's imagination as thoroughly as Wieland, but while Theodore's motives are as clear as Abraham's, Carwin's are so elementary as to defy analysis. Just the same, Brown, having divided his identity between Wieland and Carwin, was at pains to explain the biloquist. His name had figured in the list of titles Brown included with his outline of *Wieland*, clearly legible though canceled by a stroke of the pen (a subtitle following it is more thoroughly obliterated and illegible: *possibly* it reads "the road of crime"). Hard upon the completion of *Wieland*, the novelist began ***The Memoirs of Carwin the Biloquist***, breaking it off after he had written enough to fill some sixty printed pages.

Both before and after the composition of the novel, then, Carwin had enjoyed a shaky existence independent of *Wieland*. This is as it should have been, for

Carwin's fictional origin is significantly different from that of the Wieland children. Clara and Theodore were first-generation Americans, highly conscious of their European ancestry and steeped in the neoclassical culture of eighteenth-century Europe. Carwin is more truly a native American. Unlike the Wielands, whose rural home in southeastern Pennsylvania lay but a few miles from what was America's most cosmopolitan metropolis, Carwin was raised on a farm in a "western district of Pennsylvania." His father was a hostile stranger to knowledge outside the farm, his ideas never ranging "beyond the sphere of his vision," and young Carwin's insatiable—even Faustian—"thirst of knowledge" was met by the stern farmer with scorn and "stripes" (247).

One evening, in his fourteenth year, the boy was sent to bring his father's cows in from a distant meadow. He had been "menaced with severe chastisement" if, as was the youth's inquisitive custom, he lingered beyond a strict time limit. He reached the meadow only to discover that the cows had broken the fence and run off. "It was my first duty to carry home the earliest tidings of this accident, but the first suggestion [of an unappeasable curiosity] was to examine the cause and manner of this escape." Soon absorbed in speculative reverie, young Carwin grows heedless of the passing time until "some accident" calls to mind the painful consequences of delay. He resolves not to return home by the "beaten path," but by a wilderness shortcut that would take him through a landscape anticipating *Edgar Huntly,* a "sublime" scene of precipitous cliffs and swirling water. Presently "entangled in a maze" of "abrupt points" and "gloomy hollows"—thoroughly "bewildered," as Edgar Huntly was to say of himself—Carwin discovers a glen through which passage would be shorter and safer than the path he had first proposed to follow. But even this is steep and narrow, so overshadowed by a great cliff that all is plunged into midnight, though the sun has just set. Fearful of "goblins and spectres," Carwin tries to distract himself "by hallowing as loud as organs of unusual compass and vigour would enable me." He calls to the errant cows "in the shrill tones of a Mohock savage"—perhaps he had heard such cries in western Pennsylvania—and the rocks of the wilderness landscape reverberate, though their echo is at first indistinct.

But at one particularly treacherous turn, after a short pause, he calls out again. "In a few seconds a voice, as I then imagined, uttered the same cry from the point of a rock some hundred feet behind me." Carwin casts "a fearful glance behind . . . The speaker, however, was concealed from my view." Again giving voice to the "Mohock" cry, the boy is treated to a "new occasion for wonder." His "ditty" is repeated, a perfect imitation, after a few seconds, but from "a different corner"—the imitator, as before, invisible.

When the quick-witted boy realizes that he has discovered "an echo of an extraordinary kind" he is delighted and, forgetting the prospect of his father's punishment, amuses himself for an hour in talking to the cliffs. He returns frequently to what he now calls his "vocal glen" until he hits upon the idea of producing the echo without aid of the cliffs. "From speculation I proceeded to experiment." And in the wilderness of America, Carwin's biloquism—a talent (he admits) "too liable to perversion for a good man to desire to possess"—is in the most literal sense born (248-53).

Like Edgar Huntly, then, Carwin discovers in the wilderness a hitherto unknown elementary—radical and primitive—aspect of himself. The conditions of the wilderness, of the New World, provoke such discoveries, and the story of *Wieland,* however fleshed out by German, Roman, Greek, and biblical sources, is, as John Neal said of Brown himself, American to the backbone.

Born in and of the wilderness, Carwin's biloquism is the child of confusion's own landscape. As usual, the landscape of the novel is abstract; but if Brown intellectualized the details of the scene into mere emblems, he could not dismiss the intellectual and emotional fact embodied in those emblems. Clara repeatedly presents her situation through metaphors drawn from the landscape. At the beginning of her narrative she pictures herself placed upon a "dreadful eminence" (6) by a train of events unparalleled in the experience of any other human being. Later she sees herself set upon the "brink of danger" (189) and upon the "brink of fate" (22). The revelation of her brother's atrocity threatens to push Clara to the "brink of the same abyss" into which Theodore has already fallen (180). Pleyel, fearful and jealous of what he takes to be her clandestine affair with Carwin, tells Clara how he felt compelled to interfere: "Should I see you rushing to the verge of a dizzy precipice, and not stretch forth a hand to pull you back?" (129). But it is just such a verge that invites Clara as she is about to write of her brother's suicide. Why recall such a horrible scene? Why even continue to live? "Why not terminate at once this series of horrors?—hurry to the verge of the precipice, and cast myself for ever beyond remembrance and beyond hope?" (228). Despite a paucity of picturesque landscape, the wilderness, of which Carwin is product and personification, permeates *Wieland.*

Such figures of speech as those in *Wieland* would be melodramatically banal in the civil scenes of Europe's great cities. Uttered in the American wilderness, they take on crucial significance as evidence of an interpenetration of mind and landscape, an absorption in the spirit of the place. The wilderness was for Brown the territory of the mind's most obscure recesses. Huntly sleepwalks and dreams there, fully awakening into what seems yet another dream. Clara falls asleep in a remote wilderness spot only to dream of the wilderness, a dream within a seeming dream. Given the almost casual equation Brown formulated between mind and landscape, it is not surprising that, along with images of light and dark, the wilderness provides a source of figures through which Brown defines his novel's moral and epistemological themes.

The very epigraph resolves the moral content of *Wieland* into the opposing figures of "Virtue's blissful paths" and the "mazy paths" of deceit. This figure is repeated throughout the novel, from its opening page—where Clara disdains "supplication to the Deity," declaring that the "power that governs the course of human affairs has chosen his path"—through a description of the "austerer and more arduous path" of study Wieland pursued (23). It is continued through Carwin's assurance to Clara that she is under the protection of a divine power so that her "path will be without pits to swallow, or snares to entangle" her (92); and through Pleyel's assertion that Carwin has chosen to conduct his life along an "obscure path" (126). Numerous additional examples might be cited, and frequently these figures of speech are counterpointed to the occasional glimpses Brown affords of the actual paths, narrow and obscure, that run through a sketchily rendered Pennsylvania wilderness. On several occasions the figurative and the physical are not merely counterpointed, but actually dissolve into one another. "There is danger in your path," Carwin warns Theodore, who is at that moment walking the literal, physical path to the temple (33, 46). Although Theodore does turn from the temple and walk back down the path, he of course continues along a metaphorical path to the catastrophe that his father's temple represents.

Long "has been the march," young Brown wrote in his 1794 **"Devotion: An Epistle,"** "And weary, through the thorny tracts that lead / To nothing in the metaphysic wilderness." This might well serve to describe the intellectual journey the novelist took in *Wieland* four years after writing the poem. In a sense, *Wieland,* a book of the metaphysic wilderness, does lead to "nothing"—at least to the frustration of knowledge and revelation. Like the story of Abraham and Isaac, *Wieland* is an epistemological fable; but the biblical episode affirms man's capacity for attaining absolute truth, whereas Brown's novel denies the human capacity for attaining any truth absolutely. In *Edgar Huntly* the wilderness functions both as metaphor and as place, while in *Wieland*—as in Poe's "The Pit and the Pendulum"—the wilderness is realized almost exclusively as metaphor. Because the physical facts of *Edgar Huntly's* wilderness force the sleepwalker to call upon "natural" instincts beyond (or beneath) his civilized reason, Huntly finds within himself an untapped reserve of strength and cunning. Although the wilderness defines the limit of knowledge born in the lightsome chamber of civi-

lized existence, it also reveals a truth outside that chamber. In *Wieland,* however, the wilderness is not present as a *place* of revelation, but only as a *metaphor* of limitation. Essentially, the novel's characters remain lost along figurative paths, tottering on the emotional verge of this or that intellectual abyss.

The discovery of limits, of the "nothing" at the end of thorny tracts, is itself a crucial truth, though. The abrupt and anticlimactic ending of *Wieland*—in which Pleyel, time, and Europe have quite healed Clara's emotional wounds—precludes any divine revelation of the sort Theodore craved. Ironic revelation there is, however, couched in figures of paths, abysses, precipices, darkness, and light. It is the novel's unremitting and unresolved ambiguity, a paradoxical revelation of the absolute limit of revelation.

One of the topics we shall take up in the next chapter is Brown's failure to realize his youthful plan of writing an epic on Christopher Columbus. We may anticipate that discussion here by observing that, in one important sense, Brown did not completely fail. In his four major novels he continued the Navigator's exploration of America, not as a geographical entity, but as a phenomenon of mind. By adding a New World to the geographical and intellectual cosmogony of Europe, Columbus forced the Old World to define its limits. J. H. Elliott, in *The Old World and the New,* quotes Etienne Pasquier, a Parisian lawyer of the early 1560s:

> "It is a striking fact that our classical authors had no knowledge of all this America, which we call New Lands." With these words [Pasquier] caught something of the importance of America for the Europe of his day. Here was a totally new phenomenon, quite outside the range of Europe's accumulated experience and of its normal expectation.[38]

The writings of Columbus himself reveal both the newness of the "New Lands" and the inadequacy of Europe's limited experience fully to comprehend it. Howard Mumford Jones criticizes the letter Columbus wrote to describe the New World as "vague," nonspecific, with little "beyond the repetition of a few simple formulas" common to conventional Renaissance evocations of nature. Later writers and compilers of voyages, particularly Peter Martyr in the early sixteenth century, "translated reports of Columbus, Vespucci, and others" even more deliberately into Renaissance terms, drawing desperately upon classical authors for inadequate formulaic imagery. To be sure, the United States of Brown's century was not Columbus's Europe. But the wilderness, upon whose frontier Brown and his countrymen lived, was yet New Land, and Brown, like Columbus three hundred years before him, struggled to comprehend it, to encompass it within the narrow bounds of his experience. Howard Mumford Jones said, "The nightingale, by the by, which does not exist in the

New World, haunted Columbus: twice on his outward voyage, when the weather was especially fine, he noted in his journal that nothing was wanting for perfection but the song of the nightingale."[39]

Nor do European dungeons exist in America, until Edgar Huntly projects one into the Pennsylvania landscape. Or if the wilderness lacks the temples of ancient Rome, men like Thomas Jefferson and the senior Wieland readily supply Palladian equivalents. As late as 1835 Washington Irving would suggest that the American prairies "only want here and there a village spire, the battlements of a castle, or the turrets of an old family mansion"—as foreign to the New World as a nightingale—"rising from among the trees, to rival the most ornamented scenery of Europe."[40] Brown, like Columbus and like Irving, participates in Europe's dialogue with America, the dialogue that is (according to J. H. Elliott) the history of the Old World and the New. On the one hand, there is "the attempt of Europe to impose its own image, its own aspirations, and its own values on a newly discovered world"; but on the other hand, "a growing awareness of the character, the opportunities and the challenges represented by the New World of America helped to shape and transform an Old World which was itself striving to shape and transform the New" (Elliott, 7).

In the case of a writer like Thoreau, who tells us that the "frontier" exists wherever a man "fronts" a "fact," we can be certain of a conscious awareness of America as an epistemological metaphor. It would be asking too much to expect that degree of self-consciousness from Brown. Although it is difficult to believe him unaware of his own obsession with epistemological themes, it is just as difficult to believe that Brown was fully cognizant of the role America played in working them out. The epistemological metaphors of *Wieland* seem more the inevitable emanations of the spirit of the American place than the carefully wrought products of conscious design. Just the same, at least one of Brown's fellow Americans exhibited an acute awareness of his country as a phenomenon crucial in the world's intellectual cosmogony. Jeremy Belknap, biographer, historian, and novelist, was also a minister. Called upon by the Massachusetts Historical Society in 1792 to deliver a commemorative discourse upon Columbus's discovery of America, Belknap began with a text from Scriptures: "Many shall run to and fro and knowledge shall be increased" (Daniel 12:4).

For, Belknap said, Columbus's voyages "opened to the Europeans a new world; which gave a new turn to their thoughts." The Navigator's heroism consisted in his fulfillment of Daniel's prophecy. Columbus was a divinely inspired but thoroughly empirical scientist: "not a closet projector, but an enterprising adventurer [who,] having established his theory on principles . . . was deter-

mined to exert himself to the utmost to demonstrate its truth by experiment." America was the place of empirical truth; Europe, the closed land of abstract dogmatic belief. "Ignorance and error were canonized" by Europeans, such as St. Augustine, who "doubted the diurnal motion of the earth, or the existence of antipodes." The philosophers of the Old World judged—prejudged—the "torrid and frigid zones" uninhabitable: "It is now known by experience, that the human constitution is capable, by proper management, of enduring all the vicissitudes of heat and cold, of moisture and dryness, to which any accessible part of the earth is subject; and that its health may be preserved in all climates and situations."[41] With dead aim, a battered and exhausted Edgar Huntly hurled an Indian tomahawk between the eyes of a panther. Huntly observed: "No one knows the powers that are latent in his constitution"—until they are discovered "by experience."

How commonplace Belknap's notions of America and Columbus were is impossible to determine exactly. Certainly, American audiences were capable of enjoying the likes of the British playwright Thomas Morton's *Columbus,* little more than the thinnest of excuses to find an exotic setting for the thinnest of love stories, and without the slightest intellectual pretensions.[42] But Belknap's more thoughtful interpretation did circulate well beyond the Massachusetts Historical Society when, two years after the commemorative address was delivered, he included an altered version of the piece in his encyclopedic *American Biography,* a work reviewed in Brown's *Monthly Magazine.*[43] A more significant indication of the currency of Belknap's views is their affinity with Joel Barlow's genial and popular vision of America. At bottom, Barlow's utopian vision rests upon the New World's epistemological status. Both Belknap and Barlow argue that the American "experiment," in revealing a new world of God's creation, brought man to a greater knowledge of God himself, so that America serves the Old World as, in effect, the book of the Lord. The ramifications of this revelation are, of course, not only intellectual but social and political.[44]

For Barlow, America was the land of light; but through the dark pages of *Wieland* light is a fugitive thing. The brightest and steadiest, which bursts only upon the mind of Theodore, is the least real. As the novel perverts the idea of Abrahamic revelation, so it inverts the values represented in Barlow's metaphors of enlightenment. The enduring revelation of the New World is not of light, but of darkness, the limit of knowledge. Joel Barlow summons up Hesper, the genius of the Western world, to guide Columbus through his vision. Brown substitutes a flesh-and-blood native of western Pennsylvania. Carwin's double tongue proclaims the relativity of man's knowledge, even as the discovery of a New World some three hundred years before Brown wrote *Wieland* revealed the relative nature of truths long held sacred by the Old. At the end of *Wieland,* Brown's "genius" returns to his place of origin, retiring to a farmer's life in the wilderness of western Pennsylvania in order to elude Ludloe.

Clara Wieland, however, abandons America for Europe. We leave her in the penultimate chapter longing for death; her entire family, after all, has died, and died horribly. But, summarily, in the final chapter—"written three years after the foregoing and dated at Montpellier"—she flatly declares: "Such is man. Time will obliterate the deepest impressions" (234). Clara confesses that, three years earlier, with the catastrophe fresh in her mind, she was "enamoured of death." Indeed, she fully expected to die, "yet here am I, a thousand leagues from my native soil, in full possession of life and of health, and not destitute of happiness" (234). What is more, she has married that avatar of neoclassical enlightenment, Henry Pleyel! A conventional comic token of the restoration of cosmic order, the marriage ends the tragedy on a note of comedy.[45]

Clara's removal to Europe is not merely a "happy ending" thrown as a sop to a smiling American public. It is a purgation, and more for Brockden Brown than Clara Wieland. After she finished her narrative of the Wieland family tragedy Clara betook herself to bed, "in the full belief that my career in this world was on the point of finishing." She apparently languished for several days until, one night, "after some hours of restlessness and pain, I sunk into deep sleep." She dreamed:

> My fancy became suddenly distempered, and my brain was turned into a theatre of uproar and confusion. It would not be easy to describe the wild and phantastical incongruities that pestered me. My uncle, Wieland, Pleyel and Carwin were successively and momently discerned amidst the storm. Sometimes I was swallowed up by whirlpools, or caught up in the air by half-seen and gigantic forms, and thrown upon pointed rocks, or cast among the billows. Sometimes gleams of light were shot into a dark abyss, on the verge of which I was standing, and enabled me to discover, for a moment, its enormous depth and hideous precipices. Anon, I was transported to some ridge of Aetna, and made a terrified spectator of its fiery torrents and its pillars of smoke.
>
> (236)

At first this seems another of Brown's wilderness dreams, replete with images of abyss, verge, and precipice. There is even the dissolution of the boundary between dream and waking reality that is also a feature of Huntly's wilderness experience and Clara's earlier dream in the woods: "I was conscious," Clara reports, "even during my dream of my real situation" (236). However, here the wilderness images have undergone a subtle but crucial transformation. There are not only abysses and precipices in this dream, but the whirlpool,

rocks, and billows of an ocean and, more significantly, a smoke-belching Mount Aetna. The wilderness has become European, a Dantesque landscape with the addition of classical overtones in Aetna and its *pillars* of smoke. Just as Edgar Huntly preferred the more familiar horror of a European dungeon to the entirely new terror of an American wilderness, so Clara's dreaming mind molds the images of the American wilderness into European, even classical, shape. The horror is vivid; but it has been fashioned into a form familiar to the experience of the Old World.

The dream that purges Clara's mind, and Brown's book, of New World images is a dream of combustion. And for good reason: due to a servant's carelessness in disposing of some live embers, Clara's bedroom is actually aflame as she dreams, and she narrowly escapes a fate that recalls her father's. But escape she does, and more: "This incident, disastrous as it may first seem, had, in reality, a beneficial effect on my feelings. I was, in some degree, roused from the stupor which had seized my faculties. The monotonous and gloomy series of my thoughts was broken." Not only does the fire cauterize Clara's emotional wounds, it sends her packing off to Europe: "My habitation was levelled with the ground, and I was obliged to seek a new one" (237). The "new" habitation, however, is "the shore of the ancient world," where, although the memory of catastrophe does not leave her, "the melancholy which it generated, and the tears with which it filled my eyes, were not unprofitable." This catharsis, an *affective* forgetfulness, is due largely to the influence of the European "spectacle of living manners and the monuments of past ages" which Clara contemplates "with ardour." The "ancient world" reinstates in Clara's heart "its ancient tranquillity" (237).

The empiricism of John Locke took especial root in America most likely because the demands of New World experience were themselves so eminently empirical. The further revelation of *Wieland,* itself rooted in the Lockean soil of America, is the inadequacy of human perception and understanding to interpret the reality the New World so immediately represents. Clara's removal to an ancient world of ancient tranquillity was doubtless an emotional and intellectual necessity for Brown. Reversing the utopian stereotype, he pictures a Europe in which forgetfulness approaches innocence, and an America made guilty by its discovery of the frontier of knowledge itself. The novelist allowed his unconscious and speculative "literary" self full expression in *Wieland,* pushing his characters through a territory of paradoxical revelation. But Charles Brockden Brown could not live wholly in the revealed gloom of this American "literary mood." Having used her to probe the New World's primeval darkness, he returns Clara to the civilized sunshine of Europe. Her name, after all, means "light."

Notes

1. "An Account of a Murder Committed by Mr. J———Y———, upon this Family in December, A.D. 1781," in *New York Weekly Magazine 2,* nos. 55 and 56 (July 20 and 27, 1796), pp. 20 and 28; rptd., *Philadelphia Minerva 2,* nos. 81 and 82 (August 20 and 27, 1796), n. pag. An anonymous reviewer of *Wieland* recognized the Tomhannock murder as a source for the novel in the *American Review and Literary Journal* 1 (January, 1801), pp. 333-9. J. C. Hendrickson, in "A Note on *Wieland,*" *American Literature* 8 (November, 1936), pp. 305-6, identifies J———Y——— as James Yates.

2. Carl Van Doren, "Early American Realism," *Nation* 99 (November 12, 1914), pp. 577-8.

3. A facsimile of the outline is reproduced together with a transcription in the Kent State *Wieland* [edited with an introduction by Sydney J. Krause and S. W. Reid (Kent, OH: Kent State University Press, 1978)]. Page references hereafter will be cited in the text.

4. Michel Guillaume Jean de Crèvecoeur, *Letters from an American Farmer* (1782; rptd., New York: Dutton, 1957), p. 35.

5. In *Posthumous Works of Ann Eliza Bleecker* (New York: T. and J. Swords, 1793). *The History of Maria Kittle* was also published in a separate edition in 1797 by Elisha Babcock, Hartford. All references are to the 1793 edition and will be cited in the text.

6. Edwin Fussell, *Frontier: American Literature and the American West* (Princeton: Princeton University Press, 1965), p. 10.

7. See Kendall B. Taft, ed., *Minor Knickerbockers* (New York: American Book, 1947), p. 378, n. 3.

8. "Though it has been virtually ignored by literary historians, the amazing influence that [C. M. Wieland's] *Oberon* evidently exerted would seem to make this pioneer metrical romance easily the most influential foreign literary work of the time. . . . In a steady stream [Wieland's] writings . . . appeared in countless editions and *well over 375 translations into no less than 14 other languages!*" (Werner W. Beyer, *The Enchanted Forest* [New York: Barnes and Noble, 1963], pp. ix and 2). See also Harry R. Warfel, "Charles Brockden Brown's German Sources," *Modern Language Quarterly* 1, no. 2 (September, 1940), pp. 357-65.

9. John McCarthy, *Fantasy and Reality: An Epistemological Approach to Wieland* (Bern and Frankfurt: Lang, 1974), pp. 9 and 12.

10. See the Warfel article cited in note 8. For more on Brown's use of C. M. Wieland, see John G. Frank, "The Wieland Family in Charles Brockden Brown's *Wieland,*" *Monatshefte* 42, no. 7 (November, 1950), pp. 347-53.

11. Christoph Martin Wieland, *The Trial of Abraham. In Four Cantos. Translated from the German* (Norwich, Conn.: John Trumbull, 1778), p. 28. Page references hereafter will be cited in the text.

12. See the entries under "Albigenses" and "Waldenses" in Ephraim Chambers, *Cyclopaedia; or, An Universal Dictionary of the Arts and Sciences,* 5th ed. (London: D. Midwinter, 1741-3), and in the second volume of the 1753 *Supplement* (London: Printed for W. Innys, 1753). Accounts by later authorities are found in Samuel Macaulay Jackson et al., eds., *The New Schaff-Herzog Encyclopedia of Religious Knowledge* (New York: Funk and Wagnalls, 1910); James Hastings et al., eds., *Encyclopaedia of Religion and Ethics* (New York: Scribner's, 1958); and Edwin H. Palmer et al., eds., *The Encyclopedia of Christianity* (Wilmington: National Foundation for Christian Education, 1964), vol. 1.

13. Larzer Ziff, "A Reading of *Wieland,*" *PMLA,* 77 (March, 1962), pp. 51-7; see pp. 51 and 54.

14. Charles Chauncy, "Enthusiasm Described and Cautioned Against: A Sermon Preach'd at the Old Brick Meeting House in Boston, the Lord's Day after the Commencement, 1742" (Boston: J. Draper and S. Eliot, 1742), p. 3. Page references hereafter will be cited in the text.

15. Erasmus Darwin, *Zoönomia; or, The Laws of Organic Life* (Philadelphia: T. Dobson, 1797), pt. 2, vol. 1, p. 444.

16. William L. Hedges, "Charles Brockden Brown and the Culture of Contradictions," *Early American Literature* 9 (Fall, 1974), pp. 107-42 (see pp. 110 and 112).

17. [Charles Brockden Brown,] *An Address to the Congress of the United States, on the Utility and Justice of Restrictions upon Foreign Commerce* (Philadelphia: C. and A. Conrad, 1809), p. vi.

18. William Smith, *History of New-York, from the First Discovery to the Year 1732* (1757; rptd., Albany: Ryer Schermerhorn, 1814), pp. 201-3 and 202n. A second edition was issued by Mathew Carey in Philadelphia, 1792.

19. Except where noted otherwise, the information that follows is drawn from Charles West Thomson, "Notices of the Life and Character of Robert Proud, Author of 'The History of Pennsylvania,'" in *Memoirs of the Historical Society of Pennsylvania* (Philadelphia: McCarty and Davis, 1826; rptd., Philadelphia: Lippincott, 1864), vol. 1, pp. 417-35.

20. Robert Spiller et al., *The Literary History of the United States,* 4th ed. (New York: Macmillan, 1974), p. 137.

21. Although Proud affixed the date of the "Plaintive Essay" in good Quaker fashion, substituting the simple "6 mo." for the pagan June, he dated the "Vox Naturae" from "Philadelphia, Christmas Day, 1782." Quaker practice, as set out in *Rules of Discipline, and Christian Advices of the Yearly Meeting of Friends for Pennsylvania and New Jersey* (Philadelphia: Samuel Sansom, Jr., 1797), enjoins against distinguishing days and months by pagan names and condemns "Fasts and Feast Days and Times, and other human Injunctions and Institutions relative to the Worship of God." From all appearances temperamentally unsuited to the spirit of Woolman and Penn, Proud, in the privacy of manuscript, was also capable of heterodoxy in a significant detail of Quaker practice.

22. "Letters of Robert Proud," *Pennsylvania Magazine of History and Biography* 34 (January, 1910), p. 62-73; see p. 63.

23. [Charles Brockden Brown], review of Proud's *History of Pennsylvania, Monthly Magazine* 1 (June, 1799), pp. 216-7. For authorship see Bennett, p. 129.

24. Robert Proud, *History of Pennsylvania* (Philadelphia: Zachariah Poulson, Jr., 1797), vol. 1, pp. 7-8. Page references hereafter will be cited in the text.

25. See Herman Melville, *Redburn: His First Voyage* (1849; rptd., New York: Doubleday, 1957), pp. 236-7. For a discussion of Melville's possible borrowing from the spontaneous combustion scene in *Wieland,* see note 17, Introduction.

26. So the Reverend Charles Chauncy questioned the metaphor of illumination employed by proponents of The Great Awakening. He doubted the validity of any "joy" or "assurance" vouchsafed by "a *direct Light shining in*" the mind of an enthusiast rather than by "Evidence . . . from the *Word of GOD.*" Chauncy warned that "the Joy of these Times [the decade of the Awakening] is too generally the Effect of this *sudden Light,* and not of a *strict* and *thorow Examination.*" It is "infinitely dangerous for Men to trust to *this light,* and depend upon the *Joy* arising from it, without the concurring *Testimony* of their own *Consciences,* upon clear and full evidence." (Charles Chauncy, *Seasonable Thoughts on the State of Religion* [Boston: Printed by Rogers and Fowle for Samuel Eliot, 1743], p. 123.)

27. Joel Barlow, *The Vision of Columbus: A Poem in Nine Books* (Hartford: Hudson and Goodwin, 1787), bk. 7, p. 204

28. See Kenneth Silverman, *A Cultural History of the American Revolution* (New York: Crowell, 1976), passim and p. 232, for a discussion of the "rising glory" motif. Brown wrote his own "Rising Glory of America" (1787), a poem transcribed in his father Elijah's manuscript journal (Historical Society of Pennsylvania: AM03399, item 4).

29. Hugh Blair, *Lectures on Rhetoric and Belles Lettres,* 2d ed., corrected (London: W. Straham, T. Cadell, and W. Creech, 1785), vol. 2, pp. 204-13. Page references hereafter will be cited in the text. On the great popularity of Blair in America, see William Charvat, *The Origins of American Critical Thought, 1810-1835* (Philadelphia: University of Pennsylvania Press, 1936), pp. 29-31.

30. [Charles Brockden Brown,] "The Difference between History and Romance," *Monthly Magazine* 2 (April, 1800), pp. 250-3.

31. "Read Brown's 'Carwin,' as far as he has written it" (Smith, August 8, 1798, p. 460).

32. Two articles summarize the controversy: Robert Hobson, "Voices of Carwin and Other Mysteries in Charles Brockden Brown's *Wieland,*" *Early American Literature* 10 (Winter, 1975-76), pp. 307-9; and David Lyttle, "The Case against Carwin," *Nineteenth-Century Fiction* 26 (December, 1971), pp. 257-69.

33. Howard Mumford Jones, *O Strange New World* (New York: Viking, 1967), pp. 227-72.

34. Plato, "Apology," in Benjamin Jowett, trans., *The Dialogues of Plato* (Boston: Houghton Mifflin, 1962), pp. 66-7.

35. Jean Brun, *Socrates,* trans. Douglas Scott (New York: Walker and Co., 1962), pp. 66-7

36. Darwin, *Zoönomia,* pt. 2, vol. 1, p. 444.

37. Anthelme Chaignet quoted in Brun (see note 35, above).

38. J. H. Eliott, *The Old World and the New* (Cambridge: At the University Press, 1972), p. 8.

39. Jones, *New World,* p. 14; cf. Anne Bradstreet's "sweet-tongu'd Philomel" in stanza 26 of the *Contemplations.*

40. Washington Irving, *A Tour on the Prairies* (1835; rptd., Norman: University of Oklahoma Press, 1956), p. 108.

41. Jeremy Belknap, *A Discourse Intended to Commemorate the Discovery of America by Christopher Columbus . . .* (Boston: Apollo Press, 1792), p. 34.

42. Thomas Morton, *Columbus; or, The Discovery of America. An Historical Play. As Performed at the*

Theatre-Royal, Covent-Garden, London (Boston: William Spotswood, 1794). The play had its American premiere in New York, September 16, 1797. William Dunlap praised the production. See George C. D. Odell, *Annals of the New York Stage* (New York: Columbia University Press, 1927), vol. 1, p. 463; and William Dunlap *History of the American Theatre and Anecdotes of the Principal Actors* (1832; rptd., New York: Burt Franklin, 1963), vol. 1, p. 372.

43. [Charles Brockden Brown?], review of Jeremy Belknap, *American Biography* . . . (Boston: Isiah Thomas and Ebenezer T. Andrews, 1794), *Monthly Magazine* 1 (July, 1799), pp. 282-7. See note on authorship, Chapter 1, note 1.

44. Alexander Martin wrote an addendum to Morton's *Columbus* entitled "A New Scene Interesting to the Citizens of the United States of America, Additional to the Historical Play of Columbus, by a Senator of the United States." Published in 1798 by Benjamin Franklin Bache at Philadelphia, the fragment sounds a utopian theme closely resembling Barlow's; Martin even borrows Barlow's Hesper—albeit adorned in "Roman cap"—to guide Columbus through a vision of the United States. See Richard Walser, "Alexander Martin, Poet," *Early American Literature* 6 (Spring, 1971), pp. 55-61.

45. Wayne Franklin, in "Desperate Imagination: Tragedy and Comedy in Brown's *Wieland*," *Novel* 9 (Winter, 1975), pp. 147-63, shows how Brown was influenced by Shakespeare in the mixture of tragic and comic modes in *Wieland.*

Roberta F. Weldon (essay date 1984)

SOURCE: Weldon, Roberta F. "Charles Brockden Brown's *Wieland*: A Family Tragedy." *Studies in American Fiction* 12, no. 1 (spring 1984): 1-11.

[*In the following essay, Weldon explores* Wieland *as the tragedy of an entire family and an entire society, rather than of one man.*]

In *Wieland* Charles Brockden Brown creates a family and shows how its flaws lead to its tragic fall. The elements of the novel direct the reader away from a concentration on any one character and towards a consideration of the basic unit of society, the family. Although the title character of the novel may be Wieland, his tragedy and fall affect Clara, Catherine, and Pleyel and are caused partly by his family history—the tragic lives of both his father and grandfather. This perspective allows Brown to emphasize a conception of man as pri-

marily a social being, and yet the social order in *Wieland* is one near collapse where the promise of restoration seems remote. Moreover, the history of the Wieland family, one of the first literary American families, with its ghastly murders and undercurrents of incest, rivals that of the most bizarre Roman tragedy and causes the Wielands to become finally not a model for emulation but a standard of failure. The nature of this family, the reasons for its failure or fall, and the tragic consequences make up the central concerns of the novel and reveal a work that, while it has at its center a strong pattern of classical allusions and resonances, uses the pattern to show that the classical ideals are ultimately flawed and not viable for an American social model.

Identifying the central character in *Wieland* has caused some disagreement among critics. Most of the earlier interpretations of the novel accept Wieland as the central figure, but later criticism devotes more attention to the role of the narrator, Clara, Wieland's sister.[1] The interpretations that emphasize one character and diminish the significance of the role of the others can tend to distort an understanding of the main concerns of the novel. From the start, Clara is careful to establish that the story she relates is not simply hers or her brother's; it is instead a narrative of the events "that have lately happened in my family."[2] Her personal despair is subsumed by her sense of the enormity of the tragedy as it has altered the history of an entire family. She describes "the storm that tore up *our* [emphasis added] happiness, and changed into dreariness, and desert the blooming scene of *our* [emphasis added] existence" (pp. 5-6). The title does not refer only to the patriarch of the family, Theodore Wieland, as much as it does to the entire Wieland family—grandparents, husband, wife, sister, children, and even future in-laws (Pleyel).

Early in the novel Clara relates a discussion between Wieland and Pleyel concerning Cicero's *Oration for Cluentius* that first establishes the emphasis on the family. The oration uses the crimes of one family to present a disturbing picture of Roman life in the final days of the Roman republic. In defending Cluentius against the charge of murder, Cicero recounts a long list of depravities—mainly incest and murder—committed for political and financial gain by one member of Cluentius's family against another. In this way, Cicero succeeds in creating a strong impression of the corruption and depravity caused by the breakdown of the family structure and its values in Roman society. Significantly, Wieland and Pleyel are concerned with determining whether the oration's account mirrors "the manners of the time" (p. 30). Pleyel is reluctant "to make the picture of a single family a model from which to sketch the condition of a nation" (p. 30), while Wieland is apparently willing to accept Cluentius's history as representative, in a microcosmic way, of Roman life.

The conversation between Wieland and Pleyel provides an allegory from which to view the history of the Wieland family. Clara's narrative contains many of the same sordid details that are related in the *Oration for Cluentius*. Wieland's mania is so appalling because it is so unnatural; it causes him to seek to destroy those most closely related to him—his wife, children, sister, and dearest friend. To win sympathy for Cluentius, Cicero describes the heinous crimes of Sassia, Cluentius's mother, and Oppianicus, his mother's husband and Cluentius's enemy. Under Sassia's influence, Oppianicus also murders his wife, children, and brother, while Sassia attempts to destroy her son, Cluentius. The unnatural crimes described in these two narratives are quite similar, but while Oppianicus murders for personal gain, Wieland's motives, as Clara understands them, have "lost none of their claim to the homage of mankind"; he seeks only the "supreme good" and is directed by the "boundless energy of Duty" (p. 230) to God. Still, in spite of the apparent differences in motivation of the criminals, Brown implies that there is reason to associate the two narratives. The Wieland family is destroyed not solely because of the insanity of its patriarch but also, like the Roman family that Cicero describes, because of its morally erroneous foundation.

On the surface, most of what the Wielands uphold include those values that would make them a model family and which would even link them to the classical ideal. Cicero is "the chief object of his [Wieland's] veneration" (p. 24). Significantly, Wieland is not content just to read and study Cicero's works. He must also imitate his style and manner: "He was never tired of conning and rehearsing his productions. To understand them was not sufficient. He was anxious to discover the gestures and cadences with which they ought to be delivered" (p. 24). He and his family re-create on the banks of the Delaware a society modelled on classical virtues or values. They accept the classical emphasis on reason as the cornerstone of society and value leisure because it affords them the opportunity to develop their intellect. The temple is the center of their life, and they place in it a marble bust of Cicero, whose presence oversees their daily occupations—reading and studying literature, especially the Latin classics, engaging in discussion, enjoying music and poetry. They believe that reason makes one human and is also the agency which deduces truth from sensory evidence (p. 35). Moreover, they accept, just as Cicero does in the *Oration for Cluentius,* that the power of reason alone prevents the fearful descent into the "dark abyss" of uncontrolled passions. Of course, reason fails them; Wieland and his family are destroyed by dark emotions, "cowardly rashness" and "criminal despair" (p. 225). After Wieland has murdered his wife and children, Clara returns to find the temple in disrepair, overrun by shrubs and weeds. The Apollonian spirit, represented by Cicero, has been dispelled from the temple by the Dionysian force for disorder and chaos. Cicero is the god that failed, for reason, equity, and fortitude, the virtues of his religion, give way to new powers.

Barbarity and savagery claim the world of the Wieland family. And yet, the cause of this family's downfall has always troubled the book's readers,[3] the more so because in some ways its members should be best suited to prevent the overthrow of the ordered world they have taken pains to create. In the earlier section of the novel, they do approach in their conduct the Roman ideal that they study. Their familial love and devotion are strong, and they cherish one another's company and try to foster each other's intellectual and moral growth. Because of the near flawlessness of their conduct, it is almost tempting to claim that there is no assignable cause for the tragedy that ensues. The expulsion from their "blooming . . . existence" to the "desert" (p. 6) despair is simply an inevitable part of the human condition. The movement from the world of innocence to the world of experience is inexorable. Or it might be suggested that the family fails because of an excess of a basically positive impulse, the desire that the Wielands share for reason and order to pattern their lives. The failure of the empirical method of the Lockean tradition may contribute to their fall, but their expectation that reality should be rational and reasonable may be a more significant cause. The Wielands deny the power that the forces of irrationality and disorder have to shape and determine their lives. Like Vere in *Billy Budd,* the Wielands have taken from the story of Orpheus and his lyre the idea that "forms measured forms are everything" and neglected the lesson of the second part of the myth that the forces of irrationality cannot be permanently repressed or eventually they will break forth in disorder against the repressor. In this interpretation, the Wielands are overthrown by those powers they have tried so strongly to banish from their world precisely because they have almost succeeded in banishing them. While this interpretation is satisfying on a certain level, especially to the post-Freudian reader, Brown stresses that the Wielands fail primarily because of moral shortcomings. Wieland becomes a "man of sorrows" and his family is destroyed because its moral and social vision is warped.

Brown establishes in the "Advertisement" to the novel that the events of the book "took place between the conclusion of the French and the beginning of the revolutionary war" (p. 3). In the body of the novel Clara mentions that "the sound of war had been heard. . . . The Indians were repulsed on one side, and Canada was conquered on the other" (p. 26). And yet, the Wieland family has enjoyed six years of "uninterrupted happiness" despite this "sound of war" (p. 26). In fact, Clara is close to smugness when from her protected vantage point she observes that war "was at such a distance" that it seemed "to enhance our enjoyment by affording objects of comparison" (p. 26). It is rather disconcerting that the Wieland family lacks any substantial feeling about the Colonial crisis and about the fate of those involved in the war. That Clara can assert that "revolutions and battles, however calamitous to those who occupied the scene, contributed in some sort to our happiness, by agitating our minds with curiosity, and furnishing causes of patriotic exultation" (p. 26) is somewhat disturbing and indicates that the kind of insularity the Wielands embrace can lead to a dangerous myopia.

Ironically, the strength of the Wieland family bond is also the source of its fatal weakness. The Wielands isolate themselves in a somewhat remote area of Pennsylvania, and, except for the companionship of Pleyel, they are not dependent upon or desirous of outside relationships. They apparently flourish in the rarefied atmosphere of each other's company, enjoying intercourse. They are removed from the discord and the concerns of Colonial society and exist in a comparatively unreal world of reason, benevolence, and justice. In a perceptive article on the novel, William Manly suggests that excessive introspection forms the basis for the novel's tragedy: "The central drama of the novel lies . . . in Clara's consciousness as she copes with a growing isolation from the sane and normal preoccupations of daily life."[4] But the isolation she experiences is also a particular manifestation of the larger problem which dominates the novel. The isolation of Wieland, Catherine, and Clara serves as a metaphor for the equally significant alienation of an entire family who are pursuing the philosophy of individual perfection as a social model. Clara's thoughts on the war first suggest the family's insularity, and the strong intimations of incestuous desires only provide another manifestation of the same problem. The members of the family have cherished what has come to be identified as an American belief in the supreme power of the individual. They have made this principle, which has its roots in Roman classicism, the basis of the familial order, and because of it the family they have formed is as insular and inward looking as its members. It is not the individual experience of the characters that threatens to divorce them from reality as much as their collective response to experience.

In a review of a Fourth of July oration published in *Monthly Magazine* in 1798, Brown comments on the decline of society. In the first part of the review he summarizes the conclusions of the author of the oration, Mr. Quincy, about the reason for the decline. According to Brown, Mr. Quincy argues that the main cause of "our present danger" is the excessive individualism of the people.[5] He chastises those who are indifferent to the public welfare and who selfishly pursue "private gain."[6] He calls for "genuine love of the public good"[7] as the foundation for a new society. Apparently in agreement with Mr. Quincy, Brown concludes his re-

view by asserting that "every good man must unite with Mr. Quincy in deploring these evils and in deprecating their ruinous consequences."[8] Since the review was written during the period in which Brown was working on *Wieland,* it seems reasonable to conjecture that some of the "ruinous consequences" of excessive individualism are dramatized in the story of the Wieland family. The Wieland family story is in one important way an American tale, as the subtitle suggests. By focusing on the error of the Wieland family, the novel examines the flawed design underlying the American ideal. The Wielands believe with Emerson that "the individual is the world" but experience the danger of self-absorption and are destroyed by it. Brown seems to suggest that a family can be, as Wieland argues in the discussion of the *Oration for Cluentius,* "a model" of the national character. Like the Roman family in the *Oration,* the Wielands represent the failed ideals of a society. Perhaps this may help to explain the reason why Brown sent a copy of *Wieland* along with a letter to Thomas Jefferson. Brown can argue in the letter that the merit of fictitious narratives is comparable to that of "social and intellectual theory . . . the history of fact in the processes of nature and the operations of government"[9] precisely because his novel *Wieland* has as its basis the same sort of preoccupation with the national character that marks the work of the social, intellectual, and political theoretician, a preoccupation which would certainly appeal to Jefferson.

Still, if the family is so decidedly a model of failure, the happy ending of the novel becomes a problem.[10] In fact, after reading the ending, the reader is tempted simply to conclude that Brown, in finishing *Wieland, or the Transformation* as he does, shares Hawthorne's desire in the original edition of *The Marble Faun,* entitled *Transformation,* "to send the reader away happy."[11] Brown's ending, though, is much more elaborate and fully developed than Hawthorne's. In a long concluding section Clara relates that she recovers from the despondency which she experiences after learning of her brother's mania and witnessing his suicide. "All's well that ends well," or so it seems. Clara has joined the world of the present; she leaves her destructive isolation to experience the world. Earlier in the novel Pleyel speaks to Wieland about returning to Europe as returning to social responsibilities, responsibilities Wieland does not want. Thus, in journeying eastward Clara may be making a choice for structure, authority, and responsibilities that extend beyond the scope of the private.

Yet the conclusion is not as straightforward as the simple retelling and analysis of plot implies. Even examining the associations with Europe that the novel establishes leads to a recognition of the complexities of the conclusion. In journeying eastward to Europe Clara is both leaving America and returning to the place of origin, a locale that her grandfather had left two generations earlier full of confidence that his dream of converting the Indians in the New World could be fulfilled. Her departure implies a belief in the future at the same time that it symbolically reflects a reaching back to the past. Ironically, the promise that she sees in the future is to be found in the Old World, not the new, and, granted her family history, has to be based upon a strong recognition of the possibility of failure. A similar sort of complexity is also apparent in the conversation between Pleyel and Wieland about returning to Europe. Pleyel has argued rationally that Wieland should return to Europe to assume his social position, but the narrative implies that Pleyel's deeper reason for trying to influence his friend's decision is personal and emotional, so that Pleyel can be among the company of friends when he weds the European Baronness Therèsa de Stolberg.

Brown's fictional method makes the reader aware of the complexity of reality. He takes extraordinary care to make the reader attentive to different versions of the truth, and to the necessity for recognizing "the little lower layer," especially when trying to understand human conduct. This technique is most obviously evident in the way in which he handles the character of Carwin, "the double tongued deceiver," or more subtly in his consideration of the motives of Wieland's father or of Wieland himself. The *Oration for Cluentius* once again provides further insight into Brown's vision of the nature of reality. Pleyel attempts to dismiss the merits of the oration on the basis that Cicero "had embraced a bad cause; or, at least, a doubtful one" (p. 30). Apparently, this oration was tainted for Pleyel because Cicero's motives for arguing on Cluentius's behalf were questionable. Cicero had previously argued against Cluentius and contended that he had bribed a jury. And yet, three years later Cicero is using the same defense on Cluentius's behalf. In the oration he attempts to prove that Oppianicus, Cluentius's enemy, had been guilty of bribery. It is important, too, that Cicero had boasted in Quintilian's *Institutio Oratoria* that in the Cluentius case he succeeded in "pulling the wool over the eyes of the court."[12] Consequently, even in the reference to Cicero, Brown is exploring different versions of the real. Cicero, the ideal, is tainted by false motives. The episode is full of a somewhat troubling complexity that marks the entire novel, and especially its conclusion.

Brown ties the knot of his story with the marriage of Clara and Pleyel. But clearly in ending the novel in this way he does not use this marriage to reaffirm a belief in the social order based upon an acceptance of the national character as represented by the Wielands. Brown is not part of the group of Gothic novelists who clear up all the darkness at the conclusion of the book and suggest, as Leslie Fiedler describes, "in the very technique of fiction a view of the world which insists that though fear is real, its causes are delusive."[13] The mar-

riage ends the story but also marks a beginning, a beginning of a new family in the Wieland line. Because of this double impulse, it is difficult to describe unambiguously the significance of the final revelation of the book. The marriage, while it fixes the characters in a new relation, also raises the question of the future of the family. As in most novels that end in marriage, there is a twofold response by the reader to the conclusion: the ending gives pleasure because the tensions are resolved so successfully but causes a certain amount of concern and wonder about the future of the union. When Pip marries Estelle in the second version of the ending to *Great Expectations,* the reader is both glad and somewhat dismayed when he considers Pip's choice of a marriage partner. The satisfying release that the marriage provides for the reader is a difficult pleasure for the nineteenth-century novelist to deny his audience, and Brown is no exception. The marriage in **Wieland** is an occasion for celebration. Clara has chosen life rather than death, and her marriage affirms that decision. But when Clara's choice of a marriage partner and her own mental condition at the conclusion of the novel are examined the joy is tempered.

The Clara of the concluding section of **Wieland** is remarkably similar to the Clara whose perceptions make up the central portion of the novel. There is a time in the novel when Clara undergoes a radical change in her outlook. Immediately after the recognition that her brother is a demented murderer, Clara's usual belief in reason and its power to inform the will seems sorely shaken. She sadly confesses that she was not rescued from her deep despondency and death wishes by "fortitude or the capacity for instruction" or by her belief in "the exercise of the social and beneficent affections, the contemplation of nature and the acquisition of wisdom" (p. 235). In short, she was not comforted by the consolations of the rationalist but by the passage of time and fate. When she is rescued from the fire and brought to the hut, the new locale seems to suggest, on a psychological level, the utter simplicity and vulnerability of the character at this point. Her world view is almost primitive in some respects. She accepts the reality of fate and time as forces that shape the individual. Socially, her rescue to the hut suggests her removal to a much simpler order, an almost natural state. But from the hut she journeys to Europe, and all that is said of her travels, that she "contemplated, with ardor, the spectacle of living manners and the monuments of past ages" (p. 237), indicates a dramatic change in Clara from the simple self of the hut to the more complex self of the structured and sophisticated European social world. Clara's marriage to Pleyel, the individual most associated with the Roman model and most enamoured of reason, only reconfirms what her journey eastward implies. Pleyel has been betrayed by his belief in reason. Depending upon the evidence of the senses to inform his will correctly, he has wronged Clara when, thinking he hears Carwin and Clara talking, he incorrectly assumes Clara is guilty of a serious indiscretion. His final injunction to Clara before his separation from her, "may adversity instruct you in that wisdom, which education was unable to impart to you" (p. 135), becomes an almost ironic commentary on the possible means of his own illumination. But it is important to note that the reader has no reason to believe that Pleyel changes or that his old beliefs are at all questioned. In marrying him, Clara seems to be falling back upon a reliance on her original ideas that reason and equanimity are mainstays. With these beliefs as its foundation, the new social order which Clara and Pleyel will establish promises to be much like the old—a social order based upon the philosophy of individual perfection, which threatens to become excessive self-involvement and thus to isolate its members from society and reality in a world of delusion. It is remarkable that a story about the American family should conclude with an eastward migration, and yet it is fitting, since in this movement Brown reconfirms the initial impression suggested by the pattern that is revealed in the section on the *Oration for Cluentius*. The values that Clara and the Wielands have cherished have failed, and in the failure of this family it is possible to see a failure of the national experiment if the society does not change the emphasis of its philosophy and values. The eastward movement confirms the failure; Clara's journey does mark a new beginning but, more significantly, it signals an end, an end to the American experiment of the Wieland family.

The conclusion of the novel underscores Brown's technique of making the reader aware of the complexity of reality and human conduct that he has used throughout the novel. Clara is journeying eastward to the future and to a more sophisticated world, but she is also trying to return to a simpler past, one where, as the Wieland family's tragedy reveals, the answers to the moral and social questions, though ironically more sophisticated, are also more certain and unequivocal and in that sense less complex. At the conclusion, Clara seems only a little darkened by the tragedies of her life, and in her decision to marry Pleyel she chooses to confirm a belief in the future, in the possibility of establishing a new family. But the reader feels much less confident about this future than Clara does. R. D. Laing's observation that "'family' space and time is akin to mythic space-time, in that it tends to be ordered round a center and runs on repeating cycles,"[14] if used to comment on Clara's situation, seems to indicate that the patterns of the Wieland family, running in tragic cycles, promise only tragedy again. Despite Clara's hopes for the future, it is clear that the ghosts of past families have been internalized by Clara and will take up residence with the family at Montpelier. Unless Clara can come to terms with the "internalized family" and gain a sav-

ing recognition that will disrupt the cyclic pattern, the family of the future will be like that of the past, and the social order will not be reaffirmed.

Although the marriage of Clara and Pleyel concludes the history of the Wieland family on a seemingly happy note, Brown suggests that the failings which precipitated the family tragedy have not been overcome and will continue to affect the new family and possibly future generations. There is no indication the inheritance from the Wieland side will not be despondency and madness, growing out of a dangerous myopia and social isolation; the Pleyel strain, with its complete reliance on the classical standard of reason, will only exaggerate the tendencies of the Wieland line, as it has in the past. Clara does not break the tragic cycle. The conclusion of *Wieland* promises both continuance and failure of the family, a blessed and terrifying possibility both for the Wielands and for society.

Notes

1. Fred Lewis Pattee, in his introduction to *Wieland*, argues that "despite the fact that Clara and Carwin dominate the first half of the book to the almost total exclusion of the title character, Wieland is the central figure, and his 'transformation' is the central motif" (*Wieland, or the Transformation: An American Tale,* ed. Fred Lewis Pattee [New York: Hafner Publishing Company, 1958], p. x1). David Lee Clark's approach to the theme of the book is based upon his assumption that Wieland is the central character. See *Charles Brockden Brown: Pioneer Voice of America* (Durham: Duke Univ. Press, 1952). Joseph Soldati, in his study of the Faust motif in the novel, focuses on the character of Wieland ("A Study of Charles Brockden Brown's *Wieland*," *ESQ* [*A Journal of the American Renaissance*], 20 [1974], 115). Another group of critics have, however, not accepted the view that the title character is the central character and have concluded instead that the story revolves around the narrator, Clara. Among this group are Arthur Kimball in *Rational Fictions: A Study of Charles Brockden Brown* (McMinnville: Linfield Research Institute, 1968); John Frank, "The Wieland Family in Charles Brockden Brown's *Wieland*," *Monatshefte,* 42 (1950), 347-53; Donald A. Ringe, *Charles Brockden Brown* (New York: Twayne, 1966); William M. Manly, "The Importance of Point of View in Brockden Brown's *Wieland*," *AL* [*American Literature*], 35 (1963), 309-12; Harry Warfel in *Charles Brockden Brown* (Gainesville: Univ. of Florida Press, 1949); and Norman Grabo in *The Coincidental Art of Charles Brockden Brown* (Chapel Hill: Univ. of North Carolina Press, 1981). Finally, although David Lyttle focuses on the role of Carwin in "The Case

Against Carwin," *NCF* [*Nineteenth-Century Fiction*], 26 (1971), 257-69, he also acknowledges the centrality of Clara.

2. Charles Brockden Brown, *Wieland or the Transformation, An American Tale,* volume 1 of the bicentennial edition of *The Novels and Related Works of Charles Brockden Brown,* ed. Sydney J. Krause and S. W. Reid (Kent: Kent State Univ. Press, 1977), p. 5. The text of the bicentennial edition is based on the first printing: the book edition of *Wieland* printed by T. and J. Swords in New York and published by Hocquet Caritat in 1798. Subsequent references to this edition will be placed within the text of the article.

3. Assigning a cause for the failure of the Wielands has been one of the major critical concerns of the novel. On this question most of the critics fall into one of two groups: those who see the failure of reason as the source of the calamities, and those who locate it in the disorder of the imagination or emotions. Although Arthur Kimball emphasizes the "utterly inscrutable nature" of the causes of the tragedy, he does not agree that the fall is simply an inevitable part of the human condition but links the Wieland tragedy to Brown's protest against "enlightenment optimism with its assumption of man's innate virtue and its overly optimistic hopes for the New World" (*Rational Fictions,* pp. 214-15). Larzer Ziff, in "A Reading of *Wieland,*" *PMLA,* 77 (1962), 54, thinks that *Wieland* shows Brown's growing dissatisfaction with eighteenth-century optimistic philosophy and his "latent sympathy with some sort of doctrine of inherited depravity." For Donald Ringe in *Charles Brockden Brown* (p. 39), the tragedy of *Wieland* shows "that human beings are a lot more complex than the contemporary psychology assumed and that their motives and actions are not so simply explained." While William Hodges agrees that reason fails the Wielands, he does not believe, as Larzer Ziff does, that Brown retains sympathy with a Calvinistic conception of the human personality ("Charles Brockden Brown and the Culture of Contradictions," *EAL* [*Early American Literature*], 9 [1974], 107-41). Other critics, however, trace *Wieland's* downfall to his imagination, which creates destructive delusions. Fred Lewis Pattee, in the introduction to *Wieland,* argues that the source of Wieland's downfall is the voices that he hears which come "from his own imagination deluded by years of brooding on the ancestral tragedy" (p. xli). David Lee Clark stresses that it is Brown's intention to show "the evil effects of credulity and superstition thus early lodged in the mind of young Wieland" (*Charles Brockden Brown: Pioneer Voice of America* [p. 167]). For Michael Davitt Bell, "what destroys the Wielands' idyllic American community is the force of imagination, of voices heard and visions seen in dreams," which Bell links to "the force of literary art and literary imagination" ("The Double Tongued Deceiver: Sincerity and Duplicity in the Novels of Charles Brockden Brown," *EAL,* 19 [1974], 144). The assumption underlying both of these interpretations is that psychological exploration and an examination of faculty psychology are the primary concerns of Brown's fiction. While not denying this assumption, my interpretation stresses that an important concern for Brown and his late eighteenth- and early nineteenth-century readers would also have been estimating the moral and social significance of the Wielands' downfall.

4. William Manly, "The Importance of Point of View in Brockden Brown's *Wieland,*" *AL,* 35 (1963), 320. Also, Norman Grabo argues persuasively that the story is Clara's and takes place in "the theater of her musings, the chamber of her memories" (p. 24) where she confronts two aspects of the self, represented by Carwin, "her own self-generated sexuality—raw, irrational, irresponsible, violent, even criminal . . . a personification of an impulse in Clara that is essentially antinomian," and Theodore, Carwin's "obverse twin, the replica of his father's duty, obedience, and guilt" (p. 27).

5. *The Monthly Magazine and American Review,* I (June, 1799), 220.

6. *The Monthly Magazine and American Review,* p. 220.

7. *The Monthly Magazine and American Review,* p. 220.

8. *The Monthly Magazine and American Review,* p. 220.

9. As cited in David Lee Clark, p. 163.

10. Norman Grabo considers the ending of *Wieland* to be an important part of the "pattern of significance" (p. x) that the novelist establishes in his work.

11. Hershel Parker and Henry Binder present this interpretation of the ending of *The Marble Faun* in "Exigencies of Composition and Publication: *Billy Budd, Sailor,* and *Pudd'nhead Wilson,*" *NCF,* 33 (1978), 132.

12. David Stockton, *Cicero: A Political Biography* (London: Oxford Univ. Press, 1971), p. 61.

13. Leslie Fiedler, *Love and Death in the American Novel* (New York: Criterion Books, 1960), p. 126.

14. R. D. Laing, *The Politics of the Family and Other Essays* (New York: Pantheon Books, 1969), p. 6.

Marietta Stafford Patrick (essay date 1984)

SOURCE: Patrick, Marietta Stafford. "Romantic Iconography in *Wieland*." *South Atlantic Review* 49, no. 4 (November 1984): 65-74.

[*In the following essay, Patrick argues against critics who claim that* Wieland *is an unsophisticated novel dependent on the conventions of Gothic and sentimental novels. According to Patrick, the novel questions the process of transformation, perception, and personal identity, suggesting that it has far more in common with the later works of American literature than with earlier ones.*]

Charles Brockden Brown's **Wieland** has been treated by older critics as a derivative novel. Pattee in an early introduction considers the novel in light of such popular eighteenth century literary forms as the sentimental, the Gothic, and the social novel in England.[1] **Wieland** does illustrate certain motifs of the sentimental and Gothic forms, but as Herbert Ross Brown observes, these trappings, especially the use of the epistolary form, seem incidental rather than primary; in **Wieland,** as Brown notes, no effort is made to sustain an illusion of actual correspondence.[2] More to the point, it becomes obvious early in the novel that Brockden Brown is not concerned with the seduction theme. The Gothic properties, though remarkable in features of setting and atmosphere, are similarly played down. The most significant factor in considering Brown's use of the Gothic and the sentimental forms is that he manages to transcend their surface and limited concern with what will happen next by internalizing action.

Criticism, however, attempting to note a psychological complexity in **Wieland** has done so at the expense of the work's total thematic and aesthetic context. Leslie Fiedler, for example, pushes a theory of the novel as "a projection of Brown's distrust of religiosity and his obsession with the destructive aspects of the brother-sister relationship."[3] David Brion Davis' theory of the "underlying guilt of an incestuous wish" leads to a similar distortion of the novel's meaning.[4] More recently David Lyttle has set forth a reductive theory of Carwin as "above all the rebellious son who seeks revenge against the father."[5] Lyttle, working within this framework, then concludes that Clara is not seduced by Carwin because she is an extension of his mother.[6] Lyttle sees the writing of the novel as therapeutic.[7] Paul Witherington similarly concludes that Brown was "purging himself rather than his heroes."[8] Sydney Krause explains the novel in terms of polarities which are projected from Brown's own divided personality.[9]

Richard Chase makes a less pretentious and more meaningful claim for the psychological experience in **Wieland**: "Brown's true forte was melodrama of a sort that allowed him to advance beyond the Gothic novel and to inaugurate that peculiar vision of things we often find in American fiction—a vision of things that might be described as a heightened and mysteriously portentous representation of abstract symbols on the one hand and on the other the involutions of the private psyche."[10] Chase acknowledges the depth of Brown's work by indicating the interior world of his characters, but he does not address himself to the question of how Brown expresses the "involutions of the private psyche." One way to show how Brown does do so is to recognize that in Brown may be found the imagery of the collective unconscious. Thus Jung's theory of transformation or individuation[11] may provide a viable pattern for seeing development in Brown's characters. The subtitle of the novel, *The Transformation,* suggests that a change occurs not just for the female protagonist but for the male protagonists Wieland and Pleyel as well. Jung's theory of rebirth seems to provide a workable approach to the internal change that occurs in the major characters in the novel. In Jungian theory the transformation is characterized by an essential change in the nature of the ego through the encounter with the archetype of the shadow. This transformation is the beginning of the higher spiritual man. The interaction suggested above between ego and shadow involves another class of archetypes which Jung calls archetypes of transformation. "These are not personalities but rather typical situations, places, ways, animals, plants and so forth that symbolize the kind of change whatever it is."[12] Archetypes of transformation featured in landscape and setting, such as the temple, Clara's house, and her summer house by the river, argue for a more carefully structured novel than most critics have acknowledged. As Jung indicates "knowledge of the symbols is indispensible for it is in them that the union of the conscious and unconscious contents is consummated."[13] The symbols of transformation signified here in the image of enclosure provide a viable approach to the significant level of action in the novel because they may be interpreted as mind symbols as well as isolation signs. A movement toward these enclosures or symbols of transformation initiates and defines the conflict in the novel as a journey inward. A circular movement of withdrawal and return develops in the novel around the symbols of transformation and dramatizes the theme of self-discovery.

That the enclosure of the temple is a mind symbol or symbol of transformation for both Wieland men has been suggested by Donald A. Ringe in his chapter on Brown in *Major American Writers.*[14] The dramatic encounters that occur within the temple lend credence to such an interpretation. The temple, furnished with a bust of Cicero, is primarily associated with the mind of Wieland rather than that of Clara. The problem of perception that Brown suggests in the symbolic withdrawal of the elder Wieland into the temple is explored dramatically as a search for identity in the character of the younger Wieland, who experiences a withdrawal that becomes thematically significant. The action of the novel is primarily concerned with this cycle of withdrawal and return because it is this movement that brings about the transformation in Wieland and the other major characters in the novel. The temple as a symbol of transformation is essential in this process of self-discovery because it is here that Wieland first hears the "voices" projected by Carwin that lead to his moral awareness.

Carwin appears in the novel as the Jungian archetype of the shadow. The shadow contains all those qualities which the ego condemns as "negative values." But the shadow "only half belongs to the ego, since it is part of the personal unconscious and as such part of the collective. Its effect on the personality as a whole lies in compensating the ego."[15] This image of Carwin is inviting because it explains his character and his function in relation to the female protagonist. In fact his presence in the world of the novel can be justified by viewing him in archetypal terms as the shadow figure in relation to all the main characters who appear as developing egos.

The characterization of Carwin suggests this interpretation. He is presented from several perspectives as a shadowy criminal figure, anticipating in this respect his more modern counterparts in world literature such as Dostoevsky's Svidrigailov and Conrad's Secret Sharer.

The shadow is, like all the archetypes, ambivalent. Thus Carwin is "on the one side regrettable and reprehensible weakness, on the other side healthy instinctivity and the prerequisite for higher consciousness."[16] Because of this ambivalence, he is, in Erich Neumann's phrase, not just the hostile brother, but the companion and friend: "The way to the self lies through him . . . only by making friends with the shadow do we gain the friendship of the self."[17] Significantly Carwin's dramatic function is limited to his night conferences with Wieland and Clara and Pleyel. He figures as an active presence in those areas in the novel that might be described as mind symbols or symbols of transformation, such as the temple, Clara's closet, and her summer house. Carwin's appearances occur primarily at night in darkness except for Clara's first meeting with him which precipitates internal storm and darkness in her and the others. Moreover Carwin's actions in the novel are not guided by reason. Instead he lets his passions dominate and control his behavior. His "amorous contagion" for the servant girl is an affair controlled neither by moral nor rational restraints. His careless intervention in the lives of others is irrational and perverse. A curious combination of typical trickster or shadow motifs can be found in the character of Carwin; for instance his fondness for sly jokes and malicious pranks, his powers as a shape shifter, his dual nature.[18] As trickster or shadow figure, his ability to change his shape seems to be one of his chief characteristics.

A transformation occurs in the novel through the agency of Carwin in the character of Clara Wieland. Though affinities exist between Clara and the sentimental and Gothic heroines, more significant parallels might be considered between the psychological complexities of Clara and the mythic hero. She too experiences a spiritual transformation that brings a qualitative change. The hero myth develops into the myth of self-transformation which can only be realized through the union of the ego with the self.[19] At the beginning of the narrative Clara seems to fluctuate between the ego qualities of frivolity and self-assurance. The action of the novel, which involves a series of withdrawals, works toward a stripping away of her frivolity and self-assurance.

Through Clara Wieland, Brown explores the problem of perception and identity with a depth and intensity that is not sustained in his treatment of Pleyel and the Wieland men. The reader becomes actively engaged in the psychological exploration of Clara Wieland's character for several reasons. Her first-person narration adds dramatic force to her transformation. This point of view creates a distance between the reader and Wieland. Though the multiple point-of-view technique has been noted by critics, Wieland is in fact the narrator for only one chapter. The reader views the cycle of his development from Clara's angle of vision. Furthermore, Wieland's errors, though involving the same problems of perception and understanding as Clara's, are the errors of a madman and thus seem remote and abstract from the experience of the reader. More significant here, however, is the fact that Brown uses the symbol of transformation more successfully in exploring Clara's withdrawal and return. The pattern of her development gives form to the novel. The symbol of transformation seems to be most clearly a structural and thematic device in the characterization of Clara. The problems of perception and identity are most fully realized as Brown taps Clara's psychic level of experience through this archetypal symbol.

It can be argued that Clara Wieland shares the egotism of her brother. In Neumann's terms she appears in the novel as ego-hero. There is a strain of personal pride in her self-assurance, her self-sufficiency. Independent of all institutions of authority, Clara relies completely on her own personal perceptions. The tension in the novel might be described on one level as the inevitable intrusion of the Absolute on such a relative and thus limited point of view.

Clara Wieland is quite clearly isolated from the realities of life. In the opening chapters she seems to exist outside of time: "In the midst of present enjoyment no thought was bestowed on the future."[20] ". . . time had no other effect than to augment our impatience in the absence of each other . . ." (p. 21). Clara is detached, it seems, from the realities of suffering and death that time involves. As ego, her interest in war, for example, is a rational intellectual kind of curiosity, remarkable because of a lack of emotional and moral consciousness.

Clara's description of her family's religious rituals indicates a similar emotional and moral vacuity: "Our devotion was a mixed and casual sentiment, seldom verbally expressed, or solicitously sought, or carefully retained." (p. 22). As ego, Clara responds to the first "problem" that confronts her serene world, the voices heard by Wieland and Pleyel, with intellectual detachment and self-assurance. Her attempts at rational interpretations are ironically undercut by the actual circumstances. The authoritative tone in which Clara asserts her speculation and theorizing about the voices smacks of egotism in light of her error and the awful consequences that ensue.

It is when Carwin impinges on the world of Clara that her rational ego views are exposed to question and her self-assurance and frivolity give way. Carwin is characterized as belonging to the non-ego by the fact that he is a stranger.[21] Clara's first encounter with Carwin is highly charged with symbolic meaning. Her fascination with Carwin's image is thematically relevant because it suggests the process of active imagination, "a certain way of meditating imaginatively by which one may deliberately enter into contact with the unconscious and make conscious connection with psychic phenomena."[22]

Clara's alternate view of the storm and Carwin is significant because the symbolic shadow properties of Carwin are suggested by the blackness and violence of the storm. With the appearance of Carwin the sunny afternoon gives way to an "uproar of the elements." Fascination with Carwin's image activates a similar "uproar of the elements" in the mind of Clara. Storm and blackness, that is, the dark realities of time and change, death, anxiety, and guilt, are internalized, as it were, in Clara's mind during the period of her withdrawal after seeing Carwin.

By gazing so intensely at the image of Carwin, Clara seems to have activated his dark imager in herself. To borrow a Hopkins coinage Carwin "selves" that in Clara which is "altogether involuntary and uncontrollable" (p. 52). As Jung explains, "such irruptions are uncanny because they are irrational and inexplicable to the individual concerned. They signify a momentous alteration of the personality in that they immediately constitute a painful personal secret that estranges the human being from his environment and isolates him from it."[23] Clara's symbolic meeting with Carwin precipitates her withdrawal and thus her interior dialogue with herself. That

Carwin is essential to Clara's self-discovery is signalled in a variety of ways. The ladder which Carwin uses to first gain entry into Clara's closet establishes an essential link between Clara and Carwin or between the two halves of Clara's self: ". . . I found a ladder and mounted to your closet window" (p. 202). As Jung suggests, the ladder is a typical symbol in the individuation process: ". . . the steps and ladder theme points to the process of psychic transformation with all of its ups and downs."[24] The closet or the inner recess of Clara's bedchamber to which she is drawn has symbolic value as a mind symbol or symbol of transformation not merely because Clara's books and papers rather than household implements or clothes are deposited there, but because the privacy of the enclosure and the intricacies involved in reaching it suggest the remote recesses of the mind. Significantly, the link between Clara and Carwin is established through this enclosure. This link to Carwin exposes Clara to the first of a series of severe tests that will finally lead to self-discovery. The test involves Clara's response to evil or guilt in the form of the murderous dialogue in the closet. The effect of Clara's encounter with evil is to challenge her as ego, that is, to challenge her veneer of self-assured prim repose and to bring forth the irrational shadow qualities of fear and anxiety and cowardice that center around her knowledge of evil. It is essential to note that Clara sees evil as an external threat. The burden of the novel and Carwin's symbolic relationship to Clara is to make her morally and emotionally aware of this dark force as a threat from within.

Through Carwin, Clara is exposed to a series of severe tests as she moves inward. Carwin himself finally comments on the purpose of his visits to Clara's closet as a challenge or test to her control and mastery of herself: ". . . a vague project occurred to me, to put this courage to the test. A woman capable of recollection in danger, of warding off groundless panics, of discerning the true mode of proceeding, and profiting by her best resources, is a prodigy. I was desirous of ascertaining whether you were such an one" (p. 202). Clara's pattern of withdrawal seems to clearly involve a test or challenge that finally leads to self-discovery as each withdrawal augments her progress toward self-knowledge.

A necessary step in Clara Wieland's understanding of herself is a transformation of the ego which involves a recognition of affinity with Carwin, that he is in a symbolic sense part of her. This is achieved by a final visit to the inner recesses of the closet in the bedchamber at Mettingen. Clara visits the closet in order to retrieve her personal journal before leaving the country with her uncle. Clara's final visit to Mettingen activates a pattern similar to previous patterns of withdrawal. Images of enclosure and darkness mark this solitary journey as a movement inward intellectually as well as physically. Darkness, silence, isolation, and enclosure signal a climactic journey into the interior of Clara's mind.

This journey inward marks Clara's most severe test. The risk involved is the disintegration of Clara's own mind. The scene dramatizes a temporary loss of ego qualities. Her hatred transforms her into that which she has feared: ". . . my soul was bursting with detestation and revenge" (p. 217), and: "I thirsted for his blood and was tormented with an insatiable appetite for his destruction . . ." (p. 221). Significantly the blackness that pervades the scene comes not from Carwin, but from within Clara and Wieland. Activated here is the evil which Clara herself is capable of. This evil includes the blasphemous damnation of her invocation to heaven, her attempts to take her own life, her readiness to take the lives of Carwin and her brother.

The effect of this scene is to bring Clara face to face with her own shadow qualities. This necessitates the presence of Carwin, her shadow self, and the symbolic exchange of their roles. It is of importance that Clara herself seems responsible for the advent of Carwin. She seems to invoke his presence as if he were a disembodied spirit, by her curses: "The name of Carwin was uttered, and eternal woes, woes like that which his malice had entailed on us, were heaped upon him. I invoked all-seeing heaven to draw to light and punish the betrayer . . ." (p. 193).

Carwin's function is to save Clara literally and symbolically. He intervenes twice to save her life: his presence checks her preparation for suicide and the projection of his voice saves her from the maniacal homicide of Wieland. Symbolically, he assures the unity of the self by forcing her recognition of evil as a threat from within rather than without. Clara is no longer obsessed with Carwin when she perceives her own shadow qualities, that is, when she understands her own complicity in what has happened: ". . . my heart was black enough to meditate the stabbing of a brother . . . my hands were sprinkled with his blood as he fell. . . ." (p. 232). When Clara is able to see herself and her brother as active agents in the course of events, Carwin is no longer an enigma. She can place him, assimilate him, and finally let him go: ". . . thenceforth he was nothing to me. . . ." (p. 232). The scene in the enclosure has worked toward a stripping away of Clara's pride (consciousness) by making her aware of her own dark nature. The peculiar freedom that Carwin comes to enjoy in Clara's "house" signifies that he is indeed her secret sharer. He explains to Clara in their last interview: ". . . my knowledge of you was of that kind which conjugal intimacies can give, and in some respects more accurate" (p. 205).

Clara insists on remaining at Mettingen after Wieland dies. She betakes herself to her bed in the belief that her career in this world is on the point of ending. This final withdrawal into the chamber, that is, the inner recesses of Clara's mind, marks the change in Clara from passive to active suffering which prepares for her transformation. The scene complements the preceding ones because it marks the fruition of Clara's journey inward. There is no relief here because Clara suffers the agony of awareness of her own guilt. This final withdrawal dramatizes the psychological hell which self-knowledge brings. The images signify the deep anguish Clara suffers as she comes to grips morally and emotionally with her own capacity for evil and error.

Though Clara has discovered essential truths about herself, integration cannot be achieved until she breaks out of the trap of her own mind. Return is essential to wholeness and integration. The self-absorption implicit in her decision to remain isolated in the bedchamber of her house, that is, locked up inside her own mind, suggests her father's obsession. Clara does finally struggle to "break the spell," but her own efforts are not sufficient to awaken her, that is, bring her back into the world of time and moral responsibility. Her release is finally effected by something physical and external to herself, ". . . someone shaking me with violence put an end to my reverie. My eyes were unsealed and I started from my pillow. . . ." (p. 236). She is awakened from a delirious dream[25] by a loud voice and smoke in her chamber. Fire expresses an intense transformation process.[26] The fire forcing Clara outside brings transformation and thus purgation and release. Clara's physical and spiritual awakening leads to integration and the identity imaged in seeking a new habitation, a new form of being. Clara's transformation involves a movement from an ego-centered subjective attitude to objective awareness of the limitations of the ego and of the existence of the greater psyche which Jung designates as the self.

Fullness of being is achieved when Clara can extend herself beyond the past into the present and future: "A new train of images disconnected with the fate of my family, forced itself on my attention . . ." (p. 237). The writing of the story becomes another means of Clara's release and integration into the world. Like the Ancient Mariner, she seems compelled to narrate her story and from the very telling of it, she experiences a community with the world outside herself. A communion between her private world and the public world is established by the telling of the tale. As Neumann explains, the creative act signifies an ordering of the self.[27] Clara, then, having travelled through the depths of the self, finally achieves a kind of tranquility and stillness through the catharsis of fire which has forced her to construct a new "house" and the creative act of telling the story. She has come full circle, however, when she is able to extend herself by loving Pleyel again.

The symbolic value of the archetype of the enclosed space is complex in Brockden Brown for it leads to an analysis of the process of transformation and finally relates to the problem of perception and identity, projecting *Wieland* beyond the limited range of Gothic and sentimental prototypes. This technical device which becomes Brown's method of figuring "the involutions of the private psyche," links *Wieland* to later significant American fiction and indicates sophistication of technique and structural unity in a novel which has been denigrated for a lack of these qualities.

Notes

1. Fred Lewis Pattee, Intro. *Wieland: or the Transformation,* by Charles Brockden Brown (New York: Harcourt, Brace and World, 1962), pp. xxv-xli.

2. Herbert Ross Brown, *The Sentimental Novel in America, 1789-1860* (Durham: Duke Univ. Press, 1940), pp. 69-70.

3. Leslie Fiedler, *Love and Death in the American Novel* (New York: Criterion Books, 1960), p. 150.

4. David Brion Davis, *Homicide in American Fiction, 1798-1860: A Study in Social Values* (Ithaca: Cornell Univ. Press, 1957), pp. 88-94. Carl Bredahl, Jr., "Transformation in *Wieland,*" *Early American Literature,* 12 (1977), 182, echoes Fiedler and Davis in assuming the theme of incest in *Wieland.*

5. David Lyttle, "The Case Against Carwin," *Nineteenth Century Fiction,* 26 (Dec. 1971), 267.

6. Lyttle, p. 268.

7. Lyttle, p. 258.

8. Paul Witherington, "Benevolence and the Utmost Stretch," *Criticism,* 14 (1972), 191.

9. Sydney J. Krause, "Romanticism in *Wieland:* Brown and the Reconciliation of Opposites," *Artful Thunder,* eds. Robert J. DeMott and Stanford E. Marovitz (Kent, OH: Kent State Univ. Press, 1975), p. 18.

10. Richard Chase, *The American Novel and Its Tradition* (New York: Doubleday, 1959), p. 30.

11. Carl G. Jung, *The Archetypes and the Collective Unconscious* (New York: Random House, 1959), p. 130.

12. Carl G. Jung, *Integration of the Personality* (New York: Farrar and Rinehart, 1939), p. 89.

13. Jung, *Archetypes,* p. 289.

14. Donald A. Ringe, "Charles Brockden Brown," *Major Writers of Early American Literature,* ed. Everett Emerson (Madison: Univ. of Wisconsin Press, 1972), pp. 273-94.

15. Erich Neumann, *The Origins and History of Consciousness* (Princeton: Princeton Univ. Press, 1954), p. 353.

16. Carl G. Jung, *Aion* (Princeton: Princeton Univ. Press, 1959), p. 255.

17. Neumann, *The Origins,* p. 353.

18. Jung, *The Archetypes,* p. 255.

19. Neumann, *The Origins,* p. 252.

20. Charles Brockden Brown, *Wieland: or the Transformation,* ed. with an introduction by Sydney J. Krause and S. W. Reid (Kent, OH: Kent State Univ. Press, 1978), p. 22. All subsequent references to *Wieland* are to this text.

21. Carl G. Jung, *Psychology and Alchemy* (Princeton: Princeton Univ. Press, 1953), p. 108; see also Jolande Jacobi, *Man and His Symbols,* ed. Carl G. Jung (Garden City, New York: Doubleday, 1964), p. 279.

22. Marie-Louise von Franz, *Man and His Symbols,* ed. Carl G. Jung (Garden City, New York: Doubleday, 1964), p. 206.

23. Jung, *Integration of the Personality,* p. 103.

24. Jung, *Psychology and Alchemy,* p. 60.

25. James R. Russo, "The Chimeras of the Brain: Clara's Narrative in *Wieland,*" *Early American Literature,* 16 (1981), 60-80, begs the question in arguing that Clara imparts an inconsistent narrative throughout the novel because of her insanity.

26. Jung, *Psychology and Alchemy,* p. 382.

27. ". . . creativity in all its forms is always the product of a meeting between the masculine world of ego consciousness and of the feminine world of the soul." Neumann, *Origins,* p. 355.

Thomas Pribek (essay date 1985)

SOURCE: Pribek, Thomas. "A Note on 'Depravity' in *Wieland.*" *Philological Quarterly* 64, no. 2 (spring 1985): 273-79.

[*In the following essay, Pribek refutes the notion that the characters of* Wieland *are inherently evil, suggesting instead that they should be read as rational characters who are undone by the villainy of an outsider.*]

The reading of Charles Brockden Brown's *Wieland* as a rationalist tract has been questioned thoroughly by recent critics. For example, the narrator Clara Wieland's capacity for accurate perception, judgment, and narration has been called into doubt so far as to accuse her of unknowingly murdering her brother.[1] Even more critics read the novel with a kind of Calvinist approach: Brown suspects, they say, some form of original sin because of which human beings, Theodore Wieland being the most emphatic example, are inherently incapable of fully rational thought and deliberate action.[2]

Perhaps the most influential of the Calvinist readings (if citations in bibliographies of critical works and editions of the novel are an accurate indication) is Larzer Ziff's "A Reading of *Wieland*."[3] Ziff emphasizes Clara's observation about the "depravity" of her brother's senses, thus suggesting, Ziff says, some irremediable corruption of human perception analogous to moral degeneracy: "Wieland's mania . . . is not to be explained through ventriloquism, through delusion, but rather through an inherited depravity which preceded it."[4]

However, an investigation of the contemporary definitions of the term and of its several uses in *Wieland* indicates that Ziff may be reading too much into Clara's observation—or, more precisely, reading it too narrowly in a typically modern sense that associates "depravity" almost exclusively with moral culpability and understands it to mean "inherently evil." In fact, the more accurate reading of the term by contemporaneous dictionaries and usage actually tends to support the earlier critical view that *Wieland* is a drama of essentially reasonable and uncorrupted minds ruined by villainous tampering—people whose senses are not inherently unreliable and self-deceiving but, unfortunately, capable of being deceived. That Wieland shows no clear indications of insanity until Carwin's meddling begins may still be the fairest way to read his character.

To Brown's late eighteenth-century audience, "depravity" indeed recalls New England's Puritan origins, then still nourishing some pre-Enlightenment notions of man as a necessarily evil creature. The dictionaries indicated, however, that while this is one connotation of the term, it is perhaps not its primary or exclusive meaning. Moreover, an audience familiar with sentimental novels might read "depraved" with a more worldly meaning (sexual license) which accepts innocence as the natural human condition.

James Mulqueen has suggested that Brown meant "depraved" as a medical term, describing illness in the senses brought about by circulatory disorder. He notes Brown's association with Elihu Smith and Benjamin Rush, and his reading in medical journals, although he does not provide any quotation that actually uses the term. And while Mulqueen's suggestion apparently removes the Calvinistic echoes by providing a physical, not psychological, cause of madness, it still preserves the concept of an internal cause that makes original sin

a possible symbolic interpretation.[5] Wayne Franklin has pointed critics in the right direction by asserting that Ziff overlooks Carwin's role as "depraver." Although he cites Samuel Johnson's *Dictionary* in a footnote, Franklin does not report specifically on what meanings Brown's contemporary readers might attach to the term, nor does he study connotations that emerge from Brown's text.[6] To do so is to challenge, in part, the Calvinist readings.

The one passage that Ziff cites is in fact the only one using a form of the word "depravity" and applying the word to Wieland: "Perhaps a voice had been heard," reasons Clara after Carwin's first use of ventriloquism at Mettingen, "but Wieland's imagination had misled him" (34):[7]

> The will is the tool of the understanding, which must fashion its conclusions of the notices of sense. If the senses be depraved, it is impossible to calculate the evils that may flow from the consequent deductions of the understanding.
>
> I said, this man is of an ardent and melancholy character. . . . He is, in some respects, an enthusiast, but is fortified in his belief by innumerable arguments and subtilties.
>
>   (35)

To Ziff, this is evidence that Brown suggests human perception has some "inherited" defect that makes one the victim of delusions. And taking "depravity" to mean "naturally wicked" (the moral connotation we tend to give it today), Ziff contends that Brown "ends his journey through the mind by approaching the outskirts of Edwards' camp."[8]

However, this is the only passage Ziff cites in this connection, giving it heavy thematic weight. Furthermore, we should note that at this point Clara does not genuinely believe her brother has heard any real voice. She attributes it to the touches of the mystic in Wieland that mirror their father's delusions. By the end she holds Carwin primarily responsible; and the kinds of "depravity" in *Wieland* support her attempt to locate a villain rather than to blame innate deficiencies of human nature.

Samuel Johnson's *A Dictionary of the English Language* lists six related forms of the term, the common ones being the transitive verb "to deprave," the agent-noun "depraver," and the noun "depravity" (other forms include the rarer nouns "depravement" and "depravation" and the participial adjective "depraved").[9] The definition of the verb is most important, of course, since all other inflectional forms are derived from it. To deprave is "to vitiate, to corrupt, to contaminate"; and as a transitive verb, its usage requires a subject and object; that is, "he that causes depravity" is responsible, and "depravation" is understood to have an external agent.

Noah Webster's first American dictionary, *A Compendious Dictionary of the English Language* (1806), heavily based on Johnson's *Dictionary,* has the same entries, emphasizing the verb, participial adjective, and most common noun form (deprave, depraved, depraver). His definitions are almost identical to Johnson's. To deprave is "to corrupt, vitiate, taint, spoil"; a depraver is "one who depraves." Webster's dictionary contains no quotations for illustrating usage, as Johnson's does. Johnson, for example, quotes Shakespeare, Milton, Swift, Richard Hooker, and John Dryden; and while Milton may be read as a Puritan, the others—especially Hooker—as certainly cannot. Furthermore, the quotes support the general definitions, indicating that "depravity" is not an exclusively theological term and certainly not the property of any particular sect. The *Oxford English Dictionary,* prepared when etymology was considerably more a science than it was in Johnson's day, notes that a verb form meaning "to vilify, defame, decry" is the root of its English usage.

In *Wieland* (1798) Brown uses forms of the word only eight times (some close together in essentially the same scene), and most of the instances argue against giving it any strongly theological connotations. Most of the time, as noted above, Wieland is not the subject, nor is any kind of madness or defect of the senses being described. In fact, the subject and meaning are rather general in its first several uses, which are historical references that describe a whole class of people and provide part of the social background of the novel. Wieland's father's missionary efforts among the Indians were frustrated by "the license of savage passion, and the artifices of his depraved countrymen" (11). Clara is likely echoing a common criticism of her day about the pernicious effects of double-dealing traders who brought Indians the worst of civilization: rum.[10] In this case, the "depravity" that keeps the Indians unredeemable is product of their environment rather than inherent savagery, and the greed of the White savages is likewise a social phenomenon.

Then when Wieland considers whether he should claim the family's European properties, he reasons with his family thus:

> [W]as it laudable to grasp at wealth and power even when they were within our reach? Were not these the two great sources of depravity? What security had he, that in his change of place and condition, he should not degenerate into a tyrant and voluptuary? Power and riches were chiefly to be dreaded on account of their tendency to deprave the possessor.
>
> (38)

A good American patriot here, he is concerned about becoming some Old World aristocrat: tyrannical, self-absorbed, and devoted to pleasure. However, his worry is entirely worldly. It is not his immortal soul that Wieland fears for in this instance. In addition, the rhetorical questions are phrased as a general proposition of human behavior, nothing he need worry about more than anyone else. Furthermore, the last sentence uses "deprave" as the transitive verb: "riches . . . deprave the possessor"; that is, corruption comes from an outside influence. "Depravity" is an acquired trait of civilization, not something innate.

Clara Wieland is accused of a certain form of depravity. In these instances, however, the context is literary, the novel of seduction. Pleyel, when he adopts the cliché responses of the wounded lover—he thinks he has overheard Clara's dalliance with Carwin—self-pityingly he tells her, "I have not arms with which to contend with so consummate, so frightful a depravity" (104). He bemoans "thy fall" and fears that some "wretch" has ruined her honor. Clara denies the accusation, responding that "There is a degree of depravity to which it is impossible for me to sink" (113). Pleyel is fair enough to recognize that, if Clara has been dishonored, it was at the temptation of another, the supposed seducer Carwin. Pleyel grants her original innocence, if only to make her "fall" the more wounding to his sensibilities.[11]

Besides noting that once again the meaning does not directly hint at inherent corruption, we should also note that the corruption here refers explicitly to sexual conduct, not some primal sin, that the real sin—as far as Pleyel is concerned—is betrayal of his affection, and that neither Pleyel nor Clara is arguing about the loss of her eternal soul, only his respect and eligibility as a suitor. Thus, in this scene "depravity" must be read as the diction of the sentimental novel, not a theological or psychological treatise, even though the charge of depravity is clearly a moral judgment on Clara.

Pleyel, of course, actually heard only Carwin's feigned seduction scene, one of his "black catalogue of stratagems" (211). When he confesses to Clara, he tells her that "I had depraved the imagination of Pleyel; I had exhibited you to his understanding as devoted to brutal gratifications and consummate in hypocrisy" (211). Here is the only other example of the term used in connection with sensory perception and processing, and it is important that it is another transitive verb form. Carwin fooled Pleyel, who may have been gullible and predisposed to jealousy because of his shy love for Clara, but Carwin never explicitly says that Pleyel's "imagination" or "understanding" is naturally defective in all instances. And in context, the term is used as a self-condemnation: Pleyel is an innocent victim of Carwin's meddling.

There is only one instance in *Wieland* that I can find in which the term seems to carry the simple meaning Ziff reads into it. This instance is the condemnation of "Maxwell's depravity" (242) in one of the last paragraphs of the story, when Clara is tying up some loose ends in the narrative. Maxwell may be purely evil—we get only the sketchiest biography—and if so, he is the only such character in the book. Carwin and Wieland are sufficiently humanized that they gain a certain degree of reader sympathy. But I am inclined to doubt the importance of the word here, since it does not describe one of the main characters whose actions carry the thematic weight of the novel; furthermore, Maxwell's crimes, seduction and duelling, are just the kind of Old World degeneracy that Clara and her brother might have had in mind when they decided against claiming their family's European holdings. Maxwell is just the kind of man who is depraved by a corrupt civilization that good American patriots often condemned, particularly in sentimental novels.

That Brown was aware of human fallibility cannot be doubted, but to say that his ideas about human nature make **Wieland** a condemnation of optimistic theories of Enlightenment psychology and a tract that argues for a return to something like a Calvinist interpretation of human nature is too extreme a reading. Whatever arguments Brown may have had with the optimism of empirical psychology or American Protestantism after the Enlightenment, his criticism is not carried by an explicit accusation of sensory "depravity." By an examination of dictionary denotation and literary connotations in **Wieland,** we see that it is not a key term in support of a Calvinist reading of **Wieland** and, in fact, offers evidence for a more complex social reading of the novel.

Notes

1. See, for example, Cynthia Jordan, "On Rereading *Wieland*: 'The Folly of Precipitate Conclusions,'" *Early American Literature* 16 (1981): 154-74; and James Russo, "'The Chimeras of the Brain': Clara's Narrative in *Wieland*," *Early American Literature* 16 (1981): 60-88.

2. See, for example, Michael Gilmore, "Calvinism and Gothicism: The Example of Brown's *Wieland*," *Studies in the Novel* 9 (1971): 107-18; Paul Levine, "The American Novel Begins," *American Scholar* 35 (Winter 1965-66): 134-48; and Kenneth Bernard, "Charles Brockden Brown," in *Minor American Novelists,* ed. Charles Alva Hoyt (Southern Illinois U. Press, 1970): 1-9. Donald Ringe, "Charles Brockden Brown," in *Major Writers of Early-American Literature,* ed. Everett Emerson (U. of Wisconsin Press, 1972): 273-94, has a related interpretation, since he reads *Wieland* and other novels as a systematic questioning of some of the fundamental ideas of the Enlightenment.

3. Larzer Ziff, "A Reading of *Wieland*," *PMLA,* 77 (1962): 51-57.

4. Ziff, 54.

5. James Mulqueen, "The Plea for a Deistic Education in Charles Brockden Brown's *Wieland*," *Ball State University Forum* 10 (1969): 70-77.

6. Wayne Franklin, "Tragedy and Comedy in Brown's *Wieland*," *Novel* 8 (1975): 147-63.

7. Charles Brockden Brown, *Wieland and Memoirs of Carwin* (Kent State U. Press, 1977). All citations to this edition are included in parentheses in my text.

8. Ziff, 54.

9. I have used the 1773 edition of Johnson's *Dictionary.*

10. By coincidence, Crevecoeur also accused backsettlers of "depravity": "They get drunk with them, and often defraud the Indians." J. Hector St. John de Crevecoeur, *Letters from an American Farmer* (New York: E. P. Dutton, 1957): 50-51. In the historical setting of the novel (just before the Revolution) Clara could count on people recalling Cresap's War (also called Lord Dunmere's War) in 1774, which Crevecoeur cites as an example of the effects of degenerate civilization.

11. See Susanna Rowson's *Charlotte: A Tale of Truth* (Columbus: Charles E. Merrill, 1970): 73 and 83, for similar use of "depravity" in describing the heroine's ruin.

Bill Christophersen (essay date 1986)

SOURCE: Christophersen, Bill. "Picking Up the Knife: A Psycho-Historical Reading of *Wieland*." *American Studies* 27, no. 1 (spring 1986): 115-26.

[*In the following essay, Christophersen focuses on Clara's transformation as a metaphor for the transformation of America from British colony to young nation.*]

> Literature . . . has a relationship to social and intellectual history, not as documentation, but as symbolic illumination.[1]

Edwin S. Fussell, in his essay "*Wieland*: A Literary and Historical Reading," goes far toward establishing a political/historical context for Charles Brockden Brown's **Wieland, or The Transformation** (1798). He identifies the transformation of *patria* that Brown and his generation had experienced as the real antecedent of the subtitle. Suggesting that, figuratively speaking, the newly nationalized writer of Brown's era was, like Carwin, a biloquist—a British "speaker" become American—and stressing the almost causal role writing had played in the American Revolution, Fussell sees this novel that pivots on biloquial voices and the writing act as embodying a revolutionary/postrevolutionary tension. With Clara Wieland as a "daughter of the American Revolution" in conflict with Carwin, an "American revolutionary and postrevolutionary writer," Carwin's destruction of the Wieland family becomes an image of America's revolutionary devastation—even as Brown's "horror and contempt" for the author's powers becomes a "product of postrevolutionary backlash." Fussell concludes by noting a paradox: "Writing is both the cause and the effect of action: . . . the American Revolution . . . , at least partly caused by writers, . . . necessitates an American literature to justify it and to ensure its fruits to posterity."[2]

Fussell, in highlighting a historical context for Brown's melodramatic plot, gives new resonance to Carwin and to several of the book's motifs. His fertile reading, however, skirts the central drama—Clara's transformation and confrontation with her deranged brother Theodore. Fussell concentrates to good effect on Carwin, but Carwin is, at last, more red herring than protagonist. If *Wieland* is the American tale Fussell says it is, the transformation Clara undergoes even more than Carwin's biloquist transformations ought to reflect the nation's revolutionary/postrevolutionary tensions. This essay suggests that such is the case. It further suggests that Wieland himself reflects both Clara's and the young republic's dangerous potentialities writ large—hence the nationalism of Brown's "American Tale."

I

From the start Brown's favorite writers were epic poets. "National songs," Brown wrote in a letter to William Dunlap (November 28, 1794), "strains which have a particular relation to the political or religious transactions of the poet's country, seem to be the most precious morcels [sic]. . . ."[3] Brown set out, indeed, to write an American epic in 1794 (he had planned several). I believe this epic ambition that Brown failed to realize in verse informs his fiction—especially *Wieland*—revealing itself in story lines with national as well as dramatic and psychological dimensions: story lines that generally feature a society under siege by an ineluctable evil.[4]

Brown's background adds credence to a nationalistic reading of his works. Fussell rightly notes that Brown, a young, liberally educated Philadelphian during the formative years of the new republic, had firsthand exposure to the political and philosophical tradewinds of the time. Brown avidly read the French Encyclopedists and the English "novelists of purpose," especially Godwin and Wollstonecraft. On the other hand, Brown's association, during the 1790s, with various New York conservatives in the Friendly Club no doubt counter-

weighted an ideological dialogue that, as Alan Axelrod has suggested, may have begun years earlier when Brown was tutored by Tory Quaker Robert Proud.[5] Proud's explicit denunciations of revolution, augmented by the Quaker's moral opposition to violence, may well have heightened Brown's sensitivity to the violent potential of individuals and nations, and (as Fussell suggests) to the paradox of a purportedly God-fearing republic conceived in blood and insurrection.[6]

Wieland, not surprisingly, bears early indications of historical intent on Brown's part. Not only is the tale set on the eve of the American Revolution (as Fussell notes): its protagonist is also equipped with a family history that reads like America's. Brown sets the stage for his drama by detailing the elder Wieland's history and death and introducing the family circle that has succeeded him at Mettingen. As David Bryon Davis points out,

> The story thus far is almost an allegory of American colonial history. It includes disrupting economic changes in Europe, religious fervor which was not unrelated to these changes, frequent references to predestination and to stern self-analysis, the vision and failure of spreading truth among the savages, unexpected economic success, and even the well-known figure of a temple (or city) on the hill. The parallel continues with the disorganization and self-consumption of the original religious fanaticism and with the appropriation of the temple by rationalistic descendants. Finally, the continental Enlightenment appeared [*sic*] in the character of Henry Pleyel, 'the champion of intellectual liberty . . . who rejected all guidance but that of his reason.'[7]

Such suggestions of historical allegory may seem farfetched or gratuitous. Yet Brown, judging by his prefaces, his fictions "Thessalonica" and "The Death of Cicero," his historical sketches and his "political" pamphlets (as much literary as political artifacts), was intrigued by a literature in which history and fiction intersect. Indeed, his narrator in "Walstein's School of History" finds "the narration of public events, with a certain license of invention, the most efficacious of moral instruments."[8] Nor was the strategy of allegorizing contemporary history, of making "the picture of a single family a model from which to sketch the condition of a nation," absurd to Brown—however so it may have seemed to Pleyel.[9] Jeremy Belknap, in *The Foresters* (1796), a book subtitled, like *Wieland,* "An American Tale," and reviewed by Brown in his *Monthly Magazine and American Review* (April 1799), had allegorized the colonization, rebellion and confederation of America. Brown, in praising Belknap, alludes to the "pleasing and popular form" of allegory.[10] Davis' suggestion of an allegorical level to *Wieland,* then, is perhaps less far-fetched than it might seem. Like Fussell's reading, however, it skirts the main drama. To that drama we must, by degrees, turn.

In all Brown's major romances, naive young protagonists undergo transformations in which a dark side of their personalities comes to the fore and they become capable of horrendous acts. These characters, however, are unaware of their evil propensities: fundamentally, they do not know themselves. Brown's early novel *Skywalk* (a lost precursor to *Edgar Huntly*) was, in fact, subtitled *The Man Unknown to Himself: An American Tale.* In *Arthur Mervyn* and *Edgar Huntly*—especially the latter, a tale in which the "concerns of this country" find expression in a sleepwalker-protagonist—this ignorance of self assumes startling proportions.

For Brown such lack of self-awareness apparently characterized America. In *An Address to the Government* . . . Brown, in the elaborate guise of a French Counsellor of State urging France to deploy troops in Louisiana, seeks, through reverse psychology, to goad America into seizing the territory herself. America, claims the French Counsellor, has too many political and social problems to permit her to act effectively in her own interest. The problems the French Counsellor lists—the presence of suppressed populations (blacks and Indians), capitalist greed, a political system prone toward faction—are so ironic in an "enlightened" republic that they suggest a nation unknown to itself. Reiterating the image he had used in *Edgar Huntly,* Brown has his French Counsellor lecture Napoleon as follows: "It is time to awaken. Should this fatal sleep continue . . . fortune will have smiled in vain. . . ."[11] But the letter, of course, is a device; there is no French Counsellor. Brown is writing to America. And his words, I propose, may be taken as the theme, not only of his pamphlet, but of his fiction in general.

With Brown's apparent doubts about America's self-awareness in mind, consider *Wieland,* Brown's first romance of troubled sleep and traumatic awakening. Clara Wieland in a horrible flash discovers her brother's homicidal mania. Only by degrees, however, does she discover her own propensity for comparable violence. This transformation, which critics have explored but never fully clarified,[12] is central to our understanding of *Wieland.*

Clara, prior to her tragedy, is both sane and sensible. This, indeed, is what makes her transformation matter. In contrast to her brother, whose brooding, obsessed mien suggests the potential psychotic, Clara is not easily swayed by superstition, nor is she given to solitary pursuits. Rather, she is strong-minded: fearing an intruder in her closet, she tries the door. Nevertheless, she soon finds herself plagued, then driven, by irrational forces she cannot control. Critics have noted the sexual alliances she unconsciously contemplates. Ambivalent about all three men in her life, she sleepwalks and dreams that her brother beckons to her from across a gulf, but awakens instead to the voice of Carwin—who

no sooner disappears than Pleyel appears, calling to her "from the edge of a precipice" (*Wieland,* 64). Less apparent, though, are the aggressive impulses Clara betrays.

Clara's fears and fantasies are perhaps more violent than sexual. Deciding to grant Carwin a midnight interview, she resolves to arm herself, then reflects on the moral as well as physical danger she is courting: "Whoever has pointed steel is not without arms; yet what must have been the state of my mind when I could meditate, without shuddering, on the use of a murderous weapon, and believe myself secure merely because I was capable of being made so by the death of another!" (*Wieland,* 144). Given Clara's evolution, Pleyel's wrongheaded tirade depicting her as "the colleague of a murderer" (*Wieland,* 113)—a murderer once removed—assumes ironic significance. Clara herself muses aloud: "Yesterday and today I am the same. . . . yet in the apprehension of another I had ceased to be the same. . . . What was it that swayed me? . . . What purpose did I mediate?" (*Wieland,* 113, 140, 146). The point is that she is not the same; she meditates all kinds of things. Metaphorically she not only pursues her own brother, but discovers murderers in her own closet.

Clara's psychodrama is temporarily interrupted by the slaughter that devastates her brother's family. Clara bears up as well as can be expected following the murders, but her discovery of her brother's agency leads to "a new dread . . . more insupportable than the anguish . . . lately endured." Revolving her brother's transformation, Clara writes: "Had I not equal reason to tremble? What was my security against influences equally irresistible? . . . Was I not transported to the brink of the same abyss? Ere a new day should come, my hands might be embrued in blood . . ." (*Wieland,* 179-180). In fact, as her subsequent acts show, a frightening propensity for violence *has* dawned on Clara. Its first fruits include a flirtation with suicide: "Death is a cure which nature or ourselves must administer. To this cure I now looked forward with gloomy satisfaction" (*Wieland,* 180).

Clara recovers under her uncle's care. She cannot, however, dispel the suspicion that Carwin has prompted her brother's conduct, and, with uncharacteristic vehemence, remarks, "I thirsted for knowledge and for vengeance" (*Wieland,* 190). Twice more Clara reiterates the sentiment: "The milkiness of my nature was curdled into hatred and rancour"; "my soul was bursting with detestation and revenge" (*Wieland,* 216, 217). Her craving for vengeance soon leads to blasphemy: "I invoked all-seeing heaven to drag to light and punish this betrayer, and accused its providence for having thus long delayed the retribution that was due to so enormous a guilt" (*Wieland,* 193). During the final visit to her old house despair overtakes her, and she again premeditates, then resolves upon suicide. She is preparing to execute her design, in fact, when Carwin appears. These mortal sins, however, are only preliminaries.

The final episode finds Clara confronted by her deranged brother come to kill her. "All that I have said [thus far] is preparatory to this scene," Clara specifies, italicizing the significance of what is to follow (*Wieland,* 221). That final scene is crucial not merely because Wieland's fanatical passion is brought to a climax, but because here Clara finds herself ready to commit the mythic equivalent of Wieland's crime:

> Yes, I acknowledge that my guilt surpasses that of mankind. . . . What shall I say? I was menaced, as I thought, with death, and, to elude this evil, my hand was ready to inflict death upon the menacer. . . . O insupportable remembrance! hide thee from my view for a time; hide it from me that my heart was black enough to meditate the stabbing of a brother!
>
> (*Wieland,* 223)

Circumstantial justification notwithstanding, Clara's readiness to commit fratricide, the crime in which "every form of guilt is comprehended" (according to Cicero's *Pro Cluentio,* a text Wieland refers to earlier in the tale), suggests the enormity of her transformation. Brown spares Clara (and us) this final horror, arranging, as one critic has noted, for Clara to drop the knife and for Wieland to pick it up and kill himself.[13] But Clara, acutely aware of her own implication in this tragedy, underlines its wider significance: ". . . my hands were sprinkled with his blood as he fell" (*Wieland,* 232). Nor does Brown leave matters here.

II

The Maxwell-Stuart-Conway subplot, in which Brown describes Maxwell's semi-successful seduction of Mrs. Stuart and enunciates what Clara's tale has dramatized—that "no human virtue is secure from degeneracy" (*Wieland,* 241)—provides a bridge, however unlikely, to the historicity of *Wieland.* Regarding Mrs. Stuart's transferal of affection, though not of favors, Brown writes: "This revolution in her sentiments was productive only of despair. Her rectitude of principle preserved her from actual guilt, but could not restore to her her ancient affection, or save her from being the prey of remorseful and impracticable wishes" (*Wieland,* 241). Mrs. Stuart "falls," in other words, even though she stops short of committing the deeds she thinks about. The same kind of guilt tarnishes Clara: though she does not actually wield the knife against her brother, the realization that she has verged on doing so traumatizes her and constitutes a virtual "fall." The point of the digression, however—that a "revolution in . . . sentiments," even if not taken to the limit, carries irrevocable consequences—bears not only on Clara, but also on postrevolutionary America. Brown's use of the term

"revolution" evokes, however fleetingly, the consequences of political "revolutions." In conjuring this dimension, it invites us to examine the drama of family confrontation we have just witnessed in a broader light.

Colonial America, like Clara, had, in maturing, undergone a change; had found her new self alienated from and threatened by her former self; had picked up the knife, as it were, however reluctantly and justifiably, and squared off against her former self—that elder-kinsman-turned-antagonist, Great Britain. Fortunately, while our revolution triumphed (thanks to France), our republicanism (unlike France's) remained within bounds. But, Brown seems to warn his readers, even if we hadn't, like our ideological brother France, become a fanatical butcher (and this, I submit, is the second historical antecedent of Wieland's mania), we ought not be blind to the residual possibility, or to the violent transformation we *had* undergone. For as Mrs. Stuart (who also stopped short of infamy) discovers, a "revolution in . . . sentiments" *anticipates* the worst.

The violent transformation dramatized in Brown's climax, I am suggesting, echoes a complex national transformation (though, let me stress, I am speaking of echoes, not equivalences). Wieland's threatening posture conjures two contrasting historical moments: first, the revolutionary era, during which America, like Clara, was obliged to take up arms against her former protector and kinsman; and second, America's postrevolutionary era, whose haunting spectre was that of our zealot-'brother'-turned-indiscriminate-murderer, revolutionary France. Brown, I am suggesting, does indeed make "the picture of a single family a model from which to sketch the condition of a nation"—a literary strategy that he explicitly discusses earlier in the novel (*Wieland,* 30).

At the risk of redundancy, let me put the matter another way. Behind the book's final brother-sister confrontation, two opposite sides of the American psyche resonate: our volatile, revolutionary self, ready to resist an elder kinsman and former protector, if need be, to survive; and our postrevolutionary self, afraid of being "transported to the brink of the same abyss" as our crazed political brother, France—perhaps even needing, paradoxically, to "kill" that lunatic, revolutionary self. (Brown, indeed, characterizes Wieland's lunacy with the politically-loaded words "overthrow" and "anarchy" as well as "revolution" [*Wieland,* 162, 171, 154].)

But which self deserved to be heeded? Brown confounds the two: Clara's knife-wielding posture suggests both revolution *and* reaction; Wieland's menacing attitude recalls both Britain's mid-century arrogance *and* France's late-century fanaticism. Brown thus not only evokes a turn-of-the-century American dilemma, he also implies that each self poses a comparable danger.

"Murderers lurked in my closet," says Clara, midway through the tale. "One resolved to shoot, and the other menaced suffocation" (*Wieland,* 58). This icon of two-fold danger such as Clara will face during the climax (and once after that—see p. 13) also reflects the nation's political juncture in the years prior to Brown's writing of *Wieland.* America in the mid-1790s was factionalized, torn almost to the point of civil war between an explosive republicanism and a Federalist reaction. This factional strife, kindled by the French Revolution, among other things, and fanned by international cross-winds (Britain's war with France exacerbated as well as mirrored America's domestic split), threatened, during the years 1794-1797, to become a conflagration. During the summer of 1798, a Federalist administration, reacting to a new wave of republican discontent, passed the Alien and Sedition Acts, decrees that sought to stifle anti-Federalist criticism and the growth of republicanism. Republicans, in turn, drafted the defiant Virginia and Kentucky Resolutions—accompanied, apparently, in Virginia's case, by arms appropriations to resist federal troops bent on enforcing the Acts.[14] America was, in brief, a family at odds with itself, not only in the years prior to, but even during the months when Brown was completing *Wieland.*

Nor were America's problems merely internal. France, a dangerous other as well as a projected self, menaced war. This real, external threat lends further resonance to Brown's confrontation scene. America's outrage over the XYZ Affair—a French diplomatic insult—peaked in June, 1798. By July, France's declaration of war on the United States was considered imminent. Because America owed France her very existence (and perhaps assistance under the Treaty of Paris, though we had denied this on legalistic grounds), this bitter pass must have been regretted with a mixture of guilt, fear and mortification not unlike that by which Clara, confronting her formerly solicitous brother, is paralyzed.

Essentially, though, these political crises—France's hostility, faction at home—reflected a more profound identity crisis: America's need to come to terms with her revolutionary heritage. The French Revolution had mirrored our republican sentiments, then made us rue the likeness. The 1790s saw George Washington denounce committee-of-correspondence-type Democratic Clubs as diabolical; saw John Adams sponsor laws that threatened the first amendment; saw Patrick Henry come out of retirement to back the Federalists in their most illiberal hour. This suggests the scope of the transformation America in 1798 was experiencing: our elder self, our long-revered revolutionary self, had suddenly begun to look like a crazy relative. Or perhaps our accusatory postrevolutionary self was the crazy relative. Who could be sure? In either case, that lunatic was us; to dispatch him, moreover, was, in a sense, to become him.

Brown's America was—to borrow a motif from *Wieland*—a temple on a cliff. Her primary challenge was to retain her balance, to avoid being toppled by European wars or domestic crises. Hence George Washington's admonition to shun faction at home and "entangling alliances" abroad. But as crises erupted and faction increased, a studied balancing act must have seemed more and more difficult, even futile. "My mind seemed to be split into separate parts," says Clara, "and these parts to have entered into furious and implacable contention" (*Wieland,* 140). Perhaps decisive action—even a figurative fratricide—was necessary.

Brown does not answer this dilemma in *Wieland* (though he does in *Ormond*); he merely dramatizes it. *Wieland,* Brown's Scylla and Charybdis myth for the young republic, is primarily a plea that she wake up to the danger on either hand. The conclusion repeats this motif: Clara, literally asleep in her bed, barely escapes when her house catches fire. Simultaneously menaced by flames and by suffocating smoke, she is unable to break the "spell" that stupefies her (*Wieland,* 236). And though Brown contrives a *deus ex machina* to save her, her house burns to the ground.

This apocalypse and Clara's consequent expatriation suggests grave doubts on Brown's part toward America's prospects. Even Clara's fairy-tale preservation (carried through the flames to safety in the arms of a dark stranger, she is soon reunited, then eventually united with Pleyel) is rendered ironic by the change she undergoes. Once in Europe Clara adopts a moralistic, phony-sounding—one is tempted to say a "thrown"—voice, and, with it, a habit of rationalizing—indeed, of transforming—troublesome truths. Regarding the feelings she harbors for Pleyel even after he has married another, she says: "I continued to love him, but my passion was disguised to myself; I considered it merely as a more tender species of friendship, and cherished it without compunction" (*Wieland,* 238). Such explicit rationalizing forms an ironic coda to a tale that has hinged on the importance of discerning the truth behind appearances, of knowing oneself.

Clara's "biloquism" (so Carl Nelson, at least, has called it[15]) recalls a tack taken earlier by her uncle: that self-deception, ironically, may be necessary for survival. It proves so, at least, for Wieland, whose delusion sustains him even as it subverts his mind. And for America? Was America up to the task of self-confrontation? Considered in this context, Fussell's paradox takes on an almost tragic necessity, the revolution/writing act necessitating, as it were, a postrevolutionary rewriting act, a biloquial transformation of past deeds into palatable "history," of present lunacy into functional "sanity."

Vying with this disheartening possibility, however, is a still grimmer one: that the American experiment—the New, Improved Jerusalem, the Enlightened Republic on a Hill—may simply be doomed beyond recall. Allusions to the crumbled glories of Rome, for instance—

and particularly to Wieland's revered Cicero, whose death in an insurrection signified the triumph of anarchy and darkness—bode ill for the Wielands' neoclassical polity. Brown's occasional allusions to *Macbeth,* moreover,[16] melodramatic though they seem, remind the American reader that for centuries striking at a king meant nothing less than upending nature, and that hands thus bloodied defied cleansing. In addition, Brown's intimations elsewhere in the book that fire signifies divine displeasure (consider the elder Wieland's death) makes the burning down of Clara's house smack of divine mandate rather than mishap.

In short, Brown, in his "American Tale," has traced depravity not merely to an Old World villain (Carwin) or to an overwrought zealot (Theodore Wieland), but to his normative, rational, eminently American protagonist, Clara Wieland; has recorded her progress toward infamy culminating in an ironic confrontation with her brother/self that carries overtones of America's own ironic confrontation with her revolutionary self; has suggested that even a limited "revolution" contains the seeds of future blight; and has hinted that America, the figurative protagonist as well as the setting of *Wieland,* may be doomed, even as Clara is doomed, twice-over: first, by a fatal ignorance of self, and second—ironically—by self-knowledge, once it has been afforded. By sending his surviving characters back to Europe, Brown as good as denies the possibility of rectifying the New World's "fall," of returning a still-adolescent America to a state of bliss. Even any *apparent* resumption of sanity, of balance, Brown seems to say, will come about through Old World artifice (New World art?), not genuine convalescence. Ironically, the most genuine hope *Wieland* extends is that Clara and America may, in time, learn, as Carwin perhaps learns by the tale's end, to use a revolutionary, transforming power with discretion.

III

Wieland criticism during the past generation has generally taken a psychological or philosophical tack—either bringing Freudian insights to bear on the characters' behavior (particularly Clara's) or examining the ways in which the novel questions Enlightenment assumptions it was formerly thought to dramatize. Studies along these lines by Larzer Ziff, Donald Ringe, Arthur Kimball, Alexander Cowie and others have become basic to our understanding of *Wieland.*[17] Several recent critics, however, have remarked increasingly on the novel's Americanness. Roberta F. Weldon, for instance, in an article characterizing the Wieland family as a microcosm of American individuality and insularity, proposes that "in the failure of this family it is possible to see a failure of the national experiment."[18] Cynthia S. Jordan, stressing the extent to which *Wieland* renders all narrative endings—especially happy ones—suspect, con-

cludes: "Brown's message to a young nation, nurtured from its infancy on stories promising its own happy ending . . . has only too recently begun to be heard."[19] Alan Axelrod's *Charles Brockden Brown: An American Tale* proposes that all of Brown's fictions "attempt to establish an American identity,"[20] which Axelrod associates with a frontier mind-set. And Edwin Fussell, his preoccupation with Carwin notwithstanding, wonders, at one point, "whether or not Clara is in some of her permutations the young nation herself."[21] These readings offer at least perceptive alternatives to the one developed above, if not collateral credibility for its nationalistic tack. Axelrod's thesis in particular—that the complex tension of opposites they generate (reflect?) makes Brown's novels "American tales"—reifies, I think, the revolutionary/post-revolutionary hypothesis that Fussell and I propose.

So, too, do other of Brown's writings. *An Address to the Government* . . . , besides suggesting a nation wrapped in "fatal sleep," also corroborates the concern with a politically polarized America inferred from *Wieland.* In this pamphlet Brown refers to the "great weakness of these States"—that "Their form of government and the state of the country is a hot-bed for faction and sedition."[22] Brown's short fictions **"Thessalonica"** and **"The Death of Cicero,"** furthermore, investigate the social psychology of anarchy and political upheavals in an earlier republic.

Brown, moreover, in an otherwise forgettable work entitled *The Man At Home,* hints at political/historical concerns like those inferred from *Wieland. The Man At Home* was published in installments in the *Weekly Magazine* during February and March of 1798 (when Brown was beginning *Wieland*). A tale rhetorically obsessed with "revolution," it features a box with a false bottom concealing a manuscript that "unfolds the causes and exhibits the agents in a transaction of high importance in the American Revolution." Characterizing this manuscript, Brown's narrator Bedloe says, in words that could almost apply to the confrontation scene in *Wieland,* "It is a sort of picture of the age at that period, and displays remarkable features in the condition of France, England and America."[23] (*The Man At Home* also draws an indirect parallel between the plague of 1793 in Philadelphia and the political plague of "faction in an ancient republic"—a conceit that both reiterates Brown's concern with the dangers posed by political strife and adumbrates a symbolic motif Brown uses in *Ormond.*)

These external referents lend incidental support to the reading of *Wieland* proposed above. The most compelling indirect argument, though, for reading *Wieland* as a fable about America's revolutionary/postrevolutionary tensions comes in *Ormond,* the novel that followed *Wieland* by a scant four months. In *Ormond* Brown re-enacts the *Wieland* fable, but heightens and simplifies its political overtones. Again the protagonist, threatened by a murderous aggressor who is both an other and a self ("Is there no part of me in which you discover your own likeness?" Ormond at one point asks Constantia[24]), takes up the knife. Here, however, the resonating ambivalence of the *Wieland* climax, with its simultaneous echoes of two different moments and mindsets, becomes something close to straightforward historical allegory. Ormond, a Frenchman and revolutionary[25] with whom the young, enlightened American adolescent, Constantia Dudley, has been infatuated, who has killed her father—purportedly on her behalf—and who, after courting her affections, has returned, transformed and violent, to extort unwarranted "dues," clearly personifies France. (The book's first half, in which a yellow fever plague sweeps Philadelphia, almost carrying off the heroine, adumbrates this crisis—"plague" being a metaphor for revolution both in the rhetoric of the time and elsewhere in Brown's work.) The climax, in which Constantia stabs Ormond, postfigures America's spurning of France and, ultimately, of her radical, "French" self.[26]

IV

Before all else, Brown's fictions are dramas of the human heart: dramas of traumatic self-discovery and compulsive self-denial, of young men and women who don't know the evils they are capable of and don't understand the true nature of the deeds they commit. Yet because the young republic was going through similar crises of identity, survival, self-assertion and self-understanding at the time Brown was writing, Brown's gothic fictions remain essentially "American Tale[s]" that portray the country itself, not just a few of its inhabitants. This is especially true of *Wieland,* the work that most thoroughly dramatizes the dark underside of Enlightenment optimism and the schizophrenia of Federalist America.

Notes

1. Robert E. Spiller, *The Cycle of American Literature* (New York, 1955, rpt. 1957), ix.

2. Edwin S. Fussell, "*Wieland*: A Literary and Historical Reading," *Early American Literature,* 18 (Fall, 1983), 171-186, especially 184.

3. William Dunlap, *The Life of Charles Brockden Brown: Together With Selections From The Rarest of His Printed Works, From His Original Letters, And From His Manuscripts Before Unpublished,* 2 vols. (Philadelphia, 1815), 2:92.

4. I am in some ways more comfortable terming *Wieland* a modern prose epic than an historical allegory because "epic," while denoting a literature rooted in national/social history, nevertheless suggests multiplicity of meaning rather than simple equivalence; myth rather than metaphor. But the generic term hasn't been invented that fully characterizes the hybrid *Wieland.*

5. *Charles Brockden Brown: An American Tale* (Austin, Texas, 1983), 73.

6. Fussell, 172.

7. *Homicide in American Fiction, 1798-1860* (Ithaca, New York, 1957), 89.

8. Charles Brockden Brown, "Walstein's School of History," *Monthly Magazine and American Review,* (April, 1799), 407.

9. Charles Brockden Brown, *Wieland and Memoirs of Carwin the Biloquist,* Eds. S. W. Reid, Sydney J. Krause, and Alexander Cowie. Bicentennial Edition (Kent, Ohio, 1977), 30. Future references will be included parenthetically in the text.

10. Charles Brockden Brown, Review of *The Foresters, Monthly Magazine and American Review* (April, 1799), 432.

11. Charles Brockden Brown, *An Address to the Government of the United States on the Cession of Louisiana to the French; and on the Late Breach of Treaty by the Spaniards, including the Translation of a Memorial, on the War of St. Domingo, and the Cession of Mississippi to France, drawn up by a Counsellor of State* (Philadelphia, 1803), 18.

12. Cynthia S. Jordan presents the most detailed reading of Clara's dark side. She sees no transformation, only chronic untrustworthiness in Clara's behavior. Nonetheless, she notes the evidence and argues, indeed, that Clara may actually have killed her brother and fabricated his suicide, so suspect is her narrative ("On Rereading *Wieland*: 'The Folly of Precipitate Conclusions,'" *Early American Literature,* 16 [1981], 154-174). Other critics who have beaten the same bushes are Scott Garrow and John Cleman. Both highlight Clara's stated fear that she too might become prey to the forces that have transformed her brother. Garrow fails, however, to adequately trace such a transformation, and identifies it, somewhat disappointingly, as merely a "lapse into senseless depression and irrational action motivated by fear," while Cleman too timidly concludes that "the question of Clara's innocence is not clear-cut." ("Character Transformation in *Wieland,*" *Southern Quarterly,* 4 [1966], 316; "Ambiguous Evil: A Study of Villains and Heroes in Charles Brockden Brown's Major Novels," *Early American Literature,* 10 [1975], 207.)

13. Leslie A. Fiedler, *Love and Death in the American Novel* (London, 1960), 142.

14. John C. Miller, *The Federalist Era* (New York, 1960), 164, 241. As Miller notes, "Most Virgin-

ians denied these measures were directed against the Federal government: the enemy, they declared, were the French and Indians. But William Branch Giles and John Randolph later asserted that the purpose of Virginia's warlike preparations was to resist Federal Troops."

15. Carl Nelson, "The Novels of Charles Brockden Brown: Irony and Illusion," Diss., State University of New York at Binghamton, 1970, 75.

16. Carwin's most frequently thrown command, "Hold, Hold!" is only the most obvious echo of *Macbeth* in *Wieland*. Consider also the bloodied hands motif, the supernatural overtones of the first dramatic scene and the witchcraft motif traced by Carl Nelson ("Irony and Illusion," 48-58). And the sleepwalking Clara? Does Brown mean to make her an ironic counterpart to Lady Macbeth?

17. See Ziff, "A Reading of *Wieland*," *PMLA* 77 (1962), 51-7; Ringe, *Charles Brockden Brown* (New York, 1966); Kimball, *Rational Fictions: A Study of Charles Brockden Brown* (McMinnville, Oregon, 1968); and Cowie, Introduction to the Bicentennial *Wieland* (See Note 9 above).

18. "Charles Brockden Brown's *Wieland*: A Family Tragedy," *Studies in American Fiction,* 12 (Spring, 1984), 8.

19. Jordan, 171.

20. Axelrod, xix.

21. Fussell, 183.

22. *An Address,* 45.

23. Charles Brockden Brown, *The Rhapsodist and Other Uncollected Writings,* Harry R. Warfel, ed. (New York, 1943), 69.

24. Charles Brockden Brown, *Ormond, or The Secret Witness,* Eds. S. W. Reid, Krause and Cowie. Bicentennial Edition (Kent, Ohio, 1982), 167.

25. Ormond is linked to a society patterned on the Illuminati, an eighteenth century cabal credited, in the popular mythology, with fomenting the French Revolution. See John Robison, *Proofs of a Conspiracy Against All the Religions and Governments of Europe, Carried on in the Secret Meetings of Free Masons, Illuminati, and Reading Societies* (New York, 1798), 9-10.

26. Constantia's deed, though boldly performed, is not without its own ambivalence. Instead of liberating her, it seems to confine and isolate her irrevocably. Our final image of Constantia is Sophia's keyhole portrait of her, "trapped" alone in her old house, distraught with horror and what looks like guilt. Constantia/America, in killing her French

self, has, in a sense, amputated the ideological possibilities that had brightened her "coming out." By contrast, the old house in which she has taken refuge has become a prison.

Shirley Samuels (essay date 1990)

SOURCE: Samuels, Shirley. "*Wieland*: Alien and Infidel." *Early American Literature* 25, no. 1 (1990): 46-66.

[*In the following essay, Samuels explores the connections between family and nation and the threat to both from outsiders as a prominent theme of* Wieland.]

An eighteenth-century New England minister who wrote a history of the American Revolution once described the need to "dress" his history modestly: "laboured elegance and extravagant colouring only brings her into suspicion, hides her beauty, and makes the cautious reader afraid lest he is in company with a painted harlot" (Gordon 393). While it seems understandable that a minister would not want his reader to keep "company with a painted harlot," the conjunction of history and harlotry here appears rather striking. Such nervousness about licentious sexuality in language—specifically language that depicted the still-volatile topic of the American Revolution—extended to other writers, ministers, orators, and politicians in the young republic. They protected themselves by claiming to use a conservative rhetoric in their efforts to extradite the "alien" dangers of both deism and radical democracy. They proceeded, however, by emphasizing the dangers of the loose woman and, in attempting to educate the American people about the contagion of her infidelity, paradoxically enhancing the sexual associations they claimed to be protecting themselves against.[1]

One of the most famous of these educators, known today for his aggrandizing *Life of Washington*, was "Parson" Weems, who spent thirty years peddling books and tracts with titles like *The Bad Wife's Looking Glass* and *God's Revenge Against Adultery*. Presented as moral lessons, rooted in an idealized concept of sexuality and the family, these tracts also discussed political issues, a mixture common in eighteenth- and early nineteenth-century writings to the point that the rhetoric of sexuality and the family became nearly interchangeable with that of religion and politics. Such interchangeability is a direct concern of the early American novel. While concentrating on gothic sensationalism and sentimental seduction,[2] the novel in the early republic displays contemporary social and political anxiety about the stability of the family and its freedom from unfaithfulness, often figured as the contamination of the outside world.

I

In *God's Revenge Against Adultery* (1815), Weems presents two exemplary cases of the dangers of infidelity:

the "accomplished Dr. Theodore Wilson, (Delaware) who for seducing Mrs. Nancy Wiley, had his brains blown out by her husband," and the "elegant Mr. James O'Neale, Esq. (North Carolina) who for seducing the beautiful Miss Matilda d'Estrange, was killed by her brother" (143). At first glance, the moral for adulterers seems to be to stay clear of family members; at second, to beware of women with disturbing names. But, as Weems unfolds them, the crucial problem with these scenes is that neither seducer has been educated to control his excessive desires. One professes himself a deist, and the other joins in religious revivals; both transgress the controlled confines of religious thought while violating the confines of the family. And despite the specifics of geography in Weems's account, it also becomes clear that the problem of uncontrolled desire is a national one, and that this pamphlet is finally as much about political and religious education in the new republic as about adultery.

Dr. Theodore Wilson deceives his wife because "he was infected with that most shameful and uneasy of all diseases, an incurable lust or itching after strange women." His "disease" is not from natural causes, however: "this elegant young man owed his early downfal to reading 'PAINE'S AGE OF REASON'" (146). This "libertine publication" sets loose Wilson's "boundless ardour for animal pleasures" and encourages him with "bold slanders of the bible" so that Wilson "threw aside his father's good old family bible, and for a surer guide to pleasure took up the AGE OF REASON!" (147). Paine's incitement to deism has not been uniformly treated as a "guide to pleasure," but religious infidelity becomes more than metaphorical as Wilson's disease spreads.

Wilson begins a liaison with the wife of a tavern keeper. Nancy Wiley has been poorly educated; she overvalues her own beauty and "neglect[s] those immortal beauties of the mind WISDOM and PIETY" (150). They seem well matched, until her husband finds them together and kills Wilson, whereupon Wilson's wife dies of grief. The only beneficiary in Weems's account is Wilson's younger brother, who forsakes the "strenuous idleness" of a study of the law to study divinity "and is now the pastor of the first Presbyterian church in Philadelphia" (166).

The moral here appears to be that religion provides surety against Paine's dangerous excesses, but "Case the Second" provides a countering example. Here, a "rich old gentleman, whose name was L'Estrange" has found wealth but not happiness: "In spite of my money, I find I am growing old and crazy . . . I'll go to the BIBLE and see if I can find happiness there." He learns, curiously enough, that "religion, properly defined, is only the ART OF HAPPINESS," and therefore opens his home to religious revivalists, especially embracing young Mr. O'Neale, who "professed himself a CONVERT!" (169).

Unfortunately, young O'Neale's education, like that of Nancy Wiley, has been "worldly minded" and he has sought "his happiness in the concupiscences of the FLESH, the chief among which is the appetite for SEX" (170).

Looking for this happiness, in spite of his "conversion," O'Neale attempts to seduce Miss Matilda L'Estrange, "but her sense of natural modesty, strengthened by education," (171) helps her resist him until she too experiences a religious conversion. She reaches a "transport" of "convulsive joy; her breasts heaving and panting—her color alternately coming and going, now crimsoned with joy and delight, and now pale and exhausted as if near overcome with fatigue" (172). In this sexual "holy extacy," Matilda seeks out O'Neale and throws "her arms around his neck," "fondly pressing him to her swelling breasts." These "virgin caresses" "served to kindle higher the fever of brutal passion"; O'Neale takes advantage of the moment, and "Miss L'Estrange was ruined . . . by a villain under the sacred garb of religion" (173-4). Inevitably she becomes pregnant and her family casts her out. Her brother shoots O'Neale, whose dying lament is, "Oh had I but been early brought up to religion and some good trade, I had never come to this miserable end!" (187).

O'Neale's lame regrets, and these case histories generally, emphasize the importance of a careful upbringing, safe from the introduction of false texts and desires that exceed the bounds of marriage and the family. Purportedly a pamphlet about the dangers of adulterous sex, this turns out to be a tract that insists on a concept of education conservatively cordoned off from either deism or revivalism. Why are both of these extremes of religious discourse linked with illicit sexual desire? Put another way, why did post-Revolutionary writers see both religious and political excesses as threats to the family?

The most notorious deist was Thomas Paine, whose Age of Reason was vilified for making religious infidelity accessible to the masses. In other words, the language was straightforward and any one could afford to buy it, since Paine subsidized its publication.[3] Thirty-five replies to Paine's Age of Reason were published within a decade of its appearance (1794-1796), suggesting the alarm with which it was received.[4] Far more than the document itself, these replies link an "infidelity" of religious thought with infidelity within the family and, by implication, the state. Timothy Dwight, the conservative New England minister and Yale president, mounted several prominent attacks on Paine and other deists with his satirical "The Triumph of Infidelity" and sermons like "A Discourse on Some Events of the Last Century" (1801). In the latter, Dwight attacks infidelity as a composite of "opposition to Christianity, devotion to sin and lust, and a pompous profession of love to

Liberty" (265). Deism as a threat to institutionalized Christianity here becomes inseparable from a sexuality that erodes the boundaries of the family and a version of democracy that endangers the state.

If the exponents of deism had presented a "candid and logical opposition to Christianity," Dwight claims, "no reasonable objection [could] be made." But they insist on insidious rhetoric: the "infidels have neither labored, nor wished, to convince the understanding, but have bent all their efforts to engross the heart." The reader, "engaged by the ingenuity of the writer, is lost in a mist of doubtful expressions and unsettled sentiments. His faith is constantly solicited to gravely described dreams; and his eye is required to fix on the form of a cloud." Like Weems, Dwight appears to be describing a process of seduction. The "ingenuity of the writer" is focused on the method rather than the matter of persuasion, so that "from the highway of common sense [the reader] is invited into bypaths" (265-67). Implicitly, Dwight suggests that if Paine had stuck with "Common Sense," he would find no fault with his "ingenuity." But Paine, and other deists, have strayed "into bypaths," and the former efficacy of attempts to "convince the understanding" is now channeled into "engrossing the heart."

The dangerous character of infidels manifests itself in their talents and the diversity of their application: "Their writings have assumed every form, and treated every subject of thought." From "lofty philosophical discourse," they have "descended . . . to the newspaper paragraph; . . . from regular history to the anecdote; from the epic poem to the song." The influence of deism is everywhere: "in a note subjoined to a paper on criticism or politics; in a hint in a book of travels." What is most insidious about deism, then, is its omnipresence and the hapless plight of the reader who must assent despite himself, "to yield his judgment before he was aware that he was called to judge" (268). Since infidelity may be at work in the most innocuous writing, all forms of writing become suspect.

The nervousness that Dwight displays about the omnipresence and diversity of deistic writings may help explain why he finds infidelity a political as well as a sexual and religious threat. The notion of infidelity penetrated political disputes in several ways. Religious boundaries were patrolled by the politically and professionally dominant Federalists who claimed to hold a monopoly on religion and who opposed what they saw as Democratic deism. Subsequently, as the historian Clifford Griffin has shown, many of the so-called benevolent associations that appeared during the early nineteenth century—the Bible Society, for example, or the American Tract Society, which distributed almost two million pamphlets in the first half of the century— were Federalist-inspired attempts to maintain social order. These associations saw the Bible as a "moral po-

lice" that kept "guard over property and life" and was "better than every measure of secret espionage to which a Napoleon or a Nicholas might resort." Finally, claimed the Home Missionary Society, "*The Gospel is the most economical police on earth.*"[5] The Bible was unabashedly the most visible symbol of a conservative political order.

The kind of policing that was carried out in the name of the Bible extended from the benevolent societies to other institutions such as schools, and particularly to the relatively new American institution of literature. At the heart of these gestures of containment was a model of social control that took the form of a clearly defined family order. Since the French Revolution had introduced a model of revolution that seemed to undermine this order, writers of the period frequently worked to keep the notion of revolution contained politically and metaphorically as a "family affair," a process that became linked with the desire to confine and institutionalize the family.[6]

Even such apparently innocuous terms as the "sacred honor" of the nation point to the conjunction of religious and sexual beliefs at the heart of national and familial identity. They may also shed a new light on the literature of the early Republic. Novels like Charles Brockden Brown's **Wieland** in many ways *because* of their gothic concern with incest, repressed desires, and lurid crimes, successfully "make the picture of a single family a model from which to sketch the condition of a nation" (33-34). That is, by so luridly depicting the threat posed to the family by the outside world, these novels encouraged and promoted a conservative, closed model of the family, though at the same time, in the closed circle of incestuous violence of **Wieland,** we can see that concentration on the family produces its own threats. The representative family-as-nation that was portrayed in numerous political pamphlets of the Revolutionary War found a fictional form in novels of the early Republic. National concerns were portrayed as domestic dilemmas, since in order to preserve the nation, it was conceived necessary to preserve the family as a carefully constituted supporting unit. Therefore, the sexual infidelity that represented the greatest threat to the family was presented as a national threat, especially after the French Revolution when women were popularly understood to be the instigators of the dread mob that came to stand for democratic rule, and Liberty came to be depicted as a whore.

As Timothy Dwight, among others, saw it, the French Revolution had unleashed Infidelity as the loose woman of the barricades:

> Emboldened beyond every fear by this astonishing event, Infidelity . . . walked forth in open day, and displayed her genuine features to the sun. Without a blush

she now denied the existence of moral obligation, anni-hilated the distinction between virtue and vice, chal-lenged and authorized the indulgence of every lust, trod down the barriers of truth [and] lifted up her front in the face of heaven.

(269)

In other words, Democracy appears as a bold prostitute. Dwight again conflates the abhorrent possibilities of al-lowing infidelity to have a recognized place in religious discourse, allowing "democracy" to control the affairs of state, and allowing the "genuine features" of prosti-tutes to be exposed "to the sun." Each act again in-volves the others; and each spells out destruction to church, state, and family. What Dwight seemed to fear most was that the loose morals introduced by this loose woman might be accompanied by a dread contagion, perhaps venereal, and he preached against whatever would "spread the disease," suggesting that Jacobin de-mocracy was a form of the yellow fever plague that had so terrorized Americans at the time of the Terror in France.

II

The fear of contamination by the French in general, though perhaps one might argue by French women in particular, led Federalists to propose the Alien and Se-dition Acts as a means of "quarantining" America from the "vile and loathsome embrace" of the French (Miller 43). Shortly before Congress was to vote on the mea-sures, Senator Humphrey Marshall, who supported the Alien Act, turned to poetry to explain its necessity. Marshall begins "The Aliens, A Patriotic Poem," by praising the qualities of the United States that attract aliens. But the wrong aliens are being attracted. A troop of "venal wretches," the French, have come to the United States because they were "At home involv'd in horrid war, / And all the vices, that curse the mind." The proper recourse:

> For Aliens, who've crossed the seas,
> In language strong, and firm accost them;
> The innocent—be they at ease,
> The guilty—make haste and arrest them.

Not surprisingly, the poem tries to cordon off the "safe" alien from the potentially contagious one, but the para-dox of America, epitomized by Philadelphia as the cen-ter of both government and aliens, is that its very order, especially its "laws, like those divine, / Calleth the Alien, from afar." Attracting those "Aliens" it wishes to repel, America must act to contain the threat of the Alien, who is perversely attracted by the order that his coming threatens to disrupt.

Invoking the same model of attracting and even pro-moting disorder while producing a desire for familial and social order, Charles Brockden Brown's *Wieland;*

or The Transformation, published the year the Alien and Sedition Acts were passed, might be read as their novelistic response, but also counterpart. Like the quali-ties of America that attract the "alien," the very charm of the Wieland's idyllic community has attracted Car-win, the alien called from afar. In each case, the attrac-tiveness of order invites the intrusion of disorder. How-ever, the novel does not unilaterally assign guilt to Carwin as the alien intruder, and indeed often questions whether we should instead blame, as the narrator, Clara, sometimes believes we should, the interior of the home itself, or, more particularly, "the immeasurable evils that flow from an erroneous or imperfect discipline" (5). *Wieland* presents alternative versions of educa-tional and religious beliefs but frames the presentation with this announcement of a moral to be derived from the effects of such an "imperfect discipline": these very "freedoms" of thought and belief may have caused the destruction of the Wieland family. Despite its gothic sensationalism, the novel, like Weems's pamphlet, often appears more significant as an educational tract, one which contains lessons about the contemporary disputes over religious infidelity, a strictly circumscribed educa-tion, the chastity of women, and the status of institu-tions, preeminently the institution of the family.

After the death of their parents, Clara and Wieland have a premature and, in Federalist terms, unnatural indepen-dence. They are "subjected to no unreasonable re-straints," indeed are virtually free from any external re-straints at all, and are "saved from the corruption and tyranny of colleges and boarding schools," becoming "superintendants of [their own] education" (20, 21). Clara's terms for her upbringing could have been taken from colonial pamphlets about the benefits of indepen-dence from Britain.[7] The dangers of infidelity, however, would have been apparent to anxious contemporaries: "Our education had been modelled by no religious stan-dard. We were left to the guidance of our own under-standing and the casual impressions which society might make upon us. . . . We sought not a basis for our faith" (22). In other words, the Wieland children are educated in the style of the Enlightenment, a style derived in the eighteenth century from the formulations of Locke and Rousseau. One function of the novel might be to ques-tion how successfully this style functions on American soil.

Clara's utopian upbringing has created a hazardous situ-ation both because it has attracted Carwin and because it has not been supplemented by the kind of institutions that were increasingly perceived as necessary in the young republic. Indeed, Clara judges that she has had a "perverse and vicious education," especially because she has not been "qualified by education or experience to encounter perils" (80, 140). In *The Discovery of the Asylum,* David Rothman asserts that the late eighteenth-century American fear of contamination by France was in the process of becoming a fear of contamination by anything in the "world"; to counter this fear, the family had to be protected and protective and to "inoculate" the child against society. As we have seen, the rise of institutions of social control in this period, like the orphan asylum and even the school, is modeled on and supported by such an insular notion of the family. The institution compensated for the failure of the family, supplemented and even instructed the family, from which it was presumed to have derived (85, 121, 234, 152-53). One of *Wieland*'s functions as a tutelary tract might be to prepare the way for the notion that institutions are a necessary supplement to the family. Without the formal institutions of education, religion, "benevolent societies," orphanages, or prisons, the new republic would be susceptible to the chaos unleashed within the Wieland family.[8]

In *Wieland*, that chaos is blamed on Carwin, whose intrusion has excited sexual tensions in Clara and Pleyel and an insane and murderous religious enthusiasm in Wieland. Published while the fear of contagion by the alien was at its height, the novel foments and yet tries to explain away the threat by both blaming Carwin for introducing sexuality, disorder, and violence into the Wieland family, and explaining that introduction as nothing more than an enhancement of sexual and familial tensions already present.[9] Carwin is an intruder, an alien called "from afar" by what he perceives as the almost "divine" qualities of Clara and her brother. But he also embodies an instability already present within the Wieland family. Introduced as an external threat, the alien, Carwin, instead stands (in) for an internal one, the infidelity of religious and institutional beliefs that the novel at first appeared to celebrate.[10] If the family had been properly inoculated against him, he could have had no effect on them.

The extent to which the family can be seen as a haven from the outside world is made problematic on the historical front as well. Although *Wieland*'s action takes place "between the conclusion of the French and the beginning of the revolutionary war," Clara finds that "revolutions and battles, however calamitous to those who occupied the scene, contributed in some sort to our happiness, by agitating our minds with curiosity, and furnishing causes of patriotic exultation. Four children . . . exercised my brother's tenderness" (3, 26). The unabashed segue between the "scene" of war and the family scene does not disturb Clara and would pass by the reader were it not that what seems continuous to her appears discontinuous to us. While Clara apparently intends that the violence outside should emphasize the harmony within the family, the introduction of the children is instead the introduction of violence: they are to be the object not of Wieland's "tenderness," but of violence "calamitous to those who occupied the scene." Both the absent battles and the present children myste-

riously "contributed in some sort to our happiness," while both agitate minds with curiosity about violence. If Clara conflates the revolutions of nations and the transformations of families, this conflation of national and familial violence further confirms the extent to which the novel registers contemporary national concerns in its depiction of familial turmoil. The novel emphasizes the violence within the family while ascribing that violence to the intrusion of a violent force, but that very force seems immanent rather than intrusive, and the efforts to name it as "alien" only emphasize its immanence.

The clearest instances of the intrusion of the alien into the family may be the explicit "otherworldly" experiences of the novel, the spontaneous combustion of the elder Wieland and the "inspiration" of the younger. While the younger Wieland begins by seeking a "ground of his belief" in the "history of religious opinions," Clara finds in the Calvinist "ground" her brother stands on nothing but "props" that can be only a temporary support: "Moral necessity, and calvinistic inspiration, were the props on which my brother thought proper to repose" (23, 25). Unfortunately for Wieland, the shakiness of his "ground" points to an "obvious resemblance between him and my father" (23). In other words, we are warned that his attempt to reason toward faith by combining "calvinistic inspiration" with the "history of religious opinion" will produce infidelity and madness. The conflation of Wieland's attempt to reason toward faith (apparently an oblique reference to Paine) and the horrific effects of his sudden access to God (reminiscent of some of the excesses of the Great Awakening) appears as a reference to the conflict earlier described between Timothy Dwight, the grandson of that arch-Calvinist Jonathan Edwards, and Thomas Paine, the archdeist. Paralleling the twin downfalls of the Weems pamphlet, the novel shows the pitfalls of either position. Neither the inspired Wieland nor the rationalist Pleyel represents a form of belief that can effectively function against the hazards of the early Republic. By demonstrating the weakness of either extreme, the novel enacts a desire for the norm. And the champion or hero of this enactment may finally be not the reasonable Pleyel, or even Clara, but Carwin. His voice forces a questioning of perceived realities and underscores the abnormalities already present within the Wieland family. Carwin can be seen as an "alien" who introduces himself surreptitiously into households and exposes abnormalities as part of a regularizing or normalizing strategy.

III

Before examining further the effects of Carwin's presence in *Wieland*, I want to examine the context of this presence by returning to the terms of the pairing established in Weems's pamphlet, where deism and revivalism were both excesses that led to disaster. Specifically, I want to trace the religious, legal, and sexual implications of Wieland's destruction of his family by looking at the crime both in the novel and in two possible sources for the novel. The novel's presentation of Wieland's brutal murders brings together, in the arena of the family, anxieties about law and religion. Set in a period when the nation was haunted alike by fears of the removal of an institutionalized God perceived in deism and of the direct access to Him promised in the revivalism of the Great Awakening, the novel also works effectively to collapse the difference between these categories and to relocate the threat as an intrusive violation into the family.

When Clara reads Wieland's confession, which she transcribes as evidence within her own first-person narrative, she discovers his belief that in murdering his family he has obeyed a personal call to faith. Like the court he appears in, Wieland once wanted to "settle the relation between motive and actions, the criterion of merit, and the kinds and properties of evidence" (23). Now he professes to be thankful for the chance "to testify my submission to thy will" (165). Incongruously presenting a personal narrative of conversion in the world of the court, Wieland represents himself and his motives for the murder of his family in the terms of the conversion narrative that was required for admittance into the Puritan congregation.[11] But his story of conversion, instead of gaining him admittance into the "congregation," causes him to be cast out, and in a way that emphasizes the conflict between "legal" and "religious" explanations that the novel examines.

Wieland's appeal to a transcendent deity was soon to become, in the eyes of the law, an insanity defense. Even in the 1790s, as the novel presents the case, Wieland's perceived madness saves him from the gallows, although not from institutionalization. David Brion Davis has discussed the change in the early republic from the Calvinist concentration on sin or sinful thought as worthy of punishment to the focus on actual crime and its origin in "parental neglect and faulty emotional growth [rather than] inherent depravity or a conscious choice of evil." According to this view, the early republic witnessed a basic shift in notions of responsibility and communal legitimations and also a shift in notions of character. The structure of social institutions, modeled on the family, becomes the locus of the moral and emotional "nurture" and formation of the subject: "there was a growing conviction that crime was a disease . . . to be prevented by improved education and social reform" (*Homicide* 9, 22). Adapting to this shift to the jurisdiction of the family, Timothy Dwight preached that "murder in the proper sense is begun in . . . the early and unrestrained indulgence of human passions. This indulgence, therefore, Parents, and all other Guardians of children, are bound faithfully to re-

strain" (*Theology* 3:356). The conversion narrative has given way to the legal confession, innate character to education and growth, and penitence to the penitentiary. In one respect this transformation was itself dramatically ratified in the separation of church and state represented by the ratification of the Constitution and the dispersal of the authority of the church into the related institutions of education, law, and the family. The novel plays out the anxieties that this change in jurisdiction has produced.

More particularly, the novel dramatizes the change from judging Wieland's crime according to his faith (Wieland castigates his judges for their failure to recognize divine rather than legal jurisdiction: "Impious and rash! thus to usurp the prerogatives of your Maker!") to judging it according to a legal conception of sanity. Still the novel betrays a rather uncertain jurisdiction over the topic of madness. In part this is due to the uncertainty of causal relations in a novel that foregrounds the problem of cause and effect.[12] The notion that madness is both motive and cause for Wieland's crime poses rather than solves the problem of motive, complicating what it means to have motives. Clara's uncle reassures her that "there could be no doubt as to the cause of these excesses. They originated in sudden madness, but that madness continues, and he is condemned to perpetual imprisonment" (177). Rather than solving the crux of Wieland's motives, the weak causal links of this statement beg the question. What is the connection between the continuation of Wieland's madness ("but") and his imprisonment ("and")? If the "cause" or origin of Wieland's "excesses" is "madness," does his imprisonment represent an attempt to cure him or to contain the effects of his delusions? The notion that character can change is exhibited most problematically here: if Wieland's madness no longer continued, would he be freed?

An excess of belief has led to Wieland's crimes, but what may appear as a simple conflict between religious and legal explanations is further complicated by references to the family. Curiously, in addition to his marked submission to a divine vision, Wieland appeals to the community, and he makes that appeal in terms that suggest he recognizes yet another version of the constituted self. Turning to the audience at his trial, he asks, "Who is there present a stranger to the character of Wieland? Who knows him not as an husband—as a father—as a friend?" (164). His appeal to the community's "knowledge" of him in familial terms is at once an escape from the confines of legal and religious definitions of the citizen or congregant and a move to the heart of those definitions. If Wieland is "known" as a member of his family, he is placed safely within both legal and religious discourses. His actions in murdering his family have been as much a confirmation of his belief in the value of family as a denial.

IV

Wieland contains a family destroyed from within, though agency is ascribed to outside forces. A similar displacement occurs in one of the presumed sources for *Wieland*. James Yates was sitting in front of his fire in 1781 reading the Bible when he suddenly heard a voice commanding him to destroy his idols. He threw his Bible into the fire; then, upon further admonition from the voice, he killed his wife and four children. His next thought was to set the house on fire so that it would appear that the Indians had done the deed ("I shall be called a murderer for destroying my idols—for obeying the mandate of my father—no, I will put all the dead in the house together, run to my sister's and say the Indians have done it!"),[13] but he was thoroughly convinced that his actions were justified since they had been dictated by a divine voice and decided that it was better to have the deed known as a confirmation of his devoutness. Axelrod has argued that by taking "'communion' with the wilderness" Yates internalizes the threat of the Indians and acts as they would presumably have acted (59).[14] But if Yates, as a sort of afterthought, displaces his violence onto the Indians, his justifications for his actions, and indeed the acts themselves, explicitly invoke a rather different perspective. Yates's justifications, and his presentation of himself as wavering between a family of "idols" and "divine" injunctions to destroy them (reminiscent of Puritan iconoclasm), suggest that he has not so much incorporated the threat of the Indians as violently externalized the closely linked internal problems of belief and the family.

Another analogue for *Wieland* may be the *Narrative for William Beadle* (reprinted several times in the 1790s), which gives an account of a murder-suicide that took place in the last year of the American Revolution. This analogue has not been heretofore noted and is worth looking at in some detail for the clues it may provide about *Wieland.* Beadle was a retailer ruined because of the failure of continental species toward the end of the war. One morning in 1782, he killed his wife and four children and then himself. Beadle left letters in which "he professes himself a deist" and claimed that "the deity would not willingly punish one who was impatient to visit his God and learn his will from his own mouth face to face": "That it is God himself who prompts and directs me . . . I really believe" (20, 21, 31). Conflating the concepts of deism and revivalism, Beadle apparently meant that the promise of direct access to God enabled him to perceive his premeditated murders as righteous acts, and hence his mind, like Wieland's "was contemplative" before the murders (15).[15]

The narrative of Beadle's life was presented by its editor as a testament to the "shocking effects of pride and false notions about religion," but it also and perhaps more strikingly shows the power of the unstable tension between family and world in the early Republic (10). When Beadle originally began to fail, "he adopted a plan of the most rigid family economy, but still kept up the outward appearance of his former affluence" (6). More than an understandable attempt to retain status, Beadle's version of "family economy" is transformed into the necessity of family sacrifice. Beadle's family went hungry because "he was determined not to bear the mortification of being thought poor and dependent," but his considerateness did not stop there: "since it is a father's duty to prepare for his flock, he thought it better to consign them over to better hands" (21, 24). His wife had been having premonitory dreams of the murders, perhaps because Beadle had been in the habit of bringing a butcher knife and an axe to bed with him every night. Beadle wrote of her premonitions, but claimed that "heaven" thought "his purpose was right": God "now directs me and supports me" (18). He wondered whether he could justify killing his wife; finally he decided that it "would be unmerciful to leave her behind to linger out a life in misery and wretchedness which must be the consequence of the surprising death of the rest of the family, and that since they had shared the smiles and frowns of fortunes together, it would be cruelty to her, to be divided from them in death" (15).

Beadle's fear of being alienated from the community, through poverty, or the family, through death, was dramatically realized when the community had to dispose of his body. No one wanted to be responsible: "at last it was performed by some Negroes, who threw him out of the window, with the bloody knife tied on his breast" (20). Having found suitably marginal characters as undertakers and a thoroughly marginal means of egress, the community became perturbed about interring the body: "After some consultation, it was thought best to place it on the banks of the river between the high and low water mark; the body was . . . bound with cords upon a sled, with the clothes on it as it was found, and the bloody knife tied on his breast, without coffin or box, and the horse he usually rode was made fast to the sled." After a gruesome funeral procession, "the body was tumbled into a hole dug for the purpose like the carcase of a beast" (12). Despite the communal attempts to eliminate Beadle and even to eradicate his identity as a human being, the multiply outcast Beadle returned yet again: some children discovered his body washed up by the river, and it was finally reburied by a crossroads.

Finally, then, the difference that Beadle enforces between outward appearance and an inner "rigid family economy" sets up an unbearable distinction between the family and the world. Although Beadle's explanation of his actions invokes a peculiar form of deism, in fact the confusion between revivalism and deism he exhibits appears equivalently in the Weems pamphlet and in other discussions of the early republic that create a striking correspondence between the effects of these religious excesses. The editor of Beadle's account, Stephen Mix Mitchell, asks, in terms reminiscent of *Wieland,* if it is possible that "a man could be transformed from an affectionate husband and an indulgent parent to a secret murderer, without some previous alteration, which must have been noticed by the family or acquaintance?" (16). The "previous alteration" that effected a transformation in Beadle seems again, as with Yates and Wieland, to have been caused by exposure to religious excess. What appears in these accounts to be on the one side an affirmation of devout Calvinist orthodoxy and on the other an affirmation of deistic reasoning that curiously allows for direct access to God turns out to be much the same thing when put into practice: deism and Calvinist revivalism are represented as significant, and significantly similar, threats to the family. What may be most disturbing, however, about these "alterations" is that they cannot finally be blamed on an alien intrusion; instead, the family-republic, like the Wieland family that serves as its "model," is caught in the grip of transformations in which it discovers that the alien is already within.

V

In *Wieland,* the direct result of excessive styles of belief is not only the violence we have been discussing, but also, and perhaps more importantly in terms of the scene of the family, irregular sexual desires. Specifically, as several critics have noted, incest appears as an almost unmistakable element of both Wieland's actions and Clara's responses. In this final and most disturbing version of naming inner desires as alien in order to expel them, Clara performs a double action, at once projecting the violence of her brother's actions onto Carwin, and discovering Carwin in threatening scenes (with sexual overtones) where she has anticipated her brother.

Wieland and Carwin are repeatedly linked by Clara. Even the possibility of a connection between the antinomian beliefs that Wieland appeals to when he explains the murder of his family (by which one may be freed from moral law by virtue of grace) and the Albigensian beliefs for which her father apparently died (in which God and Satan are manifestations of the same force) provides a link between what Clara perceives as godlike qualities in Wieland and the apparently satanic qualities of Carwin. Both Carwin and Wieland undergo "transformations," though their characters remain ambiguous and even interchangeable.[16] When Clara opens closets expecting to find her brother, or steps back from pits her brother has beckoned her toward, she finds Carwin. When she discovers the murders her brother has committed, she blames Carwin. Although she explains them as antipodes, the "virtues" of her brother may not finally be distinguishable from those of Carwin: the alien and the infidel are the same.

Further, Clara's obsessive concern with the placing of responsibility, the assumption of guilt, and the assignation of blame, her attempts to discover who is guilty

and how that guilt shall be determined and judged, appear connected to her own displacement of a sense of guilt. Near the end of her narrative, Clara "acknowledge[s] that my guilt surpasses that of all mankind" (223). One critic asserts plausibly that Clara's "repressed guilt and incestuous desires provide her with motivation" for the crimes that Wieland commits, and argues that she "writes our story with a pen sharpened by a knife steeped in her brother's blood" (Hesford 239). Clara's fascination with Carwin as he interferes with her fantasy life, mingled with her immediate assumption of his agency in the destruction of her family, points to her desire to have a scapegoat for her own desires. She identifies with Wieland's "transformation" to the extent that she asks, "Was I not likewise transformed from rational and human into a creature of nameless and fearful attributes? Was I not transported to the brink of the same abyss? Ere a new day should come, my hands might be embrued in blood" (179-80). In spite of her attempt to maintain Carwin as a supernaturally gifted "double-tongued deceiver," Clara manages to castigate herself. Though she calls Carwin the "phantom that pursued my dreams," she suspects that he might be one of the "phantoms of my own creation" (159, 83).

Clara responds immediately to Carwin's voice: her eyes fill with "unbidden tears" and are later "rivetted" upon the portrait she makes of him (52, 53). Though his features are "wide of beauty," it seems curiously their very characteristic of being "outside" beauty and the inversion of usual standards in the "inverted cone" of his face that attracts her, so that she "consumed the day in alternately looking out upon the storm and gazing at the picture" (53, 54). She cannot "account for [her] devotion to this image"—though she allows the reader to suppose it a sign of the "first inroads of a passion incident to every female heart"—and similarly cannot explain why, although the outside storm passes, "thoughts ominous and dreary" overwhelm her as she continues to look at the picture (54). Rather than pointing to a romantic infatuation, these signs point to her participation in or even invocation of Carwin's existence at the same time as the associations she makes with him seem importantly connected to her own desires. Looking at Carwin's portrait, she thinks of death, specifically dwelling upon the foreshadowed deaths of her brother and his children. This oscillation between the portrait and the storm is reiterated when, in her retrospective tracing of the events that led to the deaths of her brother's children, she remembers Carwin as "the intelligence that operated in this storm" (190). The storm that raged outside has been internalized. Still, she does not finally know whether Carwin is "an object to be dreaded or adored" and moves to blame him with a tentative assertion: "Some relief is afforded in the midst of suffering, when its author is discovered or imagined" (71, 190).

Indeed, Clara's attempts to "discover" or "imagine" (activities that she appears to confuse in the novel) the "author" of the deeds she has been so appalled by seem finally rather disingenuous. Like Beadle, she has tried to separate the "inviolate asylum" of the home from the dangers of the world, and, like Beadle, she finds that the scene of the home is already the scene of destruction. (It seems quite telling that Clara hears murderers in her closet.) While she claims that "that dwelling, which had hitherto been an inviolate asylum, was now beset with danger to my life," her mistake is to think that it has ever been an "inviolate asylum" (60).[17]

Clara's efforts to fix blame and determine judgments are part and parcel of the attempts to maintain familial and social boundaries that may be seen to structure the action of *Wieland.* Although Clara and Wieland turn their father's restrictive and rigidly regulated retreat (the temple where he meets his demise) into a haven for free discourse (a new infidelity), it quickly becomes a place where transgressions are foregrounded. Carwin turns the temple into a zone of terror by his voice projections, but his intrusion should have been expected. Clara speaks of the meetings that take place there as free from societal interference and of Carwin as the destroyer of their peace, but rather than being simply the double-tongued deceiver that she calls him, rather than being simply an intruder or foreign violator of the pastoral American scene, Carwin's very abnormalities expose the shaky underpinnings of the family "asylum." By his intrusion into what Clara has presented as normal domestic scenes, he emphasizes or highlights underlying incongruities and potent desires. Although he systematically invades all Clara's retreats, including her body (albeit through the surrogate servant Judith, and through the ventriloquized sexual conversation that Pleyel "overhears"), Carwin might be seen as exposing Clara's general policy of concealment. In her shaded retreat by the river, Clara dreams of terrifying incest; Carwin wakes her. Clara's bower already resembles a sexual recess; Carwin forces her to confront the mingled invitation and threat of her brother's and her own sexuality.

In *Wieland,* then, the family is initially presented as a retreat, or "sweet and tranquil asylum" (193), from the intrusions of the outside world, but the distinction between home and world, radically personified by the figure of the intruding Carwin, gets blurred as the destruction seen to lurk without gets discovered within. Clara concludes her account of her family with a typically mixed acknowledgment of the flaw that lay within: "the evils of which Carwin [was] the author, owed their existence to the errors of the sufferers." No violence could have been introduced into the family "if their own frailty had not seconded these efforts" (244). What Clara still manages to assume in this statement is Carwin's "authorship" of an account which she herself has writ-

ten. Even as Clara cannot fully recognize the implications of her involvement as the author of the account of her family or see the family as the source of its own destruction, the novel presents her failed perceptions as part of a prevailing faulty perception in the early republic. For the family to keep its identity as an "asylum," the outside world must be posited as a threat. At the same time, the imitation of the family in social institutions designed to assume or supplement its functions provides a way out of the unbearable tension created between inside and outside by such an insular view of the family. *Wieland*'s message may finally be that for the family to be a haven from the excesses of radical democracy, deism, and revivalism, it must be inoculated, by way of these social institutions, at once with and against the "outside" world. Following the lead of Charles Brockden Brown, the American novel continued to explore the boundaries of the family and to suggest styles of education that would be appropriate for maintaining the family as the support for such an "outside" world, a world represented as all that is alien to the tranquil space, the "inviolate asylum," of the family.

Notes

1. A version of the first part of this essay appeared previously in *Early American Literature* 22 (1987), in a special issue devoted to talks from the Early American Literature Division meeting at the 1986 Modern Language Association convention.

2. Davidson asserts that the "Gothic exhibited a particular genius" for exploring the "transitional culture" of the early republic (218).

3. Paine's work cost threepence, while Godwin's *Political Justice* was prohibitively expensive at three guineas, as reported in Grylls (16).

4. Mason Weems even peddled a version of Paine's *Complete Works* that contained a reply instead of the *Age of Reason*; reported in Skeel (296).

5. The first phrases are from a speech by Emory Washburn on the Bible Society in 1847, the last from the publications of the Home Missionary Society in 1837; cited by Griffin (95, 91, 94).

6. For an excellent discussion of the relation between the family and the institution in the period, see Rothman. Fliegelman provides a useful and intriguing account of attitudes toward the family in the literature of the late eighteenth century. See also Grossberg's discussion of the "republican family." The two Samuels essays discuss the connections of family and state in the fiction of the early republic. For the classical background of family and nation imagery in Wieland, see Weldon.

7. Cf. Fliegelman's discussion of the relation of novels and political programs in the eighteenth century.

8. While Tompkins finds a "plea for the restoration of civic authority" in *Wieland* (61), I do not find the novel quite so programmatic; still, I concur with her emphasis on political and historical context.

9. There has been much critical attention to the sexual attraction Clara feels for Carwin and for her brother. Davis, for example, claims that "Carwin had saved Clara from an incestuous relation with her brother" (*Homicide,* 90). What has not been focused on is the parallel between that sexual tension and the representations of deism and revolution in sexual terms during this period. Instead, many critics read the novel as psychological or moral commentary. Cowie, for example, asserts that "at times *Wieland* seems more like an exposure of the author's unconscious than a reasoned attempt to communicate with the reader logically" (327). For other standard critical treatments of the novel, see Bell, Gilmore, or Ziff. For a suggestive reading of incest in other novels of the period, see Dalke.

10. Suggesting the unlocatable threat of the Bavarian Illuminati (with which secret organization he is often linked, especially because of his apprenticeship under Ludloe in *Carwin the Biloquist*), it is Carwin's mysterious appropriation of voices, voices that are "inexplicably and unwarrantedly assumed," and, even more importantly, his assumption of the desires that go along with those voices, that makes Clara fear him most. Pleyel has already accused Clara of being in love with Carwin when he hears the conversation between them that Carwin projects. Wieland has already prepared himself to hear the voices that he hears. For the history of the threat of the Illuminati in America, see Stauffer.

11. The language of Wieland's account of his journey to God also incongruously echoes several passages in Jonathan Edwards's "Personal Narrative." In this conversion narrative, Edwards reports that as he "walked abroad alone . . . for contemplation . . . God's excellency appeared in every thing" (60). Wieland too reports walking outside alone: "My mind was contemplative. . . . The author of my being was likewise the dispenser of every gift with which that being was embellished" (166).

12. For interesting discussions of the frailty of cause and effect relations in the novel see Scheick and also Seltzer. For a history of nineteenth-century American treatments of insanity, see Caplan.

13. *New York Weekly Magazine,* July 1796, vol. 2, no. 55, p. 20. Blaming the Indians has a long history in the United States. In a perhaps similar way, William Bradford blamed internal problems in the Plymouth colony on the external threat of the Indians, who usefully alleviated the psychological threats of faith by posing a physical one. As long as he could blame the Indians for tensions within the colony, he could ignore the divisive internal battles over commerce, settlement, and religion. See also Slotkin: "The crowning irony of the witchcraft delusion is that the Puritans' hysterical fear of the Indian devils led them to behave precisely like the Indians" (142).

14. This source was recognized as early as 1801 by an anonymous reviewer in the *American Review and Literary Journal.* Axelrod comments further that "the blackest irony of James Yates's actions is that in performing what he sees as God's will he commits an atrocity worthy of the stereotyped godless American Indian" (58).

15. Another parallel to *Wieland* occurs with a servant girl who survives the massacre of the family: Beadle sends her on an errand during his murderous activities at home; in *Wieland,* she hides in the closet.

16. Pleyel mentions Carwin's "*transformation* into a Spaniard" (68).

17. These reactions again seem directly connected to the contemporary American fears of Revolution. For an interesting treatment of the novel in this historical context, see Fussell.

Works Cited

"An Account of a Murder Committed by Mr. J———Y———, upon His Family, in December, A. D. 1781." Reprinted in *Philadelphia Minerva* 2.81, 82 (August 20 and 27, 1796).

Axelrod, Alan. *Charles Brockden Brown: An American Tale.* Austin: Univ. of Texas Press, 1983.

Bell, Michael Davitt. "'The Double-Tongued Deceiver': Sincerity and Duplicity in the Novels of Charles Brockden Brown." *Early American Literature* 9 (1974): 143-63.

Bradford, William. *Of Plimoth Plantation, 1620-47.* Ed. Samuel Morison. New York: Modern Library, 1981.

Brown, Charles Brockden. *Wieland, or The Transformation; an American Tale.* Bicentennial ed. Ed. Sydney Krause, S. W. Reid, and Alexander Cowie. Kent, Ohio: Kent State Univ. Press, 1977.

Caplan, Ruth. *Psychiatry and the Community in Nineteenth-Century America.* New York: Basic Books, 1969.

Cowie, Alexander. "Historical Essay." In Charles Brockden Brown, *Wieland.* Kent, Ohio: Kent State Univ. Press, 1977.

Dalke, Anne. "Original Vice: The Political Implications of Incest in the Early American Novel." *Early American Liberature* 23 (1988): 188-201.

Davidson, Cathy. *Revolution and the World: The Rise of the Novel in America.* New York: Oxford Univ. Press, 1986.

Davis, David Brion. *Ante-Bellum Reform.* New York: Harper and Row, 1967.

———. *Homicide in American Fiction, 1798-1860.* Ithaca: Cornell Univ. Press, 1957.

Dwight, Timothy. "A Discourse on Some Events of the Last Century." New Haven, 1801. Rpt. in *American Thought and Writing.* Ed. Russel Nye and Norman Grabo. Boston: Houghton Mifflin, 1965. 262-72.

———. *Theology Explained and Defended, in a Series of Sermons.* New York, 1846. Cited by Davis (*Homicide* 8).

Edwards, Jonathan. "Personal Narrative." *Representative Selections.* Ed. Clarence Faust and Thomas Johnson. New York: Hill and Wang, 1965. 57-72.

Fliegelman, Jay. *Prodigals and Pilgrims: The American Revolution Against Patriarchal Authority, 1750-1800.* Cambridge: Cambridge Univ. Press, 1982.

Fussell, Edwin. "*Wieland*: A Literary and Historical Reading." *Early American Literature* 18 (1983): 171-86.

Gilmore, Michael. "Calvinism and Gothicism: The Example of Brown's *Wieland.*" *Studies in the Novel* 9 (1977): 107-18.

Gordon, William. *The Letters of William Gordon.* Rpt. in Massachusetts Historical Society, *Proceedings* 62 (1929-30): 393.

Griffin, Clifford. "Religious Benevolence as Social Control, 1815-1860." Rpt. in David Brion Davis, *Ante-Bellum Reform.* New York: Harper and Row, 1967. 81-96.

Grossberg, Michael. *Governing the Health.* Chapel Hill: Univ. of North Carolina Press, 1985.

Grylls, Rosalie. *William Godwin and His World.* London: Odham's, 1953.

Hesford, Walter. "'Do You Know the Author?': The Question of Authorship in *Wieland.*" *Early American Literature* 17 (1982/83): 239-48.

Marshall, Humphrey. "The Aliens: A Patriotic Poem." Philadelphia: May 15, 1798.

Miller, John. *Crisis in Freedom: The Alien and Sedition Acts.* Boston: Little, Brown, 1952.

Mitchell, Stephen Mix. *Narrative of the Life of William Beadle.* Windsor, Vt.: Spooner, 1795.

Paine, Thomas. *The Life and Major Writings of Thomas Paine.* Ed. Philip Foner. Secaucus, N.J.: Citadel, 1974.

Rothman, David. *The Discovery of the Asylum: Social Order and Disorder in the New Republic.* Boston: Little, Brown, 1971.

Samuels, Shirley. "Plague and Politics in 1793: *Arthur Mervyn.*" *Criticism* 27 (1985): 225-46.

———. "The Family, the State, and the Novel in the Early Republic." *American Quarterly* 1986: 381-95.

Scheick, William. "The Problem of Origination in Brown's *Ormond.*" *Critical Essays on Charles Brockden Brown.* Ed. Bernard Rosenthal. Boston: G. K. Hall, 1981. 126-41.

Seltzer, Mark. "Saying Makes it So: Language and Event in Brown's *Wieland.*" *Early American Literature* 13 (1978): 81-91.

Skeel, E. E., ed. *Mason Locke Weems, His Works and Ways.* New York: privately printed, 1929.

Slotkin, Richard. *Regeneration through Violence: The Mythology of the American Frontier, 1600-1860.* Middletown, Conn.: Wesleyan Univ. Press, 1973.

Stauffer, Vernon. *New England and the Bavarian Illuminati.* New York: Columbia Univ. Press, 1918.

Tompkins, Jane. *Sensational Designs: The Cultural Work of American Fiction, 1780-1860.* New York: Oxford University Press, 1985.

Weems, Mason. "God's Revenge Against Adultery." (1815) Rpt. in *Three Discourses.* New York: Random House, 1929.

Weldon, Roberta. "Charles Brockden Brown's *Wieland*: A Family Tragedy." *Studies in American Fiction* 12.1 (1989): 1-11.

Ziff, Larzer. "A Reading of *Wieland.*" *PMLA* 77 (1962): 51-57.

Toni O'Shaughnessy (essay date 1990)

SOURCE: O'Shaughnessy, Toni. "'An Imperfect Tale': Interpretive Accountability in *Wieland.*" *Studies in American Fiction* 18, no. 1 (spring 1990): 41-54.

[*In the following essay, O'Shaughnessy examines the deliberate manipulation of readers' interpretive responses to events in the plot of* Wieland.]

In the "Epistle to the Reader," which prefaces his *Essay Concerning Human Understanding* (1690), John Locke describes his own authorship in ambiguous and suggestive language. Authors, he says, are those "who let loose their own Thoughts," as hunters release hounds or hawks, "and follow them in writing."[1] The understanding searches for "Truth" like a dog after "Quarry," making new and temporarily delightful discoveries. Although the possibility of final apprehension of truth is always apparently assumed in Locke's discussion, in fact Locke's hunter "cannot much boast of any great Acquisition." Truth is never finally caught. This is not, however, a significant problem for Locke, since "the very pursuit makes a great part of the Pleasure." An author, though he may not arrive at truth, enjoys "the Hunter's Satisfaction" as he passively follows his thoughts in their pursuit of truth.[2]

Locke further claims that the creative submission of the author to his understanding is equally available to readers, who are encouraged to follow their own thoughts while reading and thus to be, at one remove, like the author following truth.[3] With this move, Locke seems to relieve writers of responsibility for the interpretations placed on their texts. Readers cannot hold authors accountable for meanings that they themselves create, especially when in the process they become much like writers themselves. The specific use to which Locke's own text will be put, and indeed whether it seems to have anything to offer a reader or not, is up to the reader. "Thou art not," Locke charges his reader, "to blame me for it."[4]

Perhaps it is because Locke is self-consciously considering his own authorship in the prefatory epistle that he there emphasizes authors' comparative blamelessness for the interpretations readers make of texts (though he is careful to say that all that he has written is true to the best of his knowledge). For in the *Essay* proper, as is well known, Locke is at pains to prevent the interpretive anarchy such emphasis might encourage if it were presented without qualifying caveats. He makes it clear in Book III that authorial freedom from interpretive responsibility is never separate from authors' moral responsibility to "take care to *apply their Words,* as near as may be, *to such* Ideas *as common use has annexed them to.*"[5] He goes on to say that

> for Words . . . being no Man's private possession, but the common measure of Commerce and Communication, 'tis not for any one, at pleasure, to change the Stamp they are current in; nor alter the *Ideas* they are affixed to; . . . Men's Intentions in speaking are, or at least should be, to be understood.[6]

While insisting that "the very nature of Words, makes it almost unavoidable, for many of them to be doubtful and uncertain in their significations,"[7] Locke also insists that this does not excuse those who are "guilty" of a "*wilful*" abuse of words.[8] For Locke, final judgment on a text, and indeed its very meaning, are up to the reader; nevertheless, the author should represent his ideas in words that readers are likely to construe according to the author's intentions. When authorship is thus responsible, and readers emulate authors in judging for themselves by following their own understandings, interpretation is as reliable as possible.

Complicated and equivocal as Locke's interpretive model certainly is, it depends nevertheless on traditional, and from a contemporary perspective somewhat optimistic and even contradictory, assumptions. Locke supposes that authors write in order to transmit communicable meanings; that readers read to discover those meanings; and that it is possible, though very difficult, for a text to transmit the author's meaning to a reader who is thinking for himself. The inherent unfixedness of language, Locke suggests, may be controlled if an author takes pains to clarify meaning and if a reader agrees to "follow his own thoughts" in the same passively creative way that an author does when writing. A reader who can assume a well-meaning and conscientious author behind a text can be trusted to interpret reliably on his own and to accept responsibility for his own interpretation. Both author and reader are directly accountable at distinct stages in the interpretive process.

The matter of interpretive accountability is as pressing a concern in Charles Brockden Brown's **Wieland** (1798) as it is in Locke's essay. But Brown's novel explodes Locke's vulnerable categories of responsibility and exploits the fearful possibilities implied in the mirrored relationship Locke posits between author and reader and in his recognition of the instability of language itself. In **Wieland,** authors engage in willful abuse of representation and manipulate readers' customary interpretive strategies not for purposes of community and communication but for purposes of power. Readers are suspicious and confused and refuse to accept the responsibility that, according to Locke, goes along with the "Liberty" of forming their own interpretations.[9] Authors cannot be trusted as acting in good faith; readers cannot interpret authoritatively but cannot escape interpretation. The author's position becomes a morally indecipherable one; his intentions have no direct relation to the effects of his voice.[10]

The members of the Wieland household respond in various ways to this interpretive crisis. In particular, Clara Wieland's ideas about interpretive accountability undergo significant transformations as she is forced repeatedly to recognize the inadequacy of her interpretive strategies. Clara's problem is that she believes that language is necessarily and monolithically interpretable and that authors hold the key to correct interpretations. In Carwin, Clara encounters an author who will not be accountable for the uninterpretable text attributed to him. Clara finds this situation deeply troubling, and tries out a number of responses to it, without ever effectively abandoning the hermeneutic assumptions that make Carwin's discourse problematic in the first place.

From the time of her father's mysterious death, Clara Wieland is preoccupied with questions of interpretation and accountability. "What," she asks after narrating this incident, "is the inference to be drawn from these facts?" (p. 19).[11] Clara's language reveals her assumption that there is a single correct interpretation of the event, that the death of her father has some specific, identifiable cause. She is "anxious to explain" her father's death definitively: "Was this the penalty of disobedience? . . . Or, was it merely the irregular expansion of the fluid that imparts warmth to our heart and our blood, caused by . . . fatigue? . . ." (p. 19). The agent responsible for the elder Wieland's death remains inscrutable, Clara believes, because the data remain incomplete. She implies that her father "chose to give" only part of the "information" needed for correct interpretation of the event: "There was somewhat in his manner that indicated an imperfect tale" (p. 18). Later, although she will not quite deny the apparently miraculous nature of her brother's having heard his wife's voice when she was nowhere near, Clara claims to be "invincibly averse" to a "method of solution" that relies on the "miraculous" (p. 34). Like her brother Theodore, Clara seems to believe that it should be possible to locate the direct cause of an event with "certainty" (p. 36); unlike Theodore, however, she is initially unwilling to accept that the cause may be rationally inexplicable.

Accordingly, when Theodore first reports hearing a mysterious voice, Clara responds by adopting a rational hypothesis: her brother's senses, she supposes, are "the victims of . . . delusion" (p. 35).[12] But when the rationalist Pleyel hears the voice, and it delivers a message Clara is unconscionably happy to hear ("The Baroness de Stolberg is dead!" [p. 42]), she changes her mind. Now the voice is "unquestionably superhuman" (p. 45), a "mysterious, but not . . . malignant agency" (p. 46). With this, Clara has shifted the source of the voice from the "depraved" (p. 35) senses of her brother to an unknown, outside agent. She now feels responsible to find the correct interpretation of the "information" provided by this supernatural voice (p. 45).

At this juncture, Carwin appears. His first entrance (or more precisely, the first entrance of his voice) precipitates a new experience in Clara.

> I cannot pretend to communicate the impression that was made upon me by these accents. . . . The voice . . . imparted to me an emotion altogether involuntary and incontroulable. . . . I dropped the cloth that I held in my hand, my heart overflowed with sympathy and my eyes with unbidden tears
>
> (p. 52).

Clara's language reveals the change: not only are her sense impressions beyond her control but so, she thinks, are the emotions she feels in response to them. Clara

sees herself as the passive victim, not the active agent, of her sudden infatuation. The voice, and not Clara's own interpretive judgment, is responsible for her overwrought response.

At first, Clara tries to impose her usual interpretive strategies on Carwin's discourse. She attempts to take his words as efforts at communication but finds them indecipherable. Of his appearance, Clara says, "my fancy had conjured up a very different image. . . . Strange as it may seem, I could not speedily reconcile myself to this disappointment" (p. 52). She tries to contain Carwin by studying a sketch of him that she has drawn (pp. 53-54). But the original of the image she creates is impossible for Clara to reduce according to her familiar formulae. Her interpretation of Carwin is frustrated: "He afforded us no ground on which to build even a plausible conjecture" (p. 72). Carwin is an author who refuses to make concessions to society and communication, who does not seem interested in the meaning his interpreters discover in his discourse, or in whether they discover any meaning there or not. He does not use his voice to communicate but to elicit an effect.

Clara feels alienated from Carwin's discourse. Seeking perhaps to force the authorial hand, she responds by becoming increasingly passive. She begins to see herself as a helpless victim, unable to interpret for herself: "All unaware, and in a manner which I had no power to explain, I was pushed from my immovable and lofty station, and cast upon a sea of troubles" (p. 69). Unable to decipher Carwin (p. 72), she becomes unable to distinguish truth from fiction (p. 74), or even to know dreams from waking thoughts (pp. 86-87). Before long, her actions are "dictated" not by sense but by "phrenzy" (p. 88). "My reason had forborne," she says. "Surely I was utterly bereft of understanding" (p. 88). Even when alone and in physical danger, she considers herself "wholly at the mercy" of her attacker and makes no effort to resist him: "The resources of my personal strength, my ingenuity, and my eloquence, I estimated at nothing" (p. 90). "Invaded" by "a sentiment like despair," she will assume no authority over language or events: "I was silent in my turn. What could I say? I was confident that reason in this contest would be impotent. I must owe my safety to his own suggestions" (p. 91). This insistence on seeing her words and actions as entirely out of her own control frees Clara from the interpretive responsibility of a reader who has been given the right sort of data. If she can believe herself to be entirely helpless against Carwin's physical and hermeneutical assaults she will not have to feel guilty about her own lack of active resistance. In order to avoid responsibility for the tragedy she narrates, Clara needs to blame Carwin not only for sending out false signs but also for the way the Wielands interpret those signs. Clara blames the illegibility of Carwin's text on its author, not on its readers' interpretive habits. If her family cannot interpret this discourse according to the rules of "Commerce and Communication,"[13] the fault, Clara insists, is not theirs. "Thou art the author of these horrors!" she shrieks at Carwin. "What have I done to deserve thus to die?" (p. 227).

Clara's belief in Carwin's accountability finds what she takes for incontrovertible supporting evidence in their final interview. Clara has returned to her house, ostensibly for her secret journal, but also for "vengeance" (p. 190) on Carwin, the "author" of her family's misfortunes (p. 189).[14] Perhaps it is because she approaches the meeting with this predisposition that Clara does not seem to notice the equivocal language of Carwin's explanation. What seems to Clara to be a clear confession of guilt may as easily be read as a defense of victimized innocence:

> Great Heaven! what have I done? . . . I am innocent. I intended no ill . . . but I was destined perpetually to violate my resolutions. By some perverse fate, I was led into circumstances in which the exertion of my powers was the sole or the best means of escape
>
> (pp. 195-96, 206).

Carwin pictures himself as a Lockeian author who follows his own "powers" with a kind of creative passivity. The "expedient" of ventriloquism was never quite Carwin's own idea: it "suggested itself" (p. 208). Carwin's narrative becomes less the confession of a malevolent criminal than the testimony of a bewildered junkie unable to control a habit.[15] As such, it is at once a statement of guilt ("I cannot convey to you an adequate idea of the kind of gratification which I derived from these exploits . . .") and of innocence ("yet I meditated nothing" [p. 201]), complicated at every turn by the juxtaposition of antitheses. For instance, it is impossible to tell whether ventriloquism was Carwin's "sole" alternative or the "best" among several. By including both alternatives, Carwin creates space for his own agency while at the same time refusing accountability. "My actions," he concedes, "have possibly effected more than I designed" (pp. 195-96); nevertheless, "I am not this villain; I have slain no one; I have prompted none to slay" (p. 198). Carwin refuses to accept the responsibility Clara wants to assign to him. Instead, he shifts accountability onto Clara herself: "The unexpected interpretation which you placed upon my former proceeding, suggested my conduct on the present occasion" (p. 203).[16]

The niceties of Carwin's elocution, however, make little impression on Clara, determined as she is to assign accountability:

> It is enough that he owns himself to be the agent; his tale is a lie, and his nature devilish. As he deceived me, he likewise deceived my brother, and now do I behold the author of all our calamities!
>
> (p. 216).

But Clara does not realize that even when she is directly accusing Carwin, her language betrays her: "If Carwin's were the thrilling voice and the fiery visage which I had heard and seen, then was he the prompter of my brother, and the author of these dismal outrages" (p. 197). By making synonymous "prompter" and "author," Clara undercuts her own position. A prompter, after all, only reminds an actor of lines he already knows and must choose to say; he is responsible neither for the actor's performance nor for the words themselves. Clara attempts to fix accountability on a single cause, but her use of the equivocal notion of "prompting" to describe the activity of the author undermines her own thesis.[17]

What finally forces Clara away from an easy equation of agency and accountability is the surreal "spectacle" of her brother's death (p. 232). Clara's use of theatrical language is again significant. By calling Theodore's "last deed" a "spectacle," Clara attempts to place herself outside the action, offstage; she is not involved in Theodore's death but is merely a spectator.

But Clara is an odd kind of spectator in this scene. Just a moment before, she had identified so closely with Theodore that "my state was little different from that of my brother. I entered, as it were, into his thought. My heart was visited and rent by his pangs" (p. 231). Clara experiences such strong sympathy with Theodore that she almost *becomes* him; the two are strangely indistinguishable. This situation complicates and frustrates the reader's desire to attribute to either Clara or Theodore the crucial and implicating lines that follow: "Oh that thy phrenzy had never been cured . . . that death would cover thee with his oblivion! What can I wish for thee? . . . . Can I wish for the continuance of thy being? No" (p. 231). It is impossible to attribute these words exclusively to either Clara or Theodore. Clara seems to be addressing her brother, but if she has just "entered into his thought," it is possible that Theodore himself thinks thus. If these are Theodore's thoughts, they could be directed at himself or at Clara; they may be spoken aloud or voiced internally. If Clara's, the words could suggest that she is wishing death on Theodore; then again, this would not be the only occasion in which she wishes death for herself. Now that Clara has somehow "entered" into Theodore, it is impossible to be sure who is Theodore and who is Clara, or who is wishing death on whom.

This indistinguishability of Clara from Theodore suddenly becomes very dangerous when Theodore, according to Clara, kills himself. "Engaged" by his "demeanour," Clara says, she dropped the knife; Theodore "seized it with the quickness of thought" and "plunged it to the hilt in his neck" (p. 231). The narrative seems straightforward, but the uncanny sympathy between brother and sister in the previous moment considerably complicates any attempt to determine who is acting and who is watching. Accountability for an action performed "with the quickness of thought" cannot be assigned to a single person when another has just "entered" the "thought" of the ostensible actor and become "little different" from him.

Clara needs, at this critical moment, to separate herself from Theodore and to make sure that he alone is the agent of his own death. She attempts to do so through the use of theatrical language. By defining the action in which she has played an integral part as a "spectacle," Clara reduces her own role to that of a passive viewer, apparently forgetting the possibility she recognized earlier that one may be at once actor and audience: "I stand aside, as it were, from myself. . . . I listen to my own pleas, and find them empty and false" (pp. 222-23). She attempts to find a place outside of the action, from which she can watch without being implicated.

This is not to say that Clara killed Theodore.[18] What matters is not whether Clara or Theodore actually wielded the knife but the fact that one cannot know for sure what happened or who was responsible. The action is confused in this scene; the agents are not clearly distinguished. Clara is not quite guilty, but she is not quite innocent either; she is not fully responsible, but, more terrifying to one who needs to find a single cause for every effect, she is implicated. Clara describes her willingness to take "any means of escape" from Theodore, "however monstrous" (p. 222), her readiness "to inflict death upon the menacer [Theodore]" (p. 223), her "criminal despair" (p. 225), her loss of "power to reason" (p. 230), and her enormous guilt (pp. 222-23). She comes very close to stabbing her brother at least once.[19] At the moment of Theodore's death, Clara finds herself in the position Carwin has occupied alone until now. Her involvement indubitable, her motives questionable, it is difficult to determine the extent to which she is accountable for her brother's death.

Faced with her own implication, with the suggestion that she herself may have been the "prompter" of this terrible scene, Clara gives up her frantic search for accountability. She adopts a theatrical metaphor, taking herself offstage as though she had had no part in the drama; and she completely revises her ideas about Carwin's accountability:

> I ceased to upbraid or accuse. His guilt was a point to which I was indifferent. . . . I care not from what source these disasters have flowed; it suffices that they have swallowed up our hopes and our existence
>
> (pp. 232-33).

Now that the location of agency has become a threatening activity, Clara recognizes that accountability, cause, and effect are entangled and indecipherable, and she re-

fuses, for the first time, to engage in the search for a definitive cause. The meaning of Carwin's discourse and the exact nature of her own involvement in Theodore's death now seem relatively insignificant, overshadowed by the effect they have brought about. Assignment of blame has become dangerous at the same time that it suddenly seems trivial. Clara refuses to "listen" or to "answer," to interpret or to speak (p. 232). Her gaze is fixed, with a strangely distanced sympathy, on Theodore's dead body, an alien image of herself.

David Marshall has suggested that representative eighteenth-century authors, anxious about their exposure before the world as "a spectacle before spectators," posited within their works an alternate theatrical relation between themselves and a carefully limited hypothetical audience with whom they could pretend to realize "the dream of an act of sympathy."[20] The intolerable situation of theater is thus, Marshall contends, transformed into a strategy for authorial control. The author continues as an actor on stage, but he defines and addresses a select, sympathetic audience.

Clara, too, is an author afraid to act before an audience. But in her case, even the "small number of friends" to whom the book is addressed is too threatening (p. 3). Clara is unwilling to expose herself as an actor even to the judgment of the kind of self-created audience which, as Marshall demonstrates, enables other authors to perform; instead, she altogether rejects the idea of her own involvement in the action and casts herself as a spectator on events with which she has nothing to do. Clara turns to the theatrical metaphor as an escape from implicating sympathy, not to sympathy as an escape from theatricality. At the same time, she constructs a unique theatrical image: she imagines herself as audience, not actor. Both sympathy *and* theatricality threaten Clara; she seeks to escape the implications of her identification with Theodore by placing herself outside the drama altogether.

Ironically, the safe new position Clara chooses for herself dissolves the moment she assumes it. Just as she gives up all desire to act and takes a seat in the gallery, the last player disappears from the stage. Clara continues to hang around "the scene" (pp. 232, 233, 234), but there is nothing more to watch. She is a spectator in an empty theater; the play is over. Clara's defensive strategy collapses the moment she adopts it. Clara attempts to resolve her new predicament by resuming a speaking role; she writes again, three years later, still attempting to interpret her family's tragedy. This was not her first intention. She had imagined, as she says, "that I had forever laid aside the pen" (p. 234); but she finds it impossible to live without engaging in interpretation (p. 235) or to die before her efforts have brought interpretive closure (p. 228).

Unfortunately, Clara knows only one method of interpretation: the assignment of accountability. When personally threatened by accountability at the scene of Theodore's death, she gave up interpretation altogether; now, forced again to interpret, she returns to the quest for cause, modifying her method in order to protect herself, but keeping her familiar object in place. Having seen the inadequacy and danger of her former belief that responsibility for interpretation lies with the discursive agent, Clara now posits a new, safer thesis: "The double-tongued deceiver" could not have succeeded, she decides, if the "frailty" of his victims had not "seconded these efforts" (p. 244). Theodore failed to construct right definitions of duty and divinity; she herself, not having been "gifted with ordinary equanimity or foresight," was not equal to extraordinary interpretive situations yet is somehow to blame for her failure to interpret correctly (p. 244). Whatever text may be offered, she seems to say, responsibility for its use lies with the audience, even if that audience fails or is constitutionally unable to interpret reliably. This depiction of readers as both responsible for the effects of interpretation and incapable of interpreting provides a bleak context for Clara's comment to her readers: "I leave you to moralize on this tale" (p. 244).

Whether Clara is really capable of leaving interpretive accountability in the hands of the reader remains in doubt, however, since in the process of presenting her new model, she cannot help but direct her readers:

> I leave you to moralize on this tale . . . but it will not escape your notice, that the evils of which Carwin and Maxwell were the authors, owed their existence to the errors of the sufferers
>
> > (p. 244).

It is exactly the same move she had made in the first paragraph of the narrative, supposedly written three years before:

> Make what use of the tale you shall think proper. If it be communicated to the world, it will inculcate the duty of avoiding deceit. It will exemplify the force of early impressions, and show the immeasurable evils that flow from an erroneous or imperfect discipline
>
> > (p. 5).

For all Clara's talk about having "changed" (p. 235), she seems still to retain in practice her belief that a text contains a single correct interpretation, determined by the author, who is responsible for its transmission. Regardless of the perspective from which Clara interprets the text of her family's history, she cannot do without her fundamental belief that to read is to look for a correct meaning. She continues to assume with Locke that "men's Intentions in speaking are, or at least should be, to be understood."

Wieland exposes the inadequacy of Clara's interpretive efforts and, by analogy, of other interpretive efforts that rely on similar assumptions. The kind of discourse Carwin introduces (and is himself powerless to control or explicate) destabilizes Locke's taxonomy of accountability and commodification of meaning. Authors and readers are no longer either active producers or passive receivers of meaning; there is no moment in which the text and its correct interpretation, as fixed commodities, change hands. Instead, language becomes an agent in itself, more important for its power to effect behavior than for its source or meaning. It is a force none of its wielders can control.

At the end of his second sequel to *Robinson Crusoe,* Daniel Defoe includes a tale remarkably suggestive of *Wieland.* The involved plot may be summarized briefly: a student with atheistic leanings is prevented from attending a meeting of the godless society to which he belongs by a tremendous bolt of lightning which strikes the pavement before him, barely missing him. Shaken by the thought that there may be a God after all, the student returns home, where he is visited by a devout friend, and is subsequently converted. Meanwhile, a second atheistic student comes to the house to accompany his friend (the first atheist) to the meeting. He knocks on the door and is answered, not by his friend, but by the evangelizing visitor, who

> opened the door a little way, so as he was not very distinctly seen, and spoke aloud in the person of his friend thus: "O sir, beseech them all to repent; for, depend upon it, there is a God; tell them I say so."[21]

The second atheist proceeds on his way, "filled . . . with horror" and "confusion,"[22] and is himself overtaken by a thundershower. Taking refuge in a bookshop, he meets a pious student who insists that he read a particular poem, the words of which echo his troubled thoughts:

> But if it should fall out
> That there may be a God
> Had I not best consider well, for fear
> 'T should be too late?[23]

The atheist is further terrified when the pious student echoes word for word the message given at the doorway of the house.[24] At a loss to determine who could "dictate" the identical words, the atheist guesses that the source must be the devil.[25] The pious student insists, however, that the source must rather be God: "You must . . . distinguish," he says, "what proceeds from heaven, what from hell, the voice of God, and the voice of the devil."[26] Together they call on the first atheist and learn that he did not speak to his friend at the doorway. They decide that the second atheist must have heard "some voice from heaven,"[27] and he faints away.

The story ends there, but the narrator (Robinson Crusoe) continues to moralize upon it.[28] He calls the story "a visible evidence of God," even though "there was nothing in it but the voice of a man unseen and mistaken. . . . Here was neither vision or voice, but that of an ordinary person, and one who meant well and said well."[29] "Many a voice," Crusoe insists, "may be directed from heaven that is not immediately spoken from thence."[30] The event shows "a great superintendency of divine Providence in the minutest affairs of this world."[31] The final sentence of Defoe's book, however, reveals a nagging uncertainty about impersonation: "I hope I have said nothing of it to misguide anybody, or to assist them to delude themselves, having spoken of it with the utmost seriousness in my design, and with a sincere desire for a general good."[32] Like the Christian visitor who deceived the atheistic student at the doorway, the narrator has what he interprets as good motives; but still there is the problem of how an impersonator can be sure his words will be used by providence and not by the devil. The difficulty of distinguishing the two is dramatized in the story itself, and the moralizing narrator seems only too aware of the arbitrary nature of his own interpretations. His easy deduction of providential control deconstructs in the book's final, uneasy sentence.

Like the atheist in Defoe's tale, Theodore Wieland believes the voices he hears to be from God. But his belief transforms him into a fiend, not a Christian. If Defoe's story is, as Marshall argues, a defense of the lying novelist who speaks in voices not his own, a "justification . . . of ventriloquy,"[33] Brown's novel interrogates Crusoe's vulnerable insistence that the effect of fictional impersonation will necessarily be good if the lying author means well. What, *Wieland* asks, if the impersonator does not mean well? Who can say whether an author means well or not, or even what it might mean to "mean well?" *Wieland* shows that it may be possible for an author to have no particular intention at all, or to have intentions so confused that their morality may not be determined. "My purpose was not prescribed by duty," Carwin admits, "yet surely it was far from being atrocious and inexpiable" (p. 204). The author's intentions no longer have any direct connection with the effects of his voice.

Brown himself denies accountability for the results of authorial impersonation. Just as Clara protects herself through the use of theatrical language, calling Theodore's death a "spectacle," so Brown, in the *Advertisement* to *Wieland,* calls his novel a "performance," a drama in which he does not participate, not even (ostensibly) as narrator (p. 3). Brown rejects both Locke's self-exculpatory taxonomy of accountability and the dubious faith of Defoe's nervous narrator. In one breath he claims to have a specific intention in writing *Wieland* ("the illustration of some important branches of the moral constitution of man" [p. 3]); in the next, he insists that the intention is not pertinent:

"Whether this tale will be . . . ranked with the few productions whose usefulness secures them a lasting reputation, the reader must be permitted to decide" (p. 3). Brown seems to place final responsibility for the text with the reader but in the process undermines his own authority to grant the reader this autonomy. Readers are "permitted to decide," but the author, who is presumably doing the permitting, is not quite a free agent himself, since he "must" permit the audience to make what use of his tale they will. The phrase circles in on itself, denying final authority and accountability. Brown further invalidates the reader's autonomy by (like Clara) specifying correct interpretation: "It is hoped that intelligent readers will not disapprove. . . ." He spends most of the *Advertisement* telling readers how to read his book, then ends by insisting on their autonomous power over it and by placing responsibility for his continued literary production onto them. Although he acknowledges the role of readers as interpreters of texts, Brown cannot resist the impulse to guide interpretation, to keep it from straying too far from his own intentions. Brown envisions both author and reader as contributing toward interpretation but will not quite locate interpretive accountability decisively and exclusively in either.

Decisive placement of interpretive accountability, however, is exactly what Clara Wieland consistently seeks, despite the fact that her own narrative denies its possibility. Clara's misfortune lies, in part, in the conflict between her interpretive assumption of single, definitive responsibility and her inability to achieve on the basis of this assumption even a superficially satisfying explanation for the dreadful results of impersonation in the history of her family. There is no superintending Providence, no final source for the deceptions, no way of assigning responsibility without being implicated herself. The "cause" of the Wieland tragedy is really many causes, all of which may also be interpreted as effects. Likewise, the "transformation" of the book's subtitle is not a single event but a plural process, artificially arrested at the novel's close. Locke's anxiety "that any one . . . should mistake, or not comprehend my meaning"[34] is radically insufficient here; there is no stable distinction between "real" and "barely imaginable" interpretations.[35] Language itself has been transformed from a passive container of meaning to an active agent, with power to transform a society.

Notes

1. John Locke, *An Essay Concerning Human Understanding,* ed. Peter H. Nidditch (Oxford: Clarendon Press, 1975), p. 6. All citations to Locke come from this edition.

2. Locke, p. 6.

3. Locke, p. 7. The passage discussed in this paragraph appears on pp. 6-7 and reads as follows:

"This, Reader, is the Entertainment of those, who let loose their own Thoughts, and follow them in writing; which thou oughtest not to envy them, since they afford thee an Opportunity of the like Diversion, if thou wilt make use of thy own Thoughts in reading. 'Tis to them, if they are thy own, that I referr my self: But if they are taken upon Truth from others, 'tis no great Matter what they are, they are not following Truth. . . . For though it be certain, that there is nothing in this Treatise of the Truth whereof I am not fully persuaded; yet I consider my self as liable to Mistakes, as I can think thee; and know, that this Book must stand or fall with thee. . . . If thou findest little in it new or instructive to thee, thou art not to blame me for it."

4. Locke, p. 7.

5. Locke, p. 514.

6. Locke, p. 514.

7. Locke, pp. 475-76.

8. Locke, p. 490.

9. Locke, p. 373.

10. Many of these observations have been made before in the by-now voluminous literature on *Wieland.* Edwin Sill Fussell notes that in *Wieland,* "the concept of author is raised to almost infinite powers but with no commensurate responsibility or benevolence." See "*Wieland*: A Literary and Historical Reading," *EAL* [*Early American Literature*], 18 (1983), 175. Walter Hesford says that "if Brown gives us in Carwin a portrait of an author, it is of one who has not even authority over his own fiction." "'Do you know the author?': The Question of Authorship in *Wieland,*" *EAL,* 17 (1983), 244. Most recently, Roland Hagenbuchle has reiterated the fact that "it is . . . a hopeless undertaking to search for clearly defined causes and intentions in *Wieland*" and that "it remains unclear to the end in how far he [Carwin] is actually responsible for the disastrous events." See "American Literature and the Nineteenth-Century Crisis in Epistemology: The Example of Charles Brockden Brown," *EAL,* 23 (1988), 128, 125. As a continuation of the discussion carried on in these important studies of the notorious interpretive and epistemological problems in studying the novel, I make central to my reading of *Wieland* two related issues which I believe are pivotal to the novel itself: the difficulties Clara Wieland experiences in her attempts to assign interpretive accountability, and her inability to find any other method for reading and writing except such assignment. In "On Rereading *Wieland*: 'The Folly of Precipitate Conclusions'," *EAL,* 16 (1981), 154-

74, Cynthia S. Jordan remarks that Clara Wieland has a "constitutional need to believe" in "fictions with endings that seem absolute" (p. 166). I wish to suggest further that Clara needs to believe that responsibility for the interpretations of such fictions may be definitively and finally placed. It seems to me that she looks for interpretive closure not only in Jordan's sense of neat narrative endings but also in a more personal sense: Clara needs to find a person in whom accountability for meaning resides.

11. All citations are to Charles Brockden Brown, *Wieland or The Transformation: An American Tale,* ed. Sydney J. Krause, S. W. Reid, et al. (Kent: Kent State Univ. Press, 1977). Citations appear parenthetically by page number.

12. In a sense, of course, Clara is correct. Theodore *is* deluded, and before long, so are most of the principal actors on the Wieland stage, especially Clara herself. Indeed, a major subject of interrogation in *Wieland* is the assumption, fundamental to Locke's *Essay,* that reliable knowledge of the world is based on the interpretation of data transmitted via the senses; in *Wieland,* information obtained by means of the senses is contradictory and untrustworthy. It is worth noting, however, that at this important juncture Theodore's delusion does not occur in actual sensual experience but in the interpretation he places upon the evidence of his senses. He is not deluded in hearing the voice (as Clara initially thinks) but in assigning its source (in this case, Catherine Wieland). Pleyel suggests perceptively that "perhaps a voice had been heard, but Wieland's imagination had misled him in supposing a resemblance to that of his wife and giving such a signification to the sounds" (p. 34). But Theodore himself is unable to accept such an explanation. Theodore's dogged response ("I must deny credit to your assertions, or disbelieve the testimony of my senses" [p. 32]) prefigures Clara's later determination to place interpretive accountability definitively, and signals the weakness of the Wielands' rigid interpretive categories.

13. Locke, p. 514.

14. Clara's exact words at this juncture clearly state her need to locate accountability in authors: "Some relief is afforded in the midst of suffering," she says, "when its author is discovered or imagined; and an object found on which we may pour out our indignation and our vengeance" (p. 190).

15. As Norman S. Grabo points out in *The Coincidental Art of Charles Brockden Brown* (Chapel Hill: Univ. of North Carolina Press, 1981), "Carwin . . . is desperate, scared . . . rightly aware that he has set into motion a series of actions over

which he has no control and, in a sense, no responsibility" (p. 10).

16. Brown uses a similar tactic in the *Advertisement* to *Wieland*: "The following Work is delivered to the world as the first of a series of performances, which the favorable reception of this will induce the Writer to publish" (p. 3).

17. Hesford notes that if readers wish to "claim Carwin as a prototypical author, we need to grant that human authorship is a matter of compiling, imitating, or translating sources—not of authentically beginning or generating something new" (p. 244).

18. James R. Russo makes this argument in "'The Chimeras of the Brain': Clara's Narrative in *Wieland*," *EAL*, 16 (1981), 81-82. I find Jordan more convincing when she tempers her suggestion that "Clara might have killed her brother and suppressed half the truth in the later telling" with a recognition that the thesis that Clara killed Theodore remains only one interpretive "possibility" (p. 165). For me, the important point is that responsibility for Theodore's death cannot be definitively determined.

19. Clara says that when she felt herself "menaced . . . with death" at the hands of Theodore, she drew out the knife she had brought to the house "against the machinations of Carwin." "I now see that my state of mind would have rendered the deed inevitable if my brother had lifted his hand. This instrument of my preservation would have been plunged into his heart" (p. 223).

20. David Marshall, *The Figure of Theater: Shaftesbury, Defoe, Adam Smith and George Eliot* (New York: Columbia Univ. Press, 1986), p. 2.

21. Daniel Defoe, *Serious Reflections During the Life and Surprising Adventures of Robinson Crusoe, with His Vision of the Angelic World,* vol. 3 of *The Works of Daniel Defoe,* ed. G. H. Maynadier (New York: Crowell, 1903), p. 311.

22. Defoe, p. 311.

23. Defoe, p. 313.

24. Defoe, p. 316.

25. Defoe, p. 318.

26. Defoe, p. 320.

27. Defoe, p. 323.

28. Marshall provides a perceptive discussion of the ironies and anxieties involved in Defoe's impersonation of a fictional voice in this story. See especially pp. 94-103. I am indebted to Marshall's discussion for my own awareness of this tale.

29. Defoe, p. 324.

30. Defoe, pp. 324-25.

31. Defoe, p. 325.

32. Defoe, p. 325.

33. Marshall, p. 102.

34. Locke, p. 9.

35. Locke, p. 373.

Andrew J. Scheiber (essay date 1991)

SOURCE: Scheiber, Andrew J. "'The Arm Lifted Against Me': Love, Terror, and the Construction of Gender in *Wieland*." *Early American Literature* 26, no. 2 (1991): 173-94.

[*In the following essay, Scheiber explores the ambiguity of Clara's characterization, attributing that ambiguity to her status within masculine and patriarchal institutions of the time.*]

A persistent locus of critical contention in Charles Brockden Brown's **Wieland** has been the character of Clara, the novel's narrator. Nina Baym has argued that "Clara is not a character in any traditional sense," but rather "serves only as a vantage point from which events are misapprehended and experienced in their fullest capacity to shock and terrify" (95). J. V. Ridgely, puzzled by what he sees as some crucial lacunae in Clara's narration, finds it "unaccountable" that she fails "to ponder the process by which she and Pleyel have been able to restore themselves" (12). Even Bernard Rosenthal, one of the recent champions of Brown's work, admits that at one key juncture of the story Clara's responses border on unintentional farce (111). Finally, Michael Kreyling, in a Derridean sortie on the novel, claims that Clara's narrative deconstructs the very rubrics on which it is founded, including such familiar notions as "voice" and "the unity of character" (50).

To be sure, there are disturbing paradoxes—some would say outright contradictions—in Clara's character and in her narration. On the one hand she professes to trust in the powers of the intellect and the evidence of the senses; yet on the other she is all too willing to subscribe to superstitious, even ridiculous, interpretations of events. Despite her claim to be a modern, independent woman, she nevertheless looks to masculine figures of authority—even her brother, who threatens to destroy her—as sources of power and approval; and her stubborn impulse to trust in the benignity of the gods seems, in light of the catastrophes that befall her, to mock at the idea that she represents anything more than an incoherent nexus of conflicting signifiers.

But these contradictions and incoherencies are not, as some have suggested, the result of authorial confusion or incompetence. Rather, they inscribe a pattern of conflict which defines Clara's problematical identity; this pattern is reflected in, and in turn affects, the language and structure of her narration. Clara's struggle for inner coherence of self and story may largely be traced to schizophrenic definitions of late eighteenth-century womanhood which are evoked by the extraordinary events of her narrative. Though the gender system in which Clara finds herself trapped is complex and multilayered, it may in essence be summarized thus: though nominally a child of the age of rationalism and political self-determination, Clara is by virtue of her sex a second-class citizen whose identity is contingent on the support and corroboration of authoritarian, masculine-centered institutions of power: the patriarchal family, the life of the intellect, and the religion of her ancestors. The origin of Clara's difficulty—and, I would argue, of the many contradictions which mark the text of *Wieland*—is her ambiguous and precarious status with respect to these institutions which at once subsume and marginalize her identity as a woman.[1]

This pattern of simultaneous enclosure and exclusion is signaled by the rhetoric of the text itself. While her brother Theodore achieves full identification with the family name (indeed, throughout her narration Clara refers to him simply as "Wieland"), her own relation to it is somewhat more ambiguous. As the daughter in the family she is excluded from the patrilineal line of authority and identity; she is thus merely a provisional Wieland, who in marriage will forfeit her surname and who cannot, in contrast to her father and brother, continue it through her children. Yet even unmarried, Clara is less than an integral factor in the Wieland equation, as the novel's title suggests. The primacy of her individual ordeal is occluded by the naming of her text—a signal that her narrative, like her identity, is the franchise of her family and her brother, under whose banner she exists in a state of conditional erasure—at once present and, in the system of patriarchal nomenclature, uncounted.

Other aspects of Clara's situation show her to be at once member and subject of this familial confederacy, where in relation to her brother she is a mere second among equals.[2] Though the Wieland fortune is divided evenly between herself and Theodore, it is he who occupies the patriarchal homestead, with Clara living by herself, in a smaller house on the edge of the estate. Her own explanation of this arrangement betrays an ambivalence about her "separate" and independent identity that typifies her ambiguous status within the family: on one hand she professes to be "desirous of administering a fund, and regulating a household of my own" (22); but her avowal that this separation from her brother and his family is a form of "self-denial" (22)

undercuts this professed desire for self-determination. Clara apparently feels compelled to deny that there is any egoism attached to her assumption of this separate status; in portraying her independence as a sacrifice to propriety (an acceptable "feminine" reason) rather than a condition of personal preference, Clara subordinates her personal desires and ambitions to the primacy of the family in general and of her brother in particular.

Clara's identity is thus contingent on her status as a Wieland, an identification which entangles her in a relation both necessary and dangerous. She tries to negotiate her paradoxical position by denying there is a problem; for her the Wieland name becomes identified with such positive values as power, security, and benevolence, while its more threatening associations—the trauma of her parents' deaths, even her brother's incipient madness—are repressed. This pattern of repression dominates the early phases of Clara's narrative. Referring to her father's bizarre demise, she claims that "[t]he impressions that were then made upon me can never be effaced" (19); but she also avers that the years following his death were "tranquil and happy," and that she and Theodore "were molested by few of those cares that are incident to childhood" (20). Similarly, she finds nothing disturbing either in her brother's sinister melancholia, which she describes as "thrilling," or in his "obvious resemblance" to their blasted father (23). Even the advent of the mysterious voices (which, as she herself admits, bear "a resemblance" to the circumstances of her father's catastrophe) she interprets as being "not of malignant agency" (19, 46).

Yet perhaps most difficult to digest is her matter-of-fact account of their conversion of the temple, the scene of the elder Wieland's ruin, into a pleasure dome of intellectual and artistic pursuits. This place, which ought to be rife with dire connotations, becomes a site of song, conversation, and even feasting, and evokes for Clara "[e]very joyous and tender scene most dear to my memory" (24). Nina Baym has criticized this aspect of the story, observing that "[o]ne cannot say much for Brown's acuity as a psychologist in permitting the children to overlook, entirely, the way in which they are feasting on the spot where their father was struck down by his malady" (90). But it is consistent with the motif, firmly established elsewhere in the novel, of the double-edged nature of the patriarchal family environment, in which worship and terror, protector and destroyer, lie enfolded within one another.

It is, in short, the cruel paradox of Clara's existence that she depends for approval and protection on an order of power and authority—represented by her father's fatal eccentricities and her brother's murderous imperatives—which views her existence as conditional, marginal, sacrificeable. For her in particular the willful imposition of carefree, Arcadian bliss upon the scene of her father's ruin has a psychological as well as a symbolic aptness; like the family itself, the summerhouse has become for Clara a locus of denial, an illusory proof against the very dangers it evokes. (It is worth noting that in the summerhouse one finds the intersection of the three main patriarchal institutions—the family, scholarship and the life of the intellect, and religious worship—which at once generate and dissolve Clara's sense of self.)

But because the notion *human,* like that of **Wieland,** is metaphorically male, as are the attributes proper to it, Clara occupies a marginal position not only in her family, but in the broader landscape of her culture as well. This is most evident in her struggle to reconcile herself to her epoch's glorification of intellect as the primary human faculty. As a member of the "second sex," Clara's prescribed relation to the life of the mind is negative and circumscribed; she is marked by her femaleness as less "rational" than (and therefore subordinate to) the male of the species. And though her peculiar upbringing has given her aspirations and expectations to the contrary, Clara is extremely sensitive to what Mary Wollstonecraft indicts as "the prevailing opinion" that "man was made to reason, woman to feel" (61, 63).[3]

Wollstonecraft was early, but not alone, in perceiving this distinction as a false one, and in insisting on education as the primary method of eradicating such artificial distinctions; and indeed Clara's education, however undisciplined, seems at first to have enabled her to transcend this gender barrier. When she describes herself and her brother as "left to the guidance of our own understanding and the casual impressions which society might make upon us" (22), the noteworthy fact is that her own desultory course of study appears to have been indistinguishable from Theodore's. She describes her own intellect as, like her brother's, "enriched by science and embellished with literature" (23), and she seems as comfortable as the men in their self-styled temple of learning, with its harpsichord, its bust of Cicero, and the group's recreations of "the performances of our musical and poetical ancestors" (24)—ancestors who (need we say it?) are presumably male. In other words Clara's education has (in however disorganized a fashion) embraced a curriculum deemed normal and desirable for citizens of the new: Republic—that is, for men. To be sure, post-Revolutionary America saw the necessity for women's intellectual cultivation; but, as Linda Kerber notes in her discussion of the "Republican mother" ideal, the focus of women's educational development remained narrowly domestic, and "[a]cademic study, a meritorious male pursuit, seemed self-indulgent when found among women" (Kerber 190). For example, Benjamin Rush insisted that any plan of female education "be calculated to prepare [young women] for the duties of social and domestic life" (39),

and defined the benefits of such education in terms of service to the family males; "it has been remarked," he notes, "that there have been few great or good men who have not been blessed with wife and prudent mothers" (37). Noah Webster, noting that women's education "should be particularly guarded," opined that "education is always *wrong* which raises a woman above the duties of her station" (69, 70)—her "station" comprising, of course, the offices of wife and mother. Such opinions lend credence to David Lee Clark's assertion that the closing years of the eighteenth century actually saw an ascendancy of Rousseau's reactionary views, which defined a woman's "proper education" as one in which "delicacy, softness, sensibility, obedience, and sexual attraction were considered the cardinal virtues" (111).

There is nowhere any hint that Clara's training has partaken of these "domestic" matters which were thought an appropriate focus for women's mental energies in her time. Nor is there any evidence that Clara sees her education as having any reference to conjugal or maternal responsibilities; even her romantic inclinations toward Pleyel seem unconnected to any thoughts of their natural conclusion, marriage and motherhood. In short, she aspires toward full participation in the life of the intellect, and in the history of her culture and family, while circumventing that core of "womanly" duties to which, for her, these interests are to be subordinated.

At the same time Clara has internalized a "second-sex" construction of the feminine, which persuades her not only of the subversive nature of her intellectual aspirations, but of her unfitness to carry them out. Thus her own lapses of rationality become at once a judgment on herself and a fulfillment of her nature; she continually ascribes such failures to her womanhood itself, apologizing for her susceptibility to the "female" weakness of passion. Her feelings of love are deemed "hateful and degrading impulses" (82); her sexual awakening makes her "a victim of imbecility," traceable to "a fatal passion,—a passion that . . . was alone sufficient to the extermination of my peace" (83). And, in speaking of her response to Carwin's appearance, she muses that perhaps the reader "suspect[s] that such were the first inroads of a passion incident to every female heart" (54)—a phrasing that suggests that Clara sees such lapses of reason as generic to her sex as well as specific to herself.[4]

Thus the pattern of enclosure and marginalization that defines Clara's status in her family is reprised in her uncertain relation to the early Republic's normative value of intellectual cultivation. Though the Age of Reason invites her to identify herself with the life of the mind, Clara is barred by her womanhood from fully achieving such an identification, since the gender ideology of the time defines the intellect as secondary, rather than primary, to the essence of "feminine" nature. Her query to the reader, "Was I not likewise transformed from rational and human into a creature of nameless and fearful attributes?" (179-80), reveals the powerful self-condemnation that Clara derives from the gender system, which places "rational" and therefore "human" at one pole—the masculine—and its negation at the other, feminine, end of the gender axis.

And yet the norms of "femininity" by which she finds herself judged are themselves shot through with ambiguity, contradiction, and danger. This is most clearly evident in her relationship with Pleyel, whose attitudes have a reactionary undertow that belies his role as the novel's putative apostle of New World rationalism. As A. Carl Bredahl observes, "Pleyel sees perfect virtue, an Old World ideal in Clara" (188)—which is less than all to the good. His view simply reinstates the traditional role of the woman as symbol of virtue, purity, and propriety; as he tells Clara, "Not a sentiment you uttered, not a look you assumed, that were not, in my apprehension, fraught with the sublimities of rectitude and the illuminations of genius" (116); to him she is "a being after whom sages may model their transcendent intelligence, and painters, their ideal beauty. Here is exemplified, that union between intellect and form which has hitherto existed only in the conceptions of the poet" (121); she is to him "a model . . . devoid of imperfection" (122-23).

When examined closely, these declarations reveal a curious double focus. Certainly what Pleyel sees in Clara is at least in part the perfection of a creature of rationalism and intelligence; but implicit in his description is the idea that her essence is not merely rational but sublime—that of an angel, or, more precisely, of an art work. She is in his paradigm less a participant in the life of the mind and the imagination than an exemplar which stimulates it—not a painter or a poet or a sage herself, but an unearthly muse, an inspiration and object of cultural consciousness rather than author or agent. Thus Pleyel's adoration takes away as much as it gives; his worshipful definition preserves his culture's traditional dynamic of perception, which defines the male as the active perceiver and the female as the passive entity, whether as muse or as model.[5]

Clara is acutely aware of her role as a passive signifier of these etherealized values. As a mere object of Pleyel's perception, she may not act on her own feelings for him, but must instead play on the intricate codes which signify female virtue and propriety: "He must not be assured that my heart is his, previous to the tender of his own; but he must be convinced that it has not been given to another. . . . The delicate line of propriety,—how hard it is to fall short and not to overleap it!" (79); she believes that a "confession" of love to Pleyel "would be the most remediless and unpardon-

able outrage upon the dignity of my sex, and utterly unworthy of that passion which controuled me" (82). The codes' requirement that she stifle her own feelings, and respond only to Pleyel's, enforces Clara's status as a trope of masculine desire; the "dignity" and "worthiness" of her sentiments depend upon their remaining tacit unless called forth by some initiating gesture from Pleyel—as if he were not their object, but their author.

But these codes of female purity are, like Pleyel's worship, closely intertwined with their antithesis, a negative image of womanhood which Nancy Cott has characterized as "the tradition of Christian mistrust based on women's sexual treacherousness" (168). Here the stereotypically "feminine" virtues of purity, modesty, and accomplishment are replaced by a set of equally stereotypical female vices: concupiscence, duplicity, and susceptibility to irrational passion. The latent power of this inverted, negative idea of womanhood surfaces when Pleyel overhears what he believes to be a romantic tryst between Clara and Carwin. Despite Clara's heretofore irreproachable behavior, and despite the suspicious nature of the other voices that have invaded the Wieland household, Pleyel is quick to conclude that she has "fallen." In a sudden reversal of sentiment he accuses her of "consummate depravity," and brands her "most specious, and most profligate of women" (104). Clearly, the suggestion that Clara has given herself to Carwin strikes an expectant chord in Pleyel.

Although Clara is shocked and confused by this sudden revolution in Pleyel's feelings, his attitude presents her with the by now familiar demand that in order to command respect as a woman, she must somehow transcend her culture's definition of womanhood itself. Pleyel's worship is contingent on her being "accomplished and wise beyond the rest of women" (116), an exception to rather than a representative of her sex; but her supposed assignation with Carwin shows Clara to be "only a woman" after all, and allows Pleyel to conclude that her nature is not "angelic," but that of Eve the temptress and deceiver. As he says in accusing Clara of having forfeited her honor to Carwin, "Nothing *in the shape of a man* can vie with thee!" (118, emphasis mine). This accusation is, as its wording implies, typical of and specific to womanhood. Clara's fault is double; she has failed in Pleyel's eyes to "surpass her sex"; in fact she has fulfilled his worst suspicions about the degraded nature of womanhood itself. To be simply "what she is" is not enough; her "worthiness" in Pleyel's eyes depends upon her fidelity to an ideal which the social codes themselves insist is impossible for a "mere woman."

So, with respect to her culture's horizon of expectations and Pleyel's more particular set of demands, Clara at once fulfills and violates the two-sided, ambiguous definitions placed on her as a woman. Her awareness of her own "womanly" feelings places her constantly at odds with her view of herself as a creature ruled by rationality, and her identification with her own sex is further complicated by the self-contradictory Eve/angel symbology which Pleyel brings to bear upon her. Clara's identity is thus a site of intense confusion and conflict, its integrity dissolved by the corrosive chemistry of these destructive significations. Given this, it is not surprising that to some readers she seems not to have an identity at all—nor should it be incredible that, in such a state of confusion, she should turn to embrace the very source of her affliction, the patriarchal order which she looks to for approval, self-confirmation, and even protection.

Yet the issue of Clara's paradoxical and painful status as a female is most dramatically joined in what Bernard Rosenthal has identified as the principal focus in the novel—that of the religious fanaticism pervading the Wieland family (Introduction 10-11). For Clara religion—particularly the family religion—extends the pressure of male-identified authority and power to the theological plane. Her relationship to the Divine is inextricably entwined in her relationship to the other systems of family and culture which inscribe her identity as a woman; as with them, she is invited to identify with the Wieland version of worship, even though it judges her as marginal and—ultimately—expendable.

As with other loci of patriarchal force, religion is for Clara a site of manifest repression. At the beginning of the novel she characterizes the religious sentiment governing the family circle in the most innocent and benign of terms; for the Wielands, she claims, religion "was the product of lively feelings, excited by reflection on our own happiness, and by the grandeur of external nature" (22). But this is, at best, revisionist history on her part. What she has described is a species of religion centered in the "feminine" powers of communal and earthly feeling; but such a characterization has few points of contact with actual practice in her family.

It is clear, for instance, that the Wieland spiritual ethos is allied much more closely with the opposing "masculine" values of the self-sufficient intellect and its frequent corollary, ideological fanaticism. In Theodore, particularly, the privileging of such "masculine" traits as intellect and will over the "feminine" emotions is evident. He believes that his subduing of his "emotions" is the gateway to spiritual triumph; his horror and remorse at the murder of his wife are considered "degeneracy" (173) when balanced against the imperative of fulfilling his spiritual mandate; his "moment of triumph" consists in his "successfully subdu[ing] the stubbornness of human passions" and making of his wife "the victim which has been demanded" by the mysterious voices (172).

Other aspects of the family religion testify to its masculine character as well. It is authoritarian (the emphasis on "obedience" to divine commands), and its authority descends patrilineally, with the male heir assuming the role of self-anointed priest, prophet, and scribe. Both father and son share an obsession with sacred texts of one kind or another, indicating a "scholastic" dimension which, as we have seen, is discouraging of female participation. And though the elder Wieland does not ask that his wife or anyone else conform to his mode of worship, neither does he invite them to share in it; for him "devotion was not only a silent office, but must be performed alone" (11), a practice which requires a being fully "independent" and intellectually self-sufficient—that is, generically male.

As a woman trapped within this field of masculine religious power, Clara is subject to its effects without being able to participate fully in its conduct. The meanings and imperatives of the family religion are mediated through the presiding males, first father and then brother—and both times with devastating results. Yet in spite of these disasters she worships and memorializes both the elder and younger Wieland as spiritual paragons; her narrative becomes by turns a denial of, and an apology for, the horrors they have wrought. Bredahl has observed that Clara's "narrative stance is that of the traditional female admiring the dominant male in the family" (178); but this admiration is not simply daughterly or sisterly. For Clara the masculine is the face of the Divine, and her brother Theodore a figure in whom all her hopes and anxieties about supernatural authority and power are focused; the physical signifier through whom the divine itself is expressed, Theodore is for Clara as inseparable from God as Mohammed is from Allah.

Walter Hesford has usefully discussed Theodore's identification with the Divine, observing that in the Judeo-Christian tradition of which the Wieland family religion partakes, "God is 'he,'" and "the author of our being and authoritative center and disseminator of meaning is masculine"; and Clara's acceptance of Wieland's identification of the Divine will with his own certainly supports Hesford's thesis that she represents the "feminine" side of the equation—"the passive recipient of the seed of meaning, the passive reader of the given script" (246). But her situation is still more complex than this. Clara is both reader *and* script, her identity as a subordinate being inscribed for her, upon her, by the same act of signification that marks her brother as authoritative, normative, and (metaphorically at least) divine. She must read herself in and through Theodore, in terms of a difference which presents itself to her as authoritative and unquestionable.

Clara's confused and contradictory responses to Theodore's slaughter of his family proceed from her attempt to preserve the integrity of the symbolic nexus between her brother and the Divine. Her idolatry at first prevents her from seeing Theodore's will as separate from God's; in her compulsion to "retain all my former affection for this person, and veneration for the purity of his motives" (186), Clara insists that he has been "acquitted at the tribunal of his own conscience" and that "none but a command from heaven could have swayed his will" (181). And yet to believe in Theodore's claim of divine authority for his acts is to accuse the God whose decrees he has supposedly executed—a theory which leads to the conclusion that the gods themselves are hostile, if not actually insane, and blasts Clara's presumption, present from the early stages of her narrative, that the world is governed by forces both benign and comprehensible.

Naturally enough, Clara attempts to preserve the corrupted ideology which has authored her nightmare by displacing the blame on outside elements—namely, Carwin. By identifying his human trick of ventriloquism as the source of the voices, she is able at once to absolve Theodore and the gods he serves. Thus Carwin, not Theodore, becomes the one whose "malice had entailed [woes] upon us" (193); she rejects Carwin's explanations, insisting that "his tale is a lie, and his nature devilish" (216). Even as Theodore threatens her own life, Clara's horror is neatly deflected from her brother to Carwin: "I firmly believed that Carwin's was the instigation" (218); she even names him as the object of her vengeance, asserting that she "thirsted for his [Carwin's] blood" (221).

What Clara forgets—or perhaps represses—is that her terror of her brother, and her need to displace that terror onto some other object, precedes Theodore's murderous rampage. A dream early in the novel presents Theodore to Clara as her destroyer, beckoning her into the abyss (62), and she is only rescued by a warning, "Hold! Hold!"—later to become associated with Carwin. Later, tormented by the premonition that there is someone within her closet "whose purposes were evil," she fastens on "[t]he frantic conception that my brother was within," and asks herself "what emotion should possess me when the arm lifted against me was Wieland's?" (88, 87). Clearly, the murders are the ultimate evidence of what Clara has intuitively known all along, but has been loath to admit to herself or others: namely, that the brother she worships and whose benevolence she depends upon is anything but benign or protective. But her need to believe otherwise abides throughout; in a striking denial of the true source of her terrors, Clara lumps these dreams and premonitions together with the actuality of Wieland's deeds, and finds these images all "unavoidably connected with that of Carwin" (190).

Still, blaming the mysterious stranger will not help Clara salvage the nexus of divine and patriarchal moral authority; as satisfying as it may seem at first glance, it is an unworkable gambit on two counts. First, it robs her horrific experience of any coherent spiritual import, transforming her tale from one of dark tragedy to one of mere grisly absurdity; but more importantly, it diminishes the status of her brother, reducing him from demigod to a pathetically fallible human dupe, no longer the agent of a "heavenly prompter," but a victim of mere "human treachery" (219). When she sees Theodore, temporarily dispelled of his belief in his divine mandate and "transformed . . . into the *man of sorrows*" (230), she instantly wishes his delusions—and hers—had never been dispelled. She laments the loss of his "sanctity of motives" and of his "elevation above the sensual and the selfish" (231). Significantly these reflections occur only moments before Theodore, having threatened to kill her, instead plunges the penknife into his own heart.

Wieland's suicide may be read in part as prophecy, as Brown's vision of the collapse of a patriarchal system whose presumption of authority conceals its own inner spiritual bankruptcy. The justification for patriarchal power rests on a semiotic confusion in which the normative values of virtue, intelligence, and self-mastery are signified by the male; but Theodore's deranged deed reveals the arbitrary nature of the sign in which these normative values are joined with their masculine signifier. In his final attack on his sister the mask of masculine authority is stripped away, denuded of its pretensions of any inherent moral or natural basis, and revealed in the full horror of its raw, naked power.[6]

A corollary point must be insisted here. It is important for a full appreciation of Brown's thesis to understand that Theodore's moral derangement is not merely an individual psychological aberration, but an extreme instance of more general patterns of male-identified pioneer values that characterized the America of the author's time, and which are focused in the Wieland family history itself. Indeed, the Wieland legacy is marked by two characteristic American traits, strong enough in isolation but incendiary when mixed: the penchant for viewing one's life in terms of a divine, even apocalyptic, quest; and the cult of individual independence and self-sufficiency—values which show the "domestic" world of women and family as insignificant and irrelevant, if not a downright obstacle.

Wieland's egoistic spirituality has both precedent and antecedent in the American cultural cavalcade. It may be incipiently glimpsed in the neo-Puritanism of Jonathan Edwards, who in his "Personal Narrative" finds God not in the social religiosity of the meetinghouse but in solitude with nature; it is extended and modified in the writings of traveler-naturalists such as Audubon, where, as Annette Kolodny has shown in *The Lay of the Land,* the experiencing "I" constructs a relation, at once loving and destructive, between the lone "masculine" quester and the "feminine" wilderness he penetrates. More broadly, Constance Rourke has observed how American legend of Brown's time and afterward glorified lone questers devoid of familial ties (104); and in her book *The American Narcissus,* Joyce Warren has mounted a sustained critique of the all-absorbing egoism implicit in American culture from Franklin to Twain, characterizing this ethos as inscribing "a world of the inflated self" in which others—particularly women—"exist only as objects to be ignored or destroyed . . . or to be made use of or absorbed into the self" (17).

The male Wielands clearly engage this individualistic—and occasionally messianic—construction of the self; but they are most marked by torment over their failure to fulfill its mandates. The elder Wieland initially comes to America to proselytize the Indians, but instead marries and becomes a prosperous farmer; he is afterward tormented by the idea that he has abandoned his "duty," and that there must be a "penalty" paid "in consequence of his disobedience" (10, 13). His "disobedience" consists in his choosing the civilized arrangements of family, social status, and economic wealth over the challenges of that archetypically masculine American dream, the solitary wilderness quest—a choice which the canonical American hero, from Cooper's Natty Bumppo and Twain's Huck Finn to the muted protagonists of Hemingway, has regarded as a surrender and a betrayal of the male self's spiritual destiny.[7]

In this light, Theodore's actions make most sense if considered as the fulfillment of his father's original abortive attempt to atone for his abandonment of his divinely ordained mission. The sin of this surrender to domesticity must be avenged, purged from the family; and Theodore accomplishes this awful purification through the slaughter of his own wife and children. His act at once eliminates the "domestic" influence in his life and also enables him to reclaim the privilege of a Divine commission which his father had forfeited, as Walter Hesford observes, Theodore has "conjure[d] up a voice that commands him to sacrifice his bourgeois domestic version of happiness in order to ratify his true destiny" (242).

Significantly, his program of murder does not include Pleyel, but confines itself to women and children—a "final solution," as it were, that eliminates all obstacles to solitary male spiritual apotheosis. "Purity," it would appear, demands the elimination of all that is unmasculine in a man's horizon of vision—a logical extension of patriarchal symbology, which sees male as normative and female as inferior, aberrant. As he prepares to murder her, Theodore tells Catharine, "I pity the weakness of thy nature; I pity thee, but must not spare" (171). His conviction that she must be destroyed is at least partially authorized by the Edenic parallel: for if Man is

Adam, then Eve is the agent of spiritual fall, and Eden can only be restored by purging her from the landscape.

As we have seen, Clara's own construction of the world—and of herself—internalizes this aggressive pejoration of the feminine, which devalues and punishes her for being "only a woman," while barring her from acquiring or displaying those normative "human" qualities which are assigned to the masculine pole of the gender system. She thus exists in a nexus of values which simultaneously grant and refuse her a justification for existence, generating idealized versions of womanhood while devaluing and threatening to destroy the actual woman present in her. Small wonder, then, that she finds that her consciousness "seemed to be split into separate parts, and these parts to have entered into implacable contention" (140); as we have shown, she is a divided self—both Wieland and not-Wieland, both self-sufficient creature of the intellect and the two-faced angel/Eve, both faithful acolyte and disposable victim of a god-brother who repays her worship with terror and murder. On this divided ground Clara can find no place to stand where she is not in conflict with herself and with the cultural norms which inscribe her; the "inconsistencies" which Brown's critics find in Clara are symptoms not of the author's faulty technique or understanding, but of the self-contradictory identity imposed on her by her social and familial environment.

These contradictions form the axis of her narration, which by turns challenges and accepts the terms of her fate. On the one hand she questions her auditor, demanding to know "what it is that has made me deserve to be placed on this dreadful eminence" (6), while on the other she holds that her condition "squares with the maxims of eternal equity" (5): "I estimated my own deserving: a hatred, immortal and inexorable, is my due" (222-23). These contradictory sentiments may be explained by the following crucial distinction: that as a Wieland and as a noble human being Clara cannot accept her fate—but that as a woman, whose humanity is by definition morally and intellectually qualified, she is congenitally guilty, somehow responsible for the various horrors perpetrated upon her.

In the final chapter, which papers over the conflict with superficial platitudes derived from the Stuart-Conway-Maxwell subplot, Clara fully and unambiguously embraces the notion of her own responsibility and guilt. The lesson she finally derives from her tale—namely, that the evils suffered by the victims in both the Conway strand and her own story "owed their existence to the errors of the sufferers" and in particular to the "disastrous passions" of those involved (244)—shows that she has achieved closure only by aligning herself totally with the typology of patriarchal force, and inverting the true implication of her experience. (After all, we have seen how Theodore's subjugation of his own "unruly passions" is precisely what enables him to carry out his horrible mandate.) By accepting her role as victim and ascribing authorship of her fate to her own "feminine" faults, Clara absolves both Theodore and Carwin, and shoulders the ultimate burden of guilt herself.

But as with her identity, Clara's final narrative solution is marked by discontinuity and incoherence. Norman Grabo has emphasized the break between the main part of her narrative and the final chapter, which contains some striking discontinuities with the rest of her tale: related at both temporal and geographical distance from the main body of the story, it concentrates on the vapid Stuart-Conway-Maxwell subplot rather than the substance of Clara's own experience. Grabo sees this last chapter as Clara's attempt to "conventionalize" both the content and moral of her ordeal, in effect "turn[ing] her experience into formula fiction" after her first, more direct attempt has failed (25).

But this is a distinction of degree rather than of kind, since even in the first narrative Clara's interpretive efforts are circumscribed by the axioms of culture that produce her conflict. Because in both sections she addresses herself to male auditors (and, by extension, a "public" audience whose attitudes reflect the masculinist bias of culture), she finds herself compelled to frame her argument in the same self-defeating terms that govern the experience she is trying to rationalize; she is unable to confront the true source of her terrors—the significations of patriarchal culture—because it defines the terms of the public discourse which she has chosen as her medium of narration.

What Clara needs is an alternative channel of expression, some private vocabulary, through which she might subvert or resist the conventions that frustrate her other attempts to justify or explain herself. I would suggest that there is indeed such an alternative channel, a third "version" of Clara's tale; but like Clara herself it is enclosed and marginalized within the structure of her more "public" narrative acts. This third "text" is that of Clara's journal, written in cipher, which as she herself admits "contained the most secret transactions of my life" (191). This private document may be distinguished from the other two versions by the fact that its audience is not the world at large, but Clara herself; and as such it represents, as Carwin insists, "the key to your inmost soul" (206), expressing as it must an uncensored Clara, a counterimage to the "official" document of the story itself, which she uses as an attempt (ultimately unsuccessful) to "compose" an acceptable public version of herself and her actions.

It is significant that Carwin is the only other person—and a man at that—to glimpse the contents of the journal. In his mercurial, serial self-invention, he is the perfect representative of the chaos that looms beyond the corrupted ideological battlements behind which Clara finds herself at once imprisoned and protected. And, as a number of critics have observed, he like Clara fabricates strategic fictions which confront and play upon entrenched cultural values. Edwin Fussell sees Carwin primarily as an agent of deconstructive chaos, "a veritable model of . . . literature out of control," one "who [has] wrought great evil—but maybe in the fullness of time he will wreak some good—without quite willing it" (183, 182); on the other hand, Cynthia Jordan argues that Carwin's primary role is to provide Clara with an illusory narrative closure, and that his "specific evil . . . is that he is an artful storyteller, one who fashions tidy fictions with endings that seem absolute" (92).

But with respect to Clara, Carwin is less author than *reader,* one who accesses and decodes the secret text that is occluded by her culturally authorized identity. In reading Clara through her journal rather than through her "official" discourse, he corroborates the private, lawless self which looks within rather than without for validation; as Bredahl says, she becomes in his eyes a creature whose powers have no reference to "external standards of justice" (188). He tells her, "[M]y knowledge of you was of that kind, which conjugal intimacies can give" (205)—a phrase that suggests his discovery, in the journal, of Clara's suppressed sexual self-awareness as well as other secrets of the heart.

So why are Clara's "private" writings not shared with her reader, even though she openly discusses the effort she makes to destroy them? Quite simply, because in her view they are of no use in her defense; in fact, quite the contrary. She is already struggling to conceal or transcend her pejorated womanhood, and cannot help but feel that such "intimacies" as Carwin has discovered must be a source of shame, an exposure of the impermissible "real" woman that lies behind her public image. I have already suggested how Clara feels impelled to deny or transcend her emotional responses, since they suggest the "feminine" identity which her culture at once constructs and condemns. Her recurrent attempts to deny or purge herself of such passions show how these powers of feeling, aligned as they are with the pejorated "feminine," strike her as indecent, unpresentable; and, since she is convinced that "those sentiments which we ought not to disclose it is criminal to harbour" (80), even the intimate, private self must be throttled when it conflicts with the demands of one's public persona.

This, I would suggest, is the principle governing the fate of the journals, and a clue to the nature of their contents: since the personal, individual Clara has no place in the eyes of her brother or Pleyel—or, by extension, in the culture at large—it can have no place in her "official" narrative either. The journal, a locus of private and secret signification, inscribes a Clara not "authorized" by the patriarchal norms which generate her public identity and by which, inescapably, she feels herself to be judged. Her destruction of the journal, like the cozy fiction of her final chapter, emblematizes Clara's ultimate sacrifice of her individual selfhood to the onerous cultural constructions of her identity as a female.

But destroying the document does not erase its presence from the text; like her father's bizarre death and her brother's murderous insanity, it remains a fact repressed but not erased, an errant datum that even Clara's most willful interpretation cannot absorb. It is the reality on which the first narrative founders, and which the second one attempts to conventionalize through its airy analogy with the Louisa Conway case. But the final chapter, so formulaic in tone and structure when compared to the disintegrative entropy of her first narrative, is nevertheless marked by the same repressions; in essence it reprises Clara's strategy for dealing with the hostile fate which circumscribes her, as it erects a new fiction, a new temple of belief, on the very site where the threatening older truth lies entombed.

So the true wonders of the invisible world in **Wieland** are not the mysterious voices, but the axioms of culture, whose narrow and self-contradictory terms cripple those who, like Clara, must live within their constraints. The beasts in the closet—whom Clara variously identifies as Theodore, Carwin, and other males of threatening hue—are instruments of nightmarish epiphany through which the full horror, irrationality, and prodigious power of these axioms are revealed.

Of those in the novel, Carwin alone sees clearly what Clara can only glimpse obscurely in the dark recesses of her consciousness; as the tale's outsider and its trickster/harlequin figure, he eagerly plays the deconstructor of these hidden cultural norms, including the unnatural ideal of womanhood which inscribes Clara's self-contradictory public identity. Having been privy to the "real" Clara of the journals, he stands ready to liberate her from this discredited ideology; but she, unwilling or unable to countenance the disintegration of the patriarchal order through which she has defined herself, once again makes a fortress of her prison and (through marriage to Pleyel) an intimate of her enemy.

There are suggestive parallels between **Wieland** and another work with a similar dynamic which Brown is known to have admired and emulated—Godwin's *Caleb Williams*. Both novels use first person apologias to dramatize the insufficiency of individual experience as a basis for action; like Godwin's narrator, Clara is torn between idolatry of an authority figure and her experience of that figure's persecution; and Clara's story, like Caleb's, is founded on contradictions that make its telling an act of simultaneous narrative creation and destruction. Both novels show the Oedipal turmoil of at once loving the father and seeking to escape his destructive powers; but *Caleb Williams* shows this paternalistic ideology in class terms, while **Wieland** shows it in terms of gender struggles within the culture and within its essential unit, the nuclear family.

But a more telling parallel might be with Richardson's *Clarissa,* in which the captive female heart undertakes its ultimately doomed negotiation with a hostile system of social significations. Frequently finessed in discussions of **Wieland** is the fact that it is, after all, an epistolary novel, but one in which the writer's entire presentation is subjected to standards of propriety and veracity that have their roots in public, rather than private, codes of belief. What finally distinguishes Clara's narrative is the absence of sustaining intimacy which assists other women, from Richardson's Clarissa Harlowe to Alice Walker's Celie in *The Color Purple,* in their efforts to resist, subvert, or finally triumph over the patriarchal codes that are the source of their misery. Brown's novel is ultimately a testament to the destructive powers of the codes by which a culture generates and enforces its hierarchies of power—particularly gendered ones—as Clara, finally trapped and defeated, embraces the ideology that has been the source of her torment, and retreats into a cozy fiction that shields her from the terrifying implications of her own tale.

Notes

1. Clara's status is illustrative of the category which Simone de Beauvoir has identified as that of "the second sex." As de Beauvoir argues, culture's representation of "human" as metaphorically if not biologically male creates an asymmetry in the masculine/feminine opposition; woman, now a "second sex" after primary and integral male, becomes "the negative, defined by limiting criteria" (xv); "Humanity is male and man defines woman not in herself but as relative to him; she is not regarded as an autonomous being. . . . He is the Subject, he is the Absolute—she is the Other" (xvi).

   Although the phrase "the second sex" had not yet been coined in Brown's time, he would not have found de Beauvoir's formulation at all alien. Concerns over the gender system's inequitable asymmetries were central for the Enlightenment feminists whose work Brown both admired and emulated; and for Brown himself it seems of crucial interest to the young Republic's destiny to determine how inclusively, in terms of gender and otherwise, fundamental assertions such as "all men are created equal" ought to be interpreted and enforced.

2. My use of political language here is conscious. As Jay Fliegelman has pointed out, in Brown's time

issues of family governance were often metaphorically applied to those of national governance. The enshrinement of Washington as "the father of his country" (discussed in Friedman, 44-78, as well as by Fliegelman) neatly conflated questions of "patriotism" and patriarchy (note the masculine root of both words)—but failed to resolve the issue, implicit in *Wieland,* of a woman's filial obligation to institutions (both political and familial) which had neglected to provide for her full enfranchisement and selfhood.

3. One cannot emphasize too strongly the influence of Wollstonecraft's work on Brown's formulation of, and commitment to, what would become known as "the woman question" (see Clark, 110-14). This influence, which is most baldly evident in Brown's tract *Alcuin; or the Rights of Women* (1798), is also palpable, though implicit, in *Wieland.* Of the three emphases that one may discern in this novel—the nuclear family, education and the life of the intellect, and religion—the first two in particular evoke Wollstonecraft's concerns in *A Vindication of the Rights of Woman,* which first appeared on American shores in Philadelphia in 1792.

4. Clara's pejorative attitude toward her own "passions" reflects the heavy price at which women of her time purchased the privilege of being regarded as "intellectual" creatures. As D'Emilio and Freedman observe, Clara's time was one marked by "increasing suspicion about the expression of female passion" (44); and Nancy Cott has argued that "passionlessness" as an ideal of feminine deportment was "on the other side of the coin which paid, so to speak, for women's admission to moral equality" (168).

5. The historical persistence of this male subject / female object opposition is eloquently discussed by Gilbert and Gubar. In this dynamic, they argue, the female object of perception "becomes herself an embodiment of . . . extremes of mysterious and intransigent Otherness which culture confronts with worship or fear, love or loathing"; she "mediates between the male artist and the Unknown, simultaneously teaching him purity and instructing him in degradation" (19, 20). It seems to me that Gilbert and Gubar here describe precisely the sort of angel/Eve duality that governs Pleyel's perceptions of Clara.

6. Bernard Rosenthal has suggested that Catharine has been raped as well as murdered (107); though his thesis points more to Carwin than to Theodore as the violator, I would suggest that ascribing the act to the latter produces the more potent interpretation. For if Rosenthal's suggestion is viable (and I am inclined to accept his argument, with the

qualification mentioned above) the rape of Catharine by her husband would constitute the final outrage of sexual violence, completing and emblematizing the domination and victimization of the female by pure, unjustified masculine force.

7. Leslie Fiedler has observed how the American mythos abhors this process of domestication, since it tethers masculine ambition to a world of "responsibility and drudgery and dullness" whose principal feature is the presence of familial women—notably wives. As Fiedler sees it, the "acceptance of the status of father" requires the male's "abandonment of the quest" as well as his "assumption of the role of the ogre who holds her [the beloved] in captivity" (338); interestingly, in *Wieland* this process is multi-generational, with the father's abandonment of the quest completed in the son's transformation into the monster who goes beyond the mere act of captivity to the actual destruction of his wife and children.

Works Cited

Baym, Nina. "A Minority Reading of *Wieland*." *Critical Essays on Charles Brockden Brown.* Ed. Bernard Rosenthal. Boston: G. K. Hall, 1981. 87-103.

Beauvoir, Simone de. *The Second Sex.* 1949. Trans. H. M. Parshley. New York: Bantam, 1961.

Bredahl, A. Carl, Jr. "Transformation in *Wieland*." *Early American Literature* 12 (1977): 177-192.

Brown, Charles Brockden. *Wieland, or the Transformations.* 1798. Vol. 1 of *The Novels and Related Works of Charles Brockden Brown.* Ed. Sydney J. Krause et al. Kent, Ohio: Kent State Univ. Press, 1977.

Clark, David Lee. *Charles Brockden Brown: Pioneer Voice of America.* Durham, N.C.: Duke Univ. Press, 1952.

Cott, Nancy F. "Passionlessness: An Interpretation of Victorian Sexual Ideology, 1790-1850." *A Heritage of Her Own: Toward a New Social History of American Women.* Ed. Nancy F. Cott and Elizabeth L. Pleck. New York: Simon and Schuster, Touchstone, 1979. 162-181.

D'Emilio, John, and Estelle B. Freedman. *Intimate Matters: A History of Sexuality in America.* New York: Harper and Row, 1988.

Fiedler, Leslie. *Love and Death in the American Novel.* 2nd ed. New York: Stein and Day, 1966.

Fliegelman, Jay. *Prodigals and Pilgrims: The American Revolution Against Patriarchal Authority, 1750-1800.* Cambridge: Cambridge Univ. Press, 1982.

Friedman, Lawrence J. *Inventors of the Promised Land.* New York: Alfred A. Knopf, 1975.

Fussell, Edwin Sill. "*Wieland*: A Literary and Historical Reading." *Early American Literature* 18 (1983-84): 171-86.

Gilbert, Sandra M., and Susan Gubar. *The Madwoman in the Attic: The Woman Writer and the Nineteenth-Century Literary Imagination.* New Haven: Yale Univ. Press, 1979.

Grabo, Norman S. *The Coincidental Art of Charles Brockden Brown.* Chapel Hill: Univ. of North Carolina Press, 1981.

Hesford, Walter. "'Do You Know the Author?': The Question of Authorship in *Wieland.*" *Early American Literature* 17 (1982-83): 237-48.

Jordan, Cynthia S. *Second Stories: The Politics of Language, Form, and Gender in Early American Fictions.* Chapel Hill: Univ. of North Carolina Press, 1989.

Kerber, Linda K. *Women of the Republic: Intellect and Ideology in Revolutionary America.* Chapel Hill: Univ. of North Carolina Press, 1980.

Kolodny, Annette. *The Lay of the Land: Metaphor as Experience and History in American Life and Letters.* Chapel Hill: Univ. of North Carolina Press, 1975.

Kreyling, Michael. "Construing Brown's *Wieland*: Ambiguity and Derridean 'Freeplay.'" *Studies in the Novel* 14 (1982): 43-54.

Ridgely, J. V. "The Empty World of *Wieland.*" *Individual and Community: Variations on a Theme in American Fiction.* Ed. Kenneth H. Baldwin and David K. Kirby. Durham, N.C.: Duke Univ. Press, 1975. 3-16.

Rosenthal, Bernard. Introduction. *Critical Essays on Charles Brockden Brown.* Ed. Bernard Rosenthal. Boston: G. K. Hall, 1981. 1-21.

———. "The Voices of *Wieland.*" *Critical Essays on Charles Brockden Brown.* Ed. Bernard Rosenthal. Boston: G. K. Hall, 1981. 104-25.

Rourke, Constance. *American Humor: A Study of the National Character.* New York: Harcourt Brace, 1931.

Rush, Benjamin. "Thoughts upon Female Education, Accommodated to the Present State of Society, Manners, and Government in the United States of America." 1787. *Essays on Education in the Early Republic,* Ed. Frederick Rudolph. Cambridge: Belknap Press (Harvard Univ. Press), 1965. 25-40.

Warren, Joyce. *The American Narcissus: Individualism and Women in Nineteenth-Century American Fiction.* New Brunswick: Rutgers Univ. Press, 1984.

Webster, Noah. "On the Education of Youth in America." 1790. *Essays on Education in the Early Republic.* Ed. Frederick Rudolph. Cambridge: Belknap Press (Harvard Univ. Press), 1965. 41-77.

Wollstonecraft, Mary. *A Vindication of the Rights of Woman.* 1792. Ed. Carol H. Poston. New York: Norton, 1975.

Elizabeth Jane Wall Hinds (essay date 1997)

SOURCE: Hinds, Elizabeth Jane Wall. "*Wieland*: Accounting for the Past." In *Private Property: Charles Brockden Brown's Gendered Economics of Virtue,* pp. 99-131. Newark: University of Delaware Press, 1997.

[*In the following essay, Hinds discusses issues of class and inheritance in* Wieland.]

Within the unfolding drama of international capitalism, **Wieland, or The Transformation: An American Tale** appears less than interested in a growing market economy or in any private world modeled on the contingencies of exchange in the public sphere, in part because **Wieland,** Brown's first novel, is set in the country, far away from the immediate pressures of such a market. Yet I will argue that Brown establishes in this novel a context for the interchange of market and private values, for in its idyllic setting, **Wieland**'s cast of characters enacts a drama of "upper-class" suffering brought on by the isolation and insularity their inherited luxury has enabled. Brown's Arthur Mervyn and Constantia Dudley, actors on an urban stage, are called to action by the peculiar demands of a city in time of crisis: in order to survive, these two must interact to varying degrees with a public world of labor and exchange, and as a result their private values, not to mention private virtues, reflect in social terms what Habermas calls "exchange relations."[1] For Arthur and Constantia, virtue merits success and security insofar as virtue is gained by participation in a world outside their houses.

By contrast, Brown's Wieland family, out on its country estate, has turned in on itself as it has turned its back on a public world of exchange. By virtue of their inheritance, the Wielands are excused from the necessity of work, and thus their private values are a little too private, establishing them in a leisure class, since they take no part in the principles of reciprocity involved in the virtues of the marketplace. Incestuous in its behavior, this family is poised from the beginning to take a great fall—to suffer from a disease of isolation embodied in a species of Calvinist neurosis seemingly inherited along with its property. For the third time in as many generations, the male of the Wieland household has fallen victim to sensory delusions. Acting on command from a mysterious voice, Theodore Wieland murders his wife and children, sets out to complete his "duty" by killing his sister Clara, and finally commits suicide in a moment of clarity and remorse. Sister Clara, no less susceptible to intimations of the supernatural than Theodore in spite of her claims to rationality, suffers from a tormented apprehension of threat to both body and spirit, eventually succumbing to a nervous breakdown from which she recovers only minimally when forced to abandon her home.

The suffering visited on the house of Wieland grows directly out of its isolated social class, for the Wielands are defined equally by their inheritance of superstition and their inheritance of property, both of which ground them in a world of materiality, of biological determinism, and of a land-based economy that reaches far beyond the physical setting of its houses. In short, the house of Wieland is haunted by its past, and in this third generation of self-destruction, that inheritance comes close to annihilating the family for good. The only remaining Wieland is the one telling the tale, and in her story, Clara evidences both the close bond with her past and the double-bind of her class and gender: as an "aristocratic" woman, Clara is placed beyond the possibility of virtue in its late-eighteenth-century gendered social definition. Nancy Armstrong and Leonard Tennenhouse define the virtues of "domestic" womanhood in the late eighteenth century as combining "psychological depth" and "femaleness"—"the qualities that differentiate her from the male rather than [as previously and as would be the case for leisure-class women] in terms of her father's wealth and title."[2] In other words, as domesticity came to define women during this period, the "virtuous" woman was something of a Constantia Dudley—a hard-working, saving, and essentially conservative personality.

Clara Wieland, on the other hand, partakes too much of the aristocratic. "As femaleness was successfully redefined in [domestic] terms," Armstrong and Tennenhouse argue, "the woman exalted by an aristocratic tradition of letters ceased to appear so desirable. In becoming the other side of a new sexual coin, the aristocratic woman in turn represented surface instead of depth, embodied material rather than moral values, and displayed idle sensuality where there should be constant vigilance and tireless concern for the well-being of others."[3] Clearly, a good deal of Clara's definition as a character results from a poisonous combination of class and gender. Brown's virtuous Constantia occupies something of a "middle-class," though, as Stuart M. Blumin reminds us, "the middle class had not already emerged by the end of the eighteenth century."[4] Still, Blumin writes, there *did* exist something like a class system with a "recognizable 'middling rank,'" even in Brown's 1790s Philadelphia.

> "Class," including variants of "middle class," was by then appearing with somewhat greater frequency, especially in the pages of the more radical newspapers, but even at the end of the century it was still far more common to express social levels in terms of ranks, sorts, stations, conditions, orders, or even estates. . . .

Terms such as "the better sort" and "people of middling rank," according to this argument, reveal the imprint of aristocratic Europe, despite the absence or attenuation in America of clearly bounded "interests."[5]

Indeed, Brown's sensitivity to "class" or "rank" is apparent in his careful handling of the hard-working Constantia Dudley and Arthur Mervyn, characters whose virtue is inseparable from "labor" values as opposed to inherited wealth, and whose plots are essentially comic. With *Wieland,* Brown offers the other side of this class-virtue matrix: the leisured Wieland family, tethered to the past by way of inheritance, participates in an existence too materially grounded for virtuous behavior, resulting in a plot more tragic than comic. If *Ormond* and *Arthur Mervyn* suggest an affinity on Brown's part for the "middling orders," even with some evident doubts about the mercurial nature of the entrepreneur, *Wieland* provides a resounding critique of an aristocratic class enabled by an overtly material and private set of values.

At bottom, this most classically gothic of Brown's tales is haunted by inheritance, and a good portion of Clara's haunting is just this: as a woman she is defined by her house and body, but as inheritor of gentried values she cannot perform the labor necessary to fulfill the role of domestic womanhood. Clara's position, then, realizes in little what the house of Wieland suffers at large. Doomed to fulfill the inherited role of her class, her insulated, materially determined virtues cannot enter into the values defined by the publicity of market exchange in the 1790s.

INHERITANCE AND INCEST, REPETITION AND CLASS

Wieland is still Brown's most popular novel, to judge from the array of critical assessments given to social, psychological, and historical readings.[6] Whatever their differences, on one score most twentieth-century readers of Brown seem to be in agreement: *Wieland* seems to foreground a barely suppressed impulse to incest, dramatized most fully in Clara's dream of her brother beckoning to her across an abyss, surrounded with an atmosphere of foreboding running to terror. In his Historical Essay for the Kent State edition of *Wieland,* Alexander Cowie takes the position that Clara's "abnormal" psychological state points to "latent incestuous longings for" Theodore—that her overactive sexual state at the moment has brought on such a lust-filled dream.[7] Norman Grabo would agree, arguing that as characters in this novel substitute for one another in the most coincidental of patterns—as Pleyel shows up when Carwin is expected, Catharine is murdered in Clara's bed, Carwin's thrown voice appears with all the authority of Deity—so too does Theodore Wieland substitute in both dream and night terrors for the lusted-after Carwin and Pleyel.[8] Or is it the other way around? Clara's dream, this line of argument suggests, may embody the "true" lust—the lust for brother Theodore—that has been disguised in the light of day by ostensible desire for the more appropriate Pleyel and at least marginally acceptable, because unrelated, Carwin. Most recently, Christophersen writes of an incestuous substitution of brother for lover; looking into Clara's fear of someone hiding in her bedroom closet, Christophersen notes that "She both loves [Theodore] and fears him sexually."[9]

Nearly a century of critics probably can't be altogether wrong—indeed there is something vaguely incestuous about the family situation of this novel, what with its conjunction of closer-than-usual kinship ties and overheated desire on the part of more than one character. However, I'd like to study three scenes closely one more time, the scenes of so-named incestuous longing, before deciding the limit of what they offer. In the midst of a satisfying and innocent existence, to hear Clara tell it, comes first a "signal of the ruin which impended over" her in the form of voices in her closet in the middle of the night, two voices in hot argument over the better method of killing "her" (54), a "her" Clara assumes to be herself. She's been prepared, as it happens, for this upsetting happenstance by spending the preceding evening in fantastic imaginings ranging from sexual desire to death to war. This very day, in fact, Clara has encountered the mysterious Carwin, he of the mellifluent voice, whose simple phrase "for charity's sweet sake" (51), modulated with passion, has reduced Clara to trembling: "It imparted to me an emotion altogether involuntary and uncontrollable. . . . I dropped the cloth that I held in my hand, my heart overflowed with sympathy, and my eyes with unbidden tears" (52). "Sympathy" indeed. Clara thus begins a long ride on the pheremone train, a state of mind and body throwing her into a disequilibrium quite intense for the rest of the evening. She sits up late, drawing portraits of Carwin and studying them, only to venture later into morbid death fantasies, as though her sexual desire has simmered down into a corrupted sludge.

After such preparation, no wonder the mysterious closet voices send her running in panic to brother Theodore's house for protection. But later, a second visitation of voices in the closet sets up an oddly inverted chain of interpretations for Clara, as she this time in fancy makes her brother the threatening rather than protecting figure. Again Clara has spent an agitated evening, the object of her love, Pleyel, having missed an appointed time to join the Wieland clan for a bit of play-acting. And again, Clara's love-thoughts have turned to death-fantasies: believing now that Pleyel is indifferent to her, she imagines him dead, lost to an angry river he must have crossed. Worked up to this frenzy, Clara takes to reading her dead father's memoirs and is, around the midnight hour, seized with an overwhelming fear of her closet, only to be struck by a terrible shriek and a cry

of "Hold! Hold!" (85) as she touches its lock. This time, her imagination leads her to her brother as the culprit. "Who was it whose suffocating grasp I was to feel, should I dare to enter it? What monstrous conception is this? my brother!" (87). The associations on this occasion have begun, of course, with a memory of the dream she's had between the first and second visitations of the voice, a dream most commonly read as symbolically incestuous. Nodding off to sleep at the summerhouse, a "slight," open, and airy spot Clara usually enjoys in solitude, she "imagines" herself drawn by Theodore's voice and gestures to cross an open pit on her way to his house; "He stood on the opposite edge of the gulph. I mended my pace, and one step more would have plunged me into this abyss, had not some one from behind caught suddenly my arm, and exclaimed, in a voice of eagerness and terror, 'Hold! hold!'"[10]

This memory in place, Clara then fears her brother in her closet at the second visitation of voices here, and to the degree that the novel's climax reveals Theodore as a vicious killer, her fears do make sense: on all three occasions of early terror and foreboding, Clara is afraid someone will kill her. Given her sexually charged state during the two closet scenes, it seems legitimate, on the one hand, to read Clara's anxieties as sexually motivated, as indeed incestuous longings for and/or fears of brother Theodore. On the other hand, nothing particularly sexual takes place in either dream- or closet-scene. On the face of it, Clara is threatened with death, precisely the subject of her recurrent fantasies once they have refocused away from the nebulously sexual.

In fact, Clara interprets her dream much later as a premonition of the death her brother does eventually bring to their household. After she learns that the murders of his wife, children, and servant were not enough to complete Theodore's imagined duty to his God, that he has been repeatedly breaking out of prison to try and kill her, too, she glosses the dream and closet-experience thus: "I recollected the omens of this destiny; I remembered the gulf to which my brother's invitation had conducted me; I remembered that, when on the brink of danger, the author of my peril was depicted by my fears in his form: Thus realized, were the creatures of prophetic sleep, and of wakeful terror!" (189-90). For Clara, the meaning of her dream and her upsetting fear of Theodore lies in threat of personal injury, not specifically in incestuous entanglement.

Naturally, Brown's readers aren't obligated to read as Clara does, and one can't help but recall the symbolic imagery of the penknife with which Clara threatens herself and Theodore kills himself, the heightened sexual charge Clara sustains through much of the novel, and the "passion more than fraternal" (185) Theodore bears for his sister. On a broader scale, however, I would argue that the recurrent interpretation of incestuous relations in *Wieland,* while not beknighted misreadings of a pure sister-brother relationship, may be prompted not so much by these threats to Clara's person so much as by the familial and economic matrix established by the position of the Wieland household within a growing market economy surrounding the Wieland's author, an economy in many ways still rooted in property-ownership run by a somewhat aristocratic class on the European model but also with a young, internationally directed capitalism getting a firm foothold in Brown's Philadelphia.

The Wielands live in an insulated setting, both economically and familially: their inherited estate supports Clara and Theodore, and their daily associates likewise comprise a small family—wife Catharine, brother-in-law Pleyel, and Louisa Conway, a servant raised from a young girl with the Wieland family. Absent the need to go beyond their own estate for either financial support or company, the Wieland clan does not give and take in exchange of any sort. Indeed, their economic class is as "incestuous" as the family situation appears to be; that is, as one brother and sister attach themselves to another brother and sister (Theodore marrying Catharine Pleyel and Clara eventually marrying brother Pleyel), keeping the "stock" of marriage exchange as narrow as possible without literal incestuous marriage, so too does the stock of property come from and remain within the family. At least for this generation of Wielands, the family tree barely forks: any threat of an attraction or marriage outside the close circle that might come to fruition is stifled, seeing that Pleyel's baroness is handily killed off, and Carwin—the outsider to whom Clara is powerfully attracted—is rejected, not later when he proves to be a villain, but much sooner, as soon as Clara finds herself attracted to him. This scenario of locked-in familial closeness, I maintain, Brown stages in a play of the insular property-sustained ease and security of the Wielands' inheritance, a legacy literally embodied in the various houses at Mettingen. Within these structures, the Wielands come into their inheritance; sustained by the wealth of previous generations, they are secured from any risky, free-market exchange beyond the estate, exchanges of either kinship or finance; and finally, locked behind the doors of such sustaining, inherited wealth, the Wielands suffer retribution poetically appropriate for the insular, nonvirtuous leisure class—their inheritance, indeed their own property, comes to haunt and destroy them.

Taking *Wieland*'s cue and studying whether Brown might "make the picture of a single family a model from which to sketch the condition of a nation" (33-34), Shirley Samuels asserts that the novel poses a "conservative, closed model of the family" in secure opposition to a "luridly" depicted "outside world."[11] Yet, the incest Samuels herself discovers haunting the novel

suggests just the opposite, I believe, since the "lurid" world of incestuous relations takes place within the home, within the very "closed model of the family" supposedly designed to protect and support. In avoiding exchange of both familial and economic sorts, the Wielands, like their famous descendants the Ushers, are terrorized by their own past, materially destroyed by a type of biologically determined neurosis coupled with the physical spaces of their own homes. The nearly complete destruction of the family dramatizes a warning against these several insularities of an aristocratic class.

Such insularities Claude Lévi-Strauss has defined as having both economic and kinship bases to the extent that a system of "reciprocity" within many cultures "is not merely nor essentially of an economic nature," but instead more generally constitutes an impulse to exchange embracing both the economic and the familial; breaking this "rule" of reciprocity, then, constitutes "incest" of types going beyond the kinship taboo.[12] One might note that however broadly "reciprocity" applies to cultures, the ethos of the late-eighteenth-century United States, with its fast-growing economy newly invested in international markets, would necessarily support a social and economic principle of reciprocity indispensable to market interests; Habermas would suggest a similar ethos on the social level, given that the "public" sphere of growing exchange systems, in his analysis, was generating a kind of "publicity" within the "private" domain of the household: in effect, the market concept of reciprocity would, then, mirror and support a system of kinship exchange.

Thus, Lévi-Strauss is able to discuss a general system of exchange supporting the incest taboo in specifically economic terms: "Generalized exchange establishes a system of operations conducted on credit. . . . The belief' that one family's investment of a marriage partner will be "returned" not by the family invested in but by a third, unrelated family, "is the basis of trust, and confidence opens up credit. In the final analysis, the whole system exists only because the group adopting it is prepared, in the broadest meaning of the term, *to speculate.* But the broad sense also implies the narrow sense: the speculation brings in a profit, in the sense that with generalized exchange the group can live as richly and as complexly as its size, structure and density allow, whereas with restricted exchange . . . it can never function as a whole both in time and in space."[13] To define exchange and its taboo, incest, in both economic and kinship terms highlights the problem of the Wieland family, for its class—a sociocultural position affecting both economic and familial behavior—sets it apart from the give-and-take of public exchange embodied, for instance in Arthur Mervyn's commitment to speculation, in the end predetermining, so to speak, the Wieland family's demise.

Within his four major novels, the house of Wieland represents Brown's only experiment with a gentrified class of characters. Compared to the pestilential poverty surrounding *Ormond* and *Arthur Mervyn,* the Wielands have it easy; compared to the disinherited Edgar Huntly, doomed to look upon wealth but never to touch it, Clara, Theodore, and the family surrounding them are economically secure for life. The entire cast of *Wieland* rests easy in their inherited country estate, far from the demands of the city and the class of characters Brown negotiates in his "city" novels. Unlike Constantia Dudley and Arthur Mervyn, the Wielands do not have to labor for their hasty pudding. Indeed, when Theodore is approached with the prospect of going to Germany with Pleyel to take possession of land he can now claim as his own. Theodore demurs, and in terms that bespeak an aristocratic birthright. He might lay claim to these ancestral lands, now that the Prussian wars have returned them to the ancient race of "noble Saxons."

Theodore, however, declines to exercise his privilege—an aristocratic gesture in the very refusal—even though Pleyel touts a favorite scheme, evidently, of Theodore's, claiming "the privileges of wealth and rank" may be exercised in "benevolence" (37-38) towards the poor. Young Mr. Wieland's reasoning upon wealth, here, is interesting for its consciousness of rank: "was it laudable to grasp at wealth and power even when they were within our reach?" Further, one has no reason to "grasp" so. Secure in his inherited plenitude, Theodore refuses to risk his present happiness for uncertain, "distant and contingent" (38) possibilities. In short, he refuses the speculative behavior of an Arthur Mervyn, even with much more secure outcomes than any offer Arthur ever enjoys. His sister and wife, too, will concur with this conservative reading of the situation, preferring present security to the risk of losing their friend.

The Wieland household is moneyed, then—more than moneyed. They have property, and it appears to be all they need or want. Living on their gentrified country estate, keeping company with a tight-knit family clan, Theodore edits his Cicero and engages in sprightly disagreement over matters philosophical with Pleyel while the ladies attend their needlework; all engage in the decidedly aristocratic activities of play-acting, reading, and conversation (not to mention Clara's journal-keeping), a scene of leisure far removed from the merchant-class Philadelphia of *Ormond* and *Arthur Mervyn.* Theirs is not the country as rural setting, however, but instead, to use Raymond Williams' words, "a rural landscape emptied of rural labor and of labourers," in which "the facts of production" are removed to the degree that even the servant girl, Louisa, is embedded in the family narrative as a friend warranting her own story.[14]

Idyll that it is, the Wieland household does suffer more than its share of hardship, and its particular genre of suffering embeds the twin modalities of property and kinship converging in a doomed suggestion of incest pervading the novel. Here on the Wieland estate—the combined houses of Mettingen, including the main house Theodore resides in with wife, children, and Louisa, Clara's home, her "summerhouse" and the Temple built by father Wieland for worship but now the scene of leisured family activity—on this estate the family plays out its seemingly inherited proclivity to self-destruct, and to self-destruct in fiery responses to real or imagined calls from the supernatural world intruding into its private and insular world.

The fate of the Wielands bespeaks a powerful critique of an aristocratic class set off from the exploding free market, complete with all the risks of exchange, surrounding Brown at the end of the 1790s. In a novel that Carroll Smith-Rosenberg might classify as a discourse of the "emergent middle class," Brown's Wieland family and the fate reserved for it highlights the growing class-consciousness of the decade consequent on the "ideological battle between classical republicanism [with its power-base in property] and the rhetoric of economic and political laissez-faire."[15] Brown's 1790s had not reached a full embrace of market capitalism, as Smith-Rosenberg suggests in describing a still-hot ideological struggle between market and political ideals. Gordon Wood likewise relates that "The ties that bound people together in this society were still explained and given meaning by terms that looked to the past more than the future, to the personal world of the family as much as the impersonal world of commerce," a statement highlighting the fluctuating nature of a social practice not yet attuned to a market economy not yet fully in place.[16] In spite of Brown's ambiguous treatment of the capitalist par excellence, Arthur Mervyn, his treatment of the Wielands' aristocratic tendencies, their insularity bordering on incest, works to disparage an inherited economy of landed gentry much more critically characterized than any suspicions he may have had regarding the coming capitalist class. Such a terrible fate created for the Wielands—the multiple murders, the suicide, Clara Wieland's degeneration as she is physically and psychically persecuted—especially given the repetition through generations of spiritual neuroses linked to grisly deaths (it isn't Carwin, after all, who destroys the family, but its own patriarch) speaks to a sense of the "vicious, nonproductive elegance of the aristocracy" Brown invented for the Wielands, what J. V. Ridgely has noted as a murderous detachment of family members in *Wieland* from larger social bodies.[17]

The family's insularity provides impetus for both the novel's incestuous undertones and for the characters' destiny, for the incest implied in their way of living comes about primarily from their inheritance—an inheritance of secured property with the isolation it encourages. This patrimony comes in the form of what we might call a neurosis of spirituality in addition to property inherited: both Wieland "children," that is, the present generation of Clara and Theodore, replicate their ancestors' belief in a spirit world and to some degree act out in damaging behavior such belief. Engaging in few exchanges beyond the confines of their property, the Wieland family is thus unprepared for Carwin's descent upon them: he takes up an extraordinary amount of their mental energy, as the whole group tries to fathom the mysteries of this late addition to their group ("These incidents, for a time, occupied all our thoughts," Clara writes [48]). Likewise, without their knowledge of Carwin as the culprit, the mysterious voices introduced into their insular idyll so much upset the family's stability that the entire group begins to disintegrate. Clara lives alternately in fear for her life and in awe of what she determines to be a "protecting" benefactor who warns her away from danger; Theodore sinks into himself, withdrawing from the family as his predisposition to melancholy is encouraged by the voices; and Pleyel undergoes the torments of hell as the voices first tell him his fiancée is dead and then enact a false performance of his friend and idol, Clara Wieland's, supposed sexual interlude with Carwin.

This interloper—a mysterious stranger if there ever was one—in effect shifts the careful balance of the Wielands' self-enclosed, private world. Clearly an emissary from the public world beyond the Wieland estate, Carwin's mystery in part stems from his involvement in the public arena; Pleyel has known him from an earlier time in Spain, and one of Carwin's mysteries is his ability to appear as Englishman, Spaniard, or American rustic as the situation may demand. Chameleonlike, he intrigues by virtue of his contact with these other cultures, a contact so complete as to change him, literally, into his surroundings, creating a more malicious but parallel character to Arthur Mervyn, the Protean man. There seems to be, as the Wielands see it, no there there: as they don't know Carwin, he appears as only his public personae, and his appearance on the scene of familial, private closeness begins the family's decline.

One has to wonder why the Wielands overlook Carwin as a possible source of the voices, since he is the only new element introduced into their otherwise unchanging lives and since they find him such a mystery. Though surprised by this figure from the outside world, the family isn't entirely unprepared for the upcoming events, however, for both Clara and Theodore seem to have inherited a predilection for the mysterious along with their property. With a grandfather who without warning jumped off a cliff to his death and with a father whose concentration on his duty to God led to a seeming spontaneous combustion in the Temple devoted to his God, the present generation of Wielands, however

different from each other in temperament, dwell on the possibility of a Divine Hand directing their behavior and their duty. Clara and Theodore essentially agree that the voices they've begun to hear must have a supernatural origin, and though Clara more than once accuses her brother of having an overly mystical sensibility, what with his insistence that their father's death derived "from a direct and supernatural decree," with his being something of an "enthusiast," a believer in "the system of divine government" (35), she herself frequently displays all the signs of this rather Calvinistic inclination. Clara unfailingly sees "a shadowy resemblance" (34) between the mysterious voices she and her brother hear and her father's death. More than that, Clara finds a kind of sublime pleasure in contemplating a supernatural world perhaps interfering in her own: "It begat in me a thrilling, and not unpleasing solemnity" (35).

Neither Clara nor Theodore is able to conceive of a human explanation for the voices, and Carwin's plan merely to test this little group—to have some fun at their expense and nothing more—falls on a very willing audience. Carwin, as Norman Grabo suggests, is in fact a rather "shabby" villain, one whose actual interference is mild compared to the havoc it generates.[18] For the destruction of this family results not so much from Carwin—as he says at the scene of Theodore's return in search of another sacrifice in sister Clara, he has merely set the action in motion ("my only crime was curiosity. . . . The perpretrator of Catharine's death was unknown to me" [205-6, 216])—but rather from the Wielands' own predisposition to believe in the reality of a spirit who demands obeisance in return for favor. It is this sense of *duty* toward the divine, of course, that undoes the Wieland family, not merely a belief in divinity, since the call to duty prescribes action, in Theodore's case the action of sacrificing his family in a repeat performance of the Abraham and Isaac story but without the happy ending. Clara, too, sees herself as directed from above by a "hand invisible and of preternatural strength . . . selecting my life for its aims" (84-85). When a voice warns her away from the summerhouse, Clara reveals her belief in a spirit as exacting as Theodore's and her father's "daemon," one who may "award" (66) her with death if she fail to keep quiet, as ordered, about the incident there.

Duty owed to such a demanding God has ruined both father and (possibly) grandfather Wieland; now in this third generation, both son and daughter imagine an equally deterministic universe, or as Theodore expresses it, "We seem to be led hither by a kind of fatality" (43). The necessity claimed by such imagined duty calls up, too, a material determinism infused into what seems like every space of *Wieland*'s framework. One of the novel's most discussed emphases, for instance, is the Lockean notion of sense data as the primary source of knowledge.[19] A premise, in fact, of the Wielands' situation as it develops is the unreliability of the senses, their sensory "depravity," so to speak, which allows false information to appear as truth when the "evidence" of a supernatural being may well turn out to be only human machinations.[20] For Clara and Theodore, however, "proof" lies in the "material" world of sense data, a belief that disallows any radical distinction between physical and spiritual worlds—the spirit, here, takes some kind of "form" in the material world humans inhabit.

More consequentially, a materialism underpins the Wieland universe in the biological determinism operating upon the family. Brother and sister have both inherited all their father's spiritualism, including his deadly sense of duty and sacrifice—this, in spite of the fact that their father didn't raise or educate them. Clara mentions, for one thing, that she and her brother have been raised without religion, and yet both have a deep belief in a God as exacting as any institution might have taught them. Further, the family seems doomed not only to believe but to perish in the ecstacy of belief, a very specific set of familial traits traceable only to congenital predisposition Brown may have considered as inherited "blood." Of course, Clara's belief in a "genius of [her] birth" (95) and Theodore's acting out his depraved delusions guarantee nothing; readers have often disagreed as to the import of *Wieland*'s seeming determinism. Larzer Ziff, for example, writes that Brown had both an attraction to and repulsion from such a notion; others argue that the Calvinism lies only in the characters' fancies and that the novel dramatizes the evil consequences of the delusions—not real depravity.[21] We may not get to the bottom of Brown's own persuasion about this issue, but the novel does bear out, whether Calvinistic or not, a biological determinism and materiality behind its actions in the generational repetition of events. Whether the Wielands' depraved senses are real or imagined, whether their belief in a Divine Hand is warranted or not, the novel makes clear that these beliefs, at least, crop up in each generation, destroying physically those who believe imaginatively.

With this material basis of judgment and action, with the prompting to delusion or duty to God growing out of a familial connection to past generations, the Wieland saga describes a parabola of inherited, material consequences no less than it dramatizes an inheritance of property and a suggestion of incestuous, gentried isolation. John Irwin's study of doubling and incest provides insight into the Wieland family's apparently predetermined fate and its isolationist economics of property, for the repetition through time enacted at least by the male Wielands (remember that father and son even share the same given name) with their melancholy spiritualism, Irwin might argue, illustrates an "incestous" family situation wherein the isolation supporting repeated generations of behavior likewise encourages incest.[22] Specifically, "doubling and incest are both images of the self-enclosed—the inability of the ego to break out of the circle of the self and of the individual to break out of the ring of the family."[23] In the Wieland case, I would add that self-enclosure is enabled by the family's economic and social class, literally embodied in the property it inherits along with its blood.

The houses in *Wieland* in effect double the family to the degree that, to invoke the later "Fall of the House of Usher" and its incestuous brother and sister, the "house of Wieland" calls up "both the family and the family mansion."[24] The fate of the Wielands is inextricably bound together with their various properties, as Clara herself seems to indicate: "All happiness and dignity must henceforth be banished from the house and name of Wieland" (151). The elder Wieland's death is unthinkable without its setting in the Temple, for instance, given all the attention paid to this structure built for worship but repeatedly the theater of death and mystery. Though the structure itself changes very little, it represents quite various activities remarkably well. First designed as a spartan dwelling to house lonely worship, the Temple shows amazing transformative power when the younger generation adds its musical instruments, sofas, and bust of Cicero to create an appropriate scene for its activities. For all of its changes, the Temple acts as a lightning rod for each generation's demise. Likewise, scenes of terror seem to attach to particular dwellings in *Wieland*: Clara's dream and one altercation with the voices take place at the summerhouse, Clara overhears voices plotting her death in her private closet, she discovers sister-in-law Catharine dead in Clara's own bed, and the climactic scene of Theodore's return to kill his sister takes place in Clara's bedroom.

More than mere setting, the Wieland houses are haunted. In one sense, the novel is a ghost story, complete with inherited depravity, incestuous shadowings, and houses that hide mysterious persons and voices. And like other ghost stories (one recalls *The Turn of the Screw*), the action of terror centers on the house as the seat of private and domestic activity. The terror of these stories threatens the home, not just the house, in that the values of domesticity—privacy, chastity, family—are challenged by an outsider. While Theodore's wife and children are murdered by their own patriarch, destroying the family and its supposed mutual protectiveness, Clara is threatened in the most private of spaces with loss of life *and* virtue; discovering Carwin in her closet at one point, she believes he has come to rape her, and earlier, when she imagines Theodore in the closet, it's not clear just what she fears from him. In *Wieland,* the privacy of domesticity comes to be attacked by the elements of the domiciles themselves, which have taken on attributes of the public world in that they provide a theater for the shape-shifting, mercantile type—Carwin—

and since the structures can themselves accommodate changes in their appearance and function so readily. Like the public spaces of mercantile exchange described by Agnew as theatrically mercurial, the Wielands' properties allow for an interpenetration of the public world into supposedly private space.

Tricia Lootens's study of *The Haunting of Hill House* may gloss the Wieland haunted house as well, for Lootens describes a matrix of the familial and sexual, or private and "public" modes of exchange, wherein terror is "simultaneously familial and erotic," where nuclear families "kill where they are supposed to nurture."[25] What makes *Wieland* a story of terror as well as a story of psychological disintegration is that the danger comes from inside the house, that the characters do not lose a struggle "with the forces of the next world" but instead lose to their own intimate associates, though, importantly, those familial associates have been affected by the outsider—the "public" man—Carwin.[26] That the home should be a place of security goes without saying, but the home, especially as embodied in fiction, is more often than not an icon of absolute protection from the outside world and all its "public" values. As Marilyn Chandler writes, "the biblical notion of the 'world' as the devil's domain reinforced the idea that the home was a place of protection where one could be 'in the world but not of it.'"[27]

Ironically, the worldly domain outside the home calls to mind not only the demonic associations of much gothic fiction, but just as importantly suggests a market configuration of "dangerously" public values—a public "psychology" associated with the *spectral* consciousness of Adam Smithian exchange values. The "ghost" in Arthur Mervyn's public, spectacular frame of reference, what I have earlier called an indwelling "specter," is shadowed forth here in *Wieland* as a trace of the past, coupled with the intrusion of Carwin-the-public-man, to make of the novel something of a traditional ghost story at the same time the specter of public values likewise haunts the premises in a specifically market-oriented fashion. In other words, while the literal threat in *Wieland* does indeed come from inside the house, that private space has already been infused with the taint of publicity in the form of Carwin, bearing with him the spectral values of a world outside. It seems the Wieland family is "of the world" as well as "in" it. The Wielands' insularity, their refusal of reciprocity with a world beyond the home, even when (perhaps because?) that involvement might prove profitable, does not in the end insulate them from the ghosts of a public world.

As with the more standard-variety ghost story; *Wieland* portrays houses as "value-laden, animated agents of fate looming in the foreground, not the background, of human action."[28] Clara maintains an intimate connection with her "places," noting the summerhouse has been her private retreat and declaring sometimes that she has no need to fear her own closet. Yet her house she describes in frightening terms fairly often: during the second voices-from-the-closet scene, Clara notes the moonlight showing on the walls with "chequered" and "shadowy forms" (86). Returning to her house after the murders to collect her journal, soon to be threatened by brother Theodore, Clara experiences in slow motion her approach to the closet: "I passed the entry, mounted the stair, and unlocked the door of my chamber. It was with difficulty that I curbed my fancy and smothered my fears. Slight movements were transformed into beckoning shadows and calling shapes" (193). Servants on the property—"inhabitants of the *Hut*"—don't hesitate to say Clara's house is "haunted by a thousand ghastly apparitions" (192).

This haunting takes on a typical character of fear, with the shadows and the vaguely animate settings. More than that, the various dwellings, not content to be part of the "foreground" of the novel, take on an agency of their own, at least in Clara's gothic imagination. At the summerhouse, it is the "lulling sounds of the waterfall, the fragrance and the dusk" that "sink [her] into sleep" (62). The dwellings in general work upon her, the voices giving both cottage and summerhouse a "spirit," one she persists in claiming is personally interested and protective. Within this ghost story, Clara doesn't differ much from other heroines who, according to Lynette Carpenter and Wendy K. Kolmar, can view the supernatural activity of their houses as friendly. Women writers especially, they contend, "seem more likely to portray natural and supernatural experience along a continuum. Boundaries between the two are not absolute but fluid, so that the supernatural can be accepted, connected with, reclaimed, and can often possess a quality of familiarity."[29] Carpenter and Kolmar suggest that *Wieland* stands as legitimate forebear to later women writers, since the narrative is Clara's—"its heroine embattled and terrorized in her own home"—but one should also note that Theodore feels a similar familiarity with "spirits" in the temple.[30] In spite of her comfort with the supernatural, however, it is clear that Clara is released from the terrors resident in her house only when it burns: so fully invested in her home and its history is she, even after that home has ceased to enjoy only a system of private values after the intrusion of Carwin with his contagion of publicity, that she can only begin a recovery and go far away to Europe when the house is gone.

So mutually sustaining is Clara and her property that she has suffered, like the characters at Hill House, "a literal kinship with the house."[31] As long as her house is safe, impenetrable from the outside, so is Clara, such that the intact house replicates her intact body; once the house is invaded, Clara goes into a psychological decline from which she escapes only with many scars. The house, in its gothic, private, and insular configuration, "inhabits" Clara through the mechanism of her inherited past, but the ghosts of this house operate doubly, representing the public specter after Carwin's intrusion as well as a private past; Clara maintains her "kinship" with her property in both of its ghostly manifestations. If the house in this novel is a trope of the body, so too is the body a trope of the house. *Wieland* is filled with reminders of materiality at its gothic core: its houses, therefore, move beyond figuring the Wielands' fates—fates undeniably detrimental to body *and* spirit. The impenetrable link between body and property describes a fictional calculus wherein inherited houses perform the same haunting function toward the Wieland family as does their inherited, punishing "religion." The bodies of the family, then, come to be a locus of retribution, like their houses carrying the germ of their own destruction.

Inheriting property and mystical-neurotic "blood" equally, the Wieland family enacts a drama of class prerogatives as each member bears the fruit of previous generations behind the screen of the insular country estate. The material base of this haunting—its location in the body and the property—calls up an "incestuous" form of behavior for brother and sister Wieland, whose fast bond with past family members persists into closeness with each other so tight it includes them in shared biological inheritance, shared nightmares, and what appears to be shared bodies. If James Wilson is correct in assessing fictional brother-sister incest as symbolic of solipsism, *Wieland* carries solipsism to an extreme, working into the family's past and present both a self-enclosed economy of upper-class seclusion and a physicality of inheritance purveying bodies, spirits, and houses.[32]

The destruction of Theodore's family and near-destruction of Clara indicates more than a little criticism on Brown's part of a class of characters whose insularity and naiveté has so little protected them from themselves that any visit from the world outside upsets their fragile equilibrium explosively. Privacy itself appears to come under fire, therefore—a privacy so absolute as to be incestuous, since it's in the most intimate of ways that the family is threatened. What the world of *Wieland* lacks is a regulating contact with the public world, a publicity coming fully into being alongside an international market economy at the eighteenth century's end. In "proportion to the increasing prevalence of the capitalist mode of production, social relationships assumed the form of exchange relationships" at this time, Habermas writes, a mode of association having ambiguous consequences socially and psychically, to be sure, as Brown was to explore shortly in his *Arthur Mervyn,* but also functioning as a spectral, social eye to assure reciprocal exchange economically and familially.[33] Such exchange-based relations would reinforce an incest taboo as well, encouraging exchange of family along with capital and underscoring a sense of the Wieland family as incestuous simply by virtue of its seclusion from public oversight.

In *Wieland,* inheritance destroys, perhaps because in this scene of leisure-class suffering, what is lacking is publicity, and thus the virtues of a Constantia Dudley or an Arthur Mervyn are likewise missing. And given the brutal treatment of Clara by her author—given that Brown has her suffer the fires of lust, the spontaneous combustion of her father, the murder of nearly everyone close to her, and finally the burning of her own house without any consequential growth—Brown evidently took a low view of the upper crust, having them hoist on their own petard as the houses they inhabit and the blood they inherit turn on them to all but obliterate their kind. Compared to his successful and virtuous Constantia and Arthur, the Wielands' insularity might establish a pattern of virtue across Brown's novels wherein the striving-capitalist sort—the poor, needy, but ambitious youth—grows into virtue by way of labor, not unlike the author himself, furiously laboring with his pen to establish a name for himself in an era in which, as Blumin reminds us, a "middle class," not to mention an "authorial class," was not quite yet a viable category.[34] Yet Brown's view of the striving *lower* class, at the production of *Wieland* and its unfinished sequel *Memoirs of Carwin the Biloquist,* at any rate, is equally acidic. And surprisingly so, given his more measured treatment in *Arthur Mervyn* of what Theodore Wieland might call the "grasping" class, which appeared in two volumes in the two years following *Wieland.* In 1798, however, in *Carwin,* Brown generated a view of the merchant-class Carwin no less hateful than the insular and aristocratic Wielands.

In the juxtaposed narratives of *Wieland* and *Carwin the Biloquist,* an opposition of two styles of economies and the class structures they support evidence an at least semiconscious awareness, on Brown's part, of the class structures he embodied in his familiar narratives. Carwin, an early incarnation of the successful Arthur Mervyn, comes from ignorance and poverty: his father, a farmer like Arthur's, abuses Carwin for his ambitions, continually pressing his notion that the only education needed for farm work is reading enough to understand the Bible and math enough to calculate earnings. Carwin wants more, though, and is eventually sent to live with his aunt in the city and taught to expect an inheritance from her. When this scheme fails, Carwin is taken in by the shady Ludloe, a distinct parallel to Arthur's surrogate father, Welbeck, who promises Carwin all the wealth and comfort he could want if he would study to join a mysterious secret society, a little-disguised Illuminati.

Carwin bears an uncanny likeness to Arthur Mervyn, and in light of the later-created Arthur's success and relatively gentle handling on the part of his creator, this early incarnation of the poor, ambitious youth is instructive. Like Arthur, Carwin detests labor and studies to generate a living otherwise. Yet, though Carwin worries over his ability to keep the secrets of the Illuminati as demanded by Ludloe, it isn't a worry grown of virtue; he states clearly, in fact, that his "moral principles had hithero been vague and unsettled"; his later career as we see him in *Wieland* proves him more immoral than unsettled as he takes the lives of perfect strangers in his hands and destroys them for a lark.[35] Brown took great pains to develop Carwin as a lower-class youth striving beyond his class, and his villainy cannot be dissociated from his class in this fragment, just as Arthur Mervyn's virtue is a direct outgrowth of his own striving class. Judith, the treacherous servant who "acts" the part of Clara in Carwin's scene of lovemaking manufactured to ruin Clara's reputation is likewise a representative of the truly lower classes in this novel. By comparison to Louisa Conway, a nominal servant-become-family-member, Judith is not a credit to her rank; coupled as she is with Carwin, Judith reinforces a portrait of a most unvirtuous lower order.

At the time of *Wieland's* creation, then, Brown's critical examination seems to have cut both ways, since Carwin falls prey to the lowest sort of immorality as a result of his protectorless poverty at the same time his Wieland family is victimized by the inherited securities of its class. In theory "against kings and privilege and in favor of equality," Cowie remarks of Brown's attitude toward the upper class, he likewise harbored "an instinctive patrician scorn for the uncouth, unwashed mob."[36]

It comes as no surprise that Brown would have mixed reactions to what might have appeared the only two class options at large: one with the incestuous tendencies of the aristocracy and the other a groveling crowd dependent for favors upon its betters. As he again and again pointed out, the United States had not yet developed a literature nor had it provided a "place" for literary types, writers who fell into neither class. As Gordon Wood argues, the era of the 1790s offered more economic and social risk than security, what with a prevailing view that an economy based entirely in credit capital would cast its lot with the merely imaginary. As a result, according to Smith-Rosenberg, even basic definitions of class categories were in flux, allowing simultaneously a held-over conservative, classical republican ideal of the propertied upper class as "virtuous" at the same time that a newer, "commercial-republican" ideal of virtue as "frugality" and "application" was coming along to replace the previous era's idea of virtue.[37] Brown bore two distinct responses to his contemporary class options: as Watts explains, while Brown saw de-

mocracy as allowing more wealth to more people, wealth in a democracy is spread out thin, leaving little excess to patronize arts and letters, though the other option—a European-style aristocratic system—provides for cultural support only through excess money gained in abuse of the lower orders.[38] Suspicions about both extremes seem to prevail in Brown's *Wieland* and *Carwin,* though *Arthur Mervyn* would soon evidence an order of virtue aligned with the public world of commercial enterprise.

The private world of *Wieland,* then, a world aristocratically insular, familially enclosed, and psychologically damaging, comes under fire for its very privacy, for as Habermas explains of the growing "publicity" of the late eighteenth century, the "Law of Opinion judged virtues and vices; virtue, indeed, was measured precisely in terms of public esteem" to a degree that "secularized morality" was taking the place of "privatized religious faith."[39] If Brown was even semiconsciously describing an economy of property ownership in *Wieland* by comparison with a cash- and credit-economy in *Carwin the Biloquist,* with perhaps a growing notion of the Arthur Mervyn who would make *morality* conversant with a market economy, I would argue that he likewise defined Clara Wieland in gendered terms of property and virtue by comparison with a standard of moral activity embodied in the "Republican wife."[40] While Brown's Constantia Dudley may be virtuous only by careful dissociation from the marketplace, such dissociation is not enough for Brown's fictional females: Clara Wieland, refusing the role of domestic womanhood, falls prey to every species of terrorism. As a woman whose home is unsuitably removed from the publicity that regulates, a woman inappropriately following the male habits of intellect rather than the domestic calling of virtuous, laboring womanhood, Clara's virtue is constantly questioned. For Clara, the economic class that sets her apart from the world of work likewise defines her as less than virtuous.

VIRTUE AND VOICE: AN ECONOMICS OF GENDER

If the Wieland family is torn asunder at least in part because its insular class structure implodes the family in on itself, it is also the case that Wieland brother and sister encourage one another's inward-looking delusions and protect one another from the public world. Indeed, Theodore and Clara double one another's personality in a resemblance uncanny except for the legitimating cause of their patrimony, an inheritance equally controlling of and damaging to both. That brother and sister behave similarly is one thing; that they so consistently replicate one another's thoughts is quite another. Clara enters so much into Theodore's state of mind that at the crisis of her story, even though she has herself pled with Carwin to simulate a divine voice to stay Theodore's hand against her, she shares Theodore's experience of the

(5[1791]:142). Less favorable opinions on novel-reading in the same magazine appeared in the issue of October, 1792 (6:225-26, 262).

26. Perhaps some such regret that *Female Quixotism* could not be taken quite seriously was expressed in the *Monthly Anthology*: "Many of us have doubtless dwelt with great sympathy on the pathetick story of the unfortunate Dorcasina Sheldon, and have been inclined to believe that the ingenious author had almost out-quixoted Don Quixote" (5[1808]:499).

Bibliography

[Brown, William Hill.] *The Power of Sympathy; or, The Triumph of Nature.* 2 vols. Boston, 1789 (R). Subsequent editions: Edited by Walter Littlefield. Boston, 1894; edited by Milton Ellis. New York: Facsimile Text Society, 1937; with an introduction by Herbert Brown. Boston: New Frontiers Press, 1961; definitive edition edited by William S. Kable. Columbus: Ohio State University Press, 1969.

[Foster, Hannah Webster.] *The Boarding School; or, Lessons of a Preceptress to her Pupils.* Boston, 1798.

Hitchcock, Enos. *Memoirs of the Bloomsgrove Family.* 2 vols. Boston, 1790.

Mitchell, Isaac. *The Asylum; or, Alonzo and Melissa.* 2 vols. Poughkeepsie, N.Y., 1811.

[Neal, John.] *Keep Cool.* 2 vols. Baltimore, 1817.

[Read, Martha.] *Monima; or, the Beggar Girl.* 2d ed. New York, 1803.

[Relf, Samuel.] *Infidelity, or the Victims of Sentiment.* Philadelphia, 1797.

Rowson, Susanna Haswell. *The Inquisitor; or, Invisible Rambler.* 3 vols. Philadelphia, 1793.

[Tenney, Tabitha.] *Female Quixotism: Exhibited in the Romantic Opinions and Extravagant Adventures of Dorcasina Sheldon.* 2 vols. Boston, 1801.

[Tyler, Royall.] *The Algerine Captive; or, The Life and Adventures of Doctor Updike Underhill.* 2 vols. Walpole, N.H., 1797 (R). Subsequent edition: With an introduction by Jack B. Moore. Gainesville, Fla.: Scholars' Facsimiles & Reprints, 1967.

Wirt, William. *The Old Bachelor.* Richmond, Va., 1814.

Sally C. Hoople (essay date 1984)

SOURCE: Hoople, Sally C. "The Spanish, English, and American Quixotes." *Anales Cervantinos* 22 (1984): 1-24.

[*In the following essay, Hoople traces the influence of Miguel de Cervantes's* Don Quixote *on Charlotte Lennox's* The Female Quixote *and Tenney's* Female Quixotism.]

Tabitha Tenney's novel *Female Quixotism,* which was published in Boston in 1801, is, as Duyckinck says, "one of the numerous literary progeny of Cervantes' immortal satire."[1] Moreover, in many ways Tenney is closely related to two other early authors whose work reflects the influence of *Don Quixote.* Although Charlotte Lennox was born in New York in 1720, she moved to England in 1735, where her novel *The Female Quixote* was published in 1752. In spite of tenuous claims that she was the first American novelist[2], generally she is regarded as an English writer. Her novel, like the greater *Don Quixote* and the made-in-U.S.A. *Female Quixotism,* humorously attacks the negative effects of reading romances. While *Modern Chivalry* (published in numerous parts between 1792 and 1815), by Hugh Henry Brackenridge[3], does not specifically satirize the reading habits of young girls, it does deal topically with a broad range of subjects which Brackenridge subjects to his critical scrutiny.

M. F. Heiser, who traces *Don Quixote*'s American literary offspring, notes that "the flowering of the creative influence of Cervantes in the United States came early, between 1790 and 1815."[4] In a similar study Harry Levin observes that "the profoundest tribute to Cervantes is that which other writers have paid him by imitation and emulation."[5] Washington Irving's keen interest in Cervantes, an enthusiasm which included extensive early research for a biography of *Don Quixote*'s creator, offers evidence of the popularity of Cervantes during the period of the early Republic. James Russell Lowell, including among Cervantes' imitators such writers as Sterne, Fielding, Smollett, Irving (in *Knickerbocker*), and Dickens (in *Pickwick Papers*), indicates that he does not mention his list of imitators "as detracting from *their* originality, but only as showing the wonderful virility of *his*."[6]

Providing a central theme for Lennox and Tenney, Cervantes creates in Don Quixote a character whose derangement springs from excessive study of books. Influenced primarily by Spanish romances such as the works of sixteenth-century author Feliciano de Silva, "whose lucid prose style and involved conceits were as precious to him as pearls"[7], Quixote revels in fictional tales of chivalry and love. Charlotte Lennox's heroine, Arabella, overindulges in seventeenth-century French romances which, while they have, often, some basis in history, deal with extravagantly improbable exploits of heroism and virtue. Swayed by the English romances, such as Samuel Richardson's *Sir Charles Grandison,* of the eighteenth century, Tenney's heroine, Dorcasina becomes obsessed with a diet of straight sentimental fiction. The common factor which Arabella and Dorcasina inherit from Don Quixote is the mental aberration which results from their fictional journey away from mundane but trustworthy reality.

Linked to Cervantes' hero, Don Quixote, by their common separation from reality and their eccentric entrance into an unreal world of imagination, Dorcasina and Arabella share with Quixote another quality: not one is completely devoid of sanity, and all possess under certain circumstances a high degree of humanitarianism and lucidity. Dorcasina's maid Betty and Arabella's "favorite woman" Lucy, like Captain Farrago's Irish servant Teague O'Regan in *Modern Chivalry,* function as foils to their superiors. However, whereas Betty and Lucy in their usual common-sense responses to their mistresses' aberrations reflect Sancho Panza, Teague possesses qualities of both Don Quixote and Sancho. Lacking the intellect and imaginative powers of Sancho's master, he could hardly be called a composite of the two characters, but he does combine Don Quixote's self-delusions with the rollicking earthiness of Sancho. The three books mirror the conflict between illusion and reality which their literary Spanish forebear discloses, frequently adopting Cervantes' device of developing this conflict through the use of disguises and masquerades. Acting out their dreams within an episodic structure, these quixotic characters and their companions bumble through a strange world of distorted realism and outrageous humor.

A tutelary forerunner of the derangement of Arabella and Dorcasina, Don Quixote's mania springs from an inordinate reading of romances, in his case Renaissance. Even Captain Farrago, whom Brackenridge portrays as a comparatively stable personality, is "in some things whimsical, owing perhaps to his greater knowledge of books than of the world."[8] Setting a precedent for Tenney, Cervantes states in his Prologue that one purpose for writing his book "is that of undermining the ill-founded edifice that is constituted by those books of chivalry, so abhorred by many, but admired by many more" (p. 16)[9]. According to Cervantes' novel, Don Quixote becomes so immersed in fantastic books of chivalry that he neglects his hunting and his estate, and even sells much of his land to provide funds for purchasing his beloved books:

> In short, our gentleman became so immersed in his reading that he spent whole nights from sundown to sunup and his days from dawn to dusk in poring over his books, until, finally, from so little sleeping and so much reading, his brain dried up and he went completely out of his mind. He had filled his imagination with everything that he had read, with enchantments, knightly encounters, battles, challenges, wounds, with tales of love and its torments, and all sorts of impossible things, and as a result had come to believe that all these fictitious happenings were true; they were more real to him than anything else in the world.
>
> (p. 27)

The canon, however, recognizes in Don Quixote the vacillation of his mental faculties: he "could not but be struck by the strange nature of his madness and was as-tonished at the extremely sensible manner in which the knight talked and answered questions, losing his stirrups, so to speak, only when the subject of chivalry was mentioned" (p. 437).

Attempting to convince Don Quixote that his reading habits are the cause of his separation from reality, just as the people close to Dorcasina will chide her for reading illusion-breeding novels, the canon reasons with his besotted friend:

> Is it possible, my good sir, that those disgusting books of chivalry which your grace has read in your idle hours have had such an effect upon you as to turn your head, causing you to believe that you are being carried away under a magic spell and other things of that sort that are as far from being true as truth itself is from falsehood?

Describing his own contact with such "mendacious and frivolous" books, the canon declares that when he reflects "upon their real character", he flings "the best of them against the wall and would even toss them into the fire, if there happened to be one at hand[10]; for they are deserving of the same punishment as cheats and imposters." Disturbed that "these audacious works even upset the minds of intelligent and wellborn gentlemen like" Don Quixote, he pleads with his friend to "return to the bosom of common sense, and wisely make use of the many gifts with which Heaven has seen fit to endow" him "by applying" his "fertile mind to reading" books that will improve his conscience and reputation (437-38). Later the canon reiterates his tribute to Don Quixote's fundamental intelligence and his grief that such an intellect should yield to the corruptive influences of bad reading: "nor is it any reason why a man like your Grace, so worthy and respected and endowed with so fine a mind, should permit himself to believe that all the mad things described in those nonsensical books of chivalry are true" (p. 441).

Cursing the books of chivalry that have turned his head, Don Quixote's housekeeper declares that "such books as those" should "be consigned to Satan and Barabbas, for they have sent to perdition the finest mind in all La Mancha" (p. 50). Whatever her qualifications for judging character may be, critic Thomas Mann obviously does not completely concur with her evaluation. Nevertheless, he does show reverence for Don Quixote's positive qualities:

> Don Quixote is of course a simpleton; that is clear from his mania of knight-errantry. But his obsolete whimsy is also the source of such true nobility, such purity of life, such an aristocratic bearing, such winning and respect-compelling traits, physical and mental, that our laughter over his grotesque and doleful countenance is always mingled with amazed respect. No one can know him and not feel drawn to the high-minded and pathetic man, mad in one single point but in all others a blameless knight.[11]

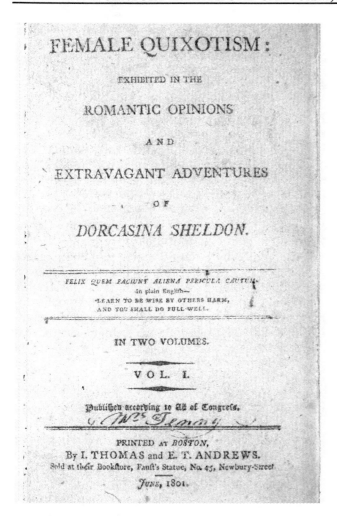

FEMALE QUIXOTISM:

EXHIBITED IN THE

ROMANTIC OPINIONS

AND

EXTRAVAGANT ADVENTURES

OF

DORCASINA SHELDON.

FELIX QUEM FACIUNT ALIENA PERICULA CAUTUM.
In plain English.
"LEARN TO BE WISE BY OTHERS HARM,
AND YOU SHALL DO FULL WELL."

IN TWO VOLUMES.

VOL. I.

Published according to Act of Congress.
Mrs Tenney

PRINTED AT BOSTON,
By I. THOMAS and E. T. ANDREWS.
Sold at their Bookstore, Faust's Statue, No. 45, Newbury-Street.

June, 1801.

A number of critics, like Mann, have wrestled with the seemingly paradoxical juxtaposition of Don Quixote's lunacy and nobility. In his Introduction to Henry Fielding's *Joseph Andrews,* for example, Maynard Mack discusses the ambiguity attendant upon interpretation of the Quixotic character. Linking Parson Adams and the collision of his dream world with the real world to Don Quixote's impractical, even crackbrained idealism, Mack observes that naïve Adams is, "like his forebear, partly hero and partly dupe."[12] Tracing the development of criticism on *Don Quixote* before 1800, Anthony Close notes an increasingly sympathetic approach to Quixote's madness and the stress on his positive human attributes: "Another step in this direction is the widespread, and just, recognition of the qualities of humanity, charity, and goodness in the character of Cervantes's hero."[13]

Aptly describing Quixote's erratic mental condition "as a checkerboard of lucidity and insanity", Vladimir Nabokov discusses the "mystery of his dual nature" in which "he appears as a crazy sane man, or an insane one on the verge of sanity; a striped madman, a dark mind with lucid interspaces."[14] Just as for Don Quixote

"reality and illusion are interwoven in the pattern of life"[15], similarly Mrs. Lennox's Arabella experiences a monomania which renders her irrational, but is a fixation only in the realm of romantic love in fiction. Like Don Quixote, who has imbibed Spanish romances of knight-errantry, Arabella has suffered mental aberration from exposure to such seventeenth-century French heroic romances as Madeleine de Scudéry's *Artamenes* and *Clelia*[16], yet passage after passage of *The Female Quixote* describes a beautiful young woman of outstanding intelligence, elegance, and compassion. Recognizing these characteristics, Glanville, Arabella's cousin, who is in love with her, sorrows at her eccentric behavior in banishing him for the offense of declaring his passion for her, but cannot ascribe her actions to rudeness because of "the Elegance of her Manners, in every other respect." Examining her intelligence, he also concludes that it is not "possible to doubt she had a great Share of Understanding; since her Conversation, singular as some of her Sentiments seemed to him, was far superior to most other Ladies" (p. 37).

Although the victimized Glanville hardly passes for an objective observer, one cannot ignore his testimony completely. Cognizant of Arabella's idiosyncrasies, he thinks to himself: "One would swear this dear Girl's Head is turned . . . if she had not more *Wit* than her whole Sex besides" (p. 41). Critic M. F. Heiser supports Glanville's evaluation by noting that Arabella is "like Don Quixote possessed of wit and sense in all but this her one foible."[17] When Arabella compels Glanville to read her favorite romances, he ponders the incongruity of her devotion to the ideas which have imprisoned the imagination of the woman whom he considers "one of the most accomplished Ladies in the World" (p. 50). Surely this sentiment is reminiscent of the regret which Don Quixote's loyal housekeeper expresses about the corruptive influence of books upon "the finest mind in all La Mancha" (p. 50). Even Glanville's skeptical father, Sir Charles, becomes somewhat convinced of the superiority of Arabella's merits in spite of her strange romantic whimsy. When they do not discuss Romances, he finds her conversation "fine, easy, and entertaining" (p. 65).

Not only does Arabella under normal circumstances function with comparative sanity and display considerable intelligence, but when she is not in the silly romantic throes of self-centeredness and outrageous expectations, she becomes, as Maynadier observes, "a lady of true delicacy, lovable and charming in spite of her illusions."[18] When Sir Charles, rankled by Arabella's request that he leave the room after he has scolded her about her whimsies of the imagination, complains to his son about her rusticity, Glanville protests that she

has as little of the Rustic as if she had passed all her Life in a Court. Her fine Sense, and the native Elegance of her Manners give an inimitable Grace to her Behaviour; and as much exceed the studied Politeness of other Ladies I have conversed with, as the Beauties of her Person do all I have ever seen.

(p. 64)

She also displays superior personal qualities in contrast to her new acquaintance, Miss Groves, whose conversation, lacking the refinement of Arabella's, is limited to "Fashions, Assemblies, Cards, or Scandal." Arabella, on the other hand, treats the woman with a civility that reflects "native Elegance and Simplicity of . . . Manners . . . accompanied with so much real Benevolence of Heart, such insinuating Tenderness, and Graces so irresistible" that Miss Groves is "quite oppressed with them" (p. 68).

The illness and death of Arabella's father elicits his daughter's compassion and tenderness of character. As he lies dying, she assumes all of the care for him, performing her duties with the utmost solicitude and watching by his bedside throughout each night: "As the Marquis's Indisposition increased, so did her Care and Assiduity: She would not allow any one to give him any thing but herself; bore all the pettish Humours of a sick man with a surprising Sweetness and Patience" (p. 58). Later her response to the terms of her father's will, leaving one-third of his estate to Glanville if Arabella does not marry him, confirms her natural good nature and benevolence. Instead of becoming disturbed by her own loss of property, she expresses pleasure at these conditions and wishes Glanville "Joy of the Estate that was bequeathed to him, with a most inchanting Sweetness" (p. 66). Her immediate reaction to the Marquis's death, however, while it reveals the depth of her love for him, displays such an extravagant degree of bathos and melodrama that one cannot dispute Lennox's satirical intentions. After reviving from her perilous illness, which has prevented her from attending the funeral, she mourns her loss in an inordinate complaint which surely mocks the romantic convention of the complaint, and suggests emotional instability:

> Merciless Fate! said she, in the most moving Tone imaginable, Cruel Destiny! that, not contented with having deprived my Infancy of the soft Cares, and tender Indulgences, of a Mother's Fondness, has robbed me of the only Parent I had left, and exposed me, at these early Years, to the Grief of losing him, who was not only my Father, but my Friend, and Protector of my Youth!
>
> Then, pausing a Moment, she renewed her Complaints with a deep Sigh: Dear Relics of the best of Fathers! pursued she, Why was it not permitted me to bathe you with my Tears? Why were those sacred Remains of him, from whom I drew my Life, snatched from my Eyes, ere they had poured their Tribute of Sorrow over them? Ah! pitiless Women! said she to her Attendants, you prevented me from performing the last pious Rites to my dear Father! You, by your cruel Care, hindered me from easing my sad Heart, by paying him the last

Duties he could receive from me! Pardon, O dear and sacred Shade of my beloved Father! pardon this unwilling Neglect of thy afflicted Child, who, to the last Moment of her wretched Life, will bewail thy Loss.

(pp. 59-60)

In spite of Glanville's explanations that these complaints are not uncommon for a person who is mourning, his father questions Arabella's basic lucidity, concluding that these "are the strangest complaints" that he has "ever heard, and favour so much of Phrensy" that he fears "her Head is not quite right" (p. 60).

In the midst of Arabella's pathetic expressions of grief, Charlotte Lennox inserts sly humor in her description of Sir Charles who, when he meets Arabella, gazes upon "her with as much Admiration as his Son, though with less Passion" (p. 60). When Glanville chides her for harming herself by the extremity of her grief, Arabella retorts by citing examples of exaggerated mourning in seventeenth-century French literature and thus incurs Sir Charles's disapproval of her indulgence in "such Romances" that "only spoil Youth, and put strange Notions into their Heads" (p. 61). These elements of mockery in the midst of sorrow reveal a modified form of the reaction to the original Don Quixote's death which leads Thomas Mann to remark that "it is easy to give a comic turn to the description of sincere sorrow." Describing the wholehearted mourning at Don Quixote's passing, Mann nevertheless notes "the grotesque description of 'the sluices of their swollen eyes when the news that he must die forced a torrent of tears from their eyes and a thousand groans from their hearts.'" Mann reinforces this comic turn by acknowledging the inevitable intrusion of mundane creature needs and desires into the midst of elevated emotions:

> "Human nature is human nature", "life must go on", and so forth . . . We are told that during the three days of Don Quixote's agony, though "the whole house was in confusion, yet the niece ate, the housekeeper drank, and Sancho Panza made much of himself; for this business of legacies effaces, or moderates, the grief that is naturally due to the deceased". A mocking tribute to realism, an unsentimental attitude which may once have caused offence.[19]

Like Don Quixote and Arabella, their descendant Tenney's Dorcasina is an ambiguous character who, but for her addiction to novels and their illusory realm, is "in every respect a sensible, judicious, and amiable girl" (*Female Quixotism,* I, 4), who "had received from nature a good understanding, a lively fancy, an amiable cheerful temper, and a kind and affectionate heart. What a number of valuable qualities were here blended" (I, 7). While Mrs. Tenney lists these "engaging endowments" as a contrast to Dorcasina's negative characteristics—"she was unfortunately of a very romantic turn, had a small degree of obstinacy, and a spice too much of vanity" (I, 7)—the essentially moralizing author stresses repeatedly that in the midst of the heroine's monomania, qualities of intelligence and benevolent humanity shine forth. In spite of her inordinate reading, Dorcasina devotes much time to "the superintendance of" her father's "domestic concerns" (I, 9), and when her first suitor, Lysander, visits the Sheldon family with his father for several weeks, he falls in love with her as each day he discovers "new beauties" and sees "so many proofs of her sweetness of temper, condescension to the servants, and duty and affection to her father" that he finally regards her unusually "well calculated to render a man happy" (I, 20-21). During their conversations "her usual intelligence sparkled in her countenance" (I, 20), a clear indication that though her mind may be distorted, she exhibits a high degree of intellectual perspecuity. Her values, however, become warped to the point that, instead of rejoicing in Lysander's letter of proposal and tribute to her goodness, she is mortified that he has not expressed rapture over her personal and physical charms.

For four years after her rejection of Lysander, Dorcasina lives in comparative seclusion, frightening away suitors by her obsessive dedication to novels. This compulsive distraction notwithstanding, paradoxically she also devotes much time to "attendance upon her father, and acts of piety and charity", and Tenney describes her as "really pious, but not ostentatious; and the mild, charitable, and liberal complexion of her religion, was one of her greatest ornaments" (I, 27). In fact she becomes so notable for her charitable deeds that the indigent come to her from many miles around with assurance of assistance, "for it was her invariable rule to send none away empty handed; and the poor and weary traveller was sure to find entertainment and refreshment under this hospitable roof" (I, 28). At the end of *Female Quixotism* in her letter to her friend Harriot Stanly Barry, Dorcasina describes her plan to use her considerable fortune in seeking out "proper objects of charity . . . and to bestow on them what I have no occasion to use myself" (III, 224)[20].

Not only is Dorcasina charitable toward the poor, but like Arabella she is so solicitous of her father that when he becomes ill, she is unable to eat and experiences great distress. When he suffers a relapse after seeing her in O'Connor's arms, she expresses a willingness to lay down her life for her father. When he questions her about her compromising situation, "her pure mind, unused to deceit, disdained even on this occasion to equivocate", (I, 96). Later Mr. Sheldon laments his daughter's silly infatuation and the injurious effect it has had upon her judgment and values: "Your moral principles have been carefully formed, and your conduct has ever been a model of the purest virtue: what then would have been your distress to have found yourself allied to vice, profligacy and meanness?" (I, 194).

After she has finally become convinced of the deceitfulness of her false suitors O'Connor and Philander, she conducts her life with relative sanity for a number of years, devoting her time to family duties and to the happiness of her father (II, 77). When her father is stricken with his final illness, Dorcasina reacts, as Arabella does, with terrified distraction: "She wrung her hands in the deepest distress; hung over her senseless father, in speechless agony; then, turning her eyes to heaven, fervently prayed that he might be restored" (III, 12). While she does not indulge in extravagant complaints after her father's death, she does spring "forward to embrace the breathless corpse". Like Arabella, she faints, and succumbs to "a universal weakness, which" deprives "her of the melancholy satisfaction of following the remains of her beloved parent to the grave" (III, 15), and renders her incapacitated by severe illness for many months. Although Tenney describes Dorcasina's mourning in its extreme manifestation, the author's terseness in dealing with its effects affords a higher degree of realism and of sincerity, albeit with a hint of gentle mockery, than Lennox's protracted passage setting forth her Arabella's complaints.

In the intervals between her ridiculous infatuations and emotional traumas climaxed by her father's death, Dorcasina seems to attain a balanced perspective between her fictional illusions and the real world about her, although these illusions have so powerful a grasp that a new incident fraught with romantic potential topples the balance in an instant. Thus Tenney as creator shrewdly portrays a character whose derangement, like Quixote's, alternates precariously with lucidity. Dorcasina conducts herself with propriety and becomes "as rational a woman in regard to love and marriage, as she was in every other respect" (II, 191). She impresses Mr. Cumberland with her industriousness, yet it is primarily her romantically unrealistic expectations about courtship that cause her to reject his prosaic advances. Finally, however, shorn of her illusions, she visits her friends Mr. Stanly and Mr. and Mrs. Barry for two weeks, "conducting, during the whole time, and conversing with so much propriety and good sense, unmixed with any of her former extravagance, that they were extremely delighted with her, and thought her a most valuable and agreeable companion" (III, 218). Later, finding herself virtually alone in the world, she expresses to Betty chagrin about her former conduct, embarrassed that she "cannot look back without blushing for" her "follies". Betty, however, comforts with these observations: "I am sure, ma'am. . . . I don't know whose conduct will bear reflection, if yours won't; so good, and kind, and charitable, and dutiful as you have always been" (III, 219). Instead of anger at the Stanlys for their masquerades and other deceptions in attempting to rid her of her delusions, she is grateful to them for enlightening her. Thus the blunt statement which Thomas Mann makes about Don Quixote may also apply to Arabella and Dorcasina: "Don Quixote is a bit cracked but not in the least stupid."[21]

In another clear parallel to Cervantes' immortal Don Quixote, lesser mortals like Arabella, Dorcasina, and Captain Farrago have serving companions who, to a certain extent, are patterned after Sancho Panza, but also, in varying degrees, function as mirrors of their leaders. Heiser refers to Lucy as "akin to, if not as humorous as, the realist Sancho Panza"[22], and Maynadier labels her as "a Sancho Panza changed in sex."[23] Closely aligned with Lucy, Betty is, according to Duyckinck, "a female Sancho Panza"[24], whom Alexander Cowie describes as an "extremely realistic Sancho-Panza-ish maid."[25] Although Fred Lewis Pattee sees in the book an acute lack of humor and an unrealistic "treatment of the Sancho Panza character, Betty"[26], I tend to agree with Ola Elizabeth Winslow's assessment of Betty "as a more original creation than the mistress", one that "might even have amused Cervantes in moments."[27] While Carl Van Doren sees in Captain Farrago "a new Don Quixote" and in Teague "a grotesque and witless Sancho Panza"[28], Heiser claims that "Captain Farrago is not a Don Quixote", and although Teague "has Sancho's appetites and is governed by his five senses . . . the situation is somewhat reversed: the servant is quixotic, and the master a judicial devotee of reason and common sense."[29] To a certain extent each subordinate character contains the complexity and ambiguity that Henry Grattan Doyle, in his Introduction to *Don Quixote,* perceives in Sancho Panza: "Don Quixote's other self . . . who represents the earthy 'when do we eat' side of our dual nature."[30]

The primary characteristic which Lucy and Betty share with Sancho is obedience, though reluctant at times, and ridiculous at others. Forsaking his wife and children, Sancho consents to become Don Quixote's squire. Although his motives are mercenary and questionable— Don Quixote has promised to make him governor of an island—he accepts his duties and his master's idiosyncrasies with a resigned "God's will be done" and modified concessions such as the one he makes after Quixote's disastrous encounter with the windmills: "I believe everything that your Grace says; but straighten yourself up in the saddle a little, for you seem to be slipping down on one side, owing, no doubt, to the shaking-up that you received in your fall" (*Don Quixote,* p. 64). Sancho's obedience is perhaps suspect when he, like Don Quixote, refuses to pay an innkeeper, "even though it cost him his life" (p. 127), arguing that he will not violate Quixote's avowed code of knight-errantry which precludes payment for lodgings. However, in spite of his vocal disagreements with his master and threats to leave him, Sancho expresses admiration of Quixote's bravery—"in all the days of my life I have never served a more courageous master than your Grace" (p. 76)— and weeps when the Knight proposes to set out alone

on a hazardous task. Even in this event Sancho obviously has ulterior reasons for his grief, fearing that he will lose his island. Whatever his motives, Sancho resolves to remain with his master to the very end, even when Quixote strikes his servant as punishment after Sancho ridicules him. In his discussion of Don Quixote's purity of spirit, Thomas Mann finds

> it exquisite that Sancho Panza the pot-bellied, with his proverbs, his mother wit, his shrewd peasant judgment of human nature, who has no use for the "idea" that results in beatings, but rather for the skin of liquor— Sancho Panza has feeling for this spirit. He loves his good albeit ridiculous master despite all the hardship that loyalty to him incurs; does not leave him nor stir from his side, but serves him with honest and admiring fealty—even though sometimes he may lie to him at need.[31]

Less rebellious than Sancho or Betty, Lucy obeys passively nearly every order which Arabella issues and accepts almost completely her mistress's every whim. When Arabella attributes the departure of the gardener, Edward, to "some new Design he had formed to obtain her . . . *Lucy* who always thought as her Lady did, was of the same Opinion" (*The Female Quixote,* p. 26), although the other servants more realistically link his withdrawal to his alleged theft of a carp and his fear of detection. Even the docile Lucy, however, deviates from total passivity under extreme circumstances. When, for instance, Arabella commands her to relate her mistress's history, complete with the minutest words, actions, thoughts, gestures, "Smiles, Half-smiles, Blushes, Turnings pale, Glances, Pauses, Full-stops, Interruptions; the Rise and Falling of my Voice, every Motion of my Eyes", Lucy in despair perceives the impossibility of the task and retorts, "Lord bless me! Madam . . . I never, till this Moment, it seems, knew the hundreth, thousandth Part of what was expected from me: I am sure, if I had, I would never have gone to Service; for I might well know I was not fit for such Slavery" (p. 122). Nevertheless, in spite of her mild protests, Lucy serves her mistress with a high degree of obedience, especially in light of Arabella's fantastic behavior and demands, and credulously believes most of her mistress's delusions about men who are perishing from infatuation with her. Believing Arabella's stories about Edward, Lucy sobbingly tells Glanville, "You must know, Sir . . . that there came a Man here to take away my Lady: A great Man he is, though he worked in the Gardens; for he was in Love with her: And so he would not own who he was" (p. 97). Even when she scolds her mistress after Arabella receives a letter from the conniving Bellmour in which he falsely claims he will die for love of her, Lucy acts under the illusory apprehension that Arabella has placed upon her:

> Oh! Madam! cried *Lucy* . . . Never was such a sad mournful Letter in the World: I could cry my Eyes out for the poor Gentleman. Pray excuse me, Madam; but,

indeed, I can't help saying, You are the most hardheart-edest Lady I ever knew in my born Days: Why, to be sure, you don't care, if an hundred fine Gentlemen should die for you, tho' their Spirits were to haunt you every Night!

(p. 175)

According to Heiser, just as Dorcasina, is "a much closer counterpart of Don Quixote than Arabella"[32], so Betty is modeled more closely after Sancho Panza than Lucy is. Certainly Heiser's comparison of Betty's situation, in which she "suffers many indignities in the comedy of errors inevitably the result of her mistress' blind singleness of mind"[33], to that of Sancho applies also to Lucy's dilemma. It is true also that Lucy, like Betty and Sancho, initially perceives clearly and literally the actions which surround her. When Lucy reports to Arabella that Mr. Hervey laughed at his own mistake after opening the letter that he thought was Arabella's answer to his, only to discover that she had returned his note unopened, Arabella interprets his laughter as the disturbance of his reason resulting from the shock to his system. When Lucy hears Arabella's fears that Mr. Hervey might die from unrequited love, she begins "to think there was something more, than she imagined, in this Affair" (p. 15).

Betty, however, remains more skeptical about Dorcasina's charms—to a certain extent for good reason, because Dorcasina lacks Arabella's physical beauty—and frequently attempts to reason with her mistress. When Dorcasina entertains romantic notions about Lysander before ever meeting him, Betty suggests realistic moderation: "Perhaps you and the young gentleman wont fall so violently in love with each other as you imagine; and perhaps you never will become his wife" (I, 15-16). Not trusting O'Connor, Betty then also attempts to reason with Dorcasina and suggests that Mr. Sheldon perhaps has justification for turning against the Irishman. While her argument is simplistic—"Well ma'am, isn't it as likely you should be deceived as your father? He is older than you, and ought therefore to know more" (I, 161)—her innate common sense correctly tells her that Dorcasina's impetuosity could lead only to a disastrous union with O'Connor. However, in spite of her arguments with her mistress and her more open rebelliousness in, for example, such incidents as her protest against dressing in Mr. Sheldon's clothes in a mock romantic imitation of O'Connor, Betty, like Sancho and Arabella, in most instances finally declines comment and adheres obediently to the wishes of Dorcasina.

Although all three books stress the down-to-earth realism and the saving common sense of these three subordinates, certain elements undermine this seemingly characteristic quality. Also weak willed and credulous, Lucy absorbs Arabella's illusions and responds to her mistress's foibles accordingly. Doyle makes the observa-

tion that "Sancho becomes more and more like his master, his master more and more like his squire—even to quoting proverbs."[34] While Betty is more successful than Lucy in retaining her integrity in the face of her mistress's romantic delusions, she, like Sancho, who shakes "like someone who had had a dose of mercury" and whose teeth chatter "like those of a person who has the quartan fever" (pp. 139-140), quails before what appears supernatural to her, consequently performing with Dorcasina an alternating game of illusion versus reality.

Referring to the "strange and subtle interechoes between the knight and his squire . . . two heroes, their shadows merging in one and overlapping, forming a certain unity that we must accept"[35], Nabokov discusses the alterations that take place in the two characters as *Don Quixote* progresses. In the beginning Nabokov perceives in Cervantes the intention "to give his lionhearted lunatic a witless coward for squire, in manner of contrapuntal contrast: lofty madness and low stupidity."[36] Tracing Sancho's decline from lucidity to absentmindedness, and from his attempts to cure his master's illusions to his role of enchanter in reinforcing Quixote's delusions about Dulcinea, Nabokov alludes to various commentators' conclusions "that both Don Quixote's madness and Sancho's common sense are mutually infectious, and that while, in the second part of the book, Don Quixote develops a sanchoid strain, Sancho, on the other hand, becomes as mad as his master." Quoting Salvador de Madariaga, who "sees Sancho as a kind of transposition of Don Quixote in a different key"[37], Nabokov notes that master and servant "seem to swap dreams and destinies by the end of the book, for it is Sancho who returns to his village as an ecstatic adventurer, his mind full of splendors, and it is Don Quixote who drily remarks, 'Drop those fooleries'". Stressing the link between Sancho's ignorant simplicity and Don Quixote's childishness, in spite of his superior intellect, Nabokov remarks that Sancho, like Betty, "trembles before the unknown and the supernatural, but his shudder is only one step removed from his master's quiver of gallant delight." Ironically, however, perhaps suggesting the concept of divine madness, Madariaga equates the decline of illusion to a loss of exalted spirit:

> While Sancho's spirit rises from reality to illusion, Don Quixote's descends from illusion to reality. And the two curves cross in that saddest of adventures, one of the cruelest in the book, when Sancho enchants Dulcinea, bringing the most noble of knights, for love of the purest illusion, to his knees before the most repulsive of realities: a Dulcinea coarse, uncouth, and reeking of garlic.[38]

Betty's and Dorcasina's curves cross, also, at one point within the context of romantic illusion, but there is no spirit of exaltation in Betty's ascension into the realm of unreality. When Dorcasina's suitor Mr. Cumberland compliments Betty, the servant's head becomes hopelessly turned: "her ideas were now as wild and extravagant as ever those of her mistress had been" (II, 205). She becomes so transported by the belief in his love for her that she spills the warming coals in Dorcasina's bed, responds insolently to her mistress's reprimand, and concludes with a threat of leaving: "I don't intend to be your drudge much longer" (II, 211). However, when she discovers her error about Mr. Cumberland's affections, she immediately reverts to subservient normalcy, suffering enormous mortification. In sum, her kind of flights from reality are short-lived, instigated by specific incidents rather than springing from a morbidly overactive imagination and resultant long-term mania.

Although Brackenridge's Teague O'Regan, like Betty, is, to a certain extent, modeled after Sancho Panza, particularly in the realm of unrealistic aspirations, he "never", according to Henri Petter, "assumes the function of the guardian at times attributed to Sancho or to such an American counterpart as Betty, Dorcasina's maid in Mrs. Tenney's *Female Quixotism.*"[39] Instead, Captain Farrago repeatedly and sometimes unsuccessfully attempts to draw Teague into the confines of propriety and rationality. Seeing the bogtrotter as a "representative" of "erratic impulsiveness . . . often at its most amoral and irresponsible", Petter notes that "later Teague becomes increasingly a mere representative of the irrational masses."[40] This contrast between the Captain and Teague extends to the realm of their verbal expression. As William C. Spengemann says,

> The contest between Captain Farrago's educated English and O'Regan's Irish brogue in *Modern Chivalry* re-enacts the Enlightenment debate between the hierarchical theory of language as a civilized acquisition that separates human beings farther and farther from bestial nature as they rise in society and the more democratic idea of language as a natural gift that unites people of all stations in a classless human bond.[41]

Expressing a similar view, M. F. Heiser states that "Teague represents the unenlightened and impetuous many; the Captain represents the rational few" and observes that Teague's "quixotism is incurable, but not more so than that of the democratic populace who are on most occasions eager to elevate him to the eminence he so brashly desires."[42] Thus Teague lacks the fundamental obedience of Sancho, Lucy, and Betty, even if he shares with them *and* their owners their somewhat inconsistent and ambiguous qualities of self-delusion. Teague, though, tends to be more successful than the others in the at least temporary realization of his ambitions, but only because paradoxically he has, if only clumsily, the ability to delude the very irrational masses that he in his own irrationality embodies. Unequipped with the cleverness of a Melvillean confidenceman, he practices self-delusion as he deludes others.

Betty's unattainable Mr. Cumberland, Lucy's gullibleness about her mistress, and Teague's misplaced confidence in his own ability to be a leader of men are all reflections of Sancho's elusive island, which is a facet of his creator's attempt to come to terms with the conflict between illusion and reality. One of the many manifestations of this conflict appears in the significance of names and name changes. Ironically assuring the reader of his intention not to "depart one iota from the truth" (*Don Quixote,* p. 26), Cervantes attempts to establish the authenticity of his story by referring to differing opinions about his hero's real surname. Whether it was Quijada, Quesada, or Quejana, however, the hero, influenced by visions of knight errantry, settles upon "Don Quixote de la Mancha." According to the *OED* [*Oxford English Dictionary*], "Quijote" in Spanish literally denotes a "cuisse", or a plate of armor for covering the thigh. Thus not only does the name provide a title implying gentlemanly distinction by alluding to the armor which he wears, but it also offers a suggestion of covering, or veiling, the true identity of the hero. For the object of his infatuation, Aldonza Lorenzo, he selects the romantic and mellifluous "Dulcinea del Toboso."

In similar fashion, Tenney's heroine, Dorcas, under the influence of her reading of novels, expands her name to the more fanciful and musical "Dorcasina." At the end of *Female Quixotism,* however, when disenchantment flings her back into mundane reality, she reverts to the Biblical "Dorcas", just as Don Quixote proclaims that he is "no longer Don Quixote de la Mancha but Alonso Quijano" (p. 984). Reference to Acts 9:36 reveals an interesting link with Dorcas' creator: "Now there was at Joppa a certain disciple named Tabitha, which by interpretation is called Dorcas: this woman was full of good works and almsdeeds which she did."[43] Even as Dorcasina, the heroine practices charitable deeds; at the end of the book she turns "all that enthusiasm, which love formerly inspired, to acts of benevolence and charity. In the exercise of these heavenly virtues, she became more cheerful, and more resigned" (*Female Quixotism,* III, 221). The connection between the names "Tabitha" and "Dorcas" seems more than coincidental in light of a biographical account of Mrs. Tenney's later years which she spent, after her husband's death, "consoling herself in charitable works" and "producing exquisite pieces of needlework toward the end of her life."[44] Carrying the connection still one step further, there is a reference in the *OED* to the "*Dorcas Society,* a ladies' association in a church for the purpose of making and providing clothes for the poor." Also in the realm of speculation, when the Biblical Dorcas dies, Peter the Apostle prays by her body and resurrects her with his command, "Tabitha, arise" (Acts 9:40). Perhaps Tenney is suggesting that Dorcas, who loses her original identity and sanity when she becomes Dorcasina, experiences a revival into the real world when she once again assumes her Biblical name.

Not only do these victims of self-delusion assume new names to mirror their new identities, but they also don clothing which suggests their quixotic whimsies. Don Quixote wears armor from his great-grandfather's era, and Arabella, copying "the fashion of the divine Mandana and other heroines of romance" (*The Female Quixote*, p. 389, note 3), dresses in a becoming, but singular way. Reflecting the anachronistic nature of Quixote's wearing apparel, particularly his headpiece, Arabella wears an unfashionable "Headdress . . . over which she wore a white Sarsenet Hood, somewhat in the Form of a Veil, with which she sometimes wholly covered her fair Face, when she saw herself beheld with too much Attention" (p. 9). Ironically, this veil which she employs to conceal herself from others obscures her true identity from herself. Paradoxically, Arabella appears ravishingly beautiful, if somewhat bizarre, whereas Dorcasina appears merely grotesque as a result of her too slavish attempt to adhere to current high fashion. While her jacket and skirt are proper, her turban looks "like a caricature of a fashionable head dress", and her hair, which Betty has "papered and pinched", is "snarled up into two large bunches, above her ears, almost half as big as her head, loaded with powder." Thus, by arraying herself in what she considers the latest fashion, Dorcasina deludes herself into thinking that she is as "charming . . . as the goddess of beauty"; instead, her appearance is "so outré" that her friend Harriot can scarcely refrain from "laughing in her face" (II, 133). On another occasion, when Dorcasina is nearly fifty, but looks older than sixty, she covers her hair with powder "to conceal its natural whiteness" and dresses "herself in a delicate muslin robe" in order "to appear upon this occasion, young and airy." Thus comically she attempts to disguise her age and deceive herself with unbecoming apparel, "so unsuitable to her age and present situation" (III, 32).

An exceptionally keen satire dealing with confusions of identity which result from change in body covering appears in *Modern Chivalry* when a protesting crowd tars and feathers Teague O'Regan, who is acting as an excise officer. Disguised by his covering, he is captured and exhibited as a curiosity, while naïve members of the American Philosophical Society thoroughly examine him and convey their findings in what they consider a scientific, scholarly report. Characteristically Teague emerges as the catalyst who, through no cleverness on his part, becomes a dupe or victim as he instigates in others distorted perceptions.

Don Quixote, of course, is a victim of his own distorted perceptions. His disastrous bout with the windmills, and his conviction that the Benedictine friars are enchanters who have captured a princess, surely find an echo in Arabella's delusions that infatuated suitors are pursuing her to abduct her. Just as Quixote mistakes the pig-salting Aldonza for a princess with supreme beauty,

Arabella imagines that the new gardener, Edward, is a gentleman, "a Person of *sublime Quality*, who submits to this Disguise only to have an Opportunity of seeing" her daily (p. 23). In like manner Dorcasina, under the influence of her recent reading of Smollett, foolishly concludes that her servant John Brown, by association of his name with Roderick Random's pseudonym, John Brown, "must likewise be a gentleman in disguise" (III, 17). In each case the one who labors under self-deception is the only one who is really deluded. When Teague, however, decides that he is qualified to run for the legislature, he wins support of the crowd who tend "to favour his pretensions"[45], and who resent Farrago's insistence that their candidate is an ignorant servant, a mere "bog-trotter."

Offering a key to the self-delusions of these characters, Lennox, in describing Arabella's consternation at the news that Edward has been stealing carp, notes her heroine's "most happy Facility in accommodating every Incident to her own Wishes and Conceptions" (*The Female Quixote*, p. 25). In a similar observation about Don Quixote, Anthony Close, in discussing the knight's "crazy but life-like world-view", explains in part this ability to accommodate, since Quixote's

> view of the world around him is at least partly congruent with reality, as is shown by the fact that much of his discourse is a defensive apologia designed to paper over the cracks between what is and what he believes should be. He often reveals a disconcerting perspicacity; occasionally he appears to be aware of his own madness or to divine other people's judgements of his motives, before revealing that the appearance was merely an appearance. He continuously adapts to his experience and self-justifyingly rationalises it.[46]

When Quixote arrives at an inn and sees two prostitutes in the doorway, his powers of adaptation, overstimulated by romantic storybooks, easily transform the inn into a stately castle with all the customary appurtenances, and the fallen women into highborn beauteous damsels. As Coleridge remarks, "Don Quixote is not a man out of his senses, but a man in whom the imagination and the pure reason are so powerful as to make him disregard the evidence of sense when it opposed their conclusions."[47] Dorcasina rationalizes about O'Connor, persistently believing that he is a man of honor and rejecting as lies overwhelming evidence to the contrary. Inspired by self-deception about his own qualifications for the ministry, Teague O'Regan, with "a great deal of what is called Blarney" and affected prayers, manipulates the adaptive imaginations of the Presbyterian clergy, insinuating "himself into their good graces" and convincing them that he is a worthy "candidate for holy orders."[48]

Intensifying this blurring of imagination and reality is the prevalence of masquerades throughout these quixotic stories. Although the motivations for assuming disguises vary from the malicious drive to gain one's personal ends to the more positive desire to help a deluded character, the overall purpose is, of course, some form of deception. Teague O'Regan obtains entrance into the fashionable circles of Philadelphia and into the hearts of its young ladies by posing as "Major O'Regan." In fact, so potent is the "Teagueomania" which he inspires "amongst the females . . . that all idea of excellence, personal, or mental" is "centered in" this ignorant bogtrotter, "and all common lovers" are "neglected, or repulsed on his account."[49]

This employment of deception appears also in *Don Quixote* and its transatlantic descendant *Female Quixotism.* In an attempt to persuade Don Quixote to suspend his adventuring for awhile, Sanson Carrasco, in collusion with the curate and the barber, assumes first a disguise as the Knight of the Mirrors and challenges Quixote to a duel, claiming that his woman, Casildea de Vandalin, is the most beautiful in Spain and that he has already overcome Don Quixote in previous combat. The conditions of the match require the loser to return to his village and remain there for two years. Unexpectedly defeated by Quixote, Carrasco, now masquerading as the Knight of the White Moon, resumes the challenge, this time mingling an evil motive for revenge for his defeat with his original laudable desire to cure Quixote of his knight-errantry and madness. In *Female Quixotism* Harriot Stanly, with the magnanimous intention of enticing Dorcasina away from the fortune-hunting John Brown, affects the identity of a militia officer, Captain Montague, who seems passionately in love with Dorcasina. Unsuccessful in her endeavor, she even enlists her father, ordinarily a pillar of integrity, who also assumes a disguise in order to abduct the woman before a marriage to Brown can take place. While this scheme ultimately succeeds and the motivation is generous, a trace of cruelty emerges in Harriot's gleeful participation in the venture and her mock amorous farewell to Dorcasina in which she covers her with kisses and concludes "by biting her cheek so hard as to make her scream aloud" (III, 126).

Even crueller are Philander's masquerades, first as Dorcasina's lovesick suitor and later as a jealous woman. In the former role he woos her with ridiculously extravagant epistles for the purpose of mocking her and thus succeeds in winning her warmest sympathy, if not her love. What Heiser says about Harriot's masquerade applies also to Philander's efforts: "Miss Stanly . . . is the more successful the more she burlesques it, for, ironically, a burlesque of love is Dorcasina's ideal."[50] In a scene of low comedy reminiscent of much in *Don Quixote,* Philander, disguised as a jealous woman, first tears off Dorcasina's hat and pulls her hair, and then turns upon Betty, who is trying to defend her mistress: Betty

was held, cuffed, pulled by the hair, twirled round and round like a top, shaken, and pushed up against the trees, without mercy . . . the enraged virago would not suffer her to go till she [Philander] had stripped off her upper garments . . . torn them to rags . . . , telling her . . . that, if ever she caught her engaged in the same business again, she would not only divest her of her clothes, but strip off her old wrinkled hide.

(I, 236-37)

Surely this violent mistreatment, as well as the tarring and feathering of Teague O'Regan, is reminiscent of Don Quixote's beating when the muleteers, not without good cause in response to the knight's furious charge against them, proceed

to belabor him so mercilessly that in spite of his armor they milled him like a hopper of wheat . . . the mule driver by this time had warmed up to the sport and would not stop until he had vented his wrath, and, snatching up the broken pieces of the lance, he began hurling them at the wretched victim as he lay there on the ground.

(*Don Quixote,* pp. 46-47)

These elements of cruelty which tend to make a sensitive reader squirm uncomfortably rather than laugh heartily, raise the question of tone in these quixotic novels, a quality of satire which consists largely of good fun. Perhaps Daniel Marder provides a key to the problem in his seemingly inconsistent statements about *Modern Chivalry.* Introducing his discussion of Brackenridge's book, he says, "The satirical mood approaches the geniality of Horace rather than the severity of Juvenal."[51] Later, however, he notes that "the tone of Brackenridge's satire", aimed always at social reform, "can never be taken as congenial."[52] The dual nature of satirical humor often amuses and disturbs the reader simultaneously, thus fulfilling the author's intention, but blurring the dividing line between Horatian and Juvenalian tone.

James Russell Lowell attests to the Horatian tone of *Don Quixote* when he speaks of "the optimism of its author" and says, "I can think of no book so thoroughly good-natured and good-humored."[53] Thomas Mann, however, speaks of being, "at odd times . . . appalled at Cervantes's intemperate cruelty"[54] and Nabokov devotes an extended discourse to the "cruelty theme" in *Don Quixote.* Observing that both parts of the book "form a veritable encyclopedia of cruelty", Nabokov concludes that "from that viewpoint it is one of the most bitter and barbarous books ever penned", offering "samples of cheerful physical cruelty in part one" of the book and of the "mental cruelties of part two."[55] Referring to the events in *Female Quixotism* which trigger Dorcasina's romantic delusions, Petter comments that "these situations are increasingly absurd, too, given Dorcasina's aging, and are increasingly cruel."[56]

Although evidence suggests that no reform takes place in Teague O'Regan, whose fate after his arrival in France and his liberation from his cage by a mob mistaking him for a *sans culotte* remains uncertain, Don Quixote, and later his heirs Dorcasina and Arabella, undergo radical changes which hint, in varying degrees, of a kind of cruelty or at least a modulation into a minor key. Mortally ill with a fever, Don Quixote discards his assumed name, condemns the stories of knight-errantry that have deranged him, and acknowledges his return to sanity:

> The mercy that I speak of . . . is that which God is showing me at this moment—in spite of my sins, as I have said. My mind now is clear, unencumbered by those misty shadows of ignorance that were cast over it by my bitter and continual reading of those hateful books of chivalry. I see through all the nonsense and fraud contained in them, and my only regret is that my disillusionment has come so late, leaving me no time to make any sort of amends by reading those that are the light of the soul.
>
> (p. 984)

Such critics as Mann and Nabokov, however, do not share this elation. As Mann says, Quixote's mental healing, attended by death, "rejoices us strikingly little, it leaves us cold, and to some extent we regret it . . . It is the deep dejection of seeing shipwrecked his mission as knight-errant and light-bringer that killed him." Mann perceives a necessity in Quixote's death: "To make him live after his return to sanity would not do either; that would be to make the husk survive beyond the soul; would be a degradation of the character below its lofty height."[57] Nabokov sees Quixote's recantation as "an abrupt surrender, a miserable apostasy, this, when on his deathbed he renounces the glory of the mad romance that made him what he was."[58]

Arabella and Dorcasina undergo similar though of course not deathbed cures, but the mood of each novel's ending is quite different. Still retaining her youthful beauty, Arabella humbly and joyfully consents to marry Mr. Glanville after an extended dialogue with a learned divine who converts her by appealing to reason. Lacking Arabella's physical charms, the now elderly Dorcasina comes to her senses abruptly when Seymore, in disgrace, informs her that he has wooed her only for her money and ridicules her unattractive old age. After a day of reflection, "her eyes seemed to be opened, and the romantic spell, by which she had been so many years bound, all at once broken" (III, 208). Revolted by her former fancies and behavior, she settles into a solitary existence, practising resignation and alleviating the loneliness by performing charitable deeds. The conclusion of *Female Quixotism* with Dorcasina's unrealistically swift return to sanity does not echo the sad solemnity of Don Quixote's demise—of course, Tenney's Dorcasina lacks the fascination of his lofty madness—

but in its unsentimental realism, it reflects more closely than *The Female Quixote* the spirit of its Spanish original.

This immortal literary original has afforded a wealth of insights into human nature, a richness of characterization, and a diversified array of events which have reverberated down through the centuries in numerous fictional offspring. Like Don Quixote, the characters struggle with the confusions, embarrassments, attempts to make their lives imitate fictional art, and ambiguities inherent in the conflict between illusion and reality. All of these characters are worthy of redemption; besides their fundamental intelligence, sanity, and decency, they have likable traits that win a portion of the reader's sympathy. They are also delightfully amusing in their aberrations. The complexity of their confusion increases during their encounters with other characters who have, by means of masquerade, invaded their illusory realm and have, in a number of cases, tinged the narratives with disconcerting hues of cruelty. Don Quixote, Arabella, and Dorcasina are assisted on their pilgrimage through irrationality to ultimate sanity by their caring servants and companions who ordinarily exemplify reality and common sense, but who either assume occasional touches of their superiors' distorted perception or act with them contrapuntally, experiencing their own individual separation from reality.

Except for the comparatively happy conclusion of *The Female Quixote,* which leaves no doubt about the value of sanity, the endings—Teague's disappearance, Dorcasina's lucid but lonely old age, and Don Quixote's death—leave the reader with certain unanswered questions. For instance, does Teague continue to thrive under his self-delusions, in spite of his mishaps, acting as a representative of the irrational mob that he has infected with the contagion of his misconceptions? Do Dorcasina's and Don Quixote's reversion to reality present a positive case for staying firmly in the real world? Is the dividing line between illusion and reality as clear as it seems to be at the end of these books? One point *is* clear, the English and American quixotic efforts reflect that of Cervantes not only in structure, plot elements, and characterization, but also in the fundamental human questions which they present.

Notes

1. Evert A. and George L. Duyckinck, *Cyclopaedia of American Literature,* Vol. I of 2. Philadelphia, Wm. Rutler, 1854; republished Detroit, Mich., Gale Research, Book Tower, 1965, p. 521.

2. See Gustavus Howard Maynadier, *The First American Novelist?* Cambridge, Mass., Harvard Univ. Press, 1940.

3. Hugh Henry Brackenridge, *Modern Chivalry,* ed. Claude M. Newlin. New York, American Book C., 1937.

4. M. F. Heiser, "Cervantes in the United States", *Hispanic Review,* Vol. XV, Núm. 4, Oct., 1947, 410.

5. Harry Levin, "*Don Quixote* and *Moby Dick*", *Cervantes Across the Centuries,* ed. Ángel Flores and M. J. Benardete. New York, Dryden Press, 1947, p. 217.

6. James Russell Lowell, "Don Quixote", *The Writings of James Russell Lowell in Prose and Poetry,* Vol. VI, *Literary and Political Addresses.* Boston, Houghton Mifflin, Riverside Press, 1890, pp. 135-36.

7. Miguel de Cervantes, *The Ingenious Gentleman Don Quixote de la Mancha,* ed. and trans. Samuel Putnam. New York, Modern Library, 1949, p. 26. Subsequent references to *Don Quixote* will appear in the text.

8. Brackenridge, p. 6.

9. Samuel Miller in *A Brief Retrospect of the Eighteenth Century,* p. 157, discusses *Don Quixote*: "This performance was expressly intended to pour ridicule on those masses of absurdity and impurity which had so long maintained an influence over the world . . . It destroyed the reign of chivalry; produced a new modification of public taste; occasioned the death of the old romance; and gave birth to another species of fictitious writing."

10. Tenney and Lennox have borrowed the idea of book burning from Cervantes. See *Don Quixote,* p. 50: "I should have advised your Worships of my uncle's nonsensical actions so that you could have done something about it by burning those damnable books of his before things came to such a pass; for he has many that ought to be burned as if they were heretics."

    "'I agree with you', said the curate, 'and before tomorrow's sun has set there shall be a public *auto de fe,* and those works shall be condemned to the flames that they may not lead some other who reads them to follow the example of my good friend'."

    See Tabitha Tenney, *Female Quixotism: Exhibited in the Romantic Opinions and Extravagant Adventures of Dorcasina Sheldon,* 3 vols. Boston, George Clark, 1841, Vol. I, p. 182: Mr. Sheldon "was upon the point of committing to the flames every novel within his daughter's reach." Subsequent references to *Female Quixotism* will appear in the text.

    See also Charlotte Lennox, *The Female Quixote or the Adventures of Arabella,* ed. Margaret Dalziel. London: Oxford Univ. Press, 1970, pp. 55-56: (Subsequent references to this work will appear in the text.) Arabella's father, the Marquis, disturbed by his daughter's strange words, threatens to burn the books that "have turned her Brain". Left alone, Arabella bewails "the Fate of so many illustrious Heroes and Heroines, who, by an Effect of a more cruel Tyranny than any they had ever experienced before, were going to be cast into the merciless Flames". The Marquis offers Glanville the opportunity to burn the books himself. Glanville, however, ingratiates himself with Arabella by rescuing the books and restoring them to her.

11. Thomas Mann, "Voyage with Don Quixote", *Essays by Thomas Mann,* trans. H. T. Lowe-Porter. New York: Vintage Books, 1958, p. 335.

12. Maynard Mack, Introduction to *Joseph Andrews,* by Henry Fielding, pp. x-xi.

13. Anthony Close, *The Romantic Approach to 'Don Quixote': A Critical History of the Romantic Tradition in 'Quixote' Criticism.* Cambridge, Cambridge Univ. Press, 1977; first pub. 1978, pp. 12-13.

14. Vladimir Nabokov, *Lectures on Don Quixote,* ed. Fredson Bowers. New York, Harcourt Brace Jovanovich, 1983, pp. 13, 16-17. See also Arturo Serrano-Plaja, *"Magic" Realism in Cervantes: "Don Quixote" as Seen Through "Tom Sawyer" and "The Idiot",* trans. Robert S. Rudder. (Berkeley, Univ. California Press, 1970), p. 17: "Don Quixote reasons logically about everything except in a certain direction on his compass: the north-north-west of his notions about chivalry."

15. Nabokov, p. 17.

16. Madeleine de Scudéry, *Artamenes; or, the Grand Cyrus. That Excellent Romance,* 1690-91, and *Clelia, an excellent new Romance,* 1678.

17. Heiser, p. 410.

18. Maynadier, p. 43.

19. Mann, p. 368.

20. It appears that Mrs. Tenney herself occupied the remainder of her life after her husband's death in 1816 "consoling herself in charitable works". See *American Authors: 1600-1900: A Biographical Dictionary of American Literature,* ed. Stanley J. Kunitz and Howard Haycraft. New York: The H. W. Wilson Co., 1938, p. 734. See also Duyckinck, p. 523: "Among" Mrs. Tenney's "practical good services to the place of her residence, was the establishment of an old colored servant of her family in a house which became a popular place of entertainment as a rural retreat, with its 'cakes and ale', and was known as 'Dinah's Cottage'".

21. Mann, p. 344.

22. Heiser, pp. 410-11.

23. Maynadier, p. 42.

24. Duyckinck, p. 522.

25. Alexander Cowie, *The Rise of the American Novel.* New York, American Book, 1951, p. 27.

26. Fred Lewis Pattee, *The First Century of American Literature: 1770-1870.* D. Appleton, 1945; rpt. New York, Cooper Square, 1966, pp. 93-94: "A hodgepodge of adventure follows. Built after the *Don Quixote* model, the novel cries aloud for humor, cries aloud for realistic treatment of the Sancho Panza character, Betty, for fights ferocious that will stir the reader to sympathy; but none are vouchsafed by the gentle novelist. The *motif* borrowed from Mrs. Lennox, who years before had written *The Female Quixote, or the Adventures of Arabella,* is excellent, but nothing else."

27. Ola Elizabeth Winslow, in *Notable American Women 1607-1950: A Biographical Dictionary,* Vol. III, ed. Edward T. James. Cambridge, Mass: Harvard Univ. Press, Belknap Press, 1971, p. 439.

28. Carl Van Doren, *The American Novel: 1789-1939.* New York, Macmillan, 1940, p. 6.

29. Heiser, p. 414.

30. Henry Grattan Doyle, Introduction, *The Ingenious Gentleman Don Quixote de la Mancha,* by Miguel de Cervantes, Ozell's rev. of trans. of Peter Motteux. New York, Modern Library, 1950, p. xiii.

31. Mann, p. 335.

32. Heiser, p. 412.

33. *Ibíd.*

34. Doyle, p. xiii.

35. Nabokov, p. 24.

36. *Ibíd.,* p. 20. Acknowledging the link between Quixote and Sancho, Samuel Taylor Coleridge, in "Don Quixote", Lecture VIII, *The Literary Remains of Samuel Taylor Coleridge,* Vol. I, collected and ed. Henry Nelson Coleridge. London, William Pickering, 1836; New York, AMS Press, 1967, p. 120, says, "Don Quixote grows at length to be a man out of his wits; his understanding is deranged; and hence without the least deviation from the truth of nature, without losing the least trait of personal individuality, he becomes a substantial living allegory, or personification of the reason and the moral sense, divested of the judgment and the understanding. Sancho is the converse. He is the common sense without reason or imagination; and Cervantes not only shows the excellence and power of reason in Don Quixote, but in both him and Sancho the mischiefs resulting from a severance of the two main constituents of sound intellectual and moral action. Put him and his master together, and they form a perfect intellect; but they are separated and without cement; and hence each having a need of the other for its own completeness, each has at times a mastery over the other."

37. Nabokov, pp. 22-23. Nabokov quotes Salvador de Madariaga's discussion in *Don Quixote: An Introductory Essay in Psychology.* Oxford at the Clarendon Press, 1935, pp. 96-97, of the "complicated and delicate parallel" between Don Quixote and Sancho:

"Both are men endowed with abundant gifts of reason, intellectual in Don Quixote, empirical in Sancho, who at a certain moment become possessed of a self-delusion which unbalances their mind and life. But while in Don Quixote this self-delusion gathers round a nucleus of glory symbolized in Dulcinea, in Sancho it gradually takes form around a kernel of material ambition, symbolized in an island . . . we shall see a drift of this machine of absurdities, of such a Knight and such a squire, who, one would think, were cast in the same mould; and indeed the madness of the master, without the follies of the man, would not be worth a farthing.

"For indeed Don Quixote and Sancho are true brothers and their maker planned them after the same pattern."

38. *Ibíd.,* p. 23. Quotation is from MADARIAGA, p. 120.

39. Henri Petter, *The Early American Novel.* Columbus, Ohio State Univ. Press, 1971, p. 127.

40. *Ibíd.*

41. William C. Spengemann, "Early American Writing and English Literary History", paper presented at the MLA Convention, New York, December 29, 1983.

42. Heiser, p. 414.

43. King James, Version.

44. See *American Authors: 1600-1900,* p. 734: Tenney "evidently gave her full attention to the needle instead of the pen, producing exquisite pieces of needlework toward the end of her life".

45. Brackenridge, p. 15. Emory Elliott, *Revolutionary Writers: Literature and Authority in the New Republic, 1725-1810.* New York, Oxford Univ. Press, 1982, p. 185, believes that the expression of Brackenridge's purpose is more complex than a simplistic reading of *Modern Chivalry* seems to

indicate. Instead of furthering the author's ideals by repressing Teague's aspirations, Farrago, in his "pretensions and self-interest" that hold Teague back, fears "the democratic impulses that provide new opportunities for O'Regan" (p. 189). This attempt to keep everyone in his own place and to cling to the past "is directly contrary to Brackenridge's principles" of democracy (p. 185).

46. Close, p. 18.

47. Samuel Taylor Coleridge, "August 11, 1832: Hesiod.—Virgil.—Genius Metaphysical.—Don Quixote", *Table Talk,* in *The Table Talk and Omniana of Samuel Taylor Coleridge.* London, Oxford Univ. Press, 1917, p. 197.

48. Brackenridge, p. 38.

49. *Ibíd.,* p. 230.

50. Heiser, p. 413.

51. Daniel Marder, *Hugh Henry Brackenridge.* New York, Twayne, 1967, p. 86.

52. *Ibíd.,* p. 94. Elliott suggests that Brackenridge's humor is primarily Horatian when he says that the author's "tone is neither strident nor condescending" (p. 175) and that "Brackenridge's own laughter, verbal trickery, and his ironic detachment from his narrator-author soften the social satire" (p. 190). Elliott does indicate, however, that "the satire" in Volume II becomes "more heavy-handed and the tone more Juvenalian than in any passage in the first volume" (p. 191). A satirical work of the magnitude of *Modern Chivalry* can certainly, without inconsistency, encompass a broad range of seemingly contradictory tones.

53. Lowell, p. 118.

54. Mann, p. 346.

55. Nabokov, pp. 51-52.

56. Petter, p. 300.

57. Mann, pp. 366-67.

58. Nabokov, p. 18.

Cathy N. Davidson (essay date 1986)

SOURCE: Davidson, Cathy N. "The Picaresque and the Margins of Political Discourse: The Female Picaresque." In *Revolution and the Word: The Rise of the Novel in America,* pp. 179-92. New York: Oxford University Press, 1986.

[*In the following excerpt, Davidson examines the female picaresque novel and its appropriation of a literary form which celebrates male social mobility, claiming that Tenney's employment of the picaresque and her marginalized status as an author expose the restrictions of women of the period.*]

A woman on horseback, presents her form to advantage; but much more at the spinning wheel.

—*Modern Chivalry*

[The] circumscription of the female character within the domestic sphere constitutes a defining feature of sentimental fiction. In contrast, the picaresque novel defines itself by its own mobilities—formalistic and on the level of plot and characters, too. The picaresque hero can comment upon slavery, class disturbances, party politics, and different immigrant groups precisely because his travels carry him into encounters with diverse segments of the population and across those dividing lines that mark out the contours of the society. His journey is also the reader's journey and his freedom the reader's freedom. Whenever a particular episode might become too constraining and threatens to fix the action in, say, prison or matrimony, the logic of the plot still requires that the novel move on, and freedom (the protagonist's and the reader's) is regularly retained through evasive action. Furthermore, such exercises in independence, unlike comparable ventures on the part of female characters in the sentimental novel, are sanctioned in the plot. So if the picaresque explicitly celebrates an essentially male freedom, then just where do women come in—as characters, authors, and readers? Can *Modern Chivalry,* for example, prefatorially addressed explicitly to the male reader ("If you are about to chuse a wife, and expect beauty, you must give up family and fortune; or if you attain these, you must at least want good temper, health, or some other advantage" [p. 31]) even be read by women, and, if not, then what kind of chivalry is it? One might claim that just as the sentimental novel examines women's issues, why could not the picaresque form fairly be written only for men? But I would argue that, in a patriarchical society in which resources (income, books, status, freedom, and the rest) are inequably divided, what is sauce for the gander rarely serves the goose as well.

As the quotation from *Modern Chivalry* with which this section began illustrates, merely reversing the terms of an argument by no means reverses its underlying assumptions. The woman on horseback is still subordinated to her more typical position behind a spinning wheel. Both postures, moreover, are appropriated as service to a proper master. Why ride a horse? To get from hither to yon or to show one's form to advantage? In short, Brackenridge's surveyed woman is precisely the antithesis of his surveying hero. When she is not invisible in the text or entirely omitted from the narration, she exists adjunctive to his good, his ends. Therefore, to create a female picaresque novel in which a woman on horseback traverses, assesses, and describes town and countryside almost necessarily, given the culture in which it is read, devolves into self-parody. The female simply does not have the same freedoms—to journey, to judge, to have her judgments heeded—as does the male, and that is a fact of picaresque fiction almost as much as it is a fact of sentimental fiction.

Not surprisingly, in those novels in which a woman comes closest to enacting the role of the standard male picaro, she does so only in male dress. Both the Martinette-goes-to-war sequence in *Ormond* and the whole of Herman Mann's *The Female Review* allow a woman male freedom: first, because all of her companions think of her as him; second, because that deception itself serves a larger redeeming cause, patriotism, the good of her country. A feminized picaresque fiction, consequently, requires both justification and narrative deception. While the reader is in on the ruse, the characters the picara meets are not, and most of the interest of the book derives from a continual but covert textual dialectic of knowledge and ignorance, of male and female, of power and powerlessness. For once the picara's true (i.e., female) identity is revealed, her power no longer exists. In short, her very role in the fiction is specious and surreptitious, is conditional upon its being asserted in ways that challenge neither the status quo nor the double standard. Personal power without political power can provide a momentary fantasy but is no solution to the larger dilemma of female disenfranchisement within the *polis.*

Since the crossdressed picara retains her power only as long as its inauthentic basis is not revealed either literally or figuratively, the novels often flirt, almost pornographically, with the threat of exposure.[1] For example, in *The Female Review* (and, remember, most of the subscribers to the novel were men of substance) Deborah Sampson at one point suffers not only a head wound, but also a wound to her right thigh, just (we are specifically told) below her groin. To reveal the second injury would reveal her sex, so much so that the wound can be seen as an obvious stand-in for the hidden sex. She allows a doctor to remove the one bullet, but she herself secretly extracts the other one with a penknife (and, it might also be added, with obvious Freudian implications). Her sex, however, does not go entirely undiscovered. Later, lying unconscious with yellow fever, a doctor feels for her heartbeat to find if she is still alive and finds also something else. Breasts prove the woman, but a woman's wiles soon bring the doctor to promise silence, and Deborah is off again, this time westward, to travels on the frontier, encounters with Indians, and to still more narrow escapes from women who find this "blooming soldier" irresistible. A curious amalgam of stereotypically masculine and feminine attributes, the young soldier, as a kind of Revolutionary Michael Jackson, enchants most of the females s/he meets. What do women want? Deborah Sampson

knows. But it is not so clear that Herman Mann, the author, does. Although the novel recounts several incidents of her exemplary courage (and courage in the exploitative masculine model: She must kill an Indian in self-defense before she is truly "manly"), Sampson's chief occupation is to keep men from uncovering her hidden femininity while simultaneously preventing women from falling in love with her covering masculinity. The title page, too, hints equally of patriotism ("she performed the duties of every department, into which she was called, with punctual exactness, fidelity and honor") and prurience (she "preserved her chastity inviolate, by the most artful concealment of her sex").

Yet the doctors, colonels, merchants, majors, and captains (as well as Miss Hannah Wright, Miss Alice Leavens, Miss Hannah Orne, and the other misses whose names were included in the volume) apparently saw themselves as supporting through their subscriptions a purely pious tale. In contrast to the lists bound with all other early American novels, the one found in *The Female Review* is unusual in that it contains no pseudonyms such as "A Friend to the Publication" or "A Young Lady of Massachusetts," phrasings obviously intended to hide the patron's true identity.[2] But consistent with its transvestite plot, *The Female Review* crossdresses generically too. Nowhere announcing itself as a novel, this fiction masks its own fictionality by passing itself off as a proper history of the Revolution.

Another novel of crossdressing, also set during the Revolution, further underscores the inherent contradictions between female, on the one hand, and picaresque, on the other. *The History of Constantius and Pulchera; or Constancy Rewarded: An American Novel* was one of the best-selling novels of the early national period. Originally published in brief installments from June of 1789 to January of 1790 in the American monthly periodical, *Gentleman and Ladies Town and Country Magazine,* the novel also went through eight editions in English between 1794 (its original date of book publication) and 1802, was translated into German for the Pennsylvania market, was reprinted again in 1821 and 1831, and was then published in a plagiarized edition, under the title *History of Lorenzo and Virginia; or, Virtue Rewarded,* by one T. H. Cauldwell, D.D., in 1834. It was available in a pirated paperbound edition that sold for a quarter and in a handsome, calfbound duodecimo that sold for over a dollar. Despite its popularity, however (or perhaps because of it), the book has baffled contemporary critics. It is surprisingly brief (some copies are only twenty-five or so pages long) and extremely episodic (as if with each installment, the author had mostly forgotten what he or she had written last month). A number of critics have even insisted that the book is so discontinuous, its plot so ludicrous, its rhetoric so preposterous, and its moral so muddled that it must surely have been originally intended as a *parody* of the sentimental or picaresque forms, for "it is impossible to take [it] . . . seriously."[3]

Yet apparently the original readers of *The History of Constantius and Pulchera* did just that. Nothing in the twenty-one copies of the novel that I have inspected suggests that they were read any differently than, say, romantic novels such as *The Coquette* or *Charlotte*. Most are signed in the usual fashion and using the usual formula, "Elizabeth Smith, her Book." Others, however, are signed several times, sometimes by members of the same family, sometimes (judging by the dates and inscriptions) by different generations of the same family, sometimes shared among friends or relatives with different family names. Most striking for my purposes, however, in one copy of the cheap, poorly printed edition pirated by Edward Gray in 1801, there is clear evidence of a reader who not only saw nothing funny in the work but who obviously valued it and drew connections between it and her own view of the world. As noted in chapter 4, she embellished the book itself with fine handmade covers and a delicate drawing of flower buds, and, at crucial points in the text, supplied her own poetic and philosophical gloss on the events of the nebulous plot.

Why, we must ask, is the book virtually unreadable today or readable only as a parody of itself? Robert Darnton addresses essentially the same question when he sorts through Jean-Jacques Rousseau's mailbag and finds dozens of fan letters addressed to "l'Ami Jean-Jacques" from readers enraptured by *Julie, ou la nouvelle Héloïse*—"six volumes of sentiment unrelieved by any episodes of violence, explicit sex, or anything much in the way of plot"; in short, by today's standards, an unreadable book. Yet this unreadable book, with its overinflated prose and its overheated didacticism, went through a minimum of seventy editions before 1800, as many editions as any other novel in any country by that date.[4] Perhaps we read differently today than we did in 1800.

In 1800, many Americans—and there is no way of knowing just how many—read *The History of Constantius and Pulchera,* and what they read, starting with the frontispiece with its evocation of Romeo and Juliet, was a sentimental story of star-crossed lovers conjoined with a female picaresque adventure tale. At first the sentimental predominates. The first appearance of the heroine is standard romance: "In the suburbs of the city of Philadelphia, in the soft season of the year, about one o'clock, on a moon shining morning, on the terrace of a high building, forty feet from the ground, appeared a most beautiful lady of the age of sixteen—she was clad in a long white vest, her hair of a beautiful chestnut colour, hanging carelessly over her shoulders, every mark of greatness was visible in her countenance, which was overcast with a solemn gloom, and now and then, the unwilling tear unnoticed, rolled down her cheek."[5] Yet in the novel's preface, explicitly addressed to the "Daughters of Columbia," prospective readers are promised "novelty" that will be "like a new Planet in the solar System" of "the Ladies' Libraries." They are also assured that the novel will not arouse "party spirit" and the "many emotions" of the divided "political world" but, rather, will focus on women's concerns and is designed for the "Amusement of the Fair Sex." That statement, in itself, is, of course, a political statement, one that recognizes women's exclusion from or indifference to official party politics. The book opposes the world of men's politics to the world of the lady's library—different planets in the same (or, perhaps, not the same at all) universe.

Although, to say the least, much shorter than *La Nouvelle Héloïse, The History of Constantius and Pulchera* mimics the strained language of feeling that Rousseau deploys throughout his six-volume novel: "O transcendently propitious heaven! thrice bountiful, inexhaustible, magnificent Providence! inexpressible, benevolent, and superlatively beneficent fates! The most exalted language is more than infinitely too inexpressive to give an idea of the grateful sensations which occupy my breast" (p. 94). Just as recent authors run up against the limitations of language in one way, early novelists did so in another way. Pulchera, still disguised as Lieutenant Valorus, has just tested her lover's constancy and his exclamations follow upon her revealing her true identity. No words—not even *these* words—can capture his joy. But notice that his effusive language would normally be her language. Pulchera is in control. She contrives the meeting, the test, the revelation. Constantius's role is essentially passive, responsive, in a word, "feminine." The novel focuses on Pulchera's prowess and adventures, and Constantius, consistent with the passive connotations of his name, is finally reduced, rhetorically, to the role traditionally occupied by a woman, that of the grateful heroine overwhelmed by good fortune and the capable attentions of another. One almost expects the fellow to swoon.

The narrative transvestism or emotional role reversal, however, does not overtly challenge the status quo, and that consideration may well explain the "secret" to the novel's success. The heroine rushes from harrowing adventure to even more harrowing adventure, but she does so "innocently" because, ostensibly, she proceeds in opposition to her own more proper desires. The novel essentially grafts the typical picaresque adventure story (such as *Fortune's Foot-ball*) onto a sentimental novel through the ingenious device of captivity (a device to be explored at greater length in a subsequent section on the female Gothic novel). Because Pulchera is repeatedly abducted and thus, by definition, deprived of volition in the matter, she cannot really be held responsible for breaking virtually every imaginable restriction placed upon the eighteenth-century American woman. She is, happily, *forced* into her different unlikely roles as picara, world traveler, crossdressing soldier, prizemaster on a brigantine captured by pirates, and sole woman stranded with a group of men on a remote desert island. In her assumed role as Valorus, she is constantly thrown into the company of disreputable men and, just as constantly, she overpowers or outwits or otherwise triumphs over them all. She is transformed, onomastically and metaphorically, from Pulchera—suggesting a typically feminine beauty, pulchritude—to Valorus, a hero. As Lillie Deming Loshe has noted, there is a certain "cheerfulness" in the way the narration lurches from one unlikely and outlandish adventure to another, with Pulchera/Valorus thoroughly enjoying her successes in situations no eighteenth-century woman had any business even fantasizing.[6] And then her exhilarating trials all end in the domesticity she would have entered on page 1 except for the intervention of her parents (who, of course, had wanted to marry her to a designing French aristocrat). She has her adventures and her Constantius, too. He is, indeed, a final triumph and also an appropriate reward (playing the role of the traditional heroine again) for all of her other earlier triumphs.

It is, in short, a wonderful fantasy. Pulchera/Valorus violates all of the restrictions placed upon eighteenth-century women, but still ends up, thanks to her unflagging ingenuity and overall capability, safe at home again and at last in possession of her constant American lover. No wonder the novel was a best-seller! This American heroine saw the world, proved her mastery of it by triumphing over a whole host of designing men, and then returned home to an America that had won its independence (her own story of independence, like Deborah Sampson's, is set during the Revolutionary War) to enter into a marriage which, mercifully, is left undescribed at the novel's end. Like all good escapist literature, *The History of Constantius and Pulchera* allows the reader a temporary reprieve from her own situation but never requires her to question its governing assumptions. Catharsis arises precisely from the novel's lack of realism—signaled by its exuberant rhetoric—which allows the reader freely to imagine freedom without in any way having to pay the personal or public price that any effort to realize that freedom necessarily entails.

Another factor probably contributed to the popularity of this curious little tale. It is among the shortest, sparest, and simplest of early American novels. Even when the vocabulary is at its most florid ("transcendently . . . propitious . . . bountiful . . . inexhaustible . . . benevolent . . . superlatively"), the "words of three, four, and five syllables" are those that are found in Dilworth's, Perry's, and Webster's spelling books. In effect, rote vocabulary lessons have become enlivened into plot and words have gained significance by being incorporated into story. What to us seems like a highly erratic, episodic, and undeveloped plot may, therefore, have seemed almost like magic to an inexperienced reader making her way from her speller to a novel in which those long lists of words memorized in the schoolroom suddenly transported a girl very much like herself about the globe and through a whole series of adventures while Constantius waited mostly at home. The novel is simple in its disjunctive vocabulary and it is simple, too, in its disjunctive story, calling upon the reader's ready imagination to fill in the lacunae in the notably undelineated plot. In what is almost a child's ordering ("this happened and then this happened and then this happened . . ."), impetus and excitement derive not from the narrative skills of the author but from the reader being able to recreate a tale of utter implausibility and to participate thereby in the global derring-do of a sixteen-year-old girl from the suburbs of Philadelphia.

Only in crossdressing or captivity do a few women characters find something of the same full freedom that the picaresque regularly grants to its male protagonists. Moreover, that freedom, it must be emphasized, is conditional and temporary, and definitely not for domestic consumption. Clearly, "Mrs. Constantius" (née Pulchera), back in "the suburbs of Philadelphia," may wistfully recall her life as Valorus, ship's mate and soldier, but she will not swashbuckle through the marketplace. As Arabella, the satirized heroine in British novelist Charlotte Lennox's *The Female Quixote* (1752), aptly observes, when a woman "at last condescends to reward [a man] with her Hand . . . all her Adventures are at an End for the Future."[7] Returned to female dress and mien again, Deborah and Pulchera presumably live happily ever after. But such an ending does not elicit the imagination of the author, and both the "happiness" and the "after" can be appropriately left to the readers who will all have their own experiences on that same score.

Tabitha Gilman Tenney, in *Female Quixotism: Exhibited in the Romantic Opinions and Extravagant Adventures of Dorcasina Sheldon* (1801), portrays a protagonist whose adventures are hardly as extravagant as those of Pulchera or Deborah Sampson. Perhaps Dorcasina's wildest act is to dress up her previous name, which was the more mundane Dorcas. In this novel the picara never strays more than thirty miles from her place of nativity. Her adventures are mostly in reading and are all emphatically and stereotypically female. A devotee of romances, she reads to imagine herself the object of male adoration. Theoretically, she need imagine no further than that essentially passive state. Love should conquer all, which means she need conquer nothing—not enemy soldiers, not pirates, not even the more difficult nonfictional books in her father's library. Tenney's genius is to tie the form that most emphasizes freedom from society back to limitation (read: female limitation) and society (read: patriarchal society). The protagonist's "romantic opinions" and "extravagant [albeit mental] adventures" only circumscribe the fixity of her place.

An intelligent woman, an heiress of a thousand pounds a year (rightly designated in the novel as "a great fortune"), Dorcasina renders herself pathetic not just by her novel reading, but by her willingness to believe in the whole fantasy of love perpetrated in the novels she reads. She takes "happy ever after" at face value and sets out to discover the man who will render her so. She is consequently victimized by both her own delusions and by men who calculatingly exploit those delusions and see in her only a windfall profit to be easily won by passionately declaiming a few romantic phrases plagiarized from those same novels in which her delusions are grounded. She reads too trustingly, both the books and the men she meets. Just as *The History of Constantius and Pulchera* was a kind of elementary how-to-read-a-novel novel, *Female Quixotism* is a more subtle how-not-to-read-a-novel novel. Tenney allegorizes the reading process and turns it upon itself; one must be a resisting reader, a critical reader, a reader able to read other readings of the fiction, able to read the context in which the text is read.

Dorcasina emblemizes the passive consumer who presents no critical opposition to the texts she reads. She reads her life the same way—postulating a gentleman behind an uncouth, illiterate servant (she has just finished *Roderick Random*), seeing true love in the faces of false men whose dissembling is motivated by the materialistic consideration of her fortune. She is saved from the most calculating of these men only by his fortuitous arrest for outstanding debts. Mr. Seymore, a dubious schoolmaster of uncertain past, intends to rise in the world through a fortunate match despite the fact that he is already married. His plan was to wed Dorcasina and then to have the middle-aged woman incarcerated in an insane asylum so that he could enjoy her cash unencumbered by her company. Bilked of the real prize at the last moment, his revenge is to tell his ostensible prize just where she stands in his regard: "Ridiculous vanity, at your age, with those grey locks, to set out to make conquests! I . . . assure you that any man would be distracted to think of marrying you except for your money."[8] The veil is lifted, and Dorcasina sadly recognizes the delusions under which she has long labored. Even sadder, she realizes that it did not have to end that way: "Had my education been properly directed . . . I believe I might have made acquirements, which would have enabled me to bear a part, perhaps to shine, when thrown among people of general information" (2:212).

An emphasis on female education begins even with the novel's epigraph: "Felix Quem Faciunt Aliena Pericula Cautum. In plain English—Learn to be wise by others harm, / and you shall do full well." As in many early works, the Latin quotation is translated into "plain English" for those who do not have the benefit of a classical education—for, more specifically, the "Columbian Young Ladies, who Read Novels and Romances" and to whom the volume is dedicated. This epigraph, along with the novel's preface, reiterates the eighteenth-century assumption that narrative directly addresses questions on the conduct of life. By reading of Dorcasina's delusions and consequent suffering, the reader should "learn to be wise" and "do full well" in her own personal existence. The key, then, is not for women to stop reading—but for women to read the right kinds of books, the right kinds of novels even, not the novels Dorcasina reads but the novel in which she reads them. It is all a matter of choice, and Tenney, moreover, makes clear the grounds of her protagonist's unfortunate propensity to mislead her fancy with bad fiction. Had Dorcasina's mother lived, we are told, the daughter's education would have been well regulated, sensible. Instead, her father has indulged his own appetite for bad novels and nourished his daughter's. In the process, the widower has also insured that his only child will remain at his side, a devoted daughter who is also his housekeeper and companion.

The importance of female reading, Tenney insists, is all the greater given the intellectual climate of the time in which *any* female reading was seen as suspect. After Dorcasina rejects her first suitor because he does not, in his speech or letters, sound like Werther or Harrington, no more male attention disturbs her novelistic retreat for many years. "Notwithstanding the temptation of her money, and her agreeable person," most men who knew of Dorcasina's love of novels avoided her, "wisely forseeing the inconveniences which would result from having a wife whose mind was fraught with ideas of life and manners so widely different from what they appear on trial." The author seems to endorse such prudent reservations but not the baser doubts of men put off simply by Dorcasina's love of books: "Others there were, who understood only that she spent much time in books, without any knowledge of the kind which pleased her. It was sufficient to keep them at a distance, to know that she read at all. Those enemies to female improvement, thought a woman had no business with any book but the bible, or perhaps the art of cookery; believing that everything beyond these served only to disqualify her for the duties of domestic life" (1:17). This double-edged focus makes *Female Quixotism* more than a satire of one silly woman who reads too many equally silly books. The novel is also a larger different satire on a whole society in which a deficient educational system and dubious sexual politics render women devoid of judgment by deeming judgment, in a woman, a superfluous quality.

One early incident in the novel effectively epitomizes the dual focus of its pervasive satire. When the father attempts to marry his daughter to the only son of his best friend, Dorcasina anticipates "a sensible pain at quitting my dear and affectionate father, and this delightful spot where I have passed all my life, and to which I feel the strongest attachment. But what gives me the greatest pain," she continues, "is that I shall be obliged to live in Virginia, be served by slaves, and be supported by the sweat, toil and blood of that unfortunate and miserable part of mankind" (1:9-10). Her condemnation of slavery continues for another page and a half. She is articulate, moral, intelligent; she denounces slavery in all of its forms and goes considerably beyond her father's reservations on the matter, for while he believes slavery is evil, he also insists it is an "inherited" evil now so entrenched as to be, perhaps, beyond cure. That prognosis is not good enough for Dorcasina. She refuses to accept "inheritance" as any adequate justification for perpetrating an immoral system, and the author obviously concurs with her judgment. But note the impossibly romantic solution Dorcasina devises for what she rightly sees as America's most serious problem. She will marry the Virginian (whom she styles Lysander) with the express purpose of convincing him, through his ardent love for her, that he has no choice—no wish—but to free his slaves. Love, she fondly imagines, should conquer all, even social injustice, and even on the largest social level: "Wrapt in the glow of enthusiasm," she envisions "his neighbors imitating his example, and others imitating them, till the spirit of justice and humanity should extend to the utmost limits of the United States, and all the blacks be emancipated from bondage, from New-Hampshire even to Georgia" (1:11). With such effusions from her protagonist, Tenney brilliantly captures the excesses of sentimental rhetoric. Yet the excess of romantic posturing that renders this solution ridiculous is surely no less suspect than the excess of social hypocrisy and injustice that requires it. Dorcasina, however, is not so naive as not to know that the first decisive action toward her envisioned emancipation of the slaves must be taken by her husband. She might be his prime mover but his will still be the prime move. In short, Dorcasina grotesquely mirrors the status quo even as she questions it. But by subjugating all of her opinions to a notion of romanticism and domestic love, she would be, at one and the same time, both a secret revolutionary and a standard *feme covert*. Yet, one well might ask, what other alternatives has she? The only political solution Dorcasina can envision is a hopelessly romantic one—perhaps because hopeless romanticism decently obscures the fact that the very position from which she plans to act, the subservient domestic helpmeet, is itself a form of slavery.

The picaro adventures on the margins of social possibility; the picara either ends up ensconced in domesticity or, like Dorcasina, never really leaves it, which makes the female picaresque a fictional form fundamentally divided against itself. We have, on the one hand, extravagant escapist fantasies typically dependent upon a woman's cross-dressing (the male picaresque in drag) and, on the other, a woman's picaresque adventures as a mostly imagined escape that both counterbalances and weighs the public and private constraints under which her fantasy labors. Dorcasina is no Don Quixote, for the simple reason that even if he challenges only windmills, he still traverses the landscape he misreads and validates that misreading by his various misadventures. The carnivalesque elements in *Don Quixote,* borrowed largely from Rabelais, thus serve to question the official cultural and political hierarchies, in some ways to reverse them completely—which is precisely what also happens in *Modern Chivalry* or *Mr. Penrose, Seaman* when convention is turned topsy-turvy.[9] But in **Female Quixotism,** Dorcasina's excursions in her quixotic mental world do not trouble the status quo. Only after she awakens to see the "real" world does she begin to question such fundamental matters as the nature of matrimony or the nature of men. "I begin to think all men are alike," Dorcasina confides to her faithful womanservant, Betty, after she has been released from her romantic notions of life, "false, perfidious, and deceitful; and there is no confidence to be put in any of them" (2:201).

When Dorcasina finally sees how the rest of the world views her and how, using that view, Seymore intended also to use her and her money, she seeks refuge with her friend Harriot Stanly, now married to the same Captain Barry who earlier pretended to woo Dorcasina out of some twisted desire to show her what the "real" world was like. Coming to this domestic refuge, however, Dorcasina is surprised to encounter not the wedded bliss which she had expected (and which she feared might contrast too painfully to her own lonely state) but sadness and disharmony. Dreams and delusions still. As the protagonist confesses to her now married friend, she had formerly thought that "in a happy union, all was transport, joy, and felicity; but in you I find a demonstration that the most agreeable connection is not unattended with cares and anxieties." The new Mrs. Barry must concur in that evaluation: "I have been married a twelvemonth, to the man whom of all the world I should have chosen. He is everything I wish him to be; and in the connection I have enjoyed great felicity. Yet, strange to tell, I have suffered more than I ever did before, in the whole course of my life" (2:207). As Dorcasina notes, the once "sprightly Harriot Stanly" has been "metamorphosed, by one year's matrimony, into a serious moralizer" (2:207) and a diminished version of her former self. This second realization parallels the first as a liberation from fantasy. "The spell is now broken," Dorcasina can proclaim, referring equally to the fictions of her novels and the fictions of her society, which were not, after all, that different from one another.

Almost triumphantly, Dorcasina takes control of her life and of the final words of the text. Only the end of the novel is in the first person. Her concluding letter to Harriot announces that she will spend the rest of her days in assisting others less fortunate than herself, in sewing, and in reading novels. She also informs Harriot, who has never read even one novel, that "I [still] read them with the same relish, the same enthusiasm as ever; but, instead of expecting to realize scenes and situations so charmingly portrayed, I only regret that such unallayed felicity is, in this life, unattainable" (2:212). Her life has allegorized her reading, just as the lives of those who do not read novels allegorizes the bleakness of a life without any imaginative escape (i.e., romantic fantasy or picaresque adventures). Given those alternatives, Dorcasina chooses fiction.

In a perceptive analysis of the romance as a genre and, more specifically, of Charlotte Lennox's *The Female Quixote,* Laurie Langbauer has recently argued that Lennox's book "associates the dangers of romance with sins of women, and through this association clinches its derision of the form. Romance's faults—lack of restraint, irrationality, and silliness—are also women's faults." As Langbauer also notes, this same connection was early drawn by Henry Fielding who, in a review of Lennox's novel, observed that he preferred *The Female Quixote* to *Don Quixote* precisely because it was more plausible that a woman, not a man, would be ruled by romances:

> As we are to grant in both Performances, that the Head of a very sensible Person is entirely subverted by reading Romances, this Concession seems to me more easy to be granted in the Case of a young Lady than of an old Gentleman. . . . To say Truth, I make no Doubt but that most young Women . . . in the same Situation, and with the same Studies, would be able to make a large progress in the same Follies.[10]

Fielding's logic is as circular as it is androcentric. Women read silly books because women *are* silly or vice versa (it really does not matter). Cervantes missed the point in his classic; no man, surely, would really succumb to fiction's influence as "most young Women" are wont to do. In contrast, Tenney denies Dorcasina Everywoman status. Every woman who reads *Female Quixotism* is encouraged to see herself as different from what Dorcasina was, and, indeed, Dorcasina becomes different too. Furthermore, Tenney refuses to hang both the satire and the blame, as Fielding conveniently does, on the ostensible folly of women. Why, she wants to know, are women so susceptible to the fantasies of romance they encounter in novels? Maybe it is because the world outside of novels holds so little else for a capable, intelligent woman.

Female Quixotism runs counter to the male picaresque, to the sentimental romances affirming a patriarchal status quo, and also to another trend already under way in 1801 and one that became increasingly popular throughout the first half of the nineteenth century despite (or, perhaps, concomitant with) the highly restrictive legal and social conditions of women. I refer to the fad for female adventures starring women in their plots and almost always in their titles—*The Female Fishers, The Female Marine, The Female Robinson Crusoe, The Female Spy. A Domestic Tale, The Female Wanderer, The Female Spy; or, The Child of the Brigade*—even *The Female Land Pirate*. In contrast to these female picaresque fantasies, Tabitha Tenney's book provides a hard core of realism—and it does not paint a very pretty picture of women's lives. Dorcasina retreats to fiction at the end of her life because, first, her education has been so elementary that she simply cannot read anything more challenging than popular fiction, and, second, because fiction itself is finally far more satisfactory than anything she has found in the world at large. She prefers, not unreasonably, a happy fantasy life to an unhappy actual one.

I would here add a brief epilogue—an appropriately marginal allegory on the marginality of women's lives—to this discussion of the politics of the female picaresque. Although a best-selling novelist (and one of the best early American novelists), Tabitha Tenney remains virtually unknown as an individual. In the *History of Exeter,* her husband, Dr. Samuel Tenney, is accorded almost two pages of fulsome comment: "He was a man of fine presence, and of much dignity. His domestic and social relations were of the happiest character. He was universally esteemed and respected, and in his death, his townsmen felt that they had met with no ordinary loss." The novelist, in contrast, receives four lines: "Dr. Tenney's wife was Tabitha, daughter of Samuel Gilman, a highly accomplished lady. She was the author of two or more published works, the chief of which was *Female Quixotism* which had much popularity in its time, and went through several editions." The Tenney family history contains the same prescription—"wife of," "daughter of," "a highly accomplished lady"—and, ironically, so, too, does the history of the Gilman family. There are letters reproduced in the Gilman volume from Dr. Samuel Tenney to Tabitha's father, but they do not mention the daughter. In contrast, I know of only one letter by Tabitha, but it, too, is about Samuel Tenney. On October 25, 1823, she wrote the Honorable William Plumer who was seeking information for his proposed biography of Dr. Tenney. "It would certainly be most gratifying," the wife observes, "to see some account of my late husband appear in the way which you propose." The letter reveals virtually nothing of Tabitha's own life or thoughts, but, then again, Mr. Plumer was not interested in those. The historical record here affirms the vision of women that Tenney criticized. Woman's place is as daughter or wife or mother; she passes unnoticed in the written record, except, of course, in novels.[11]

In only two sources have I found any record of Tabitha Gilman Tenney that goes beyond the usual and formulaic "highly accomplished lady" encountered in practically all dictionary entries on the author. One account is an amusingly idiosyncratic personal memoir, *A Few Reminiscences of My Exeter Life,* by Elizabeth Dow Leonard. Writing in 1878, Leonard particularly remembers the earlier "authoress" because novelists then "did not grow as now, plenty [sic] as blackberries, but were as hard to find as a real phoenix or one-horned unicorn." Novelty, however, did not assure esteem or even notice. As Leonard confesses: "I blush to say, with all my pride in the rich achievements of my native village, I never read [**Female Quixotism.**] . . . Those who did read it pronounced it superlatively silly, and [Tabitha Tenney] tried in after years to recall it without success." I have not uncovered elsewhere any evidence to corroborate this report of authorial regret, but, valid or not, Leonard's account constitutes a sad postscript to the long neglect of one of America's first best-selling novelists.[12]

The only other information on Tenney appears in the private record, not the public. I refer to a diary by Patty Rogers, which has never been published, a marvelously detailed account of the reading and romances of an eighteenth-century American young woman. The diarist, an expansive young woman who was apparently well known in the town of Exeter for both her volubility and her love of fiction, was one of Tabitha Gilman's contemporaries. The two, however, apparently, did not much care for one another. Patty found Tabby too reserved, but then, as Patty directly and indirectly records, others, including her beau (the preceptor, William Woodbridge), found Patty too excitable. This opinion may also have been shared by Patty's second suitor (or would-be seducer: the issue is unclear), a former doctor in the Revolutionary army, the thirty-seven year old Samuel Tenney who had apparently returned to Exeter with the dual intentions of marrying and entering politics.

The diary records in intimate detail Patty Rogers's love for novels, how her various suitors "seduce" her with fiction, the way Woodbridge (she styles him Portius in her diary) eventually forsakes her for a girl of more sense and less "sensibility" ("He said some persons had too much sensibility!"). She also describes how Dr. Tenney, her father's friend, begins to ply her with billets, poetry, and, above all, novels. On one occasion, he gallants both her and Tabby Gilman home. At another time (she has now renamed him Philamon) he takes "liberties" with her in a carriage and later he takes "liberties" (the same ones? different?) on her doorstep ("You treated me ill," she reprimands him, "as if you thot me a bad girl—Nobody else treats me so ill"). And all the while he also publicly courts Tabitha Gilman, a sober, serious, quiet young woman, a year younger than

Patty and, the latter records, "a person peculiarly disagreeable to me—not from any injury she ever did me, but there is a Certain something, in her manner, with which I am ever difficulted." The older doctor, a former soldier in the Revolutionary War, denies that he favors Tabby and regularly flirts with Patty, who just as regularly sets down their exchanges in her diary, interweaving the sentimental plot of her small life with the plots of the various novels she reads (*History of the Human Heart, Ganganelli, A Sentimental Journey,* etc.). Of course, the ambitious doctor presently marries the more sensible Tabby, and, since Patty's diary ends here, we learn no more from her of her rival.[13]

With the arrival of the husband on the scene, the official record takes over. He was elected to Congress for three terms, and the couple lived, during his term of office, in Washington, D.C. They had no children. In 1801, a year after moving to Washington, Tabitha wrote **Female Quixotism,** a novel in which there is little mention of the world of masculine politics but which does feature Dorcasina Sheldon, a young woman who in personality, in voice and style, and in her passion for novels remarkably resembles Patty Rogers. In 1816, after Samuel's death, Mrs. Tenney returned to Exeter where Patty Rogers, yet unwed and now renowned for her sewing, her piety, and her charitable works, still resided. In her later years, Tabitha Tenney stopped writing, took up sewing, and she, too, was esteemed for the originality and intricacy of her needlework. There is no more to tell, and even this inconclusive account exists only in fragments, suggesting other stories that operate equally on levels of history and fiction: Is **Female Quixotism** a satire against the writer's old rival? Or did the author, married, thirty-nine years old, and childless when she published her novel, recognize a bond between herself and Patty that she may not have been willing to acknowledge in 1785 when Dr. Tenney played each woman's virtues off against the other's shortcomings? For even though Patty does seem to provide the inspiration for Dorcasina in **Female Quixotism,** we should also remember that the biblical name Dorcas is simply the Greek version of the Aramaic Tabitha (as we are specifically told in Acts 9:36), and, moreover, that biblical reference to the good, charitable Dorcas/Tabitha of Joppa whom Peter raised from the dead applies equally to the older character and the older author.[14]

The politics implicit in this possible conjoining of writer and rival transcends the fractious and almost exclusively masculine debate on what shape the new nation should take. It is the same politics that can be observed in the life, letters, and literary legacy of Tabitha and Patty. One imagines the two old women—Tabitha died in 1837 at the age of seventy-five and Patty in 1840 at seventy-nine—living on in Exeter, both esteemed by the community, each engaged in charitable works and spinning tales of her youth in the early years of the Republic while she also plied her needle. It is a world of women's lives as far removed from the world of *Modern Chivalry* or *The Algerine Captive* as from *The Female Review* or *The Female Land Pirate* but not that different from the final days of one Dorcasina Sheldon, who emerges, when viewed from the end of both her original and her author, as a most representative female picaresque hero.

Notes

1. Henri Petter, *The Early American Novel* (Columbus: Ohio State Univ. Press, 1981), p. 381, notes rightly that Mann's exploitation of Sampson's sexual identity is analogous to the Richardsonian prurience over a woman's virginity.

2. *The Female Review: Or, Memoirs of an American Young Lady* (Dedham, Mass.: Nathaniel & Benjamin Heaton, 1797), frontmatter.

3. Percy H. Boynton, *Literature and American Life* (Boston: Ginn, 1936), pp. 195-96; Alexander Cowie, *The Rise of the American Novel* (New York: American Book Company, 1948), p. 30; and Petter, *Early American Novel,* p. 290. Special thanks to Jack B. Moore for sending me a copy of his unpublished essay, "Our Literary Heritage: A Justly Neglected Masterpiece," which documents the magazine publishing history of this bizarre novel.

4. Robert Darnton, *The Great Cat Massacre and Other Episodes in French Cultural History* (New York: Basic Books, 1984), p. 242.

5. *The History of Constantius and Pulchera; or Constancy Rewarded: An American Novel* (Boston: [no pub.], 1794), p. 1. Future references to this edition will be made parenthetically within the text.

6. Loshe, in Henri Petter's *The Early American Novel,* (Columbus: Ohio State Univ. Press, 1971) calls *Constantius and Pulchera* a "cheerful and animated tale" with a "cheerful conglomeration of improbabilities" (p. 64).

7. Charlotte Lennox, *The Female Quixote* (London: Oxford Univ. Press, 1970), p. 138.

8. Tabitha Tenney, *Female Quixotism: Exhibited in the Romantic Opinions and Extravagant Adventures of Dorcasina Sheldon,* 2 vols. (Boston: I. Thomas and E. T. Andrews, 1801), 2: 201. All future references to this edition of the novel will be cited parenthetically within the text.

9. Walter L. Reed, *An Exemplary History of the Novel: The Quixotic Versus the Picaresque* (Chicago: Univ. of Chicago Press, 1981), pp. 74-75.

10. Laurie Langbauer, "Romance Revisited: Charlotte Lennox's *The Female Quixote,*" *Novel,* 18 (1984), 39. The Fielding review was recently republished in Henry Fielding, "The Covent Garden Journal, No. 24, March 24, 1752," in *The Criticism of Henry Fielding,* ed. Ian Williams (London: Routledge & Kegan Paul, 1970), p. 193. For a fuller discussion of Lennox, see also Gustavus Howard Maynadier, *The First American Novelist?* (Cambridge: Harvard Univ. Press, 1940); and Philippe Sejourne, *The Mystery of Charlotte Lennox: First Novelist of Colonial America* (Aix-en-Provence: Publications des Annales de la Faculté des lettres, 1967). And, for a comparison of Lennox and Tenney, see Sally Allen McNall, *Who Is in the House? A Psychological Study of Two Centuries of Women's Fiction in America, 1795 to the Present* (New York: Elsevier, 1981), esp. pp. 15-18.

11. Charles H. Bell, *History of [the Town of] Exeter, New Hampshire* (1888; repr. Bowie, Md.: Catholic Heritage Press [Heritage Books], 1979), pp. 382-84; Arthur Gilman, *The Gilman Family* (Albany, N. Y.: Joel Munsell, 1869), pp. 97-98; and Mary Jane Tenney, *The Tenney Family, or the Descendants of Thomas Tenney of Rowley, Massachusetts, 1638-1890* (Boston: American Printing and Engraving Co., 1891), p. 57. The letter from Tabitha Gilman Tenney to the Honorable William Plumer (October 25, 1823) is reprinted courtesy of the Plumer Papers, New Hampshire Historical Society, Concord, N.H. My special thanks to Dr. Sally Hoople for sending me a photocopy of this letter.

12. Elizabeth Dow Leonard, *A Few Reminiscences of My Exeter Life,* ed. Edward C. Echols (Exeter, NH: 2 X 4 Press, 1972), pp. 46-48. Leonard also relates an amusing anecdote about how, when Washington's death was announced in Exeter, "many ladies thought it was necessary to faint, Mrs. Tenney among the number. She had a valuable mirror in her hand when she received the terrible news of [Washington's] fate. She walked leisurely across the room, laid the mirror safely down, placed herself in a proper attitude . . . and then fainted away" (p. 48). Certainly this anecdote corroborates the rather sober, sensible Tabby Gilman portrayed by Patty Rogers in her diary. Sally Hoople, in her fine doctoral dissertation, *Tabitha Tenney: "Female Quixotism,"* Fordham Univ., 1984, p. 291, also quotes from one other source, a letter in the Duyckinck Collection, Manuscripts and Archives Division of the New York Public Library, which notes that Tenney was "perhaps more remarkable for her domestic qualifications than for her literary performances," another sad commentary on one of the best of the early novelists.

13. Diary of Patty Rogers, Manuscript Department, AAS. See especially the entries for 1785 on January 9 and 10, May 29, June 20, August 1, 2, and 4, and September 14 and 21.

14. Hoople, *Tabitha Tenney,* p. 112.

Cynthia J. Miecznikowski (essay date 1990)

SOURCE: Miecznikowski, Cynthia J. "The Parodic Mode and the Patriarchal Imperative: Reading the Female Reader(s) in Tabitha Tenney's *Female Quixotism.*" *Early American Literature* 24, no. 1 (1990): 34-45.

[*In the following essay, Miecznikowski considers the parodic functions of* Female Quixotism *in relation to the eighteenth-century sentimental novel and Miguel de Cervantes's* Don Quixote.]

Tabitha Gilman Tenney's novel *Female Quixotism: Exhibited in the Romantic Opinions and Extravagant Adventures of Dorcasina Sheldon,* first published anonymously in 1801 and widely reprinted thereafter, is underestimated by twentieth-century scholars of early American literature.[1] Only two recent studies offer readings of the novel—one as social satire, the other as collusive criticism of the novel as genre.[2] While both of these readings of the novel are useful for their study of its extratextual implications, neither addresses the ways in which the text's radical and conservative tendencies interplay *within* the text itself; that is, neither interpretation accounts for the ways in which the novel both conforms to and deviates from the conventional norms of the romance novel and what is gained by this duality. Moreover, Cathy Davidson's classification of the novel as "the female picaresque" effectively marginalizes this "revolutionary" novel and perhaps secures its position outside the canon of early American literature. At second glance, Tenney's novel, like its prototype *Don Quixote,* appears more parodic than "picaresque" or satiric, for it seems to appropriate conventions of the romance and to invert them only to reinscribe them differently. In *A Theory of Parody,* Linda Hutcheon distinguishes between parody, "an 'intramural' form with aesthetic norms," and the "'extramural' norms" of satire that are "social or moral" (Hutcheon 25). This is a crucial distinction that suggests that parody implies a relationship between one text and another, while satire implies a relationship between a text and the world. Since Hutcheon's theory posits a relationship of art to art, parody becomes characterized by intertextuality. But parody is not simply imitative or derivative; it forces an awareness of the difference and the distance between art and experience. Hence, parody is characterized by a "doubleness of form" that arises out of its "transcontextualization" of aesthetic norms (Hutcheon 32) in a text that always implies its original. The dual nature of parody, its "complicity and distance," underlies its apparently paradoxical nature. Read as parody, Tenney's novel perpetuates continuity of the novelistic genre through, in Hutcheon's words, "repetition with a difference" that derives from the "critical distance" between the work in question and the text, or genre, that it implies (Hutcheon 32). In other words, Tenney's novel seems, *primarily,* to "inscribe the mocked conventions [of the romance novel] onto itself, thereby guaranteeing their continued existence" (Hutcheon 75). Working within a form that is not highly regarded in order to re-form it, Tenney's novel parodies the romance by calling attention to its aesthetic norms and marking the difference between her novel and its implied text, or texts. By deviating from its norms, *Female Quixotism* dispels the mythical truth of the romance which its authors claimed, its readers invested in, and its critics repudiated.

Consideration of the adverse critical climate in which Tenney wrote and published ought to demonstrate that the novel's double-edged, satirical indictment of both its readers and its critics would not have been a viable primary aim. The mimetic imperatives of the eighteenth-century literary aesthetic had prompted early novelists to fashion prefatory truth claims.[3] But critics of the new genre saw the novel's lack of truth, or worse, its artifice, as a threat to social and political stability. Moreover, the new genre was thought to reflect social conflict between the classes in its dramatization of "man in the contemporary scene" (Beasley 13). The English romance, in particular, promulgated a vision of Christian heroism in an evil world and thus, from the perspective of the dominant culture, was accused of presenting its readers with a "dangerous vision of life" (Beasley 42).[4] Tenney's parody of the romance, however, allowed her to satirize both contemporary criticism of the novel—the prevailing, misconceived attitudes toward fiction that her "real" and "implied" readers knew too well—and the conventions of the genre from which these criticisms derived. As Davidson has suggested, the novel is best read as an "allegory of reading," a phrase which implies its self-reflexive, intratextual elements and parodic inversions.

My reading of Tenney's novel begins with the dedicatory preface "To All Columbian Ladies, Who read Novels and Romances" (1:iii). These implied readers are addressed "Dear Girls" by an anonymous "Compiler" who claims to be their "Friend and Admirer" (1:iv) and whose persona betrays a certain masculinity.[5] As dictated by eighteenth-century novelistic convention, the preface describes the novel as a "true history of a romantic country girl" (1:iv)—not a "mere romance" (1:iii) such as the heroine herself reads, but a "true picture of real life" (1:iv). The claim to truth is presumably authenticated by the promised similarity to "the most extravagant parts of the authentic history of the celebrated hero of La Mancha, the renowned Don Quixote" (1:iv). Tenney's allusion to Cervantes locates the novel's parody in its allegory of reading or interpreting texts, particularly romances. Her allusion is a parodic gesture that implies complicity between her novel and Cervantes's, but also distance, or difference, from it.[6] The similarity between Dorcasina and Don Quixote is that both are "readers," or "misreaders," of their experience because of their previous encounters with romantic texts. Saturated with the values and conventions taught by the romances they have read, both readers attempt to impose their own textually constituted romantic visions upon a recalcitrant reality. Their respective impressions of experience are thus fictionalized, textualized, not only in obvious ways by their authors (Tenney and Cervantes), but by the codes and conventions of the romantic texts with which they as readers are inscribed. The crucial difference between Quixote and Dorcasina, however, may be expressed in terms of their gender, and herein lies the novel's satiric impulse which we may be tempted to privilege in our reading. For while Quixote is depicted as an errant knight who actively seeks adventure far from home, Dorcasina is portrayed as a young, marriageable woman, and this entails her clinging close to home, practicing domestic "virtues" and waiting for her "adventures" (if she has any) to "happen *to*" her. If Tenney's parody of the romance also intimates criticism of women's roles in eighteenth-century American culture, her textual inversion of Cervantes works *inter*textually first by drawing on reader's and writer's shared knowledge of the codes and conventions of the novel's parodic prototype as well as of the romance in general. That is, the novel's "story" is primarily that of woman as *reader,* not simply as "woman." Satire intervenes only after this bond has been established in order to address "the text's situation in the world" (Hutcheon 116).

The compiler's prefatory appeal to the novel's implied readers situates the text within the world of its readers: "I hope you will be induced to read it, as well for my sake, who have spent much time in compiling and cash in publishing it, as for your own, for whose particular use it is designed" (1: iii). Implicit in his appeal is the implied author's identity as a "compiler," not a "novelist." This work is "truth" not fiction. But Tenney undermines her implied author's credibility in his commitment to the veracity of *Don Quixote.* The compiler seems to be no better reader than either the subject of his study or her male predecessor whose exploits are invoked, yet the voice of the compiler is undoubtedly manipulative, both seductive and authoritarian. The preface thus seems to invite a certain skepticism about reading not only romantic novels but purported histories as well, which can be just as corrupted by the lack of perception or the mercenary ends of their authors as novels may be by sentimentality. Moreover, the skeptical reader will observe that the two genres—history and romance—are elided in the connection made between *Female Quixotism* and *Don Quixote,* the latter of which Tenney's reader knows to be more romance than history. Another strategy Tenney employs which provokes a reader's skepticism and supports the author's deployment of irony later in the text is to distinguish herself (the text's "real" author) from its "implied author" (the compiler), who is further distinguished from the narrator.[7] With this move, Tenney accomplishes two things. First, the distinction among authorship, implied authorship, and narrative persona exempts Tenney herself from complete authority over what happens in the narrative. This strategy calls attention to the fictionality of her text and frees her from responsibility for judging Dorcasina's character or moralizing about the novel's parodic ending. Second, this distinction allows Tenney to invest her implied author's persona with the conventional attitudes toward reading that the novel then calls into question. The strategic use of an implied author thus enables subtly subversive references to Dorcasina's passion for romances, the novel's parodic focus.

For example, in the novel's early pages, the narrator explains that prospective suitors who knew of Dorcasina's reputation for novel reading were put off, "notwithstanding the temptation of her money, and her agreeable person, [and so] were too prudent to think of seeking her in marriage; wisely foreseeing the inconveniences which would result from having a wife whose mind was fraught with ideas of life and manners so widely different from what they appear to be on trial" (1:17). There were other men, too, "who understood only that she spent much time in books, without any knowledge of the kind which pleased her" (1:17). And lest the observation be taken optimistically, the narrator informs the reader, "it was sufficient to keep them at a distance, to know that she read at all" (1:17). Through the unallied voice of the narrator, Tenney presents a view of women's reading upheld by Dorcasina's male peers—a view that does not even distinguish among genres, but which assimilates and condemns women's reading of all kinds of texts. In a shift in persona from narrator to author, Tenney then denigrates "those enemies of female improvement" who "thought a woman had no business with any book but the bible, or maybe the art of cookery" (1:17). The author's intrusive criticism runs the risk of redirecting the text toward social satire. But Tenney immediately retreats after this and relies instead on the narrative itself and its various disclosures of *mis*reading to challenge her own reader's interpretive judgment.

Throughout the novel, Dorcasina's misreadings of her relationships with men are lamented by her widowed father whose "taste in books" is precisely the opposite of his daughter's, for "novels were her study, and history only her amusement" (1:7). That Dorcasina was raised from the age of three solely by her father is implicated as an indirect cause of her unhealthy proclivity toward sentimental fiction, for had her mother lived, the narrator suggests, she would have "pointed out to her the plain rational path of life; and prevented her imagination from being filled with the airy delusions and visionary dreams of love and raptures . . . with which the indiscreet writers of that fascinating kind of books, denominated Novels, fill the heads of artless young girls, to their great injury, and sometimes to their utter ruin" (1:13). This "historical" note helps establish a basis for Dorcasina's naïveté and for her reluctance to take advice, for with the figure of maternal authority absent from her life, she is in some sense on her own in a men's world; she is her own mother. Her father blames himself, in part, for "having indulged her in perusing those pernicious books, . . . that seemed to have, beyond cure, disordered every faculty of her mind" (1:39). Sheldon thus represents the voice of the eighteenth-century novel's contemporary critics who lamented the "dangers of novel reading" (Petter 52). His own reading of novels, therefore, implies a double standard, one which is expressed in the novel's preface by the condescending voice of the compiler: men are better readers than women. Hence, men can read novels without damage to their minds; women cannot without committing intellectual suicide. What becomes apparent as the novel progresses is that Dorcasina is doomed not only because she is motherless, not simply because she reads novels, but also because she *mis*reads them by taking them for truth. Because her whole identity is consumed with "the etiquette and ritual of the romance novel" (Petter 52), she is a poor reader, even of her own experience, which is inscribed by the textualized "reality" of the romance. But the reader of Tenney's novel soon recognizes better "readers" than Dorcasina among the novel's other characters.

Betty, Dorcasina's maid and confidante, who plays "Sancho" to her "Quixote" and whose own reading competence is a mystery, echoes Sheldon's complaint that his daughter has read too many novels for her own good. By the astute judgments of character which Betty and other female nonreaders of novels repeatedly level against Dorcasina's false suitors, Tenney's reader is perhaps persuaded that novel reading is indeed detrimental to the female mind. But the reader is also acutely aware that Dorcasina tends to fictionalize, to contextualize her experience within the panorama of the sentimental novel, and to project a textualized identity upon an incongruous reality. Dorcasina, because of her novel reading, cannot make as accurate judgments (or "readings") of character as the women in the novel who do *not* indulge in fiction or the women readers of Tenney's book who *do*. Although this gesture exposes the novel's satiric undercurrent, it is secondary, I want to

suggest, to the text's parodic impulse which discloses its textuality and which renders specious any criticism of fiction's lack of truth.

Among the readers in the novel who turn out to be more expert than Dorcasina are its two most literate men. They are also the most vicious impostors she encounters and better readers of her than she is of them or even herself; and they soon know her "like a book." In book one, "the scholar" Philander, alias Mr. Smith, poses as "the scoundrel" O'Connor, the first fortune hunter to win Dorcasina's heart and nearly her hand.[8] Philander exchanges love letters pinned to a tree in the grove where the lovers used to meet, abducts Dorcasina (much to her ambivalent fear and delight) when she refuses to "leave" O'Connor for him, and involves her in one scheme after another only to beat a hasty retreat to Connecticut when his own exposure is threatened. Throughout book one, verbal irony, in the form of sentimental language spoken or written, mocks Dorcasina's romantic blindness, her "quixotism." Disguise and mistaken identity provide instances of dramatic irony that distinguish Tenney's novel from the romance by providing comic moments at the expense of the norms of her own text.[9] Thus, the novel becomes, at times, almost self-parodic. For example, O'Connor first poses as Dorcasina's lover. When O'Connor flees, Smith appears in his place, first posing as O'Connor, then disguising himself as Philander and concocting plot after plot entailing still more fraud and deceit. Dorcasina herself, in O'Connor's absence, enlists Betty (her maid) to dress in Sheldon's clothes and to pretend to woo her in O'Connor's place. One important instance of mistaken identity occurs when Dorcasina arrives at her father's summer house in the middle of the night, intending to meet O'Connor there but finding Scipio, the family's black servant, instead. Dorcasina mistakes him for O'Connor and kisses him while he sleeps. At the same time, O'Connor, encountering Miss Violet on her way to Scipio, mistakes her for Dorcasina. When Scipio awakens, he takes O'Connor for a thief, and chaos briefly ensues.

The tone of the novel is more serious, however, in the second book where conventional expectations of the romance are inverted. Mr. Seymore, having abandoned his wife and family in Charleston to avoid debtors' prison, is posing as a teacher when he is introduced to Dorcasina by well-intentioned friends. Described as amiable enough on the outside but "all manner of vice and hypocrisy" within (2:170), Seymore hopes to marry Dorcasina and then commit her to an asylum. He is the last of her fortune-hunting seducers and comes along when she is well into her fifties. It is Seymore who confronts Dorcasina with the pathetic truth about herself in his parting words to her as he is hauled off to prison:

[I]t was your money, and my necessities that induced me to deceive you; and you credulous old fool, so greedily swallowed the grossest flattery, that it would have been difficult to avoid imposing on you. Ridiculous vanity, at your age, with those grey locks, to set out to make conquests! I . . . advise you to give up all thoughts of that kind, and . . . assure you that any man would be distracted to think of marrying you except for your money.

(2:201)

Seymore is exactly right about Dorcasina; he "reads" her correctly. He makes ill use of what he has gained through his "reading" perhaps, but had Dorcasina been a better, more critical reader, she would not have needed his revelatory remarks. Tenney's novel, then, warns less against the "dangers of reading" than against the dangers of reading uncritically, and offers other, more legitimate readers—both of books and of character—besides the fortune-hunting dissemblers. These include Dorcasina's father, Betty, Scipio, and the Stanlys, family friends who look out for Dorcasina, coddling her, humoring her, and keeping her from the hard truth about herself by engaging her in what they consider to be playful deceptions. Because there are so many levels of reading in the novel, so many "texts," and so many kinds of readers, if the novel is a satire on reading or interpretation, then it implicates and condemns itself as well. If we read Tenney's novel as parody, however, it unmasks its own textuality, suspending satiric judgment, deferring moral didacticism, and leaving its readers to judge the text on its own terms. The novel's intertextual nature and intratextual ironies divert it from satire and deflect any ameliorative aim its readers may apprehend.

"Dorcas" Sheldon is eighteen at the beginning of her story when she decides to change her name to suit her romantic inclinations, a gesture towards self-definition that her father finds whimsical but harmless. In her twentieth year, she receives a proposal of marriage from the son of Sheldon's "old esteemed friend in Virginia" whose "ideas of domestic happiness were just and rational" (1:8), in obvious contrast to Dorcasina's, and so the two are never married. Dorcasina's commitment to romance persists almost to the novel's end and is gradually rendered more and more absurd by the pitiful facts—physical, emotional, and social—of her predicament. She is not the epitome of feminine beauty even in her youth, but neither is she wholly unattractive. The narrator concedes: "She had received from nature a good understanding, a lively fancy, an amiable cheerful temper and a kind and affectionate heart" (1:6). In short, she is rather "like the greater part of her countrywomen; such as no man would be smitten with at first sight, but such as any man might love upon intimate acquaintance" (1:6-7). This narrative ploy effectively identifies the novel's implied readers with Dorcasina, intimating these readers' own susceptibility to sentimentality, both in novels and in men. But the endorsement of mimesis implied by the narrator as well as the implied author is suspect, given Dorcasina's own all-too-trusting approach to a "text." For Tenney's narrator to seduce his readers into investing themselves in his text would be to commit the same crime against them of which novelists are implicitly accused in the novel's preface and throughout its story.[10] The text's solicited reader-identification thus undermines the intentions of both the implied author and the narrator and ultimately subverts the mimetic implications of the text.

Tenney partially redeems Dorcasina at the end of *Female Quixotism* by relegating her to the margins of society in the role of a philanthropic spinster, a rather conventional fate. She is thus rescued from her pathetic state—"sallow and full of wrinkles, [her] front teeth . . . all gone, and her hair . . . quite white" (2:103)—but is still in vicarious pursuit of dreams of connubial bliss through her continued, though now changed, reading of romances. The novel's final pages consist of a letter to Harriet Stanly, now Mrs. Barry, in which Dorcasina blames her father's ineptness as well as her own ignorance and romantic "turn of mind" (2:210) for her situation. Her suggestion that all young women are "ignorant of the world" and "naturally" romantic echoes the novel's prefatory warning to its implied readers. The implied author's double-edged indictment of reading and readers resurfaces in Dorcasina's wistful allusion to the disparity between the real and the ideal. Yet, the ending of the novel seems also to suggest that there is a sense in which what is "untrue" is not inherently bad or necessarily dangerous, or that what may make fiction so is not its lack of truth. If (mis)taken for truth, fictions are dangerous, but they can also be playful amusement; they may even be benevolent. But perhaps never to be deceived is preferable, Dorcasina ponders at the novel's close, and she advises Harriet that her daughters might be better off never having the opportunity to confront the difference between the real and the imagined. The ending, however, seems also to attribute some value to reading, even novel reading, at the same time that it criticizes, or cautions, the would-be reader. For in the end, although Dorcasina has learned to separate art from life, she continues to retreat to the visionary world of the romance novel, a world which she knows now does not exist, not even for Harriet whose marriage to Captain Barry suffers early from the death of her mother and soon after from the stillbirth of the Barrys' first child. The elimination of the novel's only chance for the conventionally "happy" ending reinforces Dorcasina's altered perspective and resituates the role of fiction in the world.[11]

Female Quixotism, then, may be regarded as a satiric parody of the eighteenth-century romance that is also a parody of a parody, *Don Quixote*. The text imitates the romance, working within its boundaries, both including and excluding its conventions, conserving and subverting its form. What is gained by this intertextuality is the creation of a new genre, as Hutcheon suggests, "out of the questioning of the very act of aesthetic production" (Hutcheon 10), a genre that self-consciously and self-critically "satirize[s] the reception and creation of [a] certain kind of art" (Hutcheon 16), namely the romance or sentimental novel. If parody is a "symptom of historical processes which invalidate the normal authenticity of primary forms" (Kiremidjian 241), Tenney's novel demonstrates parody's both nostalgic and revolutionary impulses, for it glances backward in order to rehabilitate the novelistic form. We ought to resist, then, the temptation to see the novel as a "female picaresque," for to do so is to relegate it to the margins of the patriarchal tradition whose conventions it seems to challenge successfully. To claim a place for the novel at once within and outside of the picaresque tradition is to situate our reading of the novel *within* that tradition instead of along side of it. Such a reading threatens to limit the scope of the novel's indictments to satire. Consequently, such a reading disregards the dissonance between form and content that is the essence of parody as a "revolutionary" form and ultimately dismisses the novel's radical critique of traditional theories of representation.

Notes

1. There are five editions of *Female Quixotism.* The first four two-volume editions were published in 1801, 1808, 1825, and 1829. One three-volume edition was published post-humously in 1841. All references to the text are to the 1801 edition printed in Boston by Thomas and Andrews.

2. In *Revolution and the Word,* Davidson identifies Tenney's novel as a subgenre of the picaresque tradition that she names "the female picaresque." For Davidson, the novel is a satire on women's education and conventional attitudes towards novel reading in the early national period. Conversely, in *Early Novel,* Petter deems the novel an indictment of the new genre itself which reflects Tenney's sensitivity to and complicity with her contemporary critical climate. Thus, Davidson foregrounds the novel's subversive impulses while Petter emphasizes its conservatism, but both scholars address the novel's extratextual, or "extramural," context and aim.

3. Beasley explains that ethical and mimetic imperatives of the times led to these early texts' prefatory "claim of truth" but that these were "usually only subterfuges" (6). He attributes this tactic to the influence of French and Spanish novels in translation, citing *Don Quixote* ("Cervantes' great assault on the idealized nonsense of chivalric romance") as most important (10).

4. Beasley identifies two subgenres of the English romance: the heroic and the didactic (25). He claims that the former was "dead" by the early eighteenth century, and that while both "types of avowedly invented narrative exploit unashamedly the chivalric conventions of noble action and inflated sentiments," the "primary reason why the didactic romance enjoyed an open respect . . . lies in the different degree to which they emphasize a moral function" (25). Major (i.e., canonical) writers (Richardson, Smollett, Fielding), however, exploited and mocked the conventions of the English romance, including its sentimentality, and created parodic romances that served to indict contemporary perceptions of fiction in general and the novel in particular. My contention is that Tenney's method is akin to that of these canonized authors.

5. I am suggesting that Tenney strategically employs a male persona for the dedicatory preface who voices eighteenth-century attitudes toward women's novel reading and patronizes, even attempts to seduce, his readers.

6. Hutcheon reminds us that the etymology of the term "parody" implies duality. The Greek prefix *para* means not only "counter" or "against"—the meaning which informs the common view of parody and which leads to its confusion with satire. *Par,* she points out, also means "beside" and suggests "an accord or intimacy instead of contrast" (32). Thus, she suggests, parody is "double-coded," "double-directed," and so "double-voiced" (70-72).

7. Taking a cue from Booth, Chatman further delineates levels of authorship and readership. The "real author" (the writer who sits down to write), the "implied author" (the "posture" or ideology that the real author assumes or adopts to write and which changes from one text to another), and the narrator (the storyteller) have their counterparts in the reader who plays the roles of "real reader," "implied reader," and "narratee" (148-52). The implied author, Chatman suggests, is "reconstructed by the reader from the narrator" (148), for "unlike the narrator, the implied author . . . has no voice" (148). I am suggesting that in Tenney's novel, as in many early novels, the prefatory "voice" is distinguishable from the voice of the narrator as that of a disembodied implied author. The real author and real reader are, of course, absent from the narrative exchange in the presence of the implied ones (151). This technique draws attention to the text *as a text* and thus a fiction.

8. Tenney's choice of an Irish pseudonym for the impostor shows her sensitivity to the prejudices of

her contemporary sociopolitical milieu, as does her characterization of the Sheldons' black servant and his lady love.

9. Hutcheon suggests that the deployment of irony in a parodic text is a "conservative" strategy that helps to establish the necessary "critical distance" between the parodic text and its "target" (68). "Parody, like irony," she writes, "can be said to require a certain institutionalized set of values— both aesthetic (generic) and social (ideological)—in order to be understood, or even to exist" (95). That is, a reader has to understand what a romance is, for example, in order to recognize a parody of one, just as a reader (or auditor) must believe she knows a writer's (or speaker's) intention in order to suspect irony. In a vivid analogy, Hutcheon reveals the distinction between the object of satire and the object of parody. She explains that "the mock-epic did not mock the epic: it satirized the pretensions of the contemporary as set against the ideal norms implied by the parodied text or set of conventions" (44). Similarly, Tenney's novel does not satirize the romance any more than the mock-epic satirized the epic. The text primarily parodies the conventions of the romance, imitates them "with a difference," but secondarily satirizes its contemporary readers' attitudes towards fiction.

10. Chatman distinguishes between "story" (content) and "discourse" (form) in narration (154). Point of view, he suggests, resides in the story, voice, or expression in the discourse (154). In parody, however, the distinction between form and content is obscured, for parody "separates form and content to demonstrate their relatedness and even their identity in the primary work, and, in the parody itself, to dramatize the pathos of their dissonance" (Kiremidjian 241-42). Parody is thus characterized by an "instability" that reflects its role as "a major mode of expression for a civilization in a state of transition and flux" (Kiremidjian 242).

11. The rather harsh, "realistic" impulse behind this somewhat melodramatic depiction of Harriet's marital woes marks the parodic distance between the world of the romance novel and the world outside of it. Kiremidjian explains that since "parody acknowledges the recalcitrance of matter to form, . . . it is used by . . . artists not as a sign of resignation but as the only means of expressing modes of experience that will otherwise not yield to form" (240) because of the dissonance between primary aesthetic modes and the experience to be represented to an audience. Tenney's abrupt defiance of the mythical image of the happily ever after effectively "expresses the inexpressible" and, from the perspective of an American woman at the turn of the nineteenth century, raises to a whisper, at least, women's perhaps otherwise silent skepticism toward the romance novel.

Works Cited

Beasley, Jerry C. *Novels of the 1740s.* Athens: Univ. of Georgia Press, 1982.

Bjornson, Richard. *The Picaresque Hero in European Fiction.* Madison: Univ. of Wisconsin Press, 1977.

Blackburn, Alexander. *The Myth of the Picaro: Continuity and Transformation of the Picaresque Novel, 1554-1954.* Chapel Hill: Univ. of North Carolina Press, 1979.

Booth, Wayne C. *The Rhetoric of Fiction.* 2nd ed. Chicago: Univ. of Chicago Press, 1983.

Cervantes, Miguel de. *The Adventures of Don Quixote.* Trans. J. M. Cohen. 1950. Middlesex: Penguin, 1984.

Chatman, Seymour. *Story and Discourse: Narrative Structure in Fiction and Film.* Ithaca: Cornell Univ. Press, 1978.

Davidson, Cathy N. "Flirting with Destiny: Ambivalence and Form in the Early Sentimental Novel." *Studies in American Fiction* 10 (1982): 17-39.

———. *Revolution and the Word: The Rise of the Novel in America.* New York: Oxford Univ. Press, 1986.

Friedman, Edward H. *The Anti-Heroine's Voice: Narrative Discourse and Transformations of the Picaresque.* Columbia: Univ. of Missouri Press, 1987.

Guillén, Claudio. "Toward a Definition of the Picaresque." *Literature as System: Essays Toward the Theory of Literary History.* Princeton: Princeton Univ. Press, 1971. 71-106.

Hutcheon, Linda. *A Theory of Parody.* New York: Methuen, 1985.

Kiremidjian, G. D. "The Aesthetics of Parody." *Journal of Aesthetics and Art Criticism* 28 (Winter 1969): 231-42.

McDowell, Tremaine. "Sensibility in the Eighteenth-Century American Novel." *Studies in Philology* 24 (July 1927): 383-402.

Miller, Stuart. *The Picaresque Novel.* Cleveland: Case Western, 1967.

Monteser, Frederick. *The Picaresque Element in Western Literature.* University, Ala.: Univ. of Alabama Press, 1975.

Petter, Henri. "The Pernicious Novels Exposed: *Female Quixotism.*" In *The Early American Novel.* Columbus: Ohio State Univ. Press, 1971. 46-59.

Tenney, Tabitha Gilman. *Female Quixotism: Exhibited in the Romantic Opinions and Extravagant Adventures of Dorcasina Sheldon.* Boston: Thomas and Andrews, 1801.

Jean Nienkamp and Andrea Collins (essay date 1992)

SOURCE: Nienkamp, Jean, and Andrea Collins. Introduction to *Female Quixotism: Exhibited in the Romantic Opinions and Extravagant Adventures of Dorcasina Sheldon*, by Tabitha Gilman Tenney. 1801. Reprint, pp. xiii-xxviii. New York: Oxford University Press, 1992.

[*In the following essay, Nienkamp and Collins provide an overview of the historical and cultural influences on Tenney's novel as well as a biographical sketch of Tenney that offers insight into her literary achievement.*]

When *Female Quixotism* was first published in 1801, the United States was engaged in building a national identity. All aspects of life—not just the laws inherited from England—were scrutinized for their suitableness for Americans. What literature, entertainment, and fashions were most appropriate for a people who were distinguishing themselves culturally and commercially from their British roots? What extent and kind of education would promote civic responsibility among men who had never previously had a voice in government and women who would be rearing future generations of the citizenry? What, after all of the wartime rhetoric concerning freedom and natural rights, should America do about its slaves? While *Female Quixotism* addresses all of these concerns, the novel touches on them in the context of its central concern, what books good citizens "should" read.

Particularly at issue was the growing popularity of novels, a genre that troubled the molders of early American society. First, in a nation not too far from its Puritan origins, novels came up against the charge that fiction was immoral because it was tantamount to lying. Readers today usually wouldn't make this observation, because they use other standards of "truth" for judging literature, but the charge carried great moral weight during the eighteenth and nineteenth centuries. Many writers of novels of the period, Tabitha Tenney included, tried to avoid this charge by asserting in their titles or prefaces that their books were "true histories."

Furthermore, people in Federalist America prided themselves on their no-frills practicality, and they often associated entertainments with frivolous European luxuriousness. Many novels were imported or pirated from England, so a patriotic distrust of those works was a natural extension of the boycott of British goods encouraged during the Revolution. Robustly nationalistic works such as Royall Tyler's play, The Contrast (1787), Joel Barlow's poem, *The Vision of Columbus* (1787), and William Hill Brown's novel, *The Power of Sympathy* (1789), contended that European culture was inappropriate and debilitating for the rigorous necessities of American life.

Particularly important during a time when a majority of the population was quite young was the purported effect of novels on young people. Most of the era's criticism directed against novel reading—criticism in sermons, pamphlets, books, newspapers, and magazines—argued that reading novels impaired the education of the nation's youth. Novels, it was thought, made immoral actions seem more interesting than virtuous ones. By emphasizing romance and adventure, some critics argued, novels gave young people false ideas of life and particularly made women unsuited for and unhappy with the domestic roles for which society destined them. Such are the primary arguments *Female Quixotism* explicitly offers in its criticism of novel reading.

Many authors of novels written during this period attempted to exempt their works from the criticisms directed at novels by criticizing novel reading—of other kinds of novels, of course. William Hill Brown, in *The Power of Sympathy,* argued that American women were harmed by reading English novels just as Charlotte Lennox in *The Female Quixote* (1752) claimed that English women were harmed by reading French romances. Tabitha Gilman Tenney attempted to distinguish *Female Quixotism* from the romances it criticized in a much more thoroughgoing way. While most of the novels deploring novel reading had sentimental, if not romantic, endings, *Female Quixotism* was consistently anti-romantic to the very end. Instead of portraying the ultimate marriage of the central characters who go off to live "happily ever after," instead of concluding with a sentimental death scene in which a woman dies while still young and beautiful with a crowd of relatives, friends, and her true love mourning her, *Female Quixotism* follows its protagonist, Dorcas Sheldon, to her unmarried old age, to physical deterioration, disillusionment, and ultimate loneliness.

But this ironic denouement is not the only difference between *Female Quixotism* and its contemporaries. Like *Don Quixote,* and unlike the sentimental novels written by Tenney's contemporaries, *Female Quixotism* is a comic, boisterous anti-romance. The novel's cutting wit spares hardly any segment of society: droll servants, earnest merchants, scheming scholars, and self-deluding gentry all get their fair share of ribbing.

Female Quixotism takes place in the isolated village of L———, Pennsylvania, up the Delaware River from Philadelphia. The central character, Dorcas Sheldon, restyles herself "Dorcasina" to accord better with the romantic notions she has acquired from her naive reading of too many romances. These romantic notions occasion a series of misadventures as Dorcasina searches in vain for the passionate love portrayed in her beloved books. After rejecting the honorable advances of her first suitor, "Lysander," who fails to act or write like the heroes of her favorite novels, Dorcasina has a number of hairsbreadth escapes from unscrupulous men who want to marry her only for her money.

The first of these escapades involves the Irishman O'Connor, portrayed as a rascal who easily captures Dorcasina's heart by imitating the romantic language of novels. O'Connor, having forged letters of introduction to insinuate himself into the Sheldon household, is discovered and run out of town by Dorcasina's father, Mr. Sheldon. Dorcasina becomes convinced of O'Connor's villainy only after she sees him in the pillory on felony charges. Dorcasina shifts her attentions to the wounded Captain Barry, who is recuperating from a war injury in the Sheldon household. But Dorcasina's marriage plans are foiled again. After a nighttime elopement, she discovers her beau is actually the Captain's servant, James. Mr. Sheldon provides a more "suitable" suitor to his now forty-five-year-old daughter in the person of the merchant Mr. Cumberland, but for once Dorcasina's romantic notions serve her well as Mr. Cumberland also turns out to be more interested in money—any woman's money—than in Dorcasina herself.

After Mr. Sheldon dies, Dorcasina's close neighbors and friends the Stanlys assume the responsibility of preventing Dorcasina from marrying foolishly. Throughout the novel, the Stanlys have served as the counterpoint to Dorcasina's misguided education as they keep their daughter Harriot from reading novels and provide her with the social skills Dorcasina lacks. Their first challenge after Mr. Sheldon's death is to stop Dorcasina from marrying her servant, John Brown, whom she romantically and stubbornly insists is a gentleman in disguise. In rollicking scenes featuring cross-dressing and sexual innuendo, Harriot masquerades as the dashing Captain Montague to woo Dorcasina away from Brown. But even Harriot's combined efforts with Scipio, the Sheldons' faithful and resourceful African-American servant, fail. Finally, kidnapped from L——by the Stanlys and kept on an isolated farm to separate her from both Brown and her novels, Dorcasina almost marries a supposed widower, Seymore, before he is imprisoned as a debtor and reveals to Dorcasina that no one would marry her except for her money.

Amidst all of these escapades, Dorcasina is variously kidnapped, molested, and tricked by both disguise and circumstance in her search for true love. Dorcasina ends up alone at fifty, bereft of her attractiveness and romantic delusions—a singular fate indeed for the "heroine" of a novel, although a far from singular fate for such a "middling" American woman as Dorcasina.

Remarkably, Dorcasina's misadventures seem to be the only upheavals in L——, even though the fifty-year period represented in the novel encompasses the Revolutionary War, its economic precursors, and the subsequent politics of nation-building. Few of these momentous changes agitate or inconvenience the lives of the Sheldons and their neighbors. But not all of the developments evolving on the larger national scene are excluded from this isolated setting. Many of the social issues being debated in public arenas directly affected women's domestic lives, so even the microcosmic world of *Female Quixotism* had to cope with issues of gender, race, and class—issues as volatile then as they are today.

Relations between the sexes during this period were determined by women's economic dependence on men, a dependence completely controlling their lives in the latter half of the eighteenth century. In this pre-industrial age, religious and legal tenets confined most women to domestic duties, either in their own households or (as ill-paid labor) in the homes of others. The low wages and scarcity of suitable work for women continued an economic subjugation that reflected the disadvantageous legal status of women. A woman's legal status at this time depended on her marital status in a system of coverture inherited from British common law. While an unmarried woman—a *feme sole*—lacked political rights such as the right to vote, a married woman, or *feme covert,* was even more constrained by her lack of property rights. Wives could not keep the wages they had earned; they could not own property separately from their husbands—or make wills or sign legal documents or even have custody of their own children.

In this context, the absurd comedy of Dorcasina's search for a husband is a novelistic rendering of an ominous reality. The novel suggests that Dorcasina's fate as a single woman might be preferable to the potential misery of her life with an ill-suited husband. Women's single career choice—who and whether to marry—determined their lifelong felicity and their livelihoods. In practice, *whether* to marry was hardly a matter of choice. Social consensus assumed any marriage was preferable to "spinsterhood," contrary to Mrs. Stanly's position that the single life is a reasonable and positive choice for women. On the other hand, Tenney—careful to portray no "happily-ever-afters"—provides that even the suitable and loving marriage of Dorcasina's neighbor, Harriot Stanly, is punctuated with misfortunes.

Female Quixotism depicts romance novels as pernicious precisely because they incapacitate women for making critical choices about marriage. Dorcasina is educated at home by her father, who allows her to read novels that "fill the heads of artless young girls" with "airy delusions and visionary dreams," "sometimes to their utter ruin," instead of having the benefit of a mother's guidance, which "would have pointed out to her the plain rational path of life" (3). Mrs. Stanly, on the other hand, sends Harriot to Philadelphia for her education, admonishing Harriot's governess not to allow the child to read novels.

Tenney's case against novel reading seems to concur with that of many advocates of education for women. No doubt, Tenney would have agreed with educators like Benjamin Rush and even Judith Sargent Murray, who argued that women must be trained in subjects that would allow them to conduct the primary education of their children (both male and female) and to converse intelligently in polite society. This attitude was far from universal, as the narrator of *Female Quixotism* suggests in the condemnation of those "enemies to female improvement" who "thought a woman had no business with any book but the bible, or perhaps the art of cookery; believing that every thing beyond these served only to disqualify her for the duties of domestic life" (13). On the contrary, *Female Quixotism* portrays no necessary conflict between learning for women and the fulfillment of domestic duties.

Women are not the only socially disadvantaged group limned in *Female Quixotism.* The novel offers a depiction of the ambiguous social relations between African-Americans and the ruling white elite during the period when the northern states began the gradual emancipation of their slaves. Representative of the changing status of African Americans in the North, Scipio is bought as a young boy by Mr. Sheldon, but he appears to be a free servant late in the novel, when he anticipates having to seek a new position if Dorcasina marries John Brown. Dorcasina's diatribe against slavery early in the novel illustrates the strong feelings raised by the institution from the beginning of the Republic, and it suggests the leading role women played in abolitionism.

A change in the legal status of African-Americans does not, however, bring about an immediate change in the racial attitudes of Anglo-Americans. *Female Quixotism* suggests both the older stereotypes white Americans held and a newer sympathy toward African-Americans. Scipio is an African-American version of the age-old "wise fool" character in literature, a character not unlike the fool in Shakespeare's plays. Although typified as an "African wag" who is frequently described in terms relative to other "persons of his complexion" (210, 238), Scipio is one of the most fully and sympathetically drawn characters in a novel in which many of the servants' antics are pure buffoonery. Furthermore, ambiguous attitudes about race relations emerge in Dorcasina's behavior: Dorcasina pontificates at length about the evils of slavery, but she is scandalized by her own inadvert "familiarity" one evening with Scipio, "when, with her snowy arms, she encircled Scipio's ebony neck" (58).

Sentiments toward characters of other nationalities are not so ambiguous. Concomitant with the nationalistic fervor gripping the United States after the Revolution was the rejection of anything or anyone foreign. The two nationalities coming in for much of the negative critique in the novel are the Irish and the French. The stereotype of the "Irish rogue"—represented in Book I by O'Connor and the "shrewd Irish servant" who tries to rape Dorcasina—was carried over to the new nation from eighteenth century British novels and culture. Strong anti-French sentiment arose in the United States after the perceived hellish excesses in the name of republicanism during the Reign of Terror. French influence is thus attributed to the moral depravity of Seymore and Mr. M. of the village of L——in Book II. In general, the novel advocates a morally based isolationism to protect America from corrupting European influences.

In addition to the depiction of gender, ethnic, and international relations, *Female Quixotism* offers a rich portrayal of class structure in the United States at this period. Dorcasina's whole search for romantic love is premised on her status as a wealthy woman: to Dorcasina, marriage is not a necessity of economic survival, because she is of the landed class. But hers is not the only social level portrayed. Class distinctions are evident in the obviously hierarchical relationship between the wealthy Dorcasina and her maid Betty. Even finer detail, though, is achieved in the episode in which Mr. Cumberland courts Dorcasina, while Betty believes he is actually courting her. The distinctions between the landed elite, the *nouveau riche* merchant class, and the lower-class servants provide the source for an abundance of misunderstanding and farcical humor. Later in the novel, when Dorcasina plans to marry John Brown, the kitchen antics of the servants and the friendly guidance of Mrs. Stanly take on a new, urgent tone, as all attempt to restore the threatened social order in the Sheldon household. Tenney brings these issues alive without pretending any panacea is available in this comedic, but realistic, world.

Female Quixotism responded not only to its post-Revolutionary American social setting, but also, parodically, to a literary culture that spanned the Atlantic. Tenney's familiar and sometimes irreverent use of English literature reflects both her support for the reading of literature by women and her critique of naive reading of romance novels. In *Female Quixotism,* Tenney makes direct references to Samuel Richardson's *Sir Charles Grandison* (1753-54) and Tobias Smollett's *Roderick Random* (1748); and she quotes other writers such as Shakespeare, Milton, Dryden, Pope, and Sterne. Given such evidence of Tenney's broad reading and literary interests, it is not surprising to find extensive parodic allusions in her work to other novels popular at the time—even as she condemns many of them for giving women false expectations of life.

The title *Female Quixotism* suggests immediately that Tenney places her novel in the context of Cervantes's *Don Quixote.* The pair consisting of Dorcasina and

Betty is one of the more lively echoes of Don Quixote and his servant Sancho Panza among the many literary offshoots of *Don Quixote.* The dependence of the plot on Dorcasina's "novel-mania" is the most striking parallel with Don Quixote, but Dorcasina also exhibits the latter's moments of intelligence and bravery. Each of these novels, too, portrays its protagonists in their growing decrepitude: compare Dorcasina's being "deprived of all the flesh her bones were ever clothed with; and her skin . . . sallow and full of wrinkles . . . her front teeth . . . all gone" (233) with Don Quixote having "little flesh on his bones and a face that was lean and gaunt."[1]

Likewise, Dorcasina's servant Betty is equally a counterpart to Sancho Panza in her superstitions and her propensity for taking the physical abuse stemming from Dorcasina's adventures. Like Sancho Panza, Betty is initially the voice of reason and common sense against Dorcasina's quixotic delusions. But Betty's realism gradually becomes tainted with Dorcasina's illusionary world to the point that Betty imagines romantic possibilities between herself and first Mr. Cumberland (an aspiring man of a higher social class) and then John Brown (a man young enough to be her son). Just as Sancho Panza seems eventually to trade places with Don Quixote in clinging to romantic dreams, Betty attempts to recreate the hope after Dorcasina's disillusionment: "'Oh, never worry about that now, ma'am; you may yet get a good husband, and live as happy as the days are long'" (321).

While *Female Quixotism* is structured episodically, like *Don Quixote* and the popular picaresque novels of the mid-eighteenth century, the similarity between individual episodes is limited by the fact that the protagonist in *Female Quixotism* is a woman: respectable women at this time did not have the kind of footloose mobility characteristic of the picaresque hero. One situation common in the picaresque novel is the use of masquerade by a friend in order to lead the protagonist away from his or her delusions. In *Don Quixote,* Sanson Carrasco dresses up as the Knight of the Mirrors and then the Knight of the Moon, in order to defeat Don Quixote in battle and require that the old "knight" return to his native village. In *Female Quixotism,* Harriot dresses as Captain Montague to woo Dorcasina away from her imminent marriage to John Brown, and Harriot collaborates with her father's protective abduction of Dorcasina when milder measures fail. In both *Don Quixote* and *Female Quixotism,* the friends' motives are not purely altruistic: Carrasco, as the Knight of the Moon, wants revenge for being defeated by Quixote as the Knight of the Mirrors; and Harriot expects to be amused by her deception.

Other situations in *Female Quixotism* parody those common to many eighteenth-century British novels, which were popular in America and available in cheaply pirated or imported editions. The masquerades and cross-dressing practiced with great earnestness in *Pamela, Sir Charles Grandison,* and *Roderick Random* are spoofed in the high-jinks of Philander, Betty, Harriot, Seymore, and the barber Puff. The contrived abduction scenes are likewise evocative of other novels, but self-consciously so:

> The very same accident had formerly happened to Harriot Byron [of *Sir Charles Grandison*], though she was, to be sure, rescued in a different manner; and Dorcasina's satisfaction would have been complete, had O'Connor chanced to have been her deliverer.
>
> (139)

The contrived nature of the abduction scenes in *Female Quixotism* reduces to an absurdity the abductions in *The Female Quixote, Pamela,* and *Joseph Andrews.* Similarly, Dorcasina's mistaken elopement with James undermines the seriousness of such scenes in *Clarissa* and *Tom Jones.*

The fact that *Female Quixotism* parodies the literary milieu in which it was conceived does not belittle the original twists Tenney gives to each situation, or the broad humor with which she delineates them. Suggesting that the summerhouse scene between Dorcasina and Scipio, O'Connor and Miss Violet is Shakespearian in its use of multiple mistaken identities and twisted romances does not preclude appreciation of its farcical humor and sly hints of miscegenation. On a grimmer note, nothing in all of Pamela's or Clarissa's fainting fits or Sophia Western's night-time peregrinations over England conveys the dread of Harriot's first night-time walk as Captain Montague, or the real threat and disgrace of Dorcasina's attempted rape and its consequences.

A final question about literary influences might be an obvious one, of how much Tenney owes to Charlotte Lennox's *The Female Quixote,* a similar parody published half a century earlier. Certainly, many of the situations are the same: like Lennox's heroine Arabella, Dorcasina lost her mother at an early age and was raised and educated by her father in a secluded setting. They each have a faithful female servant and *confidante,* although Betty is a much more lively and Panza-like foil to the vagaries of her mistress than Arabella's Lucy. They both have genuine, suitable suitors, as well as impostors who are after their wealth; both imagine potential lovers in servants (not to mention almost all men they meet); and both adopt peculiar modes of dress that serve as visible signs of their mental peculiarities. Finally, the understanding of each is "corrupted" through the reading of literature foreign to their own countries: Arabella is obsessed with the French heroic romances of the previous century, while Dorcasina pictures herself the heroine of books like *Sir Charles Grandison* and *Roderick Random.* Thus, they both serve as nationalistic warnings as well as anti-romance warnings.

Otherwise, Tenney has created a very different female Quixote, based on a more thorough anti-romanticism. Lennox, although her basic tenet is to criticize romance reading, creates a romantic heroine who is "conventionally young, well-born, lovely, intelligent, and virtuous" and who ends up marrying her original suitor, Glanville, and living happily ever after, "united . . . in every Virtue and laudable Affection of the Mind."[2] Tenney, in contrast, more realistically portrays Dorcasina as being "a middling kind of person, like the greater part of her countrywomen" (4). The novel follows Dorcasina over a time period of fifty years, during which time her delusions become increasingly absurd and pathetic. Instead of the conventional marriage and happy ending, Dorcasina finds herself a disillusioned old maid, resigned to a life of charity and novel reading. Thus the parodic and hence didactic nature of Tenney's novel is much more consistent than that of Lennox's.

Moreover, Arabella undergoes relatively few adventures and spends a disproportionate amount of time lecturing her cousins (and anyone else she meets) on the romantic precedents for her behavior and expectations. As we have already seen, Tenney sketches most of Dorcasina's life and skips from adventure to adventure. In doing so, she follows the example of Henry Fielding:

> When any extraordinary Scene presents itself, (as we trust will be often the Case) we shall spare no Pains nor Paper to open it at large to our Reader; but if whole Years should pass without producing any thing worthy of his Notice, we shall not be afraid of a Chasm in our History; but shall hasten on to Matters of Consequence, and leave such Periods of Time totally unobserved.[3]

This selective focus is one of the reasons why Tenney's narrative is a much more rollicking, funny tale than Lennox's. Dorcasina's escapades engage the reader in a way that Arabella's monologues cannot possibly. So while Tenney may have derived her original conception from Lennox's *The Female Quixote*, which was available in America (although there is no external evidence Tenney read it), in transmuting her material Tenney creates a portrait of "female quixotism" having all the vitality and slapdash humor of a new nation attempting to find a cultural identity.

Female Quixotism thus provides a window on both the social and literary worlds of the late eighteenth century in America. Popular and timely in its own day, the novel offers today's readers a new perspective on eighteenth century literature and on many of our own social issues. Just as *Female Quixotism* served as an anti-romance for its readership in the early nineteenth century, today it can serve to de-romanticize our notions of the early American republic, which was not only peopled by larger-than-life heroes such as Washington and Jefferson, but by women of all classes and other disadvantaged groups trying to live the best life they could—and vying among themselves in their efforts.

BIOGRAPHICAL SKETCH

What we need for a discovery of the life of Tabitha Gilman Tenney is a faithful *confidante,* one of whose functions is to relate the history of her companion to all sympathetic inquirers, like Arabella expects of Lucy in *The Female Quixote*:

> To recount all my Words and Actions, even the smallest and most inconsiderable, but also my Thoughts, however instantaneous; relate exactly every Change of my Countenance; number all my Smiles, Half-smiles, Blushes, Turnings pale, Glances, Pauses, Full-stops, Interruptions; the Rise and Falling of my Voice; every Motion of my Eyes; and every Gesture which I have used for these Ten Years past; nor omit the smallest Circumstance that relates to me.[4]

Instead, we have only the formulaic mentions of Samuel Tenney's "highly accomplished" wife; the brief, gossipy details afforded by diarist Patty Rogers and memoirist Elizabeth Dow Leonard; and the imprecise and didactic fables of writers like Evert A. Duyckinck, who claims "her father died in her infancy, and she was left to the sole care of her pious and sensible mother,"[5] even though her father lived until Tabitha was sixteen and had six younger brothers and sisters.[6] Piecing together these sources still leaves a tantalizingly incomplete picture of "a woman," as Elizabeth Dow Leonard says, "who had written a book, punctuated and printed it."[7]

Tabitha Gilman was born on April 7, 1762, in Exeter, New Hampshire, to Samuel Gilman and his second wife, Lydia (Robinson) Giddings Gilman, the eldest of their seven children.[8] According to surviving reports, Tabitha seems to have had the strong maternal role model her novel's heroine lacks. Her mother, "an educated and forceful woman," is said to have raised Tabitha in a "Puritanical, bookish, and secluded" manner.[9] Duyckinck credits Tabitha's interest in literature as providing her with "a facility and correctness of language which gave her noticeable freedom and elegance in conversation," so perhaps "Tabby" Gilman's upbringing was not entirely secluded.[10]

Certainly, in 1785, she was "courted" by Dr. Samuel Tenney, who had served as a surgeon in the Revolutionary War. This is noted by Martha ("Patty") Rogers, another resident of Exeter whose diary for that year has been preserved. Rogers's antipathy to Tabby Gilman—"a person pecularly [sic] disagreeable to me—not from any injury she ever did me, but there is a certain something, in her manner, with which I am ever disgusted"—perhaps stems from the fact that Dr. Tenney seems to have been courting Patty Rogers at the same time he courted Tabitha Gilman. Samuel Tenney walked Rogers home from church, gave her romance novels to read, and took "liberties" with her at her own house.[11] If

Tabitha's life bore any similarity to Patty's—an assumption that may not be as safe as it sounds, since Patty seems to have been known as a girl with "too much sensibility" in contrast to the sober Tabitha—then her young adulthood was probably filled with work at the home, frequent visits to friends, meetings on Sundays, and assemblies on Thursday nights.

Tabitha married Samuel Tenney in 1788, when she was 26 and he 40 years old, trading the invisibility of a young single woman for the social and legal invisibility of a wife. We have few facts about Tabitha after her marriage: she evidently published a reader for young women, *The New Pleasing Instructor,* in 1799; she accompanied her husband to Washington on his election to the Senate in 1800; and she published *Female Quixotism* in 1801. This sketchy outline can again be supplemented through anecdotal information from various sources. What a shame it is that we don't have the letters she wrote from Washington, which Duyckinck says "are specimens of her talent at graphic description, as well as illustrative of the fashion and manners of the times."[12]

One window we do have into Tenney's "public" life (that is, after her books were published anonymously) is provided by Elizabeth Dow Leonard. Leonard's reverence for the "real live authoress" does not survive her lively sarcasm, however, and the picture Leonard offers of Tenney verges on the comical:

> She was the lawful wife of Judge Tenney, a brawny, raw-boned and awkward but very good man, with more law in his pocket than in his head. Tabitha affected the dignified and the delicate and sentimental, also the statuesque. Her motions were slow and solemn as of one "who lived apart and reasoned high," and her speech the words of an oracle. "You talk as slowly as Tabby Tenney" was an Exeter proverb.[13]

The reserved nature that was probably the result of Tenney's "Puritan, bookish, and secluded" upbringing, then, is seen by Leonard as an affectation. She supports this accusation with a wonderful "description" of Tenney's reaction to George Washington's death:

> She had a valuable mirror in her hand when she received the terrible news of G. W.'s fate. She walked leisurely across the room, laid the mirror safely down, placed herself in a proper attitude, adjusted her garments like Caesar when he fell, and then fainted away, and so paid her patriotic tribute to the great man's memory and did not sacrifice her looking glass, as a less sensible and discreet woman would have done.[14]

Tenney evidently maintained an extremely proper social front, behind which it is difficult to discern her real feelings. This socially proper reverence for Washington is again reflected in an existing fragment of a letter by Tenney, which appears to be addressed to a younger woman: "You must not broach any of your tory sentiments, for the memory of Washington is greatly venerated here."[15]

Dr. Tenney was at Washington for three terms as a congressman, during which time he opposed on every single vote the election of Jefferson as president. He also voted for the continuation of the Alien and Sedition Act, used to suppress political dissent during the Federalist era. The Tenneys had no children, although they did have in their household during some part of their marriage Anne Gilman, a distant younger cousin of Tabitha's and the daughter of a close friend of Samuel's. After Samuel Tenney's death on February 6, 1816, Tabitha returned to Exeter and is said to have applied herself to needlework. She does not seem to have written for publication after *Female Quixotism.* She died in Exeter on May 2, 1837.

Notes

1. Miguel de Cervantes Saavedra, *The Ingenious Gentleman Don Quixote de la Mancha,* trans. Samuel Putnam (1604; New York: The Modern Library-Random House, 1949) 25.

2. Charlotte Lennox, *The Female Quixote or The Adventures of Arabella,* ed. Margaret Dalziel (1752; London: Oxford Univ. Press, 1970) xiii, 383.

3. Henry Fielding, *The History of Tom Jones,* ed. Martin C. Battestin and Fredson Bowers (1749; Middletown, Conn.: Wesleyan Univ. Press, 1975) 76.

4. Lennox 121-122.

5. Evert A. Duyckinck and George L. Duyckinck, *Cyclopaedia of American Literature,* ed. M. Laird Simons, 2 vols. (Philadelphia: Rutter, 1877) I: 521.

6. C. H. Bell, *History of the Town of Exeter* (Boston, 1888) 383; Martha Jane Tenney, *The Tenney Family* (Boston: American Printing and Engraving, 1891) 57. Arthur Gilman, author of *The Gilman Family,* does not even say that much about her, but gives almost a full page to her husband, even quoting a letter from him to a different Gilman.

7. Elizabeth Dow Leonard, *A Few Reminiscences of My Exeter Life,* ed. Edward C. Echols (Exeter, N. H.: Two By Four Press, 1972) 47.

8. Arthur Gilman, *The Gilman Family,* (Albany: Joel Munsell, 1869). The Gilman genealogy is confused on the point of how many elder half-siblings she had. On p. 70, it says that Samuel Gilman had 2 children by his first wife, Tabitha Gilman; on pp. 96-97 it names 6 children born prior to his marriage to Lydia.

9. Jessica Hill Bridenbaugh, "Tabitha Gilman Tenney," *Dictionary of American Biography,* ed. Allen Johnson et al. 22 vol. (New York: Scribners, 1928-37) 18: 374.

10. Duyckinck I: 521.

11. Martha "Patty" Rogers, diary for 1785, The American Antiquarian Society, Worchester. Entries of note include the June 20th reference to "Miss T—G-m—"; Rogers begins to give Samuel Tenney the pseudonym "Philammon" on April 21; reference to Philammon courting Miss Gilman, July 13; liberties referred to August 4 and September 21 (the same day he "absolutely denied . . . courting Tabby"). Samuel Tenney must have been quite a gallant at the time: when Patty asked him about Tabitha, he replied "I like her as well as the rest of you girls and no better." See also Cathy N. Davidson, *Revolution and the Word: The Rise of the Novel in America* (New York: Oxford Univ. Press, 1986) 191-92. The diary had long been of interest to the staff of the American Antiquarian Society, but Cathy Davidson was the first to connect its references to "Miss T—G-m—" and "Tabby" with the author of *Female Quixotism.*

12. Duyckinck I: 521.

13. Leonard 47.

14. Leonard 48.

15. Tabitha Gilman Tenney, letter fragment, date and recipient unknown, Boston Public Library.

Sevda Çaliskan (essay date 1995)

SOURCE: Çaliskan, Sevda. "The Coded Language of *Female Quixotism.*" *Studies in American Humor* 3, no. 2 (1995): 23-35.

[*In the following essay, Çaliskan considers the subversive humor of* Female Quixotism.]

In her witty article titled "What Can a Heroine Do? Or Why Women Can't Write" (1972), Joanna Russ, the author of the highly provocative *The Female Man*, makes a list of very familiar situations or story lines which seem very funny when "the sex of the protagonist (and correspondingly the sex of the other characters)" is changed. Here are a few examples of these odd transformations:

a. Two strong women battle for supremacy in the early West.

b. A young girl in Minnesota finds her womanhood by killing a bear.

c. Alexandra the Great

d. A young man who unwisely puts success in business before his personal fulfillment loses his masculinity and ends up as a neurotic, lonely eunuch.

e. A beautiful, seductive boy whose narcissism and instinctive cunning hide the fact that he has no mind (and, in fact, hardly any sentient consciousness) drives a succession of successful actresses, female movie produceresses, cowgirls, and film directresses wild with desire. They rape him

Joanna Russ's point is that "there are very few stories in which women can figure as protagonists" because Western (and Eastern) "culture is male" and the myths this culture produces and the stories these myths give rise to are all conceived and enacted from a male point of view. Since "Our literary myths are for heroes, not heroines" (7), a woman writer, she claims, may either use the only three myths, and the stories built on these myths, available to her (the Abused Child Story, the Love Story, and the Story of How She Went Crazy), or she may use male myths with male protagonists. This second path, however, leads to the falsification of herself and her experience as a woman:

> A woman who refuses to write about women ignores the whole experience of the female culture (a very different one from the official, male culture), all her specifically erotic experiences, and a good deal of her own history. She falsifies her position both artistically and humanly: she is an artist creating a world in which persons of her kind cannot be artists, a consciousness central to itself creating a world in which women have no consciousness, a successful person creating a world in which persons like herself cannot be successes. She is a Self trying to pretend that she is a different Self, one for whom her own self is Other.
>
> (10)

According to Joanna Russ, the third and the most sensible alternative is to abandon male culture's myths altogether and to use the lyric mode, which "exists without chronology or causation (whose) principle of connection is *associative*" and which makes it possible to "*(organize) discreet elements* (images, events, scenes, passages, words, what-have-you) *around an unspoken thematic or emotional center*" (author's emphasis), instead of desperately trying to make sense, using the narrative and dramatic modes, which are of no use to a woman writer because they are formed by the principles of voluntary actions, chronology and causation (12). From a feminist point of view, the lyric mode challenges the patriarchal motto "Make something unspeakable and you make it unthinkable." "The lyric structure . . . can deal with the unspeakable and unembodyable as its thematic center" (16).

The points raised in this brilliant essay gain a new vitality in Dana A. Heller's *The Feminization of Quest Romance: Radical Departures* (1990). Heller points to the fact that the mythical-literary quest motif is closely bound to the idea of identity, to self-discovery, which is "an exclusively male attribute" (4):

> Women have been blocked from identifying themselves with the active subject of quest-romance because they have internalized an image of themselves as passive

objects, framed by the classic structure of the myth, removed from the very symbols and activities the quest
traditionally evokes.

(6)

Men, on the other hand, Heller points out, remain heroes even when they fail the quest. They become anti-
heroes like Huck Finn or Holden Caulfield: "No matter
how futile his gestures for salvation, no matter how de-
moralizing his initiation, the male hero remains heroic
by dint of the mobility and capacity for action granted
him by gender" (8).

Like Joanna Russ, Heller also emphasizes the uselessness of myths produced and perpetuated by patriarchal
culture for women writers and shows that with the
changes in the image, status, and role of women in society in the "feminized" twentieth century, the quest-
romance, a genre which used to be exclusively male,
also changed and became "feminized," bringing with it
the strong need to redefine the concept of heroism.

However, the transformation of the passive heroine to
the active subject of the quest-romance was a slow process: "Rejecting contrived public images in favor of
personally enabling patterns, courageous literary protagonists who dared to take their quests out into the
world remained largely unheard of until the twentieth
century" (13).

For a woman writer, one very effective and safe way of
coping with the restrictions imposed on her art is to
subvert these myths, rituals, and archetypes through humor. A very common technique of the art of subversion
is to change traditionally defined gender roles and expose their arbitrariness and, while appearing to make
fun of the characters, actually make the social and cultural institutions that assign these roles objects of ridicule. Joanna Russ's list of plots with changed subjects
is a perfect example of this. In reading "The Short
Happy Life of Francis Macomber," for instance, "one
cannot stop to ask . . . why killing a large animal will
restore Macomber's manhood—(it is) already explained
by the myth" (Russ, 12), but in a story that features "a
young girl in Minnesota who finds her womanhood by
killing a bear" the myth behind the Macomber story,
which is its very foundation, is rendered absurd and
ridiculed.

Similarly, but in a much subtler way, in early nineteenth
century, before it was possible to talk about such issues
openly, some women writers chose to mock these myths
that were supposed to be universal when they saw their
inapplicability to the female psyche. One of the genres
in which women could not produce meaningful works
without betraying themselves for reasons mentioned
above was the adventure romance. A title like Tabitha
Tenney's *Female Quixotism* (1801), for instance, was a

contradiction in terms and was bound to be humorous
in order to be taken seriously. The book was subtitled
The Extravagant Adventures of Dorcasina Sheldon,
which was meant to remove any shadow of doubt as to
the true nature of this work. Since women lacked the
freedom of movement and the capacity for action required by the conventions of adventure romance, it was
impossible to imagine a female protagonist seriously
engaged in any extravagant adventure. The concept of
idealism, however impractical it may be, implied by the
term "quixotism" itself was also incompatible with the
idea of femininity which prevailed at the turn of the
century. The kind of idealism that prompts Don Quixote
to action was unthinkable in the case of a heroine.

Thus, *Female Quixotism* was humorous not because it
borrowed its name from and was loosely modeled on
Cervantes's *Don Quixote,* which is a satirical romance,
and thus positioned itself as the parody of a parody, but
because its title implied an incongruity. For historical
reasons this work has remained an essentially humorous
work, while the original *Don Quixote* underwent a series of transformations from a comic romance to a serio-
comic work, or even a work of tragic dimensions as
each age read it differently, and as it continues to inspire both new readings and new imitations.[1]

But the immediate predecessor of Tenney's novel was
not Cervantes's *Don Quixote*; it was *The Female Quixote: or the Adventures of Arabella* by Charlotte Lennox,
which was published in England in 1752 and was available in America during Tenney's time. Although both
works follow the same pattern, which centers around a
young, inexperienced heroine whose perceptions and
expectations from life are severely distorted by her
reading of romantic stories, as Cathy N. Davidson points
out, they differ in their portrayal and treatment of their
heroines.[2] Lennox's Arabella is sane enough at moments when she declares that her preference for reading
romances is prompted by the dullness of her life, which
is the lot of women in her time:

> What room, I pray you, does a lady give for high and
> noble Adventures, who consumes her Days in Dress-
> ing, Dancing, listening to Songs, and ranging the Walks
> with People as thoughtless as herself? How mean and
> contemptible a Figure must a Life spent in such idle
> Amusements make in History? Or rather, Are not such
> Persons always buried in Oblivion, and can any Pen be
> found who would condescend to record such inconsid-
> erable Actions?

(279)

The limitations of her life as a woman reduce Arabella's own life story to the familiar pattern of being born,
educated, and married, and Arabella is painfully aware
of this.

Such moments of recognition make Arabella a different
character than Tenney's Dorcasina, whose intense dissatisfaction with her own boring life is not stated but

implied through her seemingly foolish thoughts and actions. For this very reason, Tenney's criticism is more powerful and consistent and the book's subversive power is greater than that of *The Female Quixote*. Unlike Lennox's novel, which is inevitably tainted by the very characteristics it sets out to criticize, and thus gives a confusing message about the heroine, the message of Tenney's novel is cleverly concealed but clear throughout, and it does not create doubts about the writer's attitude towards either the subject or the heroine.[3]

Of the various subversive strategies *Female Quixotism* employs, the first is to pretend to satirize its own genre and thus escape the criticisms of "moralists who feared the harmful effect of novel reading on the female character."[4] In fact, what *Female Quixotism* attempts to do is not to mock romance as a genre, nor is it a warning "against the dangers of reading uncritically," as Miecznikowski asserts (40). As a parody of a parody, it mocks those who mock romance when its hero is a woman.

Thus, its concern is far more serious than its "compiler" proclaims. The dedication "To All Columbian Young Ladies Who Read Novels and Romances," which begins with "Dear Girls," and ends with "your Friend and Admirer, the Compiler," warns them against the dangers of reading novels and romances and expresses the "sincere wish" that they may learn from the example of Dorcas Sheldon and "avoid the disgraces and disasters that so long rendered her despicable and miserable" (I, 3-4). The historical fact that the book was written by a woman but was published anonymously with a preface by a fake compiler who adopts a male persona undermines the seriousness of this intent and gives it an ironic twist.

Miecznikowski's excellent analysis of the distinction among authorship, implied authorship, and narrative persona in *Female Quixotism* is extremely helpful for understanding Tenney's intention "to invest her implied author's (the compiler's) persona with conventional attitudes toward reading that the novel calls into question" (37). Thus, the ironic distance between herself and the implied author enables Tenney to disclaim responsibility for his views. However, the question of authorship is more complex than this analysis suggests. The implied author does not deny that he has a moralistic purpose in compiling the book, but he does not claim responsibility for the events in it, for he insists that it is "a true picture of real life," "a biography," instead of "a mere romance," a fiction (3-4). He admits to having heard bits and pieces of the story from other sources, but "her whole story," "the minute account of her adventures, with a generous permission to publish them" comes from Dorcasina herself (I, 3).

Thus, Dorcasina Sheldon is made the writer of her own story in two senses: first, as the female quixote, she imagines things and creates adventures out of ordinary situations; second, as the narrator of her own story to the compiler after she survives her own quixotism. The moral coloring of the story is obviously given to it by the compiler, not by Tenney, who sides with her character in *writing* the story. This is evident in Tenney's identification with her character by naming her Dorcas, the Greek version of her own name, Tabitha (Acts 9, 36).

So, the claim to truth is not only used to mock the novelistic convention of creating an illusion of reality but also serves to disconnect the real author and the implied author. *Female Quixotism* is a perfect example of what happens to "her story" when it is framed by "his moral." As such, it is a story about writing, or rather the dangers of writing one's own story as opposed to reading, which is a passive act.

Superimposing such a narrative on the exclusively masculine "text" of adventure romance provides Tenney with the opportunity to expose the double standards that are at work in her culture. Both Cervantes' and Tenney's characters follow the same pattern: they read books which distort their perception of reality, they begin to live in a world of their own creation, imagining themselves to be different than what they really are. After a series of adventures, they become sane again and understand their foolishness and blame it on the books they read. However, Don Quixote nevertheless becomes an immortal hero and writes his name in golden letters in literary history, while Dorcasina remains a comic character, who is more to be despised than pitied.

This is because the roles cast for men and women in the myth behind these stories are very different. In such stories men are the actors and women are the silent spectators. Therefore, Don Quixote's actions, however impractical and ridiculous they may seem, are nevertheless noble actions; they are not incompatible with the underlying myth, which is powerful even in its absence. Romantic idealism is not a bad thing in itself; alas, times have changed and there is very little room for it in Don Quixote's world. He is not a fool, but pitifully out of date. There is a dominant nostalgic tone in Cervantes' book.

In Dorcasina's case it is very different. One cannot talk about nostalgia in connection with *Female Quixotism,* because women's past does not offer anything to be nostalgic about. Instead of looking back and glorifying long-lost values using pre-existing myths, it attempts to create its own myth, the myth of the female quixote, which is new because it does not have a history.[5] What Dorcasina attempts to do is equally incompatible with her times, not because it is out of date, but because it is new. In this sense it is truly revolutionary. She becomes a threat to society when she decides to "act out" the scenarios of the books she reads. In other words, she stops being a silent reader and starts writing her own story, with the role of the protagonist cast for herself.

Unfortunately, unlike Don Quixote, who has a variety of role models to choose from, Dorcasina has very limited choices, all within the boundaries of love and marriage. Dorcasina's father has a big library "furnished with the best histories, ancient and modern; and every novel, good, bad and indifferent, which the bookstores of Philadelphia afforded" (I, 9). While history is her father's favorite reading and novels his amusement, the reverse is true for Dorcasina. Her insatiable appetite for reading novels can be explained by the fact that these are the only books in which a young, impressionable girl could find role models. Since history books rarely feature women center stage, she naturally identifies with the heroines of love stories. These, however, are almost always "distinguished by the elegant form, delicately turned limbs, auburn hair, alabaster skin, heavenly languishing eyes, silken eyelashes, rosy cheeks, acquiline nose, ruby lips, dimpled chin, and azure veins" quite unlike Dorcasina, whose physical appearance is far from striking (I, 8). Just as Quixada determines to become a knight-errant and changes his name to Don Quixote of La Mancha, so does Dorcasina change her "unfashionable and romantic" name Dorcas to Dorcasina to "give it a romantic termination" and launches out into the world as an irresistable romantic heroine ready to make amorous conquests (I, 10). Except once, when she imagines herself as the savior of Southern slaves, her thoughts never waver from the idea of falling violently in love. Don Quixote, on the other hand, sallies forth to "redress all manner of wrongs, exposing himself to continual dangers" with the intention of winning "everlasting honor and renown" (59).

Nevertheless, Dorcasina's attempt to change her position as a reader to that of a "writer" is an important step, and it explains the need to write stories that feature female quixotes. Reading women must have become a threat in both Lennox's and Tenney's times to make it necessary to write cautionary tales. As in Arabella's and Dorcasina's case, the books that women read at the time were largely romantic love stories and sentimental novels, and the majority of these books were written by "scribbling women" for a largely female audience. The popularity and abundance of such books testifies to a need among the female population, but there is another side of the matter. Culturally speaking, these books serve a double purpose. On the one hand, with their representations of passive or victimized women they perpetuate the patriarchal myth that women are weak and fragile and that their only purpose in life is to find good husbands and become wives and mothers; on the other hand, they provide excitement for

women who crave for intense emotional experience. Patriarchal culture allows for, and even supports, this as long as women get the patriarchal message. The danger begins when the difference between fact and fiction is blurred and women start to demand from life what writers promise in fiction. A woman who demands more from love and marriage than what reality offers is stepping out of her traditional submissive role and defying male authority. She is "literalizing" everything she has been fed by books of romantic love stories. When seen from this angle, such books even help raise consciousness about the limited role relegated to women in society; but this may not always be a conscious effort on the part of the writer or the reader. As in the case of Dorcasina, it may be a cumulative effect of reading such books that leads to an intense dissatisfaction with life.

This is where moralists begin to talk about the dangers of novel reading for women. This is also when the writing of such books as *The Female Quixote* and **Female Quixotism** becomes necessary. But while Lennox seems to partly agree with these moralists, Tenney uses their discourse to negate their argument.

By deliberately refraining from making her protagonist a conscious figure who recognizes and rebels against the seclusion and the limitations of a woman's life in her society, Tenney is able to make a stronger statement about the frustrations of women than her predecessor. This strategy of employing a completely foolish character who is totally blind to the situation allows her to put a stronger emphasis on the objections to her behavior and expose them in a much brighter light. The people who try to "save" Dorcasina appear just as, if not more, foolish than Dorcasina herself. Harriot's disguise as Montague and courting of Dorcasina, and Mr. Stanly's abduction and forced imprisonment of her to prevent her from marrying Brown are no less extravagant or ridiculous than Dorcasina's own actions. In fact, what these "friends" are trying to protect are Dorcasina's family name and family fortune—things that do not really belong to her. While they recognize and fight against several rogues who are after Dorcasina's money, they fail to understand the essential injustice of a system that makes a woman dependent on male authority. If this system did not allow the husband to take full possession of his wife's fortune, there would be no fortune-hunters in the first place. But it is too early for women to talk about such things openly in the 1800's.

However, Tenney does make her point when she refuses to finish her story with the conventional happy ending: an approved marriage. Unlike Arabella, at the end of her story Dorcasina is already an old maid with grey hair, wrinkled skin, missing teeth, and no hopes for marriage. The surface story presents this picture as an irredeemable loss, a pitiful waste; but the subtext, which is cleverly disguised in Dorcasina's lamentations has a different story to tell:

> . . . instead of being a matron, rendering a worthy man happy, surrounded by a train of amiable children, educated in virtuous principles, and formed by our mutual cares and examples to virtuous habits, and of promoting and participating the happiness of the social circle, in which we might be placed, I am now, in the midst of the wide world, solitary, neglected and despised.
>
> (III, 225)

In this picture of an ironic ideal Dorcasina appears not as a unique individual but in her triple role as wife, mother, and a virtuous member of society. Although she mentions happiness twice, it is interesting to note that in neither case is it her own happiness. Women marry to make their husbands and society happy. Besides, as it is demonstrated in the life of Harriot, even "the most aggreeable connection is not unattended with cares and anxieties" (III, 216). Harriot admits, "I have been married a twelvemonth to the man whom of all the world I should have chosen. . . . Yet, strange to tell, I have suffered more than I ever did before in the whole course of my life" (III, 216). This is why, even after she realizes her foolishness, Dorcasina cannot dispense with her novels. She continues to read "with the same relish, the same enthusiasm as ever, but," she adds, "instead of expecting to realize scenes and situations so charmingly portrayed, I only regret that such unalloyed felicity is, *in this life,* unattainable" (III, 225, my emphasis).

The bracketed expression "in this life" secretly points to an afterlife, not in a religious sense, but in the sense of a time yet to come when women will realize that marriage is not essential to happiness and that there is no such thing as a happy marriage unless they take part in it as fulfilled individuals. The picture of married life for a woman as it is portrayed by Dorcasina and confirmed by Harriot must have been too dreary even for the Columbian Young Ladies of the time. By making Dorcasina sound as if she accedes to the premise that marriage, however dull and painful it may be, is the only alternative for a woman, Tenney manages to provoke anger and resentment to such a fate and delivers a different message between the lines.

Reading early women's writing is like deciphering an elaborate coded language. This is particularly so in the case of women humorists, both because humor is traditionally thought to be exclusively male and because women usually use self-deprecating humor not to offend the promulgators of the dominant culture. However, as Nancy Walker and Zita Dresner point out in the introduction to their anthology of women's humor, *Redressing the Balance*:

> . . . laughing at one's own shortcomings is not only a way of diminishing their importance and potentially overcoming them but is also a technique for cleansing

them of pejorative connotations imposed by the dominant culture and, thereby, turning them into strengths . . . the use of humor by women against women, when it is used to advance ideas that might conflict with those of the male establishment about women's roles and prerogatives, represents a step toward empowerment rather than capitulation.

> (xxiii)

Female Quixotism is a perfect example of the subtlety of early women's humor, which disguises itself as the voice of the dominant ideology while it undermines that ideology by delivering metamessages that are inherent in it. Such books as *Female Quixotism* will take their well-deserved place in the literary canon when these metamessages are carefully decoded.

Notes

1. See the chapter titled "The Fortunes of Don Quixote" in E. C. Riley's *Don Quixote,* (London: Allen and Unwin, 1986).

2. Davidson mentions this only in passing in a biographical note about Tenney in *American Women Writers,* Vol.4, p.218.

3. For moral confusion in *The Female Quixote* see Deborah Ross, "Mirror, Mirror: The Didactic Dilemma of *The Female Quixote*" in *Studies in English Literature: 1500-1900,* (Summer 1987, 27): 455-73.

4. Ola Elizabeth Winslow, in a biographical note on Tenney in *Notable American Women: 1607-1950,* says *Female Quixotism* satirizes its own genre. My understanding is that it only pretends to do so.

5. Sandra M. Gilbert and Susan Gubar observe that women writers are "precursors of 20th century modernists, the *avant garde* of the *avant garde,*" because they express exuberance rather than anxiety at the breaking down of traditional structures. "Introduction: The Female Imagination and the Modernist Aesthetic," *Women's Studies,* (1986, 13) pp. 1-10.

Works Cited

American Women Writers. Vol.4. Ed. Lina Mainiero. New York: Frederick Ungar, 1982.

Cervantes, Miguel de. *Don Quixote of La Mancha.* Trans. Walter Starkie. New York: New American Library, 1964.

Gilbert, Sandra M. and Susan Gubar. "Introduction: The Female Imagination and the Modernist Aesthetic." *Women's Studies* 13 (1986): 1-10.

Heller, Dana A. *The Feminization of Quest-Romance: Radical Departures.* Austin: University of Texas Press, 1990.

Lennox, Charlotte. *The Female Quixote: or the Adventures of Arabella.* New York: Oxford University Press, 1989.

Miecznikowski, Cynthia J. "The Parodic Mode and the Patriarchal Imperative: Reading the Female Reader(s) in Tabitha Tenney's *Female Quixotism.*" *Early American Literature* 25 (1990, 1): 34-45.

Notable American Women 1607-1950: A Biographical Dictionary. Vol.3. Cambridge, MA: The Belknap Press of Harvard University Press, 1971.

Riley, E. C. *Don Quixote.* London: Allen and Unwin, 1986.

Ross, Deborah. "Mirror, Mirror: The Didactic Dilemma of *The Female Quixote.*" *Studies in English Literature 1500-1900* 27 (Summer 1987): 455-73.

Russ, Joanna. "What Can a Heroine Do? Or Why Women Can't Write." *Images of Women in Fiction: Feminist Perspectives.* Ed. Susan Koppelman Cornillon. Bowling Green, Ohio: Bowling Green University Popular Press, 1972.

Sharon M. Harris (essay date 1997)

SOURCE: Harris, Sharon M. "Lost Boundaries: The Use of the Carnivalesque in Tabitha Tenney's *Female Quixotism.*" In *Speaking the Other Self: American Women Writers,* edited by Jeanne Campbell Reesman, pp. 213-28. Athens: The University of Georgia Press, 1997.

[*In the following essay, Harris argues that Tenney's employment of the carnivalesque in* Female Quixotism *exposes the limitations of the purportedly democratic government of the United States during the early years of the new nation.*]

When Tabitha Gilman Tenney's novel *Female Quixotism* was published in 1801, it joined a national voice of lament over the dangers of novel reading. The typical antinovel argument was that the genre's romantic allurements would lead women away from the realities of their domestic responsibilities. In *Female Quixotism,* however, Tenney used a comic, anti-romantic stance in relation to novel reading to demonstrate the failed sense of democracy in the new republic. No element of the citizenry escapes her comic examination; as the editors of the recent Oxford edition of *Female Quixotism* note, "The novel's cutting wit spares hardly any segment of society: droll servants, earnest merchants, scheming scholars, and self-deluding gentry all get their fair share of ribbing."[1] The argument I am presenting examines Tenney's novelistic use of the carnivalesque as a means of exposing the realities of the new nation's social or-

der, especially as it oppressed and segregated its citizens by race, class, and gender. But I also want to address the bifurcated argument embedded in this text, an argument that both exposes the failed sense of democracy in the new republic and simultaneously perpetuates the dominant culture's encoding of racial and ethnic difference.

The concept of the carnivalesque was made available to critical studies by Mikhail Bakhtin. The historical significance of carnival is that it has always been linked to moments of social or political crisis. Thus, it is not surprising that carnivalesque images reemerge in post-Revolutionary U.S. literatures as the nation begins to define not only its role in international affairs but equally the roles of its various citizens. In denoting the carnivalesque as a mode aligned with "the peculiar culture of the marketplace and of folk laughter with all its wealth of manifestations," Bakhtin outlines three distinct forms these manifestations take: first, ritual spectacles, such as carnival pageants and comic marketplace shows; second, parodies, both oral and written, either in the vernacular or with an invocation of classical standards; third, the use of curses and oaths as a means of explicitly challenging classical language standards.[2] Most prevalent in medieval and Renaissance literatures, the carnivalesque exposes the "two-world condition" of those cultures: officialdom and a world outside that officialdom, that is, a world of the people. It is important to note that, while carnival resembles the spectacle, it is different in one important way. As Bakhtin reminds us, "carnival . . . does not acknowledge any distinction between actors and spectators. . . . Carnival is not a spectacle seen by the people; they live in it. . . . During carnival time life is subject only to its laws" (7). Freedom is embraced and all hierarchies are suspended; in its way, then, carnival is intended to constitute a true democratic moment.

Central to an understanding of the carnivalesque is its engagement with grotesque imagery, and Tabitha Tenney's main character in *Female Quixotism* may certainly, within her culture, be defined as a grotesque. She immerses herself in novel reading, deludes herself about a series of doomed romances, and at the novel's conclusion opts for spinsterhood and contrition. She may be wiser, but she is still single, and for women, in the new nation's emphasis on republican motherhood, that is a form of grotesque. Yet it is crucial to our understanding of how Tabitha Tenney employs the carnivalesque to recognize an important point, emphasized by Bakhtin but too often overlooked in subsequent analyses, namely, the historically evolving nature of the carnival-grotesque form. In the era of Molière and Swift, this form functioned "to consecrate inventive freedom, . . . to liberate from the prevailing point of view of the world, from conventions and established truths." In the late eighteenth century, however, a radical change took place. It began as a German literary controversy over the character of Harlequin but soon became "a wider problem of [aesthetic] principle: could manifestations such as the grotesque, which did not respond to the demands of the sublime, be considered art?" What evolved was a movement away from the broader concepts of Rabelais and Cervantes to what Bakhtin terms "the new subjective grotesque"; he cites *Tristram Shandy* as the "first important example" of this evolution (34-36).

Tabitha Tenney was well aware of the changes in the carnival-grotesque and contributed to its transformation. In the late eighteenth century the carnival-grotesque became not a festival of all the people but rather "a private 'chamber' character. It became, as it were, an individual carnival, marked by a vivid sense of isolation" (Bakhtin, 37). In the years leading up to publication of *Female Quixotism,* the United States, under Federalist rule, pursued an extreme isolationist ideology; the carnivalesque not only fit Tenney's artistic needs but also engaged her political inclinations, as will be outlined in detail below. What is critical in this transformation of the genre is that the "principle of laughter which permeates the grotesque" (especially in relation to the bodily life) lost its regenerative power; the grotesque becomes an object of fear to be relayed by the author and assumed by the reader. One example of this change is the mask: originally, the mask was "connected with the joy of change and reincarnation"; it celebrated difference rather than uniformity. In the late eighteenth century, however, the mask was "stripped of its original richness and acquire[d] other meanings alien to its primitive nature" (37-40). It became an instrument of deceit and secretiveness. The carnival-grotesque evolved into a nocturnal event, evoking themes of darkness rather than embracing the symbolic implications of sunrise and morning as the original carnival had.

This latter sense of the carnivalesque is explored by Julia Kristeva. "Carnivalesque discourse," she observes, "breaks through the laws of a language censored by grammar and semantics and, at the same time, is a social and political protest. There is no equivalence, but rather, identity between challenging official linguistic codes and challenging official law."[3] As Mary Russo has argued, we must embrace the carnivalesque with caution, since it can be employed as a panacea by a dominant culture rather than as a truly liberating vehicle.[4] Yet it is a tool of authorities only when the carnival is a ritual sanctioned by them. In *Female Quixotism,* it is precisely when Dorcasina Sheldon, the "private 'chamber' character," stops reading and breaks with officialdom (literally, with her father's house) that Tenney depicts her as secretly engaging in the carnivalesque as a means of moving from the role of the subjected to that of the subject, of reinscribing her world on her own terms. It is in the episodes that occur outside Mr. Shel-

don's house that Tenney interjects the issues of gender, race, and class, leading the reader into a recognition of how limited the so-called democratic reforms of the eighteenth century had actually been.

In *Revolution and the Word,* Cathy N. Davidson recognizes *Female Quixotism* as a picaresque novel. Typically, Davidson notes, the picaresque's loose narrative form "allows a central character . . . to wander the margins of an emerging American landscape [and] to survey it in all its incipient diversity," but since women's mobility was severely restricted in the early federal period, the female picara cannot meet these narrative criteria. Davidson asserts, therefore, that Dorcasina's story does not challenge the status quo until the novel's conclusion, when she questions the nature of matrimony.[5] I would argue, however, that the status quo for Anglo American women is challenged throughout the novel; first, because the picaresque is itself a carnivalization of the novel's form, and second, because Dorcasina takes many "journeys" outside her domicile. Granted, these journeys may be only to an isolated grove or to a nearby town, but distance itself is insignificant in relation to the alternative experiences she encounters. In these journeys, the upper-class Dorcasina engages in relationships with members of every class of U.S. society, including her own Anglo American household servants, African American servants whose domain lies within the Sheldon estate but not within the household itself, an Irish rogue, an enterprising prostitute, schoolteachers, and a barber. It seems to me far more radical to assert that this diversity lies within one's own neighborhood than to assume an audience will translate so-called "foreign" experiences to a sense of the American polis.

In some respects, *Female Quixotism* foreshadows feminist and postmodern challenges to Enlightenment philosophies, especially the Enlightenment privileging of reason and science. In an era deemed the "Age of Reason," Tabitha Tenney's employment of the carnivalesque challenges cultural definitions of rationality itself, not only by depicting the chaos that surrounds the aristocratic Sheldon domicile but equally by exposing the class biases internalized in the celebration of "reason," as defined by the dominant culture. In the United States at the turn of the century, the voice of rationality was always deemed that of the white male aristocrat. Mr. Sheldon personifies this voice and Dorcasina's first love, Lysander, represents its perpetuation in the next generation of young, privileged males: "His person was noble and commanding . . . and his address manly and pleasing. . . . His ideas of domestic happiness were just and rational" (7). Tenney depicts Lysander as the ideal of absolute patriarchy. The gendering of reason by Enlightenment philosophies is also satirized by Tenney. In contrast to Lysander, Tenney presents an alternative voice of reason in that of the Anglo American servant

Betty, Dorcasina's life-long companion. Throughout the novel, Betty's intellectual, reasoning abilities are not aligned with issues of philosophy or overt politics but rather with her power to penetrate beneath the actions and the masks of propriety displayed by various characters in the novel; it is neither Dorcasina nor Mr. Sheldon but rather Betty who discerns individuals' "unmasked" natures and their degrees of reliability. It is Betty's voice, far more than Mr. Sheldon's, that Dorcasina needs to hear in order to escape her repeated cycle of misapplied love that results in emotional abuse and trauma. While the comic spirit of the carnival prevails, the pathos of Dorcasina's repeated traumatic experience suggests the very real consequences of the gendering of reason and the marginalization of women, even in their own homes and their own country.

Mr. Sheldon is never fully aware of his daughter's beliefs and not aware at all of her adventures, while Betty not only knows of Dorcasina's experiences but also attempts to guide her away from self-defeating actions into a better sense of social reality. Tenney pushes the boundaries of rationality further, however, when she exposes the class-based consequences of Betty's knowledge. The prevailing ideology of the Age of Reason held that rational thought and action will lead to the best possible political and social orders; yet in spite of her wisdom and social astuteness, Betty's social class does not allow her to conquer prevailing misconceptions. The automatic devaluation of any expression by a person of her class is rendered both through her employers' lack of adherence to her cautionary voice and, more explicitly, through a physical (bodily) suppression of Betty herself. In episode after episode, when Betty cautions her against a particular action, Dorcasina pursues her own desires—to her detriment, surely, but it is almost always Betty who must endure physical abuse for Dorcasina's foolish actions. This abuse is rendered most explicitly when Dorcasina insists that Betty dress in Mr. Sheldon's clothing and pretend to be Dorcasina's lover. Betty has barely begun her impersonation when "she was interrupted . . . by the sudden appearance of Scipio, the gardener, Patrick, the boy, a white servant, and two or three labourers from the field," all of whom chase her about the grounds, believing that she is "some evil minded person" who intended to steal Mr. Sheldon's belongings (99). The episode ends when Dorcasina herself appears and exposes Betty's identity, but Betty is left as the mortified object of her peers' mirth, and she is seen at the end of the scene "sinking with shame and vexation" (99). In other, similar episodes, Betty is repeatedly abandoned by Dorcasina in moments of physical combat that Dorcasina's actions have created: several times Betty is beaten; in one episode her upper garments are stripped off of her; and in another, the servant of Dorcasina's latest lover "laid violent hands upon [Betty], pulled her hair, shook her, pinched her, and mauled her" (132). While there is al-

ways supposed to be a comic element to such scenes in the novel, the carnivalesque nature of these scenes exposes real consequences for the servant class due to antics perpetuated by the upper-class. Dorcasina may be humiliated when she loses lover after lover, but it is Betty whose body is mauled and appropriated for her mistress's use.

These episodes lead us to one of the most significant aspects of Tenney's engagement with the carnivalesque in *Female Quixotism*. In an era of denial and suppression of female sexuality, the carnivalesque by its very nature allows for its exploration. It is on this avenue of sexual exploration, too, that class and race distinctions are momentarily lost. The carnival is the time for cross-dressing and masquerading, and *Female Quixotism* is rife with instances of both activities, which allow Tenney to explore themes of sexuality that are banned in the father's house and by the father's law. The scenes that allow the issue of sexuality to be raised most often depend upon the eighteenth century's shift from open, daylight carnival celebrations to dark, surreptitious couplings, and this shadow culture, as it were, allows Tenney to explore racial and class "crossings" as well. In one instance, Dorcasina finds herself in the summer house and in the arms of Scipio, the African American gardener, whose own partner, the African American servant Miss Violet, is at the same moment being embraced by Dorcasina's white Irish lover, Patrick O'Connor. Both couples are quite delighted in their sexual explorations—until their true identities are exposed and their recognition of racial difference forces them to consider the false strictures of their usual "intercourse."

In another instance of masquerade, a prostitute presents herself as Dorcasina and rather than the expected narrative suggestion that no one could mistake a prostitute for an upper-class white woman, the women are easily mistaken for each other by people in the neighborhood. Other scenes of cross-dressing titillate the reader with images of women loving other women, not in the culturally sanctioned mode of female loving that Carroll Smith-Rosenberg has described, but in overt sexual play.[6] For instance, Dorcasina insists that Betty dress as Patrick O'Connor and imitate his sexual play with her, and later the very proper Miss Harriot Stanly dresses as a young officer, Captain Montague, and secretly takes on the part of Dorcasina's lover. This cross-dressing episode is especially significant for its exposure of women's sexual desires and equally so for its breaches of gender stereotypes. Harriot dresses as a captain, and one of Dorcasina's later lovers is also a captain, who has his servant masquerade as himself; the servant/captain is accepted by Dorcasina as her lover; the cycle of this episode is completed when Harriot later marries the captain whom the servant was imitating. If the reader becomes lost in this chain of masqueradings, that is precisely the point. The failure of language to distinguish the cyclical recasting of characters here exposes the false bases of social hierarchies and of gender stereotypes.

What the carnivalesque allows Tabitha Tenney to do, ultimately, is twofold: to expose the gender biases and prejudices still rampant in a nation that depicts itself as the ideal of democracy, and to address the suppression of (white) female desire. This is decidedly the late-eighteenth-century version of the carnivalesque, however, for the ending of this novel does not depict radical social or political change; in many ways Dorcasina is left in the dark, as it were, in the final chapter of *Female Quixotism.* Although she chooses to remain single and, importantly, to reclaim her nonromanticized name, Dorcas, she is left at the novel's conclusion a self-described isolate: "I am now, in the midst of the wide world, solitary, neglected, and despised" (324). She is, by her culture's standards, a grotesque. As a single woman, her experiences cannot lead her to the regenerative power once linked to carnival participation. No social freedom has been attained; all of officialdom's laws remain intact. Dorcas Sheldon thus represents the woman who has turned from romantic visions to reason, but her fate is not that of her male compatriots who make the same journey. Like Betty, she is not elevated to the realm of philosopher or statesman. Yet Tenney's conclusion emphasizes the fact that Dorcas has gained two important features: self-knowledge and an ability to inscribe herself as subject. These features are rendered through carnivalesque discourse as Kristeva defined it, acting as a social and political protest through its damning indictment of the American republic's falsified representations of equality.

The challenges to the Anglo American woman's pattern of marital servitude should not be ignored or belittled. Such challenges were necessary steps in the prelude to the women's rights movements of the nineteenth and twentieth centuries. Nor should we ignore the fact that Dorcas Sheldon's carnivalesque conversion is dependent upon hierarchical structures and acts of racial and ethnic oppression. While Betty manifests the figure of the wise woman throughout the novel, and we see Dorcasina transformed from the fool into the isolate-sage, no such status or transformation is afforded the African American characters in the novel.   .

The carnivalesque is a means of disrupting the symbolic order, the production and representation of reality according to the Law of the Father. Tenney's narrative achieves that disruption and exposes "reality" as an ideology that must be perpetuated in order to sustain the realm (here, quite literally, the house) of the Father. While *Female Quixotism* succeeds in its disruptive practices in relation to the central white female character, it in fact reinscribes the dominant ideology in terms

of class and race and does so especially with *women* characters. What appears to be a "feminization" in fact aids in the perpetuation of patriarchal hierarchies by dividing women (rather than articulating difference), by creating class and race conflicts, and thereby limiting resistance to the real source of domination, patriarchy itself. That Tabitha Tenney cannot fully write Dorcasina into a "happy ending" suggests her recognition of this dilemma.

Tzvetan Todorov's study of the colonization of the Americas emphasizes the significance of predetermined conceptualizations in the colonizer's interpretation and representation of the "Other."[7] This process is not, of course, limited to fifteenth-century cultural encodings of race. For all that Dorcasina is willing to experience the world anew, to discover "new worlds" for herself, her prior conceptualizations of class and race privilege are never abandoned. As she seeks to de-colonize herself from the control of her father and from patriarchal conventions, she does so through a process that recolonizes all non-white, non-upperclass individuals. That Betty and Miss Violet are most forcefully recolonized suggests the privileged woman's preconception of "other" women as dangerous. Mary-Louise Pratt has exposed the processes by which "frontier" propaganda literature acts as a "normalizing force . . . [that] serves, in part, to mediate the shock of contact on the frontier."[8] For Dorcasina, the novels she has been reading are the normalizing force through which she (mis)represents *to herself* her adventures in the grove-frontier. Every experience she has outside her father's house is read through her preconceived expectations formed from novel reading. Thus, ironically, while Tenney presents novel reading as dangerous, she elides the normalizing force not only of the texts Dorcasina reads but of her own imaginative text as well. The power of preconceptualization is evident in its subsequent and multifold misrepresentations in *Female Quixotism.* On the one hand, preconceived ideas lead Dorcasina to misinterpret her own demeaning experiences as romances while, on the other hand, it allows her to continue to read herself into a position of privilege, what Edward Said terms "positional superiority," over white servants and all people of color in spite of her own repeated foolish actions and subsequent humiliations. Indeed, the recovery of her sense of self against the normalizing forces surrounding gender in a patriarchal society is dependent upon her learned conceptions of race and class.

An examination of the masquerade, an integral feature in the production of the carnival, exposes Tenney's disruption of the patriarchal symbolic order as a disruption accessible only to the upper-class white woman. Unlike Bakhtin and Kristeva, Luce Irigaray is able to see beyond the phallocentric discourse of psychoanalysis and in that process exposes the vast plain of female desire behind "the *masquerade of femininity*." And desire with no adequate means of expression drives, shall we say, Dorcasina's life. As Irigaray observes, "The masquerade has to be understood as what women do in order to recuperate some element of desire, to participate in man's desire, but at the price of renouncing their own. In the masquerade, they submit to the dominant economy of desire in an attempt to remain 'on the market' in spite of everything. But they are there as objects for sexual enjoyment, not as those who enjoy.'"[9] Ultimately, the masquerade (like the dominant culture itself) cannot posit viable difference, and Tenney's apparent discomfort is exposed at a crucial point in the narrative, the summer-house escapade.

The scene in the summer house is an example of the bifurcated argument Tenney presents. Early in the text, Tenney has Dorcasina mouth an antislavery position that reflects the changing attitudes in the northern United States. Although Dorcasina desperately desires marriage to Lysander, she laments that "what gives me the greatest pain, is, that I shall be obliged to live in Virginia, be served by slaves, and be supported by the sweat, toil, and blood of that unfortunate and miserable part of mankind. . . . Slavery and happiness are, in my opinion, totally incompatible; 'disguise thyself as thou wilt, still, slavery, thou art a bitter pill'" (8). As noted above, Tenney challenges many cultural assumptions about race and gender in the summer-house scene, yet her representations of African Americans, especially of African American women, are often complicit in those assumptions. As Dana Nelson has pointed out, in this era the dominant culture racially encoded the African in specific ways that helped to perpetuate and justify a slave society.[10] To unpack the complexities of this encoding is to understand its cultural tenacity as well. Africans were depicted as at the bottom of the human evolutionary chain, indeed as only partially human (the "founding fathers" registered Africans as only three-fifths human). Thus Africans were represented as "primitive" in all facets of their lives—emotional development, social institutions, religious practices—and this primitivism was joined with the assertion that Africans were sexually uninhibited. It is important, too, to realize that, in this "Age of Reason," reason itself was absolutely linked with written discursive abilities; therefore, the African's oral rather than written traditions were deemed evidence of an inability to reason. Further, reason was equated with selfhood and since, as the perverted syllogistic reasoning unfolded, Africans could not reason, they were not therefore individuals and could not have status as self or exert agency. It is not difficult to comprehend the necessity of such reasoning in order to perpetuate the extraordinary *system* of abuse against African Americans inherent in slavery. While Tabitha Tenney exposes the presence of African Americans in U.S. society, something that few of her contemporary novelists acknowledged, she perpetuates a discourse of racial difference that elides the necessity of addressing change in the characterizations of Scipio and Miss Violet and, indeed, that erases their presence from the end of the novel.

Tenney's depiction of Scipio as a careful and talented servant/gardener is diminished by her depiction of Miss Violet as the stereotypic lazy and promiscuous person of color. The latter characterization, however, also reveals the Anglo American woman's fear of disruptions to assumed race and class superiority. The rendering of that fear through the female figure (literally and representatively) further reveals and complicates her text's embodiment (em/"body"/ment) of cultural difference.

As in any good carnival, all characters in the novel play the fool at some point. It is when the masks are removed and the carnival ends that we note Tenney's process of differentiation. During the scene in the summer house, Scipio is comically rendered, but his depiction is less characterization than simply a tool necessary to forward the narrative transformation of Dorcasina Sheldon. Scipio has fallen asleep; when Dorcasina enters the darkened summer house, she assumes he is her Irish lover, O'Connor, and is able to realize her desire for physical contact before he awakens: "[Dorcasina] approached him softly, sat down by his side, and, putting one arm round his neck and resting her cheek against his, resolved to enjoy the sweet satisfaction which this situation afforded her, till her should of himself awake. This liberty, in his waking hours, her modesty would have prevented her from taking; but, with a heart thrilling with transport, she blessed the accident, which, without wounding her delicacy, afforded her such ravishing delight" (53). The comedy of the scene is dependent upon the reader's shock at the contact between a white woman and a black man, as Tenney explicitly records their racial difference: "with her snowy arms, she encircled Scipio's ebony neck" (59). Tenney also makes explicit Dorcasina's shame at such contact when she discovers the truth: "Mortified and disappointed beyond measure, she crept into the house, and got to bed undiscovered: where, between her own personal chagrin, and distress for her lover, she lay the whole night in sleepless agitation. . . . Her delicate mind could hardly bear to reflect on her familiarity with her father's servant" (54-55).

When Scipio awoke and discovered O'Connor sneaking into the summer house, he immediately darted forth and cuffed the intruder several times; that is, he performed his legitimate duty of protecting the grounds from intruders. In Tenney's description of Miss Violet, however, we are exposed to an extended representation of uninhibited sexuality and "primitiveness" that encapsulates the racial coding of those white men whose inscriptions of white women's lives Dorcasina is supposed to reject in order to effect her own transformation from fool to sage. When O'Connor sees Miss Violet enter the garden and head for the summer house, he assumes it is Dorcasina. A reader's initial reaction is probably that this failure to distinguish identity is intended to expose race biases in the same manner that biases surrounding class and female sexuality were exposed through the confusion of identity between Dorcasina and the prostitute. However, we are told that "O'Connor, seeing a person *in white* advancing towards him, thought, *naturally enough,* that it could be no other than his mistress" (53, emphasis added). The racial coding here is evident: whiteness signifies sexual purity, the primary trait of womanhood in True Woman ideology, which was identified solely with white women and indeed, as Sidonie Smith has observed, was dependent upon "keeping black women in their place."¹¹ Tenney's purpose in this construction has less to do, at this point, with Miss Violet than it does with the exposure of O'Connor as a fool. (As will be noted more fully below, all of the Irish characters in this novel are as unredeemed as are the African American characters.)

A careful examination of the encounter of Miss Violet and O'Connor, however, will reveal how deeply internalized are Tenney's concepts of racial difference. When O'Connor met Miss Violet and mistakenly assumed she was Dorcasina, "he dropped on one knee, and poured forth a torrent of words in the usual style, blessing his supposed angelic mistress, for her goodness and condescension, in thus favouring him with an interview. Miss Violet was at first struck with astonishment, and could not divine the meaning of those fine compliments; but, perceiving by his manner and address, that it was a gentleman who thus humbled himself before her, and having a spice of the coquette in her disposition, she had not objection to obtaining a new lover; but, being totally at a loss what to reply to such a profusion of compliments, delivered in a style so new to her, she very prudently remained silent" (53). This passage exemplifies the racial encoding of the era. In spite of Tenney's previous satirization of Dorcasina as a foolish and easily duped woman, she is depicted here as "angelic" in contrast with Miss Violet's sexual indiscrimination ("a spice of the coquette"). Further, the failure of language is predominant. Because, as an African American, Miss Violet is assumed to have no reasoning ability, she cannot "divine the meaning" of O'Connor's compliments; his words constitute "a style so new to her" that she is rendered silent.

It is not enough that Miss Violet be rendered mute; her sexuality is explored and implicated in this scene again and again. We are told, for example, that after Scipio tosses O'Connor out of the garden, Miss Violet does not lament the loss of her new admirer. She simply excuses her behavior to Scipio so she may regain his attention, because she "could as easily change a white lover for a black, as receive the addresses of a new one" (53). Thus while Dorcasina is in her room, giving "herself up to sighs, tears and lamentations" (55) over her mistaken liaison with Scipio, Miss Violet is depicted as promiscuity personified. Indeed, as the figure of *willful* sexual discovery in the garden, Miss Violet becomes the body onto which the blame for Eve's indiscretions is transferred. Since Eve was the figure most often cited by religious and civil leaders in this period as the reason that women were to be subjected to men, it is a significant transformation: the blame for womankind's fate is now placed on the black woman while the white woman is exonerated through her shame and repentance.

Tenney's intent that we note this sexual and racial difference between Dorcasina Sheldon and Miss Violet is made even more pointed by her use of the masquerade to break the silence about female desire in a *positive* manner, through her characterization of Dorcasina's young white contemporary, Harriot Stanly. Whereas Miss Violet becomes the racially stereotyped figure of sexual promiscuity, Miss Stanly becomes the female figure in control of her sexuality, who can use it to her benefit and who is rewarded (to some extent) with marriage at the novel's conclusion.

Dorcasina's lack of a mother's influence is designated in the opening pages of **Female Quixotism** as the cause of her near-fatal attraction to novels: "At the age of three years, this child had the misfortune to lose an excellent mother, whose advice would have pointed out to her the plain rational path of life; and prevented her imagination from being filled with the airy delusions and visionary dreams of love and raptures, darts, fire and flames, with which the indiscreet writers of that fascinating kind of books, denominated Novels, fill the heads of artless young girls, to their great injury, and sometimes to their utter ruin" (4-5). In contrast, Harriot is not an "artless" young woman. Not only did she have an attentive mother but—an act that also reveals the very grave failure of the Mr. Sheldons of the world— she was afforded a proper female education that guided her away from Dorcasina's failings. Tenney's introduction of issues of desire into the characterization of a young woman is to be commended. Through masquerade, Harriot can express sexual longings under the guise of teaching Dorcasina a lesson about the folly of romanticizing relationships. Harriot's "play" goes far beyond mere titillation, and it recalls Irigaray's notion that the masquerade is necessary because, for women to "recuperate some element of desire, [they must] participate in man's desire, but at the price of renouncing their own." Thus, in order to express desire, Harriot must masquerade as a male. Dressed as a captain, she may take on aggressive (masculine) sexual behavior; notably, she directs her amorous acts toward another female: "She then threw her arms round Dorcasina's neck, and almost stopped her breath with kisses, and concluded by biting her cheek so hard as to make her scream aloud" (278). Significantly, this scene occurs at night, observing the transformation of the carnival in the late eighteenth century to a nocturnal event. When Harriot later marries a real-life captain, we might be tempted to see this alliance as both a comic moment, a (masked) captain marrying another captain, and as a regenerative one; but whereas Tenney is unable to inscribe racial difference, she is able to challenge the idea that heterosexual couplings are any more transformative than was the embrace between the masked Harriot and the duped Dorcasina. When Dorcasina visits Harriot (now Mrs. Barry) at the novel's end, the novel shifts from carnival time back to "real" time. After having observed Harriot's married life for a few days, Dorcasina addresses her friend:

> "I find that, in my ideas of matrimony, I have been totally wrong. I imagined that, in a happy union, all was transport, joy, and felicity; but in you I find a demonstration that the most agreeable connection is not unattended with cares and anxieties." "Indeed, Miss Sheldon," replied Mrs. Barry, "your observation is just. I have been married a twelvemonth, to the man whom of all the world I should have chosen. He is everything I wish him to be; and in the connection I have enjoyed great felicity. Yet, strange to tell, I have suffered more than I ever did before, in the whole course of my life."

(320-21)

Thus Tabitha Tenney exposes the disenfranchised status even of upper-class white women in the new republic. In important ways, Tenney critiques the gendered nature of existence in the new democracy and condemns the nation's failure to properly educate and employ its female members.

Yet at the same time, she exposes her own ironic alliance with class and racial prejudices. Her contemporary Thomas Jefferson also struggled with such issues, ultimately arguing in *Notes on the State of Virginia* for the creation of laws supporting a combination of slave emancipation and "distant colonization." Similarly, Tenney casts Betty as the privileged Dorcas's supportive and wise but naturally (read: by class) inferior servant-friend, and she follows Jefferson's ideal to its "logical" conclusion by removing the African American characters from the last portion of the novel: that act of removal/erasure is, of course, the very real effect of "distant colonization." As Dana Nelson observes, the failure of Jefferson's text to accomplish "'rational management' of the issue of slavery is a signpost to the Enlightenment philosophers' profound inability to master the incongruity between slave system and legal contract, between arbitrary power and 'natural' authority."[12] Similarly, for Tenney, her inability to create a narrative that fully allows the disruption of the social order intended through the depiction of carnival or to rationally

manage the reining in of carnival by the privileged class (as Mary Russo cautioned) leads to her own text's failed conclusion. Tenney cannot write into her own text a full vision of democracy.

That she is (perhaps unwittingly) aligned with Jeffersonian ideologies concerning race is particularly ironic, since Tenney's political alliances were distinctly opposed to Jefferson's in most ways. As noted above, all the Irish characters in this novel are as unredeemed as the African American characters. Tenney's political views are rendered through her depiction of immigrants in the novel, most notably in the characterization of the disreputable and dangerous Irishman Patrick O'Connor, who wants to marry Dorcasina only to have access to her wealth and privilege. In the years during which Tabitha Tenney wrote *Female Quixotism,* her spouse, Samuel Tenney, was a Federalist senator in Washington, D.C., representing their home state of New Hampshire. During the volatile election of 1800, the extraordinary power of the Federalists was diminished under charges of unconstitutional use of their powers and, most notably, of the intentional suppression of political dissent. Of special concern to the party was "foreign subversion." In 1798 alone, the Federalists enacted the Naturalization Act, the Alien Enemies Act, and the Sedition Act. These enactments are of special significance in relation to *Female Quixotism.* The Federalist position was bluntly clarified by Harrison Gray Otis, who cautioned that the United States should not "invite hordes of Wild Irishmen, nor the turbulent and disorderly parts of the world, to come here with a view to distract our tranquility."[13]

Two famous New England trials of 1799 may also have influenced Tenney's class and ethnic characterizations, those of David Brown and Luther Baldwin. Both men were working-class individuals who dared to criticize the Federalist government. Opposed to the centralized government established by the new constitution, Brown asserted that the only goal of government was to steal from its citizens and to claim the new nation's western lands for the Federalist leaders' personal wealth. Brown was tried under the newly established Sedition Act, found guilty, fined $480, and sentenced to eighteen months in jail. Since it was impossible for a working-class individual to pay such a fine, the sentence inevitably resulted in continued imprisonment for speaking against the government. It was only after the Federalists were defeated in the election of 1800 that Brown was freed. A satiric comment against President John Adams by Luther Baldwin (rendered orally, unlike Brown's pamphleteering) also resulted in a conviction for sedition, with fines and imprisonment. The Jeffersonians picked up Baldwin's case and used it to expose what they saw as the Federalists' abuse of power and antidemocratic actions.

It is precisely such nationalistic and classist attitudes that pervade Tenney's depictions of the characters surrounding Dorcasina. At the point in the novel in which O'Connor appears, we are told of the power of her father's word: "It had always been her pleasure to conform, in every instance, to the wishes of her parent, whose mild commands had ever been to her a law" (48). And the law of the father, as with the Federalists, is isolationist. When Dorcasina persists in her love of O'Connor, the Irishman, over Lysander, an American and her father's preferred mate for his daughter, Mr. Sheldon admonishes her, "Alas, my dear! I grieve to see you thus infatuated. Will you persist in giving less credit to one of your own countrymen, whose character for probity is well known and acknowledged, than to a foreigner, whom nobody knows, and who has nothing to recommend him but his own bare assertions?" (76).

That Tenney aligns nationalism with patriarchal values is evident when Dorcasina finally accepts her father's views and rejects the "foreigner": her father's reward is expressed explicitly in terms that return her to the father's house, "Thank you, my dear, you are now again my daughter" (95). That is, she is given the only means of "enfranchisement" available to women: the protection of the "fathers." This is the issue that Tenney cannot reconcile in **Female Quixotism.** She seeks to challenge the erasure of difference in the new republic, but she depends upon difference—and acceptance of difference—in order to effect what changes do occur in Dorcasina Sheldon's struggle for subjectivity.

It is in the juxtaposition of Dorcasina, Miss Violet, and Harriot Stanly that Tenney most overtly reveals her own complicity with certain elements of patriarchy. If she characterizes Dorcas at the end of the novel as rejecting the limited role of the True Woman in turn-of-the-century America, Tenney maintains most heartily the encoding of racial difference. In fact, there is a necessary hierarchy of women in her vision. Harriot may not have a perfect life, but she does have significant status as conveyed by the title of "Mrs." Dorcas, in comparison, "found herself alone, as it were, on the earth. The pleasing delusion which she had all her life fondly cherished, of experiencing the sweets of connubial love, had now entirely vanished, and she became pensive, silent and melancholy" (322). She has rejected her former ways and turned from romance to realism, but she is self-condemning: "I have not charms sufficient to engage the heart of any man" (322). Her transformation is, at best, one of repentance. Yet Dorcas Sheldon's ostensible transformation at the novel's conclusion is, in turn, dependent upon a contrast not only with Harriot but also with Miss Violet. Whereas the African American woman has been depicted as indiscriminately gliding from man to man and is ultimately silenced by her status, and thereby easily erased from the text itself, Dorcas Sheldon has risen above the dominant culture's

expectations of her as a woman. Because she remains single, she may be considered a grotesque by her culture, but she can still claim a certain status in the community because of her wealth. She uses her money for "acts of benevolence and charity" (323), thus gaining the status of Good Woman if not of Married Woman. It is Miss Violet who is cast as the inherently and unredeemed grotesque figure through the negative depiction of her sexuality and ultimately through her textual elision. What began as a novel notable for its exposure of the diverse nature of difference in eighteenth-century U.S. culture descends into an unresolved fracturing of narrative perspective. Ironically, when the carnival ends and Tenney seeks narrative closure, she cannot put all the pieces back together again. She cannot manage to fully liberate Dorcas from patriarchal strictures precisely because the decolonization process meant to be effected by the instigation of carnival has been predicated upon a return to colonialist measures.

Notes

1. Jean Nienkamp and Andrea Collins, introduction to Tabitha Gilman Tenney, *Female Quixotism: Exhibited in the Romantic Opinions and Extravagant Adventures of Dorcasina Sheldon,* ed. Nienkamp and Collins (New York: Oxford University Press, 1992), xiv-xv. Subsequent references to *Female Quixotism* will be given in the text.

2. Mikhail Bakhtin, *Rabelais and His World,* trans. Helene Iswolsky (Cambridge: MIT Press, 1968), 4-5. Subsequent references to this work will be given parenthetically in the text.

3. Julia Kristeva, "Word, Dialogue and Novel," in *The Kristeva Reader,* ed. Toril Moi (New York: Columbia University Press, 1986), 36.

4. Mary Russo, "Female Grotesques: Carnival and Theory," *Feminist Studies/Critical Studies,* ed. Teresa de Lauretis (Bloomington: Indiana University Press, 1986), 213-29.

5. Cathy N. Davidson, *Revolution and the Word: The Rise of the Novel in America* (New York: Oxford University Press, 1986), 132, 188.

6. See Carroll Smith-Rosenberg, "The Female World of Love and Ritual," *Disorderly Conduct: Visions of Gender in Victorian America* (New York: Oxford University Press, 1985), 53-76.

7. See Tzvetan Todorov, *The Conquest of America,* trans. Richard Howard (New York: Harper and Row, 1984).

8. Mary-Louise Pratt, *Imperial Eyes: Travel Writing and Transculturation* (New York: Routledge, 1992), 121.

9. Luce Irigaray, *This Sex Which Is Not One,* trans. Catherine Porter with Carolyn Burke (Ithaca: Cornell University Press, 1985), 133-34.

10. Dana D. Nelson, *The Word in Black and White: Reading "Race" in American Literature 1638-1867* (New York: Oxford University Press, 1993).

11. Sidonie Smith, *Subjectivity, Identity, and the Body: Women's Autobiographical Practices in the Twentieth Century* (Bloomington: Indiana University Press, 1993), 39. Barbara Welter's important essay casts its dates as 1820 to 1860 (see "The Cult of True Womanhood: 1820-1860," *American Quarterly* 18 [Summer 1966]: 57-70); texts such as *The Coquette* (1797) and *Female Quixotism* (1801) suggest that the ideology emerged in the late eighteenth century.

12. Nelson, 18.

13. Quoted in Gary B. Nash, et al., eds., *The American People: Creating a Nation and a Society* (New York: Harper and Row, 1986), 1: 254.

Bryce Traister (essay date 2000)

SOURCE: Traister, Bryce. "Libertinism and Authorship in America's Early Republic." *American Literature* 72, no. 1 (2000): 1-30.

[*In the following essay, Traister compares some of Tenney's male characters in* Female Quixotism *to the stereotypical American libertine male and his representation in Charles Brockden Brown's novel* Arthur Mervyn.]

Late in the first book of Tabitha Tenney's **Female Quixotism** (1801), the novel's heroine, Dorcasina Sheldon, "calling herself the most wretched of women" because her unreasonable father has prohibited her marriage to Patrick O'Connor, rejects the novels "in which she had formerly taken such delight" and turns for comfort to the letters O'Connor had written her during their clandestine courtship. Dorcasina "had got them arranged in perfect order, tied with a silken string, and wrapped in a cover, upon which was written these words, *Letters from my dearest O'Connor before marriage*."[1] One of the great novel-reading heroines of the eighteenth-century Anglo-American antinovel tradition, Dorcasina has already arranged her paramour's letters into the form of her favorite genre and has even given them a title. **Female Quixotism** then presents what must have been for late-eighteenth-century readers a hilariously caricatured scene of female novel reading: "Taking the first [letter] in order she kissed the seal, and the superscription; then, after opening it, and pressing the inside upon her heart, she read it three times over. This done, she folded it up again and laid it on her bosom, with that she had received in the morning" (**FQ**, [**Female Quixotism**] 93). Full of "all the ardour of counterfeited passion" (**FQ**, 44-45), the letters have permanently unmoored Dorcasina from the world of rational understanding in precisely the manner pernicious novels were believed to set the innocent female mind afloat in a sea of chaotic sensibility. Tenney's satire images female novel reading as a kind of parodic sexual expenditure in which the artless feminine mind and body exhaust themselves in the libertine's artful designs.

Female Quixotism thus warns against the dangers lurking in bad novels by dramatizing Dorcasina's repeated undoing by a series of false men, all of whom ventriloquize the stilted melodramatic language of sentimental novels as part of their design to acquire Dorcasina and her considerable estate.[2] Not only the fortune-hunting O'Connor but also the trick-playing "Philander," the class-crossing James, and the merchant Cumberland parrot the sentimental locutions of the seduction novel in order to advance their designs on the aging heroine. In this respect, Tenney's novel could be said to imagine a relation between masculine sexual agency and narrative agency, a relation that suggests that the ability to counterfeit genuine sentiment posed a significant threat not only to young females but also to a young nation besieged, according to former president John Adams, by smooth-talking libertine males: "The time would fail me to enumerate all the Lovelaces in the United States. It would be an amusing romance to compare their actions with his."[3] Whether whispering the self-interested nonsense of love or of democracy, the American libertine was linked to a capacity to persuade or absorb his listener using only words.

Former president Adams's wish for this "amusing Romance" was realized not only in Tenney's gallery of rogues but in Charles Brockden Brown's 1799-1800 novel *Arthur Mervyn: or, Memoirs of the Year 1793*, one of the period's most sustained treatments of the male libertine imagination and its effects on the credulous female reader. A novel of "plague and politics," *Arthur Mervyn* has been read as a register of early national political turmoil and institutional change, as a negotiation of the relation between political self-understanding and print ideology, and as a meditation on the two "radically different" Americas (republican and liberal) available to novel-reading Americans.[4] In such "political" accounts of *Arthur Mervyn*, the novel's historical aspects—particularly its depiction of the 1793 cholera epidemic—take interpretive precedence over its narrative or textual features, one of which is a remarkably sustained focus on libertines, actual and imagined, and on the ways in which transgressive male sexual and narrative licence paces nearly all of the novel's competing and complementary voices, which is to say that libertine narrative structures the novel's plot. In the case of the libertine-forger Thomas Welbeck, for example, illicit sexual exploits complement his other criminal acts (forgery, fraud, and murder) in the novel's dissection of his character. Another of the novel's libertine figures, the tavern-haunting Wallace, turns out to have been the faithless suitor of Susan Hadwin, whose death by plague occurs simultaneously with Wallace's disappearance in the vicinity of a country brothel. Female illness and death repeatedly result from acts of male licentiousness. And, of course, the novel's eponymous protagonist, as many critics have remarked, spends much of the novel defending himself from various charges of unsavory forms of behavior. Among other things, he is accused of engaging in a "criminal intimacy" with his servant-cum-stepmother, Betty Mervyn; of entertaining a suspicious interest in the hapless debauchée, Clemenza Lodi; of falling in and out of love with no fewer than four women; and of emotionally abusing the novel's emotional sponge, Eliza Hadwin.[5] Each object of Arthur's "interest" embodies a different aspect of American femininity under assault by libertine masculinities, both confessedly real and (perhaps) merely imagined. As an analysis of urban plague, *Arthur Mervyn* thus circulates ideas about masculine identity that coincide disturbingly with postrevolutionary ideas of contagion understood as both social and physiological danger. The plague in *Arthur Mervyn,* as in Brown's earlier novel of urban epidemic, *Ormond* (1799), is a sickness of gender relations symptomatic of fundamental problems within the young republic.[6]

To the extent that *Arthur Mervyn* embodies the age's political anxieties about the decay of virtuous self-restraint into self-interested rapacity, the novel adds to our knowledge of early American literature's participation in and contribution to the nation's political historiography. But what interests me here is the novel's investment in literary—specifically authorial—modes of national agency, a preoccupation evidenced in *Arthur Mervyn*'s obsession with its status as a narrative told by a series of young American men and with the power of male-authored narrative to forge (or fracture) sympathetic lines of sociality through and across barriers of class and gender. At stake in Brown's last "major" novel is the capacity of male narrative to render social standing authoritatively; that is, the novel considers the extent to which authorial discourse can indicate or represent an individual male author or character with reasonable claims to social presence and masculine gender privilege. Against charges of various forms of libertinism Arthur Mervyn answers with and through narrative; against the claim that he is a sexual maniac, Arthur answers that he is an author and that his self-indemnification will follow from his sincere acts of narrative persuasion. The problem that quickly emerges, however, is that both authors and libertines are creators of narrative. More specifically, they produce unverifiable narratives, which is to say that both libertines and authors generate fiction, a type of discourse ambiguously connected to the "real" world.[7] Brockden Brown in *Arthur Mervyn*—and perhaps postrevolutionary cul-

ture more generally—understood literary authorship and sexual libertinism to be linked categories of masculine agency because both authors and libertines inhabit and are perceived to deploy a language of artful fabrication profoundly connected to male self-interest. Brown's novel of narrative self-fashioning thus registers the troubled cultural status of the early American literary author, even as it attempts to fashion a respectable account of male authorship independent of the libertinism that animates it.

Judging from the early republican periodical record, it seems fair to say that many Americans of differing political persuasions worried that the new American man was a libertine. The titles of serialized essays, moral tales, and reviews indicate a cultural preoccupation with the libertine male, while the texts themselves present the libertine as the negative, often viciously satirized foil of postrevolutionary American masculinity. In April 1796 the *Philadelphia Minerva* ran "The Man of Dissipation; or, a Warning to Libertines. Founded on Facts," followed six weeks later by "The Libertine Reclaimed. A Tale." The first recounts the adventures of the aptly named "Loverule," who possessed "every art" necessary to win "the attention of the softer sex";[8] the second narrates the debauchery and ultimate conversion of Mr. Fairfax, "a man of fashion, vivacity and dissipation."[9] Both tales plot the rake's rise, ruin, and redemptive transformation into a loving and repentant husband and father. A portion of "The School for Libertines," which also voices the theme of debauchery undone, first appeared in the 1789 *Gentlemen and Ladies Town and Country Magazine,* was printed in its entirety in the October 1795 issue of the *New York Magazine,* ran again in the November issue of *Philadelphia Minerva,* and was published yet again in the 1797 *New-York Weekly Magazine.*[10] Attributed to Thomas Bellamy, the story focuses on a young rake "possessing every art of genteel address," who, having seduced a friend's wife, flees his own pregnant wife and son and travels to Italy, where he assumes the name Freeman and marries a young heiress. During his second life, he encounters a young girl in a convent and makes the acquaintance of a young libertine named Eastman; the young girl and Eastman fall in love, of course, and turn out to be the children of Freeman's first marriage, of course. Freeman reveals himself as their miserable and repentant father ("thankful to mysterious Heaven!"), and Freeman's old family is restored within his new one in this more optimistic rendering of the libertine-driven incest plot seen earlier in William Hill Brown's *Power of Sympathy.*[11] A pedagogical tale (as so many were during the period), "The School for Libertines" is one of many multiply reprinted pieces specifically concerned with libertinism, such as the 1794 "The Sentimentalist" (from the *Massachusetts Magazine*), which focuses on the activities of the libertine and the virtuous American's best means of guarding against the rake's progress.[12]

In reading "The Sentimentalist" and similar tales and essays, one might be tempted to argue that the postrevolutionary periodical scene records the emergence of a new literary genre, the libertine confession narrative, whose focus on a dissipated libertine renouncing his evil ways becomes something close to a literary fantasy of the period. In "The Sentimental Libertine; A Story Founded upon Fact," published in the March 1790 issue of the *Massachusetts Magazine,* the lasciviously named "Richard Bumper" recounts his recent conversion from libertine to married man, noting that the libertine's "passion will hurry him imperceptibly from liberty to liberty" (173), while the husband's "virtue is its own reward" (174).[13] In "The Sentimentalist," an unnamed narrator waxes elegiac over the expiring body of a libertine named Harwood in a sentimentalized drama of sickly, homosocial fraternity later restaged in *Arthur Mervyn*'s various narrations of morally vitiated men and their interlocutors. "Thy associates were vicious," intones the narrator of "The Sentimentalist," "and they hurried thee into scenes of dissipation, which debased the natural dignity of thy mind and enfeebled the energy of thy virtues." The narrator laments a familiar catalogue of masculine failings, an "unthinking head" and the "pampering of . . . appetites," yet he finds in Harwood's confession of past sin expiation sufficient to restore an optimistic view of the future: "I think on these things, my friend, and hope comforts my soul."[14] John Adams's equation of libertinism with the radical individualism feared by Federalists as the ultimate consequence of representative democracy thus reflects the nature of both imported and local literary culture. In libertine confessionals of the 1790s, the rake's rise, reign, ruin, and redemption supply a subjunctive literary postmortem on the Revolution's potential inversion of personal and social identity, as the rhetoric of optimistic masculinity undone attached itself seamlessly to a rhetoric of impending national collapse, only to later reassert a hopeful vision of masculine virtue strengthened by its temporary interruption. These libertine confessions from the periodical literature of the period find powerful elaboration in the expressively obsessed and repressed narratives of *Arthur Mervyn.*

To be sure, by 1798 the libertine was a throwback to a much earlier and largely superseded English social geography, but this inconvenient historical fact did not, as we have seen, stop postrevolutionary Americans from stealing, producing, and consuming a literature dominated by the libertine-maiden seduction plot. While much critical attention has been paid to the plight of the young woman and her negotiation of the period's sex-gender system,[15] little has been focused on the seduction plot's other principal actor: the libertine. The critical focus on the innocent woman and on concomitant issues of female gender is understandable in light of feminist literary historiography's own development within the field of early American cultural studies. Then, too,

gender-based criticism of American literature has rightly identified the representation and social status of women as a major source of anxiety during this period, as well as a suppressed issue within American literary studies. Julia Stern's recent analysis of early American literature's investment in "an arresting feminization of narrative voice," for example, finds in Hannah Foster's *Coquette* (1797) an "ultimately misogynistic feminization of middle-class culture in late-eighteenth-century America," a gender betrayal that issues from the novel's depiction of one woman's social ostracism at the hands of a female "chorus" ultimately aligned with the self-interested masculine privilege of the libertine.[16] The sexual and social status of young women, as depicted in the novel's tale of a young woman's seduction, abandonment, and death, registers a variety of sociopolitical fears intimately connected to nascent mythologies of America's founding and development. The libertine's participation in the seduction plot as a character proceeds simultaneously with his presence outside the plot as its primary agent. That is, the "artful villain" is the plot's creator as well as its antagonist.

To the degree that literary seduction plots register profound currents in colonial and early national cultural practices, the libertine was necessary to the unfolding of an America whose possible corruption heavily inflected developing rhetorics of national self-fashioning.[17] Indeed, Foster's *Coquette* registers the libertine's necessary presence in society in the aggressively genteel Lucy Freeman's complaint that "the assassin of honor; the wretch, who breaks the peace of families, who robs the virgin innocence of its charms, who triumphs over the illplaced confidence of the inexperienced, unsuspecting, and too credulous, is received, and caressed, not only by his own sex, to which he is a reproach, but even by ours, who have every conceivable reason to despise and avoid him."[18] America's insufficiently rebuked libertine paradoxically becomes a fascinating spectacle binding his onlookers together in fluent if ineffectual outrage. As Stern remarks, the libertine assault is a necessary cultural fantasy because he embodies a threat that "makes it possible for the gentry to identify precisely where the boundaries of their class and comportment begin."[19] The libertine thus functions as a catalyst for social and even national cohesion. So imagined, the role of the libertine resembles that of the printed text of modern nationalism; his circulation enables a national body whose identity inheres in its collective repudiation of him.[20]

In addition to mediating and reflecting certain aspects of American national identity, libertinism represented a cultural fantasy in which Americans witnessed the contradictory constructions of individualism operative in the postrevolutionary and early republican periods. Ostensibly, libertinism signified a form of radical individualism unfettered by the restraints of institutionalized social mores and dedicated to the freedom paradoxically conferred by the total submission of self to sensualism. For Federalists, of course, such radical individualism presented the greatest threat the new nation had yet faced, though both Federalists and Republicans subscribed to and promoted a nascent mythology of (properly regulated) American individualism.[21] Blessed, as it were, with the "sacred flame of liberty," the libertine nonetheless questioned the very ideology of libertarian individualism that underwrote his exploits. Libertinism, as James Grantham Turner has argued, vacillated between "a fierce individualism that underestimates the power of social forces, and a compliance to social conventions which, though intended to be ironic and self-liberating, eventually traps the self within the mask"; in the end, "the geography of libertinism," rather than the libertine self, directs the libertine's actions.[22] The paradox of libertinism thus challenged the very notion of autonomous male individualism, revealing the extent to which the supposedly free self turned out to be a representational aftereffect of socially determinative forces. Apparently free by virtue of unrestrained indulgence, the libertine remains nonetheless a slave to his passions, passions originating in the "mechanical" world of physiological determinism that render the libertine an automaton. According to the "Letter of a Reformed Libertine" (1790), libertines "are slaves to the irregular motions of passion"; "Ned Gayless," the rake of the *South Carolina Weekly*'s "Ruinous Gradation to Vicious Habits" (1797), is "ravished with the allurements of fashionable life."[23] Americans thus found their own fascination with the paradoxes of revolutionary agency embodied in the figure of the oddly passive yet still animated libertine, a male figure at once radically free and disturbingly bound, fiercely independent but insufficiently so.

As literary trope, the American libertine embodied the political anxieties of the age; libertinism negotiated the tensions between republican and liberal visions of the United States. If, as J. G. A. Pocock has argued, the political experiment that is the United States initiated a politics of pretended disinterest through its recovery of classical republican thought,[24] the libertine trope imagined the masking of certain kinds of "interest" beneath a veneer of studied virtue. Furthermore, the libertine's sense of sexual and social privilege recalled the repudiated body of the English aristocrat, even as the libertine's apparent submission to a republican order of representation lodged a principle of social hierarchy within republican social space. The attack on the libertine was in part an attack on conservative republicanism's desire to retain the principle of aristocracy within the new political and social order of America. As any number of the periodical accounts of libertinism make clear, the fallen man's value lay in his ability to exemplify the dangers of virtue corrupted; the melancholy expiration of the solitary and abandoned debauch images the lapse of "public virtue" into self-interested dissolution.[25]

More often than not, however, the American libertine came from the middling or even poorer ranks of American society, suggesting that cultural concern about the libertine ultimately associated the figure with the forces of political liberalism and social enfranchisement—officially ushered in with the Jeffersonian ascendancy—thought to be responsible for revolutionary agitation. Liberal democracy enabled the rapacity of the lower orders, as Tenney's *Female Quixotism* suggests in its depiction of the "enterprising and persevering" rake Patrick O'Connor (*FQ*, 20), whose antisocial rhetoric furthers his self-interested designs: "'Come, my adorable angel, let us despise the censures of an ill-judging world; let us follow the dictates of all-powerful love; let us be united and happy, and bid defiance to its malice'" (*FQ*, 22). The liberty of pursuit available to an interloping Irishman like O'Connor energized an American language of masculine sexual persuasion in which "attraction" demanded a self emancipated from the strictures of social discipline. In this sense the libertine was a creature born of natural rights and the human quest for freedom. Thus his chief function was to illustrate the dangers of rational self-interest gone wrong.[26]

Central to the early American construction of the libertine-as-automaton was the discourse of sensibility, a language of capacious emotional experience that was, like the libertine's sexual desire, often physiological in its expression. A discourse intrinsically resistant to rationalization (in part because it was understood to oppose the power of reason), sensibility was a hotly debated topic for discussion and literary dramatization in early American culture.[27] "But you call me, with some degree of truth, a strange medley of contradiction—the moralist and the amoroso—the sentiment and the sensibility—are interwoven in my constitution, so that nature and grace are at constant fisticuffs," writes *The Power of Sympathy*'s Harrington Jr., whose short life encompassed a still shorter career as would-be libertine.[28] The future suicide then discloses more fully the powerful inspiration to the self supplied by sensibility: "But come thou spirit of celestial language, that canst communicate by one affectionate look—one tender glance—more divine information to the soul of sensibility, than can be contained in myriads of volumes" (*PS*, [*The Power of Sympathy*] 9). Here, the protagonist imagines his soul engaged in an unmediated transaction with a spirit akin to the divine, imagines that a wordless language of sympathy exists between simultaneously vibrating souls. The novel's analysis of American sympathetic relations also explores writing and reading in the new nation, "'a matter of more importance,'" intones the censorious Worthy, "'than is generally imagined'" (*PS*, 27). Harrington's dismissal of texts in favor of the unmediated (if theatricalized) interchange of affectionate energies was a fairly standard conceit of the novel of sensibility, whose suspicion of language often took the form of registering the inability of language to represent powerful feeling adequately, as is the case here, or of representing sensibility's extra-linguistic nature as a failure of the instrumentality of language itself, as in Harrington's incoherent and ungrammatical final farewell to the world: "[D]rop one tear on the remembrance of a friend, of a brother—but I cannot allow you to be grieved—grieve for me! Wretch that I am—why do I delay————" (*PS*, 178). Sensibility hurries the subject, animating expressivity to the point that the fragmentation of language commemorates agency's disappearance; that is to say, the sensibility imagined here potentially makes the Harringtons of early America objects within a circulation of sympathy that proceeds independently of the individual's will. The sensible male becomes passive within an economy of sympathy whose linguistic representation effectively dispenses with the feelingful self. Like Turner's impassioned libertine, Harrington becomes the victim of his own emotional liberty.[29]

It should be remembered that early in *The Power of Sympathy* the antitextuality attributed to sensibility by Harrington informs his still unabandoned libertine plot to seduce Harriot. The theatricalized if wordless drama he imagines issuing from an uncorrupted "celestial" sphere is part of his confessed "design," which is to say that sensibility and related eighteenth-century discourses not only fail to segregate the libertine from virtuous society but guarantee his continued circulation as a character necessary for social relations keyed to the language of sentiment. Moreover, insofar as the discourse of sensibility promised authentic personal relations animated by the disinterested forces of emotion, Harrington's incorporation of sensibility into his libertine "design" betrays the textual capacity inherent in the discourse of sensibility itself: that is to say, the "artless," to borrow the vocabulary of *The Power of Sympathy*, can always be circumscribed by the "artful"—emotion can be faked. Harrington's transformation from would-be libertine into suicidal author thus comes as no surprise (William Hill Brown's incest plot notwithstanding). A less morbid but no less suspicious author figure, Brockden Brown's Arthur Mervyn, reveals the slippage between libertine and authorial sensibility in a passage that signals the inconstancy of agency associated with both sexual and literary masculinity: "Move on my quill! Wait not for my guidance. Reanimated with thy master's spirit, all-airy light! An heyday rapture! A mounting impulse sways him: lifts him from the earth" (*AM*, 413). Because this passage comes near the novel's conclusion, the writing of sexual agency

(Arthur's approaching marriage to Ascha Fielding) not only becomes coterminous with the writing of the narrative but seems to proceed independently of Arthur himself.

That *The Power of Sympathy* dramatizes early American culture's preoccupation with inflamed male sensibility through a libertine author's suicide narrative is in keeping with its explication of the status of literature—specifically of novels—in the early republic. American culture understood both the libertine and the author to be animated by a language of sensibility either ultimately or easily subservient to the interests of an "artful [male] villain."[30] The novel discloses a critical discourse operative in the period's literary culture that linked libertine and author through the pernicious agency of novels. Just as the "artful fictions" of the libertine might seduce the "artless" innocence of the young girl, so might the authored novel seduce, at least figuratively, the guileless, usually female, young, and often silly reader. "'[M]any fine girls have been ruined by reading novels,'" summarizes Mrs. Holmes in *The Power of Sympathy* (*PS*, 33), a sentiment shared by Tabitha Tenney in her attack on the genre responsible for "the disgraces and disasters" endured by artless girls "turned by the unrestrained perusal of Novels and Romances" (*FQ*, 3). Even critics who appreciated the form noted the "power [it] exercised over the reader's heart" through its ability to fill readers "with the emotions of love, pity, joy, anguish, transport, or indignation."[31] Samuel Miller's *Brief Retrospect of the Eighteenth Century* (1803) describes the consequences of a prolonged sequestration with novels as a "depraved moral taste" and "a mass of crime and misery too great for the ordinary powers of calculation." In the same passage Miller denounces even those few novels "which contain no licentious principles or indelicate descriptions" because "though they be not chargeable with making a direct attack on the fortress of virtue, they are only fitted to mislead. To fill the mind with unreal and delusive pictures of life, is, in the end, to beguile it from sober duty, and to cheat it of substantial enjoyment."[32] Novels not only represent seduction, abandonment, and death, they—and by extension their creators—are responsible for the actual tragedies afflicting the young female reader, who, "unsuspicious of deceit, . . . is easily deceived" (*PS*, 32).

The relation established in *The Power of Sympathy* between illicit sexual conduct and masculine literary agency reappears in "The Rhapsodist," Charles Brockden Brown's well-known meditation on authorship. Brown's essay, which appeared in four successive issues of the *Universal Asylum and Columbian Magazine* in 1789, defines the poet as "one who delivers the sentiments suggested by the moment in artless and unpremeditated language," a definition of authorship that places Brown in the rhetorical tradition of European romanticism even as it recalls the language of sexual artifice operative in the eighteenth-century seduction plot.[33] Yet the description depends on the equation of authorship with delivery, thereby identifying the agency of the author with the idea of the premodern auctor, "an instrument for the immanent workings of the divine, articulating rather than formulating or creating."[34] From this point of view, the Rhapsodist is a spokesperson for sentiment, the conduit for a sensibility he neither creates nor controls. In creating a space for authorial identity by suspending the creative agency of the author, Brown deepens authorship's connection to sensibility, in this case a sensibility masculinized by virtue of its itinerary: "[The author] pours forth the effusions of a sprightly fancy, and describes the devious wanderings of a quick but thoughtful mind" (*R*, 5). Opposed to the relative passivity of the rhapsodist's channeling of artless sentiment is the itinerant activity of an author "remarkable for sudden transitions in his subjects, and hasty discussions" (5). Yet this wandering, spontaneous, and effusive figure is also "devious" (5), suggesting that the "sincerity" derived from spontaneity carries with it a darker, less transparent disposition, one marked by an antisocial "fondness for solitude . . . when he shall be left to the enjoyment of himself, and to the freedom of his own thoughts" (*R*, 6). Brown later locates this "wandering imagination" geographically "in the wilds of the Columbian woods, and in the seraglios of the East" (*R*, 16), thereby aligning his literary expressiveness with a male rhetoric of territorial wandering and sexual conquest. "The Rhapsodist" could be said to counter the loss of agency occasioned by the auctor's receptive instrumentality with a vocabulary of sexual territoriality usually associated with willful masculinity. Although "The Rhapsodist" supplies a less immediately threatening conjunction of male sexual and expressive capacity than that found in *The Power of Sympathy*, Brown nonetheless advances a logic of early American authorship that foregrounds sexual capacities as foundational to the male author.

If sex underwrites the literary achievement of male authors, we might reasonably wonder if the same could be said of texts written by and about women. Early in *Female Quixotism*, Dorcasina wishes that her first meeting with a new suitor, the virtuously boring Lysander, had been "more to her taste, that some resolute fellow, in love with her to distraction, but who had made no impression on her heart, had carried her off by force to marry her, and that Lysander had rescued her by his gallantry" (*FQ*, 7). Enamored both with the letters of the "artful adventurer" O'Connor (*FQ*, 27) and with the adventurous romance of her own imagination, Dorcasina crosses and recrosses the divide between passive consumer of novelistic sentiment and active producer of the narratives that ultimately leave her a spinster. Indeed, *Female Quixotism* implies that the female creation of the kind of narrative found in seduction novels

intensifies the plight of the female reader. Eventually Dorcasina's creation of the seduction plots denied her in life produces a cross-dressing vignette in which her servant Betty, dressed in Dorcasina's father's clothes, recreates the scene "where [Dorcasina] had first beheld the adored youth, in order to recal [*sic*] the rapturous moments she had passed in [his] company" (*FQ*, 96). Instructed by Dorcasina to "call [her] angel, goddess, and . . . divine Dorcasina" (97), Betty attempts to reenact O'Connor's wooing, hilariously botching the script demanded by Dorcasina: "Dear soul, intosticating [*sic*] charmer, celestial deity; Mars, Junos, Venis; my very marrow is burnt up from the fire of your dazzling eyes. I have gone about, since I saw you, like a roaring lion; there has been neither sleep to my eyes, nor slumber to my eyelids" (*FQ*, 98). In this class-inflected caricature of the artifice of wooing, the efforts of the female imagination to recreate the scene of seduction result in a scene of gender transgression and violently imaged masculine sexual licence. (Indeed, Dorcasina observes that Betty's speech "is more like the incoherent ravings of a madman, than the address of an ardent lover" [*FQ*, 99], and she insists that Betty try again.) As the cross-dressed servant continues to woo her female mistress, the stilted artifice of the sentimental novel descends further into outrageous parody. Betty tries to "act her part, in the worst manner possible, that she need not again be forced into so disagreeable a situation" (*FQ*, 99), and the farce becomes too "outre" for the narrative to represent. The problem with the female imagination and the plots it envisions, Tenney's text suggests, is not only the seduction plot's inevitable connection to moral outrage but also the female mind's inability to police what it imagines. Even in this caricatured plot of female cross-dressing and theatrical literary imitation, the threat of male sexual interest emerges as an unwanted, intrusive voice, suggesting that the would-be female author lacks the rational self-regard necessary to regulate the imaginative agency she has assumed.

The gender ambiguity of Dorcasina's cross-dressed recreation of her own seduction recalls the paradox of gender that emerges in Brockden Brown's account of the rhapsodical author, a paradox captured in his enigmatic conclusion to the first installment of his series: "In short, he will write as he speaks, and converse with his reader not as an author, but as a man" (*R*, 5). To speak the language of the author is to forgo the language of man, a logic that, if we read "man" as specifically masculine, makes masculinity and authorship opposed aspects of selfhood. The potential gender inversion inherent in male authorship is apparent also in the claim of "artlessness" in "The Rhapsodist," a quality attributed to the innocent girl in the standard seduction plot. Thus *The Power of Sympathy*'s Harrington, whose authorial pronouncements conclude and commemorate as epitaph the libertine-driven narrative of incestuous tragedy, is believed to have been unmanned—that is, de-stroyed—by his "too nice sensibility" (*PS,* 179); he is considered by his friends to have been "the dupe of Na-ture, and the sacrifice of Seduction" (*PS,* 180). Indeed, one might argue that Harrington becomes the feminized victim of an authorial power that he both deploys and is deployed by in his suicide: "The pensive and melan-choly will muse over the ordinary accidents of life, and swell them, by the power of imagination, to the heavi-est calamities" (*PS,* 170). Harrington thus becomes the overly involved reader of a tragic design he delivers yet doesn't construct, expresses yet fails to circumscribe. In relinquishing rational agency to an imaginative force he doesn't control, he becomes the tragic "dupe of Na-ture, . . . the sacrifice of Seduction"—the innocent girl of the seduction plot or its guileless reader. Read in these terms, Harrington's suicide becomes a parable of male gender inversion inaugurated with the suggestion in "The Rhapsodist" that to occupy the position of au-thor is to relinquish masculine agency.

It is in the loss of agency that characterizes both liber-tine and author that the paradoxical gendering of both male authorship and the libertine may be seen. Richard-son's Lovelace, as many critics have pointed out, is an extremely "feminine" character, evincing a delicate sen-sibility and fashion sense; according to James Turner, "[t]he great seducer disappears in a cloud of Brussels lace and primrose-coloured paduasoy."[35] Libertine sexual agency depends on a female cultural sensibility whose deciphering the rake undertakes as a matter of professional self-advancement. Overly delicate and de-pendent on the feminine, the libertine emerges as a womanly man. One of the early republican period's most powerful readings of libertinism, Foster's *Co-quette,* has as its chief libertine the penniless Peter San-ford, who discloses his helplessness before the power of his own sexual and sensible arousal: "I never knew I had so much sensibility before!" he writes to his inter-locutor, Charles Deighton. "Why, I was as much a woman as the very weakest of the sex."[36] John Adams's recasting of *Clarissa* in America, in which the interac-tion of male sexual aggression and female sensibility produces a vision of America as "Anarchiad," reveals a subtext that focuses on Lovelace as a potential embodi-ment of effeminate masculinity.[37] Like the suspension of authorial agency imaged in Brockden Brown's "The Rhapsodist," Sanford's near-helpless avowal of passion represents a subordination of self to sensualism, a po-tential disavowal of the autonomous self-sufficiency un-derstood as prerequisite to republican masculinity. The sentimental libertine disturbed republican social rela-tions as much through his ambiguous gendering as through his simulation of virtue. Indeed, the two were the same. As Philip Gould has suggested, republican masculinity was articulated through a "quasi-feminized

ethos of feeling and benevolence," making the liber-tine's embodiment of overwhelming sensibility akin to a dangerous ventriloquization, or counterfeit, of republi-can virtue.[38]

It is worth remarking that the discourses of sensibility and sentimentality may not have been unequivocally gendered as feminine during this period. Gould's dis-cussion of republican masculinity, for example, indi-cates that sentimental male expression was not merely normal but exemplary of virtuous republican manhood. Furthermore, the dual nature of sensibility—its status as both moral feeling and sexual desire—bespeaks a gen-der multiplicity within the discourse itself. As a lan-guage of early republican self and nationhood, sensibil-ity appealed to both "masculine" and "feminine" natures. To be sure, the incorporation of the sentimental into women's fiction and the proliferating ideologies of female domesticity—well underway by the beginning of the nineteenth century—have contributed to the femi-nization of sentiment in both critical and historical nar-ratives. But during the late eighteenth and early nine-teenth centuries, American sentimentality was not exclusively or even preponderantly gendered female, as has for some time been believed.[39]

As a potential gender traitor, the libertine-author trans-gresses not so much through his corrupt use of senti-mentality as through an effeminacy derived from the surrender of masculine agency to the forces of fashion-able convention. Indeed, to the degree that male effemi-nacy is an imitation of female behavior, both effemi-nacy and its rhetorical simulation indicate a similar sort of unseemly male behavior. A humorous piece of dog-gerel that appeared in the May 1786 edition of the *Worcester Magazine* captures this uneasy conjunction of effeminacy and suspect male expression:

> The puppy-beaux and macaronies,
> Who ape our manners, lisp and sigh,
> If frighten'd, faint—if troubled, die—
> Who dress in silk—paint—perfum'd are,
> And beat us out in loads of hair,
> Let us the females out of hand,
> With sword equip'd, compose a band,
> To wage continual war with all those.
> Whose monkey tricks disgrace the smallclothes;
> For all the world will call that plan good,
> Which beats such reptiles back to manhood.[40]

A satire on "puppyism," the poem not only criticizes the "effeminacy of manners in many of the young mer-cantile bucks of the present day" but suggests that women become warriors in retaliation.[41] We thus see the blurring of gender on both sides of the sexual divide, as men take too keen an interest in fashion and women in military exploits. The lisping of effeminacy indicates the folly of affection, defined by the Reverend Joseph Lathrop of Springfield, Massachusetts, in the October

1790 *American Museum* to be "an attempt to be, or appear to be, something different from ourselves, and to assume graces, in our behaviour and conversation, of which we are not capable."[42] "Philo" defines affectation as "a certain artificial gloss upon manners and external appearance" by which the self-fabricator (anticipating *Arthur Mervyn*'s libertine forgery artist Thomas Welbeck) attempts "to palm upon [our] senses the basest counterfeits for the purest coin."[43] The links between affectation, expression, and effeminacy in early American codes of male gentility indicate not merely that the fop is an effeminate "puppy" but that the speech habits of foppish self-fashioning are constitutive of the literary author's ambiguous masculinity.

It was partially through the construct of the libertine-author that early American literary culture enacted the drama of masculine gender formation being played out in a wide variety of cultural theaters. In *Arthur Mervyn* we see the vicissitudes of what might be called the poetics of masculine self-witnessing in one of the novel's competing narrative voices, that of Mrs. Althorpe, a former country neighbor of Arthur. In one of the novel's first and most damning counternarratives, we learn that Arthur Mervyn was "feeble" as a boy, that "he became the mother's favorite . . . and loved to stroll in the woods more than to plow or sow" (*AM*, 233). In addition to his shirking of labor and discipline, this young rhapsodist isn't even interested in the normal pursuits of young men: "They ride, or shoot, or frolic; but this being moped away his time in solitude, never associated with other young people . . . never fired a gun or angled for fish in his life." His adolescent failures are presented as episodes in the confounding of masculine gender, a confusion culminating in Althorpe's picture of Arthur Mervyn "busily engaged in *knitting stockings*!" (*AM*, 234; italics in original). "As spruce a fellow as ever came from dancing school or college" (*AM*, 232), Arthur Mervyn is compounded of effeminate behaviors alternately connected to genteel and intellectual modes of refinement. "Perhaps he was addicted to books," offers Dr. Stevens, the interlocutor of the Althorpe narrative. Stevens registers the novel's sustained interrogation of the relation between intellectual activity and social standing, a relation Althorpe's testimony characterizes negatively in the seamless, perhaps causative connection articulated between Arthur's dreamy sensibility and his "criminal intimacy" with Betty, a family servant who later becomes Arthur's stepmother. At issue isn't sexuality per se but sex outside wedlock and across class lines—Arthur Mervyn's "perverse and singular conduct" (*AM*, 233). Sexual and linguistic perversity merge in Arthur's bizarrely contradictory behavior. The Althorpe counternarrative, which makes a strong case for the view that Arthur is not the virtuous young man he pretends to be, insists that the investigation of his identity proceed through an interrogation of gender; in other words, the problem of Arthur's moral credibil-

ity is the problem of assessing his worth as a man. As Arthur's antagonists accuse him of libertinism and still worse behavior, and as this accusation undermines his credibility as a narrator, the scene triangulates the discourses of libertinism, authorship, and gender as the central epistemological puzzle that the novel, if not early American literary culture more generally, labored to solve.

Brockden Brown's novel repeatedly, perhaps even obsessively, stages encounters between tale-telling libertines and their usually innocent dupes. These encounters reflect the period's conservative view of novels and their beguiled readers. The first such dupe is Arthur himself, who meets "a young man, expensively and fashionably dressed" in a Philadelphia tavern (*AM*, 31). A convivial stranger whose "conversation was chiefly characterized by frankness," the tavern patron melts Arthur's initial reserve with "[e]very new act of kindness," until Arthur agrees to leave the tavern with him in search of a "chamber and a bed which he would insist on [Arthur's] sharing with him" (*AM*, 32). As Arthur revels in the stranger's "solicitations for [his] company" (*AM*, 33), the scene develops an erotic of homosocial encounter into an imitation of the seduction plot, and the two men retreat into a darkened house unseen save by the servants. Sex is at once uppermost in and removed from the stranger's machinations, as he tricks Arthur into a closet, locks the door, and vanishes, rendering a decidedly "queer" seduction plot an elaborate practical joke. An unwilling if fascinated spectator of a second deceitful male, this one trying to pass off his illegitimate infant as a foundling. Arthur again witnesses the confounding of virtue and scheming, the display and disguise of sexual interest experienced in his tavern encounter. He eavesdrops on this second male (the merchant Thetford, business partner of Welbeck and part of the novel's chorus of Arthur detractors) bending over a sleeping woman and an infant he has placed by her side: "Smiling cherub! Safe and sound, I see. Would to God my experiment mayest succeed and that thou mayest find a mother where I have found a wife!" (*AM*, 37). Fleeing a family destroyed by illness and reconstituted by male treachery and lust (his father, Sawny Mervyn, succumbs to the temptations of the "profligate" Betty Lawrence), Arthur covertly witnesses an urban rehearsal of his own family's moral subversion. Yet familial corruption paradoxically becomes familial construction as a successfully disguised libertine-father forges a sentimental narrative of family building out of a narrative of male philandering.[44] Libertinism and authorship thus coalesce in this uncanny tableau of domestic (un)making.

The novel further complicates Arthur's spectatorial dilemma, since his own (admittedly unintentional) agency in the affair could easily be considered the true crime committed that night: "The light in which such a visitant would be probably regarded by a woman's fears, the precipitate alarms that might be given . . . might pollute a spotless reputation or furnish fuel to jealousy" (*AM*, 36). The first of many such encounters staged by the novel between Arthur and fabricated domestic configurations, the scene clearly suggests that one possible consequence of undisciplined masculinity might be a kind of licence at once sexual and imaginative. In this sense, the libertine father's scheming and Arthur's covert witnessing are linked; Arthur's "innocent" participation in one scheme of seduction, that of the stranger in the tavern, makes him a potentially culpable witness to another.

With a precision unremarked in any scholarly consideration of *Arthur Mervyn*, Brockden Brown restages this scene of ambiguous masculine sexual, fictive, and readerly agency later in the narrative, when Arthur has removed to the mansion of Thomas Welbeck, the as yet undetected libertine forger. Along with Mervyn, Welbeck is, like Thetford, a master of narrative, specifically, of sentimental narrative. Welbeck's mastery of both libertine and sentimental narratives of masculinity speaks powerfully to the period's worry that the two might well be the same—that the feelingful language of desexualized virtue is the libertine's most persuasive tool. To take a final example from the periodical record, according to "The Libertine Reclaimed," a 1789 dialogue published in the *Christian Scholar's and Farmer's Magazine,* the libertine is known variously for "Professing virtue;—but practicing vice! . . . Shining talents! Fashionable accomplishments! And literary attainments, embellished by the wisdom of virtue!"[45] No scene in *Arthur Mervyn* demonstrates more powerfully the fictive dynamic of sentimental libertinism than Arthur's initial encounter with Clemenza Lodi. Descending to the breakfast room of Welbeck's mansion, Arthur is instructed to ignore "any emotion" that "A Lady" about to enter the room "may betray at the sight of" Arthur (*AM*, 52), a lady whom Welbeck claims is his daughter but who is, Arthur later realizes, the seduced sister of the dead brother whom Arthur coincidentally resembles. "She did not immediately notice me," relates Arthur. "When she did she almost shrieked with surprise. She held up her hands, and gazing upon me, uttered various exclamations which I could not understand." Frankly uninterested in the reason for Clemenza's astonishment, Arthur instead provides a physical description of the woman, a "celestial vision" with "snowy hues" whose "accents were thrillingly musical." He revels in his newly acquired power to influence a beautiful woman. Making a claim familiar in literary sentimentalism—the inability to "execute her portrait" (*AM*, 52), Arthur belies his claim to linguistic incapacity by sketching an evocatively stylized vision of her, a vision made possible by an appreciative spectatorial eroticism. Just as Welbeck's scheming counterfeits a "brother" for his "daughter," Arthur's portrait of Clem-

enza similarly, if unintentionally, replaces Clemenza's actual, still undisclosed sexual and filial history with an affective vision of beautified maidenhood. He "spontaneously" articulates a sentimental narrative determined in advance by Welbeck's orchestration of the encounter. Welbeck thus constructs a "family," as his friend Thetford did, by manipulating the affective mechanisms that make familial intimacy so powerful. Arthur's "interest" in Clemenza, delivered in an erotically charged language of sentimental portraiture, thus correlates mimetically with Welbeck's sexual violation of her, a predation that appears to Arthur, after the closet scene at Thetford's, as a proprietary form of paternal protection. Clemenza's stuttering confusion and Arthur's sentimental fluency cohere through Welbeck's carefully orchestrated simulacrum of a family unit. Authoring the familial fiction is a disguised and predatory male sexuality possibly shared by Arthur Mervyn, whose sexual history with the "artful profligate" (*AM*, 231) is such that it "cannot be discredited" (*AM*, 236). This structural relationship indirectly links the familial fabrications of Welbeck's sexual libertinism to the fabrications of Arthur's sentimentalized eroticism, the agency of which, like that of the Rhapsodist, remains questionable.[46]

A second anti-Mervyn counternarrative, this one provided by Williams, a friend of Dr. Stevens, questions Arthur's "innocent" participation in yet another Welbeck-authored counterfeiting of family. In this testimony, Williams offers a second look at one of Arthur's early exploits, in which he conveyed a message to Mrs. Wentworth, a widow "connected by some ties of tenderness" to a youth named Clavering, who died, according to Arthur Mervyn, in Mervyn's own house (*AM*, 66). Mediating the Mervyn-Wentworth encounter are two aesthetic artifacts: a portrait of Mrs. Wentworth bearing "an actual resemblance between the strokes of the pencil which executed the portrait and that of Clavering" (*AM*, 64) and a miniature of Clavering, lost by Arthur his first night in Philadelphia but now sitting on Mrs. Wentworth's mantle. The scene arrays a series of connections along family lines—between Mrs. Wentworth and her artist nephew, between the artist's self-portrait and his aunt's house—that ultimately bring Arthur in as supplement to the sundered family relations commemorated not only by the two portraits but also by the visage of Arthur, who physically resembles the missing Clavering. This resemblance doubles the portrait/miniature homology as Arthur/Clavering comes to stand "innocently" in the parlor of his "aunt."[47]

The scene's arrangement of art and people thus establishes a mimesis not just between the family's representation in art and the family itself but between family relations and their organization as a kind of art, a mechanism Williams later asserts is yet another Welbeckian simulation of family: "In due time, and after the lady's mind had been artfully prepared by Welbeck, the pupil made his appearance; and, in a conversation full of studied ambiguities, assured the lady, that her nephew was dead" (*AM,* 249-50). Welbeck's interest here, according to the Williams counternarrative, is to substitute Clemenza Lodi, "whom he had molded for his purpose, in place of the lost youth, in the affections of the lady while living," thereby securing Mrs. Wentworth's estate for Clemenza, which is to say, for her seducer, Welbeck (*AM,* 249). The language of artifice is by now familiar, yet here it is intensified by its references to the manipulation of aesthetic artifact and response on display in Mrs. Wentworth's parlor, and it is now attributed causally to Welbeck and Mervyn. The scene and its counter-narrative restage the confounding of family undertaken by Thetford, whose twinned vocations as libertine and merchant are shared by Welbeck, to whom a third might be added—"artist." The Williams counternarrative brings this artistic temperament one step closer to the literary artist through the language it uses to describe Welbeck's and Mervyn's fraudulent agency. Williams refers to "the plot" going forward and to the trouble encountered by its "plotters" (250). The narrative voice refers to the artifice of the plot to confuse and confound Mrs. Wentworth, a deception presumably not intended by the portraits, whose ultimate significance lies in their ability to further libertine self-interest.

Many critics have remarked that *Arthur Mervyn* is a novel of multiple narrative interpolations and that its narrative polyvocality is, in its very overdetermination, a characteristic the novel puts to formal and political use.[48] Fewer have remarked the literalization of this narrative-within-narrative structure, the mysterious manuscript that Arthur steals from Thomas Welbeck, who acquired the text through the sexual conquest of the manuscript author's sister, the hapless Clemenza Lodi. Sewn between the pages of the book is $20,000 in paper currency. The manuscript thus images what must have been any early American novelist's professional fantasy: the literal translation of a narrative into money. As it turns out, the act of fictional narration is even more literally and disturbingly reflected by the act of producing money when the hidden money turns out (perhaps) to have been as artfully fabricated as any narrative: the currency is counterfeit. But the novel is not content merely to link the art of putting words on a page to the art of counterfeiting. It gives the screw of authorial authenticity one last turn by undermining even the story of the currency's forgery, when Arthur Mervyn, prodded by Welbeck's claim to have made the currency himself, hurls the manuscript, and its false(?) notes, into a fire. "Maniac!" screams Welbeck. "Miscreant! To be fooled by so gross an artifice! The notes were genuine. The tale of their forgery was false" (*AM,* 210). That the tale of forgery, a narrative accompanied by "every token of sincerity" (*AM,* 209), is itself a forgery, locates the novel's epistemology of narrative in the vaporous domain of libertinism.[49] The potentially infinite logical regress of the currency-cum-narrative forgery reflects the libertine's loss of self either to the sensibility of his passion or to the multiple masks donned and discarded during the rake's progress. Moreover, the manuscript's imbrication within the discourse of libertinism confounds many of the oppositions structuring both the language of the libertine and the language of late-eighteenth-century literary convention: art and artlessness, simulation and original, translation and invention, sentimentalism and the feeling it is "designed" to connote.

The manuscript's chain of transmission further reflects its status as a commemoration of sexual predation, neatly rehearsing the dialogue of libertine artifice and authorial capacity. For the authorship of the manuscript is called into question as both Arthur and Welbeck imagine schemes by which they might become the author of the text. A "profound and elegant" work, the manuscript represents a business opportunity for the ever-scheming Welbeck, as we have seen, but it also calls forth the author in Arthur, who admits that his "ambition had panted, with equal avidity, after the reputation of literature and opulence. To claim the authorship of this work was too harmless and specious a stratagem, not to be readily suggested" (*AM,* 100). If Welbeck would become the manuscript's "author" through his counterfeiting of currency, Arthur would do so through the scarcely less reprehensible means of theft and plagiarism. The problem is that both libertine and dupe, forger and translator, imagine authorship as a self-interested endeavour structured by interests independent of both the text and its circulation within society.[50] Authors, like libertines, create fictions that refer back to a self whose interests the text does not actually reflect. In the case of the author (and particularly Brockden Brown), this self is *homo economicus,* whose financial interests are irrelevant to the content of his "literary" narratives. The predatory libertine's self-interest is masked by fictions designed to satisfy sexual appetite, fictions consisting chiefly of professions of virtue and true love. In the struggle over the manuscript's control, the novel dramatizes authorial self-making in early America as a contest between economic and libertine ambition, a contest characterized by a lack of interest in the object of his labors on the part of both the author and the libertine. The ultimate status of literary authorship, as envisioned in *Arthur Mervyn,* is understood less by determining which of the novel's competing narrators is more innocent than by determining which character/author narrates male virtue most convincingly.

James Russo has suggested that in *Arthur Mervyn,* "the narrator is the novel,"[51] a formulation that helpfully recalls the equation of novelistic agency and libertine linguistic skill in early American culture. For to some extent it is the control of language, or, as in *The Power of*

Sympathy, the lack thereof, that defines the limits of normal masculine behavior and marks its transgression.[52] The sentimentalism both celebrated and upbraided in the 1790s did not elicit an anxious cultural response because male sentimentality automatically committed the crime of effeminacy by identifying with a discourse associated exclusively with the feminine, as most critics have maintained;[53] rather, the sentimental male, like the libertine and the author, occupied a disturbing linguistic position: "unmanned" either by sentiment's agentless sensibility (as in *The Power of Sympathy*) or by a kind of verbal overextension, by the exercise of a too artful, too disingenuous, too self-conscious and self-interested investment in his discursive performances. Thus what makes Arthur Mervyn a "chameleon," as several critics have called him, is not merely the perversity of his actions but their calculated use as explanatory narrative. As narrative agent he embodies the paradox produced by the search for a "natural language" in the early national period, when the crafting of language was seen as suspicious because it wasn't natural, while the natural expression of sincere feeling could and, indeed, had to be articulated carefully.[54] It is in the slippage between sincere craft and crafted sincerity, between feeling expressed and feeling imagined, between accidental art and the achievement of artlessness that early American culture witnessed and elaborated a logic of the authorial libertine and the sentimental man of letters as twin embodiments of some of the young nation's most pressing sociopolitical fears. The imaginative conjoining of libertine and author partially explains why the intensifying calls for a national literature did not do much to legitimize authorship as a profession. There was just something too artful about it.

In typical Brockden Brown fashion, the impossibility of solving conclusively the epistemological riddle posed by the cash-between-the-pages episode reflects the novel's narrative unverifiability, suggesting that *Arthur Mervyn* fails to untether literary authorship from its libertine origins. While one might be tempted to offer a more optimistic reading of the novel's elaboration of the social struggles of male authorship—on the grounds, perhaps, that Brockden Brown was searching for a way to depict authorship as a socially legitimate profession—the connection of literary authorship to sensibility and its "liberated" masculine embodiments keeps the author within the discursive precinct of the libertine.

Notes

1. Tabitha Tenney, *Female Quixotism: Exhibited in the Romantic Opinions and Extravagant Adventures of Dorcasina Sheldon,* ed. Jen Nienkamp and Andrea Collins (1801; reprint, New York: Oxford Univ. Press, 1992), 93, italics in original; subsequent quotations from this novel are cited parenthetically in the text as *FQ.*

2. It is worth noting that as *Female Quixotism* begins, Dorcasina has already been "filled with the airy delusions and visionary dreams of love and raptures, darts, fires and flames" that constitute the bulk of the misadventures to come (4). That is, novels have already ruined her, making the picaresque narrative that follows a series of illustrations or restagings of a downfall that has already occurred. I should note here as well that Tenney's novel, as Jean Nienkamp and Andrea Collins observe in the introduction to their 1992 edition, is indebted to Charlotte Lennox's *Female Quixote* (1752), another picaresque novel of overheated female sensibility.

3. John Adams to William Cunningham, 15 March 1804, *Correspondence between the Honorable John Adams, Late President of the United States, and the Late William Cunningham, Esquire* (Boston: E. M. Cunningham, 1823), 19.

4. On the institutionalizing aspects of the novel, see Shirley Samuels, "Plague and Politics in 1793: *Arthur Mervyn,*" *Criticism* 27 (summer 1985): 225-46; on the novel's relation to early American print ideology, see Michael Warner, *Letters of the Republic: Publication and the Public Sphere* (Cambridge: Harvard Univ. Press, 1990), 151-76; and on *Arthur Mervyn*'s negotiation of republican and liberal political cultures, see Cathy Davidson, *Revolution and the Word: The Rise of the Novel in America* (New York: Oxford Univ. Press, 1986), 251-53.

5. Charles Brockden Brown, *Arthur Mervyn; or, Memoirs of the Plague Year 1793,* ed. Sydney Krause (Kent, Ohio: Kent State Univ. Press, 1980), 230; subsequent references to *Arthur Mervyn* are to this edition and are cited parenthetically in the text as *AM.*

6. Several critics have considered the novel's use of illness as metaphor for the young nation's social problems, including Samuels, "Plague and Politics in 1793," and William L. Hedges, "Benjamin Rush, Charles Brockden Brown, and the American Plague Year," *Early American Literature* 7 (winter 1973): 295-311. Samuels considers the gendered aspects of illness more particularly in her "Infidelity and Contagion: The Rhetoric of Revolution," *Early American Literature* 22 (summer 1987): 183-90.

7. Catherine Gallagher argues that fiction is a textual practice whose lack of referentiality serves as the basis of novelistic realism, and that it is the lack of referentiality that enables readers of fiction to identify with novelistic characters. In other words, fiction is rendered "persuasive" not in spite of but because of its unverifiability; see *Nobody's Story:*

The Vanishing Acts of Women Writers in the Marketplace, 1670-1820 (Berkeley and Los Angeles: Univ. of California Press, 1994), xv-xvii. See also Gallagher's discussion of the "originality" of fiction in Charlotte Lennox's *Female Quixote,* 158-62.

8. *Philadelphia Minerva,* 23 April 1796.

9. *Philadelphia Minerva,* 4 June 1796.

10. The publication history of "The School for Libertines" is somewhat mysterious. Its June 1789 printing in the *Gentleman and Ladies Town and Country Magazine* (vol. 1) was presumably intended to be the story's first installment in the magazine, ending as it does with the customary promise of the periodical cliff-hanger—"(to be continued)" (259). Yet the magazine did not follow through on its promise, and not until the October 1795 edition of the *New York Magazine* did the story appear in its entirety.

11. [Thomas Bellamy], "The School for Libertines: A Story Founded on Facts," *New-York Weekly Magazine,* January 1797, 237, 246. No doubt the incest plot shared by *The Power of Sympathy* and "The School for Libertines" influenced the editors of the *New York Magazine* to run the latter immediately following an extract from the well-known novel in their October 1795 issue, 688-89.

12. Many other libertine tales appeared in the wide variety of magazines that constitute the postrevolutionary periodical record, including "The Duelist and Libertine Reclaimed," *Massachusetts Magazine,* April 1789; "The Progress of Vice," *Massachusetts Magazine,* September 1789; "The Voluptuary's Soliloquy," *Columbian Magazine,* January 1790; "Letter of a Reformed Libertine," *American Museum,* October 1790; "Letter upon Fashionable Libertinism," *New Hampshire Magazine,* June 1793; "The Rake Reformed in the House of Mourning," *The Experienced Christian Magazine,* March 1797; "Picture of a Libertine," *New York Magazine,* September 1797; and "The Effects of Libertinism," *The Rural Casket,* 12 June 1798. Some of these pieces were stolen from English sources; "The Rake Reformed" is attributed to Isaac Watts, while the "Progress of Vice" has been traced to the *European Magazine.* Others are excerpted from longer American works; "Picture of a Libertine," for example, is from Foster's *Coquette.* While it is impossible to catalogue, much less adequately discuss, all such works here, I do want to suggest how voraciously the postrevolutionary authorial, editorial, and readerly imaginations produced, arranged, and consumed the body of the libertine.

13. "The Babbler. No. V.: The Sentimental Libertine; A Story Founded upon Fact," *Massachusetts Magazine,* March 1790, 173, 174.

14. "The Sentimentalist. No. II," *Massachusetts Magazine,* July 1794, 422.

15. A fine example of criticism focused on the maiden is Carroll Smith-Rosenberg's, "Domesticating 'Virtue': Coquettes and Revolutionaries in Young America," in *Literature and the Body: Essays on Populations and Persons,* ed. Elaine Scarry (Baltimore: Johns Hopkins Univ. Press, 1988).

16. See Julia A. Stern, *The Plight of Feeling: Sympathy and Dissent in the Early American Novel* (Chicago: Univ. of Chicago Press, 1997), 13, 15. While focused largely on the early American novel's negotiation of the feminine, Stern's fine study does touch on the representation of libertinism; see 107. David Shields also mentions libertinism at points in *Civil Tongues and Polite Letters in British America* (Chapel Hill: Univ. of North Carolina Press, 1997); see in particular Shields's analysis of the "jest," whose status as "liberty in expression" could become a kind of elocutionary libertinism (70).

17. On the seduction plot's importance to postrevolutionary politics, see Jay Fliegelman, *Prodigals and Pilgrims* (Cambridge, Eng.: Cambridge Univ. Press, 1982), 97, 235-40. As Cathy Davidson remarks in her definitive discussion of William Hill Brown's *Power of Sympathy,* "Seduction . . . becomes a metonymic reduction of the whole world in which women operated and were operated upon" (*Revolution and the Word,* 106).

18. Hannah H. Foster, *The Coquette,* ed. Cathy Davidson (1797; reprint, New York: Oxford Univ. Press, 1986), 63.

19. Stern, *The Plight of Feeling,* 107.

20. On an imaginatively shared reading experience as central to modern nationalism, see Benedict Anderson, *Imagined Communities: Reflections on the Origin and Spread of Nationalism* (London: Verso, 1983), 35-37. I would note here that "Mrs. Richman" and John Adams are members of the same nation in their shared imagining of each other imagining the necessary presence of the libertine.

21. For a discussion of the threat contained in radical (male) individualism, see Fliegelman's treatment of Brockden Brown's *Wieland* in *Prodigals and Pilgrims,* 237-41.

22. James Grantham Turner, "Lovelace and the Paradoxes of Libertinism," in *Samuel Richardson: Tercentenary Essays,* ed. Margaret Anne Doody and

Peter Sabor (Cambridge, Eng.: Cambridge Univ. Press, 1989), 74, 85.

23. "Letter of a Reformed Libertine," *American Museum,* October 1790, 163; "Ruinous Gradation to Vicious Habits," *South Carolina Weekly Magazine,* March 11, 1797, 309.

24. J. G. A. Pocock argues that within the republican political tradition of dissenting Whig historians resided a notion of "natural aristocracy" that would arise to replace the aristocratic order overthrown by the revolution. See Pocock, *The Machiavellian Moment: Florentine Political Thought and the Atlantic Republican Tradition* (Princeton, N.J.: Princeton Univ. Press, 1975), 515.

25. The phrase "public virtue" is from Gordon Wood, *The Creation of the American Republic, 1776-1787* (1968; reprint, New York: Norton, 1972), 68-69.

26. For a recent treatment of the liberal tradition in American political thought, see Joyce Appleby, *Liberalism and Republicanism in the Historical Imagination* (New York: Cambridge Univ. Press, 1992). It would be a mistake to suppose that the literature of early American libertinism supports either the republican synthesis or the liberal pluralism model of American historiographical theory, for the ideology of American libertinism supported neither unequivocally. Rather, one might say that American libertinism registered the ongoing transformation of American culture from one characterized by a politics forged in the shadow of Whig historiography to one increasingly defined by the political economy of market capitalism and the liberalized social relations it engendered. For a treatment of this transformation as it relates to the fiction of Charles Brockden Brown, see Stephen Watts, *The Romance of Real Life: Charles Brockden Brown and the Origins of American Culture* (Baltimore: Johns Hopkins Univ. Press, 1994), 1-26.

27. Sensibility was alternately celebrated, derided, advanced, or cautioned against throughout the 1790s. Its ambivalent status is succinctly captured in this aphorism: "Sensibility, although the source of our most exquisite enjoyments, yet, by exposing us to danger from every quarter, and rendering us vulnerable on every side, too often occasions our most lasting inquietudes" ("Sentiments," *Massachusetts Magazine,* May 1795, 118).

28. William Hill Brown, *The Power of Sympathy,* ed. William S. Kable (1789; reprint, Columbus: Ohio State Univ. Press, 1969), 7-8; subsequent references to this novel are cited parenthetically in the text as *PS.*

29. I am indebted here to Catherine Gallagher's discussion of how sympathy "dispenses with its original 'object,' the original sufferer" (*Nobody's Story,* 171).

30. The prevalence of the terms *art, artful,* and *artless* in descriptions of libertine speech is as overwhelming as it is underremarked. Thus the just-seduced Alicia, heroine of "The Duelist and Libertine Reclaimed," finds herself "by art deprived of" her virtue (*Massachusetts Magazine,* April 1789, 206). Alton/Freeman, graduate of the "School for Libertines," possesses "every art of genteel address" ("The School for Libertines," *New-York Magazine,* January 1797, 237). Mrs. Richman, the matron figure of Foster's *Coquette,* warns the protagonist against the "artful intrusions" of the libertine Sanford: "Beware, my friend, of his arts" (38). The natural foil for the artful libertine, of course, is the girl who lacks artifice: the "innocent artless girl" of Rowson's *Charlotte Temple,* for example. In her study of late-eighteenth-century seduction fiction, Elizabeth Barnes asks the question: "[H]ow, for instance, is one to distinguish between the seducer's and the author's craft?" (*States of Sympathy: Seduction and Democracy in the American Novel* [New York: Columbia Univ. Press, 1997], 48); see also 52 and 55.

31. [Mrs. Barbauld], "On Novel Writing," *Literary Magazine and American Register,* December 1804, 694. Charles Brockden Brown was the editor of this magazine.

32. Samuel Miller, *A Brief Retrospect of the Eighteenth Century,* 2 vols. (1803; reprint, New York: Lenox Hill, 1970), 2:176.

33. Charles Brockden Brown, *"The Rhapsodist" and Other Uncollected Writings,* ed. Henry R. Warfel (1789; reprint, New York: Scholars' Facsimiles and Reprints, 1943), 5; subsequent quotations from this work are cited parenthetically in the text as *R.*

34. Grantland Rice, *The Transformation of Authorship in America* (Chicago: Univ. of Chicago Press, 1997), 53. Rice's discussion of the changing status of authorship, from a person believed to "arrange" ideas to one credited with "inventing" them, derives from Donald Pease's account of how the premodern auctor—instrument of divine revelation—became the early modern author, one who "claimed authority for his words" ("The Author," in *Critical Terms for Literary Study,* ed. Frank Lentricchia and Thomas McLaughlin [Chicago: Univ. of Chicago Press, 1990], 107).

35. Turner, "Lovelace and the Paradoxes of Libertinism," 74. Other critics who discuss Lovelace's feminine attributes include Terry Eagleton, *The*

Rape of Clarissa: Writing, Sexuality, and Class Struggle in Samuel Richardson (New York: Oxford Univ. Press, 1982); William Warner, *Reading "Clarissa": The Struggles of Interpretation* (New Haven: Yale Univ. Press, 1979); and Terry Castle, *Clarissa's Ciphers: Meaning and Disruption in Richardson's "Clarissa"* (Ithaca, N.Y.: Cornell Univ. Press, 1982).

36. Foster, *The Coquette*, 124.

37. I refer again to Adams's 1804 letter to William Cunningham, in which Adams declares, "Democracy is Lovelace and the People are Clarissa" (*Correspondence between the Honorable John Adams . . . and . . . William Cunningham*, 19).

38. Philip Gould, *Covenant and Republic: Historical Romance and the Politics of Puritanism* (Cambridge, Eng: Cambridge Univ. Press, 1996), 27. Many critics, both recent and less so, maintain a somewhat unbreakable link between the feminine and sensibility, among them Julia Stern in *The Plight of Feeling.*

39. See Claudia Johnson's *Equivocal Beings: Politics, Gender, and Sentimentality in the 1790s: Wollstonecraft, Radcliffe, Burney, Austen* (Chicago: Univ. of Chicago Press, 1995), which argues that the gendering of sentiment as feminine must be reconsidered because there was an accepted rhetoric of male sentimentality operative in 1790s English political culture (4-8).

40. "Effeminacy," *Worcester Magazine,* May 1786, 66. The poem is attributed to a female "correspondent."

41. Ibid.

42. [Joseph Lathrop], "The Folly of Affectation," *American Museum,* October 1790, 164. *American Museum* reprinted the piece seven months later in its May 1791 issue (270-1).

43. "Philo. No. VII," *Massachusetts Magazine,* March 1790, 179-80.

44. In "Plague and Politics," Shirley Samuels provides an alternative but compatible interpretation of this scene, suggesting that the father's scheme points to "the unnatural constitution of this family group," a constitution reflected in Mervyn's secret presence inside the Thetford home (237).

45. "Clericus," "The Libertine Reclaimed: A Dialogue," *Christian Scholar's and Farmer's Magazine,* August/September 1789, 326, 327.

46. David Marshall suggests that eighteenth-century notions of sympathy entailed an epistemology of overdetermined "sameness" or resemblance that disturbingly linked the "effects" of seduction to the "effects" of sympathetic communion: "indeed . . . the Richardsonian novel of sensibility designed to move and touch its readers might be dangerous as well as deceptive" (*The Surprising Effects of Sympathy: Marivaux, Diderot, Rousseau, and Mary Shelley* [Chicago: Univ. of Chicago Press, 1988], 86). *Arthur Mervyn*'s association of Welbeck's schemes and Mervyn's dreams recapitulates this problem quite dramatically.

47. This scene is discussed in James Russo's "The Chameleon of Convenient Vice," *Studies in the Novel* 11 (winter 1979): 381-405, in which Russo argues that "Mervyn" is, in fact, Clavering, who has killed the actual Arthur Mervyn and assumed his identity. A brilliant reading of the novel's forensic evidence, it ultimately fails to persuade because no reason is given for Mrs. Wentworth's failure to recognize her nephew and because the novel does not sustain itself as a hoax.

48. Kenneth Bernard focuses on how the novel's narrative complexity reflects, "to a degree, the complexity of life itself" ("Arthur Mervyn: The Ordeal of Innocence," *Texas Studies in Literature and Language* 6 [winter 1965]: 443). Shirley Samuels argues that the novel "tells a story of social regulation, but it tells it by way of a proliferation of stories and narratives" ("Plague and Politics," 226).

49. The term *vaporous* is one James Turner suggests is particularly appropriate to Lovelace; see "Lovelace and the Paradoxes of Libertinism," 70.

50. Grantland Rice notes in his analysis of early American attitudes toward copyright, "Many writers noted with approbation that the disinterested workings of the marketplace countered the vain ambitions of authors toward immortality" (*The Profession of Authorship in America,* 94), a notion that further separates textual from authorial interests.

51. Russo, "The Chameleon of Convenient Vice," 382.

52. In his discussion of Franklin's *Autobiography,* Christopher Looby suggests that early American authorship was a matter of controlling the disruptive capabilities of language inherent in the Revolution's status as linguistic event; see Looby, *Voicing America: Language, Literary Form, and the Origins of the United States* (Chicago: Univ. of Chicago Press, 1996), 99-144.

53. A recent example of this tendency is Stern's *Plight of Feeling.*

54. The most sustained meditation on this contradictory notion of "natural theatricality" is Jay Fliegel-

man's *Declaring Independence: Jefferson, Natural Language, and the Culture of Performance* (Stanford, Calif.: Stanford Univ. Press, 1993).

FURTHER READING

Bibliography

White, Devon. "Contemporary Criticism of Five Early American Sentimental Novels, 1970-1994: An Annotated Bibliography." *Bulletin of Bibliography* 52, no. 4 (December 1995): 293-305.

> Provides an annotated bibliography of scholarship pertaining to five early American sentimental novels, including Tenney's *Female Quixotism.*

Criticism

Brown, Herbert Ross. *The Sentimental Novel in America 1789-1860.* Durham, N.C.: Duke University Press, 1940.

Defines and contextualizes the sentimental novel with references to Tenney.

Frost, Linda. "The Body Politic in Tabitha Tenney's *Female Quixotism.*" *Early American Literature* 32, no. 2 (1997): 113-34.

> Analyzes the protagonist in *Female Quixotism.*

Hoople, Sally. Introduction to *Female Quixotism,* by Tabitha Gilman Tenney. 1801. Reprint, pp. 3-9. Delmar, N.Y.: Scholars' Facsimiles & Reprints, 1988.

> Examines Tenney's novel as illustrative of the cultural shifts during her lifetime.

Loshe, Lillie Deming. *The Early American Novel, 1798-1830.* 1907. Reprint. New York: Frederick Ungar Publishing Company, 1958, 131 p.

> Traces the early development of the novel in American literature and briefly acknowledges Tenney.

Additional coverage of Tabitha Gilman Tenney's life and career is contained in the following source published by the Gale Group: *Dictionary of Literary Biography,* Vols. 37 and 200.

Ivan Turgenev
1818-1883

Russian novelist, novella, short story, and sketch writer, playwright, poet, and essayist.

The following entry presents criticism on Turgenev from 1920 through 1996. For further discussion of Turgenev's life and career, see *NCLC*, Volume 21; for a discussion of the novel *Fathers and Sons*, see *NCLC*, Volume 37.

INTRODUCTION

Called "the novelist's novelist" by Henry James, Ivan Turgenev was the first Russian author to achieve widespread international fame. Although he was originally linked with Fyodor Dostoevsky and Leo Tolstoy as a member of the triumvirate of great Russian novelists of the nineteenth century, Turgenev's reputation began to diminish during the course of the twentieth century. He produced numerous works in a variety of genres but is most famous for his narrative prose, particularly *Ottsy i deti* (1862; *Fathers and Sons*), a work that was denounced by his contemporaries, both liberal and conservative.

BIOGRAPHICAL INFORMATION

Turgenev was born on October 28, 1818, in the city of Orel into a family of wealthy gentry. He spent his childhood at the family's estate with his father, a charming but ineffectual cavalry officer, and his mother, a strong-willed but eccentric heiress whose extensive land holdings included the estate at Spasskoye and its 5,000 serfs. Turgenev's biographers note that his many fictional representations of strong female characters and weak-willed male characters replicate the personal dynamics of the Turgenev family. During Turgenev's early childhood French was the primary language spoken in his household, though his mother later permitted the use of Russian as well. Her library was extensive and her son spent much of his childhood reading literature in several languages. In 1824 the family moved to Moscow where Turgenev began his formal education, consisting of a combination of local schools and private tutors. In 1833 he entered Moscow University and a year later transferred to the University of St. Petersburg, where he began writing poetry. After graduation he went to Germany, enrolled at the University of Berlin, and studied philosophy for the next several years. In 1841 Turgenev returned to Russia and for the remainder of his life divided his time between his homeland and Western Europe.

Turgenev's first published work was a narrative poem that received little attention. Although he continued to write poetry and drama, he soon turned to narrative prose, producing short stories and sketches—many of them on the injustice of Russian serfdom—for the radical periodical *The Contemporary*. These stories were enormously popular with the public but attracted unfavorable attention from government officials. The publication of twenty-two of these sketches in the collection *Zapiski okhotnika* (1852; *A Sportsman's Sketches*), together with an admiring obituary of Nikolay Gogol that same year, resulted in Turgenev's arrest and imprisonment. After a month in jail, he was confined to

Spasskoye, where he remained under house arrest for nearly two years.

In 1856 Turgenev began writing novels and in 1862 produced *Fathers and Sons,* now considered his master-piece. Reaction among the various political factions within Russia was immediate, and the novel was denounced from all sides. Distressed by the unfavorable reviews, Turgenev began to spend more and more time in Western Europe in the company of such renowned authors as Gustave Flaubert, Henry James, and George Sand. His absence from his homeland only increased the attacks on his work, and his subsequent novels were offered as proof by his critics that he was out of touch with his native country. With the publication of his last novel, *Nov',* (1877; *Virgin Soil*), Turgenev abandoned any attempt to deal with the Russian political scene and turned to the production of prose poems and stories that were philosophical and nostalgic. Turgenev, after a lengthy illness, died in 1883 near Paris. His body was returned to Russia, where he was widely mourned despite attempts by the government to discourage and restrict memorials.

MAJOR WORKS

A Sportsman's Sketches exposed the miserable conditions of Russia's serfs and is often compared with Harriet Beecher Stowe's anti-slavery novel *Uncle Tom's Cabin,* although Turgenev's message was far more understated. Some years later, when the serfs eventually won their freedom, Turgenev's text was credited with helping to secure their emancipation. In 1856 Turgenev produced his first novel, *Rudin,* introducing themes and character types that would inform his subsequent novels and stories, including such characters as the political idealist given to words rather than action, the strong heroine willing to risk everything for love, and the passive, ineffectual suitor who abandons the heroine at the first sign of opposition. Turgenev's next two novels, *Dvoryanskoe gnezdo* (1859; *A House of Gentlefolk*) and *Nakanune* (1860; *On the Eve*), deal with similar themes of fatalism and frustration.

Turgenev's most famous novel, *Fathers and Sons,* features a protagonist who represented a new political type in Russia at the time—the nihilist. The character Bazarov rejects all elements of Russian politics and culture and believes in nothing except empirical science. His next novel, *Dym* (1867; *Smoke*), was a pessimistic appraisal of Russia's political scene, and his final novel, *Nov',* represented the Russian Populist Movement of the 1870s.

In addition to his six novels, Turgenev produced shorter works that attained great popularity, among them the short story "Mumu" (1852), and the novellas *Pervaya lyubov'* (1860; *First Love*), and *Veshnie vody* (1872; *The Torrents of Spring*). Turgenev's last published work during his lifetime was *Stikhotvoreniya v proze* (1882; *Poems in Prose*).

CRITICAL RECEPTION

In the nineteenth century, scholarship on Turgenev centered around his six novels and the storm of controversy surrounding them in Russia, whereas elsewhere they were considered illuminating representations of Russia's sociopolitical scene. In the twentieth century, scholars began to concentrate more and more on Turgenev's shorter fiction, which consists of the sketches in *A Sportsman's Sketches,* as well as approximately 35 other stories and novellas. Vladimir Fisher, for example, suggesting that the stories have been unjustly overshadowed by the novels, concentrates on the autobiographical and historical elements in the shorter works, as well as their pessimism and fatalism. Thomas Eekman has also studied the shorter prose and maintains that Turgenev's "stock theme" in the stories, as in the novels, is love, and James B. Woodward argues that the "essential impotence of man is the most basic and consistent theme in Turgenev's fiction."

Many late twentieth-century scholars focused on the role of women in Turgenev's work. Among them are Christine Johanson, who has studied the historical accuracy of Turgenev's female characters, and Jane T. Costlow, who examines the heroines of the novels, particularly Odintsova in *Fathers and Sons.* According to Costlow, "Turgenev's heroines have been creatures of passion, not sensibility; they have been defiant and exultant, not carefully resigned." Walter Smyrniw discusses Turgenev's part in the creation of the nineteenth-century iconic representation of the femme fatale. Suggesting that the author was influenced by similarly-themed representations in the paintings of Dante Gabriel Rossetti, Smyrniw explains that Turgenev created sensual female characters who are endowed with the same erotic physical features Rossetti gave to his female subjects.

Many scholars acknowledge that Turgenev's reputation during and following the twentieth century has been overshadowed by that of his more famous countrymen, Tolstoy and Dostoevsky. Richard Freeborn, however, insists that Turgenev's work remains valuable since the author, as an eyewitness to the 1848 revolution in France, possessed a unique perspective on the political pressures and changes leading to the Russian revolutions of 1905 and 1917. Elizabeth Cheresh Allen, studying *Poems in Prose,* acknowledges both the uneven quality of Turgenev's final effort as well as the author's declining reputation in the twentieth century. She concludes that in his ambitious attempt to secure Russia's place in literary history, Turgenev succeeded in securing his own.

PRINCIPAL WORKS

*Parasha (poetry) 1843

"Dnevnik lishnego cheloveka" ["The Diary of a Super-fluous Man"] (short story) 1850

"Mumu" (short story) 1852

Zapiski okhotnika [*Russian Life in the Interior*; also published as *A Sportsman's Sketches*] (sketches and short stories) 1852

Rudin (novel) 1856; enlarged edition, 1860

Asya (novella) 1858

Dvoryanskoe gnezdo [*A House of Gentlefolk*; also published as *A Nobleman's Nest*] (novel) 1859

"Gamlet i Don Kokhot" ["Hamlet and Don Quixote"] (criticism) 1860

Nakanune [*On the Eve*] (novel) 1860

Pervaya lyubov' [*First Love*] (novella) 1860

Ottsy i deti [*Fathers and Sons*; also published as *Fathers and Children*] (novel) 1862

Dym [*Smoke*] (novel) 1867

†*Mesyats v derevne* [*A Month in the Country*] (drama) 1872

Veshnie vody [*The Torrents of Spring*] (novella) 1872

Nov' [*Virgin Soil*] (novel) 1877

Stikhotvoreniya v proze [*Poems in Prose*] (poetry) 1882

Polnoe sobranie sochinenii. 10 vols. (novels, novellas, short stories, dramas, poetry, criticism, and letters) 1891

The Novels of Ivan Turgenev. 15 vols. (novels, novellas, short stories, and poetry) 1894-1899

The Novels and Stories of Iván Turgénieff. 16 vols. (novels, novellas, and short stories) 1903-1904

The Plays of Ivan S. Turgenev (dramas) 1924

Polnoe sobranie sochinenii i pisem. 28 vols. (novels, novellas, short stories, dramas, poetry, criticism, and letters) 1960-1968

Turgenev's Letters (letters) 1983

*Most of Turgenev's works were originally published in periodicals.

†This work was written in 1850.

CRITICISM

Vladimir Fisher (essay date 1920)

SOURCE: Fisher, Vladimir. "Story and Novel in Turgenev's Work." In *Critical Essays on Ivan Turgenev*, edited by David A. Lowe, pp. 43-63. Boston: G. K. Hall & Co., 1988.

[*In the following essay, originally published in 1920, Fisher discusses features found in Turgenev's short stories and novels that reveal the author's experiences and observations.*]

THE AUTOBIOGRAPHICAL ELEMENT

Turgenev's novels have overshadowed his stories. And in general, the latter were somehow unlucky. The critics, in the person of Belinsky, met the first story[1] rather coldly. The success of **Notes of a Hunter** at the end of the 1840s and the beginning of the 1850s prevented the public and the critics from appreciating the great merits of the stories. The reflected light of the fame of **Notes of a Hunter** fell on two of the stories—**"Mumu"** and **"The Inn."** But after that began the era of the novels, which happened to coincide with the blossoming of the Turgenev story. But the vivid social significance of the novels crowded the stories out of the foreground. True, our socially minded critics noted some stories, but more was said apropos of them than about them (Chernyshevsky's article about **Asya**[2]); some stories provoked bewilderment (**"Phantoms," "Enough," "The Dog"**); others enjoyed success among the public as entertaining reading (**"The Song of Triumphant Love"**); they were always published enthusiastically in journals, they were translated, but they were little studied.

In the scholarly literature that has arisen recently, the stories have been addressed in order to treat questions of one sort or another that occur in connection with the study of the writer's worldview (Ovsyaniko-Kulikovsky)[3] or of his "manner" (Istomin).[4]

But the Turgenev story has its special interest if only because it is the product of the writer's pure inspiration, which does not lay claim here to the solution of any social questions, for which solution, in the opinion of certain people, Turgenev had no gift.

The autobiographical significance of Turgenev's stories, however, has been established, although hardly studied thoroughly. The writer's declaration that his entire biography is in his works relates primarily and especially to his stories. He himself pointed especially to the story **First Love.** But that does not mean that the Turgenev story is of purely subjective origin. On the contrary, its interest is more objective, and the subjective image in the story stands not in the foreground, but, for the most part, at a double or triple remove: the person in whom we recognize the author is often the witness in a story, the observer, the narrator, but not the hero. The author draws not so much on experiences from his own life as on observations.

If one looks at Turgenev's stories from the biographical point of view, one will have to single out, in the first place, those that treat family legends and the author's family recollections; the first such story in time is **"Three Portraits,"** which treats the author's ancestors on his maternal side; the figure of his mother is encountered, as is well known, in the stories **"Mumu," "A King Lear of the Steppe,"** and **"Punin and Baburin"**; that of his father, in the story **First Love.**

Other stories shed light on the author's school years: the narrator or hero is a university student or preparing to be one, and, moreover, at Moscow University; the author's brief stay at the latter left an incomparably greater mark on his artistic memory than did his stay at Saint Petersburg University, about which so much is said in **"Memoirs of Literature and Life."** But a Moscow coloration prevails in a great number of Turgenev's stories, beginning with **"Andrey Kolosov"** and ending with **"Klara Milich,"** and also forms an organic part of the majority of his novels.

The stories in a third category cover the "years of wandering": the narrator or hero travels abroad, as Turgenev himself travelled after finishing his education; these are **"Three Meetings,"** *Asya,* and **"Spring Freshets,"** the autobiographical nature of which has been established.

The other stories are probably also autobiographical to a certain degree, although that is more difficult to establish, so varied is their coloration.

Establishing the autobiographical element in Turgenev's stories is extraordinarily important for elucidating the process of their creation, but not for elucidating their essence: Turgenev's stories do not give a sequential history of the author's inner life, as do Tolstoy's works. Personal recollections, meetings, and observations only gave Turgenev the material out of which there arose something, but in its essence something different from poetic autobiography.

Even more insignificant and incidental is the autobiographical element in the novels. Certain features of Lavretsky's joyless childhood ("Woe to a heart that has not loved in youth!"), the student life of Lezhnev, who had written "an entire drama in imitation of *Manfred*" (Turgenev's *Steno*), the character Shubin, which reproduces in part Turgenev in his youth, with his eccentricity, self-analysis, and childish playfulness—that is approximately all of the autobiographical details that the existing evidence about Turgenev allows one to establish in the novels.

The Narrators of the Stories

The autobiographical origin of the majority of Turgenev's stories affects their form noticeably: the majority of them (twenty-five out of thirty-four) are narrated in the first person, while in the novels, whose plots are for the most part invented, that form of narration is not encountered. At the same time, the first person in the story is not the main person, and often is quite peripheral. But the author needs him for the form, and he, the author, expends considerable energy to create him, and in such a way that the reader does not confuse him with the author. . . .

Thus, Turgenev, while needing the fiction of narrators, is anxious in every way to leave him in the shade, not to introduce him into the plot if at all possible, and not to restrict himself with his manner. In fact only in a few stories is the narrator the main person, for instance, *Asya*; in the majority of instances he plays a secondary role, as in the story **"Yakov Pasynkov,"** or he plays no role at all other than that of a viewer, observer, witness, for instance, **"The Brigadier."**

And nonetheless in the corpus of Turgenev's stories autobiographical or subjective traits appear every now and then; now we see a young master, the son of a female estate owner, then a young university student, now a traveller, then a hunter, now simply an elderly tall gentleman with graying hair. From time to time the narrator is a mouthpiece for the author's worldview or the author's artistic credo.

But there are quite objective narrator characters too: such is the Kaluga estate owner Porfiry Kapitonych (**"The Dog"**), the priest (**"Father Alexey's Story"**), and the old man (**"The Watch"**). There are absolutely undistinguished, fictional narrators, for instance, Mr. X (**"A Strange Story"**).

Turgenev's lack of desire to imitate a narrator's manner does not come, of course, from an inability to create experiments such as Karl Ivanovich's story in Tolstoy.[5] A superb authority on mores, Turgenev has a masterful command of other people's speech and knows how to convey its slightest nuances, including pronunciation.[6]

But poetic autobiography is present in Turgenev's stories only as an element and does not comprise their essence. Cultural realia,[7] which saturate many of Turgenev's stories, are an element and a material, too, but cultural realia do not comprise their essence either. . . .

The Historical Background of the Stories

One additional surface aspect of Turgenev's stories that ought to be recognized as such is the socio-historical element. In telling about Sanin and Gemma's love (**"Spring Freshets"**), the writer notes the awkwardness that Sanin feels when the prospect of selling his peasants presents itself to him. It is clear that this has very slight relation to the story's plot. But it is remarkable that Turgenev always dates his narratives precisely and indicates the place of action precisely. In general, that is the accepted practice in historical novels; it is also understandable that Turgenev indicates the years in his novels, which depict a specific moment in the history of educated Russian society. But what need have we to know that the action of the story **"Klara Milich"** transpires precisely in 1878?

In Turgenev the reader almost always learns in what year, or at least in what decade the action transpires. We learn that the action of **"The Desperado"** takes place in 1829, that of *First Love* in 1833, that of **"A Misfortunate Girl"** in 1835, that Sanin meets Gemma in 1840, and that he is 22 then, that **"A Correspondence"** relates to the years 1840-42, the action of **"Faust"** to 1850. The separate parts of the story **"Punin and Baburin"** are headed with figures: "1836," "1837," "1849," and "1861." Moreover, the time is marked by historical and historico-literary information. The story **"The Jew"** coincides with the forays abroad after the War of 1812; **"The Watch,"** with Alexander I's ascension to the throne; Baburin's exile, with the arrests that raged in 1849. The action of *First Love* occurs right "at the height of romanticism"; that of **"A Misfortunate Girl,"** at the time when Pushkin's Onegin is fresh in everyone's memory; **"Knock—Knock—Knock"** relates to the time of Marlinsky's great renown; Gemma reads Malss, a Frankfurt writer of the 1840s; the reader always knows what the heroes of a story read and what their literary tastes are: that characterizes them and the time. But, of course, only in part. So be it that Sanin was born in 1818, loves Gemma in 1840, reads Malss with her and contemplates selling his peasants. But if he had been born in 1848 and in 1870 loved a Gemma who was born later, the essence of their love would remain the same: the only difference would be that they would read someone other than Malss, and Sanin would have had to sell his estate instead of live people. Why does Turgenev need this chronology and illusion?

It is an almost unprecedented phenomenon. . . . This "historicity" of Turgenev's stories is only a surface aspect, an element, material, like autobiography and cultural realia. It is not an artistic necessity, but it is, for Turgenev, a psychological one.

In order to understand this, one must turn to those stories that happen to lack this chronology.

Pessimism

These are primarily those stories that are the almost unmediated expression of the author's worldview—**"Phantoms," "Enough,"** and **"A Dream."** Here Turgenev's creativity is bared; here those "surface aspects" that were mentioned earlier do not turn up.

First, there is nothing autobiographical here: the author conveys his own attitude and worldview, true, but a general one that is not linked to any particular moment in his personal life.

Second, there are no conditions of place here, that is, cultural realia. In this regard, an especially interesting example is the story **"A Dream,"** where there is not even a single name, but human relations are shown in their essence.

Third, there are no conditions of time here: no dates, no historical or historico-literary information.

And in order to understand the Turgenev story at all, one has to disengage oneself from the autobiographical element, from cultural realia, from the historical background, because none of these things is of the essence; it is essential to contemplate human relations presented by Turgenev in the purity in which they are shown in the story **"A Dream."**

Thus, a Turgenev story's main interest is psychological and philosophical, although only in a few cases are the philosophy and psychology not made up in the colors of place and time.

In the story **"Phantoms"** precisely the absolute freedom from the fetters of time and space is observed. Ellis carries the hero off to distant places and distant eras. The result is horror, melancholy, despair. . . .

Of course the essence of Sanin and Gemma's relations would remain the same in another era as well, but Turgenev wants to see them alive; and for that he needs specifically Frankfurt, specifically 1840, Gemma's Italian gestures, and the reading of Malss, specifically Malss, not of Sudermann.

Nature as an elemental force, as a substance, is horrible. And life in its essence is petty, boring, flat, and terrifying in that there is nothing terrifying in it. But

> Look around—and the everyday world
> Is multicolored and marvellous

And so, fettering a person to a place, fixing him in the framework of chronological dates, and observing him in that little corner, after forgetting about the infinity that surrounds him—that is Turgenev's artistic mission.

"Stay!" he exclaims in the *Poems in Prose,* "remain forever in my memory as I now see you!"

Fatalism

Another feature of Turgenev's worldview that influences the concepts of his stories in a specific way is a distinctive fatalism. While seeing only a phenomenon in the individual human, Turgenev sees a substance in human life, in the life of the masses. The aggregate life of people is such a complex combination of individual wills, such an interweaving of intersecting aspirations, that it is ruled by chance, which is not envisioned by any individual consciousness and for which no individual principle can establish norms. An individual thrown into the mass is powerless, like a straw in the wind, like a raindrop in a current: the drops create the current, but each individual drop is completely in the power of the current. Turgenev's most powerful poem, **"The Crowd,"** expresses this sad capitulation of the individual to the mass.

An individual in an elemental mass of other individuals is given up to chance. The story **"Three Meetings"** is built on the play of chance. But in portraying life in general, Turgenev often ponders *the mysterious play of fate* that we blind ones call blind chance" (**"Faust"**). "Neither can one alter one's *fate,* nor does anyone know himself, and besides, it's also impossible to foresee the future. In reality, nothing else happens in life except the *unexpected,* and we spend our whole lives doing nothing but accommodating ourselves to events" (**"A Correspondence"**).

Chance rules in life. Chance sends Vyazovnin to Paris, where he so stupidly runs up against a sword; chance brings Alexey Petrovich (**"A Correspondence"**) to the ballet, where he falls in love with a ballerina; chance brings N. N. together with Asya, Sanin with Gemma; chance turns Ridel's joke into the fatal reason for Teglev's suicide (**"Knock—Knock—Knock"**); chance governs the watch that invades the lives of the boys (**"The Watch"**); but fate often peeps out from behind chance. . . .

Therefore the life of an individual is not defined by his character. By virtue of his position an individual is inevitably passive; the active principle is the reality surrounding him. The perceived opinion about a weakness of will as the main trait of Turgenev's heroes has begun to waver recently. It is not weakness of will that makes many of Turgenev's heroes impotent in life and "superfluous," but something else, located outsides themselves—fate.

In the story **"The Watch,"** the narrator's father, a minor business agent, after quarreling with his friend Latkin, curses him. "Fate itself seemed intent upon discharging my father's last wish. Soon after the rupture . . . Latkin's wife, who, true, had been ill a long while, died; his second daughter, a three-year-old child, went deaf and dumb from terror in a single day: a beehive had gotten stuck around her head; Latkin himself had an apoplectic stroke and fell into extreme poverty." No matter how Lavretsky's break with his wife may be motivated psychologically, one should not forget his Aunt Glafira's curse: "You won't make a nest for yourself anywhere!" In the story **"The Inn"** there is also the fickle finger of fate: Naum, who gets the inn through deceit, keeps being lucky; but "after being a successful manager for some fifteen years, he arranged to sell his inn at a profit to another petty bourgeois. He would never have parted with his fortune if the following apparently insignificant circumstance had not occurred: for two mornings in a row his dog, sitting in front of the windows, howled long and plaintively; he went out onto the street for the second time, took a good look at the howling dog, shook his head, set off for town, and on that very day agreed on a price with the petit bourgeois who had long wanted to buy the inn. A week later

he left for somewhere far away—outside the province; the new owner moved in, and what do you think? That same evening the inn burned down, not a single closet survived, and Naum's successor was left a beggar." Fate sends Porfiry Kapitonych, a Kaluga estate owner with a bald spot and a belly, a dog who perishes after playing a definite role in his life (**"The Dog"**). The same fate sends Lukeria (**"Living Relics"**) a disease and turns her from a "giggler, singer, dancer" into a saint.

Lukeria believes that that is God; but it is an unjust god who at the same time has a beehive get stuck to an innocent child's head; it is a god who gives Naum success in unfair business practices but punishes the innocent petty bourgeois who buys the inn from him; it is a god who manifests incomprehensible sympathy for Porfiry Kapitonych; it is a god who listens attentively to the curses of evil people, not the prayers of the good. His whims resemble those of the crotchety old woman who causes the mute Gerasim suffering (**"Mumu"**).

In Turgenev there are no people who forge their own happiness: all are blamelessly guilty, lucky without reason. All are doomed.

THE COMPOSITION OF A STORY

That is precisely what a Turgenev story tells about. Generally speaking, it tells about how an outside force irrupts into a person's life, takes him into its universe, throws him here and there according to its arbitrary rule, and, finally, casts the shipwrecked person up unto his bank as a pathetic piece of debris. Moreover, fate does not reckon with a given person's predisposition toward one thing or another, but imposes a role upon him that is often beyond his strength. You would think him a Gogolian hero, but an adventure in the spirit of Pechorin[8] happens to him.

So, Lieutenant Yergunov, a blood brother of Gogol's Zhevakin, has an adventure reminiscent of Lermontov's story "Taman."

Aratov, a relative of Podkolyosin,[9] experiences a mysterious poem of love with a mystical ending (**"Klara Milich"**).

Porfiry Kapitonych, the Kaluga estate owner, "a middle-aged man of average height, with a belly and a bald spot," experiences "something supernatural," before which "common sense" completely retreats.

Turgenev portrays the contact of tawdry people with the romance of life, of shallow and weak people with the mystery of love, and of sober people with the mysteries of nature.

In accordance with this, three moments are distinguishable in a Turgenev story:

(1) The norm. The depiction of an individual in the ordinary conditions of life in which another writer would in fact leave that person, for instance, Goncharov.

(2) The catastrophe. The violation of the norm thanks to the incursion of unforeseen circumstances that do not arise from the given situation.

(3) The finale. The end of the catastrophe and its psychological consequences.

The moments are laid out in just such a sequence in, for instance, the story *Asya,* where N. N.'s trip is the norm; the catastrophe, his love for Asya; and the finale, N. N.'s lonely old age.

But these moments may follow in reverse sequence: the finale, that is, the depiction of the consequence of the catastrophe, may be at the beginning; then follows the story of the norm and of the catastrophe that came after it. The story **"A Correspondence,"** for instance, is composed in that way, where the hero's death is told at the beginning, and then the norm unfolds from his correspondence—his relations with Marya Alexandrovna; and the catastrophe—his affair with the French singer.

The repetition of similar moments sometimes occurs in one and the same story: a finale turns into a norm which, in turn, is violated by a second recurrent catastrophe, which leads to a new finale.

That is how the story **"A Dream"** is constructed. The first norm here is the narrator's parents' happy, easygoing trip, about which his mother tells him later (chapter 9); the catastrophe is the appearance of the stranger, who becomes the narrator's father; the finale is the ruined life described at the beginning of the story, in the first chapter. That finale has turned into a norm. The new appearance of the stranger and his death comprise the second catastrophe in the story, which brings with it a new finale that comprises the contents of the last fragment of the story (beginning with the words "My mother and I never spoke of him").

It remains to make a separate analysis of each of these moments.

THE NORM

The moment in a Turgenev story that I have called the norm consists of a realistic depiction of the hero's circumstances of life. These norms can be reduced to several types. The main ones are the following:

(1) The narrator of the hero of the story is a student or preparing to be one; he lives in Moscow more or less independently, more or less sociably.

(2) The narrator or hero of the story travels abroad, without definite aims.

(3) The narrator or the hero of the story arrives in his village on business or as a consequence of the absence of business.

The transition from the norm to the catastrophe is accomplished by Turgenev with the help of a plot that provides the story's surface interest. The appearance of a female character usually serves to put the plot in motion. The moment of the appearance by the woman—usually the one who enters the room—is a very important turning point in the story. If the norm is portrayed for the most part realistically, then the plot intrigue is distinguished by its romantic character. The female character who appears in Turgenev is almost always full of enigmatic, mysterious, enticing beauty. Moreover, she stands in contradiction to the surrounding milieu. . . . The question of how that creature could turn up in this milieu arises; interest is aroused, the story's tempo increases. This tension is already felt in the conveying of the impression made by the heroine's appearance: it stuns, amazes, strikes, and rivets the narrator to the spot. The center of attention from that moment on is the female character, and the narrator's role is unimportant: he may be the hero of the story, like Sanin, or the hero of *Asya,* or he may remain an accomplice, a go-between, a witness, as in the stories **"A Misfortunate Girl," "Punin and Baburin."**

And so, the realistic exposition in a Turgenev story represents a sort of thesis; the romantic plot intrigue, which thanks to the realistic grounding, accounts for the whole effect of the story, an antithesis.

The further transition to the catastrophe form the synthesis. The female character does not remain a romantic daydream: having surprised the reader, she gradually stands out in bolder and bolder relief, becoming persuasive and lifelike. The realistic writer comes into his own. Upon the hero or narrator's close acquaintance with the heroine, the realistic and almost always wretched, sometimes difficult conditions of her life come to light. At home Zinaida (*First Love*) has decay, slovenly poverty, and a vulgar mother with an inclination to malicious litigation. Asya is the illegitimate daughter of an estate owner and has grown up in extremely abnormal conditions. It is depressing at the Zlotnitskys' home (**"Yakov Pasynkov"**): "The very furniture, the red wallpaper with yellow cracks in it in the living room, the multitude of wicker chairs in the dining room, the faded worsted pillows depicting maidens and dogs on the sofas, the horn lamps and gloomy portraits on the walls—everything instilled in one an involuntary melancholy. . . ." And girls who know how to love only once in life grow up in those surroundings. Finally, the enchanting Gemma (**"Spring Freshets"**), a representative of the petit bourgeoisie, the fiancée of the solid merchant Klyber, called upon to use her beauty to save her impoverished family's situation, and later—the wife of an American businessman. When her mother discusses quite practically the benefits of her marriage to Sanin, in the presence of the latter, Gemma feels extremely awkward.

However, a female character does not always initiate the intrigue in a Turgenev story; sometimes an animal (twice a dog, once a horse), sometimes things (**"The Watch"**) are the instrument of fate that brings on the catastrophe. But no matter what, the plot intrigue is always romantically unexpected; as is well known, Turgenev took special pains with it, finding that the absence of "invention" was the weak side of Russian writers. As Gutyar notes quite justly, the outline of a Turgenev work "is suggested only in part by the fate of those people who served as the protoypes of the story's protagonists."

The Catastrophe

As applied to a Turgenev story, the term "catastrophe" does not have quite the same meaning as in a tragedy.

There is little of the tragedic in Turgenev, or the tragic in his works consists of the absence of tragedy where it ought to be, of the fact that the most terrible thing in life is that there is nothing terrible. But the term "catastrophe" is applicable here because what happens to Turgenev's protagonists bears the imprint of fate: both good fortune, which they are incapable of apprehending adequately, and misfortune, which turns out to be beyond their powers. The mother's story in **"The Dream"** is characteristic in this regard.

She is alone in a hotel room—her husband has gone to the club; she goes to bed. "And suddenly she felt so awful that she even turned cold all over and began to shiver. She thought she heard a light knocking behind the wall—the way a dog scratches—and she began watching that wall. An icon camp burned in the corner; the room was hung all around with damask. Suddenly something moved over there, rose a bit, opened up. And all black, long, that horrible man with the evil eyes came right out of the wall! She wanted to cry out and could not. She froze in fear. He came up to her quickly, like a beast of prey, threw something over her head, something stifling, heavy, white."

And so, that is how fate functions. Its emissaries penetrate walls covered with damask in which unclean doors are revealed. The turning point in the story is quite unreal. But Turgenev's devices are bared in general in **"A Dream,"** and if one ponders the essence of life's phenomena, the stranger's emergence from the wall is not the least bit any stranger than the appearance first of Gemma in Sanin's life, and then of Marya Nikolaevna; it is just that in the latter instance a realistic motivation is given such as is lacking in the first.

It has already been noted more than once that for Turgenev the supreme confirmation of the individual is love, and that at the same time love is a pernicious, destructive, and dangerous force. Fate lures Turgenev's heroes into a whirlwind of passion, and whether they want that or not, it leaves them no choice: if they meet it head on, ruin and devastation threaten them; if they lack courage, they will be punished—by the misery of later regrets, like the hero of *Asya,* by the horror of emptiness and the fear of death, like Sanin, or a rejected love will make its claims on them from beyond the grave, as happens to the hero of **"Klara Milich."**

However, there are people on whom fate does not bestow its attention. There is a certain level of life, a fullness of sensations, to which not everyone is capable of rising. Only a person who rises to that point will experience life in full measure, but he will also drink the bitter cup of suffering; only with the level of passion do life and beauty begin. The idyll that Turgenev paints in the story **"Old Portraits,"** an idyll of old-world land owners, does not move him; Malanya Pavlovna's impenetrable stupidity, which her loving husband is also aware of, does not increase the delight of the idyll; and the fact with which the story ends destroys the idyll. In the story **"Two Friends"** that tranquil life is established in the finale: good Verochka, with her phlegmatic right, remains deaf to the language of passion, marries a husband once "without rapture," then marries a second time, to a person more comprehensible to her. "Pyotr Vasilievich, his wife, and all their domestics spend the time very monotonously—peacefully and quietly; they enjoy their happiness, *because on earth there is no other happiness.*" A specter of life, however, arises above theirs, and that is the memory of Vyazovnin; but he, himself incapable of rising to the level of passion, has flashed by in their life like a shadow, and they remain on the bottom. No catastrophe has occurred.

A catastrophe is possible only for those people who have the attributes necessary for reaching life in its fullness, even though they may have no desire to do so: passion nevertheless will pull them into the whirlpool. In the story **"Faust,"** Vera, thanks to her mother's efforts, has been seemingly insured against the element of passion since childhood. Its most powerful conductor, art, was removed. Vera leaves for the canopy of a marriage "without rapture," like Verochka; but a person from another world, with a copy of Goethe's *Faust* in his hands, turns up and "ploughed up raging voices" in the young woman. . . .

Real life prudently creates one marriage; fate, the romance of life, erects above it its own mighty superstructure, which crushes that marriage.[10]

But the topic here has been individuals unwillingly carried away by passion, who shun it out of "fear" or good sense. There are those who play with fire, who set out into the ocean of passion without worrying about an anchor. Such is Zinaida (*First Love*). But the highest degree is to accept the cup of life without faint-hearted fear, but to limit oneself to the lofty commands of duty. Such is Yakov Pasynkov, who has made denial his principle. Those who have not stood at the necessary height also come to this conclusion. "Life is hard work. Denial, constant denial—that is its secret meaning, its unriddling: not the fulfilling of favorite ideas and dreams, no matter how elevated they might be, but the fulfilling of duty—that is what a person should worry about; without putting chains on himself, the iron chains of duty, he cannot reach the end of his days without falling." Only if a person is anchored to duty will he not be swept away by a catastrophe.

That is the meaning of Liza Kalitina's ideal.[11]

THE FINALE

The catastrophic nature of events in Turgenev's stories is often overshadowed by descriptions of storms; they are rather frequent (**"A Quiet Spot," "Faust," "Spring Freshets," "A Dream"**). And where there is no storm or tempest, it is overshadowed with the help of similes and metaphors. . . .

The storm of life, the storm of passion does its work and leaves debris. The debris of life's storm includes Chulkaturin, the heroine of **"Three Meetings,"** Alexey Petrovich of **"A Correspondence,"** the hero of **"Faust,"** Zinaida of *First Love,* the Brigadier, King Lear of the Steppe, and Sanin. Others perish, like the baron in the story **"A Dream,"** or Vera (**"Faust"**), or the hero of the story **"Klara Milich."** Others remain debris; moreover, something from the past remains in their hands, a romantic recollection. . . .

FROM STORY TO NOVEL

Turgenev began his literary activity in the era of romanticism's decline. . . . Turgenev himself was profoundly imbued with romanticism, enthusiastic about its very important representatives Goethe and Byron. But in the 1840s Turgenev surrendered his romantic individualism. That capitulation can be heard in his first narrative poems, *Parasha* and *A Conversation,* and especially in the poem **"The Crowd,"** which has a greater significance for Russian literature than is usually imagined. It is a sad rejection of Byronism. The individual who has proudly torn himself away from the crowd cannot hold out in his solitary position, becomes conscious of his weakness, and recognizes the victory of the crowd. It was not easy for Turgenev to accomplish that rejection. The poem echoes with sadness and resignation. The young Turgenev, himself broken inside, given to excessive analysis, lacking in will, began his search for a strong, integrated, beautiful person. But how and where

to look? The Byronic method had been rejected. The Byronic heroes married their Parashas and began living happily on their estates. The romantic phantasmagoria had been dispelled. . . .

In his early stories, too, he angrily condemns romanticism. It is enough to read **"Andrey Kolosov"** and **"The Diary of a Superfluous Man"** to get an idea of that anger.

The poet feels that there is no room for him in the crowd, but neither is there room outside it. And he escapes to simple people, to nature, to the heroes of *Notes of a Hunter,* who have extracted wholeness and simplicity from the innermost depths of mother nature. But here too he remained an outside observer: there was no point even in talking of a return to nature for Turgenev, of taking to plain living—it was not for nothing that he had broken with romanticism. He will return to a higher arena of life; he needs to determine the relationship of the individual to society, to the people, to humanity. After all, romanticism was a temporary cutting away of the individual; he has to be reunited with the society around him, because it is impossible to live outside it. So that the individual personality will not be swallowed up, like a speck of dust, in infinity, Turgenev will try to attach it more firmly to the moment, to tie it to societal evolution, and only then to raise the question of what to do. Because the individual, torn away from the conditions of time and place, seemed to Turgenev to be so horrifyingly impotent that in reply to the question of what to do, he said: "After crossing one's useless arms on one's empty chest, preserve the last and only virtue accessible to him [to man], that of the recognition of one's own insignificance" (**"Enough"**).

It was from that state that Turgenev in fact fled to the world of his novels, where the broadly understood feeling of duty was, on the one hand, to persuade a person that "his arms" were not "useless," but that, on the contrary, mankind needs their work; on the other hand, that very feeling of duty was to safeguard a person against the storms of the universe of passion threatening him on all sides.

That is how the novel grew out of Turgenev's story. And in the majority of those novels one can distinguish with greater or lesser clarity the layerings that turned the story into a novel.

At the same time as Natalya's love for Rudin arises, develops, and is concluded on Lasunskaya's estate, conversations about Rudin are being held on a neighboring estate, the story of his youth is being told, about the milieu that produced him. The first element is a typical Turgenev story; the second gives this story a sociohistorical background; a third element—Rudin's story about his activity—deepens the sociohistorical aspects of the novel.

In *A Nest of Gentlefolk* two stories can be found: the heroine of the first is Varvara Pavlovna; the heroine of the second, Liza. Lavretsky's genealogy, his conversations with Panshin and Mikhalevich, and his life in the countryside create a social novel.

The novel *Fathers and Sons* consists of three episodes: (1) Bazarov at the Kirsanovs', (2) Bazarov at Odintsova's, (3) Bazarov at his parents'; the first episode has sociohistorical interest; the two others, universally human.

Smoke includes the story of Litvinov's student love for Irina; the episode in Baden makes up the sociohistorical aspect of the novel.

Hence the inserted episodes, biographical digressions, genealogies that are so typical for Turgenev. There he is unburdening his heart, talking about the universal while creating a novel; on the other hand—the chronological dates and historical background.

However, while depicting the personal side of his heroes' lives in his novels, Turgenev feels at home, but he seems to avoid portraying them on a wide arena of activity, although that apparently was in fact supposed to provide the basis of the novel's design. Rudin at Lasunskaya's estate is drawn graphically and vividly; we hear only a fleeting account of his years of study and activity. Lavretsky's love for and life with his wife, Lavretsky and Liza's love are drawn vividly; but the fact that Lavretsky realizes his goal of "plowing the soil" and what he does for the peasants are related in a general way, casually. The author is passionately interested in how Yelena comes to love Insarov and how she leaves with him; but Insarov's preparation for future activity is spoken of in passing, and the author decides not to depict that activity and kills off the hero. And Bazarov is depicted not where he developed, not in the milieu of which he is a representative, but on gentry estates, where he argues, loves, and dies. The same goes for Litvinov.[12] Only in *Virgin Soil* is an attempt made to depict the activity itself, but here too the arena of the novel's action is a gentry estate, and moreover, the depiction of the activity itself does not belong to Turgenev's best pages.

How Tolstoy's Nekhlyudov,[13] Levin, and Vronsky[14] manage their estates—that we know clearly and definitely; how Lezhnyov, Lavretsky, Litvinov[15] manage their estates—Lord only knows.

They simply manage them.

Obviously, Turgenev the artist needs his heroes' social activity only as an outside force that defines a human in a certain way. His attention is concentrated on individuals; everything else is kept at a distance. What is interesting is how an individual lives, loves, and dies; for the sake of fullness and expressiveness of image conditions of time and place that are in and of themselves perhaps not very important are taken into account. Such is the writer's unconscious worldview.

Consciously, Turgenev may have had claims to the solution or raising of questions of the day; that was precisely what the critics looked for in his novels. And all the misunderstandings that have arisen because of that have occurred because critics were unable to appreciate what Turgenev had to offer, and demanded what he could not offer, although he tried. Perhaps unaware of it himself, he transferred these questions to a completely different plane.[16] Recent criticism, not without grounds, has expressed doubt about Turgenev as a social writer. But the desire to be one cost Turgenev dearly; he had to seek new devices, more or less successful ones, in order to give the novel social significance; he had to write such a decidedly weak work as *Virgin Soil.*

DIALOGUE IN THE NOVEL

In the Turgenev novel, as compared to the story, dialogue plays a large role. Avoiding depicting his contemporary heroes in deed, the writer portrays them marvelously in word. It is no accident that the hero of the first novel is an orator; and all the succeeding heroes speak interestingly and expressively. Turgenev conveys the charm of Rudin's speech, who speaks out against scepticism and who by striking certain strings of the heart forces others to sound at the same time; Lavretsky's speech about Russia echoes with sober sense; Bazarov's speech echoes with sharp and casual expressiveness. And many interesting and sensible conversations are related on the pages of Turgenev's novels. And the subject of these conversations is always Russia, the current moment, the contemporary generation's view.

Of course, there are dialogues of a purely personal character, just as in the stories; in them Turgenev is an incomparable master, now conveying Liza's sometimes simply unclear but profound speech, now Homerically reproducing the speech of secondary characters—Marfa Timofeevna, N. A. Astakhov, or Bazarov's parents.

But the dialogues on contemporary topics that constitute a peculiarity of Turgenev's novels can be subdivided into the categories of debates and didactic dialogues. . . .

We shall call didactic dialogues those whose ideal nature can in no way be concealed: the speech of the author himself can be heard—what in the old days was called that of a spokesman for the author. The presence of such dialogues, interesting as they may be in and of themselves, cannot be considered a virtue in a novel: Turgenev falls back on them when he lacks power of invention. That can be especially felt in **Rudin,** where Lezhnyov provides an evaluation of Rudin on the reader's behalf. There is no concern for the style of the person speaking here; there is no debate here—the listeners offer only the necessary responses; the voice of the author can be heard distinctly.

This device, which subsides in Turgenev's best novels (**A Nest of Gentlefolk** and **Fathers and Sons**), is repeated in the others. In **On the Eve** we again hear authorial speech in Shubin, when he talks to Yelena about Uvar Ivanovich. In **Smoke** Potugin speaks for the author; in **Virgin Soil** it is Nezhdanov, in his poem about Russia. . . .

DIDACTIC CHARACTERS

This Lezhnyov, who plays the role of a chorus in **Rudin,** has another importance as well. "Here's the sort of person we need more of," the writer seems to want to say. Indeed, Lezhnyov puts into practice ahead of time the activity that Turgenev, using Lavretsky as a mouthpiece, will later proclaim the most necessary and greatest one: he plows the soil and apparently does so as well as possible. For that Turgenev rewards him with personal happiness: the novel ends with Lezhnyov's idyll. . . .

In **On the Eve** a didactic character again appears, the one least successful in an artistic sense but most successful in a didactic one—Insarov. That character is put together mechanically from traits that Russians lack but that are desirable and are essential, the very first condition for any action, without which even the quality of genius will turn out to be barren. Turgenev deprives Insarov of everything human: the absence of any spiritual struggle when deciding to leave Yelena, on the grounds that she is a person who does not correspond to his goals, the examination for the rank of wife that he gives her—those things alienate one; and one refuses to believe that Insarov will accomplish something great, because greatness is also accomplished through passion and feeling—and Turgenev knows that perfectly well.

Litvinov is the new result of Turgenev's "search for a man." His goal is the same as Lezhnyov's and Lavretsky's. He is more alive than Lezhnyov because he is more subject to the effect of the passionate element; but he is deader than Lavretsky. His gesture when he indicates to Irina the place beside him in the train car is splendid, but it is didacticism. Turgenev seems to have sensed a certain betrayal of artistic truth here and wrote the story **"Spring Freshets"** after **Smoke**; Sanin experiences approximately the same thing as Litvinov, but he ends in a more Turgenevian fashion; he remains in the company of the temptress, enduring all the humiliation of his false position and, after the need has passed, breaks free. But what is allowable in a story of his is impermissible in a Turgenev novel.

Turgenev the didactic strives generously to award his businesslike "good" people with personal happiness, leads them solicitously to the family idyll with the beloved; sometimes he sets obstacles for them—passion, but he helps them overcome delusive temptations. But where Turgenev remains a pure artist, in the stories, those temptations turn out to be insuperable. . . .

PSYCHOLOGY

Didacticism, satire, philosophizing—all these devices result from Turgenev's desire to make a social statement. But the eternal triumphs over that element, and the artist defeats the social critic. No matter what practical means the writer proposes, no matter how he calls for "small deeds," no matter how he rewards his "good people" with prosperity and happiness, he knows at the bottom of his heart that this is all "smoke"; that a lost life is lost, even though its experience was useful for the future generation; that the proud individual is threatened by the monster of death; that in life the individual is manipulated by fate; that man is insignificant. This profound consciousness of the individual's helplessness determines Turgenev's special manner of depicting individual psychology. That manner is absolutely contrary to Dostoevsky's. The latter extremely individualizes every psychological experience; Turgenev sadly makes it part of a general law, seemingly devaluing the personal in this way. He does this with the help of experienced aphorisms that he always seems to have ready. . . .

This basic view of Turgenev's gives rise to two peculiarities of his psychological manner: laconicism or negligence in the depiction of psychological experiences. Turgenev's laconicism is often distinguished by great power; he uses it when he has an especially solicitous attitude toward the person being portrayed, as though afraid of reducing him to a category, sparing him.

After receiving the news of the death of his wife, "Lavretsky dressed, went out into the garden, and walked up and down a single lane until morning."

After Varvara Pavlovna's arrival and Liza's meeting her, "Marfa Timofeevna sat up all night long at the head of Liza's bed."

Lavretsky's last meeting with Liza, at the monastery:

> Making her way from choir to choir, she walked past him close by, walked past in the even, hurryingly humble tread of a nun—and did not look at him; the lashes of the eye directed at him just trembled slightly, she just inclined her emaciated face even more—and the fingers of her compressed hands, wrapped round with rosaries, pressed against each other even more tightly. What did they both think, what did they feel? Who can know? Who can say? There are certain moments in life, certain feelings. One can only point at them—and pass on by.

Here is supreme economy of means, supreme solicitude for feeling. And along with that extreme negligence of human psychology turns up in Turgenev. . . . Hence the total ignoring of individual psychology in many characters unattractive to Turgenev. . . .

THE ELEGY

The pessimism of Turgenev's consciousness, which manifests itself in the conclusions of his novels and in his psychological manner, finds, however, a distinctive antidote in his creative intuition. There are forces that he counterposes to the individual's helplessness and insignificance in the face of death. Those forces are love and simplicity. This surmounting of pessimism is expressed in Turgenev lyrically, and his best novels conclude with solemn lyric chords.

If, as has been pointed out, Turgenev flees the horror of eternity by escaping to the temporal, then the dissatisfaction with the temporal and the limited awaken in him, on the other hand, an elevated longing for the eternal, the nontransitory. Although Rudin has not accomplished anything, he has left in young souls some sparks of enthusiasm, love, and truth, and those sparks will live; Rudin's temporal existence stretches into eternity, and he is spoken of in Lezhnyov's cozy home. Although Lavretsky and Liza have left the walk of life without touching "the cherished goblet in which the golden wine of enjoyment bubbles and plays," in the worlds he addresses to the young generation there is no bitterness: he gives them a blessing, and there is something Pushkinian in these reconciling chords of his speech.

Although Bazarov has died, and his mighty, proud powers turned out to be fruitless, he is silently present at the festival of life in the Kirsanovs' home, he lives in their memories and in his parents' tears. "Can it really be that their prayers, their tears are fruitless? Can it really be that love, sacred, devoted love is not all-powerful?" Turgenev asks. As a thinker, he should have answered: "Yes, fruitless and powerless." But the lyric poet answers: "Oh, no! No matter how passionate, sinful, and rebellious a heart is hidden in the grave, the flowers growing on it look at us serenely with their innocent eyes; they speak to us not only of eternal peace, that great peace of 'indifferent' nature; they also speak of eternal reconciliation and of life eternal."

Turgenev's creative thought has made its circle from the horror of infinity to the framework of the temporal; from the temporal it stretches its wings toward the infinite.

The result is an elegy in the form of a novel.

THE PICTORIAL AND MUSICAL ASPECT OF THE TURGENEV NOVEL

One of the means of overcoming Turgenev's elegiac longing that is developed in his novels is beauty. He needs colors and sounds in order to justify life, and he generously scatters moonbeams and the sounds of the piano throughout his novels. The action of his novels always occurs in the spring or summertime, the sun shines brightly during the day, at night the moon and stars come out, and in the gentry manors pianos are heard. . . .

The sounds of the piano and the cello that are always heard in Turgenev's manor houses give a musical charm to his images. But *A Nest of Gentlefolk* is especially noteworthy in this regard. Here music sets off the contents of the novel. When his unrecognized love for Liza begins in Lavretsky, the old man Lemm dreams of composing a cantata about the stars. On that wonderful night when Lavretsky's mouth brushes against Liza's pale lips, the old musician's dream is fulfilled; inspired, he plays his piece for Lavretsky, a "song a triumphant love." But on the following days these sounds die down in order to give way to the more bravura melodies played by Varvara Pavlovna and Panshin. The years pass. Lavrestky visits the Kalinin estate, where everything has changed, where a new generation is having a good time. He goes up to the piano, plays a chord—it is the first chord of the piece by the deceased Lemm. It rings out like a memory, and then falls silent.

That chord of recollection can be heard in all of Turgenev's stories. Past experience is dear to him. Like shadows, like smoke, everything temporal passes, but the eternal is left—and we are allowed to fell that eternal by the poet, who, like Lavretsky, goes up to the piano in a gentry manor and plays a memorable chord.

Notes

1. ["Story" as used in the title seems the best rendering of the Russian *povest* in this context. Readers unfamiliar with Russian, however, should be aware that in the final analysis, *povest* lacks an adequate English equivalent, primarily because the Russian term is a very slippery one. In the twentieth century it has come to indicate a work of prose fiction longer than a short story and shorter than a novel, but in many cases a writer's choice between *povest* and *roman* (novel) can only strike one as subjective and even arbitrary. Moreover, in the nineteenth century the term was applied to such disparate works as Pushkin's short stories and Dostoevsky's *Crime and Punishment*.]

2. [For information about Chernyshevsky and his article, see the introduction to this volume.]

3. [D. Ovsyaniko-Kulikovsky, "I. S. Turgenev," vol. 2, *Sobranie sochinenii* (St. Petersburg: Prometey, 1910-1911).]

4. [K. K. Istomin, "'Staraya manera' Turgeneva (1834-1855). Opyt psikhologii tvorchestva," *Izvestia Otdelenia russkogo yazyka i slovesnosti Akademii nauk* 2 (1913):294-347; 3 (1913);120-194.]

5. [Reference to Tolstoy's *Childhood.*]

6. Yu. I. Aykhenvald reproaches Turgenev for mocking errors in French pronunciation. Turgenev does not mock, but, rather, conveys the errors in any pronunciation—the accent of Germans speaking Russian or French, the accent of Frenchmen pronouncing Russian names, the accent of an Italian speaking French. Turgenev hears his heroes' speech, he hears how the heroes of the novel *Fathers and Sons* pronounce the same word, "principle." Not to mention the speech of the masses, one can point out Bersenev's involved, academically meandering speech (*On the Eve*), the speech of Kollomeytsev, who pronounces "brrr" the French way, as remarkable masterpieces of this sort.

7. [The Russian word that Fisher uses here, *byt,* is notoriously difficult to render into English. In this context the word suggests the sorts of sociocultural details that anchor a literary work in a specific time and place.]

8. [Hero of Lermontov's novel *A Hero of Our Time* (1840).]

9. [Hero of Gogol's comedy *The Marriage* (1842).]

10. This motif is outlined sketchily in the narrative poem *The Priest*, published at the beginning of 1917.

11. [Reference to the heroine of *A Nest of Gentlefolk.*]

12. [The references in the paragraph are to *Rudin, A Nest of Gentlefolk, On the Eve,* and *Fathers and Sons,* in that order.]

13. [Hero of *Resurrection.*]

14. [Major protagonists in *Anna Karenina.*]

15. [Characters from *Rudin, A Nest of Gentlefolk,* and *Smoke,* respectively.]

16. A strange fact, it would seem: for a half-century Russian criticism has viewed Turgenev's novels as historical criticism of the Russian intelligentsia; over the course of the same half-century Western Europe has been interested in those novels and has been reading them avidly; it is not the fate of the Russian intelligentsia, after all, that interests Western Europe!

Christine Johanson (essay date 1984)

SOURCE: Johanson, Christine. "Turgenev's Heroines: A Historical Assessment." *Canadian Slavonic Papers* 26, no. 1 (March 1984): 15-23.

[*In the following essay, Johanson examines Turgenev's female characters as realistic representations of contemporary Russian women.*]

"Kukshina . . . that progressive louse which Turgenev combed out of Russian reality": thus Dostoevskii decried the false emancipée in *Ottsy i deti.*[1] Dmitrii Pisarev, the literary critic whose radical social views disgusted the great novelist, thought differently: "Between Kukshina and the emancipated woman, there is nothing in common."[2] He went on to explain that Turgenev could not possibly portray an emancipated woman "in the finest sense" because such women did not yet exist in Russia.[3]

Both critic and novelist judged the fictional heroine not according to artistic criteria, but as a historical portrait of the contemporary Russian woman. So did the Russian reading public.[4] Since the time of Belinskii, reader and critic had become accustomed to viewing fictional characters and situations as reflections of social reality. The tendency to discuss the literary heroine as representative of contemporary women, however, became particularly pronounced after the Crimean War when the "woman question" emerged as an issue of public debate.[5] Did she accurately reflect the role and status, the attitudes and aspirations of women in contemporary society? Could she indeed serve as a model for Russian women and an inspiration for social reform?

Turgenev's heroines became part of this public controversy, although the novelist never elevated the "woman question" to a central issue in his work. He went to great lengths to demonstrate that his literary creations were drawn from contemporary life. This is particularly evident in his numerous defences and explanations of his first four novels: *Rudin* (1856), *Dvorianskoe gnezdo* (1859), *Nakanune* (1860), and *Ottsy i deti* (1862). With specific reference to them, Turgenev declared: "During this entire period, I have sought . . . conscientiously and impartially to portray and embody that which Shakespeare calls the 'body and pressure of time' and that quickly changing physiognomy of Russians of the cultured stratum. . . ."[6] Whether the women in these novels accurately depict the "changing physiognomy" of women of the "cultured stratum" is my main concern here. This paper will assess the historical authenticity of Turgenev's portrayal of the social position, family life, and marital relations of gentry women in mid-nineteenth-century Russia. Particular emphasis is given to the changing attitudes, aspirations, and activities of gentry women during the reform era that followed the Crimean debacle. I should add that, although Turgenev established the settings of two of the novels—*Rudin* and *Dvorianskoe gnezdo*—as the 1840s, I treat them here as contemporaneous with the time of their publication.

The emancipation of the serfs deprived the gentry of bonded labour and much land. Resulting economic pressures prompted many young women to abandon the country estate in search of employment or education in the city. More important, the reforming spirit of the time raised women's aspirations for a larger role in society—a society which they saw in the throes of radical transformation. Relaxation of state control over educational affairs pending the formulation of a new university statute allowed women to audit university lectures, formerly an exclusively male preserve.[7] In 1859-60, young women flocked to university towns, particularly to the northern capital. Ekaterina Iunge, who attended St. Petersburg University, testified to the buoyant confidence of her generation:

> Everything was clear to us. . . . Russia will enter a new era, will go hand in hand with the rest of the world along the road of human progress and happiness. And we saw our ardent desires coming true, our dreams becoming a reality.[8]

Meanwhile, public debate over the "woman question" encouraged women to challenge social convention and traditional institutions, including the family.[9] Sofiia Kovalevskaia, the famous Russian mathematician, recalled the family discord and youthful rebelliousness of the postwar decade:

> Ask any gentry family of the time and you will hear one and the same thing: parents quarrelled with their children. And these arguments arose not out of material, pecuniary causes. . . . Children, especially girls, seemed at the time to be possessed by a kind of epidemic—to flee the parental home.[10]

This led to new social tensions during the "'sixties" (as the period from 1855 to 1866 has come to be known in Russian historiography).

It is this conflict between the generations that underlies the action in Turgenev's novels. Rebellious daughters precipitate major confrontations in *Rudin, Dvorianskoe gnezdo,* and *Nakanune*; they reject the suitors chosen by their parents or select spouses without parental consent. Natal'ia's declaration of love for Rudin prompts her mother to exclaim that she would rather see her daughter dead than married to him. Liza's refusal to be Panshin's wife provokes an outburst of tears and anger from her mother. When Elena secretly marries Insarov, her father threatens to divorce them and send his daughter to a nunnery. Such parental outrage is, of course, not surprising given the hierarchical structure of the family and its social and economic significance in nineteenth-century Russia.

Tradition entrenched the father as ruler of the household, with the wife as his assistant and the children in complete submission. What custom enshrined, the legal code endorsed.[11] In Turgenev's novels, then, rebellious daughters were defying not only tradition, but the law as well. Elena's offence was particularly grave. The Russian legal code expressly forbade marriage without parental consent.[12] Thus, the father's threat to divorce

the newly-weds and to cloister his daughter was not unfounded, though the latter punishment was more typical of adulterous wives.[13] By marrying Insarov, moreover, Elena had threatened the wealth and status of her family. These material considerations were not peculiar to Elena's father, but were traditional for gentry parents. It was customary, then, for parents to exert stringent control over daughters of marriageable age.[14]

Such vigilance contrasts sharply with the absence of direct parental supervision during childhood and youth. Turgenev's novels illustrate the emotional and physical distance that characterized parent-child relations in gentry families of Imperial Russia.[15] Natal'ia, Liza, and Elena pass through infancy, childhood, and puberty in relative isolation from their parents. Wet-nurses, nannies, and governesses prevent them from intruding upon the parental domain. Frequently business matters and service obligations separated the nobleman from his family for significant periods of time,[16] thereby inhibiting the development of relations between father and child. Indeed, constraint and fear distinguish the daughter's relationship with her father not only in *Dvorianskoe gnezdo,* but also in the memoirs of Russian women of the period.[17] Similarly, household management and social commitments prevented gentry women from devoting much time or attention to their children.[18] In both fictional and real family life, expressions of maternal affection were often confined to allowing daughters to kiss their hands in the morning and to blessing their offspring at night.[19] Only when daughters approached marriageable age did a mother begin to exercise personal and sustained supervision over them. Like the gentry father, she too tried to influence the daughter's choice of spouse.

In theory, Russian law forbade forcing a child into an unwanted marriage.[20] In practice, however, family pressures, threats of disinheritance, or simply fear or respect for one's parents brought not a few reluctant brides to the altar. Turgenev portrayed such a woman in *Ottsy i deti,* although he never explained why Arina Vlas'evna married against her will. In this case, forced marriage resulted in a relatively contented, albeit poor and uncultured, existence, but it was not always so. Elizaveta Vodovozova recalled the physical abuse and mental anguish suffered by her sister who married the man of her mother's choosing.[21] Admittedly, such brutal consequences were uncommon among the gentry.[22] Both law and custom, however, prescribed a wife's subservience to her husband. Russian law not only sanctioned the husband's absolute authority over his wife,[23] but gave him the means to control her movements. No married woman could obtain an internal passport, necessary for travel and city residence, without his permission.[24] Given his broad legal powers, the Russian husband could make his wife a virtual prisoner. Parental interference in the choice of spouse, then, could have grave implications for daughters. Turgenev's novels reflect, in a limited manner, the various responses of women to an ill-chosen husband and the ensuing marital discord.

Wives had little opportunity to escape an unhappy marriage. Such was the plight of Elena's mother, Anna Vasil'evna. Social convention bound her to an adulterous husband. Russian law offered no easy deliverance for, although adultery constituted legal grounds for divorce, it was extremely difficult to prove.[25] The prospect of public scandal, moreover, acted as a further deterrent. In some cases, a wife could leave her husband and establish a separate residence, but because Russian law decreed that spouses live together,[26] a disagreeable husband could bring an errant wife to court. Kukshina's husband proved exceptionally agreeable: cohabitation with his silly, self-indulgent wife involved far greater risk of social embarrassment than did separation. Anna Vasil'evna's husband, on the other hand, would not have agreed to separation under any circumstances: he had married for money, and his wife's property helped him maintain his mistress. Anna Vasil'evna's independent wealth, however, reveals that in one important respect, namely property-rights, women were equal to men before the law.[27] In most other areas, male superiority was written into the legal code.

Fathers wielded the same control over the movements of unmarried daughters as a husband exercised over his wife. A single woman under twenty-one was registered on her father's passport.[28] Thus when the twenty-year old Elena decided to elope with Insarov, she required a false passport. Forged passports became relatively common among women in Russian revolutionary circles during the late 1870s and 1880s.[29] In other cases, a "fictitious marriage" provided freedom of movement. A suitable bachelor would marry a young woman in order to free her from paternal control. After the wedding, he would renounce his marital "rights" and grant her permission to travel and reside wherever she wished. For Sofiia Kovalevskaia, a "fictitious marriage" opened the way to a brilliant career in mathematics. None of Turgenev's heroines enters a "fictitious marriage." Admittedly, such unions did not gain widespread popularity among Russian youth until after the publication of these novels.[30] A "fictitious marriage," however, would never have appealed to Natal'ia, Liza, or Elena, since it was not the yearning for freedom, but love for a particular man that precipitated their rebellion against parental authority and social convention. Without him, they withdraw or vanish from active life: Natal'ia resigns herself to a quiet marriage with a gentry neighbour whom she had earlier rejected; Liza enters a nunnery; and Elena disappears in the Balkans. This is not to imply that Turgenev's heroines are not exceptional women. In their strength, moral purity, and capacity for self-sacrifice, they tower above those who surround them.[31] Indeed, they are not so much products of the reform period as

embodiments of the ideal of Russian womanhood which had captured the literary imagination since Pushkin's Tat'iana.

Turgenev's heroines, as models of feminine strength and courage, perhaps inspired young gentry women striving for freedom in the "'sixties." But as women who sought fulfillment in a love-relationship, they hardly offered any guidance in the struggle for advanced education or economic independence.[32] The women of fiction had neither marketable skills nor formal education. In fact, their essential beauty—their purity and naturalness—developed precisely because their childhood and youth had remained untutored and unspoiled by formal training.[33] Turgenev's Natal'ia, Liza, and Elena, then, had little relevance for the hundreds of women who flocked to the cities in search of employment or education in the post-war decade.

In these novels only Kukshina represents the "new" woman of the "'sixties." This unconventional character mimicked the manners and views of the "progressive" woman who read contemporary journals and sometimes smoked cigarettes. Just as the studious woman preferred a simple dark dress and short haircut to the crinoline, curls, and other feminine adornments which, the public insisted, rendered her unfit for university study,[34] so too did Kukshina fly in the face of feminine fashion. She attended a ball "without any crinoline, in dirty gloves, but with a bird of paradise in her hair."[35] After the Russian government banned women from Russian universities in 1861, many went abroad to continue their education,[36] and so Kukshina appeared at the University of Heidelberg where she and other Russians shocked professors "by their complete inactivity and absolute idleness."[37]

This absurd dilettante, as Pisarev argued, constituted "a splendidly executed caricature of . . . the Russian emancipated woman."[38] Turgenev agreed, and rebuked those who claimed that Kukshina accurately depicted the contemporary Russian woman.[39] Nevertheless he had made the progressive woman a subject of comic disdain, thereby contributing to the negative stereotype of women striving for education and independence in the "'sixties." But even this caricature did not capture the full extent of public ridicule and scorn suffered by such women. Kukshina emerges as an innocuous and almost endearing idiot when compared to the foul and venal "liberated" women created by more conservative writers. For example, Dostoevskii's "emancipated" women, such as Madame Virginskaia in *Besy,* tend to wallow in hypocrisy and deceit, while the newspaper *Vest'* portrayed the "new" woman as careless about personal hygiene, very familiar with men, and preoccupied with anatomy.[40]

Turgenev's novels, in fact, offer little insight into the early feminist movement of those years. His heroines do not reflect the attitudes and ambitions of the "new" woman who sought a larger role in society. Instead, his novels depict the marital and family relationships of gentry women in pre- and post-reform Russia. His descriptions of family life illustrate the male supremacy enshrined in custom and law, and its implications for wives and daughters.

Above all, however, Turgenev's novels reveal that it was not the tensions based on sex, but the profound divisions between classes or estates that constituted the most fundamental reality of Russian society. Social rank alienated the gentry heroine from the peasant woman far more than sex separated her from the nobleman. Female peasants impinged upon the world of privileged women only as servants or objects of occasional charity. In the opening scene of **Rudin,** Aleksandra Pavlovna brings soup to a dying peasant woman, but then, distracted by the attentions of a local noble and her brother's unrequited love for Natal'ia, forgets all about her. Elena expresses sympathy for the peasantry and gives alms to the poor, yet she has as much in common with a peasant woman as she does with the stray animals she brings home. Nor, of course, did the noble judge the peasant woman according to gentry standards of feminine virtue. In **Ottsy i deti,** for example, Nikolai Petrovich seems not so much ashamed of his liaison with Fenechka, who bore his illegitimate child, as embarrassed by the presence of this social inferior in the family home during his son's visit.[41]

Turgenev's novels show dramatically that the nest of the gentry loomed far above the peasant hut. While he achieves little in depicting the "changing physiognomy" of gentry women during the reform era, his novels are most informative in revealing the profound social stratification in nineteenth-century Russia.

Notes

1. Fyodor M. Dostoevsky, *Winter Notes on Summer Impressions,* transl. Richard Lee Renfield (New York, 1955), p. 68.

2. D. I. Pisarev, "Bazarov (*Ottsy i deti,* roman I. S. Turgeneva)," in D. I. Pisarev, *Sochineniia v chetyrekh tomakh* (Moscow, 1955), II, p. 35.

3. *Ibid.*

4. The relation of Turgenev's fictional characters to contemporary youth dominates the informal discussion of *Ottsy i deti* in E. N. Vodovozova, *Na zare zhizni i drugie vospominaniia,* 2 vols., ed. V. P. Koz'min (Moscow-Leningrad, 1934), II, pp. 141-47. A good sampling of contemporary reactions, translated into English, is found in Ivan Turgenev, *Fathers and Sons,* ed. and transl. Ralph E. Matlaw (New York, 1966), pp. 169-236.

5. "Ukazatel' literatury zhenskago voprosa na russkom iazyke," *Severnyi vestnik,* 1887, No. 7,

pp. 1-32 [separate pagination], and *ibid.,* 1887, No. 8, pp. 33-35, lists a total of 1,785 articles on the woman question.

6. I. S. Turgenev, "Predislovie k romanam," in I. S. Turgenev, *Polnoe sobranie sochinenii i pisem v dvadtsati vos'mi tomakh* (Moscow-Leningrad, 1960-68), XII, p. 303 (hereafter cited as *PSSP*). The novels under discussion are found in volumes 6, 7, and 8 of this collection.

7. Christine Johanson, "Autocratic Politics, Public Opinion, and Women's Medical Education During the Reign of Alexander II, 1855-1881," *Slavic Review,* 38, no. 3 (September 1979), 427-29.

8. E. F. Iunge, *Vospominaniia* (Moscow, 1933), p. 215.

9. For further discussion of this debate, see Richard Stites, *The Women's Liberation Movement in Russia: Feminism, Nihilism, and Bolshevism, 1860-1930* (Princeton, N. J., 1978), pp. 29-63.

10. S. V. Kovalevskaia, *Vospominaniia detstva i avtobiograficheskie ocherki* (Moscow, 1945), p. 68.

11. Russian law stipulated: "Personal parental authority does not cease, but is limited . . . when daughters marry, because one individual is unable to satisfy two such unlimited powers as parent and spouse." See Ia. A. Kantorovich [ps. Orovich], *Zhenshchina v prave* (St. Petersburg, 1895), p. 145.

12. *Zhenskoe pravo. Svod uzakonenii i postanovlenii otnosiashchikhsia do zhenskago pola* (St. Petersburg, 1873), p. 98.

13. Dorothy Atkinson, "Society and the Sexes in the Russian Past," in Dorothy Atkinson, Alexander Dallin, and Gail Warshofsky Lapidus (Eds.), *Women in Russia* (Stanford, Calif., 1977), p. 21.

14. Russian law established the minimum age for marriage as sixteen for girls and eighteen for boys. See *Zhenskoe pravo,* p. 99.

15. Memoirists who recall the remoteness of their mothers during childhood include: Iunge, *Vospominaniia,* pp. 14, 17, 19, 193; Kovalevskaia, *Vospominaniia detstva,* pp. 10-13; Vodovozova, *Na zare zhizni,* I, pp. 127-29; and Ekaterina Zhukovskaia, *Zapiski,* ed. K. Chukovskii (Leningrad, 1930), p. 19. Vera Figner, *Zapechatlennyi trud. Vospominaniia v dvukh tomakh* (Moscow, 1964), I, pp. 67-68, developed strong emotional ties to her mother although the latter devoted little time to her. Useful discussions of mother-daughter relationships in nineteenth-century Russia are: Jessica Tovrov, "Mother-Child Relationships among the Russian Nobility," and Barbara Alpern Engel, "Mothers and Daughters: Family Patterns and the

Female Intelligentsia," in David L. Ransel (Ed.), *The Family in Imperial Russia. New Lines of Historical Research* (Urbana, Ill., 1978), pp. 15-59. The childhood and youth of gentry boys is examined by Marc Raeff, "Home, School, and Service in the Life of the Eighteenth-Century Russian Nobleman," in Michael Cherniavsky (Ed.), *The Structure of Russian History: Interpretive Essays* (New York, 1970), pp. 212-23.

16. Raeff, "Home, School, and Service," p. 213.

17. See Turgenev, *PSSP*, VII, p. 242; O. K. Bulanova-Trubnikova, *Tri pokoleniia* (Moscow-Leningrad, 1928), p. 136; Figner, *Zapechatlennyi trud*, I, p. 58; and Iunge, *Vospominaniia*, p. 19. A notable exception is Vodovozova's relationship with her father. See *Na zare zhizni*, I, pp. 74-124 *passim*.

18. Engel, "Mothers and Daughters," pp. 48-49, shows that frequent pregnancy often diminished the opportunity for maternal devotion to an individual child. Turgenev's heroines, however, do not come from large families.

19. Turgenev's portrayal of Agafokleia Kirsanova's relationship with her children bears a marked resemblance to Vodovozova's description of parent-child contact in gentry families. See *Na zare zhizni*, I, p. 128.

20. *Zhenskoe pravo*, p. 99.

21. Vodovozova, *Na zare zhizni*, I, pp. 343-403 *passim*.

22. In the early nineteenth century, the legal code specifically forbade, for the first time, the beating and mutilation of wives. The new law, however, had little impact on the peasantry among whom wife-beating was sanctioned by customary law. See Atkinson, "Society and the Sexes," p. 33.

23. The legal code decreed: "A woman must obey her husband as the head of the family, reside with him in love, respect, and unlimited obedience, and offer him every pleasantness and affection as master of the household." See *Zhenskoe pravo*, p. 110.

24. Kantorovich, *Zhenshchina v prave*, p. 249.

25. *Zhenskoe pravo*, pp. 118-19.

26. *Ibid.*, p. 110.

27. For the property rights of women, see *ibid.*, pp. 168-208.

28. Kantorovich, *Zhenshchina v prave*, pp. 248-49. Boys, on the other hand, received their own passports at age seventeen.

29. For example, see "Olga Liubatovich," in Barbara Alpern Engel and Clifford N. Rosenthal (Eds. and transls.), *Five Sisters: Women Against the Tsar* (New York, 1977), p. 157.

30. Largely responsible for public awareness of the "fictitious marriage" as a means to women's liberation from parental control was the publication of N. G. Chernyshevskii's novel, *Chto delat'?*, in *Sovremennik,* March, April, and May 1863.

31. For further discussion of the heroic female type in nineteenth-century Russian literature, see Vera Sandomirsky Dunham, "The Strong-Woman Motif," in Cyril E. Black (Ed.), *The Transformation of Russian Society: Aspects of Social Change Since 1861* (Cambridge, Mass., 1960), pp. 459-83.

32. Henri Granjard, *Ivan Tourguénev et Les Courants Politiques et Sociaux de son Temps* (Paris, 1954), p. 468, asserts that Elena not only represented a social phenomenon of the 1860s, but also served as a model for contemporary youth. None of the female memoirists that I have studied, however, mentions any of Turgenev's heroines as a model or source of inspiration. On the other hand, in the twentieth century there are some indications that male writers tended to evaluate real women according to the standards set by Turgenev's heroines. See S. A. Esenin to G. A. Panfilov, July-August 1912, *Voprosy literatury,* 1960, No. 3, pp. 130-31; and Alexander Svobodin, "The Artist, the Woman and the Time: The Turgenev Girl," *Soviet Woman,* 1961, No. 7, p. 30.

33. A notable exception is the title character of the story, *Asia* (1858). The young heroine's home-life, however, offset any influence that formal education might have had on her character.

34. V. D. Sipovskii, "Polozhenie u nas voprosa o vysshem zhenskom obrazovanii," *Zhenskoe obrazovanie,* No. 1 (August 1876), pp. 258-60.

35. Turgenev, *PSSP,* VIII, p. 264.

36. Johanson, "Autocratic Politics," pp. 433-34.

37. Turgenev, *PSSP,* VIII, pp. 400-401.

38. Pisarev, "Bazarov," p. 33.

39. I. S. Turgenev to K. K. Sluchevskii, 14 April 1862, in Matlaw, *Fathers and Sons,* p. 186.

40. See the excerpt quoted by Charles A. Moser, *Antinihilism in the Russian Novel of the 1860's* (The Hague, 1964), p. 44.

41. His readiness to change Fenechka's accommodations prompts this interpretation. See Turgenev, *PSSP,* VIII, p. 204.

Richard Freeborn (essay date 1984)

SOURCE: Freeborn, Richard. "A Centenary Tribute to Turgenev." *Journal of European Studies* 14, no. 3 (September 1984): 155-71.

[*In the following essay, Freeborn discusses Turgenev's literary legacy one hundred years after his death.*]

Ivan Sergeevich Turgenev was born in 1818 and died in 1883. He was born into the privileged, serf-owning world of the Russian nobility, educated at the universities of Moscow and St Petersburg and abroad, at Berlin. The experience of Western Europe turned him into a devotee of European civilization, so that he became known as a Westernist or *zapadnik*. For forty years of his life, from 1843 until his death, he was a devoted admirer of the singer Pauline Viardot. He never lived far from her during most of those years (save for a period in the 1850s when he was confined by the authorities to his estate in Russia) and he became a close, irreplaceable member of the Viardot family. For the last twenty years of his life he resided more or less permanently outside Russia, first in Germany and, then, for the last decade or so of his life in Paris and Bougival, so that there was some justice in Henry James's decision to include him among *French Poets and Novelists*. But for all his European connections he remained a Russian writer, the author of the famous Sketches of Russian rural life, variously translated as *A Sportsman's Sketches* or as I have preferred to entitle them (in my selection) *Sketches from a Hunter's Album,*[1] and the first Russian novelist to achieve European renown with such works as *Rudin, Home of the Gentry, On the Eve,* and *Fathers and Children* (or *Fathers and Sons*), the best known of his novels. Nowadays we may look back at Ivan Turgenev and feel that his reputation has been overshadowed by the achievement of his great Russian contemporaries, Dostoevskii and Tolstoi. His literary work was of lesser note, there is no denying that fact; but it has certain characteristics that can still claim our attention a hundred years after his death, and I would like to mention one circumstance which may cast Turgenev's achievement in a different light.

No one who reads Turgenev can fail to realize that somewhere in the background, like a distant heart-beat or perhaps the chiming of a clock, is the awareness that political pressures and political changes were in the offing in his lifetime. Those pressures and changes were to culminate in Russian life in the revolutions of 1905 and 1917. What was Turgenev's attitude to these pressures? To quote from the Preface to Leonard Schapiro's biography:

> There have been attempts to claim Turgenev as a radical at heart. I am not convinced by these attempts—though there was a short period in his life when this was almost true. What makes him exceptional and remarkable on the Russian scene is that he cannot be readily labelled—unless love of liberty, decency, and humanity in all relations can be called a 'label'. Everything in Russian conditions conspired to force people into categories. . . . Turgenev was one of the very few nineteenth-century Russian figures who rejected this typically Russian tyranny of categories and labels, which is one reason why his political outlook is more acceptable to a Western European liberal than that of Dostoevsky, or Tolstoy. But Turgenev was no Western European liberal in the accepted sense.[2]

This judgement is unquestionably right, in my view. Yet I am inclined to go slightly further. In examining Turgenev's attitude to the political pressures of his time, it is important to recognize that he was the only nineteenth-century Russian novelist to have first-hand experience of revolution. The scenes which he witnessed during the June days in the revolutionary Paris of 1848—"it was a frightful, it was an agonizing time" as he described it[3]—anticipated similar scenes in Moscow in 1905 or in Petrograd in 1917, whether they involved the destruction of insurgent barricades or the indiscriminate killings associated with urban insurrection. Turgenev's description in **"Our People Sent Me"** (**"Nashi poslali"**) (which he included among his *Literary Reminiscences*) has the veracity and power of good on-the-spot reporting. It described a truth which for Turgenev involved a lifelong commitment and became a theme gradually accommodated in his work as a writer to the point where we may pass over it unnoticed, perhaps scarcely discern it, yet it is the essence of Turgenev's special, individual picture of the world and what differentiates his realism, I suggest, from the realism of his greatest literary contemporaries.

"Impartiality and a desire to seek only the Truth are two of the good qualities for which I am grateful to nature for having given me", he wrote to Druzhinin in 1856.[4] The claim may seem pious, but it acknowledges, if only by implication, one significant differentiating characteristic: the fact that Turgenev made no appeal to divine provenance in arguing a case for his impartiality. He never supposed that the truth had a divine origin or sought divine approval for its existence. Turgenev's impartiality, as an ideal, subsumed a world without God. His impartiality was not therefore Olympian, strictly speaking; it was objective, distanced, realistic. In the last decade of his life, summarizing his achievement in response to an importunate request for a definition of his personal philosophy of life, he conceded that "I am first and foremost a realist and am interested more than anything else in the living truth of the human physiognomy. I am indifferent to everything supernatural; I do not believe in any absolutes or any systems; most of all I love freedom."[5] When he was being coy, he would simply concede, in a spirit of truthfulness, that "I am a writer, as I told the Tsar himself, albeit an independent one, but a writer with a conscience and of moderate opinions—and that's all".[6] The conscience was most certainly inseparable from the writer in Turgenev's case. That his opinions were moderate is not always so obvious. His love of freedom made him politically incline towards liberalism, but he was, he insisted, "a dynastic liberal who recognizes that no reforms are possible except those which *come from above,* and if such reforms do not take place I repeat to my young friends that they must wait, and wait, and wait; for is not revolution unthinkable in Russia, and against our whole historical tradition?"[7] And when he posed that question, he was not posing it idly, I suggest, but as one who knew very well what "a frightful", what "an agonizing time" revolution could mean. He also recognized that his liberalism, however dynastic, had its origins in Europe and was a symptom of his Westernism and to that extent could never be wholly separated from the spirit of 1789 and the democratic turmoil of Europe which manifested itself most clearly in his own lifetime in the Paris barricades of the June days of 1848.

If he took Herzen to task for betraying that revolutionary spirit which was politically so important to his own understanding of Westernism, he was of course even more outspoken in his condemnation of the violence which followed in the wake of the emancipation of the serfs and which accompanied the Populism of the 'seventies as it degenerated into terrorism. The condemnation of the revolutionaries in *Virgin Soil* was directed mostly at their immaturity and disrespect for the complexities, social and historical, of Russian life. Their dedication, however, was acknowledged and perhaps even enhanced by the way in which, for all the sketchiness of their characterization, their portraits were contrasted with the much fuller and more wickedly drawn portrayals of the artificially liberal establishment figures in the novel. The balance, therefore, was what mattered. If he was not always successful in achieving such a balanced representation of views or attitudes in his fiction, the fact remains that his quest for truth, his realistic vision of the world, his love of freedom and his writer's conscience obliged him to acknowledge the need for checks and balances, for that compromise between the many pressures exerted by his time. I do not seek to represent Turgenev as one who "virtually created in his own image . . . the figure of the well-meaning, troubled, self-questioning liberal, witness to the complex truth . . .",[8] as Sir Isaiah Berlin has claimed, since his self-questioning superfluous Hamlets, from Rakitin, say, of *A Month in the Country* through to Rudin and Lavretskii, can in no sense be regarded as conspicuous for their political liberalism and are generally flawed as character-studies through their failure to appreciate, let alone bear witness to, the complex truth of their situations, their natures and their relationships; but Sir Isaiah is right and just in his appraisal of Turgenev's personal commitment to the West and his understanding of the political pressures at work in its midst:

> Civilization, humane culture, meant more to the Russians, late-comers to Hegel's feast of the spirit, than to the blasé natives of the West. Turgenev clung to it more passionately, was more conscious of its precariousness, than even his friends Flaubert and Renan. But unlike them, he discerned behind the philistine bourgeoisie a far more furious opponent—the young icono-

clasts bent on the total annihilation of this world in the certainty that a new and more just world would emerge. He understood the best among these Robespierres, as Tolstoy, or even Dostoevsky, did not. He rejected their methods, he thought their goals naïve and grotesque, but his hand would not rise against them if this meant giving aid and comfort to the generals and bureaucrats. He offered no clear way out: only gradualism and education, only reason.[9]

Turgenev's single most important contribution to a fuller understanding of these "young iconoclasts" was his portrait of Bazarov in *Fathers and Children.* In all popular assessments of Turgenev it is Bazarov who is best known, the one great achievement on which his fame as a writer rests; it is of course also the most controversial of his portraits and the most influential. How are we to interpret Yevgeny Bazarov? A young man, representative of the generation of the 'sixties, training to be a doctor, an embodiment of scientific man whose principal concern is to reject all precepts and authorities that are not based on the natural sciences. As a type there is no doubt that Bazarov was new. His challenge to the older generation, in its rejection of aestheticism and romanticism, was hard-headed, rational and brutal. Perhaps the older generation, the sour cream, as it were, of the Russian nobility, scarcely offered stiff opposition to Bazarov's challenge, but the *implication* of Bazarov's iconoclasm is what matters and has tended to reverberate and expand into a threat posed by a technocratic Jacobinism to the liberal ethos of bourgeois Western society. The nub of the matter is how we interpret Bazarov's nihilism. Is it no more than a particularly extreme example of a kicking against the pricks, of one generation's rebellion against another, of the denial of existing authority in the name of a new and more just world? And though these are different questions all mustered behind the one question mark, they advance towards a standard bearing another device, that of Revolution. "And if he calls himself a Nihilist, one should read: Revolutionary", Turgenev insisted to Sluchevskii in his famous letter of April 1862.[10] Though there is no real evidence deducible from the novel that Bazarov is portrayed as a revolutionary, and we may assume that Turgenev was more keenly aware than any of his contemporaries of the annihilating, uncivilizing implications of Bazarov's nihilism, what Turgenev knew also at first hand was the fact of revolution. Bazarov's portrayal must have sprung from this background as well as from the polemics of the 'sixties, from two revolutionary situations, in short. For, to Turgenev, the meaning of revolution, as he experienced it in Paris, was annihilating. In **"Nashi poslali"** he wrote:

> A frightful, tormenting time began; he who has not experienced it cannot have an accurate idea of it. For the French, of course, it was horrible, since they could well think that their own country, their whole society was being destroyed and collapsing into the dust; but the anxiety of a foreigner, condemned to involuntary inac-

tivity, was, if not worse, then was certainly more agonising than their outrage and despair. The heat was intense; one couldn't go out; a fiery stream of air poured unimpeded through the open windows and the sun was blinding; any activity, reading or writing, was unthinkable. . . . Five, ten times a minute resounded the roar of canonfire; sometimes one could hear the rattle of rifle fire and the confused din of fighting. . . . Nothing stirred in the streets; the burning cobblestones turned yellow, the burning air glowed incandescent in the rays of the sun; and along the sidewalks stretched the embarrassed faces and motionless figures of national guardsmen—and there wasn't single ordinary living sound! All around was space and emptiness, but you felt yourself hemmed in, as if you were in a coffin or a prison.[11]

The spirit of tragedy hangs over this scene, just as the implications of Bazarov's fictional life are tragic. In the end, we may think of Bazarov as a tragic hero, dying accidentally of typhus when it seemed that his life promised so much. But the tragic concept was there at the beginning of Bazarov's portrayal, if we are to believe Turgenev's testimony. If he was a revolutionary at all, he was a doomed Pugachev, though perhaps he was just as doomed to superfluity as all the other Turgenevan heroes. His challenge can be construed ultimately as no more and no less than that of the healer who seeks to alleviate rather than change, to revive rather than revolutionize. This is the muted but very real force for change in life which Turgenev observed as a foreigner might observe a revolution occurring in another country, more aware of its agonising effect than the natives themselves, without experiencing their outrage and despair, but conscious all the while of being confined and imprisoned by the smelting processes of the revolution as they were occurring outside in the streets and knowing that the immediate victim of it all was freedom itself.

Turgenev was a chronicler, but he chronicled in terms of portraits, of physiognomies, and though the revolution may be occurring out there in the streets what matters to us about his achievement is what he referred to in his first short story **"Andrey Kolosov"**, quoting Byron, as "the music of the face". Politics as such were a lesser priority for him. ". . . I have never engaged in political activity, nor shall I ever do so. Such matters are alien to me and uninteresting and I concern myself with them only insofar as I need to as a writer who deals with contemporary life", he wrote to Countess Lambert.[12] But he always emphasized the importance he attached to *characters* rather than *ideas* (". . . I have always, throughout my literary career, started not from *ideas* but from *characters* . . .", letter to Polonskii, 1869)[13] and he must be regarded as a writer who sought to interpret the changes in life through characters while recognizing man's twofold limitations as a rational being who aspires to put his ideas to the service of realizable ideals and as the insignificant creature of a single

day, at the mercy of nature and eternity. Within this philosophical frame, which necessarily imposes a pessimistic and tragic shading upon the portrayal contained within it, the study of character is what immediately attracts the eye in Turgenev's work. And the power to make the portrayal recognizable as living, one with which we may identify and even sympathize, however much we may reject nihilism or the Hamletism of the superfluous man or the formidable and strong-minded virtuousness of his defiantly youthful heroines, is what constitutes the truth of Turgenev's picture of the world. But it is a truth animating the portrayal essentially in motion, in a movement towards change, at a point where, after its own fashion, an individual life suddenly confronts an essential challenge. Take Chulkaturin, for example, the Mr Stocking of **"The Diary of a Superfluous Man."**[14] His portrayal depends essentially upon two phases, both of which involve a kind of change in his awareness of himself that amounts to a revolution in his life. The change that results is irrevocable and total. The first phase consists of ecstasy and is the occasion of one of the most dazzling passages of nature description in the whole of Turgenev's work. It is the moment when Chulkaturin, who has already fallen in love with Liza, believes that he discerns the sudden arousal of a matching ecstasy in her. They have gone out for an evening walk:

> At that time she was seventeen years old. . . . And yet, on that very evening, in my presence, there began within her that calm inner ferment which anticipates the transformation of a child into a woman. . . . I was witness to this change in her whole being, this innocent confusion, this anxious thoughtfulness; I was the first to notice the sudden softening of the gaze, the ringing nervousness of the voice—and, O fool! O superfluous man! for the length of a whole week I didn't even feel ashamed of supposing that I, *I* was the cause of this change.
>
> This is how it came about.
>
> . . . Liza and I were the first to come out of the woodland; Bizmyonkov remained behind with the old lady. We came out, stopped and were both forced to screw up our eyes, for directly ahead of us, in a molten mist, an enormous blood-red sun was setting. Half the sky was aflame and glowing red; red rays of light struck out across the meadows, casting crimson reflections even into the shadowy sides of the gullies, and lay like a fiery lead on the surface of the stream (where it wasn't hidden by overhanging bushes) and literally pressed themselves into the very bosom of the ravine and the woodland. We stood there inundated by the fierce radiance. I am incapable of conveying all the impassioned majesty of this scene. They say that to a blind man the colour red is like a trumpet voluntary; I have no idea how correct this analogy is, but there was definitely some kind of invocation in the burning gold of the evening air, in the purple brilliance of the sky and the earth. I cried out in excitement and turned instantly to Liza. She was gazing directly at the sun. I remember how the conflagration of the sunset was re-

flected in her eyes in tiny spots of burning fire. She was overwhelmed and deeply moved.[15]

The reflection of the sunset in Liza's face ironically and ambiguously reflects the ecstatic change occurring in the narrator himself when he supposes—though it is a false supposition, a hopeful self-deception at best—that she has experienced something shared by him. He is witness to her complex emotions much as Turgenev was a witness to revolution, though, in the end, the superfluous man was the one most deeply affected, if only through being forced to recognize that he was in all essentials superfluous both to her and to life. The greater part, of course, of the Superfluous Man's story is devoted to an agonized, static appraisal of his superfluous condition. But what he offers to us as the central and most significant episode in his life is the short period of three weeks, no more, when he was ecstatically in love with Liza.

The quality of the emotion most emphasized by Turgenev is its unexpectedness, accompanied by its power to change irreversibly. In this latter aspect it tends to resemble a sickness which emphasizes human mortality. There is no doubt that, in a way bordering on cliché, Turgenev associated love with death, the one being opposed to the other at either end of the spectrum of human experience. In those works of his which most clearly mirror his own life he laid special emphasis on the incongruity of the ecstasy itself, its abnormality and its infectious, transforming power. *Asia* is one example. The hero's love for Asia is scarcely articulated, except as a sudden awareness of happiness. Its suddenness and its power are what matter most. As he returns by boat across the Rhine after dancing with Asia in the cottage high above the town, the sensation of delight overwhelms him like a supernatural epiphany:

> Looking about me, listening and recalling what the day had been like, I suddenly felt a secret unease in my heart and raised my eyes to the sky, but even in the sky there seemed to be no tranquility. Dotted with stars, it constantly quivered and danced and shivered. I leaned down to the surface of the river, but even there, even in those dark, cold depths, the stars flickered and shimmered. A feeling of agitated life seemed to surround me and I felt a similar agitation rising within me. I leaned on the boat's edge. . . . The whisper of the breeze in my ears, the soft murmuring of the water along the boat's stern irritated me, and the quick fresh breathing of the waves against the boat did not cool my feelings. A nightingale started singing on the bank and infected me with the sweet poison of its song. Tears gathered in my eyes, but they were not tears of abstract ecstasy. What I felt was not so much a vague, still recently experienced sensation of all-embracing desire, such as when the soul expands, resounds and seems to be aware that it understands everything and loves the whole world. . . . No! It was a fierce yearning for personal happiness that had ignited within me. I still didn't dare give it a name, but it was happiness, happiness to saturation point, that I desired and longed for. . . .[16]

He does not dare actually speak the name of love when he meets Asia for the last time. If he had overcome for that moment what he defines as "my unkind genius of ineptitude"[17] he might have persuaded her that he loved her as she was ready to love him. But ripeness is all, that is the motto for such moments, for as the hero reminds himself: "Happiness has no tomorrow. It has no yesterday. It does not remember the past, it does not think of the future. It only has a present time—and that's not a whole day, but only an instant."[18] The sediment of melancholy which remains as the lasting memorial of such Turgenevan studies of the ephemeral, fleeting quality of love and happiness seems to be relished in a maudlin way even more strongly than the ecstasy of the experience, but the ecstasy is what transforms, if only by offering its momentary promise of some ideal conditions of things, that instant of happiness when humanity recognizes its potential.

In Turgenev it is always surrounded by nostalgia. And the nostalgia is that of age for youth. All literary realism is arguably a form of reminiscence. Subjectivity is therefore a dimension essential to it and an enhancement of it, but the realism is largely determined by the extent to which the narrator succeeds in objectifying the experience of the past. Turgenev's is a gift matching Tolstoi's in this respect and surpassing Dostoevskii's, I suggest. With the possible exception of Chekhov there is no Russian writer of the last century or this who can outshine Turgenev's mastery in evoking nostalgia for youth. His masterpiece of such confessional reminiscence is *First Love* and it marvellously illustrates through the two central portraits how first love can change, not only in an encounter between sexes but also in the need of the younger for the older, of the narrator for Zinaida and Zinaida for the father, thus showing how love devours as well as sacrifices itself and, despite being the privilege of youth, seeks to shed its own youthfulness in an act of sacrifice to age and impotence and death. This remarkable short story is by far the most complex of Turgenev's studies of love. Its complexity derives, on the one hand, from the fact that the boy's viewpoint seems simple and all-embracing in its immediate emotional receptivity but is in fact only partial, and, on the other, from the fact that Zinaida herself becomes much more than a heroine observed, as Natalia might be said to be principally a heroine observed by Rudin or Liza a heroine observed by Lavretskii. Zinaida seems to achieve her own independence of the narrator's reminiscence; she seems to transcend the limits of the narrator's memory of her—and she possesses such transcendent independence quite paradoxically through the way in which the mature narrator exploits the boy's partial and immature understanding of her. Her impoverished, socially questionable background, brought close to burlesque through the wickedly funny characterization of her mother, the little court of suitors over which she exercises such despotic sway, her Wagnerian dreams of Romantic self-sacrifice which have their emotional counterpart in the boy's loving and sacrificial devotion to her and her own secret but wanton infatuation for the boy's father, these complex aspects of her portrait meet and are invested with the supreme fascination of the unattainable through the boy's ecstatic, idealizing love for her. Her portrayal is faultless insofar as it develops within the frame of the—admittedly partial—reminiscence. Of course, we are given no more than intimations of the supreme change occurring in her or the way in which her life was completely altered by the experience. The mature procrastinating narrator rings the curtain down upon his "first love" by invoking Pushkin's inimitably sardonic, bittersweet lines:

> Iz ravnodushnykh ust ia slyshal smerti vest'
> I ravnodushno ei vnimal ia.

> *From lips indifferent heard I news of death*
> *And indifferently attended to them.*[19]

His "first love" thus closes not only with the loved one's death but also with the most splendid of all Turgenev's addresses to youth. It summarizes all that he meant by nostalgia, all that sense of its fleeting arrogance—"O youth! youth! you have no concerns, you possess, as it were, all the treasures of the universe, even grief is a comfort to you, even sadness suits your looks, you are self-assured and bold, you say: 'Look, I'm the only one alive!' while the very days of your life run away and vanish without trace and without number and everything in you disappears like wax, like snow in the heat of the sun . . ."[20]—and secreted within that ephemeral experience is the single instant of ecstasy, as momentary and swift as a ghost, of the "first love" to which Turgenev himself said goodbye "with no more than a sigh, a nagging sense of loss":

> As for me—what did I hope for, what did I expect, what rich future did I look forward to when—with no more than a sigh, a nagging sense of loss—I said goodbye to the fugitive and momentary ghost of my first love?[21]

Indeed, what had Turgenev hoped for? Writing his story early in 1860, perhaps he had hoped by evoking the past to suggest that the future held greater promise, or that at least the childhoods of those who came after would not have to be filled with such stories of first love as his narrator Vladimir Petrovich had to tell. For the Epilogue to *First Love* which Turgenev added to the French and German translations in 1863 invited the reader to reflect on the conditions under which his, Turgenev's generation, had grown up and to sense in it all "some overall, national guilt, something akin to crime" and a recognition that "Something is rotten in the state of Denmark".[22] No doubt this was an inappropriately serious, heavyweight judgement to make on a reminis-

cence of first love which had no overt political significance at all. Therefore Turgenev never included it in the Russian version of *First Love.* But it underlines something that is implicit in the greater part of his work, especially in all his major fictional portraits and their settings: the fact that the ecstasy of first love acquires its power to transform as much from the morally corrupt circumstances of the world Turgenev depicts for us as from the unexpectedness of its coming and the abnormal state, the sick condition, which it induces.

Turgenev's greatness, I suggest, is in knowing the agony of this fact but in hardly ever making it explicit. He can observe revolution from his room on the fourth floor and sense the agony of what is happening more keenly than those at street level. But he is no part of that revolution, he is a foreigner to it in a literal sense. His writer's conscience gives him an awareness of the frightful, agonizing time it was while simultaneously making him an impartial transmitter of the truth as he senses it. The revolution itself, like first love, is the principal agent of change in this picture of the truth and it is only when that agent is at work that Turgenev's true powers as a writer really engage with it to create their own transformation. A moral sense of the corrupt circumstances must always be subsumed in this process, no matter how inexplicit the moralizing may be.

We cannot appreciate fully his portrayals of Khor and Kalinych, of Pavlusha and the other boys from **"Bezhin Lea"**, of Kasian or Lukeria, for example—or indeed any of the portrayals in *Zapiski okhotnika*—without this awareness. If as readers we are not made aware that "Something is rotten in the state of Denmark" after experiencing his studies of rural Russian life, then the moral intent of the fiction has eluded us and it is our loss. The portrayals themselves are masterpieces of juxtaposition. They are word pictures of peasant figures visualized as physiognomies set in a framework of nature, juxtaposed with a natural scene, and caught in one moment of summer like some graven challenge to human mortality and eternity. Their vitality is of a particular instant, the product of one encounter. Rescued ephemerally from the anonymity of serfdom, they are unchanging and brilliant as vivid Repin portraits. The portrayals of their masters, the serfowners, have a similar confined, static quality, though in their cases the country-house settings and the internal narratives provide a frame of reference, both socially speaking and in time, that explains them, gives room for parody and emphasizes where necessary their moral fallibility. But in no case can it be said that they change, for there are no ecstasies there, no revolutions in their lives, to change them.

Far-fetched and over-simple though it may be to claim it, there are grounds for thinking that it was not until Turgenev had had time to assimilate the meaning of the revolutionary events of 1848 that he came to regard human experience as revolutionized and transfigured by love, by its ecstasy and its madness. His own love for Pauline Viardot may of course be reflected in such studies of love as that between Rakitin and Natalia Petrovna in *A Month in the Country* and echoes of it, we may assume, are to be found in so many of the weak hero-strong heroine relationships that form the basis of his mature fiction. Such biographical fact does little, however, to explain the study of first love we find in *Rudin,* or in any of the novels, for that matter, with the possible exception of *Smoke.* Natalia's "first love" for Rudin presumably leaves its mark indelibly on her life, but the shock of the experience to Rudin himself tests him morally to the limit and forces him to look at himself, just as the Superfluous Man stares at himself in the mirror and is horror-struck to realize that he is superfluous above all to the object of his love. In contemplating himself, he changes: it is where solipsism collapses before the pressures of reality. Turgenev 'revolutionized' Rudin in a final epilogue which endows him with the futile but bold self-sacrifice of a Quixote. Though not Quixotic, Lavretskii nevertheless undergoes an experience of change which forces him to acknowledge that the only moral choice open to him is a sacrifice of self. The fundamental change worked in the most obviously Quixotic of his portraits, that of Elena of *On the Eve* and Bazarov, has a revolutionary connection—protest against the moral corruption of the past, of an older generation, of outworn ideas, though it is love which acts as the principal agent of transformation. These studies in what Turgenev called "the rapidly changing physiognomy of Russians of the cultured stratum"[23] are each concerned with change brought about by love, but in each case the moral challenge posed by heroine to hero or vice-versa highlights the corrupt moral circumstances of the world to which they belong. Turgenev's own Hannibal's Oath against Serfdom, like his commitment to the West and his liberalism, were challenges to a morally bankrupt social system and a political tyranny which, for all his gradualism, he would have wished to see changed, provided of course that did not result in its replacement by a Jacobinist tyranny of young revolutionary nihilists. Because it has to be stressed that Turgenev knew what such revolution could mean and he did not wish anything of the kind for Russia.

What, then, is Turgenev's legacy? We may rehearse his achievements as the first Russian novelist to have an international reputation, the chronicler of the Russian intelligentsia, the champion of the Russian peasantry, renowned as the creator of Bazarov and supreme as a master of Russian prose whose word pictures of the Russian countryside are among the finest ever written. We may point to his cultural role as a leading representative of Russian Westernism, his self-appointed ambassadorial role as an intermediary between Russia and Europe and, for the greater part of his adult life, his

role as devoted friend and admirer of the singer Pauline Viardot. Yet related so closely as he was to his time, and offering us such a clear and realistic image of it in his best works, he was not a profoundly inventive writer. Formulae, coincidences, narrative contrivances, stereotypical characterizations and stereotypical phrases mar and sometimes distort his work to the point where, on re-reading it nowadays, it occasionally appears not only old-fashioned but inherently clumsy as well. As a man perceived through his letters, of which we have such an abundance, he was almost without exception likeable, considerate, level-headed and very often his raconteur's brilliance, his wit, his sharpness of observation and his candour are seen at their best in that setting. He practically never wrote without humour, even though satire tended to degenerate into spitefulness and embittered sarcasm in his hands. The humour was usually laconic, summoning a smile rather than laughter at its most successful. It served as an enrichment to his shrewd, truthful observation. Turgenev's eye, so sensitive to changes in the natural scene and so refreshing in its perception of the vivid surfaces of the natural world, was always keenest in its observation of human foibles and those moments when, in the relationship of one person to another, the emotional interaction literally brought into being a kind of poetry.

The poetry of the relationship is made poignant and memorable to us by its brevity. So short-lived is the happiness celebrated by such poetry that it seems to be scarcely more than an instant's duration in a total lifetime's experience. Yet it is the real agent of change in Turgenev's picture of life; and Turgenev himself, while knowing the anguish of it, tends in his objectivity to relate to it no more closely than might a perspicacious observer of a revolution in a foreign country. The moment of revolution, like the "secret alchemy" of poetry, in Shelley's description of it, "strips the veil of familiarity from the world",[24] so that for the Turgenevan hero and heroine the world is no longer familiar. Each is momentarily changed in his or her view of selfhood and to that extent the world is no longer familiar to them. The lifetime of acceptance that follows, to which in Turgenev's pessimistic view of the human condition they may seem to be fated, encompasses the happy-ever-after of marriage and is therefore a conventional, familiar ending to their lives; or they are solitary wanderers, living out their superfluity in vain introspection and unhappy failure; or they simply have to learn that stoical lesson of renunciation, expressed by the epigraph to **"Faust"** in Goethe's words "Entbehren sollst du, sollst entbehren", which is all Turgenev allows man to feel as he faces his own mortality.

Turgenev's was a limited philosophy. All too easily in the last twenty years of his life he succumbed to pessimism and tended to represent life as menaced by supernatural powers. Though such essays in the penetration of reality point towards Symbolism, they are in fact lesser items in Turgenev's achievement. Turgenev did not possess that transcendent power as a writer which passes, like Shakespeare's or Dostoevskii's, across the temporal limits of centuries and exercises the appeal of a prophecy as relevant to the future as to its own day. Turgenev may have perceived the dangers of Russian nihilism more clearly than his contemporaries, but it cannot really be claimed on his behalf that he foresaw the advent of demagogic political tyrannies as did Dostoevskii; nor was he as profound a thinker or psychologist. He was upholstered by his wealth, generally comfortable in his circumstances for all his protestations of personal inadequacy. In the final years of his life he was beset by the improperly diagnosed agonies of cancer and he bore them with great courage and as much humour and dignity as he could muster. But he was never rawly naked to life in his writer's sensibilities as was Dostoevskii.

If that was not part of his legacy, he presents to us in this centenary year of his death another model or example as a writer which is not without merit. He believed all his life in freedom. No doubt it seems glib to state it as simply as that, and perhaps Turgenev's life displays the eternal paradox of man's intellectual yearning for freedom while being always emotionally in thrall, chained as he was by his passionate attachment to Pauline Viardot. But the uniqueness of Turgenev when compared with all other Russian writers of his time was his quite conscious devotion, both emotional and intellectual, cultural as well as political, to Europe and European civilization. That devotion was inseparably bound up with what he referred to in his ***Literary Reminiscences*** as "that freedom and awareness towards which I aspired"—a freedom and awareness ("toi svobody, togo soznaniia, k kotorym ia stremilsia") that did not exist in his native Russia:

> I had to get far away from my enemy so that I could fall upon him all the more powerfully from a distance. In my eyes this enemy took a definite form and bore a particular name: this enemy was—serfdom. Under this heading I gathered and concentrated everything against which I had decided to fight to the bitter end, with which I had sworn never to come to terms. . . . This was my Hannibal's oath; and I was not the only one to make such an oath at that time. I went to the West in order the better to fulfil it.[25]

The freedom permitted him by the West allowed him to fulfil his Hannibal's oath not only through the writing of his famous ***Sketches,*** but also by giving him a perspective on his own country's problems that enabled him to bear witness to the changes in the Russian intelligentsia from the 'forties to the 'sixties with the same critical, objective clarity he brought to his observation of the revolutionary events in Paris in 1848. The freedom mattered to him in several very personal senses—in

the sense, perhaps negative, that he was free of immediate domestic responsibilities, free of censorship, if not of the literary kind then of the kind imposed by the coteries of the literary worlds of Moscow and St Petersburg, free to cultivate friendships with so many of the most outstanding personalities of his time, so that his correspondence became a litany of European celebrities as well as a kind of Who's Who of his own Russian contemporaries. Unlike any other Russian of his time, he enjoyed the freedom to be European, to be at home in Europe; his only real exile took the form of confinement to his estate of Spasskoye. In short, he exemplified the freedom enjoyed by the well-off nineteenth-century European, though he never ceased for a moment to be Russian.

But there was another freedom which he treasured more highly, and it is the most important of his legacies, I suggest. It was his freedom as a writer to employ his talent as he wished. In his Preface to his novels of 1880 he concluded by addressing himself to the problem of the constraining and destructive influence of contemporary criticism. His final words are scathing. They are also a reminder that the freedom for which he was appealing could so easily be imperilled and lost:

> Believe me, a real talent never serves aims outside itself and always finds its satisfactions within itself. The life surrounding a writer gives him his content—he is its *concentrated reflection;* but he is just as incapable of writing a panegyric as he is of writing a lampoon. In the last resort, it is beneath him. To submit to a given theme or to promote a particular programme is for those who can do no better.[26]

As he quoted more than once, his motto in these matters was the line and a half from Pushkin's poem "To the Poet" ("Poetu") of 1830, which in his article on ***Fathers and Children*** (**"Po povodu *Ottsov i detey*"**) he explained in the following way:

> Nothing liberates a person as much as knowledge, and nowhere is knowledge more necessary than in the matter of art, of poetry: it's not for nothing that in bureaucratic language the arts are called 'free'. Can a person 'get hold of', 'capture' what surrounds him if he is not free within himself? Pushkin understood this profoundly; it is not for nothing that in his immortal sonnet, in the sonnet which every beginning writer should learn by heart and remember as his motto, he said:
>
>   . . . dorogoiu *svobodnoi*
> Idi, kuda vlechet tebia *svobodnyi* um . . .
>
>   . . . *following a* free *path*
> *Go wherever your* free *mind leads you* . . .[27]

Pushkin's "free mind", his "free intellect" was what Turgenev most treasured. In his Pushkin speech of 1880, less famous though it may now be than Dostoevskii's, he celebrated Russia's national poet for having been the first, as he put it, to have "driven the banner of poetry deep into Russian soil" and he went on to claim:

And as it has been said of Shakespeare that everyone who learns to read inevitably becomes a new reader of his, so we will hope that every descendant of ours who stands with love before this monument to Pushkin and understands the meaning of this love will, by this very act, show that he like Pushkin has become more Russian, more educated and more free! Ladies and gentleman, don't let this last word surprise you! In poetry there is a liberating, because there is an uplifting, moral force.[28]

Turgenev, witness to his age, observer of revolution, the most European Russian of his time, knew as a writer the moral force of his art, but he recognized that it could only uplift if it were free. The greatest compliment we may pay to him as a writer is to adapt his own words in celebration of Pushkin and to say of him that, in the hundred years since his death, the reading of his work, whether in his own tongue or in translation, has helped all readers of his to become more Russian, more educated and more free.[29]

Notes

1. I. S. Turgenev, *Sketches from a Hunter's Album*, by Richard Freeborn (Harmondsworth: Penguin Classics, 1967 and subsequent editions).

2. Leonard Schapiro, *Turgenev: His Life and Times* (Oxford, 1978), p. xii.

3. I. S. Turgenev, *Sochineniia*, xiv (Moscow and Leningrad, 1967), 142.

4. *Turgenev's Letters*, selected, edited and translated by A. V. Knowles (London, 1983), 57.

5. *Ibid.*, 209.

6. *Ibid.*, 112.

7. *Ibid.*, 250.

8. Isaiah Berlin, *Fathers and Children: The Romanes Lecture* (Oxford, 1972), 58.

9. *Ibid.*, 59.

10. *Letters* (ref. 4), 105.

11. *Sochineniia*, xiv, 140.

12. *Letters* (ref. 4), 113.

13. *Ibid.*, 159.

14. My own translation of the name in *Love and Death: Six Stories by Ivan Turgenev* (London, 1983).

15. *Ibid.*, 40-41.

16. *Ibid.*, 126.

17. *Ibid.*, 141.

18. *Ibid.*, 139.

19. The words are taken from A. S. Pushkin's poem of 1825, "Beneath the Blue Skies of My Native Land".

20. *Ibid.*, 201.

21. *Ibid.*, 202.

22. *Ibid.*, 20.

23. *Sochineniia*, xii (Moscow and Leningrad, 1966), 303.

24. Percy Bysshe Shelley, "A Defence of Poetry", quoted from *Revolutions, 1775-1830*, ed. by Merryn Williams (Harmondsworth: Penguin Books, 1977), 591.

25. *Sochineniia*, xiv, 9.

26. *Ibid.*, xii, 310.

27. *Ibid.*, xiv, 107.

28. *Ibid.*, xv (Moscow and Leningrad, 1968), 76.

29. This paper is a modified version of one given at the Turgenev centenary conference held at the University of Liverpool in October 1983.

Thomas Eekman (essay date 1987)

SOURCE: Eekman, Thomas. "Turgenev and the Shorter Prose Forms." In *Text and Context: Essays To Honor Nils Åke Nilsson*, edited by Peter Alberg Jensen, Barbara Lönnqvist, Fiona Björling, Lars Kleberg, and Anders Sjöberg, pp. 42-52. Stockholm: Almqvist & Wiksell International, 1987.

[*In the following essay, Eekman discusses the recurring love theme in Turgenev's short stories as well as his repeated use of first person narrators and framed story-within-a-story structural devices.*]

Few books in world literature have such a misleading title as Turgenev's *Zapiski ochotnika*. The actual hunting is restricted to just a few paragraphs, and usually the narrator, before he has caught even one woodcock, has arrived at some country house or somewhere else where he meets people, whose outward appearance and character he describes, whose life history he tells us and whose conversations he renders. No matter how important the function of nature is in his stories, as decoration and as a means to create the atmosphere—Turgenev is primarily a hunter of people, a fascinated observer of human characters, human passions, life vicissitudes, and the mutual relationships of men.

One peculiarity of the *Zapiski* is that they are all written in first person narration. This can be explained, at least partly, by Turgenev's wish to approach living reality as closely as possible, to strengthen the ties between literary imagination, fiction, and reality. Presumably the *Huntsman's Sketches* do contain Turgenev's own experiences, meetings, observations and contemplations. Telling a story in the "I"-form has the advantage of diminishing the distance between the author and the reader: the former takes the latter by the hand ("Dajte mne ruku, ljubeznyj čitatel', i poedemte vmeste so mnoj"—thus begins **"Tat'jana Borisovna i ee plemjannik"**), he turns directly to him, involves him in the events described; that immediate contact apparently was an attractive point for Turgenev. Especially when speaking of nature he likes to confide to the reader his enthusiasm and admiration, as in the concluding story **"Les i step'"**. And the "I" is the living tie that binds the stories together.

An additional reason that may induce an author to choose the first person narration is the urge to disclose his inner life, to communicate his intimate thoughts, to make confessions. That confessional character is traditionally inherent in much first person narration. In fact, every writer has a certain need to exhibit his inner I, to confess his intimate thoughts: without that need he would remain silent. And for testimonies about oneself "I"-narration seems the most natural, sincere and believable method.

However, in the *Zapiski ochotnika* the role of the "I" is different. This "I" never speaks about himself, he always encounters other people and directs our attention toward them; he rarely expresses his own feelings—only when talking about nature and in rare cases when people are concerned (at the end of **"Svidanie"** he remarks: ". . . no obraz bednoj Akuliny dolgo ne vychodil iz moej golovy . . ."). The narrator is the observer and recorder, the reporter who interviews others and who by his questions and remarks provokes other people to speak, to make their confessions and to expose their character. His words are, as a rule, neutral, informative. Sometimes he is simply the witness of events that happen to other people, or of their personal relations. Only in **"Birjuk"** he himself actively intervenes in the action; and in **"Stučit!"** (which was written much later than the original series) the narrator himself has an adventure; however, in this story, too, the attention is mainly directed towards other persons: the narrator's coachman, the alleged robbers they meet.

Yet Turgenev sometimes uses the "I"-procedure in a different way. In the story **"Ermolaj i mel'ničicha"** the landowner Zverkov tells the story of his maid Arina, whom he had refused permission to get married and whom he had chased away when it turned out that she was pregnant. Here it is not the narrator who is talking, but the landowner Zverkov whom he puts on the stage. This story acquires its bitter taste and is so impressive exactly because Turgenev does not retell the story, but

we hear it directly from the mouth of the "I", a feudal lord who is not even aware of the injustice he and his wife have inflicted upon a subordinate.

A different case we find in **"Uezdnyj lekar'"**, in which the narrator plays again a very limited role—the pith of the story is the tale told by the doctor about a woman patient. It is not a tendentious story, but a love story, and one of an intimate, very personal and tragic character. Our huntsman did not experience the events himself, he is merely the man who takes notes; yet the story is in first person narration, and this way the intimate, confession-like character is reinforced.

The two latter stories belong to the type of frame stories, containing a story which is woven into another story and forming a more or less significant part of that framing story, or at least distracting our attention for some time from that story. This interpolation of secondary stories, figures, and descriptions, which break the strict, simple thread of the narrative, split it, stop it, deflect it and make it more colorful and diversified, is what is happening all the time in the *Zapiski.* In some instances, as in **"Uezdnyj lekar'"**, that inner story is so predominant that it acquires primary importance and overgrows the frame. In **"Petr Petrovič Karataev"**, too, the story this Karataev tells us forms the main part of the text—a story in which both the love element and the anti-feudal element play a role. In **"Gamlet ščigrovskogo uezda"** the reader is first, for six to seven pages, confronted with various types of landowners until finally the "Hamlet" enters the scene, whose narrative constitutes the kernel of the story; and here again, the inner story is in the first person.

Next to the 25 *Huntsman's Sketches,* Turgenev left us approximately 35 other stories and novellas of various form, size and character and from various periods in his literary career. To them belong **"Ivan Kolosov"**, his very first writing to appear in print (1844), as well as the story with the ominous title **"Konec"**, which he on his deathbed dictated to Pauline Viardot in French, German and Italian. As is well known, he changed the composition of the *Huntman's Sketches* several times. Among the stories that never figured among the *Zapiski* there are a few that would perfectly fit among them. They, too, deal with characters (both peasants and landowners), situations, relations and events in the Russian country: **"Poezdka v Poles'e"**, for example, **"Brigadir"**, or **"Stepnoj korol' Lir"**, one of his most powerful stories. **"Punin i Baburin"** also portrays characters from the Russian countryside, but it exceeds the scope of the *Huntsman's Sketches.* The first chapter contains childhood reminiscences—of Turgenev himself, or so it seems. The second and third take place later in Moscow and St. Petersburg, where the "I" meets the same Punin and Baburin again (there is a fourth chapter, which is actually a short epilogue). On the other hand, **"Konec"** could as to its form, length, subject matter, atmosphere and style be one of the ***Huntsman's Sketches.*** Consequently, no sharp dividing line can be drawn between Turgenev's ***Zapiski ochotnika*** and his other shorter prose works. It may be mentioned here that, when size is the criterium, no clear dividing line can be drawn between the stories and novels either. There are stories of 10 to 16 pages, but ***Vešnie vody*** has 112 pages, whereas ***Rudin*** has only 102 pages.[1]

However, size is not the only or the most essential distinction that can be made between a short story or novella and a novel. As a rule, the novel is more elaborate in its structure, its theme and plot, as well as in its delineation of the hero's or heroes' character, often encompassing the whole life or a significant part of the life of one or more persons; whereas the novella does not admit deep psychological analysis and is mostly limited to one episode or moment in the hero's life. Goethe mentioned in his well known conversation with Eckermann "das Unerhörte" as the element characteristic of any novella.[2] In most definitions or discussions of the genre since then this occurrence of an unheard of, extraordinary event was put forward as a requirement of a good novella. Ludwig Tieck held that the novella "puts a big or small occurrence in the brightest possible light" and presents it as "extraordinary, perhaps unique"; the story should make "an unexpected turnabout", by which "it will impress itself the deeper in the reader's imagination".[3] Turgenev's older contemporary Nikolaj I. Nadeždin did not recognize this demand of the unusual central event: "The novella [povest'] is an episode from the limitless poem of human vicissitudes."[4]

However, contemporary theoreticians generally confirm that the novella "depicts a single event with the appurtenances necessary to understand it well".[5] "Thus one can recognize the novella by the fact that a chain of motifs leads to a central event, and then possibly away from it again";[6] "the occurrence that takes shape in it has the character of the surprising, the unexpected, the incalculable".[7] A crisis, a reversal of fortune, a conflict, a *pointe* is postulated by several writers on the subject.[8] Such a claim would not apply to some of Čechov's longer stories. But in Turgenev's case, the required central event or climax is usually there. It is reached when the "I" rushes to the place where he expects to find Asja, but she has disappeared; or when the "I" discovers the love affair between Zinaida and his father (**"Pervaja ljubov'"**); or when Fustov finally returns to the town to find out that Susanna has died (**"Nesčastnaja"**). In **"Klara Milič"** at least three such culmination points have been established.[9]

Such a climax is usually absent or much less dramatic in the ***Huntsman's Sketches.*** The novels do have a crisis, an apogee, or more than one. But what distinguishes Turgenev's novels thematically from the shorter forms

is that the novels have two centers: the hero and society, with which he is in close contact and, at the same time, in conflict.[10] In the novels, the hero is socially involved, and in some cases even a social ideologist—whereas the novellas focus on the hero's personal emotional conflict, his love affair in the majority of cases; the reasons of his defeat are psychological, not social. This is a distinction in epic horizon between novel and novella; and here, too, Turgenev's novellas are closer to the typical romantic, traditional patterns.

In the light of this, we have to reconsider our above remark that the novella does not admit deeper psychological analysis and often deals with just one episode or critical point in the hero's life. Turgenev's shorter prose works are exactly characterized by their *not* being confined to just that: in them, by means of introductions, by inserting reminiscences or elaborations on the previous lives of the characters, and notably by adding an epilogue which gives glimpses of their later fortunes, he evokes a more or less complete picture of the main protagonists and their fate. And that is a feature which tends to efface the just established distinction between the novel and the novella.

In just seven out of the 25 ***Huntsman's Sketches*** is love introduced; rarely is a love affair the main theme of a story (as in **"Uezdnyj lekar'"**). In the novels love is, of course, a dominating element, except for ***Otcy i deti.*** In the novellas, too, love is a momentous factor in the life and the adventures of the heroes—with the exception of a story like **"Mumu"**, where love appears only in an episode, and of two stories where love is absent: **"Sobaka"** and **"Rasskaz otca Alekseja"**, both belonging to Turgenev's "mystic" or mysterious stories in which hallucinations are described.

Thus we see (in case we did not know yet) that love is Turgenev's stock theme, which he handles, elaborates and varies with consummate skill. It is his deeply felt, true to life depiction of the rising stream of love which becomes more and more powerful and carries the hero away, combined with his subtle evocation of atmosphere and fine character analysis that make these stories into such smart, moving, if not gripping, works of literature, even in our times, although the contemporary reader may be used to far more provocative, overtly erotic ways of dealing with the love theme.

Both on the ***Huntsman's Sketches*** and related stories and on the series primarily based upon the love motif Turgenev worked during his entire career as a writer. One similarity between the two groups of stories is that most of them are narrated in the first person. Typically, in the beginning of the love story a young man (a military man who arrives in a new garrison or a civil servant on a tour of duty, or simply a traveler) comes into contact with a milieu that is unknown to him, in a small provincial town, on an estate, sometimes in a foreign country, where the love adventure then develops. Recent occurrences or memories are never the subject matter; the narrator always goes back to his adolescence, or even his childhood—cf. stories like **"Stepnoj korol' Lir"**, **"Punin i Baburin"**, **"Časy"**, **"Son"**, in which he views the events with the candidness, the fresh and sharp observation of a boy. In those cases, however, the narrator himself is not taking part in the love relationship. More frequent are the stories in which the narrator is one of the partners, thinking melancholically back to an episode in his life, which, however, did not have a fatal result for him: he apparently recovered pretty soon from the shock and now he lives on; maybe he has had some other love adventures since then. *Vešnie vody* is an example: the memory which forms the contents of the story is evoked by a small garnet cross which the hero finds among love letters that came out of a drawer. That memory strikes him strongly, it is true—but apparently he had been able for years to repress it. The epigraph to the story is from an old romance, in which the moments of happiness are being compared to a swiftly fleeting brook in the spring. This mirrors the philosophy Turgenev seems to express. It is a philosophy of resignation, a consciousness that feelings and passions, happiness and sorrow are transient experiences which man is unable to change or to retain. Man, basically a weak, insecure and lonely being, is unable to master the forces of nature that work within him and upon him and set traps for him: he is "being lived" instead of actively shaping and directing his own life, until, before he realizes it, old age descends upon his head like snow (a favorite image of Turgenev), and solely the memory of so many missed opportunities remains.

A large part of these novellas employs the frame structure in some variety, although not all of them are *Rahmenerzählungen* in the strict, classical sense. From 1855 onward *all* of Turgenev's stories are provided with a frame, with two exceptions: **"Prizraki"** and **"Klara Milič"**. But it is already present in his very first prose work, **"Ivan Kolosov"**, in its most usual, conventional form: somewhere a small group of gentlemen is conversing, one of them takes the floor and obliges the company with his story; towards the end this company reappears for some concluding comments. In **"Andrej Kolosov"** we find this classical Turgenevian device in its most complete, most consistently sustained form. "Odin nebol'šoj, blednyj čeloveček" addresses a group of people at the fireside, suggesting that each of them in his turn will tell something about an unusual character. He is urged to begin himself, and thereupon we hear the story of Ivan Kolosov. This introduction occupies approximately a page; during the little gentleman's relation, at least in the beginning, the framing element is not forgotten: the listeners from time to time interrupt the narrator, he asks for a cigar, one of those present

twice interrupts him with a quotation from Byron, the little gentleman repeatedly addresses his audience. Such interruptions occur less frequently once the story is well on its way, but even there they are not completely absent. When it is finished one of the listeners asks: "'And what happened to Varja?'—'I don't know', answered the narrator. We all rose to our feet and went home." Thus the story is concluded by the embracing frame, albeit merely with a few short sentences. The idea that all in turn would tell a story about an unusual personality is not taken up any more. It might be pointed out that this firstling of Turgenev is actually a double first person story, because not only the inner story is told in the first person, but in the framing story, too, the "I" (supposedly the author) takes part ("ja tože byl v čisle sporivšich").

Two years later (still before his first *Huntsman's Sketch*) appeared **"Tri portreta"**. This portrait story is a frame story in an even more extensive sense. It is this time a hunting company to which the "I" also belongs: a double first person narrative again. The actual central story begins after four pages. The narrator hardly plays a role in it: the main characters are his grandfather and some of his contemporaries; yet he throws in a remark from time to time and occasionally addresses his audience. At the end of the story, however, Turgenev fails to lead us back to the company of hunters under the three portraits: he leaves the frame open.

In the years that follow, Turgenev is very much occupied by his *Zapiski ochotnika.* But in 1850 two non-*Zapiski* stories are created, and both are frame stories again, in which both the framing and the inner story are narrated in the first person; but the pattern is somewhat diversified. In **"Dnevnik lišnego čeloveka"** the hero, Čulkaturin, relates his love story, which is a story of the type Turgenev wrote more often, ending in a negative, unhappy way. Čulkaturin's superfluity is not socially indicative, but purely personal, it is a powerlessness, generated by his character, his nature, to gain the respect and concern of other people, and finally also the love of his chosen one: life goes on and gives him the cold shoulder, just like it does other figures from Turgenev's stories. The frame element consists merely of the fact that towards the end, after the last page of the diary, a "Note from the Editor" follows, which informs us that Čulkaturin did pass away the night after he wrote his last note.

The other story from 1850 (published only in 1856), **"Perepiska"**, has the well known letter form, also used in **"Faust"** (1855). This time Turgenev has left out the frame altogether (about how the letters were found and published etc.). Yet the framing element is present: it is not a straight narrative, but a story couched within the framework of these nine letters, in which the letter-writer also communicates to his friend other things that have nothing to do with the actual story.

Asja (1857) does have the classical frame structure, although in a reduced form. It is again a story about somebody who is unsuccessful in the decisive moments of his life, who is worried and hampered by his own half-heartedness. He first makes some remarks about himself; then he starts his story. The first printing, in the *Sovremennik* of 1858, bears the subtitle "Rasskaz N. N.". But that is all that remained of the frame story idea. It looks like Turgenev got tired of coming out with that party of friends every time and starting the real story only after several introductory pages or paragraphs. It should be mentioned parenthetically that N. N.'s story contains a framed-in story, namely that which Asja's half-brother Gagin tells about her and himself; and in that story again the story is couched relating how Asja came into the world, as told by the man-servant.

The next novella, however, **"Pervaja ljubov'"**, written three years later (*Dvorjanskoe gnezdo* and *Nakanune* came in between), shows again the company of gentlemen, one of whom is talked into telling his love story, with a variation in that he does not start out immediately, but prefers first to write his account down and to read it at the company's next meeting. A concluding return to the company is again lacking. More traditional and complete in their frame structure are **"Sobaka"** (in which some persons of the listening company are described and called by their names, they repeatedly interrupt the narrator, a good-natured landowner from Kaluga, and come to the front again at the end to express their amazement at the inexplainable events) and **"Istorija lejtenanta Ergunova"**, a story which is not told once, but which the lieutenant repeats each month for the same group of people ("we"). The "I" of the framing text retells Ergunov's tale, and therefore we find in this inner story, as an exception, not first, but third person narration. The actual story is, in this manner, three times removed from the reader.

Next came **"Nesčastnaja"**, a frame story in its ideal form, so to speak. This time the framing story has just as much significance, content and dramatic climax as the framed one, with which it is organically connected. The inner story is placed approximately in the middle of the work (which is about 66 pages long) and constitutes more or less the clue to it. It was followed by Turgenev's most extensive novella, *Vešnie vody,* which does contain love reminiscences and possesses the characteristics of a frame story, but is not written in the first person. Sanin lets the events pass his mind's eye; subsequently the external story is taken up again, we see him returning to the place where thirty years ago the described events took place. All subsequent novellas: **"Son"**, **"Otryvki iz vospominanij svoich i čužich"** (consisting of two stories), **"Pesn' toržestvujuščej ljubvi"** and **"Klara Milič"** either are complete frame stories or at least contain some frame elements.

Now that we have ascertained how often Turgenev used these devices and procedures, we might ask *why* he did it. Every writer can have his own designs when using certain methods, or he can be led by certain motives without even being aware of them. As mentioned above, the "I"-procedure will lend a greater directness and verisimilitude to a story.[11] The effect seems to be that the author/narrator is drawn as closely as possible to the reader and the convincingness of the story is maximalized. The other device, the frame, has the opposite effect: that of removing the author from the reader, putting up a screen between them. It seems as if the author "pushes his responsibilities further and further away from himself", as Percy Lubbock put it: "this is not my story, says the author: you know nothing of me."[12]

Other reasons for using the frame structure include the author's wish to stylize, to embellish a story by providing it with an extra dimension; and his wish to write in the hero's own language, to render the speech of a person who does not use the regular literary language, but a dialect, an argot, children's language, or who speaks with a foreign accent. That is certainly a reason why Turgenev's contemporary Nikolaj Leskov so frequently used the device. In Turgenev's case this does not seem a strong motivation. It is true, the narrator of **"Sobaka"** has a parlance that is somewhat more juicy and jovial than Turgenev usually put into the mouths of his heroes from the landowning class; and the pope Aleksej, in **"Rasskaz otca Alekseja"**, tells his story, as he announces in the framing text, in his own simple words. However, by and large all Turgenev's heroes talk just like Turgenev wrote: a grammatically and stylistically impeccable and well constructed Russian. Of course, where Turgenev introduces a peasant, he will let him speak in his own way; Hirschel in the story **"Žid"** speaks with Jewish particularities, and the words of Pantaleone in *Vešnie vody* are interspersed with Italian. But if we take the main characters, and particularly the narrators in his shorter prose, they express themselves, as a rule, in Turgenev's own language; their usage of language can therefore not have been a compelling reason to avail himself of the frame device.

More momentous than all this was, in all likelihood, the literary tradition of which he was part and which he followed. As was indicated above, Turgenev did not invent the novella-with-frame, it was widely used before him—in fact, the novella as a literary genre was born with the frame structure: generated by Boccaccio, further developed by Chaucer etc. In Germany, the habit of clothing a story (novella) in a frame was very general; only after Goethe this form became less stereotyped, but it was by no means totally abandoned. Theodor Storm wrote his "Immensee" and several other works as frame stories. Turgenev, during the years he lived in Germany, met Storm and read and admired his writings. Likewise, in France he knew and appreciated

Prosper de Mérimée, whose novella "Carmen" had the frame structure. Even more important may have been the literary tradition in which Turgenev was brought up. It is characteristic that some of the most famous and influential love stories of the late 18th and early 19th centuries all had the frame form: "Manon Lescaut" by l'abbé Prévost, Goethe's "Leiden des jungen Werthers", Richardson's "Pamela" and "Clarissa Harlowe", Benjamin Constant's "Adolphe". Some of these consist of framed letters. "Adolphe", "une anecdote trouvée dans les papiers d'un inconnu", deeply impressed many Russians. By its theme (the tragedy of a love which extinguishes) and its atmosphere it is undoubtedly related to Turgenev's work and must have influenced him. In his dealing with the love theme, he continued preromantic and romantic traditions in form and fabula, spirit and style.

Aside from these international literary factors, however, there is the factor of personal disposition. Some writers are by nature more frank and unreserved, others more inhibited. Turgenev was not a person who would easily expose himself, either in daily life or as an author. Doesn't Henry James tell us that Turgenev would sometimes blush like a sixteen year old boy? From his correspondence, even with intimate friends, it also appears that he would be very careful not to exceed certain sexual and other decency norms. A certain prudery may well have contributed to his endeavor to erect screens between him and the reader. The class conventions and precepts in middle-19th century Russia were pretty rigorous: traditions, habits, decency rules played an important role in social life. And Turgenev was not a revolutionary in the realm of morals, not somebody to snap his fingers at all taboos. In European literature, certainly including Russian literature, it was not yet generally acceptable to delve deep into erotic questions in literary works, even though the romanticists had brought the individual emotional element and psychological analysis into the depiction of love.

If he nevertheless wanted to describe love, the most intimate human feelings, relations and situations, perhaps partly experienced by himself, he could do that no better than by writing in the first person and therewith stressing the personal and intimate character of the narrative, but at the same time, in order to avoid a shameful feeling and to keep a certain distance, by indicating that it was not he himself, but somebody totally different. This is no demonstrable truth, but a hypothesis which seems almost to force itself upon the reader of stories like *Asja* or *First Love.* And it would at least to a certain extent explain the fact that Turgenev so strikingly often applied a definite pattern or scheme (that of the company and the narrator). One could object, of course, that there are a few frame stories in which love does not play a role (**"Sobaka"**) or a very subordinate one (**"Stepnoj korol' Lir"**), so they would not require

the frame. On the other hand, one might object, there are a few stories that do have the erotic element but are missing the encompassing frame (like **"Zatiš'e"** or **"Klara Milič"**), or that are framed love stories, but do not have the first person narration (*Vešnie vody*). But we do not propose an absolute rule, just a tendency; it would be strange and contradict Turgenev's many-sidedness if he would have moulded all his shorter prose works in exactly identical forms.

When the inner story is relatively slight or merges with the dominating frame, our hypothesis does not apply; the function of the inner story may then be to give a character some background, to clarify a situation or somebody's action, or sometimes just to vivify or retard the action. To heighten the interest, to make the story more colorful, Turgenev had, of course, more means at his disposal. One of his typical methods is to start out with an extensive description of the surroundings in which the action is going to take place, and subsequently of the dramatis personae—a description not always indispensable for our understanding of the course of events (in **"Brigadir"**, for example). The counterpart of this lengthy, leisurely introduction is his urge to inform us about the lives of his protagonists after the story or novel is finished—as if he is unable to take leave of them, as if an urge for completeness makes it impossible for him to suddenly leave them alone, without communicating anything about their further lot. Perhaps he was of the opinion that the reader, who was so intensively engaged in the lives of these heroes, has the right (and must have the desire) to learn about their later fortunes. "I konec?", sprosit, možet byt', neudovletvorennyj čitatel'. "A čto že stalos' potom s Lavreckim? S Lizoj?"—that's how he starts the brief epilogue to *Dvorjanskoe gnezdo,* and similar words are used in the epilogue to *Otcy i deti.* This phenomenon is, of course, not restricted to Turgenev—it has to do with the quiet flow and elaborateness of 18th-19th century prose and of life in general in those times. All Turgenev's novels (with the exception of *Nov'*) possess—each in its own way—such a "perspectivistic" ending. But epilogues appear also in his shorter works. Strangely enough, he has one even in his very first play, **"Neostorožnost'"** (1843): it ends with a separate scene that takes place "ten years after", with its own decoration etc., in which only two short sentences are being pronounced. Virtually all his novellas are "epilogical". Even when a correspondence is rendered (**"Perepiska"**, **"Faust"**), the last letter has a conclusive, more or less philosophical character. In **"Tri vstreči"** and **"Jakov Pasynkov"**, one might say the whole last chapter serves as an epilogue. In **"Bretter"**, which climaxes toward the end with a duel of the two male heroes (and a duel is a very common apogee in many stories), during which the *bretter* (fighter) kills the tragic hero Kister—Turgenev cannot refrain from adding a last sentence: "Maša . . . vse ešče živet"—a sentence which seems, at least to us, modern readers, an anticlimax after the dramatic finale and could better have been left out.

In short, frames and epilogues, together with nature descriptions and milieu evocations, personal portraits and biographies, interpolated addresses to the reader of a general, philosophical or contemplative nature, belong to Turgenev's stock of attributes which he used to build up and clothe the skeleton of his works and to make them more appealing, livelier and more personal.

Notes

1. In the edition I. S. Turgenev, *Sobranie sočinenij,* 11 vols., Moskva: Pravda, 1949.

2. See Joseph Kunz, ed., *Novelle.* Darmstadt: Wissenschaftliche Buchgesellschaft, 1968, p. 4.

3. Quoted by Arnold Hirsch, *Der Gattungsbegriff "Novelle".* Berlin: E. Ehering, 1928, p. 42.

4. Cf. G. B. Kurljandskaja, *Struktura povesti i romana I. S. Turgeneva 1850-ch godov.* Tula: Priokskoe kn. izdatel'stvo, 1977, p.3.

5. Hans Hermann Malmede, *Wege zur Novelle,* Theorie und Interpretation der Gattung Novelle . . . Stuttgart, 1966, p. 155.

6. Ibid.

7. Joseph Kunz, *op.cit.,* pp. 229-231.

8. Ibid., pp. 10-14.

9. Reinhold Trautmann, "Turgenjew als Novellist", a valuable text for this theme; in his *Turgenjew und Tschechow,* Leipzig: Volk und Buch Verlag, 1948, p. 21.

10. G. B. Kurljandskaja, *op.cit.,* pp. 229-231.

11. Cf. T. Eekman, "The 'Frame Story' in Russian Literature and A. P. Čechov", *Signs of Friendship,* To Honour A. G. F. van Holk . . . , ed. J. J. van Baak, Amsterdam: Rodopi, 1984, p. 404.

12. Percy Lubbock, *The Craft of Fiction,* New York: Jonathan Cape & Harrison Smith, 1931, p. 147.

13. Of course, not every reader is equally charmed by Turgenev's shorter prose works: Vladimir Nabokov thought that "As a story-teller, he is artificial and even lame . . . His literary genius falls short on the score of literary imagination." (In his essay "Turgenev", *Lectures on Russian Literature,* New York-London: Harcourt Brace Jovanovich, 1981, p. 70).

James B. Woodward (essay date 1988)

SOURCE: Woodward, James B. "Determinism in the Novels of Turgenev." *Scando-Slavica* 34 (1988): 17-27.

[*In the following essay, Woodward discusses Turgenev's consistent treatment in his novels of characters who are powerless and unable to direct their own lives.*]

The essential impotence of man is the most basic and consistent theme of Turgenev's fiction. In the works of no other major Russian writer is the individual portrayed as so limited by the very nature of his being in his freedom of choice, in the opportunities allowed him to shape his own destiny. He is perpetually prey to the influence of "forces" which he is usually powerless to resist or comprehend. Thus the hero of the story **"Son"** describes a typical experience: "Only then did I realise that from morning onwards I had been led by unknown forces, that I was in their power, and for several moments there was nothing in my soul except the incessant lapping of the sea and a mute terror before the fate that had taken possession of me."[1]

Experiences of this kind, as this story illustrates, are particularly prominent in the shorter works, especially those written, like **"Son"** itself, in the last two decades of Turgenev's life, and indeed it has been argued that the novels were written as a kind of refuge from the view of life which such experiences reflect. According to this argument, the hero as Everyman is replaced in the novels by the hero as social man; the dimensions of time and space are restored; released from the timeless realm of the short fiction, in which he confronts the mysteries of life in helpless isolation, he is transposed to a particular society at a particular moment in its history with needs to which he can respond and which inspire him with a sense of purpose and duty, with a belief in his ability to influence events which "protects him from the storms of the passionate elements".[2] But the difference is plainly more apparent than real. For Rudin, Lavreckij, Insarov and Bazarov there is no "protection" in the social arena. The role of Everyman is not relinquished by the heroes of the novels, and they accordingly emerge as no less exposed. "He had a single feeling", we read of Litvinov in **Dym**: "the blow had fallen, his life was snapped like a rope, and with his whole being he was drawn forward and seized by something unknown and cold" (IX, 257).

Thus no such distinction can reasonably be made between the heroes of the novels and those of the tales. They are equally prey to "unknown forces". Yet there is nevertheless a difference between them which critical comment has not fully clarified. It is that the fateful "forces" which invade their lives have a precise and consistent significance in the novels which Turgenev enables the reader to determine. The reader is not left, as he is in the tales, simply to reflect on the mysteries described. Such mysteries in the novels are always presented as effects deriving from specified causes. These causes are usually "unknown" to the characters, and their effects are consequently likewise "unknown", but both are "known" to Turgenev himself. The events and catastrophes experienced by the characters as the disruptive incursions of irrational "forces" are expressions in the novels of a conception of life which, if highly personal and contentious, is nevertheless rational. It thus follows that the characters' interpretations of events are rarely to be taken as reflecting the true state of affairs. Between author and characters there is always a distance which implies divergent levels of understanding. This divergence may not always be immediately apparent, for the author's understanding is seldom made explicit and has usually to be inferred from oblique indications. But it always exists, and to overlook it is invariably to misinterpret the situation.

A pertinent example of such misinterpretation is the usually unquestioning acceptance by criticism of the reason given for the disasters that overtake them by the heroines of *Dvorjanskoe gnezdo* and *Nakanune.* In both cases they are attributed to divine intervention. The "resurrection" from the dead of Lavreckij's wife and the fatal illness that strikes Insarov are viewed by them as punishments inflicted by God for the "sin" of aspiring to personal happiness. They accordingly conclude from their experiences that self-renunciation is the law of God's world and that man's duty on earth is to work for others, and this conclusion is normally regarded as expressing the view of Turgenev himself. But obvious questions are immediately triggered. Thus if God insists on self-renunciation, why is Rudin, who so eloquently preaches this gospel, so brutally dispatched on the Parisian barricade? Moreover, if the love of Elena and Insarov is criminal, why is it initially declared by a shrine, as if with the blessing of the God who destroys them? And similarly, how is the God who punishes Lavreckij and Liza to be reconciled with the "force" that brings them together? Unless these contradictions are meant to suggest that the world is ruled by a fickle God, they can only be regarded as challenging the assumption that Elena and Liza are speaking for Turgenev. A brief examination of the last of these episodes will confirm that his view is really quite different.

The reference is to the episode in chapter 34 of *Dvorjanskoe gnezdo* in which Lavreckij, after taking his leave of Liza, sets off for a stroll in the warm night air. In the course of the walk he encounters "a narrow path" which leads him to "a long fence and a small gate", and "without knowing why", we read, "he tried pushing it". Turgenev continues:

> It creaked faintly and opened just as if it had been waiting for the touch of his hand. Lavreckij found himself in a garden, took a few steps along an avenue of limes and suddenly stopped in amazement: he recognized the Kalitins' garden . . . "This was intended", he thought.

The episode culminates in his meeting in the garden with Liza, his declaration of love and their embrace. "Something brought me here", he says to her, and on returning to the gate to leave, he finds that it is locked and is obliged to jump over the fence (VII, 235-6).

Like Litvinov, therefore, Lavreckij is "seized by something unknown", and it is similarly implausible to equate this "force" with the vengeful Creator invoked later in the novel. Far from impeding his pursuit of happiness, it is evidently intent on propelling him towards it, overcoming in the process his psychological resistance. Three chapters earlier he had asked himself: "Can it be that at thirty-five years of age I have nothing better to do than once again place my soul in the hands of a woman?" (VII, 226). Like Liza he is torn between will and conscience, between the competing claims of happiness and duty. But now the conflict is abruptly resolved, and his power of decision is mysteriously preempted. He is led to the gate (*kalitka*) which admits him to Liza (Kalitina) "as if it had been waiting for the touch of his hand", and after he has passed through it, it promptly locks itself, as if to bar his withdrawal from the world that he has entered—from the garden and its gift of love and happiness.

Thus again questions are prompted: if this "unknown force" is not Liza's God, what is it? And what happens to make Lavreckij susceptible to its influence so soon after voicing his profound inhibitions? The answers are implicit in the description of the scene, for Lavreckij succumbs to the "unknown" influence on emerging from the house into the world of nature. Nature, the "greatest character in all Turgenev's works",[3] is the "force" that leads him irresistibly to the gate. The episode recalls the scene in chapter 20 in which pensively he gazes at the surrounding landscape and is moved to remark by his sense of nature's power: "Whoever enters its circle must submit" (VII, 190). His experience in chapter 34 is a demonstration of this truth, and it demonstrates, in addition, what "submission" means. Paradoxically it means the assertion of the self. It means the submission of reason to the subconscious will, the merging of the will with the will of nature and the consequent eclipse of reason and conscience. This process is conveyed by the description itself. On this night, it is noted, "there was no moon" (VII, 235). The gloom is at once the darkness of the night and the darkness of Lavreckij's unillumined subconscious, while the fence and the gate are the symbols of his inhibitions which now lose in the darkness their power to deter him. And the effect of this combination of the two levels of meaning is to evoke subtly a sense of the interaction between them. To the will of nature that leads him to Liza his subconscious will instinctively responds, and like Litvinov, who is similarly drawn to Irina and impelled to betray his fiancée Tanja, he becomes momentarily deaf to duty's call.

But between the two episodes there is the notable difference that Lavreckij's experience is described by the author. The invasion of his mind is presented, in short, as an objective reality, not a subjective impression, and the result is an unusually direct revelation of Turgenev's personal understanding of life. The episode announces that, contrary to the belief of Elena and Liza, the God who presides over human affairs is the God whose will is reflected in nature—a God who demands of man not altruistic self-sacrifice but precisely the opposite: the pursuit of self-interest. Human nature, it proclaims, is fundamentally egoistic and, as such, is the expression of a universal law to which man, as a part of nature, is unalterably subject. *This* is the law, it states, to which man must submit, and it is on those who defy *this* law that punishment is visited. Hence the punishment inflicted later on Lavreckij and Liza in the appropriate form of the egoistic Varvara, who duly returns to destroy their happiness as the symbol incarnate of nature's law. Liza's "crime" is not her surrender to love but, on the contrary, the sense of guilt which this surrender inspires, her inability to commit herself totally to it, to banish the consciousness of her obligations to others. And while blessing Elena's declaration of love, God inflicts on Insarov, as earlier on Rudin, the punishment of death for the similar "crime", for "sacrificing self-interest to the common good" (VI, 267).

The episode, therefore, not only confirms the distance that exists between Turgenev and his characters; it also prompts a notably different view of his thought in the novels from that which is usually taken. Affirming the primacy of the will, it proclaims obedience to the will as a "law" of life, as the law imposed by an active God conceived as one with the will of nature. As a result it prompts also a revision of the judgement that he lacked a conception of "universal life". Thus the Soviet scholar V. M. Markovič writes in this connection:

> The novels of Turgenev do not reveal a higher purpose in life. The category of "universal life", which is characteristic of Tolstoj and also, in a particular variant, of Dostoevskij, is plainly alien to the thought of Turgenev in his art. Yet in the Russian novel the idea of a possible harmonious reunification of the individual and the world, the idea of interaction between the individual and the general, is connected precisely with this category. Turgenev was evidently far from such ideas.[4]

The episode certainly substantiates the first of these comments. It confirms that Turgenev did indeed differ from Tolstoj and Dostoevskij in having no vision of a higher purpose in life, of a transcendent moral principle operating in the universe. It indicates also, however, that the "category of 'universal life'" is not "alien" to his thought, that he had a vision of a transcendent *amoral* principle operating in the universe. And it indicates, in addition, that he was no less concerned than his two great contemporaries with "the idea of interaction between the individual and the general". Indeed, this "idea" lies so crucially at the heart of the Turgenevan novel that unless it is recognised, his main purpose is obscured. For it may certainly be argued, at least in respect of the first four of his novels, not only that their major episodes, like the episode described, all hinge on

"interaction" of precisely this kind, but that the consequences of resisting it are their central theme. Each novel essentially poses the same question. As M. O. Geršenzon puts it, Turgenev asks: should man be "nature", or should he be an individual?[5] Should he, in other words, "submit", or should he rebel? Should he simply obey his "natural" instinct and commit himself totally to the pursuit of self-interest, or should he assert his individuality by suppressing this instinct and "sacrificing self-interest to the common good"? Turgenev's heroes make the latter choice. They are all "individuals" or rebels in this sense, and nature's interventions are thereby explained. The invasions of their minds by "unknown forces" are nature's attempts to bring them back into the fold, to re-forge the severed link between "the individual" and "the general". They are the manifestations of their "interaction". And if "harmonious reunification" does not result, then nature secures it by inflicting death, thereby achieving the "eternal reconciliation" announced by the flowers on Bazarov's grave (VIII, 402). Herein lies the reason why in Turgenev's novels the only characters to die are the altruistic heroes, the characters who are guided not by nature's "logic" but by the "logic" which Turgenev contrasts as "human". "Nature takes no account of logic", he states in *Dym,* "of our human logic; it has its own logic which we do not understand and do not acknowledge until it runs over us like a wheel" (IX, 287). Such is the customary fate of his heroes.

The episode in *Dvorjanskoe gnezdo,* therefore, illuminates the deterministic understanding of life that lies at the basis of the Turgenevan novel. The intervention of the "force" to which Lavreckij submits is not a fortuitous or illogical event but the active response of Turgenev's God—identified, as stated, with the universal will—to the inhibitions which deter him from observing His "law". And we may now understand why Lavreckij is propelled in the episode towards love and why the experience of love in the Turgenevan novel is of such central importance for all the heroes. For the desire for love to which they all succumb is the most potent and disruptive of nature's interventions. Hence the open-air setting in which love is declared in *Rudin* (VI, 311) and *Nakanune* (VIII, 93-4) as well as *Dvorjanskoe gnezdo.* It is the primary expression of nature's "logic", a manifestation of the "natural" self, whereby nature most insistently contrives to shake the "unnatural" foundations of "human logic", to assert its authority over rebellious "individuals" and reintegrate them with the unity of "universal life". The coincidences in the novels are thus explained. Elena's chance meeting with Insarov by the shrine (VIII, 91) and Litvinov's second meeting with Irina in Baden-Baden (IX, 199) are no less the work of nature's will than Lavreckij's meeting with Liza in the garden.

We observe that for the rebels love is always a shock, an alien, disconcerting, disorienting "force", as the ineptitude of Rudin so vividly demonstrates in his tragicomic relationship with Natal'ja Lasunskaja. Both Insarov and Bazarov struggle to resist it. "I don't need the love of a Russian girl", cries the Bulgarian hero to Bersenev's astonishment, and he refuses to grant Elena's request for a final meeting before his departure (VIII, 86-7). Bazarov likewise reacts with dismay and irritation to the feelings aroused by the imperious Odincova (VIII, 270, 285). And Liza's response to Lavreckij's kiss is similarly anguish, even "terror". "I am terrified", she cries. "What is this that we are doing?" (VII, 237). Her question encapsulates the sense of disorientation induced by the collisions between the two kinds of "logic" represented as collisions between two kinds of love. "She loved everyone", we read of Liza, "and no one in particular" (VII, 234), and Rudin, Insarov, Bersenev and Bazarov are similarly characterised by this impersonal love, by the same general concern for the "common good" that Bersenev defends at the beginning of *Nakanune* (VIII, 14). But all are seduced from this selfless concern by the irresistible attractions of "someone in particular". All succumb to the temptations of "love-delight" which Bersenev contrasts with his ardent "love-sacrifice", and the result is the crises which herald the failure of their noble rebellions against nature's "logic".

The love-relationship, therefore, in the Turgenevan novel, as the episode in chapter 34 of *Dvorjanskoe gnezdo* confirms, is itself a reflection—indeed, the principal reflection—of its creator's deterministic conception of life. But the contrast developed between the two kinds of love has an additional dimension which explains the complexity of Turgenev's attitude both to life and to the rebels whom he plainly admires. For they are contrasted not only as egoistic and altruistic, but also as irrational or sensual and cerebral. "Love-delight" is experienced by the Turgenevan hero not only as submission to the demands of the will, but equally as an irrational submission to beauty. Itself irrational, the beauty of the heroine duly evokes his irrational response. It is an expression, like the landscapes, of nature's beauty and thus likewise an instrument of nature's will. And the same is true of all the other forms of beauty inspired by the beauty of nature and love which habitually bombard the Turgenevan hero—above all, of course, the beauty of art. Hence Insarov's exposure to the art of Venice on the eve of the "fisherman's" intervention to claim him.[6] The beauty of the landscapes, woman and art is the weapon which nature consistently deploys in its battle to convert the cerebral idealist.

Thus as the embodiment of the essential reality of life nature presents itself in the novels in two contrasting forms: in the form of the coercive universal will, which links the individual with the whole of creation, and in the form of rationally inexplicable beauty. Turgenev depicts it as a two-faced Janus, as the source of conflict in all its forms (including social conflict and the "conflict" of love)[7], and as the source of man's most sublime experiences, of the value that he regarded as transcending all others. Hence the characteristic ambivalence of his attitude to life—an ambivalence reflected in the two types of character that he contrasts in the novels with his "unnatural" heroes. On the one side are the egoists, the incarnations of the will, on the other the devotees of nature's beauty. Occasionally the two types are fused into one, as in *Rudin* in the figure of the loathsome Pandalevskij who declares "the enjoyment of nature" to be his "passion" (VI, 245); more usually they are presented as quite distinct and consequently appear to have little in common. But in relation to the hero they perform a uniform role, illuminating by contrast his alienation from reality in one or the other of its two distinct forms. Thus Rudin, who is keenly responsive to beauty but suffers from a crippling weakness of will, is confronted with an indomitably powerful will in the person of Dar'ja Michajlovna Lasunskaja, while Bazarov, who possesses a powerful will but regards nature as nothing more than a "workshop" for man (VIII, 236), is similarly "exposed" by the nature-lover Arkadij. Lasunskaja and Arkadij, for all the differences between them, are essentially the two sides of a single coin, performing a role that may now be seen to be directly comparable to that of the heroines. They too exist as personified comments on the limitations or incompleteness of the "unnatural" idealists and similarly as instruments of nature's will directed against the rebels who dare to defy it. No less than the beauty of the heroines and the landscapes, they too embody the "unknown force" which the heroes engage in futile combat.

But the determinism which lies at the basis of the novels is still more extensive than these comments have suggested, for the hero's fate is determined in two distinct senses. Not only is he doomed as a rebel to defeat; he is also doomed to be a rebel. For Turgenev represents as a coercive "force" not only the irresistible "logic" of nature but equally the contrasting "human logic", the spirit of commitment to altruistic self-sacrifice. His heroes are not rebels of their own volition. They are propelled into their futile conflicts with nature by a "force" which they are equally powerless to control—by the "unknown force" of their genetic inheritance. Their rebellions may express a moral protest, but they are not the result of free moral choices. They are fundamentally expressions of inherited traits and, as such, explain why Turgenev is accustomed to introduce at least one of his heroes' parents. "Everyone remains as nature made him", Ležnev remarks to the hero in *Rudin* (VI, 367), thus implicitly ascribing Rudin's challenge to nature less to the influence of Hegelian thought than to the inherited influence of his self-sacrificing mother. In the words of Neždanov, "the whole crux of the matter is not one's convictions but rather one's character" (XII, 229).[8] Like the Slavophilism of Lavreckij and the materialism of Bazarov, whose mothers are similarly unpretentious and self-effacing, Rudin's ideas are merely the particular form in which the genetic imperative expresses itself.[9] Hence the paradox that even in his capacity as rebel the Turgenevan hero is still "submissive". His fatal disregard for the imperative of nature is the result of his unconscious, instinctive obedience to the bequeathed imperative to work for others which, as Rudin puts it to Ležnev, is the "worm" that "gnaws" him (VI, 357).[10] And it is precisely the conflict between the two imperatives that the introduction of *both* parents in the novels implies, as in the stories of Lavreckij, Elena and Bazarov. The two parents contrast as living embodiments of "human logic" and the "logic" of nature, as the sources of the conflict experienced by their children between conscience and will or between reason and the irrational. As a result Lavreckij's "submission" to nature may be aptly described in different terms—as denoting the "submission" of the legacy of his mother to that of his father, the self-assertive Ivan, while conversely his devotion to the well-being of his serfs is plainly an expression of Malan'ja's influence. His story is the record of his continual oscillation between the "forces" bequeathed by his contrasting parents.[11]

Viewed in this light, therefore, the entire story of the typical Turgenevan hero can be seen to be determined from the outset. He is the victim of a conflict that is not of his making. His actions result in the final reckoning not from consciously or laboriously formulated decisions but from the balance of "forces" in his own personality. Hence Lavreckij's "submission" in the episode described. The "interaction" takes place because it is genetically determined, because he is the "son of nature" whom his father created (VII, 163) as well as the son of Malan'ja whom his father destroyed. And this conception of man's destiny as implacably decreed has clear implications for Turgenev's technique, explaining those features of his character-portraits which distinguish him sharply from Dostoevskij and Tolstoj. Most notably, it explains why motives are rarely subjected to analysis, for there can be no analysis if there is no motive, if action is the result not of motive but of impulse or, as Bazarov puts it, merely of "sensation", of the "structure" of the "brain".[12] Instead of analysis there is oblique explanation—the explanations provided by the portraits of the parents, by the hero's relations with the secondary characters and by the manner in which he responds to beauty in the variety of forms in which it confronts him.

The view of personality as formed from birth[13] explains also why the novels' characters do not develop.[14] It is commonly argued in this connection that Turgenev presents only the final "results of the psychological pro-cess" as distinct from its preparatory or formative stages,[15] but the term "process" is misleading for the reasons stated. For neither Rudin nor Bazarov can easily be imagined as subjecting their ideas to critical assessment, as engaging in a preliminary inner debate. Their ideas are embraced not as the fruits of intellectual enquiry but instinctively as expressions of their determined "sensations".[16] It is true that development appears to take place as a result of the heroes' characteristic inconsistency. While expounding their ideas, they all succumb, as stated, to the temptation represented by the beauty of the heroine and thus appear to depart from their established image. Hence Markovič's contention that there is usually a contradiction between the portrait of the hero presented at the beginning and the image that emerges later from "the dynamics of the plot".[17] But the contradiction is not only itself determined by the conflict of "forces" within his personality; it is also invariably foreshadowed from the start—by the contradictions, for example, in Rudin's physical portrait (VI, 258),[18] by the portraits of Lavreckij's contrasting parents, by the reference to the "hollow chest" of the powerful Insarov (VIII, 37) and by the "something" which "to some people was even repellent" that coexists in Elena with her altruistic zeal (VIII, 32). And even in the absence of a detailed initial portrait the inconsistency of the hero is clearly predicted. Thus Bazarov's relationship with the aptly named Arkadij alludes from the beginning to the acute inner conflict signalled later by his reaction to nature's charms in the form of the beauty of the cold Odincova. In each case the plot is basically a dramatisation of the psychological conflict initially conveyed. In this sense the role of the static portraits is comparable to that of such episodes or omens as Insarov's dream of his death in chapter 24 of *Nakanune* (VIII, 117). Just as such omens "are always fulfilled",[19] so the portraits anticipate the conflicts that follow.

Thus between thought and technique there is a clear correspondence. The characters are presented in a manner which reflects their creator's deterministic conception of life. To the "forces" which dictate their attitudes and actions corresponds the "force" represented by their predictive portraits. Their freedom is as limited in the fiction as in life, and in this sense the form is a mirror of the content.

Notes

1. I. S. Turgenev, *Polnoe sobranie sočinenij i pisem: Sočinenija* 9, Moskva-Leningrad 1966, p. 285. All subsequent references to Turgenev's works are to the fifteen volumes of works in this edition and are hereafter entered in the text by volume and page numbers.

2. V. M. Fišer, "Povest' i roman u Turgeneva", in *Tvorčestvo Turgeneva,* edited by I. N. Rozanov and Ju. M. Sokolov, Moskva 1920, p. 23.

3. S. A. Andreevskij, *Literaturnye očerki,* 4th supplemented edn., Peterburg 1913, p. 259.

4. V. M. Markovič, *Čelovek v romanach Turgeneva,* Leningrad 1975, p. 69.

5. M. O. Geršenzon, *Mečta i mysl' I. S. Turgeneva,* Moskva 1919, p. 111.

6. Cf. the comparison of death in *Nakanune* to "a fisherman" who "has caught a fish in his net" (VIII, 166).

7. Cf. his definition of the relationship between lovers in his story *Perepiska* as a relationship between "master" and "slave" (VI, 190).

8. Cf. V. M. Markovič's comment: "The vital aim of Turgenev's heroes and the heroines has no positive basis outside their own personalities. The aim is set for the hero by his inner aspirations and needs; all the bases that come from without are plainly 'secondary'" (Markovič, *op. cit.,* p. 102).

9. Cf. his remark to Ležnev: "I was born a rolling stone . . . I cannot stop" (VI, 366).

10. Cf. the "mysterious inner worm" that "gnaws" and "preys upon" Neždanov (XII, 80).

11. Cf. Neždanov's remark to Marianna in *Nov'*: "There are two men in me, and the one does not allow the other to live" (XII, 279).

12. Cf. his remarks to Arkadij: "Why do I like chemistry? Why do you like apples? It's all a matter of sensation. It's all the same. Deeper than that men will never penetrate" (VIII, 325).

13. Cf. Potugin's comment in *Dym*: "A man enters the grave as he entered the cradle" (IX, 238).

14. On the difference between the characters of the novels and those of some of the shorter works in this respect cf. R. E. Matlaw, "Turgenev's Novels: Civic Responsibility and Literary Predilection", *Harvard Slavic Studies* 4, 1957, p. 258.

15. G. B. Kurljandskaja, *Chudožestvennyj metod Turgeneva-romanista.* Tula 1972, p. 228. Cf. the comment on Turgenev's portrait of Bazarov in D. I. Pisarev, *Sobranie sočinenij* 2, Moskva 1955, pp. 30-1.

16. For this reason, as V. M. Markovič has observed (*op. cit.,* p. 96), it is impossible to accept L. V. Pumpjanskij's argument that the Turgenevan hero is the product of a particular "culture" (L. V. Pumpjanskij, "Romany Turgeneva i roman 'Nakanune'. Istoriko-literaturnyj očerk", in I. S. Turgenev, *Sočinenija* 6, Moskva-Leningrad 1930, p. 17).

17. Markovič, *op. cit.,* pp. 52-4, 58-9.

18. Cf. G. A. Bjalyj, *Turgenev i russkij realizm,* Moskva-Leningrad 1962, p. 79.

19. M. A. Petrovskij, "Tainstvennoe u Turgeneva", in *Tvorčestvo Turgeneva,* edited by I. N. Rozanov and Ju. M. Sokolov, Moskva 1920, p. 96.

David A. Lowe (essay date 1988)

SOURCE: Lowe, David A. "Turgenev and the Critics." In *Critical Essays on Ivan Turgenev,* pp. 1-15. Boston: G. K. Hall, 1988.

[In the following essay, Lowe provides an overview of the critical response to Turgenev's work.]

TURGENEV AND THE CRITICS

As an artist, Ivan Turgenev has long since acquired the reputation of an apostle of moderation. As Dmitry Merezhkovsky noted in a presentation delivered in 1909, "In Russia, in a land of every sort of maximalism, revolutionary and religious, a land of self-immolations, a land of the most frenzied excesses, Turgenev is practically our only *genius of the right measure* after Pushkin. . . ."[1] Predictably, however, especially in a Russian context, Turgenev's perceived moderation and minimalism evoked extreme responses in his lifetime and continue to produce partisan reactions even today.

The major issues in Turgenev criticism revolve around a few fundamental polarities, most of them interrelated and several of them having perhaps more to do with Turgenev's biography than with his art. One area of dispute concerns Turgenev's perceived, alleged, or proclaimed geopolitical stance with regard to Russia's centuries-old uncertainty about her national identity. The question may be summarized as Turgenev the Russian versus Turgenev the European. During Turgenev's lifetime, Western Europe generally saw him as piquantly Russian, while as far as someone like Dostoevsky was concerned, Turgenev compromised himself all the way around by showing a slavish devotion to Europe, especially to Germany. By regularly emphasizing Russia's status as a European nation, Turgenev himself strove for a synthesis on this point, but few of his critics have shown a desire to erase any boundaries, metaphoric or real, between Europe and Russia.

Although Turgenev always described himself as apolitical, a second, related motif in the literature about him emphasizes his political sympathies. Dostoevsky, for instance, saw Turgenev as an archetypical Westernizing Russian liberal of the 1840s. As part of his dramatization of the thesis that the liberals of Turgenev's generation had given metaphoric birth to the radicals and revolutionaries of the 1860s, Dostoevsky lampooned Turgenev in at least two characters in *The Possessed*—Karmazinov, the "famous writer," and the elder Verkhovensky, an amoral, fatuous windbag. A quite contrary view of Turgenev's politics informs a Soviet article from the 1950s, wherein the author maintains that Soviet children should not be encouraged to read a novel as reactionary as *Fathers and Sons*.[2]

In his remarks on Turgenev, Merezhkovsky makes use of one of his favorite devices, the paradox, to explain the contradictory readings of Turgenev's political stance: "Turgenev, as opposed to our great creators and destroyers Tolstoy and Dostoevsky, is our only guardian, our only conservative, and like any true conservative, is at the same time a liberal" (58). Few other of Turgenev's critics have attempted to see both sides of this question, and much commentary on Turgenev, especially in the nineteenth century, assigns the writer praise or blame on the primary basis of the presumed political judgments expressed overtly or implicitly in specific works.

Whether Turgenev even lends himself to discussion in terms of geography or politics depends on the resolution of another major question in Turgenev criticism, namely, that of the nature of his subject matter. Critics tend to operate from one or the other of two presumptions—either that Turgenev's works reproduce Russian reality or that his writings reflect and treat universal, timeless human concerns. In the past century, critics of virtually all stripes paid the greatest heed to those works inviting or at least permitting discussion based on perceived similarities or discrepancies between the world portrayed in them and Russia at large. In practice, that meant a primary focus on the cycle *Notes of a Hunter* and on Turgenev's six novels. Few critics took cognizance of Turgenev's poetry, short stories, and plays, all of which offer relatively ungrateful material for interpreters who see literature as a branch of photojournalism.

An allied topic contrasts Turgenev the novelist with Turgenev the short story writer, poet, or playwright. During his lifetime, Turgenev's acclaim, though certainly due in no small part to *Notes of a Hunter,* ultimately rested on his novels. Since then, however, many of his stories and at least one of his plays, *A Month in the Country,* have captured the serious attention of both the critics and the public. Indeed, in the twentieth century, as influential a critic as D. S. Mirsky has argued that the sociopolitical aspect of Turgenev's oeuvre, the "stuffing" in his novels, has grown more and more stale, while the essential poetry and lyricism, especially of the stories, emerge with a freshness and purity that earlier critical stances and readers' attitudes in fact hin-

dered.[3] Not everyone would agree with that assessment, of course, and Turgenev's novels continue to generate studies with such titles as "Turgenev: The Politics of Hesitation."[4]

A fifth major controversy in the literature about Turgenev arises from disagreement over whether Turgenev's manner of writing represents realism or something other than realism. In the Anglophone world, such influential critics as William Dean Howells and Henry James promoted Turgenev as a founding father of realism. Until quite recently, Soviet criticism, which made a fetish of realism and treated romanticism as an ideological malady not far removed from outright sedition, also proclaimed Turgenev one of the fountainheads of Russian realism. Many of Turgenev's contemporaries, however, observed that his art had deep roots in romanticism, a fact that Western scholarship has begun emphasizing in the last twenty years or so. Meanwhile, at the beginning of the twentieth century several Russian poets and prose writers of the modernist persuasion cited Turgenev as an important influence on their styles or themes. Contemporary Turgenev scholarship continues to try to distinguish the romantic or symbolist from the realistic elements in Turgenev's style. As a consequence, few critics nowadays, even in the Soviet Union, label Turgenev a realist without swathing that epithet in several layers of qualifications.

Although modern literary theory has considerably discredited the notion of style and content as discrete entities, much Turgenev criticism continues the nineteenth-century tradition of distinguishing the medium from the message in Turgenev's works. Radical critics in Turgenev's day almost completely discounted questions of style, while the so-called aesthetic critics discussed the perceived apparatus of Turgenev's art. In the early decades of this century, the Russian Formalists penned several important studies of Turgenev's poetry, plays, stories, and novels that evince little or no interest in hermeneutics, while post-Formalist criticism has tended to concern itself with the political, sociological, historical, or philosophical contexts of Turgenev's writings. In short, Turgenev criticism remains divided over what matters more in Turgenev's oeuvre—the "how" or the "what." Turgenev himself wanted it both ways. In the foreword to his novels he maintains that in art the question of how is always more important than the question of what, but he also averred that there were times in the life of a nation when art had to give way to other, more important considerations.

A final major point of contention concerns Turgenev's general merit as a writer. Although his reputation both at home and abroad fluctuated dramatically during the major part of his career, by the end of his life the world at large had declared Turgenev a classic. Almost immediately upon his death, however, voices began to question the scale and relevance of Turgenev's art. Merezh-kovsky summed up the situation in the early years of the twentieth century: "Turgenev, they say, is outmoded. The two gigantic caryatids of Russian literature—Tolstoy and Dostoevsky—really have overshadowed Turgenev for us. Forever? For long? Aren't we fated to return to him through them?" (58). Merezhkovsky's queries remain very much to the point today. Critics continue to argue about whether Turgenev belongs to the ranks of the geniuses or the journeymen.

All the polarities that shape discussion of Turgenev have their precedents in nineteenth-century criticism. Twentieth-century histories of Russian literary criticism generally identify three major groupings or schools of Russian criticism in the last century: radicals, conservatives, and aesthetic critics. These designations, a product of Russian cultural history and Soviet literary historiography, clearly demonstrate the confusion between political journalism and literary art characteristic of much nineteenth-century Russian writing about belles lettres. Furthermore, these conventional labels conceal important similarities between the radicals and conservatives and differences within individual camps. Nonetheless, as with the equally problematic terms *realism* and *romanticism,* the notion of nineteenth-century Russian critics as radicals, conservatives, or aesthetes has become such a fixture of literary discussion that it makes more sense to draw on it, albeit with reservations and disclaimers, than to attempt an entirely new system of classification.

In Soviet parlance the tag "radical democrats" almost always accompanies the radical critics. By and large, these literary commentators exerted the greatest influence of any critics of the age, and their views and general approach to literature have played a decisive role in the evolution of Soviet criticism as well. Few Soviet sources make any attempt to conceal the favored status granted the radicals. On the contrary, reference works often force the radicals upon the reading public in the same unsubtle way that Stalin made the poet Vladimir Mayakovsky a secular icon by dubbing him the "best and most talented poet" of the era and declaring indifference to his memory a crime. In Ye. Yefimov's *I. S. Turgenev: Seminar,* for instance, a standard guide for teachers, mention of nineteenth-century criticism of *On the Eve* is accompanied by the following unambiguous note of caution: "The treatment of the question of the appraisal of *On the Eve* by reactionary and liberal critics is to be limited to a few examples. The main attention is to be devoted to the criticism of the revolutionary democrats."[5]

The radical critics generally continued a mode and style of civic-minded criticism founded by Turgenev's friend and mentor, Vissarion Belinsky (1811-48). In Turgenev's mind, and not only in his, Belinsky represented many of the noblest strivings and best traits of the "men of the 1840s." That term, crucially important for any survey of the evolution of Russian culture in the last century, refers to the educated Russians of Turgenev and Belinsky's generation, men who helped shape modern Russian culture. Although the generation of the 1840s embraced both conservatives and revolutionaries, Slavophiles and Westernizers, theologians and atheists, virtually all the movers and shakers of the era shared a gentry provenance (the plebeian Belinsky being a major exception) and a dual commitment to art and the life of the mind. Thanks to their immersion in German idealism, the men of the 1840s in fact viewed art as the primary vehicle for describing and understanding the world.

Belinsky occasionally showed remarkable acumen, especially in spotting the talent of Lermontov, Dostoevsky, and Turgenev early on. One cannot overlook several lamentable aspects of his legacy, however. He boasted a leaden style, and as Mirsky observed, "It was Belinsky, more than anyone else, who poisoned literature by the itch for expressing ideas, which has survived so woefully long" (175). Mirsky means the Russian tendency, especially pronounced in the nineteenth century, to attempt to compensate for the lack of a free press by using writing about literature as an Aesopian forum, or even pulpit, from which to address the burning issues of the day. In this connection, a remark that Pushkin made in 1820 bears repeating: "We have literature of a sort, but we have no criticism."[6] Pushkin's complaint remained largely valid for the rest of the century. Russia's literary criticism, particularly in the nineteenth century and especially as practiced by Belinsky and his heirs, often reads like what the rest of the world would probably consider heavily politicized journalism on mostly nonliterary topics.

In his **"Recollections of Belinsky,"** Turgenev had the following to say about Belinsky's attitude toward his works: "As for me, I have to say that after the first salute that he made to my literary activity, he rather soon—and quite rightly—grew cold toward it; he could not have encouraged me in the composition of those verses and narrative poems which I had given myself up to at that time."[7] Turgenev is referring here to Belinsky's initial enthusiasm for such works as *Parasha* (1843), which the critic praised for their appeal to the intellect (the dread "ideas" to which Mirsky alludes) and for their "hints at Russian life."[8]

As for Belinsky's reaction to Turgenev's first efforts in prose, Turgenev recalls: "Although he was more satisfied with my prose works, he placed no special hopes on me" (Vol. 14, 52). Turgenev somewhat understates the case here. Belinsky in fact identified the initial sketches of *Notes of a Hunter* as among the best works of 1847 and argued that in them Turgenev had "approached the people [the peasantry] from a side from which no one before him had yet approached them."[9] Moreover, said Belinsky in a letter to Turgenev, the sketch **"Khor and Kalinych"** showed Turgenev's "true forte."[10] In the final analysis, however, Belinsky left no significant critical writing about Turgenev, and his views had no appreciable influence on the poetry and short stories that Turgenev produced during Belinsky's sadly short life. In his novels, however, whose appearance Belinsky did not live to see, Turgenev clearly heeded Belinsky's implicit demand for a socially conscious art. Turgenev admitted as much when he dedicated his supreme novelistic achievement, *Fathers and Sons,* to Belinsky.

While Belinsky distinguished art from bald propaganda, such was not the case with his spiritual progeny of the 1850s and 1860s, Nikolay Chernyshevsky (1828-89), Nikolay Dobrolyubov (1836-61), and Dmitry Pisarev (1840-68), who lacked Belinsky's grounding in German idealism. The evolution of the radicals' views on art, from the stingy utilitarianism propounded by Chernyshevsky in his notorious M.A. thesis, "The Aesthetic Relation between Art and Reality," to the wholesale destruction of aesthetics undertaken by Pisarev, follows an ascending curve of violence to the very concept of art as a legitimate form of human expression. Chernyshevsky launched the assault on art by declaring it at best a substitute for reality, and Pisarev brought the naive savagery to a simple-minded logical conclusion by declaring chemists always more useful than poets.

The arrival of the radicals on the literary scene in the late 1850s produced a dramatic change in the critical reception of Turgenev's works. Until then his stories and novels had garnered generally admiring reviews, but as a consequence of the radicalization of educated Russian society, Turgenev's works suddenly became the subject of vituperative polemical articles. Chernyshevsky's major contribution to the fray, a review of the story *Asya* (1858), bore the title "A Russian at the *Rendezvous.*"[11] Although Chernyshevsky sometimes showed himself capable of genuine insights into specific works of literature, especially Tolstoy's trilogy, *Childhood, Boyhood,* and *Youth,* "A Russian at the *Rendezvous*" sheds no light at all on Turgenev's story. Instead, in a manner typical of Russian literary criticism at its most irrelevant, this classic article uses Turgenev's utterly apolitical story as an opportunity to flail liberals in general and Turgenev in particular.

René Wellek points out that Chernyshevsky's junior colleague and protégé, Dobrolyubov, applied Chernyshevsky's views on aesthetics more systematically than did the senior critic himself.[12] As a consequence, Dobrolyubov occupies a position, modest, to be sure, in the evolution of a sociology of literature. In his articles he often dwelt on the differences between two genera-

tions of the Russian intelligentsia: the men of the 1840s and those of the 1860s. In Dobrolyubov's opinion, the representatives of Turgenev's generation suffered from a fatal attraction to endless and pointless philosophizing, while the radicals of the 1860s felt that the time had come to translate words into acts. In just that spirit Dobrolyubov wrote his most famous piece on Turgenev, a review of the novel *On the Eve* bearing the title "When Will the Real Day Come?"[13]

The hero of *On the Eve,* Insarov, is a Bulgarian freedom fighter. Reading Turgenev's novel as a documentary record of social history, Dobrolyubov accuses Turgenev's generation of an inability to produce men of action and resolve such as Insarov. In a passage that invites interpretation as a call to revolution, Dobrolyubov predicts the imminent appearance of a Russian Insarov:

> We shall not have to wait long for him; the feverishly painful impatience with which we are expecting his appearance in real life is the guarantee of this. We need him; without him our lives seem to be wasted, and every day means nothing in itself, but is only the eve of another day. That day will come at last! At all events, the eve is never far from the next day; only a matter of one night separates them.
>
> (226)

Of the radical critics of the 1850s and 1860s who addressed themselves to Turgenev's works, Pisarev alone demonstrated genuine insight. For all his usual extremism and iconoclasm, Pisarev's "Realists" and "Bazarov," both about *Fathers and Sons,* offer observations about the novel and its protagonists that even today may be accepted almost without reservation.[14] Pisarev understands, for instance, that as personalities, the nihilist Bazarov and the aristocrat Pavel Petrovich "are made of the same material."[15] More importantly, Pisarev sees what escaped many of his contemporaries—that the question of where Turgenev's sympathies lie in the novel lacks a pat answer.

All in all, in fact, Pisarev's articles on *Fathers and Sons* rank among the best nineteenth-century criticism of the work. Nevertheless, it should be noted that by their very perspicacity, "Realists" and "Bazarov" represent an exception within Pisarev's oeuvre, most of which sacrifices profundity for effect. Generally speaking, the radicals' criticism of Turgenev tells one much more about Russian cultural history than about Turgenev's works. However, an acquaintance with Chernyshevsky's and Dobrolyubov's otherwise irrelevant pieces on Turgenev serves as a valuable introduction to twentieth-century Turgenev criticism, much of which either continues the traditions of civic criticism or, conversely, rejects them in a frankly polemical manner.

The refusal to treat Turgenev's works as sociopolitical documents had its advocates among Turgenev's own contemporaries. By concentrating on Turgenev's stories of the 1850s and 1860s, the most important of the aesthetic critics, Alexander Druzhinin (1824-64), Vasily Botkin (1810-69), and Pavel Annenkov (1812-87)—all friends of Turgenev's—tried to divorce his art from politics. Druzhinin's major effort in that direction, the long article "*Stories and Tales by I. Turgenev*" (1857), attempts to counter earlier readings of Turgenev by radical critics or critics close to the radicals. Drawing on the nineteenth-century cliché that inanely dubbed Alexander Pushkin (1799-1837) an art-for-art's sake poet devoid of a civic conscience and Nikolay Gogol (1809-52) a nitty-gritty realist, Druzhinin maintains that critics writing before him

> . . . see a realist artist in the most charming idealist and dreamer who has ever appeared among us. They hail a creator of objective works in a person full of lyricism and impetuous, uneven subjectivity in his art. They dream of a continuer of Gogol in a person raised on Pushkin's poetry and too poetic to seriously tackle the role of anyone's continuer. . . . They expected from him what he could not give; they were not satisfied with what of his could and should have given true pleasure. . . .[16]

In Druzhinin's conception, then, Turgenev emerges as a pure artist unsullied by and unsuited for any sociopolitical orientation.

Annenkov shares with Druzhinin a determination to disassociate Turgenev's art from any burning social issues. In spite of the title of his "About Thought in Works of Fiction (Remarks on the Latest Works of Turgenev and Tolstoy)" (1855), Annenkov's article in fact analyzes Turgenev's poetics. Focusing on the stories from the 1850s, Annenkov distinguishes a new subtlety in Turgenev's art, a transformation that Turgenev himself was to describe as a move away from his "old manner" to "a new one." Annenkov finds the growing sophistication of Turgenev's narrative technique especially apparent in rounded characterization, gentle humor, and all-embracing lyricism.[17] Annenkov's observation has since become a cliché of Turgenev criticism, as has the remark, made in another article from 1855, that Turgenev's lyricism bears comparison with that of the poet Fyodor Tyutchev (1803-73): "He [Turgenev] is a poet of the sun, summer, and only somewhat of autumn, just like Mr. Tyutchev, with whom he has much in common in his view of nature and his understanding of it."[18]

Unlike aesthetic critics such as Druzhinin and Annenkov, who rejected the notion of Turgenev as an ideological writer, conservative critics did not dispute the radicals' contention that Turgenev's works encapsulated specific ideas and ideologies. The most important of these conservative critics, Apollon Grigoriev (1822-64) and Nikolay Strakhov (1828-95), represented a school of thought known as *pochvennichestvo*. This term, created from the Russian word *pochva,* "soil," lacks any

reasonable English equivalent but suggests links both with nature and with one's native soil. Attempting to reconcile Westernizing and Slavophile strands in Russian culture, the theorists of *pochvennichestvo,* who included Dostoevsky, drew on Belinsky's organic view of aesthetics, itself a heritage of German idealism, in their conception of a work of art as a biological organism of sorts, and of art in general as a way of understanding life and the world.[19]

Despite its considerable longueurs, Grigoriev's classic "*A Nest of Gentlefolk* by Ivan Turgenev" remains one of the most insightful nineteenth-century articles on the writer.[20] In charting the evolution of Turgenev's art, Grigoriev identifies important early influences on the writer, especially romanticism and the so-called natural school. Of the Russian romantics, Grigoriev points to Mikhail Lermontov and his hero Pechorin, from the novel *A Hero of Our Time* (1840), as especially significant sources of inspiration for Turgenev. The natural school, its role, and, indeed, its very existence, have become topics open to considerable debate among twentieth-century scholars and critics. Nonetheless, for Grigoriev the term clearly refers to Russian writers of the 1840s whose works echoed Gogol's. First among them, at least as far as posterity is concerned, is Dostoevsky, and Grigoriev anticipated twentieth-century scholarship that has drawn attention to the links between Turgenev's early works and Dostoevsky's.

The ideologist in Grigoriev comes to the fore when he analyzes Lavretsky, the hero of *A Nest of Gentlefolk.* In Grigoriev's treatment, Lavretsky's return from abroad to his family estate represents an instance of *pochvennichestvo* in action. All in all, Grigoriev sees Lavretsky as an authentic and positive Russian type. Both conservative and radical critics indulged in a nearly fanatical pursuit of positive heroes in works of literature, by the way, and they bequeathed this naive but potentially dangerous sport to socialist realism and its commentators.

Strakhov made his most important contribution to Turgenev criticism with a brilliant analysis of *Fathers and Sons* originally published in Dostoevsky's journal *Time.*[21] In his lengthy review, Strakhov insists that Turgenev's poetic novel treats life, not politics, that it rises out of the particular to address the universal. Strakhov does not deny that Turgenev's poetry has ideological overtones, however. True to *pochvennichestvo,* Strakhov sees *Fathers and Sons* as a dramatization of the triumph of living life over arid theory: "Turgenev stands for the eternal foundations of human life, for those basic elements which may perpetually change their forms, but in essence always remain unchanged."[22] Here Strakhov admires both Turgenev's artistry and his ideological commitments, but that was not always so. Elsewhere Strakhov applauds the novelist's talent but deplores his Westernizing Weltanschauung.[23]

The division of critics into radicals, aesthetes and conservatives reflects the overheated political climate of the 1860s. In that decade and atmosphere, Turgenev's determination to remain an ostensibly objective artist-observer made him enemies on virtually all sides. The publication of **Fathers and Sons** in 1862, a novel now generally regarded as one of the supreme masterpieces of Russian literature, spelled the end of Turgenev's popularity in Russia for nearly two decades, until the very last years of his life.

While Turgenev's reputation suffered in his homeland, however, it gained considerably abroad. Turgenev in fact was gaining an international following—the first Russian writer ever to do so. In 1869, writing to Pyotr Vasiliev, the compiler of *A Bibliographical Note on Translations of I. S. Turgenev's Works into Foreign Languages* (Kazan, 1868), Turgenev noted:

> Almost everything that I have written has been translated into *French,* under various titles. Besides *Notes of a Hunter, A Nest of Gentlefolk,* about ten stories, as well as *Smoke,* have been translated into German; the bookseller Behre in Riga has begun an edition of selected works of mine—the first volume includes *Fathers and Sons,* the second—**"An Unfortunate Girl"** and three other stories. *Notes of a Hunter, Smoke, Fathers and Sons,* and *A Nest of Gentlefolk,* have been translated into *English.* . . . *Smoke* and *Fathers and Sons* have been translated into *Dutch; Smoke, A Nest of Gentlefolk,* and several stories—into *Swedish;* a few stories have been translated into *Czech, Serbian,* and Hungarian. I have also been informed that *Notes of a Hunter* has been translated into *Spanish* and will soon be published. . . .[24]

Toward the end of his life, Turgenev was gratified to see his reputation in Russia recover. By the late 1870s, Russian readers, critics, and the public in general reacted to his person and works at least with respect, and often with exaltation. On his visits to Russia in 1879, 1880, and 1881, Turgenev found large, enthusiastic crowds turning out for his readings. Upon his death, commentators both at home and abroad mourned the passing of one of the very greatest writers of the age.

In France, where Turgenev had enjoyed cordial relations with the literary community, especially in the last two decades of his life, Melchior de Vogüé's *Le roman russe* (1886) served to alert the non-Russian world in general to the virtues of Russian novelists, Turgenev not the least among them. The French critic especially admired the compassion that Turgenev demonstrated in his works and which seemed so lacking in French works of the era.[25] Writing at approximately the same time, Paul Bourget, in his *Essais de psychologie contemporaine,* generally agreed with de Vogüé about the essential healthiness of Turgenev's literary world. True, Bourget saw Turgenev as disillusioned, weak-willed, and pessimistic, but not decadent and despairing.[26]

In the Anglophone world, the evolution of American and English critical attitudes toward Turgenev displayed an affinity to the contrapuntal pattern known as contrary motion. The elevation of Turgenev to the ranks of the classics occurred first of all thanks to American critics. As Royal Gettmann has demonstrated, until the mid-1880s, English critics either remained indifferent to Turgenev or treated his writings not as works of literature but as sources of documentary information about Russian life.[27] Meanwhile, in the United States, critics took an intense interest in Turgenev from the early 1870s on. Gettmann observes: "They approached the novels . . . as serious, artistic narratives. . . . In the effort to refine public taste and to raise the level of fiction, a group of writers associated with W. D. Howells deduced from the works of Turgenev a form of the novel they called 'dramatic.' This anticipated in several respects—withdrawal of the author, singleness of theme, restriction of time and place—the 'well-made' or 'dramatic novel' described by Percy Lubbock and J. W. Beach" (185).[28] Adding to the American chorus of praise for a great realist, Henry James, in the 1880s and 1890s, published several famous appreciations of Turgenev. Summing up his art, which James admired for its subtle combination of moral vigor and refined technique, James wrote: "Turgenev is in a peculiar degree what I may call the novelists' novelist,—an artistic influence extraordinarily valuable and ineradicably established."[29]

In spite of the advocacy of such an influential figure as James, however, Turgenev's reputation in the United States began to slip from the 1890s on, as the novels of his great contemporaries—first Tolstoy, then Dostoevsky—became generally known. Meanwhile, in England, as though to make up for earlier ill-use, and no doubt taking the lead from James, critics and fellow novelists created a veritable Turgenev cult. To quote Gettmann again: "The English were compelled to admit the sickly condition of their fiction, and they could no longer deny the existence of French realism. Using Turgenev as a shield against the French, the English moved toward what I have called the post-Victorian compromise—an ideal which accommodated Flaubert's care for art with Russian concern for the spirit" (186). As examples of the reverence with which Turgenev was treated, one might cite Arnold Bennett, who applauded Turgenev for having "uttered the last word of pure artistry,"[30] or Ford Madox Ford, who opined: "We are pretty certain that Turgenev was greater than Shakespeare . . . his characters are more human than Shakespeare's were."[31]

In the years following World War I, the English at last joined in the reappraisal long since under way in America. Turgenev was measured against other Russian writers and found wanting. Often asking of him and his art what neither could give or even intended to, critics expressed doubts about Turgenev's reliability as a social historian, a hunger for richer subject matter, and objections to Turgenev's pessimism.

A reevaluation of Turgenev's art by Russian critics paralleled the one that occurred abroad. This reorientation was accomplished in two stages, both of which went against the traditional notion of Turgenev as a realist concerned with depicting Russian social reality. In the first, critics and writers associated with the turn-of-the-century phenomenon known in Russian cultural history as decadence or symbolism, claimed Turgenev as their own.[32] In a famous programmatic article, "On the Reasons for the Decline of and the New Currents in Contemporary Russian Literature" (1893), Merezhkovsky identified three basic elements of the new art—mystical content, symbols, and a wider vision of reality—that are foreshadowed in Turgenev's works.[33] The poet Konstantin Balmont declared that symbolist poetry owed its primary inspiration to Turgenev:

> The path from Pushkin to the refined and tender poetry of our days runs not so much through Lermontov and Nekrasov, not so much even through the sternly nocturnal Tyutchev and the starry-glowing Fet, as precisely through Turgenev, who educated our language, our singing reverie, who taught us to understand, through beautiful lover, that the best and truest essence . . . in art is the Maiden-Woman.[34]

Other critics noted an affinity between symbolist prose and Turgenev's *Poems in Prose* and so-called mysterious tales. In general, symbolism and decadence proclaimed Turgenev a kindred spirit by focusing on his stories and ignoring the novels.

The second stage of reorientation came with Russian Formalism, a school of criticism that came to the fore at approximately the time of World War I and exerted an overwhelming influence on Russian criticism until the mid-1930s.[35] Generally speaking, the Formalists went against the nineteenth-century tradition of literary criticism as civic-minded journalism. In place of politicized commentary more or less totally divorced from the text, the Formalists hoped to forge an exact science based on close—even microscopic—attention to the text. In the process, the Formalists made many important contributions to the fields of literary theory, literary history, comparative literature, and the sociology of literature. In the case of Turgenev criticism, the Formalists and critics closely allied to the Formalists adopted a frankly polemical stance toward one of the most sacred tenets of nineteenth-century Turgenev criticism by flatly denying that Turgenev pursued political goals in his art. Having attempted to sweep that notion aside, Formalist critics went on to produce landmark studies of Turgenev's technique in the novel and short story and magisterial works on Turgenev's place in the evolution of Russian and European literature.

In the years since World War II Turgenev criticism, both in the Soviet Union and abroad, has proceeded along the parallel tracks of formal analysis and more or less traditional literary scholarship. The formal studies have forced a reappraisal of the nature of Turgenev's realism and an accompanying reinterpretation of many of this works. Scholars have made tremendous strides in the areas of textology and biography. The major achievements in this regard are the *two* complete editions of Turgenev works and letters undertaken by Leningrad's Institute of Russian Literature (Pushkin House), the first completed in 1968, the second in progress. Such scholarly largesse is entirely unprecedented, even for the Soviet Union. It testifies, however, to the continuing vitality of Turgenev criticism and scholarship in the late twentieth century. Turgenev's reputation may not be what it once was, but to judge by both the quantity and the quality of criticism published in the major European languages over the last few decades, the awareness that Turgenev is not a Tolstoy or a Dostoevsky has hardly spelled an end to the attraction that one of Russia's finest artists holds for critics. On the contrary, the healthy state of Turgenev criticism merely confirms the accuracy of Mirsky's assessment that it is "impossible to imagine a time when **'The Singers,' 'A Quiet Spot,'** *First Love,* or *Fathers and Sons* will cease to be among the most cherished of joys to Russian readers" (208). One can only assume that Mirsky did not consciously intend to exclude non-Russians from the ranks of Turgenev's future admirers, because as we approach the twenty-first century, Turgenev's appeal has never seemed more universal and timeless.

Notes

1. D. S. Merezhkovsky, "Turgenev," vol. 18, *Polnoe sobranie sochinenii* (Moscow: Sytin, 1914), 58; hereafter cited in the text.

2. V. Arkhipov, "K tvorcheskoy istorii romana I. S. Turgeneva *Ottsy i deti,"* *Russkaya literatura* 1 (1958):132-62. For a discussion of Arkhipov's article and published responses to it by Soviet critics and scholars, see Zbigniew Folejewski, "The Recent Storm around Turgenev as a Point in Soviet Aesthetics," *Slavic and East European Journal* 6, no. 1 (1962):21-27.

3. See D. S. Mirsky, *A History of Russian Literature,* ed. Francis J. Whitfield (New York: Knopf, 1958), 207; hereafter cited in the text.

4. Irving Howe, "Turgenev: The Politics of Hesitation," in *Politics and the Novel* (New York: Horizon Press, 1957), 129-33.

5. Ye. Yefimov, *I. S. Turgenev: Seminar* (Leningrad: Gosuchpedizdat, 1958), 131.

6. A. S. Pushkin, *Polnoe sobranie sochinenii,* vol. 10 (Moscow: AN SSSR, 1956-58), 145.

7. I. S. Turgenev, *Polnoe sobranie sochinenii i pisem,* vol. 14 (Moscow-Leningrad: AN SSSR, 1960-68), 52; hereafter cited in text.

8. See Turgenev, vol. 1, 506, 515.

9. See Turgenev, vol. 4, 494, 511.

10. V. G. Belinsky, *Polnoe sobranie sochinenii,* vol. 12 (Moscow: AN SSSR, 1956), 336.

11. An English translation of Chernyshevsky's "A Russian at the *Rendez-vous"* is included in Belinsky, Chernyshevsky, and Dobrolyubov, *Selected Criticism,* ed. Ralph Matlaw (New York: Dutton, 1962), 108-29.

12. René Wellek, *A History of Modern Criticism,* vol. 4, (New Haven, Conn.: Yale University Press, 1965), 249.

13. An English translation of Dobrolyubov's "When Will the Real Day Come?" may be found in Belinsky, Chernyshevsky, and Dobrolyubov, 176-226; hereafter cited in the text.

14. A substantial excerpt from "Bazarov," translated into English by Lydia Hooke, may be found in Ivan Turgenev, *Fathers and Sons,* edited with a substantially new translation by Ralph Matlaw (New York: Norton, 1966), 195-218.

15. D. I. Pisarev, "Realisty," in *Bazarov; Realisty* (Moscow: Khodozhestvennaya literatura, 1974), 109.

16. Alexander Druzhinin, *"Povesti i rasskazy I. Turgeneva,"* *Sobranie sochinenni,* vol. 7 (St. Petersburg: Tip. Imp. Akademii nauk, 1865-67), 288.

17. See Pavel Annenkov, "O mysli v proizvedeniyakh izyashchnoy slovesnostyi (Zametki po povodu poslednikh proizvendenii g. Turgeneva i. L. N. T.)," *Sovremennik* (1855): section 3, 10-11.

18. Annenkov, in *Sovremennik* no. 1 (1855), quoted in *Sobranie kriticheskikh materialov dlya izucheniya proizvedenii I. S. Turgeneva* vol. 1, ed. V. Zelinsky (Moscow: Tipografiya Malinskogo, 1884), 111. For Annenkov in English, see the memoirs *The Extraordinary Decade,* ed. Arthur Mendel, trans. Irwin Titunik (Ann Arbor: University of Michigan Press, 1968), and the 1858 article "The Literary Type of the Weak Man (Apropos of Turgenev's Story 'Asya')," trans. Tatiana Goerner, *Ulbandus Review* 1, no. 1 (Fall 1977):90-104, and 2, no. 2 (Spring 1978):74-85.

19. On Belinsky, Grigoriev, and Strakhov as organic critics, see Victor Terras, *Belinskij and Russian Literary Criticism: The Heritage of Organic Aesthetics* (Madison: University of Wisconsin Press, 1974), 99.

20. Apollon Grigoriev, *"Dvoryanskoe gnezdo I. S. Turgeneva," Russkoe slovo,* nos. 4, 5, 6, 8 (1859); for an English translation, see A. A. Grigor'ev, "A *Nest of Gentlefolk* by Ivan Turgenev," in *Literature and National Identity,* trans. and ed. by Paul Debreczeny and Jesse Zeldin (Lincoln: University of Nebraska Press, 1970), 65-118.

21. Nikolay Strakhov, *"Ottsy i deti," Vremya* no. 4 (1862); for a substantial excerpt from the article, in an English translation by Ralph Matlaw, see Turgenev, *Fathers and Sons,* 218-29.

22. Strakhov, quoted in *O Turgenev: Russkaya i inostrannaya kritika,* ed. P. P. Pertsov (Moscow: Kooperativnoe izd., 1918), 42-43.

23. The best treatment of Strakhov in English is Linda Gerstein, *Nikolai Strakhov* (Cambridge, Mass.: Harvard University Press, 1971).

24. I. S. Turgenev, *Polnoe sobranie sochinenii i pisem* (Moscow-Leningrad: Nauka, 1960-68), *Pisma* 8, no. 55. See p. 430 of the same volume for bibliographical information about the translations.

25. Melchior de Vogüé, *Le roman russe* (Paris: Plonnourrit, 1886), 133-202.

26. Paul Bourget, "Ivan Tourguénev," *Nouveaux Essais de Psychologie contemporaine* (Paris: A. Lemerre, 1886), 199-250.

27. Royal Gettmann, "Turgenev in England and America," *Illinois Studies in Language and Literature* 27, no. 2 (1941); 185; hereafter cited in the text. For my remarks on English-language Turgenev criticism I have drawn extensively on the excellent study Gettmann compiled with Rissa Yachnin and David Stam, *Turgenev in English: A Checklist of Works by and about Him,* introduction by Marc Slonim (New York: New York Public Library, 1962); Allan Urbanic and Barbara Urbanic, "Ivan Turgenev: A Bibliography of Criticism in English, 1960-83," *Canadian-American Slavic Studies* 17, no. 1 (Spring 1983); 118-43; and Donald Davie, "Turgenev in England, 1850-1950," in *Studies in Russian and Polish Literature in Honor of Waclaw Lednicki,* Zbigniew Folejewski et al. (The Hague: Mouton, 1962), 168-84.

28. For a detailed discussion of Howell's views on Turgenev, see Gettmann, "Turgenev in England," 53-61.

29. Quoted in Gettmann, "Turgenev in England," 131. For an extensive treatment of James's evaluation of Turgenev and of Turgenev's influence on the American novelist, see Gettmann, 66-77, and Dale Peterson, *The Clement Vision: Poetic Realism in Turgenev and James* (London; Pt. Washington, N.Y. Kennikat, 1975).

30. *Academy* 57 (4 November 1899); 516; quoted in Gettmann, "Turgenev in England," 156.

31. Ford Madox Ford, *The Critical Attitude* (London: Duckworth, 1911), 156-58; quoted in Gettmann, "Turgenev in England," 165.

32. For a detailed study of Turgenev's links to symbolism, see Marina Ledkovsky, *The Other Turgenev: From Romanticism to Symbolism* (Würzburg: Jal-Verlag, 1972), 125-38, to which I am greatly indebted for my own remarks on Turgenev and symbolism.

33. Merezhkovsky, *Polnoe Sobranie Sochinenii,* Vol. 12, 249.

34. Konstantin Balmont, "Rytsar Devushki-Zhenshchiny," in N. L. Broksy, ed. *Turgenev i ego vremya* (Moscow-Leningrad: Gosizdat, 1923), 16-17.

35. The most important English-language studies of Russian formalism are Victor Erlich, *Russian Formalism: History and Doctrine* (The Hague: Mouton, 1969); Krystyna Pomorska, *Russian Formalist Theory and its Poetic Ambiance* (The Hague: Mouton, 1968); and Ewa Thompson, *Russian Formalism and Anglo-American New Criticism* (The Hague: Mouton, 1971).

A. V. Knowles (essay date 1988)

SOURCE: Knowles, A. V. "The Last Two Novels." In *Ivan Turgenev,* pp. 89-103. Boston: Twayne, 1988.

[*In the following excerpt, Knowles discusses Turgenev's novels* Smoke *and* Virgin Soil, *both poorly received in Russia but acclaimed by critics elsewhere in the world.*]

SMOKE

Smoke, Turgenev's fifth completed novel, appeared in Katkov's *Russian Herald* in the early part of 1867. The idea for the book probably first occurred to him in 1862, immediately after the publication of *Fathers and Sons.* Apparently he originally thought of writing a love story, but his reaction to the reception of *Fathers and Sons* and two developments inside Russia led to a change of emphasis. On a personal level, he became so upset at the hostility directed toward the previous novel and against him personally that he wished to justify himself and perhaps even to pay back his attackers. He was also concerned about the increasingly apparent difficulties with the implementation of the emancipation and over the growing radicalism of the opposition to the czarist government.

Turgenev began writing **Smoke** in November 1864, while staying in Germany at the spa in Baden-Baden. He knew the town extremely well, and in setting his novel there captured its atmosphere very skillfully, depicting the summer visitors, the weather, the surroundings, the hotels and casinos, the avenues and restaurants, as well as the interminable arguments among the Russian residents and holiday-makers. As usual with Turgenev, the plot is uncomplicated. The action occurs over a period of less than a fortnight, from the tenth to the twenty-second of August 1862. The hero, the thirty-year-old Gregory Litvinov, is considered by some of the monstrously conservative Russians there to be "a rebel and free-thinker," but he is actually rather an average man. Litvinov is returning to Russia from Western Europe, where he has been completing his education. He stops in Baden-Baden to await his fiancée Tatyana, who is on her way home with her aunt from holiday. Litvinov meets by chance the novel's heroine, Irina Ratmirova, whom he had known and loved some ten years before and who has since married. He falls in love with her again, and his love is reciprocated. He breaks with Tatyana and begs Irina to go away with him. After much anguish and indecision on both their parts, especially hers, Irina cannot summon the courage to leave the life she knows, and consequently refuses to go. Litvinov returns to Russia a heartbroken and desolate man, despairing about both his own future and that of his country. A few years later, when he has settled down to become a successful farmer, he recovers enough from the episode with Irina to renew his relationship with Tatyana, who forgives him and they marry.

Interspersed throughout **Smoke** are numerous satirical passages describing on the one hand members of the Russian left-wing intelligentsia and on the other reactionary army officers and other influential figures in the social and governmental hierarchy. The counterbalance to them is Potugin, a mouthpiece for many of Turgenev's own most cherished beliefs. Whereas characters, ideas, social background, and behavior were convincingly melded in *Fathers and Sons,* Turgenev never managed to repeat this success in his novels. **Smoke** might mark a significant point in the development of Turgenev's view of life and his opinions about Russia, but in the final analysis it is a rather unfortunate mixture of love story and polemics where neither has much to do with the other. To be sure, almost all the events and the discussions that take place either involve Litvinov or are related through him, and this method does bestow some unity on the novel, but it also imposes serious limits on the scope of the characterization not only of Litvinov but also of the other characters, who, with the exception of Irina, remain rather flat and underdeveloped and tend to become the caricatures with which Turgenev supposedly populated *Fathers and Sons.* Unlike that novel, however, which is a unified and satisfying whole, **Smoke** once again illustrates the difficulties Turgenev had in combining his skill as a storyteller with his wish to comment on contemporary events in his native country.

While the controversy over *Fathers and Sons* was still at its height, and the intensity of the abuse directed at him showed little signs of diminishing, Turgenev wrote to the writer Marko Vovchok on 27 August 1862 that his position inside Russia had become quite untenable, for "despicable generals praised me and the young insulted me." He told the socialist thinker and activist Petr Lavrov that the radicals' attitude to him was unfair and completely unjustified. He saw himself, as he later wrote in **"You Will Hear the Judgment of a Fool,"** one of the late *Prose Poems,* rather like one of his own characters: "Honest souls turned away from him. Honest faces went red with indignation at the very mention of his name." Turgenev patently felt that although he had been misunderstood, he had got himself into rather a false position and did not know how to extricate himself from it except by stopping writing altogether or by leaving Russia for good. Caring less about the opinions of the right-wing although utterly rejecting them (he continually rejected Katkov's suggestions during the writing of *Smoke* that he make all his generals and high-ranking civil servants paragons of virtue), he still thought of himself as a progressive, one of the growing group of people who were determined to change Russia's social and political systems. Yet he could not accept either the behavior displayed by the active radicals or the open contempt in which they held him and his opinions, even though he wanted to portray these same radicals sympathetically too. His exasperation at them was such that all his sympathy for them had evaporated by the time he wrote *Smoke,* in which he attempts to show that his own ideas are important and those of the opposition of little value.

Turgenev told Katkov on 25 December 1866 that *Smoke* would touch on many questions of serious concern to him, and that it would be a tremendously significant work. He would conclude that neither the left nor the right, neither what he saw as the foolish, superficial, muddle-headed, and irresponsible representatives of the young intelligentsia nor yet the unintelligent, ill-informed, blinkered, and pompous bureaucrats and senior army officers, were capable of offering any efficacious remedy for the malaise that gripped Russia. All their talk was just smoke. The despairing Litvinov, on his way back to Russia, muses: "Everything is smoke . . . everything is ceaselessly changing, everywhere there are new forms, event follows event, but essentially everything remains the same; everything rushes and hurries somewhere and everything vanishes without trace, without anything being achieved; another wind may blow and everything then rushes in the opposite direction, and the same ceaseless, restless—and unnecessary—game begins all over again."

Turgenev thought he had a better answer, and when further insults were heaped on him, he was not at all surprised. He told Herzen on 4 June 1867: "They are all attacking me, Reds and Whites, from above and below, and from the sides." He was hardly mistaken, but he himself contributed to his misfortune. Turgenev was, after all, a fine writer of love stories but a poor political pamphleteer, however much he himself thought otherwise while writing the novel. The attempt to combine a pamphlet with a love story proved beyond his capabilities. Yet although *Smoke* does have some faults in construction and characterization, and though some of its conversations and monologues are tedious to read, did it deserve such hostility in Russia? Can it not be read primarily as a love story?

If Turgenev's success at integrating a love story with social and political comment reached its apogee in *Fathers and Sons,* then *Smoke* clearly showed that he was beginning to lose that touch—but he remained as beguiling as ever in composing a love story. The story of Litvinov's passion for Irina, and its unhappy outcome, remains fascinating.

As Litvinov is, as it were, the narrator of everything that happens during that fateful fortnight in Baden-Baden, almost everything that occurs is seen only through his eyes, and consequently his own personality is a little understated. He is a good but very ordinary man, perhaps even rather dull. He is similar in some ways to other male characters of Turgenev's, to Lezhnev, or Lavretsky, or Arkady Kirsanov, and like them is from the lower ranks of the landowning nobility. His father was a retired civil servant who had married a woman some twenty years younger than he. She had tried to turn him into a landowner rather than a government official (Turgenev always prefers the former to the latter). But neither his mother nor his father did very much about the estate, which remained to all intents and purposes neglected for years. Litvinov was sent to Moscow to study but left before completing his course and returned home, where he developed a passion for farming. Soon realizing that he knew nothing about it, he spent the next four years in Germany, Belgium, and England studying agriculture and technology. He had become engaged to be married to the young Tatyana Shestova, whom he sincerely loved and deeply respected, and at the beginning of the novel is waiting for her arrival in Baden-Baden. He is happy, even serene; his future looks settled and he is proud of his plans for the family estate. But then Irina enters his life for the second time.

Chapters 7-9, in typical Turgenev fashion, depict their previous relationship in Moscow. Some ten years before Litvinov had fallen in love with Irina, the seventeen-year-old daughter of an aristocratic family that had fallen on hard times. Irina was then tall, graceful, intelligent, very beautiful but also temperamental. There was something passionate and self-willed about her, something "that spelled danger for herself and for others." Litvinov fell in love with her at once, but she was slow to return his affection. At the very moment when he decides that his love is hopeless and is about to leave her for ever, she pleads with him to stay. Litvinov always remembered that first occasion when he learned that his love was returned, nor did he forget the days "that came after when still trying to doubt and afraid to believe he clearly saw with a thrill of rapture and almost of awe how the unexpected happiness arose, grew and, sweeping everything before it, flooded his heart at last. There followed the radiant moments of first love, which are not, and indeed ought not to be, repeated in the same life." Weeks and months flew by, not without misunderstandings between the two of them, caused mainly by an apparent inconsistency in Irina's character, coupled with the shame she felt at the comparative poverty in which she and her parents lived. Their relationship ended when Irina attended a ball at which the court was present and made a deep impression on everyone there. Her parents grasped the opportunity, through her, of raising themselves once again into the ranks of the wealthy and influential. They moved to St. Petersburg, where Irina wrote to Litvinov that, however unhappy she felt, all was over between them. "Forgive me, forget me," she urged. "I am not worthy of you. Be generous and do not attempt to see me." Litvinov is heartbroken, for Irina has put material considerations before her love for him. Litvinov abandons his university studies and returns to his father's estate. He gradually loses touch with her and pays no attention to the gossip that reaches his ears from time to time. Irina finally marries general Ratmirov, and Litvinov grows to love Tatyana.

However, the love that flares up again between them becomes an all-consuming passion, especially for Litvinov. For him it is quite simply an obsession, one further complicated by the guilt he feels at rejecting Tatyana, who with both pain and resignation accepts her fate. Finally, after much soul-searching, Litvinov decides he can do nothing but ask Irina to go away with him and share his future, whatever it may bring. Irina is both overjoyed and frightened, but her fear overcomes the uncertain hope of happiness, and she suggests to Litvinov that their commitments are such that they should part. Having resolved to ask Irina to join her life with his, Litvinov is dismayed by her decision, but is prepared to accept it "even if I die afterward." However, later in the day Irina changes her mind and writes to him: "my life is in your hands, do with me what you will. I don't want to hamper your freedom, but if need be I will throw up everything and follow you to the ends of the world." Litvinov then has further doubts himself and entertains dark forebodings at the thought of what happened between them ten years earlier. "Obviously one can't love twice; another life has entered into you—you have allowed it in—and you will never rid yourself of that poison."

The idea of love as sickness is, of course, nothing new in Turgenev, though normally he views the experience of love as an ennobling one. But here the sickness that will pass has become a poison for which there is no antidote. All Litvinov's hopes and ideals, all his plans for the future are destroyed by his passion for Irina. He cannot sleep, he cannot eat, and his powers of rational thought disappear. Things are even worse after their love is passionately consummated. When he makes one last effort to convince her, she, true to her character, first agrees but then tells him that she cannot go with him. She proposes an alternative: that Litvinov come to St. Petersburg, where her influential friends will find him suitable work and they may continue seeing each other. Irina is incapable of living without the support of the society she inhabits, however much she despises many of its values. Such a solution, though, is unacceptable to Litvinov. He leaves for Russia without Irina, not knowing what he will do. "Practical men like Litvinov," as Turgenev sums it up, "should not be carried away by passion; it destroys the very meaning of their lives."

Of all Turgenev's heroines, Irina is certainly the most intriguing. Since readers see her almost entirely through Litvinov's eyes, she remains as mysterious to them as she does to him. She is the first of Turgenev's heroines to possess a demonic quality that clouds her judgment even as it entraps others. More strikingly, she is also the first heroine who ultimately proves weaker than the hero. As she is the most finely drawn and perceptively observed of Turgenev's major heroines, many readers have never forgiven Turgenev for endowing her with the wrong values and yet making her so irresistible. As Edward Garnett wrote: "Irina will stand for ever in the gallery of great creations. Turgenev has in her perfected her type till she reaches a destroying witchery of fascination and subtlety. She ardently desires to become nobler, to possess all that ideal of love . . . but she has only the power given her of enervating the man she loves. She is born to corrupt, but never to be corrupted. Her wit, her scorn, her beauty preserve her from all the influences of evil which she does not deliberately employ."[1]

Remarkably, *Smoke* has a happy ending. After a few years pass Litvinov renews his friendship with Tatyana and asks her to marry him. Her self-sacrifice in releasing him from his earlier promise yields to forgiveness, and she accepts. This strikes the reader as contrived. Turgenev invests all his skill at characterization into Irina, by far the most arresting character in the whole novel. By contrast, Tatyana is a very thinly painted portrait. If Litvinov is distinguished by his mediocrity, then Tatyana seems only virtuous, patient, and long-suffering. Her presence in the novel is largely superfluous, except that she is first the passive cause of Litvinov's mental torment, and then gives him a happy marriage at the last. This does not fit well with what has preceded it. Nor does it contradict Turgenev's generally pessimistic outlook on life. Its artificiality merely demonstrates his inability to believe that any love between a man and a woman can bring anything better than brief happiness. The idea that Tatyana and Irina offer Litvinov the choice between a sacred and a profane love is valid,[2] but it is far too one-sided a contrast to be artistically convincing. It may be not illogical for Litvinov and Tatyana to settle down to an uneventful life together, but Turgenev knew very well that "nature takes no account of logic, of our human logic; she has one of her own, which we do not understand or acknowledge until we are crushed under its wheel." That is the author's authentic voice.

The ideas that Turgenev wished to discuss in *Smoke* have to do either with the future of Russia after the emancipation of the serfs or with the Russian character. Turgenev saw three main options. The first involved major changes suggested by the radical intellectuals and the methods to be employed for their realization; the second was the retention at all costs of the situation as it was thought to be before 1861, the aim of the reactionary generals and bureaucrats; and the third was the middle course that Turgenev himself favored and that he advocated through the character of Potugin. The first two are dismissed with the most biting satire. In the very first chapter Turgenev exposes the boredom, pretentiousness, and emptiness of the Russian upperclass expatriates in Baden-Baden. They fill their time with gambling, gossip, popular music, and meaningless conversations. The opinions of such people—to some of whom Turgenev gives ridiculous names (Prince Koko, Princess Zizi, Princess Zozo) or simply a letter (Countess S, Baron Z, Prince Y)—are fully revealed in chapter 10. Litvinov is taking a leisurely breakfast on the terrace of the Old Castle when a party of Russians arrives. They are all elegantly dressed and converse in French. "Their importance showed itself in everything," Turgenev writes. "The very sound of their voices seemed to be amiably thanking a crowd of subordinates. . . . Each seemed to be deeply conscious of his own dignity and the importance of the part he was to play in the state. . . ." Irina and her husband are among the company, which Litvinov joins, and a conversation develops. A friend of theirs has had to resign his post because he felt he had to justify his high-handed treatment of some tradesman, out of fear of ridicule in the press. A general retorts that if he had his way he would allow the papers to print nothing more than the prices of corn and meat and advertisements for fur coats and boots. "And for the sale of the nobles' estates at auction," adds Irina's husband. This leads on to complaints that the nobility has been ruined by the emancipation, and that it is the job of people such as themselves to stick to their principles and warn the country to stop heading for disaster through reforms. What has been done must be undone, and especially the emancipation, which has brought the landowners nothing but impoverishment. And the peasants? They do not even enjoy their freedom. One of the generals maintains:

> "I am not an enemy of so-called progress, but all those universities and seminaries and elementary schools, those students, sons of the clergy, men of no class, all that rabble. . . . Yes, we must draw the line. Bear in mind no one in Russia asks for anything or makes any demands. Self-government, for instance, is anyone asking for it? Do you ask for it? Or you? Or you? You rule not only over yourselves, but over all of us as it is." (The general's face was lit up by an amused smile.) "Democracy is glad to welcome you, it flatters you, it is ready to serve your ends, but it is a double-edged weapon. Much better to have things done in the old, well-tried way. Don't allow the mob to get presumptuous but trust to the aristocracy, which alone is strong. . . . And as for progress—I really have nothing against it. Only don't give us all those lawyers and juries and elected rural officials—and above all don't interfere with discipline—as for the rest, you may build bridges and wharves and hospitals, and there is no harm in lighting the streets with gas."

In other words, keep things exactly as they used to be, but allow a little social improvement. Turgenev's contempt for such people and their opinions is expressed not only in the satirical presentation but also through Litvinov, who, we read, "could not have picked out a single sincere word, a single sensible idea or new fact from all that dull and incomprehensible babble. There was no real excitement in their shouts and exclamations, no passion in their censure; only sometimes the fear of financial loss. And not a drop of living water under all that litter and rubbish. What stale trash, what worthless trifles, what barren futilities. . . . And at bottom, what ignorance!" Even Irina agrees with him. The people in her world, she tells Litvinov, "understand nothing, they have no sympathy for anything, they haven't even intelligence, only *savior faire* and cunning, [and] they don't care a scrap for music or art or poetry." Litvinov's honest plebeian pride is aroused and he wonders what he, the son of a petty official, could possibly have in common with these St. Petersburg military aristocrats. Everything he believed in was diametrically opposed to their views: Litvinov "thought their jokes flat, their tone unendurable, their movements affected. The very softness of their speech suggested to him a revolting contemptuousness." And clearly Turgenev agreed with his hero.

If Turgenev dismisses the reactionary view, he does the same for the radicals. If the left-wing had criticized Bazarov for being a caricature when he was not, then here Turgenev shows what he was capable of in this area. His contempt for the radical stance emerges most clearly in chapter 4, describing a group led by Gubarev (whose prototype is probably Herzen's friend and collaborator Ogarev), who voices their political aims. They must study the peasantry, he says, unite with it, and find out what it really thinks. Gubarev considers the peasantry a revolutionary force. But Turgenev ridicules Gubarev and his ideas no less energetically than he does those of the right-wing. His view of the peasantry is shown as absurdly romantic; he and his followers are drawn as insincere, shallow, and wrong-headed. Turgenev surrounds Gubarev with a motley crew of nonentities as if to stress that point: there are the empty-headed Bambaev, the glory-seeking Bindasov, the gossiping and opinionated Voroshilov (who, Turgenev told Annenkov, casts dust in people's eyes by quoting the latest pronouncements of science without knowing what went before), the misguided Pishchalkin, and the silly Madame Sukhanchikova, who exists on a diet of half-baked ideas, ill-digested opinions, and the juiciest of scandals. Turgenev is as severe on these characters and what they purport to stand for as he is on the reactionaries. Both camps are equally ridiculous but, in Turgenev's opinion, if not shown up for what they really are, both are equally dangerous for the future well-being of Russia.

Potugin advocates a middle way. His position in the novel is as artistically tenuous as Tatyana's, and although Turgenev tries to integrate him into the love story by casting him as Irina's selfless and devoted admirer who carries out her every wish (including spying on Litvinov), he does not succeed. Potugin has no real place in the story of Litvinov's passion for Irina, and his long speeches on Russia and its future simply delay the development of the narrative. But as a mouthpiece for Turgenev's own ideas, he is of prime importance.

Potugin comes from the *raznochintsy*. The son of a priest, he is full of down-to-earth common sense, and has had long experience of the workings of the bureaucracy. Life, however, has not treated him at all kindly, and he is now a lonely and embittered man. But he is also a man of conviction, a Westernizer. Turgenev wrote to Pisarev on 4 June 1867 from Baden-Baden: "In common with most of my Russian readers you do not like **Smoke**. In the face of such a unanimous response I cannot but doubt the qualities of my creation. . . . But from the heights of European civilization one can still survey the whole of Russia. You think that Potugin is Arkady all over again. I cannot but say that here your critical sense has deserted you—these two characters have absolutely nothing in common. Arkady has no convictions whatsoever, while Potugin will die an inveterate and passionate Westernizer, and my writings will all have been in vain if this fierce and inextinguishable fire does not come through."

According to Potugin, Russians have two major difficulties. They have an innate need to be led, and it has not mattered much by whom. That is why the left-wing has its Gubarevs: the important thing is not his ideas as such, but rather his strength of will and ability to convince others of the correctness of his opinions. The second problem is the Russian attitude toward Western Europe. The Russians might argue that Europe has run its historical course, but it still provides the intellectual nourishment on which Russia will survive and flourish. Neither the generals' wish to return to some mystic Russia of long ago—preferably as long ago as possible—nor the left-wing's romantic dreams of the revolutionary potential of the peasantry, will help. What is needed is a selective borrowing from the very best that Western Europe has to offer. Russians cannot help themselves by their own resources. History, according to Potugin, emphasizes this simple fact, however much most of his countrymen fail to recognize it. What has Russia ever produced of any lasting value to mankind? In painting, only the insignificant Bryullov; in music, Glinka is perhaps the exception, which only shows up the poverty of his predecessors; in science and industry, nothing. Even the samovar, bast shoes, and the knout, those apparently quintessentially Russian items, were all imported from abroad. Russians must show more humility. Unable to understand simple facts, they concoct theories that lead only to idealistic conclusions of no help to anyone, least of all the Russians themselves. "We must thank civilization," Potugin says, "not only for knowledge, art, and law but even for the idea of beauty itself and of poetry . . . and the people's so-called naive and unconscious art is all stuff and nonsense."

At the very end of the novel, as Litvinov sets out for Russia, Potugin bids him farewell with the advice: "Each time you begin something new, ask yourself whether you are serving civilization . . . whether your activity is of the educative, European kind, which alone is useful and fruitful in our times and for us." That is Potugin's message, and also Turgenev's, one he delivered consistently throughout his life.

VIRGIN SOIL

Turgenev's last and longest novel is usually regarded as a *roman à thèse*, and so largely disregarded. D. S. Mirsky, for example, dismisses it in the following words: "**Virgin Soil** is a complete failure and was immediately recognized as such. Though it contains much that is in the best manner of Turgenev . . . the whole novel is disqualified by an entirely uninformed and necessarily false conception of what he was writing about. His presentation of the revolutionaries of the seventies is like an account of a foreign country by one who had never seen it."[3] Richard Freeborn entitles his chapter on the novel "The Failure of **Virgin Soil**."[4]

Turgenev was well aware of the difficulties of writing about Russia while living abroad. He admitted that one cannot attempt to expose the essence of Russia while living almost permanently abroad. He had taken up a task far beyond his powers. He thought that the fate of any Russian writer of prominence contained a tragic element. His was absenteeism. Such opinions engendered many forebodings. Was Turgenev really out of touch with Russia? Had his ability as a novelist declined even further after *Smoke*? Must *Virgin Soil* be discounted as ill-informed, poorly written, and adding nothing of interest to our knowledge of Turgenev? Most of his readers have been rather disappointed in it, despite its immediate popularity outside Russia. They think they perceive an evident decline in his powers as a writer, as a commentator on contemporary events in Russia, as a creator of unforgettable characters, and as a weaver of stories, especially love stories. Yet Turgenev himself, despite the volume of negative critical comment, was convinced that ultimately his novel would be useful to his country.

Virgin Soil springs from Turgenev's interest in the early stages, dating from the late 1860s, of the so-called movement to the people and his judgment upon it. The purpose of the movement, which culminated in a massive exodus from the towns to the countryside by idealistic young students and others in the summer of 1874, was to spread revolutionary propaganda amongst the ordinary people by attempting to share their lives and thus their problems. Ultimately they hoped to incite the peasantry to oppose the landowners, factory owners, the authorities, and the czarist government. Their ideas of what would replace the established social, political, and economic order were couched in rather vague and even inconsistent terms, including utopian socialism, anarchism, even a form of enlightened, but temporary, dictatorship. Initially the call "go to the people; that is where you belong" had come from Herzen—and is critically reflected in Gubarev's beliefs in *Smoke*. Bakunin had thought the conditions of the peasantry so awful and their hatred of the government so deep that they could easily be stirred into revolt with the right leadership. Petr Lavrov added fuel to the fire through his *Istoricheskie pisma* (*Historical Letters*), published at the end of the 1860s, in which he wrote of the debt owed to the people by the intelligentsia, or in other words the gentry. This was the birth of the concept of the "repentant nobleman." But by the end of 1874 the enthusiasm, idealism, and dedication of youth lay in ruins. Government authorities employed all the means at their disposal in retaliation and arrested well over a thousand people for spreading revolutionary propaganda. More important, perhaps, was the often suspicious attitude of the peasants themselves, who rejected the young intellectuals who tried to dress as they did and live with them. The mutual misunderstanding was pronounced, as the peasants either refused to listen to the strangers in their midst or handed them over to the police. The movement culminated in the "Trial of the 193" which marked the end of this particular phase of Russian populism. Turgenev reflects all of this in *Virgin Soil.*

Turgenev first mentioned a book on this latest phenomenon in Russian society as early as July 1870, when he sketched out a short list of characters contrasting a "romantic revolutionary" (Nezhdanov) with a more realistic man who goes calmly about his work (Solomin). For the next few years the idea germinated gradually, until on 27 July 1876 he wrote to his editor Mikhail Stasyulevich (by this time he had fallen out with Katkov), publisher of the journal *Vestnki Evropy* (*Messenger of Europe*), that his new novel would be called *Virgin Soil* and bear the epigraph: "To turn over virgin soil it is necessary to use a deep plow going well into the earth, not a surface one gliding lightly over the top." Turgenev insisted, however, that his plow was a metaphor not for revolution but for enlightenment. The manuscript was completed in November 1876. Turgenev feared that the novel would be badly received, and that if he had been beaten for *Fathers and Sons* with sticks then it would be tree-trunks this time. He was not mistaken. At the end of 1876 Turgenev wrote to Stasyulevich:

> Up until now the younger generation has either been represented in our literature as a gang of crooks and rogues, which is false and could only insult the young reader as a lie and a libel, or it has been idealized, which again is false, and, besides, harmful. I decided to approach the truth along the middle way—to depict young people, most of them good and honest, and to show that notwithstanding their disinterestedness the task that they had set themselves was so artificial and untrue to life that it could only end in fiasco. . . . Whatever happens, the young cannot possibly complain that they have been depicted by an enemy; on the contrary, I think that they cannot but feel the sympathy I have if not for their aims then at least for them personally. It is in this way that a novel written for them and about them can be useful to them.

For all that, when the novel appeared in the early part of 1877 it was received as Turgenev had feared. Almost no one in Russia liked it. The right wing attacked him for his adverse comments on Russia, and for his highly satirical portrayal of the Sipyagin family and of Kallomeytsev. The left wing could not countenance his making his "hero" Nezhdanov so irresolute and feeble, or Marianna not determined enough and prey to her emotions, or Solomin too "bourgeois." But there was another and more justifiable reason for the attacks. In 1877 *Virgin Soil* could be thought several years out of date, for the Populist movement, upon recovering from the debacle Turgenev describes so well, had entered a more radical and violent stage.

The "story" in *Virgin Soil* is the most complex Turgenev ever attempted; the book contains many minor characters and subsidiary plots. It combines two romantic love stories with Turgenev's analysis of the revolutionary movement of the late 1860s (although much of what he wrote applied equally well to the mid-1870s).

The love elements, though, do appear to be rather a side issue and have very little to do with the novel's main message. *Virgin Soil* opens at the lodgings of some Russian revolutionaries. One of them, Mashurina—an intense, rather unattractive young woman—is shown as a dedicated follower of a certain Vasily Nikolaevich, a shadowy figure who never appears but who is clearly modeled on the revolutionary Sergey Nechaev, whose long trial in 1871-73 Turgenev followed closely. Not all the group, however, obey his every command. Nezhdanov, the ostensible hero (with whom Mashurina is obviously although secretly in love), is far too introspective and skeptical to follow anyone blindly. The illegitimate son of a wealthy nobleman, he is employed by Sipyagin as tutor to his son. Sipyagin is portrayed throughout the novel in disapproving terms. He is an influential, ambitious government official, determined to appear liberal but actually ever loyal to the government. Clearly he lives by self-interest, and is at heart a hypocrite and snob.

Sipyagin's neighbor Kallomeytsev is painted with particular venom as an out-and-out reactionary with pretensions, and at times his characterization lapses into caricature. Sipyagin's wife Valentina Mikhaylovna is a self-possessed, cold-hearted, vain, and capricious woman. She has pretentions to culture just as her husband has to liberalism, but she is merciless toward those of weaker character than she and at a loss with those of stronger character. Her brother, Markelov, is markedly different. He is a fanatical revolutionary, convinced that the Russian peasantry only need a "spark" to set off the fires of revolt. When his activities inevitably lead to his arrest (his brother-in-law, far from helping him, actually assists in the process) he refuses to name any of his collaborators and acts with admirable courage and dignity. He is in love with Marianna, the novel's heroine, but his affection is not returned. Marianna, Valentina Mikhaylovna's niece, has been brought up in her household. Never allowed to forget the generosity of the Sipyagins, she dislikes and despises her "benefactors" and yearns for freedom and activity. She and Nezhdanov are immediately attracted to each other although she loves the cause he is fighting for more than she loves him, and wants to join her life to his in order to serve the people. She is typical of many young women of the period—idealistic, dedicated, and rather naive—but Turgenev fails to make her other than a representative type or to endow her with the psychological depth of his great heroines. She is certainly not as pale a creation as Natalya in *Rudin* but she does not begin to compare with either Liza (*Home of the Gentry*) or, especially in this context, with Elena (*On the Eve*). Similarly, Nezhdanov recalls some of Turgenev's earlier ineffectual heroes. He is as unsure of his dedication to the revolutionary cause as he is of his love for Marianna.

From the very earliest drafts of the novel Turgenev intended that Nezhdanov should end his life in despair and by his own hand. The weakness in the characterization of Nezhdanov—who remains nonetheless the most interesting character in the whole novel—is a weakness of *Virgin Soil* as a whole. In his plan of 1872 Turgenev describes him as "a tragic nature with a tragic destiny." He should have embodied the tragic destiny of a whole generation, but as things turned out his tragedy is not that of his generation but a personal one. It is almost as if Turgenev reverted one last time to the "superfluous man." He is as Paklin describes him in the last chapter: a "splendid fellow" but an "idealist of realism." He was simply not fit to be a revolutionary. He was rather an aristocrat manqué who longed to be a peasant democrat, a poet not an activist. Nezhdanov should dominate the novel, but, to its detriment, he never does.

Nezhdanov and Marianna finally escape together from the Sipyagin household. They are offered help by the novel's real hero, Solomin, the manager of a local factory who provides them with shelter and contact with the local peasantry. Solomin himself has little faith in revolutionary activity but is prepared to protect and assist those who do. From the start Turgenev wanted to contrast Solomin and Nezhdanov, the practical man and the dreamer. The son of a clergyman, Solomin studied science and mathematics and worked in England. He remains aloof from those who preach revolution because he does not think the ordinary people either understand it or want it. He believes in slow and patient work, as Turgenev stresses in contrasting his way of life with Nezhdanov's. When the latter dresses as an ordinary workman and distributes revolutionary literature among the peasants, his misguided efforts end in abject failure. Enticed into the local taverns, he quickly becomes hopelessly intoxicated and is brought home in a state of collapse. The sight of him even shakes for a time Marianna's belief in the people: "She was not disturbed but depressed. It seemed as if a breath of the real atmosphere of the world to which she was striving had blown upon her suddenly, making her shudder at its coarseness and darkness. What Moloch was this to which she was going to sacrifice herself?"

This is, however, only a temporary lapse. Solomin even persuades her that she can be of far more use to the people, not by becoming "simplified" herself, in the words of a peasant employee of his (an expression that Turgenev had heard from one of his own peasants at Spasskoe) or by handing out literature to illiterate peasants, but by undertaking something far humbler: nursing the local children and teaching them to read. Marianna is disappointed but agrees with the practicality of his suggestion. When, later, Markelov is arrested, suspicion falls upon Nezhdanov, Marianna, and Solomin, with no little help from Sipyagin. Nezhdanov finally capitulates to his doubts, writes a letter to Solomin and

Marianna urging them to marry each other, and shoots himself. His motivation has nothing to do with fear of arrest or its consequences, but stems from the continual indecision he had shown throughout his short life, his inability to convince himself of the rightness of his cause, his guilt at being (at least partially) from the aristocracy, and his uncertainty as to whether his love for Marianna is genuine. There are also a few hints to show that he suspects Solomin, who loves Marianna himself, is the better man for her. After his death Marianna and Solomin go into hiding until the affair dies down. They will shortly marry and, presumably, continue to work together for the cause to which Solomin has dedicated himself.

Although *Virgin Soil* is occasionally tedious to read—some repetitive pages could easily have been omitted without detriment to the rest—and the characterization less full and more stereotyped than is normally the case with Turgenev, it is clear that Turgenev has finally abandoned the belief that his own class would produce the likely leaders of reform in Russia. Earlier he had repeatedly argued that Russia's educated class was her only hope of salvation. He always rejected violence as pointless, indeed positively harmful, and believed Russia could never be reformed except from above. His high hopes for the emancipation of the serfs ten years later were disappointed. *Virgin Soil,* despite its defects, shows that his faith now lay in men and women from a different social background from his own, men like Solomin, practical, enterprising, and ambitious, but also patient, realizing that change will take time. As he points out: "The main thing about [Solomin] is that he is no instant healer of all our social ills. Just look at us Russians—we are always waiting. Something or someone will always turn up—and cure everything at a stroke. Who will this magician be? Darwinism? The village? A foreign war? Anything you like." But Solomin is prepared to wait and to work for gradual but certain improvement.

Although Turgenev portrays the "movement to the people" as naive and a little absurd, he also believed that those who participated in it were redeemed by their devotion to their beliefs. Although the young disliked his portrayal of them, he was surely sympathetic to them—for their faith, their sincerity, and their willing self-sacrifice. As Paklin puts it at the very end of the novel, it is people like Solomin who will make the future, they are the real men. "They're strong, colorless, dull men of the people. But now they're the only kind that's needed." He is a man with an ideal and yet sensible; an educated man, yet one from the ordinary people. Turgenev could admire such a man and prophesy that the future was his. It might be said that he was right.

Notes

1. Edward Garnett, *Turgenev: A Study* (London [: Collins,] 1917), 133-34.

2. Freeborn, [Richard] *Turgenev [: The Novelist's Novelist.* Oxford: Oxford University Press, 1963], 157.

3. Mirsky, [D.S.] *History of Russian Literature,* [(London: Routledge and Kegan Paul, 1949)], 195.

4. Freeborn, *Turgenev,* 162.

A. D. P. Briggs (essay date 1993)

SOURCE: Briggs, A. D. P. "One Man and His Dogs: An Anniversary Tribute to Ivan Turgenev." *Irish Slavonic Studies* 14 (1993): 1-20.

[*In the following essay, Briggs examines the importance of dogs in Turgenev's life and literature.*]

TURGENEV'S DOGS

I wish to honour the name of Ivan Sergeyevich Turgenev in a curious way—though it is one which certainly would have appealed to him—by drawing attention to his interest in dogs.[1] Dogs played a significant role for him, both in real life and in literature. He grew up surrounded by them at Spasskoye; one of his earliest recorded memories is of going out hunting with his father at the age of nine or ten and observing the behaviour of a bird defending its young against their dog, Trezor. This incident was recorded twice by Turgenev, in the autobiographical sketch entitled **'The Quail'** (1880) and in an earlier *Poem in Prose* (May 1878), **'The Sparrow'**, which is a fictional adaptation of the same event. From then on his biography is punctuated with continual references to dogs of one kind or another, though mainly in connection with hunting. In 1857 one of his reasons for visiting England was to acquire a pair of dogs for the summer shooting back home in Russia. Patrick Waddington refers to this interest of Turgenev's as an 'obsession with dogs'. Pauline Viardot apparently implored Ivan Sergeyevich not to send any more to Courtavenel where they created bloody havoc among the Viardots' own hounds.[2] The obsession extended beyond hunting dogs. In 1871, again in England, Turgenev was vastly amused by a dog in a circus acting the part of a clown and doing so with what he described as an 'undoubted flair for comedy'.[3] He wrote a famous essay describing the redoubtable qualities of the best dog he ever owned, Pegasus, a cross between an English Setter and a German Sheepdog.[4] Pegasus was a fine animal who seems to have gained a European reputation for the excellence of his nose and the precision of his professional behaviour. In this essay Turgenev also waxes eloquent about dogs in general. Surveying the age-old history of the man—dog relationship he comes to this conclusion:

> Envy, jealousy and—a capacity for friendship; desperate bravery, devotion to the point of self-sacrifice and—ignominious cowardice and fickleness; suspiciousness, spitefulness and—good nature, cunning and straightforwardness—all these qualities manifest themselves—sometimes with astonishing force—in the dog that has been re-educated by man and that deserves more than the horse to be called the noblest of all man's conquests. . . .[5]

He goes on to remind us of the breadth of his own experience in this field:

> Like many another 'inveterate' sportsman, I've had many dogs, bad, good and excellent—I even had one that was positively mad and that committed suicide by jumping out of the dormer window of a drying room on the fourth floor of a paper mill.

Pegasus aged before his time. By his ninth year his famous old skills had atrophied and Turgenev, who was beginning to feel that this was true of himself also in 1871, took his leave of the dog that had been in these words which close his essay:

> I took leave of him not without a feeling of sadness. 'Goodbye' I thought, 'my incomparable dog! I shall never forget you, and I shall never have such a friend as you!' I don't suppose I shall go hunting any more either.[6]

These sentiments call to mind similar ones voiced famously three-quarters of a century earlier by Lord Byron. Burying his beloved Newfoundland at Newstead Abbey in November 1808, he described him in a protracted inscription as

> . . . the poor dog, in life the firmest friend,
> The first to welcome, foremost to defend . . .

and brought the epitaph to a rousing conclusion with these phrases:

> To mark a friend's remains these stones arise;
> I never knew but one—and here he lies.

For good measure, one can see a fine portrait of this dog, Bosun, still hanging in Newstead. It will not escape notice that Byron's grandiloquence is left resonating in the Nottinghamshire air whereas Turgenev's valediction is lowered in tone immediately after its utterance by a sentence which, as well as achieving that purpose, also associates the writer with the dog in a personal and genuine-sounding way.

The difference is important. There is no doubt that Lord Byron loved his dog. What is in doubt is whether he could possibly have known anything like the deeply ex-

perienced, lifelong attachment to the canine species that was ineradicable from the character of Ivan Turgenev. The Russian makes countless references to dogs throughout his career as a writer—as we shall see—but there is never anything theoretical, sentimental, hyperbolical or in the slightest way rhetorical about them.

SOME DOGS IN RUSSIAN LITERATURE

Turgenev was not the first, last or only Russian writer to know and love dogs, or to make references to them in his work. In this respect he is working within a well-established and still living tradition. It is not clear how far back this tradition goes, although it probably began in Russia with fables such as those of Khemnitser and Dmitriev in the eighteenth century ('The Dog and the Lions' and 'The Dog and the Quail' are two examples). Krylov develops the idea early in the nineteenth century with such fables as 'The Elephant and the Pug', 'The Sheep and the Dogs' and 'The Two Dogs'. In the last-named poem the animals are personalised by being given the names Barbos and Zhuzhu.

Griboyedov makes intelligent use of a dog reference in *Woe from Wit*. His hero, Chatsky, reminds the audience of a landowner who repaid his serfs for years of devoted care by swapping some of them for three borzois! (This was a reference on an actual recent event.) Pushkin was no stranger to the dog world, as we can remind ourselves by glancing at a number of the lyrics; for instance, the barking of dogs echoes through the sleeping autumn woods to particular effect in *Osen'*. Dogs are referred to in *The Gypsies* and in *The Tale of the Dead Princess;* in *Count Nulin* the borzois and an anonymous yard dog who appear early on are eclipsed by the maid's pet Pomeranian who is given a decisive role at the climax of the story. In *Eugene Onegin* dogs come out (in the Turgenevan manner) to welcome Tatyana as she approaches Onegin's manor house in Chapter 7 (XXI), and, earlier on, in her nightmare one of the monsters is a horned creature with a dog's snout (5, XVI). It will also be remembered that when Masha visits the Imperial Park at the end of *The Captain's Daughter* to plead for Grinev, the presence of the unrecognised Empress is announced first of all by 'a little white dog of English breed' running ahead of her.

Gogol is probably the first Russian writer to have made a serious story out of the canine species. The demented Proprishchin (in *Notes of a Madman*) believes he can understand both the spoken and written language exchanged between two dogs, Madgie and Fidèle. Eventually he comes to imagine he is no less than the King of Spain, which possibly lends credence to the proposal that Gogol may have borrowed his basic idea from Cervantes's story 'The Dialogue of the Dogs'. Meanwhile in *Dead Souls* Gogol has fun with the name Sobakevich, which is derived from the Russian for 'dog', and perhaps with Nozdrev, a sniffing word derived from 'nostril'; much is also made of a dogs' chorus when Chichikov arrives at Korobochkina's house in Chapter 3.

Later in the century the modern fabulist Saltykov-Shchedrin gives us a fable in prose entitled *Faithful Trezor*—the sad story, with thinly veiled political overtones, of three dogs, Trezor, Kutka, Arapka, and their city fraternity. Before that Nekrasov presented the world with *Hunting with Dogs,* which appeared to celebrate that sport but used the occasion to satirise the nobility. Again, the dogs are personally identified and there are plenty of them: Zmeyka, Nabat, Sokol, Khandra, Nakhal, Svirep, Terzay, Rugay, Ugar, Zamashka and Pobedka. (Nekrasov's mid-century rival, Fet, wrote a less successful, less interesting poem with precisely the same title.)

In the case of Tolstoy we are dealing with a countryman who knew his dogs almost as intimately as did Turgenev. Bulka, Terza, Karay, Lyam, Lyubin, Milka, Milton, Rugay, Trunila, Ulyashin, Viflyanka, Voltorn, Zhiran and Zhuchka—there are a dozen and a half named animals populating his prose from *Childhood* onwards. The best known are, of course, in *War and Peace* and *Anna Karenina*. In the latter, memorable moments occur between Levin and his dog Laska, who always welcomes him home from the city; and on a famous occasion he and Stiva go hunting together, striving to outshoot each other and setting Laska in competition with Oblonsky's dog, Krak. Tolstoy's best-known dog of all comes on the scene towards the end of *War and Peace* and he has not one name but four. Platon Karatayev adopts an anonymous, unprepossessing mongrel, named Azor by the French soldiers and Femgalka by the Russian story-teller. Karatayev calls him Seryy or Vislyy (Grey or Floppy), according to his mood.

This dog is used by Tolstoy to create a powerful and lasting impression, in fact a double impression: of unselfconscious, spontaneous enjoyment of life, notwithstanding its disadvantages and setbacks, and of fidelity. When Karatayev is shot by the French and left behind in the snow his little friend remains there howling over the body, and that is our last memory of him as we march away with the semi-conscious Pierre. Nothing is incredible or even exaggerated in this moving scene but there is a sense of Tolstoy's exploiting his rich material, as on so many other occasions, for his own symbolic and didactic purposes. Turgenev will never use his own dogs in that manner.

Dostoyevsky's dogs, as one might expect, are a rundown, mistreated lot. At the beginning of *The Insulted and the Injured* the old man Smith has a dog, Azorka, who is said to look about eighty years old, older than any other dog on earth and, sure enough, he expires be-

fore our eyes, quietly, not long before his master does the same. In *The Idiot* we come across the bitch Norma and hear of a lapdog thrown out of a train window. In *The Brothers Karamazov* the young Ilyusha keeps a dog called Perezvon and recalls an awful trick played on another dog, Zhuchka. Earlier Dostoyevsky has recalled the cruelty meted out to dogs by the prisoners in *Notes from the House of the Dead*; Sharik is treated with indifference, Belka is ridiculously deformed and poor Kul'pyaka is quietly disposed of by an inmate who later emerges with a luxurious dog-skin lining to his boots.

Dogs continued to attract the attention of Russian writers down to the end of the century. Among Kuprin's animal stories at least three are devoted wholly or partly to dogs: *A Slav Soul, The White Poodle* and *Dogs' Happiness*. Stephen Graham says of this writer: '. . . it is part of Kuprin's sentiment to love dogs almost as much as men and he tells no tales at dogs' expense'.[7] With Chekhov several tales come immediately to mind, such as *The Lady with the Little Dog, Kashtanka* and perhaps even *Whitebrow*.

This tradition continues in the twentieth century. Leonid Andreyev wrote a story about a dog called *Snapper* and a play called *The Waltz of the Dogs*. An important figure in Blok's famous poem *The Twelve* is a mangy cur. Bulgakov's *The Heart of a Dog* and Nazhivin's *The Dogs* belong to the 1920s. In later years Zoshchenko and Ilf and Petrov include dog stories in their satirical pieces: in particular *Dog Scent* and *Ich Bin from Head to Foot,* starring the wonderful talking dog, Brunhilde. Just when one might have thought the tradition was dying out it was given a boost more recently with a dog story which is assured of lasting fame, Vladimov's *Faithful Ruslan* (a title which perhaps looks back to Saltykov-Shchedrin's *Faithful Trezor*).

This survey is anything but exhaustive. It is the result of arbitrary recollection, some desultory hunting along a few bookshelves and a little help from one or two colleagues. (Perhaps there is an appetising research topic here for a dog-loving Russophile.) Nevertheless it is very interesting. It shows that one has little difficulty in discovering twenty Russian authors who have used dogs in their writings, and determining the personal names of about fifty such fictional animals. And this provokes one or two pointed questions. Can there be any other European literature which has been as rich in dog stories (or references) over the last couple of hundred years? Where do we British now stand in regard to our claim to pre-eminence as animal-lovers? Finally, in the present context, what was Ivan Turgenev's contribution to this rich national tradition?

TURGENEV'S NOVELS

We should begin by stating clearly that he is the major contributor, outranking everyone else in both the range and the numerical extent of his dog references—there are at least a hundred of them—and in sheer quality. To put it simply, Turgenev wrote the finest dog story in Russian literature, and one of the finest to be found anywhere.

The outstanding characteristic of Turgenev's dogs is that, although they are ubiquitous, they are normally so unobtrusive as to be almost transparent. In literature as in life dogs were his natural companions; sometimes you noticed them, usually you did not, but they were nearly always there at your side. How many readers, for instance, retain a conscious recollection of any dogs at all in Turgenev's novels? Most likely, very few. Yet they are there in abundance.

Let us look first at the six novels. In *Rudin* there is one example of a merely decorative role for three unnamed dogs when, in Chapter 12, Lezhnev arrives home in his carriage. We are informed that 'Two enormous house dogs were running in front of his horse, one yellow, one grey; he had recently acquired them.' But not all dogs look and behave like aristocrats. Turgenev adds, 'An old mongrel came out at the gate to meet them, opened his mouth as if he was going to bark but ended up yawning and turning back again with a friendly wag of his tail.' Writing like this, although of modest significance, is based on close observation of the species, and a deep affection for it. Earlier in the novel, dogs are used more functionally, to demonstrate Pigasov's silliness. He treats the company at dinner to a flatulent commentary on human nature, dividing mankind into two sorts, like dogs, the long-tailed (who are self-confident and successful whatever their actual qualities) and the bob-tailed (who are timid creatures and born losers). Rudin dismisses this as turgid nonsense and Volyntsev attacks him for his lack of charity. The embarrassment is dispelled only by Darya Mikhailovna's plunging into a distracting story—about another dog belonging to her friend, the Minister X.

In both *A Nobleman's Nest* and *On the Eve* dogs are used in symbolic roles. Lavretsky returns to Vasilevskoye after a long absence (Chapter 18). The all-too-evident run-down character of the place is emphasised by the fact that 'not even a dog appeared' as he drove up. Then, in fact, we do hear a funny croaky barking from some hidden place. In the next chapter the uselessness and backwardness of the whole estate is summarised in the figure of the decrepit dog responsible for this miserable noise: he has been worn down by being heavily chained to his kennel for an entire decade. Elsewhere the lassitude and indifference of everything and everyone is epitomised in a single phrase: 'even the dogs barked indifferently'. At the beginning of Chapter 20 Lavretsky performs the inevitable symbolic action of releasing the dog from his chain, although, realistically enough, the poor chap does not recognise his newly found advantage and stays in his kennel, sunk in a

peaceful torpor. Resonating against this experience is an interesting moment described in the epilogue. Lavretsky makes another return visit, not to Vasilevskoye but to the Kalitins' household, where everything has changed. The old folk have died off and been replaced by youngsters; the replacement is expressed symbolically by the presence of new, young houseboys and the fact that 'where once the podgy Roska [the old house-dog] used to waddle solemnly, two setters raced frantically about, jumping over the sofas . . . running and barking . . .'. Then in Turgenev's next novel, *On the Eve,* Yelena's tenderness, charity and potential for positive activity are twice epitomised in her relations with dogs. In Chapter 6 we learn of her propensity for extending succour and protection to 'every underfed dog' and, in case the reader should imagine that this remark is mere rhetoric, at the outset of Chapter 14 he is informed that 'The next day, shortly after one o'clock, Yelena was standing in the garden in front of a box in which she was rearing two mongrel puppies.' (The gardener had found them abandoned . . . and brought them to her, the washer-woman having told him that the young lady was fond of any sort of animal. He had not erred in his calculation; she had rewarded him with a quarter of a rouble.)

In *Fathers and Children* the mutual suitability between Katya and her dog amounts to an association not far short of symbolism. At Odintsova's, Katya is preceded into the room (in Chapter 15) by a splendid young dog, a borzoi brimming with vitality and sporting a sky-blue collar. Her name is Fifi. She is still close to Katya in Chapter 25, where emphasis is placed upon her shapeliness, graceful attitude and connection with hunting. Her obvious aristocratism accords well with Katya's love of Mozart and the natural world, and places her well within the camp of the traditionalists, despite her youth, rather than that of the nihilists. Fifi is not far from her mind when she tells Arkady, also in Chapter 25, that Bazarov is a wild creature, whereas he and she are tame animals. The dog has also a minor functional role in the earlier chapter when Arkady begins stroking her in order to cover his growing embarrassment. Fifi may not be very noticeable in the novel but she is sweetly integrated and well observed.

Turgenev's last novel *Virgin Soil* resembles *A Nobleman's Nest* in its use of canine symbolism. In Chapter 16 Nezhdanov and Markelov look round the factory where Solomin works as manager. The place is busy but neglected and dirty, such is the emphasis on profit-making and the disregard for the needs of the people. Among the numerous details evinced to emphasise how run-down the whole place is we cannot fail to notice 'some shaggy hungry-looking dogs [which] wandered to and fro, too listless to bark'. By Chapter 23, however, the emphasis has changed. Much is now being made of Solomin's closeness to the people. He walks four miles back to the factory and is admitted with pleasure and respect by the watchman, who is followed by 'three house dogs wagging their tales with great delight'. The most pointed use of the dog in this novel, however, comes later still, in Chapter 29. Nezhdanov's failure in his attempt at 'going to the people' is recorded in its every last detail. The particularity which concerns us is that, among the several misadventures which he suffered on this occasion, he was bitten by a dog.

These references to dogs in Turgenev's novels are unassertive, almost unnoticed. They range from the purely decorative to the overtly symbolic and they are handled with a natural ease and discretion. If anything is remarkable it is merely that there are rather a lot of them—and we make no claim to have made a comprehensive survey which searches out every last one.

EARLY AND LATE WORKS

Another measure of Turgenev's enduring interest in dogs may be taken from allusions appearing in both his earliest and his last works. Three of the four narrative poems by which his name was first established in the early and mid-1840s bring dogs unobtrusively into the story. Only one of them is named—inevitably, perhaps, as Trezor, in **'The Landowner'**. At the other end of his career, in the late 1870s, Turgenev put together a series of sketches and meditations known as *Senilia*, or *Poems in Prose*. We have already observed that one of these, **'The Sparrow'**, is a fictionalised version of a hunting incident involving the real-life Trezor; he, or someone very like him, also appears in **'The Partridges'**. Much the most interesting of these pieces, however, is one which bears the title **'Sobaka'** (**'The Dog'**). The master and his dog are sitting looking at each other indoors on a stormy evening. The man is struck with a sudden awareness of the similarity between the two of them. Both embody the precious spirit of life, and this unique similarity makes the differences between them seem unremarkable. The two huddle together in spirit, sharing the short-lived and doomed sensation of being in existence. In view of his abiding sympathy for the species it is neither inappropriate nor the least bit surprising that Ivan Sergeyevich should choose a dog for this expression of sudden spiritual illumination. Incidentally, this moving little sketch should not be confused with a story of the same name in which the ghost of a dog is exorcised by the purchase of a puppy; despite recent attempts to suggest that we should take this tale seriously[8] it remains what the author described it as, a mere trifle.

The narrative poems and *Senilia* represent the relatively feeble beginning and end of Turgenev's literary career. In between, there are occasions when one might expect to meet dogs and others when it is less likely. It seems improbable, for instance, that there will be many allusions to dogs in the plays, and they probably do not exist there. On the other hand, anyone asked to select a work where dogs might be expected to abound would be likely to suggest *A Sportsman's Sketches*. One would be right to do so. The standard collection of these sketches numbers twenty-five; no fewer than twenty-three of these contain dog references. (Only the strongly narrative indoor story **'The Country Doctor'** and **'Two Landowners'**, with its static portraiture, are entirely devoid of them.) No fewer than eleven named animals appear before us: Ammalat, Astronom, Dianka, Esperans, Konteska, Milovidka, Saiga, Seryy, Valetka, Venzor and Zhuchka. Numberless anonymous fellow-travellers accompany them throughout the sketches. The amount of detail accorded to each specimen varies from the merest mention to the most intimately detailed portrait. The breed of dog ranges from the scruffiest, scraggiest mongrel to the lordliest hound. There are tiny puppies and ageing patriarchs. Every conceivable canine posture and behaviour pattern is represented and also one or two which might hitherto have been considered inconceivable.

In some sketches all we are given is a passing reminder that the narrator is a hunter and is therefore accompanied by a dog. In **'The Meeting'**, for instance, we learn that 'my dog and I' passed through a spinney, entered a birch wood and lay down to sleep. The rest of the sketch tells of what was observed when they awoke. Complete silence was needed in order not to be discovered by Akulina and Viktor; the dog is not mentioned again but we know he is there and his patient attitude is a tribute to that master-to-dog bonded relationship from which both participants derived such pleasure and pride. At the other end of the scale **'Yermolay and the Miller's Wife'** gives a detailed picture of the pointer, Valetka, a typical exemplar of that canine devotion which survives even in the face of maltreatment by humans. The first thing we learn of him is that Yermolay never fed him. 'Why should I?' he argued. 'A dog's a clever beast and ought to be able to find its own food.' We see Valetka for the last time in a later sketch, **'The Rumble of Wheels'**, when Yermolay failed to say goodbye because he was too busy beating the daylights out of his dog. Despite everything—including his ugliness—Valetka never complained or ran away, and his life, if not deliriously happy, was meaningful and long.

The sketch with the greatest number of dogs in it is **'Chertopkhanov and Nedopyuskin'**. One after another they come, mongrels, borzois, hounds and beagles, packs of dogs, puppy dogs, a dog trodden by a clumsy horse and, strange to relate, even a poodle by the name of Venzor who is being taught, albeit with little success, to read. Another amusing example of human rather than canine absurdity occurs when Pyotr Petrovich Karatayev, in the sketch that bears his name, tells of his experiences with dogs. He once kept a dozen pairs of the finest hounds and his best companion was a pointer called Konteska. Not only did she—like Turgenev's real-life Pegasus—possess the best nose in the business, but her capabilities ran to the most sophisticated of behaviour indoors. 'Give her a bit of bread with your left hand and say "A Jew ate it" (*zhid yel*) and she would refuse it. But give it to her with your right hand and say "A lady ate it" (*Baryshnya kushala*)—and she'd snap it up at once.'

It is well established that throughout the *Sketches* the land-owning class emerges as vulgar and brutal whereas the lower orders are depicted with sympathy. What has not been noticed so far is that something similar occurs in the relationship between men (those of all classes and stations) and their dogs. True, the understanding and love which exists between a hunter and his dog remains something special. As for the rest, however, if the owner is not thrashing his pitiful mongrel without sense or mercy, he is probably dressing him up in gaudy collars or silken leads or otherwise treating him as something more precious than humankind. In **'Ovskyanikov the Freeholder'** we read of a bitch with the agreeable name of Milovidka (Nice-looker) who rode in her master's carriage during her lifetime and who, when she died, was given a funeral with music in his park and an inscribed headstone on her grave.

In the course of *A Sportsman's Sketches* Man's best friend attracts scores of references. Almost all of them are literal rather than figurative. On only two occasions are dogs used in any oblique sense; both are deliberate and memorable. At the end of **'The Bailiff'** the narrator asks one of the peasants what he thinks of the bailiff in question. 'He's not a man, he's a dog', comes the reply. This bitter denunciation of a cruel brute is repeated no fewer than three times, which sharpens Turgenev's attack on those who control the peasants' destinies, though the quadruple reference does no service to the animal which he loved so much. In that moving sketch entitled **'The Living Relic'** the cheerful but moribund Lukerya has a nightmare in which she is threatened by a large, mad, fierce, red dog—an original and frightening representation of what she herself recognises as her own illness.

Elsewhere the references are all literal and, of course, exact in the observation of detail. Dogs are seen and heard, walking, running, lying, barking, growling, dozing, sneezing, yawning and performing those half-and-half actions which begin in one form (as a bark or a growl) and end in another (a cough, a yawn, a whine or a smile). We are treated to the occasional passing generalisation about the canine species, and it is clear that the generaliser knows whereof he speaks. In **'Yermolay and the Miller's Wife'** he tells us, 'It is well known that dogs can smile, and smile very sweetly too.' 'All borzois are extraordinarily stupid', he says in **'Cher-topkhanov and Nedopyuskin'**. And in **'L'gov'** he turns an expert eye on an occasion when dogs first meet each other, describing the whole curious wary and sniffy business as 'that Chinese ceremonial which is the special custom of their kind'.

Turgenev is knowledgeable and confident enough not to have to resist the temptation from time to time to invest his dogs with apparently human characteristics. His animals are credited with 'a constrained smile', 'a dignified growl', 'noble self-importance' and so on. There is no danger here of sentimentalising his dogs through tasteless anthropomorphism. Human-like behaviour is observed in, rather than forced upon, the non-human creatures. We have all seen these same characteristics in canine behaviour. Dogs do positively invite and deserve depiction as imitators of men. Turgenev recognises a basic truth about them: that they are themselves voluntary anthropomorphists, inveterate and unrepentant. The one sure conclusion about his treatment of this subject, in general terms and particularly in *A Sportsman's Sketches,* is that it suffers from not a single lapse of knowledge, judgement or taste.

Mumu

Up to this point our subject has been only semi-serious. It may be of interest that Turgenev was a lover of dogs and that this affection found in his work a broader reflexion than has been generally observed: but where does this discovery lead us? Is there no special significance in his fascination and close knowledge which might validate our otherwise rather ponderous consideration of a small corner of the great man's work? In point of fact there is good reason to direct attention towards this area, since it includes what may safely be described as one of Turgenev's finest and most significant works, a story of some ten thousand words, **'Mumu'**. It is true that this story is not usually described in quite such generous terms, but there is a strong case for asserting that the work has been undervalued. It is certainly worth reconsidering, especially in the light of what we have learnt about Turgenev's general fascination for dogs.

The facts about the writing of the story, and the details of the tale itself, although fairly well known, are worth repeating. When Nikolai Gogol died in 1852 Turgenev wrote an appreciative obituary which was turned down by the censor in St Petersburg. The authorities wanted as little publicity as possible given to the memory of a man who had written a good deal of critical, anti-establishment literature. Turgenev reacted by giving it a new title, **'A Letter from St Petersburg'**, and sending it to a Moscow journal. For this he was imprisoned for a whole month and then exiled to his estate at Spasskoye. The sentence was served in the house of a police chief and the conditions of imprisonment were hardly draconian. It was during this spell that he wrote **'Mumu'**, which turned out to be by far his most revealing and persuasive condemnation of the serf system.

The story tells of Gerasim, a giant of a man who is also a deaf-mute. (We say 'giant', although at six feet five he was only two inches taller than Turgenev himself.) At the whim of the mistress-landowner he is brought from his native countryside into the city, where eventually he settles down and falls in love with one of the house laundrymaids, Tatyana. She, alas, is married off to a drunken shoemaker in an attempt to reform him. Gerasim is consoled on the very day of her departure by his chance discovery of a tiny spaniel puppy whom he rescues from drowning in the river. He raises her and they become devoted companions. He calls her by the only kind of name he can pronounce—'Mumu'. All goes well for a time, but the little dog manages to offend the mistress and she orders them to get rid of the spaniel. The first attempt fails when Mumu, who has been sold down at the market without Gerasim's knowledge, chews through her rope and returns home. From then on he keeps her hidden away, but to no avail. The mistress discovers the trickery and now insists that the dog be put down. Rather than entrust this solemn task to anyone else Gerasim takes Mumu out on the river and drowns her himself. This is not quite the end of the story, however. Instead of returning home, Gerasim walks all the way back to his old village, and even the tyrannical mistress makes only the feeblest attempt to get him back. The embarrassing situation is, in any case, shortly resolved by the death of the old woman.

This ending is of critical importance, indicating as it does a kind of breaking-point beyond which even the traditionally submissive Russian serf cannot safely be pushed. For the middle-of-the-road Turgenev this is strong stuff, amounting almost to a prediction of revolution or even a disguised call to arms. He seems to be saying that Russian society must either mend its ways or risk pushing its lower orders eventually into determined resistance. With Mumu herself safely dispatched a little earlier, it is clear from this conclusion that we are dealing with something more than a lachrymose animal story. All the more important then that critics should get the details right. A. V. Knowles has things the wrong way round when he sets down Mumu as an example of 'the admirable quiet submission of the Russian peasant to his unhappy lot'; it is not true that Gerasim, in his words, 'continues to serve the widow faithfully despite her actions'.[9] Similarly, Leonard Schapiro leads us in the wrong direction by this summary of the story: 'The man drowns the dog, and after a period of wandering returns to his post and continues to serve his mistress.'[10] He does no such thing. These writers have confused the real-life prototype, Andrei, with Turgenev's fictional character, Gerasim. Of the former we are told by Mme V. Zhitova, a ward of Turgenev's

mother, that 'Everyone knows the unhappy fate of Mumu, with this difference only, that the devotion of Andrew to his mistress remained unchanged . . . he loved her very much. He even forgave her for Mumu's death.'[11] Turgenev will have none of this. He tells us that when the old lady found out where Gerasim had gone 'at first she gave orders for him to be sent straight back to Moscow; then she declared that such an ungrateful man was of no use whatever to her. However, she died soon after this. . . .' Gerasim's defiance, and the old lady's unprecedented impotence in the face of it, are clearly expressed.

It may be seen from the circumstances under which the story was written, and the nature of the tale itself, that it bristles with dangers, political and artistic. Turgenev is not simply writing a story: he is wreaking vengeance upon the government and society that have afflicted him, taking issue with a sworn enemy—the system of serfdom, castigating his own mother for her well-documented brutality and dabbling in details with the most tremendous potential for sentimentality. Can it be possible for the literary art to survive and succeed in such adverse circumstances?

Some people have thought not. The story of Mumu has been neglected by most critics, usually being dismissed by them in a few passing words. One of the best known and most reliable among them, Prince Mirsky, however, claims that 'Mumu . . . is a "philanthropic" story . . . where an intense sensation of pity is arrived at by methods that strike the modern reader as illegitimate, working on the nerves rather than on the imagination.'[12] The use of the word 'modern' here is interesting. It seems to suggest that new standards had come into literary criticism which might invalidate certain excesses to which earlier generations had been prone. And there were such apparent excesses. Annenkov, who attended the first reading, claimed that the story had a 'truly moving effect because of its calm yet distressing narrative tone';[13] Herzen said that it made him tremble with rage[14] and, in England, Christina Rossetti described it as 'consummate, but so fearfully painful'[15] and Thomas Carlyle went so far as to say it was the most beautiful and touching story he had ever read.[16] How are we to decide whether Mirsky is right, or whether he has misread the story and undervalued it?

We must first acknowledge that **'Mumu'** is an unusual creation for Ivan Turgenev. It is more energetic, filled with greater narrative interest and altogether more compelling than any of his other stories. It is not a love story *tout court*. It does not work with gradual persuasion on the reader's imagination and sensitivity, but rather commands attention. It is the strongest story that he ever wrote. There can be no doubt as to its ability to evoke powerful passions in its readers, now as then: pathos, hatred, admiration, disgust and fury. We may reasonably suggest that it does so by literary means which remain entirely legitimate, even for the so-called 'modern reader'. If we are dealing with a strong story, skilfully told, also fulfilling a socio-political purpose and capable of moving the reader to a variety of passions, it may be that this is one of Turgenev's finest literary achievements.

Mirsky's point about 'illegitimate' narrative methods amounts to a suggestion that Turgenev works on the heartstrings of his readers (or his 'nerves') by exploiting sentimental material in a meretricious way. This is an unfair accusation—unless one is prepared to accept that the very choice of the subject matter is self-disqualifying. Turgenev's treatment of it can hardly be described as indelicate, insensitive or in any way cheap. To begin with, the story, despite its title, is not about Mumu; it is about Gerasim. The spaniel herself appears in less than half of the narrative. And the first purpose of the story is not to move us to tears: it is to mobilise all available narrative skill and literary art in order to expose the cruelty and injustice of contemporary Russian life. Thus the sad moments in the story—the destruction of Gerasim's relationship with Tatyana and the drowning of his dog—are not the reason for its existence nor its highest achievement: they are stages in a long, progressive argument. Turgenev has manifestly avoided the temptation to write a self-enclosed tear-jerker.

The same kind of discipline attends also the manner in which the story is told. Here there are two temptations to be resisted: the narrator must not overdo the pathos and must not overemphasise the social injustices which it is his aim to portray. Turgenev proceeds with the greatest of restraint. He adopts a narrative attitude which is light-hearted rather than portentous and he spares us details which a lesser artist might well have found irresistible. The casual tone is everywhere apparent. It is achieved by the narrator's renouncing of omniscience. 'What they talked about is something we do not know . . .', he admits on one occasion, and on others he shares a friendly generalisation with the reader, such as 'To think what trifles will upset a person!' or 'But a man can get used to anything and . . .', 'Now you can understand why the butler was so upset . . .' and so forth. The ordinariness and good sense of the narrator establish a tone of moderation from which there are no lapses, not even when the dirtiest of details have to be recounted. Gerasim's agonising move from the country to the town is expressed in the simplest of terms: 'the mistress had him taken from the village where he lived alone'. Her unlimited power over all her vassals is never overstated. Referring to Kapiton, the shoemaker, she asks her butler 'Now then, Gavrila—perhaps we ought to marry him off. What do you think?' Gavrila says later to Kapiton 'You don't get beaten enough!' We learn that Gerasim was about to ask permission to marry

Tatyana—not *her* permission but the mistress's. Tatyana herself submits to her marriage with eloquent taciturnity. When the experiment of reforming her husband fails we are simply told 'Kapiton had gone to the dogs with his drinking and so, since he was a person of no use, he was despatched along with his wife on a convoy going to a remote village.' Such instances could easily be multiplied. The moving around of ordinary people at the whim of their mistress, marrying them off, rearranging their personal destinies, ordering their punishment, the expecting and receiving of no opposition—all of this is depicted as lightly and easily as it came to the mistress herself, as if it were natural and normal. Not once does the narrator lose his temper, or even his objectivity. Thus the socio-political purpose which is the real point of the story achieves a tremendous thrust from the delicate artistry with which it is handled. Turgenev knows well that no argument gains by being overstated.

If he does not err in narrative manner, selection of detail or the pursuance of a political argument, does Turgenev perhaps fail in the characterisation of '**Mumu**'? Bryusov saw the difficulty here. '"**Mumu**",' he said, '[is] classically simple and clear; the only criticism to be made of it would be a tendency towards caricature in the figure of the mistress.'[17] Yes indeed, and in some of the other characters, too. Tatyana stands for submissiveness, Kapiton for depraved conduct, the house doctor for sycophantic quackery, and so on. Perhaps they do tend towards the one-dimensional. They are, however, minor characters. If this had been a novel, no doubt Turgenev would have given us half a chapter on the doctor Khariton, nicely establishing him as a rounded figure. Instead, all we have is the following: 'This doctor, whose entire art consisted in wearing soft-soled shoes, had a light touch when taking the pulse, slept fourteen hours a day and spent the rest of the time sighing and treating the mistress with drops of laurel water.' This is not much of a character-sketch but what it loses in complexity or verisimilitude it gains in sheer flippancy—a much-needed commodity in a story of this nature. (There is, incidentally, a good deal of humour in '**Mumu**', another of its saving graces, but, as is commonly the case elsewhere, Turgenev has been given little credit for it).

The major characters in this story—setting aside the eponymous spaniel—are Gerasim and the mistress. Is it possible to determine, in her case, whether 'a tendency towards caricature' ever becomes caricature itself? For that would also be an 'illegitimate' literary method and Mirsky's charge would be upheld. One suspects that the real-life Varvara Petrovna had her own very authentic tendency towards self-dramatisation, which must have been all too familiar to those who had to live with it but which must also have seemed over-dramatic to visiting outsiders. Are we really to believe that the mistress of this story—she is not named—displays a capriciousness or a cruelty beyond the reality on which she is founded? Edmund Wilson took her very seriously in his essay on Turgenev, and saw her as motivated in an entirely understandable way. 'The bitterness of the mistress at not being loved herself', he suggests, 'figures here as a motive, and we appreciate the story more if we have some independent knowledge of Varvara Petrovna's life.'[18]

As for Gerasim, no one has ever seen fit to diminish his gigantic physical, moral or literary stature. His behaviour throughout this story, through one undeserved misadventure after another, is nothing short of magnificent. People expect him to display rage and tantrums, using some of that enormous energy to express his disappointment. He will not give them that satisfaction. His dignity and grandeur remain intact. Understated indications prove the depths of his emotion but neither he nor the narrator of his story is prepared to be belittled or cheapened by any overt display of feeling. On the cruel day of Tatyana's marriage to Kapiton we are told that 'he did not change his deportment. Only he returned from the river without any water—somehow his barrel had got broken on the way. And that evening in the stable he brushed and wiped down his horse so vigorously that she swayed about like grass in the wind and rocked from one foot to another under his iron fists.' Once again hints and suggestions stand in place of turgid explication, and understatement serves the story well. Gerasim is an unusual character, but his reality has never been questioned. He is one of Turgenev's greatest successes in characterisation, belonging to that gallery of archetypes by which this writer's name is known, an equal to Rudin, Bazarov, Lukerya, the Hamlets and Don Quixotes whom he depicted in such elemental and substantive terms. Ivan Aksakov saw Gerasim as a metaphorical representation of the Russian people, filled with a terrifying energy, yet impotent and inarticulate.[19] In a broader sense he stands for the rare human capacity to withstand adversity with dignity and to wait for the proper moment and manner to resist.

Mumu herself presents no problem. We have seen in some detail the extent of Turgenev's expertise in the matter of dogs. Without going into further detail we may state with every confidence that each particularity of Mumu's character and behaviour is accurately represented. Perhaps it is the very introduction of a dog as a central character that Mirsky regards as an illegitimate method. The danger arises from the likelihood of exaggerated sentimentality or anthropomorphism. The facts are simple. Ivan Turgenev knew his dogs so well and brought them into his work with such frequency that he is on the surest of grounds. He simply did not sentimentalise his dogs, in real life or in literature, and his only anthropomorphism is that small amount which is cultivated, as we all recognise, by dogs themselves.

Thus it emerges that the chief qualities of this story—its restraint, light tone, mild and sad humour, and the certainty deriving from Turgenev's close personal knowledge of the actual protagonists, including the dog—safely discharge the tension of embarrassment or prurience which might build up if a lesser artist were to approach the same subject. Even the details of those awful, last-minute preparations made by Gerasim, grooming his dog and giving her a final meal, and the sparing account of the actual execution on the river, are so authentic, economical and under-assertive that they pass before us without the slightest trace of bad taste. With all the respect due to a great man, Mirsky here is barking up the wrong tree.

This story is not about dogs. It is about unfair arrangements in human society, the abuse of power, the need for humanitarian generosity, the inevitability of suffering while we wait for that to emerge, and the hope of dignity while ever adversity has to be endured. If the story has been neglected, this may be because it is far from typical of the Turgenev with whom we are familiar. It is more energetic, suspenseful and optimistic than anything else he wrote. It is also full of literary quality.

When Turgenev died, a hundred and ten years ago, he was remembered by many people in Britain who had come to know him personally or by reputation. One of the wreaths which found its way to Russia to be placed upon his grave was addressed 'To the author of **"Moomoo"**'. It was sent by the Society for the Prevention of Cruelty to Animals.[20] If these well-meaning people seriously believed that **'Mumu'** was written with something like their own purposes in mind they were mistaken. If, on the other hand, they wished merely to pay tribute to one of Russia's greatest writers, who was also a great dog-lover and more successful than any other at incorporating dogs and using them in his work, the committee members who sent the wreath were not far from the truth.

Notes

1. In 1983 the centenary of Turgenev's death was marked at a weekend conference of the British Universities Association of Slavists at the University of Liverpool. This paper was given on that occasion, but not published. It is now re-presented to mark the 110th anniversary.

2. Patrick Waddington, *Turgenev and England,* New York University Press, New York, 1981, p.24.

3. See footnote to *Pegaz,* the last essay in Литературные и житейские воспоминания; Turgenev, Собрание сочинений, Gosudarstvennoe izdatel'stvo khudozhestvennoi literatury, Moscow, 1962, Vol.10, p.192.

4. Ibid. An excellent translation of this essay (*Pégas*) may be found in David Magarshack (translator

and editor), *Turgenev's Literary Reminiscences and Autobiographical Fragments,* Faber & Faber, London, 1957, pp.238-44.

5. Op.cit., p.192 (Magarshack, p.238).

6. Ibid., p.197 (Magarshack, p.244).

7. A. Kuprin, *A Slav Soul and Other Stories,* Constable, London, 1916, p.x.

8. See, for example, Frank Friedeberg Seeley, *Turgenev: A Reading of his Fiction,* Cambridge University Press, Cambridge, 1991, pp.258-62.

9. A. V. Knowles, *Ivan Turgenev,* Twayne, Boston, 1988, pp.40-41.

10. Leonard Schapiro, *Turgenev: His Life and Times,* Oxford University Press, Oxford, 1978, p.86.

11. V. Zhitova, *The Turgenev Family,* Harvill Press, London, 1947, pp.87 and 89.

12. D. S. Mirsky, *A History of Russian Literature,* Knopf, New York, 1972, p.189.

13. See N. Bogoslovsky, Жизнь замечательных людей: Тургенев, Molodaya gvardiya, Moscow, 1964, p.186.

14. I. S. Turgenev, Собрание сочинений, Vol.5, p.331.

15. Waddington, op.cit., p.197.

16. Ibid.,p.87.

17. V. Bryusov, letter of 25 July 1896, in M. P. Alekseyev, ed., Тургенев и его современники, Nauka, Leningrad, 1977, p.179.

18. Edmund Wilson, 'Turgenev and the Life-giving Drop', in Magarshack, op.cit., p.21.

19. Quoted in Schapiro, op.cit., p.88.

20. A. Yarmolinsky, *Turgenev: The Man, his Art and his Age,* Collier, New York, 1961, p.368.

Peter I. Barta (essay date 1993)

SOURCE: Barta, Peter I. "Superfluous Women and the Perils of Reading 'Faust.'" *Irish Slavonic Studies* 14 (1993): 21-36.

[*In the following essay, Barta discusses Turgenev's short story "Faust" in conjunction with the author's 1856 review of a translation of Goethe's* Faust.]

Both Turgenev's fiction and his criticism reveal an unusually strong interest in great literary works of the past: *Hamlet, Don Quixote, King Lear* and *Manon Lescaut* mark important stages in Turgenev's career. At times, Goethe's *Faust* in particular preoccupied Turgenev. He translated part of the drama into Russian, wrote a detailed review of Mikhail Vronchenko's translation of the first part of *Faust* in 1844 and published his own story, entitled '**Faust**', in the literary magazine, *Sovremennik.*[1] '**Faust**' appeared in 1856, the same year as *Rudin.* The volume of *Sovremennik* in which it was published also contained A. Strugovshchikov's translation of the first part of Goethe's *Faust.*

Turgenev's story was highly praised by Nekrasov and Tolstoy, and a French translation appeared as early as 1856; a German translation followed in 1862.[2] The story is intriguing for several reasons. In the first place it occupies a position between two prose forms—the short story and the novel: Turgenev himself referred to it as 'a novel in letters'.[3] '**Faust**' is also the first work by Turgenev to contain 'mysterious' elements.[4]

If a conventional and 'obedient' reader were to focus on the issues which the author places in the foreground, Turgenev's '**Faust**' could be regarded as typical of fiction based on the figure of the so-called 'superfluous man'. Such a reading would be limiting, however. The reader's selection of relevant details for the formation of a *gestalt* according to authorial specifications would leave on the fringes such issues as the connection between the fate of the story's heroine, Vera Nikolaevna, and the female characters in the numerous allusions to literary works in the story's plot. Turgenev's own biases and his identification with many features of the male protagonist, Pavel Aleksandrovich, are smoothly silenced in the *Rahmenerzählung*: the framework of the letters distances the author from the plot. However, the *Ich-Erzählung* format provides a strong sense of personal involvement on the part of the writer.[5]

This article will study Turgenev's '**Faust**' in connection with Turgenev's review of the Vronchenko translation of Goethe's drama (in reality, an extensive critical study of Faust). Furthermore, we shall deal with the numerous literary texts which provide background to the story's plot. Turgenev's story and his essay on Faust reflect the ideological assumptions inherent in the texts to which the story alludes: they entrap and destroy Turgenev's heroine whose function is to throw light on the suffering, catharsis and new-found, albeit trite, wisdom of the weak and egoistic man whom she loves and who, of course, survives her. (We shall assume a broad familiarity with the content of Turgenev's novella.)

The plot, embedded in a carefully constructed *fabula,* contains a spatial frame: the narrator and protagonist, Pavel Aleksandrovich, keeps paying visits from his home to the neighbouring estate where Vera Nikolaevna and her family live. Semiotic signifiers abound in Pavel Aleksandrovich's estate, and these, together with his comments about the past, provide the history of his inactive and dull life. He is only in his mid-thirties but he already feels like an old man. The vicarious experiences through the literary works with which he surrounds himself help to alleviate his boredom and influence his two activities: writing long letters to his friend in St Petersburg and playing a game of seduction with the innocent and provincial Vera. With the help of fictional works, Pavel Aleksandrovich dismantles the pillars of Vera's upbringing and attempts to present himself as the romantic, fictional lover. The story his letters narrate places him in the centre of the action; we learn almost nothing about the addressee of the letters, and none of the letters Pavel Alexandrovich *receives* is included in this one-sided 'epistolary novel'. We learn that his correspondent's name is Semen Nikolaevich; he formerly studied together with Pavel Aleksandrovich, and at the time of the story's action he runs an office in the capital. Pavel Aleksandrovich expresses no interest in him in the letters: his sole concern is his own emotional life. Whilst his description of himself as a lover is reminiscent of the fictional characters he reads about, it is uncertain whether at any stage of the story he is really in love with Vera: it *is* certain, though, that he is sorry for himself and preoccupied with his own emotions. He is unwilling to entertain the thought of accepting Vera's love for him; nevertheless he seems fascinated with himself in the role of the lover.

As a reader of Goethe's *Faust,* the idea of seduction in the play intrigues Pavel Aleksandrovich.[6] Vera—married to a kind but torpid man—also finds this aspect of the drama fascinating. Pavel and Vera engage in richly ambiguous conversations about their readings: he suggests that great pleasure awaits her as they explore the world of literature, and he supposedly refers constantly to aesthetic and not sexual pleasure. He does not seem to comprehend what Vera means when cautioning that once on 'this road, no return is available'. She, of course, talks about the seductive game whose logical conclusion is adultery. The reading of Pushkin's *Eugene Onegin* marks the beginning of the last phase in Pavel Aleksandrovich's game.[7] As they are reading together, Pavel kisses Vera's hand, and in response she blushes and rushes away.[8] It still does not suit him to acknowledge what the process is leading to. Their different interpretations of the relationship remain obscure until the end of the story where the *peripeteia* occurs. As Vera asks him what he has done to her, he still feigns surprise, taking the question as one pertaining to the discovery of aesthetic delights. Vera, however, can take it no longer and informs him that she is in love with him.

Pavel Aleksandrovich is clearly not innocent: he has consciously made Vera fall in love with him. This fact is disguised, however, by the way information is presented in the text. Since Pavel Aleksandrovich uses Goethe's *Faust* to arouse Vera's interest in him, it is help-

ful to study his particular interpretation of the play, which reflects Turgenev's own essay on the translation of *Faust*. Turgenev writes that *Faust* is beyond the reach of people who have a mind solely for practical matters: they will understand *Hamlet* and *Macbeth* but not *Faust*.[9] Thus, having met the members of Vera's circle, Pavel Aleksandrovich deliberately selects *Faust* for a public reading in the belief that everybody in the company except Vera will fail to keep up with the text. In particular, he knows that Priimkov, Vera's husband, will be unable to share the aesthetic experience that will affect him and Vera, since the reading is in the original German and Priimkov's German is poor. In this way, Vera will see that her husband is inferior to Pavel Aleksandrovich. Priimkov, true to the specifications of Turgenev's *Faust* essay, demonstrates that his mind is good only for practical banalities: he asks Pavel Aleksandrovich at an inappropriate moment when he is about to begin the reading of *Faust* whether he would like some sweetened water to drink. His heart filled with condescension for Priimkov, Pavel Aleksandrovich addresses his performance to the lady of the house.

But the manipulation of Vera's feelings does not end here. Pavel Aleksandrovich reads out a meticulously compiled selection of passages from Goethe's *Faust*. For instance, Pavel, like Turgenev, dismisses the second part of Goethe's drama because of its supposed artistic flaws. He explicitly says that he is to omit from his reading such parts as the 'Walpurgisnacht' and the 'Intermezzo'. What he does not mention, however, is that he will be presenting a substantially more abbreviated version even than that. This becomes clear in the atmospheric detail provided by Turgenev. Thus, we know that the reading in the garden pavilion got under way as it was getting dark since, as they were walking towards the pavilion, a pink hue covered the cloud in front of them as the sun was setting. The reading took place on 19 June, which even according to the old calendar, is one of the longest evenings in the year. In the Orlov province in the central part of European Russia, where the estate (strongly reminiscent of Spasskoe) presumably is located, the sun would be setting some time between 8:30 and 10:00 at the present time; but in the nineteenth century this would have been two hours earlier, between 6:30 and 8:00 p.m.: St Petersburg time was one, and not two, hours ahead of Central European time and there was no daylight-saving time in the summer. We know that behind them there was an ominous black cloud, suggesting that a storm was approaching. We also know that after the reading they returned to the house for supper and there was lightning outside. Even for an experienced reader surrounded by a well-prepared audience, the first part of Goethe's *Faust* will take at least five and a half, perhaps six, hours of reading. If this had been the case, the company would have gathered for supper after midnight in the small hours of the morning. According to the customs which prevailed among the provincial gentry in households like Vera Nikolaevna's, this would have been rather unlikely. Nor does a giant storm cloud normally wait for six hours in north-eastern Europe in June before lightning and thunder occur. Most probably what happened was that Pavel Aleksandrovich read out an assortment of highlights from *Faust,* taking no more than one and a half, at the most two, hours. His intention was to steer Vera's thoughts to seduction and so he focused on those portions of the text that related to Faust and Gretchen, skipping the rest.

Pavel Aleksandrovich's attempts to make Vera fall in love with him face no obstacles. Vera is free to give in to what she mistakenly supposes to be his intention: to run away with her, or make love to her in secret. Her husband is well-meaning and unsuspecting, and can safely be ignored. In the past, her mother, Yeltsova, had forbidden Pavel Aleksandrovich to marry Vera after he limply asked for her hand, regarding him as weak and not really in love with Vera. She is now dead, and Pavel admits in a letter his satisfaction at overcoming the dead woman's will. However, his irresolute actions after being turned away by Yeltsova confirmed that she had been correct about him: he took her rejection without opposition, failed to inform Vera about his desire to marry her, departed and forgot her. During their first acquaintance, he chose not to remain alone with Vera after he noticed that she loved him. He even admits in one of his letters that Vera's type does not attract him, so presumably he proposed to marry her merely because he thought that that was the appropriate thing to do. The wise and experienced Yeltsova must have sensed that he did not love her daughter. During his second 'courtship' he fancies that he is in love, although he hastens to add in his letter to his friend that he knows that his love is hopeless. He fails to elaborate, however, upon the fact that the relationship is doomed not because of Vera's unwillingness, but rather his own. He is too conventional to contemplate the violating of social norms which would undoubtedly be involved were he to return Vera's love. Therefore, having falsely raised her expectations, he fails her a second time too.

In assuming the role of the romantic lover, the sentimental educator of the naive Vera, Pavel Aleksandrovich is encouraged to identify with Faust himself. In his seventh letter, he addresses Mephistopheles in a theatrical manner: О МеФистоФель! и ты мне не помогаешь.'[10] Yet, while Turgenev's **'Faust'** contains a large number of allusions to the first part of Goethe's *Faust,* Pavel Aleksandrovich himself has almost no Faustian qualities to speak of.[11] A good case in point is the occasion when Vera fails to turn up to a night-time rendezvous by the lake. Pavel Aleksandrovich wanders by her house, which has lights blazing even though it is before midnight. The reason for this is that Vera is very ill and the family are about to send for the doctor: yet

Pavel tells himself that they must surely be entertaining guests and that this is the reason Vera did not come to their meeting. He ought to have realised, of course, that the determined and resourceful Vera would not stay away from their meeting merely because of guests. He probably invents reasons for himself not to have to be involved in unpleasantness inside the house for which he knows he is responsible. This scene, indeed, exhibits certain similarities with the 'Walpurgisnacht' episode which Pavel Aleksandrovich so carefully skipped in his reading of the play. In that episode Faust is unaware that Gretchen is in great trouble. He displays callousness, having seduced Gretchen and then left her, killed her brother and put her mother to sleep for good with the aid of the devil. But Faust is not hypocritical and untrue to himself as Pavel Aleksandrovich is. It is noteworthy that on her deathbed Vera identifies Pavel Aleksandrovich not with Faust but with Mephistopheles: as she catches sight of him, we read in Pavel Aleksandrovich's ninth letter, she quotes Gretchen's words from the final scene of Part I of *Faust*: 'Чего хочет он на освященном месте, / Этот . . . вот этот'.[12] Gretchen's original words, 'Der! Der! Schicke ihn fort! / Was will er an dem heiligen Ort?' (4602-3) are uttered when she catches sight of Mephistopheles as Faust implores her to escape with him from the prison cell.[13]

Indeed, Pavel Aleksandrovich's analogy with Faust is an unflattering one. Faust wants to understand the mysteries of life and seeks to experience the fullness of existence and infinity: it is because of the powerful thirst for knowledge and experience that he gives away his soul and sacrifices his salvation. Pavel Aleksandrovich pales by comparison: whereas Faust leaves Gretchen beautiful jewels to tempt her, Pavel Aleksandrovich merely points out to Vera a pinkish-coloured cloud in the sky. Instead of rebelling against human limitations, the lacklustre Pavel Aleksandrovich never violates his sense of boring propriety.[14] Instead of the Faustian thirst for knowledge, boredom propels Pavel Aleksandrovich to disrupt the lives of those around himself.

In fact, Pavel Aleksandrovich seems to be unsuccessful at everything he does. Thus, he states that he prefers not to discuss why, upon his return to Berlin after the first courtship of Vera, his plans to be active *failed* to materialize. He also *failed* in Moscow society: even his own butler intimidated him and made him feel insecure. His estate is in ruins, while his servants and his house are neglected and are in a state of decay. And as he takes Vera Nikolaevna on an outing on the lake, it is Schimmel, the old German, who has to take control of the boat when the wind starts gusting and Pavel cannot handle the vessel. His very language is unoriginal and heavily cliché-laden: he came home to 'find himself'; he complains about the impossibility of 'starting life over again'. He writes in the seventh letter: 'должно зить с пользой, с целью на земле, исполнять свой долг, свое дело. И я принялся было за работу . . . Вот опять все развеяно, как вихрем!'[15] Even his quotation from Pushkin's poem, 'Разговор книгопродавца с поэтом', is incorrect: he says 'Я содрогаюсь—сердце больно— / Мне стыдно идолов моих' instead of the correct 'Я так и вспыхну, сердцу больно: / Мне стыдно идолов моих'.[16]

The narrative, however, disguises Pavel Aleksandrovich's mediocrity. It is his viewpoint that dominates and marginalises information which could mar the desired image of the world around him. He presents himself as an exhausted, liberal Russian intellectual, paralysed by the socio-political realities of an oppressive and dictatorial Russian society, which has no room for people of his kind. His vital energies have been spent: therefore, even when he is in love, he fails to deliver the promise and disappoints the beloved woman.[17] In short, he is a 'superfluous man', at least from the viewpoint of the dominant school of criticism in Russia.

However, I have argued elsewhere that the conventional critical concept of the 'superfluous man' is not useful. Its understanding as a 'reflection' of a social type oversimplifies the process of mimesis in writing: texts reflect other texts rather than serving as an attentive and subservient mirror, offering a thoroughly compiled copy of some kind of 'real world'.[18] Rather, it is social behaviour that reflects ideology generated by discourse in places such as novels. Calling a man such as Pavel Aleksandrovich or Rudin 'superfluous' implies that personal behaviour is a direct result of socio-political reality. So, whilst it lacks psychological subtlety and has firmly sexist implications, 'superfluous man' is convenient as a term by which an egoistical and mediocre person can be depicted more positively.

Pavel Aleksandrovich wants the recipient of his letters to think highly of him. In one letter he implicitly compares himself to Hamlet, by addressing Semen Nikolaevich as 'Horatio'. He implies that there is some analogy between his return to his home and Odysseus's *nostos* to Ithaca: he complains that his dog had died and failed to wait for him as Argos did for his master. His generalisations suggest that he is a wise man of the world: he pontificates without any hesitation that the second part of *Faust* is worthless, that every old German smells of chicory and that married women with children should show visible signs of ageing: he expresses displeasure that Vera Nikolaevna has not lost her looks as he has. Nevertheless, being with her is pleasant for him. Vera gratifies Pavel Aleksandrovich's vanity, for, rather than reminding him of his useless life, she makes him feel important by allowing him to 'educate' her. He looks after his own mental well-being with meticulous care: he objectifies his feelings, concerns and hopes in his letters, oblivious of the fact that Vera, on the other hand, has no one to talk or write to about her feelings.

And he shows little interest in the consequences of his own behaviour for Vera: when the friend, Semen Nikolaevich, offers to come and take him away to prevent a possible tragic ending to the relationship, he turns the offer down. He asks his friend to spare his feelings, which is more than he does for Vera.

A conventional reading, which follows the important signposts placed along the reader's path, will concede that the story's basic concern is an ethical one.[19] Pavel Aleksandrovich's comments at the end of the story suggest that he has matured into a wise and sad man with a sense of duty and moral integrity, an 'Ancient Mariner' of the nest of the gentry. According to the story's 'message', confirmed in numerous scholarly articles, he has learnt from his affair with Vera Nikolaevna that 'duty' is more important than personal aspirations.[20]

The story's epigraph is a quotation from Goethe from the scene entitled 'Faust's Study': 'Enthbehren sollst du! Sollst entbehren!' (1549). The old scholar, Faust, utters these words with a sense of bitterness: in response to Mephistopheles's advice to don a youthful mask 'to find out what life is all about', he says that nothing can alter the human predicament of infinite imagination locked into transience. An aged man, he is expected to renounce the ways of the world yet he is in no mood to do so. In Turgenev's story, Pavel Aleksandrovich's last letter, set against the allusions to Goethe, implies that he has risen above supposed Faustian egoism.[21] However, Pavel Aleksandrovich's repeated suggestions about having understood the paramountcy of duty are unconvincing if we consider his pattern of behaviour. His trite and cliché-ridden discourse does not change between the beginning and the end of the story and it is highly questionable whether his behaviour does either. In fact, by 'performing one's duty' what Pavel Aleksandrovich (and Turgenev) means is the performance of useful activities in the spirit of Belinsky's 'sociality'.[22]

The epigraph is not, in fact, particularly relevant in the story.[23] Its inclusion overtly invites comparisons between Faust and Pavel Aleksandrovich, yet I have implied above that the limp Pavel Aleksandrovich and Faust really have nothing in common. This fact contradicts Turgenev's apparent intention to have the story **'Faust'** illustrate his theory about Goethe. Turgenev's essay seems to imply that Goethe is an 'egoistic' Romantic who sings about beauty, but this is not what Russia needs in the 1840s. Rather, according to Turgenev, this is a time for activists who are willing to effect social and political changes.[24] Consistent with this vision, Pavel Aleksandrovich is supposed to mature into this activist at the end of the story. As a result of his personal loss, the narrative suggests, he reaches a more advanced state of human life than Faust: he aspires to a higher purpose.[25] This is not altogether convincing, and we need to examine Turgenev's own character and views in order to understand why.

Features of Turgenev's own character inform Pavel Aleksandrovich's personality, and this may partly explain why he is presented with so much sympathy in **'Faust'**. For example, elements from Turgenev's essay on Goethe's *Faust* enter Pavel Aleksandrovich's discourse directly. Comments about the *sui generis* features of the old German teacher, Schimmler, echo Turgenev's own comments about Goethe's Wagner in *Faust* as a 'немец par excellence'.[26] Turgenev skips 'Walpurgisnacht' and 'Intermezzo' in his essay, just as Pavel Aleksandrovich omits these in his own reading. Both the author and the character enthuse about Goethe's 'Earth Spirit' scene,[27] and they similarly disregard the entire second part of *Faust.* Pavel Aleksandrovich's loving memories of reading *Faust* in his youth in Berlin echo those of Turgenev.[28] Pavel Aleksandrovich's estate and its surroundings resemble the Turgenev estate at Spasskoe and his relationship with Vera Nikolaevna recalls aspects of Turgenev's friendship with Maria Nikolaevna Tolstaya, Lev Tolstoy's sister.[29] Indeed, Turgenev corresponded with Maria Tolstaya concerning Goethe's *Faust,*[30] and it is also of interest that Maria Tolstaya did not like to read literary works.[31]

Again like Turgenev, Pavel Aleksandrovich is condescending about unsophisticated women and is drawn to Platonic relationships with married noblewomen.[32] Pavel Aleksandrovich's comments and Turgenev's essay on Goethe's *Faust* both reflect these attitudes. The general positive evaluation of Mephistopheles in Turgenev's essay (and story) is oblivious of Mephistopheles's role in Gretchen's fate and reflects only his impact on Faust's life.[33] In this context, Turgenev is sufficiently biased against Gretchen to overlook specific textual evidence in Goethe's *Faust*: he suggests in his article on *Faust* that Gretchen is stupid in that she immediately falls in love with Faust as he decisively approaches her: 'Фауст знакомится с ней решительно и смело, как все гениальные люди; Гретхен в него влюбляется тотчас.'[34] If we look at the scene which Turgenev analyses, it becomes evident that his reading distorts it:

FAUST:

> Mein schönes Fräulein, darf ich wagen,
> Meinen Arm und Geleit Ihr anzutragen?

MARGARETE:

> Bin weder Fräulein, weder schon,
> Kann ungeleitet nach Hause gehn. (Sie macht sich
> 　los
> und ab)

(2605-8)

Faust indeed makes a strong impression on Gretchen but she unambiguously rejects his initial approach rather than showing any obvious sign of 'immediately falling in love'.

Turgenev's condescending attitude about her is blatantly obvious in his article:

> О самой Гретхен мы не будем много распространяться: она мила, как цветок, прозрачна, как стакан воды, понятна, как дважды два-четыре; . . . она, впрочем, несколько глупа. Но Фауст и не требует особенных умственных способностей от своей возлюбленной.[35]

Turgenev even admonishes the Russian translator, M. Vronchenko, for suggesting that Gretchen is bright:

> мю теперь же не можем не заметить г-ну переводчику, что он, при первой встрече Фауста с Гретхен, напрасно заставляет его говорить про нее:

> > Как недоопустна и скромна,
> > И, кажется, притом умна!

> В подлиннике сказано: 'Und etwas Schnippisch doch zugleich . . .' Schnippisch—непереводимое слово: оно скорее значит—жеманна в хорошем смысле . . . но не в коем случае не умна.[36]

In spite of Turgenev's criticism, 'schnippisch' *does* imply wit and intellect and not 'affectedness' as жеманство does, even though the short form of the adjective умный does indeed put greater emphasis on intellectual potential than the original German text calls for.

As Turgenev discusses the final scene of Goethe's *Faust,* he suggests that Gretchen in her stupidity is morally superior to Faust: 'Гретхен, этот бедный, глупый, обманутый ребенок, в этой сцене не в тысячу ли раз выше умного Фауста . . .'.[37] This argument strongly reminds one of the conclusion of Turgenev's article, 'Гамлет и Дон Кихот': Hamlet is brilliant but weak and inactive and ruins everything, whereas Don Quixote is positive and strong, albeit insane. The Russian Hamlet, a petty demon, stands for the Turgenevian superfluous man and Don Quixote represents the type of strong and loving female involved with the superfluous man. Her quixotic element lies in her passion and self-sacrificing heroism which take the upper hand over practical, *comme-il-faut* behaviour. The critical tradition which identifies Pavel Aleksandrovich as the superfluous man and Vera Nikolaevna as the strong woman accepts the ideological moorings of Turgenev's study on Hamlet and Don Quixote. In his famous article, 'Русский человек на рандеву', Chernyshevsky confirms Turgenev's theory of the superfluous man. Describing Pavel Aleksandrovich, Chernyshevsky writes that his indecisiveness in matters of love reflects his attitude to socially useful activities. He is such an impossible lover, Chernyshevsky argues, that it is the woman who must confess her love first. Then he goes on: 'Не удивительно, что после такого поведения любимого человека, у бедной женщины сделалась нервичекая горячка.'[38]

In addition to the sexist assumption of the passage (namely, that nice women expect to assume a passive role in courtship), Chernyshevsky also ignores the possibilities, first, that Pavel Aleksandrovich may not have a great deal to contribute to society and, secondly, that it is Vera and not he who is superfluous. He uses Vera to the maximum: more than the object of his love, she is a means of allowing him to experience love. She gives him much-needed self-esteem and her death provides him with a purpose in life: now he can see himself as a tragic figure who, after a great crisis, will devote himself solely to the call of duty (the implication here is, of course, misleading, as Pavel Aleksandrovich did not preoccupy himself with frivolous or bohemian undertakings at the expense of 'duty' before the events described in the story: he was merely leading a boring life). Having made her confession to him, Vera fulfilled her useful task in complementing the male protagonist; she is now superfluous and the only useful thing for her to do is die. Were she to live, further humiliations would await Pavel Aleksandrovich instead of the opportunity to parade as a wise man of tragic grandeur.

Male mediocrity and vanity, then, destroy the female character. 'Strong' woman is a misnomer in such fiction as *Rudin* or **'Faust'**: the odds are so much against women in their male-dominated society that they cannot prevail. A good illustration of this is the relationship between Pavel Aleksandrovich and Vera's determined mother, Yeltsova. Pavel Aleksandrovich recalls: 'я как-то сказал ей, что все мы, современные люди, надломленные . . . Надламывать себя не для чего,—промолвила она,—надо всего себя переломить или уж не трогать . . .'.[39] Yeltsova's comments indicate that she sees all too clearly that Pavel Aleksandrovich attempts to put the blame for his weakness and indecisiveness on socio-political factors and also that she is not impressed by Pavel Aleksandrovich's complaints.[40] From Pavel Aleksandrovich's viewpoint, of course, it is Yeltsova who is 'superfluous', since her presence prevents him from luring Vera into a hopeless relationship.

Pavel Aleksandrovich's harmful influence manifests itself in the literature to which he exposes Vera and through which he counters the dead mother's wish to keep her daughter from him. There is a further interesting issue here, concerning Vera's reading matter. Her mother, Yeltsova, insisted on educating Vera solely in the exact sciences and not in literature. Moreover, so long as she obeyed her mother and stayed away from books she was contented; but once she gave in to Pavel Aleksandrovich's urgings and read the books he recommended, her demise ensued.

In order to appreciate this point, it is necessary to specify what the characters mean by 'literature'. The influential books in question include such famous works as *Faust, Eugene Onegin* and the novels which surround Pavel Aleksandrovich at his estate: Prévost's *Manon Lescaut,* Vicomte d'Arlincourt's *Le Solitaire,* Restif de la Bretonne's *Le paysan perverti* and Voltaire's *Candide*. The importance of each of these texts within the consciousness of Turgenev's **'Faust'** merits a closer look. The narrator refers to one of the pictures on the wall of his room as 'Manon Lescaut'. The portrait of Vera's grandmother, an Italian peasant woman who wanted to elope with the man she loved and was killed for this, also reminds him of Manon. Prévost's heroine resists parental tyranny, and clearly this is also a feature of Vera, her mother and her grandmother. In Prévost's novel, the character Des Grieux, like Vera's grandfather and father, suggests that Manon should elope with him to avoid a life of restrictions. However, their life together is fraught with tremendous hardships and in the end Manon dies and is survived by a now wise, if saddened, Des Grieux. In what seems like a direct parallel, Pavel Aleksandrovich is similarly wise and sad after the untimely death of Vera.

Furthermore, the curtains in Pavel Aleksandrovich's room show scenes from Arlincourt's *Le solitaire,* in which a boorish-looking hermit is abducting a young woman. The hermit loves Eloide, although he has killed her father, destroyed her uncle and seduced her cousin. Faust, it will be recalled, similarly destroyed the family of the woman he loved. In Pushkin's novel, too, Eugene Onegin's boredom-induced flirtation leads to Lensky's death and Tatyana's unhappiness. The mediocre and lacklustre Pavel Aleksandrovich has killed nobody, nor is he a boor; but, like the protagonists of his readings, he thoroughly disrupts peaceful lives to no purpose. From a different perspective, *Le Paysan perverti* and *Candide* relate how wordly adventures unsettle the foundations of one's early education. In **'Faust'**, Pavel Aleksandrovich offers to Vera merely vicarious adventures from books; but these nevertheless destroy her peace of mind, founded in the education she had received from her mother. When she realises that Pavel Aleksandrovich is unwilling or unable to offer anything in return for the tranquillity she has sacrificed, her life loses its meaning. In the fictional world of the story **'Faust'**, as in Turgenev's own society, books are believed to reflect 'reality' mimetically, that is by imitation.[41] The world the books in the story project centres on the Fausts, Onegins and Des Grieux, for whom the purpose of female figures is to illuminate and complement the males. Once they have done that, they die or disappear in boring marriages, because they have become superfluous. Why do books entrap such young female readers as Tatyana in *Eugene Onegin,* Natasha in *Rudin* or Vera in **'Faust'**?[42] The narratives in these women's readings first of all confirm a world order which denies them their space as individuals and then induce them to accept their own position as superfluous women whose task is to admire the men who reject or destroy them before learning their lessons.

At the very moment Vera allows passion to take over, she seeks protection under her mother's lifelike portrait. She admits that she never wanted to be free from the protection of her mother, Yeltsova, who knows from her own and her mother's experience that whenever women give way to passion tragedy strikes. Yeltsova advises her daughter to be like ice and never to reveal her desire. She bans books whose plots confirm their own ideological moorings. Woman's desire is thus seen as a threat to the male-dominated social order: it is not allowed to be realised, but is to be depicted as a means for a better description of male desire. Women who, like Yeltsova, show real strength and rebel will be turned into frightening creatures with supernatural powers. Thus, rather than accusing Pavel Aleksandrovich alone of destroying Vera, the narrative implies that the mother, propelled by dark forces, like a witch, came back from the dead to haunt her daughter in order to stop her from ignoring her injunction never to read novels.

Turgenev's **'Faust'** deals therefore with the consequences of violating authority, three forms of which inform the story: patriarchal, matriarchal and narratorial. This study has focused on the realist narrative's attempt to disguise the text's ability to lead the reader to reconsider socially naturalised ideological assumptions which are, by their nature, artificial constructs. They minimise the inconsistencies of the patriarchal order and marginalise matriarchal values: grandmother, mother and daughter die before their strong will and determination can change the world in which self-serving male interests prevail.

Notes

1. The review appeared anonymously; however, there seems to be little doubt that Turgenev was the author: see Elias Rosenkratz, 'Turgenev und Goethe', *Germanoslavica,* Vol.2, nos.1-4 (1932), pp.76-90 (p.77).

2. Peter Thiergen, 'Iwan Turgenews Novelle "Faust"', in Günther Mahal, ed., *Faust-Rezeption in Rußland und in der Sowjetunion.,* Knittlingen: Faust-Museum, 1983, pp.65-9 (p.66).

3. Ivan Turgenev, Полное собрание сочинений и писем в дваддати восьми томах, Izdatel'stvo Akademii Nauk SSSR, Moscow and Leningrad, 1960-64, vol.6 (1964), pp.357-8.

4. D. Zsuzsa Zöldhelyi, *Turgenyev prozai költemenyei,* Tankönyvkiadó, Budapest, 1991, p.38. Under Belinsky's influence, in the years preceding 'Faust', Turgenev rejected mysterious elements in literature. Because he regarded such elements as characteristic of the German 'soul' it is hardly surprising that the writing of his own 'Faust' should inspire him to change his mind about transcendental motifs: see ibid., pp.39-40.

5. Thoma Eekman, 'Turgenev and the Shorter Prose Forms' in Peter Alber Jensen (ed.), *Texts and Contexts: Essays to Honor Nik Åke Nillson,* Almqvist & Wiksell International, Stockholm, 1987, pp.42-52 (p.48).

6. E. Steffensen, 'Гете и Тургенев (анализ рассказа Тургенева "Фауст")' in S. V. Martselev, ed., Славянская культура и мировой культурный процесс, Nauka i tekhnika, Minsk, 1985, pp.226-30 (p.228).

7. Ibid.

8. *Eugene Onegin* is yet another story in which seduction is attempted. Here, however, Onegin, who rejected young and innocent Tatyana the first time, is in turn rejected by her a few years later when she is a dignified and unhappily married woman.

9. Turgenev, op.cit., vol.1 (1960), p.213.

10. Ibid., vol.7 (1964), p.40.

11. A. Bem, 'Faust bei Turgenev', *Germanoslavica.* 1932-33:2 (1-4), pp.359-68 (p.365). We find many direct allusions to Goethe's Faust. For example, as Vera Nikolaevna and Pavel Alexandrovich prepare for the reading of Faust in the Chinese pavilion in the park, Vera's daughter, Natasha, is frightened by a spider. In Faust, Mephistopheles appears before Faust for the first time in the form of a poodle. Vera is not frightened; rather, she takes the spider into her hands. Later, she explains that Mephistopheles does not terrify her as the devil but as a natural force present in humans. Schimmel's and Priimkov's trivial comments remind one of Wagner and Martha. Schimmel's presence by the side of Vera irritates Pavel Alexandrovich as Martha's company frustrated Faust in courting Gretchen. But as Schimmel is in charge of the boat carrying Pavel and Vera and sings sexually suggestive songs, he is reminiscent of Mephistopheles too.

12. Turgenev, op.cit., vol.7, p.49.

13. It is noteworthy that the young Turgenev translated the final scene of Part I of Goethe's *Faust* into Russian. Entitled 'Последняя сцена первой части Фауста Гете', the translation, signed by 'Т. Л.', appeared in Отечественные записки, June 1844, vol. 34, part 1, pp.220-26. It is clearly not accidental that Turgenev is preoccupied with Gretchen. The 'women's question' was of great interest among Western-oriented liberal writers at the time: cf. Herzen's Кто виноват?

14. V. N. Tikhomirov, 'Традиции Гете в повести Тургенева "Фауст"', Вопросы русской литературы, 1977, 1 (29), pp.92-9 (p.95); Stefenson, op.cit., p.229.

15. Turgenev, op.cit., vol.7, p.39.

16. I. A. Bityugova, 'Фауст', in I S. Turgenev, Полное собрание сочинений . . . , vol.7 (1964), pp.395-414 (p.413). Inaccurate quotations are frequent both in Turgenev's letters and in his fiction. While, undoubtedly, carelessness accounts for some of these, Zsuzsa Zöldhelyi suggests that such 'mistakes' are frequently purposeful. Slightly altered quotations thus turn into powerful allusions: see Zsuzsa Zöldhelyi, 'A puszta Lear Királya', *Filológiai Közlöny,* 1979, nos 3-4, p.264.

17. The well-articulated ideological charge of the narrative is obediently decoded by some critics. P. A. Kropotkin writes in *Idealy i deistvitel'nost' v russkoi literature* (St Petersburg, 1907, 102: '[В Фаусте] слышится почти отчаяние в образованном русском интеллигенте, который даже в любви оказывается неспособным проявить синнное чувство . . .; даже при самых благопиятных обстоятельствах, он может принести любящей его женщине только печаль и отчаяние' (cited from Bityugova, op.cit, p.409).

18. Peter I. Barta, 'Closure and Cracks in the Mirror: Narrative and Ideology in Turgenev's *Rudin*', *Scottish Slavonic Review,* Autumn 1990, pp.31-41 (p.33).

19. See, for instance, L.N. Tokarev, '"Фауст" Гете в оценке И.С. Тургенева', Вестник московского университета, серия ВИИ, Филология, Журналистика, 1961, no.1, pp.65-74 (p.72).

20. Katharina Schutz, *Das Goethebild Turgeniews,* Bern, Verlag Paul Haupt, 1952, p.108; Tikhomirov, op.cit, pp.72-3; Bityugova, op.cit, p.402). R. L. Jackson suggests that Pavel Aleksandrovich's comment, 'Вера погибла, а я уцелел', is a parody on the beginning of the second part of Faust: 'Das Lebens Pulse schlagen frisch lebending / Ätherische Dämmerung milde zu begrüßen': see Robert Louis Jackson, 'Взаимосвязь *Фаусма* Гете и *Комедии* данте в замысле рассказа Тургенева "Фауст"' in Paul Debreczeny (ed.), *American Contributions to the Ninth International Congress of Slavists,* Kiev, September 1983, Vol.2, Columbus, OH: Slavica, p.242.

21. Faust's interests in his personal happiness rather than the good of society has become a standard critical commonplace in Russia: see V. M. Zhirmunsky, Гете в русской литературе, Nauka, Leningrad, 1981, p., 282; he quotes Turgenev's views on the subject extensively.

22. Andre von Gronicka, 'Goethe's Influence on I. S. Turgenev's "Faust" and "Asia" Novellae', in John A. McCarthy (ed.), *Aufnahme-Weitergabe: Literarische Impulse um Lessing und Goethe,* Hamburg, Helmut Buske Verlag, 1982, pp.193-204 (p.198).

23. Bem, op.cit, p.366.

24. Zhirmunsky, op.cit., p.284.

25. Jackson, op.cit., p.241.

26. Turgenev, op.cit., vol.1, p.227.

27. Gronicka, op.cit., p.194; Schutz, op.cit, p.111.

28. See Gronicka, op.cit., p.203, note 8.

29. Bityugova, op.cit., pp.397, 399.

30. Thiergen, op.cit., p.67.

31. Bityugova, op.cit., p.399.

32. Barta, op.cit, pp.35-6.

33. Turgenev, op.cit, vol.1, p.226.

34. Ibid., p.231.

35. Ibid.

36. Ibid.

37. Ibid., p.233.

38. Cited from Bityugova, op.cit, p.408.

39. Turgenev, op.cit., vol.7, p.17.

40. All the women in Vera's family are determined in pursuing their passion and even if they fail they are stronger in their death than the men who survive them. The attempts of Vera's grandmother and mother to attain their freedom ended tragically. The grandmother, an Italian peasant woman, fell in love with a Russian nobleman and gave birth to his daughter, Vera's mother. Her jealous Italian fiancé killed her as she was fleeing with the Russian, Vera's grandfather. Bereft, Yeltsova's father devoted his life to spiritualist experiments. He did not want his daughter to leave and she had to flee from him with Yeltsov. Endowed with supernatural powers, he predicted that his daughter's life would be unhappy: sure enough, Yeltsov was accidentally shot while hunting and Yeltsova failed in her attempt to save Vera from her demise. The details about the family's past in the story's fabula contain many mysterious elements. In the *sujet,* too, mysterious elements play a significant role: Yeltsova seems 'alive' on her portrait. Furthermore, Vera's daughter shows a striking resemblance to her grandmother, as if Yeltsova were present in her granddaughter.

41. Christine Johanson, 'Turgenev's Heroines: A Historical Assessment', *Canadian Slavonic Papers,* vol.27, no.1 (1984), pp.15-23 (p.15).

42. Tatyana in Pushkin's *Eugene Onegin* and Francesca in the fifth canto in Dante's *Divine Comedy* so strongly believe what they read that they confuse the world of fiction with the reality of their own lives, suggests Riccardo Picchio: see Ricardo Picchio, 'Dante and J. Malfilatre as Literary Sources of Tat'jana's Erotic Dream (Notes on the Third Chapter of Puskin's Evgenij Onegin)', in Andrej Kodjak and Kiril Taranovsky (eds), *Alexander Pushkin: A Symposium on the 175th Anniversary of His Birth,* New York, New York University Press, 1976, p.46.

Elizabeth Cheresh Allen (essay date 1995)

SOURCE: Allen, Elizabeth Cheresh. "Turgenev's Last Will and Testament: Poems in Prose." In *Freedom and Responsibility in Russian Literature: Essays in Honor of Robert Louis Jackson,* edited by Elizabeth Cheresh Allen and Gary Saul Morson, pp. 53-68. Evanston, Ill.: Northwestern University Press, 1995.

[*In the following essay, Allen considers Turgenev's* Poems in Prose *as the appropriate conclusion to a great literary career in an attempt to reassert the author's position in literary history.*]

Turgenev's final published work, *Poems in Prose* (***Stikhotvoreniia v proze***), can prove puzzling—and even somewhat discomfiting—to those of his current readers who encounter it. In contrast to the preponderance of his earlier works, this last collection of writings appears, to put it charitably, uneven, whether judged aesthetically, psychologically, or philosophically. Except for brevity, it is difficult to discover any common thread, any unifying force for coherence among these brief sketches. Nor do strong underlying affinities between them and Turgenev's other compositions readily make themselves manifest. What is more, on the surface they display no achievement in either form or contents meriting their placement alongside the best Western representatives of this genre—the prose poems of Baudelaire, Rimbaud, Mallarmé, and Rilke. In this essay, therefore, I attempt to establish these seeming trifles as a fitting conclusion to what, at the time they were written, was generally viewed in both Russia and the West as Turgenev's masterly, triumphant literary career. In so doing, I also seek to reaffirm the importance of that career today, since its reputation has gradually diminished during the course of the twentieth century, especially in comparison with the reputations of Turgenev's foremost Russian contemporaries, Dostoevsky and Tolstoy.

To achieve these goals, I will argue that close study of the *Poems in Prose,* accompanied by efforts to place them in relation to their nineteenth-century Western European counterparts, at the very least leads to an appreciation of what Turgenev was *trying* to accomplish by writing them as, so to speak, his literary last will and testament. Although one need not wholly subscribe to the maxim "To understand all is to forgive all," this appreciation of Turgenev's *Poems in Prose* may foster a willingness to forgive any inadequacies in their execution and to respect their intentions.[1] After all, not failure but low aim is crime, and in the *Poems in Prose,* Turgenev was aiming very high indeed. For in them, my study suggests, Turgenev aspired to nothing less than the fulfillment of what he took to be his responsibility to Russian literature by demonstrating for all time the expressive depth and breadth, or, in a word, the freedom, of the Russian literary tradition.

The first step in arriving at an appreciation of Turgenev's prose poems is to recognize that his turn to this literary mode at the end of his career can be seen, if not as a logical development, then not altogether as an anomaly either. With his health deteriorating, Turgenev undoubtedly found the formal brevity and flexibility of prose poems more manageable aesthetically, conceptually, even physically, than longer narrative works. Indeed, the prose narratives he composed while writing the *Poems in Prose* approximate collections of prose poems in the compactness of their chapters: in **"A Song of Triumphant Love" ("Pesn' torzhestvennoi liubvi")** of 1881, for instance, several of the fourteen chapters are no more than a few dozen words long, each chapter in effect constituting a prose poem by virtue of its conciseness and evocative power. In fact, it can be said that Turgenev had mastered the form of the prose poem years before he explicitly began employing it, through the process of mastering longer genres: numerous passages in his earlier works could themselves stand alone as prose poems (e.g., the deathbed scene at the conclusion of *First Love* [***Pervaia liubov'***] or the description of Bazarov's gravesite at the end of *Fathers and Sons* [***Otsy i deti***]). Turgenev's final move to the poem in prose can also be seen to complete the circle of his professional career, whether one takes that circle to start with the lyric poems Turgenev wrote in his youth or with the prose pieces—some so concentrated and poetic that they are almost prose poems themselves—for which Turgenev first received widespread attention and acclaim, *A Sportsman's Sketches* (***Zapiski okhotnika***).

Viewed from yet another angle, Turgenev's prose poems can be seen to continue a distinctive component of the Russian literary tradition. Although it was Turgenev who formally introduced to Russia what the Symbolist poet Valerii Briusov dubbed this "hermaphrodite" genre, generic precursors had appeared in some fragments, short works, and segments of longer works by

Karamzin, Pushkin, and Gogol decades earlier; subsequently even Dostoevsky has Ivan Karamazov note that his tale of the Grand Inquisitor is itself tantamount to a prose poem. As many critics have observed, innovative conflations of genres are arguably a characteristic feature of most major nineteenth-century Russian fictional works. Turgenev's prose poems thus play out both an individual inclination and a national literary tendency.

At the same time, it is undeniably odd that Turgenev chose at the end of his career to abandon the genre of which he was a past master and upon which his great fame rested, narrative prose fiction. And Turgenev's turn at this point to a new genre is all the more odd given that, by taking up the prose poem, he embraced what most writers and critics of the day considered a revolutionary genre, the weapon wielded by then-notorious authors in their assault upon the aesthetic sensibilities and moral values of their readership. Such confrontation was anathema to Turgenev both temperamentally and philosophically—so why did he select a literary form usually deployed for that very purpose?

It is possible that Turgenev actually sensed this confrontational aspect of prose poems and therefore feared that his collection of them would indeed provoke an openly antagonistic response, or at least an unenthusiastic one. This may be why he first entitled the collection *Posthuma* (using the Latin term for posthumous works), apparently intending it to be published only after his death. Having caught wind of Turgenev's newest creative endeavor, however, the editor of the *European Herald* (*Vestnik Evropy*), M. M. Stasiulevich, urged Turgenev to release a group of the prose poems to him for publication. Succumbing to this flattering pressure, Turgenev himself submitted to Stasiulevich fifty-one of the eighty-three short, lapidary sketches he would write between 1877 and 1882. Having made this decision, Turgenev changed the title from *Posthuma* to *Senilia* (again using a Latin term for works of old age), since, as he wrote to Ludwig Pietsch with characteristically protective self-deprecation, the sketches were merely "the last heavy sighs of . . . an old man."[2] Fifty of the sketches appeared with Turgenev's consent in 1882 under the title recommended by Stasiulevich, which he confessed he stole from Baudelaire, *Poems in Prose.* (The censors withheld **"The Threshold"** [**"Porog"**], for its allegedly admiring depiction of a female revolutionary, and it was published separately in 1883.) The other thirty-two of his poems in prose subsequently became, as Turgenev had originally conceived of them, "posthumous works": discovered amid Turgenev's papers after his death, they were published by André Mazon in 1929.[3]

Turgenev's possible fears of a negative response to these works proved unfounded—at first. Upon reading a sampling, Stasiulevich enthused, "They are brief, like lightning, and like lightning, suddenly illuminate vast perspectives before you." Indeed, Stasiulevich initially wanted to entitle the collection *Zigzags* (*Zigzagy*) to suggest these lightninglike effects.[4] Pavel Annenkov, chronicler and promoter of the literary life in Russia at the time and a close friend of Turgenev's, hailed the *Poems in Prose* as "material from the sun, the rainbow, diamonds, female tears, and noble male thought."[5] And both Lev Tolstoy and Ivan Goncharov liked these pieces very much (although Turgenev did remark sarcastically that Goncharov's admiration, coming as it did from this usually vitriolic rival, probably foreshadowed "a weak public reception" for the compositions[6]). The only important critical voice raised against the *Poems in Prose* upon their publication came, not surprisingly, from the often vituperative Nikolai Chernyshevskii, who asserted that "not one of Turgenev's *Poems in Prose* was worthy of being published."[7] But publishers in France, Germany, and even Denmark did not agree with Chernyshevskii, and translations of the *Poems in Prose* appeared in those countries within five years of publication in Russia.

Early twentieth-century critics also found much in the *Poems* to admire. In 1917, Edward Garnett, in the first full-length study in English of Turgenev's works, devoted as many pages to the *Poems in Prose* as to several of Turgenev's novels, averring that "this exquisite collection of short, detached descriptions, scenes, memories, and dreams, yields a complete synthesis in brief of the leading elements in Turgenev's own temperament and philosophy." Garnett even went so far as to extol the *Poems* as "unique in Russian literature, one may say unsurpassed, for exquisite felicity of language and for haunting, rhythmical beauty."[8] Eminent early Soviet critics such as Mikhail Gershenzon and Leonid Grossman shared Garnett's admiration for the literary and philosophical merits of the *Poems,* and Grossman wrote a lengthy essay in 1918 analyzing their form and content, declaring them to be no less than "the most beautiful pages of rhythmical prose in all of Russian literature."[9]

But the critical tide turned by the middle decades of the twentieth century. Increasingly, commentators dismissed Turgenev's *Poems in Prose* as bereft of either the aesthetic delights or the metaphysical profundities earlier critics had discovered in them. Even critics generally friendly to Turgenev, such as Avram Yarmolinsky and V. S. Pritchett, derided the prose poems as sentimental and sophomoric: Yarmolinsky affirmed that "the personal lyrical quality which [the *Poems*] possess is generally blighted by a weakness for the allegorical and the sententious," and Pritchett claimed that "the Poems strike one as being poetically vapid and self-conscious."[10]

Soviet critics of the mid-twentieth century were on the whole slightly less hostile to Turgenev's prose poems than were their Western counterparts, although, predictably, the former largely ignored those prose poems deemed most "personal" and restricted their approval to those they considered most "socially relevant," such as **"The Village" ("Derevnia"), "Cabbage Soup" ("Shchi"), "The Threshold" ("Porog"),** and **"The Russian Language" ("Russkii iazyk").**[11] Among works of Soviet criticism, Dmitrii Shatalov's laudatory monograph on the *Poems in Prose,* published in 1961, stands virtually alone among recent critical studies in according any major significance whatsoever to them.[12]

To comprehend the literary and historical significance of Turgenev's *Poems in Prose* it is first necessary to consider the history and the nature of the prose poem itself. The history of the prose poem's emergence as a distinctive genre is fairly straightforward.[13] It was conceived during the cultural war begun in the seventeenth century, the so-called Quarrel of the Ancients and the Moderns, over the inflexibility of neoclassical strictures on versification and genre division; the prose poem was one outcome of the subsequent battles periodically waged against the purity and separation of literary genres. Victory for the opponents of this purity was presaged by the "deversification" of poetic texts by Horace, Tasso, and Milton, which were translated into French prose, as well as by the popularity of MacPherson's fraudulent prose epic attributed to Ossian. And Rousseau's wildly adored *The New Heloise (La nouvelle Héloïse)* was touted as a model of *la prose poétique,* that is, narrative prose that boldly incorporates rhythmic, phonic, and rhetorical devices of poetry.

During the eighteenth century, the way of the prose poem was also paved, as René Wellek points out, by "the success of genres for which [neoclassical] theory made little or no provision: the novel, the periodical essay, the serious play with a happy ending, and so on."[14] Thus by the late eighteenth century the theoretical and practical ground had been laid for programmatic departures from "pure" genres in works interweaving lyric, dramatic, and narrative passages, of which Friedrich Schlegel's *Lucinde,* published in 1799, was a notable example. Romantic demands for experiences of synesthesia, the fusion of separate sensory impressions, and for aesthetic productions unifying all the arts *(Gesamtskunstwerke),* furthered the cause of genre integration. By the mid-nineteenth century, with the publication of *Gaspard of the Night (Gaspard de la nuit)* by Aloysius Bertrand, which caused him to be dubbed "the father of the prose poem," followed in 1869 by Baudelaire's formal titular affirmation of an established genre, *Small Poems in Prose (Petits poèmes en prose),* the prose poem became a full-fledged literary form and achieved a permanent place in Western literary history as the signal of the irrevocable overthrow of the doctrine of the purity and separation of genres.

The establishment of the prose poem as an independent if hybrid genre also signaled elemental changes in the conceptions of poetry and prose themselves. For the appearance of the prose poem betokened the conceptual emancipation of "poetry" from verse form. Theoretical statements of numerous Romantics illustrate and affirm this emancipation, not describing the formal configurations of poetry but rather advocating the forum it gives to imagination, or will, or spirit. Percy Bysshe Shelley, for instance, in his "Defense of Poetry," defines poetry as "the expression of the imagination," without reference to any requisite verse format. Indeed, he declares inadmissible the "popular division" of prose and verse and labels the distinction between poets and prose writers "a vulgar error," because both poetry and prose can convey "the very image of life expressed in its eternal truth."[15] Such a conception of poetry suggests that its creative vision of beauty can be invested in any literary form, including prose.

The emancipation of poetry from the constraints of verse not only liberated poetry; it also helped to elevate the cultural status of prose. Before and even during the nineteenth century, prose was often perceived to be inferior to poetry, as prose in general and prose fiction in particular were largely associated with the narration of particulars and objective externals, rather than with the expression of universals or subjective truths. Shelley's wife, Mary, was among those who shared this condescending view of prose: in her introduction to *Frankenstein,* she contrasts poetry's "radiance of brilliant imagery" and "the music of the most melodious verse that adorns our language" with "the machinery of a story" and "the platitude of prose."[16] But this kind of condescension gradually disappeared, as the prose novel became the literary form of choice for the nineteenth century and as the expressive capacities of prose equaling or even surpassing those of poetry became ever more apparent.

At least those capacities seemed apparent to the likes of Joris-Karl Huysmans, who in 1884 (one year after Turgenev's death) had his decadent protagonist Des Esseintes in *Against Nature (A rebours)* hail the prose poem as his favorite form of literature. "Utterly exasperated" by verse's "stiff and starchy lines in their formal attire and their abject subservience to the rule of grammar" and by "the way in which each and every line" of poetry is "mechanically bisected by the inevitable caesura and finished off with the invariable shock of dactyl striking spondee," Des Esseintes finds himself in "unspeakable torment" over traditional poems as "pegs that fitted only too foreseeably into corresponding holes." Hence he rhapsodizes over the prose poem as "an aesthetic treat available to none but the most discerning" and maintains that, "handled by an alchemist of genius," the prose poem should "contain within its small compass and in concentrated form the substance of a novel, while dispensing with the latter's long-winded analyses and superfluous descriptions. The words chosen for a work of this sort," he goes on, "would be so unalterable that they would take the place of all the others; every adjective would be sited with such ingenuity and finality that it could never be legally evicted, and would open up such wide vistas that the reader could muse on its meaning, at once precise and multiple, for weeks on end, and also ascertain the present, reconstruct the past, and divine the future of the characters in the light of one epithet."[17] By Huysmans's day, the prose poem had indubitably arrived.

Given the fairly clear historical evolution of the prose poem, it is surprising that a clear theoretical definition of it turns out to be extremely hard to come by. It is simple enough to describe what the prose poem is not—not traditional poetry and not traditional prose—but infinitely harder to explain what the prose poem is. Commentators have been reduced to apostrophizing it in terms ranging from "a complex and controversial" genre to "an oxymoronic monster" and simply "a mess."[18] The closest thing to a precise definition I have come across is provided by Michel Beaujour: "The prose poem is a text where the verbal density approaches that of regular metrical forms while eschewing the anaphoric servitudes of prosody."[19] The trouble is, this definition only describes what condition the prose poem "approaches," not what condition it distinctively achieves. Even the usually helpful Princeton *Encyclopedia of Poetry and Poetics* offers little more in the way of substantive definition, remarking only the formal attributes of a prose poem as "a composition able to have any or all features of the lyric except that it is put on the page—though not conceived of—as prose." Observing that only length distinguishes a prose poem from "more or less" poetic prose, the entry is suggestive only in noting that the term should be used solely to designate "a highly conscious (sometimes even self-conscious) artform."[20] Exactly what the prose poem is conscious, or self-conscious, about, though, remains unspecified.

If self-consciousness does constitute a definitive feature of the prose poem—and I would argue that it does—it is expressed by the author's deliberate decision to create a work belonging to what, borrowing a term from Gary Saul Morson, might best be labeled a "boundary genre." Morson coins this term to signify a genre in which "two mutually exclusive sets of conventions govern."[21] And in composing a poem in prose, to be sure, an author can at once evoke and defy readers' mutually exclusive expectations about prose fiction and lyric poetry; the author of prose poems can draw upon both sets of expectations without satisfying all the expectations of either set. This author need not provide the dominant narrative line of a plot developed chronologically and the dominant voice of a narrator that are expected of prose fiction—but can do so, at will. This au-

thor need not provide the rhythmic, phonic, or syntactic patterns encapsulating a static moment that are expected of lyric poetry—but can do so, at will.

Free to unite the flexibility of prose fiction with the intensity of lyric poetry, the author creating poems in prose can challenge readers to abandon their preconceived notions about the expressive potential—and the expressive limits—of either genre on its own. Moreover, to expand upon Morson's basic definition of a "boundary genre," this author can focus readers' attention on the very idea of "boundaries" themselves, since both their generic conformity and their generic violation are made into explicit issues by the choice of this particular genre. Thus the very act of creating prose poems suggests that their authors understand, as Morson and Caryl Emerson have recently shown Bakhtin to do, that genres have intellectual content embedded in their very forms.[22] The prose poem, as a boundary genre, would therefore carry within itself the intellectual assumption that the unconsciously accepted constraints engendered by boundaries—existential and psychological as well as literary ones—must be consciously recognized and appropriately handled, whether by their continued acceptance or consequent rejection. Thus the author of prose poems can compel readers to reconceive the value and validity not only of particular literary genres but of some forms of human experience as well. For this genre can expose certain experiences as too unique, too complex, or too expansive to fit within the confines of one single, traditionally defined, and therefore constrained manner of comprehending and portraying them.

The causes and effects of the need to reassess boundaries, in any event as that need is manifested in Turgenev's prose poems, are perhaps best elucidated by comparing those works with Baudelaire's *Small Poems in Prose,* also entitled *Paris Spleen* (*Le spleen de Paris*). The comparison may at first seem odd, because Baudelaire so deliberately cultivated, personally and literarily, what Turgenev so deliberately avoided—extravagance and controversy. Yet there are both striking similarities and striking differences between the two groups of prose poems that set in useful relief the conception of literary genres and the vision of human experience Turgenev employed this boundary genre to convey. Although there is no concrete evidence to show that Turgenev ever read Baudelaire's prose poems, he maintained a residence in Paris much of his adult life and could hardly have failed to encounter them, so famous, not to say infamous, was their author. Moreover, the similarities between the two authors' collections of prose poems would seem to reach beyond the coincidental. Baudelaire's collection contains fifty prose poems plus a free verse epilogue; Turgenev's contains fifty-one prose poems. Both authors prefaced their works with suggestions about the nature of their creations and the best way to read them. Both authors treat the subjects of death, evil, nature, beauty, dreams, and time. Both authors end many of their prose poems with philosophical epigrams. And both conclude their cycles with tributes to cultural phenomena dear to them—for Baudelaire, Paris, and for Turgenev, the Russian language. These similarities suggest that, like Baudelaire, Turgenev was trying to take readers along a wide-ranging intellectual and emotional course full of sudden, sharp twists and turns that both writers deemed the prose poem alone agile enough to negotiate.

Notwithstanding these similarities between the prose poems of Baudelaire and Turgenev, though, there are also distinctive differences. Although each author published the same number of poems in prose, Baudelaire's are significantly longer: only eighteen of them occupy one printed page or less, whereas thirty-three of Turgenev's are that short. Baudelaire's collection thus runs to over one hundred printed pages, Turgenev's to only fifty. The greater expanse of his texts affords Baudelaire the greater poetic potential: although he eschews verse form, he constructs his prose poems upon a base of phonic and rhythmic patterns that impart a continuous lyricism to these compositions, even when that lyricism is periodically combined, as only Baudelaire could combine it, with an ironic detachment from the subject matter. Their diction is ceaselessly evocative, their rhetorical devices consistently arresting. Baudelaire was clearly coming to this genre primarily as an author of poetry, completely at ease employing intricate poetic devices in the broader arena afforded by prose.

Turgenev, by contrast, came to the genre primarily as an author of prose fiction. His prose poems are more "prosy" than Baudelaire's, composed of short phrases and succinct sentences generally lacking the pronounced rhythmicity and sonority of Baudelaire's works. Turgenev's diction is relatively explicit and concrete, his use of rhetorical devices relatively limited. Thus Turgenev's prose poems, as different as they are from one another stylistically, share a simplicity and clarity of expression that stands in stark contrast to the complexity and occasional obscurity of Baudelaire's.

A comparison of just a few lines from each collection treating the same subject illuminates their divergent qualities. The subject is a mundane one: a dog. In Baudelaire's "The Faithful Dogs" ("Les bons chiens"), the narrator declares, "I sing the luckless dog who wanders alone through the winding ravines of huge cities, or the one who blinks up at some poor outcast of society with his spiritual eyes, as much as to say: 'Take me with you, and out of our joint misery we will make a kind of happiness.'"[23] In Turgenev's **"The Dog"** (**"Sobaka"**), its narrator records:

> My dog is sitting in front of me, looking me straight in the eyes.
>
> I'm looking back, straight into her eyes.

> She seems to want to tell me something. She's mute, she has no words, she doesn't understand herself—but I understand her.
>
> I understand that the same feeling exists within each of us at this moment, that there's no difference between us.

(10: 129)

Baudelaire employs a single, mellifluous sentence to portray the wordless communication of beast and human being. His sentence is marked by the pairing of adjectives and nouns—"luckless dog," "winding ravines," "huge cities," "poor outcast," "spiritual eyes," "joint misery"—that linguistically prefigures the coupling of ostracized man and solitary dog. Baudelaire also conveys the spiritual equivalence of man and beast by poetically attributing the powers of language and intellect and even imagination to the dog, who appears to apprehend a common existential dilemma. Baudelaire thus relies on the eloquence of powerful imagery to animate and expand on his idea of the estrangement caused by modern urban existence.

Turgenev conveys an existential message as well, but that message is couched in four unadorned, predominantly single-sentence paragraphs in which no nouns are modified by adjectives and in which no imaginary vision of reciprocal verbal communication is presented. The locus of consciousness stays firmly fixed in the narrator; the dog remains an animal, one not poetically personified as a similarly sensitive fellow traveler. The narrator suggests later on that an elemental spiritual commonality in the fear of death is shared by the two living creatures but offers no hint of a shared conscious conception of life. Turgenev lets the eloquence of simplicity communicate his belief in the estrangement felt by all isolated living beings.

Whence these differences? The fact that both Baudelaire and Turgenev chose to write poems in prose indicates they both subscribed to the view that some aspects of human experience are better captured by this boundary genre than by either prose or poetry alone. But they differ dramatically in their views about the kind of human experiences that can and cannot be so captured. At the time he wrote his prose poems, Baudelaire was drug-addicted, poverty-stricken, and alone, convicted of obscenity and blasphemy, having witnessed his name equated with depravity and morbidity. Oppressed by middle-class mores and values, Baudelaire found in the boundary genre of prose poems a means with which to tout the virtues of what might be termed boundary experiences, that is, thoughts, feelings, and behavior at the extremes farthest from the ordinary, tedious routine of the everyday life of average individuals. Escape from that life of any kind—dreams, drunkenness, exotic travel, even crude entertainment—any departure from spirit-deadening normalcy as defined by the bourgeoisie, is lauded as a morally superior act. Superior, too, is the artist who dares to rebel against conventionality, deliberately trying to shock that bourgeoisie out of its habitual, complacent acceptance of anything traditional, including traditional genres. In this effort, Baudelaire thus codifies a new genre that is not only unconventional but anticonventional, able to depict extraordinary emotions and events that ordinary modes of expression and ordinary genres are all too often unable to transmit.

The anticonventionality of Baudelaire's artistic enterprise is nowhere more representatively illustrated than in the splendid prose poem "The Bad Glazier" ("Le mauvais vitrier"). In it the narrator invites a glazier hawking his wares on the street to climb six flights of stairs and display those wares, only to dismiss him on the grounds that the glazier has "no colored glass, no pink, no red, no blue! No magic panes, no panes of Paradise?" Sending the disappointed salesman away, the narrator then announces, "Going out on my balcony, I picked up a little flower pot, and when the glazier appeared at the entrance below, I let my engine of war fall down perpendicularly on the edge of his pack. The shock knocked him over and, falling on his back, he succeeded in breaking the rest of his poor ambulatory stock with a shattering noise as of lightning striking a crystal palace." Baudelaire's narrator heartlessly assaults the hardworking, honest laborer as if attacking that middle-class icon to science, progress, and rationality, the Crystal Palace, which Dostoevsky's underground man likewise verbally assaults so vehemently. And this narrator does so on the same grounds as the underground man—that this palace really constitutes a monument to the self-deceptive self-congratulation of human beings blinded to the loss of their own humanity by the rationally organized, repetitious dullness of their lives. Baudelaire's narrator then records that, "drunk with my madness, I shouted down at him furiously: 'Make life beautiful! Make life beautiful!'"[24] This cry implies that conventional morality not only can but must be violated in favor of anything that will transform colorless actuality and thereby enable the transcendence of that actuality. Rejecting social standards of civilized behavior, the narrator thus allies his seemingly amoral pursuit of self-gratification with the righteous indignation of a defender of the downtrodden in desperate need of an aesthetic escape from a spiritually oppressive existence.

His defiant gesture carries certain risks, the narrator concedes, for he concludes by granting, "Such erratic pranks are not without danger and one often has to pay dearly for them. But what is an eternity of damnation compared to an infinity of pleasure in a single second?"[25] At this point, Baudelaire's narrator departs from the values of the underground man, who makes clear that he prizes "suffering" over "happiness" by labeling the former "noble" and the latter "cheap."[26] This narra-

tor, by contrast, unapologetically exalts pleasure, rejecting not only traditional religious precepts concerning sin and punishment but also traditional scientific assumptions about the nature of reality by imagining an endless expanse of time occurring within an abbreviated chronological moment; eternity here becomes the province of the artist's creative mind rather than the domain of socially sanctioned institutions. This is the same sort of creative mind that envisions an endless expanse of expressive potential within the abbreviated space of a prose poem.

Turgenev's prose poems stand in striking contrast to Baudelaire's, precisely because while Baudelaire was endeavoring to be radical, even revolutionary, in the context of French literature and culture, Turgenev was seeking to be conservative in the context of Russian literature and culture. Unlike Baudelaire (or Dostoevsky, too, for that matter, born in the same year as Baudelaire, 1821, three years after Turgenev), who was a social outcast rebelling against what he took to be centuries of aesthetic constraints that French traditions had imposed upon the artist, Turgenev was accepted and admired by much of his society, as well as by the international literary community. A defender rather than an opponent of the Russian literary tradition, which was so much younger than the French, Turgenev tried to be neither unconventional nor anticonventional. Indeed, if anything, his prose poems are hyperconventional, each a short exemplar of a readily identifiable literary type. For Turgenev discovered in this distinctive genre the perfect vehicle to demonstrate the freedom of Russian literature—its freedom to encompass the range of expressive potential equal to that of European literatures, not within the space of a single prose poem, but within an assemblage of individual prose poems. And in demonstrating that freedom, Turgenev chose to praise not the virtues of boundary experiences, as Baudelaire does, but the virtues, if you will, of the experience of boundaries. Whereas Baudelaire detests and transgresses boundaries, Turgenev appreciates them, affirms them, and finds freedom within them.

Throughout his literary career, Turgenev aesthetically advocated the preservation of boundaries, that is, of limitations, of constraints, by his reliance on delimited images of time and space, on circumspect language, on narrowed points of view, and on reserved characterizations. He did so on the moral grounds that limitations—or well-defined boundaries—protect and support psychologically vulnerable individuals from a variety of threats to their autonomy and integrity. These boundaries impart the psychic shape and strength necessary to ward off forces promoting enslavement and disintegration. In creating prose poems at the end of his literary career, then, Turgenev discovered yet another reason to value boundaries—and another means to commend them. Within the confined bounds of a single prose poem, Turgenev could draw upon the conventions of one traditional genre (limits in themselves) to illustrate formally as well as substantively the merits of boundaries, and then shift to a new prose poem to draw upon other conventions for the same purpose. Thus the inherent flexibility of prose poems that gave Baudelaire the freedom to explore the varieties and virtues of unconventional experience granted Turgenev the freedom to explore the varieties and virtues of conventional experience.

Turgenev thus draws upon a wide variety of literary genres in doing so. Unlike the prose poems of the French, which are more nearly *sui generis,* Turgenev's prose poems invoke elements of myth, fairy tale, satire, romance, drama, reminiscence, horror story, fable, eulogy, dream fantasy, legend, prayer, and extended epigram. No single narrating persona imposes one consciousness, one style of perceiving, upon all recorded events; narrative points of view shift from text to text, alternating among first-person observer, first-person participant, and impersonal third-person observer. Pure monologue, pure dialogue, straightforward reportage, and various admixtures of narrative modes also appear, as does a cornucopia of subjects ranging from a sparrow's defense of its offspring to the ways that rumors circulate, from the true nature of charity to the ripples a thrown rock makes in a still pond and the type of thoughts one might entertain before dying.

But through all of this rich variety, Turgenev's **Poems in Prose** are for the most part unified by a certain theme, one shared with his other works. This is the sanctioning of boundaries, be they physical or metaphysical—and the condemnation of their violation—in recognition of the supports for psychological and spiritual autonomy that they provide. To be sure, a few of Turgenev's prose poems are pure études, miniature genre studies and nothing more, such as **"An Eastern Legend"** (**"Vostochnaia Legenda"**), the retelling of a traditional fairy tale about deceptive appearances, and **"The Correspondent"** (**"Korrespondent"**), which repeats a joke about an assault on a newspaper reporter. But the majority either openly celebrate individuals who acknowledge and maintain limits on themselves and their experiences, either by lauding the existential and emotional independence they achieve as a result or by criticizing individuals who ignore or exceed such limits.

In advancing this cause, Turgenev's prose poems differ dramatically from Baudelaire's. Indeed, their ethos is antithetical to the kind of radically rebellious self-indulgence endorsed by the narrator of "The Bad Glazier." For instance, in the panegyric prose poem **"N.N.,"** the narrator extols the woman identified only by these initials thus: "You are good and wise . . . and everything is separate from you . . . and no one is necessary to you. . . . You are compassionless yourself—and do not require compassion." Wholly self-controlled and self-sufficient, N.N. has so insulated herself from trivial earthly cares as to suggest the "shapely shades" who inhabit the Elysian Fields and who "pass by without sadness and without joy" (10: 170). This independent mode of existence earns her the narrator's respect and admiration.

A narrator in the fablelike prose poem **"Cabbage Soup"** (**"Shchi"**) also bestows admiration upon an old peasant woman who calmly consumes the soup that she has seasoned with expensive—for her, at least—salt she cannot afford to waste, although she has buried her only son hours earlier. Her rigorous constraint is placed in vivid contrast to that of the lady landowner offering her condolences, who, the narrator observes, had been so stricken at "having lost her nine-month-old daughter, that in her grief she had refused to rent a wonderful dacha outside of Petersburg, and had spent the entire summer in the city!" (10: 152). The narrator's disdain (punctuated by an exclamation point at the end of this observation) for the lady's melodramatic sense of self-deprivation is unmistakable. The moral high ground clearly belongs to the peasant, whose quiet self-containment betrays no need for any overt expression of despair. Her reticence certainly contrasts markedly with the public display of hostility evinced by the narrator of "The Bad Glazier" when he is unhappy.

Respect for the constraints and boundaries that affirm individual autonomy and integrity while ensuring that individuals act in accordance with traditional standards of civility and decency elicits the approbation of various narrators; disregard of such constraints and boundaries evokes antagonism. In the satirical **"Two Quatrains"** (**"Dva chetverostishiia"**), for instance, Turgenev portrays the moral degradation of a young poet who steals a quatrain from another young poet. Making a few minor alterations in the text—changing "Friends! Comrades! Lovers of poetry! / Admirers of all that is well-formed and beautiful!" to "Lovers of poetry! Comrades! Friends! / Admirers of all that is well-formed, melodious, and tender!" (10: 140-41)—the thief shamelessly presents the quatrain as his own and garners great public acclaim as a result. Although he is received like a hero by adoring crowds, the reader's knowledge of the truth and of the real author's sufferings makes clear the wrong done by the thief's indifference to integrity—his own as well as his colleague's—and to the right of individuals to the products of their own labors. These are the same rights, of course, that Baudelaire's narrator blithely violates when he destroys the glazier's glass panes.

That narrator obviously revels in the violation of the ordinary constraints of civilized behavior as a form of brazen self-assertion in the face of social responsibility.

By contrast, Turgenev sanctions those constraints for fostering both social responsibility and individual fulfillment in the eulogistic **"To the Memory of Iu. P. Vrevskaia" ("Pamiati Iu. P. Vrevskoi")**, to cite but one example. Here the narrator salutes the uncomplaining self-sacrifice and silent suffering of a recently deceased society woman who had forsaken her comfortable life to serve as a nurse in Bulgaria. This narrator regretfully notes, "It's sad to think that no one voiced any gratitude even to her corpse, although she herself was embarrassed by and foreign to all gratitude." To compensate for this failure, the narrator decides to create a prose poem in her honor in hopes that "her dear shade [will] not be offended by this belated little wreath that I'm daring to lay upon her grave!" (10: 146). Sacrifice, gratitude, affection, respect—emotions largely alien to Baudelaire's prose poems, and inimical to the narrator of "The Bad Glazier"—are virtues in Turgenev's artistic and moral vision. For they impose salutary limits upon the expression and satisfaction of human needs and desires—the limits that nurture self-mastery and self-expression freed from debilitating diversions.

In a sense, then, Turgenev demonstrated his self-mastery by embracing the limits of the prose poem and employing them to illuminate the very value of adherence to limits. But why employ such a variety of styles, tones, and narrative points of view in this pursuit? And why root so many of the prose poems so obviously in such well-established literary conventions?

Turgenev himself hinted at the answers to these questions in a speech he gave in Moscow at the dedication of the monument erected to Pushkin in 1880, in the midst of the period during which he was writing his prose poems. Turgenev took advantage of this occasion not simply to celebrate Pushkin as a founder of the modern Russian literary tradition but to assess the contemporary status of that tradition as well. Lavishing praise upon Pushkin for having established a Russian literary language and for having provided models of literary characters and images inspirational to generations of Russian writers, Turgenev is nonetheless careful to designate Pushkin as an "initiator" or founder, rather than a "completer," of the Russian literary tradition. Turgenev claims Pushkin was unable "by himself to fulfill the two tasks that in other countries are shared by an entire generation and more," namely, "to compose a language and to create a literature." Pushkin was not, therefore, "a national poet in the sense of a universal poet . . . as we name Shakespeare, Goethe, Homer" (12: 345). The task was too great, the time too short, for Pushkin single-handedly to bring Russian literature to full aesthetic and intellectual maturity and thus enable him to achieve the stature of a "universal" author. While honoring Pushkin's accomplishments, Turgenev asserts that Russia still needed "a new, as yet unknown,

chosen individual . . . who will surpass his teacher and will fully deserve the appellation of a national and universal poet, which we have not resolved to bestow upon Pushkin, although," Turgenev adds, "we do not dare to deprive him of it, either" (12: 349).

What difference did it make whether Pushkin had universal stature or not? To Turgenev, a national that possesses a universal author has achieved "a consciously complete, unique expression of its art, its poetry," which Turgenev defines as "its living, individual spirit, its idea, its language in the highest meaning of the word." This art "becomes the property of all humanity even more than does science, precisely because art is a vibrant, human, thinking spirit, an immortal spirit that can survive the physical existence of its body, its people. What has remained to us from Greece? Its spirit has remained to us!" (12: 341-42). A universal author, to Turgenev's mind, confirms that a nation has completely discovered "its spiritual contents and its voice" and can "enter into the fraternity of nations who have recognized" it. Such a poet therefore enables a nation to "assert its absolute right to its own place in history" (12: 341).

Turgenev deeply desired Russia to secure its own place in history, and he saw literature as an indispensable means of doing so. This was the implicit point of his final published prose poem, **"The Russian Language" ("Russkii iazyk")**, in which Turgenev asserts that Russian is a "great, powerful, righteous, and free" language and avers that "it is impossible to believe that such a language was not given to a great nation!" (10: 172). Pushkin had established this language in order to commence the mission that Turgenev deemed utterly essential at the end of his career—the mission of giving the Russian spirit a lasting voice through its literature and thereby confirming Russia's rightful place in history. And so it may well be that Turgenev saw his own explorations of the prose poem as his final contribution to that mission, hence as his ultimate moral responsibility. What Pushkin began, by codifying the Russian literary language, Turgenev would complete by exposing—with the most compact of models—the total range and hence the expressive freedom of Russian language and literature, thus proving that Russia had truly found "its spiritual contents and its voice." Turgenev endeavored to demonstrate that the discrete boundaries of prose poems, joined together, could trace the shape and disclose the strength of the entire Russian literary tradition in all its poetic and prose fullness as no other, traditional genre could do. That Turgenev could conceive of performing this highly conservative task by utilizing one of the most radical modern literary forms, the prose poem, bears witness to the extraordinary verbal capacity of this briefest of boundary genres. And even if Turgenev did not exploit that capacity as adventurously as did some of his contemporaries, he apparently recognized its potential—and as a result perhaps died a happier man, whether or not the "universal author" he may secretly have hoped that he himself would be acclaimed.

Notes

1. See Gary Saul Morson's essay "Anna Karenina's Omens," in this volume, for reasons *not* to forgive all, however.

2. Letter to L. Pietsch, Dec. 25/13, 1882, in I. S. Turgenev, *Polnoe sobranie sochinenii i pisem, Pis'ma,* 13 vols. (Moscow: Akademiia nauk SSSR, 1961-68), 12: 128-29.

3. I. Tourguénev, "Nouveaux poèmes en prose," *Revue des Deux Mondes* 4 (1929): 289-311.

4. Letter to A. N. Pypin, Aug. 12/July 31, 1882, quoted in Turgenev, *Polnoe sobranie sochinenii i pisem, Sochineniia,* 12 vols. (Moscow: Nauka, 1979-86), 10: 454. Subsequent page references to Turgenev's *Sochineniia* are included in parentheses in the essay. For a history of the process of entitling these works, see 10: 453-56.

5. Letter to M. M. Stasiulevich, quoted in Turgenev, *Sochineniia* 10: 456.

6. Letter to A. V. Toporov, Jan. 9, 1883/Dec. 28, 1882, in Turgenev, *Pis'ma* 12: 355.

7. Letter to A. N. Chernyshevskii, Feb. 18/6, 1885, quoted in Turgenev, *Sochineniia* 10: 457.

8. Edward Garnett, *Turgenev: A Study* (London: W. Collins Sons and Co., 1917; rpt., Port Washington, N.Y., 1966), 195.

9. Leonid Grossman, "Posledniaia poema Turgeneva: Senilia," in *Sobranie sochinenii,* 5 vols. (Moscow: N. A. Stolliar, 1927-28), 3: 74.

10. Avram Yarmolinsky, *Turgenev: The Man, His Art, and His Age* (New York: Orion Press, 1959), 348; V. S. Pritchett, *The Gentle Barbarian: Life and Work of Turgenev* (New York: Random House, 1977), 236.

11. See, for instance, E. V. Petukhov, "'Stikhotvoreniia v proze' I. S. Turgeneva," *Slavia,* no. 13 (1931): 699-717; P. Pustovojt, *Turgenev* (Moscow: Prosveshchenie, 1957), 130-34; and S. M. Petrov, *I. S. Turgenev* (Moscow: Khudozhestvennaia literatura, 1968), 312-18.

12. Dmitrii Shatalov, *"Stikhotvoreniia v proze" I. S. Turgeneva* (Arzamas, USSR, 1961).

13. For the standard history of the prose poem, especially in France, see Suzanne Bernard, *Le poème en prose de Baudelaire jusqu'à nos jours* (Paris: Librairie Nizet, 1959).

14. René Wellek, *A History of Modern Criticism, 1750-1950* (New Haven, Conn.: Yale University Press, 1955), 20.

15. Percy Bysshe Shelley, "A Defense of Poetry," in *Complete Works of Percy Bysshe Shelley,* 10 vols., ed. Roger Ingpen and Walter E. Peck (New York: Scribner, 1926-30), 7: 109, 113-15ff.

16. Mary Wollstonecraft Shelley, "Author's Introduction," in *Frankenstein; or, The Modern Prometheus* (1818, Mattituck, N.Y.: Penguin, 1983), ix.

17. Joris-Karl Huysmans, *Against Nature,* trans. Robert Baldick (New York: Penguin, 1959), 198-99.

18. Mary Ann Caws, "Preface," in *The Prose Poem in France: Theory and Practice,* ed. Mary Ann Caws and Hermine Riffaterre (New York: Columbia University Press, 1983), vii; Michel Beaujour, "Short Epiphanies: Two Contextual Approaches to the French Prose Poem," in Caws and Riffaterre, *Prose Poem,* 50.

19. Beaujour, "Short Epiphanies," 55.

20. Alex Preminger, Frank J. Warnke, and O. B. Hardison, eds., *Princeton Encyclopedia of Poetry and Poetics,* enlarged ed. (Princeton, N.J.: Princeton University Press, 1974), 664.

21. Gary Saul Morson, *The Boundaries of Genre: Dostoevsky's "Diary of a Writer" and the Traditions of Literary Utopia* (Austin: University of Texas Press, 1981), 48.

22. Gary Saul Morson and Caryl Emerson, *Mikhail Bakhtin: Creation of a Prosaics* (Stanford, Calif.: Stanford University Press, 1990), esp. 271-305.

23. Charles Baudelaire, *Paris Spleen,* trans. Louise Varese (New York: New Directions, 1947), 105.

24. Ibid., 14.

25. Ibid.

26. F. M. Dostoevsky, *Polnoe sobranie sochinenii,* 30 vols. (Leningrad: Nauka, 1972-85), 5: 178. To be sure, the observation is phrased as a rhetorical question.

Jane T. Costlow (essay date 1995)

SOURCE: Costlow, Jane T. "'Oh-là-là' and 'No-no-no': Odintsova as Woman Alone in *Fathers and Children*." In *A Plot of Her Own: The Female Protagonist in Russian Literature,* edited by Sona Stephan Hoisington, pp. 21-32. Evanston, Ill: Northwestern University Press, 1995.

[*In the following essay, Costlow discusses Turgenev's treatment of female characters, particularly Odintsova, in his most famous novel.*]

Turgenev Women discuss events,
know about actors,
look for oil,
talk about medicine,
perform on the stage . . .
Turgenev Women in the morning mist,
Turgenev Women right beside you . . .[1]

"Turgenev Women," the contemporary song suggests, look for oil and go to sea, descend into subways and peel potatoes—asking us to believe that the superachieving, inexhaustible (and exhausted) women of late- and post-Soviet Russia are the spiritual and literal daughters of Ivan Turgenev's heroines. Can there truly be a connection? Surely ironic, rather than direct, to imagine Natalya, Liza, and Elena, among others, as Heroines of Labor (or Heroines of Love)? To pose the question as Vasily Shumov does is to ask, in a slightly offbeat way, what the legacy of Turgenev is for Russia; what connection there is between classical Russian culture and contemporary daily life (*byt*); and for our own purposes—as American and not Russian readers—how we can "read" these novels of more than a century ago, from a culture not our own. For in reading nineteenth-century novels we ourselves head out to sea a bit, or set off in search of black gold: compelled (or repelled) by figures who are both familiar and distant to us, convinced that there are ways in which their lives and identities, despite historical distance and difference, nonetheless reflect for us some of our own dilemmas. Who are these Turgenev women, and how can we read them? How can we let them read us?

The central heroines in each of Turgenev's first three novels—Natalya in **Rudin,** Liza in **A Nest of Gentle Folk,** and Elena in **On the Eve**—are young women of great conviction and courage, qualities that at the novels' beginnings seem to exist only *in potentio,* but are elicited and actualized by the appearance of the novels' central heroes: Rudin, Lavretsky, and Insarov. To some extent the heroines' convictions are negative, at least initially: they are convinced that the world into which they have been born (the affluent and refined world of Russia's Europeanized, landowning gentry) is lacking; they are endowed with a kind of negative clairvoyance that allows them to discern, despite their relative innocence, the hypocrisy and emptiness of those around them. Their positive convictions—religious, political, and moral—emerge in and through their experience of love. These heroines become touchstones of virtue and valor, helping the reader to perceive the inadequacies of the microcosm of Russian society we enter when we move into Turgenev's drawing rooms. The heroines' courage—their willingness to act rashly, in defiance of convention, risking parental and societal approprium— saves them from being the frail and too-often victimized embodiments of virtue we encounter in the Victorian tradition.[2] These are no pale and withering lilies; they are passionate, defiant rebels constrained by con-

ventional roles for women, and ultimately, by the lack of worthy heroic partners.

Turgenev's heroines are also typically women "on the threshold" of adulthood; in their encounters with leading figures of Russian (and Bulgarian) thought and politics, they step across that threshold into a world of more momentous ("adult") sensual, moral, and political life. In a prose poem written at the end of his life Turgenev presented this heroinic figure for one final time: the young woman is challenged by a "ponderous, muffled voice" that depicts for her the sufferings that await her, once she steps across the threshold. She responds to that litany resolutely; when she steps across, she is proclaimed a fool by some, a saint by others.[3] The figure of the woman on the threshold is articulated here as a kind of secular icon, a figure toward whom Turgenev directs enduring reverence and expectation. As more than one critic has pointed out, Turgenev invested great hope in these impassioned and relatively innocent women, as though an "Amazonian" spirit of rectitude and courage could take Russia by storm and turn her toward a more promising future. The "heroines" of the Shumov song would, alas, have despaired long ago of any such expectation.[4]

Having sketched some of the features of this Turgenevan "iconic" womanhood, however, we must acknowledge that it is harder to find her—or it—in the novel generally viewed as Turgenev's greatest, **Fathers and Sons.** There is a rich cast of female characters in this novel, one that occasioned stormy disagreement in Russian society. It is a novel in which encounters with women serve as fulcrums to the plot, and in which the challenges of passion are at least as unsettling as the critiques of ideology.[5] It is also a novel in which the "woman question"—the extensive public discussion of women's role in society, their rights to education and work—is explicitly if parodically addressed.[6] It is, in short, a novel in which the emblematic hero Bazarov (and the society whose tensions he may seem to embody and evoke) passes through the worlds and minds of women, on his way to an encounter with stark destiny. Surely, then, it is legitimate to wonder who these women are, what we can know and say of their lives and worlds and minds.

We begin with the odd but perhaps illuminating fact that the canonic English translation of the title errs: Turgenev's title refers to fathers (*ottsy*) and *children* (*deti*), thus at least allowing for the possible importance of female offspring to the ideational intentions of the novel.[7] The English title urges our concentration on the relationships of male generations: Kirsanov father and son, Bazarov father and son, the men of the sixties and the men of the forties, the father within the son (Nikolai within Arkady) who will unravel the momentary idolatrous bond to Bazarov the ideologue. If we consider the novel's women, however, other familial relationships will emerge as significant: the bonds of mothers and sons (Bazarov's mother's passionate, unrequited affection; Fenichka's maternal, "Marian" beauty, bespeaking a renewal of the sacred mother Mariia Kirsanova, a departed but vivifying presence at the Kirsanov estate); the nurturing labor of peasant nannies; the cycles of birth and death that women preside over in their wedding and laboring and mourning (Fenichka and Katya join the company of such women in the novel's epilogue). But we will also become attentive to what is perhaps the most important feminine familial relationship, one that informs in its divergence from the maternal: the novel's most significant female character is Anna Sergeevna Odintsova, a woman of "oh-là-là!" (150) and "no-no-no" (144);[8] a solitary, regimented woman who both discovers and retreats from her kinship with Bazarov; a nihilist of passion; a motherless child; a daughter—like the goddess Athena—of men, of her father and of a husband old enough to claim paternity; a woman who is *odin* (one, alone; masculine form), not *odna* (one, alone; feminine form). Surely it is Odintsova whom Turgenev had in mind in calling the novel **Fathers and Children,** not **Fathers and Sons**: there are mothers aplenty and mothers important in Turgenev's fourth novel, but it is the motherless daughter who most compels and confounds our attention, whose mind and body and denials rivet the narrator and Bazarov—and us. Who are these women? Who is Odintsova? Who are we, reading and responding to these women?

Odintsova is, in a profound sense, a woman *alone,* as her name suggests; we as readers must grapple with the question of what her solitude means, and why she chooses to perpetuate it. Her solitude stands in contrast, however, to all the other women in the novel, who are drawn as creatures of context, of relationship, of imitation; women who are representative or emblematic of larger social and symbolic groups. This is most obviously true of the mothers in the novel (Mariia Kirsanova, Fenichka, Arina Bazarova, Katya at novel's end), but it is also true of Kukshina (who is presented as emblematic of "emancipated women") and of the enigmatic Princess R. (who is perhaps trapped in her identity as a "society woman" [*svetskaia dama*]). Bazarov, ever the rigorous natural scientist, suggests in conversation with Odintsova that individuality is illusory; that humans, like trees, are essentially alike (277). While Turgenev no doubt takes issue with his naturalist hero on this matter, it is nonetheless true that all of the women characters *except* for Odintsova are presented as "typical," a typicality that grounds their identity and suggests how they are placed in Russian and more broadly human society. Bazarov makes repeated attempts to "classify" Odintsova: when he meets her at the provincial ball he wonders what species of mammals she belongs to (151), but he also notes that she is unlike the other "dames" (*baby*) there (148). Turgenev's

novel presents its own classification of women, a psychic and symbolic taxonomy that contextualizes Odintsova's ambivalently "odd" position.

In thinking of the novel's mothers, one automatically thinks of Arina Bazarova, chin in hand, weeping at the sight of her long-absent, now returned son; or of Fenichka's tender concern for the infant Mitya. These two women present us with the novel's most powerful images of maternity, invoking a semantics of mothering that is grounded in intense and unwavering attention, and in forms of labor that nurture and protect—quite literally—the body. We first see Fenichka as she herself keeps watch over her baby; Nikolai hasn't yet introduced her to his son, but we glimpse her as "now listening, now dozing," framed by the open door through which she watches her son. She is lovely, "with a white kerchief thrown over her dark hair" (89), and we will come to know in ever greater detail the beauty and awkward grace of this young mother, who waddles and blushes (95). "Is there anything in the world," asks the narrator—wholly rhetorically—"more captivating than a beautiful young mother with a healthy child in her arms?" (109). This is Turgenev's narrator as Raphael, portraitist/iconographer of blooming, abundant maternity.

Fenichka (and later Katya) are both *young* mothers, women in their early twenties who charm and beguile with their intense and innocent attentions to the very young. Bazarov's mother, on the other hand, is maternity in its aged aspect, verging on the ridiculous when she directs at her grown son the same adoring gaze we imagine in Fenichka's eyes. "[Bazarov's mother] paid no attention to Arkady, . . . propping her round face on her little first—her full cherry-coloured lips and the moles on her cheeks and over her eyebrows gave her a most benign expression—she never took her eyes off her son and kept sighing" (200). Whether we are to imagine that Fenichka could *become* someone like Arina Vlasyevna is debatable; the narrator suggests, ruefully, that "nowadays such women as she have ceased to exist" (203). Fenichka enchants, not just Nikolai but his brother Pavel and ultimately Bazarov himself; she is a blooming rose (as Bazarov suggests in the tête-à-tête that provokes the duel), a "small wild animal" half-hidden in a field of rye when Nikolai calls out to her (112); a maker of gooseberry jam (her husband's favorite); and a seamstress whose pincushion eclipses the fierce General Yermolov, whose picture hangs in her room (108-9). Arina Vlasyevna, on the other hand, is a "true Russian gentlewoman of the old school" (202), preoccupied with signs and portents, devout and superstitious, kindhearted and unquestioning of the world around her. Maternity has lost its charms in her; its limited concerns with fleshly sustenance come nearer to engulfing the spirit—as Bazarov will be "engulfed" by disease, by Russia, by the earth itself. For all her charms and all the narrator's efforts at approval, Arina Vlasyevna is part of a domestic world that encloses and stultifies, and serves as Bazarov's last stop en route to death. This is the obverse of the sentimentalized maternity of the Kirsanov homestead.

Fenichka and Arina Vlasyevna are both associated with highly articulated domestic spaces; Fenichka's room in particular stands as a wonderful emblematic rendering of the woman, seen through the eyes of Pavel, a man who, we come to find out, loves Fenichka and surely laments his own solitude. Fenichka's room is "clean and snug," with smells of a freshly painted floor, "of camomile and lemon balm." There is an icon of St. Nikolas the Miracle-Worker (appropriately enough, since Nikolai has worked a kind of "miracle" in Fenichka's life), hung with an easter egg; it nicely figures the comfortable mixture of Christian and pagan, Orthodox and popular religiosity, that the narrator will suggest is characteristic of Arina Vlasyevna as well. There are jars of her own jam; a cage with a goldfinch; bad photographs and the picture of Yermolov—objects that convey labors of love, gentle enclosure, and the domestication of the political. They are also a series of objects that *enclose,* just as the room itself does; but Turgenev's implication, surely, is that such enclosure is benign, creative, productive, and capable of beauty. Fenichka has come from the rye into a domestic world; she is a kind of "caged bird," but she bears her taming freely and lightly. This is a room that articulates all the novel's fondest virtues, the values it most longs to embrace and perpetuate.[9] And it is a woman's world, a room that bears the marks of her affectionate labors and many connections: affectional, religious, national. Loving labor has created this room and these objects (those jam jars), and it is that evocation of love bodied forth in fingers as well as eyes that touches most deeply here. When Arkady returns to his father's house he sleeps under a quilt that his peasant nanny made: these quilts and jam are emblems of the real labors and loves of maternal women in the novel.

Fenichka's room is, however, only one place in the world of *Fathers and Children,* and we pause there quite briefly. If we look beyond the novel's mothers we will acknowledge two other female figures who provide important context for Odintsova: Avdotya (Yevdoxia) Kukshina[10] and the mysterious Princess R. Both women are associated with other kinds of rooms and enclosures, much less benign: Kukshina with a disorderly, ash-strewn study; Princess R. with the drawing rooms and ballrooms of high society; Kukshina with the "excesses" of emancipated women, the Princess with the excesses of passion. Both women are associated with destruction, rather than with the creation and nurturing of life: Kukshina with the destructive fires that periodically burn down sections of provincial Russian towns,[11] and the Princess with the immolations of the Cross. If

the novel's mothers define a spectrum of maternal affection, Kukshina and the Princess establish realms of excess; *both* groups of women seem to establish a range of alternatives for women in Russian society—none of which Odintsova herself will adopt. It is Kukshina and the Princess, however, who represent the most potent "dangers" for a solitary woman.

The Princess R.'s story is told by Arkady to Bazarov, as a way of explaining Pavel to the radical newcomer. The Princess is an "enigma" (Pavel himself called her a "sphinx" [101]), whose life is represented as an increasingly tormented alternation between the coquetry of drawing rooms and the "wringing anguish" of solitary prayer. The Princess might in fact seem to be a pale version of one of Dostoevsky's "infernal woman," or an unlikely combination of women from Turgenev's second novel, *A Nest of Gentlefolk*: the seductress of that novel, Varvara, plays out her manipulative melodramatic scenes in a country drawing room; its heroine, Liza Kalitina, ultimately leaves the world for the solace and solitude of monastic prayer.[12] The main function of the Princess R. story in *Fathers and Children* seems to be to "explain" Arkady's uncle; but in a larger sense it is a cautionary tale of the perils of passion: perils lived out to the death in the case of the Princess herself, and lived out to near madness in Pavel Kirsanov. The Princess is a woman who has in some profound sense *lost control of herself:* "She seemed to be in the grip of mysterious forces, unknown even to herself, which played with her at will, her limited intelligence being unable to cope with their caprices" (101). The Princess is the woman in the novel who seems most nearly to accede to certain codes of convention; she is to all appearances "a lady of fashion" (100). But the constraints of such convention-bound existence are seen to be powerless against the darker forces that take her as their prey.

Kukshina, on the other hand, is the victim less of dark and impassioned forces than of her own silliness, and of an ideology that Turgenev ridicules quite ruthlessly in his depiction of the "femme émancipée" (139). We meet her in a room that is as emblematic of the woman as was Fenichka's: it is, significantly, "more like a working study than a drawing-room" (and certainly not the repository of any homemade gooseberry jam). The study is filled with dust, cigarette butts, and uncut journals; the lady of the house reclines on a leather couch, "her blonde hair was rather dishevelled and she was wearing a crumpled silk dress, with heavy bracelets on her short arms and a lace kerchief on her head" (140). This room provides a symbolic and literal counterpoint to Fenichka's tidy domesticity and the elaborately constrained drawing rooms of polite society. It is also, however, a "study" in loose sexuality and intellectual pretensions: since the journal pages are uncut and the woman's pose readily suggests "loose" behavior. Turgenev reiterates *and* perpetuates in his portrait of Kukshina some of the charges that were leveled against women of the 1860s who challenged convention: such women's efforts at obtaining an education or entering traditionally male professional domains were repeatedly smeared with insinuations of flightiness and sexual misconduct.[13] If the Princess R. represents the excesses of passion, Kukshina is made to embody the purported excesses of emancipation; she is a woman who celebrates her independence (143), but "freedom" in Kukshina is represented as disintegrative and physically repulsive. One senses Turgenev the aristocrat in the narrator's aversion to a woman rolling a cigarette: "[Kukshina] rolled a cigarette between her fingers which were brown with tobacco stains, put it to her tongue, licked it up and started to smoke" (143). The energy of Turgenev's prose works to induce a moral repulsion in the reader that is grounded in visceral disdain; we have left Raphael far behind, and come closer to the debauched intimacies of Toulouse-Lautrec's brothels.

What is striking about both Princess R. and Kukshina is the extent to which their stories provide foils for Odintsova's; we are meant in part, I believe, to read the accounts of their lives as roads that a woman like Odintsova might take but doesn't. It defies the reader's imagination to imagine Odintsova a mother (she is eight years older than her sister, but very much a sororal, and not a maternal, figure to Katya). Princess R., on the other hand, and Kukshina represent quite credible options for, or versions of, Odintsova. Odintsova is certainly a woman of the drawing room or study, not a woman of the nursery or kitchen; she is a woman with intellectual pretensions, articulate and well-read (her journal pages are cut); she is intensely desirable, even erotic (as both the "oh-là-là" of Bazarov's first account and the narrator's repeated admiration of her body remind us); she is independent, without children, a woman slandered by many of her neighbors as a (sexually) "emancipated woman" (153-54). She is, finally, a woman who flirts with passion, who seems to glimpse within herself some of the forces that prey on the Princess R. But she is also a woman of negation, introduced with a string of negatives, insisting that Bazarov misunderstood her and that she misunderstood herself, a woman who says no to Bazarov and to whatever it is within herself that she glimpses in the course of her encounters with him. She is sister to both Kukshina and Princess R. (Kukshina claims she's a friend and in fact "introduces" her to the reader [144]), and her story can be read as a refusal of their excesses. But that refusal is, I believe, one of the most compelling enigmas of this novel, at least as compelling and problematic as Bazarov's "succumbing" to love and death—the narrative turn whose explanation has formed the focus of virtually all critical discussion of the novel. But who is Odintsova, and why does she refuse Bazarov? How can we read such refusal: as cause for celebration or la-

ment? What, finally, does this solitary woman in a world of mothers and excess have to say to us?

The question is, on one level, not difficult to answer: Odintsova is an affluent and accomplished landowner, orphaned early, married to a "hypochondriac" much older than she, widowed after six years. She lives on her estate in the company of her sister Katya and her maternal aunt; she is a woman who has with care and calculation constructed a world of order and routine; she is a woman of "independent and determined" character (154). She is characterized from the first as a woman of great beauty and sensuality (Bazarov's first comment is "I say, what a splendid body!" [155]), but as a woman of quite chill demeanor: images of coldness follow Odintsova from Arkady and Bazarov's first conversation about her through to the epilogue. She is, in Arkady's words, "charming . . . but so cold and reserved"; Bazarov counters, "You say she is cold; that just adds to the flavour. You like ice-cream, don't you?" (150). We are told in the last chapter of the novel that she ultimately remarries, a man "kind-hearted and cold as ice" (292).

The effect of such imagery is to suggest that beneath Odintsova's calm, chill demeanor there lie some sort of subterranean forces, a strength of passion that is generally repressed: this is implied in Bazarov's initial proverbial comment ("Still waters . . . you know" [150; ellipsis in original]) and in the plot itself, in which Odintsova draws Bazarov into increasing intimacy, playing a kind of risky and flirtatious game that she herself ultimately disclaims responsibility for. "I did not understand you—you did not understand me, . . . I did not understand myself either" (183).

On a warm, almost sultry summer evening Odintsova invites Bazarov into her private chambers, alone. These chapters are among the most compelling of the novel; they begin on the ideological terrain of Bazarov's discussions with Pavel Kirsanov (Odintsova asks about a chemistry text, and challenges Bazarov's taxonomic disrespect for individuality), but they move into the realm of charged eroticism and a complicated dance (both verbal and physical) of desire and repression. Their conversation moves from chemistry to the possibilities of "being carried away" (175); from the rejection of individual difference to a game of confession: Odintsova volunteers that she is "unhappy because . . . I have no desire"; Bazarov suggests she's "longing to fall in love" but can't; Odintsova asks if he thinks it would be "easy to surrender oneself completely" (176-77; ellipsis in original).

Bazarov accuses Odintsova of "playing the coquette" (177), but it is clear that they have moved from the "objective" world of classification and rationality into a much murkier realm. And part of its murkiness is the difficulty of attribution of will: it is not clear what Bazarov himself wants, just as it is unclear what Odintsova herself desires to happen. In this languid evening encounter, however, they *both* move beyond the strictly ordered existences they have set themselves, and *both* are challenged—perhaps by those "unknown forces" that victimized the Princess R. The effect of Turgenev's prose in these chapters is, moreover, to submit the reader to some of the same experiences of sensuality and confusion as Bazarov and Odintsova themselves feel: we follow the currents and undercurrents of their words and gestures (the sudden, crashing opening of the window as Bazarov trembles with emotion [174]; the swaying blind and the "pungent freshness of the night"; Odintsova's "agitation," which communicates itself to Bazarov [175]; the mantilla Odintsova draws across her bare arms; her flush at meeting Bazarov's eyes [176]). Turgenev presents this encounter with a cinematographer's attention to gestural detail; he evokes a desire in the reader that echoes that of his characters.

Our desire, however, like Odintsova's and like Bazarov's, is frustrated: not just by her rejection of his embrace, but by the closure of their first discussion, when warm sensuality gives way to Odintsova's more accustomed chill: "A maid came into the room with a decanter on a silver tray, Madame Odintsova stopped short, told the maid she could go, and sat down again, deep in thought. Her hair slipped loose and fell in a dark coil over her shoulders. The lamp went on burning for a long while in her room while she still sat there motionless, only from time to time chafing her hands which were now beginning to feel the chill of the night air" (178). The moment is emblematic of much of what we know about Odintsova: the elegance and comfort of her well-appurtenanced life; the lovely body, with the implication of sensuality in her loosened hair; the juxtaposition of heat and chill—the burning lamp and the chilling body—and through it all the enigma of the thoughts that roil within the woman herself. Odintsova, too, is a sphinx: but her enigmatic presence will not be resolved for us by a single word, as was that of Pavel's beloved Princess.

Why does Odintsova refuse Bazarov? And, in refusing him, does she not refuse a part of herself? The novel offers some answers: Odintsova herself justifies the rejection (immediately after the fact) by suggesting that "various vague emotions—the sense of life passing by, a longing for novelty—had forced her to a certain limit, forced her to look behind her—and there she had seen not even an abyss but only a void . . . chaos without shape" (184; ellipsis in original). Bazarov himself implies that she is a woman who might flirt out of boredom or curiosity, but that she is incapable of falling in love (176-77). The narrator faults her wealth: "If she had not been rich and independent she might perhaps have thrown herself into the struggle and experienced

passion . . ." (165; ellipsis in original). Do such explanations suffice? May we not still want to interrogate what is at work here, precisely in an *independent* woman's rejection of a passion she obviously experiences? (This is, after all, a woman created by an author whose women are shown repeatedly to take risks, and to act on their passionate impulses.) Might we not want to interrogate the ways in which Odintsova is emblematic of larger forms of refusal—both in the Russian literary tradition and in our own world? Let us recontextualize her "enigma" and ask why (and to what) women say no.

In purely legal terms, it would be considerably easier for Odintsova to say yes to Bazarov than it was for some of her literary sisters: the most famous refusal in Russian literature, Tatiana's refusal of Onegin, is enunciated by a married woman; Pushkin makes sure that we know the depth of Tatiana's feeling for Onegin, an emotion that makes her refusal that much harder, but that much more programmatic: the strength of passion will *not* overcome the bonds of matrimony.[14] The most famous counterexample in Russian literature is, of course, Anna Karenina's: she reverses Tatiana's submissive but deeply painful refusal, with disastrous results. One notes two things about Odintsova in such company: (1) that she is not bound, as are her sisters, by marriage bonds; and (2) that Tolstoy's novel—contra his own intentions—is an argument for the absolute necessity of honoring the desires of a passionate heart. Anna's dilemma is tragic precisely because to have honored her marital vows would have accomplished a different kind of suicide: slower, more hidden, but still suicide.[15] Turgenev's novel is positioned chronologically between the Pushkin and Tolstoy texts; it may also occupy a quite different ideological terrain, acknowledging the primacy of the heart, but playing out suicide in a different fashion. Bazarov is the novel's most obvious "suicide": his death is a bitter acknowledgment of the inability of science to encompass the enigmas and conflicts of human hearts and human souls. But Turgenev implies that there are two other metaphoric corpses in the novel: Pavel Kirsanov ("In the glaring daylight his handsome emaciated head lay on the white pillow like the head of a dead man . . . And, indeed, to all intents and purposes, so he was" [253; ellipsis in original]) and Odintsova herself. I would submit, then, that the *refusal* of passion (of bodies "carried away" erotically and emotionally) marks for Turgenev the inverse of what it does for Pushkin and Tolstoy: to refuse love is to refuse life—which both Odintsova and Bazarov, for different reasons and in different ways, do.

It is significant, I believe, that Odintsova is drawn as a "motherless" child, a woman whose life and order and place are legacies of her father and of a husband who was nearly the age of her father. The estate she rules is a world constructed (in more ways than one) at the wishes of her late husband; his portrait presides iconically over that world (156-57). Odintsova's name, as noted earlier, derives from the Russian word for "one": *odin.* But it is the masculine form of that word, a root I take as suggestive of something essential to her character. She is, as I proposed at the beginning of this essay, an Athena figure: woman *odin,* alone, for herself—in the masculine sense. Athena is the great goddess born not of woman but of man, burst from the head of Zeus—suggesting that Odintsova, like Bazarov, is a creature of the head, and not of the heart. The opposing figure in the Greek pantheon was Artemis: a virginal goddess who is also a woman alone, but *odna,* for herself—in the feminine sense.[16] Where lies the difference? In the imbalance of intellect and eroticism; in the advocacy of authoritarian order at the expense of a wilder, impassioned existence; in the allegiance to men rather than to women; in the denial of the relationship to the body and its cycles—Artemis (or Diana, to the Romans) was the goddess of childbirth and death, as well as of the hunt.

In an earlier essay on *Fathers and Children* I argued that Bazarov, as he is dying, alludes to the myth of Actaeon and Artemis: he has a vision of himself consumed by hunting dogs. Artemis, in that story, is bathing with nymphs in the forest, when Actaeon the hunter happens upon them.[17] He sees Artemis in her nakedness, her beauty, at her most revealing; and for that he is punished. His "transgression" elicits Artemis's anger; she turns him into a stag, and his own hounds turn on him, devouring him in their frenzy. This tale suggests the wildly destructive energies that ensue from a kind of "transgressive" intimacy, from the aggressive hunter's vision and knowledge of the sacred goddess. And what does the story suggest in the context of Turgenev's novel? Surely Odintsova is no Artemis. Both she and Bazarov, the narrator tells us, are "indifferent" to nature (169); she, unlike her sister Katya, fears garden snakes (265); she is a creature of the manor—of rules, order, regularity—not of the wilder *loci* of creation. But that is perhaps the point. The plot of Turgenev's novel brings Odintsova to a glimpse of herself as an impassioned, "animalistic" being:[18] no longer as the chill, intellectual Athena, but as Artemis, whose virginity is wild. The agent of that transformation is Bazarov: the twist on Ovid's story is that it is not just Actaeon/Bazarov who "sees" Artemis/Odintsova; it is Odintsova herself who transgresses the boundaries she has so carefully constructed. "She had seen not even an abyss but only a void . . . chaos without shape" (184; ellipsis in original). That is Odintsova's ex post facto rationalization of her action; it is "Athena" speaking. We can only speculate on whether the energies within her that a liaison with Bazarov would have unleashed could have been creative (rather than destructive).

It is worth noting, though, that there is a long tradition in Western culture of depicting female sexual energy as inherently dangerous, and Russian literature generally follows that tradition.[19] Russian literary texts that narrate the refusal of passion might be read in company with cautionary tales (such as Leskov's "Lady MacBeth of the Mtsensk District," Turgenev's *Smoke,* Ostrovsky's *The Storm*): both kinds of narrative imply the danger of giving "free rein" to women's sexuality; they also suggest that women themselves would prove unable or unwilling to restrain it. Maternity is traditionally the only "safe" form of female sexuality, an institution and practice that has confined women and directed their erotic energies toward nurturance. In this sense one might read the "mothers" of Turgenev's novel as bearers of such convention; Fenichka's sexuality is innocent and directed toward children. But we also remember the more threatening, ambivalent figure of the archaic mother who devours the spirit: the superstitious, aging, slightly pathetic mother of Bazarov, who stands at his grave as a final reminder of the devouring "maternal" earth.

One might still find allies for opposing voices in unexpected places: Does not Tolstoy, in his crazed and murderous Pozdnyshev, suggest that the brilliant *dialogue* of creativity and eroticism, of masculine and feminine, that we find in Beethoven's "Kreutzer" Sonata will be possible only when men no longer fear women and their sexuality; that is, when men take responsibility for their own hostilities, their own "fall"? Odintsova, however, will never play the piano with the passion and brilliance of Pozdnyshev's wife; she will never break with her routines and journey to Venice and Bulgaria in service of revolutionary change (as does Elena in *On the Eve*); she will never experience the emotion that consumes Anna Karenina and drives her, tragically, to extinguish the very fire of life that had made her a passionate being; she will never follow Artemis into places of wildness and risk. We might imagine quite "sensible" reasons for not doing any of these things, but Turgenev's heroines have been creatures of passion, not sensibility; they have been defiant and exultant, not carefully resigned. Odintsova avoids the excesses of Kukshina and Princess R., but she does so at great cost. Bazarov is "consumed" at the end by the great maternal earth, which brings regeneration at the price of anonymity. One can only wonder what other ending there might have been, had Artemis and Actaeon been able to forge a new vision and order, grounded not in repression but in passionate acceptance of the hearts and souls and bodies they and we all are.

Notes

1. The song "Turgenev Women" (Turgenevskie zhenshchiny) is written by Vasily Shumov and performed by the rock group "Tsentr"; it appears on their 1988 album "Made in Paris" ("Sdelano v Parizhe") [Melodiia]. Shumov's reference to Tur-

genev Women in the morning mist (v utrennem tumane) reveals his familiarity with Turgenev's own verse—the lyric "Ultro tumannoe, utro sedoe," best known and much beloved in its musical setting. Many thanks to my colleague Dennis Browne for bringing this contemporary piece of Turgeneviana to my attention.

2. I am thinking here of the image of the virtuous woman as an "angel in the house," a pernicious image with which English women writers in particular had to come to terms. Nina Auerbach, in *Woman and the Demon: The Life of a Victorian Myth* (Cambridge: Harvard University Press, 1982), discusses both the myth and its multiple subversions in late nineteenth-century British writing.

3. "The Threshold" ("Porog"), in I. S. Turgenev, *Stikhotvoreniia* (Leningrad: Sovetskii pisatel', 1955), 362-63.

4. In his discussion of *On the Eve* Victor Ripp addresses the paradox and problematics of investing great expectations in women whose virtue derives largely from inexperience: they are perhaps innocent (since relatively isolated from corrupting institutions), but how then are they to act forcefully on precisely those institutions without losing their innocence? *Turgenev's Russia* (Ithaca: Cornell University Press, 1980), 159-86.

5. For a discussion of the novel that gives generous attention to polemic occasioned and addressed by it, see David Lowe, *Turgenev's Fathers and Sons* (Ann Arbor: Ardis, 1983), especially chapter 4. For a discussion of the connections of intimate and political relationships in the novels, see chapter 5 of my *Worlds within Worlds: The Novels of Ivan Turgenev* (Princeton: Princeton University Press, 1990).

6. The standard work in English on the woman question (*zhenskii vopros*) is Richard Stites, *The Woman's Liberation Movement in Russia: Feminism, Nihilism, and Bolshevism, 1860-1930* (Princeton: Princeton University Press, 1978). See also G. A. Tishkin, *Zhenskii vopros v Rossii v 50-60 gg. XIX v.* (Leningrad, 1984). I examine women writers' contributions to the discussion in "Love, Work and the Woman Question in Mid Nineteenth-Century Women's Writing," in *Women Writers in Russian Literature,* ed. Toby Clyman and Diana Greene (Westport, Conn.: Greenwood, 1994), 61-75.

7. Actually there are more faithful English renditions of the title: both Constance Garnett's and Isabel Hapgood's turn-of-the-century translations are entitled *Fathers and Children,* as are Richard Hare's (Collier, 1949) and Avril Pyman's (Dutton, 1968). But most translators have opted for *Fathers and Sons.* Rosemary Edmonds is no exception, even though her widely used translation is introduced by Isaiah Berlin's classic essay, "*Fathers and Children*: Turgenev and the Liberal Predicament." Russians themselves seem to have some awareness of the English speaker's dilemma: a Petersburg entrepreneur whose company goes by the name "Ottsy i deti" professed some uncertainty as to whether his English business card should read "Fathers and Children" or "Fathers and Sons." He assumed that Americans would recognize the latter, but not the former. Since Americans today know the work largely in the Edmonds translation, I expect his hunch is correct.

8. In Russian these evocative syllables go like this: "oi-oi-oi." See I. S. Turgenev, *Polnoe sobranie sochinenii i pisem* (Moscow and Leningrad: Izdatel'stvo Akademii nauk, 1964), 8:268; hereafter cited as *PSS.* Rosemary Edmonds appropriately translates these syllables with approving male gallicisms better suited to the drawing room than a machismo grunt. The "no" sequence is actually Kukshina's, when she speaks of her "friend" Odintsova in the following terms: "Vprochem, eto by nichego, no nikakoi svobody vozzreniia, nikakoi shiriny, nichego . . . etogo" (*PSS,* 8:261; ellipsis in original). Edmonds's translation makes the best of the negative challenge: "she has no independence of outlook, no breadth, nothing . . ." (144; ellipsis in original). This repeated negation introduces the "nihilist" of love. All quotations from the novel are taken from Rosemary Edmonds's translation of *Fathers and Sons* (New York: Viking Penguin, 1965) and are cited in the text. In Russian, family names of women normally end in "a," and I have adhered to this practice throughout the essay.

9. Gary Saul Morson argues this point compellingly in a recent essay on the novel. See "Genre and Hero/*Fathers and Sons*: Intergeneric Dialogues, Generic Refugees, and the Hidden Prosaic," in *Literature, Culture, and Society in the Modern Age: In Honor of Joseph Frank,* Stanford Slavic Studies, ed. Edward J. Brown, Lazar Fleishman, Gregory Freidin, and Richard Schupbach, no. 4 (Stanford: Stanford University Press, 1991), 336-81.

10. The slight confusion regarding her given name seems to echo parodically the "enigmas" of the Princess R. and Odintsova herself.

11. Turgenev's association of Kukshina with fire is oddly premonitory of the fires that accompanied political disturbances in St. Petersburg in the summer of 1862, the year after the emancipation of

the serfs (and the publication of the novel). See Abbott Gleason, *Young Russia* (Chicago: University of Chicago Press, 1980), 166-76.

12. There is a hint of symbolism at work in these heroines' names: Varvara (the seductress) is a "barbarian"; Liza (the future nun) takes the way of the biblical "narrow gate," her family name Kalitina echoing the Russian *kalitka,* or gate.

13. It is assumed that Turgenev drew his portrait of a "femme émancipée" from one woman in particular: Evgeniia Petrovna Kittara, whom he met through Marko Vovchok, a Ukrainian woman writer whose work Turgenev had translated. Kittara emerges in Vovchok's correspondence as a somewhat flighty woman of sudden and diverse enthusiasms. See G. B. Stepanova, "O prototipe Kukshinoi v romane Turgeneva 'Ottsy i deti'," *Russkaia literatura,* no. 3 (1985): 152-54.

14. Dostoevsky's Pushkin Speech of 1881 articulates clearly the programmatic force of such refusal.

15. Amy Mandelker argues compellingly for reading the novel as a tragedy; her discussion of literary traditions of suicide is also germane to my reading of Odintsova. See her *Framing "Anna Karenina": Tolstoy, the Woman Question, and the Victorian Novel* (Columbus: Ohio State University Press, 1993), 93-98.

16. Robert Bell suggests that Artemis and Athena, as virginal goddesses, are both "less human" as well as "more awesome" than Hera, Aphrodite, or Demeter. See his *Women of Classical Mythology: A Biographical Dictionary* (New York: Oxford University Press, 1993), 72. I am indebted in my imagination of Artemis to Nor Hall, who speaks of the goddess in archetypal terms: "She is a wild mountain woman, woman alone, fighter, hunter, dancer, lover of animals, protectress of all newborn sucking and roving creatures, a sister to men and teacher of women. . . . Artemis knew the ways of woman's animal body without being taught. . . . Artemis brings certain caged aspects of feminine nature out of exile." *The Moon and the Virgin: Reflections on the Archetypal Feminine* (New York: Harper and Row, 1980), 109, 122, 123.

17. Ovid provides one of the better-known versions of the myth of Artemis/Diana and Actaeon; *Metamorphoses,* trans. Rolfe Humphries (Bloomington: Indiana University Press, 1955), 61-64. See my discussion of the myth with more specific regard to Bazarov in *Worlds within Worlds,* 134-35. As I suggest in that essay, there are moments within the text that echo the particularities of the myth: when, for example, the narrator himself "watches" Odintsova in the bath (165).

18. "She had caught sight of herself in the glass; the image of her head thrown back, with a mysterious smile on the half-closed eyes, half-parted lips, told her, it seemed, in a flash something at which she herself felt confused . . ." (183; ellipsis in original).

19. The literature on this topic is extensive. See, among others, John A. Phillips, *Eve: The History of an Idea* (San Francisco: Harper and Row, 1984), and Margaret R. Miles, *Carnal Knowing: Female Nakedness and Religious Meaning in the Christian West* (New York: Vintage, 1989). Russian instances of the problem are addressed in the introduction and many of the essays in Jane T. Costlow, Stephanie Sandler, and Judith Vowles, eds., *Sexuality and the Body in Russian Culture* (Stanford: Stanford University Press, 1993).

Walter Smyrniw (essay date 1995-96)

SOURCE: Smyrniw, Walter. "Turgenev's Femmes Fatales." *Germano-Slavica* 9, nos. 1-2 (1995-96): 135-53.

[*In the following essay, Smyrniw explores possible sources for Turgenev's representation of treacherous women in his novels.*]

> Nimm dich in acht vor ihren schönen Haaren,
> Vor diesem Schmuck, mit dem sie einzig prangt.
> Wenn sie damit den jungen Mann erlangt,
> So läßt sie ihn so bald nicht wieder fahren.
>
> Goethe

In her comprehensive study of femmes fatales in literature and art, Virginia Allen has ascertained that the phrase "femme fatale" came into usage at the turn of our century, whereas the concept and the "erotic icon" of a seductive woman evolved in the previous century. She also discovered that the term femme fatale "has crept into history and criticism in the fields of literature and art history . . . with very little examination of the icon as such."[1]

Quite analogous was the reception of the femmes fatales in the works of Ivan Turgenev. Such women were neither perceived nor discussed by the critics of the nineteenth century. Only in recent times, literary scholars began to identify some women in Turgenev's works as femmes fatales.[2] Although not inappropriate *per se,* such designations are hardly illuminating, inasmuch as they are often made in passing and not duly linked to the evolution of the "erotic icon" in European literature and art. For a more comprehensive insight into Turgenev's depiction of femmes fatales, it is essential to take into account both the physical attributes of femmes fatales, and the historical circumstances which gave rise to these character types.

During the nineteenth century a number of variations of the femme fatale icon appeared in literature and in visual arts. Nevertheless, certain common traits can be discerned among them. As a rule, femmes fatales were portrayed as beautiful, erotic, enchanting, manipulative, seductive and destructive. Such women were "not only amorous and lovely, but indulged [in their] sexuality without concern for [the] lover of the moment. . . ." The instruments of enticement and erotic arousal entailed "sculptured lips . . . , full and pouting . . . , lowered eyelids . . . , a partially opened mouth, thrown-back head, and long flowing hair."[3] And the destructive traits of these women were highlighted through comparisons to vampires, sirens, mythological and historical women of antiquity who had proved lethal to their lovers. In many instances femmes fatales were cast to represent the evil nature of women, i.e. their role in temptation, sin and damnation. Such depictions served often as a contrast to women's role in the redemption and salvation of mankind, representing thereby the so-called Mary and Eve dichotomy, the opposite poles of the "dual concept of the Eternal Feminine."[4]

By the 1860's the femme fatale typology reached its full development in European literature and visual arts. However, the incipience of the femme fatale concept and its inherent imagery dates back to the preceding century, or more precisely, to the plays of Johann Wolfgang von Goethe. In his early play *Götz von Berlichengen* (1773) Goethe cast the prototype of the femme fatale in the role of Countess Adelheid. Manipulative, seductive and evil, Adelheid is endowed with the inverse traits of Götz's sister Maria who is gentle, compassionate and docile. As Virginia Allen puts it, "the polar opposition of Maria and Adelheid" represents "the ancient dual concept of the Eternal Feminine."[5] Goethe's *Faust* contains a further elaboration of the above concept as well as the introduction of the Jewish legend about Adam's first wife Lilith in the Walpurgisnacht scene. Although brief, this part of Goethe's play had a substantial influence on the incipience of the femme fatale icon, as it became an important source of inspiration for several writers and painters.

In the wake of Goethe's writings, English poets and painters made further contributions to the evolution of femme fatale typology. Percy Bysshe Shelley's translations of scenes from *Faust,* particularly the Walpurgisnacht scene and the depiction of Lilith, and his poem "On the Medusa of Leonardo Da Vinci in the Florentine Gallery" (1824) endorsed the emerging view of women's erotic and destructive propensities. John Keats also dealt with this very theme in his ballad "La Belle Dame sans Merci" (1819), and in the poem "Lamia" (1819) he introduced the image of a "snake woman" which later became an important component of the fully-developed icon of femmes fatales. Amidst English painters, Henry Fuseli and Theodor von Holst became the

foremost contributors to the evolution of the erotic portrayal of women. Of considerable influence were Fuseli's painting's "The Nightmare" (1781) and "The Daughter of Herodias with the Head of John the Baptist" (c. 1779) and von Holst's "A Scene from Goethe's *Faust*" (1833) or, alternatively entitled, "Faust and Lilith."

All of the aforementioned conceptions and attributes of femmes fatales were assimilated by Dante Gabriel Rossetti, a painter, a poet, and the founding-member of the Pre-Raphaelite Brotherhood, a group of English painters, poets and critics, established in 1848. Thanks to Rossetti's efforts, femmes fatales became what Virginia Allen calls the "full-bodied, full-throated long-haired . . . versions of lethal womanhood."[6] In his paintings Rossetti repeatedly underscored that the erotic and deadly traits of femmes fatales represent but one aspect of the diadic concept of the Eternal Feminine. The other concept can be discerned in a number of his paintings of saints and various emblems of salvation. As a poet Rossetti had the propensity of writing some poems on the very themes of his painting, as though he wanted to emphasize verbally the visual statements about the sensual and spiritual beauty and the powers of temptation and salvation held by the women representing the diadic concept of the Eternal Feminine. The most striking examples of this creative wont are Rossetti's paintings *Lady Lilith* (1868) and *Sibylla Palmifera* (1866-1870) and their companion sonnets with the title "Body's Beauty" for the former, and "Soul's Beauty" for the latter.

No one understood Rossetti's intention better than Algernon Swinburne, his close friend and fellow poet. As Rossetti had a major influence on Swinburne, many of his poems entailed outright descriptions of Rossetti's paintings. Moreover, in his essays and reviews Swinburne alluded to the prevalence of the dualistic concepts in Rossetti's works, and Swinburne was the first to employ the term "fatal" in reference to Rossetti's depictions of "deadly desirable women."[7] In sum, thanks to the mutual efforts of Rossetti and Swinburne "the English version of the full-fledged femme fatale" was well established by 1871 when Robert Buchanan attacked both Swinburne and Rossetti for their on-going depictions of sensuous women which gave rise to what he called "The Fleshy School of Poetry."[8]

Many of the above-mentioned developments have a bearing on Turgenev's portrayal of femmes fatales, because he had the opportunity of becoming personally acquainted with both Rossetti and Swinburne during his sojourn in England between 1870 and 1871. But no less significant is the fact that since his student days at the University of Berlin, Turgenev valued highly Goethe's writings, especially his *Faust*. The first published evidence of this was his translation of the last scene from

Faust, published in 1844. This was followed by Turgenev's long review of M. Vrochenko's translation of *Faust* which appeared in 1845.

The translation and the review were but a prelude to Turgenev's adaptations and transformations of certain motifs from Goethe's play. The foremost example of this wont is the epistolary story **"Faust,"** penned by Turgenev in 1856. It contains an interesting account of the diverse receptions of the erotic motifs in *Faust* and of the psychological impact that the play can have on certain personalities.

As Goethe's *Faust* was being read aloud in Turgenev's story, Herr Schimmel, an old teacher of German, kept exclaiming "How sublime! . . . How profound! . . . How wonderful!" Whereas his Russian neighbour, Priimkov, found it rather boring, his wife, Vera Nikolaevna, listened attentively to the reading and then decided to peruse the play herself. As for the reader himself, Pavel Aleksandrovich, who was "under the influence" of *Faust,* felt it prudent to skip a few passages from the "Night on Brocken."[9] His reluctance to read them is understandable, for this part of Goethe's play contains an erotic pageant, featuring such exotica as naked witches and the appearance of Lilith, Adam's first wife. Moreover, Faust's dancing and conversation with the Young Witch and Mephistopheles' chat with the Old Witch further underscore the erotic and sexual notions of the play. Later, when she reads the work herself, Vera Nikolaevna beholds the erotic and seductive motifs of the "Night on Brocken," but they do not seem to make an impression on her. Instead, she is struck by the lot of Gretchen and identifies herself with Gretchen to such an extent that she appropriates some aspects of her behaviour and utterances. Thus prior to telling Pavel Aleksandrovich that she loves him, Vera Nikolaevna asks him to read aloud the scene where Gretchen asks Faust whether he believes in God (the very scene where Gretchen promises to sleep with him); and similarly, on her death bed Vera Nikolaevna utters Gretchen's words "Was will er an dem heiligen Ort" and "throughout her illness, she raved about *Faust* and her mother whom she called sometimes Martha and sometimes Gretchen's mother."[10]

From the above passages it is indicative that Turgenev was well aware of the "dual concept of the Eternal Feminine" in the summer of 1856 when he wrote the story **"Faust,"** but chose not to develop this notion in his story. It would seem that Turgenev decided to reserve such a compositional mode for a novel which he started writing in the fall of 1856. Consequently, Turgenev's novel *Dvorianskoe gnezdo (A Nest of Gentry,* 1859) contains his first exposition of the temptation and salvation syndrome (the Mary and Eve dichotomy), which Goethe introduced in his plays *Götz von Berlichengen* and expounded further in *Faust.*

Fedor Lavretskii, the protagonist of *A Nest of Gentry,* first falls in love with a sensuous, seductive and a manipulative woman, and later with a woman exemplifying purity and religious values. The former is his wife, Varvara Pavlovna, and the latter is his distant relative, Liza Kalitina. When he met Varvara, Lavretskii was overwhelmed by her physical beauty: "her pretty face", her "marvellous eyes", "thin eyebrows," "expressive lips," "the posture of her head, arms and neck."[11] On marrying this voluptuous woman, Lavretskii had no inkling that Varvara was using her sensuous beauty to manipulate him. He managed to escape from her control only after discovering that she was unfaithful to him.

Lavretskii was the first but not the only victim of Varvara's amorous exploits. She allured men not only through her physical attractiveness, but aggressively by way of sensuous gestures and allusions. These enticing actions entail flirting with Gedeonovskii by placing "the tip of her little foot on his foot," by making eyes at him and giggling while he was giving her a lift in his carriage.[12] In the case of Vladimir Panshin, Varvara Pavlovna resorted to such enticements as "holding her white hands at the level of her lips" while he was playing a romance on the piano, suggesting that they sing songs with sensuous contents, as well as her "habit of touching very slightly the sleeve of her collocutor" and "these instantaneous touches excited Vladimir Nikolaevich very much."[13] In view of all these sensuous and alluring signals, Panshin could not help but accede to Varvara Pavlovna's invitation to visit her at the Lavriki estate and spend a lot of time there. In a few months she gained complete control over Panshin: "Varvara Pavlovna had enslaved him, literally enslaved him: there is no other word to express her unlimited, irrevocable, irresponsible power over him."[14] Although Varvara Pavlovna is repeatedly identified in the novel as a "lioness" and a coquette, some literary scholars have concluded that Varvara Pavlovna is "worthy of the appellation femme fatale . . . ," and that she is portrayed as a "treacherous *femme fatale.*"[15] Although such inferences are not inappropriate, they should be qualified by the understanding that the portrayal of Varvara Pavlovna, the first femme fatale in Turgenev's novels, was predicated on the prototypes of femmes fatales which Turgenev beheld in Goethe's plays, and particularly in *Faust.*

Cast as an antipode to Varvara Pavlovna, Liza Kalitina is not lacking in beauty. Lavretskii finds her physically attractive and reflects on her enchanting features,[16] and Panshin too found her captivating till Varvara lured him away. Although Liza's good looks are mentioned, they are less conspicuous than her proclivity to truth, purity, altruism and religious devotion. In spite of the piety instilled since childhood by her nurse Agafiia, Liza is capable of falling in love and admits this to Lavretskii.

But at the same time she subordinates everything, including her desire for personal happiness, to the will of God. Consequently, when she realizes that such happiness cannot be attained because the news about the death of Varvara Pavlovna was false, Liza quickly concludes that God must be punishing her for falling in love with Lavretskii and resolves to enter a convent in order to expiate not only her personal sins, but also those of her family members.[17]

The details of the portraits of Varvara Pavlovna and Liza are too numerous to be mentioned here in toto, but suffice it to state that the contrasts in these personages have seldom escaped the attention of literary critics. Some have perceived the depiction of the above women as "utterly diadic, an almost perfect enactment of the virgin/whore polarity,"[18] and others have asserted that "Liza and Varvara are in a very real sense two aspects of Pauline Viardot, in so far as they represent the two sides of his ideal woman, the twin faces of the eternal feminine."[19] Such explications are unsatisfactory in several respects: they do not relate the diadic mode of characterization to Turgenev's keen interest in character types (as exemplified in his essay **"Hamlet and Don Quixote"**), and they do not mention the source from which Turgenev could have derived the concept of Eternal Feminine.

In 1858 Turgenev worked almost simultaneously on the essay entitled **"Hamlet and Don Quixote"** and on the novel *A Nest of Gentry.* In view of this it is not surprising that by the end of the last century some critics managed to discern Turgenev's conception of Quixotic traits in the behaviour of Mikhalevich, a minor personage in *A Nest of Gentry.*[20] Turgenev does not exclude women from the Hamletic and Quixotic typology, for he asserts that "two fundamental, antipodal traits of human nature are embodied in these two types . . . ," and that "all people belong more or less to one of these types."[21] To be sure, some of Turgenev's heroines were cast as feminine variants of the Hamletic and Quixotic character types, or else combinations of both, but one would be hard put to perceive Turgenev's femmes fatales in terms of this typology. There is, however, an alternate possibility. From the analogy between Hamlet and Mephistopheles which Turgenev makes in the essay[22] it is plain that he reflected not only on the works of Shakespeare and Cervantes, but also on Goethe's *Faust* while he was working on the "Hamlet and Don Quixote" essay and on the novel *A Nest of Gentry.*

On comparing the first part of *Faust* with *A Nest of Gentry* one can readily discern that both contain a diadic portrayal of women—a siren and sibyl syndrome—and also note the similarities between Gretchen and Liza and between Varvara Pavlovna and Lilith. Both Gretchen and Liza are young, innocent and profoundly religious; they are attracted to older men who intrude into their world of piety; both Gretchen and Liza lose the tranquility of life by falling in love, and eventually they accept the tragic consequences of their affairs and submit themselves to the judgement of God. The parallels between Lilith and Varvara are fewer, but they are equally striking: both seek only sensuous gratification, and both tempt and seduce men in order to keep them under complete control. From these and other similarities which can be discerned in *Faust* and *A Nest of Gentry* it is evident that Goethe's play provided Turgenev with a model for the diadic feminine typology which he utilized in *A Nest of Gentry* and in several subsequent works. In view of the above factors, it is surprising, however, that the various parallels in Goethe's play and Turgenev's novel were not previously observed by the scholars who had explored Goethe's influence on Turgenev.[23]

In spite of being only an episodical character in the novel *Ottsy i deti* (*Fathers and Sons,* 1861), Turgenev's next femme fatale represents an important phase in the author's treatment of the Eternal Feminine concept. In this novel Turgenev decided to cast Princess R—— as both a siren and a sibyl. As a siren, the Princess had "the reputation of a frivolous coquette" who "laughed and jested with young men whom she received before dinner in her dimly-lit drawing room. . . ." Although "no one would have called her a beauty," Princess R—— managed to allure men with two remarkable features: "her hair, gold coloured and as heavy as gold, which fell below her knees" and her eyes which had an unusual and "an enigmatic glance." Whereas in the role of a sibyl the Princess would weep and pray during the night and "often paced the room till morning, wringing her hands in anguish, or sat, pale and cold, reading the Psalter."[24] And without attaining it herself, Princess R—— pointed out to Pavel Kirsanov how salvation could be achieved by returning the ring he had given her, by drawing on it "lines in shape of a cross over the sphinx" and by conveying the message to him "that the cross is the solution."[25]

Although the depiction of the siren and sibyl duality is quite brief, it contains new and significant elements in respect to Turgenev's subsequent renditions of femmes fatales. One of them entails such attributes as long and gold coloured hair and the impressive and powerful eyes. The other pertains to the city of Baden which serves as the setting for Pavel Kirsanov's last romantic encounter with Princess R—— as well as the setting for Turgenev's next novel, *Dym* (*Smoke,* 1867), featuring a major femme fatale figure.

In *Smoke* Turgenev made no attempt to depict the traits of both a siren and a sibyl within the same person, as he had in the case of Princess R——. Instead, he reverted to a diadic exposition of the temptation-salvation syndrome. However, he decided to reverse the emphasis that he had used previously. Whereas in the *A Nest of Gentry* Turgenev adhered to the pattern inherent in *Faust* by developing to a greater extent the traits of the sibyl, i.e. the character of Liza, in *Smoke* he chose to deviate from Goethe's model and emphasize the role of the siren. Therefore, in the latter novel the portrayal of Tatiana Shestova, the sibyl and saviour, is kept to a bare minimum. Her fiancé, Grigorii Litvinov, thinks of her as "his sweet, kind, holy Tatiana . . . ," as his "guardian angel" and a "good genius. . . ." Litvinov's friend, Sozont Potugin, also observes that Tatiana "has a golden heart, a truly angelic soul." But apart from these attributes, the portrayal of Tatiana is so minimal that it resembles the photograph of her which Litvinov contemplates prior to yielding to a Russian siren called Irina Ratmirova.[26] In all, the reader discerns nothing about Tatiana's childhood, her education, how and when she met her fiancé, and for that matter why she loves him, and even more importantly, why she eventually forgave Litvinov for succumbing to a femme fatale.

Quite the contrary is Turgenev's depiction of Irina's character. He presents the reader with an abundance of details about her life, ranging from the experiences as a young girl to those of a woman in her early thirties. It would seem that Turgenev strove to show thereby how Irina had acquired the mentality of a femme fatale, i.e. the propensity of sensually attracting certain males and then keeping them under complete control. In Irina's case this inclination can be traced to her "love of power" (*vlastoliubie*), first exemplified during her sojourn at the boarding school, and later having "an almost unlimited freedom in the home of her parents."[27] This enabled Irina to gain complete control over Litvinov when he was courting her in his student days, then terminate their relationship and later subjugate him once again while she was married to another man. Moreover, Irina also enticed Potugin to fall in love with her and then controlled his life to the extent that he was willing to marry Irina's pregnant friend and to bring up her daughter. And even when she turned thirty, Irina was "just as charming as ever" and "a countless number of young men fell in love with her . . . ," but others did not fall in love with her, as they were "afraid of her 'malevolent' mind" (*boiatsia ee "ozloblennogo" uma*).[28]

As a highly successful femme fatale, Irina attracts men primarily by her physical beauty. At seventeen Irina was already an unusual woman, a very striking figure. Turgenev depicts it with great skill and in such detail that he renders an accomplished verbal portrait.

> She was a tall young woman with a good figure, with somewhat small breasts and young narrow shoulders, and for her age an unusually pale and smooth skin, as clear and smooth as porcelain, and thick blonde hair with its darker strands mingling uniquely with lighter ones. Her features were elegant, almost artificially regular and had not lost the artless expression of early youth; but in the slow movements of her beautiful neck, in her smile, seemingly either an absent-minded or a weary smile which revealed that she was a nervous young lady, and in the very outlines of the thin, faintly smiling lips, of her small, aquiline, slightly compressed nose, there was something self-willed and passionate, something dangerous both for others and for herself. Striking, truly striking were her eyes, which were dark-grey shot with green, languishing eyes with unusually long and radiating lashes, like those of Egyptian goddesses, and boldly sweeping brows. Those eyes had a strange expression: they seemed to be looking attentively and thoughtfully from an unknown depth and distance.[29]

That is how Litvinov perceived Irina when he first met her during his days at the university of Moscow. When he saw her ten years later in Baden Irina not only retained all her youthful features, but seemed even more beautiful. "How lovely, how strong is the femininity of her young body!"[30] thought Litvinov. However, he soon discovered that Irina had changed in one respect: she became very skilled at using the strength of her femininity and her beauty to enchant and to control men. With this intent she would bedazzle men by her "white shoulders," the "beautiful curve of her gleaming neck," the "whiteness of her face," by the "birthmark on her cheek," by her "thirsting lips" and "extraordinary eyelashes."[31] Even more enticing were her "splendid eyes," for her "bewitching eyes pierced into his [Litvinov's] heart. . . ."[32] But the most powerful arsenal was her beautiful, blonde hair. Irina used it as the means of keeping Litvinov under her control. Thus when he began to have doubts about their relationship, "she caught him with both hands, pressed his head to her breast, her comb jingled and started rolling, and her falling hair enveloped him in a fragrant and soft wave."[33]

From the examples cited above and from other textual details in *Smoke*, it is evident that by means of the elaborate depiction of Irina's sensuous beauty and the various means she had employed to entice men and to keep them under her control. Turgenev succeeded in rendering an accomplished portrait of a typical femme fatale. As such it bears a close resemblance to the femme fatale icon at the apex of its development in European literature and art in the 1860's. However, the image of the siren in Turgenev's novel differs in some respects from its European counterparts. Whereas in West European visual arts and literature the seductive traits of femmes fatales were often underscored through specific symbols and allusions to mythological figures or to famous seductresses in the annals of antiquity, Turgenev's depiction of the femme fatale in *Smoke* is confined to contemporary reality and a fidelity to a realistic writing technique that excludes a deliberate utilization of symbolism.

In 1870 Turgenev embarked again on the writing of a short novel which he subsequently called *Veshnie vody* (*Torrents of Spring,* 1872). As Turgenev put it in a letter to Ia. P. Polonskii of 18 December 1871, his novel contains "a love theme which has no bearing at all on social, political or contemporary issues." Moreover, in the above letter Turgenev also stated that as an author he knew "what [he] *wanted* to achieve" by it (chto *khotel* sdelat'), but he was not certain that the public would perceive it.[34] And indeed the contemporary readers and critics alike failed to discern the significance of the main theme in *Torrents of Spring.* Not only Turgenev's fellow countrymen, but even such Western literary figures as Gustave Flaubert, who was greatly impressed with *Torrents of Spring* and praised Turgenev's skill in the depiction of the contrasting types of women, did not seem to realize that the two women were cast as a sibyl and a siren which comprise the opposite poles of the Eternal Feminine theme in the novel. It would seem that not only Turgenev's contemporaries, but also readers in our time fail to discern the sibyl and siren dichotomy and its relevance to the love theme due to a literal reading of the text and a disregard of the inherent symbolism and figurative language of the novel.

At the literal level, *Torrents of Spring* contains an account of two diverse experiences of love which Dmitrii Sanin had when he travelled through Germany in the summer of 1840. The first took place during a stop in Frankfurt (on Main). Sanin fell in love with Gemma Roselli, the daughter of an Italian confectioner who immigrated to Germany. In every respect this was a spiritual and a Platonic relationship. But quite unexpectedly, two days later he had a sensuous affair in Wiesbaden with Maria Polozova, a rich Russian woman, to whom Sanin wanted to sell his estate in order to have enough money to marry Gemma. Thereafter Sanin abandoned Gemma and became Polozova's love-slave. Even at a literal level *Torrents of Spring* is an intriguing novel with several ironic developments. But Turgenev does not confine the exposition of the love theme to a realistic level. By way of an authorial comment he encourages the readers to reflect on a deeper level of meaning of this novel by decoding some of its inherent symbols. For example, Turgenev states parenthetically that "in Italian Gemma means, of course, a precious stone."[35] This comment is made shortly before Gemma gives Sanin "a little garnet cross" that she had worn on her neck and says: "If I am yours, then your faith is now also my faith!"[36] Thus the authorial remark as well as Gemma's gesture and comment are meant to prompt the reader to reflect on the symbolic significance of the cross and its relevance to Gemma's role in the novel.

Both the garnet cross and Gemma's declaration underscore the spiritual nature of the love between Sanin and Gemma. In view of this it is not surprising that Sanin and Gemma do not even exchange a single kiss throughout their brief relationship. Instead, they communicate their affection for each other symbolically by exchanging several times the rose which a German officer had taken impudently from their table in a restaurant after making a toast to Gemma's beauty.[37] Inasmuch as Gemma's surname, Roselli, signifies in Italian a "small rose," both the rose and the gernet cross which Sanin received from Gemma are in essence a form of symbolic communication which Turgenev calls "the giving of one's soul to another."[38] Moreover, both in the traditional sense and in *Torrents of Spring,* the cross encompasses symbolically such interrelated human experiences as treachery, suffering, forgiveness and salvation.

All of the above notions are not only expressed through the symbol of the cross, but developed as striking motifs of the novel. For example, on responding to Gemma's query at the time of his departure for Wiesbaden Sanin states: "I'm yours . . . I'll come back," but betrays her two days later by succumbing to Maria Polozova's sensuality. Consequently, Sanin is denounced by Pantaleone who calls him an *"infame traditore"* (a vile traitor).[39] By way of this betrayal Sanin brought a lot of suffering to Gemma and her family. However, he did not fare much better himself, as he had to endure the ignominy of being a sex-slave of Polozova, of having to wear an iron ring as a sign of his bondage. And even after severing his relationship with her, Sanin was not able to marry and in later years suffered from a "spiritual and physical" fatigue and loneliness.

At first the reader has the impression that Gemma's garnet cross was not a potent talisman. Although Sanin had "kissed a thousand times the little cross,"[40] it did not ward him against Polozova's sexual ploys. But from the framework of the novel it is plain that the little cross played a vital role in the reawakening of Sanin's memories about the spiritual intimacy with Gemma, in his salvation from a *taedium vitae,* a fear of death and lonely old age. In her letter Gemma forgave Sanin for his betrayal and the suffering he had brought her, and "wished him above all peace of mind and a calm spirit. . . ."[41] As Gemma also desired to see him, Sanin was able to look forward to a spiritual salvation, ie. a reunion with her in America.

At the end of the novel Sanin underscores the symbolic value of the little garnet cross by having it "set in a magnificent pearl necklace" and sending it as a wedding present to Gemma's daughter. In several respects the setting of the cross is analogous to the architectonics of *Torrents of Spring.* In the novel Turgenev employs a number of symbols in order to accentuate the symbolic roles of the major personages and the motifs associated with them. Thus the symbolic meaning inherent in Gemma's given name and surname, the subtle symbolism of the rose that was exchanged between Sanin and Gemma, and, above all, the garnet cross bring to the fore Gemma's role of a sibyl and saviour. And similarly, an array of impressive symbols highlights Polozova's role of the siren and femme fatale.

In comparison with the sirens in his previous works, Maria Polozova is obviously Turgenev's most accomplished portrait of a femme fatale. However, a number of the attributes of her physiognomy are similar to the author's previous castings of femmes fatales. Polozova is portrayed as "a young, beautiful lady" with "a marvellous figure," "a charming neck, marvellous shoulders." And "when she smiled, not one or two, but three little dimples appeared on each cheek, and her eyes smiled more than her lips, more than her long, bright red, delicious lips with two tiny moles on the left side."[42] Like Irina Ratmirova in *Smoke,* Polozova had very striking eyes, and "when she opened them wide, something evil came through their bright, almost cold gleam. . . ." But the most powerful feature by far was Polozova's "thick blonde hair [which] fell down on both sides of her head—braided but not pinned up."[43]

Although Turgenev does not state it explicitly, the reader can nevertheless discern without difficulty the symbolic significance of Polozova's "snake-like braids" [*zmeevidnye kosy*]. And in a further passage, the semblance to a snake is not confined to the hair, but extended to Polozova herself: "'A snake! Ah, she is a snake!' thought Sanin . . . 'but what a beautiful snake!'"[44] And indeed, on the following day Polozova proves herself a true snake-woman—a highly skilled temptress and seductress—when Sanin agrees to go riding with her. During this outing Polozova was riding ahead of Sanin, and the snake-like braids were continually flying before his eyes, luring him into temptation. The image of a snake appears also in the description of Polozova's triumphant smile after her seduction and subjugation of Sanin. However, as it is conveyed through a Russian idiom which cannot be translated literarily into English, this image can only be discerned in the Russian text: "*na gubakh zmeilos' torzhestvo.*"[45]

Less obvious, but no less effective, is the symbolic significance of Polozova's name and the place she chose to seduce Sanin. At first sight the surname Polozova appears to be based on the Russian word *poloz,* meaning a runner of a sledge. But *poloz* has another meaning in Russian, namely, a grass-snake. It would seem, therefore, that Turgenev intently chose this surname to underscore symbolically the seductive propensity of this femme fatale. And by the same token, it would seem that he picked Wiesbaden as an appropriate setting for the sexual ploys of the grass-snake-woman, not only because it was a fashionable spa frequented by Russians at the time, but also because in German the name of the city connotes both a grass meadow (Wiese) and water or spa (Bad). In view of this, it is also symbolically significant that en route to the place of seduction Polozova decided to turn off the main highway and proceed along the path leading to a "meadow which was at first dry, but then wet, and then completely swampy. The water seeped through everywhere, stood in puddles.

Maria Nikolaevna rode her horse deliberately through these puddles, laughed loudly and repeated: 'Let's do some school-pranks!'"[46]

Although the exact place of the seduction of Sanin is not given in the novel, it can be approximated from a number of references to the local topography. For example, on leaving the city of Wiesbaden, Polozova told Sanin that she wanted to ride to the "wonderful mountains," to the "wonderful forest." In the given local this can only refer to the forests of the Taunus Mountains which lie north of Wiesbaden. Further, when they reach the forest, Polozova asked Sanin whether he could see "a red wooden cross." When Sanin replied in the affirmative, she stated "'Ah, great! I know where we are.'"[47] This is obviously a reference to a road sign, and in the Taunus Mountains, a sign with a red cross could pertain to the mountain called Rotekreuzkopf (Red-Cross-Head) which lies not far from Wiesbaden.

The sign with a red cross and the Rotekreuzkopf mountain have a twofold symbolic significance. Not far from the Rotekreuzkopf mountain (about a kilometre from it) there is a village spa called Schlangenbad (Snake-Spa). As the name suggests, this is the true domain of all water-snakes, and, therefore, it is not surprising that Polozova knows this place well. And by the same token, those who were familiar with the vicinity of Wiesbaden (and in the nineteenth century many Russians knew it well, as they frequented both the spa and the gambling tables of Wiesbaden) would recognize without difficulty the relevance of the Snake-Spa to the recurring snake symbolism in the novel. And in the context of *Torrents of Spring* the wooden red cross can also be linked to the symbolic significance of Gemma's little garnet cross which Sanin was kissing most ardently only a day before succumbing to Polozova's seduction in the forest at the foot of Red Cross Mountain.

As the allusion to the red cross occurs shortly before Sanin's seduction by the beautiful snake-woman, it adds more than a touch of irony to the symbolism of the novel, inasmuch as for Sanin the Red Cross Mountain did not signify a salvation, but a fall and damnation. And not for Sanin alone, for Polozova likely used this very place for the seduction of the German officer, Baron von Dönhof, who like Sanin had to wear Polozova's ring of bondage. No less ironic is the symbolism conveyed by Polozova's first name, Maria. Traditionally this name conveys symbolically such notions as purity, virginity and salvation. It is, therefore, an ironic, indeed an incongruous name for a woman like Polozova who is in every respect the antithesis of a spiritual being. Indeed, in the novel Polozova is not only identified as "an immoral woman," but cast as a predatory creature. Not only her wont to dominate over men's bodies and souls, but Polozova's ardent desire to possess the whole world can be readily surmised from the descriptions of her facial expressions during the wild gallop to the mountains:

> What a face it is! It seems as though it is wide open: the wide open eyes, greedy, bright and wild; the lips, the nostrils also wide opened and breathing greedily; she is staring straight, fixed in front of her, and, it seems, that her soul wants to possess everything it sees—the earth, the sky, the sun, and the air itself—and it regrets only one thing: there are not enough dangers—it would have overcome them all![48]

From the above depiction of Polozova as well as from her seductive role it is plain that by assigning the name Maria to an obvious femme fatale Turgenev had the objective of creating a portrait of a false virgin, a false saviour, indeed, the very icon of an Anti-Maria.

In contrast to Turgenev's previous works, the exposition of the Eternal Feminine theme in *Torrents of Spring* entails not only a skilful utilization of realistic details, but also an array of symbols which are meant to underscore the inherent Mary and Eve syndrome. A further contrast with Turgenev's previous depictions of femmes fatales are also the allusions to various literary and mythological figures of antiquity. In the rendition of Polozova during the "mad gallop" Turgenev likens her to an Amazon and a Centaur: "This is no horsewoman [*Eto uzh ne amazonka*][49] putting her horse to a gallop—this is a galloping young female Centaur, half beast, half god. . . ."[50] Further, inasmuch as her braids were previously likened to snakes, the reader can also associate Polozova with other figures in Greek mythology, namely the Gorgon sisters, famous for their snake-hair and mortal glances. But the dominant and the recurring allusion in Turgenev's novel is to Virgil's *Aeneid*. First, on chatting with Sanin, Polozova extols Book IV as the best part of the epic and mentions it again during their horse ride. As Sanin "had only a vague idea of the *Aeneid*," he was not aware that Polozova identified herself with the passionate queen of Virgil's epic and based some of her schemes on her favourite part of this work. Therefore, it is hardly a coincidence that the reader can discern several parallels between the erotic episodes in the *Aeneid* and *Torrents of Spring*. For example, in Book IV of the *Aeneid* Dido invites Aeneas to go hunting on horseback. During the hunt they are caught in a severe thunderstorm in a forest on a mountain and seek refuge in a cave where they make love. Polozova also asks Sanin to go horse riding with her, and they too face a thunderstorm on a mountain. Delighted by this coincidence Polozova says to Sanin "'Remember, I told you yesterday about the *Aeneid*? You know a storm also caught *them* in the woods.'" Polozova obviously knew where to find cover from the rain, for they soon reached "a humble warden's hut" under "an overhanging grey cliff." At the entrance to the hut Polozova "turned around to Sanin and whispered: 'Aeneas!'"[51]

On comparing the femmes fatales cast by Turgenev in the novels *A Nest of Gentry, Fathers and Sons, Smoke* and *Torrents of Spring* one can discern some recurring similarities and the emergence of new traits among these figures. In all of the above novels the femmes fatales are always depicted as a component of the temptation/salvation syndrome encompassing the concept of the Eternal Feminine. All of the temptresses have the propensity to attract men by their physical beauty and sensuality, of keeping in bondage the men who succumb to their charms. Moreover, in the novels written after 1860 Turgenev's femmes fatales have such common instruments of enticement as very prominent and bewitching eyes, and long blonde hair. Although she is endowed with all of the above mentioned traits, Maria Polozova differs from the previous femme fatales by indulging in sexuality more overtly and for the sake of personal enjoyment. Indeed, Polozova not only marries a man willing to tolerate her extramarital sexual liaisons, but makes wagers with her husband on the men that she plans to seduce.

A chronological comparison of Turgenev's depiction of femmes fatales reveals more than the similarities and differences among the protagonists. It also brings to light the facts that Turgenev was preoccupied with Goethe's *Faust* when he embarked in *A Nest of Gentry* on the exposition of a diadic typology predicated on the Mary and Eve syndrome, and that he concluded the exposition of this typology in his last novel by invoking both Goethe's name and his father's house and by setting *Torrents of Spring* in Frankfurt and Wiesbaden, Goethe's ancestral domain. Do these facts suffice to sustain the inference that Turgenev developed the femme fatale typology solely on the basis of the Eternal Feminine concept derived from Goethe? At first sight, this would not seem unreasonable, inasmuch as Turgenev strove to depict in his works the various phenomena of life through certain character types, a number of which he derived from the works of such men of letters as Shakespeare, Cervantes, Schiller and Goethe. However, it is also plain that Turgenev did not restrict himself to the works of the foremost authors, but paid close attention to the contemporary literal and cultural trends in Europe.

As he spent most of his life abroad, Turgenev was not only well-aware of the literary and cultural developments in Germany and France, but also in England. Consequently, Turgenev was obviously cognisant that the femme fatale typology was well established in literature and visual art during the 1860's. Furthermore, he was personally acquainted with some of the poets and painters whom Virginia Allen identified as the major contributors to the evolution of the femme fatale icon: Théophile Gautier, Dante Gabriel Rossetti, Algernon Swinburne[52] and several members of the Pre-Raphaelite Brotherhood. Evidently, Turgenev read some of Rossetti's poems as early as 1852, and later, during his 1871 sojourn in England, he also became acquainted with Rossetti's controversial collection of verses, which appeared in 1870 under the title *Poems*. But it is also evident from his letters that Turgenev did not understand some of Rossetti's poems, and that on the whole, he did not appreciate Rossetti's poetic works.[53] However, it is equally obvious that Turgenev greatly admired Swinburne's poetry, extolled his "great lyrical talent," and proclaimed him "the most remarkable contemporary English poet."[54] Although Turgenev did not identify the edition of poetry that appealed to him most, he was likely referring to Swinburne's *Poems and Ballads* (1866) which contained many of his best and most notorious poems, including those which feature his versions of femmes fatales. Quite likely Turgenev was also aware of the fact that the appearance of this volume caused a major uproar in the literary world, as it was deemed by some both insulting and blasphemous to womanhood.[55]

Turgenev's first encounter with the visual art of the Pre-Raphaelites dates back to 1857 when he attended the Art Treasures Exhibition in Manchester. This exhibition featured a large display of English paintings, and, according to Patrick Waddington, Turgenev "must at least have been visually excited by the often stunning freshness of the Pre-Raphaelite paintings sent in by proud industrialists."[56] It is not clear whose paintings Turgenev may have seen at the exhibition in Manchester, but it is known that in 1871 Turgenev met many Pre-Raphaelites in London. In fact they held a party in his honour at the house of Ford Mardox Brown. Although "at Brown's house Turgenev will have had the chance to examine a vast range of Pre-Raphaelite pictures and objects d'art . . . ," he was nevertheless keenly interested in seeing Rossetti's paintings. Such an opportunity presented itself on 23 June 1871 when Rossetti invited Turgenev for dinner. There is reason to believe that Turgenev's curiosity about Rossetti's painting was duly appeased on that occasion, since "Rossetti's house . . . was a veritable museum."[57] Among other things, Turgenev may have caught a glimpse of some of Rossetti's numerous painting and sketches from Goethe's *Faust*.[58] Turgenev could have seen a number of Rossetti's paintings and sketches of femmes fatales, and possibly one of several studies known as "La Belle Dame sans Merci" that feature a young woman, whose long, golden hair is woven around the neck of the man riding with her on horseback.[59] Furthermore, inasmuch as he read Rossetti's recently published *Poems* which contained a number of "Sonnets for Pictures," (ie. poems written on the same themes as his paintings), Turgenev may have been keenly interested in seeing some of these paintings, particularly *Lady Lilith* (1868) and *Sibylla Palmifera* (1866-1870) for which Rossetti wrote the companions sonnets "Body's Beauty" and "Soul's Beauty". It is not likely that Rossetti had shown Turgenev *Sibylla Palmifera,* because this painting was commissioned by George Rare and delivered to him after it was completed.[60] But Rossetti could have shown *Lady Lilith* to Turgenev, or else a watercolour variation of this painting, for both were still in his possession at the time. It is worth noting that on the back of the watercolour version of *Lady Lilith* the following lines were written "in the artist's handwriting":

> "Beware of her hair, for she excels
> All women in the magic of her locks
> And when she twines them round a young man's neck
> She will not ever set him free again."[61]

On this very label Rossetti acknowledged that these verses had been composed by Goethe. They pertain of course to Goethe's rendition of Adam's first wife Lilith in the Walpurgisnacht scene of *Faust.*

Even if Turgenev had not seen the above annotation on the watercolour version of *Lady Lilith,* he would have readily surmised from the reading of the sonnet "Body's Beauty" that Rossetti's poem did not entail a mere recapitulation of the Jewish legend about Adam's first wife, but a variation of Goethe's depiction of Lilith. This can be discerned from Rossetti's reference to Lilith's "enchanted hair" which "Draws men to watch the bright web she can weave, / Till heart and body and life are in its hold."[62] Further, Turgenev would likely have noticed Rossetti's major deviations from Goethe's model. Whereas in *Faust* Goethe made no mention of the colour of Lilith's hair, Rossetti bestowed his Lilith with "strangling golden hair" in both the sonnet "Body's Beauty" and in the painting *Lady Lilith.*[63] Moreover, Rossetti introduced the image of a snake in his depiction of Lilith. Thus in the sonnet he asserted that Lilith's "sweet tongue could deceive" even before Eve was tempted by "the snake," whereas in the painting he integrated the image of the snake into Lilith's "strangling golden hair."[64] Consequently, it is a striking feature of the painting that on the left side of Lady Lilith's head the hair is braided, forming a twisting, snake-like braid along her neck and shoulder, whereas the hair on the right side, unbraided and stretched out by a comb that she holds in her hand, has retained the snake-like waves formed by the braiding, and hence this creates the impression of a twisting locomotion of several snakes.

From Turgenev's correspondence it is evident that he was working on **Torrents of Spring** throughout his 1871 sojourn in London. Is there reason to presume, therefore, that the reading of Rossetti's *Poems* and the possible viewing of his paintings had an influence on Turgenev's novel? In the opinion of Patrick Waddington, **Torrents of Spring** "had little if any relation to his stay in England, being full of nostalgia for his lost happiness in Germany, coloured by his lifelong love of Italy and—more superficially—by his unfulfilled ambition to see America."[65] But one is inclined to reach quite the contrary conclusion on comparing Turgenev's depiction of a femme fatale in *Torrents of Spring* with Rossetti's treatment of this subject both in the poem "Body's Beauty" and in the painting *Lady Lilith.* There is a striking similarity between Rossetti's femme fatale figures in the above works and Turgenev's depiction of Polozova with "snake-like braids" and with "thick blonde hair" which is during the course of the novel either flowing free, as during the wild gallop to the mountains, or being braided and arranged. Moreover, like Rossetti, by way of the snake-like hair Turgenev strove to convey the convergence of the notions of seduction and destruction. This is most apparent in a variant pertaining to the seductive and destructive actions of Polozova which Turgenev deleted from the final version of *Torrents of Spring*: "The soft and strong rings of the 'beautiful snake' were sliding down, and barely audibly and unceasingly coiling around the rabbit."[66] The image of a beautiful snake, in essence a boa constrictor choking its victim, corresponds both to the "strangling golden hair" of Lilith in the poem "Body's Beauty" and to the golden hair strangling the young rider in Rossetti's sketch "La Belle Dame sans Merci."

The similarity of the femme fatale imagery in the works of Rossetti and Turgenev suggests that on seeing them Turgenev must have been impressed with Rossetti's paintings to such an extent that he chose to utilize some of the imagery in his novel. Moreover, from the reading of Rossetti's poems "Soul's Beauty" and "Body's Beauty" Turgenev was no doubt able to surmise that Goethe's *Faust* had served as the primary source of the femme fatale notions expounded by both Rossetti and other Pre-Raphaelites, and that the femme fatale icon was not only linked to Lilith, but also to Goethe's conception of the Eternal Feminine.

In view of the above factors, there is reason to believe that the experiences in England during the summer of 1871, rather than a "nostalgia for his lost happiness in Germany" had prompted Turgenev to revise a short story that he began writing in the previous year, and to augment it to such an extent that it became a short novel which he eventually called the *Torrents of Spring.*[67] Written in the wake of personal acquaintances with several leading members of the Pre-Raphaelite Brotherhood, *Torrents of Spring* contains not only Turgenev's most accomplished portraits of a sibyl and a siren—the diadic counterparts of the Eternal Feminine concept—, but also an impressive portrayal of Polozova, a femme fatale bearing the closest resemblance to her counterparts in European literature and visual arts in the nineteenth century by way of her keen interest in sensual experiences and indulgence in sexuality, and by way of such erotic features as "sculptured lips . . . opened mouth . . . , and long flowing hair" all of which are used to entice, to seduce, to manipulate and ruin her lovers.

Notes

1. Virginia M. Allen, *The Femme Fatale: Erotic Icon* (Troy, N. Y., 1983), p. ix.

2. Ivan Turgenev, *Dvorianskoe gnezdo,* edited with notes by Patrick Waddington (Oxford-New York, 1969), p. 227; see also Eva Kagan-Kans *Hamlet and Don Quixote: Turgenev's Ambivalent Vision* (The Hague, 1975), pp. 52-55; see also Marina Astman "Obraz 'inferal'noi zhenshchiny' v russkoi literature," in *Otkliki: sbornik statei pamiati Nikolaia Ivanovicha Ul'ianova (1904-1985),* edited by Vsevolod Sechkarev, (New Haven, 1986), pp. 91-93; see also Elizabeth Cheresh Allen, *Beyond Realism: Turgenev's Poetics of Secular Salvation* (Stanford, 1992), p. 204; see also Rolf-Dieter Kluge, *Ivan S. Turgenev: Dichtung zwischen Hoffnung und Entsagung* (München, 1992), p. 133.

3. Virginia M. Allen, *The Femme Fatale: Erotic Icon,* pp. 2, 4.

4. Virginia M. Allen, *The Femme Fatale: Erotic Icon,* p. 6.

5. Virginia M. Allen, *The Femme Fatale: Erotic Icon,* p. 20.

6. Virginia M. Allen, *The Femme Fatale: Erotic Icon,* p. 99.

7. Virginia M. Allen, *The Femme Fatale: Erotic Icon,* pp. 124-25.

8. Virginia M. Allen, *The Femme Fatale: Erotic Icon,* p. 139.

9. I.S. Turgenev, *Polnoe sobranie sochinenii i pisem v dvadtsati vos'mi tomakh,* VII (Moscow, 1964), p. 25. Henceforth the references to this edition shall be cited as *Works* or *Letters.*

10. *Works,* VII, p. 49.

11. *Works,* VII, p. 166.

12. *Works,* VII, pp. 256, 267.

13. *Works,* VII, p. 265.

14. *Works,* VII, p. 287.

15. Elizabeth Cheresh Allen, *Beyond Realism: Turgenev's Poetics of Secular Salvation,* p. 204; see also Ivan Turgenev, *Dvorianskoe gnezdo,* edited with notes by Patrick Waddington, p. 217; Waddington's italics.

16. *Works,* VII, p. 184.

17. *Works,* VII, pp. 272, 285-86.

18. Joe Andrew, *Women in Russian Literature 1780-1863* (New York, 1988), p. 145.

19. Ivan Turgenev, *Dvorianskoe gnezdo,* edited with notes by Patrick Waddington, p. 216-17.

20. *Works,* VII, p. 467.

21. *Works,* VIII, p. 172.

22. *Works,* VIII, p. 182.

23. Eva Kagan-Kans has observed in passing the similarity between Goethe's Gretchen and some of Turgenev's heroines, see *Hamlet and Don Quixote: Turgenev's Ambivalent Vision,* pp. 42-43; see also A. Bem, "Faust bei Turgenev," *Germanoslavica,* II (1932-33), pp. 359-68; see also Elias Rosenkrantz "Turgenev und Goethe," *Germanoslavica,* II (1932-33), pp. 76-90; see also Katharina Schütz, *Das Goethebild Turgeniews* (Bern, 1952).

24. *Works,* VIII, pp. 221-22.

25. *Works,* VIII, p. 224.

26. *Works,* IX, pp. 208-209, 250-51, 275.

27. *Works,* IX, pp. 180-81.

28. *Works,* IX, pp. 326, 327.

29. *Works,* IX, p. 180.

30. *Works,* IX, p. 216.

31. *Works,* IX, pp. 216, 242, 255.

32. *Works,* IX, pp. 246, 252.

33. *Works,* IX, p. 304.

34. *Letters,* IX, p. 195. Turgenev's italics.

35. *Works,* XI, p. 96.

36. *Works,* XI, p. 97.

37. *Works,* XI, pp. 42, 43, 45, 57.

38. *Works,* XI, p. 86.

39. *Works,* XI, p. 149.

40. *Works,* XI, p. 125.

41. *Works,* XI, p. 156.

42. *Works,* XI, p. 111.

43. *Works,* XI, pp. 109, 115.

44. *Works,* XI, pp. 126, 136.

45. *Works,* XI, p. 148. The Russian idiomatic expression "*po ee litsu zmeilas' ulybka*" (a smile stole across her face) is predicated on the Russian verb *zmeit'sia,* derived from *zmei/zmeia* (snake).

46. *Works,* XI, p. 143.

47. *Works,* XI, p. 146.

48. *Works,* XI, p. 144.

49. In Russian the term *amazonka* has several meanings; it can signify a legendary female warrior, a strong woman, a horsewoman or a woman's riding-habit. In this context the word may be read to mean both an Amazon and a horsewoman.

50. *Works,* XI, p. 144.

51. *Works,* XI, p. 147.

52. Virginia M. Allen, *The Femme Fatale: Erotic Icon,* p. 254.

53. Patrick Waddington, *Turgenev and England* (London, 1980), p. 186.

54. *Letters,* IX, p. 125; see also *Letters,* X, pp. 8, 128.

55. Virginia M. Allen, *The Femme Fatale: Erotic Icon,* p. 206.

56. Patrick Waddington, *Turgenev and England,* p. 56.

57. Patrick Waddington, *Turgenev and England,* pp. 193-95.

58. Virginia Surtees, *The Paintings and Drawings of Dante Gabriel Rossetti (1828-1882): A Catalogue Raisonné,* I (Oxford, 1971), pp. 239-40.

59. Virginia Surtees, *The Paintings and Drawings of Dante Gabriel Rossetti (1828-1882): A Catalogue Raisonné,* II (Oxford, 1971), plate 93 (Cat. no. 76B).

60. Virginia Surtees, *The Paintings and Drawings of Dante Gabriel Rossetti (1828-1882): A Catalogue Raisonné,* I (Oxford, 1971), p. 116.

61. Virginia Surtees, *The Paintings and Drawings of Dante Gabriel Rossetti (1828-1882): A Catalogue Raisonné,* I (Oxford, 1971), p. 118.

62. *The Collected Works of Dante Gabriel Rossetti,* I (London, 1886), p. 216.

63. *The Collected Works of Dante Gabriel Rossetti,* I (London, 1886), p. 216; see also Virginia Surtees, *The Paintings and Drawings of Dante Gabriel Rossetti (1828-1882): A Catalogue Raisonné,* I (Oxford, 1971), p. 116.

64. *The Collected Works of Dante Gabriel Rossetti,* I (London, 1886), p. 216; see also Virginia Surtees, *The Paintings and Drawings of Dante Gabriel Rossetti (1828-1882): A Catalogue Raisonné,* II (Oxford, 1971), plate 293 (Cat. no. 205).

65. Patrick Waddington, *Turgenev and England,* p. 145.

66. *Works,* XI, p. 336.

67. *Works,* XI, p. 456-57.

Robert Lagerberg (essay date 1996)

SOURCE: Lagerberg, Robert. "The Open Frame and the Presentation of Time in Turgenev's *First Love*." *Australian Slavonic and East European Studies* 10, no. 2 (1996): 111-20.

[*In the following essay, Lagerberg discusses the structure of* First Love, *which contains an opening, but not a closing, frame story.*]

In terms of structure Turgenev's story *First Love* is unusual, if not unique, in Russian literature, since the frame used to open the story is not repeated at its end, as would normally be expected. A brief summary of the story's structure will make this clearer. *First Love* is told from the viewpoint of a middle-aged bachelor, Vladimir Petrovich, who sits after dinner late at night with his host and another acquaintance, Sergei Nikolayevich. The host asks each of his guests to tell the story of his first love. Sergei Nikolayevich confesses that he has little of interest to tell, his first (and last) love being his nanny when he was six years old. The host himself also has no story he considers worth telling, his first love being the wife to whom he was married by arrangement and with whom he fell in love subsequently. Finally Vladimir Petrovich, who admits to being a poor story-teller, agrees to write down the unusual story of his first love and read it one evening for the entertainment of the two men. This then represents the opening frame and the remainder of the story is provided by what is written in his notebook.

The majority of Vladimir Petrovich's story is in fact largely static in terms of plot development as it tells of his passive love at the age of sixteen for a certain Zinaida, who is the daughter of an impoverished princess and some five years older than himself. Volodya falls in love with her almost instantaneously: the central part of the story is about his blissful suffering in love without any significant change in his feelings for Zinaida. Gradually he begins to realise that Zinaida does not love him, or indeed any of the five other men who make up her entourage and who also have aspirations of winning her love, but another. Who it is, though, Volodya does not know. The first of the two concluding dramatic moments in the story occurs when Volodya, now imagining himself to be the vengeful jealous lover, or Othello as he ironically calls himself, waits up at night to catch and kill his rival as he goes to his tryst with Zinaida, but he is stunned and humiliated when he sees that his intended victim is none other than his own father. He drops his knife and runs home still not able to fully comprehend what all the evidence suggests. The second climax occurs when, some months later, Volodya rides out of town with his father, who leaves him waiting while he meets Zinaida. Volodya follows his father and is surprised to see him talking with Zinaida, but frustrated by her words, Pyotr Vasilyevich strikes her hand with his riding crop. Volodya watches aghast as Zinaida kisses her scarlet wound in silent submission. Soon after this incident Vladimir's father dies of a stroke in St Petersburg, and his mother sends a sum of money to Moscow, the implication being that it is payment for Zinaida's confinement with Petr Vasilyevich's child, or perhaps to keep this scandal a secret.

The story ends some four years later. Vladimir learns that Zinaida is now married and in St Petersburg, but he turns down the opportunity of visiting her, and when he eventually calls on her, learns that she has recently died while giving birth. The final passage contains the pessimistic thoughts of Vladimir concerning youth, love and death. In the final paragraph, Vladimir, who has been berating himself for not feeling sufficient emotion immediately upon hearing of the death of Zinaida, recalls that in fact some days after Zinaida's death he stood by the bed of a poor old woman, who dies in abject poverty and terrible suffering, and finally felt the full tragic force of death. The final words of the story are:

> И помню я, что тут, у одра этой бедной старушки, мне стало страшно за Зинаиду, и захотелось мне помолиться за нее, за отца—и за себя.[1]

The framing technique used at the beginning of the story is not repeated and thus there is no return to the three men in the dining-room.

That the story *First Love* is largely autobiographical has never been in doubt. Turgenev himself regarded it with special affection throughout his life:

> Это единственная вещь, которая мне самому до сих дор доставляет удовольствие, потому что это сама жизнь, это не сочинено . . . «Первая любовь»—это переято.[2]

However, there was surprisingly little that was known about the events which occurred during the summer of 1833 until the painstaking detective work of N. Chernov shed some light on this subject.[3] It now seems clear that the real name of Zinaida can be ascertained as Yekaterina Lvovna Shakhovskaya, a poetess of some talent but little fame, who was born on 10 September 1814 and who died in St Petersburg on 28 June 1836, some nine months after the death of Turgenev's own father, all of which, of course, corresponds to the circumstances recounted in *First Love.* Yekaterina's age during the summer of 1833 would have been eighteen, and Turgenev's fourteen. Turgenev increased the ages of Zinaida and Vladimir Petrovich to twenty-one and sixteen respectively. This slight alteration of the facts seems to have been occasioned by the need to make the complex feelings of his young hero more credible, which in turn necessitated the increase in Zinaida's years so as to maintain the significant gap in years between the young 'page' and the more mature princess. It is curious to note that Turgenev's own grave in the Volkov Cemetery in St Petersburg lies not far from Belinksy, the first influential person to acknowledge his talent as a prose writer, and that of his first love, Yekaterina Lvovna Shakhovskaya.

What then are we to make of the final pages of *First Love* and its absent frame? Why did Turgenev decide not to end his story with a return to the persons who began it? In adducing reasons for the ending which has remained in the standard version of *First Love* (there is another version, mention of which will be made shortly) moralistic considerations are often mentioned. In particular mention is made of a letter which Turgenev wrote to Fet dated 1 June 1860, in which he says this about the episode of the dying woman:

> Приделал же я старушку на конце—во-первых потому, что это действительно так было—а во-вторых потому, что без этого отрезвляющего конца крики на безнравственность были бы еще сильнее.[4]

There has, on account of this quotation, been a tendency to downgrade the story's existing ending, but this one statement is insufficient to dismiss the artistic qualities of the concluding passage, particularly when one is dealing with a writer like Turgenev, whose capacity for inconsistent and even contradictory statements regarding his own work is well documented. Attention has also been paid to the inclusion in the French edition of *First Love* published in 1863 (three years after the first publication in 1860) of a concluding frame (the so-called *рибавленный хвост для Французского издания в «Первой любви»*).[5] As mentioned earlier, in the final (Russian) version of *First Love* the story begins with a gathering of three men, one of whom, Vladimir Petrovich, agrees to write down the story of his own first love and read it to the two other men some days later, but at the conclusion of his narrative the story itself ends and we never hear their comments. In the conclusion to the French edition of 1863 each of the characters present at Vladimir Petrovich's reading expresses his less than enthusiastic opinion with regard to the events of the story, the dialogue ending as follows:

> 'We do not mean by this that you are perverse—on the contrary. We mean that the social conditions in whose midst we have all grown up have formed in our country in a way that is unique and which had never existed previously and probably never will exist again. Your simple and uncontrived story has inspired in us a kind of dread. Not that it shocked us as immoral: it conceals something darker and more profound than mere immorality. Personally, you are clear of any reproach, not having done anything wrong. But in each line of your story, there comes through some general fault common to a whole nation that I would venture to call a national crime.'

> 'Oh, what a big word for so small a matter!' commented Vladimir.

> 'The case is small, but the matter is certainly not. There is, I repeat, and you feel it yourself, there is as a certain soldier says in *Hamlet*: "Something (is) rotten in the state of Denmark."'

> 'Let us hope in any case that our children will have something else to relate from their youth and that they will tell it in a different way.'[6]

So ends the closing frame of the French edition and it is not hard to see why Turgenev found this rather forced dialogue unsatisfactory. As E. I. Kiiko has demonstrated, the addition of this frame was occasioned not so much from a feeling that the story as it stood in its Russian version was in some way deficient artistically, as from pressures which Turgenev felt upon him as a result of criticism of the story's alleged immoral content and lack of any social message. Kiiko concludes:

> Очевидно, заключительные страницы «Первой любви», появившиеся во Французском издании 1863 года (. . .) были написаны в ответ на критические замечания, высказанные по поводу этой повести. Тургеневу важно было отвести оба обвинения критика: упрек в безнравственности и упрек в обшественной индиФФерентности повести.[7]

It appears, therefore, that the author himself felt that in terms of the story as a work of art the incomplete framing technique was better suited than the complete one, and critics of *First Love* have been entirely justified in generally viewing this *рибавленный хвост* as lacking in artistic value.[8] It would be wrong, however, to equate the literary merits of the existing final passage of the story (the episode of the dying woman) with the later unsuccessful concluding frame in the French edition solely on the basis of Turgenev's reference to moralistic considerations in his letter to Fet which was mentioned above.

What then is the role of the opening frame of the story? There are three basic functions of a frame in a work of literature: first, of course, the frame sets the scene and establishes the theme of the inner narrative, as well as presenting a discussion of the events in the main narrative; second, it embeds the inner narrative in certain external circumstances;[9] and third, a frame comments on how it is that a literary work evolves from a given situation, that is to say that it is a form of metanarrative.[10] In *First Love* the opening frame undoubtedly establishes the theme of the story—first love—without which it would be somewhat understated. It also comments on how the story itself comes about, that is to say it is a metanarrative. However, the particular structure of *First Love,* in view of its absent concluding frame, means that the inner narrative is not embedded in the outer one, but rather stands in juxtaposition to it. The relationship between the outer and inner texts then is syntagmatic. What is also important for frames is that they establish two sets of protagonists, the before and after as it were.[11] In the case of *First Love* we have two heroes: Vladimir Petrovich and his younger self, Volodya. For Vladimir Petrovich the act of writing down his story is ostensibly a means to entertain his two friends, but it is also a means by which the older man is able to understand and come to terms with what happened in his childhood.[12] In addition it is a means by which Turgenev manages to distance himself from his own rather risqué subject matter: thus, even though the story is told in the first person, by creating the person of Vladimir Petrovich who narrates the story, the author himself becomes indirectly connected, something important bearing in mind Turgenev's concerns about the moral content of this story.[13] I shall return to this aspect of the frame in connection with the story's conclusion.

As mentioned earlier, the major part of the narrative is largely static in terms of plot development. It is though towards the end of the story that important developments take place and together with this the presentation of time also changes: in the last few chapters of the book there occur several jumps forward in time, each one larger than the previous. The first climax of the story is the mock patricide (the episode when Vladimir waits outside to catch and kill Zinaida's lover but is astounded to see his own father). It is directly after this episode that the passage of time becomes more rapid. After this mock killing Vladimir notes that his former state of anxiety has passed leaving a feeling of death: 'точно что-то во мне умирало'.[14]

For the next week he is in a kind of daze after which his parents have a terrible quarrel, his mother having been informed from one of Zinaida's admirers that her husband is having an affair with Zinaida. Volodya and his parents now move back to central Moscow, another month passes and the story's second climax occurs when Volodya sees his father strike Zinaida across the arm with his whip. Volodya's father, previously a figure whom he much admired and strove to take after, is now diminished in Volodya's eyes. By hurting Zinaida he exposes his own pain and suffering, and thus weakness, this the man who has boasted to his son:

> 'Умей хотеть—и будешь свободным, и командовать будешь.'[15]

These two dramatic moments are vital stages on Volodya's journey from youth to adulthood during which he comes to understand love as something other than pure and pleasurable. He now notes:

> Последний месяц меня очень состарил—и моя любовь со всеми своими волнениями, и страданиями, показалась мне самому чем-то таким маленьким, и детским, и мизерным перед тем другим, неизвестным чем-то, о котором я едва мог догадываться и которое меня пугало, как незнакомое, красивое, но грозное лицо, которое напрасно силишься разглядеть в полумраке.[16]

Volodya enters university two months later, and six months later the family moves to St Petersburg where Volodya's father dies of a stroke a few days after receiving a letter of extortion from Moscow, presumably from Zinaida's mother. The story then moves forward four years in the final chapter. Zinaida is now married and in St Petersburg. Volodya turns down the opportunity of visiting her and finds out a few weeks later that she has died. The story closes with a passage which can be divided into three parts. First, Volodya or rather Vladimir Petrovich, as the voice here is that of the older narrator, bemoans the inability of youth to feel the urgency of life and the tragedy of death. Second, he speaks of the evening shadows falling on his life and the fact that memories of his first love are still his dearest possession. Third, there is the passage in which he witnesses the death of the old woman. These three reflections represent the narrator's understanding of his path in life from naive but happy youth to disillusioned adult knowledge and finally death. The link between the three is provided by love.

The story *First Love* then is concerned with the passage from youth to adulthood, or innocence to knowledge. Indeed the theme of first love is itself inseparable from this evolution. As the narrative comes to an end, Volodya also grasps what he has been straining so hard to see for the last months, and Vladimir Petrovich is able to understand these events in the wider context of his whole life. In effect then what happens is that the two protagonists—Volodya and the adult Vladimir Petrovich—are united by the act of storytelling, or rather story-writing. Sixteen-year-old Volodya is naive; initially he is unaware of love, then he perceives love but does not understand it, and finally he comprehends the suffering that comes from love, and the close connection between love and death, and because he comprehends he can write the story—or is it because he writes the story that he knows?[17] Since the figure at the story's end is united with the figure in the opening frame a concluding frame is not needed: the circle is complete—childhood to adulthood via first love. The rapid chronological progressions at the end of the story both represent Volodya's too hasty departure from adolescence and form stepping stones in time between the events of the narrative and the opening frame: one month later, two months, six months and four years. In this way the lack of a closing frame takes the reader by default back to the opening frame. It is also worth noting that by using a written version of events rather than a spoken one, the motivation to return to a spoken mode of communication (i.e. a closing frame) is reduced.

The main role of the opening frame is therefore to provide the possibility for Vladimir to overcome his traumatic experiences through art. The story is used not so much to retell the past as to interpret it, and the opening frame therefore becomes an integral part of the narrative. One must remember though that Turgenev is the most pessimistic of writers, heavily influenced by the philosophy of Schopenhauer: by telling his story Vladimir Petrovich gains the paradoxical knowledge that love elevates one to great heights of beauty, but simultaneously destroys the will and ultimately leads to death. Thus Pyotr Vasilyevich's entire philosophy of life and physical being are destroyed by his falling in love, the same fate that befalls Turgenev's greatest character, Bazarov, in *Fathers and Sons.*

Another striking aspect of the opening and closing sections of *First Love* is the contrast between the masculine world of the dining-room in the opening frame and the feminine world at the story's end where both Zinaida and the old woman die. In fact elements of the Oedipus myth make *First Love* fertile ground for psychoanalytic interpretation.[18] Zinaida in effect becomes both a surrogate mother for Volodya (through the fact that his father woos her) and the object of his own desire. Volodya, as in the Oedipus legend, kills his father, but a mock version of this takes place in *First Love* with Volodya dropping the knife and running. The symbolic loss of his own mother through his father's affection for Zinaida, the death of Zinaida, his surrogate mother, and the death of his father, his will crushed by his passion, in addition to the final advice Volodya receives from his father in the form of a letter which he began to write on the day of his stroke:

> Сын мой,—писал он мне,—бойся женской любви, бойся этого счастья, этой отравы . . .

culminate in a harrowing quasi-religious experience at the deathbed of an impoverished old woman. In fact we know little about the Vladimir Petrovich who sits with his friends after dinner in the opening frame: he is about forty years old, a bachelor, and a poor story-teller. The picture does suggest however a kind of masculine refuge from the danger of passion, a haven in rather bland amicability, and the notion that Vladimir's first love has produced an archetypal superfluous man is surely not misplaced.[19] One is also reminded of the conclusion to *Fathers and Sons* which offers a not wholly convincing picture of domestic bliss in the Kirsanov household as an alternative to the more dangerous adventures of Bazarov and Anna Odintsova.

Finally, it is possible that Turgenev used the frame in another way. As mentioned earlier, by introducing his story through the medium of Vladimir Petrovich he manages to distance himself from the less than respectable (at least for the times) content of his narrative. Can it be that at the story's end the absence of a closing frame is intended, amongst the other things already mentioned, to reduce this distance? One notes in particular the last word of the story:

> И помню я, что тут, у одра этой бедной старушки, мне стало страшно за Зинаиду, и захотелось мне помолиться за нее, за отца—и за себя.[20]

The use of the reflexive pronoun along with the absence of any express mention of the 'intermediate' Vladimir Petrovich by means of a closing frame weakens the illusion of the opening frame and unites not only Volodya and his adult narrator, but perhaps the real narrator Turgenev also. A mild admission of guilt therefore is achieved without the heavy-handedness of a concluding analysis as in the French edition, while the special balance between inner and outer narrative which Turgenev sought is also accomplished.

Notes

1. Turgenev 1965, p. 76.

2. *Русские ведомости,* 1883, No 270, 2 October.

3. See Chernov 1973.

4. Turgenev 1962, p. 86.

5. The background to this circumstance has been dealt with comprehensively by E. I. Kiiko (1964).

6. Translated from the French by the present author as it appears in Kiiko 1964, p. 67.

7. Kiiko 1964, p. 64.

8. See, for example, Zweers 1984, p. 589.

9. See Isenberg 1993, p. 24. Isenberg's excellent analysis of *First Love* (pp. 22-49) offers numerous new insights into the story to which the present paper adds a particular angle first attempted in a previous article (Lagerberg, 1994).

10. See Grübel 1984, pp. 153-56 and Isenberg 1993, p. 23.

11. Isenberg 1993, pp. 27-28.

12. *Ibid.,* p. 29.

13. *Ibid.,* p. 33.

14. Turgenev, 1965, p. 61.

15. *Ibid.,* p. 31.

16. *Ibid.,* p. 72.

17. See Isenberg 1993, pp. 46-47.

18. Isenberg 1993, gives a detailed outline of this aspect of the story, for instance pp. 34-36.

19. See Oloskey Mills 1971, for such a reading.

20. Turgenev 1965, p. 76.

Words Cited

(Chernov). Чернов, Н. 'Повесть И. С. Тургенева «Первая любовь» и ее реальные источники', *о росы литературы,* 9, 1973, 225-41.

Grübel, Rainer. 'Narrative Aisthesis der "Ersten Liebe": Erinnerung vs. Wiederholung: Zur Topik und Intertextualität der Erzählungen "Pervaja ljubov'" von Turgenev und "Vymysel" von Gippius,' in: *Russische Erzählung—Russian Short Story: Utrechter Symposium zur Theorie und Geschichte der russichen Erzählung im 19. und 20. Jahrhundert,* ed. Rainer Grübel, Amsterdam, 1984, pp. 153-94.

Isenberg, Charles. *Telling Silence: Russian Frame Narratives of Renunciation,* Evanston, Illinois, 1993.

(Kiiko). Кийко, Е.И. 'Окончание повести «Первая любовь»', *Литературное наследство,* 73, 1964, 59-68.

Lagerberg, R. 'Images of Night and Day in Turgenev's *Pervaia liubov'*", *New Zealand Slavonic Journal,* 1994, 57-68.

Mills, Judith Oloskey. 'Theme and Symbol in "First Love"', *Slavic and East European Journal,* 15, 1971, 433-40.

(Turgenev). Тургенев, И.С. *Полное собрание сочинений и чсем в двадцати восьми томах* (Москва-Ленинград, 1960-1968): *Письма,* т. IV, Moscow-Leningrad, 1962.

———. 'Первая любовь', *Полное собрание сочинений исем в двадцати восьми томах* (Москва-Ленинград, 1960-1968), т. IX, Moscow-Leningrad, 1965, pp. 7-76.

All references to the text of *First Love* are to this edition.

Zweers, A. F. 'First Love: Ivan Turgenev's description of dawning loves', in: *Signs of Friendship: To Honour A. G. F. van Holk, Slavist, Linguist, Semiotician,* ed. J. J. van Baak, Amsterdam, 1984.

Sander Brouwer (essay date 1996)

SOURCE: Brouwer, Sander. "Literary Character in Turgenev's Prose." In *Character in the Short Prose of Ivan Sergeevič Turgenev,* pp. 31-73. Amsterdam: Rodopi, 1996.

[*In the following excerpt, Brouwer studies elements of Romanticism and Realism in Turgenev's short stories, suggesting that the author creates a tension between the two styles in his short prose.*]

2.1 SOME PROBLEMS OF TURGENEV'S PROSE

As P. Brang noted (Brang: 50), Turgenev's prose, especially the short stories, reveals a tension between the Realist and the Romantic style. Turgenev himself first indicated this tension in his 1870 draft for the novel *Virgin Soil,* whose main character is called a 'romantic of Realism', a term which would be applicable to a greater or lesser degree to the protagonists in all of his novels. S. I. Rodzevič (1918) adopted the term and regarded it as a key to Turgenev's oeuvre as a whole, but especially to the short stories. Various other critics see Turgenev's poetics as related to German 'poetic Realism' (Peterson). Still others regard him as a straightforward Romantic author (Granjard; Pahomov). In my view, this latter approach does not do justice to important aspects of Turgenev's poetics, for it is precisely the *tension* between the two principles that I see as important. Thus I find the attempt to divide his works into a Romantic, a Realist and a pre-Symbolist period (Koschmal) equally artificial and deductivist, despite the fact that Romantic qualities may be dominant in the earlier works (mainly in the poems and in the drama) and certain tendencies toward Symbolism may be discerned in the later stories (especially the 'supernatural' ones).

Another rather rigid dividing-line which critics often draw when speaking of Turgenev's oeuvre is one between different groups of his works, i.e. between the novels and the stories, especially the 'supernatural tales'. This tradition came into existence as soon as the supernatural tales were published. Radical critics, from Herzen and Ogarev to Saltykov-Ščedrin, praised the novels and almost unanimously rejected the supernatural tales, which were found to "mark the author's break with the social problem, his turn towards mysticism, to 'pure poetry'" (Zel'dcheji-Deak 1973: 351; this article gives a short survey of the critical reception of the supernatural tales). The influence of this position can still be felt in Pumpjanskij's treatment of the supernatural tales in the twenties, and in Šatalov's in the sixties. The representatives of another line of criticism, the so-called 'aesthetic line', were, on the contrary, favourably disposed towards these stories: for Družinin, Botkin and Annenkov, for example, the story **"Faust"** meant a victory of the 'Puškinian' over the 'Gogolian' principle (idem: 352). Both positions coincide, however, in the sharp distinction they draw between the supernatural tales and the novels, in which the social problem is seen to be central. The same line is later expressed by Merežkovskij, who found that

> the development of political themes, the burning current issues, the apprehension of the various trends of the day in Turgenev's great novels (. . .) begin to wear out (. . .) and another Turgenev, not fashionable, and therefore not wearing out, begins to appear before us (. . .) who continues Puškin's tradition, the author of such works as **"Living Relics," "Bežin Meadow," "Enough," "Ghosts," "The Dog,"** and especially **"The Song of Triumphant Love."**
>
> (quoted from: ibidem)

From the beginning of the century, this concept influenced scholarly critics such as Geršenzon, Rodzevič, and V. M. Fišer (1920, cf. especially p.8) and through them later critics like Ledkovsky, who posits a sharp contrast between the stories and the so-called Realist works:

> It is rather significant that Turgenev's 'realistic' works, in which he exposed the latest political and social trends of the contemporary Russian scene, have tended to become outdated at different periods since their publication (. . .) The true measure of Turgenev's achievement rests in his concern with the eternal themes of individual existence in an impersonal universe, on which he concentrates exclusively in his novellas and 'mysterious tales'.
>
> (Ledkovsky: 137-8)

Although Ledkovsky remarks that these eternal themes "can be detected in all his works" (idem: 138), her assertion is scarcely backed up; apart from in the supernatural tales, it seems that such themes are for her no more than foreign bodies.

I would prefer to treat Turgenev's prose works as having a common poetics, though different accents may be placed depending on period and genre. Jumping a little ahead, I would agree with Lotman (1986: 20) that the plots of Turgenev's prose works are laid on three levels: the contemporary and everyday, the archetypal and the cosmic. Each of these levels is present in every work, but their correlation to one another may differ. To this we shall return presently.

The sharp distinction between Turgenev's novels and his stories on thematic grounds is counterbalanced by the difficulties many scholars have in distinguishing between them on structural grounds. And this is no coincidence. It is worth pausing to reflect at greater length on the principal difference between short and long prose form when touching on this problem in connection with Turgenev.

As is argued by Hansen-Löve (1984) and Schmid (1991: 26-35), an important structural quality of modern short prose lies in the fact that the motivation for crucial deeds performed by characters and for aspects of their psychological make-up is not made explicit to a greater or lesser degree. Lacunae at the motivational level (such as chronological or linear-causal gaps; and psychological, sociological, biological or cultural motivation for the behaviour as displayed by the deeds and utterances of the characters) are compensated by more articulated segmentation at the level of narration ('sjužet'), where the more or less conspicuous accumulation of parallellisms, repetitions, leitmotivical variation of isomorphous segments enhances the role of equivalences. Additional meaning (additional, that is, to the meaning generated at the level of interpretation of the events—let us remember that the choice of the events and the concretization of qualities of agents and setting already

generates meaning) is thus generated by operations that involve that 'paradigmatical' axis of meaning generation in language, the metaphoric mechanism (cf. Jakobson 1960/1971).

The laconism of the short form is thus seen as functionally connected with an expected thematical complexity, which is only partly made explicit: extremely few details are given relating to a very broad range of thematical material that could be expected to generate an almost infinite wealth of detail.

The relative shortness of Turgenev's *novels* thus appears in a new light: their poetics reveals important characteristics of the poetics of the short prose form. Not only are the novels relatively short, which leads some critics to regard them as long stories, or novellas (повести), rather than as novels[1]—while conversely, some stories, like **Spring Torrents,** are sometimes treated as novels—but there is also a strong tendency to 'orchestrate' (a term of Pumpjanskij's; see below) the actions and the psychology of the characters by means of metaphor: by highlighting details of the natural setting in such a way as to suggest not biological/causal relations, but metaphorical equivalences.

The strongly schematic construction of the *events* in all the six novels, which appear to be almost six variations of a common fable (Gippius; Peterson: 74; Brang: 120-122) points to a conception of these events as being enacted according to some underlying pattern, and as being determined by a certain set of regularities—however little they are made explicit—rather than by the arbitrary chaos of empirical reality. In other words, the characters' deeds are apparently motivated not only by their specific individual psychological make-up, but also by a pre-determined conception of human fate and human existence.

It is therefore not coincidental that in the last two decennia there has been a greater critical interest in the 'aesthetic' qualities of Turgenev's novels, that is, in the aspects that have more to do with an active, metaphorical shaping of the characters' fate than with their 'historical value' as recordings of 'slices of life', or chronicles, as it were, of the Russian liberal aristocracy and radical intelligentsia. The interest has been most noticeable in the West. In Russia, the same approach has been less outspoken, undoubtedly for ideological reasons. (One of its representatives is V. M. Markovič, cf. Markovič 1975 and 1982; Erofeev 1982). The modern interest in the West has emerged partly as a reaction to a previous tendency to regard the socio-political aspect as the most relevant and to neglect Turgenev as a writer of lyrical prose, a "poet of nature and love" (Børtnes: 31-32). Nowadays, it is the mechanism of creating sets of interconnected images that generate additional meaning on a metaphorical plane, which attracts most interest[2]. This is precisely the mechanism that I find to be of central importance in the image of the characters in the short prose, and it is this that I will concentrate on in my analyses of Turgenev's stories. Above, we have adopted Jakobson's general model of meaning-generation in which the metaphorical and metonymical principle are seen as reciprocally related and mutually dependent in any artistic text. Hansen-Löve (1984) argues that mechanisms of equivalence, which generate metaphorical meanings, tend to be more prominent in short stories, but we see them at work in Turgenev's novels as well—a feature which is undoubtedly connected with their relative shortness.

A similar phenomenon has been observed in Turgenev's drama. Here the unity of action dissolves as a consequence of the interweaving of secondary chains of action and more or less independent episodes. The accent is more on character depiction, while separate scenes tend to mask the unity of the main action. As Klein states, this process may largely be due to the influence of the poetics of the Natural School in Russian literature of the thirties and forties, with its predilection for (pseudo-) objective rendering of 'slices of life'. Towards the end of the forties, however, the novelty of this device had already begun to wear off. According to Klein, Turgenev searched for a way to replace the lost unity of his drama with a unity of a different kind. This he found by "creating an overall field of reference, which accommodates numerous motifs and stylistic elements and joins them into a semantic whole" ([es gelingt] Turgenev, seinem Stück ein übergreifendes Bezugsfeld zu schaffen, das zahlreichen Elementen motivischer und stilistischer Art Raum bietet und zu einem Bedeutungsganzen zusammenfügt) (. . .) "the unity of the drama that he thus regains is the unity of an occasional field of associations" (Die wiedergewonnene Einheit des Stücks ist die Einheit eines okkasionell geschaffenen Assoziationsfeldes; Klein 14).

All this leads to the conclusion that the poetics of Turgenev's prose—both novels and stories—may in many respects be regarded as a single whole, and that these poetics are in important measure determined by the prominent role played by mechanisms of 'verbal art' interfusing with those of 'narrative art'.

It has been observed that Turgenev's short stories differ typologically from the earlier "Ereignis-novellen" (Brang: 50): they give prominence to the psychological penetration into character rather than to the description of events—a fact which for some would be a proof of their Realist strain (for instance, Mersereau 1973). It is undoubtedly true that the clash of events in Romantic prose is based upon the dramatic opposition between characters, which are conceived largely in one dimension only. They tend to be schematic ('flat', in E. M. Forster's terminology), so as to facilitate a sharp

'peripeteia' (which was very early recognized as something typically 'Romantic' by Puškin in his letter to Bestužev of May-June, 1825[3]). Compared to this one-dimensionality, the characters in Realist prose, including those in Turgenev's stories, certainly appear as psychologically more convincing. They are 'deeper', more 'rounded', and there is a keener eye for inner conflict and contradiction. Still, it is obviously an illusion to think that they are 'modelled after reality' more than their Romantic counterparts, that they are any less the result of artistic and ideological operations and choices, or that they depend less on a creative consciousness. Paradoxically, the illusion of Realism in Turgenev's short stories (due to the characters being psychologically convincing) is accompanied by a weakening of both the internal logical-causal coherence of the event-structure and the explicit explanation for psychological processes. On the other hand, it is compensated by the strengthening of the level of (authorial) associations and allusions.

However, the weakening of the logical-causal coherence of the events in Turgenev's stories should not be merely interpreted as a sign of their Realism—in which 'character dominates over event instead of event over character', according to an often-heard definition of Realism as contrasted to Romanticism. Authoritative Russian critics who advanced Realism in literature indeed called for a probing into the human psyche, a making explicit of all its mechanisms, especially the more hidden ones. Belinskij expected from an author that he "illuminate with the torch of his fantasy all the bends of his heroes' hearts" . . . and Černyševskij wrote in his doctoral thesis that "one of the qualities of a poetic genius is his ability to understand the essence of a real person's character, to look at him with a penetrating eye" . . . quoted from Šatalov 1980: 56). However, in Turgenev's prose such penetration is missing—something which is quite fundamentally connected with his poetics as a whole. As Jane Costlow (1990: 30-54) has argued, there is a basic mistrust underlying all Turgenev's narration relating to the ability of language to render life as it really is. Such narration prefers not to explicate the depths of a character's psyche, but to present it as an enigma.

2.2 STATE OR UNDERSTATE?

In order to illustrate this, let us first turn to Turgenev's review of S. T. Aksakov's *Notes of a Rifle Hunter*. This review is of fundamental importance for an understanding of Turgenev's conception of nature and the principles of its description (Kagan-Kans calls it his "credo"; Kagan-Kans 1975: 84). I hope to show, however, that the method discussed is characteristic not only of Turgenev's descriptions of Nature, but also of his rendering of human character. If this is true, then it suggests that in the first place this method is connected with his general worldview and his poetics as a whole, and that secondly, in that worldview, human existence indeed obeys much the same laws as unconscious Nature.

For Ėjchenbaum (1919), the way Turgenev depicts nature reminds one of Tjutčev and Fet, whose manner Turgenev himself described as follows: . . .

> [There exist subtly developed, nervous, excitable-poetic personalities, who have some kind of special view of nature, a special flair for its beauties; they observe many of its nuances, many often hardly noticeable details, and they succeed in expressing them with utmost felicity, acuity and grace; it is true that the general lines of the picture either escape them, or they have not enough strength to grasp and to retain them. One could say that what is most accessible to them is the scent of beauty, and their words are fragrant. Details are predominant with them, at the expense of the general impression.]
>
> (IV: 519[4])

I think that Ėjchenbaum here gives only half of the picture. In his own descriptions of nature Turgenev is far clearer and simpler than the above-mentioned poets. A few lines later Turgenev accuses such poets of trying to "eavesdrop" and to "peep into" nature (. . . idem: 520). In fact, this manner of depicting nature is for him one of the two extremes between which a good artist should steer a middle course. Exponents of the other extreme are the Romantic nature poetry of Victor Hugo and the Russian Romantic poet Benediktov. Let us look at this opposition in some more detail.

In the first place, Turgenev states that man's interest in nature is more than just an arbitrary one. Man cannot but love nature; love for nature is something that is given in the 'human condition': "Man cannot but be interested in nature, he is bound with her by a thousand threads: he is her son" (. . . IV: 516). But then he goes on to condemn a false kind of love for nature, a love that is based on a transplantation of the field of culture to the field of nature. Hugo and Benediktov are taken as paradigmatic for the kind of description that goes with this kind of love: . . .

> [In this love for nature one often detects much egoism. To be specific: we love nature in relation to ourselves: we regard it as our own pedestal. By the way, this is why, in so-called nature descriptions, comparisons with human emotions incessantly creep in ('and the whole inviolable cliff roars with laughter', etc.), or else the simple and clear communication of impressions of sight is substituted for by treatises on the occasion. [And he adds in a note:] The main representative of this kind of poetry is V. Hugo (cf. his 'Orientales'). The number of imitators and worshippers of this false manner is hard to enumerate, and yet not one of its images will last: everywhere one sees the author instead of nature; but only when nature firmly supports him can man develop strength.] (the quotation is from Benediktov's poem *Ymec* [The cliff]—SB)
>
> (ibidem)

As we see, Turgenev reproaches writers like Hugo and Benediktov for not rendering nature, but merely expressing their own thoughts and emotions. They regard nature from a distance, interpret it, as if its meaning were clear to them. On the other hand, he reproaches the Tjutčevs and Fets for having a fine ear for the subtleties of individual details, but not being able to capture or render the broad sweep of the picture. For Turgenev, nature should be described in such a way that it keeps a *balance* between entering into detail and rendering the general picture. Such a description would be consonant with the sense and meaning of nature itself: . . .

> [No doubt, it [nature—SB] constitutes one great, harmonious whole—every point in it is connected with all the others—but at the same time it shows a tendency to make every point, every single entity want to exist exclusively for itself, regard itself as the centre of the universe, turn everything it is surrounded by into something that can be used, the independence of which is denied, that can be seized as property. For the mosquito that sucks your blood you are just nourishment, and it uses you just as quietly and guilelessly as the spider, whose web he has been caught in, would use it in its turn; just as the root, digging in the dark, uses the moisture of the earth. Direct your attention for a few moments to the fly, that easily flies from your nose to a piece of sugar, to a drop of honey in the heart of a flower, and you will understand what I intend to say, you will understand that it is definitely just as self-contained as you yourselves are.]
>
> (IV: 516-17)

It seems that Turgenev sees the task of the artist as being to surmount this natural self-sufficient existence. Not by 'stepping aside' from it: that would lead to either a subjective description à la Hugo, which is tantamount to 'seizing something as property', only in a linguistic sense; or it would lead to a soulless rhetorical description à la Buffon (see idem: 518). The artist should surmount this self-contained existence by looking at nature "with full sympathy" (. . . idem: 517). He has to "separate from himself and reflect upon the phenomena of nature" (. . . idem: 518). Only then does nature "disclose itself and allow one to 'take a peep' at it" (. . . idem: 517).

This programmatical passage bears a remarkable resemblance to some passages in Turgenev's review of Ostrovskij's *Poor Bride,* written some eight months before his review of Aksakov's book (IV: 663 and 671), in which he reproaches Ostrovskij for having rendered his characters in far too much detail: "such an elaboration of the petty details of a character is untruthful—artistically untruthful" (. . . idem: 494). Not coincidentally, he compares this method with that of "a landscape-painter, who would undertake to work out the smallest fibres of the leaves, the smallest grains of sand in the foreground of his paintings" (. . . ibidem). Turgenev reproaches Ostrovskij for "having cut up his characters into small pieces to such an extent, that as a result the separate detail escapes the reader" (. . . idem: 495). Finally, Turgenev states his own position with unequivocal clarity: . . .

> [Mr. Ostrovskij, in our opinion, steals, as it were, into the mind of each personality he creates; but we allow ourselves to remark that an author should accomplish that undoubtedly useful operation as a preliminary step. He should already have full command over his personalities before he shows them to us. 'But that's psychology!' some will say; perhaps so, but the psychologist has to disappear into the artist, like a skeleton is hidden from the eyes in a living, warm body, which it serves as a firm, but invisible support.]
>
> (ibidem)

For Turgenev, explicit psychology should give way to psychology implicitly suggested by the artistic texture. Perhaps Costlow overstates the case slightly when she writes that "the attempt to constitute wholeness and purity of speech" is the "ideal which governs his antipathy to the verbal psychologizing of Tolstoy and Dostoevsky" (Costlow: 33)—not least because Tolstoj's manner of "verbal psychologizing" should not be too easily bracketed with Dostoevskij's. However, if she means that the image of a character in Turgenev's prose is the result of explicit statements about the character's thoughts and feelings (and inexplicit 'showing' of these thoughts and feelings through his behaviour) as well as of more understated, allusive forms of speech, then her point is quite valid.

Below I will argue not only that Turgenev's general method of presenting character in his prose follows the same pattern as his treatment of nature, but also that the dominant feature of the natural and human entities on which he focuses his attention is for him of the same kind. In broad terms, this feature represents, as we have seen, the collision between the centripetal force of the individual entity, asserting its rights as an individual[5], and the centrifugal force of the environment in the widest sense—for a human being this would include both the socio-cultural environment and unconscious nature. First, however, I should like to make a few general remarks on Turgenev's technique of perspectivation.

2.3 NARRATOR AND CHARACTER

The specifics of the mutual relation between the perspectives of narrator, character and implied reader (narratee) in Turgenev's first four novels have been treated by V. M. Markovič (1975). Markovič discusses only Turgenev's novels, and then only the first four, because he finds the poetics of the last two, *Smoke* and *Virgin Soil,* to differ somewhat from these four. But I believe that his results are of great value for our insight in the poetics of the short prose as well. Firstly, this is because Markovič's method is typological: he treats the

specifics of the interplay of character- and narrator-perspective in Turgenev's work as contrasting with those of Dostoevskij and Tolstoj. Secondly, I think that the structural qualities of the novels that Markovič has uncovered can be modified so as to be applicable to the short stories. So I will first outline Markovič's observations on the novels before proceeding to modify them for the short prose.

The central 'poetic law' that Markovič formulates for the construction of the interrelation of perspectives in Turgenev's novels is that "the narrator finds himself on one level . . . with the reader (I take it that Markovič must mean the 'implied' reader here; SB) and is principally at a distance from the characters" (Markovič 1975: 9). The perspective of the narrator shows different degrees of penetration into the inner world of the characters. Markovič distinguishes three main types. When narrating concrete behaviour of one or more characters over relatively short periods presented in relatively great detail, the narrator hardly ever comments on the psyche of the characters. He records only what he could have heard and seen, had he been present, and resembles an outside observer. However, in passages in which a shorter or longer period is summarized (from the length of a conversation to that of a few days or even weeks) the narrator is capable of informing the reader about the inner state of the characters, their thoughts, emotions, even those that are hidden from themselves. And in the generalized characterizations . . . there is a maximum degree of penetration; the narrator may oversee a whole life or its central episodes and formulate final conclusions about a character and revealing 'who he or she is'. These oscillations between a position that resembles that of a real life observer on the one hand and that of an all-knowing and all-seeing viewpoint on the other seem to contradict and mutually exclude each other. But, as Markovič convincingly argues, they are really different realizations of one and the same basic position. In all three cases, the narrator takes the position (and the narration follows the logic) of "an 'other' unique person, who is able to understand (. . .) a given unique person, observing the restrictions of real life's . . . possibilities" (Markovič 1975: 23). It should be added, that this personal narrator not only analyses his characters, but also judges them (. . . idem: 24). In the long-term surveys this understanding is voiced in the tone of a person who after the event has had the opportunity to establish what has really happened, who is in a position to judge or at least convincingly draw his conclusions. It is justified by the retrospective viewpoint of the narrator. In the generalizations the narrator speaks in a tone analogous to that of a long-standing acquaintance who has had the opportunity to observe the character during that part of his life which preceded the events narrated, or at least long enough to form a judgment as to his long-term character traits and his deeper motives. Nowhere, however, does the narrator exceed the limits life sets to a 'real life' observer, whose evaluation is necessarily subjective. On the other hand, as has been said, his subjectivity is not made concrete; no data are given which would allow us to envisage the narrator as a particular individual; we cannot put our finger on any concrete psychological or ideological limitations of his perspective.

In Turgenev's stories with a third-person narrator too, the distance of the narrator from the narrated characters, the fact that he finds himself, as it were, in another dimension, . . . is his main specific quality. Though the narrator may present the characters and their actions in a subjective individual (for instance elegiac or ironical) tone, this tone nowhere allows us to imagine him as a concrete individual; his perspective nowhere betrays a psychologically concrete countenance. His knowledge of the events and situations of the related world is nowhere motivated by a personal acquaintance with (one or more of) the characters. Where the narrator gives personal comments or judgments, these always have a rather self-evident validity; even if they are emotionally coloured, they seem to express 'what anybody would think of it'. Characteristic of Turgenev's method is that even in the (many) cases when an I-narrator is used, the language of this narrator is not stylized as the language of someone with some outspoken individually or socially characteristic viewpoint (Bachtin 1975.2: 221-2). In the few instances where there is such 'skaz', eg. in **"The Dog"** (see below), its function is not to characterize the narrator as having a limited viewpoint, but rather to give an extra convincing tone to the supernatural story: "Turgenev needed a narrator for the oral narrative form, but that form served the purpose of directly expressing his thoughts" (Bachtin 1975: 223).

Thus we see that the more the narrator is removed from the world of the characters, the greater is his penetration into the meaning of events; and, conversely, the closer he is, the less he seems able to grasp that meaning. This confirms the principle mentioned above that the perspectives of the characters in their world necessarily fall short of yielding an adequate insight into their situation in life and of seeing it in some meaningful context. In Turgenev's universe, the more one's perspective is limited to the world of everyday events, of history, or to the clash of personal interests, the more one fails to grasp the tragic truth of one's situation: to understand that tragedy, one needs detachment, distance. In the case of an I-narration, it is striking how often a retrospective position, removed as far as possible from the events related, is chosen[6]. This is the case in many of Turgenev's key stories, starting with **"A Hamlet of the Ščigry District,"** in which the Hamlet has already parted from society life, through *First Love* (for the importance of the retrospective position, see Grübel 1984) to **"Punin and Baburin"** (where the narrator presents himself in the story's opening lines as

an old and disillusioned man[7]). But we find it most clearly stated in **"Diary of a Superfluous Man,"** which is narrated from the standpoint of death: Culkaturin makes it clear from the beginning that he already has one foot in the grave, and the reader is constantly reminded of this fact thanks to the diary form, in which almost each entry opens with a reminder of approaching death. Many other stories tell of events from childhood (from the perspective of old age), or at least from a long time past (20 years seems to be a favourite span: we find it in several stories).

In Turgenev's novels there is a balance between a plain 'showing' of unique, concrete, individual characters with no narratorial comment, and emotionally lyrical or detached philosophical comment, in which the characters and their fate are placed in the context of universal laws of natural and human existence. Turgenev's predilection for this type of narration is no coincidence. It is best designed to bring to the fore those aspects of human character that are of central importance in his worldview: the discrepancies between individual ambition, self-realization, and the debt one has to pay to human society and Nature as a whole. Indeed, the task that the narrator seems to have set himself is to understand the "mutual dependence of antithetical qualities" (. . . Markovič 1975: 30) in the characters. Turgenev's main characters show a tension between certain qualities that in most cases can be broadly categorized as strength of reflection versus the will to act, or practical sense versus inspired enthusiasm: if one of the two qualities is more developed, this is achieved at the cost of diminishing the other. In the world of the characters themselves, the antithetical qualities are felt as tragic inner discord (for instance, as a paralyzing awareness of the uselessness of all human strivings in the face of all-pervading death) or else acted out as a conflict between self-realization and social existence[8]. As a rule, this results in the failure of the strivings of the individual, a failure which deprives the character's actions of meaning, for he fails not so much to achieve personal happiness, material well-being or social standing, but to shape his life as historically useful or as ideologically meaningful. It is only in the comment of the narrator (at least in a conscious form) that this tension is given shape as a general law. That is, it is something the given character shares with other historical, literary or mythological characters, for example. Alternatively, it may be evident on a 'metaphysical' plane: the character is seen as falling under the common law of nature (which is an objective law for the narrator, although not necessarily for the reader: for him, it is part of the author's individual worldview, the result of interpretative operations). Thus there is a gap between that which is unique, concrete and seemingly coincidental, and the general laws which it obeys. Nonetheless, because of the narrator's personal, 'individual' tone, his comments and his references to the general laws of human nature never form a straightforward explanation of the personage's character. Furthermore, when the narrator puts the unique and concrete fate of the character in the context of historical or cosmic order, this does not result in it acquiring any more intrinsic meaning than it already has from the point of view of the character himself.

2.4 INDIVIDUAL EXISTENCE AND THE PROBLEM OF MEANING

In his introduction to Turgenev's novel **On the Eve,** L. V. Pumpjanskij defined Turgenev's novels as "novels of character", aimed at giving a "judgment on the social significance of the character" (. . . Pumpjanskij 1929: 9⁹). Central to the novels is the "judgment" not so much of some action of a character, but rather of certain qualities belonging to that character. These are first and foremost his ideological qualities, understood in the widest sense, to which psychological qualities, cultural-historical determination and details of his everyday life . . . are subsidiary. Indeed, Turgenev's central characters struggle to achieve some positive, meaningful, relevant position in life (a struggle, in which they do not as a rule succeed). The most important criterion for the judgment of a character in Turgenev's novels is that of his social productivity as opposed to his unproductivity. Turgenev criticism has come to use the term 'superfluity' for this last category, after the term he himself coined in his **"Diary of a Superfluous Man."** The latter, however, is not a novel, which already indicates that there is good reason not to restrict Pumpjanskij's definition too strictly to the novels alone. Indeed, Pumpjanskij's observations touch on the central thematic categories of Turgenev's narrative prose as a whole. In a more recent period, Ju. Lotman formulated these categories on a more abstract level: "the plots of Turgenev's narratives . . . are founded on the collision of meaningfulness and meaninglessness [of the characters' existence; SB]" (Lotman 1986: 17).

What is implied in Pumpjanskij's and Lotman's definitions is of quite far-reaching importance for the image of character in Turgenev's prose. Character is central in his prose works, but how is the "social significance" and "meaningful existence" of a character to be presented? In order to do this, it is my conviction that Turgenev used metaphorical means of characterization rather than, or at least alongside, metonymical means.

However, in the first place Turgenev's descriptions of his characters are based on metonymic relationships: a character's outward appearance is mostly indicative of his psychological make-up and his social status—see, for instance, the initial description of the boys in **"Bežin Meadow"**[10]—and so are his dress, his manners, the cigars he smokes, his home, his carriage, and so forth. Metonymical relations exist as a rule between a character's psychology and ideological position on the one hand, and his social and historical background, including the education he has received on the other. The same can be said of a character's words and actions, that are usually logical results of characterological (emotional, instinctive, volitional), intellectual and moral dispositions and/or conscious choices. However, the relation of character to meaning is of a totally different nature. The question of whether the life of a character has meaning is answered not by the absence or presence of a relation of that character to something contiguous with his existence in the world (e.g. esteem in the eyes of others, personal satisfaction), but it of necessity requires a position outside of that world[11]. Even the disappearance of all relations between the character and his world—his death—does not answer that question, for death may give meaning. In order to establish whether an individual existence has or has not been meaningful, it must be asked whether that existence has been[12] in tune with the laws of the cosmic whole (be they of a teleological or of a static, immanent nature), which laws essentially escape relations of contiguity with that existence. And this is indeed the aspect that is most central to the life of Turgenev's characters.

In Turgenev's narratives such a cosmic order is felt to be present although it is mostly made explicit in reviews and letters and in a few stories like **"Enough,"** or passages in **"A Journey into Poles'e,"** for instance. This order is present 'in the background' and it can only be reconstructed tentatively, requiring a "poetic lecture" of the text (Schmid 1992: 26-27). Such a reconstructed cosmic order can with some reason be called a "personal myth", to borrow a term Jakobson introduced for a group of Puškin's texts that share a common plot-structure (Jakobson 1975). For such a myth belongs to a conception of human life that relates individual existence, self-sufficient and contained in the illusion that actions lead to lasting results, to archetypes and ever-recurring patterns. In other words, every individual life essentially repeats the old tragedy of a hopelessly doomed struggle with all-pervading death. This is the light in which I would interpret Turgenev's frequent comparison of his characters to cultural archetypes (Faust, King Lear, Chor'-Socrates [in the 1847 version in **"The Contemporary"** Chor' and Kalinyč were further compared to Goethe and Schiller—III: 447], Hamlet, Don Quixote, Jeanne d'Arc [in **"Living Relics,"** cf. Droblenkova] and others). Furthermore, many plots are reminiscent of plots and situations from European literature and culture: Lavreckij's life recalls that of the holy martyr he is named after, Theodorus Stratilatus (Markovič 1982: 165-166; Costlow: 61-63), Insarov's that of Tristan (Masing-Delic 1987) and his relationship with Elena brings to mind that of Aeneas with Dido (Costlow: 86, 92). Bazarov recalls Oedipus (Masing-Delic 1985) and his relationship with Odincova reflects that of Actaeon with Diana (Costlow: 105-137; her book offers still other interesting parallels). Below I will show parallels between the figure of Gerasim in **"Mumu"** and the epic hero Vasilij Buslaev as well as between him and St. Christopher. Porfirij in **"The Dog"** will be seen to replay the myth of, again, Actaeon. This side of Turgenev's poetics is still under-investigated, despite it being in the centre of interest in recent times, and shows him to be a forerunner of Modernism in not unimportant respects (cf. Schmid 1992: 25).

Furthermore, in Turgenev's texts there is, as a rule, no personal perspective (of either character or personal narrator) that can be detected as the carrier of this personal myth, something which would also be linked with a paradigmatical and 'mythological' mechanism of meaning-generation (idem: 25-26). In general, Turgenev's prose thus shows traits of that 're-mythologizing' tendency in nineteenth- and twentieth-century European literature that has been pointed out by Lotman and Minc 1981, among others (cf. below, section 2.6).

Before we proceed to indicate the main lines along which 'added', metaphorical qualities of the narrated world are generated (of which the first among them are the narrated characters), I should like to make a few general remarks on the world-picture that is sensed in the background of practically all of Turgenev's works. Of course, I cannot go into all the details and aspects of that view—the reader is referred to Kagan-Kans' study (1975), which, though arguable in some matters of detail, still remains a valuable survey of the 'philosophy' that formed a characteristic background to Turgenev's works and remained basically unchanged throughout his life.

It could be said that, paradoxically, in Turgenev's world-view the common law governing all being is an absence of meaning, in the sense of some occult, eternal principle of being that goes beyond that being itself. Costlow convincingly argues that it is the "attempt to jump out of causality—to escape consequence and temporality" for which Rudin is condemned by Turgenev's text (Costlow: 16). Still, causality and consequence are equally inadequate for an understanding of human life: Turgenev seems convinced that human life is totally subdued to blind fate: "the secret game of fate, which we, blind mortals, style 'blind chance'" (. . . V: 128); "the secret forces on which life is built, and that occasionally, but suddenly, break through the surface" (. . . idem: 98). These "secret forces", that sometimes suddenly break through the surface are of great importance for the later 'supernatural' stories, in which that "breaking through" is realized as the occurrence of supernatural phenomena. But for his work as a whole too this forms an indication that Turgenev's narrated world is not solely to be understood as being ruled by causality, one of the main categories of metonymic relations. Let me repeat that this by no means implies that it is pos-

sible in that world to escape the visible, factual world, ruled by causality: where any attempt to do so is made, it inevitably fails. Just as Actaeon was immediately punished by a terrible death when he had beheld the unveiled divinity[13], so any direct contact with the occult in Turgenev's world inevitably leads to death or at least despair. It is not even necessary for man to take the initiative: fate will overtake him gratuitously. In Turgenev's later work, approximately from the time of **"A Journey into Poles'e"** (see Chapter 6), this blind fate is generally identified as 'all-levelling nature', which is why the descriptions of nature often acquire gloomy undertones. The fables of most of Turgenev's works have been summarized (in the rather felicitous wording of Ju. Lotman) as:

> the continuous incursion of nature with its law of death and birth, its expelling of the old in favour of the young, the weak in favour of the strong, the refined in favour of the rude, and with its indifference to human aims and ideals, to everything that brings order in the life of man.

> (Lotman 1986: 19)

This intrusion makes human life "meaningless and therefore tragic. But this is not the lofty tragedy of meaning, but the hopeless tragedy of meaninglessness" (ibidem). This tragedy, from the point of view of the character and his strivings, often comes in the shape of the unexpected and unmotivated death of the central character, which strips his life's activities of all meaning, but which for the author, in contrast, seems inherent to existence and wholly in tune with the laws of the universe. It is of pivotal importance for Turgenev's worldview that death renders life senseless. Here, again, there is no consolation whatsoever to be gained from some 'higher' layer of meaning; in Turgenev's world, there is no cause which is worth dying for. Consequently, the martyr as a type is unthinkable in that world, for a martyr's death could crown a life and give it a deep religious significance. Also, Turgenev's tragic characters are not like the hero from Classical tragedy, who dies for a higher cause. In Gogol's *Taras Bul'ba* the death of Taras and his son serves the liberation of the Ukraine and thus provides a sense of fulfilment. But there is never any such pathos in Turgenev—Rudin dies nameless on the barricades for a lost cause; Insarov dies before he has even attempted a great deed; Bazarov's death serves no purpose; Neždanov kills himself from disappointment in his own ideals, and so on.

Human existence thus seems caught between the illusion of "causality and consequence" (Costlow) on the one hand—the belief that will, purpose, rational and emotional aims can effect definitive changes—and an irrational, hostile, blind fate that dooms every individual to a death which makes all his strivings meaningless on the other. This indeed is the cornerstone of Turgenev's image of man.

2.4.1 Hamlet and Don Quixote

I refer, of course, to the well-known dichotomy of 'Hamlet' and 'Don Quixote', which Turgenev elaborated in a speech given in 1860 (V: 330-350)—a dichotomy which plays a role, in one form or another, in practically all of his narrative works. His first thoughts on the subject occurred as early as 1847, and it can be said that almost all of the more important characters in any of Turgenev's works show some traits that allow us to relate them to the Hamlet/Don Quixote dichotomy. This was shown by Kagan-Kans (1975), who discusses many aspects of the dichotomy and its place in Turgenev's personal worldview as well as showing how it is reflected in his work. Let us briefly outline the meaning of this opposition.

For Turgenev, on the one hand there is the coldly reasoning, self-analytical Hamlet, whose main energy, in his lack of faith, is directed towards himself. Doubting everything, including himself, his basic attitude is one of realism: he takes life as it is, without any illusion, fully aware of the gaping abyss that awaits man at the end of the road; he is therefore ironical about any 'higher truth'. This attitude paralyzes his will and renders him incapable of action. Though he may clearly distinguish the rights and wrongs of human life, of his own situation, or of the world, he denies that there is any higher truth that might be the key to bringing about happiness. On the other hand, there is Don Quixote, the unselfish enthusiast, always in action, who uncalculatingly follows an ideal, confident of a truth that is outside of himself. Unfortunately, this is at the expense of lacking a sufficient measure of practicality and a clear sense of reality and discrimination. This opposition is at the heart of Turgenev's work, in which there is an indissoluble bond between heroic enterprises or even intentions and the way these come to a meaningless end. In his plots the failure of the main hero is standard; a failure that is always unexpected and senseless. A strong or gifted individual, who stands out from the rest, is equipped with a personality structure such as to render him doomed to accomplish nothing.

Kagan-Kans points out that the origins of this dichotomy lay with the Romantic recognition of modern man's self-alienation, of the predominance of sterile intellectual reflection, which torments him, and of self-analysis, which cripples him. However, she seems to be of the opinion, which I do not share, that Turgenev actually gave more weight to the 'Don Quixote' side of human nature, and that at various stages of his career he found this ideal human type embodied in various contemporary types. In this she seems to be influenced by the concept of Geršenzon (1919), who was, to my knowledge, the first to rediscover the importance of Turgenev's lecture **"Hamlet and Don Quixote"** for his views on the essence of human life[14]. He holds that Tur-

genev's hopes were all set on the Don Quixotes, on 'heart' instead of 'head', on enthusiasm which is directed towards an ideal outside of the ego rather than cold analytical self-analysis and concentration on the self. Similarly, Kagan-Kans posits: "there is no doubt that, disturbed as he was by the Mephistopheles in him, Turgenev set before himself the ideal of the integrated (. . .) harmonious being" (Kagan-Kans: 16). I believe that Turgenev's worldview was much more tragic. True, he admires the Don Quixotes for their unselfish activity, their enthusiasm, and their strength of will. But he also calls them . . .

> [crack-brained Don Quixotes, who are only useful to humanity and can set its feet marching because they see but one sole point on the horizon, a point whose nature is often not at all what it seems to their eyes. Involuntarily the question arises: does one then really have to be insane to believe in truth? and is the mind that has taken full control of itself for that very reason really deprived of all of its strength? Even a superficial discussion of these questions would lead us very far indeed.]

> (V: 340-341)

This is why Ju. Lotman very rightly remarks that in Turgenev's works heroic deeds may be highly valued, but "even the value of the heroic deed does not attach meaning to it" (Lotman 1986: 18)[15].

Furthermore, condensing his characters into certain types, like Hamlet and Don Quixote, is a means of raising them to the plane of a higher conflict: the individual, historically concrete characters are, on a higher level, actors who play out the historical world drama of human existence in their own age. But for Turgenev, this eternal drama in its turn reflects an eternal, cosmic drama. The Hamlets and Don Quixotes are mere human incarnations of two cosmic forces that can be observed in another form in nature itself. The following passage is worth quoting at length:

> [in that separation, that dualism, of which we have spoken, we have to acknowledge the fundamental law of all human life; that the whole of that life is nothing other than the eternal reconciliation and the eternal strife between two principles that are continuously being separated and continuously merge. If we were not afraid to frighten your ears with philosophical terms, we would be ready to say that the Hamlets are the expression of the fundamental centripetal force in nature, that makes every living being regard itself as the centre of creation and everything else as existing only for its own purpose (thus the mosquito that sat on Alexander the Great's forehead, quietly convinced of its right to do so, fed on his blood as his due food; just so Hamlet, despising himself, unlike the mosquito, which has not risen to such a level, just so Hamlet, we were saying, regards things always as they are relevant to himself). Without this centripetal force (the force of egoism) nature could not exist, and nor could it without that other,

centrifugal force, according to which everything that exists, exists only for the other (this force, this principle of devotion and sacrifice [. . .] is represented by Don Quixote). These two forces of stagnation and movement, of conservatism and progress, are the basic forces of all existence. They explain the growing of a flower to us, but also give us the key to understand the development of the most powerful peoples.]

(V: 341)

These words cannot fail to bring to mind Turgenev's review of S. T. Aksakov's *Notes of a Rifle Hunter,* in which nature is also presented as dominated by two main forces: the centripetal, according to which "every single entity wants to exist exclusively for itself, regards itself as the centre of the universe, turns everything it is surrounded by into something that can be used", and the centrifugal, according to which "every point is connected with all the others" (. . . IV: 516). The same centripetal and centrifugal forces we recognize in the two fundamental human types described in **"Hamlet and Don Quixote"**; the image of the mosquito sucking human blood occurs in both texts, though in the later one the mention of Alexander the Great makes it especially telling. In all, I believe it is justified to compare Turgenev's artistic method of presenting human characters with that of his depiction of nature. In both, the artist should on the one hand avoid going into all too subtle details, yet on the other he should refrain from bare subjectivism or soulless rhetoric. As we have seen, this middle position between aloofness and involvement is indeed characteristic of Turgenev's narrators (cf. section 2.3).

Of course, there is an important difference between the natural and the human spheres. Hamlet feels self-contempt, to which level the mosquito "has not risen"—that is, he has raised the natural principle to the level of consciousness and moral awareness; while the altruistic Don Quixote embodies, however unconsciously, the unifying tendency that seems to exist in nature only as a principle. Still, the underlying mechanism is the same: individual existents, be they natural or human, function in the world of Turgenev's texts only as the relative poles of an opposition[16]. Ultimately, it is the author's aim to present the individual existent—the character—as part of the total whole. We have Turgenev's own words as evidence that this whole is of an aesthetic nature: it is "that general, endless harmony, in which everything that exists—exists for the other" (. . . IV: 517). The detached position of the narrator, of which we have spoken, is analysed by Grübel (1984) in *First Love* as precisely this position of *aesthetic* distance resulting from the retrospective viewpoint of old age which offers a way out of life's dilemma between will and knowledge, the ethical and the epistemological. In the story it is presented as the contrasting and consecutive stages of rash youth and disillusioned maturity.

2.5 NOVELS AND STORIES

Such is the fatal dichotomy that Turgenev sees in human nature. Up to now we have treated this worldview and important features that are related with it, like the relation between character and narrator, and between character and narrated world, without any regard to the question of narrative genre. This is on the one hand justifiable in view of the relative shortness of Turgenev's novels, which makes them more than usually similar to the story. But on the other hand, differences between the image of character as shown in the novel as opposed to the story may not be overlooked. I will now briefly state my position in this matter.

The poetics of Turgenev's short prose has up till now been investigated too little (Muratov 1985: 3) to be able to give more than a tentative general characterization of what distinguishes it from that of the novels. However, Pumpjanskij's proposition, quoted above, that what is central to Turgenev's novels is the "judgment on the social significance of the character", may give us a clue as to how to proceed with the stories. It is true that the central character in the novels is depicted in his social and historical surroundings. However, this does not mean, of course, that in his so-called 'realist', 'social-critical' novels, Turgenev objectively reflects some given social reality (even though he does at the same time comment on and criticize it). At the root of these works there lies a personal ideology (in the broadest sense), which principally *organizes* this reality, which constructs it anew, and projects its own coordinates onto it. This ideology I regard as a kind of personal myth—which in the novels is expressed on levels other than in the stories. As Ju. Lotman remarks: "the plots of Turgenev's works develop . . . on three levels: firstly, the level of contemporary reality, secondly, the archetypal level, and thirdly, the cosmic" (Lotman 1986: 20). It may be said that the specific weight attached to these mutually interdependent levels varies according to the genre (and the period). In the novels, the central character is depicted first of all in his social and cultural-historical dimensions. Central here is his social failure: his superfluity, inability to enter into productive relations with society. Details in his image do in fact point to a metaphoric layer of meaning, but this layer 'remains in the background' more than in the stories: there the metaphorical, paradigmatical features of the central character 'compete', so to say, more strongly with the image built on relations of contiguity: social, historical, cultural, even biological determination, psychological (emotional, volitional and so on) consistency, and causality in the relations between character and actions[17].

In his book on the *Tales of Belkin* (1991), Schmid discerns three devices based on the interaction of the paradigmatical structure with the causal-narrative structure. Two of them may be recognized in Turgenev's stories, as well, the first being the construction of intratextual equivalences and paradigms. The second is the "focusing and decontextualisation of separate motifs by allusion to other (fremde) texts and the activation of intertextual equivalences" (Schmid 1991: 49). The third device analyzed by Schmid (in the work of Puškin) is the realisation and unfolding of set phrases and sayings. This device, however, is of practically no importance for Turgenev.

For Turgenev's artistic method in his short prose, Pumpjanskij has used the term "orchestration":

> The fundamental specific trait of the Turgenevian story is its powerful 'orchestration', which works through the depiction of the scenery and is 'philosophical'. . . . Herein lies its main difference from the 'Tales of Belkin', from 'Taman', from the stories of Gogol and the young Dostoevskij, and this is why it has had such an enormous influence on West European (especially German and English) literature.
>
> (Pumpjanskij 1929.2: 5)[18]

The term "orchestration" fairly well covers that layer of metaphorical features of the image of character that I find so important in Turgenev's stories. The term "philosophical" is more difficult to accept. Pumpjanskij himself slightly chides Turgenev for the lack of "methodology" in his "philosophy":

> Of special interest is the 'method' of this philosophizing: from the single observation, from a connection discovered, thought soars to a general judgment on life, omitting all intermediate steps, and so a tremendous flight of thought unites the fragmentary 'episode' with the general 'doctrine'. (. . .) Thus, between the perfectly single observation and the highly consequential (ответственнейшим) generalization there is no inner barrier, no 'methodological space' at all.
>
> (Pumpjanskij 1929.2: 8)

It will be clear that Pumpjanskij here requires something of Turgenev's "philosophy" that cannot be expected from it, and that it does not pretend to give. Turgenev's worldview cannot be reconstructed as a systematic "philosophy", but rather as what I have called a personal myth. Neither can I therefore agree with Kagan-Kans' reassessment of Turgenev as a "philosophical" author (Kagan-Kans: 7). All the same, it is true that whereas in the novels Turgenev's worldview is expressed more in the "judgment" passed on the social unproductivity of the character, in the short works the various forms of orchestration do highlight the character's 'existential' failure, i.e. the meaninglessness of his existence against the background of life in general, or the cosmic life often embodied in Nature[19]. It is significant that Kagan-Kans came to her reassessment on the basis of an examination of Turgenev's short works rather than of the novels, where the social aspect is more prominent. But, as I hope to have shown, the social and the 'existential' in Turgenev's works are actually interrelated, uniting on an abstract level in what Ju. Lotman has called the opposition of meaningfulness versus meaninglessness.

2.6 THE PARADIGMATIC IMAGE OF CHARACTER

In the previous chapter I introduced the various ways in which the paradigmatic image of character can be constructed. I will now discuss some mechanisms that are of special relevance for Turgenev's short prose.

In general, such a paradigmatic relation is constituted by creating a thematical or formal equivalential relation between particular elements of the text, be they details of the description of a character's outward appearance or certain inner qualities, details of objects, space- and time-characteristics, thematic elements, names, and so on. These equivalences form a structure, a network of their own, adding new layers of meaning to the temporal-causal sequence of events. In the analyses in the following chapters this mechanism will be shown as it operates Turgenev's stories. We will see that as a result of creating equivalential relations between various elements of the characters' environment, this environment is metaphorically shaped to consist of two opposed semantic fields; the central character's action then constitutes a transgression of the boundary between these fields.

This makes it possible to place many of Turgenev's characters in Ju. Lotman's well-known categories of 'mobile' versus 'immobile' characters. For Lotman, only those actions can be considered narrative events that form a transgression by a character of the border between semantic fields, that themselves in one way or another reflect categories active in the cultural conceptual system (Lotman 1970: 282). The characters fall into two main classes: firstly, characters who are tied to a certain semantic field (for instance: the town versus the countryside, civilized Europe versus an uninhabited island, the woods versus the castle, etc) or class (for instance: rich versus poor, friends versus foes, dead versus living, representatives of Nature versus those of Society of Civilization) and who remain within its borders; they serve mainly as the exponents of the semantic field and may therefore be called 'classificators'. The second main class of characters are the "active characters" . . . , who are 'mobile' and can transgress these borders. A third class may be recognized in those characters who help or hinder the active ones to cross the border, but they may also be seen as a subgroup of the first class. Since the type of text *with* a 'narration'[20] is constructed on the basis of texts without narration as their negation, the 'mobile' character is introduced as a person who has freed himself from a certain convention, and is thus able to cross the semantic boundary in spite of the usual prohibition of such an action[21].

2.6.1 INVARIANT EVENT-STRUCTURE

Most of Turgenev's stories reveal a remarkable similarity in their basic plot skeleton. In general, the stories do not concentrate on the presentation of a psychological development, which may to a certain extent be connected with the generic nature of the short prose work as such. For example, the novella "is deliberately plotted to concentrate on one central conflict which, in turn, illuminates the inherent disposition of an already fully developed character" (Silz: 6). Moreover, however strictly the characters in Turgenev's works are seen in metonymic relation with their world, and their actions in a strictly temporal and causal relation with themselves and with the characters' psychology, still, in the course of the careers of many central characters, an invariant fable may be detected without great difficulty. Again, the specific poetics of the prose story may play a role here: short narratives (of novella length) "are likely to approach the conditions of poetry (. . .) The shorter the work of fiction, the more likely are its characters to be simply functions and typical manifestations of a precise and inevitable sequence of events" (Mudrick: 214-215). Though this statement may seem to refer more to an earlier type of short story, in which 'plot' was dominant over 'character', and not to Turgenev's stories, in which the narration concentrates more on the motivation for the characters' action—and, conversely, the effect of their action (and that of other characters' actions) on their inner life—the recurrent pattern of these actions is nonetheless evident. In general, planning the protagonists' career as a fixed pattern already indicates that human life is thought of as dependent on more than just contiguous relations with the ever-changing environment of concrete circumstance.

Once more I should like to approach the invariant structure of the stories on the basis of an analysis of the novels—which in this respect, as we have seen, structurally do not differ essentially from the stories on account of their shortness. Dale Peterson has called attention to a "recurrent formulaic structure within the basic fable that constitutes the central symbolic action in Turgenev's six novels" (Peterson: 74[22]). This "basic scenario" Peterson describes as "the injection, or more commonly the return, of an ex-provincial protagonist into the heartland of what Turgenev labels, in the last words of his last novel, *Bezymjannaja Rus'*, 'Anonymous Russia'"; this appearance, in what is for the protagonist a new milieu, results in a clash with the environment, which "coincides with his meeting a heroine who emerges from that same milieu"; both the protagonist and the "indigenous heroine who is an overreacher in her environment (. . .) usually prove to be totally incompatible once suspended in the resident culture surrounding them" (Peterson: 76-77). I quite agree with Peterson that the result is

a novel in which psychological and characterological causation and sequence are less important than perceived analogies and contrasts with and among other life postures. The fully developed idea of such a novel often crystallizes in the form of an illustrative scene or an archetypal portrait of cultural relations as embodied in an apprentice figure confronting an inevitable initiation.

(idem: 81)

Thus at the root of the novels lies the protagonist's transgression of a boundary, whereby he enters an alien milieu in which his character is tested. He is subsequently met by a (female) representative of that milieu who is going in the opposite direction, out of that milieu, into which she no longer fits. All this is even more the case for Turgenev's short prose work, with the main difference that, as I said in the preceding section, it is not so much the social confrontation which is central in the short prose, but the 'existential'. It may be added that, whereas in the novels various narrative lines may interweave, such as the social and the amorous line (and with less intensity the confrontation of the protagonist with nature), the stories tend to concentrate on a single narrative line. In the majority of the stories, the movement of the protagonist into peasant Russia is often central, and his meeting with peasant types who are not really representative of that milieu (or at least, of what is commonly thought to be representative of it). This is the case in most of the stories from *Notes of a Hunter,* and in **"Father Aleksej's Story,"** while we find an interesting inversion of this scheme in **"Mumu"** (see Chapter 5). Alternatively, there is a movement into and a confrontation with Nature itself: **"A Journey into Poles'e"** (see Chapter 6), **"Bežin Meadow"** (which combines elements of both types, as do other stories— see Chapter 4). Or again, the protagonist may be immersed in the deeper regions of inner life, another unknown realm: the unexpected power of passion (be it love: **"Faust,"** *Asja, First love, Spring Torrents,* **"The Brigadier,"** among other stories, or greed, as in **"King Lear of the Steppes"**). Yet again, an intrusion into another reality may be felt: that of the irrational, threatening, supernatural, in the so-called 'supernatural tales' (among them **"The Dog,"** see Chapter 7).

On the level of story, the characters of Turgenev's prose works are thus already 'characterized' by their fate, which repeats the common pattern of all individual life striving for some measure of self-affirmation. Those events in their lives are selected that demonstrate their failure. In the novels this is predominantly their social failure, in the short prose more often their existential failure, often somehow connected with their amorous hesitancy—their 'amorous unproductivity', to play on Pumpjanskij's term 'social unproductivity'[23].

This failure is in general shaped as the character's incapacity to adjust to the alien environment in which he has been placed. Next I should like to examine how the opposing 'environments' and the border between them which has been transgressed by the character are constructed.

2.6.2 THE TRANSGRESSION-SCHEME IN TURGENEV'S SHORT PROSE

One of the aims of this book is to show the importance for the study of Turgenev's work of taking into account the folkloric connotations displayed by many motifs in his short prose. Data concerning Turgenev's knowledge of Russian folklore and popular religion and superstition have been collected (e.g. Azadovskij 1960 and Maslennikova 1976), but the relevance of folkloric images in his work has hardly been acknowledged, and certainly not elaborated upon. And it is often through the folkloric or popular religious connotation of certain details that equivalential relations are made possible. This is shown in the analyses of **"Bežin Meadow,"** **"Mumu,"** **"A Journey into Poles'e"** and **"The Dog."** One of the most important equivalential relations in these stories is that between details of the different spaces the characters move in; as a result these spaces acquire the traits of the opposition, well known from Russian folklore, between 'this', 'our' . . . and the 'other' . . . land, whereby that other land is identified as the realm of spirits, the supernatural, the irrational, threatening and horrifying 'yonder'. But in the meantime, the sharp opposition between the two spaces also models that between other semantic categories: that between civilization and uncivilized Russia, between culture and nature, between everyday reality and the supernatural.

On the one hand, the method of constructing this classification of space and of characters and their actions through the use of folkloric connotations—which make equivalential relations between elements possible—is quite specific for the work of Turgenev, but on the other hand the occurrence of such a classification, thanks to which the actions of the characters acquire the quality of transgressing a boundary, is not unique for his work, nor, for that matter, for Russian literature.

It has been observed that the depicted world in modern prose increasingly tends to resemble the arbitrary chaos of empirical reality, and the narrative point of view to restrict itself to an individual perspective. However, on the plane of event-structure and personage-constellation, this process has been accompanied by a tendency to "convert major segments of the narration and whole plots into stereotypes" (Lotman 1987: 106). While the fictional world was becoming as diverse and manifold as reality, the acts of its inhabitants were not. Why was this so? Let us follow Lotman's thoughts in more detail.

Lotman sees as a new and central phenomenon of the modern novel[24] the fact that "elements of the text, such as the names of the objects, the action, the names of the personages etc., as they appear in the work, are already marked by the socio-cultural and literary semiotic environment" (idem: 105[25]). The connotations that these elements carry in the extra-textual semiotic reality, and which they preserve in the work, influence the development of the plot: they "function as coding mechanisms, which cut off certain possibilities of plot-development and stimulate others" (ibidem). For instance, the plot of *The Queen of Spades* would have been impossible with a cavalry officer instead of an engineer as its main hero; if the ulan and the treasurer in Lermontov's *The treasurer's wife from Tambov* had fought it out in a regular duel instead of at the card table, the plot would have been entirely different. In contrast, when an element of extra-textual reality enters into a folk-tale (for instance, Ivan kills the dragon with a rifle), then this does not alter the plot at all. I presume that Lotman here points to the phenomenon described by Bachtin as the 'being under discussion', the "disputed nature" . . . of the object in a modern work of literature. Of course, this disputed nature can have various effects, depending on other factors. It may become the dominant principle of the work, as in Dostoevskij's polyphonic novels, or it may be tuned down and submit to the lyrical intonation of the author's word, as in the works of Turgenev.

This question is not unimportant for our problem, literary character. In modern literature, what are possible or impossible actions for a given personage is in large measure determined by who he 'is', that is, what social, cultural, ideological, or other semiotic codes characteristic for his culture he incorporates. As Lotman says: "the poetics of the plot in the novel are in important measure the poetics of the hero, since a certain type of hero is connected with certain fixed plots" (idem: 104-105). Since every object, situation or character, retaining its extra-textual semiotic context, brings with it a whole spectrum of possible lines of plot development, there seems to exist an extraordinary wealth of possible transformations and combinations of plot structures. We get the impression that an author could construct his plot as he pleases. But this is not the case. As Lotman explains:

> The sharp increase of differentiation of plots in the nineteenth century would have led to the total destruction of narrative structure, had this not been compensated for, at the other pole of organization of the text, by a tendency to convert major segments of the narration and whole plots into stereotypes. . . . This stereotyping leads to the activation of archaic plot models which are stored in cultural memory.

> (idem: 106)

In other words, modern narrative has recourse to mythological patterns (cf. Lotman, Meletinskij and Minc 1988). For Lotman and Minc, the history of the development of artistic literature can to an important extent be seen as the process of translating mythological, that is, non-discrete and cyclical texts, into the discrete and linear language of narration. One of the four major periods when mythology influenced art is that of the rise of the novel, during which mythological models were carried over into the discrete world of artistic texts (Lotman and Minc 1981: 42). I think that we would be right to understand the period of the rise of the novel not as the relatively short period in which the modern novel acquired its definitive shape, but as a more prolonged process, closely connected with other cultural changes: it is the process of 'novelization' . . . of which M. Bachtin speaks. Thanks to the dialogical structure of the novel that has been unveiled by Bachtin in the novels of Dostoevskij, but which can be said to be characteristic of whole types of artistic texts[26], a new and unique combination becomes possible of the typologically conflicting 'central' and 'peripheral' mythological text-generating systems, given form as correlating elements of one and the same structure.

The central mythic text-generating system fixes the world as a single, constantly repeated, cycle. The peripheral generates texts which fix accidental deviations from the norm, that is, excesses and anomalies that do not unite in some orderly, lawful whole. With the disintegration of mythic culture, texts from the central mythic system came to be 'translated' into discrete linear language, that is, they partly adopted the form of the texts from the peripheral system i.e. linear narrative with an elementary plot. Qualities that belonged to one personage were now distributed among several, who formed pairs and opposites. Furthermore, since beginning and end were now marked, change was introduced, the simplest variant being the chain 'entering a closed space and then leaving it', a process which may be said to represent temporal death followed by resurrection. But as texts from the central system established homomorph equivalences between entities from different spheres, an elementary semiotic situation was created around them. The narrative had to be interpreted, what was told about some particular events had a personal meaning for every member of the audience: "The myth always tells about me. A 'novelty', an anecdote, tells about the other. The first organizes the world of the listener, the seconds adds interesting details to his knowledge of that world" (Lotman 1973: 13).

Historically, modern prose developed from 'peripheral' texts (idem: 12). These 'novella's', which tell of the unexpected and the excessive, absorbed elements of the central mythological texts, that is, they modelled the unexpected along the lines of the plot scheme 'temporal death followed by resurrection'. Simultaneously, the semiotic, 'modelling' capacity of modern prose increased: it projected these unexpected events onto the world of the audience.

In modern prose, the unexpected and the death-resurrection plot scheme are united through interrelation, not through hierarchical ordering. A personage in a modern prose work can combine poles of different oppositions and thus of different micro-plots (on the other hand, one opposition may be distributed over different personages). He may thus be at one and the same time a member of semantic fields which in the general system of oppositions of the work are seen as each other's opposites. This combination of different qualities may be modelled over time as a metamorphosis, and this is done with the help of the mythological model of temporal death followed by resurrection. Or it may be modelled as the simultaneous existence of contradictory qualities in one person. Such a personage unites 'personalities' that in a mythological text would have been distributed over two personages, who are each other's opposites. Paradigmatical for such a unity is the combination of the gentleman and the robber, which we encounter in the work of Puškin, and which plays such an important role in many works in the period of roughly 1780-1850, from Schiller to Dumas, from Zschokke to Bulwer-Lytton[27].

So far we have seen that in Turgenev's stories, with the help of equivalential relations between elements of the text, the actions of the characters are modelled according to the archetypal scheme of transgressing the boundary between semantic fields. The characters themselves fall into two classes: mobile characters and classificators. On the basis of this classification, other groupings may become possible. As a consequence, different characters may undertake parallel or opposed actions, and this will be shown in the analyses of the stories in the following chapters.

Thus in Turgenev's stories, through parallellism in characters' lives and careers, and through pairing as a result of equivalential relations between elements of the setting and of a character's own appearance, habits and so forth, the personages are classified according to the principle of analogy and contrast. This is clearly a paradigmatical, not a syntagmatical principle[28]. Now analogy and contrast have long been acknowledged as one of the fundamental building blocks of Turgenev's art. Stender-Petersen (246) speaks of the principle of "die gegenseitige Komplementarität der Charaktere" as a consistent feature in all of Turgenev's creation[29]. It is not difficult to convince oneself that pairs of characters are indeed a recurrent phenomenon in his stories: in *Notes of a Hunter* we have Chor' and Kalinyč, and Čertopchanov and Nedopjuskin; in **"Two Landowners"** Chvalynskij and Stegunov; in **"Two Friends"** Vjazovnin and Krupicyn; in **"A Quiet Spot"** Astachov and Veret'ev; in **"Three Portraits"** Lučinov and Rogačev; Fabij and Mucij in **"The Song of Triumphant Love"**; we have Punin and Baburin; of course, there are Hamlet and Don Quixote, and so on. (For an enumeration of the most important pairs in the novels, cf. Stender-Petersen: 246-254).

Furthermore, as I have already said, Turgenev's tendency to put individual characters in the perspective of archetypes and recurring schemes can be seen as linked to mythological identification. As such, it may be considered a special case of the paradigmatical principle of analogy.

Thus we see that for an understanding of the image of character in Turgenev's works, it is by no means sufficient to restrict oneself to the collection of data on the 'psychological content' of the characters. Aspects of characterization are closely connected with plot, setting, theme and with the question of perspective. Indeed, as Baruch Hochman puts it:

> the organization, or schematism (of literary character—SB), does not reside within the characters alone. It is not just a matter of what is given within the self-contained limits of the characters—that is, it is not just a matter of the patterning of their responses, commitments, traits, and other features (. . .). Even when we retrieve characters as relatively autonomous entities, we perceive them as part of an organizing structure made up of elements that are interfused with each other and that illuminate each other.
>
> (Hochman: 64)

2.7 THE CULTURAL CONTEXT

Turgenev's use of the device of analogy and contrast, and his tendency to reduce the main events in narrative texts to certain basic schemes, can, as we have seen, be connected with what we have called a personal myth, at the basis of which lies a dualistic model or structure. In the following, I should like to develop an idea of Ju. Lotman's, who suggests that Turgenev's worldview as manifested in his artistic texts takes a polemical position with regard to certain mythological schemes that lie deeply hidden at the root of conceptions of man and his role in the social environment (that is, contemporary Russia) of nineteenth-century Russian literature and culture.

In all European literature, the Romantic period saw the revival of interest in the 'hero', that figure of strength and stature who represents the society around him. As Reed shows, a new feature of the Romantic attitude towards the hero, as compared with earlier periods, is that he "is presented as the solution to a major problem of the age, the modern problem of an overly developed reflective thought" (Reed: 5). Romanticism constructed an ideal of the hero who overcomes this disease of the age, "who seemed to possess wholeness, unselfconscious passion, and the ability to act" (ibidem). However, another major theme in the Romantic attitude towards the hero is that the same ability to act brings him into conflict with the accepted social norms and values. The definition of the hero from earlier periods, as one who "represents (. . .) a socially approved norm, for representing which to the satisfaction of society he is decorated with a title" does not apply here at all (ibidem). This leads to a very complex variety of possible relationships between the hero and society and its values. The hero is never an outright antisocial being. His actions set him apart from society, but he always remains committed to it in one way or another. In his rejection of society there always remain traces of hope that it might be reorganized, whether by reviving the values of the past or by bringing about some social or moral ideal. The scale of possible attitudes manifested by the active hero thus ranges from his plundering of society to his redeeming it. On the other hand, it can be plausibly argued (see Garber 1967, for instance) that the suffering and inactive 'anti-hero', who refrains from any active engagement, stems from the same roots as the active, rebellious one, precisely because it is not the latter's own selfish desires which generate the values he adheres to, but, in the final analysis, his compassion with the sufferings of others. The active and the passive hero, one might say, differ merely in tactics, not in overall aims. Furthermore, the passive, uncommitted figures like Manfred or René are as much isolated from society as their active counterparts; they likewise transgress the boundary of accepted social values, though they do not 'act' in the technical sense.

A third main current in the Romantic attitude towards the hero is the fact that his activity acquires demoniacal overtones. On the one hand, this may be connected with the interest in the figure of the rebellious and fallen angel (together with a revival of interest in Christian mythology)—as was noted by Lotman and Minc (1981: 49). On the other hand, by transgressing the boundary of accepted norms and thereby, in the mythological world model, of Civilization, the active hero acquires a privileged relationship to Nature, which, as Reed shows, had by this period long ceased to a source of bliss (Reed: 11-14).

In Russia, Puškin was the first to use the well-known Romantic *emplois* of the gentleman-dandy and the robber, who both stand out from their social environment (the dandy in the sense that his behaviour is based on deliberately shocking the society he belongs to), in order to model his transgressors of the boundary of accepted norms and values (for the many and various examples in Puškin's work of such types, see Lotman 1979: 29-30).

At the same time in Puškin's work, yet most strongly in that of Gogol', the mechanism that we have mentioned earlier (section 2.6.2) came into effect—namely, that elements of the text retain their extra-textual sociocultural and literary semiotic connotations, this yielding additional expectations as to the probability or improbability of certain developments in the plot. The demoniacal active personage acquired traits that may be regarded as specific to the Russian cultural tradition. In his role of outsider, i.e. a personage who is related to society as someone from outside its boundaries, he shows a fundamental ambivalence: he is seen as either a redeemer of that society or as its undoer. As a matter of fact, the same ambivalence with regard to the Romantic active hero in the Western tradition had already been discovered by Garber (Garber 1967: 326; 328). But it has a special importance in the Russian situation, where it converges with a traditional popular fundamental mistrust of representatives of the cultured elite, a tradition that was still very alive in the period under discussion (see below)[30].

The importance of the ambivalent hero in the Russian situation was used by Lotman to formulate a set of possible plots that may be regarded as specific to Russian culture of the nineteenth century. He calls such a set of possible plots that are typical of a given culture typical a "plot range." . . . In his view,

> Genealogically the plots . . . of the Russian novel go back to European ones; from the eighteenth century on, they are constructed according to much the same schemes. The national specifics of the plot are confined to a certain *couleur locale* in the actions, but the plot structure itself is not affected. To create the 'Russian plot' was the work of Puškin and Gogol'.

> (Lotman 1987: 10)

In his article, Lotman traces one particular line of this Russian plot range. He postulates that the West European novel can be broadly characterized as based upon the striving of the hero who occupies a place that is unfit for him (that is, one which does not satisfy him, which is unseemly), in order to gain a better one (idem: 11). The typical West European plot is motivated by the hero's urge to change his position in life, in society. But in contrast, in one of its main lines, the Russian novel "poses the problem of a change of essence of the hero and of the life that surrounds him" (. . . ibidem). The main character, who would typically have transgressed the boundaries of social conventions, has a vocation to transform either life around him or his own self. Schmid (1992: 104) regards turns of event of this latter type as characteristic of Russian Realist prose. In Russian criticism they are known as . . . which can be translated as 'illumination', 'gaining an insight', and as 'shift of consciousness', 'an inner, mental change', 'a transgression of moral and characterological boundaries', a 'moral, religious or social insight, an inner revulsion, an ethical-moral purification and perfection' and even as the Joycean 'epiphany' (cf. Schmid idem: 104-105 and references in note 2). I am inclined to agree with Schmid on the limitation of this concept to a particular

period[31]; however, Schmid would probably agree with Lotman that the phenomenon is typologically specific to *Russian* Realism.

In the structuring of the plot and the personages in this type of Russian novel, the main personage, who has a vocation to transform the world, may, however, be cast in one of two roles: either as the 'undoer' or as the 'redeemer' . . . idem: 12) of the world he is called upon to transform. (In the case of the transformation of his own self he will undo or save himself: he will plumb the depths of crime and of sin, pass through a moral crisis and will be reborn—or not, as the case may be)[32].

The combination of elements of the redeemer and undoer in the work of Puškin is already very significant. But it is in the work of Gogol' that this dichotomy acquires its obviously mythological features. The undoer, from Gogol' onwards, assumes the characteristics of the Antichrist:

> In this quality he on the one hand inherits the image-repertoire . . . of the demoniacal hero of Romanticism, and on the other the popular and traditional notions connected with this figure. He arrives from the outside like a pernicious temptation from the devil. . . .

> (Lotman 1986: 12)

On the other hand, "the redeemer-hero, too, appears as an arrival from the outside" (idem: 13; for examples, see idem: 12-14).

This, then, seems to be the mythological scheme in the structuring of the plot and the personages (at least in this type of Russian literature) that is regenerated as a consequence of the creation of the 'Russian novel' by Puškin and Gogol', and that is continued by Dostoevskij and to some extent by Tolstoj. Transgressing a boundary—let us remember that Lotman distinguishes transgressing a boundary as the most important plot-shaping function in narrative literature—is indeed linked in this type of novel with certain notions that are inherited from Russian traditional culture, notions that are expressed in the mythological motifs and schemes of folklore. The first important notion is that—transgressing a border is thought of as stepping into an inversed world, a world absolutely, qualitatively different from the original, which consequently and of necessity involves a qualitative change in the personality of the transgressor. The second is that—this 'other' person, someone who belongs to such another world, is regarded as potentially either 'holy' or 'evil', and thus in relation to the first, 'our', world, takes the position of either redeemer or undoer. (In relation to his own fate the terms would be 'doom' and 'rebirth').

The first notion is described by Lotman and Uspenskij as typical of a culture in which there is a dominant worldview that may be described as 'mythological', as opposed to 'historical-discrete'. In such a culture,

When some object occurs in a new place, it may lose the connection with its previous state and become *another* object (in some cases this may correspond with a change of names). This explains the characteristic ability of mythological space to model *other,* non-spatial relations (semantic or axiological, among others).

(Lotman and Uspenskij 1973: 288)

Russian medieval culture (from the eleventh to the seventeenth century) retained important features of this worldview, especially in its organization of space (Lotman 1965), but also in some ideological particularities (Lotman and Uspenskij 1977: 4-5; cf. Lotman and Uspenskij 1977.2). Important mechanisms were still active in the lower cultural strata in the nineteenth century.

The second notion reflects the basic traits that are ascribed in Russian traditional culture to a figure standing outside the collective, the Old Russian outcast. . . .

The Old Russian outcast as a socio-psychological phenomenon has been described by Lotman and Uspenskij (1982). Here also, Old Russian culture retained characteristics of the mythic cultural stage, in which mastering some kind of special knowledge was regarded as sorcery, and as such was considered dangerous, "a force that disturbs the social equilibrium and that contains a potential threat for the established order" (Lotman and Uspenskij 1982: 111). This special knowledge was nevertheless felt to be indispensable to society. Therefore, any 'learned' persons, such as doctors, horse-doctors, smiths or, for that matter, clergymen, could be regarded as dangerous, as enemies or intruders. Conversely, the power of sorcery could be ascribed to strangers, for instance, to foreigners, Cossacks or robbers. Old Russian culture retained an ambiguous attitude towards all persons who in one way or another were outsiders to society. It is true that foreigners as well as persons who were masters of a special field of knowledge were regarded as enemies, but they were also treated with a certain respect mixed with fear. It is the complex attitude towards this class of persons that, according to Lotman, influenced the image of the protagonist-outsider in Russian nineteenth-century literature. His and B. A. Uspenskij's article on the outcast in Russian culture was originally meant as an introduction to a wider investigation into the cultural position of the 'intelligentsia' in Russian culture of the modern period[33]. In forming its own self-image, the intelligentsia, at first the cultured nobility, later in the nineteenth century the educated elite in general, adopted many of the semantic categories with which in Old Russian culture the outcast had been endowed. This image in its turn was reflected in the image of the protagonist in Russian literature. Central here is the dichotomy 'saviour/ undoer'.

Of course, this 'reflection' of the image of the outcast should not be understood as the more or less conscious

shaping of a literary character after the model of some Old Russian outcast type. For traditional notions connected with the outcast are stored in deep layers of the cultural memory; they can be seen as a remote . . . cultural context, defined by Smirnov as:

semantic norms of speech, consolidated in daily practice, that are in one way or another assimilated . . . by an author; they determine the intrinsic possibilities of the development of the events in the work, which are either activated or suppressed with the help of external stimuli (biographical and social); (. . .) a semantic norm, that covers the whole range of texts that are objectively commensurable in content. . . .

(Smirnov 1981: 118[34])

For Lotman, as we have seen, the main differential quality of Russian narrative prose as against its West European counterpart was its concentration on the main character, whose surroundings or whose personality were changed, while western literature concentrated on changing that character's position in life. Whether a saviour or an undoer, such a character embodied the idea that human actions could effect qualitative changes in human existence. In Turgenev's prose, this idea is forcefully denied, as we have seen. In this, however, his prose is deeply concerned with questions specific to Russian literature. The worldview it expresses should be seen in its fundamental interaction with that literature:

Turgenev's novels and stories played a demythologizing, sobering role in Russian literature of the nineteenth century. For that very reason it seemed that they fell outside the general structure of the 'Russian novel'. It was easy to conceive of them as novels of 'failure', that is, to regard them as the negative realization of the European model. Of course, this meant distorting the genuine Turgenevian structure, the essence of which lies not in the success or the failure of the hero's career, but in the meaningfulness or meaninglessness of his existence.

(Lotman 1986: 18-19)

The failure of the hero to give meaning to his life, to find a meaningful activity, then, can be seen as a dialogically shaped *denial* of a tendency in another branch of Russian literature. Turgenev's failed heroes are invariably depicted as transgressing the boundary that is for others impossible to transgress, or as 'coming from the outside', as we have seen. But Turgenev denies them the aura of saviour or undoer, that surrounded such characters in the works of that other branch.

Notes

1. Among them Turgenev himself, who wrote to Paul Heyse on March 21 (April 2), 1874: "es geschieht Ihnen wie mir: wir beide schreiben keine Romane, nur verlängerte Novellen" (Pis'ma X: 215).

2. Full-length landmark studies are, for example, Ledkovskij 1973, Kagan-Kans 1975, Peterson 1975, Costlow 1990, Allen 1992; some important essay-length studies are Fischler 1976, Thiergen 1978 and 1989, Børtnes 1984, Clayton 1984 and Masing-Delic 1985. But the list could be extended considerably.

3. "полно тебе писать *быстрые* повести с романтическими переходами—это хорошо для поэмы байронической." [You've written enough of those *fast* stories with Romantic tossings—that befits Byronic poems; Puškin X: 115].

4. In all quotations from Turgenev's works, Roman numerals indicate the volume of the second Academy edition of the *Полное собрание сочинений* (see References under Turgenev), Arabic numerals the page number.

5. cf. "every single entity regards itself as the centre of the universe, turns everything it is surrounded by into something that can be used"; quoted above.

6. A very special variant in *Notes of a Hunter* is the detached position of the narrator as a *hunter,* a figure between two worlds—see Chapter 3.

7. More or less the same position is taken by the main character of *Smoke,* which shows the importance of the device not only for the stories and not only for the I-narration.

8. This conflict can be dated back to the classical opposition 'vita activa' as opposed to 'vita contemplativa', stemming from Plutarch; Turgenev can nowhere be seen to give preference to either side: he is not inclined to particularly admire public activity, be it in the field of commerce or in civil or military service; nor does he take refuge in the comforts of idyll, as is admirably shown by Costlow: 55-82.

9. The Russian has . . . (heroic novel), but Pumpjanskij makes it clear that 'heroic' is meant not in the laudatory, but in the formal or technical sense, which is why I prefer to translate 'of character'. Some ten years later, Pumpjanskij gave a variation on this qualification, comparing Turgenev's novels with those of George Sand: both are "personal novels about culture" (Pumpjanskij 1940: 92). I agree with Costlow, who, having quoted the second passage, argues that for Turgenev, the 'Sandian' type of novel forms a contrast with the novels à la Dumas, with their "complex, melodramatic plotting", as he himself indicated in his review of Evgenija Tur's novel *The Niece* (1851) (Costlow: 11). Thus she concludes that "Turgenev elaborates a novelistic form that depends less on the complexities of plot than on the revelations of conversation" (idem: 12). She then proceeds to interpret *Rudin* as "a novel *about* talk" (idem; Costlow's italics). To my mind, such an interpretation tends to reduce too strongly to one aspect the total complex of social relations around which the novel is built.

10. Nevertheless, metaphorical elements may appear in these descriptions, as in the comparison of Kostja's face with a squirrel's (III: 92). Such comparisons are not rare and show a certain recurrent pattern. Though they may not denote a supernatural sphere, as the leitmotivic details do in the later stories—among them comparisons of details of outward appearance with animals (see Koschmal: passim)—they nonetheless tend to form an intertextual pattern (see the remark on Kostja and Kalinyč in Chapter 4). Perhaps Turgenev shows a certain 'system' in the animal-comparisons, and it would be interesting to investigate how far that system is indebted to the classification of human faces according to a resemblance with certain animals that was introduced by Lavater. In any case, the method of comparison with animals is based on a metaphorical principle.

11. One could say that 'meaning' is a *tertium comparationis* between a character and his life: speaking of the meaning of a character's life is applying a metaphor.

12. Note the present perfect tense, that projects the 'exotopic' position of the judging perspective into a temporal post hoc.

13. Cf. my analysis of *The Dog* in chapter 7.

14. Indeed, it is to be expected that for a thinker as close to Symbolism as Geršenzon, the Don Quixote type, the 'Schwärmer' and idealist, would be more to his own personal taste.

15. In the years 1840-1850, Turgenev still cherished slight hopes that moderate, 'enlightened', practical landowners, like Ležnev (*Rudin*) or Lavreckij (*A Nest of the Gentry*) might perhaps bring about lasting positive changes at least to the deplorable state of the Russian rural economy, and enlighten the burden of the peasants (see Thiergen 1989, Kurljandskaja 1980: 64-5, and my remarks in chapter 5). But Lavreckij fails, too, and no positive expectations remain.

16. We have already had the opportunity to connect this with the main direction taken by the rendering of the characters in themselves, i.e. to show the mutual interdependence of antithetical qualities: consciousness and deeper understanding of the world are accompanied by a weakening of the volitional faculty.

17. In Hansen-Löve 1984 and Schmid 1991: 72-74 the short story is described as a genre especially

suited to the interweaving of 'verbal art' mechanisms with 'narrative art' mechanisms.

18. Besides "philosophical", Pumpjanskij calls Turgenev's orchestration "elegiac" (ibidem). The elegiac orchestration may occasionally develop into direct, explicit narrator's reflections of the type described by Pumpjanskij thus: "The image of life, built by youth, is arbitrary; only old age sees life as it really is, in all its emptiness and horror. (. . .) Until the threshold of death, until old age, man lives barred from the truth; in other words, life is a chain of perceptional illusions!" (Pumpjanskij 1929.2: 10). We recognize in this passage the traits of the author's worldview, as it connects with the narrator's position, that we have treated before.

19. For the theme of nature, I refer the reader to Chapters 3 (on the *Notes of a Hunter*), 4 (on *Bežin Meadow*) and 6 (on *A Journey into Poles'e*).

20. I use the term 'narration' here as a translation of Lotman's Russian 'sjužet' in order to remain consistent with the terminology proposed in section 1.7. I do not consider, however, that Lotman here means the Formalist 'narration' as opposed to 'story'. What he means is a type of text that relates narrative events, which are themselves defined as transgressions of a (semantic) boundary.

21. "the mobile personage differs from the immobile in that he is permitted to perform certain actions that are forbidden to others (. . .). The right to some special behaviour (heroic, immoral, moral, insane, unpredictable, peculiar; but always independent of the circumstances that compulsively restrict the immobile personages) is shown by a long series of literary heroes" (Lotman 1970: 295). Characters, in Lotman's conception, are defined with respect to the function they have in the plot. It is clear that we are interested in broader aspects of character. I shall therefore use Lotman's otherwise very fruitful concept only insofar as it is of use for the analysis of peculiarities of plot in Turgenev's work, and will not discuss its merits or its possible shortcomings in themselves.

22. As a matter of fact, this recurrent structure had been described as early as 1919 by V. Gippius (see Gippius 1919/1989).

23. I hope that the reader will agree that this is more than just a play on words. The fact that Černyševskij in his famous review of *Asja,* called *A Russian man at a rendez-vous,* interpreted the amorous failure of its hero without much difficulty as a sign of his social failure, indicates how closely the amorous and the social test of Turgenev's protagonists were interrelated for the reading public.

24. In my view, the term 'novel' may here be taken to denote more than the novel in its narrow sense, viz. any narrative work in the period when literature had become 'novelized' (the term is Bachtin's). Russian nineteenth-century literature from Puškin and Gogol' on can be called 'novelized'. It is based on the hybridization and stylization of various genres, the extra-literary diversity of speech plays an essential role in it; the literary image is constructed "in maximal contact with the present, that is felt as uncompleted" (Bachtin 1975: 455). In this respect, the main development of Russian literature does not differ from that of European literature in general, a development which Bachtin described as a process of emancipation of the personages' speech from the authors'. This is connected with a growing 'self-consciousness', a growing awareness of the conventionality of language.

25. Lotman had already pointed to this phenomenon in connection with the theme of cards in Puškin's work (Lotman 1975: 120).

26. "the dialogical structure does not belong exclusively to the novels of Dostoevskij, but it rather is a quality of the novel-form as such. One could even extend the scope further and say: of certain types of artistic texts" (Lotman 1973: 29).

27. For an investigation into the transformation of this image from myth through folklore and early modern West European literature (Shakespeare, Calderón) to late Romanticism (Lermontov), see Frejdenberg 1987.

28. It can be noted that in working thus, Turgenev follows the tradition of classifying types of characters into oppositional pairs that is known from European Romanticism. In itself, it may be traced back to Schiller's well-known distinction of the 'naïve' and the 'sentimental' type (for other variants, see Potthoff: 139). Turgenev's own variant is best expressed in his 'Hamlet' versus 'Don Quixote' dichotomy.

29. Stender-Petersen also finds that classification and schematization predominate in the works of Gončarov (Stender-Petersen: 228).

30. Whether historically the same mistrust lies at the root of the ambivalence in Western Romanticism remains an open question. We should probably think that in the given period it was more pronouncedly (rather than exclusively) the case in Russia than in Western Europe.

31. Nevertheless, this type of plot can clearly be traced back to the Christian *vita* and even to pre-Christian 'metamorphosis' literature (Apuleius, Ovidius).

On the other hand, some, not unimportant, off-shoots in twentieth-century Russian prose can be found.

32. As regards the actions of such a character, Lotman notes that they may constitute a transformation of the traditional love-scheme:

> The function of the female personage 'to be undone' or 'to be redeemed' may be given to 'the world', to Russia, while the active personage assumes the masculine *emploi*—as is the case in Blok's *My Russia, my wife* . . . and Pasternak's *Life—my sister* . . . seen through the prism of Hamlet's 'Ophelia—sister—lover'.

(Lotman 1986: 12)

Cf.:

> The combination of the image of the robber with the motif of being in love is an exceptionally stable one.

(Lotman 1979: 34)

Compare, too, the entanglement of the 'social' and the 'amorous' plot lines in Turgenev's novels, mentioned above.

33. Information of B. A. Uspenskij, Moscow.

34. Approximately the same definition had already been given in Smirnov 1978: 187, but in Smirnov 1981 I find the wording more felicitous.

List of abbreviations

GPI—Gosudarstvennyj pedagogičeskij institut

GU—Gosudarstvennyj universitet

MAE—Muzej antropologii i ètnografii

SPR—Slavistic Printings and Reprintings

SSLP—Studies in Slavic Literature and Poetics

TZS—Trudy po znakovym sistemam

UP—University Press

UZ—Učenye zapiski

WSA—Wiener slawistischer Almanach

References

Aksakov, S. T., *Sobranie sočinenij* v 5-i tomach. Moskva, 1966.

Allen, E. Ch., *Beyond Realism.* Turgenev's Poetics of Secular Salvation. Stanford, Ca.: Stanford UP, 1992.

Azadovskij, M. K., 'Pevcy' I. S. Turgeneva, in: M.K.A., *Stat'i o literature i fol'klore.* Moskva-Leningrad: 395-437, 1960.

Bachtin, M. M., *Voprosy literatury i èstetiki.* Moskva, 1975.

Børtnes, Jostein, The Poetry of Prose—the Art of Parallelism in Turgenev's 'Otcy i deti', in: *Scando-Slavica* 30, 1984: 31-55.

Brang, Peter, *Studien zu Theorie und Praxis der Russischen Erzählung 1770-1811.* Wiesbaden: Otto Harrassowitz, 1960.

———, *I. S. Turgenev.* Sein Leben und sein Werk. Wiesbaden: Otto Harrassowitz, 1977.

Costlow, Jane T., *Worlds within Worlds.* The novels of Ivan Turgenev. Princeton, New Jersey, Princeton UP, 1990.

Clayton, J. Douglas, Night and Wind: Images and Allusions as the Source of the Poetic in Turgenev's 'Rudin', in: *Canadian Slavonic,* 1984.

———, *Papers/Revue Canadienne des Slavistes* Vol.XXVI, No.1 (March), 1984: 10-14.

Droblenkova, N. F., 'Zivye mošči': žitijnaja tradicija i 'legenda' o Žanne D'Ark v rasskaze Turgeneva, in: *Turgenevskij sbornik* V: 289-302, 1969.

Ėjchenbaum, B. M., The Sportsman's sketches. An introductory essay, in: *Canadian-American Slavic Studies* 17, no. 1, 1983: 7-12. (Translation of 'Vstupitel'nyj očerk' in: I. S. Turgenev, 'Zapiski ochotnika'. Petrograd 1918).

Fischler, Alexander, The Garden Motif and the Structure of Turgenev's 'Fathers and Sons', in: *Novel, a Forum on Fiction* 9, Spring 1976: 243-255.

Frejdenberg, O. M., Metodologija odnogo motiva, in: *TZS* 20 (UZ Tartuskogo GU 746), 1987: 120-130.

Garber, Frederick, Self, Society, Value, and the Romantic Hero, in: *Comparative Literature* 19, 1967: 321-333.

Grübel, R. G., Narrative Aisthesis der 'Ersten Liebe': Erinnerung vs. Wiederholung. Zur Topik und Intertextualität der Erzählung 'Pervaja ljubov'' von Turgenev und 'Vymysel' von Gippius, in: *Russkij Rasskaz*: 153-195, 1984.

Hansen-Löve, Aage A., Beobachtungen zur narrativen Kurzgattung, in: *Russkij Rasskaz*: 1-45, 1984.

Herzen, A. I. (A. I. Gercen), *Sobranie sočinenij* v 30-i tomach. Moskva, 1954-1965.

Hochman, Baruch, *Character in Literature.* Ithaca and London: Cornell UP, 1985.

Jakobson, R. O., Linguistics and Poetics, in: *Selected Writings* VI. The Hague: Mouton: 18-51, 1960/1971.

———, *Pushkin and his sculptural myth.* The Hague-Paris: Mouton, 1975.

————, Statuja v poetičeskoj mifologii Puškina, in id., *Raboty po poètike.* Moskva: 145-181, 1975a.

Kagan-Kans, Eva, *Hamlet and Don Quixote*: Turgenev's Ambivalent Vision. The Hague-Paris: Mouton (*SPR* 288), 1975.

Koschmal, Walter, *Vom Realismus zum Symbolismus.* Zu Genese und Morphologie der Symbolsprache in den späten Werken I. S. Turgenevs. Amsterdam: Rodopi (*SSLP* 5), 1984.

Kurljandskaja, G. B., *I. S. Turgenev i russkaja literatura.* Moskva, 1980.

Ledkovsky, Marina, *The Other Turgenev:* From Romanticism to Symbolism. Würzburg: jal-Verlag 1973 (Colloquium Slavicum-Beiträge zur Slavistik 2).

Lotman, Ju. M., O ponjatii geografičeskogo prostranstva v russkich srednevekovych tekstach, in: *TZS* 2, 1965 (UZ Tartuskogo GU 181): 210-216.

————, *Struktura chudožestvennogo teksta.* Moskva, 1970.

————, Proischoždenie sjužeta v tipologičeskom osveščenii, in: id., *Stat'i po tipologii kul'tury* (Materialy k kursu teorii literatury, vyp.2). Tartu: 9-41, 1973.

————, Povest' o kapitane Kopejkine (rekonstrukcija zamysla i idejno-kompozicionnaja funkcija), in: *TZS* 11, 1979 (UZ Tartuskogo GU 467): 26-44.

————, Proza Turgeneva i sjužetnoe prostranstvo russkogo romana XIX stoletija, in: *Slavica* (Debrecen) 23, 1986: 5-24.

————, O sjužetnom prostranstve russkogo romana XIX stoletija, in: *TZS* 20, 1987 (UZ Tartuskogo GU 746): 102-115.

Lotman, Ju. M., Meletinskij, E. M., Minc, Z. G., Literatura i mify, in: *Mify narodov mira* II: 58-65, 1988.

Lotman, Ju. M., Minc, Z. G., Literatura i mifologija, in: *TZS* 13, 1981 (UZ Tartuskogo GU 546): 35-56.

Lotman, Ju. M., Uspenskij, B. A., Mif—imja—kul'tura, in: *TZS* 6, 1973 (UZ Tartuskogo GU 308): 282-303.

————, Rol' dual'nych modelej v dinamike russkoj kul'tury (do konca XVIII veka), in: *UZ Tartuskogo GU* 414, 1977 (TRSF-L 28): 3-37.

————, Novye aspekty izučenija kul'tury drevnej Rusi, in: *Voprosy literatury* 3, 1977: 148-166, 1977.2.

————, Izgoj i izgojničestvo kak social'no-psichologič eskaja pozicija v russkoj kul'ture preimuščestvenno dopetrovskogo perioda ('svoe' i 'čužoe' v istorii russkoj kul'tury), in: *TZS* 15, 1982 (UZ Tartuskogo GU 576): 110-122.

Markovič, V. M, *Čelovek v romanach I. S. Turgeneva.* Leningrad, 1975.

Masing-Delic, Irene, Bazarov pered sfinksom. Naučnoe anatomirovanie i ėsteticeskaja forma v romane Turgeneva 'Otcy i deti', in: *Revue des Etudes Slaves* 57, 1985: 369-383.

Maslennikova, R. A., K voprosu o turgenevskom fol'klorizme, in: *Naučnye trudy Kurskogo GPI* 59 (152), 1976 (6-oj mežvuzovskij turgenevskij sbornik): 100-114.

Mudrick, Marvin, Character and Event in Fiction, in: *Yale Review* 50, 1961: 202-218.

Muratov, A. B., *Turgenev-novellist* (1870-1880-e gody). Leningrad, 1985.

Pahomov, George, Nature and the Use of Paradox in Turgenev, in: *Zapiski russkoj akademičeskoj gruppy v ŠA/Transactions of the Association of Russian-American Scholars in USA* 16, 1983: Turgenev Commemorative Volume 1818-1883, ed. by O. P. Ilyinsky, N. A. Natov, N. P. Poltoratzky a.o. New York: 47-56.

Peterson, Dale E., *The Clement Vision.* Poetic Realism in Turgenev and James. Port Washington, NY/London: National University Publications. Kennikat Press, 1975.

Pumpjanskij, L. V., *Dostoevskij i antičnost'.* Petrograd 1922/Bremen: Verlag K-Presse 1973 (Studien und Texte, No.1).

Romany Turgeneva i roman 'Nakanune', in: Turgenev I. S., *Sočinenija* T.6: 9-26, 1929.

Turgenev-novellist, in: Turgenev I. S., *Sočinenija* T.7: V-XXX, 1929.2.

Puškin, A. S., *Polnoe sobranie sočinenij* v 10-i tomach. Izd. 4-oe. Leningrad: Nauka 1977-1979.

Reed, Walter L., *Meditations on the Hero.* A Study of the Romantic Hero in Nineteenth-Century Fiction. New Haven and London: Yale UP 1974, 1974.

Šatalov, S. E., Prozrenie kak sredstvo psichologičeskogo analiza, in: *Čechov i Lev Tolstoj.* Red. L. D. Opul'skaja, Z. S. Papernyj, S. E. Šatalov. M.: 56-68, 1980.

Schmid, Wolf, *Puškins Prosa in poetischer Lektüre.* Die Erzählungen Belkins. München: Wilhelm Fink (Theorie und Geschichte der Literatur und der schönen Künste 82, NF Reihe A 4), 1991.

————, *Ornamentales Erzählen in der russischen Moderne.* Čechov-Babel'-Zamjatin. Frankfurt aM etc.: Peter Lang (Slavische Literaturen 2), 1992.

Silz, Walter, *Realism and Reality*: Studies in the German Novelle of Poetic Realism. (University of North Carolina Studies in the Germanic Languages and Literatures 11), 1954.

Smirnov, I. P., *Diachroničeskie transformacii literaturnych zanrov i motivov.* Wien (*WSA* Sonderband 4), 1981.

Stender-Petersen, Adolf, *Geschichte der Russischen Literatur.* München: Beck 1978[3], 1957/1978.

Thiergen, Peter, Aliis in Serviendo Consumor. Emblematische Symbolik und Bildsprache in I. S. Turgenevs 'Rudin' (Turgenev-Studien I), in: *Slavistische Studien zum VIII. internationalen Slavistenkongress in Zagreb 1978.* Hrsg. von J. Holthusen, W. Kasack und R. Olesch (Slavistische Forschungen 22). Köln-Wien: Böhlau: 509-520, 1978.

Lavreckij als 'potenzierter Bauer'. Zu Ideologie und Bildsprache in I. S. Turgenevs Roman 'Das Adelsnest'. München: Otto Sagner (Vorträge und Abhandlungen zur Slavistik 13), 1989.

Turgenev, I. S., I-VI: *Polnoe sobranie sočinenij i pisem* v 30-i tomach. Pis'ma v 18-i tomach. Izd. 2-oe, ispr. i dop. Moskva 1982-1989 (on continuation). VII-XIII: *Polnoe sobranie sočinenij i pisem* v 28-i tomach. Pis'ma v 13-i tomach. Moskva-Leningrad, 1961-1968.

———, *Polnoe sobranie sočinenij i pisem* v 30-i tomach. Sočinenija v 12-i tomach. Izd. 2-oe, ispr. i dop. Moskva 1978-1986.

———, *Sočinenija.* Pod red. K. Chalabaeva i B. Ėjchenbauma. V 12-i tomax. Moskva-Leningrad 1928-1934.

Zel'dcheji-Deak, Z., 'Tainstvennye povesti' Turgeneva i russkaja literatura XIX veka, in: *Studia Slavica Hung.* XIX, fasc.1-3, 1973: 347-364.

Jane Costlow (essay date 1996)

SOURCE: Costlow, Jane. "Abusing the Erotic: Women in Turgenev's 'First Love.'" In *Engendering Slavic Literatures,* edited by Pamela Chester and Sibelan Forrester, pp. 3-12. Bloomington, Ind.: Indiana University Press, 1996.

[*In the following essay, Costlow examines gender and power relations in Turgenev's novella* First Love.]

At the midpoint of his novella of doomed infatuation—a work acclaimed as its author's most "enchanting and brilliant story"[1]—Turgenev dramatizes the initiation into sexual knowledge that is the story's central concern. Vladimir, the story's hero, clambers onto a garden wall only to leap down at the command of his beloved Zinaida. "You keep insisting that you love me," she says. "Jump down to me on the road, if you truly love me."[2] Zinaida's word is Vladimir's command, and in the next instant the boy lies stunned and briefly unconscious on the ground. Vladimir's leap enacts the identification of sexual coming-to-knowledge with a "fall," an identification central to Judeo-Christian culture. But Vladimir's "fall" is immediately followed by a loss of consciousness, however brief. It is in this moment of lost con-

sciousness—at first real, and then feigned—that Turgenev's story shifts for a moment into a kind of blessedness, evoking everything that is lost in the larger world of the novella. Zinaida leans over the boy, addressing him for the only time in the story with the intimate "thou" (*ty*) and covering him with tender kisses. "'My dear little boy,' she said, leaning over me, and anxious tenderness sounded in her voice, 'how could you do that, how could you heed me . . . I love you . . . stand up'" (45). To address Vladimir as a little boy and cover him with gentle kisses is to bestow on him a kind of maternal concern in which tenderness and eroticism are conjoined. To speak words of love and an injunction to stand is to bring the boy back to life in a gesture not unlike a mother's toward her vulnerable child. Zinaida is hardly "maternal" in the larger story, nor does it seem that Vladimir wants from her a mother's affection. Nonetheless, *First Love* is in large part a story of a boy's education in what it means to desire. "Know how to desire," his father tells him, "and you will be free; you will command" (31). What happens in Vladimir's "fortunate fall" is a blissful escape from the violent desires of the rest of this story, an evocation of attention and connection that is gentle, tactile, loving. It is an intimation of the obverse of the world Vladimir comes to *see*—and finally to *know*: a world in which Eros is the child less of Aphrodite than of Ares, a world marked by sadistic ritual, imposing will, and a voyeuristic eye.

"The touch," Madeleine Grumet reminds us, "is older than the look."[3] We enter the world with imperfect sight and unfocused vision; we are bound to others and to life itself by touch, taste, and sound. Our eyes mature as organs of sensation only gradually, and as vehicles of knowledge and love they are at first inseparable from the patterns of touch that encircle our vulnerable bodies. To say this is perhaps to imagine origin in a way that flirts with nostalgia and romance: we are reminded of Freud's "oceanic bliss" and Kristeva's "semiotic," idealized imaginings that feminist critics have cautioned us from accepting too easily.[4] I evoke an initial state marked not by vision but by touch—and a childhood marked by vision intertwined with the other senses—not for nostalgic purposes, however, but to suggest adult alternatives to a world of spectacle and violence. *First Love* narrates the passage to knowledge as a journey of sight: what the boy sees is a woman's body—alluring, statuesque, abused. The tale Turgenev tells is a narrative of eros and the eye; of a boy's accession to the world of his father, in which desire—and "love"—will be structured as a spectacle of objectified violence. After the final revelation of desire and bodily harm—when Vladimir sees his father strike Zinaida, and Zinaida kisses the wound—the boy will profess his love for his father, his willingness, presumably, to endorse what he has overseen. But we can, I think, interrogate Vladimir's journey to knowledge and "maturity," the way his story positions woman as both fetish and mime, the inevitability of *this* vision of love. When Vladimir falls into unconsciousness and the bliss of Zinaida's tenderness, he falls into sightlessness—his eyes are closed. Does Turgenev intimate, in this moment, a place of relationship *outside* the voyeuristic contract of objectification and will? Can we see something other than bodies abused in this tale of first "love"? Can we find a kind of attention that does not reinscribe paternal law, the myth of violent will as the only path to pleasure and connection? Finally, can a woman close her eyes and remember a kind of touch that precedes, and precludes, violence?

Turgenev's story of love is obsessed with seeing. Vladimir's sentimental education is staged (quite literally) as a series of moments in which he *watches,* is transfixed, and does not understand. The story's tension is to a great extent predicated on this disjunction of knowledge and sight; "maturity" comes when understanding catches up with vision, and Vladimir finds language for what he sees: "That's what love is . . . that is passion." These are the boy's simple predicates of fact, once he has seen his father strike Zinaida. Before Vladimir can name what he sees, though, he watches with a precarious innocence. He watches a cluster of men being struck by a woman with "explosive" flowers (11); he watches as Zinaida uses one of her admirers as a pedestal to her statue-like body (26); he watches as she sticks a pin into another's finger (33-34); he watches unperceived as Zinaida reads a book (21); again unperceived, he spies on his father's nocturnal visits to the wings of the house that Zinaida and her mother rent (60-61). One of Zinaida's admirers is named Belovzorov[5]—but if there is any innocent eye in this tale, it can only be Vladimir's, for even when he himself enters the stage of debauch, it is as one who does not understand what he does. Lushin, the doctor, and the one of Zinaida's admirers who figures as a kind of moral mentor for Vladimir, is alone in urging him to an awakening of sight: "Now then, young man . . . how can you, as bright as you are, not see what's going on around you?" (39).

The novella positions Vladimir as an equivocal observer—not wholly removed, because he comes to participate in (and to enjoy) Zinaida's erotic games; and neither innocent nor damned—because, as Zinaida suggests, there is as yet "no law written for him," since "Monsieur Voldemar is with us for the first time" (24). The position Vladimir occupies vis-à-vis the world of "mature" passion and games is made quite explicit in the story's first scene of watching.[6] The boy sets out on his customary garden walk, but is suddenly stunned (the Russian, *okamenel,* reverberates with petrification, turning to stone) by what the narrator calls a "strange sight" (*strannoe zrelishche*). Several steps from where he stands, Vladimir sees a "tall, shapely girl" sur-

rounded by four men; "she hit each of them in turn on the forehead with those small gray flowers whose name I don't know, but which are well known to children: these flowers form small baglets and break with a crack when you strike them against something hard" (11). The sight of this odd ritual sparks in Vladimir the desire to be included in its apparently gentle violence: "[I] would have given everything on earth just to have those charming fingers hit me on the forehead, too" (11). He is "unmanned" as the gun he carries falls to the ground, and he surrenders to the synesthesia of desire as he consumes with his gaze (*pozhiral vzorom*) the neck, arms, hair, eyes, lashes, and cheek of this striking woman. Vladimir's voyeuristic pleasure is interrupted, however, by "someone's voice," whose abrupt scolding shifts the boy from the position of the one watching to the one watched. "'Young man, oh young man'— someone's voice suddenly said near me—'surely it's not permitted to stare like that at other people's young ladies?'" (11) The desirous gaze is checked by the voice of prohibition and propriety; Vladimir's trance ends as he is caught in the play of two glances—for at the sound of the reprimanding voice, Zinaida turns her eyes on the boy who had been watching her.[7] Vladimir is poised between the "ironic" gaze of the doctor who had scolded him, and the "huge gray eyes" of the girl, positioned both literally and symbolically between shame and pleasure—between *styd* (as the narrator puts it) and *veselost*.' "I was very ashamed and very happy" (11).

This brief passage captures—as spectacle, *zrelishche*— the complex gestures, relationships, and allegiances that drive Turgenev's story. The boy watches Zinaida engaged in erotic play, but he is in turn watched by Lushin, a kind of good father in a story that more explicitly casts paternity as distance, unconcern, and will (*volia*). The flowers that serve as weapons are marked, curiously, as "unnamed"—the first emblems of anominalism in a text that flirts with what can be said and what can't. The scene is lushly erotic, as is the whole text, but it is an eroticism of violence, spectacle, control.[8] And finally, the woman's body stands as a monument of power, but it transpires that she is already possessed—she is, as Lushin says, *chuzhaia,* someone else's goods. To call her this is to insist not merely on propriety but on property: Lushin functions in this scene as a voice of shame, but one grounded in ownership more than morality. Someone *owns* Zinaida, and the desire she seems to represent is not in truth her own.

What Turgenev tells us here is a version of what Hélène Cixous has called "the first story in the world,"[9] the story of desire, transgression, and knowledge we find in Genesis. The biblical tale, we remember, hinges on eating, sight, and the voice of an angry God; as in Genesis, Vladimir is wrenched from a delicious knowledge by an as yet disembodied voice that calls him to shame and renunciation. Turgenev's garden story is not yet ready, however, to resolve in death and exile from pleasure—that will come later. Its initial impulse is to remain poised between shame and pleasure, *before* the fall, holding onto a kind of knowledge not predicated on refusal. Vladimir wants Zinaida, and has not yet submitted to the words of prohibition that will be his father's law. The father's law—the law of will and power, of supreme egotism, but also a law that insists on its prior rights to the object of the son's affections—will be irrevocably instated only at the story's end, when Vladimir once more watches a "game" of violence and submission. But in that "game" the perpetrator will be his father, and Zinaida will kiss the wound left on her flesh by her lover's whip. "That's what love is . . . that is passion," the story insists—and we are meant, I think, to agree.

I want at this point to pose quite explicitly the issues raised by *First Love,* for if the story is Turgenev's "most enchanting," then we need to be quite clear about how this tale attempts to charm. The story is constructed of sexuality, violence, and voyeuristic pleasures—and returns to moments of erotic "play" that involve games of dominance and pain. Stated thus, Turgenev's enchanting story seems perilously to partake of the pornographic imagination—the line between eroticism and pornography being fluid at best, and deeply contextual. Turgenev is not someone we normally associate with pornography; his own inclination was to link the French master of the pornographic—the Marquis de Sade—with Dostoevsky.[10] In his more muted way, however, Turgenev equals Dostoevsky in this narrative's givenness to cruelty, and in its construction of the beloved woman's body as itself a kind of fetishized implement of pain.

The moment of cruelly inflicted pain that is revelatory for Vladimir comes at the story's end, when his father strikes Zinaida with his whip—but prior to that, the instruments of torture are mostly Zinaida's: we see her first, as I've noted, hitting her admirers on the forehead; she strikes Vladimir on his fingers when they're bound with wool she's winding (17); as Vladimir kisses her fingers he's scratched by her nails (26); Zinaida sticks a pin in the doctor's hand (33-34); Zinaida speaks of her amusements as "striking people against each other" (33); her surname, Zasekina, alludes to the verb *zasech'*, to flog to death. What such repetitions accomplish is an association of Zinaida and eroticized violence, an association in which Zinaida plays the active role—plays, if you will, the role of sadist to the cluster of masochistic males in her entourage. The role she plays is the one that *seems* to embody power and will; it is Zinaida, we remember, who calls the shots and directs the action in the raucous evening of play that introduces Vladimir to the fallen house of the Zasekin family—the fallen world of eros and flogging. In this sense, Vladimir's first vision of Zinaida is exemplary, for it frames her as powerful and controlling, and creates of her body an icon of will and strength. The older narrator twice returns to the woman's "slender body" that causes his own weapon to fall: "my weapon slipped down onto the grass" (11). If Zinaida sometimes uses implements—flowers, a pin—to inflict pain, what strikes Vladimir and brings him to submission in this first encounter is the body itself, represented as a slender tower of erotic force.

I want to turn for a moment to the work of feminist film critics—in particular, to an essay by E. Ann Kaplan—in order to understand just what it is we're looking at in this "enchanting" story. Grounding her work in psychoanalytic understandings of the film process, which assume that film mimics the processes of the unconscious, Kaplan looks carefully at the formal ways in which the camera structures what we see on the screen. Women on screen are the objects of several gazes—the gaze of the camera/director, of other men within the filmic space, of an imaginary viewer in a potential audience. Central to Kaplan's argument is the notion that these gazes are predominantly, perhaps inevitably, male, and that the effect of the male gaze is to objectify the woman's body, more precisely to fetishize that body—that is, to render it phallus-like, long and slender, thus mitigating male dread of a wholly different women's sexuality.[11] Women on camera, Kaplan argues, are objects seen by men, viewed as available for male desire, as potentially submissive to male will: "Men," Kaplan reminds us, "do not simply look; their gaze carries with it the power of action and of possession that is lacking in the female gaze" (311). Sight, even the look of love, is linked to a world of power that frames even seemingly idyllic romance; in Zinaida's world, even the carnivalesque world of her erotic evenings is framed by a powerful (male) presence beyond those walls.

To return to Turgenev: One does not have to accept the global validity of Kaplan's argument to acknowledge that a story such as *First Love* constructs moments of seeing that conform to those the film critic analyzes. The male gazes upon the slender body of a woman, a dynamic that Turgenev calls attention to when he "lays bare" the frames that contain this voyeuristic moment: Vladimir watches Zinaida, but then Lushin watches Vladimir, and of course the fireside compatriots of the older Vladimir "watch" it all, via the mechanism of his carefully crafted text.[12] What is left open in this discussion, though, is the issue of power and gender—for Vladimir, at least at first, seems *not* to have the power which Kaplan insists is crucial to the male gaze; that power (the power to impose will and derive pleasure) circulates in the story between a gendered, older pair. It seems to shift from Zinaida (powerful in the story's first half, submissive at its ending) to Vladimir's father (elusive at first, revealed finally as the instrument of will and arbiter of fate). What I want to suggest, however, is that that circulation of power is in fact illusory—that power in this story is never Zinaida's—and that the only moment in the story that is truly hers (the moment of sightlessness I opened with) returns us to the complexity of sexuality, power, and pain for Turgenev. It may also return us to the world of politics beyond love.

It is too banal to say it, but it needs to be said: There is no "real" woman here, just a figure that represents projected male desire, Zinaida as the wish fulfillment of Vladimir/Turgenev.[13] When Vladimir's father strikes Zinaida at story's end, his gesture is conclusive in a way that none of Zinaida's ever are, because he holds power in the world, because he's a man, older, richer. The structure of Turgenev's story builds toward this crucial, climactic moment, giving to this final vision an epistemological and linguistic power ("That's what love is . . . that is passion") that Zinaida's gestures do not have. The law of this father is control: the whip is an instrument of will, just as his carefully meted gestures toward his son act both to distance and to bind filial affection.[14] Lushin, I've suggested, is the story's other father—kinder, seemingly more concerned for Vladimir's moral and emotional education. It is no accident, then, that this father is present at Vladimir's first vision of Zinaida, for he reminds us that this whole transaction takes place within the world of the fathers: Zinaida's games merely mime the gestures of the truly powerful. If, as Luce Irigaray has suggested, mimesis can become for women a form of parodic and liberating repetition, Zinaida's acting out of power knows no liberatory moment.[15] Both Zinaida and Vladimir will ultimately have to submit to a patriarchy grounded in will, cruelty, and shame. Indeed, Lushin's ethos of shame seems inextricably linked to the ethics of will that Vladimir's father expounds. Vladimir stands briefly poised between Lushin's "shame" and Zinaida's apparent offer of pleasure: what intervenes is Vladimir's father, who reveals possession of Zinaida by striking her. What links shame and will is the woman: Zinaida elicits shame as she evokes vulnerable sexuality; the father's will emerges as an impulse of denial and control.[16]

To grow older, this story suggests, is to have one's eyes opened; to find a language for spectacles of cruelty; to acquiesce in the dynamic of will that is desire. "Know how to desire," says Vladimir's father, "and you will be free, you will command" (31). Even if Vladimir will never become his father, the story accepts the father's definition of love and of the world. Eros is imprisoned by spectacle and violence, and there seems no way to imagine anything else.[17]

Except for that moment of sightlessness, the moment of Vladimir's "fall" and Zinaida's tender kisses, a moment that seems to escape the objectification and violence of the rest of the story precisely *because* the boy closes

his eyes, as though only the elision of this adolescent gaze enables the woman to initiate a different kind of relationship—one that aborts the provocative gaming of so much of the story. I suggested in opening that Zinaida functions in this moment as a kind of maternal presence, and Vladimir as a not-yet-seeing, not-yet-upright child. In a larger, more literal sense, mothers seem quite absent from this story: both Vladimir's and Zinaida's mothers lurk as mildly grotesque figures, the first obsessed with propriety and her husband's infidelities, the second an illiterate impoverished princess incapable of regulating her daughter's wild ways. The only other mother in the story—we realize with some surprise—is Zinaida herself, who dies only days after childbirth (74).[18] This explicit association of mothers with the grotesque—and with death—is not unimportant; but I want to suggest that there is a larger sense in which the mother is present in this patriarchal story. The mother who is present is Turgenev's own—Varvara Petrovna Lutovinova; Zinaida is, in a sense, her progeny—if not Varvara herself.

Turgenev readily acknowledged a powerful autobiographical element in *First Love,* but he emphasized in this regard the portrait of his father: "In *First Love* . . . I depicted my father. Many have reproached me for that, and in particular reproached me for not hiding it. But I think there's nothing harmful in it. There's nothing for me to hide."[19] Turgenev's mother is absent from this account; what Turgenev "hides," though, is the genesis of his knowledge of love and pain. As April Fitzlyon reminds us, "From childhood [Turgenev] was accustomed to the idea that women could hold power and exercise it. . . . he was also accustomed to the idea that women could be cruel."[20] Varvara Lutovinova, by all accounts, was a woman of enormous capacity for cruelty, a landowner who was capricious and unsparing in her willingness to inflict pain, both emotional and physical.[21] She stands, in fact, as a kind of mythic, archetypal monster of serfdom, as the vehicle of the horrors her son was to work to abolish with his writing. Can we not imagine Turgenev's artistic work as a kind of slaying of this dragon, a battle not only with Bloomian male precursors, but with the specter of his mother, the embodiment of a cruel order and manipulative love? Are Zinaida's erotic games—her willingness to inflict physical pain and emotional anguish—not modeled on the tortures his mother inflicted? If voyeurism, for Freud, was a revisitation of a primal scene, framed in later life by the voyeur's more controlling vision, perhaps Vladimir/Turgenev's voyeuristic visitations of Zinaida's cruelties aim at controlling and expunging the terrible recognition of maternal violence. For if the textual Zinaida is implicated in a patriarchal dynamic of eros as hostility, the historical Varvara played out her role as the cruel weapon of an unjust regime. There is no place in Turgenev's biography for the nostalgic imagination of the mother, as there is, say, in Tolstoy's:

Turgenev's mother is cruel and distant, as enamored of violence as the fictional father who ultimately strikes his beloved. The deaths that close *First Love*—Zinaida's own, and the death of the unknown pauper—function perhaps as a kind of narrative retribution, punishing the mothers for not escaping the cruelty and shame of the world. The child (in all of us) would like to imagine something better.

The moment of sightlessness, of Vladimir's fall, still functions, to my mind, as a utopian figure in Turgenev's story, but as an allusion to gentleness and love that have no correlates, in either Turgenev's life or text. To be utopian is to be nowhere, but such a moment is important in its potential to pull us beyond the voyeuristic logic that seems so inevitable in this story and in the world. The father's equation of desire with command, his insistence that will (*volia*) is the greatest good, articulates a truth of our world as of Turgenev's. "What is sexually exciting in Western culture," one recent analyst suggests, "is hostility, violence and domination, especially but not necessarily directed against women."[22] One of the projects of feminist thought—a project with which I identify in my reading of *First Love*—has been to name the reality and persistence of hostility as sexuality, but to move beyond that articulation toward an imagination and enunciation that might bespeak a different kind of eros.[23] To imagine such eros is to desire a different kind of relationship to the body and to physicality itself; to hope for knowledge that doesn't objectify; to imagine gazes that are mutual and attentive, rather than charged with hostility and the desire for power.[24] *First Love* imagines such eros only briefly, elliptically; its greatest energies and strengths lie in its articulation of a story about acquiescing to power. *First Love* is anchored in the world of men, a world which exchanges and objectifies women for its pleasure. Vladimir offers up visions of Zinaida for his companions' appreciation—just as Turgenev offers the story itself to his friend Annenkov.

To suggest some link between these two of Turgenev's women—between Zinaida and Varvara Lutovinova—is to suggest a link not only between biography and text, but between the erotic aggressions of intimate life and the violence of class and economic relations. The story of Zinaida and Vladimir and his father articulates the cruelties of eros; the story of Varvara Lutovinova and her serfs bespeaks the violence of unchecked economic power. There is, however, a more specific, textual, way in which that link is effected.

In *Spring Torrents,* another of Turgenev's narratives of love, the narrator proclaims that "First love is exactly like a revolution: the regular and established order of life is in an instant smashed to fragments; youth stands at the barricade, its bright banner raised high in the air, and sends its ecstatic greetings to the future, whatever it may hold—death or a new life, no matter." This rhetoric constructs an analogic relationship between love and politics that is more specifically embodied in *First Love*: the analogy in that story emerges more visually than rhetorically, and locates the connection between sexual and economic violence in the abuse of the body. At the very beginning of his memoir, the older Vladimir recalls how he stood and watched in the wallpaper factory that occupied one of the wings of his mother's estate. There were *two* wings on that estate: the other was rented by the Zasekin family. The scene Vladimir watches in the factory is, like the scene of Zinaida's games and like his father's striking of Zinaida, a scene of physical assault: "More than once I went there to watch as ten thin, disheveled boys in greasy coats, with haggard faces, jumped incessantly on wooden levers that clamped down on the press's square blocks, thus imprinting the bright wallpaper patterns with the weight of their frail bodies" (10). This moment of sociological *realia* might strike one as anomalous in this story that is so unconcerned with the political world, that seems to reach back to childhood in nostalgic flight from Russia "on the eve" of reform. *First Love* has in fact most frequently been read as standing apart from the more historically concerned novels of the period. But this vision of young boys' bodies jumping on levers and imprinting wallpaper is not anomalous, I would suggest. These boys "jump," as Vladimir will for Zinaida, but they jump for masters' economic gain, rather than to fulfill a romantic ritual. Just as Zinaida's body becomes a kind of tool of erotic devastation, so these boys' bodies are appendages of a machine; the final emblem of erotic violence in *First Love*—the welt that Zinaida kisses—is prefigured here in the imprint of body on paper.

There are several ways we might read this scene, a scene clearly linked to the voyeuristic revelations of the rest of the story. We could read it as a sublimated erotic gaze, directed at an object—young boys—too forbidden for more explicit incorporation in the narrative. We can read it as a reminder of the vast distance that separates Vladimir from these other boys—not much younger than he—who will never know the freedom of erotic and emotional adventure he knows that summer. Or we can read it as emblematically linked to Zinaida's story, reminding us that like these boys, Zinaida is materially vulnerable to exploitation. Most compelling to me, however, is the power of this scene to make connections between the intimate world of eros and a larger political world: the hierarchy, hostility, and exploitation that flourish in "love" don't exist in a vacuum. "To the extent that either sexual relations or other power relations are structured by a dynamic of domination/submission . . . the community as a whole will be structured as domination."[25] Despite its movement toward an imagined past, *First Love* stands squarely in the world of pre-reform Russia, rent by relations of domination and abuse, in both erotic and political realms. First Love is a Revolution not because the spirit soars, but because in both the body is hideously used, and the order of master and slave that seemed to be destroyed is only turned upside down. The moment of touching tenderness is lost forever, something imaginable only in a never-never land beyond (or before) imposing will and the voyeuristic eye.

Notes

1. Richard Freeborn, *Turgenev: The Novelist's Novelist* (London: Oxford University Press, 1960).

2. I. S. Turgenev, *Polnoe sobranie sochinenii i pisem v dvadtsati vos'mi tomakh* (Moscow: Izdvo Akademii nauk SSSR, 1960-68), vol. 9, pp. 4-5. All subsequent references are to this edition and will be made in the body of my essay.

3. Madeleine Grumet, *Bitter Milk: Women and Teaching* (Amherst: University of Massachusetts Press, 1988), p. 99.

4. See, for example, Domna Stanton, "Difference on Trial: A Critique of the Maternal Metaphor in Cixous, Irigaray, and Kristeva," in Nancy Miller, ed., *The Poetics of Gender* (New York: Columbia University Press, 1986), pp. 157-82.

5. The name derives from two roots: *belyi* (white) and *vzor* (gaze or look).

6. As I will note later, this is not truly the story's first scene of watching—but it is the first to involve Zinaida.

7. Turgenev's prose seems uncannily to describe the boy's trance as aborted masturbatory pleasure, implying a physical involvement in the scene that implicates him in its violence. Vladimir is described as "turning to stone" (*okamenel*) when he sees Zinaida, only to melt (*obomlel*) when the voice intervenes.

8. There has been little, if any, serious attention to the eroticism of the story. Frank Seeley, in his recent study of Turgenev, uses the terms "masochist" and "sadism" (of Vladimir and Zinaida, respectively) without taking them seriously, and insists that the story's final blow (when Vladimir's father strikes Zinaida) "was assuredly not struck by way of asserting or establishing the man's mastery over the woman." *Turgenev: A Reading of His Fiction* (Cambridge: Cambridge University Press, 1991), p. 157.

9. Hélène Cixous, "Reaching the Point of Wheat, or A Portrait of the Artist as a Maturing Woman," *New Literary History* 19, no. 1 (Autumn 1987): 1.

10. Inspired in part by Mikhailovskii's essay on the "cruel talent" of Dostoevsky, Turgenev referred to the latter as the Russian de Sade in two letters, one to Saltykov-Shchedrin and one to Annenkov. In both letters he expressed disgust at the wild adulation expressed for Dostoevsky at his funeral: "I also read Mikhailovskii's article on Dostoevsky. He's truly noted the fundamental aspect of his work. He could have recalled that there's a similar phenomenon in French literature—i.e., the infamous Marquis de Sade. That one even wrote a book: 'Tourments et supplices,' in which with great delight he dwells on the transgressive pleasure derived from inflicting elaborate torments and suffering. In one of his novels Dostoevsky also carefully describes the pleasures of a certain lover. . . . And just think, all the Russian bishops sang funeral services [*panikhidy*] to this, our own de Sade, and even read sermons about the universal love of this universal man!" *Polnoe sobranie sochinenii i pisem, Pis'ma,* vol. 13, p. 49.

11. E. Ann Kaplan, "Is the Gaze Male?" In Ann Snitow et al., eds., *Desire: The Politics of Sexuality* (New York: Monthly Review Press, 1983), pp. 311-12. Cited hereafter within the text.

12. Elizabeth Cheresh, in her new study of Turgenev, notes the way in which Vladimir's insistence on writing his account—rather than merely telling it—is linked to a desire to control response to the story. *Beyond Realism: Turgenev's Poetics of Secular Salvation* (Stanford: Stanford University Press, 1992), p. 163.

13. Compare Kaplan: "Women in film, thus, do not function as signifiers for a signified (a real woman) as sociological critics have assumed, but signifier and signified have been elided into a sign that represents something in the male unconscious." "Is the Gaze Male?" p. 310.

14. "I loved him, I admired him, he seemed to me the model of what a man should be—and dear God, how passionately I would have been attached to him if I hadn't constantly felt his distancing [*otkloniaiushchei*] hand" (30). "Sometimes gaiety came over him, and then he was ready to play and tease with me like a boy (he loved any strong physical movement); once—only once—he caressed me with such tenderness that I almost burst into tears" (30).

15. For a critical discussion of Irigaray's notion of mimicry and its potential to "disrupt" patriarchal discourse, see Toril Moi, *Sexual/Textual Politics: Feminist Literary Theory* (London, New York: Methuen, 1985), pp. 139-43.

16. If we remember the single moment ("vsego tol'ko raz!") of tenderness expressed toward his son, then the father's is also a will determined to control his own more tender impulses.

17. The editors of the Academy edition of Turgenev's works note the consistency of Turgenev's definition of love in "First Love" with such stories as "Zatish'e" and "Perepiska": "love in the story is understood as a tragic feeling, inevitably entailing the slave-like submission of one of the parties" (462).

18. The text is inexplicit, but it is possible that Zinaida had borne an earlier child, Vladimir's illegitimate half-brother: Turgenev is careful to mark the time that elapses between Vladimir's witnessing of the meeting between his father and Zinaida, and the sudden stroke (*udar*) that leads to his father's death. The stroke is caused by a letter that upsets him enormously, received eight months after that momentous, overseen meeting (72). Maidanov, one of Zinaida's acquaintances, later recalls to Vladimir that there had been "consequences" (*posledstviia*) of the "istoriia" of that summer (74).

19. From the memoirs of N. A. Ostrovskaia, quoted in Turgenev, *Polnoe sobranie sochinenii i pisem . . . , Pis'ma,* vol. 11, pp. 459-60.

20. April Fitzlyon, "I. S. Turgenev and the Woman Question," *New Zealand Slavonic Journal* (1983), p. 164.

21. For an account of Lutovinova based largely on the memoirs of Varvara Zhitova, see Tamara Zviguilsky, "Varvara Petrovna Loutovinova (1788-1850), mère d'Ivan Tourguéniev," in *Cahiers, Ivan Tourguéniev, Pauline Viardot, Maria Malibran,* vol. 4 (Paris, 1980), pp. 42-70.

22. Nancy Hartsock, *Money, Sex and Power: Toward a Feminist Historical Materialism* (Boston: Northeastern University Press, 1985), p. 166.

23. This impulse is apparent in the work of Nancy Hartsock, Ann Ferguson, and Audre Lorde, among others. See Hartsock, *Money, Sex and Power* (New York: Longman, 1983), chapter 7; Ann Ferguson, *Blood at the Root: Motherhood, Sexuality and Male Dominance* (London: Pandora, 1989), chapter 4; and Audre Lorde, "Uses of the Erotic: The Erotic as Power," in Laura Lederer, ed., *Take Back the Night: Women on Pornography* (New York: Morrow, 1980), pp. 295-300.

24. The imagination of a gaze that is mutual rather than objectifying forms something of a leitmotif in the work of some feminist thinkers. See, for example, E. Ann Kaplan, who ends her discussion of the "male gaze" with an allusion to the "*mutual* gazing" that was part of the "mutual, pleasurable bonding that we all, male and female, enjoyed with our mothers." "Is the Gaze Male?" p. 324. Similarly, Hélène Cixous ends the essay cited above with the following ruminations: "What is the '*point of wheat*'? [It] could be defined as a kind of economy of attention." "Reaching the Point of Wheat," p. 19; and Sara Ruddick, who has elaborated a morality grounded in the practice of parenting, centers her discussion on the act of loving attention. Ruddick, "Maternal Thinking," *Feminist Studies* 6, no. 2 (1980): 342-67.

25. Hartsock, *Money, Sex, and Power,* p. 155.

Nancy H. Traill (essay date 1996)

SOURCE: Traill, Nancy H. "Ivan Sergeevich Turgenev: Tentative Beginnings." In *Possible Worlds of the Fantastic: The Rise of the Paranormal in Fiction,* pp. 74-104. Toronto: University of Toronto Press, 1996.

[*In the following essay, Traill discusses elements of the paranormal and the supernatural in Turgenev's fiction.*]

If the transformations in Dickens's fantastic tales correspond roughly to the order in which they were written, the same cannot be said of Turgenev's. Where Dickens moved fairly consistently towards the paranormal mode, Turgenev juggled with a variety of modes. For instance, in **'Knock! . . . Knock! . . . Knock! . . .'** ['Stuk! . . . Stuk! . . . Stuk! . . .'] (1871), two rather primitive supernatural incidents are, respectively, disauthenticated and made ambiguous. Yet the story appeared after **'An Unhappy Girl'** ['Neschastnayal'] (1869), where there is a suggestion of the paranormal in the dénouement. In **'Faust'** (1856), a very early tale, the secondary plot exemplifies the paranormal mode; it is concerned with the nature of a special rapport, between lovers in the main plot (the narrator and Vera) and between the living and the dead in the subplot (Vera and her mother). But his traditional 'fantasy,' as he called **'Phantasms'** ['Prizraki'] (1864), followed years afterwards.[1] **'The Dream'** ['Son'] (1877) looks further, to the psychological and genetic bonds of heredity as the channels that permit paranormal communication.

Like both Dickens and Maupassant, Turgenev wrote fantastic tales along with his realistic novels in which, incidentally, we find scattered a few allusions to the fantastic. *Smoke [Dym]* (1867) has a celebrated medium fail dismally to mesmerize a crab (ch. 15). Critic Marina Ledkovsky mentions the character Irina in *Smoke,* and Mar'ya Polozova of *Spring Torrents [Veshnie vody]* (1872), two 'predatory women' who are 'subtly presented as endowed with demonic power.' Irina is disposed by heredity towards sorcery (her ancestors were accused of witchcraft) and uses it to 'bewitch' Litvinov. The sensual Mar'ya Polozova believes in love potions and plies her 'demonic charms' lavishly to 'possess' Sanin (Ledkovsky 1973, 55, 56). The possession and bewitching are metaphorical, of course, but not less meaningful for that.

For the Russian critic Gruzinsky, Turgenev characteristically 'treads cautiously and deliberately along the edge of a precipice which separates the possible from the impossible' (1918, 212). His assessment is apt for the traditional tales **'Phantasms,' 'Father Aleksey's Tale,'** and **'The Dog,'** where the status of the supernatural is indeterminate. Like Dickens's traditional fantastic stories, they focus on the character's direct contact with the supposedly supernatural.

Seven of Turgenev's tales will be discussed in detail. There are three tales of the traditional modes, **'Phantasms,' 'Father Aleksey's Tale'** [**'Rasskaz otsa Alekseya'**] (1877) and **'The Dog'** [**'Sobaka'**] (1866). In the next three, **'A Strange Story'** [**'Strannaya istoriya'**] (1870),[2] **'The Song of Triumphant Love'** [**'Pesn' torzhestvuyushchey liubvi'**] (1881), and **'Klara Milich (After Death)'** [**'Klara Milich (Posle smerti)'**] (1883), the paranormal mode is incipient, its fictional world structure not mature. We do see, though, the beginnings of stylistic and semantic devices characteristic of the paranormal mode. **'A Strange Story'** shares with this group as a whole its treatment of the mysterious power of the will and, with **'The Dog,'** its preoccupation with sectarianism. As Turgenev's most accomplished tale of the paranormal mode **'The Dream'** will be analysed separately.

THE TRADITIONAL FANTASTIC

'Phantasms,' Turgenev insisted, is not an allegory, but a 'series of pictures' [ryad kartin], a 'series of spiritual *dissolving views*' [ryad kakikhto dushevnykh *dissolving views*] (1963b, 5: 179).[3] The narrator is transported to distant lands at various moments in history by the mysterious, hazy woman, Ellis. She shows him nature at its most terrifying off the coast of the Isle of Wight. She takes him to the Black Forest, the 'vanity fair' of a decadent Paris, the Volga of Stenka Razin, and to Lago Maggiore, where he is charmed by a beautiful singer.[4] Chased by a menacing, evil yellow mist, they fall to the ground and Ellis vanishes.

'Phantasms' has something in common with Dickens's *A Christmas Carol*. Like Scrooge, Turgenev's narrator is buoyed along on the air by a creature for whom time and space are irrelevant; both characters are unsettled and altered by their visions.[5] Unlike *A Christmas Carol*, which is a third-person narrative, Turgenev's tale is told subjectively, in the first person.

Dessaix considers **'Phantasms'** a throwback to Hoffmann, Gogol', and Poe; to *l'école frénétique,* with its 'Gothic and Romantic elements' (1979, xi). The story's structure is more complex than this, I believe. At three distinct stages, Turgenev constructs and dismantles the fictional worlds of three modes—the paranormal, the ambiguous, and the disjunctive, in that order, so that we

might loosely call **'Phantasms'** the evolution of the paranormal mode in reverse, or an inverted history of the fantastic. Keeping in mind his comment about the 'series of pictures,' I would even venture to call **'Phantasms'** a *study* of the fantastic. The features of the various modes are flaunted rather obviously.

The fantastic is triggered by a remark that seems to set the stage for paranormal events of the sort we were led to expect from the narrator's speculations in Dickens's 'To Be Taken with a Grain of Salt.' Turgenev's narrator has clearly just come from a séance on the night of Ellis's appearance. Whatever he saw or failed to see is left unsaid: 'The devil take those table-tipping idiocies! They only upset the nerves' (9: 77; ch. 1; A1).[6]

In this state of nervous sleeplessness he twice hears the sound of a chord in his room. He rationalizes the experience, without fear, by modalizing it: 'I *seemed* to hear, *as if* in the room . . .' (9: 77; ch. 1; A2; my emphasis). The second time, he is slightly alarmed but reflects: 'just see what one can bring oneself to' (9: 77; ch. 1; A3). His scepticism, already apparent from his gibe at table-tipping, provides a rational reason for the sounds—the atmosphere of the séance has excited his imagination. Here, the paranormal functions as a purely literary device for motivating the succeeding events.

The ambiguous mode is signalled by the narrator's growing doubts. Is he sane? Did he have a 'remarkable dream'? The narrator's dream is, in fact, a continuation of what he has experienced in trying to fall asleep—it is a dream within a dream. When he first heard the sound of a chord, he personified the moon. It was 'hanging low in the sky, and staring me straight in the eye. White as chalk its light lay on the floor . . .' (9: 77; ch. 1; A4). In the dream, the moonlight metaphor is literalized when the streak of light is transformed into a white, female figure who summons the narrator to join her.[7]

By acting on Ellis's request on her third visit, he in effect gives life to the phantom. He ceases to doubt and thereby brings the disjunctive mode into play, introducing the opposition between the natural and the supernatural and motivating his experience with Ellis. *Structurally,* though, neither his action nor his new-found certainty is motivated. There is no authenticating force behind the narrator's acceptance of the creature's reality, nothing that compels him to believe in it; he simply does. In other words, only the fact of the narrator's acceptance, a purely subjective device, motivates the shift from the ambiguous to the disjunctive mode.

Immediately before the narrator's adventures, two devices are used which augur this shift. The first, pathetic fallacy, recalls the Gothic motifs Dickens was fond of: 'Not only did the sky grow red—the whole air suddenly became suffused with an almost unnatural crimson; the leaves and grass, as though covered with fresh lacquer, did not stir; in their stony immobility, in the sharp brilliancy of their outlines, in that commingling of a strong glow and death-like tranquillity, there was something strange, enigmatical' (9: 80; ch. 3; A5). The words 'unnatural,' 'death-like,' 'strange,' 'enigmatical,' are dramatic and create an appropriately ominous atmosphere. The second device brings Poe to mind. A large grey bird flies silently to the window, looks at the narrator, and flies off, an apparently ordinary incident which the narrator construes as an omen. 'I seemed to have got into a charmed circle' (9: 80; ch. 3; A6), he observes, signalling the end of ambiguity and a transition to the disjunctive mode, which will culminate in his meeting Ellis.

In the part of the tale which is ambiguous, the narrator is preoccupied with epistemic questions about Ellis: how is such a phenomenon possible? where does it come from? how can an immaterial being love, and be loved by, a material being? He fears the collision of irrationality and rationality. With the transition into the disjunctive mode, Ellis acquires fictional existence. The narrator's fear dissipates and the tenor of his questions changes. He is now concerned with Ellis's identity: 'What was Ellis, as a matter of fact? A vision, a wandering soul, an evil spirit, a sylph, a vampire? Sometimes it again seemed to me that Ellis was a woman whom I had formerly known . . .' (9: 109; ch. 25; A7).

Ellis herself does not understand the narrator's questions; her only concrete answer is that she did not know him before (9: 85). As Muratov points out, Ellis's inability to reply—she herself may not know the answers—removes any possibility of solving the mystery of her identity. It is not merely undecided, but undecidable (1972, 12). None the less, Ellis's existence, and therefore the supernatural domain of the fictional world, is indirectly authenticated by the housekeeper's testimony. For the last time the narrator asks himself whether he is dreaming: 'But is it not in a dream that I am seeing all this?' ((9: 97; ch. 17; A8). His cautious phrasing and his use of particles (in the original) suggest that he doubts the validity of the question more than the visions themselves. But his housekeeper's confirmation of his nocturnal absences convinces him, finally, that his experiences are real (9: 97). Once the narrator becomes convinced that Ellis exists, he no longer feels the need to identify her.

More than one critic has called Ellis a vampire because the narrator closes his story with a complaint about anaemia.[8] Dostoevsky bemoaned this superfluous hint of vampirism in a letter to Turgenev: 'In your story, the creature that appears is explained as a vampire. In my opinion, this explanation is not necessary' (Turgenev 1967b, 12: 61; bk. 1; A9).[9] Whatever species of mythological creature Ellis might be doesn't really concern us. That is, her thematic category is of less relevance than the fact that her existence has been authenticated by the means available to the first-person narrator. She achieves full status as a supernatural entity in the fictional world, even without her precise nature or the cause of the narrator's anaemia being explained. At the same time, the narrator's speculation that Ellis may be a woman he once knew hints at a potential shift in the status of the supernatural. If this were so, Ellis might be a woman who, by some paranormal means, has managed to communicate with the narrator. Whether or not that woman is dead, the narrator's speculation brings the narrative full circle back to the séance and to the hint of the paranormal at the beginning of the story.

For Dessaix, **'Phantasms'** is 'a fantastic view of things rather than a more rational view of fantastic things,' in contrast to Turgenev's later tales (1979, 106). And yet, is **'Phantasms'** a way of looking at things, at the world? Is it not perhaps more interesting to read it, as I proposed above, as a survey, a panorama of the fantastic itself? Turgenev's own characterization seems to suggest it. Each segment of the narrative and each event, taken separately, is structurally and psychologically unmotivated. The story's coherence hinges on a purely literary motivation. Every new mode of this tale is generated from the previous one, successively laying bare the devices. Because the story begins (and, it would seem, ends) with an unelaborated paranormal episode, the paranormal mode is ranked with all the other modes. In other words, Turgenev links the paranormal to other modes of the fantastic, specifically the more traditional ambiguous and disjunctive modes. **'Phantasms'** points to the fictionality of paranormal phenomena and sets them side by side with revenants and hauntings as well as realistic sketches of the natural domain. In this way, paranormal fictional events reveal their origins: they are a specific instance of the fantastic, of the imaginary phenomena which writers have never tired of cultivating.[10]

The title of the story is a significant expression of this literary motivation. The Russian word 'prizrak' refers to anything imaginary, fantastic; it connects the table-turning of the first part with the ambiguous apparition of the second part, and then with the supernatural of the last part. Death and destruction dominate the scenes shown to the narrator, though love and beauty are alluded to—at Lago Maggiore, in Ellis's declarations of love, and in the narrator's vague sense of having known her as a woman before. According to Dessaix, these antidotes to Schopenhauerian moral pessimism may be the narrator's last bulwark against dull tedium (1980, 108). Yet the narrator does not escape the void; Ellis, the spectre of death, and everything the narrator experiences before and after the encounter, are 'prizraki.' Love, beauty, and human existence are no less elusive, or transitory, or fictional than any other 'phantasm.'

A very different story is **'Father Aleksey's Tale,'** which exemplifies the disjunctive mode. With that in mind, it will come as no surprise that it is linked intertextually to the fairy-tale and especially to Christian legend. It is a *skaz*[11] told by Father Aleksey to an anonymous enframing, mediating narrator. Many years elapse between the events and Aleksey's telling of them, and there is a further lapse of twenty years before the mediator puts Aleksey's oral story into writing. The events, then, are twice removed temporally from the version that we read, and are filtered through two narrators, neither of whom experienced them.

The tale originates *in* the act of storytelling. On one level, it is a tale about the fantastic experiences of Aleksey's son. On another, it is the self-portrait of the primary narrator, Aleksey, a holy man whose beliefs and whose very nature demand that he should tell a legend in the Christian tradition. Aleksey is 'father' in three senses: in the material sense of having a son, in the religious sense of being a priest, and, in the narrative sense, as the one who conceives the tale.

Aleksey's son, Yakov, is an intelligent and questioning man who undergoes a crisis of faith. As a clergyman, his father belonged to a special class, and Yakov was destined, as the sons of priests usually were, to become a priest himself. That is, except for his fatal inclination for the natural sciences, which leads him to abandon the seminary and take up medicine. As more than one critic has pointed out, he is one of the mid-century 'raznochintsy,' intellectuals who questioned the religious creed and adopted a rational, scientific worldview (Dessaix 1980, 116). Yakov trades Christianity for a religion of humanism.

The first allusion to the supernatural is Aleksey's report of his son having seen, as a youth, a little old green man in the forest. Yakov produced a strange nut which he said the man had given him. Later, as his religious crisis intensifies, he feels himself driven by a demon that tempts him away from faith and finally induces him to commit the sacrilegious act of spitting out the Communion bread.

Aleksey at first leans towards natural explanations for his son's transformation: drinking, gambling, and a weakness for women (11: 296). He dismisses these explanations when he finds no evidence for them, and considers instead whether his son has gone mad or is just deluded (11: 297, 298). But since ambiguity and indeterminacy are not in Father Aleksey's repertoire, he must yield to a supernatural explanation. He comes to accept the existence of the demon and opens his kit of Christian tools—prayer, incense, holy water, and a pilgrimage to Voronezh.

Nothing in Yakov's character disauthenticates the young man's claims. He was not a liar (11: 293), never worried his parents (11: 292), and was not mischievous (11:

293). He was a brilliant student, a loving son, and a humanitarian (11: 294). One of Aleksey's Christian 'tools' is Marfa Savishna, a devout and virtuous woman who Aleksey believes can help Yakov. The subplot of Yakov's relationship with her is not developed; we learn only that Marfa's piety and charity seem to have had a temporary or superficial effect on Yakov. But when Father Aleksey meets Marfa Savishna, he is shocked to see that the changes in Yakov's countenance have to some extent been transferred to hers. For him, it is proof of demoniac forces at work (11: 300).

The story of the strange nut, that first suggestion of the supernatural, establishes an intertextual link with the fairy-tale. Yakov brings the ostensibly magic object home and Aleksey examines it. He lays it aside to show the doctor, but the nut disappears and is not found again, a chance loss that is also a fairy-tale motif. This bit of objective evidence creates as well an intertext with other fantastic tales, such as the key in Villiers de l'Isle-Adam's 'Véra,' the strand of hair in Maupassant's 'The Apparition,' or the lock of hair in his 'The Hair.' The purpose of such physical (i.e., natural) objects being left behind is to authenticate the supernatural being to whom they belonged.

Christian legends about the Enemy of God are the other, and the most important, intertextual resource. On this level, the story is Father Aleksey's, not Yakov's. Aleksey's question about whether the demon appeared at the moment of his son's doubting is the first clue, implicitly, to the Enemy (11: 298), and Yakov's refusal to answer may be construed as confirmation. The tormentor's physical appearance also corresponds to legend: he is black and like a man, although the horns popularly associated with Satan are absent. And Yakov, who had once been 'a comely boy,' 'a pleasure to look at,' grows more and more devilish in his looks (11: 297). It is noteworthy, too, that the demon is usually designated (rather than named) by the pronouns 'he' [on], 'that one' [tot], and, in Aleksey's case, 'the evil power' [navazhdenie]. All of these are readily associated with taboo and the euphemisms of Russian folk speech.

In the demon's traditional, biblical function of seducer we find the connection with Christian legend made explicit: he addresses Yakov directly in the church at Voronezh and induces him to spit out the Communion bread. After Yakov's death, another feature of Father Aleksey's narration strengthens the bond with Christian legend as well as with folk legends about the possessed, or the 'undead.' His remark, 'but I do not want to believe that the Lord would judge him with his severe judgement . . .' (11: 304; A10) is reminiscent of the parable of Jesus casting the devils out of the possessed into a herd of swine. Like Jesus, Aleksey is aware that the possessed person is a victim, and therefore not responsible in the eyes of God. Yakov's face after death gives Aleksey reason to believe that God will not judge harshly. Like the possessed man in the parable of the swine, who afterwards sat 'clothed and in his right mind' (Mark 5: 15), Yakov 'seemed to have grown young again and resembled the Yakov of days gone by. His face was so tranquil and pure, his hair curled in little rings, and there was a smile on his lips' (11: 304; A11).

The enframing narrator's prologue has already prepared us for the Christian legend by a metanarrative device. Aleksey's narrative performance, as it is revealed by the enframing narrator, is predetermined by his character. We are told that Aleksey is not like most of the priests the narrator has encountered, who are 'pretty much of one pattern, and made after one model'—corrupt, in other words (11: 291). He is a holy man in the best sense, asking nothing for himself and bearing physical traces of great suffering, of the Christian tried: 'I have never seen in any human face a more sorrowful, thoroughly listless expression—what is called "downcast"' (11: 291; A12).

These traits at once give Father Aleksey individuality as a fictional person and ordain the sort of narrative that a man of his cast must spin. More than anything else, his stylistic imprint suggests that the tale is *his* story, rather than Yakov's. The enframing narrator points to the absence of 'seminary and provincial mannerisms and turns of phrase' (11: 292; A13). Aleksey's *skaz* combines the colloquial speech [prostorechie] of the folk storyteller with the Church Slavonic phraseology of Christian legend.[12] Aleksey cannot *but* tell a story which is essentially a Christian legend. That it happens to be about his own son's fate is incidental. Transposed by the storyteller onto a higher level, Yakov's life story becomes yet another legend about the workings of the Enemy of God, of the unexpected and uncalled for meddling of evil creatures into the everyday lives of innocent mortals.

'**The Dog,**' even more clearly than the two preceding tales, illustrates how the *skaz* technique inherited from Gogol' produces a fantastic tale. At first blush, the story seems to make sense only as a literary joke. It was ill received by contemporary critics and many considered it a failure. Botkin, to whom Turgenev had read the tale before its publication, wrote that '**The Dog**' was an unsuccessful mix of tragedy and comedy. 'In art, nothing is worse than something that is neither one thing nor the other' (Letter of 4 June (23 May) 1864; Brodsky, ed. 1930, 202-3).[13]

'**The Dog**' may be read as the storyteller's casual, even facetious, response to the philosophical question posed in the prologue: does the supernatural exist? Those hoping for a scientific or philosophical answer are bound to be disappointed, for the story offers a *literary* solution to the puzzle. The matter is introduced by a state councillor who asks, in the not very fitting role of philosopher, 'but if we admit the possibility of the supernatural, the possibility of its intervention in real life, then allow me to ask what role sound reason should play after this?' (9: 123; A14). This pose of the sceptical positivist is treated with irony in the enframing narrator's description of him: 'Anton Stepanych . . . served in some sort of ingenious department and, since he spoke with great care, firmly, and in a bass voice, enjoyed universal esteem' (9: 123; A15).

The 'philosophical challenge' is taken up by Porfiry Kapitonych, who narrates the apparently straightforward, humorous tale about a faithful dog who saves his master from two disasters: an attack by a rabid dog and marriage to a moody, capricious woman. He purchases 'Treasure' [Trezorushka], the dog who will rescue him, after he is visited by a supernatural dog.[14] In this way, a tale about ordinary, natural incidents is cloaked in a variety of supernatural motifs, and these are borrowed from two sources: the Russian folk-tale and the culture of the Schismatics, whose persistent mythological thinking is an important sub-context.[15] Both sources converge in the figure of Sergery Prokhorych Pervushin, who is as much a folk character as he is an Old Believer. Prokhorych, as he is known to his followers, exerts over Porfiry Kapitonych some kind of 'magnetic' influence which links him to the mythological world of superstitious belief. From their first encounter, Porfiry comments on Prokhorych's extraordinarily penetrating eyes and his own feeling of being 'cowed' by the man (9: 130). That Porfiry finds himself under the influence of a special power is clear when he is leaving Prokhorych: 'I bowed down to the ground, and didn't even rise; I felt such a fear of that man, and such submissiveness that, it seems, whatever he might have ordered I would have done at once!' (9: 131; A16).[16] The enigmatic Prokhorych correctly, as it turns out, interprets the supernatural dog's visitation.[17] It is a sign that someone is praying for Porfiry Kapitonych. Significantly, both men use the word 'vision' [viden'e] for the supernatural experience.

Dessaix finds '**The Dog**' interesting primarily as one of Turgenev's two stories (the other, in his opinion, being '**The Dream**') where 'the supernatural intrudes *unequivocally* on an equal footing with the operation of natural law' (1980, 125). But let's look a little more closely at the status of the supernatural here. Three sources apparently authenticate it: Porfiry has experienced the event and witnessed its outcome; his servant Fil'ka, after suspecting his master of drunkenness (9: 125), also hears the dog; and Vasiliy Vasil'ich, Porfiry's neighbour, both sees and hears the dog. Three witnesses, then, provide the testimony of their senses. Yet all of their experiences are mediated by Porfiry; that is, the secondary authentications of Fil'ka and Vasiliy Vasil'ich depend upon the authenticity of Porfiry's own storytelling act. And there is every reason to doubt it.

The enframing narrator explains that Porfiry had been a hussar and a landowner who gambled away his property. He has no social standing, no influential connections, and no talent, we are told. He simply lives by his spectacularly good luck. The first Schismatic he speaks with tells him that 'with luck' the famed Prokhorych will see him, and indeed he does. The happy result of that visit is Porfiry's escape from the rabid dog. His greatest good fortune, we are told, is that 'he obtained the post of overseer of public warehouses, a profitable, even honourable position, which did not require extraordinary talents: the warehouses themselves existed only in supposition, and it was not even known exactly what they were filled with' (9: 124; A17).

Porfiry's being an overseer of fictional warehouses blends perfectly with his status as a teller of tales. He is a consummate fictionalist whose skills mitigate the narrative authentication of the eyewitness accounts since, in Porfiry's storytelling, anything is possible. The distinction between 'natural' and 'supernatural' is irrelevant, for the success of his story does not depend on philosophical argument, but on his style and on the power of his performance. His digressions into the supernatural make his tale less commonplace and give it the savour of the unexpected. All the *skaz* devices are used to embroider it; colloquialisms, popular phrases, and folk expressions are mixed with poetic language, as in his description of the moon—the ordinariness of the words (round, big, yellow, flat) is in contrast to the poetic syntax (9: 136). That the *skaz* is successful is clear from the way his listeners participate. They interrupt with questions or comments, and continually reassure the storyteller that they want him to go on. At all times the narrative monologue is potentially dialogic. The listeners move the story along, encouraging the storyteller to heap detail upon detail.

The story is, as well, a comic travesty of the fantastic. A supernatural dog is introduced to explain why the narrator buys a real dog. Typically for the *skaz,* seriousness is blended with ironic humour. For instance, Porfiry dilates upon Vasiliy Vasil'ich's losses at cards, but then digresses to characteristics which have nothing to do with the tale: 'that neighbour of mine had a vast mind! He manipulated his mother-in-law, by the way, something wonderful: he palmed off an IOU on her, which means he chose the most sensitive moment! . . . Now, that's really something, pulling a fast one on a mother-in-law, eh?' (9: 127; A18). Such apparent trivialities draw attention to Porfiry as narrator and as a performer of an improvised storytelling act.

In the best tradition of Gogolian social satire, the rabid dog is killed by a soldier who has never fired a shot in his life; equally absurd is the medal the soldier received

for service in the War of 1812. But the strongest index of the comic *skaz* is a metonymic transfer, an intertextual pun or literary joke that connects **'The Dog'** with a story by Gogol': the name of the man who sells Porfiry the real dog is *Shinel'*, or *Overcoat,* which is the title of one of Gogol's most famous tales.

As a storyteller's reply to a philosopher's question, **'The Dog'** offers an interesting perspective on the fantastic, and perhaps more generally, if somewhat obviously, on literature. It seems to suggest that literature can take up philosophical questions in narrative; it can develop them stylistically, making them samples of a colourful, expressive, and national style. But fiction is neither science nor philosophy; it is play. It's all about weaving tales, not solving philosophical problems. Porfiry has told a good tale but certainly has not provided an argument for or against the supernatural. The question posed in the prologue remains unanswered; Anton Stepanych repeats it in the epilogue, while the enframing narrator closes with the remark, 'None of us found any answer, and we remained, as before, perplexed' (9: 139; A19).

THE INCIPIENT PARANORMAL

The subjection of the human will to a mysterious external power was Maupassant's particular interest, as we shall see in the next chapter. **'A Strange Story'** is Turgenev's first fantastic tale of this sort, the first too in which the narrator speculates about the conditions of domination. At the time, it would have been politically loaded, and is often read as Turgenev's response to the social and political conditions of Russia in the 1860s.

Several narrative features link it to other of Turgenev's fantastic stories. An authorial filtering voice is established in a single, brief note: 'Fifteen years ago—*began Mr "X" . . .*' (emphasis added). The reference to a Mr X using direct discourse indicates that the writer is not the person who underwent the experiences described; he is transcribing a tale told to him by Mr X, who becomes our first-person (*Ich*-form) narrator. As the 'fifteen years' reveals, a good deal of time has elapsed between the events and their telling, as was the case with Father Aleksey's tale. Since the story-line is quite complicated, I will briefly summarize it.

Mr 'X' arrives in a provincial town, on government business, and meets there a former acquaintance of his father's. He is intrigued by the man's daughter, Sofya, a childlike seventeen-year-old who plays the role of mother and housekeeper in her widowed father's household. The narrator pities her, and finds her 'enigmatic,' 'sincere,' a creature with 'a particular stamp' (10: 162). He meets her later at a ball, where they discuss her beliefs and she reveals her desire to embrace a life of humiliation (10: 176). She longs for a preceptor who will show her by his own example how to sacrifice herself. Two years later the narrator learns that Sofya has run off to parts unknown, and in the autumn he unexpectedly meets her at an inn. She has indeed humbled herself; degraded herself, rather, in becoming the servant of a filthy holy fool, the magnetizer Vasiliy. The narrator does not fail to point out his certainty that she is still 'pure.' Vasiliy—or, more precisely, his powers and their effect—is the pivot around which the narrator's and Sofya's stories revolve and where they converge.

Magnetism appears in three graduated manifestations: first as a personal experience; second, as the force that motivates the characters' interaction; and lastly, as a form of ideology. Conceptually, the term is heavily loaded. It is not just a synonym for 'Mesmerism' ('animal magnetism') or 'hypnosis.'

The narrator crosses Vasiliy's path when a waiter suggests that he go to the magnetizer for fun. Mr X's curiosity is excited when he hears that he will 'see the dead.' The local people revere Vasiliy as a mystic and 'a man of great wisdom' (10: 173), 'strong in divine things' (10; 165). Vasiliy's tippling foster mother tells the narrator to hold in his mind the thought of a dead friend and not to utter a word when her son makes his appearance. The experience is truly extraordinary: from the moment Vasiliy enters the room, Mr X is terrified. He is riveted by Vasiliy's eyes, and suffers a torpidity that makes him feel like a hare caught in the fiery gaze of a borzoi. Vasiliy is obscured by a mist, and the figure Mr X has in his mind—a long-dead tutor of unmistakable appearance—rises in his place. Byalyy has pointed out that the narrator depersonalizes Vasiliy into a force by calling him *'that one'* [*tot*] (10: 172; Turgenev's emphasis). This euphemistic pronoun and the adjectives 'persistent' [*upornyy*], 'oppressive' [*tyazhëlyy*], 'menacing' [*groznyy*], and 'sinister' [*zloveshchiy*] applied to Vasiliy's gaze heighten the sense of terror (Byalyy 1962, 215). What seems to be a taboo on naming Vasiliy may link him, Ledkovsky writes, with evil forces in much the way that the devil is first implied by the pronoun 'tot' in **'Father Aleksey's Tale'** (1973, 108).

Meditating on his experience, Mr X rejects the supernatural folk interpretation and arrives at what he deems a scientific explanation: 'Without a doubt that man possessed a remarkable magnetic power; acting, of course, on my nerves in some way incomprehensible to me, he had so clearly, so certainly evoked within me the image of the old man I was thinking of, that it seemed to me at last that I saw him before my eyes' (10: 173-4; A20). What he describes is similar to the hypnotic state as scientists came to understand it later in the nineteenth century. His explanation (seeing what his own thoughts had predetermined that he should see) is far removed from the popular notions about electro-biology and magnetism that led people to believe one could be induced to commit all sorts of improprieties. All the same, he finds it incomprehensible that Vasiliy could will him to believe that his internal thoughts were projected outward in a visible image of his dead tutor. This phenomenon Mr X calls 'metastasis' or 'the transposition of sensation' [*perestanovlenie oshchushcheniy*], a phenomenon well known to science, he claims, though its source remains 'amazing and mysterious' (10: 174).[18]

He never admits any other hypothesis. His conversation with Sofya at the ball proves that he does not incline to her mystical view of Vasiliy as 'one beloved of God' [*bogougodnyy*] (10: 175). He mocks the absence of empirical evidence for her beliefs and tries to explain to her the 'scientific' fact of magnetism. But Sofya, steadfast in her own convictions, is unmoved. Her desire for a preceptor springs from the Church's inability to satisfy her spiritual needs; she longs for higher knowledge than institutional religion offers. Vasiliy represents this higher knowledge because his superior abilities are, for her, divine in origin. From Sofya's point of view, the narrator's experience with Vasiliy is unremarkable, since the immortal souls of the dead may wander among the living unseen until they are called (10: 176).

Even though Vasiliy has no status with the official church, he is bound up with Russian popular religion: the magnetizer becomes a holy fool [*yurodivyy*] (10: 182). In this, the story has something in common with **'The Dog,'** where Turgenev explored the relation between superior powers and the sectarian beliefs of the Russian folk. In a mythological world, one encounters individuals with supernatural powers.

Magnetism is first presented as Mr X's private experience, in an episode which concerned him alone and took place, as it were, in his own mind. Its second appearance, as the motivation for interaction, has to do with Sofya. Only at the end of the story do we (along with Mr X) grasp just what was so enigmatic and otherworldly about Sofya. And only in retrospect is it clear why she reacts so strongly to the narrator's remarks about Vasiliy. Her conversation with him at the ball told us something of her creed and inclinations, yet obviously concealed a close relationship with Vasiliy. Her faith in his piety, her desire for a preceptor and for humiliation were all hints of a course decided upon, of an intention, already formed, to place herself under his influence. As the narrator himself comes to understand, Sofya did not divorce words from deeds (10: 185). She therefore allows herself to be acted upon and, by means of this submission, to be brought to degradation. An attractive, well-bred, wealthy girl leaves her family to wait on a dirty, demented magnetizer. The narrator recognizes in her actions what we now call cultism. Sofya is hypnotised not so much by Vasiliy, but by what she takes him to represent. She bears physical traces of her fanatical devotion: 'to her former meditatively wonder-stricken expression another had been added—a resolute, almost daring, concentrated ecstatic expression. In this face, no trace of childishness was left' (10: 183; A21).

Magnetism as a social, ideological force is the third manifestation and comes into play at this point. Sofya is stimulated to act by her acceptance of an ideology, her mystical-religious interpretation of Vasiliy's powers as divine. Although the narrator claims not to understand Sofya's behaviour or her motives for selecting Vasiliy, he does seem to grasp that her subjugation has a socio-ideological dimension: 'I did not condemn her, just as afterwards I did not condemn other young girls who also sacrificed everything to what *they* deemed right, in which *they* discerned their calling' (10: 185; A22).

By generalizing Sofya's experience to all such girls, Mr X makes a political statement and, perhaps more interestingly, examines the political and social 'magnetism' of ideology, the charismatic appeal by which it operates. Sofya is as good as mesmerized by an ideology and the man she has elected to represent it. The narrator's expansion of the concept of magnetism to the socio-political level and his allusion to other girls like Sofya grounds the story in the Russian social context of the 1860s, when the radical intelligentsia was drawing young people away from their homes with its revolutionary message (called populism [narodnichestvo] in the 1870s). Vasiliy is a holy fool, but his power also stands for other no less alluring ideologies.[19]

Quite strikingly, magnetism determines even the structure of **'A Strange Story,'** especially its plot composition. The two strands of the plot are the narrator's and Sofya's experiences with the 'magnetizer,' and these alternate, switching back and forth suddenly. Mr X's mention of his visit to Sofya's father and his meeting the girl is a preface to the second plot strand. For a time, the two strands seem to have little in common and run along separately. The narrator's dialogue with Sofya at the ball establishes a tenuous connection. Only when her leaving home is explained do they converge. The plot structure, then, is iconic: the two strands for a period run parallel and *repel* one another like the opposite poles of a magnet; they are finally *attracted* and joined in the story's resolution. Certain problems are caused by these compositional intricacies. To bring the threads of the narrative together, Turgenev is obliged to abuse the device of the chance encounter; in addition, he has recourse to two shop-worn plot devices. First, the friend who by coincidence knows Sofya's father is abruptly introduced for no other purpose than to supply the information that Sofya has run away, and he is just as quickly dispatched. The second rather trite device, information gathered by eavesdropping, gives us the reason for the girl's flight: Mr X stops at an inn and overhears Sofya and her preceptor Vasiliy, through a crack in the wall. In spite of these hackneyed strategies, the iconic representation of magnetic repulsion and attraction in the narrative structure itself make **'A Strange Story'** a remarkable step in Turgenev's development of the paranormal mode.

'The Song of Triumphant Love,' as Brang observes, is Turgenev's only tale to be set outside Russia (1977, 176), although **'The Dream,'** which has no geographical markers, may well be, too. Its intertextuality is explicitly established by the enframing narrator, who characterizes the text as an ancient Italian *manuscrit trouvé*. The manuscript is precisely dated 1542, and there are indirect datings as well, in the textual references to Ariosto, to the son of Lucrezia Borgia—the second Ercole, Duke of Ferrara—and to the Holy Roman Emperor Charles. Even the prominence of art in the text functions as an index, for sixteenth-century Ferrara was an important cultural centre. These markers are strong ties to Renaissance works and style. Gabel', in a brief but interesting comparison, finds that the plot structure and composition of **'The Song of Triumphant Love'** have much in common with formulaic Renaissance Italian love novellas, especially in its theme of the romantic triangle. The love of two of the characters and the obstacles they must overcome generate the story and its specific incidents. Such narratives often end with the death of one member of the triangle or the separation of the lovers. The Renaissance novellas, like Turgenev's narrative, lack psychological analysis (usually vital for Turgenev), and in both much attention is given to reproducing historical colour (Gabel' 1923, 218; see also Brang 1977, 177, and Ledkovsky 1973, 100). In the Italian Renaissance novella an enframing narrator often introduces his story by offering a reason for having written it. It has been remarked that the highly stylized language of Turgenev's story gives a sense of the period, and Koni claims that the 'tempo of the language symbolises the course of the action' (quoted in Gabel' 1923, 218). Perhaps it is more important to observe that even if Turgenev wrote this subtle, complex, and texturally dense tale under the inspiration of the Renaissance novella, he also substantially transformed the model.

As Gabel' points out, some of Turgenev's motifs are not to be found in the Renaissance novella, and he resolves the traditional plot in an original way (1923, 216-19). In this respect the 'author's' epigraph taken from Schiller, 'Dare to err and to dream!' [*Wage Du zu irren und zu träumen!*]—again an explicit intertext—may be taken as an anachronistic directive for reading this 'sixteenth-century manuscript.' The story's departures from its models, its signals of difference, make the epigraph ironic, for the dreams in **'The Song of Triumphant Love'** are nightmares, and daring leads the characters into the frightening labyrinth of the unknown.

Two friends, Fabio and Muzio, and the beautiful, sweet Valeria compose the love triangle. The story is structured in two parts. The first is a pastoral where the three ideal characters are introduced. Fabio, the painter, and Muzio, the musician are unlike in physique and temperament in spite of their friendship. There is nothing fantastic in this part of the story, yet their contrasting physiognomies come to symbolize the sinister events of the second part. Fabio is tall, fair, and blue-eyed, almost angelic in appearance and disposition. Muzio is shorter, dark-complexioned, less animated and cordial, and shares with Valeria a gift for music. Her decision to marry Fabio creates no animosity, and the love triangle is apparently resolved in a friendly way: Muzio heads for the Orient.

The second part is the core of the story. Muzio returns and strange events begin to happen soon afterwards. When Fabio encounters him by chance, his initial and brief reaction is an indefinite fear, a fear which will however take shape in Valeria. Physically Muzio is unchanged, although the Hoffmannesque cast of his features has become more pronounced: he is darker, and his eyes are more deeply set. It is primarily his expression and demeanour which are altered, his face concentrated and grave, his voice quieter. There is, as Valeria observes, 'something strange and unprecedented generally in all Muzio's ways, and in all his habits' (13: 58; A23). The completeness of his transformation is signalled even by the spicy fragrance of his garments, his hair, and his breath (13: 63). Muzio is accompanied by a devoted and keenly intelligent Malay whose tongue has been cut out. According to Muzio, this remarkable servant had 'made a great sacrifice, and in compensation now possessed great power' (13: 64; A24).

The strangeness of all of this is represented on the level of language. Words belonging to the same lexical group continually recur, the first two more frequently than others: 'mysterious' [tainstvennyy], 'strange' [strannyy], 'enigmatic' [zagadochnyy], 'marvellous' [chudnyy], 'magical' [skazochnyy]. A second and related lexical category, 'incomprehensible' [neponyatnyy], serves as a key to the story. For instance, Muzio has chests filled with precious objects collected on his travels—fabrics, rugs, spices, jewels—'objects, the very use of which seemed mysterious and incomprehensible' (13: 57; A25). The pearl necklace he gives to Valeria, obtained in return for some secret service rendered to the Shah of Persia, 'seemed to her heavy, and as though endowed with some sort of strange warmth' (13: 57; A26). Valeria and Fabio listen to Muzio's tales 'as though enchanted' [kak ocharovannye] (13: 57). He has travelled in many lands associated with mystery—Persia, Arabia, India, and China—and has learned strange conjuring tricks [fokusy] such as levitation (13: 57).[20] All these objects and skills function as indices of Muzio's transformation. They are negative indices not only because they are 'strange,' but also because Muzio uses them in a sinister way to gain ascendancy over Valeria.[21]

Three incidents foreshadow Muzio's control over Valeria: the strange sensation Valeria associates with the necklace; the drinking of the Shiraz wine, over which Muzio seems to utter an incantation; and Muzio's passionate rendition of a Ceylonese melody on an odd, three-stringed violin. This song, which sends tremors through both Valeria and Fabio, is produced with a bow whose diamond tip 'scattered ray-like sparks in its flight, as though it too were kindled with the fire of that wondrous song' (13: 59; A27). Although Muzio describes it as a song of 'happy, satisfied love,' here it is an instrument for his passionate seduction of Valeria.

Muzio sets about conquering Valeria by exercising the powers he has acquired in the East. Her first dream (if in fact it was a dream) would seem to be part of Muzio's carefully orchestrated strategy, and functions as a prolepsis of later events. In her dream, she finds herself in a strange and exotic chamber where she succumbs to Muzio. The next morning, Muzio himself recounts an almost identical dream. He does not name Fabio's wife as the woman seduced, but substitutes 'a woman I once loved,' a hint Valeria does not mistake (13: 62). The coincidence of detail in the two dreams, as well as Muzio's gaze, fixed upon Valeria while he recounts his dream, suggests that he has implanted the dream in her mind. Yet there is some evidence that Valeria was not dreaming; she seems to be drugged when she goes to bed: 'her blood was surging softly and languidly, and there was a faint ringing in her head . . .' (13: 60; A28). The chamber in which she is seduced corresponds, if not in detail, at least in style, to Muzio's room in the pavilion as we see it through Fabio's eyes much later (13: 70, 72-3). There are no precise time markers; Valeria falls asleep 'towards morning,' and the moonlight is bright when she awakens. Perhaps most telling is the face of her sleeping husband, 'pale as that of a corpse . . . more melancholy than a dead face' (13: 61; A29). Fabio, too, had drunk the Shiraz wine and may have been drugged to the point of helplessness. Of particular significance is the inverse symmetry in the wording of the two paragraphs, and the switch to the present tense. At the moment Valeria yields to Muzio (in the dream) we read, 'his dry lips consumed her utterly . . . She falls back on the cushions . . .' (13: 60; A30). When she awakens, her action and sensations are opposite those experienced in the dream: 'she raises herself up in bed a little and gazes about her . . . A shiver runs through her whole body . . .' (13: 60-1; A31). These stylistic devices give prominence to the dream episode and set it in relief, as a unit, against the rest of the text. The following morning, Muzio seemed 'contented' [dovol'nyy] and 'merry' [vesëlyy] (13: 61). The implication that Muzio's passion has been gratified is supported by both words being repeated twice in a single paragraph.[22]

Muzio's most powerful bait is the Ceylonese song. Part of its allure and potency is of course its exotic unfamiliarity, its difference from the Italian music of the period. The song is so strongly associated with Muzio that it becomes an index. Whenever something occurs between Muzio and Valeria (in dream or in waking), the song is audible. When Valeria awakens from her dream she hears it (13: 61), and Fabio hears it when Valeria returns to bed after her encounter, later, with Muzio in the garden. In these contexts, the song becomes a metaphor for consummation, Muzio's unspoken expression of triumph over Valeria's will or repressed desire. This is especially apparent in the closing episode, which is also semantically the richest. Muzio has disappeared, dead or alive after a scuffle with Fabio, who stabs him; weeks have passed and Fabio and Valeria have regained their former peace. Seated at the organ, Valeria spontaneously, uncontrollably, finds herself playing Muzio's song of triumphant love. At that instant she feels a new life within her. That the symbol for Muzio's passion is juxtaposed with Valeria's pregnancy speaks for itself. The semantic indeterminacy is just a veil over an underlying, logically coherent meaning.

Music was an essential part of Valeria's contact with Muzio before his travels and her marriage to Fabio. When Muzio and Fabio were courting her, Valeria 'loved to sing ancient songs to the strains of a lute, which she played herself' (13: 54; A32). It is consistent with Muzio's alteration that he has developed a taste for the strange music of distant lands. All the melodies he plays for his hosts are 'strange and even wild to the Italian ear,' though Muzio claims they are popular songs (13: 59). Music for Valeria is an innocent and pleasant pastime. Her husband even tries to paint her as St Cecilia, the sweet patroness of musicians. But he soon observes that Valeria has lost the 'pure, holy expression' which had inspired him. One day, when he expects her in his studio, he finds her in a remote path of the garden; behind her 'a marble satyr with face distorted in a malicious smile, was applying his pointed lips to his reed-pipes' (13: 63; A33). The noble beauty of music evident in the first part of the story is replaced with the capacity of music to rouse the passions, the eroticism symbolized by the satyr and expressed in Muzio's new repertoire.

The moon is a recurring motif that connects the events. After her dream, Valeria sees her husband's corpse-like face by the light of the moon; when the last strains of Muzio's song die away, the moon disappears behind a cloud (13: 61). When Fabio sees Valeria returning after her first rendezvous in the garden, 'moonlight was flooding everything with a harsh light' (13: 65; A34). The moon's 'harshness' corresponds to Muzio's em-

brace in Valeria's dream: 'his harsh arms twine around her waist' (13: 60; A35). The verbs 'oblivat' and 'obvivat' are phonetically similar, as well as semantically related by the prefix 'ob,' expressive of taking over, or absorption. Through such linguistic affinities as these, the proleptic dream becomes virtually inseparable from its ostensible realization.

The moon acquires an added function with Fabio's suggestive remark about Valeria's actions. When he sees Muzio and Valeria moving irresistibly towards one another, again in the moonlight, he describes her as 'like a somnambulist' [kak lunatik], a word that, literally translated, means also 'moonstruck' (13: 68). Whatever the influence she is under, the allusion is never pushed beyond this subjective interpretation.

Other explanations for the events are just as equivocal. The expression of Muzio's face, in the passage just cited, is compared to the Malay's, and one cannot avoid taking the hint that Muzio may be acting under his servant's power. The Malay's uncommon abilities have already been attested, and it is conceivable that Muzio is his apprentice. Both Valeria and Fabio have called Muzio a 'sorcerer' [chernoknizhnik] (13: 68), but it may be that the Malay is master. Certainly his skill in animating Muzio's body after the stabbing testifies to an extraordinary knowledge of the so-called black arts.

The requisite Christian explanation is also offered. Valeria's confessor, Father Lorenzo, is of the opinion that witchcraft [koldovstvo] and diabolical spells [besovskie chary] lie behind everything. Muzio may have been infected with false doctrines in the unenlightened lands of his travels (13: 67). Fabio uses the expression 'diabolical incantations' [besovskie zaklinaniya] when he observes from his place of concealment the Malay's efforts to resuscitate Muzio (13: 73).

Each of these explanations is in fact merely a subjective, unauthenticated *interpretation* of the events. At a loss to understand their experiences, the characters simply annotate them by redescribing them within the narrow framework of their respective dogmas; for Fabio, Valeria, and Father Lorenzo, locked as they are in their beliefs, the events would otherwise remain incomprehensible. For the reader, the text's indeterminacy makes certain decisions impossible. We cannot know whether Valeria loves Muzio, whether Muzio died and was resurrected after being stabbed or was just barely alive. Nor, indeed, can we ever know whether Muzio is the father of Valeria's child. The mysteries remain unsolved. But Muzio has incontestably acquired a set of extraordinary skills. What Valeria observes as the change in Muzio, his being less Italian, is nothing more than a state compatible with, perhaps necessary for, the application of the knowledge he has gained.[23] Apart from the fact that **'The Song of Triumphant Love'** is an intricate and highly readable tale, Turgenev's accomplishment lies in his successfully transforming a Renaissance narrative schema into a prototypical tale of the paranormal mode by blending a story of passion with an Oriental adventure tale.

The tale is not so much concerned with the process of solving the mysteries as it is with the possibility that occult skills may be acquired. However enigmatic they are, the story seems to suggest, strange abilities may exist. The story adds an interesting element to the fantastic by proposing that paranormal capacities may be *learned*. Fabio, Valeria, and the priest cannot acquire these skills without first embracing an episteme that would force them to repudiate their beliefs. The source of Muzio's power lies precisely in his having embraced and made use of a different episteme. In this respect, his skills and knowledge are not incomprehensible; they are simply beyond the comprehension of those who will not or cannot abandon the Western cultural tradition.

'Klara Milich (After Death)' is one of Turgenev's few fantastic tales narrated in the third person. It blends perfectly the fantastic and the realistic of everyday life. Shatalov considers **'Klara Milich'** unique in Russian literature because of its 'astounding strength of psychological analysis' (1979, 289). It has been likened to Villiers de l'Isle-Adam's 'Véra' (1874), which makes a narrative out of the expression 'love is stronger than death.'[24] Dessaix and Ledkovsky both find in it affinities with Schopenhauer's views on the survival of the will after death (Dessaix 1979, xxiii; Ledkovsky 1973, 62), while others connect it with Calderón's play *Love after Death,* whose heroine is Doña Clara Malek.

Aratov encounters Klara at a literary matinée where she will read and sing. Though she is far from his ideal of a woman, he finds himself thinking about her constantly (13: 90). Aratov is an unremarkable young man, withdrawn, gentle, and virginal, who depends entirely for society on his doting aunt. Physically he is like his mother, but his character is that of his dead father, a naturalist and mystic who claimed descendance from the supposed sorcerer Jacob Bruce (13: 76-7).[25] Klara's note to Aratov asking for a private meeting causes him to spurn her as a disreputable woman. Three months afterwards, Klara commits suicide. Only from this point do the events become fantastic. Aratov dreams of Klara, hears her and sees her in his room, and finally dies uttering the words 'love is stronger than death.'

The story is structured as two layers superimposed one on the other. Realistic descriptions, predominant in the early chapters, are overlaid with fantastic events in the last chapters. The coexistence of these two layers makes it possible for Turgenev to shift repeatedly from the realistic to the fantastic.[26]

Even in Aratov's first encounter with Klara, there is a hint of the lurking fatality that will culminate in the fantastic events. At Klara's concert, Aratov notices how she stares at him, and recalls having seen her at an earlier soirée, where she looked at him 'several times with a peculiar insistence in her dark, intense eyes' (13: 86; A36). He is struck by the immobility of her face, and likens her to a somnambulist or someone under hypnosis (13: 88), an analogy which for Gruzinsky reflects Turgenev's interest in Charcot's experiments in hypnotism (1918, 218). And Klara's somnambulism is reminiscent of Valeria's in **'The Song of Triumphant Love.'** But if Klara's physical movements are wooden, her songs and readings are not. They heighten the sense of impending tragedy with their powerful intertextual references. From Pushkin's *Evgeny Onegin* (1831), she reads Tatyana's letter with great emotion, exulting over the words 'My whole life has betokened my meeting you one day'; she herself then writes a similar letter to Aratov (13: 89). Her songs tell of suffering, and waiting, and fidelity. One of the audience connects Klara with the songs she sings by remarking on her tragic eyes (13: 86). Another intertextual reference connects her still more strongly to the tragedy she sings of, and functions as a leitmotif: Aratov finds himself haunted by the words of a poem by Krasov, based on Scott's *St. Ronan's Well*—'Poor Clara! Mad Clara! Poor Clara Mowbray!' (13: 90). Her final, most dramatic action, her suicide, is the most powerful signifying gesture and her strongest message to Aratov. While acting in a play about a girl betrayed in love, she takes poison and dies after the first act. Aratov eventually realizes that she died for him (13: 121), but he does not learn the name of the play and the intertext thus remains a mystery (13: 125). All of these increasingly potent messages— songs, letter, and suicide—are the prelude for a series of messages after death that Aratov will finally grasp. Aratov's later musings on abiding love draw upon the Bible ('death, where is thy sting?'), Schiller ('And the dead also shall live'), Mickiewicz ('I shall love until life ends . . . and after life ends'), and Villiers de l'Isle-Adam ('love is stronger than death') in order to explain and justify the strangeness of his dreams and his sense of Klara's power over him (13: 120). In combination, all of these intertextual strategies greatly help to generate the fantastic.

Klara's appearances after death follow a pattern of gradation, beginning with dreams. In the first, Aratov sees her wearing a wreath of roses, and hears her voice; he is conscious on waking that 'something had taken root in him . . . something had taken possession of him' (13: 107; A37). Klara tells him, 'if you want to know who I am, go there!' On waking, he feels compelled to travel to her home in Kazan', where her sister Anna gives him a diary and a photograph. Klara's diary is a posthumous message to Aratov. It persuades him of her purity, and gives him the key to her power: 'She was chaste, I am chaste, and that's what has given her this power!' (13: 120; A38). Spiritual belonging born of shared innocence is his mystical explanation for their link across the grave. It has its counterpart in Aratov's description of himself as 'taken' [vzyat], not by physical love but by the power of a dead woman to possess him. The second dream becomes an audible presence in the room, with the word 'roses' repeated several times; Aratov recognizes Klara's voice, but then doubts his senses and compares his experience to a hallucination (13: 122). From his last dream he awakens to Klara herself in his room. He declares his passion for her, and they exchange a kiss that leaves him weak, but with the blissful expression of a man who has solved a universal mystery. He knows that he must die, and babbles deliriously about rapture and consummated marriage, always repeating that love is stronger than death. Klara's final manifestation is left implicit. Aratov's strongest physical experience, the consummation of their 'marriage,' is never described. The only clue to her having been there at all is the lock of black hair clutched in his hand. The narrator leaves the status of this crucial motif ambiguous, arguing both for and against a natural explanation: 'Where did it come from? Anna Semënovna had preserved such a lock of Klara's, but why would she give Aratov a thing so precious to her? Could she somehow have placed it between the pages of the diary and not noticed that she had given it to him?' (13: 133; A39). The narrator is unconvinced and unconvincing. His hypothesis is a mere query, after all, and the origin of the lock of hair is never made known.

In some ways, the structure of **'Klara Milich'** seems to correspond to the ambiguous mode, especially if we privilege the narrator's final comments. Aratov, like other of Turgenev's heroes, has a psychological propensity that might explain his experiences naturally. We are told that he is 'given to the mysterious and the mystical,' like his father; he is sickly, reclusive, uncorrupted by the world, and fond of idle psychologizing. Above all, he feels guilty for having wronged Klara. His remarks belittling her talents reached her ears, as such remarks will, and he did not hide his disdain for her at their rendezvous.

The tale's ambiguity persists to the climax. The status of Klara's first brief manifestation in Aratov's room is indeterminate, much like Ellis's in **'Phantasms.'** Ledkovsky draws our attention to the conventionality of the setting, the room either dark or lighted by candles, a faint glow coming from an unknown source (1973, 113).[27] In **'Phantasms,'** Ellis takes shape from a streak of moonlight, becoming a white, misty woman; Klara, complete with the wreath of roses, materializes from the blurred door Aratov is looking at. In neither case can we decide whether the appearance is really a dream. As the narrator points out, Aratov 'once or twice closed his eyes in sleep . . . He opened them wide at once, at any rate it seemed to him that he opened them' (13: 123; A40). There is a possibility that Aratov's vision is at least half oneiric, for his aunt enters the room in a white bedjacket and a nightcap with a large red bow.

At the same time, these events, precisely because they are ambiguous, allow us to conjecture that Aratov is controlled by an unknown force that has determined his fate, just as the narrator of **'The Dream'** will find himself pushed irresistibly towards his fate. Aratov tries to account for his strange compulsion by a sort of transcendent magnetism: 'Isn't the soul immortal? Does it need an earthly organ in order to exercise its power? Has not magnetism proved to us that one living soul can influence another? Then why can't this influence continue after death as well if the soul lives on?' (13: 118; A41).

His hypothesis is plausible when applied to Klara's behaviour. Aratov's belated obsession and Klara's early obsession are indeed symmetrical. At both the matinée and the soirée, where she first sees Aratov, Klara stares insistently at him with her immobile face as though drawn to him by a force. This presumption is reinforced in a passage of her diary that refers to these episodes: '"Moscow. Tuesday . . . th June. Sang and recited at a literary matinée. This is a day full of meaning for me. *He must decide my fate.* (This sentence was underlined twice). I again saw . . ." Here followed several lines carefully blotted out' (13: 116; A42).[28] Klara's fatalism is comparable to Aratov's: they have both been sentenced, as he recognizes from her underlined words (13: 120). She is as much a prisoner of fate as he, and equally powerless to escape. They both seem to be in the grip of an identical power.

Is Klara in love with Aratov? Interestingly, there is no evidence that she is. In her songs and recitation, Klara never mentions love; each line quoted by the narrator refers only to the pain of single-minded waiting. Klara is as oddly obsessed with Aratov as he is adamant in his denials of love. Except in the few last moments of his emotionally charged meeting with her sister, Aratov is conscious of exhibiting none of the usual symptoms of a bereft lover. He feels himself always impelled by the external and incomprehensible force that he attributes to Klara's will. Klara's diary entries and Aratov's interpretations give the impression that their meeting was somehow foreordained. Both seem to be driven by an unknown, mysterious power that fastens them together. Klara's behaviour at their rendezvous is, in this respect, highly significant: she addresses Aratov as though they are already acquainted, and as though he must know her reason for wanting to meet him. She has staked everything on the conviction that Aratov is under the same spell as she (13: 96). When it becomes clear to her that Aratov has no inkling of their common destiny, Klara is first grieved, then angry at his misinterpretation of her actions. Klara's anticipation, along with her diary entry, suggests that she had seen Aratov before, or sees in him someone she knew. The revelation that Aratov does not share that vision prompts her abrupt change of attitude: the logic of fatality drives her to commit suicide.

In this reading, the ambiguity and indeterminacy of the text are explained from within its latent meaning, its allusions, fragments, and semantic connections. Perhaps Klara and Aratov knew each other in another life; more likely, just as Aratov had visions of her, so may Klara have had visions of Aratov that caused her passionate fixation on him.

Turgenev's tale transforms the realistic world of ordinary human experience into a fantastic domain governed by mysterious, transcendent bonds.[29] Klara is a step ahead of Aratov with her recognition of this bond, and with her obsession and death. In the end, it is the lack of synchronization that destroys the lives of Klara and Aratov. Because of his blindness, Aratov delays his passage from contingent actuality into the realm of fantastic necessity. Only in the timelessness of death are the two united.

The Paranormal Achieved

'The Dream' is Turgenev's most sophisticated fantastic narrative, published at the same time as *Virgin Soil*. Not unexpectedly, it was *Virgin Soil* that the critics took notice of, while those who paid any attention at all to **'The Dream'** could not agree on its worth. Anonymous contributors to the moderate liberal newspaper *News* [Novosti] and the conservative *The Russian World* [Russkiy mir], called it, respectively, a 'mere trifle' [bezdelushka], and a 'half-fantastic bagatelle' and 'literary dessert' (Turgenev 1966a, 11: 528). Another critic, V. Pechkin, praised with a great deal more shrewdness Turgenev's masterly handling of language, with which he brings out 'in a few phrases the deepest psychological phenomena' (Turgenev 1966a, 11: 528-9). Among the twentieth-century critics, Garnett found **'The Dream'** 'curiously Byronic in imagery and atmosphere, and artistically not convincing' (1917, 169). Brang considers it thematically similar to **'The Song of Triumphant Love'** (1977, 179), and Byalyy sees in both stories the author's attempt to generalize or universalize the theme of 'the mysterious' (1962, 218).

Turgenev expressed his own view in a letter to his English translator Ralston. With **'The Dream,'** he was trying 'to solve a physiological riddle' (1966b, 12: 1, 63).[30] He achieved his goal, and more, for **'The Dream'** above all solves the problem of the fantastic for the realist writer. The fictional world structure of the paranormal mode is more thoroughly constructed in **'The Dream'** than in any of his other fantastic tales. And, like **'Father Aleksey's Tale,'** a Christian tale by a Christian priest, there is an almost perfect correspondence between the form and the content of the tale.

The story is triggered by a paranormal phenomenon: the narrator has a recurring dream in which he is searching for his father. Standing in the window of a house on a narrow, badly paved street is a stranger. The narrator hears the man's 'angry, almost bear-like muttering' before the scene vanishes in a fog (11: 271). He senses that the man in the dream is his father; but the person he was raised to believe was his father (and who died when the narrator was seven), in no way resembles this dream parent. The dream is precognitive, for the narrator will meet the stranger he has dreamt about and discover that the man is indeed his biological father. The device of a recurring dream that comes true generates a narrative in which the standard logic of reason is supplanted by oneiric logic.

From his childhood, the narrator has had a penchant for solitude and reverie [mechtanie].[31] It is reverie that first leads the narrator to feel himself surrounded by a transcendent reality. His musings are indefinite, filled with feelings and longings, 'as though I were standing before a half-closed door behind which lay mysterious secrets; standing and waiting, thrilling—yet not crossing the threshold' (11: 270; A43). His disposition leads him to think of becoming a poet or a monk, but he decides against both.

The door, half-open and inviting exploration, hides a dream-like transcendence, a possible experience that is neither poetic nor religious. It is precisely the visionary, the dreamer [mechtatel'], who refuses to limit reality to empirical sensory experience and has access to such transcendence. **'The Dream'** is therefore the story of a young man with a capacity for reverie who gains admittance through his dream into a world unlike that of his everyday experience. In itself, of course, dreaming is neither supernatural nor paranormal; but it may act as a channel, or so some claim, and it is this potentiality which Turgenev brings into play.

The narrator's relationship with his mother is a 'half-open door' as well. Some of his psychological traits (avoidance of boys his own age, nervousness, shyness, and fondness for solitude and meditation) can be ascribed to his secluded life with her, to the 'merging' of their lives, as he expresses it. His mother is beautiful but melancholy, 'as though some mysterious, incurable and undeserved sorrow were constantly sapping the root of her existence' (11: 269; A44). More significantly, the narrator is conscious of his mother's occasional aversion to him, fits that he puts down to her shattered health and to his own strange, incomprehensible outbursts of wicked and criminal feelings (11: 270).

Here we find two mysteries: just who is his father, and why is his mother sad? They begin to unravel when the narrator meets his 'dream' father by chance in a café, and engages him in conversation. The man, who calls himself a baron, learns the narrator's name and address, but then eludes him in the company of a Negro [Arap]. The narrator's mother eventually tells him a transparent story about a married friend who was raped by an officer and later gave birth to a son. The narrator sees through the story, of course, and recognizes it as his mother's own. After the rape, she saw the officer lying in the street dead, or so she thought, with his skull split open. For the narrator's mother, the return of the rapist is a waking dream, a 'daymare' that parallels the narrator's precognitive dream during sleep. The psychology of the rape victim, one of those realistic details which pervade even Turgenev's fantastic tales, is finely and subtly portrayed. The mother's sense of guilt and sorrow for having withheld her secret from her husband, her sense of involuntary complicity in a crime for which she was not responsible, and, chiefly, her mixed feelings for her son, the offspring of that crime, all express her great suffering. The secrets behind her sorrow and her moments of aversion are now explained by the psychological burden she has borne for so many years. And the criminal feelings the narrator occasionally experiences are accounted for by heredity. Turgenev's exploration of what Dessaix calls the 'metabiological relationship' (1980, 127) is most interesting, for it is the genetic tie that opens the channel between the narrator and his biological father.

The narrator is driven to meet his 'dream' father again. He feels himself led through the streets by a mysterious force, with an impression of something 'extraordinary' [neobyknovennyy] and 'impossible' [nevozmozhnyy] about to happen. Oneiric logic prevails and determines the events: ahead of him suddenly appears the Negro who had been with the baron. The narrator's own will and intentions are overpowered by a force that propels him onwards. He follows the Negro and is led to the very house of his dream, where the man ahead vanishes. These dream-like events take place in an appropriate setting; a narrow, misty, cobbled street, with the mysterious house in a yard full of debris and planks. The narrator wanders on until he finds himself on the beach, where he discovers the baron, his father, drowned and washed up on shore. His recurring dream had not had this dénouement: now, it would appear, the dream is unfolding simultaneously with the events, and the narrator living and acting it out as it progresses.

At the same time, the dream-like experience is supplemented and semantically transformed by a piece of physical evidence. The narrator wrenches off the corpse's hand a wedding ring, which his mother will identify as the one taken from her when she was raped. The precognitive dream, then, couples the narrator and the baron, while the ring functions, as Dessaix has pointed out (1980, 127), as the concrete, unifying object that brings together the narrator, his mother, and the baron. Thus the ring confirms empirically that the narrator's dream is truly precognitive and that his experience is paranormal. It is fully consistent with the nature of this fictional world that the narrator, in running away from the corpse, feels himself pursued by something unnameable, something that 'rushes after me, and overtakes me and catches me' (11: 287; A45). The same holds true about another fleeting motif, which connects the narrator's mother to the ring and the baron: after showing the ring to his mother, the narrator observes that for an instant her eyes opened unusually wide 'and took on a dead look, like *his*' (11: 287; A46).

It is not surprising that a story of the paranormal mode should be open-ended, as **'The Dream'** is. When the narrator first discovered the body, he studied it to be sure the man was dead. When he returns to the beach with his mother, the corpse has vanished, leaving only traces of its having lain there. Fleetingly, a supernatural explanation is offered: 'Can he gave got up of himself and gone away?' (11: 288; A47). The narration of this episode suddenly shifts into the present tense. The narrating act is made simultaneous with the event being narrated.

The original dream does not recur. But in keeping with the indeterminacy of the last episode, there is an opening out onto another recurring dream, undeveloped and fragmentary. The narrator hears screams, groans, and mutterings that seem to emanate at once from a man and from the sea.[32] These sounds identify the new dream with the old one, but now the dreamer is aware that he is no longer searching for his father. Instead, all the sounds associated with his biological father at different stages return in the form of a new mystery surrounding that man's fate. The dead baron—the narrator's father—if indeed he is dead, continues to haunt him.

In **'The Dream'** there is no trace either of the *skaz* or of any storytelling situation such as we find in **'The Dog'** and **'Father Aleksey's Tale.'** This is the text of a poet with a gift for representing complex situations like the psychology of rape, the probing of the state of reverie, and the dramatic sequence of dream-like events. The narrator is particularly skilful in manipulating the three temporal levels which are essential to the story: (1) the past, which consists of the events that took place when the narrator was seventeen. This level is signalled by the word 'then' [togda]; (2) the present, or the time of narrating, which is marked by the word 'now' [teper']; and (3) the narrative's prehistory, in which the narrator recalls the time when he was seven and his presumptive father was dying. The narrator's recognition of his 'dream' father as his biological father (the baron) depends on his remembering the man who died when he was seven. At the same time, because the narrating act is that of a mature man relating events which occurred in his youth, the authenticating force of his discourse is strengthened.

In its narrative style, **'The Dream'** is allied with the Pushkinian tradition, whereas **'Father Aleksey's Tale'** and **'The Dog'** have more in common with Gogol'. Thematically, it owes something to Pushkin's *The Queen of Spades* [*Pikovaya dama,* 1834]. For instance, the baron is a Mephistophelean type, with sullen, piercing eyes and a hook nose (11: 271); Pushkin's hero, Germann, has flashing black eyes, 'the profile of Napoleon and the soul of Mephistopheles.' With 'at least three crimes on his conscience' (Pushkin 1962, 3: 360, 369), Germann has something in common with the baron, whose crime is the rape of the narrator's mother. Gambling, too, is fateful for both. Still more striking are the bedroom scenes. The room where the narrator's mother is attacked is 'all hung with damask' (11: 278; A48), while in the Countess's room, which Germann surreptitiously enters, chairs and divans are all 'covered with faded damask' (1962, 3: 365; A49). In both rooms, a shrine lamp burns. The baron steals into the room of the narrator's mother through a secret door hidden behind a tapestry; Germann makes his escape through a door concealed behind a tapestry.[33] The precognitive dream is the central experience of a paranormal nature in Turgenev's story. But we sense that the mysteriousness of this world is not limited to the dream alone. Just as **'Klara Milich'** studied the immutability and transcendence of attraction, so **'The Dream'** presents the strange determinism of heredity, the possibility of mysterious and irrevocable bonds between people who are genetically related but who do not know each other.

These hidden bonds find channels in the ordinary phenomena of everyday life—in dreams, or in a hypnotic, dream-like state. Whatever the force that determines and shapes the narrator's dream, that activates the biological link and drives the narrator, it is not identified. It is simply postulated. It is also worth pointing out that we cannot find a motivation for the narrator's dreams in any hidden desire to find his father, since he had no inkling that the man who died when he was seven was not his real father. In any case, why these channels are open to some and not to others is an unresolved riddle; the only precondition seems to be receptiveness, which is as much a trait of the narrator of **'The Dream'** as it was of Aratov.

With its focus on paranormal channels of communication, **'The Dream'** outstrips all the stories that precede it. In the three tales where the paranormal is incipient, the special ability is assigned to a character who acts upon others by transmitting his or her peculiar power, such as the magnetism in **'A Strange Story'** and **'The Song of Triumphant Love.'** No one, including the reader, knows the source of Vasiliy's and Muzio's powers, but what makes them effective is the susceptibility of their victims: Sofya and Valeria are as receptive in their ways as the narrator of **'The Dream'** is in his.[34] But **'The Dream'** is notably different. Here the narrator's will is subject to an *impersonal* force of indeterminate origin which is transmitted through the uncontrollable channel of a dream.

Turgenev's rational approach in the last four tales to unexplained, mysterious phenomena, and his probing of his characters' psychologies bring Pushkin once again to mind. In both his realistic and fantastic works Turgenev seems to have synthesized the Pushkinian and Gogolian trends in Russian literature, so brilliantly exposed by Belinsky (1844, 9: 75-117). But debts notwithstanding, Turgenev transcended both, to my mind, when he wrote his innovative **'The Dream.'** He resolved the indeterminacy we find in Pushkin's fantastic tales, and did so without resorting to the ambiguity of the supernatural that characterizes most of Gogol's tales. Like Dickens in 'The Signal-Man' and, as we shall see, Maupassant in 'The Horla,' Turgenev found a place for the unexplained in the natural world that even a rationalist and a realist could accept.

Notes

1. I have translated 'Prizraki' as 'Phantasms,' rather than the customary 'Phantoms' or 'Apparitions,' since the word is less directly linked with spectres or revenants, and therefore with survival after death. It should be said, though, that Turgenev himself translated the title into French as 'Les Apparitions.'

2. First published in German in 1869.

3. Letter to Botkin, 26 November (8 December) 1863. The English phrase 'dissolving views' is Turgenev's.

4. Ledkovsky likens the Lago Maggiore singer to St Cecilia who, as we shall see, is an important symbolic figure in 'The Song of Triumphant Love.' She also notes the indebtedness of 'Phantasms' to the German Romantics, for whom St Cecilia represented the 'ideal woman' (1973, 162, n. 80).

5. Brang believes Turgenev was inspired by Schopenhauer's 'Ergänzungen zum ersten Buch' of the *The World as Will and Idea* [*Welt als Wille und Vorstellung*]—'the picture of the earth,' as Turgenev called it (Brang 1977, 145). The bird's-eye view found in 'Phantasms' may indeed have been inspired by Schopenhauer, but the plot device is traditional. There are aerial 'tours' in Vélez de Guevara's *El Diablo cojuelo,* Le Sage's *Le Diable boiteux,* Dickens's *A Christmas Carol,* and, in the twentieth century, Bulgakov's *The Master and Margarita* [*Master i Margarita*] (written between 1928 and 1940, published only in 1966-7).

6. The letter 'A' followed by a number refers to Appendix A, where a transliteration of the Russian original is given.

7. In 'The Portrait' [Portret] (1834-42), Gogol' uses a similar stylistic technique. The portrait is first personified: 'Two terrible eyes bored into him as if preparing to devour him alive' (1973, 1: 491; pt. 1; A50); and again, 'This was no copy from nature, this was that same uncanny, lifelike look you would expect to find on the face of a corpse risen from the grave' (1: 492; pt. 1; A51). The portrait then apparently comes to life, leaping out of the frame into the room. But the narrator is not certain in the end whether he was dreaming or awake.

8. See especially Vetrinsky 1920, who considers Ellis an allegorical representation of Turgenev's own muse. The poet is driven by an ideal which is both muse and vampire; that is, inspiring and destroying him at the same time. For Žekulin, the 'vampire-like' Ellis has something in common with the necromancer Krakamiche of Turgenev's operetta *Le Dernier sorcier,* written jointly with Pauline Viardot between 1859 and 1869 (1984, 425). Scarborough calls it 'suggested vampirism' in contrast to the 'psychical vampirism' of Klara Milich (1917, 68, 163).

9. 23 December 1863.

10. Waddington may have had something of the sort in mind when he speculates that Turgenev, after witnessing Home's feats in 1857, was perhaps 'fascinated by the artistic and technical aspects of the thing. It seemed possible that a medium at a séance created an illusion of reality akin to that of a work of literature' (1980, 109).

11. The term *skaz,* as we saw in chapter 1, n. 15, refers to the reproduction in a literary narrative of the stylistic and rhetorical devices and other elements of spoken language characteristic of oral storytelling.

12. Turgenev remarked on the language of this tale to the historian and journalist Mikhail Matveevich Stasyulevich: 'In a perfectly devout language is rendered a tale (actually reported to me) of a rural priest . . . The tone, it seems, has been faithfully kept' (18 (30) March 1877; *Pis' ma* 1966, 12: 127; book 1; A52).

13. Later critics did not find it wanting. One of the earliest was Chekhov, who praised its 'remarkable language' (quoted in Brang 1977, 151). Henry James appreciated the story, and named it among several in which 'nothing could have more of the simple magic of picturesqueness' (1908, 219). Originally the story was a genuine *skaz,* for Turgenev told it in various forms over a period of years before it appeared in print (Turgenev 1965a, 9: 501-2, 497).

14. 'Trezorushka,' with its colloquial diminutive, is a *skaz* name. But because the French word 'trésor' is used as a root, the name becomes a humorous mix of two styles, 'high' and 'low.'

15. In the seventeenth century the Schismatics [raskol'niki] (also called 'Old Believers' [staroobryadtsy]) broke away from the official Church to create a sect of their own because they objected to the changes being made in Scriptures and Church service books under Peter's reforms. As Vinogradov notes: 'The new, European influences disturbed the semantics of Church Slavonic by shaking the ideological and mythological bases of its conceptual structure . . . The judgments of the Old Believers are very indicative of the mythological process of a *real* perception of church phraseology' (1969, 21).

16. Byalyy points out the widespread conviction that Schismatic prophets and holy fools possessed mysterious but very real powers (1962, 215).

17. When the creature makes its second appearance, Porfiry Kapitonych's servant Fil'ka uses the word 'navazhdenie' (9: 126), which we already met above and which means in Russian folk and Christian mythology 'the evil power.' The narrator grows accustomed to the supernatural dog, but a visiting neighbour reacts negatively, calling Porfiry Kapitonych 'doomed,' or 'possessed,' [oglashënnyy] and the dog a 'filthy thing' [pakost'] (9: 127). The first Schismatic the narrator addresses thinks the devil theory is nonsense and proposes his own: 'only, what do you mean, the evil power? It is a phenomenon, or a sign; but you won't be able to understand it; it's not up your alley' (9: 130; A53). Porfiry is then sent through the network of Old Believers to Prokhorych.

18. Gruzinsky argues (with regard to 'The Song of Triumphant Love') that Turgenev was familiar with Charcot's theories (1918, 219). Initially, Charcot proposed that hypnosis was an 'induced form of hystero-epilepsy' (Inglis 1986, 285; see also Ellenberger 1970, 13-45). And indeed, Mr X subtly refers to this in his final conjecture about Vasiliy: 'perhaps epilepsy has conquered him' (10: 185; A54).

19. Turgenev was clearly aware that young women were active in this revolutionary movement and that some were even arrested (Byalyy 1962, 217; Muratov 1980, 20, 26). The topic resurfaces in a somewhat different guise in *Virgin Soil [Nov']* (1877). About Sofya, Turgenev wrote to Avdeev: 'such people lived and as such have the right to be rendered by art' (13 (25) January 1879; 1964b, 8: 172; A55). To Annenkov, he wrote contemptuously of the kind of mummery Vasiliy practised,

and described a case from real life, that of a former Russian Minister, Count Bobrinsky: 'I had always known him for a dull-witted, inwardly faltering and unintelligent man, but they say he has been made into a preacher, almost a prophet; they say he has—in England, in the English language— even seduced various workers and artisans onto the path of truth' (16 (28) March 1876; 1966b, 11: 234; A56).

20. Levitation was not associated with the Orient alone. Early Christian churches took a dim view of it, believing that invisible demoniac hands were lifting the possessed person. Palmer and More cite versions of the story of Simon Magus, a reputed sorcerer whom the Apostle Peter challenged to a show of magical skills; as Simon was levitating over Rome, Peter ordered the demons to release him, and he fell to the earth (1936, 28-41). Later Church opinion was divided over whether levitation was beatific or demoniac. Inglis cites the case of the sixteenth-century Teresa of Avila who would levitate uncontrollably while praying (1986, 160). Muzio, however, is in control of what appears to be a learned ability.

21. The contrast between the high-minded innocence of Fabio and Valeria and the dark negative forces which seem to rule Muzio is symbolized by the bay and oleander trees under which they sit on the night of Muzio's return, though it may not have been deliberate on Turgenev's part (13: 57; ch. 3). From ancient times the bay laurel was associated with noble deeds and poetry, as seen in its Latin name *Laurus nobilis*. The beautiful *Nerium oleander*, in contrast, is one of the deadliest of plant species, with over 50 toxic compounds, including two cardiac glycosides.

22. Before Valeria retires on the night of her dream, Muzio displays his talent for hypnotism, a scene which led Gershenzon (1919, 107-9) to compare the story to Bulwer-Lytton's *A Strange Story* (1862), where Margrave, with his remarkable powers, masters Lillian, spirits her away, and then thwarts her husband's attempts to find her. Muzio's magnetic power is implied elsewhere: Valeria observes his 'piercing and curious eyes' [pronzitel' nykh i lyubopytnykh glaz] (13: 61), and appears to be drawn irresistibly to his open arms in their final nocturnal encounter (13: 69). Gruzinsky notes a strong resemblance between the couple's somnambulism and Charcot's experiments in hypnotic states (1918, 219). Even Muzio's diamond-tipped bow scattering its 'ray-like sparks' has a potentially hypnotic force.

23. Disregarding the story's ambiguity and fantastic features, Pustovoit naturalizes Valeria's experience with Muzio, leaping to the conclusion that Valeria does not love her husband and that Muzio's return reawakens her passion. Pustovoit does support his contention with one unarguable, if isolated, textual fact: Valeria married Fabio at her mother's wish, and herself claimed no preference for either man (1957, 130; Turgenev 13: 55). However, one has to ignore a great many other facets of the tale in order to arrive at a purely psychological explanation for Valeria's submission to Muzio.

24. See Ledkovsky (1973, 62) and Turgenev (1967a, 13: 585) for brief comparisons with Villier's story, which begins 'L'Amour est plus fort que la Mort.' The phrase is apparently taken from *Canticles* (*Song of Solomon*), but the wording in the Authorized King James Version is 'for love is strong as death' (8: 6).

25. Bruce was one of Peter I's advisers; after Peter's death, he retired from service and devoted himself to a passionate study of the sciences. Eventually he gained a reputation for sorcery and soothsaying (Turgenev 1967a, 13: 588).

26. Turgenev does not suppress the realistic narrative strain when the fantastic is introduced with Aratov's nightmares. Ledkovsky points out that the story's 'mysterious plot of love beyond death, into whose fabric are woven the fantastic motifs of premonition, visionary dreams, magnetism and ghosts, develops against a perfectly commonplace, plausible background.' She calls this technique 'neutralization' (1973, 112).

27. Quoting a passage from *Parerga and Paralipomena*, Ledkovsky observes the interesting correspondence between Aratov's experience and Schopenhauer's views on the conditions that favour supernatural visions: 'When visions occur the inner eye projects the figures into places where the outer eye does not perceive anything: into dark corners, behind curtains becoming transparent all of a sudden and in general into the darkness of the night . . . Only the dark, quiet and lonely midnight will be the time for the appearance of ghosts' (1973, 111).

28. The sentence '*He must decide my fate*' may also be translated '*it must decide my fate.*' The masculine pronoun 'on' in the Russian original may apply either to the word 'day' or to a man.

29. Turgenev's 'Faust' (1856), like 'Klara Milich,' is concerned with bonds that linger after death.

30. 10 (22) January 1877.

31. 'Mechta' is perhaps best understood as the waking dream that occurs in a state of reverie [mechtanie], while 'son' is the dream of sleep. I have translated both 'mechtanie' (the state) and 'mechta'

(the dream that occurs in that state) as either 'reverie' or 'musing.' The person who spends his time musing is both 'dreamer' and 'visionary.'

32. This textual indeterminacy is reinforced by the use of indefinite pronouns, as Brang notes (1977, 173), and by indefinite verbs and adverbs that designate both the secrets the narrator senses and the mysterious forces which drive him: 'I *seem* to hear' [mne chudilos'], '*some* far-off cries, *some* senseless, mournful complaints . . . *somewhere* beyond a high wall . . .' [kakie-to dalëkie vopli, kakie-to smolkaemye, zaunyvnye zhaloby . . . gde-to za vysokoy stenoy . . .]

33. *The Queen of Spades,* however, exemplifies the ambiguous mode, as discussed in chapter 1.

34. Ledkovsky finds several parallels between 'The Dream' and 'The Song of Triumphant Love': Muzio, like the baron, is dark and enigmatic and, in his own way, seems to have violated a woman. Both characters are accompanied by mysterious, dark men and both are, ostensibly, murdered. In 'The Dream,' the mother is 'numb with terror' and unable to resist the rapist; in 'The Song of Triumphant Love,' Valeria is made a somnambulist with magic and wine, and cannot resist her seducer. 'The Song of Triumphant Love' could be the prehistory of 'The Dream.' If Valeria were to bear a son, he might well dream of his 'real father,' and perhaps meet him one day, just as the narrator of 'The Dream' meets his (1973, 57-9). Brang also notes similarities between the two (1977, 179).

Works Cited

Belinsky, Vissarion. 1844. *Tarantas* [Review]. *Polnoe sobraniy sochineniy.* 9: 75-117.

Brang, Peter. 1977. *I. S. Turgenev: Sein Leben und sein Werk.* Wiesbaden: Harrassowitz.

Brodsky, N. L., ed. 1930. *V. P. Botkin i I. S. Turgenev: neizdannaya perepiska 1851-1869.* Moscow-Leningrad: Akademia.

Byalyy, G. 1962. *Turgenev i russkiy realizm.* Moscow-Leningrad: Sovetskiy pisatel'.

Dessaix, Robert. 1980. *Turgenev: The Quest for Faith.* Canberra: Australian National University.

Gabel', M. 1923. 'Pesn' torzhestvuyushchey lyubvi: opyt analyza.' In Brodsky, ed. 1923b. 202-25.

Gershenzon, M. 1919. *Mechta i mysl' I. S. Turgeneva* Rpt. Munich: Fink. 1970.

Gruzinsky, A. E. 1918. *I. S. Turgenev.* Moscow: Gran'.

Ledkovsky, Marina. 1973. *The Other Turgenev: From Romanticism to Symbolism.* Würzburg: Jal-Verlag.

Turgenev, I. S. 1923-34. *Sobranie sochineniy.* 12 vols. Moscow-Leningrad:

———1959. *Literary Reminiscences and Autobiographical Fragments.* Ed. and trans. David Magarshack. London: Faber.

———1960-8a. *Polnoe sobranie sochineniy.* 15 vols. Moscow-Leningrad: Nauka.

———1961-8b. *Pis'ma.* 13 vols. Moscow-Leningrad: Nauka.

———1962c. *Sobranie sochinenii.* Moscow: Gosudarstvennoe izdatel'stvo khudozhestvennoy literatury.

———1979. *The Mysterious Tales of Ivan Turgenev.* Ed. and trans. Robert Dessaix. Canberra: Australian National University.

———1986. *Perepiska I. S. Turgeneva.* 2 vols. Moscow: Khudozhestvennaya literatura.

Vetrinsky, C. 1920. 'Muza-vampir.' In Rozanov and Sokolov, eds. 1920. 152-67.

Waddington, Patrick. 1980. *Turgenev and England.* London: Macmillan.

FURTHER READING

Criticism

Bortnes, Jostein. "The Poetry of Prose—the Art of Parallelism in Turgenev's *Ottsy i dety*." *Scando-Slavica* 30 (1984): 31-55.
> Discusses the novel *Fathers and Sons* from an aesthetic perspective rather than from the traditional socio-historical approach.

Brouwer, Sander. "The Use of Folklore Elements for the Characterisation of the Personages in Turgenev's 'Poezdka v Poles'e.'" In *Dutch Contributions to the Tenth International Congress of Slavists, Sofia, September 14-22, 1988,* edited by André van Holk, pp. 45-70. Amsterdam: Rodopi, 1988.
> Studies the use of folklore as a unifying principle in Turgenev's story "Poezdka v Poles's."

Busch, R. L. "Turgenev's *Ottsy i deti* and Dostoevskii's *Besy*." *Canadian Slavonic Papers* 26, no. 1 (1984): 1-9.
> Explores similarities and differences between Turgenev's 1862 novel and Dostoevskii's 1871-72 work.

Conrad, Joseph L. "Turgenev's 'Asja': Ambiguous Ambivalence." *Slavic and East European Journal* 30, no. 2 (summer 1986): 215-29.

Discusses Turgenev's short story "Asja," insisting that the work is complex because it involves two impossible love relationships.

Gregg, Richard. "Turgenev and Hawthorne: The Life-Giving Satyr and the Fallen Faun." *Slavic and East European Journal* 41, no. 2 (summer 1997): 258-70.

Studies Turgenev's admiration for Hawthorne and suggests that although initially committed to realism, Turgenev increasingly employed elements of the supernatural and the uncanny—elements generally associated with Hawthorne—in his later fiction.

Lagerberg, Robert. "Images of Night and Day in Turgenev's *Pervaia liubov'*." *New Zealand Slavonic Journal* (1994): 57-68.

Studies the use of the open frame structure and day/night imagery in *First Love.*

Paul, Alec. "Russian Landscape in Literature: Lermontov and Turgenev." In *Geography and Literature: A Meeting of the Disciplines,* edited by William E. Mallory and Paul Simpson-Housley, pp. 115-31. Syracuse, N.Y.: Syracuse University Press, 1987.

Reviews Turgenev's landscape descriptions, which introduced Western readers to the geography and culture of the Russian heartland.

Pozefsky, Peter C. "*Smoke* as 'Strange and Sinister Commentary on *Fathers and Sons*': Dostoevskii, Pisarev and Turgenev on Nihilists and Their Representations." *The Russian Review* 54, no. 4 (October 1995): 571-86.

Discusses the controversy surrounding Turgenev's nihilist character Bazarov—a characterization that earned the author severe criticism from both ends of the political spectrum.

Silbajoris, Rimvydas. "Images and Structures in Turgenev's *Sportsman's Notebook.*" *Slavic and East European Journal* 28, no. 2 (summer 1984): 180-91.

Examines *Sportsman's Notebook* in artistic rather than political and ideological terms.

Sokolowska, Katarzyna. "Artistic Aspects of Character Creation in *Lord Jim* by Conrad and *Rudin* by Turgenev." In *Joseph Conrad: East European, Polish and Worldwide,* edited by Wieslaw Krajka, pp. 113-30. Lublin: Maria Curie-Skłodowska University, 1999.

Explores Conrad's affinity with Turgenev and their shared views of nature.

Waddington, Patrick, ed. *Ivan Turgenev and Britain.* Oxford: Berg Publishers, 1995, 302 p.

Provides a collection of reviews and critical essays, originally published in Great Britain, on Turgenev and his work.

Additional coverage of Turgenev's life and career is contained in the following sources published by the Gale Group: *Dictionary of Literary Biography,* **Vols. 198 and 238;** *DISCovering Authors;* *DISCovering Authors: Canadian Edition; DISCovering Authors Modules: Most-studied Authors, Novelists;* **Drama Criticism, Vol. 7;** *Drama for Students,* **Vol. 6,** *Short Story Criticism,* **Vol. 7;** *World Literature Criticism.*

How to Use This Index

The main references

> **Calvino, Italo**
> 1923-1985 .... **CLC 5, 8, 11, 22, 33, 39,**
> **73; SSC 3, 48**

list all author entries in the following Gale Literary Criticism series:

AAL = *Asian American Literature*
BLC = *Black Literature Criticism*
BLCS = *Black Literature Criticism Supplement*
CLC = *Contemporary Literary Criticism*
CLR = *Children's Literature Review*
CMLC = *Classical and Medieval Literature Criticism*
DC = *Drama Criticism*
HLC = *Hispanic Literature Criticism*
HLCS = *Hispanic Literature Criticism Supplement*
LC = *Literature Criticism from 1400 to 1800*
NCLC = *Nineteenth-Century Literature Criticism*
NNAL = *Native North American Literature*
PC = *Poetry Criticism*
SSC = *Short Story Criticism*
TCLC = *Twentieth-Century Literary Criticism*
WLC = *World Literature Criticism, 1500 to the Present*
WLCS = *World Literature Criticism Supplement*

The cross-references

> See also CA 85-88, 116; CANR 23, 61;
> DAM NOV; DLB 196; EW 13; MTCW 1, 2;
> RGSF 2; RGWL 2; SFW 4; SSFS 12

list all author entries in the following Gale biographical and literary sources:

AAYA = *Authors & Artists for Young Adults*
AFAW = *African American Writers*
AFW = *African Writers*
AITN = *Authors in the News*
AMW = *American Writers*
AMWR = *American Writers Retrospective Supplement*
AMWS = *American Writers Supplement*
ANW = *American Nature Writers*
AW = *Ancient Writers*
BEST = *Bestsellers*
BPFB = *Beacham's Encyclopedia of Popular Fiction: Biography and Resources*
BRW = *British Writers*
BRWS = *British Writers Supplement*
BW = *Black Writers*
BYA = *Beacham's Guide to Literature for Young Adults*
CA = *Contemporary Authors*
CAAS = *Contemporary Authors Autobiography Series*
CABS = *Contemporary Authors Bibliographical Series*
CAD = *Contemporary American Dramatists*
CANR = *Contemporary Authors New Revision Series*
CAP = *Contemporary Authors Permanent Series*
CBD = *Contemporary British Dramatists*
CCA = *Contemporary Canadian Authors*
CD = *Contemporary Dramatists*
CDALB = *Concise Dictionary of American Literary Biography*
CDALBS = *Concise Dictionary of American Literary Biography Supplement*
CDBLB = *Concise Dictionary of British Literary Biography*
CMW = *St. James Guide to Crime & Mystery Writers*
CN = *Contemporary Novelists*

CP = *Contemporary Poets*
CPW = *Contemporary Popular Writers*
CSW = *Contemporary Southern Writers*
CWD = *Contemporary Women Dramatists*
CWP = *Contemporary Women Poets*
CWRI = *St. James Guide to Children's Writers*
CWW = *Contemporary World Writers*
DA = *DISCovering Authors*
DA3 = *DISCovering Authors 3.0*
DAB = *DISCovering Authors: British Edition*
DAC = *DISCovering Authors: Canadian Edition*
DAM = *DISCovering Authors: Modules*
   DRAM: *Dramatists Module;* **MST:** *Most-studied Authors Module;*
   MULT: *Multicultural Authors Module;* **NOV:** *Novelists Module;*
   POET: *Poets Module;* **POP:** *Popular Fiction and Genre Authors Module*
DFS = *Drama for Students*
DLB = *Dictionary of Literary Biography*
DLBD = *Dictionary of Literary Biography Documentary Series*
DLBY = *Dictionary of Literary Biography Yearbook*
DNFS = *Literature of Developing Nations for Students*
EFS = *Epics for Students*
EXPN = *Exploring Novels*
EXPP = *Exploring Poetry*
EXPS = *Exploring Short Stories*
EW = *European Writers*
FANT = *St. James Guide to Fantasy Writers*
FW = *Feminist Writers*
GFL = *Guide to French Literature,* Beginnings to 1789, 1798 to the Present
GLL = *Gay and Lesbian Literature*
HGG = *St. James Guide to Horror, Ghost & Gothic Writers*
HW = *Hispanic Writers*
IDFW = *International Dictionary of Films and Filmmakers: Writers and Production Artists*
IDTP = *International Dictionary of Theatre: Playwrights*
LAIT = *Literature and Its Times*
LAW = *Latin American Writers*
JRDA = *Junior DISCovering Authors*
MAICYA = *Major Authors and Illustrators for Children and Young Adults*
MAICYAS = *Major Authors and Illustrators for Children and Young Adults Supplement*
MAWW = *Modern American Women Writers*
MJW = *Modern Japanese Writers*
MTCW = *Major 20th-Century Writers*
NCFS = *Nonfiction Classics for Students*
NFS = *Novels for Students*
PAB = *Poets: American and British*
PFS = *Poetry for Students*
RGAL = *Reference Guide to American Literature*
RGEL = *Reference Guide to English Literature*
RGSF = *Reference Guide to Short Fiction*
RGWL = *Reference Guide to World Literature*
RHW = *Twentieth-Century Romance and Historical Writers*
SAAS = *Something about the Author Autobiography Series*
SATA = *Something about the Author*
SFW = *St. James Guide to Science Fiction Writers*
SSFS = *Short Stories for Students*
TCWW = *Twentieth-Century Western Writers*
WLIT = *World Literature and Its Times*
WP = *World Poets*
YABC = *Yesterday's Authors of Books for Children*
YAW = *St. James Guide to Young Adult Writers*

Literary Criticism Series
Cumulative Author Index

Antschel, Paul 1920-1970
See Celan, Paul
See also CA 85-88; CANR 33, 61; MTCW
1

Anwar, Chairil 1922-1949 .... **TCLC 22**
See also RGWL 3

Anzaldua, Gloria (Evanjelina)
1942- .... **HLCS 1**
See also CA 175; CSW; CWP; DLB 122;
FW; RGAL 4

Apess, William 1798-1839(?) .... **NCLC 73;**
NNAL
See also DAM MULT; DLB 175, 243

Apollinaire, Guillaume 1880-1918 .... **PC 7;**
TCLC 3, 8, 51
See Kostrowitzki, Wilhelm Apollinaris de
See also CA 152; DAM POET; DLB 258;
EW 9; GFL 1789 to the Present; MTCW
1; RGWL 2, 3; TWA; WP

Apollonius of Rhodes
See Apollonius Rhodius
See also AW 1; RGWL 2, 3

Apollonius Rhodius c. 300B.C.-c.
220B.C. .... **CMLC 28**
See Apollonius of Rhodes
See also DLB 176

Appelfeld, Aharon 1932- ... **CLC 23, 47; SSC**
42
See also CA 133; CANR 86; CWW 2;
RGSF 2

Apple, Max (Isaac) 1941- .... **CLC 9, 33; SSC**
50
See also CA 81-84; CANR 19, 54; DLB
130

Appleman, Philip (Dean) 1926- .... **CLC 51**
See also CA 13-16R; CAAS 18; CANR 6,
29, 56

Appleton, Lawrence
See Lovecraft, H(oward) P(hillips)

Apteryx
See Eliot, T(homas) S(tearns)

Apuleius, (Lucius Madaurensis)
125(?)-175(?) .... **CMLC 1**
See also AW 2; CDWLB 1; DLB 211;
RGWL 2, 3; SUFW

Aquin, Hubert 1929-1977 .... **CLC 15**
See also CA 105; DLB 53

Aquinas, Thomas 1224(?)-1274 ..... **CMLC 33**
See also DLB 115; EW 1; TWA

Aragon, Louis 1897-1982 .... **CLC 3, 22;**
TCLC 123
See also CA 69-72; CANR 28, 71; DAM
NOV, POET; DLB 72, 258; EW 11; GFL
1789 to the Present; GLL 2; MTCW 1, 2;
RGWL 2, 3

Arany, Janos 1817-1882 .... **NCLC 34**

Aranyos, Kakay 1847-1910
See Mikszath, Kalman

Arbuthnot, John 1667-1735 .... **LC 1**
See also DLB 101

Archer, Herbert Winslow
See Mencken, H(enry) L(ouis)

Archer, Jeffrey (Howard) 1940- .... **CLC 28**
See also AAYA 16; BEST 89:3; BPFB 1;
CA 77-80; CANR 22, 52, 95; CPW; DAM
POP; INT CANR-22

Archer, Jules 1915- .... **CLC 12**
See also CA 9-12R; CANR 6, 69; SAAS 5;
SATA 4, 85

Archer, Lee
See Ellison, Harlan (Jay)

Archilochus c. 7th cent. B.C.- .... **CMLC 44**
See also DLB 176

Arden, John 1930- .... **CLC 6, 13, 15**
See also BRWS 2; CA 13-16R; CAAS 4;
CANR 31, 65, 67; CBD; CD 5; DAM
DRAM; DFS 9; DLB 13, 245; MTCW 1

Arenas, Reinaldo 1943-1990 .. **CLC 41; HLC**
1
See also CA 128; CANR 73, 106; DAM
MULT; DLB 145; GLL 2; HW 1; LAW;
LAWS 1; MTCW 1; RGSF 2; RGWL 3;
WLIT 1

Arendt, Hannah 1906-1975 .... **CLC 66, 98**
See also CA 17-20R; CANR 26, 60; DLB
242; MTCW 1, 2

Aretino, Pietro 1492-1556 .... **LC 12**
See also RGWL 2, 3

Arghezi, Tudor -1967 .... **CLC 80**
See Theodorescu, Ion N.
See also CA 167; CDWLB 4; DLB 220

Arguedas, Jose Maria 1911-1969 .... **CLC 10,**
18; HLCS 1
See also CA 89-92; CANR 73; DLB 113;
HW 1; LAW; RGWL 2, 3; WLIT 1

Argueta, Manlio 1936- .... **CLC 31**
See also CA 131; CANR 73; CWW 2; DLB
145; HW 1; RGWL 3

Arias, Ron(ald Francis) 1941- .... **HLC 1**
See also CA 131; CANR 81; DAM MULT;
DLB 82; HW 1, 2; MTCW 2

Ariosto, Ludovico 1474-1533 .... **LC 6; PC 42**
See also EW 2; RGWL 2, 3

Aristides
See Epstein, Joseph

Aristophanes 450B.C.-385B.C. .... **CMLC 4,**
51; DC 2; WLCS
See also AW 1; CDWLB 1; DA; DAB;
DAC; DAM DRAM, MST; DFS 10; DLB
176; RGWL 2, 3; TWA

Aristotle 384B.C.-322B.C. .... **CMLC 31;**
WLCS
See also AW 1; CDWLB 1; DA; DAB;
DAC; DAM MST; DLB 176; RGEL 2, 3;
TWA

Arlt, Roberto (Godofredo Christophersen)
1900-1942 .... **HLC 1; TCLC 29**
See also CA 131; CANR 67; DAM MULT;
HW 1, 2; LAW

Armah, Ayi Kwei 1939- . **BLC 1; CLC 5, 33,**
136
See also AFW; BW 1; CA 61-64; CANR
21, 64; CDWLB 3; CN 7; DAM MULT,
POET; DLB 117; MTCW 1; WLIT 2

Armatrading, Joan 1950- .... **CLC 17**
See also CA 186

Armitage, Frank
See Carpenter, John (Howard)

Arnette, Robert
See Silverberg, Robert

Arnim, Achim von (Ludwig Joachim von
Arnim) 1781-1831 ..... **NCLC 5; SSC 29**
See also DLB 90

Arnim, Bettina von 1785-1859 .... **NCLC 38**
See also DLB 90; RGWL 2, 3

Arnold, Matthew 1822-1888 ..... **NCLC 6, 29,**
89; PC 5; WLC
See also BRW 5; CDBLB 1832-1890; DA;
DAB; DAC; DAM MST, POET; DLB 32,
57; EXPP; PAB; PFS 2; TEA; WP

Arnold, Thomas 1795-1842 .... **NCLC 18**
See also DLB 55

Arnow, Harriette (Louisa) Simpson
1908-1986 .... **CLC 2, 7, 18**
See also BPFB 1; CA 9-12R; CANR 14;
DLB 6; FW; MTCW 1, 2; RHW; SATA
42; SATA-Obit 47

Arouet, Francois-Marie
See Voltaire

Arp, Hans
See Arp, Jean

Arp, Jean 1887-1966 .... **CLC 5; TCLC 115**
See also CA 81-84; CANR 42, 77; EW 10

Arrabal
See Arrabal, Fernando

Arrabal, Fernando 1932- ... **CLC 2, 9, 18, 58**
See also CA 9-12R; CANR 15

Arreola, Juan Jose 1918-2001 .... **CLC 147;**
HLC 1; SSC 38
See also CA 131; CANR 81; DAM MULT;
DLB 113; DNFS 2; HW 1, 2; LAW;
RGSF 2

Arrian c. 89(?)-c. 155(?) .... **CMLC 43**
See also DLB 176

Arrick, Fran .... **CLC 30**
See Gaberman, Judie Angell
See also BYA 6

Arriey, Richmond
See Delany, Samuel R(ay), Jr.

Artaud, Antonin (Marie Joseph)
1896-1948 .... **DC 14; TCLC 3, 36**
See also CA 149; DAM DRAM; DLB 258;
EW 11; GFL 1789 to the Present; MTCW
1; RGWL 2, 3

Arthur, Ruth M(abel) 1905-1979 ..... **CLC 12**
See also CA 9-12R; CANR 4; CWRI 5;
SATA 7, 26

Artsybashev, Mikhail (Petrovich)
1878-1927 .... **TCLC 31**
See also CA 170

Arundel, Honor (Morfydd)
1919-1973 .... **CLC 17**
See also CA 21-22; CAP 2; CLR 35; CWRI
5; SATA 4; SATA-Obit 24

Arzner, Dorothy 1900-1979 .... **CLC 98**

Asch, Sholem 1880-1957 .... **TCLC 3**
See also GLL 2

Ash, Shalom
See Asch, Sholem

Ashbery, John (Lawrence) 1927- .. **CLC 2, 3,**
4, 6, 9, 13, 15, 25, 41, 77, 125; PC 26
See Berry, Jonas
See also AMWS 3; CA 5-8R; CANR 9, 37,
66, 102; CP 7; DAM POET; DLB 5, 165;
DLBY 1981; INT CANR-9; MTCW 1, 2;
PAB; PFS 11; RGAL 4; WP

Ashdown, Clifford
See Freeman, R(ichard) Austin

Ashe, Gordon
See Creasey, John

Ashton-Warner, Sylvia (Constance)
1908-1984 .... **CLC 19**
See also CA 69-72; CANR 29; MTCW 1, 2

Asimov, Isaac 1920-1992 ..... **CLC 1, 3, 9, 19,**
26, 76, 92
See also AAYA 13; BEST 90:2; BPFB 1;
BYA 4, 6, 7, 9; CA 1-4R; CANR 2, 19,
36, 60; CLR 12, 79; CMW 4; CPW; DAM
POP; DLB 8; DLBY 1992; INT CANR-
19; JRDA; LAIT 5; MAICYA 1, 2;
MTCW 1, 2; RGAL 4; SATA 1, 26, 74;
SCFW 2; SFW 4; TUS; YAW

Askew, Anne 1521(?)-1546 .... **LC 81**
See also DLB 136

Assis, Joaquim Maria Machado de
See Machado de Assis, Joaquim Maria

Astell, Mary 1666-1731 .... **LC 68**
See also DLB 252; FW

Astley, Thea (Beatrice May) 1925- .. **CLC 41**
See also CA 65-68; CANR 11, 43, 78; CN
7

Astley, William 1855-1911
See Warung, Price

Aston, James
See White, T(erence) H(anbury)

Asturias, Miguel Angel 1899-1974 .... **CLC 3,**
8, 13; HLC 1
See also CA 25-28; CANR 32; CAP 2; CD-
WLB 3; DAM MULT, NOV; DLB 113;
HW 1; LAW; MTCW 1, 2; RGWL 2, 3;
WLIT 1

Atares, Carlos Saura
See Saura (Atares), Carlos

Athanasius c. 295-c. 373 .... **CMLC 48**

2, 7, 33, 249; DLBY 1987; EXPS; LAIT
5; MTCW 1, 2; NCFS 4; NFS 4; RGAL
4; RGSF 2; SATA 9; SATA-Obit 54; SSFS
2; TUS

Bale, John 1495-1563 .... **LC 62**
See also DLB 132; RGEL 2; TEA

Ball, Hugo 1886-1927 .... **TCLC 104**

Ballard, J(ames) G(raham) 1930- . **CLC 3, 6,
14, 36, 137; SSC 1, 53**
See also AAYA 3; BRWS 5; CA 5-8R;
CANR 15, 39, 65, 107; CN 7; DAM NOV,
POP; DLB 14, 207, 261; HGG; MTCW
1, 2; NFS 8; RGEL 2; RGSF 2; SATA 93;
SFW 4

Balmont, Konstantin (Dmitriyevich)
1867-1943 .... **TCLC 11**
See also CA 155

Baltausis, Vincas 1847-1910
See Mikszath, Kalman

Balzac, Honore de 1799-1850 ... **NCLC 5, 35,
53; SSC 5; WLC**
See also DA; DAB; DAC; DAM MST,
NOV; DLB 119; EW 5; GFL 1789 to the
Present; RGSF 2; RGWL 2, 3; SSFS 10;
SUFW; TWA

Bambara, Toni Cade 1939-1995 .... **BLC 1;
CLC 19, 88; SSC 35; TCLC 116;
WLCS**
See also AAYA 5; AFAW 2; AMWS 11; BW
2, 3; BYA 12, 14; CA 29-32R; CANR 24,
49, 81; CDALBS; DA; DAC; DAM MST,
MULT; DLB 38, 218; EXPS; MTCW 1,
2; RGAL 4; RGSF 2; SATA 112; SSFS 4,
7, 12

Bamdad, A.
See Shamlu, Ahmad

Banat, D. R.
See Bradbury, Ray (Douglas)

Bancroft, Laura
See Baum, L(yman) Frank

Banim, John 1798-1842 .... **NCLC 13**
See also DLB 116, 158, 159; RGEL 2

Banim, Michael 1796-1874 .... **NCLC 13**
See also DLB 158, 159

Banjo, The
See Paterson, A(ndrew) B(arton)

Banks, Iain
See Banks, Iain M(enzies)

Banks, Iain M(enzies) 1954- .... **CLC 34**
See also CA 128; CANR 61, 106; DLB 194,
261; HGG; INT 128; SFW 4

Banks, Lynne Reid .... **CLC 23**
See Reid Banks, Lynne
See also AAYA 6; BYA 7

Banks, Russell 1940- .... **CLC 37, 72; SSC 42**
See also AAYA 45; AMWS 5; CA 65-68;
CAAS 15; CANR 19, 52, 73; CN 7; DLB
130; NFS 13

Banville, John 1945- .... **CLC 46, 118**
See also CA 128; CANR 104; CN 7; DLB
14, 271; INT 128

Banville, Theodore (Faullain) de
1832-1891 .... **NCLC 9**
See also DLB 217; GFL 1789 to the Present

Baraka, Amiri 1934- .... **BLC 1; CLC 1, 2, 3,
5, 10, 14, 33, 115; DC 6; PC 4; WLCS**
See Jones, LeRoi
See also AFAW 1, 2; AMWS 2; BW 2, 3;
CA 21-24R; CABS 3; CAD; CANR 27,
38, 61; CD 5; CDALB 1941-1968; CP 7;
CPW; DA; DAC; DAM MST, MULT,
POET, POP; DFS 3, 11, 16; DLB 5, 7,
16, 38; DLBD 8; MTCW 1, 2; PFS 9;
RGAL 4; TUS; WP

Baratynsky, Evgenii Abramovich
1800-1844 .... **NCLC 103**
See also DLB 205

Barbauld, Anna Laetitia
1743-1825 .... **NCLC 50**
See also DLB 107, 109, 142, 158; RGEL 2

Barbellion, W. N. P. .... **TCLC 24**
See Cummings, Bruce F(rederick)

Barber, Benjamin R. 1939- .... **CLC 141**
See also CA 29-32R; CANR 12, 32, 64

Barbera, Jack (Vincent) 1945- .... **CLC 44**
See also CA 110; CANR 45

Barbey d'Aurevilly, Jules-Amedee
1808-1889 .... **NCLC 1; SSC 17**
See also DLB 119; GFL 1789 to the Present

Barbour, John c. 1316-1395 .... **CMLC 33**
See also DLB 146

Barbusse, Henri 1873-1935 .... **TCLC 5**
See also CA 154; DLB 65; RGWL 2, 3

Barclay, Bill
See Moorcock, Michael (John)

Barclay, William Ewert
See Moorcock, Michael (John)

Barea, Arturo 1897-1957 .... **TCLC 14**
See also CA 201

Barfoot, Joan 1946- .... **CLC 18**
See also CA 105

Barham, Richard Harris
1788-1845 .... **NCLC 77**
See also DLB 159

Baring, Maurice 1874-1945 .... **TCLC 8**
See also CA 168; DLB 34; HGG

Baring-Gould, Sabine 1834-1924 ... **TCLC 88**
See also DLB 156, 190

Barker, Clive 1952- .... **CLC 52; SSC 53**
See also AAYA 10; BEST 90:3; BPFB 1;
CA 129; CANR 71, 111; CPW; DAM
POP; DLB 261; HGG; INT 129; MTCW
1, 2; SUFW 2

Barker, George Granville
1913-1991 .... **CLC 8, 48**
See also CA 9-12R; CANR 7, 38; DAM
POET; DLB 20; MTCW 1

Barker, Harley Granville
See Granville-Barker, Harley
See also DLB 10

Barker, Howard 1946- .... **CLC 37**
See also CA 102; CBD; CD 5; DLB 13,
233

Barker, Jane 1652-1732 .... **LC 42, 82**
See also DLB 39, 131

Barker, Pat(ricia) 1943- ...... **CLC 32, 94, 146**
See also BRWS 4; CA 122; CANR 50, 101;
CN 7; DLB 271; INT 122

Barlach, Ernst (Heinrich)
1870-1938 .... **TCLC 84**
See also CA 178; DLB 56, 118

Barlow, Joel 1754-1812 .... **NCLC 23**
See also AMWS 2; DLB 37; RGAL 4

Barnard, Mary (Ethel) 1909- .... **CLC 48**
See also CA 21-22; CAP 2

Barnes, Djuna 1892-1982 .... **CLC 3, 4, 8, 11,
29, 127; SSC 3**
See Steptoe, Lydia
See also AMWS 3; CA 9-12R; CAD; CANR
16, 55; CWD; DLB 4, 9, 45; GLL 1;
MTCW 1, 2; RGAL 4; TUS

Barnes, Julian (Patrick) 1946- . **CLC 42, 141**
See also BRWS 4; CA 102; CANR 19, 54;
CN 7; DAB; DLB 194; DLBY 1993;
MTCW 1

Barnes, Peter 1931- .... **CLC 5, 56**
See also CA 65-68; CAAS 12; CANR 33,
34, 64, 113; CBD; CD 5; DFS 6; DLB
13, 233; MTCW 1

Barnes, William 1801-1886 .... **NCLC 75**
See also DLB 32

Baroja (y Nessi), Pio 1872-1956 .... **HLC 1;
TCLC 8**
See also EW 9

Baron, David
See Pinter, Harold

Baron Corvo
See Rolfe, Frederick (William Serafino Austin Lewis Mary)

Barondess, Sue K(aufman)
1926-1977 .... **CLC 8**
See Kaufman, Sue
See also CA 1-4R; CANR 1

Baron de Teive
See Pessoa, Fernando (Antonio Nogueira)

Baroness Von S.
See Zangwill, Israel

Barres, (Auguste-)Maurice
1862-1923 .... **TCLC 47**
See also CA 164; DLB 123; GFL 1789 to
the Present

Barreto, Afonso Henrique de Lima
See Lima Barreto, Afonso Henrique de

Barrett, Andrea 1954- .... **CLC 150**
See also CA 156; CANR 92

Barrett, Michele .... **CLC 65**

Barrett, (Roger) Syd 1946- .... **CLC 35**

Barrett, William (Christopher)
1913-1992 .... **CLC 27**
See also CA 13-16R; CANR 11, 67; INT
CANR-11

Barrie, J(ames) M(atthew)
1860-1937 .... **TCLC 2**
See also BRWS 3; BYA 4, 5; CA 136;
CANR 77; CDBLB 1890-1914; CLR 16;
CWRI 5; DAB; DAM DRAM; DFS 7;
DLB 10, 141, 156; FANT; MAICYA 1, 2;
MTCW 1; SATA 100; SUFW; WCH;
WLIT 4; YABC 1

Barrington, Michael
See Moorcock, Michael (John)

Barrol, Grady
See Bograd, Larry

Barry, Mike
See Malzberg, Barry N(athaniel)

Barry, Philip 1896-1949 .... **TCLC 11**
See also CA 199; DFS 9; DLB 7, 228;
RGAL 4

Bart, Andre Schwarz
See Schwarz-Bart, Andre

Barth, John (Simmons) 1930- ... **CLC 1, 2, 3,
5, 7, 9, 10, 14, 27, 51, 89; SSC 10**
See also AITN 1, 2; AMW; BPFB 1; CA
1-4R; CABS 1; CANR 5, 23, 49, 64, 113;
CN 7; DAM NOV; DLB 2, 227; FANT;
MTCW 1; RGAL 4; RGSF 2; RHW;
SSFS 6; TUS

Barthelme, Donald 1931-1989 ... **CLC 1, 2, 3,
5, 6, 8, 13, 23, 46, 59, 115; SSC 2, 55**
See also AMWS 4; BPFB 1; CA 21-24R;
CANR 20, 58; DAM NOV; DLB 2, 234;
DLBY 1980, 1989; FANT; MTCW 1, 2;
RGAL 4; RGSF 2; SATA 7; SATA-Obit
62; SSFS 3

Barthelme, Frederick 1943- ...... **CLC 36, 117**
See also AMWS 11; CA 122; CANR 77;
CN 7; CSW; DLB 244; DLBY 1985; INT
CA-122

Barthes, Roland (Gerard)
1915-1980 .... **CLC 24, 83**
See also CA 130; CANR 66; EW 13; GFL
1789 to the Present; MTCW 1, 2; TWA

Barzun, Jacques (Martin) 1907- ..... **CLC 51,
145**
See also CA 61-64; CANR 22, 95

Bashevis, Isaac
See Singer, Isaac Bashevis

Bashkirtseff, Marie 1859-1884 .... **NCLC 27**

Basho, Matsuo
See Matsuo Basho
See also RGWL 2, 3; WP

Basil of Caesaria c. 330-379 .... **CMLC 35**

Bass, Kingsley B., Jr.
See Bullins, Ed

Belser, Reimond Karel Maria de 1929-
See Ruyslinck, Ward
See also CA 152

Bely, Andrey .... **PC 11; TCLC 7**
See Bugayev, Boris Nikolayevich
See also EW 9; MTCW 1

Belyi, Andrei
See Bugayev, Boris Nikolayevich
See also RGWL 2, 3

Bembo, Pietro 1470-1547 .... **LC 79**
See also RGWL 2, 3

Benary, Margot
See Benary-Isbert, Margot

Benary-Isbert, Margot 1889-1979 .... **CLC 12**
See also CA 5-8R; CANR 4, 72; CLR 12;
MAICYA 1, 2; SATA 2; SATA-Obit 21

Benavente (y Martinez), Jacinto
1866-1954 .... **HLCS 1; TCLC 3**
See also CA 131; CANR 81; DAM DRAM,
MULT; GLL 2; HW 1, 2; MTCW 1, 2

Benchley, Peter (Bradford) 1940- .. **CLC 4, 8**
See also AAYA 14; AITN 2; BPFB 1; CA
17-20R; CANR 12, 35, 66; CPW; DAM
NOV, POP; HGG; MTCW 1, 2; SATA 3,
89

Benchley, Robert (Charles)
1889-1945 .... **TCLC 1, 55**
See also CA 153; DLB 11; RGAL 4

Benda, Julien 1867-1956 .... **TCLC 60**
See also CA 154; GFL 1789 to the Present

Benedict, Ruth (Fulton)
1887-1948 .... **TCLC 60**
See also CA 158; DLB 246

Benedikt, Michael 1935- .... **CLC 4, 14**
See also CA 13-16R; CANR 7; CP 7; DLB
5

Benet, Juan 1927-1993 .... **CLC 28**
See also CA 143

Benet, Stephen Vincent 1898-1943 ... **SSC 10;
TCLC 7**
See also AMWS 11; CA 152; DAM POET;
DLB 4, 48, 102, 249; DLBY 1997; HGG;
MTCW 1; RGAL 4; RGSF 2; SUFW;
WP; YABC 1

Benet, William Rose 1886-1950 ..... **TCLC 28**
See also CA 152; DAM POET; DLB 45;
RGAL 4

Benford, Gregory (Albert) 1941- ..... **CLC 52**
See also BPFB 1; CA 69-72, 175; CAAE
175; CAAS 27; CANR 12, 24, 49, 95;
CSW; DLBY 1982; SCFW 2; SFW 4

Bengtsson, Frans (Gunnar)
1894-1954 .... **TCLC 48**
See also CA 170

Benjamin, David
See Slavitt, David R(ytman)

Benjamin, Lois
See Gould, Lois

Benjamin, Walter 1892-1940 .... **TCLC 39**
See also CA 164; DLB 242; EW 11

Benn, Gottfried 1886-1956 .. **PC 35; TCLC 3**
See also CA 153; DLB 56; RGWL 2, 3

Bennett, Alan 1934- .... **CLC 45, 77**
See also BRWS 8; CA 103; CANR 35, 55,
106; CBD; CD 5; DAB; DAM MST;
MTCW 1, 2

Bennett, (Enoch) Arnold
1867-1931 .... **TCLC 5, 20**
See also BRW 6; CA 155; CDBLB 1890-
1914; DLB 10, 34, 98, 135; MTCW 2

Bennett, Elizabeth
See Mitchell, Margaret (Munnerlyn)

Bennett, George Harold 1930-
See Bennett, Hal
See also BW 1; CA 97-100; CANR 87

Bennett, Hal .... **CLC 5**
See Bennett, George Harold
See also DLB 33

Bennett, Jay 1912- .... **CLC 35**
See also AAYA 10; CA 69-72; CANR 11,
42, 79; JRDA; SAAS 4; SATA 41, 87;
SATA-Brief 27; WYA; YAW

Bennett, Louise (Simone) 1919- .... **BLC 1;
CLC 28**
See also BW 2, 3; CA 151; CDWLB 3; CP
7; DAM MULT; DLB 117

Benson, A. C. 1862-1925 .... **TCLC 123**
See also DLB 98

Benson, E(dward) F(rederic)
1867-1940 .... **TCLC 27**
See also CA 157; DLB 135, 153; HGG;
SUFW 1

Benson, Jackson J. 1930- .... **CLC 34**
See also CA 25-28R; DLB 111

Benson, Sally 1900-1972 .... **CLC 17**
See also CA 19-20; CAP 1; SATA 1, 35;
SATA-Obit 27

Benson, Stella 1892-1933 .... **TCLC 17**
See also CA 154, 155; DLB 36, 162; FANT;
TEA

Bentham, Jeremy 1748-1832 .... **NCLC 38**
See also DLB 107, 158, 252

Bentley, E(dmund) C(lerihew)
1875-1956 .... **TCLC 12**
See also DLB 70; MSW

Bentley, Eric (Russell) 1916- .... **CLC 24**
See also CA 5-8R; CAD; CANR 6, 67;
CBD; CD 5; INT CANR-6

Beranger, Pierre Jean de
1780-1857 .... **NCLC 34**

Berdyaev, Nicolas
See Berdyaev, Nikolai (Aleksandrovich)

Berdyaev, Nikolai (Aleksandrovich)
1874-1948 .... **TCLC 67**
See also CA 157

Berdyayev, Nikolai (Aleksandrovich)
See Berdyaev, Nikolai (Aleksandrovich)

Berendt, John (Lawrence) 1939- ...... **CLC 86**
See also CA 146; CANR 75, 93; MTCW 1

Beresford, J(ohn) D(avys)
1873-1947 .... **TCLC 81**
See also CA 155; DLB 162, 178, 197; SFW
4; SUFW 1

Bergelson, David 1884-1952 .... **TCLC 81**

Berger, Colonel
See Malraux, (Georges-)Andre

Berger, John (Peter) 1926- .... **CLC 2, 19**
See also BRWS 4; CA 81-84; CANR 51,
78; CN 7; DLB 14, 207

Berger, Melvin H. 1927- .... **CLC 12**
See also CA 5-8R; CANR 4; CLR 32;
SAAS 2; SATA 5, 88; SATA-Essay 124

Berger, Thomas (Louis) 1924- .. **CLC 3, 5, 8,
11, 18, 38**
See also BPFB 1; CA 1-4R; CANR 5, 28,
51; CN 7; DAM NOV; DLB 2; DLBY
1980; FANT; INT CANR-28; MTCW 1,
2; RHW; TCWW 2

Bergman, (Ernst) Ingmar 1918- ...... **CLC 16,
72**
See also CA 81-84; CANR 33, 70; DLB
257; MTCW 2

Bergson, Henri(-Louis) 1859-1941 . **TCLC 32**
See also CA 164; EW 8; GFL 1789 to the
Present

Bergstein, Eleanor 1938- .... **CLC 4**
See also CA 53-56; CANR 5

Berkeley, George 1685-1753 .... **LC 65**
See also DLB 31, 101, 252

Berkoff, Steven 1937- .... **CLC 56**
See also CA 104; CANR 72; CBD; CD 5

Berlin, Isaiah 1909-1997 .... **TCLC 105**
See also CA 85-88

Bermant, Chaim (Icyk) 1929-1998 ... **CLC 40**
See also CA 57-60; CANR 6, 31, 57, 105;
CN 7

Bern, Victoria
See Fisher, M(ary) F(rances) K(ennedy)

Bernanos, (Paul Louis) Georges
1888-1948 .... **TCLC 3**
See also CA 130; CANR 94; DLB 72; GFL
1789 to the Present; RGWL 2, 3

Bernard, April 1956- .... **CLC 59**
See also CA 131

Berne, Victoria
See Fisher, M(ary) F(rances) K(ennedy)

Bernhard, Thomas 1931-1989 ..... **CLC 3, 32,
61; DC 14**
See also CA 85-88; CANR 32, 57; CDWLB
2; DLB 85, 124; MTCW 1; RGWL 2, 3

Bernhardt, Sarah (Henriette Rosine)
1844-1923 .... **TCLC 75**
See also CA 157

Bernstein, Charles 1950- .... **CLC 142,**
See also CA 129; CAAS 24; CANR 90; CP
7; DLB 169

Berriault, Gina 1926-1999 .... **CLC 54, 109;
SSC 30**
See also CA 129; CANR 66; DLB 130;
SSFS 7,11

Berrigan, Daniel 1921- .... **CLC 4**
See also CA 33-36R; CAAE 187; CAAS 1;
CANR 11, 43, 78; CP 7; DLB 5

Berrigan, Edmund Joseph Michael, Jr.
1934-1983
See Berrigan, Ted
See also CA 61-64; CANR 14, 102

Berrigan, Ted .... **CLC 37**
See Berrigan, Edmund Joseph Michael, Jr.
See also DLB 5, 169; WP

Berry, Charles Edward Anderson 1931-
See Berry, Chuck
See also CA 115

Berry, Chuck .... **CLC 17**
See Berry, Charles Edward Anderson

Berry, Jonas
See Ashbery, John (Lawrence)
See also GLL 1

Berry, Wendell (Erdman) 1934- ... **CLC 4, 6,
8, 27, 46; PC 28**
See also AITN 1; AMWS 10; ANW; CA
73-76; CANR 50, 73, 101; CP 7; CSW;
DAM POET; DLB 5, 6, 234, 275; MTCW
1

Berryman, John 1914-1972 ... **CLC 1, 2, 3, 4,
6, 8, 10, 13, 25, 62**
See also AMW; CA 13-16; CABS 2; CANR
35; CAP 1; CDALB 1941-1968; DAM
POET; DLB 48; MTCW 1, 2; PAB; RGAL
4; WP

Bertolucci, Bernardo 1940- ...... **CLC 16, 157**
See also CA 106

Berton, Pierre (Francis Demarigny)
1920- .... **CLC 104**
See also CA 1-4R; CANR 2, 56; CPW;
DLB 68; SATA 99

Bertrand, Aloysius 1807-1841 .... **NCLC 31**
See Bertrand, Louis oAloysiusc

Bertrand, Louis oAloysiusc
See Bertrand, Aloysius
See also DLB 217

Bertran de Born c. 1140-1215 .... **CMLC 5**

Besant, Annie (Wood) 1847-1933 ..... **TCLC 9**
See also CA 185

Bessie, Alvah 1904-1985 .... **CLC 23**
See also CA 5-8R; CANR 2, 80; DLB 26

Bethlen, T. D.
See Silverberg, Robert

Beti, Mongo .... **BLC 1; CLC 27**
See Biyidi, Alexandre
See also AFW; CANR 79; DAM MULT;
WLIT 2

Boccaccio, Giovanni 1313-1375 ... **CMLC 13, 57; SSC 10**
See also EW 2; RGSF 2; RGWL 2, 3; TWA
Bochco, Steven 1943- .... **CLC 35**
See also AAYA 11; CA 138
Bode, Sigmund
See O'Doherty, Brian
Bodel, Jean 1167(?)-1210 .... **CMLC 28**
Bodenheim, Maxwell 1892-1954 .... **TCLC 44**
See also CA 187; DLB 9, 45; RGAL 4
Bodenheimer, Maxwell
See Bodenheim, Maxwell
Bodker, Cecil 1927- .... **CLC 21**
See also CA 73-76; CANR 13, 44, 111; CLR 23; MAICYA 1, 2; SATA 14, 133
Bodker, Cecil 1927-
See Bodker, Cecil
Boell, Heinrich (Theodor)
1917-1985 ..... **CLC 2, 3, 6, 9, 11, 15, 27, 32, 72; SSC 23; WLC**
See Boll, Heinrich
See also CA 21-24R; CANR 24; DA; DAB; DAC; DAM MST, NOV; DLB 69; DLBY 1985; MTCW 1, 2; TWA
Boerne, Alfred
See Doeblin, Alfred
Boethius c. 480-c. 524 .... **CMLC 15**
See also DLB 115; RGWL 2, 3
Boff, Leonardo (Genezio Darci)
1938- .... **CLC 70; HLC 1**
See also CA 150; DAM MULT; HW 2
Bogan, Louise 1897-1970 .... **CLC 4, 39, 46, 93; PC 12**
See also AMWS 3; CA 73-76; CANR 33, 82; DAM POET; DLB 45, 169; MAWW; MTCW 1, 2; RGAL 4
Bogarde, Dirk
See Van Den Bogarde, Derek Jules Gaspard Ulric Niven
See also DLB 14
Bogosian, Eric 1953- .... **CLC 45, 141**
See also CA 138; CAD; CANR 102; CD 5
Bograd, Larry 1953- .... **CLC 35**
See also CA 93-96; CANR 57; SAAS 21; SATA 33, 89; WYA
Boiardo, Matteo Maria 1441-1494 .... **LC 6**
Boileau-Despreaux, Nicolas 1636-1711 . **LC 3**
See also DLB 268; EW 3; GFL Beginnings to 1789; RGWL 2, 3
Boissard, Maurice
See Leautaud, Paul
Bojer, Johan 1872-1959 .... **TCLC 64**
See also CA 189
Bok, Edward W. 1863-1930 .... **TCLC 101**
See also DLB 91; DLBD 16
Boland, Eavan (Aisling) 1944- .. **CLC 40, 67, 113**
See also BRWS 5; CA 143; CANR 61; CP 7; CWP; DAM POET; DLB 40; FW; MTCW 2; PFS 12
Boll, Heinrich
See Boell, Heinrich (Theodor)
See also BPFB 1; CDWLB 2; EW 13; RGSF 2; RGWL 2, 3
Bolt, Lee
See Faust, Frederick (Schiller)
Bolt, Robert (Oxton) 1924-1995 .... **CLC 14**
See also CA 17-20R; CANR 35, 67; CBD; DAM DRAM; DFS 2; DLB 13, 233; LAIT 1; MTCW 1
Bombal, Maria Luisa 1910-1980 .... **HLCS 1; SSC 37**
See also CA 127; CANR 72; HW 1; LAW; RGSF 2
Bombet, Louis-Alexandre-Cesar
See Stendhal
Bomkauf
See Kaufman, Bob (Garnell)

Bonaventura .... **NCLC 35**
See also DLB 90
Bond, Edward 1934- .... **CLC 4, 6, 13, 23**
See also BRWS 1; CA 25-28R; CANR 38, 67, 106; CBD; CD 5; DAM DRAM; DFS 3,8; DLB 13; MTCW 1
Bonham, Frank 1914-1989 .... **CLC 12**
See also AAYA 1; BYA 1, 3; CA 9-12R; CANR 4, 36; JRDA; MAICYA 1, 2; SAAS 3; SATA 1, 49; SATA-Obit 62; TCWW 2; YAW
Bonnefoy, Yves 1923- .... **CLC 9, 15, 58**
See also CA 85-88; CANR 33, 75, 97; CWW 2; DAM MST, POET; DLB 258; GFL 1789 to the Present; MTCW 1, 2
Bontemps, Arna(ud Wendell)
1902-1973 ..... **BLC 1; CLC 1, 18; HR 2**
See also BW 1; CA 1-4R; CANR 4, 35; CLR 6; CWRI 5; DAM MULT, NOV, POET; DLB 48, 51; JRDA; MAICYA 1, 2; MTCW 1, 2; SATA 2, 44; SATA-Obit 24; WCH; WP
Booth, Martin 1944- .... **CLC 13**
See also CA 93-96; CAAE 188; CAAS 2; CANR 92
Booth, Philip 1925- .... **CLC 23**
See also CA 5-8R; CANR 5, 88; CP 7; DLBY 1982
Booth, Wayne C(layson) 1921- .... **CLC 24**
See also CA 1-4R; CAAS 5; CANR 3, 43; DLB 67
Borchert, Wolfgang 1921-1947 .... **TCLC 5**
See also CA 188; DLB 69, 124
Borel, Petrus 1809-1859 .... **NCLC 41**
See also DLB 119; GFL 1789 to the Present
Borges, Jorge Luis 1899-1986 ... **CLC 1, 2, 3, 4, 6, 8, 9, 10, 13, 19, 44, 48, 83; HLC 1; PC 22, 32; SSC 4, 41; TCLC 109; WLC**
See also AAYA 26; BPFB 1; CA 21-24R; CANR 19, 33, 75, 105; CDWLB 3; DA; DAB; DAC; DAM MST, MULT; DLB 113; DLBY 1986; DNFS 1, 2; HW 1, 2; LAW; MSW; MTCW 1, 2; RGSF 2; RGWL 2, 3; SFW 4; SSFS 4, 9; TWA; WLIT 1
Borowski, Tadeusz 1922-1951 .... **SSC 48; TCLC 9**
See also CA 154; CDWLB 4, 4; DLB 215; RGSF 2; RGWL 3; SSFS 13
Borrow, George (Henry)
1803-1881 .... **NCLC 9**
See also DLB 21, 55, 166
Bosch (Gavino), Juan 1909-2001 ..... **HLCS 1**
See also CA 151; DAM MST, MULT; DLB 145; HW 1, 2
Bosman, Herman Charles
1905-1951 .... **TCLC 49**
See Malan, Herman
See also CA 160; DLB 225; RGSF 2
Bosschere, Jean de 1878(?)-1953 ... **TCLC 19**
See also CA 186
Boswell, James 1740-1795 ... **LC 4, 50; WLC**
See also BRW 3; CDBLB 1660-1789; DA; DAB; DAC; DAM MST; DLB 104, 142; TEA; WLIT 3
Bottomley, Gordon 1874-1948 ..... **TCLC 107**
See also CA 192; DLB 10
Bottoms, David 1949- .... **CLC 53**
See also CA 105; CANR 22; CSW; DLB 120; DLBY 1983
Boucicault, Dion 1820-1890 .... **NCLC 41**
Boucolon, Maryse
See Conde, Maryse
Bourget, Paul (Charles Joseph)
1852-1935 .... **TCLC 12**
See also CA 196; DLB 123; GFL 1789 to the Present

Bourjaily, Vance (Nye) 1922- .... **CLC 8, 62**
See also CA 1-4R; CAAS 1; CANR 2, 72; CN 7; DLB 2, 143
Bourne, Randolph S(illiman)
1886-1918 .... **TCLC 16**
See also AMW; CA 155; DLB 63
Bova, Ben(jamin William) 1932- ...... **CLC 45**
See also AAYA 16; CA 5-8R; CAAS 18; CANR 11, 56, 94, 111; CLR 3; DLBY 1981; INT CANR-11; MAICYA 1, 2; MTCW 1; SATA 6, 68, 133; SFW 4
Bowen, Elizabeth (Dorothea Cole)
1899-1973 . **CLC 1, 3, 6, 11, 15, 22, 118; SSC 3, 28**
See also BRWS 2; CA 17-18; CANR 35, 105; CAP 2; CDBLB 1945-1960; DAM NOV; DLB 15, 162; EXPS; FW; HGG; MTCW 1, 2; NFS 13; RGSF 2; SSFS 5; SUFW 1; TEA; WLIT 4
Bowering, George 1935- .... **CLC 15, 47**
See also CA 21-24R; CAAS 16; CANR 10; CP 7; DLB 53
Bowering, Marilyn R(uthe) 1949- .... **CLC 32**
See also CA 101; CANR 49; CP 7; CWP
Bowers, Edgar 1924-2000 .... **CLC 9**
See also CA 5-8R; CANR 24; CP 7; CSW; DLB 5
Bowers, Mrs. J. Milton 1842-1914
See Bierce, Ambrose (Gwinett)
Bowie, David .... **CLC 17**
See Jones, David Robert
Bowles, Jane (Sydney) 1917-1973 ..... **CLC 3, 68**
See also CA 19-20; CAP 2
Bowles, Paul (Frederick) 1910-1999 . **CLC 1, 2, 19, 53; SSC 3**
See also AMWS 4; CA 1-4R; CAAS 1; CANR 1, 19, 50, 75; CN 7; DLB 5, 6, 218; MTCW 1, 2; RGAL 4
Bowles, William Lisle 1762-1850 . **NCLC 103**
See also DLB 93
Box, Edgar
See Vidal, Gore
See also GLL 1
Boyd, James 1888-1944 .... **TCLC 115**
See also CA 186; DLB 9; DLBD 16; RGAL 4; RHW
Boyd, Nancy
See Millay, Edna St. Vincent
See also GLL 1
Boyd, Thomas (Alexander)
1898-1935 .... **TCLC 111**
See also CA 183; DLB 9; DLBD 16
Boyd, William 1952- .... **CLC 28, 53, 70**
See also CA 120; CANR 51, 71; CN 7; DLB 231
Boyle, Kay 1902-1992 .... **CLC 1, 5, 19, 58, 121; SSC 5**
See also CA 13-16R; CAAS 1; CANR 29, 61, 110; DLB 4, 9, 48, 86; DLBY 1993; MTCW 1, 2; RGAL 4; RGSF 2; SSFS 10, 13, 14
Boyle, Mark
See Kienzle, William X(avier)
Boyle, Patrick 1905-1982 .... **CLC 19**
See also CA 127
Boyle, T. C.
See Boyle, T(homas) Coraghessan
See also AMWS 8
Boyle, T(homas) Coraghessan
1948- .... **CLC 36, 55, 90; SSC 16**
See Boyle, T. C.
See also AAYA 47; BEST 90:4; BPFB 1; CA 120; CANR 44, 76, 89; CN 7; CPW; DAM POP; DLB 218; DLBY 1986; MTCW 2; SSFS 13
Boz
See Dickens, Charles (John Huffam)

Brackenridge, Hugh Henry
1748-1816 .... **NCLC 7**
See also DLB 11, 37; RGAL 4
Bradbury, Edward P.
See Moorcock, Michael (John)
See also MTCW 2
Bradbury, Malcolm (Stanley)
1932-2000 .... **CLC 32, 61**
See also CA 1-4R; CANR 1, 33, 91, 98;
CN 7; DAM NOV; DLB 14, 207; MTCW
1, 2
Bradbury, Ray (Douglas) 1920- .... **CLC 1, 3,**
10, 15, 42, 98; SSC 29, 53; WLC
See also AAYA 15; AITN 1, 2; AMWS 4;
BPFB 1; BYA 4, 5, 11; CA 1-4R; CANR
2, 30, 75; CDALB 1968-1988; CN 7;
CPW; DA; DAB; DAC; DAM MST,
NOV, POP; DLB 2, 8; EXPN; EXPS;
HGG; LAIT 3, 5; MTCW 1, 2; NFS 1;
RGAL 4; RGSF 2; SATA 11, 64, 123;
SCFW 4; SFW 4; SSFS 1; SUFW 1, 2;
TUS; YAW
Braddon, Mary Elizabeth
1837-1915 .... **TCLC 111**
See also BRWS 8; CA 179; CMW 4; DLB
18, 70, 156; HGG
Bradford, Gamaliel 1863-1932 .... **TCLC 36**
See also CA 160; DLB 17
Bradford, William 1590-1657 .... **LC 64**
See also DLB 24, 30; RGAL 4
Bradley, David (Henry), Jr. 1950- .... **BLC 1;**
CLC 23, 118
See also BW 1, 3; CA 104; CANR 26, 81;
CN 7; DAM MULT; DLB 33
Bradley, John Ed(mund, Jr.) 1958- . **CLC 55**
See also CA 139; CANR 99; CN 7; CSW
Bradley, Marion Zimmer
1930-1999 .... **CLC 30**
See Chapman, Lee; Dexter, John; Gardner,
Miriam; Ives, Morgan; Rivers, Elfrida
See also AAYA 40; BPFB 1; CA 57-60;
CAAS 10; CANR 7, 31, 51, 75, 107;
CPW; DAM POP; DLB 8; FANT; FW;
MTCW 1, 2; SATA 90; SATA-Obit 116;
SFW 4; SUFW 2; YAW
Bradshaw, John 1933- .... **CLC 70**
See also CA 138; CANR 61
Bradstreet, Anne 1612(?)-1672 ... **LC 4, 30;**
PC 10
See also AMWS 1; CDALB 1640-1865;
DA; DAM MST, POET; DLB 24;
EXPP; FW; PFS 6; RGAL 4; TUS; WP
Brady, Joan 1939- .... **CLC 86**
See also CA 141
Bragg, Melvyn 1939- .... **CLC 10**
See also BEST 89:3; CA 57-60; CANR 10,
48, 89; CN 7; DLB 14, 271; RHW
Brahe, Tycho 1546-1601 .... **LC 45**
Braine, John (Gerard) 1922-1986 . **CLC 1, 3,**
41
See also CA 1-4R; CANR 1, 33; CDBLB
1945-1960; DLB 15; DLBY 1986; MTCW
1
Bramah, Ernest 1868-1942 .... **TCLC 72**
See also CA 156; CMW 4; DLB 70; FANT
Brammer, William 1930(?)-1978 ...... **CLC 31**
Brancati, Vitaliano 1907-1954 .... **TCLC 12**
See also DLB 264
Brancato, Robin F(idler) 1936- .... **CLC 35**
See also AAYA 9; BYA 6; CA 69-72; CANR
11, 45; CLR 32; JRDA; MAICYA 2;
MAICYAS 1; SAAS 9; SATA 97; WYA;
YAW
Brand, Max
See Faust, Frederick (Schiller)
See also BPFB 1; TCWW 2
Brand, Millen 1906-1980 .... **CLC 7**
See also CA 21-24R; CANR 72

Branden, Barbara .... **CLC 44**
See also CA 148
Brandes, Georg (Morris Cohen)
1842-1927 .... **TCLC 10**
See also CA 189
Brandys, Kazimierz 1916-2000 .... **CLC 62**
Branley, Franklyn M(ansfield)
1915-2002 .... **CLC 21**
See also CA 33-36R; CANR 14, 39; CLR
13; MAICYA 1, 2; SAAS 16; SATA 4,
68, 136
Brathwaite, Edward Kamau
1930- .... **BLCS; CLC 11**
See also BW 2, 3; CA 25-28R; CANR 11,
26, 47, 107; CDWLB 3; CP 7; DAM
POET; DLB 125
Brathwaite, Kamau
See Brathwaite, Edward Kamau
Brautigan, Richard (Gary)
1935-1984 ..... **CLC 1, 3, 5, 9, 12, 34, 42**
See also BPFB 1; CA 53-56; CANR 34;
DAM NOV; DLB 2, 5, 206; DLBY 1980,
1984; FANT; MTCW 1; RGAL 4; SATA
56
Brave Bird, Mary .... **NNAL**
See Crow Dog, Mary (Ellen)
Braverman, Kate 1950- .... **CLC 67**
See also CA 89-92
Brecht, (Eugen) Bertolt (Friedrich)
1898-1956 ..... **DC 3; TCLC 1, 6, 13, 35;**
WLC
See also CA 133; CANR 62; CDWLB 2;
DA; DAB; DAC; DAM DRAM, MST;
DFS 4, 5, 9; DLB 56, 124; EW 11; IDTP;
MTCW 1, 2; RGWL 2, 3; TWA
Brecht, Eugen Berthold Friedrich
See Brecht, (Eugen) Bertolt (Friedrich)
Bremer, Fredrika 1801-1865 .... **NCLC 11**
See also DLB 254
Brennan, Christopher John
1870-1932 .... **TCLC 17**
See also CA 188; DLB 230
Brennan, Maeve 1917-1993 ... **CLC 5; TCLC**
124
See also CA 81-84; CANR 72, 100
Brent, Linda
See Jacobs, Harriet A(nn)
Brentano, Clemens (Maria)
1778-1842 .... **NCLC 1**
See also DLB 90; RGWL 2, 3
Brent of Bin Bin
See Franklin, (Stella Maria Sarah) Miles
(Lampe)
Brenton, Howard 1942- .... **CLC 31**
See also CA 69-72; CANR 33, 67; CBD;
CD 5; DLB 13; MTCW 1
Breslin, James 1930-
See Breslin, Jimmy
See also CA 73-76; CANR 31, 75; DAM
NOV; MTCW 1, 2
Breslin, Jimmy .... **CLC 4, 43**
See Breslin, James
See also AITN 1; DLB 185; MTCW 2
Bresson, Robert 1901(?)-1999 .... **CLC 16**
See also CA 110; CANR 49
Breton, Andre 1896-1966 .. **CLC 2, 9, 15, 54;**
PC 15
See also CA 19-20; CANR 40, 60; CAP 2;
DLB 65, 258; EW 11; GFL 1789 to the
Present; MTCW 1, 2; RGWL 2, 3; TWA;
WP
Breytenbach, Breyten 1939(?)- .. **CLC 23, 37,**
126
See also CA 129; CANR 61; CWW 2; DAM
POET; DLB 225

Bridgers, Sue Ellen 1942- .... **CLC 26**
See also AAYA 8; BYA 7, 8; CA 65-68;
CANR 11, 36; CLR 18; DLB 52; JRDA;
MAICYA 1, 2; SAAS 1; SATA 22, 90;
SATA-Essay 109; WYA; YAW
Bridges, Robert (Seymour)
1844-1930 .... **PC 28; TCLC 1**
See also BRW 6; CA 152; CDBLB 1890-
1914; DAM POET; DLB 19, 98
Bridie, James .... **TCLC 3**
See Mavor, Osborne Henry
See also DLB 10
Brin, David 1950- .... **CLC 34**
See also AAYA 21; CA 102; CANR 24, 70;
INT CANR-24; SATA 65; SCFW 2; SFW
4
Brink, Andre (Philippus) 1935- . **CLC 18, 36,**
106
See also AFW; BRWS 6; CA 104; CANR
39, 62, 109; CN 7; DLB 225; INT CA-
103; MTCW 1, 2; WLIT 2
Brinsmead, H. F.
See Brinsmead, H(esba) F(ay)
Brinsmead, H. F(ay)
See Brinsmead, H(esba) F(ay)
Brinsmead, H(esba) F(ay) 1922- ...... **CLC 21**
See also CA 21-24R; CANR 10; CLR 47;
CWRI 5; MAICYA 1, 2; SAAS 5; SATA
18, 78
Brittain, Vera (Mary) 1893(?)-1970 . **CLC 23**
See also CA 13-16; CANR 58; CAP 1; DLB
191; FW; MTCW 1, 2
Broch, Hermann 1886-1951 .... **TCLC 20**
See also CDWLB 2; DLB 85, 124; EW 10;
RGWL 2, 3
Brock, Rose
See Hansen, Joseph
See also GLL 1
Brod, Max 1884-1968 .... **TCLC 115**
See also CA 5-8R; CANR 7; DLB 81
Brodkey, Harold (Roy) 1930-1996 .. **CLC 56;**
TCLC 123
See also CA 111; CANR 71; CN 7; DLB
130
Brodskii, Iosif
See Brodsky, Joseph
Brodsky, Iosif Alexandrovich 1940-1996
See Brodsky, Joseph
See also AITN 1; CA 41-44R; CANR 37,
106; DAM POET; MTCW 1, 2; RGWL 2,
3
Brodsky, Joseph . **CLC 4, 6, 13, 36, 100; PC**
9
See Brodsky, Iosif Alexandrovich
See also AMWS 8; CWW 2; MTCW 1
Brodsky, Michael (Mark) 1948- .... **CLC 19**
See also CA 102; CANR 18, 41, 58; DLB
244
Brodzki, Bella ed. .... **CLC 65**
Brome, Richard 1590(?)-1652 .... **LC 61**
See also DLB 58
Bromell, Henry 1947- .... **CLC 5**
See also CA 53-56; CANR 9
Bromfield, Louis (Brucker)
1896-1956 .... **TCLC 11**
See also CA 155; DLB 4, 9, 86; RGAL 4;
RHW
Broner, E(sther) M(asserman)
1930- .... **CLC 19**
See also CA 17-20R; CANR 8, 25, 72; CN
7; DLB 28
Bronk, William (M.) 1918-1999 .... **CLC 10**
See also CA 89-92; CANR 23; CP 7; DLB
165
Bronstein, Lev Davidovich
See Trotsky, Leon
Bronte, Anne 1820-1849 ..... **NCLC 4, 71, 102**
See also BRW 5; BRWR 1; DLB 21, 199;
TEA

Buckley, William F(rank), Jr. 1925- . **CLC 7, 18, 37**
See also AITN 1; BPFB 1; CA 1-4R; CANR 1, 24, 53, 93; CMW 4; CPW; DAM POP; DLB 137; DLBY 1980; INT CANR-24; MTCW 1, 2; TUS

Buechner, (Carl) Frederick 1926- . **CLC 2, 4, 6, 9**
See also AMWS 12; BPFB 1; CA 13-16R; CANR 11, 39, 64, 114; CN 7; DAM NOV; DLBY 1980; INT CANR-11; MTCW 1, 2

Buell, John (Edward) 1927- .... **CLC 10**
See also CA 1-4R; CANR 71; DLB 53

Buero Vallejo, Antonio 1916-2000 ... **CLC 15, 46, 139; DC 18**
See also CA 106; CANR 24, 49, 75; DFS 11; HW 1; MTCW 1, 2

Bufalino, Gesualdo 1920(?)-1990 ...... **CLC 74**
See also CWW 2; DLB 196

Bugayev, Boris Nikolayevich
1880-1934 .... **PC 11; TCLC 7**
See Bely, Andrey; Belyi, Andrei
See also CA 165; MTCW 1

Bukowski, Charles 1920-1994 ... **CLC 2, 5, 9, 41, 82, 108; PC 18; SSC 45**
See also CA 17-20R; CANR 40, 62, 105; CPW; DAM NOV, POET; DLB 5, 130, 169; MTCW 1, 2

Bulgakov, Mikhail (Afanas'evich)
1891-1940 .... **SSC 18; TCLC 2, 16**
See also BPFB 1; CA 152; DAM DRAM, NOV; DLB 272; NFS 8; RGSF 2; RGWL 2, 3; SFW 4; TWA

Bulgya, Alexander Alexandrovich
1901-1956 .... **TCLC 53**
See Fadeev, Aleksandr Aleksandrovich; Fadeyev, Alexander
See also CA 181

Bullins, Ed 1935- ... **BLC 1; CLC 1, 5, 7; DC 6**
See also BW 2, 3; CA 49-52; CAAS 16; CAD; CANR 24, 46, 73; CD 5; DAM DRAM, MULT; DLB 7, 38, 249; MTCW 1, 2; RGAL 4

Bulwer-Lytton, Edward (George Earle Lytton) 1803-1873 .... **NCLC 1, 45**
See also DLB 21; RGEL 2; SFW 4; SUFW 1; TEA

Bunin, Ivan Alexeyevich 1870-1953 ... **SSC 5; TCLC 6**
See also RGSF 2; RGWL 2, 3; TWA

Bunting, Basil 1900-1985 ...... **CLC 10, 39, 47**
See also BRWS 7; CA 53-56; CANR 7; DAM POET; DLB 20; RGEL 2

Bunuel, Luis 1900-1983 ... **CLC 16, 80; HLC 1**
See also CA 101; CANR 32, 77; DAM MULT; HW 1

Bunyan, John 1628-1688 ..... **LC 4, 69; WLC**
See also BRW 2; BYA 5; CDBLB 1660-1789; DA; DAB; DAC; DAM MST; DLB 39; RGEL 2; TEA; WCH; WLIT 3

Buravsky, Alexandr .... **CLC 59**

Burckhardt, Jacob (Christoph)
1818-1897 .... **NCLC 49**
See also EW 6

Burford, Eleanor
See Hibbert, Eleanor Alice Burford

Burgess, Anthony . **CLC 1, 2, 4, 5, 8, 10, 13, 15, 22, 40, 62, 81, 94**
See Wilson, John (Anthony) Burgess
See also AAYA 25; AITN 1; BRWS 1; CD-BLB 1960 to Present; DAB; DLB 14, 194, 261; DLBY 1998; MTCW 1; RGEL 2; RHW; SFW 4; YAW

Burke, Edmund 1729(?)-1797 .... **LC 7, 36; WLC**
See also BRW 3; DA; DAB; DAC; DAM MST; DLB 104, 252; RGEL 2; TEA

Burke, Kenneth (Duva) 1897-1993 ... **CLC 2, 24**
See also AMW; CA 5-8R; CANR 39, 74; DLB 45, 63; MTCW 1, 2; RGAL 4

Burke, Leda
See Garnett, David

Burke, Ralph
See Silverberg, Robert

Burke, Thomas 1886-1945 .... **TCLC 63**
See also CA 155; CMW 4; DLB 197

Burney, Fanny 1752-1840 .... **NCLC 12, 54, 107**
See also BRWS 3; DLB 39; NFS 16; RGEL 2; TEA

Burney, Frances
See Burney, Fanny

Burns, Robert 1759-1796 ... **LC 3, 29, 40; PC 6; WLC**
See also BRW 3; CDBLB 1789-1832; DA; DAB; DAC; DAM MST, POET; DLB 109; EXPP; PAB; RGEL 2; TEA; WP

Burns, Tex
See L'Amour, Louis (Dearborn)
See also TCWW 2

Burnshaw, Stanley 1906- .... **CLC 3, 13, 44**
See also CA 9-12R; CP 7; DLB 48; DLBY 1997

Burr, Anne 1937- .... **CLC 6**
See also CA 25-28R

Burroughs, Edgar Rice 1875-1950 . **TCLC 2, 32**
See also AAYA 11; BPFB 1; BYA 4, 9; CA 132; DAM NOV; DLB 8; FANT; MTCW 1, 2; RGAL 4; SATA 41; SCFW 2; SFW 4; TUS; YAW

Burroughs, William S(eward)
1914-1997 .. **CLC 1, 2, 5, 15, 22, 42, 75, 109; TCLC 121; WLC**
See Lee, William; Lee, Willy
See also AITN 2; AMWS 3; BG 2; BPFB 1; CA 9-12R; CANR 20, 52, 104; CN 7; CPW; DA; DAB; DAC; DAM MST, NOV, POP; DLB 2, 8, 16, 152, 237; DLBY 1981, 1997; HGG; MTCW 1, 2; RGAL 4; SFW 4

Burton, Sir Richard F(rancis)
1821-1890 .... **NCLC 42**
See also DLB 55, 166, 184

Burton, Robert 1577-1640 .... **LC 74**
See also DLB 151; RGEL 2

Buruma, Ian 1951- .... **CLC 163**
See also CA 128; CANR 65

Busch, Frederick 1941- ... **CLC 7, 10, 18, 47, 166**
See also CA 33-36R; CAAS 1; CANR 45, 73, 92; CN 7; DLB 6, 218

Bush, Ronald 1946- .... **CLC 34**
See also CA 136

Bustos, F(rancisco)
See Borges, Jorge Luis

Bustos Domecq, H(onorio)
See Bioy Casares, Adolfo; Borges, Jorge Luis

Butler, Octavia E(stelle) 1947- .. **BLCS; CLC 38, 121**
See also AAYA 18; AFAW 2; BPFB 1; BW 2, 3; CA 73-76; CANR 12, 24, 38, 73; CLR 65; CPW; DAM MULT, POP; DLB 33; MTCW 1, 2; NFS 8; SATA 84; SCFW 2; SFW 4; SSFS 6; YAW

Butler, Robert Olen, (Jr.) 1945- ...... **CLC 81, 162**
See also AMWS 12; BPFB 1; CA 112; CANR 66; CSW; DAM POP; DLB 173; INT CA-112; MTCW 1; SSFS 11

Butler, Samuel 1612-1680 .... **LC 16, 43**
See also DLB 101, 126; RGEL 2

Butler, Samuel 1835-1902 .... **TCLC 1, 33; WLC**
See also BRWS 2; CA 143; CDBLB 1890-1914; DA; DAB; DAC; DAM MST, NOV, DLB 18, 57, 174; RGEL 2; SFW 4; TEA

Butler, Walter C.
See Faust, Frederick (Schiller)

Butor, Michel (Marie Francois)
1926- .... **CLC 1, 3, 8, 11, 15, 161**
See also CA 9-12R; CANR 33, 66; DLB 83; EW 13; GFL 1789 to the Present; MTCW 1, 2

Butts, Mary 1890(?)-1937 .... **TCLC 77**
See also CA 148; DLB 240

Buxton, Ralph
See Silverstein, Alvin; Silverstein, Virginia B(arbara Opshelor)

Buzo, Alexander (John) 1944- .... **CLC 61**
See also CA 97-100; CANR 17, 39, 69; CD 5

Buzzati, Dino 1906-1972 .... **CLC 36**
See also CA 160; DLB 177; RGWL 2, 3; SFW 4

Byars, Betsy (Cromer) 1928- .... **CLC 35**
See also AAYA 19; BYA 3; CA 33-36R, 183; CAAE 183; CANR 18, 36, 57, 102; CLR 1, 16, 72; DLB 52; INT CANR-18; JRDA; MAICYA 1, 2; MAICYAS 1; MTCW 1; SAAS 1; SATA 4, 46, 80; SATA-Essay 108; WYA; YAW

Byatt, A(ntonia) S(usan Drabble)
1936- .... **CLC 19, 65, 136**
See also BPFB 1; BRWS 4; CA 13-16R; CANR 13, 33, 50, 75, 96; DAM NOV, POP; DLB 14, 194; MTCW 1, 2; RGSF 2; RHW; TEA

Byrne, David 1952- .... **CLC 26**
See also CA 127

Byrne, John Keyes 1926-
See Leonard, Hugh
See also CA 102; CANR 78; INT CA-102

Byron, George Gordon (Noel)
1788-1824 ..... **NCLC 2, 12, 109; PC 16; WLC**
See also BRW 4; CDBLB 1789-1832; DA; DAB; DAC; DAM MST, POET; DLB 96, 110; EXPP; PAB; PFS 1, 14; RGEL 2; TEA; WLIT 3; WP

Byron, Robert 1905-1941 .... **TCLC 67**
See also CA 160; DLB 195

C. 3. 3.
See Wilde, Oscar (Fingal O'Flahertie Wills)

C. 3. 3.,
See Wilde, Oscar (Fingal O'Flahertie Wills)

Caballero, Fernan 1796-1877 .... **NCLC 10**

Cabell, Branch
See Cabell, James Branch

Cabell, James Branch 1879-1958 .... **TCLC 6**
See also CA 152; DLB 9, 78; FANT; MTCW 1; RGAL 4; SUFW 1

Cabeza de Vaca, Alvar Nunez
1490-1557(?) .... **LC 61**

Cable, George Washington
1844-1925 .... **SSC 4; TCLC 4**
See also CA 155; DLB 12, 74; DLBD 13; RGAL 4; TUS

Cabral de Melo Neto, Joao
1920-1999 .... **CLC 76**
See also CA 151; DAM MULT; LAW; LAWS 1

Cabrera Infante, G(uillermo) 1929- . **CLC 5, 25, 45, 120; HLC 1; SSC 39**
See also CA 85-88; CANR 29, 65, 110; CD-WLB 3; DAM MULT; DLB 113; HW 1, 2; LAW; LAWS 1; MTCW 1, 2; RGSF 2; WLIT 1

Cade, Toni
See Bambara, Toni Cade

Carr, Caleb 1955(?)- .... **CLC 86**
See also CA 147; CANR 73

Carr, Emily 1871-1945 .... **TCLC 32**
See also CA 159; DLB 68; FW; GLL 2

Carr, John Dickson 1906-1977 .... **CLC 3**
See Fairbairn, Roger
See also CA 49-52; CANR 3, 33, 60; CMW 4; MSW; MTCW 1, 2

Carr, Philippa
See Hibbert, Eleanor Alice Burford

Carr, Virginia Spencer 1929- .... **CLC 34**
See also CA 61-64; DLB 111

Carrere, Emmanuel 1957- .... **CLC 89**
See also CA 200

Carrier, Roch 1937- .... **CLC 13, 78**
See also CA 130; CANR 61; CCA 1; DAC; DAM MST; DLB 53; SATA 105

Carroll, James Dennis
See Carroll, Jim

Carroll, James P. 1943(?)- .... **CLC 38**
See also CA 81-84; CANR 73; MTCW 1

Carroll, Jim 1951- .... **CLC 35, 143**
See Carroll, James Dennis
See also AAYA 17; CA 45-48; CANR 42

Carroll, Lewis ... **NCLC 2, 53; PC 18; WLC**
See Dodgson, Charles L(utwidge)
See also AAYA 39; BRW 5; BYA 5, 13; CD-BLB 1832-1890; CLR 2, 18; DLB 18, 163, 178; DLBY 1998; EXPN; EXPP; FANT; JRDA; LAIT 1; NFS 7; PFS 11; RGEL 2; SUFW 1; TEA; WCH

Carroll, Paul Vincent 1900-1968 ...... **CLC 10**
See also CA 9-12R; DLB 10; RGEL 2

Carruth, Hayden 1921- ..... **CLC 4, 7, 10, 18, 84; PC 10**
See also CA 9-12R; CANR 4, 38, 59, 110; CP 7; DLB 5, 165; INT CANR-4; MTCW 1, 2; SATA 47

Carson, Rachel
See Carson, Rachel Louise
See also DLB 275

Carson, Rachel Louise 1907-1964 .... **CLC 71**
See Carson, Rachel
See also AMWS 9; ANW; CA 77-80; CANR 35; DAM POP; FW; LAIT 4; MTCW 1, 2; NCFS 1; SATA 23

Carter, Angela (Olive) 1940-1992 ...... **CLC 5, 41, 76; SSC 13**
See also BRWS 3; CA 53-56; CANR 12, 36, 61, 106; DLB 14, 207, 261; EXPS; FANT; FW; MTCW 1, 2; RGSF 2; SATA 66; SATA-Obit 70; SFW 4; SSFS 4, 12; SUFW 2; WLIT 4

Carter, Nick
See Smith, Martin Cruz

Carver, Raymond 1938-1988 ..... **CLC 22, 36, 53, 55, 126; SSC 8, 51**
See also AAYA 44; AMWS 3; BPFB 1; CA 33-36R; CANR 17, 34, 61, 103; CPW; DAM NOV; DLB 130; DLBY 1984, 1988; MTCW 1, 2; PFS 17; RGAL 4; RGSF 2; SSFS 3, 6, 12, 13; TCWW 2; TUS

Cary, Elizabeth, Lady Falkland
1585-1639 .... **LC 30**

Cary, (Arthur) Joyce (Lunel)
1888-1957 .... **TCLC 1, 29**
See also BRW 7; CA 164; CDBLB 1914-1945; DLB 15, 100; MTCW 2; RGEL 2; TEA

Casanova de Seingalt, Giovanni Jacopo
1725-1798 .... **LC 13**

Casares, Adolfo Bioy
See Bioy Casares, Adolfo
See also RGSF 2

Casas, Bartolome de las 1474-1566
See Las Casas, Bartolome de
See also WLIT 1

Casely-Hayford, J(oseph) E(phraim)
1866-1903 .... **BLC 1; TCLC 24**
See also BW 2; CA 152; DAM MULT

Casey, John (Dudley) 1939- .... **CLC 59**
See also BEST 90:2; CA 69-72; CANR 23, 100

Casey, Michael 1947- .... **CLC 2**
See also CA 65-68; CANR 109; DLB 5

Casey, Patrick
See Thurman, Wallace (Henry)

Casey, Warren (Peter) 1935-1988 .... **CLC 12**
See also CA 101; INT 101

Casona, Alejandro .... **CLC 49**
See Alvarez, Alejandro Rodriguez

Cassavetes, John 1929-1989 .... **CLC 20**
See also CA 85-88; CANR 82

Cassian, Nina 1924- .... **PC 17**
See also CWP; CWW 2

Cassill, R(onald) V(erlin) 1919- ... **CLC 4, 23**
See also CA 9-12R; CAAS 1; CANR 7, 45; CN 7; DLB 6, 218

Cassiodorus, Flavius Magnus c. 490(?)-c.
583(?) .... **CMLC 43**

Cassirer, Ernst 1874-1945 .... **TCLC 61**
See also CA 157

Cassity, (Allen) Turner 1929- .... **CLC 6, 42**
See also CA 17-20R; CAAS 8; CANR 11; CSW; DLB 105

Castaneda, Carlos (Cesar Aranha)
1931(?)-1998 .... **CLC 12, 119**
See also CA 25-28R; CANR 32, 66, 105; DNFS 1; HW 1; MTCW 1

Castedo, Elena 1937- .... **CLC 65**
See also CA 132

Castedo-Ellerman, Elena
See Castedo, Elena

Castellanos, Rosario 1925-1974 .... **CLC 66; HLC 1; SSC 39**
See also CA 131; CANR 58; CDWLB 3; DAM MULT; DLB 113; FW; HW 1; LAW; MTCW 1; RGSF 2; RGWL 2, 3

Castelvetro, Lodovico 1505-1571 .... **LC 12**

Castiglione, Baldassare 1478-1529 ...... **LC 12**
See Castiglione, Baldesar
See also RGWL 2, 3

Castiglione, Baldesar
See Castiglione, Baldassare
See also EW 2

Castillo, Ana (Hernandez Del)
1953- .... **CLC 151**
See also AAYA 42; CA 131; CANR 51, 86; CWP; DLB 122, 227; DNFS 2; FW; HW 1

Castle, Robert
See Hamilton, Edmond

Castro (Ruz), Fidel 1926(?)- .... **HLC 1**
See also CA 129; CANR 81; DAM MULT; HW 2

Castro, Guillen de 1569-1631 .... **LC 19**

Castro, Rosalia de 1837-1885 ... **NCLC 3, 78; PC 41**
See also DAM MULT

Cather, Willa (Sibert) 1873-1947 . **SSC 2, 50; TCLC 1, 11, 31, 99; WLC**
See also AAYA 24; AMW; AMWC 1; AMWR 1; BPFB 1; CA 128; CDALB 1865-1917; DA; DAB; DAC; DAM MST, NOV; DLB 9, 54, 78, 256; DLBD 1; EXPN; EXPS; LAIT 3; MAWW; MTCW 1, 2; NFS 2; RGAL 4; RGSF 2; RHW; SATA 30; SSFS 2, 7, 16; TCWW 2; TUS

Catherine II
See Catherine the Great
See also DLB 150

Catherine the Great 1729-1796 .... **LC 69**
See Catherine II

Cato, Marcus Porcius
234B.C.-149B.C. .... **CMLC 21**
See Cato the Elder

Cato, Marcus Porcius, the Elder
See Cato, Marcus Porcius

Cato the Elder
See Cato, Marcus Porcius
See also DLB 211

Catton, (Charles) Bruce 1899-1978 . **CLC 35**
See also AITN 1; CA 5-8R; CANR 7, 74; DLB 17; SATA 2; SATA-Obit 24

Catullus c. 84B.C.-54B.C. .... **CMLC 18**
See also AW 2; CDWLB 1; DLB 211; RGWL 2, 3

Cauldwell, Frank
See King, Francis (Henry)

Caunitz, William J. 1933-1996 .... **CLC 34**
See also BEST 89:3; CA 130; CANR 73; INT 130

Causley, Charles (Stanley) 1917- .... **CLC 7**
See also CA 9-12R; CANR 5, 35, 94; CLR 30; CWRI 5; DLB 27; MTCW 1; SATA 3, 66

Caute, (John) David 1936- .... **CLC 29**
See also CA 1-4R; CAAS 4; CANR 1, 33, 64; CBD; CD 5; CN 7; DAM NOV; DLB 14, 231

Cavafy, C(onstantine) P(eter) .... **PC 36; TCLC 2, 7**
See Kavafis, Konstantinos Petrou
See also CA 148; DAM POET; EW 8; MTCW 1; RGWL 2, 3; WP

Cavalcanti, Guido c. 1250-c.
1300 .... **CMLC 54**

Cavallo, Evelyn
See Spark, Muriel (Sarah)

Cavanna, Betty .... **CLC 12**
See Harrison, Elizabeth (Allen) Cavanna
See also JRDA; MAICYA 1; SAAS 4; SATA 1, 30

Cavendish, Margaret Lucas
1623-1673 .... **LC 30**
See also DLB 131, 252; RGEL 2

Caxton, William 1421(?)-1491(?) .... **LC 17**
See also DLB 170

Cayer, D. M.
See Duffy, Maureen

Cayrol, Jean 1911- .... **CLC 11**
See also CA 89-92; DLB 83

Cela, Camilo Jose 1916-2002 .... **CLC 4, 13, 59, 122; HLC 1**
See also BEST 90:2; CA 21-24R; CAAS 10; CANR 21, 32, 76; DAM MULT; DLBY 1989; EW 13; HW 1; MTCW 1, 2; RGSF 2; RGWL 2, 3

Celan, Paul -1970 .... **CLC 10, 19, 53, 82; PC 10**
See Antschel, Paul
See also CDWLB 2; DLB 69; RGWL 2, 3

Celine, Louis-Ferdinand .. **CLC 1, 3, 4, 7, 9, 15, 47, 124**
See Destouches, Louis-Ferdinand
See also DLB 72; EW 11; GFL 1789 to the Present; RGWL 2, 3

Cellini, Benvenuto 1500-1571 .... **LC 7**

Cendrars, Blaise .... **CLC 18, 106**
See Sauser-Hall, Frederic
See also DLB 258; GFL 1789 to the Present; RGWL 2, 3; WP

Centlivre, Susanna 1669(?)-1723 .... **LC 65**
See also DLB 84; RGEL 2

Cernuda (y Bidon), Luis 1902-1963 . **CLC 54**
See also CA 131; DAM POET; DLB 134; GLL 1; HW 1; RGWL 2, 3

Cervantes, Lorna Dee 1954- ..... **HLCS 1; PC 35**
See also CA 131; CANR 80; CWP; DLB 82; EXPP; HW 1

Daly, Maureen 1921- .... **CLC 17**
See also AAYA 5; BYA 6; CANR 37, 83, 108; JRDA; MAICYA 1, 2; SAAS 1; SATA 2, 129; WYA; YAW

Damas, Leon-Gontran 1912-1978 .... **CLC 84**
See also BW 1; CA 125

Dana, Richard Henry Sr.
1787-1879 .... **NCLC 53**

Daniel, Samuel 1562(?)-1619 .... **LC 24**
See also DLB 62; RGEL 2

Daniels, Brett
See Adler, Renata

Dannay, Frederic 1905-1982 .... **CLC 11**
See Queen, Ellery
See also CA 1-4R; CANR 1, 39; CMW 4; DAM POP; DLB 137; MTCW 1

D'Annunzio, Gabriele 1863-1938 ... **TCLC 6, 40**
See also CA 155; EW 8; RGWL 2, 3; TWA

Danois, N. le
See Gourmont, Remy(-Marie-Charles) de

Dante 1265-1321 .... **CMLC 3, 18, 39; PC 21; WLCS**
See also DA; DAB; DAC; DAM MST, POET; EFS 1; EW 1; LAIT 1; RGWL 2, 3; TWA; WP

d'Antibes, Germain
See Simenon, Georges (Jacques Christian)

Danticat, Edwidge 1969- .... **CLC 94, 139**
See also AAYA 29; CA 152; CAAE 192; CANR 73; DNFS 1; EXPS; MTCW 1; SSFS 1; YAW

Danvers, Dennis 1947- .... **CLC 70**

Danziger, Paula 1944- .... **CLC 21**
See also AAYA 4, 36; BYA 6, 7, 14; CA 115; CANR 37; CLR 20; JRDA; MAICYA 1, 2; SATA 36, 63, 102; SATA-Brief 30; WYA; YAW

Da Ponte, Lorenzo 1749-1838 .... **NCLC 50**

Dario, Ruben 1867-1916 .... **HLC 1; PC 15; TCLC 4**
See also CA 131; CANR 81; DAM MULT; HW 1, 2; LAW; MTCW 1, 2; RGWL 2, 3

Darley, George 1795-1846 .... **NCLC 2**
See also DLB 96; RGEL 2

Darrow, Clarence (Seward)
1857-1938 .... **TCLC 81**
See also CA 164

Darwin, Charles 1809-1882 .... **NCLC 57**
See also BRWS 7; DLB 57, 166; RGEL 2; TEA; WLIT 4

Darwin, Erasmus 1731-1802 .... **NCLC 106**
See also DLB 93; RGEL 2

Daryush, Elizabeth 1887-1977 ...... **CLC 6, 19**
See also CA 49-52; CANR 3, 81; DLB 20

Das, Kamala 1934- .... **PC 43**
See also CA 101; CANR 27, 59; CP 7; CWP; FW

Dasgupta, Surendranath
1887-1952 .... **TCLC 81**
See also CA 157

Dashwood, Edmee Elizabeth Monica de la Pasture 1890-1943
See Delafield, E. M.
See also CA 154

da Silva, Antonio Jose
1705-1739 .... **NCLC 114**
See Silva, Jose Asuncion

Daudet, (Louis Marie) Alphonse
1840-1897 .... **NCLC 1**
See also DLB 123; GFL 1789 to the Present; RGSF 2

Daumal, Rene 1908-1944 .... **TCLC 14**

Davenant, William 1606-1668 .... **LC 13**
See also DLB 58, 126; RGEL 2

Davenport, Guy (Mattison, Jr.)
1927- .... **CLC 6, 14, 38; SSC 16**
See also CA 33-36R; CANR 23, 73; CN 7; CSW; DLB 130

David, Robert
See Nezval, Vitezslav

Davidson, Avram (James) 1923-1993
See Queen, Ellery
See also CA 101; CANR 26; DLB 8; FANT; SFW 4; SUFW 1, 2

Davidson, Donald (Grady)
1893-1968 .... **CLC 2, 13, 19**
See also CA 5-8R; CANR 4, 84; DLB 45

Davidson, Hugh
See Hamilton, Edmond

Davidson, John 1857-1909 .... **TCLC 24**
See also DLB 19; RGEL 2

Davidson, Sara 1943- .... **CLC 9**
See also CA 81-84; CANR 44, 68; DLB 185

Davie, Donald (Alfred) 1922-1995 .... **CLC 5, 8, 10, 31; PC 29**
See also BRWS 6; CA 1-4R; CAAS 3; CANR 1, 44; CP 7; DLB 27; MTCW 1; RGEL 2

Davie, Elspeth 1919-1995 .... **SSC 52**
See also CA 126; DLB 139

Davies, Ray(mond Douglas) 1944- ... **CLC 21**
See also CA 146; CANR 92

Davies, Rhys 1901-1978 .... **CLC 23**
See also CA 9-12R; CANR 4; DLB 139, 191

Davies, (William) Robertson
1913-1995 .... **CLC 2, 7, 13, 25, 42, 75, 91; WLC**
See Marchbanks, Samuel
See also BEST 89:2; BPFB 1; CA 33-36R; CANR 17, 42, 103; CN 7; CPW; DA; DAB; DAC; DAM MST, NOV, POP; DLB 68; HGG; INT CANR-17; MTCW 1, 2; RGEL 2; TWA

Davies, Sir John 1569-1626 .... **LC 85**
See also DLB 172

Davies, Walter C.
See Kornbluth, C(yril) M.

Davies, William Henry 1871-1940 ... **TCLC 5**
See also CA 179; DLB 19, 174; RGEL 2

Da Vinci, Leonardo 1452-1519 ..... **LC 12, 57, 60**
See also AAYA 40

Davis, Angela (Yvonne) 1944- .... **CLC 77**
See also BW 2, 3; CA 57-60; CANR 10, 81; CSW; DAM MULT; FW

Davis, B. Lynch
See Bioy Casares, Adolfo; Borges, Jorge Luis

Davis, Gordon
See Hunt, E(verette) Howard, (Jr.)

Davis, H(arold) L(enoir) 1896-1960 . **CLC 49**
See also ANW; CA 178; DLB 9, 206; SATA 114

Davis, Rebecca (Blaine) Harding
1831-1910 .... **SSC 38; TCLC 6**
See also CA 179; DLB 74, 239; FW; NFS 14; RGAL 4; TUS

Davis, Richard Harding
1864-1916 .... **TCLC 24**
See also CA 179; DLB 12, 23, 78, 79, 189; DLBD 13; RGAL 4

Davison, Frank Dalby 1893-1970 ..... **CLC 15**
See also DLB 260

Davison, Lawrence H.
See Lawrence, D(avid) H(erbert Richards)

Davison, Peter (Hubert) 1928- .... **CLC 28**
See also CA 9-12R; CAAS 4; CANR 3, 43, 84; CP 7; DLB 5

Davys, Mary 1674-1732 .... **LC 1, 46**
See also DLB 39

Dawson, (Guy) Fielding (Lewis)
1930-2002 .... **CLC 6**
See also CA 85-88; CANR 108; DLB 130

Dawson, Peter
See Faust, Frederick (Schiller)
See also TCWW 2, 2

Day, Clarence (Shepard, Jr.)
1874-1935 .... **TCLC 25**
See also DLB 11

Day, John 1574(?)-1640(?) .... **LC 70**
See also DLB 62, 170; RGEL 2

Day, Thomas 1748-1789 .... **LC 1**
See also DLB 39; YABC 1

Day Lewis, C(ecil) 1904-1972 . **CLC 1, 6, 10; PC 11**
See Blake, Nicholas
See also BRWS 3; CA 13-16; CANR 34; CAP 1; CWRI 5; DAM POET; DLB 15, 20; MTCW 1, 2; RGEL 2

Dazai Osamu .... **SSC 41; TCLC 11**
See Tsushima, Shuji
See also CA 164; DLB 182; MJW; RGSF 2; RGWL 2, 3; TWA

de Andrade, Carlos Drummond
See Drummond de Andrade, Carlos

de Andrade, Mario 1892-1945
See Andrade, Mario de
See also CA 178; HW 2

Deane, Norman
See Creasey, John

Deane, Seamus (Francis) 1940- ...... **CLC 122**
See also CA 118; CANR 42

de Beauvoir, Simone (Lucie Ernestine Marie Bertrand)
See Beauvoir, Simone (Lucie Ernestine Marie Bertrand) de

de Beer, P.
See Bosman, Herman Charles

de Brissac, Malcolm
See Dickinson, Peter (Malcolm)

de Campos, Alvaro
See Pessoa, Fernando (Antonio Nogueira)

de Chardin, Pierre Teilhard
See Teilhard de Chardin, (Marie Joseph) Pierre

Dee, John 1527-1608 .... **LC 20**
See also DLB 136, 213

Deer, Sandra 1940- .... **CLC 45**
See also CA 186

De Ferrari, Gabriella 1941- .... **CLC 65**
See also CA 146

de Filippo, Eduardo 1900-1984 ... **TCLC 127**
See also CA 132; MTCW 1; RGWL 2, 3

Defoe, Daniel 1660(?)-1731 .. **LC 1, 42; WLC**
See also AAYA 27; BRW 3; BRWR 1; BYA 4; CDBLB 1660-1789; CLR 61; DA; DAB; DAC; DAM MST, NOV; DLB 39, 95, 101; JRDA; LAIT 1; MAICYA 1, 2; NFS 9, 13; RGEL 2; SATA 22; TEA; WCH; WLIT 3

de Gourmont, Remy(-Marie-Charles)
See Gourmont, Remy(-Marie-Charles) de

de Hartog, Jan 1914- .... **CLC 19**
See also CA 1-4R; CANR 1; DFS 12

de Hostos, E. M.
See Hostos (y Bonilla), Eugenio Maria de

de Hostos, Eugenio M.
See Hostos (y Bonilla), Eugenio Maria de

Deighton, Len .... **CLC 4, 7, 22, 46**
See Deighton, Leonard Cyril
See also AAYA 6; BEST 89:2; BPFB 1; CDBLB 1960 to Present; CMW 4; CN 7; CPW; DLB 87

Deighton, Leonard Cyril 1929-
See Deighton, Len
See also CA 9-12R; CANR 19, 33, 68; DAM NOV, POP; MTCW 1, 2

Dekker, Thomas 1572(?)-1632 ..... **DC 12; LC 22**
See also CDBLB Before 1660; DAM DRAM; DLB 62, 172; RGEL 2

Dick, Philip K(indred) 1928-1982 ... **CLC 10, 30, 72; SSC 57**
See also AAYA 24; BPFB 1; BYA 11; CA 49-52; CANR 2, 16; CPW; DAM NOV, POP; DLB 8; MTCW 1, 2; NFS 5; SCFW; SFW 4

Dickens, Charles (John Huffam)
1812-1870 .... **NCLC 3, 8, 18, 26, 37, 50, 86, 105, 113; SSC 17, 49; WLC**
See also AAYA 23; BRW 5; BYA 1, 2, 3, 13, 14; CDBLB 1832-1890; CMW 4; DA; DAB; DAC; DAM MST, NOV; DLB 21, 55, 70, 159, 166; EXPN; HGG; JRDA; LAIT 1, 2; MAICYA 1, 2; NFS 4, 5, 10, 14; RGEL 2; RGSF 2; SATA 15; SUFW 1; TEA; WCH; WLIT 4; WYA

Dickey, James (Lafayette)
1923-1997 .... **CLC 1, 2, 4, 7, 10, 15, 47, 109; PC 40**
See also AITN 1, 2; AMWS 4; BPFB 1; CA 9-12R; CABS 2; CANR 10, 48, 61, 105; CDALB 1968-1988; CP 7; CPW; CSW; DAM NOV, POET, POP; DLB 5, 193; DLBD 7; DLBY 1982, 1993, 1996, 1997, 1998; INT CANR-10; MTCW 1, 2; NFS 9; PFS 6, 11; RGAL 4; TUS

Dickey, William 1928-1994 .... **CLC 3, 28**
See also CA 9-12R; CANR 24, 79; DLB 5

Dickinson, Charles 1951- .... **CLC 49**
See also CA 128

Dickinson, Emily (Elizabeth)
1830-1886 ... **NCLC 21, 77; PC 1; WLC**
See also AAYA 22; AMW; AMWR 1; CDALB 1865-1917; DA; DAB; DAC; DAM MST, POET; DLB 1, 243; EXPP; MAWW; PAB; PFS 1, 2, 3, 4, 5, 6, 8, 10, 11, 13, 16; RGAL 4; SATA 29; TUS; WP; WYA

Dickinson, Mrs. Herbert Ward
See Phelps, Elizabeth Stuart

Dickinson, Peter (Malcolm) 1927- .. **CLC 12, 35**
See also AAYA 9; BYA 5; CA 41-44R; CANR 31, 58, 88; CLR 29; CMW 4; DLB 87, 161; JRDA; MAICYA 1, 2; SATA 5, 62, 95; SFW 4; WYA; YAW

Dickson, Carr
See Carr, John Dickson

Dickson, Carter
See Carr, John Dickson

Diderot, Denis 1713-1784 .... **LC 26**
See also EW 4; GFL Beginnings to 1789; RGWL 2, 3

Didion, Joan 1934- . **CLC 1, 3, 8, 14, 32, 129**
See also AITN 1; AMWS 4; CA 5-8R; CANR 14, 52, 76; CDALB 1968-1988; CN 7; DAM NOV; DLB 2, 173, 185; DLBY 1981, 1986; MAWW; MTCW 1, 2; NFS 3; RGAL 4; TCWW 2; TUS

Dietrich, Robert
See Hunt, E(verette) Howard, (Jr.)

Difusa, Pati
See Almodovar, Pedro

Dillard, Annie 1945- .... **CLC 9, 60, 115**
See also AAYA 6, 43; AMWS 6; ANW; CA 49-52; CANR 3, 43, 62, 90; DAM NOV; DLB 275; DLBY 1980; LAIT 4, 5; MTCW 1, 2; NCFS 1; RGAL 4; SATA 10; TUS

Dillard, R(ichard) H(enry) W(ilde)
1937- .... **CLC 5**
See also CA 21-24R; CANR 7; CANR 10; CP 7; CSW; DLB 5, 244

Dillon, Eilis 1920-1994 .... **CLC 17**
See also CA 9-12R, 182; CAAE 182; CAAS 3; CANR 4, 38, 78; CLR 26; MAICYA 1, 2; MAICYAS 1; SATA 2, 74; SATA-Essay 105; SATA-Obit 83; YAW

Dimont, Penelope
See Mortimer, Penelope (Ruth)

Dinesen, Isak .... **CLC 10, 29, 95; SSC 7**
See Blixen, Karen (Christentze Dinesen)
See also EW 10; EXPS; FW; HGG; LAIT 3; MTCW 1; NCFS 2; NFS 9; RGSF 2; RGWL 2, 3; SSFS 3, 6, 13; WLIT 2

Ding Ling .... **CLC 68**
See Chiang, Pin-chin
See also RGWL 3

Diphusa, Patty
See Almodovar, Pedro

Disch, Thomas M(ichael) 1940- ... **CLC 7, 36**
See also AAYA 17; BPFB 1; CA 21-24R; CAAS 4; CANR 17, 36, 54, 89; CLR 18; CP 7; DLB 8; HGG; MAICYA 1, 2; MTCW 1, 2; SAAS 15; SATA 92; SCFW; SFW 4; SUFW 2

Disch, Tom
See Disch, Thomas M(ichael)

d'Isly, Georges
See Simenon, Georges (Jacques Christian)

Disraeli, Benjamin 1804-1881 ... **NCLC 2, 39, 79**
See also BRW 4; DLB 21, 55; RGEL 2

Ditcum, Steve
See Crumb, R(obert)

Dixon, Paige
See Corcoran, Barbara (Asenath)

Dixon, Stephen 1936- .... **CLC 52; SSC 16**
See also AMWS 12; CA 89-92; CANR 17, 40, 54, 91; CN 7; DLB 130

Doak, Annie
See Dillard, Annie

Dobell, Sydney Thompson
1824-1874 .... **NCLC 43**
See also DLB 32; RGEL 2

Doblin, Alfred .... **TCLC 13**
See Doeblin, Alfred
See also CDWLB 2; RGWL 2, 3

Dobrolyubov, Nikolai Alexandrovich
1836-1861 .... **NCLC 5**

Dobson, Austin 1840-1921 .... **TCLC 79**
See also DLB 35, 144

Dobyns, Stephen 1941- .... **CLC 37**
See also CA 45-48; CANR 2, 18, 99; CMW 4; CP 7

Doctorow, E(dgar) L(aurence)
1931- .... **CLC 6, 11, 15, 18, 37, 44, 65, 113**
See also AAYA 22; AITN 2; AMWS 4; BEST 89:3; BPFB 1; CA 45-48; CANR 2, 33, 51, 76, 97; CDALB 1968-1988; CN 7; CPW; DAM NOV, POP; DLB 2, 28, 173; DLBY 1980; LAIT 3; MTCW 1, 2; NFS 6; RGAL 4; RHW; TUS

Dodgson, Charles L(utwidge) 1832-1898
See Carroll, Lewis
See also CLR 2; DA; DAB; DAC; DAM MST, NOV, POET; MAICYA 1, 2; SATA 100; YABC 2

Dodson, Owen (Vincent) 1914-1983 .. **BLC 1; CLC 79**
See also BW 1; CA 65-68; CANR 24; DAM MULT; DLB 76

Doeblin, Alfred 1878-1957 .... **TCLC 13**
See Doblin, Alfred
See also CA 141; DLB 66

Doerr, Harriet 1910- .... **CLC 34**
See also CA 122; CANR 47; INT 122

Domecq, H(onorio Bustos)
See Bioy Casares, Adolfo

Domecq, H(onorio) Bustos
See Bioy Casares, Adolfo; Borges, Jorge Luis

Domini, Rey
See Lorde, Audre (Geraldine)
See also GLL 1

Dominique
See Proust, (Valentin-Louis-George-Eugene-)Marcel

Don, A
See Stephen, Sir Leslie

Donaldson, Stephen R(eeder)
1947- .... **CLC 46, 138**
See also AAYA 36; BPFB 1; CA 89-92; CANR 13, 55, 99; CPW; DAM POP; FANT; INT CANR-13; SATA 121; SFW 4; SUFW 1, 2

Donleavy, J(ames) P(atrick) 1926- .... **CLC 1, 4, 6, 10, 45**
See also AITN 2; BPFB 1; CA 9-12R; CANR 24, 49, 62, 80; CBD; CD 5; CN 7; DLB 6, 173; INT CANR-24; MTCW 1, 2; RGAL 4

Donne, John 1572-1631 ..... **LC 10, 24; PC 1, 43; WLC**
See also BRW 1; BRWR 2; CDBLB Before 1660; DA; DAB; DAC; DAM MST, POET; DLB 121, 151; EXPP; PAB; PFS 2, 11; RGEL 2; TEA; WLIT 3; WP

Donnell, David 1939(?)- .... **CLC 34**
See also CA 197

Donoghue, P. S.
See Hunt, E(verette) Howard, (Jr.)

Donoso (Yanez), Jose 1924-1996 ... **CLC 4, 8, 11, 32, 99; HLC 1; SSC 34**
See also CA 81-84; CANR 32, 73; CDWLB 3; DAM MULT; DLB 113; HW 1, 2; LAW; LAWS 1; MTCW 1, 2; RGSF 2; WLIT 1

Donovan, John 1928-1992 .... **CLC 35**
See also AAYA 20; CA 97-100; CLR 3; MAICYA 1, 2; SATA 72; SATA-Brief 29; YAW

Don Roberto
See Cunninghame Graham, Robert (Gallnigad) Bontine

Doolittle, Hilda 1886-1961 . **CLC 3, 8, 14, 31, 34, 73; PC 5; WLC**
See H. D.
See also AMWS 1; CA 97-100; CANR 35; DA; DAC; DAM MST, POET; DLB 4, 45; FW; GLL 1; MAWW; MTCW 1, 2; PFS 6; RGAL 4

Doppo, Kunikida .... **TCLC 99**
See Kunikida Doppo

Dorfman, Ariel 1942- .... **CLC 48, 77; HLC 1**
See also CA 130; CANR 67, 70; CWW 2; DAM MULT; DFS 4; HW 1, 2; INT CA-130; WLIT 1

Dorn, Edward (Merton)
1929-1999 .... **CLC 10, 18**
See also CA 93-96; CANR 42, 79; CP 7; DLB 5; INT 93-96; WP

Dor-Ner, Zvi .... **CLC 70**

Dorris, Michael (Anthony)
1945-1997 .... **CLC 109; NNAL**
See also AAYA 20; BEST 90:1; BYA 12; CA 102; CANR 19, 46, 75; CLR 58; DAM MULT, NOV; DLB 175; LAIT 5; MTCW 2; NFS 3; RGAL 4; SATA 75; SATA-Obit 94; TCWW 2; YAW

Dorris, Michael A.
See Dorris, Michael (Anthony)

Dorsan, Luc
See Simenon, Georges (Jacques Christian)

Dorsange, Jean
See Simenon, Georges (Jacques Christian)

Dos Passos, John (Roderigo)
1896-1970 ... **CLC 1, 4, 8, 11, 15, 25, 34, 82; WLC**
See also AMW; BPFB 1; CA 1-4R; CANR 3; CDALB 1929-1941; DA; DAB; DAC; DAM MST, NOV; DLB 4, 9; DLBD 1, 15; DLBY 1996; MTCW 1, 2; NFS 14; RGAL 4; TUS

Dossage, Jean
See Simenon, Georges (Jacques Christian)

Erasmus, Desiderius 1469(?)-1536 ...... **LC 16**
See also DLB 136; EW 2; RGWL 2, 3;
TWA
Erdman, Paul E(mil) 1932- .... **CLC 25**
See also AITN 1; CA 61-64; CANR 13, 43,
84
Erdrich, Louise 1954- .... **CLC 39, 54, 120;**
NNAL
See also AAYA 10, 47; AMWS 4; BEST
89:1; BPFB 1; CA 114; CANR 41, 62;
CDALBS; CN 7; CP 7; CPW; CWP;
DAM MULT, NOV, POP; DLB 152, 175,
206; EXPP; LAIT 5; MTCW 1; NFS 5;
PFS 14; RGAL 4; SATA 94; SSFS 14;
TCWW 2
Erenburg, Ilya (Grigoryevich)
See Ehrenburg, Ilya (Grigoryevich)
Erickson, Stephen Michael 1950-
See Erickson, Steve
See also CA 129; SFW 4
Erickson, Steve .... **CLC 64**
See Erickson, Stephen Michael
See also CANR 60, 68; SUFW 2
Ericson, Walter
See Fast, Howard (Melvin)
Eriksson, Buntel
See Bergman, (Ernst) Ingmar
Ernaux, Annie 1940- .... **CLC 88**
See also CA 147; CANR 93; NCFS 3
Erskine, John 1879-1951 .... **TCLC 84**
See also CA 159; DLB 9, 102; FANT
Eschenbach, Wolfram von
See Wolfram von Eschenbach
See also RGWL 3
Eseki, Bruno
See Mphahlele, Ezekiel
Esenin, Sergei (Alexandrovich)
1895-1925 .... **TCLC 4**
See also RGWL 2, 3
Eshleman, Clayton 1935- .... **CLC 7**
See also CA 33-36R; CAAS 6; CANR 93;
CP 7; DLB 5
Espriella, Don Manuel Alvarez
See Southey, Robert
Espriu, Salvador 1913-1985 .... **CLC 9**
See also CA 154; DLB 134
Espronceda, Jose de 1808-1842 ..... **NCLC 39**
Esquivel, Laura 1951(?)- ... **CLC 141; HLCS**
1
See also AAYA 29; CA 143; CANR 68, 113;
DNFS 2; LAIT 3; MTCW 1; NFS 5;
WLIT 1
Esse, James
See Stephens, James
Esterbrook, Tom
See Hubbard, L(afayette) Ron(ald)
Estleman, Loren D. 1952- .... **CLC 48**
See also AAYA 27; CA 85-88; CANR 27,
74; CMW 4; CPW; DAM NOV, POP;
DLB 226; INT CANR-27; MTCW 1, 2
Etherege, Sir George 1636-1692 .... **LC 78**
See also BRW 2; DAM DRAM; DLB 80;
PAB; RGEL 2
Euclid 306B.C.-283B.C. .... **CMLC 25**
Eugenides, Jeffrey 1960(?)- .... **CLC 81**
See also CA 144
Euripides c. 484B.C.-406B.C. .... **CMLC 23,**
51; DC 4; WLCS
See also AW 1; CDWLB 1; DA; DAB;
DAC; DAM DRAM, MST; DFS 1, 4, 6;
DLB 176; LAIT 1; RGWL 2, 3
Evan, Evin
See Faust, Frederick (Schiller)
Evans, Caradoc 1878-1945 ... **SSC 43; TCLC**
85
See also DLB 162
Evans, Evan
See Faust, Frederick (Schiller)
See also TCWW 2

Evans, Marian
See Eliot, George
Evans, Mary Ann
See Eliot, George
Evarts, Esther
See Benson, Sally
Everett, Percival
See Everett, Percival L.
See also CSW
Everett, Percival L. 1956- .... **CLC 57**
See Everett, Percival
See also BW 2; CA 129; CANR 94
Everson, R(onald) G(ilmour)
1903-1992 .... **CLC 27**
See also CA 17-20R; DLB 88
Everson, William (Oliver)
1912-1994 .... **CLC 1, 5, 14**
See also BG 2; CA 9-12R; CANR 20; DLB
5, 16, 212; MTCW 1
Evtushenko, Evgenii Aleksandrovich
See Yevtushenko, Yevgeny (Alexandrovich)
See also RGWL 2, 3
Ewart, Gavin (Buchanan)
1916-1995 .... **CLC 13, 46**
See also BRWS 7; CA 89-92; CANR 17,
46; CP 7; DLB 40; MTCW 1
Ewers, Hanns Heinz 1871-1943 ..... **TCLC 12**
See also CA 149
Ewing, Frederick R.
See Sturgeon, Theodore (Hamilton)
Exley, Frederick (Earl) 1929-1992 .... **CLC 6,**
11
See also AITN 2; BPFB 1; CA 81-84; DLB
143; DLBY 1981
Eynhardt, Guillermo
See Quiroga, Horacio (Sylvestre)
Ezekiel, Nissim 1924- .... **CLC 61**
See also CA 61-64; CP 7
Ezekiel, Tish O'Dowd 1943- .... **CLC 34**
See also CA 129
Fadeev, Aleksandr Aleksandrovich
See Bulgya, Alexander Alexandrovich
See also DLB 272
Fadeyev, A.
See Bulgya, Alexander Alexandrovich
Fadeyev, Alexander .... **TCLC 53**
See Bulgya, Alexander Alexandrovich
Fagen, Donald 1948- .... **CLC 26**
Fainzilberg, Ilya Arnoldovich 1897-1937
See Ilf, Ilya
See also CA 165
Fair, Ronald L. 1932- .... **CLC 18**
See also BW 1; CA 69-72; CANR 25; DLB
33
Fairbairn, Roger
See Carr, John Dickson
Fairbairns, Zoe (Ann) 1948- .... **CLC 32**
See also CA 103; CANR 21, 85; CN 7
Fairfield, Flora
See Alcott, Louisa May
Fairman, Paul W. 1916-1977
See Queen, Ellery
See also SFW 4
Falco, Gian
See Papini, Giovanni
Falconer, James
See Kirkup, James
Falconer, Kenneth
See Kornbluth, C(yril) M.
Falkland, Samuel
See Heijermans, Herman
Fallaci, Oriana 1930- .... **CLC 11, 110**
See also CA 77-80; CANR 15, 58; FW;
MTCW 1
Faludi, Susan 1959- .... **CLC 140**
See also CA 138; FW; MTCW 1; NCFS 3
Faludy, George 1913- .... **CLC 42**
See also CA 21-24R

Faludy, Gyoergy
See Faludy, George
Fanon, Frantz 1925-1961 .... **BLC 2; CLC 74**
See also BW 1; CA 116; DAM MULT;
WLIT 2
Fanshawe, Ann 1625-1680 .... **LC 11**
Fante, John (Thomas) 1911-1983 ..... **CLC 60**
See also AMWS 11; CA 69-72; CANR 23,
104; DLB 130; DLBY 1983
Farah, Nuruddin 1945- ...... **BLC 2; CLC 53,**
137
See also AFW; BW 2, 3; CA 106; CANR
81; CDWLB 3; CN 7; DAM MULT; DLB
125; WLIT 2
Fargue, Leon-Paul 1876(?)-1947 .... **TCLC 11**
See also CANR 107; DLB 258
Farigoule, Louis
See Romains, Jules
Farina, Richard 1936(?)-1966 .... **CLC 9**
See also CA 81-84
Farley, Walter (Lorimer)
1915-1989 .... **CLC 17**
See also BYA 14; CA 17-20R; CANR 8,
29, 84; DLB 22; JRDA; MAICYA 1, 2;
SATA 2, 43, 132; YAW
Farmer, Philip Jose 1918- .... **CLC 1, 19**
See also AAYA 28; BPFB 1; CA 1-4R;
CANR 4, 35, 111; DLB 8; MTCW 1;
SATA 93; SCFW 2; SFW 4
Farquhar, George 1677-1707 .... **LC 21**
See also BRW 2; DAM DRAM; DLB 84;
RGEL 2
Farrell, J(ames) G(ordon)
1935-1979 .... **CLC 6**
See also CA 73-76; CANR 36; DLB 14,
271; MTCW 1; RGEL 2; RHW; WLIT 4
Farrell, James T(homas) 1904-1979 . **CLC 1,**
4, 8, 11, 66; SSC 28
See also AMW; BPFB 1; CA 5-8R; CANR
9, 61; DLB 4, 9, 86; DLBD 2; MTCW 1,
2; RGAL 4
Farrell, Warren (Thomas) 1943- ...... **CLC 70**
See also CA 146
Farren, Richard J.
See Betjeman, John
Farren, Richard M.
See Betjeman, John
Fassbinder, Rainer Werner
1946-1982 .... **CLC 20**
See also CA 93-96; CANR 31
Fast, Howard (Melvin) 1914- ... **CLC 23, 131**
See also AAYA 16; BPFB 1; CA 1-4R, 181;
CAAE 181; CAAS 18; CANR 1, 33, 54,
75, 98; CMW 4; CN 7; CPW; DAM NOV;
DLB 9; INT CANR-33; MTCW 1; RHW;
SATA 7; SATA-Essay 107; TCWW 2;
YAW
Faulcon, Robert
See Holdstock, Robert P.
Faulkner, William (Cuthbert)
1897-1962 .... **CLC 1, 3, 6, 8, 9, 11, 14,**
18, 28, 52, 68; SSC 1, 35, 42; WLC
See also AAYA 7; AMW; AMWR 1; BPFB
1; BYA 5; CA 81-84; CANR 33; CDALB
1929-1941; DA; DAB; DAC; DAM MST,
NOV; DLB 9, 11, 44, 102; DLBD 2;
DLBY 1986, 1997; EXPN; EXPS; LAIT
2; MTCW 1, 2; NFS 4, 8, 13; RGAL 4;
RGSF 2; SSFS 2, 5, 6, 12; TUS
Fauset, Jessie Redmon
1882(?)-1961 .. **BLC 2; CLC 19, 54; HR**
2
See also AFAW 2; BW 1; CA 109; CANR
83; DAM MULT; DLB 51; FW; MAWW
Faust, Frederick (Schiller)
1892-1944(?) .... **TCLC 49**
See Austin, Frank; Brand, Max; Challis,
George; Dawson, Peter; Dexter, Martin;

Godden, (Margaret) Rumer
1907-1998 .... **CLC 53**
See also AAYA 6; BPFB 2; BYA 2, 5; CA 5-8R; CANR 4, 27, 36, 55, 80; CLR 20; CN 7; CWRI 5; DLB 161; MAICYA 1, 2; RHW; SAAS 12; SATA 3, 36; SATA-Obit 109; TEA

Godoy Alcayaga, Lucila 1899-1957 .. **HLC 2; PC 32; TCLC 2**
See Mistral, Gabriela
See also BW 2; CA 131; CANR 81; DAM MULT; DNFS; HW 1, 2; MTCW 1, 2

Godwin, Gail (Kathleen) 1937- ..... **CLC 5, 8, 22, 31, 69, 125**
See also BPFB 2; CA 29-32R; CANR 15, 43, 69; CN 7; CPW; CSW; DAM POP; DLB 6, 234; INT CANR-15; MTCW 1, 2

Godwin, William 1756-1836 .... **NCLC 14**
See also CDBLB 1789-1832; CMW 4; DLB 39, 104, 142, 158, 163, 262; HGG; RGEL 2

Goebbels, Josef
See Goebbels, (Paul) Joseph

Goebbels, (Paul) Joseph
1897-1945 .... **TCLC 68**
See also CA 148

Goebbels, Joseph Paul
See Goebbels, (Paul) Joseph

Goethe, Johann Wolfgang von
1749-1832 ... **NCLC 4, 22, 34, 90; PC 5; SSC 38; WLC**
See also CDWLB 2; DA; DAB; DAC; DAM DRAM, MST, POET; DLB 94; EW 5; RGWL 2, 3; TWA

Gogarty, Oliver St. John
1878-1957 .... **TCLC 15**
See also CA 150; DLB 15, 19; RGEL 2

Gogol, Nikolai (Vasilyevich)
1809-1852 .... **DC 1; NCLC 5, 15, 31; SSC 4, 29, 52; WLC**
See also DA; DAB; DAC; DAM DRAM, MST; DFS 12; DLB 198; EW 6; EXPS; RGSF 2; RGWL 2, 3; SSFS 7; TWA

Goines, Donald 1937(?)-1974 ... **BLC 2; CLC 80**
See also AITN 1; BW 1, 3; CA 124; CANR 82; CMW 4; DAM MULT, POP; DLB 33

Gold, Herbert 1924- ... **CLC 4, 7, 14, 42, 152**
See also CA 9-12R; CANR 17, 45; CN 7; DLB 2; DLBY 1981

Goldbarth, Albert 1948- .... **CLC 5, 38**
See also AMWS 12; CA 53-56; CANR 6, 40; CP 7; DLB 120

Goldberg, Anatol 1910-1982 .... **CLC 34**
See also CA 131

Goldemberg, Isaac 1945- .... **CLC 52**
See also CA 69-72; CAAS 12; CANR 11, 32; HW 1; WLIT 1

Golding, William (Gerald)
1911-1993 ... **CLC 1, 2, 3, 8, 10, 17, 27, 58, 81; WLC**
See also AAYA 5, 44; BPFB 2; BRWR 1; BRWS 1; BYA 2; CA 5-8R; CANR 13, 33, 54; CDBLB 1945-1960; DA; DAB; DAC; DAM MST, NOV; DLB 15, 100, 255; EXPN; HGG; LAIT 4; MTCW 1, 2; NFS 2; RGEL 2; RHW; SFW 4; TEA; WLIT 4; YAW

Goldman, Emma 1869-1940 .... **TCLC 13**
See also CA 150; DLB 221; FW; RGAL 4; TUS

Goldman, Francisco 1954- .... **CLC 76**
See also CA 162

Goldman, William (W.) 1931- ...... **CLC 1, 48**
See also BPFB 2; CA 9-12R; CANR 29, 69, 106; CN 7; DLB 44; FANT; IDFW 3, 4

Goldmann, Lucien 1913-1970 .... **CLC 24**
See also CA 25-28; CAP 2

Goldoni, Carlo 1707-1793 .... **LC 4**
See also DAM DRAM; EW 4; RGWL 2, 3

Goldsberry, Steven 1949- .... **CLC 34**
See also CA 131

Goldsmith, Oliver 1730-1774 .... **DC 8; LC 2, 48; WLC**
See also BRW 3; CDBLB 1660-1789; DA; DAB; DAC; DAM DRAM, MST, NOV, POET; DFS 1; DLB 39, 89, 104, 109, 142; IDTP; RGEL 2; SATA 26; TEA; WLIT 3

Goldsmith, Peter
See Priestley, J(ohn) B(oynton)

Gombrowicz, Witold 1904-1969 .... **CLC 4, 7, 11, 49**
See also CA 19-20; CANR 105; CAP 2; CDWLB 4; DAM DRAM; DLB 215; EW 12; RGWL 2, 3; TWA

Gomez de Avellaneda, Gertrudis
1814-1873 .... **NCLC 111**
See also LAW

Gomez de la Serna, Ramon
1888-1963 .... **CLC 9**
See also CA 153; CANR 79; HW 1, 2

Goncharov, Ivan Alexandrovich
1812-1891 .... **NCLC 1, 63**
See also DLB 238; EW 6; RGWL 2, 3

Goncourt, Edmond (Louis Antoine Huot) de
1822-1896 .... **NCLC 7**
See also DLB 123; EW 7; GFL 1789 to the Present; RGWL 2, 3

Goncourt, Jules (Alfred Huot) de
1830-1870 .... **NCLC 7**
See also DLB 123; EW 7; GFL 1789 to the Present; RGWL 2, 3

Gongora (y Argote), Luis de
1561-1627 .... **LC 72**
See also RGWL 2, 3

Gontier, Fernande 19(?)- .... **CLC 50**

Gonzalez Martinez, Enrique
1871-1952 .... **TCLC 72**
See also CA 166; CANR 81; HW 1, 2

Goodison, Lorna 1947- .... **PC 36**
See also CA 142; CANR 88; CP 7; CWP; DLB 157

Goodman, Paul 1911-1972 ..... **CLC 1, 2, 4, 7**
See also CA 19-20; CAD; CANR 34; CAP 2; DLB 130, 246; MTCW 1; RGAL 4

Gordimer, Nadine 1923- ...... **CLC 3, 5, 7, 10, 18, 33, 51, 70, 123, 160, 161; SSC 17; WLCS**
See also AAYA 39; AFW; BRWS 2; CA 5-8R; CANR 3, 28, 56, 88; CN 7; DA; DAB; DAC; DAM MST, NOV; DLB 225; EXPS; INT CANR-28; MTCW 1, 2; NFS 4; RGEL 2; RGSF 2; SSFS 2, 14; TWA; WLIT 2; YAW

Gordon, Adam Lindsay
1833-1870 .... **NCLC 21**
See also DLB 230

Gordon, Caroline 1895-1981 . **CLC 6, 13, 29, 83; SSC 15**
See also AMW; CA 11-12; CANR 36; CAP 1; DLB 4, 9, 102; DLBD 17; DLBY 1981; MTCW 1, 2; RGAL 4; RGSF 2

Gordon, Charles William 1860-1937
See Connor, Ralph

Gordon, Mary (Catherine) 1949- .... **CLC 13, 22, 128**
See also AMWS 4; BPFB 2; CA 102; CANR 44, 92; CN 7; DLB 6; DLBY 1981; FW; INT CA-102; MTCW 1

Gordon, N. J.
See Bosman, Herman Charles

Gordon, Sol 1923- .... **CLC 26**
See also CA 53-56; CANR 4; SATA 11

Gordone, Charles 1925-1995 .. **CLC 1, 4; DC 8**
See also BW 1, 3; CA 93-96, 180; CAAE 180; CAD; CANR 55; DAM DRAM; DLB 7; INT 93-96; MTCW 1

Gore, Catherine 1800-1861 .... **NCLC 65**
See also DLB 116; RGEL 2

Gorenko, Anna Andreevna
See Akhmatova, Anna

Gorky, Maxim .... **SSC 28; TCLC 8; WLC**
See Peshkov, Alexei Maximovich
See also DAB; DFS 9; EW 8; MTCW 2; TWA

Goryan, Sirak
See Saroyan, William

Gosse, Edmund (William)
1849-1928 .... **TCLC 28**
See also DLB 57, 144, 184; RGEL 2

Gotlieb, Phyllis Fay (Bloom) 1926- .. **CLC 18**
See also CA 13-16R; CANR 7; DLB 88, 251; SFW 4

Gottesman, S. D.
See Kornbluth, C(yril) M.; Pohl, Frederik

Gottfried von Strassburg fl. c.
1170-1215 .... **CMLC 10**
See also CDWLB 2; DLB 138; EW 1; RGWL 2, 3

Gotthelf, Jeremias 1797-1854 .... **NCLC 117**
See also DLB 133; RGWL 2, 3

Gottschalk, Laura Riding
See Jackson, Laura (Riding)

Gould, Lois 1932(?)-2002 .... **CLC 4, 10**
See also CA 77-80; CANR 29; MTCW 1

Gould, Stephen Jay 1941-2002 .... **CLC 163**
See also AAYA 26; BEST 90:2; CA 77-80; CANR 10, 27, 56, 75; CPW; INT CANR-27; MTCW 1, 2

Gourmont, Remy(-Marie-Charles) de
1858-1915 .... **TCLC 17**
See also CA 150; GFL 1789 to the Present; MTCW 2

Govier, Katherine 1948- .... **CLC 51**
See also CA 101; CANR 18, 40; CCA 1

Gower, John c. 1330-1408 .... **LC 76**
See also BRW 1; DLB 146; RGEL 2

Goyen, (Charles) William
1915-1983 .... **CLC 5, 8, 14, 40**
See also AITN 2; CA 5-8R; CANR 6, 71; DLB 2, 218; DLBY 1983; INT CANR-6

Goytisolo, Juan 1931- .... **CLC 5, 10, 23, 133; HLC 1**
See also CA 85-88; CANR 32, 61; CWW 2; DAM MULT; GLL 2; HW 1, 2; MTCW 1, 2

Gozzano, Guido 1883-1916 .... **PC 10**
See also CA 154; DLB 114

Gozzi, (Conte) Carlo 1720-1806 .... **NCLC 23**

Grabbe, Christian Dietrich
1801-1836 .... **NCLC 2**
See also DLB 133; RGWL 2, 3

Grace, Patricia Frances 1937- .... **CLC 56**
See also CA 176; CN 7; RGSF 2

Gracian y Morales, Baltasar
1601-1658 .... **LC 15**

Gracq, Julien .... **CLC 11, 48**
See Poirier, Louis
See also CWW 2; DLB 83; GFL 1789 to the Present

Grade, Chaim 1910-1982 .... **CLC 10**
See also CA 93-96

Graduate of Oxford, A
See Ruskin, John

Grafton, Garth
See Duncan, Sara Jeannette

Grafton, Sue 1940- .... **CLC 163**
See also AAYA 11; BEST 90:3; CA 108; CANR 31, 55, 111; CMW 4; CPW; CSW; DAM POP; DLB 226; FW; MSW

Grillparzer, Franz 1791-1872 .... **DC 14; NCLC 1, 102; SSC 37**
See also CDWLB 2; DLB 133; EW 5; RGWL 2, 3; TWA

Grimble, Reverend Charles James
See Eliot, T(homas) S(tearns)

Grimke, Charlotte L(ottie) Forten 1837(?)-1914
See Forten, Charlotte L.
See also BW 1; CA 124; DAM MULT, POET

Grimm, Jacob Ludwig Karl 1785-1863 .... **NCLC 3, 77; SSC 36**
See also DLB 90; MAICYA 1, 2; RGSF 2; RGWL 2, 3; SATA 22; WCH

Grimm, Wilhelm Karl 1786-1859 .. **NCLC 3, 77; SSC 36**
See also CDWLB 2; DLB 90; MAICYA 1, 2; RGSF 2; RGWL 2, 3; SATA 22; WCH

Grimmelshausen, Hans Jakob Christoffel von
See Grimmelshausen, Johann Jakob Christoffel von
See also RGWL 2, 3

Grimmelshausen, Johann Jakob Christoffel von 1621-1676 .... **LC 6**
See Grimmelshausen, Hans Jakob Christoffel von
See also CDWLB 2; DLB 168

Grindel, Eugene 1895-1952
See Eluard, Paul
See also CA 193

Grisham, John 1955- .... **CLC 84**
See also AAYA 14, 47; BPFB 2; CA 138; CANR 47, 69, 114; CMW 4; CN 7; CPW; CSW; DAM POP; MSW; MTCW 2

Grossman, David 1954- .... **CLC 67**
See also CA 138; CANR 114; CWW 2

Grossman, Vasilii Semenovich
See Grossman, Vasily (Semenovich)
See also DLB 272

Grossman, Vasily (Semenovich) 1905-1964 .... **CLC 41**
See Grossman, Vasilii Semenovich
See also CA 130; MTCW 1

Grove, Frederick Philip .... **TCLC 4**
See Greve, Felix Paul (Berthold Friedrich)
See also DLB 92; RGEL 2

Grubb
See Crumb, R(obert)

Grumbach, Doris (Isaac) 1918- . **CLC 13, 22, 64**
See also CA 5-8R; CAAS 2; CANR 9, 42, 70; CN 7; INT CANR-9; MTCW 2

Grundtvig, Nicolai Frederik Severin 1783-1872 .... **NCLC 1**

Grunge
See Crumb, R(obert)

Grunwald, Lisa 1959- .... **CLC 44**
See also CA 120

Guare, John 1938- .... **CLC 8, 14, 29, 67**
See also CA 73-76; CAD; CANR 21, 69; CD 5; DAM DRAM; DFS 8, 13; DLB 7, 249; MTCW 1, 2; RGAL 4

Gubar, Susan (David) 1944- .... **CLC 145**
See also CA 108; CANR 45, 70; FW; MTCW 1; RGAL 4

Gudjonsson, Halldor Kiljan 1902-1998
See Laxness, Halldor
See also CA 103; CWW 2

Guenter, Erich
See Eich, Gunter

Guest, Barbara 1920- .... **CLC 34**
See also BG 2; CA 25-28R; CANR 11, 44, 84; CP 7; CWP; DLB 5, 193

Guest, Edgar A(lbert) 1881-1959 ... **TCLC 95**
See also CA 168

Guest, Judith (Ann) 1936- .... **CLC 8, 30**
See also AAYA 7; CA 77-80; CANR 15, 75; DAM NOV, POP; EXPN; INT CANR-15; LAIT 5; MTCW 1, 2; NFS 1

Guevara, Che .... **CLC 87; HLC 1**
See Guevara (Serna), Ernesto

Guevara (Serna), Ernesto 1928-1967 .... **CLC 87; HLC 1**
See Guevara, Che
See also CA 127; CANR 56; DAM MULT; HW 1

Guicciardini, Francesco 1483-1540 ..... **LC 49**

Guild, Nicholas M. 1944- .... **CLC 33**
See also CA 93-96

Guillemin, Jacques
See Sartre, Jean-Paul

Guillen, Jorge 1893-1984 . **CLC 11; HLCS 1; PC 35**
See also CA 89-92; DAM MULT, POET; DLB 108; HW 1; RGWL 2, 3

Guillen, Nicolas (Cristobal) 1902-1989 .... **BLC 2; CLC 48, 79; HLC 1; PC 23**
See also BW 2; CA 125; CANR 84; DAM MST, MULT, POET; HW 1; LAW; RGWL 2, 3; WP

Guillen y Alvarez, Jorge
See Guillen, Jorge

Guillevic, (Eugene) 1907-1997 .... **CLC 33**
See also CA 93-96; CWW 2

Guillois
See Desnos, Robert

Guillois, Valentin
See Desnos, Robert

Guimaraes Rosa, Joao 1908-1967 .... **HLCS 2**
See also CA 175; LAW; RGSF 2; RGWL 2, 3

Guiney, Louise Imogen 1861-1920 .... **TCLC 41**
See also CA 160; DLB 54; RGAL 4

Guinizelli, Guido c. 1230-1276 ...... **CMLC 49**

Guiraldes, Ricardo (Guillermo) 1886-1927 .... **TCLC 39**
See also CA 131; HW 1; LAW; MTCW 1

Gumilev, Nikolai (Stepanovich) 1886-1921 .... **TCLC 60**
See also CA 165

Gunesekera, Romesh 1954- .... **CLC 91**
See also CA 159; CN 7; DLB 267

Gunn, Bill .... **CLC 5**
See Gunn, William Harrison
See also DLB 38

Gunn, Thom(son William) 1929- .. **CLC 3, 6, 18, 32, 81; PC 26**
See also BRWS 4; CA 17-20R; CANR 9, 33; CDBLB 1960 to Present; CP 7; DAM POET; DLB 27; INT CANR-33; MTCW 1; PFS 9; RGEL 2

Gunn, William Harrison 1934(?)-1989
See Gunn, Bill
See also AITN 1; BW 1, 3; CA 13-16R; CANR 12, 25, 76

Gunn Allen, Paula
See Allen, Paula Gunn

Gunnars, Kristjana 1948- .... **CLC 69**
See also CA 113; CCA 1; CP 7; CWP; DLB 60

Gunter, Erich
See Eich, Gunter

Gurdjieff, G(eorgei) I(vanovich) 1877(?)-1949 .... **TCLC 71**
See also CA 157

Gurganus, Allan 1947- .... **CLC 70**
See also BEST 90:1; CA 135; CANR 114; CN 7; CPW; CSW; DAM POP; GLL 1

Gurney, A. R.
See Gurney, A(lbert) R(amsdell), Jr.
See also DLB 266

Gurney, A(lbert) R(amsdell), Jr. 1930- .... **CLC 32, 50, 54**
See Gurney, A. R.
See also AMWS 5; CA 77-80; CAD; CANR 32, 64; CD 5; DAM DRAM

Gurney, Ivor (Bertie) 1890-1937 ... **TCLC 33**
See also BRW 6; CA 167; PAB; RGEL 2

Gurney, Peter
See Gurney, A(lbert) R(amsdell), Jr.

Guro, Elena 1877-1913 .... **TCLC 56**

Gustafson, James M(oody) 1925- ... **CLC 100**
See also CA 25-28R; CANR 37

Gustafson, Ralph (Barker) 1909-1995 .... **CLC 36**
See also CA 21-24R; CANR 8, 45, 84; CP 7; DLB 88; RGEL 2

Gut, Gom
See Simenon, Georges (Jacques Christian)

Guterson, David 1956- .... **CLC 91**
See also CA 132; CANR 73; MTCW 2; NFS 13

Guthrie, A(lfred) B(ertram), Jr. 1901-1991 .... **CLC 23**
See also CA 57-60; CANR 24; DLB 6, 212; SATA 62; SATA-Obit 67

Guthrie, Isobel
See Grieve, C(hristopher) M(urray)

Guthrie, Woodrow Wilson 1912-1967
See Guthrie, Woody
See also CA 113

Guthrie, Woody .... **CLC 35**
See Guthrie, Woodrow Wilson
See also LAIT 3

Gutierrez Najera, Manuel 1859-1895 .... **HLCS 2**
See also LAW

Guy, Rosa (Cuthbert) 1925- .... **CLC 26**
See also AAYA 4, 37; BW 2; CA 17-20R; CANR 14, 34, 83; CLR 13; DLB 33; DNFS 1; JRDA; MAICYA 1, 2; SATA 14, 62, 122; YAW

Gwendolyn
See Bennett, (Enoch) Arnold

H. D. .... **CLC 3, 8, 14, 31, 34, 73; PC 5**
See Doolittle, Hilda

H. de V.
See Buchan, John

Haavikko, Paavo Juhani 1931- .. **CLC 18, 34**
See also CA 106

Habbema, Koos
See Heijermans, Herman

Habermas, Juergen 1929- .... **CLC 104**
See also CA 109; CANR 85; DLB 242

Habermas, Jurgen
See Habermas, Juergen

Hacker, Marilyn 1942- . **CLC 5, 9, 23, 72, 91**
See also CA 77-80; CANR 68; CP 7; CWP; DAM POET; DLB 120; FW; GLL 2

Hadrian 76-138 .... **CMLC 52**

Haeckel, Ernst Heinrich (Philipp August) 1834-1919 .... **TCLC 83**
See also CA 157

Hafiz c. 1326-1389(?) .... **CMLC 34**
See also RGWL 2, 3

Haggard, H(enry) Rider 1856-1925 .... **TCLC 11**
See also BRWS 3; BYA 4, 5; CA 148; CANR 112; DLB 70, 156, 174, 178; FANT; MTCW 2; RGEL 2; RHW; SATA 16; SCFW; SFW 4; SUFW 1; WLIT 4

Hagiosy, L.
See Larbaud, Valery (Nicolas)

Hagiwara, Sakutaro 1886-1942 .... **PC 18; TCLC 60**
See also CA 154; RGWL 3

Haig, Fenil
See Ford, Ford Madox

Heilbrun, Carolyn G(old) 1926- .... **CLC 25**
See Cross, Amanda
See also CA 45-48; CANR 1, 28, 58, 94;
FW

Hein, Christoph 1944- .... **CLC 154**
See also CA 158; CANR 108; CDWLB 2;
CWW 2; DLB 124

Heine, Heinrich 1797-1856 .... **NCLC 4, 54;**
PC 25
See also CDWLB 2; DLB 90; EW 5; RGWL
2, 3; TWA

Heinemann, Larry (Curtiss) 1944- .. **CLC 50**
See also CA 110; CAAS 21; CANR 31, 81;
DLBD 9; INT CANR-31

Heiney, Donald (William) 1921-1993
See Harris, MacDonald
See also CA 1-4R; CANR 3, 58; FANT

Heinlein, Robert A(nson) 1907-1988 . **CLC 1,**
3, 8, 14, 26, 55; SSC 55
See also AAYA 17; BPFB 2; BYA 4, 13;
CA 1-4R; CANR 1, 20, 53; CLR 75;
CPW; DAM POP; DLB 8; EXPS; JRDA;
LAIT 5; MAICYA 1, 2; MTCW 1, 2;
RGAL 4; SATA 9, 69; SATA-Obit 56;
SCFW 4; SFW 4; SSFS 7; YAW

Helforth, John
See Doolittle, Hilda

Heliodorus fl. 3rd cent. - .... **CMLC 52**

Hellenhofferu, Vojtech Kapristian z
See Hasek, Jaroslav (Matej Frantisek)

Heller, Joseph 1923-1999 . **CLC 1, 3, 5, 8, 11,**
36, 63; TCLC 131; WLC
See also AAYA 24; AITN 1; AMWS 4;
BPFB 2; BYA 1; CA 5-8R; CABS 1;
CANR 8, 42, 66; CN 7; CPW; DA; DAB;
DAC; DAM MST, NOV, POP; DLB 2,
28, 227; DLBY 1980; EXPN; INT
CANR-8; LAIT 4; MTCW 1, 2; NFS 1;
RGAL 4; TUS; YAW

Hellman, Lillian (Florence)
1906-1984 .. **CLC 2, 4, 8, 14, 18, 34, 44,**
52; DC 1; TCLC 119
See also AAYA 47; AITN 1, 2; AMWS 1;
CA 13-16R; CAD; CANR 33; CWD;
DAM DRAM; DFS 1, 3, 14; DLB 7, 228;
DLBY 1984; FW; LAIT 3; MAWW;
MTCW 1, 2; RGAL 4; TUS

Helprin, Mark 1947- .... **CLC 7, 10, 22, 32**
See also CA 81-84; CANR 47, 64;
CDALBS; CPW; DAM NOV, POP;
DLBY 1985; FANT; MTCW 1, 2; SUFW
2

Helvetius, Claude-Adrien 1715-1771 .. **LC 26**

Helyar, Jane Penelope Josephine 1933-
See Poole, Josephine
See also CA 21-24R; CANR 10, 26; CWRI
5; SATA 82

Hemans, Felicia 1793-1835 ...... **NCLC 29, 71**
See also DLB 96; RGEL 2

Hemingway, Ernest (Miller)
1899-1961 .... **CLC 1, 3, 6, 8, 10, 13, 19,**
30, 34, 39, 41, 44, 50, 61, 80; SSC 1, 25,
36, 40; TCLC 115; WLC
See also AAYA 19; AMW; AMWC 1;
AMWR 1; BPFB 2; BYA 2, 3, 13; CA
77-80; CANR 34; CDALB 1917-1929;
DA; DAB; DAC; DAM MST, NOV; DLB
4, 9, 102, 210; DLBD 1, 15, 16; DLBY
1981, 1987, 1996, 1998; EXPN; EXPS;
LAIT 3, 4; MTCW 1, 2; NFS 1, 5, 6, 14;
RGAL 4; RGSF 2; SSFS 1, 6, 8, 9, 11;
TUS; WYA

Hempel, Amy 1951- .... **CLC 39**
See also CA 137; CANR 70; DLB 218;
EXPS; MTCW 2; SSFS 2

Henderson, F. C.
See Mencken, H(enry) L(ouis)

Henderson, Sylvia
See Ashton-Warner, Sylvia (Constance)

Henderson, Zenna (Chlarson)
1917-1983 .... **SSC 29**
See also CA 1-4R; CANR 1, 84; DLB 8;
SATA 5; SFW 4

Henkin, Joshua .... **CLC 119**
See also CA 161

Henley, Beth .... **CLC 23; DC 6, 14**
See Henley, Elizabeth Becker
See also CABS 3; CAD; CD 5; CSW;
CWD; DFS 2; DLBY 1986; FW

Henley, Elizabeth Becker 1952-
See Henley, Beth
See also CA 107; CANR 32, 73; DAM
DRAM, MST; MTCW 1, 2

Henley, William Ernest 1849-1903 .. **TCLC 8**
See also DLB 19; RGEL 2

Hennissart, Martha
See Lathen, Emma
See also CA 85-88; CANR 64

Henry VIII 1491-1547 .... **LC 10**
See also DLB 132

Henry, O. ..... **SSC 5, 49; TCLC 1, 19; WLC**
See Porter, William Sydney
See also AAYA 41; AMWS 2; EXPS; RGAL
4; RGSF 2; SSFS 2

Henry, Patrick 1736-1799 .... **LC 25**
See also LAIT 1

Henryson, Robert 1430(?)-1506(?) ...... **LC 20**
See also BRWS 7; DLB 146; RGEL 2

Henschke, Alfred
See Klabund

Hentoff, Nat(han Irving) 1925- .... **CLC 26**
See also AAYA 4, 42; BYA 6; CA 1-4R;
CAAS 6; CANR 5, 25, 77, 114; CLR 1,
52; INT CANR-25; JRDA; MAICYA 1,
2; SATA 42, 69, 133; SATA-Brief 27;
WYA; YAW

Heppenstall, (John) Rayner
1911-1981 .... **CLC 10**
See also CA 1-4R; CANR 29

Heraclitus c. 540B.C.-c. 450B.C. ... **CMLC 22**
See also DLB 176

Herbert, Frank (Patrick)
1920-1986 .... **CLC 12, 23, 35, 44, 85**
See also AAYA 21; BPFB 2; BYA 4, 14;
CA 53-56; CANR 5, 43; CDALBS; CPW;
DAM POP; DLB 8; INT CANR-5; LAIT
5; MTCW 1, 2; SATA 9, 37; SATA-Obit
47; SCFW 2; SFW 4; YAW

Herbert, George 1593-1633 ...... **LC 24; PC 4**
See also BRW 2; BRWR 2; CDBLB Before
1660; DAB; DAM POET; DLB 126;
EXPP; RGEL 2; TEA; WP

Herbert, Zbigniew 1924-1998 .... **CLC 9, 43**
See also CA 89-92; CANR 36, 74; CDWLB
4; CWW 2; DAM POET; DLB 232;
MTCW 1

Herbst, Josephine (Frey)
1897-1969 .... **CLC 34**
See also CA 5-8R; DLB 9

Herder, Johann Gottfried von
1744-1803 .... **NCLC 8**
See also DLB 97; EW 4; TWA

Heredia, Jose Maria 1803-1839 .... **HLCS 2**
See also LAW

Hergesheimer, Joseph 1880-1954 ... **TCLC 11**
See also CA 194; DLB 102, 9; RGAL 4

Herlihy, James Leo 1927-1993 .... **CLC 6**
See also CA 1-4R; CAD; CANR 2

Herman, William
See Bierce, Ambrose (Gwinett)

Hermogenes fl. c. 175- .... **CMLC 6**

Hernandez, Jose 1834-1886 .... **NCLC 17**
See also LAW; RGWL 2, 3; WLIT 1

Herodotus c. 484B.C.-c. 420B.C. .. **CMLC 17**
See also AW 1; CDWLB 1; DLB 176;
RGWL 2, 3; TWA

Herrick, Robert 1591-1674 .... **LC 13; PC 9**
See also BRW 2; DA; DAB; DAC; DAM
MST, POP; DLB 126; EXPP; PFS 13;
RGAL 4; RGEL 2; TEA; WP

Herring, Guilles
See Somerville, Edith Oenone

Herriot, James 1916-1995 .... **CLC 12**
See Wight, James Alfred
See also AAYA 1; BPFB 2; CANR 40; CLR
80; CPW; DAM POP; LAIT 3; MAICYA
2; MAICYAS 1; MTCW 2; SATA 86, 135;
TEA; YAW

Herris, Violet
See Hunt, Violet

Herrmann, Dorothy 1941- .... **CLC 44**
See also CA 107

Herrmann, Taffy
See Herrmann, Dorothy

Hersey, John (Richard) 1914-1993 .... **CLC 1,**
2, 7, 9, 40, 81, 97
See also AAYA 29; BPFB 2; CA 17-20R;
CANR 33; CDALBS; CPW; DAM POP;
DLB 6, 185; MTCW 1, 2; SATA 25;
SATA-Obit 76; TUS

Herzen, Aleksandr Ivanovich
1812-1870 .... **NCLC 10, 61**

Herzl, Theodor 1860-1904 .... **TCLC 36**
See also CA 168

Herzog, Werner 1942- .... **CLC 16**
See also CA 89-92

Hesiod c. 8th cent. B.C.- .... **CMLC 5**
See also AW 1; DLB 176; RGWL 2, 3

Hesse, Hermann 1877-1962 ... **CLC 1, 2, 3, 6,**
11, 17, 25, 69; SSC 9, 49; WLC
See also AAYA 43; BPFB 2; CA 17-18;
CAP 2; CDWLB 2; DA; DAB; DAC;
DAM MST, NOV; DLB 66; EW 9; EXPN;
LAIT 1; MTCW 1, 2; NFS 6, 15; RGWL
2, 3; SATA 50; TWA

Hewes, Cady
See De Voto, Bernard (Augustine)

Heyen, William 1940- .... **CLC 13, 18**
See also CA 33-36R; CAAS 9; CANR 98;
CP 7; DLB 5

Heyerdahl, Thor 1914-2002 .... **CLC 26**
See also CA 5-8R; CANR 5, 22, 66, 73;
LAIT 4; MTCW 1, 2; SATA 2, 52

Heym, Georg (Theodor Franz Arthur)
1887-1912 .... **TCLC 9**
See also CA 181

Heym, Stefan 1913-2001 .... **CLC 41**
See also CA 9-12R; CANR 4; CWW 2;
DLB 69

Heyse, Paul (Johann Ludwig von)
1830-1914 .... **TCLC 8**
See also DLB 129

Heyward, (Edwin) DuBose
1885-1940 .... **HR 2; TCLC 59**
See also CA 157; DLB 7, 9, 45, 249; SATA
21

Heywood, John 1497(?)-1580(?) .... **LC 65**
See also DLB 136; RGEL 2

Hibbert, Eleanor Alice Burford
1906-1993 .... **CLC 7**
See Holt, Victoria
See also BEST 90:4; CA 17-20R; CANR 9,
28, 59; CMW 4; CPW; DAM POP;
MTCW 2; RHW; SATA 2; SATA-Obit 74

Hichens, Robert (Smythe)
1864-1950 .... **TCLC 64**
See also CA 162; DLB 153; HGG; RHW;
SUFW

Higgins, George V(incent)
1939-1999 .... **CLC 4, 7, 10, 18**
See also BPFB 2; CA 77-80; CAAS 5;
CANR 17, 51, 89, 96; CMW 4; CN 7;
DLB 2; DLBY 1981, 1998; INT CANR-
17; MSW; MTCW 1

MTCW 1, 2; PAB; PFS 1, 3, 6, 10, 15; RGAL 4; RGSF 2; SATA 4, 33; SSFS 4, 7; TUS; WCH; WP; YAW

Hughes, Richard (Arthur Warren)
1900-1976 .... **CLC 1, 11**
See also CA 5-8R; CANR 4; DAM NOV; DLB 15, 161; MTCW 1; RGEL 2; SATA 8; SATA-Obit 25

Hughes, Ted 1930-1998 . **CLC 2, 4, 9, 14, 37, 119; PC 7**
See Hughes, Edward James
See also BRWR 2; BRWS 1; CA 1-4R; CANR 1, 33, 66, 108; CLR 3; CP 7; DAB; DAC; DLB 40, 161; EXPP; MAICYA 1, 2; MTCW 1, 2; PAB; PFS 4; RGEL 2; SATA 49; SATA-Brief 27; SATA-Obit 107; TEA; YAW

Hugo, Richard
See Huch, Ricarda (Octavia)

Hugo, Richard F(ranklin)
1923-1982 .... **CLC 6, 18, 32**
See also AMWS 6; CA 49-52; CANR 3; DAM POET; DLB 5, 206; PFS 17; RGAL 4

Hugo, Victor (Marie) 1802-1885 .... **NCLC 3, 10, 21; PC 17; WLC**
See also AAYA 28; DA; DAB; DAC; DAM DRAM, MST, NOV, POET; DLB 119, 192, 217; EFS 2; EW 6; GFL 1789 to the Present; LAIT 1, 2; NFS 5; RGWL 2, 3; SATA 47; TWA

Huidobro, Vicente
See Huidobro Fernandez, Vicente Garcia
See also LAW

Huidobro Fernandez, Vicente Garcia
1893-1948 .... **TCLC 31**
See Huidobro, Vicente
See also CA 131; HW 1

Hulme, Keri 1947- .... **CLC 39, 130**
See also CA 125; CANR 69; CN 7; CP 7; CWP; FW; INT 125

Hulme, T(homas) E(rnest)
1883-1917 .... **TCLC 21**
See also BRWS 6; CA 203; DLB 19

Hume, David 1711-1776 .... **LC 7, 56**
See also BRWS 3; DLB 104, 252; TEA

Humphrey, William 1924-1997 .... **CLC 45**
See also AMWS 9; CA 77-80; CANR 68; CN 7; CSW; DLB 6, 212, 234; TCWW 2

Humphreys, Emyr Owen 1919- .... **CLC 47**
See also CA 5-8R; CANR 3, 24; CN 7; DLB 15

Humphreys, Josephine 1945- ..... **CLC 34, 57**
See also CA 127; CANR 97; CSW; INT 127

Huneker, James Gibbons
1860-1921 .... **TCLC 65**
See also CA 193; DLB 71; RGAL 4

Hungerford, Hesba Fay
See Brinsmead, H(esba) F(ay)

Hungerford, Pixie
See Brinsmead, H(esba) F(ay)

Hunt, E(verette) Howard, (Jr.)
1918- .... **CLC 3**
See also AITN 1; CA 45-48; CANR 2, 47, 103; CMW 4

Hunt, Francesca
See Holland, Isabelle (Christian)

Hunt, Howard
See Hunt, E(verette) Howard, (Jr.)

Hunt, Kyle
See Creasey, John

Hunt, (James Henry) Leigh
1784-1859 .... **NCLC 1, 70**
See also DAM POET; DLB 96, 110, 144; RGEL 2; TEA

Hunt, Marsha 1946- .... **CLC 70**
See also BW 2, 3; CA 143; CANR 79

Hunt, Violet 1866(?)-1942 .... **TCLC 53**
See also CA 184; DLB 162, 197

Hunter, E. Waldo
See Sturgeon, Theodore (Hamilton)

Hunter, Evan 1926- .... **CLC 11, 31**
See McBain, Ed
See also AAYA 39; BPFB 2; CA 5-8R; CANR 5, 38, 62, 97; CMW 4; CN 7; CPW; DAM POP; DLB 1982; INT CANR-5; MSW; MTCW 1; SATA 25; SFW 4

Hunter, Kristin 1931-
See Lattany, Kristin (Elaine Eggleston) Hunter

Hunter, Mary
See Austin, Mary (Hunter)

Hunter, Mollie 1922- .... **CLC 21**
See McIlwraith, Maureen Mollie Hunter
See also AAYA 13; BYA 6; CANR 37, 78; CLR 25; DLB 161; JRDA; MAICYA 1, 2; SAAS 7; SATA 54, 106; WYA; YAW

Hunter, Robert (?)-1734 .... **LC 7**

Hurston, Zora Neale 1891-1960 .... **BLC 2; CLC 7, 30, 61; DC 12; HR 2; SSC 4; TCLC 121, 131; WLCS**
See also AAYA 15; AFAW 1, 2; AMWS 6; BW 1, 3; BYA 12; CA 85-88; CANR 61; CDALBS; DA; DAC; DAM MST, MULT, NOV; DFS 6; DLB 51, 86; EXPN; EXPS; FW; LAIT 3; MAWW; MTCW 1, 2; NFS 3; RGAL 4; RGSF 2; SSFS 1, 6, 11; TUS; YAW

Husserl, E. G.
See Husserl, Edmund (Gustav Albrecht)

Husserl, Edmund (Gustav Albrecht)
1859-1938 .... **TCLC 100**
See also CA 133

Huston, John (Marcellus)
1906-1987 .... **CLC 20**
See also CA 73-76; CANR 34; DLB 26

Hustvedt, Siri 1955- .... **CLC 76**
See also CA 137

Hutten, Ulrich von 1488-1523 .... **LC 16**
See also DLB 179

Huxley, Aldous (Leonard)
1894-1963 .... **CLC 1, 3, 4, 5, 8, 11, 18, 35, 79; SSC 39; WLC**
See also AAYA 11; BPFB 2; BRW 7; CA 85-88; CANR 44, 99; CDBLB 1914-1945; DA; DAB; DAC; DAM MST, NOV; DLB 36, 100, 162, 195, 255; EXPN; LAIT 5; MTCW 1, 2; NFS 6; RGEL 2; SATA 63; SCFW 2; SFW 4; TEA; YAW

Huxley, T(homas) H(enry)
1825-1895 .... **NCLC 67**
See also DLB 57; TEA

Huysmans, Joris-Karl 1848-1907 ... **TCLC 7, 69**
See also CA 165; DLB 123; EW 7; GFL 1789 to the Present; RGWL 2, 3

Hwang, David Henry 1957- .. **CLC 55; DC 4**
See also CA 132; CAD; CANR 76; CD 5; DAM DRAM; DFS 11; DLB 212, 228; INT CA-132; MTCW 2; RGAL 4

Hyde, Anthony 1946- .... **CLC 42**
See Chase, Nicholas
See also CA 136; CCA 1

Hyde, Margaret O(ldroyd) 1917- ..... **CLC 21**
See also CA 1-4R; CANR 1, 36; CLR 23; JRDA; MAICYA 1, 2; SAAS 8; SATA 1, 42, 76

Hynes, James 1956(?)- .... **CLC 65**
See also CA 164; CANR 105

Hypatia c. 370-415 .... **CMLC 35**

Ian, Janis 1951- .... **CLC 21**
See also CA 187

Ibanez, Vicente Blasco
See Blasco Ibanez, Vicente

Ibarbourou, Juana de 1895-1979 ..... **HLCS 2**
See also HW 1; LAW

Ibarguengoitia, Jorge 1928-1983 ...... **CLC 37**
See also CA 124; HW 1

Ibn Battuta, Abu Abdalla
1304-1368(?) .... **CMLC 57**
See also WLIT 2

Ibsen, Henrik (Johan) 1828-1906 .... **DC 2; TCLC 2, 8, 16, 37, 52; WLC**
See also AAYA 46; CA 141; DA; DAB; DAC; DAM DRAM, MST; DFS 15; EW 7; LAIT 2; RGWL 2, 3

Ibuse, Masuji 1898-1993 .... **CLC 22**
See Ibuse Masuji
See also CA 127; MJW; RGWL 3

Ibuse Masuji
See Ibuse, Masuji
See also DLB 180

Ichikawa, Kon 1915- .... **CLC 20**
See also CA 121

Ichiyo, Higuchi 1872-1896 .... **NCLC 49**
See also MJW

Idle, Eric 1943-2000 .... **CLC 21**
See Monty Python
See also CA 116; CANR 35, 91

Ignatow, David 1914-1997 .... **CLC 4, 7, 14, 40; PC 34**
See also CA 9-12R; CAAS 3; CANR 31, 57, 96; CP 7; DLB 5

Ignotus
See Strachey, (Giles) Lytton

Ihimaera, Witi 1944- .... **CLC 46**
See also CA 77-80; CN 7; RGSF 2

Ilf, Ilya .... **TCLC 21**
See Fainzilberg, Ilya Arnoldovich

Illyes, Gyula 1902-1983 .... **PC 16**
See also CA 114; CDWLB 4; DLB 215; RGWL 2, 3

Immermann, Karl (Lebrecht)
1796-1840 .... **NCLC 4, 49**
See also DLB 133

Ince, Thomas H. 1882-1924 .... **TCLC 89**
See also IDFW 3, 4

Inchbald, Elizabeth 1753-1821 ...... **NCLC 62**
See also DLB 39, 89; RGEL 2

Inclan, Ramon (Maria) del Valle
See Valle-Inclan, Ramon (Maria) del

Infante, G(uillermo) Cabrera
See Cabrera Infante, G(uillermo)

Ingalls, Rachel (Holmes) 1940- .... **CLC 42**
See also CA 127

Ingamells, Reginald Charles
See Ingamells, Rex

Ingamells, Rex 1913-1955 .... **TCLC 35**
See also CA 167; DLB 260

Inge, William (Motter) 1913-1973 ..... **CLC 1, 8, 19**
See also CA 9-12R; CDALB 1941-1968; DAM DRAM; DFS 1, 5, 8; DLB 7, 249; MTCW 1, 2; RGAL 4; TUS

Ingelow, Jean 1820-1897 .... **NCLC 39, 107**
See also DLB 35, 163; FANT; SATA 33

Ingram, Willis J.
See Harris, Mark

Innaurato, Albert (F.) 1948(?)- ... **CLC 21, 60**
See also CA 122; CAD; CANR 78; CD 5; INT CA-122

Innes, Michael
See Stewart, J(ohn) I(nnes) M(ackintosh)
See also MSW

Innis, Harold Adams 1894-1952 .... **TCLC 77**
See also CA 181; DLB 88

Insluis, Alanus de
See Alain de Lille

Iola
See Wells-Barnett, Ida B(ell)

Kotlowitz, Robert 1924- .... **CLC 4**
See also CA 33-36R; CANR 36

Kotzebue, August (Friedrich Ferdinand) von 1761-1819 .... **NCLC 25**
See also DLB 94

Kotzwinkle, William 1938- ..... **CLC 5, 14, 35**
See also BPFB 2; CA 45-48; CANR 3, 44, 84; CLR 6; DLB 173; FANT; MAICYA 1, 2; SATA 24, 70; SFW 4; SUFW 2; YAW

Kowna, Stancy
See Szymborska, Wislawa

Kozol, Jonathan 1936- .... **CLC 17**
See also AAYA 46; CA 61-64; CANR 16, 45, 96

Kozoll, Michael 1940(?)- .... **CLC 35**

Kramer, Kathryn 19(?)- .... **CLC 34**

Kramer, Larry 1935- .... **CLC 42; DC 8**
See also CA 126; CANR 60; DAM POP; DLB 249; GLL 1

Krasicki, Ignacy 1735-1801 .... **NCLC 8**

Krasinski, Zygmunt 1812-1859 .... **NCLC 4**
See also RGWL 2, 3

Kraus, Karl 1874-1936 .... **TCLC 5**
See also DLB 118

Kreve (Mickevicius), Vincas 1882-1954 .... **TCLC 27**
See also CA 170; DLB 220

Kristeva, Julia 1941- .... **CLC 77, 140**
See also CA 154; CANR 99; DLB 242; FW

Kristofferson, Kris 1936- .... **CLC 26**
See also CA 104

Krizanc, John 1956- .... **CLC 57**
See also CA 187

Krleza, Miroslav 1893-1981 .... **CLC 8, 114**
See also CA 97-100; CANR 50; CDWLB 4; DLB 147; EW 11; RGWL 2, 3

Kroetsch, Robert 1927- .. **CLC 5, 23, 57, 132**
See also CA 17-20R; CANR 8, 38; CCA 1; CN 7; CP 7; DAC; DAM POET; DLB 53; MTCW 1

Kroetz, Franz
See Kroetz, Franz Xaver

Kroetz, Franz Xaver 1946- .... **CLC 41**
See also CA 130

Kroker, Arthur (W.) 1945- .... **CLC 77**
See also CA 161

Kropotkin, Peter (Aleksieevich) 1842-1921 .... **TCLC 36**
See also CA 119

Krotkov, Yuri 1917-1981 .... **CLC 19**
See also CA 102

Krumb
See Crumb, R(obert)

Krumgold, Joseph (Quincy) 1908-1980 .... **CLC 12**
See also BYA 1, 2; CA 9-12R; CANR 7; MAICYA 1, 2; SATA 1, 48; SATA-Obit 23; YAW

Krumwitz
See Crumb, R(obert)

Krutch, Joseph Wood 1893-1970 ..... **CLC 24**
See also ANW; CA 1-4R; CANR 4; DLB 63, 206, 275

Krutzch, Gus
See Eliot, T(homas) S(tearns)

Krylov, Ivan Andreevich 1768(?)-1844 .... **NCLC 1**
See also DLB 150

Kubin, Alfred (Leopold Isidor) 1877-1959 .... **TCLC 23**
See also CA 149; CANR 104; DLB 81

Kubrick, Stanley 1928-1999 .... **CLC 16; TCLC 112**
See also AAYA 30; CA 81-84; CANR 33; DLB 26

Kueng, Hans 1928-
See Kung, Hans
See also CA 53-56; CANR 66; MTCW 1, 2

Kumin, Maxine (Winokur) 1925- ..... **CLC 5, 13, 28, 164; PC 15**
See also AITN 2; AMWS 4; ANW; CA 1-4R; CAAS 8; CANR 1, 21, 69; CP 7; CWP; DAM POET; DLB 5; EXPP; MTCW 1, 2; PAB; SATA 12

Kundera, Milan 1929- . **CLC 4, 9, 19, 32, 68, 115, 135; SSC 24**
See also AAYA 2; BPFB 2; CA 85-88; CANR 19, 52, 74; CDWLB 4; CWW 2; DAM NOV; DLB 232; EW 13; MTCW 1, 2; RGSF 2; RGWL 3; SSFS 10

Kunene, Mazisi (Raymond) 1930- ... **CLC 85**
See also BW 1, 3; CA 125; CANR 81; CP 7; DLB 117

Kung, Hans .... **CLC 130**
See Kueng, Hans

Kunikida Doppo 1869(?)-1908
See Doppo, Kunikida
See also DLB 180

Kunitz, Stanley (Jasspon) 1905- .. **CLC 6, 11, 14, 148; PC 19**
See also AMWS 3; CA 41-44R; CANR 26, 57, 98; CP 7; DLB 48; INT CANR-26; MTCW 1, 2; PFS 11; RGAL 4

Kunze, Reiner 1933- .... **CLC 10**
See also CA 93-96; CWW 2; DLB 75

Kuprin, Aleksander Ivanovich 1870-1938 .... **TCLC 5**
See also CA 182

Kureishi, Hanif 1954(?)- .... **CLC 64, 135**
See also CA 139; CANR 113; CBD; CD 5; CN 7; DLB 194, 245; GLL 2; IDFW 4; WLIT 4

Kurosawa, Akira 1910-1998 ..... **CLC 16, 119**
See also AAYA 11; CA 101; CANR 46; DAM MULT

Kushner, Tony 1957(?)- .... **CLC 81; DC 10**
See also AMWS 9; CA 144; CAD; CANR 74; CD 5; DAM DRAM; DFS 5; DLB 228; GLL 1; LAIT 5; MTCW 2; RGAL 4

Kuttner, Henry 1915-1958 .... **TCLC 10**
See also CA 157; DLB 8; FANT; SCFW 2; SFW 4

Kutty, Madhavi
See Das, Kamala

Kuzma, Greg 1944- .... **CLC 7**
See also CA 33-36R; CANR 70

Kuzmin, Mikhail 1872(?)-1936 ...... **TCLC 40**
See also CA 170

Kyd, Thomas 1558-1594 .... **DC 3; LC 22**
See also BRW 1; DAM DRAM; DLB 62; IDTP; RGEL 2; TEA; WLIT 3

Kyprianos, Iossif
See Samarakis, Antonis

L. S.
See Stephen, Sir Leslie

Labrunie, Gerard
See Nerval, Gerard de

La Bruyere, Jean de 1645-1696 .... **LC 17**
See also DLB 268; EW 3; GFL Beginnings to 1789

Lacan, Jacques (Marie Emile) 1901-1981 .... **CLC 75**
See also CA 121; TWA

Laclos, Pierre Ambroise Francois 1741-1803 .... **NCLC 4, 87**
See also EW 4; GFL Beginnings to 1789; RGWL 2, 3

La Colere, Francois
See Aragon, Louis

Lacolere, Francois
See Aragon, Louis

La Deshabilleuse
See Simenon, Georges (Jacques Christian)

Lady Gregory
See Gregory, Lady Isabella Augusta (Persse)

Lady of Quality, A
See Bagnold, Enid

La Fayette, Marie-(Madelaine Pioche de la Vergne) 1634-1693 .... **LC 2**
See Lafayette, Marie-Madeleine
See also GFL Beginnings to 1789; RGWL 2, 3

Lafayette, Marie-Madeleine
See La Fayette, Marie-(Madeleine Pioche de la Vergne)
See also DLB 268

Lafayette, Rene
See Hubbard, L(afayette) Ron(ald)

La Fontaine, Jean de 1621-1695 .... **LC 50**
See also DLB 268; EW 3; GFL Beginnings to 1789; MAICYA 1, 2; RGWL 2, 3; SATA 18

Laforgue, Jules 1860-1887 . **NCLC 5, 53; PC 14; SSC 20**
See also DLB 217; EW 7; GFL 1789 to the Present; RGWL 2, 3

Layamon
See Layamon
See also DLB 146

Lagerkvist, Paer (Fabian) 1891-1974 .... **CLC 7, 10, 13, 54**
See Lagerkvist, Par
See also CA 85-88; DAM DRAM, NOV; MTCW 1, 2; TWA

Lagerkvist, Par .... **SSC 12**
See Lagerkvist, Paer (Fabian)
See also DLB 259; EW 10; MTCW 2; RGSF 2; RGWL 2, 3

Lagerloef, Selma (Ottiliana Lovisa) 1858-1940 .... **TCLC 4, 36**
See Lagerlof, Selma (Ottiliana Lovisa)
See also MTCW 2; SATA 15

Lagerlof, Selma (Ottiliana Lovisa)
See Lagerloef, Selma (Ottiliana Lovisa)
See also CLR 7; SATA 15

La Guma, (Justin) Alex(ander) 1925-1985 .... **BLCS; CLC 19**
See also AFW; BW 1, 3; CA 49-52; CANR 25, 81; CDWLB 3; DAM NOV; DLB 117, 225; MTCW 1, 2; WLIT 2

Laidlaw, A. K.
See Grieve, C(hristopher) M(urray)

Lainez, Manuel Mujica
See Mujica Lainez, Manuel
See also HW 1

Laing, R(onald) D(avid) 1927-1989 . **CLC 95**
See also CA 107; CANR 34; MTCW 1

Lamartine, Alphonse (Marie Louis Prat) de 1790-1869 .... **NCLC 11; PC 16**
See also DAM POET; DLB 217; GFL 1789 to the Present; RGWL 2, 3

Lamb, Charles 1775-1834 ..... **NCLC 10, 113; WLC**
See also BRW 4; CDBLB 1789-1832; DA; DAB; DAC; DAM MST; DLB 93, 107, 163; RGEL 2; SATA 17; TEA

Lamb, Lady Caroline 1785-1828 ... **NCLC 38**
See also DLB 116

Lamming, George (William) 1927- ... **BLC 2; CLC 2, 4, 66, 144**
See also BW 2, 3; CA 85-88; CANR 26, 76; CDWLB 3; CN 7; DAM MULT; DLB 125; MTCW 1, 2; NFS 15; RGEL 2

L'Amour, Louis (Dearborn) 1908-1988 .... **CLC 25, 55**
See Burns, Tex; Mayo, Jim
See also AAYA 16; AITN 2; BEST 89:2; BPFB 2; CA 1-4R; CANR 3, 25, 40; CPW; DAM NOV, POP; DLB 206; DLBY 1980; MTCW 1, 2; RGAL 4

Lampedusa, Giuseppe (Tomasi) di .... **TCLC 13**
See Tomasi di Lampedusa, Giuseppe
See also CA 164; EW 11; MTCW 2; RGWL 2, 3

Lampman, Archibald 1861-1899 ... **NCLC 25**
See also DLB 92; RGEL 2; TWA

Madden, (Jerry) David 1933- .... **CLC 5, 15**
See also CA 1-4R; CAAS 3; CANR 4, 45;
CN 7; CSW; DLB 6; MTCW 1

Maddern, Al(an)
See Ellison, Harlan (Jay)

Madhubuti, Haki R. 1942- ... **BLC 2; CLC 6,
73; PC 5**
See Lee, Don L.
See also BW 2, 3; CA 73-76; CANR 24,
51, 73; CP 7; CSW; DAM MULT, POET;
DLB 5, 41; DLBD 8; MTCW 2; RGAL 4

Maepenn, Hugh
See Kuttner, Henry

Maepenn, K. H.
See Kuttner, Henry

Maeterlinck, Maurice 1862-1949 ..... **TCLC 3**
See also CA 136; CANR 80; DAM DRAM;
DLB 192; EW 8; GFL 1789 to the Present;
RGWL 2, 3; SATA 66; TWA

Maginn, William 1794-1842 .... **NCLC 8**
See also DLB 110, 159

Mahapatra, Jayanta 1928- .... **CLC 33**
See also CA 73-76; CAAS 9; CANR 15,
33, 66, 87; CP 7; DAM MULT

Mahfouz, Naguib (Abdel Aziz Al-Sabilgi)
1911(?)- .... **CLC 153**
See Mahfuz, Najib (Abdel Aziz al-Sabilgi)
See also BEST 89:2; CA 128; CANR 55,
101; CWW 2; DAM NOV; MTCW 1, 2;
RGWL 2, 3; SSFS 9

Mahfuz, Najib (Abdel Aziz al-Sabilgi)
.... **CLC 52, 55**
See Mahfouz, Naguib (Abdel Aziz Al-
Sabilgi)
See also AFW; DLBY 1988; RGSF 2;
WLIT 2

Mahon, Derek 1941- .... **CLC 27**
See also BRWS 6; CA 128; CANR 88; CP
7; DLB 40

Maiakovskii, Vladimir
See Mayakovski, Vladimir (Vladimirovich)
See also IDTP; RGWL 2, 3

Mailer, Norman 1923- ... **CLC 1, 2, 3, 4, 5, 8,
11, 14, 28, 39, 74, 111**
See also AAYA 31; AITN 2; AMW; AMWR
2; BPFB 2; CA 9-12R; CABS 1; CANR
28, 74, 77; CDALB 1968-1988; CN 7;
CPW; DA; DAB; DAC; DAM MST,
NOV, POP; DLB 2, 16, 28, 185; DLBD
3; DLBY 1980, 1983; MTCW 1, 2; NFS
10; RGAL 4; TUS

Maillet, Antonine 1929- .... **CLC 54, 118**
See also CA 120; CANR 46, 74, 77; CCA
1; CWW 2; DAC; DLB 60; INT 120;
MTCW 2

Mais, Roger 1905-1955 .... **TCLC 8**
See also BW 1, 3; CA 124; CANR 82; CD-
WLB 3; DLB 125; MTCW 1; RGEL 2

Maistre, Joseph 1753-1821 .... **NCLC 37**
See also GFL 1789 to the Present

Maitland, Frederic William
1850-1906 .... **TCLC 65**

Maitland, Sara (Louise) 1950- .... **CLC 49**
See also CA 69-72; CANR 13, 59; DLB
271; FW

Major, Clarence 1936- ... **BLC 2; CLC 3, 19,
48**
See also AFAW 2; BW 2, 3; CA 21-24R;
CAAS 6; CANR 13, 25, 53, 82; CN 7;
CP 7; CSW; DAM MULT; DLB 33; MSW

Major, Kevin (Gerald) 1949- .... **CLC 26**
See also AAYA 16; CA 97-100; CANR 21,
38, 112; CLR 11; DAC; DLB 60; INT
CANR-21; JRDA; MAICYA 1, 2; MAIC-
YAS 1; SATA 32, 82, 134; WYA; YAW

Maki, James
See Ozu, Yasujiro

Malabaila, Damiano
See Levi, Primo

Malamud, Bernard 1914-1986 .. **CLC 1, 2, 3,
5, 8, 9, 11, 18, 27, 44, 78, 85; SSC 15;
TCLC 129; WLC**
See also AAYA 16; AMWS 1; BPFB 2; CA
5-8R; CABS 1; CANR 28, 62, 114;
CDALB 1941-1968; CPW; DA; DAB;
DAC; DAM MST, NOV, POP; DLB 2,
28, 152; DLBY 1980, 1986; EXPS; LAIT
4; MTCW 1, 2; NFS 4, 9; RGAL 4; RGSF
2; SSFS 8, 13, 16; TUS

Malan, Herman
See Bosman, Herman Charles; Bosman,
Herman Charles

Malaparte, Curzio 1898-1957 .... **TCLC 52**
See also DLB 264

Malcolm, Dan
See Silverberg, Robert

Malcolm X .... **BLC 2; CLC 82, 117; WLCS**
See Little, Malcolm
See also LAIT 5

Malherbe, Francois de 1555-1628 .... **LC 5**
See also GFL Beginnings to 1789

Mallarme, Stephane 1842-1898 ...... **NCLC 4,
41; PC 4**
See also DAM POET; DLB 217; EW 7;
GFL 1789 to the Present; RGWL 2, 3;
TWA

Mallet-Joris, Francoise 1930- .... **CLC 11**
See also CA 65-68; CANR 17; DLB 83;
GFL 1789 to the Present

Malley, Ern
See McAuley, James Phillip

Mallowan, Agatha Christie
See Christie, Agatha (Mary Clarissa)

Maloff, Saul 1922- .... **CLC 5**
See also CA 33-36R

Malone, Louis
See MacNeice, (Frederick) Louis

Malone, Michael (Christopher)
1942- .... **CLC 43**
See also CA 77-80; CANR 14, 32, 57, 114

Malory, Sir Thomas 1410(?)-1471(?) . **LC 11;
WLCS**
See also BRW 1; BRWR 2; CDBLB Before
1660; DA; DAB; DAC; DAM MST; DLB
146; EFS 2; RGEL 2; SATA 59; SATA-
Brief 33; TEA; WLIT 3

Malouf, (George Joseph) David
1934- .... **CLC 28, 86**
See also CA 124; CANR 50, 76; CN 7; CP
7; MTCW 2

Malraux, (Georges-)Andre
1901-1976 .... **CLC 1, 4, 9, 13, 15, 57**
See also BPFB 2; CA 21-22; CANR 34, 58;
CAP 2; DAM NOV; DLB 72; EW 12;
GFL 1789 to the Present; MTCW 1, 2;
RGWL 2, 3; TWA

Malzberg, Barry N(athaniel) 1939- ... **CLC 7**
See also CA 61-64; CAAS 4; CANR 16;
CMW 4; DLB 8; SFW 4

Mamet, David (Alan) 1947- .. **CLC 9, 15, 34,
46, 91, 166; DC 4**
See also AAYA 3; CA 81-84; CABS 3;
CANR 15, 41, 67, 72; CD 5; DAM
DRAM; DFS 15; DLB 7; IDFW 4;
MTCW 1, 2; RGAL 4

Mamoulian, Rouben (Zachary)
1897-1987 .... **CLC 16**
See also CA 25-28R; CANR 85

Mandelshtam, Osip
See Mandelstam, Osip (Emilievich)
See also EW 10; RGWL 2, 3

Mandelstam, Osip (Emilievich)
1891(?)-1943(?) .... **PC 14; TCLC 2, 6**
See Mandelshtam, Osip
See also CA 150; MTCW 2; TWA

Mander, (Mary) Jane 1877-1949 ... **TCLC 31**
See also CA 162; RGEL 2

Mandeville, Bernard 1670-1733 .... **LC 82**
See also DLB 101

Mandeville, Sir John fl. 1350- ...... **CMLC 19**
See also DLB 146

Mandiargues, Andre Pieyre de .... **CLC 41**
See Pieyre de Mandiargues, Andre
See also DLB 83

Mandrake, Ethel Belle
See Thurman, Wallace (Henry)

Mangan, James Clarence
1803-1849 .... **NCLC 27**
See also RGEL 2

Maniere, J.-E.
See Giraudoux, Jean(-Hippolyte)

Mankiewicz, Herman (Jacob)
1897-1953 .... **TCLC 85**
See also CA 169; DLB 26; IDFW 3, 4

Manley, (Mary) Delariviere
1672(?)-1724 .... **LC 1, 42**
See also DLB 39, 80; RGEL 2

Mann, Abel
See Creasey, John

Mann, Emily 1952- .... **DC 7**
See also CA 130; CAD; CANR 55; CD 5;
CWD; DLB 266

Mann, (Luiz) Heinrich 1871-1950 ... **TCLC 9**
See also CA 164, 181; DLB 66, 118; EW 8;
RGWL 2, 3

Mann, (Paul) Thomas 1875-1955 .... **SSC 5;
TCLC 2, 8, 14, 21, 35, 44, 60; WLC**
See also BPFB 2; CA 128; CDWLB 2; DA;
DAB; DAC; DAM MST, NOV; DLB 66;
EW 9; GLL 1; MTCW 1, 2; RGSF 2;
RGWL 2, 3; SSFS 4, 9; TWA

Mannheim, Karl 1893-1947 .... **TCLC 65**
See also CA 204

Manning, David
See Faust, Frederick (Schiller)
See also TCWW 2

Manning, Frederic 1887(?)-1935 ... **TCLC 25**
See also DLB 260

Manning, Olivia 1915-1980 .... **CLC 5, 19**
See also CA 5-8R; CANR 29; FW; MTCW
1; RGEL 2

Mano, D. Keith 1942- .... **CLC 2, 10**
See also CA 25-28R; CAAS 6; CANR 26,
57; DLB 6

Mansfield, Katherine . **SSC 9, 23, 38; TCLC
2, 8, 39; WLC**
See Beauchamp, Kathleen Mansfield
See also BPFB 2; BRW 7; DAB; DLB 162;
EXPS; FW; GLL 1; RGEL 2; RGSF 2;
SSFS 2, 8, 10, 11

Manso, Peter 1940- .... **CLC 39**
See also CA 29-32R; CANR 44

Mantecon, Juan Jimenez
See Jimenez (Mantecon), Juan Ramon

Mantel, Hilary (Mary) 1952- .... **CLC 144**
See also CA 125; CANR 54, 101; CN 7;
DLB 271; RHW

Manton, Peter
See Creasey, John

Man Without a Spleen, A
See Chekhov, Anton (Pavlovich)

Manzoni, Alessandro 1785-1873 ... **NCLC 29,
98**
See also EW 5; RGWL 2, 3; TWA

Map, Walter 1140-1209 .... **CMLC 32**

Mapu, Abraham (ben Jekutiel)
1808-1867 .... **NCLC 18**

Mara, Sally
See Queneau, Raymond

Marat, Jean Paul 1743-1793 .... **LC 10**

Marcel, Gabriel Honore 1889-1973 . **CLC 15**
See also CA 102; MTCW 1, 2

March, William 1893-1954 .... **TCLC 96**

Meyer, Gustav 1868-1932
 See Meyrink, Gustav
 See also CA 190
Meyer, June
 See Jordan, June (Meyer)
Meyer, Lynn
 See Slavitt, David R(ytman)
Meyers, Jeffrey 1939- .... **CLC 39**
 See also CA 73-76; CAAE 186; CANR 54,
 102; DLB 111
**Meynell, Alice (Christina Gertrude
 Thompson)** 1847-1922 .... **TCLC 6**
 See also CA 177; DLB 19, 98; RGEL 2
Meyrink, Gustav .... **TCLC 21**
 See Meyer, Gustav
 See also DLB 81
Michaels, Leonard 1933- .... **CLC 6, 25; SSC
 16**
 See also CA 61-64; CANR 21, 62; CN 7;
 DLB 130; MTCW 1
Michaux, Henri 1899-1984 .... **CLC 8, 19**
 See also CA 85-88; DLB 258; GFL 1789 to
 the Present; RGWL 2, 3
Micheaux, Oscar (Devereaux)
 1884-1951 .... **TCLC 76**
 See also BW 3; CA 174; DLB 50; TCWW
 2
Michelangelo 1475-1564 .... **LC 12**
 See also AAYA 43
Michelet, Jules 1798-1874 .... **NCLC 31**
 See also EW 5; GFL 1789 to the Present
Michels, Robert 1876-1936 .... **TCLC 88**
Michener, James A(lbert)
 1907(?)-1997 .. **CLC 1, 5, 11, 29, 60, 109**
 See also AAYA 27; AITN 1; BEST 90:1;
 BPFB 2; CA 5-8R; CANR 21, 45, 68; CN
 7; CPW; DAM NOV, POP; DLB 6;
 MTCW 1, 2; RHW
Mickiewicz, Adam 1798-1855 . **NCLC 3, 101;
 PC 38**
 See also EW 5; RGWL 2, 3
Middleton, Christopher 1926- .... **CLC 13**
 See also CA 13-16R; CANR 29, 54; CP 7;
 DLB 40
Middleton, Richard (Barham)
 1882-1911 .... **TCLC 56**
 See also CA 187; DLB 156; HGG
Middleton, Stanley 1919- .... **CLC 7, 38**
 See also CA 25-28R; CAAS 23; CANR 21,
 46, 81; CN 7; DLB 14
Middleton, Thomas 1580-1627 ...... **DC 5; LC
 33**
 See also BRW 2; DAM DRAM, MST; DLB
 58; RGEL 2
Migueis, Jose Rodrigues 1901- .... **CLC 10**
Mikszath, Kalman 1847-1910 .... **TCLC 31**
 See also CA 170
Miles, Jack .... **CLC 100**
 See also CA 200
Miles, John Russiano
 See Miles, Jack
Miles, Josephine (Louise)
 1911-1985 .... **CLC 1, 2, 14, 34, 39**
 See also CA 1-4R; CANR 2, 55; DAM
 POET; DLB 48
Militant
 See Sandburg, Carl (August)
Mill, Harriet (Hardy) Taylor
 1807-1858 .... **NCLC 102**
 See also FW
Mill, John Stuart 1806-1873 .... **NCLC 11, 58**
 See also CDBLB 1832-1890; DLB 55, 190,
 262; FW 1; RGEL 2; TEA
Millar, Kenneth 1915-1983 .... **CLC 14**
 See Macdonald, Ross
 See also CA 9-12R; CANR 16, 63, 107;
 CMW 4; CPW; DAM POP; DLB 2, 226;
 DLBD 6; DLBY 1983; MTCW 1, 2

Millay, E. Vincent
 See Millay, Edna St. Vincent
Millay, Edna St. Vincent 1892-1950 .... **PC 6;
 TCLC 4, 49; WLCS**
 See Boyd, Nancy
 See also AMW; CA 130; CDALB 1917-
 1929; DA; DAB; DAC; DAM MST,
 POET; DLB 45, 249; EXPP; MAWW;
 MTCW 1, 2; PAB; PFS 3, 17; RGAL 4;
 TUS; WP
Miller, Arthur 1915- ...... **CLC 1, 2, 6, 10, 15,
 26, 47, 78; DC 1; WLC**
 See also AAYA 15; AITN 1; AMW; AMWC
 1; CA 1-4R; CABS 3; CAD; CANR 2,
 30, 54, 76; CD 5; CDALB 1941-1968;
 DA; DAB; DAC; DAM DRAM, MST;
 DFS 1, 3; DLB 7, 266; LAIT 1, 4; MTCW
 1, 2; RGAL 4; TUS; WYAS 1
Miller, Henry (Valentine)
 1891-1980 .... **CLC 1, 2, 4, 9, 14, 43, 84;
 WLC**
 See also AMW; BPFB 2; CA 9-12R; CANR
 33, 64; CDALB 1929-1941; DA; DAB;
 DAC; DAM MST, NOV; DLB 4, 9;
 DLBY 1980; MTCW 1, 2; RGAL 4; TUS
Miller, Jason 1939(?)-2001 .... **CLC 2**
 See also AITN 1; CA 73-76; CAD; DFS
 12; DLB 7
Miller, Sue 1943- .... **CLC 44**
 See also AMWS 12; BEST 90:3; CA 139;
 CANR 59, 91; DAM POP; DLB 143
Miller, Walter M(ichael, Jr.)
 1923-1996 .... **CLC 4, 30**
 See also BPFB 2; CA 85-88; CANR 108;
 DLB 8; SCFW; SFW 4
Millett, Kate 1934- .... **CLC 67**
 See also AITN 1; CA 73-76; CANR 32, 53,
 76, 110; DLB 246; FW; GLL 1; MTCW
 1, 2
Millhauser, Steven (Lewis) 1943- .... **CLC 21,
 54, 109; SSC 57**
 See also CA 111; CANR 63, 114; CN 7;
 DLB 2; FANT; INT CA-111; MTCW 2
Millin, Sarah Gertrude 1889-1968 ... **CLC 49**
 See also CA 102; DLB 225
Milne, A(lan) A(lexander)
 1882-1956 .... **TCLC 6, 88**
 See also BRWS 5; CA 133; CLR 1, 26;
 CMW 4; CWRI 5; DAB; DAC; DAM
 MST; DLB 10, 77, 100, 160; FANT; MAI-
 CYA 1, 2; MTCW 1, 2; RGEL 2; SATA
 100; WCH; YABC 1
Milner, Ron(ald) 1938- .... **BLC 3; CLC 56**
 See also AITN 1; BW 1; CA 73-76; CAD;
 CANR 24, 81; CD 5; DAM MULT; DLB
 38; MTCW 1
Milnes, Richard Monckton
 1809-1885 .... **NCLC 61**
 See also DLB 32, 184
Milosz, Czeslaw 1911- ...... **CLC 5, 11, 22, 31,
 56, 82; PC 8; WLCS**
 See also CA 81-84; CANR 23, 51, 91; CD-
 WLB 4; CWW 2; DAM MST, POET;
 DLB 215; EW 13; MTCW 1, 2; PFS 16;
 RGWL 2, 3
Milton, John 1608-1674 ..... **LC 9, 43; PC 19,
 29; WLC**
 See also BRW 2; BRWR 2; CDBLB 1660-
 1789; DA; DAB; DAC; DAM MST,
 POET; DLB 131, 151; EFS 1; EXPP;
 LAIT 1; PAB; PFS 3, 17; RGEL 2; TEA;
 WLIT 3; WP
Min, Anchee 1957- .... **CLC 86**
 See also CA 146; CANR 94
Minehaha, Cornelius
 See Wedekind, (Benjamin) Frank(lin)
Miner, Valerie 1947- .... **CLC 40**
 See also CA 97-100; CANR 59; FW; GLL
 2

Minimo, Duca
 See D'Annunzio, Gabriele
Minot, Susan 1956- .... **CLC 44, 159**
 See also AMWS 6; CA 134; CN 7
Minus, Ed 1938- .... **CLC 39**
 See also CA 185
Miranda, Javier
 See Bioy Casares, Adolfo
 See also CWW 2
Mirbeau, Octave 1848-1917 .... **TCLC 55**
 See also DLB 123, 192; GFL 1789 to the
 Present
Miro (Ferrer), Gabriel (Francisco Victor)
 1879-1930 .... **TCLC 5**
 See also CA 185
Misharin, Alexandr .... **CLC 59**
Mishima, Yukio ... **CLC 2, 4, 6, 9, 27; DC 1;
 SSC 4**
 See Hiraoka, Kimitake
 See also BPFB 2; GLL 1; MJW; MTCW 2;
 RGSF 2; RGWL 2, 3; SSFS 5, 12
Mistral, Frederic 1830-1914 .... **TCLC 51**
 See also GFL 1789 to the Present
Mistral, Gabriela
 See Godoy Alcayaga, Lucila
 See also DNFS 1; LAW; RGWL 2, 3; WP
Mistry, Rohinton 1952- .... **CLC 71**
 See also CA 141; CANR 86, 114; CCA 1;
 CN 7; DAC; SSFS 6
Mitchell, James Leslie 1901-1935
 See Gibbon, Lewis Grassic
 See also CA 188; DLB 15
Mitchell, Joni 1943- .... **CLC 12**
 See also CA 112; CCA 1
Mitchell, Joseph (Quincy)
 1908-1996 .... **CLC 98**
 See also CA 77-80; CANR 69; CN 7; CSW;
 DLB 185; DLBY 1996
Mitchell, Margaret (Munnerlyn)
 1900-1949 .... **TCLC 11**
 See also AAYA 23; BPFB 2; BYA 1; CA
 125; CANR 55, 94; CDALBS; DAM
 NOV, POP; DLB 9; LAIT 2; MTCW 1, 2;
 NFS 9; RGAL 4; RHW; TUS; WYAS 1;
 YAW
Mitchell, Peggy
 See Mitchell, Margaret (Munnerlyn)
Mitchell, S(ilas) Weir 1829-1914 .... **TCLC 36**
 See also CA 165; DLB 202; RGAL 4
Mitchell, W(illiam) O(rmond)
 1914-1998 .... **CLC 25**
 See also CA 77-80; CANR 15, 43; CN 7;
 DAC; DAM MST; DLB 88
Mitchell, William 1879-1936 .... **TCLC 81**
Mitford, Mary Russell 1787-1855 ... **NCLC 4**
 See also DLB 110, 116; RGEL 2
Mitford, Nancy 1904-1973 .... **CLC 44**
 See also CA 9-12R; DLB 191; RGEL 2
Miyamoto, (Chujo) Yuriko
 1899-1951 .... **TCLC 37**
 See Miyamoto Yuriko
 See also CA 170, 174
Miyamoto Yuriko
 See Miyamoto, (Chujo) Yuriko
 See also DLB 180
Miyazawa, Kenji 1896-1933 .... **TCLC 76**
 See also CA 157; RGWL 3
Mizoguchi, Kenji 1898-1956 .... **TCLC 72**
 See also CA 167
Mo, Timothy (Peter) 1950(?)- ... **CLC 46, 134**
 See also CA 117; CN 7; DLB 194; MTCW
 1; WLIT 4
Modarressi, Taghi (M.) 1931-1997 ... **CLC 44**
 See also CA 134; INT 134
Modiano, Patrick (Jean) 1945- .... **CLC 18**
 See also CA 85-88; CANR 17, 40; CWW
 2; DLB 83

Morris, William 1834-1896 .... **NCLC 4**
See also BRW 5; CDBLB 1832-1890; DLB 18, 35, 57, 156, 178, 184; FANT; RGEL 2; SFW 4; SUFW

Morris, Wright 1910-1998 .. **CLC 1, 3, 7, 18, 37; TCLC 107**
See also AMW; CA 9-12R; CANR 21, 81; CN 7; DLB 2, 206, 218; DLBY 1981; MTCW 1, 2; RGAL 4; TCWW 2

Morrison, Arthur 1863-1945 .... **SSC 40; TCLC 72**
See also CA 157; CMW 4; DLB 70, 135, 197; RGEL 2

Morrison, James Douglas 1943-1971
See Morrison, Jim
See also CA 73-76; CANR 40

Morrison, Jim .... **CLC 17**
See Morrison, James Douglas

Morrison, Toni 1931- ..... **BLC 3; CLC 4, 10, 22, 55, 81, 87**
See also AAYA 1, 22; AFAW 1, 2; AMWC 1; AMWS 3; BPFB 2; BW 2, 3; CA 29-32R; CANR 27, 42, 67, 113; CDALB 1968-1988; CN 7; CPW; DA; DAB; DAC; DAM MST, MULT, NOV, POP; DLB 6, 33, 143; DLBY 1981; EXPN; FW; LAIT 2, 4; MAWW; MTCW 1, 2; NFS 1, 6, 8, 14; RGAL 4; RHW; SATA 57; SSFS 5; TUS; YAW

Morrison, Van 1945- .... **CLC 21**
See also CA 168

Morrissy, Mary 1957- .... **CLC 99**
See also CA 205; DLB 267

Mortimer, John (Clifford) 1923- ..... **CLC 28, 43**
See also CA 13-16R; CANR 21, 69, 109; CD 5; CDBLB 1960 to Present; CMW 4; CN 7; CPW; DAM DRAM, POP; DLB 13, 245, 271; INT CANR-21; MSW; MTCW 1, 2; RGEL 2

Mortimer, Penelope (Ruth)
1918-1999 .... **CLC 5**
See also CA 57-60; CANR 45, 88; CN 7

Mortimer, Sir John
See Mortimer, John (Clifford)

Morton, Anthony
See Creasey, John

Morton, Thomas 1579(?)-1647(?) .... **LC 72**
See also DLB 24; RGEL 2

Mosca, Gaetano 1858-1941 .... **TCLC 75**

Mosher, Howard Frank 1943- .... **CLC 62**
See also CA 139; CANR 65

Mosley, Nicholas 1923- .... **CLC 43, 70**
See also CA 69-72; CANR 41, 60, 108; CN 7; DLB 14, 207

Mosley, Walter 1952- .... **BLCS; CLC 97**
See also AAYA 17; BPFB 2; BW 2; CA 142; CANR 57, 92; CMW 4; CPW; DAM MULT, POP; MSW; MTCW 2

Moss, Howard 1922-1987 . **CLC 7, 14, 45, 50**
See also CA 1-4R; CANR 1, 44; DAM POET; DLB 5

Mossgiel, Rab
See Burns, Robert

Motion, Andrew (Peter) 1952- .... **CLC 47**
See also BRWS 7; CA 146; CANR 90; CP 7; DLB 40

Motley, Willard (Francis)
1909-1965 .... **CLC 18**
See also BW 1; CA 117; CANR 88; DLB 76, 143

Motoori, Norinaga 1730-1801 .... **NCLC 45**

Mott, Michael (Charles Alston)
1930- .... **CLC 15, 34**
See also CA 5-8R; CAAS 7; CANR 7, 29

Mountain Wolf Woman 1884-1960 . **CLC 92; NNAL**
See also CA 144; CANR 90

Moure, Erin 1955- .... **CLC 88**
See also CA 113; CP 7; CWP; DLB 60

Mowat, Farley (McGill) 1921- .... **CLC 26**
See also AAYA 1; BYA 2; CA 1-4R; CANR 4, 24, 42, 68, 108; CLR 20; CPW; DAC; DAM MST; DLB 68; INT CANR-24; JRDA; MAICYA 1, 2; MTCW 1, 2; SATA 3, 55; YAW

Mowatt, Anna Cora 1819-1870 ..... **NCLC 74**
See also RGAL 4

Moyers, Bill 1934- .... **CLC 74**
See also AITN 2; CA 61-64; CANR 31, 52

Mphahlele, Es'kia
See Mphahlele, Ezekiel
See also AFW; CDWLB 3; DLB 125, 225; RGSF 2; SSFS 11

Mphahlele, Ezekiel 1919- .. **BLC 3; CLC 25, 133**
See Mphahlele, Es'kia
See also BW 2, 3; CA 81-84; CANR 26, 76; CN 7; DAM MULT; MTCW 2; SATA 119

Mqhayi, S(amuel) E(dward) K(rune Loliwe) 1875-1945 .... **BLC 3; TCLC 25**
See also CA 153; CANR 87; DAM MULT

Mrozek, Slawomir 1930- .... **CLC 3, 13**
See also CA 13-16R; CAAS 10; CANR 29; CDWLB 4; CWW 2; DLB 232; MTCW 1

Mrs. Belloc-Lowndes
See Lowndes, Marie Adelaide (Belloc)

M'Taggart, John M'Taggart Ellis
See McTaggart, John McTaggart Ellis

Mtwa, Percy (?)- .... **CLC 47**

Mueller, Lisel 1924- .... **CLC 13, 51; PC 33**
See also CA 93-96; CP 7; DLB 105; PFS 9, 13

Muggeridge, Malcolm (Thomas)
1903-1990 .... **TCLC 120**
See also AITN 1; CA 101; CANR 33, 63; MTCW 1, 2

Muir, Edwin 1887-1959 .... **TCLC 2, 87**
See Moore, Edward
See also BRWS 6; CA 193; DLB 20, 100, 191; RGEL 2

Muir, John 1838-1914 .... **TCLC 28**
See also AMWS 9; ANW; CA 165; DLB 186, 275

Mujica Lainez, Manuel 1910-1984 ... **CLC 31**
See Lainez, Manuel Mujica
See also CA 81-84; CANR 32; HW 1

Mukherjee, Bharati 1940- ..... **AAL; CLC 53, 115; SSC 38**
See also AAYA 46; BEST 89:2; CA 107; CANR 45, 72; CN 7; DAM NOV; DLB 60, 218; DNFS 1, 2; FW; MTCW 1, 2; RGAL 4; RGSF 2; SSFS 7; TUS

Muldoon, Paul 1951- .... **CLC 32, 72, 166**
See also BRWS 4; CA 129; CANR 52, 91; CP 7; DAM POET; DLB 40; INT 129; PFS 7

Mulisch, Harry 1927- .... **CLC 42**
See also CA 9-12R; CANR 6, 26, 56, 110

Mull, Martin 1943- .... **CLC 17**
See also CA 105

Muller, Wilhelm .... **NCLC 73**

Mulock, Dinah Maria
See Craik, Dinah Maria (Mulock)
See also RGEL 2

Munford, Robert 1737(?)-1783 .... **LC 5**
See also DLB 31

Mungo, Raymond 1946- .... **CLC 72**
See also CA 49-52; CANR 2

Munro, Alice 1931- .... **CLC 6, 10, 19, 50, 95; SSC 3; WLCS**
See also AITN 2; BPFB 2; CA 33-36R; CANR 33, 53, 75, 114; CCA 1; CN 7; DAC; DAM MST, NOV; DLB 53; MTCW 1, 2; RGEL 2; RGSF 2; SATA 29; SSFS 5, 13

Munro, H(ector) H(ugh) 1870-1916 .... **WLC**
See Saki
See also CA 130; CANR 104; CDBLB 1890-1914; DA; DAB; DAC; DAM MST, NOV; DLB 34, 162; EXPS; MTCW 1, 2; RGEL 2; SSFS 15

Murakami, Haruki 1949- .... **CLC 150**
See Murakami Haruki
See also CA 165; CANR 102; MJW; RGWL 3; SFW 4

Murakami Haruki
See Murakami, Haruki
See also DLB 182

Murasaki, Lady
See Murasaki Shikibu

Murasaki Shikibu 978(?)-1026(?) ... **CMLC 1**
See also EFS 2; RGWL 2, 3

Murdoch, (Jean) Iris 1919-1999 ... **CLC 1, 2, 3, 4, 6, 8, 11, 15, 22, 31, 51**
See also BRWS 1; CA 13-16R; CANR 8, 43, 68, 103; CDBLB 1960 to Present; CN 7; DAB; DAC; DAM MST, NOV; DLB 14, 194, 233; INT CANR-8; MTCW 1, 2; RGEL 2; TEA; WLIT 4

Murfree, Mary Noailles 1850-1922 ... **SSC 22**
See also CA 176; DLB 12, 74; RGAL 4

Murnau, Friedrich Wilhelm
See Plumpe, Friedrich Wilhelm

Murphy, Richard 1927- .... **CLC 41**
See also BRWS 5; CA 29-32R; CP 7; DLB 40

Murphy, Sylvia 1937- .... **CLC 34**
See also CA 121

Murphy, Thomas (Bernard) 1935- ... **CLC 51**
See also CA 101

Murray, Albert L. 1916- .... **CLC 73**
See also BW 2; CA 49-52; CANR 26, 52, 78; CSW; DLB 38

Murray, James Augustus Henry
1837-1915 .... **TCLC 117**

Murray, Judith Sargent
1751-1820 .... **NCLC 63**
See also DLB 37, 200

Murray, Les(lie Allan) 1938- .... **CLC 40**
See also BRWS 7; CA 21-24R; CANR 11, 27, 56, 103; CP 7; DAM POET; DLBY 01; RGEL 2

Murry, J. Middleton
See Murry, John Middleton

Murry, John Middleton
1889-1957 .... **TCLC 16**
See also DLB 149

Musgrave, Susan 1951- .... **CLC 13, 54**
See also CA 69-72; CANR 45, 84; CCA 1; CP 7; CWP

Musil, Robert (Edler von)
1880-1942 .... **SSC 18; TCLC 12, 68**
See also CANR 55, 84; CDWLB 2; DLB 81, 124; EW 9; MTCW 1, 2; RGSF 2; RGWL 2, 3

Muske, Carol .... **CLC 90**
See Muske-Dukes, Carol (Anne)

Muske-Dukes, Carol (Anne) 1945-
See Muske, Carol
See also CA 65-68; CAAE 203; CANR 32, 70; CWP

Musset, (Louis Charles) Alfred de
1810-1857 .... **NCLC 7**
See also DLB 192, 217; EW 6; GFL 1789 to the Present; RGWL 2, 3; TWA

Mussolini, Benito (Amilcare Andrea)
1883-1945 .... **TCLC 96**

My Brother's Brother
See Chekhov, Anton (Pavlovich)

Myers, L(eopold) H(amilton)
1881-1944 .... **TCLC 59**
See also CA 157; DLB 15; RGEL 2

O'Flaherty, Liam 1896-1984 .... **CLC 5, 34; SSC 6**
See also CA 101; CANR 35; DLB 36, 162; DLBY 1984; MTCW 1, 2; RGEL 2; RGSF 2; SSFS 5

Ogai
See Mori Ogai
See also MJW

Ogilvy, Gavin
See Barrie, J(ames) M(atthew)

O'Grady, Standish (James)
1846-1928 .... **TCLC 5**
See also CA 157

O'Grady, Timothy 1951- .... **CLC 59**
See also CA 138

O'Hara, Frank 1926-1966 .... **CLC 2, 5, 13, 78; PC 45**
See also CA 9-12R; CANR 33; DAM POET; DLB 5, 16, 193; MTCW 1, 2; PFS 8; 12; RGAL 4; WP

O'Hara, John (Henry) 1905-1970 . **CLC 1, 2, 3, 6, 11, 42; SSC 15**
See also AMW; BPFB 3; CA 5-8R; CANR 31, 60; CDALB 1929-1941; DAM NOV; DLB 9, 86; DLBD 2; MTCW 1, 2; NFS 11; RGAL 4; RGSF 2

O Hehir, Diana 1922- .... **CLC 41**
See also CA 93-96

Ohiyesa
See Eastman, Charles A(lexander)

Okigbo, Christopher (Ifenayichukwu)
1932-1967 .... **BLC 3; CLC 25, 84; PC 7**
See also AFW; BW 1, 3; CA 77-80; CANR 74; CDWLB 3; DAM MULT, POET; DLB 125; MTCW 1, 2; RGEL 2

Okri, Ben 1959- .... **CLC 87**
See also AFW; BRWS 5; BW 2, 3; CA 138; CANR 65; CN 7; DLB 157, 231; INT CA-138; MTCW 2; RGSF 2; WLIT 2

Olds, Sharon 1942- .. **CLC 32, 39, 85; PC 22**
See also AMWS 10; CA 101; CANR 18, 41, 66, 98; CP 7; CPW; CWP; DAM POET; DLB 120; MTCW 2; PFS 17

Oldstyle, Jonathan
See Irving, Washington

Olesha, Iurii
See Olesha, Yuri (Karlovich)
See also RGWL 2

Olesha, Iurii Karlovich
See Olesha, Yuri (Karlovich)
See also DLB 272

Olesha, Yuri (Karlovich) 1899-1960 .. **CLC 8**
See Olesha, Iurii; Olesha, Iurii Karlovich
See also CA 85-88; EW 11; RGWL 3

Oliphant, Mrs.
See Oliphant, Margaret (Oliphant Wilson)
See also SUFW

Oliphant, Laurence 1829(?)-1888 .. **NCLC 47**
See also DLB 18, 166

Oliphant, Margaret (Oliphant Wilson)
1828-1897 .... **NCLC 11, 61; SSC 25**
See Oliphant, Mrs.
See also DLB 18, 159, 190; HGG; RGEL 2; RGSF 2

Oliver, Mary 1935- .... **CLC 19, 34, 98**
See also AMWS 7; CA 21-24R; CANR 9, 43, 84, 92; CP 7; CWP; DLB 5, 193; PFS 15

Olivier, Laurence (Kerr) 1907-1989 . **CLC 20**
See also CA 150

Olsen, Tillie 1912- ... **CLC 4, 13, 114; SSC 11**
See also BYA 11; CA 1-4R; CANR 1, 43, 74; CDALBS; CN 7; DA; DAB; DAC; DAM MST; DLB 28, 206; DLBY 1980; EXPS; FW; MTCW 1, 2; RGAL 4; RGSF 2; SSFS 1; TUS

Olson, Charles (John) 1910-1970 .. **CLC 1, 2, 5, 6, 9, 11, 29; PC 19**
See also AMWS 2; CA 13-16; CABS 2; CANR 35, 61; CAP 1; DAM POET; DLB 5, 16, 193; MTCW 1, 2; RGAL 4; WP

Olson, Toby 1937- .... **CLC 28**
See also CA 65-68; CANR 9, 31, 84; CP 7

Olyesha, Yuri
See Olesha, Yuri (Karlovich)

Omar Khayyam
See Khayyam, Omar
See also RGWL 2, 3

Ondaatje, (Philip) Michael 1943- .... **CLC 14, 29, 51, 76; PC 28**
See also CA 77-80; CANR 42, 74, 109; CN 7; CP 7; DAB; DAC; DAM MST; DLB 60; MTCW 2; PFS 8; TWA

Oneal, Elizabeth 1934-
See Oneal, Zibby
See also CA 106; CANR 28, 84; MAICYA 1, 2; SATA 30, 82; YAW

Oneal, Zibby .... **CLC 30**
See Oneal, Elizabeth
See also AAYA 5, 41; BYA 13; CLR 13; JRDA; WYA

O'Neill, Eugene (Gladstone)
1888-1953 ...... **TCLC 1, 6, 27, 49; WLC**
See also AITN 1; AMW; AMWC 1; CA 132; CAD; CDALB 1929-1941; DA; DAB; DAC; DAM DRAM, MST; DFS 9, 11, 12, 16; DLB 7; LAIT 3; MTCW 1, 2; RGAL 4; TUS

Onetti, Juan Carlos 1909-1994 ... **CLC 7, 10; HLCS 2; SSC 23; TCLC 131**
See also CA 85-88; CANR 32, 63; CDWLB 3; DAM MULT, NOV; DLB 113; HW 1, 2; LAW; MTCW 1, 2; RGSF 2

O Nuallain, Brian 1911-1966
See O'Brien, Flann
See also CA 21-22; CAP 2; DLB 231; FANT; TEA

Ophuls, Max 1902-1957 .... **TCLC 79**

Opie, Amelia 1769-1853 .... **NCLC 65**
See also DLB 116, 159; RGEL 2

Oppen, George 1908-1984 ..... **CLC 7, 13, 34; PC 35; TCLC 107**
See also CA 13-16R; CANR 8, 82; DLB 5, 165

Oppenheim, E(dward) Phillips
1866-1946 .... **TCLC 45**
See also CA 202; CMW 4; DLB 70

Opuls, Max
See Ophuls, Max

Origen c. 185-c. 254 .... **CMLC 19**

Orlovitz, Gil 1918-1973 .... **CLC 22**
See also CA 77-80; DLB 2, 5

Orris
See Ingelow, Jean

Ortega y Gasset, Jose 1883-1955 ...... **HLC 2; TCLC 9**
See also CA 130; DAM MULT; EW 9; HW 1, 2; MTCW 1, 2

Ortese, Anna Maria 1914-1998 .... **CLC 89**
See also DLB 177

Ortiz, Simon J(oseph) 1941- .... **CLC 45; NNAL; PC 17**
See also AMWS 4; CA 134; CANR 69; CP 7; DAM MULT, POET; DLB 120, 175, 256; EXPP; PFS 4, 16; RGAL 4

Orton, Joe .... **CLC 4, 13, 43; DC 3**
See Orton, John Kingsley
See also BRWS 5; CBD; CDBLB 1960 to Present; DFS 3, 6; DLB 13; GLL 1; MTCW 2; RGEL 2; TEA; WLIT 4

Orton, John Kingsley 1933-1967
See Orton, Joe
See also CA 85-88; CANR 35, 66; DAM DRAM; MTCW 1, 2

Orwell, George . **TCLC 2, 6, 15, 31, 51, 128, 129; WLC**
See Blair, Eric (Arthur)
See also BPFB 3; BRW 7; BYA 5; CDBLB 1945-1960; CLR 68; DAB; DLB 15, 98, 195, 255; EXPN; LAIT 4, 5; NFS 3, 7; RGEL 2; SCFW 2; SFW 4; SSFS 4; TEA; WLIT 4; YAW

Osborne, David
See Silverberg, Robert

Osborne, George
See Silverberg, Robert

Osborne, John (James) 1929-1994 .... **CLC 1, 2, 5, 11, 45; WLC**
See also BRWS 1; CA 13-16R; CANR 21, 56; CDBLB 1945-1960; DA; DAB; DAC; DAM DRAM, MST; DFS 4; DLB 13; MTCW 1, 2; RGEL 2

Osborne, Lawrence 1958- .... **CLC 50**
See also CA 189

Osbourne, Lloyd 1868-1947 .... **TCLC 93**

Oshima, Nagisa 1932- .... **CLC 20**
See also CA 121; CANR 78

Oskison, John Milton
1874-1947 .... **NNAL; TCLC 35**
See also CA 144; CANR 84; DAM MULT; DLB 175

Ossian c. 3rd cent. - .... **CMLC 28**
See Macpherson, James

Ossoli, Sarah Margaret (Fuller)
1810-1850 .... **NCLC 5, 50**
See Fuller, Margaret; Fuller, Sarah Margaret
See also CDALB 1640-1865; FW; SATA 25

Ostriker, Alicia (Suskin) 1937- .... **CLC 132**
See also CA 25-28R; CAAS 24; CANR 10, 30, 62, 99; CWP; DLB 120; EXPP

Ostrovsky, Alexander 1823-1886 .. **NCLC 30, 57**

Otero, Blas de 1916-1979 .... **CLC 11**
See also CA 89-92; DLB 134

Otto, Rudolf 1869-1937 .... **TCLC 85**

Otto, Whitney 1955- .... **CLC 70**
See also CA 140

Ouida .... **TCLC 43**
See De la Ramee, Marie Louise (Ouida)
See also DLB 18, 156; RGEL 2

Ouologuem, Yambo 1940- .... **CLC 146**
See also CA 176

Ousmane, Sembene 1923- ... **BLC 3; CLC 66**
See Sembene, Ousmane
See also BW 1, 3; CA 125; CANR 81; CWW 2; MTCW 1

Ovid 43B.C.-17 .... **CMLC 7; PC 2**
See also AW 2; CDWLB 1; DAM POET; DLB 211; RGWL 2, 3; WP

Owen, Hugh
See Faust, Frederick (Schiller)

Owen, Wilfred (Edward Salter)
1893-1918 ... **PC 19; TCLC 5, 27; WLC**
See also BRW 6; CA 141; CDBLB 1914-1945; DA; DAB; DAC; DAM MST, POET; DLB 20; EXPP; MTCW 2; PFS 10; RGEL 2; WLIT 4

Owens, Rochelle 1936- .... **CLC 8**
See also CA 17-20R; CAAS 2; CAD; CANR 39; CD 5; CP 7; CWD; CWP

Oz, Amos 1939- .... **CLC 5, 8, 11, 27, 33, 54**
See also CA 53-56; CANR 27, 47, 65, 113; CWW 2; DAM NOV; MTCW 1, 2; RGSF 2; RGWL 3

Ozick, Cynthia 1928- .... **CLC 3, 7, 28, 62, 155; SSC 15**
See also AMWS 5; BEST 90:1; CA 17-20R; CANR 23, 58; CN 7; CPW; DAM NOV, POP; DLB 28, 152; DLBY 1982; EXPS; INT CANR-23; MTCW 1, 2; RGAL 4; RGSF 2; SSFS 3, 12

Ozu, Yasujiro 1903-1963 .... **CLC 16**
See also CA 112

Pushkin, Aleksandr Sergeevich
    See Pushkin, Alexander (Sergeyevich)
    See also DLB 205
Pushkin, Alexander (Sergeyevich)
    1799-1837 .... **NCLC 3, 27, 83; PC 10;**
    SSC 27, 55; WLC
    See Pushkin, Aleksandr Sergeevich
    See also DA; DAB; DAC; DAM DRAM,
    MST, POET; EW 5; EXPS; RGSF 2;
    RGWL 2, 3; SATA 61; SSFS 9; TWA
P'u Sung-ling 1640-1715 .... **LC 49; SSC 31**
Putnam, Arthur Lee
    See Alger, Horatio, Jr.
Puzo, Mario 1920-1999 .... **CLC 1, 2, 6, 36,**
    107
    See also BPFB 3; CA 65-68; CANR 4, 42,
    65, 99; CN 7; CPW; DAM NOV, POP;
    DLB 6; MTCW 1, 2; NFS 16; RGAL 4
Pygge, Edward
    See Barnes, Julian (Patrick)
Pyle, Ernest Taylor 1900-1945
    See Pyle, Ernie
    See also CA 160
Pyle, Ernie .... **TCLC 75**
    See Pyle, Ernest Taylor
    See also DLB 29; MTCW 2
Pyle, Howard 1853-1911 .... **TCLC 81**
    See also BYA 2, 4; CA 137; CLR 22; DLB
    42, 188; DLBD 13; LAIT 1; MAICYA 1,
    2; SATA 16, 100; WCH; YAW
Pym, Barbara (Mary Crampton)
    1913-1980 .... **CLC 13, 19, 37, 111**
    See also BPFB 3; BRWS 2; CA 13-14;
    CANR 13, 34; CAP 1; DLB 14, 207;
    DLBY 1987; MTCW 1, 2; RGEL 2; TEA
Pynchon, Thomas (Ruggles, Jr.)
    1937- ... **CLC 2, 3, 6, 9, 11, 18, 33, 62,**
    72, 123; SSC 14; WLC
    See also AMWS 2; BEST 90:2; BPFB 3;
    CA 17-20R; CANR 22, 46, 73; CN 7;
    CPW 1; DA; DAB; DAC; DAM MST,
    NOV, POP; DLB 2, 173; MTCW 1, 2;
    RGAL 4; SFW 4; TUS
Pythagoras c. 582B.C.-c. 507B.C. . **CMLC 22**
    See also DLB 176
Q
    See Quiller-Couch, Sir Arthur (Thomas)
Qian, Chongzhu
    See Ch'ien, Chung-shu
Qian Zhongshu
    See Ch'ien, Chung-shu
Qroll
    See Dagerman, Stig (Halvard)
Quarrington, Paul (Lewis) 1953- ..... **CLC 65**
    See also CA 129; CANR 62, 95
Quasimodo, Salvatore 1901-1968 ..... **CLC 10**
    See also CA 13-16; CAP 1; DLB 114; EW
    12; MTCW 1; RGWL 2, 3
Quatermass, Martin
    See Carpenter, John (Howard)
Quay, Stephen 1947- .... **CLC 95**
    See also CA 189
Quay, Timothy 1947- .... **CLC 95**
    See also CA 189
Queen, Ellery .... **CLC 3, 11**
    See Dannay, Frederic; Davidson, Avram
    (James); Deming, Richard; Fairman, Paul
    W.; Flora, Fletcher; Hoch, Edward
    D(entinger); Kane, Henry; Lee, Manfred
    B(ennington); Marlowe, Stephen; Powell,
    (Oval) Talmage; Sheldon, Walter J(ames);
    Sturgeon, Theodore (Hamilton); Tracy,
    Don(ald Fiske); Vance, John Holbrook
    See also BPFB 3; CMW 4; MSW; RGAL 4
Queen, Ellery, Jr.
    See Dannay, Frederic; Lee, Manfred
    B(ennington)

Queneau, Raymond 1903-1976 ..... **CLC 2, 5,**
    10, 42
    See also CA 77-80; CANR 32; DLB 72,
    258; EW 12; GFL 1789 to the Present;
    MTCW 1, 2; RGWL 2, 3
Quevedo, Francisco de 1580-1645 .... **LC 23**
Quiller-Couch, Sir Arthur (Thomas)
    1863-1944 .... **TCLC 53**
    See also CA 166; DLB 135, 153, 190;
    HGG; RGEL 2; SUFW 1
Quin, Ann (Marie) 1936-1973 .... **CLC 6**
    See also CA 9-12R; DLB 14, 231
Quincey, Thomas de
    See De Quincey, Thomas
Quinn, Martin
    See Smith, Martin Cruz
Quinn, Peter 1947- .... **CLC 91**
    See also CA 197
Quinn, Simon
    See Smith, Martin Cruz
Quintana, Leroy V. 1944- ...... **HLC 2; PC 36**
    See also CA 131; CANR 65; DAM MULT;
    DLB 82; HW 1, 2
Quiroga, Horacio (Sylvestre)
    1878-1937 .... **HLC 2; TCLC 20**
    See also CA 131; DAM MULT; HW 1;
    LAW; MTCW 1; RGSF 2; WLIT 1
Quoirez, Francoise 1935- .... **CLC 9**
    See Sagan, Francoise
    See also CA 49-52; CANR 6, 39, 73; CWW
    2; MTCW 1, 2; TWA
Raabe, Wilhelm (Karl) 1831-1910 . **TCLC 45**
    See also CA 167; DLB 129
Rabe, David (William) 1940- .. **CLC 4, 8, 33;**
    DC 16
    See also CA 85-88; CABS 3; CAD; CANR
    59; CD 5; DAM DRAM; DFS 3, 8, 13;
    DLB 7, 228
Rabelais, Francois 1494-1553 .... **LC 5, 60;**
    WLC
    See also DA; DAB; DAC; DAM MST; EW
    2; GFL Beginnings to 1789; RGWL 2, 3;
    TWA
Rabinovitch, Sholem 1859-1916
    See Aleichem, Sholom
Rabinyan, Dorit 1972- .... **CLC 119**
    See also CA 170
Rachilde
    See Vallette, Marguerite Eymery
Racine, Jean 1639-1699 .... **LC 28**
    See also DAB; DAM MST; DLB 268; EW
    3; GFL Beginnings to 1789; RGWL 2, 3;
    TWA
Radcliffe, Ann (Ward) 1764-1823 ... **NCLC 6,**
    55, 106
    See also DLB 39, 178; HGG; RGEL 2;
    SUFW; WLIT 3
Radclyffe-Hall, Marguerite
    See Hall, (Marguerite) Radclyffe
Radiguet, Raymond 1903-1923 ...... **TCLC 29**
    See also CA 162; DLB 65; GFL 1789 to the
    Present; RGWL 2, 3
Radnoti, Miklos 1909-1944 .... **TCLC 16**
    See also CDWLB 4; DLB 215; RGWL 2, 3
Rado, James 1939- .... **CLC 17**
    See also CA 105
Radvanyi, Netty 1900-1983
    See Seghers, Anna
    See also CA 85-88; CANR 82
Rae, Ben
    See Griffiths, Trevor
Raeburn, John (Hay) 1941- .... **CLC 34**
    See also CA 57-60
Ragni, Gerome 1942-1991 .... **CLC 17**
    See also CA 105
Rahv, Philip .... **CLC 24**
    See Greenberg, Ivan
    See also DLB 137

Raimund, Ferdinand Jakob
    1790-1836 .... **NCLC 69**
    See also DLB 90
Raine, Craig (Anthony) 1944- .. **CLC 32, 103**
    See also CA 108; CANR 29, 51, 103; CP 7;
    DLB 40; PFS 7
Raine, Kathleen (Jessie) 1908- ... **CLC 7, 45**
    See also CA 85-88; CANR 46, 109; CP 7;
    DLB 20; MTCW 1; RGEL 2
Rainis, Janis 1865-1929 .... **TCLC 29**
    See also CA 170; CDWLB 4; DLB 220
Rakosi, Carl .... **CLC 47**
    See Rawley, Callman
    See also CAAS 5; CP 7; DLB 193
Ralegh, Sir Walter
    See Raleigh, Sir Walter
    See also BRW 1; RGEL 2; WP
Raleigh, Richard
    See Lovecraft, H(oward) P(hillips)
Raleigh, Sir Walter 1554(?)-1618 .... **LC 31,**
    39; PC 31
    See Ralegh, Sir Walter
    See also CDBLB Before 1660; DLB 172;
    EXPP; PFS 14; TEA
Rallentando, H. P.
    See Sayers, Dorothy L(eigh)
Ramal, Walter
    See de la Mare, Walter (John)
Ramana Maharshi 1879-1950 .... **TCLC 84**
Ramoacn y Cajal, Santiago
    1852-1934 .... **TCLC 93**
Ramon, Juan
    See Jimenez (Mantecon), Juan Ramon
Ramos, Graciliano 1892-1953 .... **TCLC 32**
    See also CA 167; HW 2; LAW; WLIT 1
Rampersad, Arnold 1941- .... **CLC 44**
    See also BW 2, 3; CA 133; CANR 81; DLB
    111; INT 133
Rampling, Anne
    See Rice, Anne
    See also GLL 2
Ramsay, Allan 1686(?)-1758 .... **LC 29**
    See also DLB 95; RGEL 2
Ramsay, Jay
    See Campbell, (John) Ramsey
Ramuz, Charles-Ferdinand
    1878-1947 .... **TCLC 33**
    See also CA 165
Rand, Ayn 1905-1982 ...... **CLC 3, 30, 44, 79;**
    WLC
    See also AAYA 10; AMWS 4; BPFB 3;
    BYA 12; CA 13-16R; CANR 27, 73;
    CDALBS; CPW; DA; DAC; DAM MST,
    NOV, POP; DLB 227; MTCW 1, 2; NFS
    10, 16; RGAL 4; SFW 4; TUS; YAW
Randall, Dudley (Felker) 1914-2000 . **BLC 3;**
    CLC 1, 135
    See also BW 1, 3; CA 25-28R; CANR 23,
    82; DAM MULT; DLB 41; PFS 5
Randall, Robert
    See Silverberg, Robert
Ranger, Ken
    See Creasey, John
Rank, Otto 1884-1939 .... **TCLC 115**
Ransom, John Crowe 1888-1974 .. **CLC 2, 4,**
    5, 11, 24
    See also AMW; CA 5-8R; CANR 6, 34;
    CDALBS; DAM POET; DLB 45, 63;
    EXPP; MTCW 1, 2; RGAL 4; TUS
Rao, Raja 1909- .... **CLC 25, 56**
    See also CA 73-76; CANR 51; CN 7; DAM
    NOV; MTCW 1, 2; RGEL 2; RGSF 2
Raphael, Frederic (Michael) 1931- ... **CLC 2,**
    14
    See also CA 1-4R; CANR 1, 86; CN 7;
    DLB 14
Ratcliffe, James P.
    See Mencken, H(enry) L(ouis)

Author Index

Skelton, John 1460(?)-1529 ..... **LC 71; PC 25**
See also BRW 1; DLB 136; RGEL 2
Skelton, Robin 1925-1997 .... **CLC 13**
See Zuk, Georges
See also AITN 2; CA 5-8R; CAAS 5;
CANR 28, 89; CCA 1; CP 7; DLB 27, 53
Skolimowski, Jerzy 1938- .... **CLC 20**
See also CA 128
Skram, Amalie (Bertha)
1847-1905 .... **TCLC 25**
See also CA 165
Skvorecky, Josef (Vaclav) 1924- ...... **CLC 15,
39, 69, 152**
See also CA 61-64; CAAS 1; CANR 10,
34, 63, 108; CDWLB 4; DAC; DAM
NOV; DLB 232; MTCW 1, 2
Slade, Bernard .... **CLC 11, 46**
See Newbound, Bernard Slade
See also CAAS 9; CCA 1; DLB 53
Slaughter, Carolyn 1946- .... **CLC 56**
See also CA 85-88; CANR 85; CN 7
Slaughter, Frank G(ill) 1908-2001 ... **CLC 29**
See also AITN 2; CA 5-8R; CANR 5, 85;
INT CANR-5; RHW
Slavitt, David R(ytman) 1935- ..... **CLC 5, 14**
See also CA 21-24R; CAAS 3; CANR 41,
83; CP 7; DLB 5, 6
Slesinger, Tess 1905-1945 .... **TCLC 10**
See also CA 199; DLB 102
Slessor, Kenneth 1901-1971 .... **CLC 14**
See also CA 102; DLB 260; RGEL 2
Slowacki, Juliusz 1809-1849 .... **NCLC 15**
See also RGWL 3
Smart, Christopher 1722-1771 . **LC 3; PC 13**
See also DAM POET; DLB 109; RGEL 2
Smart, Elizabeth 1913-1986 .... **CLC 54**
See also CA 81-84; DLB 88
Smiley, Jane (Graves) 1949- ...... **CLC 53, 76,
144**
See also AMWS 6; BPFB 3; CA 104;
CANR 30, 50, 74, 96; CN 7; CPW 1;
DAM POP; DLB 227, 234; INT CANR-30
Smith, A(rthur) J(ames) M(arshall)
1902-1980 .... **CLC 15**
See also CA 1-4R; CANR 4; DAC; DLB
88; RGEL 2
Smith, Adam 1723(?)-1790 .... **LC 36**
See also DLB 104, 252; RGEL 2
Smith, Alexander 1829-1867 .... **NCLC 59**
See also DLB 32, 55
Smith, Anna Deavere 1950- .... **CLC 86**
See also CA 133; CANR 103; CD 5; DFS 2
Smith, Betty (Wehner) 1904-1972 .... **CLC 19**
See also BPFB 3; BYA 3; CA 5-8R; DLBY
1982; LAIT 3; RGAL 4; SATA 6
Smith, Charlotte (Turner)
1749-1806 .... **NCLC 23, 115**
See also DLB 39, 109; RGEL 2; TEA
Smith, Clark Ashton 1893-1961 .... **CLC 43**
See also CA 143; CANR 81; FANT; HGG;
MTCW 2; SCFW 2; SFW 4; SUFW
Smith, Dave .... **CLC 22, 42**
See Smith, David (Jeddie)
See also CAAS 7; DLB 5
Smith, David (Jeddie) 1942-
See Smith, Dave
See also CA 49-52; CANR 1, 59; CP 7;
CSW; DAM POET
Smith, Florence Margaret 1902-1971
See Smith, Stevie
See also CA 17-18; CANR 35; CAP 2;
DAM POET; MTCW 1, 2; TEA
Smith, Iain Crichton 1928-1998 .... **CLC 64**
See also CA 21-24R; CN 7; CP 7; DLB 40,
139; RGSF 2
Smith, John 1580(?)-1631 .... **LC 9**
See also DLB 24, 30; TUS
Smith, Johnston
See Crane, Stephen (Townley)

Smith, Joseph, Jr. 1805-1844 .... **NCLC 53**
Smith, Lee 1944- .... **CLC 25, 73**
See also CA 119; CANR 46; CSW; DLB
143; DLBY 1983; INT CA-119; RGAL 4
Smith, Martin
See Smith, Martin Cruz
Smith, Martin Cruz 1942- .. **CLC 25; NNAL**
See also BEST 89:4; BPFB 3; CA 85-88;
CANR 6, 23, 43, 65; CMW 4; CPW;
DAM MULT, POP; HGG; INT CANR-
23; MTCW 2; RGAL 4
Smith, Patti 1946- .... **CLC 12**
See also CA 93-96; CANR 63
Smith, Pauline (Urmson)
1882-1959 .... **TCLC 25**
See also DLB 225
Smith, Rosamond
See Oates, Joyce Carol
Smith, Sheila Kaye
See Kaye-Smith, Sheila
Smith, Stevie .... **CLC 3, 8, 25, 44; PC 12**
See Smith, Florence Margaret
See also BRWS 2; DLB 20; MTCW 2;
PAB; PFS 3; RGEL 2
Smith, Wilbur (Addison) 1933- .... **CLC 33**
See also CA 13-16R; CANR 7, 46, 66;
CPW; MTCW 1, 2
Smith, William Jay 1918- .... **CLC 6**
See also CA 5-8R; CANR 44, 106; CP 7;
CSW; CWRI 5; DLB 5; MAICYA 1, 2;
SAAS 22; SATA 2, 68
Smith, Woodrow Wilson
See Kuttner, Henry
Smith, Zadie 1976- .... **CLC 158**
See also CA 193
Smolenskin, Peretz 1842-1885 .... **NCLC 30**
Smollett, Tobias (George) 1721-1771 ... **LC 2,
46**
See also BRW 3; CDBLB 1660-1789; DLB
39, 104; RGEL 2; TEA
Snodgrass, W(illiam) D(e Witt)
1926- .... **CLC 2, 6, 10, 18, 68**
See also AMWS 6; CA 1-4R; CANR 6, 36,
65, 85; CP 7; DAM POET; DLB 5;
MTCW 1, 2; RGAL 4
Snorri Sturluson 1179-1241 .... **CMLC 56**
See also RGWL 2, 3
Snow, C(harles) P(ercy) 1905-1980 ... **CLC 1,
4, 6, 9, 13, 19**
See also BRW 7; CA 5-8R; CANR 28; CD-
BLB 1945-1960; DAM NOV; DLB 15,
77; DLBD 17; MTCW 1, 2; RGEL 2;
TEA
Snow, Frances Compton
See Adams, Henry (Brooks)
Snyder, Gary (Sherman) 1930- . **CLC 1, 2, 5,
9, 32, 120; PC 21**
See also AMWS 8; ANW; BG 3; CA 17-
20R; CANR 30, 60; CP 7; DAM POET;
DLB 5, 16, 165, 212, 237, 275; MTCW
2; PFS 9; RGAL 4; WP
Snyder, Zilpha Keatley 1927- .... **CLC 17**
See also AAYA 15; BYA 1; CA 9-12R;
CANR 38; CLR 31; JRDA; MAICYA 1,
2; SAAS 2; SATA 1, 28, 75, 110; SATA-
Essay 112; YAW
Soares, Bernardo
See Pessoa, Fernando (Antonio Nogueira)
Sobh, A.
See Shamlu, Ahmad
Sobol, Joshua 1939- .... **CLC 60**
See Sobol, Yehoshua
See also CA 200; CWW 2
Sobol, Yehoshua 1939-
See Sobol, Joshua
See also CWW 2
Socrates 470B.C.-399B.C. .... **CMLC 27**
Soderberg, Hjalmar 1869-1941 ...... **TCLC 39**
See also DLB 259; RGSF 2

Soderbergh, Steven 1963- .... **CLC 154**
See also AAYA 43
Sodergran, Edith (Irene) 1892-1923
See Soedergran, Edith (Irene)
See also CA 202; DLB 259; EW 11; RGWL
2, 3
Soedergran, Edith (Irene)
1892-1923 .... **TCLC 31**
See Sodergran, Edith (Irene)
Softly, Edgar
See Lovecraft, H(oward) P(hillips)
Softly, Edward
See Lovecraft, H(oward) P(hillips)
Sokolov, Raymond 1941- .... **CLC 7**
See also CA 85-88
Sokolov, Sasha .... **CLC 59**
Solo, Jay
See Ellison, Harlan (Jay)
Sologub, Fyodor .... **TCLC 9**
See Teternikov, Fyodor Kuzmich
Solomons, Ikey Esquir
See Thackeray, William Makepeace
Solomos, Dionysios 1798-1857 .... **NCLC 15**
Solwoska, Mara
See French, Marilyn
Solzhenitsyn, Aleksandr I(sayevich)
1918- .. **CLC 1, 2, 4, 7, 9, 10, 18, 26, 34,
78, 134; SSC 32; WLC**
See also AITN 1; BPFB 3; CA 69-72;
CANR 40, 65; DA; DAB; DAC; DAM
MST, NOV; EW 13; EXPS; LAIT 4;
MTCW 1, 2; NFS 6; RGSF 2; RGWL 2,
3; SSFS 9; TWA
Somers, Jane
See Lessing, Doris (May)
Somerville, Edith Oenone
1858-1949 .... **SSC 56; TCLC 51**
See also CA 196; DLB 135; RGEL 2; RGSF
2
Somerville & Ross
See Martin, Violet Florence; Somerville,
Edith Oenone
Sommer, Scott 1951- .... **CLC 25**
See also CA 106
Sondheim, Stephen (Joshua) 1930- . **CLC 30,
39, 147**
See also AAYA 11; CA 103; CANR 47, 67;
DAM DRAM; LAIT 4
Song, Cathy 1955- .... **AAL; PC 21**
See also CA 154; CWP; DLB 169; EXPP;
FW; PFS 5
Sontag, Susan 1933- .... **CLC 1, 2, 10, 13, 31,
105**
See also AMWS 3; CA 17-20R; CANR 25,
51, 74, 97; CN 7; CPW; DAM POP; DLB
2, 67; MAWW; MTCW 1, 2; RGAL 4;
RHW; SSFS 10
Sophocles 496(?)B.C.-406(?)B.C. .... **CMLC 2,
47, 51; DC 1; WLCS**
See also AW 1; CDWLB 1; DA; DAB;
DAC; DAM DRAM, MST; DFS 1, 4, 8;
DLB 176; LAIT 1; RGWL 2, 3; TWA
Sordello 1189-1269 .... **CMLC 15**
Sorel, Georges 1847-1922 .... **TCLC 91**
See also CA 188
Sorel, Julia
See Drexler, Rosalyn
Sorokin, Vladimir .... **CLC 59**
Sorrentino, Gilbert 1929- .. **CLC 3, 7, 14, 22,
40**
See also CA 77-80; CANR 14, 33; CN 7;
CP 7; DLB 5, 173; DLBY 1980; INT
CANR-14
Soseki
See Natsume, Soseki
See also MJW

Soto, Gary 1952- ... **CLC 32, 80; HLC 2; PC 28**
See also AAYA 10, 37; BYA 11; CA 125; CANR 50, 74, 107; CLR 38; CP 7; DAM MULT; DLB 82; EXPP; HW 1, 2; INT CA-125; JRDA; MAICYA 2; MAICYAS 1; MTCW 2; PFS 7; RGAL 4; SATA 80, 120; WYA; YAW

Soupault, Philippe 1897-1990 .... **CLC 68**
See also CA 147; GFL 1789 to the Present

Souster, (Holmes) Raymond 1921- .... **CLC 5, 14**
See also CA 13-16R; CAAS 14; CANR 13, 29, 53; CP 7; DAC; DAM POET; DLB 88; RGEL 2; SATA 63

Southern, Terry 1924(?)-1995 .... **CLC 7**
See also AMWS 11; BPFB 3; CA 1-4R; CANR 1, 55, 107; CN 7; DLB 2; IDFW 3, 4

Southey, Robert 1774-1843 .... **NCLC 8, 97**
See also BRW 4; DLB 93, 107, 142; RGEL 2; SATA 54

Southworth, Emma Dorothy Eliza Nevitte 1819-1899 .... **NCLC 26**
See also DLB 239

Souza, Ernest
See Scott, Evelyn

Soyinka, Wole 1934- .. **BLC 3; CLC 3, 5, 14, 36, 44; DC 2; WLC**
See also AFW; BW 2, 3; CA 13-16R; CANR 27, 39, 82; CD 5; CDWLB 3; CN 7; CP 7; DA; DAB; DAC; DAM DRAM, MST, MULT; DFS 10; DLB 125; MTCW 1, 2; RGEL 2; TWA; WLIT 2

Spackman, W(illiam) M(ode) 1905-1990 .... **CLC 46**
See also CA 81-84

Spacks, Barry (Bernard) 1931- .... **CLC 14**
See also CA 154; CANR 33, 109; CP 7; DLB 105

Spanidou, Irini 1946- .... **CLC 44**
See also CA 185

Spark, Muriel (Sarah) 1918- ..... **CLC 2, 3, 5, 8, 13, 18, 40, 94; SSC 10**
See also BRWS 1; CA 5-8R; CANR 12, 36, 76, 89; CDBLB 1945-1960; CN 7; CP 7; DAB; DAC; DAM MST, NOV; DLB 15, 139; FW; INT CANR-12; LAIT 4; MTCW 1, 2; RGEL 2; TEA; WLIT 4; YAW

Spaulding, Douglas
See Bradbury, Ray (Douglas)

Spaulding, Leonard
See Bradbury, Ray (Douglas)

Spelman, Elizabeth .... **CLC 65**

Spence, J. A. D.
See Eliot, T(homas) S(tearns)

Spencer, Elizabeth 1921- .... **CLC 22; SSC 57**
See also CA 13-16R; CANR 32, 65, 87; CN 7; CSW; DLB 6, 218; MTCW 1; RGAL 4; SATA 14

Spencer, Leonard G.
See Silverberg, Robert

Spencer, Scott 1945- .... **CLC 30**
See also CA 113; CANR 51; DLBY 1986

Spender, Stephen (Harold) 1909-1995 .... **CLC 1, 2, 5, 10, 41, 91**
See also BRWS 2; CA 9-12R; CANR 31, 54; CDBLB 1945-1960; CP 7; DAM POET; DLB 20; MTCW 1, 2; PAB; RGEL 2; TEA

Spengler, Oswald (Arnold Gottfried) 1880-1936 .... **TCLC 25**
See also CA 189

Spenser, Edmund 1552(?)-1599 ..... **LC 5, 39; PC 8, 42; WLC**
See also BRW 1; CDBLB Before 1660; DA; DAB; DAC; DAM MST, POET; DLB 167; EFS 2; EXPP; PAB; RGEL 2; TEA; WLIT 3; WP

Spicer, Jack 1925-1965 .... **CLC 8, 18, 72**
See also BG 3; CA 85-88; DAM POET; DLB 5, 16, 193; GLL 1; WP

Spiegelman, Art 1948- .... **CLC 76**
See also AAYA 10, 46; CA 125; CANR 41, 55, 74; MTCW 2; SATA 109; YAW

Spielberg, Peter 1929- .... **CLC 6**
See also CA 5-8R; CANR 4, 48; DLBY 1981

Spielberg, Steven 1947- .... **CLC 20**
See also AAYA 8, 24; CA 77-80; CANR 32; SATA 32

Spillane, Frank Morrison 1918-
See Spillane, Mickey
See also CA 25-28R; CANR 28, 63; MTCW 1, 2; SATA 66

Spillane, Mickey .... **CLC 3, 13**
See Spillane, Frank Morrison
See also BPFB 3; CMW 4; DLB 226; MSW; MTCW 2

Spinoza, Benedictus de 1632-1677 .. **LC 9, 58**

Spinrad, Norman (Richard) 1940- ... **CLC 46**
See also BPFB 3; CA 37-40R; CAAS 19; CANR 20, 91; DLB 8; INT CANR-20; SFW 4

Spitteler, Carl (Friedrich Georg) 1845-1924 .... **TCLC 12**
See also DLB 129

Spivack, Kathleen (Romola Drucker) 1938- .... **CLC 6**
See also CA 49-52

Spoto, Donald 1941- .... **CLC 39**
See also CA 65-68; CANR 11, 57, 93

Springsteen, Bruce (F.) 1949- .... **CLC 17**
See also CA 111

Spurling, Hilary 1940- .... **CLC 34**
See also CA 104; CANR 25, 52, 94

Spyker, John Howland
See Elman, Richard (Martin)

Squires, (James) Radcliffe 1917-1993 .... **CLC 51**
See also CA 1-4R; CANR 6, 21

Srivastava, Dhanpat Rai 1880(?)-1936
See Premchand
See also CA 197

Stacy, Donald
See Pohl, Frederik

Stael
See Stael-Holstein, Anne Louise Germaine Necker
See also EW 5; RGWL 2, 3

Stael, Germaine de
See Stael-Holstein, Anne Louise Germaine Necker
See also DLB 119, 192; FW; GFL 1789 to the Present; TWA

Stael-Holstein, Anne Louise Germaine Necker 1766-1817 .... **NCLC 3, 91**
See Stael; Stael, Germaine de

Stafford, Jean 1915-1979 .. **CLC 4, 7, 19, 68; SSC 26**
See also CA 1-4R; CANR 3, 65; DLB 2, 173; MTCW 1, 2; RGAL 4; RGSF 2; SATA-Obit 22; TCWW 2; TUS

Stafford, William (Edgar) 1914-1993 .... **CLC 4, 7, 29**
See also AMWS 11; CA 5-8R; CAAS 3; CANR 5, 22; DAM POET; DLB 5, 206; EXPP; INT CANR-22; PFS 2, 8, 16; RGAL 4; WP

Stagnelius, Eric Johan 1793-1823 . **NCLC 61**

Staines, Trevor
See Brunner, John (Kilian Houston)

Stairs, Gordon
See Austin, Mary (Hunter)
See also TCWW 2

Stalin, Joseph 1879-1953 .... **TCLC 92**

Stampa, Gaspara c. 1524-1554 .... **PC 43**
See also RGWL 2, 3

Stancykowna
See Szymborska, Wislawa

Stannard, Martin 1947- .... **CLC 44**
See also CA 142; DLB 155

Stanton, Elizabeth Cady 1815-1902 .... **TCLC 73**
See also CA 171; DLB 79; FW

Stanton, Maura 1946- .... **CLC 9**
See also CA 89-92; CANR 15; DLB 120

Stanton, Schuyler
See Baum, L(yman) Frank

Stapledon, (William) Olaf 1886-1950 .... **TCLC 22**
See also CA 162; DLB 15, 255; SFW 4

Starbuck, George (Edwin) 1931-1996 .... **CLC 53**
See also CA 21-24R; CANR 23; DAM POET

Stark, Richard
See Westlake, Donald E(dwin)

Staunton, Schuyler
See Baum, L(yman) Frank

Stead, Christina (Ellen) 1902-1983 ... **CLC 2, 5, 8, 32, 80**
See also BRWS 4; CA 13-16R; CANR 33, 40; DLB 260; FW; MTCW 1, 2; RGEL 2; RGSF 2

Stead, William Thomas 1849-1912 .... **TCLC 48**
See also CA 167

Stebnitsky, M.
See Leskov, Nikolai (Semyonovich)

Steele, Sir Richard 1672-1729 .... **LC 18**
See also BRW 3; CDBLB 1660-1789; DLB 84, 101; RGEL 2; WLIT 3

Steele, Timothy (Reid) 1948- .... **CLC 45**
See also CA 93-96; CANR 16, 50, 92; CP 7; DLB 120

Steffens, (Joseph) Lincoln 1866-1936 .... **TCLC 20**

Stegner, Wallace (Earle) 1909-1993 .. **CLC 9, 49, 81; SSC 27**
See also AITN 1; AMWS 4; ANW; BEST 90:3; BPFB 3; CA 1-4R; CAAS 9; CANR 1, 21, 46; DAM NOV; DLB 9, 206, 275; DLBY 1993; MTCW 1, 2; RGAL 4; TCWW 2; TUS

Stein, Gertrude 1874-1946 .... **DC 19; PC 18; SSC 42; TCLC 1, 6, 28, 48; WLC**
See also AMW; CA 132; CANR 108; CDALB 1917-1929; DA; DAB; DAC; DAM MST, NOV, POET; DLB 4, 54, 86, 228; DLBD 15; EXPS; GLL 1; MAWW; MTCW 1, 2; NCFS 4; RGAL 4; RGSF 2; SSFS 5; TUS; WP

Steinbeck, John (Ernst) 1902-1968 ... **CLC 1, 5, 9, 13, 21, 34, 45, 75, 124; SSC 11, 37; WLC**
See also AAYA 12; AMW; BPFB 3; BYA 2, 3, 13; CA 1-4R; CANR 1, 35; CDALB 1929-1941; DA; DAB; DAC; DAM DRAM, MST, NOV; DLB 7, 9, 212, 275; DLBD 2; EXPS; LAIT 3; MTCW 1, 2; NFS 1, 5, 7; RGAL 4; RGSF 2; RHW; SATA 9; SSFS 3, 6; TCWW 2; TUS; WYA; YAW

Steinem, Gloria 1934- .... **CLC 63**
See also CA 53-56; CANR 28, 51; DLB 246; FW; MTCW 1, 2

Steiner, George 1929- .... **CLC 24**
See also CA 73-76; CANR 31, 67, 108; DAM NOV; DLB 67; MTCW 1, 2; SATA 62

Steiner, K. Leslie
See Delany, Samuel R(ay), Jr.

Steiner, Rudolf 1861-1925 .... **TCLC 13**

Updike, John (Hoyer) 1932- . CLC 1, 2, 3, 5, 7, 9, 13, 15, 23, 34, 43, 70, 139; SSC 13, 27; WLC
　See also AAYA 36; AMW; AMWC 1; AMWR 1; BPFB 3; BYA 12; CA 1-4R; CABS 1; CANR 4, 33, 51, 94; CDALB 1968-1988; CN 7; CP 7; CPW 1; DA; DAB; DAC; DAM MST, NOV, POET, POP; DLB 2, 5, 143, 218, 227; DLBD 3; DLBY 1980, 1982, 1997; EXPP; HGG; MTCW 1, 2; NFS 12; RGAL 4; RGSF 2; SSFS 3; TUS

Upshaw, Margaret Mitchell
　See Mitchell, Margaret (Munnerlyn)

Upton, Mark
　See Sanders, Lawrence

Upward, Allen 1863-1926 .... TCLC 85
　See also CA 187; DLB 36

Urdang, Constance (Henriette) 1922-1996 .... CLC 47
　See also CA 21-24R; CANR 9, 24; CP 7; CWP

Uriel, Henry
　See Faust, Frederick (Schiller)

Uris, Leon (Marcus) 1924- .... CLC 7, 32
　See also AITN 1, 2; BEST 89:2; BPFB 3; CA 1-4R; CANR 1, 40, 65; CN 7; CPW 1; DAM NOV, POP; MTCW 1, 2; SATA 49

Urista, Alberto H. 1947- ...... HLCS 1; PC 34
　See Alurista
　See also CA 45-48, 182; CANR 2, 32; HW 1

Urmuz
　See Codrescu, Andrei

Urquhart, Guy
　See McAlmon, Robert (Menzies)

Urquhart, Jane 1949- .... CLC 90
　See also CA 113; CANR 32, 68; CCA 1; DAC

Usigli, Rodolfo 1905-1979 .... HLCS 1
　See also CA 131; HW 1; LAW

Ustinov, Peter (Alexander) 1921- .... CLC 1
　See also AITN 1; CA 13-16R; CANR 25, 51; CBD; CD 5; DLB 13; MTCW 2

U Tam'si, Gerald Felix Tchicaya
　See Tchicaya, Gerald Felix

U Tam'si, Tchicaya
　See Tchicaya, Gerald Felix

Vachss, Andrew (Henry) 1942- .... CLC 106
　See also CA 118; CANR 44, 95; CMW 4

Vachss, Andrew H.
　See Vachss, Andrew (Henry)

Vaculik, Ludvik 1926- .... CLC 7
　See also CA 53-56; CANR 72; CWW 2; DLB 232

Vaihinger, Hans 1852-1933 .... TCLC 71
　See also CA 166

Valdez, Luis (Miguel) 1940- ..... CLC 84; DC 10; HLC 2
　See also CA 101; CAD; CANR 32, 81; CD 5; DAM MULT; DFS 5; DLB 122; HW 1; LAIT 4

Valenzuela, Luisa 1938- .... CLC 31, 104; HLCS 2; SSC 14
　See also CA 101; CANR 32, 65; CDWLB 3; CWW 2; DAM MULT; DLB 113; FW; HW 1, 2; LAW; RGSF 2; RGWL 3

Valera y Alcala-Galiano, Juan 1824-1905 .... TCLC 10

Valery, (Ambroise) Paul (Toussaint Jules) 1871-1945 .... PC 9; TCLC 4, 15
　See also CA 122; DAM POET; DLB 258; EW 8; GFL 1789 to the Present; MTCW 1, 2; RGWL 2, 3; TWA

Valle-Inclan, Ramon (Maria) del 1866-1936 .... HLC 2; TCLC 5
　See also CA 153; CANR 80; DAM MULT; DLB 134; EW 8; HW 2; RGSF 2; RGWL 2, 3

Vallejo, Antonio Buero
　See Buero Vallejo, Antonio

Vallejo, Cesar (Abraham) 1892-1938 .... HLC 2; TCLC 3, 56
　See also CA 153; DAM MULT; HW 1; LAW; RGWL 2, 3

Valles, Jules 1832-1885 .... NCLC 71
　See also DLB 123; GFL 1789 to the Present

Vallette, Marguerite Eymery 1860-1953 .... TCLC 67
　See also CA 182; DLB 123, 192

Valle Y Pena, Ramon del
　See Valle-Inclan, Ramon (Maria) del

Van Ash, Cay 1918- .... CLC 34

Vanbrugh, Sir John 1664-1726 .... LC 21
　See also BRW 2; DAM DRAM; DLB 80; IDTP; RGEL 2

Van Campen, Karl
　See Campbell, John W(ood, Jr.)

Vance, Gerald
　See Silverberg, Robert

Vance, Jack .... CLC 35
　See Vance, John Holbrook
　See also DLB 8; FANT; SCFW 2; SFW 4; SUFW 1, 2

Vance, John Holbrook 1916-
　See Queen, Ellery; Vance, Jack
　See also CA 29-32R; CANR 17, 65; CMW 4; MTCW 1

Van Den Bogarde, Derek Jules Gaspard Ulric Niven 1921-1999 .... CLC 14
　See Bogarde, Dirk
　See also CA 77-80

Vandenburgh, Jane .... CLC 59
　See also CA 168

Vanderhaeghe, Guy 1951- .... CLC 41
　See also BPFB 3; CA 113; CANR 72

van der Post, Laurens (Jan) 1906-1996 .... CLC 5
　See also AFW; CA 5-8R; CANR 35; CN 7; DLB 204; RGEL 2

van de Wetering, Janwillem 1931- ... CLC 47
　See also CA 49-52; CANR 4, 62, 90; CMW 4

Van Dine, S. S. .... TCLC 23
　See Wright, Willard Huntington
　See also MSW

Van Doren, Carl (Clinton) 1885-1950 .... TCLC 18
　See also CA 168

Van Doren, Mark 1894-1972 .... CLC 6, 10
　See also CA 1-4R; CANR 3; DLB 45; MTCW 1, 2; RGAL 4

Van Druten, John (William) 1901-1957 .... TCLC 2
　See also CA 161; DLB 10; RGAL 4

Van Duyn, Mona (Jane) 1921- ...... CLC 3, 7, 63, 116
　See also CA 9-12R; CANR 7, 38, 60; CP 7; CWP; DAM POET; DLB 5

Van Dyne, Edith
　See Baum, L(yman) Frank

van Itallie, Jean-Claude 1936- .... CLC 3
　See also CA 45-48; CAAS 2; CAD; CANR 1, 48; CD 5; DLB 7

Van Loot, Cornelius Obenchain
　See Roberts, Kenneth (Lewis)

van Ostaijen, Paul 1896-1928 .... TCLC 33
　See also CA 163

Van Peebles, Melvin 1932- .... CLC 2, 20
　See also BW 2, 3; CA 85-88; CANR 27, 67, 82; DAM MULT

van Schendel, Arthur(-Francois-Emile) 1874-1946 .... TCLC 56

Vansittart, Peter 1920- .... CLC 42
　See also CA 1-4R; CANR 3, 49, 90; CN 7; RHW

Van Vechten, Carl 1880-1964 ... CLC 33; HR 3
　See also AMWS 2; CA 183; DLB 4, 9, 51; RGAL 4

van Vogt, A(lfred) E(lton) 1912-2000 . CLC 1
　See also BPFB 3; BYA 13, 14; CA 21-24R; CANR 28; DLB 8, 251; SATA 14; SATA-Obit 124; SCFW; SFW 4

Vara, Madeleine
　See Jackson, Laura (Riding)

Varda, Agnes 1928- .... CLC 16
　See also CA 122

Vargas Llosa, (Jorge) Mario (Pedro) 1936- ... CLC 3, 6, 9, 10, 15, 31, 42, 85; HLC 2
　See Llosa, (Jorge) Mario (Pedro) Vargas
　See also BPFB 3; CA 73-76; CANR 18, 32, 42, 67; CDWLB 3; DA; DAB; DAC; DAM MST, MULT, NOV; DLB 145; DNFS 2; HW 1, 2; LAIT 5; LAW; LAWS 1; MTCW 1, 2; RGWL 2; SSFS 14; TWA; WLIT 1

Vasiliu, George
　See Bacovia, George

Vasiliu, Gheorghe
　See Bacovia, George
　See also CA 189

Vassa, Gustavus
　See Equiano, Olaudah

Vassilikos, Vassilis 1933- .... CLC 4, 8
　See also CA 81-84; CANR 75

Vaughan, Henry 1621-1695 .... LC 27
　See also BRW 2; DLB 131; PAB; RGEL 2

Vaughn, Stephanie .... CLC 62

Vazov, Ivan (Minchov) 1850-1921 . TCLC 25
　See also CA 167; CDWLB 4; DLB 147

Veblen, Thorstein B(unde) 1857-1929 .... TCLC 31
　See also AMWS 1; CA 165; DLB 246

Vega, Lope de 1562-1635 .... HLCS 2; LC 23
　See also EW 2; RGWL 2, 3

Vendler, Helen (Hennessy) 1933- ... CLC 138
　See also CA 41-44R; CANR 25, 72; MTCW 1, 2

Venison, Alfred
　See Pound, Ezra (Weston Loomis)

Verdi, Marie de
　See Mencken, H(enry) L(ouis)

Verdu, Matilde
　See Cela, Camilo Jose

Verga, Giovanni (Carmelo) 1840-1922 .... SSC 21; TCLC 3
　See also CA 123; CANR 101; EW 7; RGSF 2; RGWL 2, 3

Vergil 70B.C.-19B.C. ... CMLC 9, 40; PC 12; WLCS
　See Virgil
　See also AW 2; DA; DAB; DAC; DAM MST, POET; EFS 1

Verhaeren, Emile (Adolphe Gustave) 1855-1916 .... TCLC 12
　See also GFL 1789 to the Present

Verlaine, Paul (Marie) 1844-1896 .. NCLC 2, 51; PC 2, 32
　See also DAM POET; DLB 217; EW 7; GFL 1789 to the Present; RGWL 2, 3; TWA

Verne, Jules (Gabriel) 1828-1905 ... TCLC 6, 52
　See also AAYA 16; BYA 4; CA 131; DLB 123; GFL 1789 to the Present; JRDA; LAIT 2; MAICYA 1, 2; RGWL 2, 3; SATA 21; SCFW; SFW 4; TWA; WCH

Verus, Marcus Annius
　See Aurelius, Marcus

Very, Jones 1813-1880 .... **NCLC 9**
See also DLB 1, 243; RGAL 4

Vesaas, Tarjei 1897-1970 .... **CLC 48**
See also CA 190; EW 11; RGWL 3

Vialis, Gaston
See Simenon, Georges (Jacques Christian)

Vian, Boris 1920-1959 .... **TCLC 9**
See also CA 164; CANR 111; DLB 72; GFL
1789 to the Present; MTCW 2; RGWL 2,
3

Viaud, (Louis Marie) Julien 1850-1923
See Loti, Pierre

Vicar, Henry
See Felsen, Henry Gregor

Vicker, Angus
See Felsen, Henry Gregor

Vidal, Gore 1925- ...... **CLC 2, 4, 6, 8, 10, 22,
33, 72, 142**
See Box, Edgar
See also AITN 1; AMWS 4; BEST 90:2;
BPFB 3; CA 5-8R; CAD; CANR 13, 45,
65, 100; CD 5; CDALBS; CN 7; CPW;
DAM NOV, POP; DFS 2; DLB 6, 152;
INT CANR-13; MTCW 1, 2; RGAL 4;
RHW; TUS

Viereck, Peter (Robert Edwin)
1916- .... **CLC 4; PC 27**
See also CA 1-4R; CANR 1, 47; CP 7; DLB
5; PFS 9, 14

Vigny, Alfred (Victor) de
1797-1863 .... **NCLC 7, 102; PC 26**
See also DAM POET; DLB 119, 192, 217;
EW 5; GFL 1789 to the Present; RGWL
2, 3

Vilakazi, Benedict Wallet
1906-1947 .... **TCLC 37**
See also CA 168

Villa, Jose Garcia 1914-1997 .... **AAL; PC 22**
See also CA 25-28R; CANR 12; EXPP

Villarreal, Jose Antonio 1924- .... **HLC 2**
See also CA 133; CANR 93; DAM MULT;
DLB 82; HW 1; LAIT 4; RGAL 4

Villaurrutia, Xavier 1903-1950 ...... **TCLC 80**
See also CA 192; HW 1; LAW

Villaverde, Cirilo 1812-1894 .... **NCLC 121**
See also LAW

Villehardouin, Geoffroi de
1150(?)-1218(?) .... **CMLC 38**

**Villiers de l'Isle Adam, Jean Marie Mathias
Philippe Auguste** 1838-1889 ... **NCLC 3;
SSC 14**
See also DLB 123, 192; GFL 1789 to the
Present; RGSF 2

Villon, Francois 1431-1463(?) . **LC 62; PC 13**
See also DLB 208; EW 2; RGWL 2, 3;
TWA

Vine, Barbara .... **CLC 50**
See Rendell, Ruth (Barbara)
See also BEST 90:4

Vinge, Joan (Carol) D(ennison)
1948- .... **CLC 30; SSC 24**
See also AAYA 32; BPFB 3; CA 93-96;
CANR 72; SATA 36, 113; SFW 4; YAW

Viola, Herman J(oseph) 1938- .... **CLC 70**
See also CA 61-64; CANR 8, 23, 48, 91;
SATA 126

Violis, G.
See Simenon, Georges (Jacques Christian)

Viramontes, Helena Maria 1954- .... **HLCS 2**
See also CA 159; DLB 122; HW 2

Virgil
See Vergil
See also CDWLB 1; DLB 211; LAIT 1;
RGWL 2, 3; WP

Visconti, Luchino 1906-1976 .... **CLC 16**
See also CA 81-84; CANR 39

Vittorini, Elio 1908-1966 .... **CLC 6, 9, 14**
See also CA 133; DLB 264; EW 12; RGWL
2, 3

Vivekananda, Swami 1863-1902 .... **TCLC 88**

Vizenor, Gerald Robert 1934- .... **CLC 103;
NNAL**
See also CA 13-16R; CAAE 205; CAAS
22; CANR 5, 21, 44, 67; DAM MULT;
DLB 175, 227; MTCW 2; TCWW 2

Vizinczey, Stephen 1933- .... **CLC 40**
See also CA 128; CCA 1; INT 128

Vliet, R(ussell) G(ordon)
1929-1984 .... **CLC 22**
See also CA 37-40R; CANR 18

Vogau, Boris Andreyevich 1894-1937(?)
See Pilnyak, Boris

Vogel, Paula A(nne) 1951- ... **CLC 76; DC 19**
See also CA 108; CAD; CD 5; CWD; DFS
14; RGAL 4

Voigt, Cynthia 1942- .... **CLC 30**
See also AAYA 3, 30; BYA 1, 3, 6, 7, 8;
CA 106; CANR 18, 37, 40, 94; CLR 13,
48; INT CANR-18; JRDA; LAIT 5; MAI-
CYA 1, 2; MAICYAS 1; SATA 48, 79,
116; SATA-Brief 33; WYA; YAW

Voigt, Ellen Bryant 1943- .... **CLC 54**
See also CA 69-72; CANR 11, 29, 55; CP
7; CSW; CWP; DLB 120

Voinovich, Vladimir (Nikolaevich)
1932- .... **CLC 10, 49, 147**
See also CA 81-84; CAAS 12; CANR 33,
67; MTCW 1

Vollmann, William T. 1959- .... **CLC 89**
See also CA 134; CANR 67; CPW; DAM
NOV, POP; MTCW 2

Voloshinov, V. N.
See Bakhtin, Mikhail Mikhailovich

Voltaire 1694-1778 .... **LC 14, 79; SSC 12;
WLC**
See also BYA 13; DA; DAB; DAC; DAM
DRAM, MST; EW 4; GFL Beginnings to
1789; NFS 7; RGWL 2, 3; TWA

von Aschendrof, Baron Ignatz
See Ford, Ford Madox

von Chamisso, Adelbert
See Chamisso, Adelbert von

von Daeniken, Erich 1935- .... **CLC 30**
See also AITN 1; CA 37-40R; CANR 17,
44

von Daniken, Erich
See von Daeniken, Erich

von Hartmann, Eduard
1842-1906 .... **TCLC 96**

von Hayek, Friedrich August
See Hayek, F(riedrich) A(ugust von)

von Heidenstam, (Carl Gustaf) Verner
See Heidenstam, (Carl Gustaf) Verner von

von Heyse, Paul (Johann Ludwig)
See Heyse, Paul (Johann Ludwig von)

von Hofmannsthal, Hugo
See Hofmannsthal, Hugo von

von Horvath, Odon
See von Horvath, Odon

von Horvath, Odon
See von Horvath, Odon

von Horvath, Odon 1901-1938 .... **TCLC 45**
See von Horvath, Oedoen
See also CA 194; DLB 85, 124; RGWL 2,
3

von Horvath, Oedoen
See von Horvath, Odon
See also CA 184

von Kleist, Heinrich
See Kleist, Heinrich von

**von Liliencron, (Friedrich Adolf Axel)
Detlev**
See Liliencron, (Friedrich Adolf Axel) De-
tlev von

Vonnegut, Kurt, Jr. 1922- . **CLC 1, 2, 3, 4, 5,
8, 12, 22, 40, 60, 111; SSC 8; WLC**
See also AAYA 6, 44; AITN 1; AMWS 2;
BEST 90:4; BPFB 3; BYA 3, 14; CA
1-4R; CANR 1, 25, 49, 75, 92; CDALB
1968-1988; CN 7; CPW 1; DA; DAB;
DAC; DAM MST, NOV, POP; DLB 2, 8,
152; DLBD 3; DLBY 1980; EXPN;
EXPS; LAIT 4; MTCW 1, 2; NFS 3;
RGAL 4; SCFW; SFW 4; SSFS 5; TUS;
YAW

Von Rachen, Kurt
See Hubbard, L(afayette) Ron(ald)

von Rezzori (d'Arezzo), Gregor
See Rezzori (d'Arezzo), Gregor von

von Sternberg, Josef
See Sternberg, Josef von

Vorster, Gordon 1924- .... **CLC 34**
See also CA 133

Vosce, Trudie
See Ozick, Cynthia

Voznesensky, Andrei (Andreievich)
1933- .... **CLC 1, 15, 57**
See also CA 89-92; CANR 37; CWW 2;
DAM POET; MTCW 1

Wace, Robert c. 1100-c. 1175 .... **CMLC 55**
See also DLB 146

Waddington, Miriam 1917- .... **CLC 28**
See also CA 21-24R; CANR 12, 30; CCA
1; CP 7; DLB 68

Wagman, Fredrica 1937- .... **CLC 7**
See also CA 97-100; INT 97-100

Wagner, Linda W.
See Wagner-Martin, Linda (C.)

Wagner, Linda Welshimer
See Wagner-Martin, Linda (C.)

Wagner, Richard 1813-1883 ..... **NCLC 9, 119**
See also DLB 129; EW 6

Wagner-Martin, Linda (C.) 1936- .... **CLC 50**
See also CA 159

Wagoner, David (Russell) 1926- .... **CLC 3, 5,
15; PC 33**
See also AMWS 9; CA 1-4R; CAAS 3;
CANR 2, 71; CN 7; CP 7; DLB 5, 256;
SATA 14; TCWW 2

Wah, Fred(erick James) 1939- .... **CLC 44**
See also CA 141; CP 7; DLB 60

Wahloo, Per 1926-1975 .... **CLC 7**
See also BPFB 3; CA 61-64; CANR 73;
CMW 4; MSW

Wahloo, Peter
See Wahloo, Per

Wain, John (Barrington) 1925-1994 . **CLC 2,
11, 15, 46**
See also CA 5-8R; CAAS 4; CANR 23, 54;
CDBLB 1960 to Present; DLB 15, 27,
139, 155; MTCW 1, 2

Wajda, Andrzej 1926- .... **CLC 16**
See also CA 102

Wakefield, Dan 1932- .... **CLC 7**
See also CA 21-24R; CAAS 7; CN 7

Wakefield, Herbert Russell
1888-1965 .... **TCLC 120**
See also CA 5-8R; CANR 77; HGG; SUFW

Wakoski, Diane 1937- ...... **CLC 2, 4, 7, 9, 11,
40; PC 15**
See also CA 13-16R; CAAS 1; CANR 9,
60, 106; CP 7; CWP; DAM POET; DLB
5; INT CANR-9; MTCW 2

Wakoski-Sherbell, Diane
See Wakoski, Diane

Walcott, Derek (Alton) 1930- ... **BLC 3; CLC
2, 4, 9, 14, 25, 42, 67, 76, 160; DC 7**
See also BW 2; CA 89-92; CANR 26, 47,
75, 80; CBD; CD 5; CDWLB 3; CP 7;
DAB; DAC; DAM MST, MULT, POET;
DLB 117; DLBY 1981; DNFS 1; EFS 1;
MTCW 1, 2; PFS 6; RGEL 2; TWA

Waldman, Anne (Lesley) 1945- .... **CLC 7**
See also BG 3; CA 37-40R; CAAS 17; CANR 34, 69; CP 7; CWP; DLB 16
Waldo, E. Hunter
See Sturgeon, Theodore (Hamilton)
Waldo, Edward Hamilton
See Sturgeon, Theodore (Hamilton)
Walker, Alice (Malsenior) 1944- .... **BLC 3; CLC 5, 6, 9, 19, 27, 46, 58, 103, 167; PC 30; SSC 5; WLCS**
See also AAYA 3, 33; AFAW 1, 2; AMWS 3; BEST 89:4; BPFB 3; BW 2, 3; CA 37-40R; CANR 9, 27, 49, 66, 82; CDALB 1968-1988; CN 7; CPW; CSW; DA; DAB; DAC; DAM MST, MULT, NOV, POET, POP; DLB 6, 33, 143; EXPN; EXPS; FW; INT CANR-27; LAIT 3; MAWW; MTCW 1; NFS 5; RGAL 4; RGSF 2; SATA 31; SSFS 2, 11; TUS; YAW
Walker, David Harry 1911-1992 ...... **CLC 14**
See also CA 1-4R; CANR 1; CWRI 5; SATA 8; SATA-Obit 71
Walker, Edward Joseph 1934-
See Walker, Ted
See also CA 21-24R; CANR 12, 28, 53; CP 7
Walker, George F. 1947- .... **CLC 44, 61**
See also CA 103; CANR 21, 43, 59; CD 5; DAB; DAC; DAM MST; DLB 60
Walker, Joseph A. 1935- .... **CLC 19**
See also BW 1, 3; CA 89-92; CAD; CANR 26; CD 5; DAM DRAM, MST; DFS 12; DLB 38
Walker, Margaret (Abigail)
1915-1998 .... **BLC; CLC 1, 6; PC 20; TCLC 129**
See also AFAW 1, 2; BW 2, 3; CA 73-76; CANR 26, 54, 76; CN 7; CP 7; CSW; DAM MULT; DLB 76, 152; EXPP; FW; MTCW 1, 2; RGAL 4; RHW
Walker, Ted .... **CLC 13**
See Walker, Edward Joseph
See also DLB 40
Wallace, David Foster 1962- ..... **CLC 50, 114**
See also AMWS 10; CA 132; CANR 59; MTCW 2
Wallace, Dexter
See Masters, Edgar Lee
Wallace, (Richard Horatio) Edgar
1875-1932 .... **TCLC 57**
See also CMW 4; DLB 70; MSW; RGEL 2
Wallace, Irving 1916-1990 .... **CLC 7, 13**
See also AITN 1; BPFB 3; CA 1-4R; CAAS 1; CANR 1, 27; CPW; DAM NOV, POP; INT CANR-27; MTCW 1, 2
Wallant, Edward Lewis 1926-1962 ... **CLC 5, 10**
See also CA 1-4R; CANR 22; DLB 2, 28, 143; MTCW 1, 2; RGAL 4
Wallas, Graham 1858-1932 .... **TCLC 91**
Waller, Edmund 1606-1687 .... **LC 86**
See also BRW 2; DAM POET; DLB 126; PAB; RGEL 2
Walley, Byron
See Card, Orson Scott
Walpole, Horace 1717-1797 .... **LC 2, 49**
See also BRW 3; DLB 39, 104, 213; HGG; RGEL 2; SUFW 1; TEA
Walpole, Hugh (Seymour)
1884-1941 .... **TCLC 5**
See also CA 165; DLB 34; HGG; MTCW 2; RGEL 2; RHW
Walser, Martin 1927- .... **CLC 27**
See also CA 57-60; CANR 8, 46; CWW 2; DLB 75, 124
Walser, Robert 1878-1956 ..... **SSC 20; TCLC 18**
See also CA 165; CANR 100; DLB 66

Walsh, Gillian Paton
See Paton Walsh, Gillian
Walsh, Jill Paton .... **CLC 35**
See Paton Walsh, Gillian
See also CLR 2, 65; WYA
Walter, Villiam Christian
See Andersen, Hans Christian
Walther von der Vogelweide c.
1170-1228 .... **CMLC 56**
Walton, Izaak 1593-1683 .... **LC 72**
See also BRW 2; CDBLB Before 1660; DLB 151, 213; RGEL 2
Wambaugh, Joseph (Aloysius, Jr.)
1937- .... **CLC 3, 18**
See also AITN 1; BEST 89:3; BPFB 3; CA 33-36R; CANR 42, 65; CMW 4; CPW 1; DAM NOV, POP; DLB 6; DLBY 1983; MSW; MTCW 1, 2
Wang Wei 699(?)-761(?) .... **PC 18**
See also TWA
Ward, Arthur Henry Sarsfield 1883-1959
See Rohmer, Sax
See also CA 173; CMW 4; HGG
Ward, Douglas Turner 1930- .... **CLC 19**
See also BW 1; CA 81-84; CAD; CANR 27; CD 5; DLB 7, 38
Ward, E. D.
See Lucas, E(dward) V(errall)
Ward, Mrs. Humphry 1851-1920
See Ward, Mary Augusta
See also RGEL 2
Ward, Mary Augusta 1851-1920 ... **TCLC 55**
See Ward, Mrs. Humphry
See also DLB 18
Ward, Peter
See Faust, Frederick (Schiller)
Warhol, Andy 1928(?)-1987 .... **CLC 20**
See also AAYA 12; BEST 89:4; CA 89-92; CANR 34
Warner, Francis (Robert le Plastrier)
1937- .... **CLC 14**
See also CA 53-56; CANR 11
Warner, Marina 1946- .... **CLC 59**
See also CA 65-68; CANR 21, 55; CN 7; DLB 194
Warner, Rex (Ernest) 1905-1986 ...... **CLC 45**
See also CA 89-92; DLB 15; RGEL 2; RHW
Warner, Susan (Bogert)
1819-1885 .... **NCLC 31**
See also DLB 3, 42, 239, 250, 254
Warner, Sylvia (Constance) Ashton
See Ashton-Warner, Sylvia (Constance)
Warner, Sylvia Townsend
1893-1978 .. **CLC 7, 19; SSC 23; TCLC 131**
See also BRWS 7; CA 61-64; CANR 16, 60, 104; DLB 34, 139; FANT; FW; MTCW 1, 2; RGEL 2; RGSF 2; RHW
Warren, Mercy Otis 1728-1814 ..... **NCLC 13**
See also DLB 31, 200; RGAL 4; TUS
Warren, Robert Penn 1905-1989 .. **CLC 1, 4, 6, 8, 10, 13, 18, 39, 53, 59; PC 37; SSC 4, 58; WLC**
See also AITN 1; AMW; BPFB 3; BYA 1; CA 13-16R; CANR 10, 47; CDALB 1968-1988; DA; DAB; DAC; DAM MST, NOV, POET; DLB 2, 48, 152; DLBY 1980, 1989; INT CANR-10; MTCW 1, 2; NFS 13; RGAL 4; RGSF 2; RHW; SATA 46; SATA-Obit 63; SSFS 8; TUS
Warshofsky, Isaac
See Singer, Isaac Bashevis
Warton, Joseph 1722-1800 .... **NCLC 118**
See also DLB 104, 109; RGEL 2
Warton, Thomas 1728-1790 .... **LC 15, 82**
See also DAM POET; DLB 104, 109; RGEL 2

Waruk, Kona
See Harris, (Theodore) Wilson
Warung, Price .... **TCLC 45**
See Astley, William
See also DLB 230; RGEL 2
Warwick, Jarvis
See Garner, Hugh
See also CCA 1
Washington, Alex
See Harris, Mark
Washington, Booker T(aliaferro)
1856-1915 .... **BLC 3; TCLC 10**
See also BW 1; CA 125; DAM MULT; LAIT 2; RGAL 4; SATA 28
Washington, George 1732-1799 .... **LC 25**
See also DLB 31
Wassermann, (Karl) Jakob
1873-1934 .... **TCLC 6**
See also CA 163; DLB 66
Wasserstein, Wendy 1950- .. **CLC 32, 59, 90; DC 4**
See also CA 129; CABS 3; CAD; CANR 53, 75; CD 5; CWD; DAM DRAM; DFS 5; DLB 228; FW; INT CA-129; MTCW 2; SATA 94
Waterhouse, Keith (Spencer) 1929- . **CLC 47**
See also CA 5-8R; CANR 38, 67, 109; CBD; CN 7; DLB 13, 15; MTCW 1, 2
Waters, Frank (Joseph) 1902-1995 .. **CLC 88**
See also CA 5-8R; CAAS 13; CANR 3, 18, 63; DLB 212; DLBY 1986; RGAL 4; TCWW 2
Waters, Mary C. .... **CLC 70**
Waters, Roger 1944- .... **CLC 35**
Watkins, Frances Ellen
See Harper, Frances Ellen Watkins
Watkins, Gerrold
See Malzberg, Barry N(athaniel)
Watkins, Gloria Jean 1952(?)-
See hooks, bell
See also BW 2; CA 143; CANR 87; MTCW 2; SATA 115
Watkins, Paul 1964- .... **CLC 55**
See also CA 132; CANR 62, 98
Watkins, Vernon Phillips
1906-1967 .... **CLC 43**
See also CA 9-10; CAP 1; DLB 20; RGEL 2
Watson, Irving S.
See Mencken, H(enry) L(ouis)
Watson, John H.
See Farmer, Philip Jose
Watson, Richard F.
See Silverberg, Robert
Waugh, Auberon (Alexander)
1939-2001 .... **CLC 7**
See also CA 45-48; CANR 6, 22, 92; DLB 14, 194
Waugh, Evelyn (Arthur St. John)
1903-1966 .. **CLC 1, 3, 8, 13, 19, 27, 44, 107; SSC 41; WLC**
See also BPFB 3; BRW 7; CA 85-88; CANR 22; CDBLB 1914-1945; DA; DAB; DAC; DAM MST, NOV, POP; DLB 15, 162, 195; MTCW 1, 2; NFS 13; RGEL 2; RGSF 2; TEA; WLIT 4
Waugh, Harriet 1944- .... **CLC 6**
See also CA 85-88; CANR 22
Ways, C. R.
See Blount, Roy (Alton), Jr.
Waystaff, Simon
See Swift, Jonathan
Webb, Beatrice (Martha Potter)
1858-1943 .... **TCLC 22**
See also CA 162; DLB 190; FW
Webb, Charles (Richard) 1939- .... **CLC 7**
See also CA 25-28R; CANR 114
Webb, James H(enry), Jr. 1946- ...... **CLC 22**
See also CA 81-84

Author Index

Literary Criticism Series
Cumulative Topic Index

This index lists all topic entries in Gale's *Classical and Medieval Literature Criticism* (CMLC), *Contemporary Literary Criticism* (CLC), *Drama Criticism* (DC), *Literature Criticism from 1400 to 1800* (LC), *Nineteenth-Century Literature Criticism* (NCLC), *Short Story Criticism* (SSC), and *Twentieth-Century Literary Criticism* (TCLC). The index also lists topic entries in the Gale Critical Companion Collection, which includes the following publication: *Harlem Renaissance* (HR).

Topic Index

Topic Index

NCLC Cumulative Nationality Index

Nationality Index

NCLC-122 Title Index